A CUMULATIVE BIBLIOGRAPHY
OF MEDIEVAL MILITARY HISTORY
AND TECHNOLOGY

HISTORY
OF WARFARE

General Editor

KELLY DEVRIES
Loyola College

Founding Editors

THERESA VANN
PAUL CHEVEDDEN

VOLUME 8

A CUMULATIVE BIBLIOGRAPHY OF MEDIEVAL MILITARY HISTORY AND TECHNOLOGY

BY

KELLY DEVRIES

BRILL
LEIDEN · BOSTON · KÖLN
2002

This book is printed on acid-free paper.

Die Deutsche Bibliothek – CIP-Einheitsaufnahme

DeVries, Kelly :
A cumulative bibliography of medieval military history and technology /
by Kelly DeVries. – Leiden ; Boston ; Köln : Brill, 2002
(History of warfare ; Vol. 8)
ISBN 90–04–12227–3

Library of Congress Cataloging-in-Publication Data

Library of Congress Cataloging-in-Publication Data is also available

ISSN   1385–7827
ISBN   90 04 12227 3

PRINTED IN THE NETHERLANDS

To Dr. Bert S. Hall
My Teacher, My Mentor, My Friend

TABLE OF CONTENTS

ACKNOWLEDGMENTS

In writing, or more correctly composing, a bibliography for any subject, the author's success is determined chiefly from what resources he is able to use. While I was certainly able to begin this project using my own and nearby libraries, especially the Milton Eisenhower Library of the Johns Hopkins University, I soon realized that I would need resources far beyond these, especially to cover the areas of premodern military history and technology which had not been the focus of my own research. Fortunately, at the time that I began to think of turning into a more major project what I had until then regarded simply as my own list of articles and books, I was able to earn two grants to supplement my income of what then became an eighteen-month sabbatical leave. The first awarded me a Senior Fellowship at the Dibner Institute for the History of Science and Technology at the Massachusetts Institute of Technology, which gave me access to the wonderful library collections of Harvard University, while the second, a Professional Development Fellowship, from the National Science Foundation, division of Science and Technology Studies, enabled me to spend time at the Royal Armouries in Leeds, England, with its wonderful collection of medieval military technology resources. At both of these institutions, I was able to increase my bibliographical references by several thousand titles. Thanks should be given especially to Philip Abbott and Stephen Howe of the Royal Armouries Library, Leeds.

A bibliography is nothing more than a research reference guide, a tool which hopefully will allow users access to a number of sources, in this case solely secondary sources, which might be used to facilitate their research and/or confirm or deny their findings. Without such tools, the task of scholarship is certainly made more difficult and generally fails to be complete.

Good teachers, graduate or undergraduate, will introduce their students to these research tools, at least such was my experience. I have had a number of fine teachers who taught me well, not only in how to acquire bibliographical references, but also how to use them once they were acquired. To George Tate, Paul Pixton, and Larry Best, of Brigham Young University, and Michael Powicke, John Munro, Ambrose Raftis, William Leckie, Leonard Boyle (†), and George Rigg, of the University of Toronto,

I owe particular thanks. But it is to Dr. Bert S. Hall, my advisor and mentor at the University of Toronto, that I dedicate this book. His continual friendship, both in an academic and personal guise, has supported me in all of my endeavors, from the time I was a student, through my adjunct teaching days, and into my professorial career. It cannot have been easy — I only need mention the large numbers of letters which he has written on my behalf to garner some sympathy for that statement. Thank you.

INTRODUCTION

There is perhaps no other more lively area for study in medieval history than medieval military history, with its attendant and complementary field, the history of medieval military technology. In the past twenty years, the length of my personal academic experience in medieval military history and technology, it seems that more major scholarly inroads have been made in this field than in any other historical genre of medieval studies. (Of course, I could be biased.) What this has meant is that it is now more difficult to keep up with all of the trends and sources in the field than ever before. Hence the need for a reference work covering what has previously been written which, in turn, can assist the scholar, both the more experienced academic and the beginner, to improve his or her work in medieval military history or the history of medieval military technology.

Utilizing library catalogues, bibliographies, and footnotes, I have tried to compile the most complete list of secondary references to works in medieval military history and the history of military technology which I could. Of course, in doing this, two problems of incompleteness presented themselves. First, the references themselves are often incomplete. Article footnotes rarely contain complete references, especially as far as complete page numbers when other articles are concerned, while lately it has also become a practice, an unfortunate one in my experience, of leaving off these same article page numbers from book and article bibliographies as well. Finally, it is rare that publishers' names are ever supplied in either bibliographies or article footnotes. In short, I have included the most complete information that I can: a complete reference, with page numbers if articles, and publishers' names if books, if possible, and where not possible, as much information as I had available to me. All reference data should be complete enough to find these works in a library or to order them from an inter-library loan service.

The second problem which I, and undoubtedly any compiler of bibliographical reference works, have encountered in composing this bibliographical collection is the ultimate incompleteness of the work as a whole. No sooner is a bibliography published than new items appear which would be appropriate for it. I have tried to include everything I could up to Spring 2001 when I compiled the final draft on which this bibliography is based.

Of course, there are also the obviously missed references. No matter how thorough the bibliography compiler is in searching for references, there will always be many that are missed. (Indeed, in an earlier draft of this work, I actually missed one of my own articles!)

The plan is to provide a means whereby references, both those which represent items appearing after this work is published and those which were left out, can appear. Updates will appear! Although where yearly updates will appear has not be determined, there are plans to have these; multi-annual updates will appear in print. In each of these, both new references and those left out will appear — depending on the number of new items, these references may be annotated. I would appreciate any additions to the bibliography, with potential donors of these able to reach me through E.J. Brill Publishing or, at least for the near future, at kdevries@loyola.edu.

Finally, a few words need to be written about the geographical/chronological limitations of this work and the categories which I have used to catalogue these references. While I have kept fairly strictly to a geography which centers on conventional medieval boundaries — Europe, Byzantium, and the Middle East — the chronology does differ from the conventional medieval dates. Because of its influence on the early Middle Ages, I wanted to include references to Late Antiquity, especially to the military history and technology of the third- and fourth-century Roman Empire. For the reverse reason, the influence of the Middle Ages on the sixteenth and early seventeenth centuries, I have included references to military history and technology up to 1648 as well. This is especially important in the study of the Ottoman Turkish Wars and Arms and Armor, where the end of the fifteenth century as a chronological terminus makes little sense.

As for what categories I have used to divide these references, while some are obvious or at least indicate the interests of scholars in the past couple of centuries, I must admit that many simply reflect my own personal bias. Some categories are geographical in content (France, Spain and Portugal, Holy Roman Empire, England, etc.), some denote separate wars (Barbarian Invasions, Hundred Years War, Crusades, Dutch Revolt, Thirty Years War, etc.), and some are thematic (Chivalry, Financing, Mercenaries, Military Obligation, Military Orders, etc.) Please note that several categories have also been sub-divided into separate chronologies or military events. These different categories should be easily discerned by a simple scanning of the Table of Contents.

There are of course some anomalies. A general one is that beyond some "General," non-chronological categories, there are four major categories: "Late Antiquity;" "Medieval;" Early Modern;" and "Premodern," which refers only to "Military Technology" references. More specific anomalies are: "Barbarian Invasions" which covers all military activity of the invaders of the old Roman Empire throughout the early Middle Ages; "Bouvines" which is a category by its own and not a sub-division of "France," "the Holy Roman Empire," "England" or "Low Countries," because of the participation of military units from all of those lands; "Carolingian" which covers all military activity in central and western Europe from Charles Martel through the end of the Carolingian Kings; "Cavalry" which is different from "Knights and Knighthood," the latter being found as a sub-division of "Chivalry;" "Church" which covers all ecclesiastical miliary activities and commentaries, including the "Just War," except for the "Peace and Truce of God," references to which can be found under "Peace Movements;" "Crusades – Later" which contains references to all crusading activities referring to the Islamic lands after the "Crusade – Fourth," although the "Albigensian," "Children's," "Hussite,"and "Livonian" Crusades have their own categories; "Crusader Kingdoms" which also have a separate Crusade sub-division category; "Mongols" whose military activities are a subdivision of "Crusades" as well; Crusades against the Ottomans can be found as "Medieval/Early Modern – Ottoman Turkish Wars;" the "Eastern European" category in which both the "Medieval" and "Early Modern" periods contain all references to military activities east of the Holy Roman Empire, including Russia and Hungary; "English/Scottish Conflicts" and "English/Welsh Conflicts" which are sub-divisions of "England," although "Scotland" has its own category for references not principally directed at the Scottish Conflicts with its southern neighbor; Scottish participation in the "Hundred Years War" is categorized as a sub-division of that larger category; "Financing" references to which have their own category, unless referring to the "Hundred Years War," which has a "Financing" sub-division; "Historiography" which is a different category from "Methodology;" references to English and French Kings who ruled during the "Hundred Years War which are listed as sub-divisions of that category even if the military references do not specifically refer to that war (especially important in dealing with

"Henry VI," whose participation in the "Wars of the Roses" means that one seeking information about that king's role in that English war should look in both categories); "John of Gaunt" which has his own "Hundred Years War" subdivision, while references to the Black Prince's military activities are to be found under the "Edward III" sub-division; "Joan of Arc" which has her own "Hundred Years War" sub-division, as does the French provinces of "Brittany," "Burgundy," "Gascony and Guyenne," and "Normandy;" "France," the "Low Countries," and "Burgundy" sub-divisions of the "Hundred Years War" which also contain references to warfare occurring after the traditional date of the War's end, 1453; references to "Hundred Years War – Navies" should also be sought in "Military Technology – Premodern – Ships (inc. Warships) – Late Medieval;" the "Hungarian Invasions" category which refers only to those specific invasions, with other references to Hungary found in the "Eastern Europe" category; "Ireland" which in both the Medieval and Early Modern periods also contains conflicts fought in Ireland against the English; references to Ransoms which can be found in either "Laws of War" or "Hundred Years War – Laws of War;" "Mercenaries" which has its own category, although references to *condottieri* fighting specifically in "Italy" should also be looked for there, and mercenaries fighting in the "Hundred Years War" have a sub-division there; Recruitment and/or Feudalism references which can be found under "Military Obligation;" the "Popular Rebellion" category which contains both urban and rural rebellions; "Scandinavia" which differs from "Vikings" in its chronology, the former with references principally referring to events dated after 1100; "Renaissance" which specifically refers to general works containing that word in their titles and differs from "Early Modern – General;" the "Military Revolution" which has its own category, while "Military Revolution Abroad" refers specifically to early Colonial Warfare of European lands; the Early Modern "Italian Wars" which are included with "Italy;" "Spanish Armada" which is a sub-division of "Early Modern – Spain," although one seeking references to that conflict must also see "Military Technology – Premodern – Ships (inc. Warships) – Early Modern;" and, almost all divisions and sub-divisions of "Military Technology" which should be self-explanatory, but please note that "Courtly Engineers" appears as a sub-division here and not in "Medieval – Manuals" or "Early Modern – Military Thought."

PREMODERN MILITARY HISTORY BIBLIOGRAPHY

General

Addington, Larry H. *The Patterns of War through the Eighteenth Century.* Bloomington: University of Indiana Press, 1990.

Alexander, Bevin. *How Great Generals Win.* New York: Avon Books, 1993.

Andreski, Stanislav. *Military Organization and Society.* 2nd ed. Berkeley and Los Angeles: University of California Press, 1968.

Barrett, C.R.B. *Battles and Battlefields in England.* London, 1896.

Baumgartner, Frederic J. *From Spear to Flintlock: A History of War in Europe and the Middle East to the French Revolution.* New York: Praeger, 1991.

Black, Jeremy. *War and the World: Military Power and the Fate of Continents, 1450-2000.* New Haven: Yale University Press, 1998.

Black, Jeremy. "War and the World, 1450-2000," *Journal of Military History* 63 (1999), 669-81.

Boussel, Patrice. *Guide des champs de bataille en France.* Paris: Pierre Horay Éditeur, 1981.

Bruce, George, rev. *Harbottle's Dictionary of Battles.* 3rd ed. New York: Van Nostrand Reinhold Company, 1991.

Burne, Alfred H. *The Battlefields of Britain.* London: Methuen and Co., 1951.

Burne, Alfred H. *More Battlefields of Britain.* London: Methuen and Co., 1952.

Chaliand, Gérard. *The Art of War in World History: From Antiquity to the Nuclear Age*. Berkeley and Los Angeles: University of California Press, 1994.

Chambers, John Whiteclay. "The New Military History Myth and Reality," *Journal of Military History* 55 (1991), 395-406.

Childs, John. "Debate–A Short History of the Military Use of Land in Peacetime," *War in History* 4 (1997), 81-104.

Cockle, Maurice J.D. *A Bibliography of Military Books up to 1642*. 2nd ed. 1957; rpt. London: The Holland Press, 1978.

Cohen, Ronald. "Warfare and State Formation: Wars Make States and States Make Wars." In: *Warfare, Culture, and Environment*. Ed. R. Brian Ferguson. Orlando: Academic Press, 1984, pp. 329-58.

Contamine, Philippe, ed. *Histoire militaire de la France*. I: *Des origines à 1715*. Paris: Presses universitaires de France, 1992.

Cooney, Mark. "From Warre to Tyranny: Lethal Conflict and the State," *American Sociological Review* 62 (1997), 316-38.

Costantini, A. "D'Hannibal à Gengis-Khan: vers la suprematie de la cavalerie (216 av. J.-C.-1281)," *Revue internationale d'histoire militaire* 49 (1980), 17-32.

Corvisier, André and John Childs, ed. *A Dictionary of Military History*. Trans. Chris Turner. Oxford: Basil Blackwell, 1994.

Cowley, Robert and Geoffrey Parker, ed. *The Reader's Companion to Military History*. Boston: Houghton Mifflin Company, 1996.

Dawson, Doyne. "The Origins of War: Biological and Anthropological Theories," *History and Theory* 35 (1996), 1-28.

Dawson, Doyne. *The Origins of Western Warfare: Militarism and Morality in the Ancient World*. Boulder: Westview Press, 1996.

Débarquement à travers les âges, Le. Bayex: Comité du Débarquement, n.d.

Diamond, Jared. *Guns, Germs, and Steel*. New York: W.W. Norton and Company, 1997.

Dyer, Gwynne. *War*. New York: Crown Publishers, Inc., 1985.

Eggenberger, D. *A Dictionary of Battles*. London, 1967.

Die Fechkunst, 1500-1900: Grafik, Waffen, Kunstsammlungen der Veste Coburg. Coburg: Veste Coburg, 1968.

Ferguson, R. Brian. "A Paradigm for the Study of War and Society." In: *War and Society in the Ancient and Medieval Worlds: Asia, the Mediterranean, Europe, and Mesoamerica*. Ed. Kurt Raaflaub and Nathan Rosenstein. Washington: Center for Hellenic Studies, 1999, pp. 389-438.

Ferguson, R. Brian and Neil L. Whitehead. *War in the Tribal Zone: Expanding States and Indigenous Warfare*. Santa Fe: School of American Research Press, 1992.

Freedman, Lawrence, ed. *War*. Oxford Readers. Oxford: Oxford University Press, 1994.

Fuller, J.F.C. *The Decisive Battles of the Western World and Their Influence Upon History*. Ed. J. Terraine. 2 vols. London: Paladin, 1970.

Giorgetti, Giovanni. *Le armi antiche dal 1000 D.C. al 1800*. 3 vols. Milan: Associazione Amatori Armi Antiche, 1961.

Guest, Ken and Denise. *British Battles: The Front Lines of History in Colour Photographs*. London: HarperCollins Publishers, 1996.

Hanson, Victor Davis. "Epilogue." In: *War and Society in the Ancient and Medieval Worlds: Asia, the Mediterranean, Europe, and Mesoamerica*. Ed. Kurt Raaflaub and Nathan Rosenstein. Washington: Center for Hellenic Studies, 1999, pp. 439-54.

Harrison, Dick. *Social Militarisation and the Power of History: A Study of Scholarly Perspectives*. Lund: Nordic Academic Press, 1999.n

Hastings, Max, ed. *The Oxford Book of Military Anecdotes*. Oxford: Oxford University Press, 1985.

Higham, Robin, ed. *A Guide to the Sources of British Military History*. Berkeley and Los Angeles, 1971.

Howard, Michael. *The Causes of Wars and Other Essays*. 2nd ed. Cambridge: Harvard University Press, 1984.

Howard, Michael. "Military Experience in European Literature." In: *The Lessons of History*. New Haven, 1991, pp. 177-87.

Howard, Michael. *War in European History*. Oxford: Oxford University Press, 1976.

Howard, Michael et al. "What is Military History?" *History Today* 35 (1984), 5-13.

Iglitzin, Lynne B. "War, Sex, Sports, and Masculinity." In: *War: A Historical, Political, and Social Study*. Ed. L.L. Farrar, Jr. Santa Barbara, 1978, pp. 63-69.

Jähns, M. *Handbuch einer Geschichte des Kriegswesens von der Urzeit bis zur Renaissance*. 2 vols. Leipzig, 1878-80.

Jones, Archer. *The Art of War in the Western World*. Urbana: University of Illinois Press, 1987.

Kaegi, Walter E. "The Crisis in Military Historiography." *Armed Forces and Society* 7 (1981), 299-316.

Kagan, Donald. *On the Origins of War and the Preservation of Peace*. New York: Doubleday, 1995.

Kaiser, David. *Politics and War: European Conflict from Philip II to Hitler*. Cambridge: Harvard University Press, 1990.

Keegan, John. *The Face of Battle: A Study of Agincourt, Waterloo, and the Somme*. New York: Vintage Books, 1977.

Keegan, John. *A History of Warfare*. New York: Alfred A. Knopf, 1993.

Keegan, John. *The Mask of Command*. Harmondsworth: Penguin Books, 1987.

Keegan, John and Joseph Darracott. *The Nature of War*. New York: Holt, Rinehart and Winston, 1981.

Keegan, John and Richard Holmes. *Soldiers: A History of Men in Battle*. Harmondsworth: Viking, 1986.

Kennedy, Paul. *The Rise and Fall of the Great Powers: Economic Change and Military Conflict from 1500 to 2000*. New York: Vintage Books, 1987.

Leadman, Alex. D.H. *Proelia Eboracensia: Battles Fought in Yorkshire Treated Historically and Topographically*. London, 1891.

Liddell Hart, B.H. *Strategy*. 2nd ed. New York: Meridian, 1991.

Luttwak, Edward N. "Logistics and the Aristocratic Idea of War." In: *Feeding Mars: Logistics in Western Warfare from the Middle Ages to the Present*. Ed. J.A. Lynn. Boulder, 1993, pp. 3-8.

Luttwak, Edward N. *Strategy: The Logic of War and Peace*. Cambridge: Harvard University Press, 1987.

Lynn, John A. "The Evolution of Army Style in the Modern West, 800-2000," *International History Review* 18 (1996), 505-45.

Lynn, John A. "The History of Logistics and *Supplying War*." In: *Feeding Mars: Logistics in Western Warfare from the Middle Ages to the Present*. Ed. J.A. Lynn. Boulder, 1993, pp. 9-30.

Lynn, John A. "The Pattern of Army Growth, 1445-1945." In: *Tools of War: Instruments, Ideas, and Institutions of Warfare, 1445-1871*. Ed. John A. Lynn. Urbana, 1990, pp. 1-27.

McNeill, William H. *Keeping Together in Time: Dance and Drill in Human History*. Cambridge: Harvard University Press, 1995.

Nef, John U. *War and Human Progress: An Essay on the Rise of Industrial Civilization*. New York: W.W. Norton and Company, Inc., 1963.

Negro, Piero del, ed. *Guida alla storia militare italiana*. Naples: Edizioni Scientifiche Italiane, 1997.

Oman, Charles. "The Art of War." In: *Social England: A Record of the Progress of the People*. Ed. H.D. Traill. London, 1895, III:70-202.

Paret, Peter. "Military Power." In: *Understanding War: Essays on Clausewitz and the History of Military Power*. Princeton, 1992, pp. 9-25.

Parker, Geoffrey, ed. *The Cambridge Illustrated History of Warfare: The Triumph of the West*. Cambridge: Cambridge University Press, 1995.

Porter, Bruce D. *War and the Rise of the State: The Military Foundations of Modern Politics*. New York: The Free Press, 1994.

Preston, Richard A., Alex Roland, and Sydney F. Wise. *Men in Arms: A History of Warfare and Its Interrelationships With Western Society*. 5th ed. Fort Worth: Holt, Rinehart and Winston, Inc., 1991.

Raaflaub, Kurt and Nathan Rosenstein. "Introduction." In: *War and Society in the Ancient and Medieval Worlds: Asia, the Mediterranean, Europe, and Mesoamerica*. Ed. Kurt Raaflaub and Nathan Rosenstein. Washington: Center for Hellenic Studies, 1999, pp. 1-6.

Ropp, Theodore. "Armed Forces and Society: Some Hypotheses." In: *New Dimensions in Military History: An Anthology*. Ed. R.F. Weigley. San Rafael, 1975, pp. 41-71.

Ropp, Theodore. *War in the Modern World*. 2nd ed. New York: Collier Books, 1962.

Seabury, Paul and Angelo Codevilla. *War: Ends and Means*. New York: Basic Books, Inc., Publishers, 1989.

Seymour, W. *Battles in Britain*. 2 vols. London, 1975.

Small, Melvin and J. David Singer, ed. *International War: An Anthology*. 2nd ed. Chicago: The Dorsey Press, 1989.

Smurthwaite, David. *The Complete Guide to the Battlefields of Britain with Survey Ordnance Maps*. Exeter: Webb and Bower Books, 1984.

Stallworthy, Jon, ed. *The Oxford Book of War Poetry*. Oxford: Oxford University Press, 1984.

Townshend, Charles, ed. *The Oxford Illustrated History of Modern War*. Oxford: Oxford University Press, 1997.

Tuchman, Barbara W. *The March of Folly: From Troy to Vietnam*. New York: Ballatine Books, 1984.

Vaisse, Maurice, ed. *Aux armes citoyens! Conscription et armée de métier des grecs à nos jours*. Paris: Centre d'Etudes d'Histoire de la Défense, 1998.

van Creveld, Martin. *Command in War*. Cambridge: Harvard University Press, 1985.

Warner, P. *British Battlefields, the North*. London, 1975.

Wright, Quincy. *A Study of War*. Abr. L.L. Wright. Chicago: The University of Chicago Press, 1964.

Wylie, Neville. "Review Article–Law and War," *War in History* 3 (1996), 451-60.

Methodology

Bassford, Christopher. "John Keegan and the Grand Tradition of Trashing Clauswitz: a Polemic," *War in History* 1 (1994), 319-36.

Black, Jeremy. "Historiographical Essay: Military Organisations and Military Change in Historical Perspective," *Journal of Military History* 62 (1998), 871-93.

Boscawen, H.G.R. "'The Lessons of Yesterday!' The Relevance of Military History to the Teaching of Tactics in Today's Army," *British Army Review* (1989), 4-11.

Bucholz, Arden. "Hans Delbrück and Modern Military History," *The Historian* 55 (1993), 517-26.

Coffman, Edward M. "The Course of Military History in the United States Since World War II," *Journal of Military History* 61 (1997), 761-76.

Deutsch, Harold C. "The Matter of Records," *Journal of Military History* 59 (1995), 135-42.

Graham, Dominick. "Stress Lines and Gray Areas: The Utility of the Historical Method to the Military Profession." In: *Military History and the Military Profession*. Ed. D.A. Charters, M. Milner and J.B. Wilson. Westport, 1992, pp. 147-58.

Hacker, Barton C. "Military Institutions and World History," *The Historian* 54 (1992), 425-40.

Higginbotham, Don. "The New Military History: Its Practioners and their Practices." In: *Military History and the Military Profession*. Ed. D.A. Charters, M. Milner and J.B. Wilson. Westport, 1992, pp. 131-44.

Lynn, John A. "The Embattled Future of Academic Military History," *Journal of Military History* 61 (1997), 777-89.

Paret, Peter. "The History of War and the New Military History." In: *Understanding War: Essays on Clausewitz and the History of Military Power*. Princeton, 1992, pp. 209-26.

Pratt, Larry. "Thucydides and International History." In: *Power, Personalities and Policies: Essays in Honour of Donald Cameron Watt*. Ed. M.G. Fry. London, 1992, pp. 1-31.

Reid, Brian Holden. "Theory From Practice: Major General J.F.C. Fuller," *History Today* 39 (June 1989), 44-49.

Rodger, N.A.M. "Considerations on Writing a General Naval History." In: *Doing Naval History: Essays Toward Improvement*. Ed. J.B. Hattendorf. Newport, 1995, pp. 117-28.

Showalter, Dennis E. "Toward a 'New' Naval History." In: *Doing Naval History: Essays Toward Improvement*. Ed. J.B. Hattendorf. Newport, 1995, pp. 129-39.

Shy, John. "The Cultural Approach to the History of War," *Journal of Military History* 57 (1993 #5), 13-26.

Late Antiquity – General

Albrethsen, Svend E. "Logistical Problems in Iron Age Warfare." In: *Military Aspects of Scandinavian Society in a European Perspective, AD. 1-1300*. Ed. A.N. Jørgensen and B. Clausen. Copenhagen, 1997, pp. 210-19.

Alston, R. "Roman Military Pay from Caesar to Diocletian," *Journal of Roman Studies* 84 (1994), 113-23.

Austin, N.J.E. *Ammianus on Warfare: An Investigation into Ammianus' Military Knowledge*. Brussels, 1979.

Austin, N.J.E and N.B. Rankov. *Exploratio: Military and Political Intelligence in the Roman World from the Second Punic War to the Battle of Adrianople*. London: Routledge, 1995.

Bachrach, Bernard S. "Early Medieval Military Demography: Some Observations on the Methods of Hans Delbrück." In: *The Circle of War in the*

Middle Ages: Essays on Medieval Military and Naval History. Ed. Donald J. Kagay and L.J. Andrew Villalon. Woodbridge: The Boydell Press, 1999, pp. 3-20.

Bachrach, Bernard S. "Gildas, Vortigern and Constitutionality in Sub-Roman Britain," *Nottingham Medieval Studies* 32 (1988), 126-40.

Baradez, Jean. "L'organisation militaire romaine de l'Algérie antique et évolution du concept défensif de ses frontières," *Revue internationale d'histoire militaire* 13 (1953), 25-42.

Barker, Phil. *The Armies and Enemies of Imperial Rome*. 3rd ed. London: War Games Research Group, 1975.

Barnes, Timothy D. "Imperial Campaigns A.D. 285-311," *Phoenix* 30 (1976), 174-93.

Barnes, Timothy D. *The New Empire of Diocletian and Constantine*. Cambridge, 1982.

Baynes, N.H. "The Military Operations of the Emperor Heraclius," *United Services Magazine* 46 (1913), 526-666; 47 (1913), 30-8, 195-201, 318-24, 401-12, 532-41, 665-79.

Berger, P. *The Archaeology of the Notitia Dignitatum*. London, 1981.

Birley, Eric. *Corbridge Roman Station (Corstopitum)*. London: Her Majesty's Stationery Office, 1954.

Birley, Eric. *Roman Britain and the Roman Army*. Kendall: Titus Wilson and Son, 1953.

Blockley, Roger C. "Constantius and his Generals." In: *Studies in Latin Literature and Roman History*, II. Collection Latomus, 168. Brussels, 1980, pp. 467-86.

Breeze, David J. "The Roman Army in Cumbria," *Transactions of the Cumberland and Westmorland Antiquarian and Archaeological Society* 88 (1988), 9-22.

Brunt, Peter. "The Army and the Land in the Roman Revolution," *Journal of Roman Studies* 52 (1962), 69-86.

Brunt, Peter. "Conscription and Volunteering in the Roman Imperial Army," *Scripta classica Israelica* 1 (1974), 90-115.

Cameron, Averill. *The Later Roman Empire, AD 284-430.* London: Fontana, 1993.

Campbell, Brian. *The Roman Army, 31 B.C.-A.D. 337: A Sourcebook.* London: Routledge, 1994.

Campbell, Brian. "The Roman Empire." In: *War and Society in the Ancient and Medieval Worlds: Asia, the Mediterranean, Europe, and Mesoamerica.* Ed. Kurt Raaflaub and Nathan Rosenstein. Washington: Center for Hellenic Studies, 1999, pp. 217-40.

Campbell, J.B. *The Emperor and the Roman Army.* Oxford: Blackwell, 1984.

Carrié, Jean-Michel. "L'état à la recherche de nouveaux modes de finance-ment des armées (Rome et Byzance, IVe-VIIIe siècles)." In: *The Byzantine and Early Islamic Near East.* III: *States, Resources and Armies.* Ed. Averil Cameron. Studies in Late Antiquity and Early Islam, 1. Princeton: The Darwin Press, Inc., 1995, pp. 27-60.

Carrié, Jean-Michel. "Patronage et propriété militaire au IVe siècle: Objet rhétorique et objet réel du discours 'Sur les patronages' de Libanius," *Bulletin de correspondance Hellénique* 100 (1976), 159-76.

Cheesman, G.L. *The Auxilia of the Roman Imperial Army.* Oxford: Oxford University Press, 1914; rpt. Hildesheim: Olms, 1971.

Cleary, Simon Esmonde. "The End of Roman Britain," *History Today* 38 (Dec. 1988), 35-40.

Coulston, J.C. "Roman, Parthian and Sassanid Tactical Developments." In: *The Defence of the Roman and Byzantine East.* Ed. P. Freeman and D. Kennedy. Oxford: BAR, 1986, pp. 59-75.

Coulston, J.C. "Three Legionaries at Croy Hill." In: *Military Equipment and the Identity of Roman Soldiers: Proceedings of the Fourth Roman Military Equipment Conference.* Ed. J.C. Coulston. British Archaeological Reports International Series, 394. Oxford: BAR, 1988, pp. 1-29.

Crump, Gary A. "Ammianus and the Late Roman Army," *Historia* 22 (1973), 91-103.

Crump, Gary A. *Ammianus as a Military Historian*. Historia Einzelschriften, 27. Stuttgart, 1975.

Dixon, K.R. and P. Southern. *The Roman Cavalry from the First to the Third Century A.D.* London: Batsford, 1992.

Dobson, Brian. "The Empire." In: *Warfare in the Ancient World*. Ed. John Hackett. New York, 1989, pp. 192-221.

Dore, J.N. *Corbridge Roman Site*. London: English Heritage, 1989.

Downey, Glanville. "The Persian Campaign in Syria in A.D. 540," *Speculum* 28 (1973), 340-48.

Drinkwater, John F. "The Germanic Threat on the Rhine Frontier: A Romano-Gallic Artefact?" In: *Shifting Frontiers in Late Antiquity*. Ed. R.W. Mathisen and H.S. Sivan. Aldershot, 1996, pp. 20-30.

Drinkwater, John F. "Julian and the Franks and Valentinian I and the Alemanni: Ammianus on Romano-German Relations," *Francia* 24/1 (1997), 1-15.

Drinkwater, John F. "The Usurpers Constantine III (407-411) and Jovinus (411-413)," *Britannia* 29 (1998), 269-98.

Eadie, John W. "The Development of Roman Mailed Cavalry," *Journal of Roman Studies* 57 (1967), 161-73.

Elton, Hugh. *Warfare in Roman Europe, AD 350-425*. Oxford: Oxford University Press, 1996.

Evison, Vera I. *The Fifth-Century Invasions South of the Thames*. London: University of London, 1965.

Ferrill, Arther. *The Fall of the Roman Empire: A Military Explanation*. London: Thames and Hudson, 1986.

Ferrill, Arther. "Roman Military Intelligence." In: *Go Spy the Land: Military Intelligence in History*. Ed. K. Neilson and B.J.C. McKercher. Westport, 1992, pp. 17-29.

Foss, Clive. "The Persians in Asia Minor and the End of Antiquity," *English Historical Review* 90 (1975), 721-47.

Franzius, Georgia. "Die römischen Funde aus Kalkriese 1987-95 und ihr Bedeutung für die Interpretation und Datierung militärischer Fundplätze der augusteischen Zeit im nordwesteuropäischen Raum," *Journal of Roman Military Equipment Studies* 6 (1995), 69-90.

Franzius, Georgia. "Die römischen Funde und Münzen aus Kalkriese Ldkr. Osnabrück, Deutschland, der Jahre 1987-1996." In: *Military Aspects of Scandinavian Society in a European Perspective, AD. 1-1300*. Ed. A.N. Jørgensen and B. Clausen. Copenhagen, 1997, pp. 76-92.

French, Dorothea R. "Rhetoric and the Rebellion of AD 387 in Antioch," *Historia* 47 (1998), 468-84.

Gabba, E. "Ordinamenti militari del tardo impero." In: *Ordinamenti militari in occidente nell'alto medioevo*. Settimane di studio del centro italiano di studi sull'alto medioevo, XV. Spoleto, 1968, I:79-.

Garlan, Yvon. *War in the Ancient World: A Social History*. Trans. Janet Lloyd. London: Chatto and Windus, 1975.

Gibbon, Edward. *The Decline and Fall of the Roman Empire*. 2 vols. New York, n.d.

Grant, Michael. *The Collapse and Recovery of the Roman Empire*. London: Routledge, 1999.

Grant, Michael. *The Fall of the Roman Empire*. New York: Collier Books, 1990.

Greatrex, Geoffrey. *Rome and Persia at War, 502-532*. Leeds: Francis Cairns, 1998.

Grosse, R. "Die Rangordung der römischen Armee des 4-6 Jahrhunderts," *Klio* 15 (1918), 122-61.

Grosse, R. *Römisch Militärgeschichte von Gallienus bis zum Beginn der byzantinischen Themenverfassung*. Berlin: Weidmann, 1920.

Hanson, Victor Davis. "The Status of Ancient Military History: Traditional Work, Recent Research, and On-going Controversies," *Journal of Military History* 63 (1999), 379-414.

Hawkes, Sonia Chadwick and G.C. Dunning. "Soldiers and Settlers in Britain, Fourth to Fifth Century," *Medieval Archaeology* 5 (1961), 1-70.

Höckmann, Olaf. "Roman River Patrols and Military Logistics on the Rhine and the Danube." In: *Military Aspects of Scandinavian Society in a European Perspective, AD. 1-1300*. Ed. A.N. Jørgensen and B. Clausen. Copenhagen, 1997, pp. 239-47.

Hoffmann, Dietrich. *Das spätromische Bewegungsheer und die Notitia Dignitatum*. 2 vols. Dusseldorf, 1969-70.

Howard-Johnston, James D. "The Two Great Powers in Late Antiquity: A Comparison."In: *The Byzantine and Early Islamic Near East*. III: *States, Resources and Armies*. Ed. Averil Cameron. Studies in Late Antiquity and Early Islam, 1. Princeton: The Darwin Press, Inc., 1995, pp. 157-226.

Ilkjær, Jørgen. "Gegner und Verbündete in Nordeuropa während des 1. bis 4. Jahrhunderts." In: *Military Aspects of Scandinavian Society in a European Perspective, AD. 1-1300*. Ed. A.N. Jørgensen and B. Clausen. Copenhagen, 1997, pp. 55-63.

Isaac, Benjamin. "The Army in the Late Roman East: the Persian Wars and the Defence of the Byzantine Provinces." In: *The Byzantine and Early Islamic Near East*. III: *States, Resources and Armies*. Ed. Averil Cameron. Studies in Late Antiquity and Early Islam, 1. Princeton: The Darwin Press, Inc., 1995, pp. 125-55.

Isaac, Benjamin. *The Limits of Empire: The Roman Army in the East*. 2nd ed. Oxford: Oxford University Press, 1992.

Jones, A.H.M. *The Later Roman Empire, AD 284-602: A Social, Economic and Administrative Survey*. Oxford: Blackwell, 1964.

Jones, A.H.M. "Military Chaplains in the Roman Army," *Harvard Theological Review* 46 (1953), 239-40.

Jones, Michael E. *The End of Roman Britain*. Ithaca: Cornell University Press, 1996.

Kaegi, Walter E. "Challenges to Late Roman and Byzantine Military Operations in Iraq (4th-9th Centuries)," *Klio* 73 (1991), 586-94.

Kaegi, Walter E. "Two Studies in the Continuity of Late Roman and Byzantine Military Institutions," *Byzantinische Forschungen* 8 (1982), 87-113.

Kellner, Hans-Jörg. *Der Römische Verwahrfund von Eining*. Munich: Munchner Beiträge zur Vor- und Frühgeschichte, 1978.

Lee, A.D. *Information and Frontiers: Roman Foreign Relations in Late Antiquity*. Cambridge: Cambridge University Press, 1993.

Levillain, L. "Campus martius," *Bibliothèque de l'école de chartes* 107 (1947-48), 62-68.

Luttwak, Edward N. *The Grand Strategy of the Roman Empire: From the First Century A.D. to the Third*. Baltimore: The Johns Hopkins University Press, 1976.

MacDowall, Simon. *Late Roman Infantrymen, 236-565 A.D.* London: Osprey, 1994.

Macmullen, R. *Soldiers and Civilians in the Later Roman Empire*. Cambridge: Harvard University Press, 1963.

Malosse, Pierre-Louis. "Qu'est donc allé faire Constant 1er en Bretagne pendant l'hiver 343?" *Historia* 48 (1999), 465-76.

Mann, J.C. "Power, Force and the Frontiers of the Empire," *Journal of Roman Studies* 69 (1979), 175-83.

Mathisen, Ralph W. "Sigisvult the Patrician, Maximinus the Arian, and Political Strategems in the Western Roman Empire, c. 425-40," *Early Medieval Europe* 8 (1999), 173-96.

Maxfield, Valerie A. "The Army and the Land in the Roman South West." In: *Security and Defence in South-West England Before 1800*. Ed. R. Higham. Exeter, 1987, pp. 1-25.

McCormick, Michael. *Eternal Victory: Triumphal Rulership in Late Antiquity, Byzantium, and the Early Medieval West*. Cambridge: Cambridge University Press, 1986.

Mommsen, Theodor. "Das römischen Militärwesen seit Diocletian," *Hermes* 24 (1889), 195-279.

Olster, David M. *Roman Defeat, Christian Response and the Literary Construction of the Jews*. Philadelphia: University of Pennsylvania Press, 1994.

Parker, H.M.D. *The Roman Legions*. 2nd ed. Cambridge: Heffer, 1958.

Parker, S. Thomas. "History of the Late Roman Frontier East of the Dead Sea." In: *The Roman Frontier in Central Jordan: Interim Report of the "Limes Arabicus" Project, 1980-1985*. BAR International Series, 340. Oxford, 1987, II:793-823.

Patlagean, Evelyne. "L'impôt payé par les soldats." In: *Armées et fiscalité dans le monde antique*. Paris: Centre nationale de la recherche scientifique, 1977, pp. 303-09.

Peters, J.B. Ward. "The Career of Sex. Julius Frontinus," *Classical Quarterly* 31 (1937), 102-05.

Richardot, Philippe. *La fin de l'armée romaine (284-476)*. Paris: Economica, 1998.

Richardson, J.S. *The Romans in Spain*. Oxford: Basil Blackwell, 1996.

Ritchie, W.F. and J.N.G. *Celtic Warriors*. Princes Risborough: Shire Publications, Ltd., 1985.

Sander, Erich. "Das Recht des römischen Soldaten," *Rheinisches Museum* 101 (1958), 152-234.

Schlüter, Wolfgang. "Archäologische Forschungen zur Örtlichkeit der Varusschlacht." In: *Military Aspects of Scandinavian Society in a European Perspective, A.D. 1-1300*. Ed. A.N. Jørgensen and B. Clausen. Copenhagen, 1997, pp. 65-75.

Simkins, M. *The Roman Army from Hadrian to Constantine*. London: Osprey, 1979.

Southern, P. and K.R. Dixon. *The Late Roman Army*. New Haven: Yale University Press, 1996.

Spaulding, Oliver Lyman and Hoffman Nickerson. *Ancient and Medieval Warfare*. London: Constable, 1994.

Speidel, M.P. *Riding for Caesar: The Roman Emperor's Horse Guards.* London: Batsford, 1994.

Speidel, M.P. "The Rise of Ethnic Units in the Roman Imperial Army." In: *Roman Army Studies.* Ed. M.P. Speidel. Amsterdam: Gieben, 1984, I:117-48.

Stoneman, Richard. "The Syrian Cuckoo: Rome and the Unconquerer Sun," *History Today* 38 (Dec 1988), 29-34.

Thompson, E.A. *A Roman Reformer and Inventor, being a New Text of the Treatise De rebus bellicis, with a Translation and Introduction.* Oxford: Clarendon Press, 1952.

Tomlin, Roger S.O. "The Army of the Late Empire." In: *The Roman World.* Ed. J.Wacher. London: Routledge and Kegan Paul, 1987, pp. 107-33.

Tomlin, Roger S.O. "Christianity and the Late Roman Army." In: *Constantine: History, Historiography and Legend.* Ed. S.N.C. Lieu and D. Montserrat. London, 1998, pp. 21-51.

Tomlin, Roger S.O. "The Late-Roman Empire." In: *Warfare in the Ancient World.* Ed. John Hackett. New York, 1989, pp. 222-49.

Tomlin, Roger S.O. "The Late Roman Empire, AD 200-450." In: *Greece and Rome at War.* Ed. P. Conolly. London, 1981, pp. 249-61.

van Berchem, D. *L'armée de Dioclétian et la réforme Constantinienne.* Paris: Geuthner, 1952.

Watson, G.R. *The Roman Soldier.* London: Thames and Hudson, 1969.

Webster, Graham. *The Roman Army.* Chester, 1956.

Webster, Graham. *The Roman Imperial Army.* 3rd ed. London: A.C. Black, 1985.

Wheeler, Everett L. "Methodological Limits and the Mirage of Roman Strategy," *Journal of Military History* 57 (1993), 7-41, 215-40.

Wickenden, N.P. "Some Military Bronzes from the Trinovantian *civitas.*" In: *Military Equipment and the Identity of Roman Soldiers: Proceedings of the Fourth Roman Military Equipment Conference.* Ed. J.C. Coulston.

British Archaeological Reports International Series, 394. Oxford: BAR, 1988, pp. 234-56.

Williams, S. *Diocletian and the Roman Recovery*. London: Batsford, 1985.

Woods, David. "Julian, Arbogastes, and the *Signa* of the *Ioviani* and the *Herculiani*," *Journal of Roman Military Equipment Studies* 6 (1995), 61-68.

Zuckerman, Constantine. "Two Reforms of the 370s: Recruiting Soldiers and Senators in the Divided Empire," *Revue des études Byzantines* 56 (1998), 79-139.

Medieval – General

Abulafia, David. *The Western Mediterranean Kingdoms, 1200-1500: The Struggle for Dominion*. London: Longman, 1997.

Allmand, Christopher T. "New Weapons, New Tactics, 1300-1500." In: *The Cambridge Illustrated History of Warfare: The Triumph of the West*. Ed. Geoffrey Parker. Cambridge: Cambridge University Press, 1995, pp. 92-105.

Allmand, Christopher T. "War and the Non-Combatant in the Middle Ages." In: *Medieval Warfare: A History*. Ed. Maurice Keen. Oxford: Oxford University Press, 1999, pp. 253-72.

Angermann, H. *Ausweitung des Kampfgeschehens und psychologische Kriegführung im früheren Mittelalter*. Wurzburg, 1971.

Auer, Leopold. "Formen des Krieges im abendländischen Mittelalter." In: *Formen des Krieges: Vom Mittelalter zum "Low-Intensity-Conflict"*. Ed. Manfried Rauchensteiner and Erwin A. Schmidl. Forschungen zur Militärgeschichte, 1. Graz: Verlag Styria, 1991, pp. 17-43.

Bachrach, Bernard S. "Early Medieval Europe." In: *War and Society in the Ancient and Medieval Worlds: Asia, the Mediterranean, Europe, and Mesoamerica*. Ed. Kurt Raaflaub and Nathan Rosenstein. Washington: Center for Hellenic Studies, 1999, pp. 271-308.

Bachrach, Bernard S. "Medieval Military Historiography." In: *Companion to Historiography*. Ed. Michael Bentley. London: Routledge, 1997, pp. 203-20.

Bachrach, Bernard S. "On Roman Ramparts, 300-1300." In: *The Cambridge Illustrated History of Warfare: The Triumph of the West*. Ed. Geoffrey Parker. Cambridge: Cambridge University Press, 1995, pp. 64-91.

Bak, János M. "Delinquent Lords and Forsaken Serfs: Thoughts on War and Society during the Crisis of Feudalism." In: *Society in Change: Studies in Honour of Bela K. Király*. Ed. S.B. Vardy. Boulder, 1983, pp. 291-304.

Batany, Jean. "Du *bellator* au *chevalier* dans le schéma des 'trois ordres' (étude sémantique)." In: *La guerre et la paix: Frontières et violences au moyen âge*. Actes du 101e congrès national des sociétés savantes, Lille, 1976. Paris: Bibliothèque Nationale, 1978, pp. 23-34.

Beeler, John H. *Warfare in Feudal Europe, 730-1200*. Ithaca: Cornell University Press, 1971.

Bennett, Matthew. "The Means and Limitations of Military Power in the Middle Ages," *The Sandhurst Journal* 1 (1990), 1-19.

Bérenger, Jean. "L'influence des peuples de la steppe (Huns, Mongols, Tartares) sur la conception européenne de la guerre de mouvement et l'emploi de la cavalerie (Ve-XVIIIe siècles)," *Revue internationale d'histoire militaire* 49 (1980), 33-50.

Bergsagel, John. "War in Music in the Middle Ages." In: *War and Peace in the Middle Ages*. Ed. B.P. McGuire. Copenhagen, 1987, pp. 282-98.

Beyerle, F. "Zur Wehrverfassung des Hochmittelalters." In: *Festschrift Ernst Mayer*. Weimar, 1932, pp. 31-91.

Brand, A.J. "Ter inleiding." In: *Oorlog in de middeleeuwen*. Ed. A.J. Brand. Hilversum, 1989, pp. 9-28.

Brundage, James A. "Hierarchy of Violence in Twelfth and Thirteenth-Century Canonists," *International History Review* 17 (1995), 670-92.

Carpentier, Elisabeth. "Le combattant médiéval: problèmes de vocabulaire de Suger à Le Breton." In: *Le combattant au moyen âge*. 2nd ed. Histoire ancienne et médiévale, 36. Paris: Publications de la Sorbonne, 1995, pp. 23-35.

Contamine, Philippe. "Le combattant dans l'occident médiéval." In: *Le combattant au moyen âge*. 2nd ed. Histoire ancienne et médiévale, 36. Paris: Publications of the Sorbonne, 1990, pp. 15-23.

Contamine, Philippe. *La guerre au moyen âge*. 4th ed. Paris: Presses universitaires de France, 1994; trans. *War in the Middle Ages*. Trans. M. Jones. Oxford: Basil Blackwell, 1984.

Contamine, Philippe. "La guerre au moyen âge d'après quelques travaux recents," *Revue internationale d'histoire militaire* 61 (1985), 39-60.

Corvisier, André. "La mort du soldat depuis la fin du moyen âge," *Revue historique* 254 (1975), 3-30.

Crépin, André. "Les dépouilles des tués sur le champ de bataille dans l'histoire, les arts et la pensée du haut Moyen Âge." In: *La guerre, la violence et les gens au Moyen Âge*. I: *Guerre et violence*. Ed. P. Contamine and O. Guyotjeannin. 119e congrès national des sociétés historiques et scientifiques, Amiens, octobre 1994, Section d'histoire médiévale et philologie. Paris, 1996, pp. 15-24.

Crubezy, E. and Jean-Claude Hélas. "Le combattant à l'époque médiévale: Vers une approche archéologique et paléopathologique." In: *Le combattant au moyen âge*. 2nd ed. Histoire ancienne et médiévale, 36. Paris: Publications of the Sorbonne, 1990, pp. 297-305.

Daniels, E. *Geschichte des Kriegwesens*. II: *Das mittelalterliche Kriegwesen*. 2nd ed. Berlin and Leipzig, 1927.

Delbrück, Hans. *Geschichte der Kriegskunst im Rahmen des Politischen Geschichte*. III: *Das Mittelalter*. Berlin: Georg Stilke, 1920-32; trans. *History of the Art of War*. III: *Medieval Warfare*. Trans. W.J. Renfroe, Jr. Lincoln: University of Nebraska Press, 1990.

Delpech, Henri. *La tactique au XIIIe siècle*. 2 vols. Paris: Alphonse Picard, Éditeur, 1886.

DeVries, Kelly. *Infantry Warfare in the Early Fourteenth Century: Discipline, Tactics, and Technology*. Woodbridge: The Boydell Press, 1996.

Duby, Georges. *27 juillet 1214: Le dimanche de Bouvines*. Paris, 1973; trans. *The Legend of Bouvines: War, Religion and Culture in the Middle Ages*. Trans. Catherine Tihanyi. Berkeley and Los Angeles: University of California Press, 1990.

Duby, Georges. *Guerriers et paysans, VIIe-XIIe siècle: Premier essor de l'économie européen*. Paris, 1973; trans. *The Early Growth of the European Economy: Warriors and Peasants from the Seventh to the Twelfth Century*. Trans. Howard B. Clarke. Ithaca: Cornell University Press, 1974.

Duby, Georges. "Guerre et société dans l'Europe féodale: la morale des guerriers." In: *Concetto, storia, miti e imagini del medio evo, atti del XIV corso internazionale d'alta cultura*. Ed. V. Branca. Florence, 1973, pp. 473-82.

Duby, Georges. *The Three Orders: Feudal Society Imagined*. Trans. Arthur Goldhammer. Chicago: The University of Chicago Press, 1980.

Dunn, Diana. "Introduction." In: *War and Society in Medieval and Early Modern Britain*. Ed. Diana Dunn. Liverpool: Liverpool University Press, 2000, pp. 1-16.

Embleton, Gerry and John Howe. *The Medieval Soldier: 15th Century Campaign Life Recreated in Colour Photographs*. London: Windrow and Greene, 1994.

Erben, Wilhelm. *Kriegsgeschichte des Mittelalters*. Berlin and Munich, 1929.

Flori, Jean. "Guerre et chevalerie au moyen âge (à propos d'un ouvrage récent)," *Cahiers de civilisation médiévale (X-XIIe siècle)* 41 (1998), 353-63.

France, John. *Western Warfare in the Age of the Crusades, 1000-1300*. Ithaca: Cornell University Press, 1999.

Funck-Brentano, Frantz. *De exercituum commeatibus tertio decimo et quarto decimo saeculis post Christum natum*. Paris, 1897.

Gaier, Claude. "Combattre au moyen âge," *Revue Belge d'histoire et de philologie* 101 (1995), 489-93.

Geoz, W. "Über Fürstenzweikämpfe im Spätmittelalter," *Archiv für Kulturgeschichte* 49 (1967), 135-63.

Gillingham, John. "The Age of Expansion, *c.* 1020-1204." In: *Medieval Warfare: A History*. Ed. Maurice Keen. Oxford: Oxford University Press, 1999, pp. 59-88.

Gore, Terry L. *Neglected Heroes: Leadership and War in the Early Modern Period*. Westport: Praeger, 1995.

Guerre au moyen âge, La. Pons: Château de Pons (Charente-maritime), 1976.

Haidu, Peter. *The Subject of Violence: The Song of Roland and the Birth of the State*. Bloomington: Indiana University Press, 1993.

Halsall, G.S. *Warfare and Society in the Barbarian West, c.450-900*. London, 1998.

Hamilton Thompson, A. "The Art of War to 1400." In: *Cambridge Medieval History*. Cambridge, 1980, VI:785-98.

Harari, Yuval Noah. "Strategy and Supply in Fourteenth-Century Western European Invasion Campaigns," *Journal of Military History* 64 (2000), 297-333.

Heath, Ian. *Armies of the Dark Ages, 600-1066*. London: REG Games (Sussex) Ltd. (Wargames Research Group) and Heritage Models, Inc., 1976.

Higham, Robin. "Some Thoughts in Late Medieval Warfare." In: *XXII. Kongreß der Internationalen Kommission für Militärgeschichte* Acta 22: *Von Crécy bis Mohács Kriegswesen im späten Mittelalter (1346-1526)*. Vienna, 1997, pp. 306-12.

Hindley, Geoffrey. *Medieval Warfare*. The Putnam Pictorial Sources Series. New York: Putnam, 1971.

Honig, Jan-Willem. "Strategie in de late Middeleeuwen: of het zonderlinge geval van de afwezige militaire genieën," *Skript* 8.4 (1986-1987), 251-61.

Hooper, Nicholas and Matthew Bennett. *The Cambridge Illustrated Atlas of Warfare: The Middle Ages*. Cambridge: Cambridge University Press, 1996.

Housley, Norman. "European Warfare, *c*. 1200-1320." In: *Medieval Warfare: A History*. Ed. Maurice Keen. Oxford: Oxford University Press, 1999, pp. 113-35.

Housley, Norman. "'Pro Deo et patria Mori': le patriotisme sanctifié en Europe, 1400-1600." In: *Guerre et concurrence entre les États européens du XIVe au XVIIIe siècle*. Ed. Philippe Contamine. Fondation Européenne de la Science: Les origines de l'État moderne en Europe, XIIIe-XVIIIe siècle. Paris: Presses universitaires de France, 1998, pp. 269-304.

Hugenholtz, F.W.N. *Ridderkrieg en burgervrede: West Europa aan de vooravond van de Honderdjarige Oorlog*. Bussum: De Haan, 1973.

Jones, Martin H. "The Depiction of Battle in Wolfram von Eschenbach's *Willehalm*." In: *The Ideals and Practice of Medieval Knighthood*, II. Ed. C. Harper-Bill and R. Harvey. Woodbridge, 1988, pp. 46-69.

Kantorowicz, Ernst. *"Pro patria mori* in Medieval Political Thought," *American Historical Review* 56 (1951), 472-92.

Keen, Maurice H. "The Changing Scene: Guns, Gunpowder, and Permanent Armies." In: *Medieval Warfare: A History*. Ed. Maurice Keen. Oxford: Oxford University Press, 1999, pp. 273-91.

Keen, Maurice H. "Introduction: Warfare and the Middle Ages." In: *Medieval Warfare: A History*. Ed. Maurice Keen. Oxford: Oxford University Press, 1999, pp. 1-9.

Keen, Maurice H. *The Laws of War in the Late Middle Ages*. London: Routledge and Kegan Paul, 1965.

Koch, H.W. *Medieval Warfare*. Englewood Hills: Prentice-Hall, 1978.

Kohler, G. *Die Entwicklung des Kriegswesens und der Kriegfuhrung in der Ritterzeit von Mitte des 11. Jahrhunderts bis zu den Hussitenkriegen*. 3 vols. Berlin, 1887.

Lassabatère, Thierry. "Théorie et éthique de la guerre dans l'œuvre d'Eustache Deschamps." In: *La guerre, la violence et les gens au Moyen*

Âge. I: *Guerre et violence*. Ed. P. Contamine and O. Guyotjeannin. 119e congrès national des sociétés historiques et scientifiques, Amiens, octobre 1994, Section d'histoire médiévale et philologie. Paris, 1996, pp. 35-48.

Lejeune R. and J. Stiennon. *The Legend of Roland in the Middle Ages*. London, 1971.

Lemerle, P. "Les invasions et migrations dans le Balkans," *Revue historique* 211 (1954), 265-309.

Lewis, Archibald R. "The Closing of the Medieval Frontier, 1250-1350," *Speculum* 33 (1958), 475-83.

Lewis, Archibald R. *Nomads and Crusaders, A.D. 1000-1368*. Bloomington Indiana University Press, 1988.

Leyser, Karl. "Early Medieval Warfare." In: *The Battle of Maldon: Fiction and Fact*. Ed. J. Cooper. London, 1993, pp. 87-108.

Lochner, Karl E. *Die Entwicklungensphasen der europäische Fechtkunst*. Vienna, 1953.

Lot, Ferdinand. *L'art militaire et les armées au moyen-âge en Europe et dans le proche orient*. 2 vols. Paris: Payot, 1946.

Maso, B. "Zij dorstten niet naar het bloed van hun broeders. De onbloedige strijdwijze in de oorlogvoeringen in de 11de eeuw." In: *Oorlog in de middeleeuwen*. Ed. A.J. Brand. Hilversum, 1989, pp. 75-110.

Matthews, John and Bob Stewart. *Warriors of Medieval Times*. New York: Sterling Publishing Company, 1988.

McGlynn, Sean. "The Myths of Medieval Warfare," *History Today* 44 (January 1994), 28-34.

Morgan, Philip J. "The Naming of Battlefields in the Middle Ages." In: *War and Society in Medieval and Early Modern Britain*. Ed. Diana Dunn. Liverpool: Liverpool University Press, 2000, pp. 34-52.

Moriarty, J.R. "Ritual Combat: A Comparison of the Aztec 'War of Flowers' and the Medieval 'Melee'," *Katnob: A Newsletter-Bulletin on Meso-American Anthropology* 7.1 (Mar 1969), 25-46.

Nadolski, Andrzej. "Les fouilles archéologiques et l'histoire militaire de la Pologne au début de moyen âge." In: *Histoire militaire de la Pologne: Problèmes choises.* Ed. W. Bieganski, P. Stawecki, and W. Janusz. Warsaw: Institut d'Histoire, 1970.

Newark, Timothy. *Medieval Warfare.* London: Jupiter Books, 1979.

Nicolle, David C. "1000 Years Ago," *Military Illustrated* 139 (Dec 1989), 14-21.

Nicolle, David C. "Medieval Warfare: The Unfriendly Interchange," *Journal of Military History* 63 (1999), 579-99.

Nicolle, David C. *Medieval Warfare Source Book.* Vol. 1: *Warfare in Western Christendom.* London: Brockhampton Press, 1995.

Nicolle, David C. *Medieval Warfare Source Book.* Vol. 2: *Christian Europe and its Neighbors.* London: Brockhampton Press, 1996.

Norman, A.V.B. *The Medieval Soldier.* New York: Barnes and Noble Books, 1971.

Ohler, Norbert. *Krieg und Frieden im Mittelalter.* Beck'sche Reihe, 1226. Munich: C.H. Beck, 1997.

Oman, Sir Charles W.C. "The Art of War in the Fifteenth Century." In: *Cambridge Medieval History.* Cambridge: Cambridge University Press, 1936, VIII:646-59.

Oman, Sir Charles W.C. *The Art of War in the Middle Ages A.D. 378-1515.* Rev. and ed. J.H. Beeler. Ithaca: Cornell University Press, 1953.

Oman, Sir Charles W.C. *A History of the Art of War in the Middle Ages.* 2 vols. London: Methuen, 1924; rpt. London: Greenhill Books, 1998.

Painter, Sidney. "Castle-Guard," *American Historical Review* 40 (1934-35), 450-59.

Peyer, Hans Conrad. "Der Einfluss der Alpen auf die Strategie im Früh- und Hochmittelalter (8.-13. Jahrhundert)," *Revue internationale d'histoire militaire* 65 (1988), 57-76.

Porter, Pamela. "The Ways of War in Medieval Manuscript Illumination: Tracing and Assessing the Evidence." In: *Armies, Chivalry and Warfare in Medieval Britain and France: Proceedings of the 1995 Harlaxton Symposium.* Ed. M. Strickland. Stamford, 1998, pp. 100-14.

Puddu, R. *Eserciti e monarchie nazionale nei secoli XV-XVI.* Florence, 1975.

Puddu, R. "Istituzioni militari, società e stato tra medioevo e rinascimento," *Rivista storico Italiana* 87 (1975), 749-69.

Rautenberg, W. "Ritter und Rotten: Zur begrifflichen und funktionalen Unterscheidung des geworbenen Kriegsvolkes," *Jahrbuch der Gesellschaft für niedsächsissche Kirchengeschichte* 76 (1978), 87-121.

Raynaud, Christiane. "L'imaginaire de la guerre dans l'histoire du bon roi Alexandre (ms 456 de la collection Dutuit)," *Bulletin des sociétés d'histoire et d'archéologie de la Meuse* 28-29 (1992-93), 61-80.

Razin, A.E. *Geschichte der Kriegskunst.* II: *Die Kriegskunst der Feudalperiode des Krieges.* Berlin, 1960.

Razin, A.E. "Le langage de la violence dans les enluminures des *Grandes chroniques de France* dites de Charles V," *Journal of Medieval History* 17 (1991), 149-70.

Robards, Brooks. *The Medieval Knight at War.* London: Tiger Books International, 1997.

Robinson, H. Russell. "Warfare in the Late Middle Ages." In: *The Battle of Barnet Quincentenary, 1471-1971: Commemorative Brochure.* Ed. D. Hicks. Barnet, 1971, pp. 10-12, 27.

Sablonier, Roger. "Rittertum, Adel und Kriegswesen im Spätmittelalter." In: *Das ritterliche Turnier im Mittelalter.* Ed. Josef Fleckenstein. Göttingen: Vandenhoeck and Ruprecht, 1985, pp. 532-70.

Sander, Erich. "Der Belagerungskrieg im Mittelalter," *Historische Zeitschrift* 165 (1941), 99-110.

Scales, Len. "Medieval Barbarism?" *History Today* 49.10 (Oct 1999), 42-44.

Schaufelberger, Walter. "Montales et bestiales, homines sine domino: Der alpine Beitrag zum Kriegwesen in der spätmittelalterlichen Eidgenossenschaft," *Revue internationale d'histoire militaire* 65 (1988), 105-32.

Schmidtchen, Volker. *Kriegswesen im späten Middelalter: Technik, Taktik, Theorie*. Weinheim: VCH Verlagsgesellschaft mbH/Acta Humaniora, 1984.

Schneider, Hugo. *Adel-Burgen-Waffen*. Berne: Francke Verlag, 1967.

Showalter, Dennis E. "Caste, Skill, and Training: The Evolution of Cohesion in European Armies from the Middle Ages to the Sixteenth Century," *Journal of Military History* 57 (1993), 407-30.

Small, Carola M. "Review Article–Warfare in Later Middle Ages," *Canadian Journal of History* 31 (1996), 413-18.

Sonderegger, Stefan. "Der Kampf an der Letzi: Zur Typologie des spätmittelalterlichen Abwehrkampfes im Bereich von voralpinen Landwehren," *Revue internationale d'histoire militaire* 65 (1988), 77-90.

Spaulding, Oliver Lyman and Hoffman Nickerson. *Ancient and Medieval Warfare*. London: Constable, 1994.

Sprömberg, H. "Die Feudale Kriegskunst." In: *Beiträge zur belgische-niederländischen Geschichte*. Berlin, 1959, pp. 30-55.

Strickland, Debra Higgs. "Monsters and Christian Enemies," *History Today* 50.2 (Feb 2000), 45-51.

Tilly, Charles. *Coercion, Capital, and the European States, AD 990-1990*. Oxford: Blackwell, 1990.

Udwin, Victor Morris. *Between Two Armies*. Leiden: E.J. Brill, 1999.

Vale, Malcolm. *War and Chivalry: Warfare and Aristocratic Culture in England, France and Burgundy at the End of the Middle Ages*. Athens: University of Georgia Press, 1981.

van Leeuwen, C.G. "Denkbeelden van politieke adviseurs in de late middeleeuwen over het probleem van oorlog en vrede." In: *Oorlog in de middeleeuwen*. Ed. A.J. Brand. Hilversum, 1989, pp. 125-40.

Verbruggen, J.F. "L'art militaire en Europe occidentale du IXe au XIVe siècle," *Revue internationale d'histoire militaire* 16 (1955), 486-96.

Verbruggen, J.F. *The Art of Warfare in Western Europe During the Middle Ages from the Eighth Century to 1340.* Trans. S. Willard and S.C.M. Southern. Amsterdam: North-Holland Publishing Company, 1977.

Verbruggen, J.F. *The Art of Warfare in Western Europe During the Middle Ages from the Eighth Century to 1340.* 2nd ed. Trans. S. Willard and R.W. Southern. Woodbridge: The Boydell Press, 1997.

Verbruggen, J.F. *De krijgkunst in west-Europa in de middeleeuwen (IXe tot XIVe eeuw).* Brussels: Paleis der Academiën, 1954.

Vones, Ludwig. "Un mode de résolution des conflits au bas Moyen Âge: le duel des princes." In: *La guerre, la violence et les gens au Moyen Âge.* I: *Guerre et violence.* Ed. P. Contamine and O. Guyotjeannin. 119e congrès national des sociétés historiques et scientifiques, Amiens, octobre 1994, Section d'histoire médiévale et philologie. Paris, 1996, pp. 321-32.

Wackernagel, H.G. *Kriegsbräuche in der mittelalterlichen Eidgenossenschaft.* Basel, 1934.

Wise, Terence. *Medieval European Armies.* London: Osprey Publishing Limited, 1975.

Wise, Terence. *Medieval Warfare.* New York, 1976.

Medieval – Barbarian Invasions

Al-Azmeh, Aziz. "Barbarians in Arab Eyes," *Past and Present* 134 (Feb 1992), 3-18.

Anderson, Thomas, Jr. "Roman Military Colonies in Gaul, Salian Ethnogenesis and the Forgotten Meaning of *Pactus legis salicae* 59.5," *Early Medieval Europe* 4 (1995), 129-44.

Angermann, H. *Ausweitung des Kampfgeschehens und psychologische Kriegführung im früheren Mittelalter.* Wurzburg, 1971.

Bachrach, Bernard S. "The Alans in Gaul," *Traditio* 23 (1967), 476-89.

Bachrach, Bernard S. *The Anatomy of a Little War: A Diplomatic and Military History of the Gundovald Affair (568-586).* Boulder: Westview Press, 1994.

Bachrach, Bernard S. "Another Look at the Barbarian Settlement in Southern Gaul," *Traditio* 25 (1963), 354-58.

Bachrach, Bernard S. "The Education of the 'Officer Corps' in the Fifth and Sixth Centuries." In: *La noblesse romaine et les chefs barbares du IIIe au VIIe siècle*. Ed. Françoise Vallet and Michel Kazanski. Rouen: Association Française d'archéologie merovingienne/Musée des antiquités nationales, 1995, pp. 7-13.

Bachrach, Bernard S. "Grand Strategy in the Germanic Kingdoms: Recruitment of the Rank and File." In: *L'armée romaine et les barbares du IIIe au VIIe siècle*. Ed. Françoise Vallet and Michel Kazanski. Rouen: Association Française d'archéologie merovingienne/Musée des antiquités nationales, 1993, pp. 55-63.

Bachrach, Bernard S. "The Hun Army at the Battle of Chalons (451): An Essay in Military Demography." In: *Ethnogenese und Überlieferung: Angewandte Methoden der Frühmittelalterforschung*. Ed. Karl Brunner and Brigitte Merta. Vienna: Oldenbourg, 1994, pp. 59-67.

Bachrach, Bernard S. "The Imperial Roots of Merovingian Military Organization." In: *Military Aspects of Scandinavian Society in a European Perspective, AD. 1-1300*. Ed. A.N. Jørgensen and B. Clausen. Copenhagen, 1997, pp. 25-31.

Bachrach, Bernard S. "Logistics in Pre-Crusade Europe." In: *Feeding Mars: Logistics in Western Warfare from the Middle Ages to the Present*. Ed. J.A. Lynn. Boulder, 1993, pp. 57-79.

Bachrach, Bernard S. *Merovingian Military Organization, 481-751*. Minneapolis: University of Minnesota Press, 1972.

Bachrach, Bernard S. "A Picture of Avar-Frankish Warfare from a Carolingian Psalter of the Early Ninth Century in Light of the *Strategicum*," *Archivum eurasiae medii aevi* 4 (1986), 5-27.

Bachrach, Bernard S. "Procopius, Agathias and the Frankish Military," *Speculum* 45 (1970), 435-41.

Bachrach, Bernard S. "Some Observations on the 'Goths' at War," *Francia* 19 (1992), 205-14.

Barnwell, P. "War and Peace: Historiography and Seventh-Century Embassies," *Early Medieval Europe* 6 (1997), 127-39.

Bernet, Anne. *Clovis*. Lyon: LUGD, 1996

Bertolini, O. "Ordinamenti militari e strutture sociali dei Longobardi in Italia." In: *Ordinamenti militari in occidente nell'alto medioevo*. Settimane di studio del centro italiano di studi sull'alto medioevo, XV. Spoleto, 1968, I:429-607.

Bíró, Margit. "On the Presence of the Huns in the Caucasus: To the Chronology of the 'Ovs' Raid Mentioned in Juanšer's Chronicle," *Acta orientalia academiae scientarum Hungaricarum* 50 (1997), 53-60.

Blockley, Roger C. "Ammianus Marcellinus on the Battle of Strassburg: Art and Analysis in the *History,*" *Phoenix* 31 (1977), 218-31.

Bodmer, J.P. *Der Krieger der Merowingerzeit und seine Welt*. Zurich, 1957.

Bognetti, G.P. "L'influsso delle istituzioni militari romane sulle istituzioni longobardo del secolo VI e la natura della fara." In: *Atti del congresso internazionale di diritto romano e di storia del diritto, Verona 27-29 settembre 1948*. Milan, 1953, pp. 167-210.

Burns, Thomas S. *Barbarians Within the Gates of Rome: A Study of Roman Military Policy and the Barbarians, ca. 375-425 A.D.* Bloomington: Indiana University Press, 1994.

Burns, Thomas S. "The Battle of Adrianople: A Reconsideration," *Historia* 22 (1973), 336-45.

Burns, Thomas S. *A History of the Ostrogoths*. Bloomington: Indiana University Press, 1984.

Bury, J.B. *The Invasion of Europe By the Barbarians*. New York: W.W. Norton and Company, Inc., 1967.

Cameron, Averil. "Agathias on the Early Merovingians," *Annali della scuola normale superiore di Pisa* 37 (1968), 95-140.

Cameron, Averil. "Agathias on the Sassasians," *Dumbarton Oaks Papers* 23/24 (1969/70), 69-183.

Carnap-Bornheim, Claus von. "Zur Bedeutung der militärischen Seefahrt bei den Barbaren im 3. Jahrhundert n. Chr.–Skandinavien, die Nordsee und das Schwarze Meer." In: *Military Aspects of Scandinavian Society in a European Perspective, AD. 1-1300.* Ed. A.N. Jørgensen and B. Clausen. Copenhagen, 1997, pp. 226-38.

Chevallier, Béatrice. *Clovis, un roi européen.* Turnhout: Brépols, 1996.

Christie, Neil. *The Lombards: The Ancient Longobards.* Oxford: Blackwell, 1995.

Christie, Neil. "Longobard Weaponry and Warfare, A.D. 1-800," *Journal of Roman Military Equipment* 2 (1991), 1-26.

Claude, D. *Adel, Kirche und Königtum im Westgotenreich.* Sigmaringen, 1971.

Clover, Frank M. "A Game of Bluff: The Fate of Sicily after AD 476," *Historia* 48 (1999), 235-44.

Clover, Frank M. *The Late Roman West and the Vandals.* London, 1993.

Dallais, Francis. *Clovis ou le combat de gloire.* London: PSR Editions, 1996.

Demougeot, Émilienne. *La formation de l'Europe et les invasions barbares.* 2 vols. Paris, 1979.

Drinkwater, John F. "Julian and the Franks and Valentinian I and the Alemanni: Ammianus on Romano-German Relations," *Francia* 24/1 (1997), 1-15.

Durliat, Jean. "Le polyptyque d'Irminon pour l'armée," *Bibliothèque de l'école des chartes* 141 (1983), 183-208.

Durliat, Jean. "Le salaire de la paix sociale dans les royaumes barbares (Ve-VIe siècle)." In: *Anerkennung und Integration: zu den wirtschaftlichen Grundlagen der Völkerwanderungszeit 400-600: Berichte des Symposions der Kommission für Frühmittelalterforschung, 7. bis 9. mai 1986, Stiftzwettl, Niederösterreich.* Ed. Herwig Wolfram and Andreas Schwarcz. Vienna: Verlag der Österreichischen Akademie der Wissenschaften, 1988, pp. 21-72.

Engström, Johan. "Det vendeltida rytteriet," *Meddelande* 54 (1994), 9-34.

Fauber, L.H. *Narses: Hammers of the Goths*. London, 1990.

Ferrill, Arther. *The Fall of the Roman Empire: A Military Explanation*. London: Thames and Hudson, 1986.

Fouracre, Paul. *The Age of Charles Martel*. Harlow: Longman, 2000.

Frauenholz, E von. *Entwicklungsgeschichte des deutsche Heerwesens*. 3 vols. Munich1935-37.

Gamber, Ortwin. "Studien zum Wehrgehänge des Frühmittelalters," *Waffen- und Köstumkunde* 33 (1991), 1-14.

Garlan, Yvon. "Cités, armées et stratégie à l'époque hellénistique d'après l'oeuvre de Philon de Byzance," *Historia* 22 (1973), 16-33.

Gasparini, F. "Le armi dei Langobardi," *Diana armi*. 4/2 (1991), 96-97.

Goffart, Walter. *Barbarians and Romans, A.D. 418-584: The Techniques of Accommodation*. Princeton, 1980.

Goffart, Walter. "The Map of the Barbarian Invasions: A Longer Look." In: *The Culture of Christendom: Essays in Medieval History in Commemoration of Denis L.T. Bethell*. Ed. M.A. Meyer. London, 1993, pp. 1-27.

Halsall, G.S. *Warfare and Society in the Barbarian West, c. 450-900*. London, 1998.

Hannestad, Knud. "Les forces militaires d'après la guerre gothique de Procope," *Classica et mediaevalia* 21 (1960), 136-83.

Harmatta, J. "The Dissolution of the Hun Empire: Hun Society in the Age of Attila," *Acta archaeologica scientarum Hungaricae* 2 (1952).

Heather, Peter J. *The Goths*. Oxford: Blackwell, 1996.

Heather, Peter J. *Goths and Romans, 332-489*. Oxford: Clarendon Press, 1991.

Heather, Peter J. "The Huns and the End of the Roman Empire in Western Europe," *English Historical Review* 110 (1995), 9-41.

Heather, Peter J. "Theodoric, king of the Goths," *Early Medieval Europe* 4 (1995), 145-73.

Hildesheimer, E. *L'activité militaire des clercs à l'époque franque*. Paris, 1936.

Holland, Cecelia. "Tours: Medieval Battle Reconsidered," *MHQ: The Quarterly Journal of Military History* 11 (Winter 1999), 50-59.

Innes, M. "Franks and Slavs, c. 700-1000: The Problem of European Expansion before the Millennium," *Early Medieval Europe* 6 (1997), 201-16.

James, Edward. "The Militarisation of Roman Society." In: *Military Aspects of Scandinavian Society in a European Perspective, AD. 1-1300*. Ed. A.N. Jørgensen and B. Clausen. Copenhagen, 1997, pp. 19-24.

Jarnut, J. "Beobachtungen zur den langobardischen *Arimanni* und *Exercitales*," *Zeitschrift der Savigny-Stiftung für Rechtgeschichte, Germanischen Abteilung* 88 (1971), 1-28.

Jørgensen, Lars, Kurt W. Alt, and Werner Vach. "Families at Kirchheim am Ries: Analysis of Merovingian Aristocratic and Warrior Families." In: *Military Aspects of Scandinavian Society in a European Perspective, AD. 1-1300*. Ed. A.N. Jørgensen and B. Clausen. Copenhagen, 1997, pp. 103-12.

King, Charles. "The Veracity of Ammianus Marcellinus' Description of the Huns," *American Journal of Ancient History* 12 (1987 for1995), 77-95.

Laforest, Michèle. *Clovis, un roi de légende*. Paris: Albin Michel, 1996.

Lebecq, Stéphane. "Francs contre Frisons (VIe-VIIIe siècle)." In: *La guerre et la paix: Frontières et violences au moyen âge*. Actes du 101e congrès national des sociétés savantes, Lille, 1976. Paris: Bibliothèque Nationale, 1978, pp. 53-71.

Le Jan-Hennebicque, Régine. "Satellites et bandes armées dans le monde franc (VIIe-Xe siècles)." In: *Le combattant au moyen âge*. 2nd ed. Histoire ancienne et médiévale, 36. Paris: Publications of the Sorbonne, 1990, pp. 97-109.

Lindner, R.P. "Nomadism, Horses, and Huns," *Past and Present* 92 (1981), 3-19.

Lot, Ferdinand. *The End of the Ancient World and the Beginnings of the Middle Ages*. New York: Harper and Row, 1961.

Maenchen-Helfen, O. "The Legends of the Origins of the Huns," *Byzantion* 17 (1944-45), 244-51.

Maenchen-Helfen, O. "Huns and Hsiung-Nu," *Byzantion* 17 (1944-45), 222-43.

Maenchen-Helfen, O. *The World of the Huns*. London, 1973.

Mesnil, Commandant du. "Un guerrier Franc exhumé dans l'Orne," *Revue historique des armées* 2.2 (1946), 97-101.

Mestrallet, Eric. *Clovis ou les origines de la France*. Paris: Fagot du Maurien, 1996.

Moorhead, John. *Theodoric in Italy*. Oxford, 1992.

Mussot-Goulard, Renée. *Clovis*. Paris: Presses Universitaires de France, 1997.

Nathan, Geoffrey. "The Last Emperor: The Fate of Romulus Augustulus," *Classica et mediaevalia* 43 (1992), 261-71.

Oakeshott, Ewart. *Dark Age Warrior*. London, 1974.

Patlagean, Evelyne. "Les armes et la cité à Rome du VIIe au XIe siècle, et le modèle européen des trois fonctions sociales," *Mélanges de l'Ecole français de Rome* 86 (1974), 25-62.

Reuter, Timothy. "The Recruitment of Armies in the Early Middle Ages: What Can We Know?" In: *Military Aspects of Scandinavian Society in a European Perspective, AD. 1-1300*. Ed. A.N. Jørgensen and B. Clausen. Copenhagen, 1997, pp. 32-47.

Roma, Giuseppe. "Sulle Tracce del *limes* longobardo in Calabria," *Mélanges de l'école françaises de Rome: Moyen âge* 110 (1998), 7-27.

Rouche, Michel. *L'Aquitaine des Wisigoths aux Arabes, 418-781: Naissance d'une région*. Paris, 1979.

Rouche, Michel. *Clovis*. Paris, 1996.

Sánchez-Albornoz, C. "La caballeria visigoda." In: *Wirtschaft und Kultur: Festschrift zum 70 Geburtstag von Alfons Dopsch*. Baden bei Wien and Leipzig, 1938, pp. 92-108.

Sánchez-Albornoz, C. "La perdida de Espana, I: El ejército visigodo: su proto-feudalización," *Cuadernos de historia de España* 43-44 (1967), 5-73.

Setton, Kenneth M. "The Bulgars in the Balkans and the Occupation of Corinth in the Seventh Century," *Speculum* 25 (1950), 502-43.

Sinor, Denis. "The Outlines of Hungarian Prehistory," *Journal of World History* 4 (1958), 513-40.

Steuer, Heiko. "Germanische Heerlager des 4./5. Jahrhunderts in Südwestdeutschland (?)." In: *Military Aspects of Scandinavian Society in a European Perspective, AD. 1-1300*. Ed. A.N. Jørgensen and B. Clausen. Copenhagen, 1997, pp. 113-22.

Steuer, Heiko. "Zur Bewaffnung und Sozialstruktur der Merovingerzeit: Ein Beitrag zur Forschungsmethode," *Nachrichten aus Niedersachsens Urgeschichte* 37 (1968), 18-87.

Theiner, Augustin. *Saint Aignan, ou le siege d'Orléans, par Attila*. Paris, 1832.

Theuws, F.C.W.J. "The Integration of the Kempen Region into the Frankish Empire (550-750): Some Hypotheses," *Helinium* 26 (1986), 121-36.

Thompson, E.A. "Early Germanic Warfare," *Past and Present* 14 (1958), 2-31.

Thompson, E.A. *The Goths in Spain*. Oxford, 1969.

Todd, M. *Everyday Life of the Barbarians: Goths, Franks, and Vandals*. London, 1972.

Tóth, Z. *Attilas Schwert*. Budapest, 1930.

Verbruggen, J.F. "De Franken en hun krijgers onder de Merovingen en Karel Martel," *Genootschap voor geschied- en oudheidkunde te Vilvoorde* 4.1 (Mar 1998), 2-20.

Verbruggen, J.F. "De Franken en hun krijgers onder de opvolgers van Chlodowech," *Genootschap voor geschied- en oudheidkunde te Vilvoorde* 3.4 (Dec 1997), 2-21.

Verbruggen, J.F. "Onze voorouders: de Franken en hun krijgers," *Genootschap voor geschied- en oudheidkunde te Vilvoorde* 3.1 (Mar 1997), 2-21.

Verkamp, Bernard J. "Moral Treatment of Returning Warriors in the Early Middle Ages," *Journal of Religious Ethics* 16 (1988), 223-49.

Vernadsky, G.A. "The Eurasian Nomads and their Impact on Medieval Europe," *Studi medievale* 3rd ser. 4 (1963), 401-34.

Vyronis, Speros, Jr. "The Evolution of Slavic Society and the Slavic Invasions in Greece: The First Major Attack on Thessaloniki, AD 597," *Hesperia* 50 (1981), 378-90.

Wallace-Hadrill, J.M. "War and Peace in the Early Middle Ages," *Transactions of the Royal Historical Society* 5th ser. 25 (1975), 57-74; in: *Early Medieval History*. New York, 1976, pp. 19-37.

Werner, J. *Beiträge zur Archäologie des Attila-Reiches*. Munich, 1956.

Werner, Karl Ferdinand. "La 'Conquête franque' de la Gaule: Itinéraires historiographiques d'une erreur," *Bibliothèque de l'école de chartes* 154 (1996), 7-45.

Werner, Karl Ferdinand. "Conquête franque de la Gaule ou changement de régime?" In: *Vom Frankenreich zur Entfaltung Deutschlands und Frankreichs*. Ed. Karl Ferdinand Werner. Sigmaringen: J. Thorbecke, 1984, pp. 1-11.

White, Stephen D. "Clotild's Revenge: Politics, Kinship, and Ideology in the Merovingian Blood Feud." In: *Portraits of Medieval and Renaissance Living: Essays in Memory of David Herlihy*. Ed. S.K. Cohn Jr. and S.A. Epstein. Ann Arbor, 1996, pp. 107-30.

Wilcox, P. *Rome's Enemies: Germans and Dacians*. London: Osprey, 1982.

Wolfram, Herwig. *History of the Goths*. Trans. Thomas J. Dunlop. Berkeley and Los Angeles: University of California Press, 1988.

Wood, Ian. *The Merovingian Kingdoms, 450-751*. London: Longman, 1994.

Wood, Michael. *In Search of the Dark Ages*. London, 1981.

Woods, David. "The Saracen Defenders of Constantinople in 378," *Greek, Roman and Byzantine Studies* 37 (1996), 259-79.

Medieval – Battle Orations

Bliese, John R.E. "Aelred of Rievaulx's Rhetoric and Morale at the Battle of the Standard, 1138," *Albion* 20 (1988), 543-56.

Bliese, John R.E. "The Battle Rhetoric of Aelred of Rielvaulx," *Haskins Society Journal* 1 (1989), 99-107.

Bliese, John R.E. "The Courage of the Normans. A Comparative Study of Battle Rhetoric," *Nottingham Medieval Studies* 35 (1991), 1-26.

Bliese, John R.E. "Fighting Spirit and Literary Genre: A Comparison of Battle Exhortations in the *Song of Roland* and in Chronicles of the Central Middle Ages," *Neuphilologische Mitteilungen* 96 (1995), 417-36.

Bliese, John R.E. "Leadership, Rhetoric, and Morale in the Norman Conquest of England," *Military Affairs* 52 (1988), 23-28.

Bliese, John R.E. "Rhetoric and Morale: A Study of Battle Orations from the Central Middle Ages," *Journal of Medieval History* 15 (1989), 201-26.

Bliese, John R.E. "When Knightly Courage May Fail: Battle Orations in Medieval Europe," *Historian* 53 (1991), 489-504.

Medieval – Booty

Allmand, Christopher T. "War and Profit in the Late Middle Ages," *History Today* 15 (1965), 762-69.

Hay, Denys. "Booty in Border Warfare," *Transactions of the Dumfriesshire and Galloway Natural History and Antiquarian Society* 3rd ser. 31 (1954), 145-66; in: *Renaissance Essays*. London, 1988, pp. 285-306.

Hay, Denys. "The Divisions of the Spoils of War in Fourteenth-Century England," *Transactions of the Royal Historical Society* 5th ser. 4 (1954), 91-109; in: *Renaissance Essays*. London, 1988, pp. 265-83.

McFarlane, K.B. "The Investment of Sir John Fastolf's Profits of War." In: *England in the Fifteenth Century: Collected Essays*. London, 1981, pp. 175-98.

Veitch, John M. "Repudiations and Confiscations by the Medieval State," *Journal of Economic History* 46 (1982), 31-36.

Medieval – Bouvines (battle of)

Baldwin, John W. "Le sens de Bouvines," *Cahiers de civilisation médiévale (X-XIIe siècles)* 30 (1987), 119-30.

Ballhausen, Carl. *Die Schlacht bei Bouvines, 27. Juli 1214*. Jena: Anton Kämpfe, 1907.

Cartellieri, Alexander. *Die Schlacht bei Bouvines (27. Juli 1214) im Rahmen der europäischen Politik*. Leipzig: Dykschen Buchhandlung, 1914.

Coulson, Charles L.H. "The Impact of Bouvines upon the Fortress-Policy of Philip Augustus." In: *Studies in Medieval History Presented to R. Allen Brown*. Ed. C. Harper-Bill et al. Woodbridge, 1989, pp. 71-80.

Derville, Alain. "La bataille de Bouvines (27 juillet 1214)," *Pays de Pévèle* 22 (1986), 4-8.

Duby, Georges. *27 juillet 1214: Le dimanche de Bouvines*. Paris: Gallimard, 1973; trans. *The Legend of Bouvines: War, Religion and Culture in the Middle Ages*. Trans. Catherine Tihanyi. Berkeley and Los Angeles: University of California Press, 1990.

Dufeil, Michel-Marie. "Leuctures et Bouvines, réflexions générales." In: *Commission internationale d'histoire militaire*. Acta 6: *Montpeillier 2-6 IX 1981*. Montpellier: Commission Française d'Histoire Militaire, 1983, I:55-76.

Hadengue, Antoine. *Bouvines, victoire créatrice*. Paris: Plon, 1935.

Hiestand, Rudolf. "Von Bouvines nach Segni: Zwei Texte zur Geschichte Philipps II. Augustus," *Francia* 22/1 (1995), 59-78.

Hughes, Shaun F.D. "The Battle of Stamford Bridge and the Battle of Bouvines," *Scandinavian Studies* 60 (1988), 30-76.

Maille, Christian. "Le site de Bouvines," *Pays de Pévèle* 22 (1986), 2-3.

Verbruggen, J.F. "Le problème des effectifs et de la tactique à la bataille de Bouvines (1214)," *Revue du nord* 31 (1949), 181-93.

Victoire de Bouvines (1214), La: Une des batailles les plus importantes de l'histoire de France. Bouvines: Les amis de Bouvines, 1998.

Medieval – Byzantium [See also Medieval/Early Modern – Ottoman Turkish Wars – Fall of Constantinople]

Ahweiler, H. *Byzance et le mer: la marine de guerre, la politique et les institutions maritimes de Byzance aux VIIe-XVe siècles*. Paris: Presses Universitaires de France, 1966.

Alexander, S.S. "Heraclius, Byzantine Imperial Ideology and the David Plates," *Speculum* 52 (1977), 217-37.

André, P.J. "Occupation Byzantine et Turque en Afrique du nord," *Revue internationale d'histoire militaire* 13 (1953), 17-24.

Angold, Michael A. "The Byzantine State on the Eve of the Battle of Manzikert," *Byzantinische Forschungen* 16 (1991), 9-34.

Antonucci, Michael. "Siege Without Reprieve," *Military History* (April 1992), 42-49.

Arutyunova-Fidanyan, Viada A. "Some Aspects of the Military-Administrative Districts and of Byzantine Administration in Armenia during the 11th Century," *Revue de études arméniennes* n.s. 20 (1986-87), 309-20.

Arvites, J.A. "The Defence of Byzantine Anatolia during the Reign of Irene (780-802)." In: *Armies and Frontiers in Roman and Byzantine Anatolia*. Ed. S. Mitchell. Bar International Reports, 156. Oxford: BAR, 1983, pp. 219-37.

Bartusis, Mark C. "The *Kavallarioi* of Byzantium," *Speculum* 63 (1988), 343-50.

Bartusis, Mark C. *The Late Byzantine Army: Arms and Society, 1204-1453*. Philadelphia: University of Pennsylvania Press, 1992.

Benedikz, B.S. "The Evolution of the Varangian Regiment in the Byzantine Army," *Byzantinische Zeitschrift* 62 (1969), 20-25.

Bivar, A.D.H. "Cavalry, Equipment and Tactics on the Euphrates Frontier," *Dumbarton Oaks Papers* 26 (1972), 271-91.

Blöndel, Sigfús. *The Varangians of Byzantium*. Trans. B.S. Benedicz. Cambridge, 1978.

Bonner, Michael. *Aristocratic Violence and Holy War: Studies in the Jihad and the Arab-Byzantine Frontier*. American Oriental Series, 81. New Haven: American Oriental Society, 1996.

Bosworth, C.E. "The City of Tarsus and the Arab-Byzantine Frontiers in Early and Middle Abbasid Times," *Oriens* 33 (1992), 268-86.

Brand, Charles M. *Byzantium Confronts the West*. Cambridge, 1968.

Brown, T.S. *Gentlemen and Officers: Imperial Administration and Aristocratic Power in Byzantine Italy, AD 554-800*. London: British School at Rome, 1984.

Brown, T.S. "Settlement and Military Policy in Byzantine Italy." In: *Papers in Italian Archaeology, I: The Lancaster Seminar: Recent Research in Prehistoric, Classical, and Medieval Archaeology*. Ed. H.M. Blake, T.W. Potter, and D.B. Whitehouse. Oxford: British Archaeological Reports, 1978, II:323-38.

Browning, R. *Byzantine and Bulgaria: A Comparative Study Across the Early Medieval Frontier*. London, 1975.

Cahen, Claude. "La diplomatie orientale de Byzance face à la pousée seldjukide," *Byzantion* 35 (1965), 10-15.

Cameron, Averil. "Agathias on the Sassasians," *Dumbarton Oaks Papers* 23/24 (1969/70), 69-183.

Canard, M. "Le céremonial Fatamite et le céremonial Byzantin," *Byzantion* 21 (1951), 355-420.

Canard, M. "Les expeditions des Arabes contre Constantinople dans l'histoire et dans la légende," *Journal asiatique* 208 (1926), 61-121.

Carrié, Jean-Michel. "L'état à la recherche de nouveaux modes de financement des armées (Rome et Byzance, IVe-VIIIe siècles)." In: *The Byzantine and Early Islamic Near East. III: States, Resources and Armies*. Ed. Averil Cameron. Studies in Late Antiquity and Early Islam, 1. Princeton: The Darwin Press, Inc., 1995, pp. 27-60.

Casey, P.J. "Justinian, the *limitanei*, and Arab-Byzantine Relations in the 6th Century," *Journal of Roman Archaeology* 9 (1996), 214-22.

Cheynet, Jean-Claude. "Les effectifs de l'armée byzantine aux Xe-XIIe s.," *Cahiers de civilisation médiévale (X-XIIe siècles)* 38 (1995), 319-54.

Crow, J.G. "The Long Walls of Thrace." In: *Constantinople and Its Hinterland*. Ed. C. Mango and G. Dagron. Aldershot: Ashgate, 1995, pp. 109-24.

Dagron, Gilbert. "Ceux d'en face: les peuples étrangers dans les traités militaires byzantins," *Travaux et mémoires* 10 (1987), 207-32.

Dagron, Gilbert. "Le combattant Byzantin à la frontière du Taurus: guérilla et société frontalière." In: *Le combattant au moyen âge*. 2nd ed. Histoire ancienne et médiévale, 36. Paris: Publications de la Sorbonne, 1995, pp. 37-43.

Dagron, Gilbert. "Guérilla, places fortes et villages ouverts à la frontière orientale de Byzance vers 950." In: *Castrum 3: Guerre, fortification et habitant dans le monde méditerranéen au moyen âge*. Ed. André Bazzana. Rome: L'école Française de Rome, 1988, pp. 43-48.

Dain, Alphonse. "Les stratégistes byzantins," *Travaux et mémoires* 2 (1967), 317-92.

Dain, Alphonse. *La tactique de Nicéphore Ouranos*. Paris, 1937.

Darko, E. "La tactique Touranienne," *Byzantion* 10 (1935), 443-69; 12 (1937), 119-47.

Dedeyan, Gérard. "La contribution des arméniens à l'effort de guerre de Byzance (IVe-XIe siècle)." In: *Commission internationale d'histoire militaire. Acta 6: Montpeillier 2-6 IX 1981.* Montpellier: Commission Française d'Histoire Militaire, 1983, I: 31-54.

De Foucault, J.-A. "Douze chapitres inédits de la tactique de Nicéphore Ouranos," *Travaux et mémoires* 5 (1973), 281-311.

Dennis, George T. "Byzantine Battle Flags," *Byzantinische forschungen* 8 (1982), 51-60.

Dennis, George T. "The Byzantine-Turkish Treaty of 1403," *Orientalia christiana periodica* 33 (1967), 72-88.

Dennis, George T. "The Byzantines in Battle." In: *To empolemo Byzantio/Byzantine at War.* Ed. N. Oikonomidès. Athens: National Research Foundation, 1997, pp. 165-78.

Dennis, George T. "The Capture of Thebes by the Navarrese (6 March 1378) and Other Chronological Notes in Two Paris Manuscripts," *Orientalia christiana periodica* 26 (1960), 42-50.

Dennis, George T, ed. *Three Byzantine Military Treatises.* Washington: Dumbarton Oaks, 1985.

Diehl, C. *L'Afrique Byzantine: Histoire de la domination Byzantine (533-709).* Paris, 1896.

Dimnik, Martin. *Mikhail, Prince of Chernigov and Grand Prince of Kiev, 1224-1246.* Toronto: Pontifical Institute of Mediaeval Press, 1981.

Dölger, F. "Die Chronologie des grossen Feldzuges des Kaisers Johannes Tzimiskes gegen die Russen," *Byzantinische Zeitschrift* 32 (1932), 275-92.

Ducellier, A. *L'Albanie entre Byzance et Venise (Xe-XVe siècle).* London, 1987.

Durrieu, Comte L. "La déliverance de la Gréce projetée en France à la France du quinzième siècle," *Revue d'histoire diplomatique* 26 (1912), 333-51.

Eddé, Anne-Marie and Françoise Micheau. "Sous les murailles d'Alep: assaillants et défenseurs de 351/962 à 658/1260." In: *Le combattant au moyen âge.* 2nd ed. Histoire ancienne et médiévale, 36. Paris: Publications de la Sorbonne, 1995, pp. 63-72.

Evert-Kappesowa, H. "La tiare ou le turban," *Byzantinoslavica* 14 (1953), 245-57.

Farag, W.E. "The Aleppo Question: A Byzantine-Fatamid Conflict of Interests in Northern Syria in the Later Tenth Century A.D.," *Byzantine and Modern Greek Studies* 14 (1990), 44-60.

Fatouros, Georgios. "Bessarion und Libanios: Ein typischer Fall byzantinischer Mimesis," *Jahrbuch der Österreichischen Byzantinistik* 49 (1999), 191-209.

Forrer, Robert. "Archäologisches und Technisches zu der byzantinischen Feuerwaffe des cod. Vat. 1605 vom 11. Jahrhundert," *Zeitschrift für historisches Waffenkunde* 5 (1909-11), 115-22.

Geanakoplos, D.J. "Greco-Latin Relations on the Eve of the Byzantine Restoration: The Battle of Pelagonia, 1259," *Dumbarton Oaks Papers* 7 (1953), 99-141.

Godfrey, John. "The Defeated Anglo-Saxons Take Service with the Eastern Emperor," *Proceedings of the Battle Conference on Anglo-Norman Studies* 1 (1978), 63-74.

Goubert, O. *Byzance avant l'Islam.* 2 vols. Paris, 1951, 1965.

Greatrex, Geoffrey. "Flavius Hypatius, *quem vidit validum Parthus sensitque timendum*: An Investigation of his Career," *Byzantion* 66 (1996), 120-42.

Greatrex, Geoffrey. "Procopius and Agathias on the Defences of the Thracian Chersonese." In: *Constantinople and Its Hinterland.* Ed. C. Mango and G. Dagron. Aldershot: Ashgate, 1995, pp. 125-29.

Grunzweig, Armand. "Philippe le Bon et Constantinople," *Byzantion* 24 (1954), 47-61.

Guilland, R. "Les appels de Constantin XI Paleologue à Rome et à Venise pour sauver Constantinople (1452-1453)," *Byzantinoslavica* 14 (1953), 226-44.

Haldon, John F. "Administrative Continuities and Structural Transformations in East Roman Military Organisation, c. 580-640." In: *State, Army and Society in Byzantium: Approaches to Military, Social, and Administrative History*. Aldershot: Variorum, no. 5.

Haldon, John F. "The Army and the Economy: The Allocation and Redistribution of Surplus Wealth in the Byzantine State," *Mediterranean Historical Review* 7 (1992), 133-53.

Haldon, John F. *Byzantine Praetorians: An Administrative, Institutional and Social Survey of the Opsikion and Tagmata, c. 580-900*. Poikila Byzantina, 3. Bonn: Habelt, 1984.

Haldon, John F. "The Byzantine World." In: *War and Society in the Ancient and Medieval Worlds: Asia, the Mediterranean, Europe, and Mesoamerica*. Ed. Kurt Raaflaub and Nathan Rosenstein. Washington: Center for Hellenic Studies, 1999, pp. 241-70.

Haldon, John F. "Chapters II, 44 and 45 of *De cerimoniis*: Theory and Practice in Tenth-Century Military Administration," *Travaux et mémoires* 13 (1999).

Haldon, John F. "Ideology and Social Change in the Seventh Century: Military Discontent as a Barometer," *Klio* 68 (1986), 139-90.

Haldon, John F. "Military Administration and Bureaucracy: State Demands and Private Interests," *Byzantinische Forschungen* 19 (1993), 43-63.

Haldon, John F. "Military Service, Military Land and the Status of Soldiers: Current Problems and Interpretations," *Dumbarton Oaks Papers* 47 (1993), 1-67.

Haldon, John F. "The Organisation and Support of an Expeditionary Force: Manpower and Logistics in the Middle Byzantine Period." In: *To empolemo Byzantio/Byzantine at War*. Ed. N. Oikonomidès. Athens: National Research Foundation, 1997, pp. 111-51.

Haldon, John F. *Recruitment and Conscription in the Byzantine Army, c. 550-950: A Study on the Origins of the stratiotika ktemata*. Vienna: Austrian Academy, 1979.

44 MEDIEVAL

Haldon, John F. "Seventh-Century Continuities: the *Ajnād* and the 'Thematic Myth'." In: *The Byzantine and Early Islamic Near East*. III: *States, Resources and Armies*. Ed. Averil Cameron. Studies in Late Antiquity and Early Islam, 1. Princeton: The Darwin Press, Inc., 1995, pp. 379-424.

Haldon, John F. "Strategies of Defence, Problems of Security: The Garrisons of Constantinople in the Middle Byzantine Period." In: *Constantinople and Its Hinterland*. Ed. C. Mango and G. Dagron. Aldershot: Ashgate, 1995, pp. 143-55.

Haldon, John F. *Warfare, State and Society in the Byzantine World, 565-1204*. London: UCL Press, 1999.

Haldon, John F., ed. *Constantine Porphyrogenitus: Three Treatises on Imperial Military Expeditions. Introduction, Edition, Translation, and Commentary*. Corpus fontium historiae Byzantinae, 28. Vienna: Austrian Academy, 1990.

Haldon, John F. and Hugh Kennedy. "The Arab-Byzantine Frontier in the Eighth and Ninth Centuries: Military Organisation and Society in the Borderlands," *Zbornik radova vizantoloskog instituta* 19 (1980), 79-116.

Halton, Thomas. "Ecclesiastical War and Peace in the Letters of Isidore of Pelusium." In: *Peace and War in Byzantinum: Essays in Honor of George T. Dennis, S.J.* Ed. T.S. Miller and J. Nesbitt. Washington, 1995, pp. 41-49.

Hanawalt, Emily Albu. "Scandinavians in Byzantium and Normandy." In: *Peace and War in Byzantium. Essays in Honor of George T. Dennis, S.J.* Ed. T.S. Miller and J. Nesbitt. Washington, 1995, pp. 114-22.

Hogg, Ian. *Byzantine Armies, 886-1118*. London: Osprey, 1979.

Howard-Johnston, James D. "Heraclius' Persian Campaigns and the Revival of the East Roman Empire," *War in History* 6 (1999), 1-44.

Howard-Johnston, James D. "The Siege of Constantinople in 626." In: *Constantinople and Its Hinterland*. Ed. C. Mango and G. Dagron. Aldershot: Ashgate, 1995, pp. 131-42.

Hrochová, Vera. "Byzance et les turcs seljoukides, 1071-1204: Aspects socio-économiques," *Byzantinoslavica* 54 (1993), 142-46.

Ilieva, Annetta. "The Byzantine Image of War and Peace: The Case of the Peloponnese," *Byzantinische Forschungen* 19 (1993), 183-92.

Kaegi, Walter E. "The Byzantine Armies and Iconoclasm," *Byzantinoslavica* 22 (1966), 48-70.

Kaegi, Walter E. "Byzantine Logistics: Problems and Perspectives." In: *Feeding Mars: Logistics in Western Warfare from the Middle Ages to the Present*. Ed. J.A. Lynn. Boulder, 1993, pp. 39-56.

Kaegi, Walter E. *Byzantine Military Unrest, 471-843: An Interpretation*. Amsterdam: Hakkert, 1981.

Kaegi, Walter E. *Byzantium and the Early Islamic Conquests*. Cambridge: Cambridge University Press, 1992.

Kaegi, Walter E. "Challenges to Late Roman and Byzantine Military Operations in Iraq (4th-9th Centuries)," *Klio* 73 (1991), 586-94.

Kaegi, Walter E. "The Controversy about Bureaucratic and Military Factions," *Byzantinische Forschungen* 19 (1993), 25-33.

Kaegi, Walter E. "Initial Byzantine Reactions to the Islamic Conquest," *Church History* 38 (1969).

Kaegi, Walter E. "Patterns of Political Activity of the Armies of the Byzantine Empire." In: *On Military Intervention*. Ed. M. Janowitz and J. van Doorn. Rotterdam, 1971, pp. 4-35.

Kaegi, Walter E. "Two Studies in the Continuity of Late Roman and Byzantine Military Institutions," *Byzantinische Forschungen* 8 (1982), 87-113.

Kalmár, János. "Zur Pester Donausperrkette," *Waffen- und Kostümkunde* 12 (1970), 55-58.

Kaplan, Michel. "La place des soldats dans la société villageoise Byzantine (VIIe-Xe siècles)." In: *Le combattant au moyen âge*. 2nd ed. Histoire ancienne et médiévale, 36. Paris: Publications de la Sorbonne, 1995, pp. 45-55.

Kazhdan, A. "Armenians in the Byzantine Ruling Class: Predominantly in the Ninth and Tenth Centuries." *Medieval Armenian Culture*. Ed. T.J.

Samuelian and M.E. Stone. University of Pennsylvania Armenian Texts and Studies, 6. Chico, 1984, pp. 439-51.

Kennedy, Hugh. "The Last Century of Byzantine Syria: A Reinterpretation" *Byzantinische Forschungen* 10 (1985).

Khoury Odetallah, Rashad. "Leo Tripolites–Ghulam Zurafa and the Sack of Thessaloniki in 904," *Byzantinoslavica* 56 (1995), 97-102.

Kolia-Dermitzaki, A. "Byzantium at War in Sermons and Letters of the 10th and 11th Centuries: An Ideological Approach." In: *To empolemo Byzantio/Byzantine at War*. Ed. N. Oikonomidès. Athens: National Research Foundation, 1997, pp. 213-38.

Kolias, Taxiarchis G. "The Taktica of Leo VI the Wise and the Arabs," *Graeco-Arabica* 3 (1984), 129-35.

Kühn, H.-J. *Die byzantinische Armee im 10. und 11. Jahrhundert: Studien zur Organisation der Tagmata*. Vienna: Fassbaender, 1991.

Langdon, John S. "Byzantium's Initial Encounter with the Chinggisids: An Introduction to the Byzantium-Mongolica," *Viator* 29 (1998), 95-140.

Lewis, Bernard. "Constantinople and the Arabs." In: *The Fall of Constantinople*. London, 1955, pp. 12-17.

Lilie, Ralph-Johannes. *Die Byzantinische Reaktion auf die Ausbreitung der Araber*. Miscellanea Byzantina Monacensia, 22. Munich: Institut für Byzantine und Neogräzistik, 1976.

Lilie, Ralph-Johannes. "Des Kaisers Macht und Ohnmacht: Zum Zerfall der Zentralgewalt in Byzanz vor dem Zweiten Kreuzzug." In: *Varia I: Beiträge von Ralph-Johannes Lilie und Paul Speck*. Poikila Byzantina, 4. Bonn: Habelt, 1984, pp. 9-120.

Lilie, Ralph-Johannes. "Die Schlacht von Myriokephalon, 1176," *Revue des études Byzantines* 35 (1977), 257-77.

Loud, G.A. "Byzantine Italy and the Normans." In: *Byzantium and the West, c. 850-c. 1200*. Ed. J.D. Howard-Johnston. Byzantinische Forschungen, 13. Amsterdam, 1988, pp. 215-33.

Lounghis, T. "The Failure of the German-Byzantine Alliance on the Eve of the First Crusade," *Diptycha* 1 (1979), 158-67.

MacCoull, Leslie S.B. "'When Justinian Was Upsetting the World': A Note on Soldiers and Religious Coercion in Sixth-Century Egypt." In: *Peace and War in Byzantinum: Essays in Honor of George T. Dennis, S.J.* Ed. T.S. Miller and J. Nesbitt. Washington, 1995, pp. 106-13.

Mango, Cyril. "Heraclius, the Threats from the East and Iconoclasm, AD 610-843." In: *Byzantium: An Introduction*. Ed. P. Whitting. Oxford, 1971, pp. 39-59.

McCormick, Michael. *Eternal Victory: Triumphal Rulership in Late Antiquity, Byzantium, and the Early Medieval West*. Cambridge: Cambridge University Press, 1986.

McGeer, Eric. "Byzantine Siege Warfare in Theory and Practice." In: *The Medieval City Under Siege*. Ed. I.A. Corfis and M. Wolfe. Woodbridge, 1995, pp. 123-30.

McGeer, Eric. "Infantry versus Cavalry: The Byzantine Response," *Revue des études byzantins* 46 (1988), 135-45.

McGeer, Eric. "The Legal Decree of Nikephoros II Phokas concerning Armenian *stratiotai*." In: *Peace and War in Byzantinum: Essays in Honor of George T. Dennis, S.J.* Ed. T.S. Miller and J. Nesbitt. Washington, 1995, pp. 123-37.

McGeer, Eric. *Sowing the Dragon's Teeth: Byzantine Warfare in the Tenth Century*. Dumbarton Oaks Studies, 33. Washington: Dumbarton Oaks Research Library and Collection, 1995.

McGeer, Eric. "The *Syntaxis armatorum quadrata*: A Tenth-Century Tactical Blueprint," *Revue des études byzantins* 50 (1992), 219-29.

McGrath, Stamatina. "The Battles of Dorostolon (971): Rhetoric and Reality." In: *Peace and War in Byzantinum: Essays in Honor of George T. Dennis, S.J.* Ed. T.S. Miller and J. Nesbitt. Washington, 1995, pp. 152-64.

McQueen, William B. "Relations between the Normans and Byzantium, 1071-1112," *Byzantion* 56 (1986), 427-76.

Meyendorff, J. *Byzantine and the Rise of Russia*. Cambridge, 1981.

Mill, W. *Trebizond: The Last Greek Empire of the Byzantine Empire, 1204-1461*. Rpt. Chicago, 1969.

Moorhead, John. *Justinian*. London: Longmans, 1994.

Mullett, Margaret. "1098 and All That: Theophylact, Bishop of Semnea and the Alexian Reconquest of Anatolia," *Peritia* 10 (1996), 237-52.

Munitiz, Joseph A. "War and Peace Reflected in Some Byzantine *Mirrors of Princes*." In: *Peace and War in Byzantinum: Essays in Honor of George T. Dennis, S.J.* Ed. T.S. Miller and J. Nesbitt. Washington, 1995, pp. 50-61.

Necipoglu, N. "Economic Conditions in Constantinople during the Siege of Bayezid I (1394-1402)." In: *Constantinople and Its Hinterland*. Ed. C. Mango and G. Dagron. Aldershot: Ashgate, 1995, pp. 157-67.

Nicol, Donald M. *The Despotate of Epirus, 1267-1479*. Cambridge, 1984.

Nicol, Donald M. *The Last Centuries of Byzantium, 1261-1453*. London, 1972.

Nicolle, David C. *Yarmuk, 636 AD: The Muslim Conquest of Syria*. London: Osprey Publishing Limited, 1994.

Nordhagen, Jonas. "Harald og Bysants." In *Harald Hardråde*. Ed. A. Berg. Oslo, 1966, pp. 7-27.

Oikonomides, Nicholas. "The Concept of 'Holy War' and Two Tenth-Century Byzantine Ivories." In: *Peace and War in Byzantinum: Essays in Honor of George T. Dennis, S.J.* Ed. T.S. Miller and J. Nesbitt. Washington, 1995, pp. 62-86.

Oikonomides, Nicholas. *Hommes d'affaires Grecs et Latins à Constantinople (XIIIe-XVe siècles)*. Montreal, 1979.

Oikonomides, Nicholas. "Middle Byzantine Provincial Recruits: Salary and Equipment." In: *GONIMOS: Neoplatonic and Byzantine Studies presented to Leendert G. Westerink at 75*. Buffalo, 1988, pp. 121-36.

Oikonomides, Nicholas. "L'organisation de la frontière orientale de Byzance zux Xe-XIe siècles et le Taktikon de l'Escorial." In: *Actes du XIVe congrès internationale des études Byzantines*. Bucharest, 1974, I:285-302.

Oikonomides, Nicholas. "Tradition and Reality in the *Taktika* of Nikephoros Ouranos," *Dumbarton Oaks Papers* 45 (1991), 129-40.

Ostrogorsky, G. *The History of the Byzantine State*. Oxford, 1968.

Papacostea, Serban. "Byzance et la Croisade au Bas-Danube à la fin du XIVe siècle," *Revue Romaine d'histoire* 30 (1991), 3-21.

Pringle, Denys. *The Defence of Byzantine Africa from Justinian to the Arab Conquest: An Account of the Military History and Archaeology of the African Provinces in the Sixth and Seventh Centuries*. 2 vols. British Archaeological Report, 9. Oxford: BAR, 1981.

Ravegnani, G. *Soldati di Bisanzio in età Giustinianea*. Materiali e ricerche, n.s. 6. Rome: Jouvence, 1988.

Rémondon, R. "Militaires et civils dans une campagne Egyptienne au temps de Constance II," *Journal des savants* (1965), 132-43.

Ross, D.J.A. "The Prince Answers Back: 'Les enseignements de Théodore Paliologue." In: *The Ideals and Practice of Medieval Knighthood*. Ed. C. Harper-Bill and R. Harvey. Woodbridge, 1986, pp. 165-77.

Savvides, Alexis G.C. "Late Byzantine and Western Historiographers on Turkish Mercenaries in Greek and Latin Armies: The Turcoples/Tourkopouloi." In: *The Making of Byzantine History: Studies Dedicated to Donald M. Nicol*. Ed. Roderick Beaton and Charlotte Roueché. Ashgate: Variorum, 1993, pp. 122-36.

Shahid, Irfan. *Byzantium and the Arabs in the Fifth Century*. Washington: Dumbarton Oaks, 1989.

Shahid, Irfan. *Byzantium and the Arabs in the Sixth Century*. Vol 1, pt. 1: *Political and Military History*. Washington: Dumbarton Oaks, 1995.

Shepard, Jonathan. "Aspects of Byzantine Attitudes and Policy towards the West in the Tenth and Eleventh Centuries," In: *Byzantium and the West, c. 850-c. 1200*. Ed. J.D. Howard-Johnston. Byzantinische Forschungen, 13. Amsterdam, 1988, pp. 66-118.

Shepard, Jonathan. "The English and Byzantium: A Study of their Role in the Byzantine Army in the Later Eleventh Century," *Traditio* 29 (1973), 53-92.

Shepard, Jonathan. "Information, Disinformation and Delay in Byzantine Diplomacy," *Byzantinische Forschungen* 10 (1985), 233-93.

Shepard, Jonathan. "The Uses of the Franks in Eleventh-Century Byzantium," *Anglo-Norman Studies* 15 (1993), 275-305.

Shukurov, Rustam. "Between Peace and Hostility: Trebizond and the Pontic Turkish Periphery in the Fourteenth Century," *Mediterranean Historical Review* 9 (1994), 20-72.

Simeonova, Liliana. "In the Depths of Tenth-Century Byzantine Ceremonial: The Treatment of Arab Prisoners of War at Imperial Banquets," *Byzantine and Modern Greek Studies* 22 (1998), 75-104.

Soulis, G.C. *The Serbs and Byzantium during the Reign of Tsar Stephen Dusan*. Washington, 1984.

Strässle, Paul Meinrad. "Krieg, Kriegführung und Gesellschaft in Byzance (9.-12. Jahrhundert)," *Byzantinische Forschungen* 19 (1993), 149-69.

Stratos, Andreas N. "The Avars Attack on Byzantium in the Year 626." In: *Polychordia: Festschrift Franz Dölger zum 75. geburtstag*. Ed. P. Wirth. Amsterdam, 1967, pp. 370-76.

Stratos, Andreas N. *Byzantium in the Seventh Century*. 2 vols. Trans. M. Ogilvie-Grant. Amsterdam, 1968.

Stratos, Andreas N. "The Exarch Olympius and the Supposed Arab Invasion of Sicily in A.D. 652," *Jahrbuch der österreichischen Byzantinistik* 25 (1976), 63-73.

Stratos, Andreas N. "La première campagne de l'empereur Héraclius contre les Perses," *Jahrbuch der österreichischen Byzantinistik* 28 (1979), 63-74.

Stratos, Andreas N. "Siège ou blocus de Constantinople sous Constantin IV," *Jahrbuch der österreichischen Byzantinistik* 33 (1983), 89-107.

Strauss, Barry S. "Victory by Guile: Breaking the Siege of Constantinople," *MHQ: The Quarterly Journal of Military History* 11 (Spring 1999), 104-11.

Sullivan, D. "Tenth-Century Byzantine Offensive Siege Warfare: Instructional Prescriptions and Historical Practice." In: *To empolemo Byzan-*

tio/Byzantine at War. Ed. N. Oikonomidès. Athens: National Research Foundation, 1997, pp. 179-200.

Taft, Robert F. "War and Peace in the Byzantine Divine Liturgy." In: *Peace and War in Byzantinum: Essays in Honor of George T. Dennis, S.J.* Ed. T.S. Miller and J. Nesbitt. Washington, 1995, pp. 17-32.

Teall, John. "The Barbarians in Justinian's Armies," *Speculum* 40 (1965), 294-322.

Teall, John. "Byzantine Urbanism in the Military Handbooks." In: *The Medieval City*. Ed. H.A. Miskimin et al. New Haven, 1977, pp. 201-05.

Toynbee, A. *Constantine Porphyrogentius and His World*. London, 1973.

Trapp, Erich. *Militärs und Höflinge im Ringen um das Kaisertum: Byzantinische Geschichte von 969 bis 1118 nach der Chronik des Johannes Zonaras*. Byzantinische Geschichtsschreiber, 16. Graz: Styria, 1986.

Treadgold, Warren. *Byzantium and Its Army, 284-1081*. Stanford: Stanford University Press, 1995.

Trombley, Frank R. "War and Society in Rural Syria c. 502-613 A.D.: Observations on the Epigraphy," *Byzantine and Modern Greek Street* 21 (1997), 154-207.

Ure, P.N. *Justinian and His Reign*. Harmondsworth: Penguin, 1951.

Vasiliev, Alexander A. *Byzance et les arabes*. 2 vols. Brussels, 1934, 1950.

Vasiliev, Alexander A. *The Russian Attack on Constantinople in 860*. Cambridge: The Mediaeval Academy of America, 1946.

Verlinden, C. "Guerre et traité comme sources de l'esclavage dans l'empire Byzantine au IXème au Xème siècles," *Graeco-Arabica* 5 (1993), 207-12.

Viscuso, Patrick. "Christian Participation in Warfare: A Byzantine View." In: *Peace and War in Byzantinum: Essays in Honor of George T. Dennis, S.J.* Ed. T.S. Miller and J. Nesbitt. Washington, 1995, pp. 33-40.

Vryonis, Speros, Jr. "Byzantine and Turkish Societies and Their Sources of Manpower." In: *War, Technology, and Society in the Middle East*. Ed. V.J. Parry and M.E. Yapp. London: Oxford University Press, 1975, pp. 125-52.

Vryonis, Speros, Jr. "Byzantine Attitudes toward Islam during the Late Middle Ages," *Greek, Roman and Byzantine Studies* 12 (1971), 263-86.

Vryonis, Speros, Jr. "The Byzantine Patriarchate and Turkish Islam," *Byzantinoslavica* 57 (199), I:69-111.

Walker, P.E. "A Byzantine Victory over the Fatamids at Alexandretta (971)," *Byzantion* 42 (1972), 431-40.

Walker, P.E. "The 'Crusade' of John Tzimiskes in the Light of New Arabic Evidence," *Byzantion* 47 (1977), 301-27.

Whitby, Michael. *The Emperor Maurice and His Historian: Theophylact Simocatta on Persian and Balkan Warfare.* Oxford, 1988.

Whitby, Michael. "Recruitment in Roman Armies from Justinian to Heraclius (ca. 565-615)." In: *The Byzantine and Early Islamic Near East.* III: *States, Resources and Armies.* Ed. Averil Cameron. Studies in Late Antiquity and Early Islam, 1. Princeton: The Darwin Press, Inc., 1995, pp. 61-124.

Wortley, John. "Military Elements in Psychophelitic Tales and Sayings." In: *Peace and War in Byzantinum: Essays in Honor of George T. Dennis, S.J.* Ed. T.S. Miller and J. Nesbitt. Washington, 1995, pp. 89-105.

Zachariadou, Elizabeth A. "Holy War in the Aegean during the Fourteenth Century." In: *Latins and Greeks in the Eastern Mediterranean after 1204.* Ed. B. Arbel, Bernard Hamilton, and D. Jacoby. London, 1989, pp. 212-25.

Medieval – Carolingian

Almedingen, E.M. *Charlemagne: A Study.* London, 1968.

Anton, H.H. *Fürstenspiegel und Herrscherethos in der Karolingerzeit.* Bonn, 1968.

Bachrach, Bernard S. "Charlemagne's Cavalry: Myth and Reality," *Military Affairs* 47 (1983), 181-87.

Bachrach, Bernard S. "Early Medieval Military Demography: Some Observations on the Methods of Hans Delbrück." In: *The Circle of War in the*

Middle Ages: Essays on Medieval Military and Naval History. Ed. Donald
J. Kagay and L.J. Andrew Villalon. Woodbridge: The Boydell Press, 1999,
pp. 3-20.

Bachrach, Bernard S. "Logistics in Pre-Crusade Europe." In: *Feeding
Mars: Logistics in Western Warfare from the Middle Ages to the Present.*
Ed. J.A. Lynn. Boulder, 1993, pp. 57-79.

Bachrach, Bernard S. "Military Organization in Aquitaine under the Early
Carolingians," *Speculum* 49 (1974), 1-33.

Bachrach, Bernard S. "Was the Marchfield Part of the Frankish Constitution?" *Mediaeval Studies* 36 (1974), 178-85.

Baudot, M. "Localisation et datation de la prèmiere victoire remportée par
Charles Martel contre Muselmans," *Memoires et documents publiés par la
société de l'école des chartes* 12 (1955), 93-105.

Becher, Matthias. *Karl der Grosse.* C.H. Beck Wissen in der Beck'schen
Reihe, 2120. Munich: C.H. Beck, 1999.

Bowlus, Charles R. *Franks, Moravians, and Magyars: The Struggle for the
Middle Danube, 788-907.* Philadelphia: University of Pennsylvania Press,
1995.

Bowlus, Charles R. "Die militärische Organisation des karolingischen
Südostens (791-907)," *Frühmittelalterlichen Studien* 31 (1997), 46-69.

Bowlus, Charles R. "Warfare and Society in the Carolingian Ostmark,"
Austrian History Yearbook 14 (1978), 3-28.

Bullough, D.A. "*Europae pater*: Charlemagne and His Achievement in
the Light of Recent Scholarship," *English Historical Review* 85 (1970),
59-105.

Dannenbauer, H. "Die Freien im Karolingischen Heer." In: *Festschrift
zum 70. Geburstag von Th. Meyer.* I: *Zur allgemeinen und Verfassungs-
geschicte.* Constance, 1954, pp. 49-64.

Dopsch, Alfons. *Die Wirtschaftsentwicklung der Karolingerzeit vornehmlich in Deutschland.* 2 vols. 2nd ed. Weimar, 1922; rpt. Weimar, 1962.

Drew, Katherine Fisher. "The Carolingian Military Frontier in Italy,"
Traditio 20 (1964), 437-47.

Fouracre, Paul. "Observations on the Outgrowth of Pippinid Influence in the 'Regnum Francorum' After the Battle of Tertey (687-715)," *Medieval Prospography* 5 (1984), 1-31.

France, John. "The Military History of the Carolingian Period," *Revue Belge d'histoire militaire* 26 (1985), 81-100.

Gaier, Claude. "L'armée et les troupes de Charlemagne." In: *Charlemagne: L'empire retrouvé*. Muséobus du Ministère de la Communauté Française. Brussels, 1990, pp. 31-33.

Ganshof, François Louis. "A propos de la cavalerie dans les armées de Charlemagne," *Comptes rendus de l'Academié des Inscriptions et Belles-Lettres* (1952), 531-37.

Ganshof, François Louis. "L'armée sous les Carolingiens." In: *Ordinamenti militari in occidente nell'alto medioevo*. Settimane di studio del centro italiano di studi sull'alto medioevo, XV. Spoleto, 1968.

Ganshof, François Louis. "Zur Entstehungsgeschichte und Bedeutung des Vertrages von Verdun (843)," *Deutsches Archiv für Erforschung des Mittelalters* 13 (1956), 313-30.

Ganshof, François Louis. *Frankish Institutions Under Charlemagne*. Trans. Bryce and Mary Lyon. New York: W.W. Norton and Company, Inc., 1968.

Gillmor, Carroll. "Charles the Bald and the Small Free Farmers, 862-869." In: *Military Aspects of Scandinavian Society in a European Perspective, AD. 1-1300*. Ed. A.N. Jørgensen and B. Clausen. Copenhagen, 1997, pp. 38-47.

Gillmor, Carroll. *Warfare and the Military under Charles the Bald, 840-877*. Unpublished dissertation. Los Angeles: University of California at Los Angeles, 1976.

Goldberg, Eric J. "More Devoted to the Equipment of Battle than the Splendor of Banquets: Frontier Kingship, Military Ritual, and Early Knighthood at the Court of Louis of German," *Viator* 30 (1999).

González García, Vicente José. "La auténtica batalla de Roncesvalles y la existencia real de Bernardo del Carpio." In: *Aspects de l'épopée romane:*

mentalités, idéologies, intertexualités. Ed. Hans van Dijk and Willem Noomen. Groningen: Forsten, 1995, pp. 241-50.

Halsall, G.S. *Warfare and Society in the Barbarian West, c.450-900.* London, 1998.

Kleinclausz, Arthur. *Charlemagne.* Rpt. Paris: Tallandier, 1999.

Le Jan-Hennebicque, Régine. "Satellites et bandes armées dans le monde franc (VIIe-Xe siècles)." In: *Le combattant au moyen âge.* 2nd ed. Histoire ancienne et médiévale, 36. Paris: Publications of the Sorbonne, 1990, pp. 97-105.

Lifshitz, Felice. "La Normandie carolingienne: essai sur la continuité, avec utilisation de sources négligées," *Annales de Normandie* 48 (1998), 505-24.

Mangold-Gaudlitz, H. von. *Die Reiterei in dem germanischen und frankischen Heeren bis zum Ausgand der deutschen Karolinger.* Berlin, 1922.

Mayr-Harting, Henry. "Charlemagne, the Saxons, and the Imperial Coronation of 800," *English Historical Review* 111 (1996), 1113-33.

McCormick, Michael. "Liturgie et guerre des Carolingiens à la première croisade." In: *"Militia Christi" e crociata nei secoli XI-XIII: Atti della undecima settimana internazionale di studio, Mendola, 28 agosta-1 settembre 1989.* Miscellanea del Centro di studi medioevali, 13; Scienze storiche, 48. Milan: Vita e Pensiero, 1992, pp. 209-40.

McCormick, Michael. "The Liturgy of War in the Early Middle Ages: Crisis, Litanies, and the Carolingian Monarchy," *Viator* 15 (1984), 1-23.

McCormick, Michael. "A New Ninth-Century Witness to the Carolingian Mass against Pagans (Paris, B.N., Lat. 2812)," *Revue Benédictine* 97 (1987), 68-86.

Nicolle, David C. *The Age of Charlemagne.* London: Osprey, 1984.

Odegaard, C. *Vassi and Fideles in the Carolingian Empire.* Cambridge: Harvard University Press, 1945.

Patlagean, Evelyne. "Les armes et la cité à Rome du VIIe au XIe siècle, et le modèle européen des trois fonctions," *Mélanges d'archéologie et d'histoire* 86 (1974), 25-62.

Pohl, Walter. *Die Awarenkriege Karls des Großen, 788-803.* Militärhistorische Schriftenreihe, 61. Vienna: Bundesverlag, 1988.

Prinz, Friedrich E. "King, Clergy and War at the Time of the Carolingians." In: *Saints, Scholars and Heroes: Studies in Medieval Culture in Honour of Charles W. Jones.* Ed. M.H. King and W.M. Stevens. Collegeville, 1979, pp. 301-29.

Reuter, Timothy. "Carolingian and Ottonian Warfare." In: *Medieval Warfare: A History.* Ed. Maurice Keen. Oxford: Oxford University Press, 1999, pp. 13-35.

Reuter, Timothy. "The End of the Carolingian Military Expansion." In: *Charlemagne's Heir: New Perspectives on the Reign of Louis the Pious (814-840).* Ed. P. Godman and R. Collins. Oxford, 1990, pp. 391-405.

Reuter, Timothy. "Plunder and Tribute in the Carolingian Empire," *Transactions of the Royal Historical Society* 5th ser. 35 (1985), 75-94.

Riché, Pierre. *Charlemagne.* Paris: Perrin, 1996.

Searle, Eleanor. "Frankish Rivalries and Norse Warriors," *Anglo-Norman Studies* 8 (1985), 198-213.

Smith, Julia M.H. *Province and Empire: Brittany and the Carolingians.* Cambridge: Cambridge University Press, 1992.

Tabacco, Giovanni. *I liberi del re nell'Italia carolingia e post-carolingia.* Spoleto: Presso la sede del centro, 1966.

Verbruggen, J.F. "L'armée et la stratégie de Charlemagne." In: *Karl der Grosse: Lebenswerk und Nachleben.* Band I: *Personlichkeit und Geschichte.* Ed. H. Baumann et al. Dusseldorf, 1965, pp. 420-36.

Verbruggen, J.F. "L'art militaire dans l'empire carolingien (714-1000)," *Revue Belge d'histoire militaire* 23 (1979-80), 289-310, 393-412.

Verbruggen, J.F. "De Franken en hun krijgersonder Pepijn de Korte," *Genootschap voor geschied- en oudheidkunde te Vilvoorde* 4.2 (June 1998), 2-20.

Verbruggen, J.F. "De krijgers van Karel de Grote," *Genootschap voor geschied- en oudheidkunde te Vilvoorde* 5.2 (June 1999), 2-20.

Verbruggen, J.F. "De oorlogen van Karel de Grote (768-814)," *Genootschap voor geschied- en oudheidkunde te Vilvoorde* 5.1 (Mar 1999), 2-22.

Wachowski, Krzysztof. "Carolingian Influences on the West Slavs' Arms and Armor," *Fasciculi archaeologicae historicae* 7 (1994), 13-14.

Ziezulewicz, William. "The Fate of Carolingian Military Exactions in a Monastic Fisc: The Case of Saint-Florent-de-Saumer (ca. 950-1118)," *Military Affairs* 51 (1987), 124-27.

Medieval – Cavalry [Cf. Military Technology – Premodern – Horses (inc. Warhorses)]

Bachrach, Bernard S. "*Caballus et Caballarius* in Medieval Warfare." In: *The Study of Chivalry*. Ed. H. Chickering and T.H. Seiler. Kalamazoo, 1988, 173-211.

Bachrach, Bernard S. "Charlemagne's Cavalry: Myth and Reality," *Military Affairs* 47 (1983), 181-87.

Bachrach, Bernard S. "Charles Martel, Mounted Shock Combat, The Stirrup, and Feudalism," *Studies in Medieval and Renaissance History* 7 (1970), 47-75.

Bachrach, Bernard S. "The Rise of Armorican Chivalry," *Technology and Culture* 10 (1969), 166-71.

Bennett, Matthew. "The Knight Unmasked," *MHQ: The Quarterly Journal of Military History* 7 (Summer 1995), 8-19.

Bennett, Matthew. "The Medieval Warhorse Reconsidered." In: *Medieval Knighthood V*. Ed. S. Church and R. Harvey. Woodbridge, 1995, pp. 19-40.

Bennett, Matthew. "The Myth of the Military Supremacy of Knightly Cavalry." In: *Armies, Chivalry and Warfare in Medieval Britain and France: Proceedings of the 1995 Harlaxton Symposium*. Ed. M. Strickland. Stamford, 1998, pp. 304-16.

Bennett, Matthew. "*La règle du temple* as a Military Manual or How to Deliver a Cavalry Charge." In: *Studies in Medieval History Presented to R. Allen Brown.* Ed. C. Harper-Bill, C.J. Holdsworth and J. Nelson. Woodbridge, 1989, pp. 7-19.

Bérenger, Jean. "L'influence des peuples de la steppe (Huns, Mongols, Tartares) sur la conception européene de la guerre de mouvement et l'emploi de la cavalerie (Ve-XVIIe siècle)," *Revue internationale d'histoire militaire* 49 (1980), 33-50.

Bivar, A.D.H. "Cavalry, Equipment and Tactics on the Euphrates Frontier," *Dumbarton Oaks Papers* 26 (1972), 271-91.

Bohigas, P. *Tractats de cavalleria.* Barcelona, 1947.

Cardini, Franco. *Alle radici della cavalleria medievale.* Florence, 1981.

Cherrier, Noëlle. "Les chevaux de Philippe le Hardi (1371-1404)," *Annales de Bourgogne* 67 (1995), 107-48.

Costantini, A. "D'Hannibal à Gengis-Khan: vers la suprematie de la cavalerie (216 av. J.-C.-1281)," *Revue internationale d'histoire militaire* 49 (1980), 17-32.

Dunning, G.C. "The Horse and Knight Roof-Finial, with a Discussion of Knight Finials and Rider Finials in England on the Continent," *Bedfordshire Archaeological Journal* 9 (1974), 112-22.

Engström, Johan. "Det vendeltida rytteriet," *Meddelande* 54 (1994), 9-34.

Gaier, Claude. "La cavalerie lourde en Europe occidentale du XIIe au XVIe siècle," *Revue internationale d'histoire militaire* 31 (1971), 385-96; in: *Armes et combats dans l'univers médiéval.* Paris: De Boeck Université, 1995, pp. 299-310.

Gamber, Ortwin. "Kataphrakten, Clibanarier, Normannenreiter," *Jahrbuch der Kunsthistorischen Sammlungen in Wien* 64 (1968), 7-44.

Ganshof, François Louis. "A propos de la cavalerie dans les armées de Charlemagne," *Comptes rendus de l'Academié des Inscriptions et Belles-Lettres* (1952), 531-37.

Gillmor, Caroll. "European Cavalry." In: *Dictionary of the Middle Ages.* Ed. J.R. Strayer. New York, 1982, II:200-08.

Grabski, A.F. "La chevalerie polonaise au service de l'étranger au moyen âge." In: *Histoire militaire de la Pologne: Problèmes choises*. Ed. W. Bieganski, P. Stawecki, and W. Janusz. Warsaw: Institut d'Histoire, 1970.

Lyon, Bryce. "The Role of Cavalry in Medieval Warfare: Horses, Horses All Around and Not a One to Use," *Mededelingen van de Koninklijke Academie voor Wetenschappen, Letteren en Schone Kunsten van België* 49 (1987), 77-90.

Maglioli, Vittorio. "La cavalleria," *Armi antiche* 1 (1954), 22-28.

Marshall, Christopher J. "The Use of the Charge in Battle in the Latin East, 1192-1291," *Historical Research* 63 (1990), 221-26.

Morillo, Stephen. "The 'Age of Cavalry' Revisited." In: *The Circle of War in the Middle Ages: Essays on Medieval Military and Naval History*. Ed. Donald J. Kagay and L.J. Andrew Villalon. Woodbridge: The Boydell Press, 1999, pp. 45-58.

Morris, John E. "Mounted Infantry in Mediaeval Warfare," *Transactions of the Royal Historical Society*, 3rd ser., 8 (1914), 77-102.

Pescador, C. "La caballeria popular en León y Castilla," *Cuadernos de historia de España* 33-34 (1961), 101-238; 35-36 (1962), 56-201; 37-38 (1963), 88-198.

Pivano, S. "Lineamenti storici e guiridici della cavalleria medioevale," *Memorie della reale accademia della scienze di Torino (scienza morali)* ser. II, 55 (1905).

Powicke, Michael R. "The General Obligation to Cavalry Service under Edward I," *Speculum* 28 (1953), 814-33.

Prestwich, Michael. "Cavalry Service in Early Fourteenth Century England." In: *War and Government in the Middle Ages: Essays in Honour of J.O. Prestwich*. Ed. J. Gillingham and J.C. Holt. Cambridge, 1984, pp. 147-58.

Riquer, Martín de. *Caballeros andantes Españoles*. Madrid, 1967.

Riquer, Martín de. *Cavalleria fra realtà e letteratura nel quattrocento*. Bari, 1970.

Riquer, Martín de. *Vida caballeresca en la España de siglo XV*. Madrid: Real academia Expañola, 1965.

Rubin, B. "Die Entstehung der Kataphraktenreiter im Lichte der Choreszmischen Ausgrabungen," *Historia* 4 (1955), 264-83.

Sánchez-Albornoz, C. "La caballería visigoda." In: *Wirtschaft und Kultur: Festschrift zum 70. Geburtstag von Alfons Dopsch*. Baden bei Wien and Leipzig, 1938, pp. 92-108.

Seidel, Linda V. "Early Medieval Images of the Horseman Re-Viewed." In: *The Study of Chivalry: Resources and Approaches*. Ed. H. Chickering and T.H. Seiler. Kalamazoo, 1988, pp. 373-401.

Settia, Aldo A. "Le radici tecnologiche della cavalleria medievale: In margine ad un libro recente," *Rivista storica Italiana* 97 (1985), 264-73.

Sigal, Pierre-André. "Les coups et blessures reçus par le combattant à cheval en occident aux XIIe et XIIIe siècles." In: *Le combattant au moyen âge*. 2nd ed. Histoire ancienne et médiévale, 36. Paris: Publications of the Sorbonne, 1990, pp. 171-83.

Sotto y Montes, J. de. "La orden de caballeria en la alta Edad media," *Revista de historia militar* 4 (1960), 39-73.

Thompson, Logan. "European Armoured Cavalry, 379-1300 AD," *Classic Arms and Armour* 4 (Sep/Oct 1997), 26-30.

Vayra, P. "Cavalieri lombardi in Piedmonto nelle guerre del 1229-1230," *Archivio storico Lombardo* 10 (1883), 413-22.

Verbruggen, J.F. "De rol van de ruiterij in de middeleeuwse oorlogvoering," *Belgisch tijdschrift voor militaire geschiedenis* 30 (1994), 389-418.

Verbruggen, J.F. "La tactique militaire des armées de chevaliers," *Revue du nord* 29 (1947), 161-80.

Verbruggen, J.F. "Vlaamse gemeentelegers tegen Franse ridderlegers in de 14de en 15de eeuw," *Revue Belge d'histoire militaire* 24 (1981), 359-82.

Vernam, Glenn R. *Man on Horseback*. New York: Harper and Row, 1964.

Waley, Daniel P. "Chivalry and Cavalry at San Gimignano: Knighthood in a Small Italian Commune." In: *Recognitions: Essays Presented to Edmund Fryde*. Ed. C. Richmond and I. Harvey. Aberystwyth, 1996, pp. 39-53.

Medieval – Chivalry

Adams, Jeremy duQuesnay. "Modern Views of Medieval Chivalry, 1884-1984." In: *The Study of Chivalry: Resources and Approaches*. Ed. H. Chickering and T.H. Seiler. Kalamazoo, 1988, pp. 41-90.

Alexander, J.J.G. "The Making of the 'Age of Chivalry'," *History Today* 37 (1987), 3-11.

Altschul, Michael. "Chivalry and its Historians," *Medievalia et Humanistica* n.s. 13 (1985), 207-11.

Ascherl, Rosemary. "The Technology of Chivalry in Reality and Romance." In: *The Study of Chivalry: Resources and Approaches*. Ed. H. Chickering and T.H. Seiler. Kalamazoo, 1988, pp. 263-312.

Baker-Smith, Dominic. "'Inglorious Glory': 1513 and the Humanist Attack on Chivalry." In: *Chivalry in the Renaissance*. Ed. Sydney Anglo. Woodbridge: The Boydell Press, 1990, pp. 129-44.

Baldwin, John W. "French Chivalry Revisited: The *Guillaume de Dole* of Jean Renart," *Haskins Society Journal* 1 (1989), 183-91.

Barber, Richard. *The Knight and Chivalry*. 2nd ed. Woodbridge: The Boydell Press, 1975.

Barbero, Alessandro. "Noblesse et chevalerie en France au Moyen âge: Une réflexion," *Moyen âge*, 5th ser., 5 (1991), 431-49.

Bellitto, Christopher M. "Chivalry: A Door to Teaching the Middle Ages," *History Teacher* 28 (1995), 479-85.

Berg, Evert van den. "La littérature chevaleresque dans la Flandre du 14e siècle: épopée ou roman?" In: *Aspects de l'épopée romane: mentalités, idéologies, intertextualités*. Ed. Hans van Dijk and Willem Noomen. Groningen, 1995, pp. 331-38.

Bönsch, Annemarie. "Ulrich von Liechtenstein–seine Einkleidung für die VENUSFAHRT: Vorstellung des Ulrichprojektes: Eine Kultur-Tourismusinitiative von europäischer Dimension," *Waffen- und Köstumkunde* 40 (1998), 1-38.

Bouchard, Constance Brittain. *"Strong of Body, Brave and Noble": Chivalry and Society in Medieval France*. Ithaca: Cornell University Press, 1998.

Broughton, Bradford B. *Dictionary of Medieval Knighthood and Chivalry: Concepts and Terms*. New York: Greenwood Press, 1986.

Broughton, Bradford B. *Dictionary of Medieval Knighthood and Chivalry: People, Places, and Events*. New York: Greenwood Press, 1988.

Bryant, Arthur. *The Age of Chivalry: The Atlantic Saga*. New York: New American Library, 1963.

Burke, Peter. "Chivalry in the New World." In: *Chivalry in the Renaissance*. Ed. Sydney Anglo. Woodbridge: The Boydell Press, 1990, pp. 253-62.

Cameron, Sonya. "Chivalry in Barbour's *Bruce*." In: *Armies, Chivalry and Warfare in Medieval Britain and France: Proceedings of the 1995 Harlaxton Symposium*. Ed. M. Strickland. Stamford, 1998, pp. 13-29.

Carlson, David. "Religious Writers and Church Councils on Chivalry." In: *The Study of Chivalry: Resources and Approaches*. Ed. H. Chickering and T.H. Seiler. Kalamazoo, 1988, pp. 141-72.

Chickering, Howell. "Introduction." In: *The Study of Chivalry: Resources and Approaches*. Ed. H. Chickering and T.H. Seiler. Kalamazoo, 1988, pp. 1-39.

Chism, Christine. "Too Close for Comfort: Disorienting Chivalry in the *Wars of Alexander*." In: *Text and Territory: Geographical Imagination in the European Middle Ages*. Ed. Sylvia Tomasch and Sealy Gilles. Philadelphia: University of Pennsylvania Press, 1998, pp. 116-39.

Clough, Cecil H. "Chivalry and Magnificence in the Golden Age of the Italian Renaissance." In: *Chivalry in the Renaissance*. Ed. Sydney Anglo. Woodbridge: The Boydell Press, 1990, pp. 25-48.

Contamine, Philippe. "Points de vue sur la chevalerie en France à la fin du moyen âge," *Francia* 4 (1976), 255-85.

Cooper, Richard. "'Nostre histoire renouvelée': The Reception of the Romances of Chivalry in Renaissance France." In: *Chivalry in the Renaissance*. Ed. Sydney Anglo. Woodbridge: The Boydell Press, 1990, pp. 175-238.

Cotton, William. "Teaching the Motifs of Chivalric Biography." In: *The Study of Chivalry: Resources and Approaches*. Ed. H. Chickering and T.H. Seiler. Kalamazoo, 1988, pp. 583-610.

Coulton, G.G. *The Chronicler of European Chivalry*. London, 1930.

Dillon, Viscount. "On a Manuscript Collection of Ordinances of Chivalry of the Fifteenth Century," *Archaeologia* 62 (1900), 29-70.

Duby, Georges. *The Chivalrous Society*. Trans. Cynthia Postan. Berkeley and Los Angeles: University of California Press, 1977.

Du Puy de Clinchamps, Ph. *La chevalerie*. 2nd ed. Paris: Presses Universitaires de France, 1966.

Dürst, Hans, et al. *Rittertum*. Dokumente zur aargauischen Kulturgeschichte, 2. Schloss Lenzburg: Kantonale Historische Sammlung, 1962.

Fallows, Noel. *The Chivalric Vision of Alfonso de Cartagena: Study and Edition of the Doctrinal de los caualleros*. Newark, 1995.

Fallows, Noel. "Just Say No? Alfonso de Cartagena, the *Doctrinal de los caballeros*, and Spain's Most Noble Pastime." In: *Studies on Medieval Spanish Literature in Honor of Charles F. Fraker*. Ed. Mercedes Vaquero and Alan Deyermond. Madison: Hispanic Seminary of Medieval Studies, 1995, pp. 129-41.

Ferguson, A.B. *The Indian Summer of English Chivalry: Studies in the Decline and Transformation of Chivalric Idealism*. Durham: Duke University Press, 1960.

Fernández-Armesto, Felipe. "The Sea and Chivalry in Late Medieval Spain." In: *Maritime History*. I: *The Age of Discovery*. Ed. J.B. Hattendorff. Malabar, 1996, pp. 123-36.

Flori, Jean. *La chevalerie en France au moyen âge*. Que Sais-Je? 972. Paris: Presses Universitaires de France, 1995.

Flori, Jean. "Chevalerie et liturgie: Remise des armes et vocabulaire 'chevaleresque' dans les sources litturgiques du IXe à XIVe siècle," *Moyen âge* 84 (1978), 247-78.

Flori, Jean. "Chevalerie, noblesse et lutte de classes au moyen âge," *Moyen âge* 94 (1988), 258-71.

Flori, Jean. "La chevalerie selon Jean de Salisbury: (Nature, fonction, idéologie)," *Revue d'histoire ecclesiastique* 77 (1982), 35-77.

Flori, Jean. *Chevaliers et chevalerie au moyen âge*. Paris: Hachette, 1998.

Flori, Jean. *Croisade et chevalerie: XIe-XIIIe siècles*. Bibliothèque du Moyen Age, 12. Paris: De Boeck Université, 1998.

Flori, Jean. "Croisade et chevalerie: Convergence idéologique ou rupture?" In: *Femmes. Mariages–Lignages, XIIe-XIVe siècles: Melanges offerts à Georges Duby*. Ed. Jean Dufournet et al. Bibliothèque du Moyen Age, 1. Brussels: De Boeck-Wesmael, 1992, pp. 157-76.

Flori, Jean. *L'essor de la chevalerie, XIe-XIIe siècles*. Geneva, 1986.

Flori, Jean. "Guerre et chevalerie au moyen âge (à propos d'un ouvrage récent)," *Cahiers de civilisation médiévale (X-XIIe siècle)* 41 (1998), 353-63.

Flori, Jean. *L'idéologie du glaive: Préhistoire de la chevalerie*. Geneva, 1983.

Flori, Jean. "La notion de chevalerie dans les chansons de geste du XIIe siècle: Etude historique de vocabulaire," *Moyen âge* 81 (1975), 211-44, 407-45.

Flori, Jean. "Du noveau sur l'adoubement des chevaliers (XIe-XIIIe siècle)," *Moyen âge* 91 (1985), 201-26.

Flori, Jean. "Pour une histoire de la chevalerie: l'adoubement dans les romans de Chrétien de Troyes," *Romania* 100 (1979), 21-53.

Fowler, Kenneth. "Froissart: Chronicler of Chivalry," *History Today* 36 (May 1986), 50-54.

Funck-Brentano, Frantz. *Féodalité et Chevalerie*. Paris, 1946.

Gautier, Léon. *Chivalry*. Ed. Jacques Levron. Trans. D.C. Dunning. London: Phoenix House, 1965.

Gillingham, John. "1066 and the Introduction of Chivalry into England." In: *Law and Government in Medieval England and Normandy*. Ed. G. Garnett and J. Hudson. Cambridge, 1994, pp. 31-55.

Gillingham, John. "War and Chivalry in the *History of William the Marshal*." In: *Thirteenth Century England II*. Ed. P.R. Coss and S.D. Lloyd. Woodbridge, 1988, pp. 1-13; in: *Anglo-Norman Warfare: Studies in Late Anglo-Saxon and Anglo-Norman Military Organization and Warfare*. Ed. M. Strickland. Woodbridge, 1992, pp. 251-63.

Goodman, Jennifer R. "Caxton's Chivalric Publications of 1480-85." In: *The Study of Chivalry: Resources and Approaches*. Ed. H. Chickering and T.H. Seiler. Kalamazoo, 1988, pp. 645-62.

Goodman, Jennifer R. *Chivalry and Exploration, 1298-1630*. Woodbridge: Boydell and Brewer, 1998.

Goodman, Jennifer R. "'I Ought to be Judged as a Captain': The Chivalry of Columbus," *Medievalia et Humanistica* n.s. 19 (1992), 47-68.

Gunn, Steven. "Chivalry and the Politics of the Early Tudor Court." In: *Chivalry in the Renaissance*. Ed. Sydney Anglo. Woodbridge: The Boydell Press, 1990, pp. 107-28.

Hanning, Robert W. "The Criticism of Chivalric Epic and Romance." In: *The Study of Chivalry: Resources and Approaches*. Ed. H. Chickering and T.H. Seiler. Kalamazoo, 1988, pp. 91-114.

Huizinga, Johan. *The Autumn of the Middle Ages*. Trans. Rodney J. Payton and Ulrich Mammitzsch. Chicago: The Unviersity of Chicago Press, 1996.

Huizinga, Johan. *The Waning of the Middle Ages: A Study of the Forms of Life, Thought and Art in France and the Netherlands in the Dawn of the Renaissance*. New York: Doubleday Anchor Books, 1954.

Huizinga, Johan. "La valeur politique et militaire des idées de chevalerie à la fin du moyen âge," *Revue d'histoire diplomatique* 35 (1921), 126-38; in: *Verzamelde werken*. Haarlem, 1949, III:519-29.

Jacoby, David. "Knightly Values and Class Consciousness in the Crusader States of the Eastern Mediterranean," *Mediterranean History Review* 1 (1986), 158-86.

Jaeger, C. Stephen. *The Origins of Courtliness: Civilizing Trends and the Formation of Courtly Ideals, 939-1210*. Philadelphia: University of Pennsylvania Press, 1985.

Jourdan, J.-P. "Le langage amoureux dans le combat de chevalerie à la fin du Moyen âge (France, Bourgogne, Anjou)," *Moyen âge*, 5th ser., 99 (1993), 83-106.

Kaeuper, Richard W. *Chivalry and Violence in Medieval Europe*. Oxford: Oxford University Press, 1999.

Kaiser, Elizabeth B. and Bonnie Wheeler. "Teaching Chivalry: From Footnote to Foreground." In: *The Study of Chivalry: Resources and Approaches*. Ed. H. Chickering and T.H. Seiler. Kalamazoo, 1988, pp. 115-39.

Keen, Maurice. "Brotherhood in Arms," *History* 57 (1962), 1-17.

Keen, Maurice. "Chaucer and Chivalry Re-visited." In: *Armies, Chivalry and Warfare in Medieval Britain and France: Proceedings of the 1995 Harlaxton Symposium*. Ed. M. Strickland. Stamford, 1998, pp. 1-12.

Keen, Maurice. "Chivlarous Culture in Fourteenth-Century Europe." In: *Historical Studies, 10*. Ed. G.A. Hayes-McCoy. Dublin, 1976, pp. 1-24.

Keen, Maurice. *Chivalry*. New Haven: Yale University Press, 1984.

Keen, Maurice. "Chivalry and Courtly Love." In: *Nobles, Knights and Men-at-Arms in the Middle Ages*. London, 1996, pp. 21-42.

Keen, Maurice. "Chivalry, Heralds and History." In: *Nobles, Knights and Men-at-Arms in the Middle Ages*. London, 1996, pp. 63-81.

Keen, Maurice. "Chivalry, Nobility and the Man-at-Arms." In: *War, Literature and Politics in the Late Middle Ages: Essays in Honour of G.W. Coopland*. Ed. C.T. Allmand. Liverpool: University of Liverpool Press, 1975, pp. 32-45.

Keen, Maurice. "English Military Experience and the Court of Chivalry: The Case of Grey v. Hastings." In: *Guerre et société en France, en*

Angleterre et en Bourgogne XIVe-XVe siècle. Ed. P. Contamine, C. Giry-Deloison, and Maurice Keen. Lille, 1991, pp. 123-142.

Keen, Maurice. "Huizinga, Kilgour and the Decline of Chivalry," *Medievalia et humanistica* 8 (1977), 1-21.

Keen, Maurice. "The Jurisdiction and Origins of the Constable's Court." In: *War and Government in the Middle Ages: Essays in Honour of J.O. Prestwich.* Ed. J. Gillingham and J.C. Holt. Cambridge, 1984, pp. 159-69.

Keen, Maurice. *The Laws of War in the Late Middle Ages.* London: Routledge and Kegan Paul, 1965.

Keen, Maurice. "War, Peace and Chivalry." In: *War and Peace in the Middle Ages.* Ed. B.P. McGuire. Copenhagen, 1987, pp. 94-117.

Kennedy, Elspeth. "Geoffroi de Charny's Livre de Chevalerie and the Knights of the Round Table." In: *Medieval Knighthood, V.* Ed. S. Church and R. Harvey. Woodbridge, 1995, pp. 221-42.

Kilgour, Raymond Lincoln. *The Decline of Chivalry as Shown in the French Literature of the Late Middle Ages.* Cambridge: Harvard University Press, 1937; rpt. Gloucester: Peter Smith, 1966.

Kindrick, Robert L. "The 'Unknightly Knight': Teaching Satires on Chivalry." In: *The Study of Chivalry: Resources and Approaches.* Ed. H. Chickering and T.H. Seiler. Kalamazoo, 1988, pp. 663-82.

Kliman, Bernice W. "The Idea of Chivalry in John Barbour's *Bruce,*" *Mediaeval Studies* 35 (1973), 477-508.

Lippincott, Kristen. "The Genesis and Significance of the Fifteenth-Century Italian *Impresa.*" In: *Chivalry in the Renaissance.* Ed. Sydney Anglo. Woodbridge: The Boydell Press, 1990, pp. 49-76.

Mathew, Gervase. "Ideals of Knighthood in Late-Fourteenth-Century England." In: *Studies in Medieval History Presented to Frederick Maurice Powicke.* Ed. R.W. Hunt et al. Oxford, 1948, pp. 354-62.

Matonis, A.T.E. "Traditions of Panegyric in Welsh Poetry: The Heroic and the Chivalric," *Speculum* 53 (1978), 667-87.

Morgan, David. "From a Death to a View: Louis Robessart, Johan Huizinga, and the Political Significance of Chivalry." In: *Chivalry in the Renais-*

sance. Ed. Sydney Anglo. Woodbridge: The Boydell Press, 1990, pp. 93-106.

Newton, Stella Mary. *Fashion in the Age of the Black Prince: A Study of the Years 1340-1365*. Woodbridge: The Boydell Press, 1980.

Nicolas, Nicholas Harris. *The Controversy between Sir Richard Scrope and Sir Robert Grosvenor, in the Court of Chivalry, AD MCCCLXXXV-MCCCXC*. 2 vols. London, 1832.

Nickel, Helmut. "The Art of Chivalry," *Metropolitan Museum of Art Bulletin* 32.4 (1973-74), 57-104.

Nickel, Helmut, Stuart W. Pyhrr and Leonid Tarassuk. *The Art of Chivalry: European Arms and Armor from the Metropolitan Museum of Art*. New York: American Federation of Arts, 1982.

Noble, Peter S. "Perversion of an Ideal." In: *Medieval Knighthood, IV*. Ed. C. Harper-Bill and R. Harvey. Woodbridge, 1992, pp. 177-86.

North, Sally. "The Ideal Knight as Presented in Some French Narrative Poems, c. 1090-c. 1240: An Outline Sketch." In: *The Ideals and Practice of Medieval Knighthood*. Ed. C. Harper-Bill and R. Harvey. Woodbridge, 1986, pp. 111-32.

Orgelfinger, Gail. "The Vows of the Pheasant and Late Chivalric Ritual." In: *The Study of Chivalry: Resources and Approaches*. Ed. H. Chickering and T.H. Seiler. Kalamazoo, 1988, pp. 611-44.

Painter, Sidney. *French Chivalry: Chivalric Ideas and Practices in Mediaeval France*. Baltimore: The Johns Hopkins University Press, 1940; rpt. Ithaca: Cornell University Press, 1957.

Prestage, E., ed. *Chivalry: Its Historical Significance and Civilizing Influence*. London, 1928.

Rezak, Brigitte Bedos. "Medieval Seals and the Structure of Chivalric Society." In: *The Study of Chivalry: Resources and Approaches*. Ed. H. Chickering and T.H. Seiler. Kalamazoo, 1988, pp. 313-72.

Rousset, Paul. "La description du monde chevaleresque dans Orderic Vital," *Moyen âge* 75 (1969), 427-44.

Rudorff, Raymond. *Knights and the Age of Chivalry*. New York: The Viking Press, 1974.

Skretkowicz, Victor. "Chivalry in Spenser's *Arcadia*." In: *Chivalry in the Renaissance*. Ed. Sydney Anglo. Woodbridge: The Boydell Press, 1990, pp. 161-74.

Squibb, G.D. *The High Court of Chivalry*. Oxford, 1959.

Strickland, Matthew. "Provoking or Avoiding Battle? Challenge, Judicial Duel, and Single Combat in Eleventh- and Twelfth-Century Warfare." In: *Armies, Chivalry and Warfare in Medieval Britain and France: Proceedings of the 1995 Harlaxton Symposium*. Ed. M. Strickland. Stamford, 1998, pp. 317-43.

Strickland, Matthew. *War and Chivalry: The Conduct and Perception of War in England and Normandy, 1066-1217*. Cambridge: Cambridge University Press, 1996.

Swettenham, John. *The Evening of Chivalry*. Canadian War Museum Historical Publications, 6. Ottawa: Canadians War Museum, 1972.

Vale, Juliet. *Edward III and Chivalry: Chivalric Society and Its Context, 1270-1350*. Woodbridge: Boydell and Brewer, 1982.

Vale, Juliet and Malcom Vale. "Knightly Codes and Piety." In: *Age of Chivalry*. Ed. Nigel Saul. New York: St. Martin's Press, 1992, pp. 24-35.

Vale, Malcolm. *War and Chivalry: Warfare and Aristocratic Culture in England, France and Burgundy at the End of the Middle Ages*. Athens: University of Georgia Press, 1981.

Wetherbee, Winthrop. "Chivalry under Siege in Ricardian Romance." In: *The Medieval City Under Siege*. Ed. I.A. Corfis and M. Wolfe. Woodbridge, 1995, pp. 207-23.

Willard, Charity Cannon. "Christine de Pizan on Chivalry." In: *The Study of Chivalry: Resources and Approaches*. Ed. H. Chickering and T.H. Seiler. Kalamazoo, 1988, pp. 511-28.

Williams, Daniel. "Simon de Montfort, Earl of Leicester and the Image of Thirteenth Century Chivalry," *Transactions of the Leicester Literary and Philosophical Society* 87 (1993), 7-10.

Medieval – Chivalry – Chivalric Orders

Armstrong, C.A.J. "La toison d'or et la loi des armes," *Publications du centre europeen d'études burgundo-medianes* 5 (1963), 71-77.

Benninghoven, F. *Der Orden der Schwertbrüder*. Cologne and Graz, 1965.

Bossuat, André. "Un ordre de chevalerie auvergnat: l'Ordre de la Pomme d'Or," *Bulletin historique et scientifique de l'Auvergne* 64 (1944), 83-98.

Collins, Hugh. "The Order of the Garter, 1348-1461: Chivalry and Politics in Later Medieval England." In: *Courts, Counties and the Capital in the Later Middle Ages*. Ed. Diana E.S. Dunn. Stroud: Sutton Publishing, 1996, pp. 155-80.

Daw, Ben. "Elections to the Order of the Garter in the Reign of Edward IV, 1461-83," *Medieval Prospography* 19 (1998), 187-213.

Gillespie, James L. "Ladies of the Fraternity of Saint George and of the Society of the Garter," *Albion* 17 (1985), 261-62.

Gillingham, Harold. *Spanish Orders of Chivalry and Decorations of Honour*. New York, 1926.

Gutton, F. *La chevalerie militaire en Espagne: L'ordre d'Alcantara*. Paris, 1975.

Gutton, F. *La chevalerie militaire en Espagne: L'ordre de Calatrava*. Paris, 1955.

Gutton, F. *La chevalerie militaire en Espagne: L'ordre de Santiago*. Paris, 1972.

Jillings, Lewis. "Ordeal by Combat and the Rejection of Chivalry in *Diu Crône*," *Speculum* 51 (1976), 262-76.

Lewis, P.S. "Une devise de chevalerie inconnue, créée par le comte de Foix? Le Dragon," *Annales du midi* 76 (1964), 77-84.

Lomax, D.W. *La orden de Santiago (1170-1275)*. Madrid, 1965.

Marignac, Lucie. "Philippe le Bon et l'ordre de la toison d'or les enjeux d'une référence mythique," *Razo* 12 (1992), 87-112.

Martín, J.L. "Origenes de la Orden Militar de Santiago (1170-1195)," *Anuario de estudios medievales* 4 (1967), 571-90.

Ordre de la Toison d'or de Philippe le Bon à Philippe le Beau (1430-1505): idéal ou reflet d'une société, L'. Brussels, 1996.

Orgelfinger, Gail. "The Vows of the Pheasant and Late Chivalric Ritual." In: *The Study of Chivalry: Resources and Approaches*. Ed. H. Chickering and T.H. Seiler. Kalamazoo, 1988, pp. 611-44.

Renouard, Yves. "L'ordre de la Jarretière et l'ordre de l'Etoile: Etude sur la genèse des ordres laïcs de chevalerie et sur le développement progressif de leur caractère national," *Moyen âge* 55 (1949), 281-300.

Sotto y Montes, J. de. "La orden de caballeria en la alta Edad media," *Revista de historia militar* 4 (1960), 39-73.

Vale, M.G.A. "A Fourteenth-Century Order of Chivalry: The 'Tiercelet,'" *English Historical Review* 82 (1967), 332-41.

Medieval – Chivalry – Heraldry

Ackermann, P. "Standards, Banners and Badges." In: *A Survey of Persian Art*. Ed. A.A. Pope and P. Ackermann. London, 1939, VI:2766-82.

Adam-Even, P. "Les enseignes militaires au moyen âge et leur influence sur l'héraldique." In: *Recueil du Ve congrès international des sciences généalogiques et héraldiques*. Stockholm, 1960, pp. 167-94.

Adam-Even, P. "Les fonctions militaires des hérauts d'armes d'armes, leur influence sur le début de l'héraldique," *Archives héraldiques suisses* 71 (1957), 2-33.

Adam-Even, P. "Les sanctions militaires des hérauts d'armes, leur influence sur le développement de l'héraldique," *Mitteilungen der Gesellschaft für historische Kostüm- und Waffenkunde* 9 (1959).

Adamczewski, Marek and Zuzanna Poklewska-Patra (tr.). "The Representation of Arms and Armour in Polish Knight Heraldry," *Fasciculi archaeologicae historicae* 7 (1994), 67-75.

Ailes, Adrian. "The Knight, Heraldry and Armour: The Role of Recognition and the Origins of Heraldry." In: *Medieval Knighthood, IV*. Ed. C. Harper-Bill and R. Harvey. Woodbridge, 1992, pp. 1-21.

Allan, J.W. "Mamluk Sultanic Heraldry and the Numismatic Evidence: A Reinterpretation," *Journal of the Royal Asiatic Society* (1970), 99-112.

Anglo, Sydney. "Financial and Heraldic Records of the English Tournament," *Journal of the Society of Archivists* 2.5 (Apr 1962), 183-92.

Barraclough, E.M.C. "The Flags of the Bayeux Tapestry," *Armi antiche* (1969), 117-24.

Bourassin, Emmanuel. "La hérauderie au XVe siècle rois et hérauts d'armes." In: *Jeanne d'Arc: Une époque, un rayonnement*. Paris, 1982, pp. 107-11.

Braibant, C. *Les blasons et les sceaux*. Paris, 1950.

Bruna, Denis. "De l'agréable à l'utile: le bijou emblématique à la fin du moyen âge," *Revue historique* 301 (1999), 3-22.

Brusten, Charles. "Les emblèmes de l'armée Bourguignonne de Charles le Téméraire: Essai de classification," *Jahrbuch des bernischen historisches Museum in Bern* 37-38 (1957-58), 118-32.

Denholm-Young, N. "The Song of Carlaverok and the Parliamentary Roll of Arms as Found in Cott. MS. Calig. A. XVIII in the British Museum," *Proceedings of the British Academy* 47 (1961), 251-62.

Dennis, George T. "Byzantine Battle Flags," *Byzantinische forschungen* 8 (1982), 51-60.

Dondi, Giorgio. "Del roncone, del pennato e del cosidetto scorpione: loro origini," *Armi antichi* (1976), 11-48.

Fenske, Lutz. "Adel und Ritterum im Spiegel früher heraldischer Formen und deren Enwicklung." In: *Das ritterliche Turnier im Mittelalter*. Ed. Josef Fleckenstein. Göttingen: Vandenhoeck and Ruprecht, 1985, pp. 75-162.

Galbreath, D.L. and L. Jéquier. *Manuel du blason*. Lausanne, 1977.

Ganz, P. *Geschichte der Heraldischen Kunst in der Schweiz in XII. und XIII. Jahrhundert*. Frauenfeld, 1899.

Garcia Gómez, E. "Armas, banderas, tièndas de campaña, monturas y correos en los 'Anales de al Hakam II' por 'Isa Rāzā," *Andalus* 32 (1967), 163-79.

Gidert, Hervé. "Initiation à l'héraldique," *Militaria Belgica* 1 (1977-78), 21-28, 51-60, 85-91, 151-60, 186-92, 219-22, 248-52; 2 (1979-80), 21-28.

Gillingham, Harold. *Spanish Orders of Chivalry and Decorations of Honour*. New York, 1926.

Goodall, John A. "Heraldry in the Decoration of English Medieval Manuscripts," *Antiquaries Journal* 77 (1997), 179-220.

Goodall, John A. "Simon de Montfort (*c.* 1170-1218) and an Unusual Marshalling of Arms," *Antiquaries Journal* 78 (1998), 433-39.

Grigg, R. "Inconsistency and Lassitude: The Shield Emblems of the Notitia Dignitatum," *Journal of Roman Studies* 73 (1983), 132-42.

Harmatta, J. "The Golden Bough of the Huns," *Acta archaeologica scientarum Hungaricarum* 1 (1951), 107-49.

Khan, G.M. "The Islamic and Ghaznawide Banners," *Nagpur University Journal* 9 (1943), 106-17.

Leaf, W. "Developments in the System of Armorial Insignia during the Ayyubid and Mamluk Periods," *Palestine Exploration Quarterly* 115 (1983), 61-74.

Leaf, W. and S. Purcell. *Heraldic Symbols: Islamic Insignia and Western Heraldry*. London: Victoria and Albert Museum, 1986.

Lillich, Meredith Parsons. "Early Heraldry: How to Crack the Code," *Gesta* 30 (1991), 41-47.

Lillich, Meredith Parsons. "Gothic Heraldry and Name Punning," *Journal of Medieval History* 12 (1986), 239-51.

Llewellyn, Nigel. "Claims to Status through Visual Codes: Heraldry on Post-Reformation Funeral Monuments." In: *Chivalry in the Renaissance*. Ed. Sydney Anglo. Woodbridge: The Boydell Press, 1990, pp. 145-60.

Marks, R. and A. Payne. *British Heraldry*. London, 1978.

Mayer, L.A. *Saracenic Heraldry*. Oxford, 1933.

Nickel, Helmut. "Some Heraldic Fragments Found at Castle Montfort/ Starkenberg in 1926, and the Arms of the Grand Master of the Teutonic Knights," *Metropolitan Museum Journal* 24 (1989), 35-46.

Olivers, Stefan. *An Introduction to Heraldry*. New York: Gallery Books, 1987.

Paluka, M.H. *Heraldry and Armor of the Middle Ages*. New York, 1972.

Pardo de Guevera, E. *Manual de heráldica Española*. Madrid: Gráficas Mar-Car, 1987.

Prinet, M. "De l'origine orientale des armoires européennes," *Archives héraldiques Suisses* 2 (1912), 53-58.

Routh, Pauline Sheppard and Richard Knowles. "The Markenfield Collar," *Yorkshire Archaeological Journal* 62 (1990), 133-40.

Sander, Erich. "Deutsche Fahnen in vorheraldischer Zeit," *Zeitschrift für historisches Waffen- und Köstumkunde* 16 (1940-42), 190-200.

Solovjev, A. "Les emblèmes héraldiques du Byzance et les Slaves," *Seminarium kondakovianum* 7 (1935), 119-64.

Squilbeck, Jean. "L'iconographie de saint Guillaume et la bannière de la corporation des armuriers de Gand," *Revue Belge d'archéologie et d'histoire de l'art* 29 (1962), 103-18.

Törnquist, Leif. "Från banér till kommandotecken: En översikt över de svenska och finska fanorna och standaren genom tiderna," *Meddelande* 38 (1979), 7-158.

Vos, Luc de and Luc Duerloo. "Heraldische verkenningen," *Militaria Belgica* 2 (1979-80), 109-14, 139-44.

Wagner, Anthony Richard. *Heralds and Heraldry in the Middle Ages*. 2nd ed. Oxford, 1956.

Wright, C.E. *English Heraldic Manuscripts in the British Museum*. London: British Museum Publications Ltd., 1973.

Ziggioto, Aldo. "Le bandiere degli Stati italiani, 2: Le Repubbliche marinare: Genova e Venezia," *Armi antiche* (1968), 113-32.

Ziggioto, Aldo. "Le bandiere della Cronaca del Sercambi (seconda metà del sec. XIV)," *Armi antiche* (1981), 61-78.

Ziggioto, Aldo. "Le bandiere della marina da guerra degli Stati Italiani," *Armi antiche* (1967), 179-97.

Żygulski, Zdzisław, Jr. "Italian Arms, Armour and Insignia in Poland," *Armi antiche* 8 (1961), 19-44.

Medieval – Chivalry – Knights and Knighthood

Ackerman, Robert W. "The Knighting Ceremonies in the Middle English Romances," *Speculum* 19 (1944), 285-313.

Arnold, Benjamin. *German Knighthood, 1050-1300*. Oxford: Clarendon Press, 1984.

Ayton, Andrew. *Knights and Warhorses: Military Service and the English Aristocracy under Edward III*. Woodbridge: The Boydell Press, 1994.

Ayton, Andrew. "Knights, Esquires and Military Service: The Evidence of the Armorial Cases before the Court of Chivalry." In: *The Medieval Military Revolution: State, Society and Military Change in Medieval and Early Modern Europe*. Ed. A. Ayton and J.L. Price. London, 1995, pp. 81-104.

Bachrach, Bernard S. *"Caballus et Caballarius* in Medieval Warfare." In: *The Study of Chivalry: Resources and Approaches*. Ed. H. Chickering and T.H. Seiler. Kalamazoo, 1988, pp. 173-212.

Bachrach, Bernard S. "The *Milites* and the Millenium," *Haskins Society Journal* 6 (1994), 85-95.

Barber, Richard. *The Knight and Chivalry*. 2nd ed. Woodbridge: The Boydell Press, 1975.

Barber, Richard. "When is a Knight not a Knight?" In: *Medieval Knighthood V*. Ed. S. Church and R. Harvey. Woodbridge, 1995, pp. 1-17.

Barthélemy, Dominique. "Note sur le 'titre chevaleresque', en France au XIe siècle," *Journal des savantes* (1994), 101-34.

Barthélemy, Dominique. "Qu'est-ce que la chevalerie, en France aux Xe et XIe siècles?" *Revue historique* 290 (1994), 15-74.

Baumgartner, Frederic J. "The Final Demise of the Medieval Knight in France." In: *Regnum, Religio et Ratio: Essays Presented to Robert N. Kingdon*. Ed. J. Friedman. Sixteenth Century Essays and Studies, VIII. Kirksville, Missouri, 1987, pp. 9-17.

Bennett, Matthew. "The Knight Unmasked," *MHQ: The Quarterly Journal of Military History* 7 (Summer 1995), 8-19.

Bennett, Matthew. "The Status of a Squire: The Northern Evidence." In: *The Ideals and Practice of Medieval Knighthood*. Ed. C. Harper-Bill and R. Harvey. Woodbridge, 1986, pp. 1-11.

Blair, C.H. "The Knights of Northumberland in 1278 and 1324," *Archaeologia aeliana* 4th ser. 27 (1949), 122-76.

Boccia, Lionella Giorgio and Eduardo T. Coelho. "Colaccio Beccadelli: an Emilian Knight of about 1340." In: *Arms and Armor Annual: Volume One*. Ed. Robert Held. Northfield: Digest Books, Inc., 1973, pp. 10-27.

Böninger, Lorenz. *Die Ritterwürde in Mittelitalien zwischen Mittelalter und Früher Neuzeit: Mit einem Quellenanhang Päpstliche Ritterernennungen, 1417-1464*. Berlin: Akademie Verlag, 1995.

Borst, A. "Knighthood in the High Middle Ages: Ideal and Reality." In: *Lordship and Community in Medieval Europe: Selected Readings*. Ed. Frederic Cheyette. New York: Holt, Rinehart, and Winston, Inc., 1968, pp. 180-91.

Borst, A., ed. *Das Rittertum im Mittelalter*. Wege der Forschung, 349. Darmstadt, 1976.

Boulton, D'Arcy Jonathan Dacre. "Classic Knighthood as Nobiliary Dignity: The Knighting of Counts and Kings' Sons in England, 1066-1272." In: *Medieval Knighthood, V*. Ed. S. Church and R. Harvey. Woodbridge, 1995, pp. 41-100.

Boulton, D'Arcy Jonathan Dacre. *The Knights of the Crown: The Monarchical Orders of Knighthood in Later Medieval Europe, 1325-1520*. New York: St. Martin's Press, 1987.

Boussard, Jacques. "L'enquête de 1172 sur les services de chevalier en Normandie." In: *Recueil de travaux offerts à Clovis Brunel*. Paris, 1955, I:193-208.

Brinker, Claudia. "Ritterschaft, daz ist ein leben! oder Ritterschaft, ist das ein Leben?" In: *Die Manessische Liederhandschrift in Zürich*. Ed. Claudia Brinker and Dione Flühler-Kreis. Zurich: Schweizerisches Landesmuseum, 1991, pp. 149-55.

Broughton, Bradford B. *Dictionary of Medieval Knighthood and Chivalry: Concepts and Terms*. New York: Greenwood Press, 1986.

Broughton, Bradford B. *Dictionary of Medieval Knighthood and Chivalry: People, Places, and Events*. New York: Greenwood Press, 1988.

Bumke, Joachim. *Ministerialität und Ritterdichtung: Umrisse der Forschung*. Munich, 1976.

Bumke, Joachim. *Studien zum Ritterbegriff im 12. Und 13. Jahrhundert*. Heidelberg, 1964; trans. *The Concept of Knighthood in the Middle Ages*. Trans. W.T.H. Jackson. New York: AMS Press, Inc., 1977.

Cairns, Trevor. *Medieval Knights*. Cambridge: Cambridge University Press, 1992.

Carpenter, D. "Was There a Crisis of the Knightly Class in the Thirteenth Century? The Oxfordshire Evidence," *English Historical Review* 95 (1980), 721-52.

Chew, Helena M. *The English Ecclesiastic Tenants-in-Chief and Knight Service*. Oxford, 1932.

Church, S.D. *The Household Knights of King John*. Cambridge: Cambridge University Press, 1999.

Coss, Peter R. "Knighthood and the Early Thiteenth-Century County Court." In: *Thirteenth Century England II*. Ed. P.R. Coss and S.D. Lloyd. Woodbridge, 1988, pp. 45-57.

Coss, Peter R. *The Knight in Medieval England, 1000-1400*. Stroud: Alan Sutton, 1993.

Crane, Susan. "Knights in Disguise: Identity and Incognito in Fourteenth-Century Chivalry." In: *The Stranger in Medieval Society*. Ed. F.R.P. Akehurst and Stephanie Cain van d'Elden. Minneapolis: University of Minnesota Press, 1997, pp. 63-79.

Denholm-Young, N. "Feudal Society in the Thirteenth Century: The Knights." In: *Collected Papers on Mediaeval Subjects*. Oxford, 1946.

Duby, Georges. "Lineage, Nobility and Knighthood." In: *The Chivalrous Society*. Trans. C. Postan. Berkeley and Los Angeles, 1980, pp. 59-80.

Duby, Georges. "Les origines de la chevalerie." In: *Ordinamenti militari in occidente nell'alto medioevo*. Settimane di studio del centro italiano di studi sull'alto medioevo, XV. Spoleto, 1968, II:739-61; trans. "The Origins of Knighthood." In: *The Chivalrous Society*. Trans. C. Postan. Berkeley and Los Angeles, 1980, pp. 158-70.

Dunbabin, Jean. "From Clerk to Knight: Changing Orders." In: *The Ideals and Practice of Medieval Knighthood*, II. Ed. C. Harper-Bill and R. Harvey. Woodbridge, 1988, pp. 26-39.

Eberbach, O. *Die deutsche Reichsritterschaft in ihrer staatsrechtlich-politischen Entwicklung von den Anfängen bis zum Jahre 1422*. Dresden, 1912.

Evans, Dafydd. "The Nobility of the Knight and Falcon." In: *The Ideals and Practice of Medieval Knighthood*, III. Ed. C. Harper-Bill and R. Harvey. Woodbridge, 1990, pp. 79-99.

Feldbauer, P. *Herren und Ritter*. Herrschaftsstruktur und Ständebildung. Beiträge zur Typologie der österreichischen Länder aus ihren mittelalterlichen Frundlagen, I. Vienna, 1973.

Fenske, Lutz. "Adel und Ritterum im Spiegel früher heraldischer Formen und deren Enwicklung." In: *Das ritterliche Turnier im Mittelalter*. Ed. Josef Fleckenstein. Göttingen: Vandenhoeck and Ruprecht, 1985, pp. 75-162.

Fleckenstein, Josef. "Zur Frage der Abgrenzung von Bauer und Ritter." In: *Wort und Begriff Bauer*. Ed. R. Wenskus, H. Jahnkuhn, and K. Grinda.

Abhandlungen der phil.-hist. Klasse der Wissenschaften in Göttingen, ser. 3, 89. Gottingen, 1975, pp. 246-53.

Fleckenstein, Josef. "Friedrich Barbarossa und das Rittertum: Zur Bedeutung der großen Mainzer Hoftage von 1184 und 1188." In: *Festschrift für Hermann Heimpel*. Veröffentlichungen des Max-Planck-Instituts für Geschichte, 36.2. Gottingen, 1972, II:1023-41.

Fleckenstein, Josef. "Miles und clericus am Königs- und Fürstenhof: Bemerkungen zu den Voraussetzungen, zur Entstehung und zur Trägerschaft der höfisch-ritterlichen Kultur." In: *Curialitas: Studien zu Grundfragen der höfisch-ritterlichen Kultur*. Ed. Josef Fleckenstein. Göttingen, 1990, pp. 302-25.

Fleckenstein, Josef. "Zur Problem der Abschließung des Ritterstandes." In: *Historische Forschungen für Walter Schlesinger*. Ed. H. Beumann. Cologne and Vienna, 1974, pp. 252-71.

Flori, Jean. "Chevaliers et chevalerie au XIe en France et dans l'Empire germanique," *Moyen âge* 82 (1976), 125-36.

Flori, Jean. "A propos de l'adoubement des chevaliers au XIeme siècle: le pretendu 'pontifical du Reims' et 'l'ordo ad armandu' de Cambrai," *Frühmittelalterliche Studien* 19 (1985), 330-49.

Flori, Jean. "Qu'est-ce qu'un *bacheler*? Etude historique du vocabulaire dans les chansons de geste du XIIe siècle," *Romania* (1975), 289-314.

Föhl, W. "Niederrheinische Ritterschaft um Italien des Trecento," *Annalen des historischen Vereins für den Niederrhein* 165 (1963), 73-128.

Gies, Frances. *The Knight in History*. New York: Harper and Row, 1984.

Glubok, Shirley. *Knights in Armour*. New York: Harper and Row, 1969.

Goldberg, Eric J. "'More Devoted to the Equipment of Battle Than the Splendor of Banquets': Frontier Kingship, Martial Ritual, and Early Knighthood at the Court of Louis the German," *Viator* 30 (1999), 41-78.

Golding, Brian. "Anglo-Norman Knightly Burials." In: *The Ideals and Practice of Medieval Knighthood*. Ed. C. Harper-Bill and R. Harvey. Woodbridge, 1986, pp. 35-48.

Grancsay, Stephen V. "Knights in Armor," *Metropolitan Museum of Art Bulletin* n.s. 6 (Feb 1948), 178-88; in: *Arms and Armor: Essays by Stephen V. Grancsay from The Metropolitan Museum of Art Bulletin, 1920-1964*. New York: The Metropolitan Museum of Art, 1986, pp. 313-28.

Gravett, Christopher. *Knights at Tournament*. London, 1988.

Harper-Bill, C. "The Piety of the Anglo-Norman Knightly Class," *Anglo-Norman Studies* 2 (1979), 63-77.

Harvey, Sally. "The Knight and the Knight's Fee in England," *Past and Present* 49 (1970), 3-43; in: *Peasants, Knights and Heretics: Studies in Medieval England: Studies in Medieval English Social History*. Ed. R.H. Hilton. Cambridge, 1976, pp. 133-73.

Hindman, Sandra L. *Sealed in Parchment: Rereadings of Knighthood in the Illuminated Manuscripts of Chrétien de Troyes*. Chicago: University of Chicago Press, 1994.

Hollister, C. Warren. "The Knights of Peterborough and the Anglo-Norman Fyrd," *English Historical Review* 77 (1962), 417-36.

Holt, J.C. "The Introduction of Knight Service in England." In: *Anglo-Norman Warfare: Studies in Late Anglo-Saxon and Anglo-Norman Military Organization and Warfare*. Ed. M. Strickland. Woodbridge, 1992, pp. 41-58.

Hunt, Tony. "The Emergence of the Knight in France and England, 1000-1200." In: *Knighthood in Medieval Literature*. Ed. W.H. Jackson. Woodbridge, 1981, 1-22.

Jackson, William Henry. "Knighthood and the Hohenstaufen Imperial Court under Frederick Barbarossa (1152-1190)." In: *The Ideals and Practice of Medieval Knighthood*, III. Ed. C. Harper-Bill and R. Harvey. Woodbridge, 1990, pp. 101-20.

Jackson, William Henry, ed. *Knighthood in Medieval Literature*. Woodbridge, 1981.

Janse, Antheun. "Het leenbezit van de Hollandse ridderschap omstreeks 1475: Een analyse van het register *Valor Feodorum*," *Jaarboek voor middeleeuwse geschiedenis* 1 (1998), 163-204.

Janse, Antheun. "Ridderslåg en ridderlijkheid in laat-middeleeuws Holland," *Bijdragen en mededelingen betreffende de geschiedenis der Nederlanden* 112 (1997), 317-35.

Jefferson, Lisa. "MS Arundel and the Earliest Statutes of the Order of the Garter," *English Historical Review* 109 (1994), 356-85.

Johrendt, J. *Milites und Militia im 11 Jahrhundert: Untersuchung zur Frühgeschichte der Rittertums in Frankreich und Deutschland.* Nuremburg, 1971.

Johrendt, J. "Milites und Militia im 11. Jahrhundert in Deutschland." In: *Das Rittertum im Mittelalter.* Ed. A. Borst. Wege der Forschung, 349. Darmstadt, 1976, pp. 419-36.

Jones, Terry. *Chaucer's Knight: The Portrait of a Medieval Mercenary.* 2nd ed. London: Methuen, 1985.

Kaiser, G. "Minnesang, Ritterideal, Ministerialität." In: *Adelsherrschaft und Literatur.* Ed. H. Wenzel. Beiträge zur älteren deutschen Literaturgeschichte, 6. Bonn and Frankfurt, 1980, pp. 181-208.

Keen, Maurice. "Chaucer's Knight, the English Aristocracy and the Crusade." In: *English Court Culture in the Later Middle Ages.* Ed. V.J. Scattergood and J.W. Sherborne. New York, 1983, pp. 45-61.

Keen, Maurice. "Chivalry, Nobility, and the Man-at-Arms." In: *War, Literature and Politics in the Late Middle Ages: Essays in Honour of G.W. Coopland.* Ed. C.T. Allmand. Liverpool: University of Liverpool Press, 1975, pp. 32-45.

Keen, Maurice. "Gadifer de La Salle: A Late Medieval Knight Errant." In: *The Ideals and Practice of Medieval Knighthood.* Ed. C. Harper-Bill and R. Harvey. Woodbridge, 1986, pp. 74-85.

Kindrick, Robert L. "The 'Unknightly Knight': Teaching Satires on Chivalry." In: *The Study of Chivalry: Resources and Approaches.* Ed. H. Chickering and T.H. Seiler. Kalamazoo, 1988, pp. 663-82.

Krüger, Sabine. "Das Rittertum in den Schriften des Konrad von Megenberg." In: *Herrschaft und Stand: Untersuchung zur Sozialgeschichte im 13. Jahrhundert.* Ed. Josef Fleckenstein. Veröffentlichungen des Max-Planck-Instituts für Geschichte, 51. Gottingen, 1977, pp. 302-28.

Krüger, Sabine. "'Verhöflichter Krieger' und miles illitteratus." In: *Curialitas: Studien zu Grundfragen der höfisch-ritterlichen Kultur*. Ed. Josef Fleckenstein. Göttingen, 1990, pp. 326-49.

Leyser, Karl. "Early Medieval Canon Law and the Beginnings of Knighthood." In: *Institutionen, Kultur und Gesellschaft im mittelalter: Festschrift für Josef Fleckenstein zu seinem 65. Geburtstag*. Ed. L. Fenske et al. Sigmaringen, 1984, pp. 549-66.

Massmann, E.H. *Schwertleite und Ritterschlag*. Hamburg, 1932.

Meissburger, G. "*De vita christiana*; Zum Bild des christlichen Ritters im Hochmittelalter," *Der Deutschunterricht* 14 (1962), 21-34.

Moor, C. "Knights of Edward I," *Publications of the Harleian Society* 80-84 (1929-32).

Morris, Colin. "*Equestris ordo*: Chivalry as a Vocation in the Twelfth Century." In: *Religious Motivation: Biographical and Sociological Problems for the Church Historian*. Ed. D. Baker. Oxford, 1978, 87-96.

Mortimer, Richard. "Knights and Knighthood in Germany in the Central Middle Ages." In: *The Ideals and Practice of Medieval Knighthood*. Ed. C. Harper-Bill and R. Harvey. Woodbridge, 1986, pp. 86-103.

Nelson, Janet L. "Ninth-Century Knighthood: The Evidence of Nithard." In: *Studies in Medieval History Presented to R. Allen Brown*. Ed. C. Harper-Bill, C.J. Holdsworth and J. Nelson. Woodbridge, 1989, pp. 255-66.

Nickel, Helmut. "Sir Gawayne and the Three White Knights," *Metropolitan Museum of Art Bulletin* 28.4 (Dec 1969), 174-82.

Noble, Peter S. "Knights and Burgesses in the Feudal Epic." In: *The Ideals and Practice of Medieval Knighthood*. Ed. C. Harper-Bill and R. Harvey. Woodbridge, 1986, pp. 104-10.

Oakeshott, Ewart. *A Knight and His Armour*. London: Lutterworth Press, 1961.

Oakeshott, Ewart. *A Knight and His Castle*. London: Lutterworth Press, 1965.

Oakeshott, Ewart. *A Knight and His Weapons*. London: Lutterworth Press, 1964.

Orth, Elsbet. "Ritter und Berg." In: *Das ritterliche Turnier im Mittelalter.* Ed. Josef Fleckenstein. Göttingen: Vandenhoeck and Ruprecht, 1985, pp. 19-74.

Paterson, Linda M. "The Concept of Knighthood in the Twelfth-Century Occitan Lyric." In: *Chrétien de Troyes and the Troubadours: Essays in Memory of the Late Leslie Topsfield.* Ed. P.S. Noble and L. Paterson. Cambridge, 1984, pp. 112-32.

Paterson, Linda M. "The Occitan Squire in the Twelfth and Thirteenth Centuries." In: *The Ideals and Practice of Medieval Knighthood.* Ed. C. Harper-Bill and R. Harvey. Woodbridge, 1986, pp. 133-51.

Pietzner, F. *Schwertleite und Ritterschlag.* Heidelberg, 1932.

Pleticha, Heinrich. *Ritter, Burgen und Turniere.* 2nd ed. Wurzburg: Arena-Verlag Georg Popp, 1963.

Post, P. *Das Kostüm und die ritterliche Kriegstracht in deutschen Mittelalter von 1000-1450.* Berlin, 1939.

Powicke, Michael R. "Distraint of Knighthood and Military Obligation under Henry III," *Speculum* 25 (1950), 457-70.

Prestwich, Michael. "*Miles in armis strenuus*: The Knight at War," *Transactions of the Royal Historical Society*, 6th ser., 5 (1995), 129-53.

Rautenberg, W. "Ritter und Rotten: Zur begrifflichen und funktionalen Unterscheidung des geworbenen Kriegsvolkes," *Jahrbuch der Gesellschaft für niedsächsissche Kirchengeschichte* 76 (1978), 87-121.

Reitzenstein, Alexander Freiherr von. "Die Reiter von Mauerkirchen und Regensburg," *Waffen und Kostümkunde* 8 (1966), 61-80.

Reitzenstein, Alexander Freiherr von. *Rittertum und Ritterschaft.* Bibliothek des Germanischen Nationalmuseums Nürnberg zur deutschen Kunst- und Kulturgeschichte, 32. Munich: Prestel-Verlag, 1972.

Richter, J. "Der Ritter zwischen Gott und Welt: Ein Bild mittelalterlicher Religion bei Hartmann von Aue," *Zeitschrift für Religions- und Geistesgeschichte* 16 (1964), 57-69.

Richter, J. "Zur ritterlichen Frömmigkeit der Stauferzeit," *Wolfram-Jahrbuch* (1956), 23-52.

Ritter, J.-P. *Ministérialité et chevalerie: Dignité humaine et liberté dans le droit médiévale*. Lausanne, 1955.

Rösener, Werner. "Ministerialität, Vasallität und niederadelige Ritterschaft im Herrschaftsbereich der Markgrafen von Baden vom 11. bis zum 14. Jahrhunderts." In: *Herrschaft und Stand: Untersuchungen zur Sozialgeschichte im 13. Jahrhundert*. Ed. Josef Fleckenstein. Veröffentlichungen des Max-Planck-Instituts für Geschichte, 51. Gottingen, 1977, pp. 40-91.

Round, J.H. "The Introduction of Knight Service into England." In: *Feudal England*. London, 1895.

Rousset, Paul. "Note sur la situation du chevalier à l'époque romane." In: *Literature, histoire, linguistique: Recueil d'études offerts à Bernard Gagnebin*. Lausanne, 1973, pp. 189-200.

Rudorff, Raymond. *Knights and the Age of Chivalry*. New York: The Viking Press, 1974.

Rudorff, Raymond. *The Knights and their World*. London: Cassel, 1974.

Sablonier, Roger. "Rittertum, Adel und Kriegswesen im Spätmittelalter." In: *Das ritterliche Turnier im Mittelalter*. Ed. Josef Fleckenstein. Göttingen: Vandenhoeck and Ruprecht, 1985, pp. 532-70.

Sandberger, D. *Studien über das Rittertum in England, vornehmlich während des 14. Jahrhunderts*. Berlin, 1937.

Saul, Nigel. *Knights and Esquires: the Gloucestershire Gentry in the Fourteenth Century*. Oxford, 1981.

Scammell, Jean. "The Formation of the English Social Structure: Freedom, Knights, and Gentry, 1066-1300," *Speculum* 68 (1993), 591-618.

Schäfer, Karl Heinrich. "Deutsche Ritter und Edelknechte in Italien während des XIV. Jahrhunderts," *Quellen und Forschungen aus dem Gebiet der Geschichte* 15 (1911); 16 (1914); 25 (1940).

Schlight, John. *Monarchs and Mercenaries: A Reappraisal of the Importance of Knight Service of Norman and Angevin England*. Bridgeport: Conference on British Studies, 1968.

Schlutz, W. *Die Gleve: Der Ritter und sein Gefolge im späteren Mittelalter*. Munich, 1940.

Sprandel, R. "Die Ritterschaft und das Hochstift Würzburg im Spätmittelalter," *Jahrbuch für fränkische Landesforschung* 36 (1976), 117-43.

Strayer, Joseph R. "Knight Service in Normandy in the XIIIth Century." In: *Anniversary Essays in Mediaeval History by Students of Charles Homer Haskins*. Ed. C.H. Taylor. Boston, 1929, pp. 312-27.

Stromer, Wolfgang von. "Die Bildnisse des Ehinger und des Peter Stromair und Georg von Ehingens Reisen nach der Ritterschaft," *Waffen- und Kostümkunde* 10 (1968), 77-106.

Suttner, Gustav. *Reiterstudien*. 1880; rpt. Graz: Akademische Druck- und Verlagsanstalt, 1968.

Switten, Margaret. "*Chevalier* in Twelfth-Century French and Occitan Vernacular Literature." In: *The Study of Chivalry: Resources and Approaches*. Ed. H. Chickering and T.H. Seiler. Kalamazoo, 1988, pp. 403-48.

Tait, J. "Knight-Service in Cheshire," *English Historical Review* 57 (1942), 437-59.

Thompson, A. Logan. "The Decline of the Armoured Knight. Part 1: The Rise of the Halberd and Emergence of Gunpowder," *Classic Arms and Militaria* 5.2 (Mar/Apr 1998), 34-37.

Thompson, A. Logan. "The Decline of the Armoured Knight. Part 2: How Feudal Armoured Cavalry Became Obsolete, the Response of Feudal Aristocracy to their Defeats," *Classic Arms and Militaria* 5.3 (May/Jun 1998), 32-36.

Thompson, Colin P. "The Quixotic Knight." In: *Chivalry in the Renaissance*. Ed. Sydney Anglo. Woodbridge: The Boydell Press, 1990, pp. 239-52.

van Luyn, Pierre. "Milites et barones," *Cahiers de civilisation médiévale (X-XIIe siècle)* 36 (1993), 281-95.

van Winter, J.M. "*Cingulum militiae*: Schwertleite en miles–terminologie als spiegel van veranderend menselijk gedrag," *Tijdschrift voor Rechtgeschiedenis* 44 (1976), 1-92.

Wallhausen, Johann Jacob. *Ritterkunst*. Graz: Druck- u. Verlagsanstalt, 1969.

Williams, Ann. "The Knights of Shaftesbury Abbey," *Anglo-Norman Studies* 8 (1985), 214-.

Williams, John Bryan. "Judhael of Totnes: The Life and Times of a Post-Conquest Baron," *Anglo-Norman Studies* 16 (1993), 271-89.

Zallinger, O. von. *Ministerales und Milites*. Innsbruck, 1878.

Medieval – Chivalry – Monumental Effigies

Blair, Claude. "The de Vere Effigy at Hatfield Broad Oak," *Church Monuments* 8 (1993), 3-11.

Bridges, S.F. and J. Ward Perkins. "Some Fourteenth-Century Neapolitan Military Effigies with Notes on the Families Represented," *Papers of the British School at Rome* 24 (1956), 158-73.

Clayton, M. *Victoria and Albert Museum, London: Catalogue of Rubbings of Brasses and Incised Slabs*. 2nd ed. London, 1968.

Emmerson, Robin. "Monumental Brasses: London Design, c. 1420-85," *Journal of the British Archaeological Association* 131 (1978), 50-78.

Feldgate, T.M. *Knights on Suffolk Brasses*. Ipswich: East Anglian Magazine Ltd., 1976.

Greenhill, F.A. *Incised Effigial Slabs*. 2 vols. London: Faber and Faber, 1976.

Greenhill, F.A. *Monumental Incised Slabs in the County of Lincoln*. Newport Pagnall: Francis Coles Charitable Foundation, 1986.

Hunt, John. *Irish Medieval Figure Sculpture, 1200-1600: A Study of Irish Tombs with Notes on Costume and Armour*. 2 vols. Dublin: Irish University Press, 1974.

Lack, William, H. Martin Stuchfield, and Philip Whittemore. *The Monumental Brasses of Bedfordshire*. London: Monumental Brass Society, 1992.

Lack, William, H. Martin Stuchfield, and Philip Whittemore. *The Monumental Brasses of Berkshire*. London: Monumental Brass Society, 1993.

Lack, William, H. Martin Stuchfield, and Philip Whittemore. *The Monumental Brasses of Buckinghamshire*. London: Monumental Brass Society, 1994.

Lack, William, H. Martin Stuchfield, and Philip Whittemore. *The Monumental Brasses of Cambridgeshire*. London: Monumental Brass Society, 1995.

Lack, William, H. Martin Stuchfield, and Philip Whittemore. *The Monumental Brasses of Cheshire*. London: Monumental Brass Society, 1996.

Lack, William, H. Martin Stuchfield, and Philip Whittemore. *The Monumental Brasses of Cornwall*. London: Monumental Brass Society, 1997.

Lack, William, H. Martin Stuchfield, and Philip Whittemore. *The Monumental Brasses of Cumberland and Westmorland*. London: Monumental Brass Society, 1998.

Lack, William, H. Martin Stuchfield, and Philip Whittemore. *The Monumental Brasses of Derbyshire*. London: Monumental Brass Society, 1999.

Lankester, Philip J. "A Military Effigy in Dorchester Abbey, Oxon," *Oxonensia* 52 (1987), 145-72.

Lankester, Philip J. "Two Lost Effigal Monuments in Yorkshire and the Evidence of Church Notes," *Church Monuments* 8 (1993), 25-44.

Melville, Neil. "The Incised Effigial Stone at Foveran, Aberdeenshire," *Park Lane Arms Fair* 15 (1998), 11-17.

Norman, A.V.B. "The Effigy of Alexander Stewart, Earl of Buchan and Lord of Badenoch (?1343-?1405)," *Proceedings of the Antiquaries of Scotland* 92 (1961), 104-13.

Norman, A.V.B. "An Unpublished Fourteenth-Century Alabaster Fragment," *Journal of the Church Monuments Society* 2 (1987), 3-8.

Norris, Malcolm W. *Monumental Brasses: The Craft*. London: Faber and Faber, 1978.

Norris, Malcolm W. *Monumental Brasses: The Memorial*. 2 vols. London: Philips and Page, 1978.

Norris, Malcolm W, ed. *Monumental Brasses: The Portfolio Plates of the Monumental Brass Society, 1894-1984*. Woodbridge: The Boydell Press, 1988.

Reitzenstein, Alexander Freiherr von. "Der Ritter im Heergewäte: Bemerkungen über einige Bildgrabsteine der Hochgotik." In: *Studien zur Geschichte der europäischen Plastik: Festschrift für Theodor Müller zum April 1965*. Munich: Hirmer Verlag, 1965, pp. 73-91.

Routh, Pauline C. *Medieval Effigal Alabaster Tombs in Yorkshire*. Ipswich: The Boydell Press, 1976.

Southwick, L. "The Armoured Effigy of Prince John of Eltham in Westminster Abbey and Some Closely Related Military Monuments," *Journal of the Church Monuments Society* 2 (1987), 9-21.

Steer, K.A. and J.W. Bannerman. *Late Medieval Monumental Scupture in the West Highlands*. The Royal Commission on the Ancient and Historical Monuments of Scotland. Edinburgh: Her Majesty's Stationery Office, 1977.

Stewart, Ian. "Knights in Armour and Their Ladies: The Monumental Brasses at Cobham Church, Kent," *Country Life* (Dec 11, 1969), 1590-92.

Stothard, C.A. *The Monumental Effigies of Great Britain*. 2nd ed. London, 1876.

van Caster, E., and R. op de Beeck. *De grafkunst in Belgisch Limburg: Vloerzerken me persoonsvoorstellungen (13e tot 17e eeuw)*. Assen: Van Gorcum, 1981.

Medieval – Chivalry – Tournaments

Anglo, Sydney. "Anglo-Burgundian Feats of Arms: Smithfield, June 1467," *Guildhall Miscellany* 2.7 (Sept 1965), 271-83.

Anglo, Sydney. "Archives of the English Tournament: Score Cheques and Lists," *Journal of the Society of Archivists* 2.4 (Oct 1961), 153-62.

Anglo, Sydney. "Financial and Heraldic Records of the English Tournament," *Journal of the Society of Archivists* 2.5 (Apr 1962), 183-92.

Anglo, Sydney. *The Great Tournament Roll of Westminster*. Oxford, 1968.

Anglo, Sydney. "How to Win at Tournaments: The Technique of Chivalric Combat," *Antiquaries Journal* 68 (1988), 248-64.

Anglo, Sydney. "Jousting–The Earliest Treatises," *Livrustkammaren* 19 (1991-92), 3-23.

Anglo, Sydney. *Spectacle, Pageantry and Early Tudor Policy*. Oxford, 1969.

Annunziata, Anthony. "Teaching the *Pas d'Armes*." In: *The Study of Chivalry: Resources and Approaches*. Ed. H. Chickering and T.H. Seiler. Kalamazoo, 1988, pp. 557-82.

Baldwin, John W. "Jean Renart et le tournoi de Saint-Trond: Une conjonction de l'histoire et de la littérature," *Annales ESC* 45 (1990), 565-88.

Barber, Richard and Juliet R.V. Barker. *Tournaments: Jousts, Chivalry and Pageants in the Middle Ages*. New York: Weidenfeld and Nicolson, 1989.

Barker, Juliet R.V. *The Tournament in England, 1100-1400*. Woodbridge: The Boydell Press. 1986.

Barker, Juliet R.V. and Maurice Keen. "The Medieval English Kings and the Tournament." In: *Das ritterliche Turnier im Mittelalter*. Ed. Josef Fleckenstein. Göttingen: Vandenhoeck and Ruprecht, 1985, pp. 212-28.

Blair, Claude. "Two Toy Jousters," *Waffen- und Kostümkunde* 8 (1966), 43-47.

Carter, John Marshall. *Medieval Games: Sports and Recreations in Feudal Society*. Contributions to the Study of World History, 30. New York: Greenwood Press, 1992.

Carter, John Marshall. *Sports and Pastimes of the Middle Ages*. Lanham: University Press of America, 1988.

Clare, Lucien. *La quintaine, la course de bague et le jeu des têtes*. Paris, 1983.

Clephan, R. Coltman. *The Tournament in Periods and Phases*. London, 1919.

Contamine, Philippe. "Les tournois en France à la fin du moyen âge." In: *Das ritterliche Turnier im Mittelalter*. Ed. Josef Fleckenstein. Göttingen: Vandenhoeck and Ruprecht, 1985, pp. 425-49.

Cripps-Day, F.H. *The History of the Tournament in England and in France*. London, 1918.

Denholm-Young, N. "The Tournament in the Thirteenth Century." In: *Studies in Medieval History Presented to Frederick Maurice Powicke*. Ed. R.W. Hunt et al. Oxford, 1948, pp. 240-66.

Dillon, Viscount. "Barriers and Foot Combats," *Archaeological Journal* 61 (1904), 276-308.

Dondi, Giorgio. "Il bagordo di Ivrea: Torneo alla Corte Sabauda nel 1522," *Armi antichi* (1988-89), 3-32.

Edington, Carol. "The Tournament in Medieval Scotland." In: *Armies, Chivalry and Warfare in Medieval Britain and France: Proceedings of the 1995 Harlaxton Symposium*. Ed. M. Strickland. Stamford, 1998, pp. 46-62.

Elliott, Lois. "Le pas d'armes au XVe siècle," *Annales de l'est*, 5th ser., 45 (1993), 83-120.

Fleckenstein, Josef. "Nachwort: Ergebnisse und Probleme." In: *Das ritterliche Turnier im Mittelalter*. Ed. Josef Fleckenstein. Göttingen: Vandenhoeck and Ruprecht, 1985, pp. 624-51.

Fleckenstein, Josef. "Das Turnier als höfisches Fest im hochmittelalterlichen Deutschland." In: *Das ritterliche Turnier im Mittelalter*. Ed. Josef Fleckenstein. Göttingen: Vandenhoeck and Ruprecht, 1985, pp. 229-56.

Fradenburg, Louis Olga. *City, Marriage, Tournament: Arts of Rule in Late Medieval Scotland*. Madison: University of Wisconsin Press, 1991.

Fügedi, Erik. "Turniere im mittelalterlichen Ungarn." In: *Das ritterliche Turnier im Mittelalter*. Ed. Josef Fleckenstein. Göttingen: Vandenhoeck and Ruprecht, 1985, pp. 390-400.

Gaier, Claude. "Technique des combats singuliers d'après les auteurs "bourguignons" du XVe siècle," *Moyen âge* 91 (1985), 415-57; 92 (1986), 5-40.

Galbraith, V.H. "The Death of a Champion (1287)." In: *Studies in Medieval History Presented to Frederick Maurice Powicke*. Ed. R.W. Hunt, W.A. Pantin, and R.W. Southern. Oxford, 1948, pp. 283-95.

Gamber, Ortwin. "Ritterspiele und Turnierrüstung im Spätmittelalter." In: *Das ritterliche Turnier im Mittelalter*. Ed. Josef Fleckenstein. Göttingen: Vandenhoeck and Ruprecht, 1985, pp. 513-31.

Gaucher, E. "Les joutes de Saint-Inglevert: Perception et écriture d'un événtement historique pendant la guerre de Cent Ans," *Moyen âge* 102 (1996), 229-43.

Gravett, Christopher. *Knights at Tournament*. London, 1988.

Guichard, Pierre. "A propos de quelques témoignages écrits et figurés sur les combats singuliers équestres dans l'Espagne musulmane au XIème siècle." In: *Das ritterliche Turnier im Mittelalter*. Ed. Josef Fleckenstein. Göttingen: Vandenhoeck and Ruprecht, 1985, pp. 339-43.

Heers, Jacques. *Fêtes, jeux et joutes dans les sociétés d'occident à la fin du moyen âge*. Conférence Albert-le-Grand 1971. Montreal: Institut d'Études Médiévales, 1982.

Huizinga, Johan. *Homo Ludens: A Study of the Play-Element in Culture*. Boston: The Beacon Press, 1955.

Jackson, William Henry. "Das Turnier in der deutschen Dichtung des Mittelalters." In: *Das ritterliche Turnier im Mittelalter*. Ed. Josef Fleckenstein. Göttingen: Vandenhoeck and Ruprecht, 1985, pp. 257-95.

Jackson, William Henry. "The Tournament and Chivalry in German Tournament Books of the Sixteenth Century and in the Literary Works of Emperor Maximilian I." In: *The Ideals and Practice of Medieval Knighthood*. Ed. C. Harper-Bill and R. Harvey. Woodbridge, 1986, pp. 49-73.

Jackson, William Henry. "Tournaments and the German Chivalric *renovatio*: Tournament Discipline and the Myth of Origins." In: *Chivalry in the Renaissance*. Ed. Sydney Anglo. Woodbridge: The Boydell Press, 1990, pp. 77-92.

Jillings, Lewis. "Ordeal by Combat and the Rejection of Chivalry in *Diu Crône*," *Speculum* 51 (1976), 262-76.

Kottenkamp, F. *History of Chivalry and Ancient Armour*. Trans. A. Löwy. London: Willis and Sotheran, 1857; rpt. London: Brocken Books, 1988.

Krüger, Sabine. "Das kirchliche Turnierverbot im Mittelalter." In: *Das ritterliche Turnier im Mittelalter*. Ed. Josef Fleckenstein. Göttingen: Vandenhoeck and Ruprecht, 1985, pp. 401-24.

Lindenbaum, Sheila. "The Smithfield Tournament of 1390," *Journal of Medieval and Renaissance Studies* 20 (1990), 1-20.

Macek, Josef. "Das Turnier im mittelalterlichen Böhmen." In: *Das ritterliche Turnier im Mittelalter*. Ed. Josef Fleckenstein. Göttingen: Vandenhoeck and Ruprecht, 1985, pp. 371-90.

McNeal, Edgar H. "Fulk of Neuilly and the Tournament of Ecry," *Speculum* 28 (1953), 371-75.

Meyer, Werner. "Turniergesellschaften: Bermerkungen zur sozialgeschichtlichen Bedeutung der Turnier im Spätmittelalter." In: *Das ritterliche Turnier im Mittelalter*. Ed. Josef Fleckenstein. Göttingen: Vandenhoeck and Ruprecht, 1985, pp. 500-12.

Mölk, Ulrich. "Philologische Aspekte des Turniers." In: *Das ritterliche Turnier im Mittelalter*. Ed. Josef Fleckenstein. Göttingen: Vandenhoeck and Ruprecht, 1985, pp. 163-74.

Nickel, Helmut. "The Tournament: An Historical Sketch." In: *The Study of Chivalry: Resources and Approaches*. Ed. H. Chickering and T.H. Seiler. Kalamazoo, 1988, pp. 213-62.

Norman, A.V.B. "A Scottish Tournament of the Early 16th Century," *Livrustkammaren* 19 (1991-92), 88-103.

Parisse, Michel. "Le tournoi en France des origines à la fin du XIIIe siècle." In: *Das ritterliche Turnier im Mittelalter*. Ed. Josef Fleckenstein. Göttingen: Vandenhoeck and Ruprecht, 1985, pp. 175-211.

Parkinson, E. Malcolm. "Sir Philip Sidney on Jousting and Tilting." In: *Proceedings of the Ninth Triennial Congress of the International Association of Museums of Arms and Military History*. Quantico: Marine Corps Association, 1981, pp. 132-46.

Paterson, Linda M. "Tournaments and Knightly Sports in Twelfth- and Thirteenth-Century Occitania," *Medium Aevum* 55 (1986), 72-84.

Pfaffenbichler, Matthias. "Das Turnier als Instrument der Habsburgischen Politik," *Waffen- und Köstumkunde* 34 (1992), 13-36.

Planche, A. "Du tournoi au theatre en Bourgogne. Le pas de la fontaine des pleurs à Chalons-sur-Saone." *Le moyen âge* 81 (1975), 97-128.

Pleticha, Heinrich. *Ritter, Burgen und Turniere.* 2nd ed. Wurzburg: Arena-Verlag Georg Popp, 1963.

Role, Raymond E. "War-Games in Central Italy," *History Today* 49 (June 1999), 8-13.

Rösener, Werner. "Ritterliche Wirtschaftsverhältnisse und Turnier im sozialen Wandel des Hochmittelalters." In: *Das ritterliche Turnier im Mittelalter.* Ed. Josef Fleckenstein. Göttingen: Vandenhoeck and Ruprecht, 1985, pp. 296-338.

Sandoz, Edouard. "Tourneys in Arthurian Tradition," *Speculum* 20 (1945), 389-432.

Scherb, Victor I. "The Tournament of Power: Public Combat and Social Inferiority in Late Medieval England," *Studies in Medieval and Renaissance History* 12 (1991), 105-28.

Scibałło, Feliks. "Póznogotycka zbroja turniejowa w zbiorach wawelskich," *Studia do dziejów wawelu* 3 (1968), 335-61.

Swanson, Keith. "'God Woll Have a Stroke': Judicial Combat in the *Morte Darthur*," *Bulletir. of the John Rylands Library* 74 (1992), 155-73.

Szabó, Thomas. "Das Turnier in Italien." In: *Das ritterliche Turnier im Mittelalter.* Ed. Josef Fleckenstein. Göttingen: Vandenhoeck and Ruprecht, 1985, pp. 344-70.

Uri, S.P. "Het tournooi in de XIIe en XIIIe eeuw," *Tijdschrift voor geschiedenis* 73 (1960), 376-96.

van den Neste, Évelyne. *Tournois, joutes, pas d'armes dans les villes de Flandre à la fin du moyen âge (1300-1486).* Paris: École des chartes, 1996.

Watanabe-O'Kelly, Helen. "Tournaments and their Relevance for Warfare in the Early Modern Period," *European History Quarterly* 20 (1990), 451-63.

Watts, Karen. "Henry VIII and the Pageantry of the Tudor Tournament," *Livrustkammaren* 19 (1993), 131-41.

Webster, K.G.T. "The Twelfth Century Tournament." In: *Kittredge Anniversary Papers*. Cambridge, 1913, pp. 227-34.

Weihrauch, Hans R. "Ein verkanntes Spielzeug der Dürerzeit," *Waffen- und Kostümkunde* 5 (1963), 17-20.

Winters, Henri P.J. "Federico da Montefeltro, Duke of Urbino (1422-82): The Story of His Missing Nasal Bridge," *British Journal of Plastic Surgery* 35 (1982), 247-50.

Wozel, Heidrun. *Turniere: Exponate aus dem Historischen Museum zu Dresden*. Berlin: Militärverlag der Deutschen Demokratische Republik, 1979.

Zotz, Thomas. "Adel, Bürgertum und Turnier in deutschen Städten vom 13. bis 15. Jahrhundert." In: *Das ritterliche Turnier im Mittelalter*. Ed. Josef Fleckenstein. Göttingen: Vandenhoeck and Ruprecht, 1985, pp. 450-99.

Medieval – Church (also Just War) [See also – Crusades]

Auer, Leopold. "Der Kriegsdienst des Klerus unter den sächsischen Kaisern," *Mitteilungen des Instituts für österreichische Geschichtsforschung* 79 (1971), 316-407; 80 (1972), 48-70.

Allmand, Christopher T. "Some Effects of the Last Phase of the Hundred Years War upon the Maintenance of Clergy," *Studies in Church History* 3 (1966), 179-90.

Bainton, Roland H. *Christian Attitudes Toward War and Peace: A Historical Survey and Critical Re-evaluation*. Nashville: Abingdon Press, 1990.

Bainton, Roland H. "The Early Church and War," *Harvard Theological Review* 39 (1946), 189-212.

Barnes, J. "The Just War." In: *The Cambridge History of Later Medieval Philosophy*. Ed. N. Kretzmann, A. Kenny, and J. Pinborg. Cambridge: Cambridge University Press, 1982, pp. 771-84.

Barnes, Timothy D. "The Military Career of Martin of Tours," *Analecta Bollandiana* 1134 (1996), 25-32.

Biller, Peter. "Medieval Waldensian Abhorrence of Killing Pre-c1400," *Studies in Church History* 20 (1983), 129-46.

Bliese, John R.E. "The Just War as Concept and Motive in the Central Middle Ages," *Medievalia et Humanistica* n.s. 17 (1991), 1-26.

Bliese, John R.E. "Saint Cuthbert and War," *Journal of Medieval History* 24 (1998), 215-41.

Bliese, John R.E. "St. Cuthbert's and St. Neort's Help in War: Visions and Exhortations," *Haskins Society Journal* 7 (1995), 39-62.

Bond, Brian. "The 'Just War' in Historical Perspective," *History Today* 16 (1966), 111-19.

Brundage, James A. "Holy War and the Medieval Lawyers." In: *The Holy War*. Ed. T.P. Murphy. Columbus, 1976, pp. 99-140.

Brundage, James A. "The Limits of War-Making Power: The Contribution of the Medieval Canonists." In: *Peace in a Nuclear Age: The Bishops' Pastoral Letter in Perspective*. Ed. C.J. Reid, Jr. Washington, 1986, pp. 69-85.

Cadoux, C. John. *The Early Christian Attitude To War: A Contribution to the History of Christian Ethics*. New York: The Seabury Press, 1982.

Cardini, Franco. "La guerra santa nella cristianità." In: *"Militia Christi" e crociata nei secoli XI-XIII: Atti della undecima settimana internazionale di studio, Mendola, 28 agosta-1 settembre 1989*. Miscellanea del Centro di studi medioevali, 13; Scienze storiche, 48. Milan: Vita e Pensiero, 1992, pp. 387-401.

Cessario, Romanus. "St. Thomas Aquinas on Satisfaction, Indulgences, and Crusades," *Medieval Philosophy and Theology* 2 (1992), 74-96.

Chénon, E. "Saint Thomas d'Aquin et la guerre." In: *L'église et le droit de la guerre*. Paris, 1929.

Ciappelli, Giovanni. "A Trecento Bishop as Seen by Quattrocento Florentines: Sant' Andrea Corsini, His 'Life,' and the Battle of Anghari." In: *Portraits of Medieval and Renaissance Living: Essays in Memory of David Herlihy*. Ed. S.K. Cohn Jr. and S.A. Epstein. Ann Arbor, 1996, pp. 283-98.

Cipollone, Giulio. "Les trinitaires, rédempteurs des captifs (1198)." In: *La guerre, la violence et les gens au Moyen Âge*. I: *Guerre et violence*. Ed. P. Contamine and O. Guyotjeannin. 119e congrès national des sociétés historiques et scientifiques, Amiens, octobre 1994, Section d'histoire médiévale et philologie. Paris, 1996, pp. 311-20.

Contamine, Philippe. "L'idée de guerre à la fin du moyen âge: Aspects juridiques et éthiques," *Academie des inscriptions et belles-lettres. Comptes rendus seances* (1979), 70-86.

Contamine, Philippe. "La théologie de la guerre à la fin du moyen âge: la guerre de cent ans fut-elle une guerre juste?" In: *Jeanne d'Arc: Une époque, un rayonnement*. Paris, 1982, pp. 9-21.

Coupland, Simon. "The Rod of God's Wrath or the People of God's Wrath? The Carolingian Theology of the Viking Invasions," *Journal of Ecclesiastical History* 42 (1991), 535-54.

Cowdrey, H.E.J. "Bishop Ermenfried of Sion and the Penitential Ordinance following the Battle of Hastings," *Journal of Ecclesiastical History* 20 (1969), 225-42.

De Bruyn, Theodore S. "Ambivalence Within a 'Totalizing Discourse': Augustine's Sermons on the Sack of Rome," *Journal of Early Christian Studies* 1 (1993), 405-21.

DeVries, Kelly. "God and Defeat in Medieval Warfare: Some Preliminary Thoughts." In: *The Circle of War in the Middle Ages: Essays on Medieval Military and Naval History*. Ed. Donald J. Kagay and L.J. Andrew Villalon. Woodbridge: The Boydell Press, 1999, pp. 87-97.

Draper, G.I.A. "Penitential Discipline and Public Wars in the Middle Ages," *International Review of the Red Cross* (1961).

Dufeil, Michel-Marie. "*Miles secundum Tomam* et la découverte de l'historicité de la guerre." In: *Le combattant au moyen âge*. 2nd ed. Histoire ancienne et médiévale, 36. Paris: Publications of the Sorbonne, 1990, pp. 227-41.

Earle, William. "In Defense of War," *The Monist* 57 (1973), 551-69.

Ebbesen, Sten. "Just War?" In: *War and Peace in the Middle Ages*. Ed. B.P. McGuire. Copenhagen, 1987, pp. 179-94.

Finke, H. "Das Problem des gerechten Krieges in der mittelalterlichen theologischen Literatur." In: *Aus der Geisteswelt des Mittelalters: Martin Grabmann zur Vollendung des 60. Lebensjahr von Freunden und Schülern gewidmet*. Ed. A. Lang, J. Lechner, and M. Schmauss. Munster, 1935, pp. 1426-34.

Foot, Sarah. "Violence against Christians? The Vikings and the Church in Ninth-Century England," *Medieval History* 1.3 (1991), 3-16.

Fortin, Ernest L. "Christianity and the Just-War Theory," *Orbis* 27 (1983), 523-35.

Fournier, P. "La prohibition par le deuxième concile de Latran d'armes jugées trop meutrières," *Revue générale de droit international public* 33 (1916).

Frend, W.H.C. "The Cult of Military Saints in Christian Nubia." In: *Theologica crucis–signum crucis: Festschrift für Erich Dinkler*. Ed. C. Andersen and G. Klein. Tubingen, 1979, pp. 155-63.

Gaier, Claude. "Le destin militaire de l'abbaye de Saint-Laurent de Liège." In: *Saint-Laurent de Liège, église, abbaye et hôpital militaire: Mille ans d'histoire*. Liege, 1968, pp. 219-24.

Gaier, Claude. "Le rôle militaire des reliques et de l'étendard de saint Lambert dans la principauté de Liège," *Moyen âge* 72 (1966), 235-49; in: *Armes et combats dans l'univers médiéval*. Liege, 1995, pp. 337-48.

Gero, Stephen. "*Miles Gloriosus*: The Christian and Military Service According to Tertullian," *Church History* 39 (1970), 285-98.

Gmür, H. *Thomas von Aquino und der Krieg*. Leipzig, 1933.

Gorkum, Hendrik van. "Bijlage: De rechtvaardige oorlog." Trans. H.A. Krop. In: *Oorlog in de middeleeuwen*. Ed. A.J. Brand. Hilversum, 1989, pp. 151-72.

Grabois, Aryeh. "*Militia* and *Malitia*: The Bernardine Vision of Chivalry." In: *The Second Crusade and the Cistercians*. Ed. M. Gervers. New York, 1992, pp. 49-56.

Grant, Robert M. "War–Just, Holy, Unjust–in Hellenistic and Early Christian Thought," *Augustinianum* 20 (1980), 173-89.

Haines, Roy Martin. "An English Archbishop and the Cerberus of War," *Studies in Church History* 20 (1983), 153-70.

Hallam, Elizabeth M. "Monasteries as 'War Memorials': Battle Abbey and La Victoire," *Studies in Church History* 20 (1983), 47-57.

Hare, Kent G. "Clerics, War and Weapons in Anglo-Saxon England." In: *The Final Argument: The Imprint of Violence on Society in Medieval and Early Modern Europe*. Ed. Donald J. Kagay and L.J. Andrew Villalon. Woodbridge: The Boydell Press, 1998, pp. 3-12.

Harnack, Adolf. *Militia Christi: The Christian Religion and the Military in the First Three Centuries*. Trans. David McInnes Gracie. Philadelphia, 1981.

Harper-Bill, C. "The Piety of the Anglo-Norman Knightly Class," *Anglo-Norman Studies* 2 (1979), 63-77.

Hartigan, Richard Shelly. "Saint Augustine on War and Killing: The Problem of the Innocent," *Journal of the History of Ideas* 27 (1966), 195-204.

Head, Thomas and Richard Landes, ed. *The Peace of God: Social Violence and Religious Response in France Around the Year 1000*. Ithaca: Cornell University Press, 1992.

Heath, Peter. "War and Peace in the Works of Erasmus: A Medieval Perspective." In: *The Medieval Military Revolution: State, Society and Military Change in Medieval and Early Modern Europe*. Ed. A. Ayton and J.L. Price. London, 1995, pp. 121-44.

Hehl, Ernst-Dieter. *Kirche und Krieg im 12. Jahrhundert: Studien zu kanonischen Recht und politischer Wirklichtkeit*. Stuttgart, 1980.

Herir, J. Bryan. "The Just War Ethic and the Military Support of Science and Technology." In: *Ethical Issues Associated with Scientific and Techno-*

logical Research for the Military. Ed. C. Mitcham and P. Siekevitz. New York, 1989, pp. 99-105.

Hildesheimer, E. *L'activité militaire des clercs à l'époque franque*. Paris, 1936.

Hill, Rosalind M.T. "Undesirable Aliens in the Diocese of York." In: *The Church and War*. Ed. W.J. Sheils. Oxford, 1983, pp. 147-51.

Holdsworth, Christopher J. "'An Airier Aristocracy': The Saints at War," *Transactions of the Royal Historical Society*, 6th ser., 6 (1996), 103-22.

Holdsworth, Christopher J. "Ideas and Reality: Some Attempts to Control and Defuse War in the Twelfth Century," *Studies in Church History* 20 (1983), 59-78.

Holmes, Robert L. "On Pacifism," *The Monist* 57 (1973), 489-506.

Hornus, J.M. *Evangile et labarum: Etude sur l'attitude du christianisme primitif devant les problèmes de l'état, de la guerre et de la violence*. Geneva, 1980.

Hrabar, V.E. "Le droit international au moyen âge," *Revue de droit international* 18 (1936).

Hubrecht, G. "La juste guerre dans la doctrine chrétienne des origines au milieu du XVIe siècle," *Recueils de la société Jean Bodin* 15 (1961), 107-23.

Hubrecht, G. "La 'juste guerre' dans le décret de Gratien," *Studia Gratiana* 3 (1955), 161-77.

Jenkins, Iredell. "The Conditions of Peace," *The Monist* 57 (1973), 507-26.

Johnson, James Turner. *The Holy War Idea in Western and Islamic Traditions*. University Park: Pennsylvania State University Press, 1997.

Johnson, James Turner. *Ideology, Reason and the Limitation of War: Religious and Secular Concepts, 1200-1740*. Princeton: Princeton University Press, 1975.

Johnson, James Turner. *Just War Tradition and the Restraint of War: A Moral and Historical Inquiry*. Princeton: Princeton University Press, 1981.

Johnson, James Turner. "Toward Reconstructing the *Jus ad bellum*," *The Monist* 57 (1973), 461-88.

Kamen, Henry. "Clerical Violence in a Catholic Society: The Hispanic World 1450-1720." In: *The Church and War*. Ed. W.J. Sheils. Oxford, pp. 201-16.

Keen, Ralph. "Militant Christianity in Erasmus's *Enchiridion* and Ignatius Loyola," *Wolfenbütteler Renaissance Mitteilungen* 13 (1989), 1-8.

Kelsey, J. and James Turner Johnson, ed. *Just War and Jihad*. New York, 1991.

King, James R. "The Friar Tuck Syndrome: Clerical Violence and the Barons' War." In: *The Final Argument: The Imprint of Violence on Society in Medieval and Early Modern Europe*. Ed. Donald J. Kagay and L.J. Andrew Villalon. Woodbridge: The Boydell Press, 1998, pp. 27-52.

Krop, H.A. "De leer van de rechtvaardige oorlog in de late middeleeuwen. Hendrik van Gorkums tractaat 'De justo bello'." In: *Oorlog in de middeleeuwen*. Ed. A.J. Brand. Hilversum, 1989, pp. 111-24.

Lacroix, Benoît. "Deus le volt! La théologie d'un cri." In: *Etudes de civilisation médiévale (IXe-XIIe siècles): Mélanges offerts à Edmond-René Labande*. Poitiers: CESCM, 1974, pp. 461-70.

Leclerq, Jean. "L'attitude spirituelle de saint Bernard devant la guerre," *Collectanea cisterciensia* 36 (1974), 195-225; trans. "Saint Bernard's Attitude toward War." In: *Studies in Medieval Cistercian History*, 2. Kalamazoo, 1976, 1-39.

Lenihan, David A. "The Influence of Augustine's Just War: the Early Middle Ages," *Augustinian Studies* 27 (1996), 55-94.

Lloyd, Howell A. "Josse Clichtove and the Just War." In: *The Medieval Military Revolution: State, Society and Military Change in Medieval and Early Modern Europe*. Ed. A. Ayton and J.L. Price. London, 1995, pp. 145-62.

Loud, G.A. "The Church, Warfare and Military Obligation in Norman Italy." In: *The Church and War*. Ed. W.J. Sheils. Oxford, pp. 31-45.

Lund, Niels. "Allies of God or Man? The Viking Expansion in a Human Perspective," *Viator* 20 (1989), 45-59.

Mahaut, Marie-Claude. "Le rôle pacificateur du Pape Benôit XII dans le conflit de la Castille avec le Portugal (1337-1340)." In: *La guerre et la paix: Frontières et violences au moyen âge*. Actes du 101e congrès national des sociétés savantes, Lille, 1976. Paris: Bibliothèque Nationale, 1978, pp. 225-39.

Margolin, J.C. *Guerre et paix dans la pensée d'Erasme de Rotterdam*. Paris, 1973.

Markus, R.A. "Saint Augustine's Views on the 'Just War,'" *Studies in Church History* 20 (1983), 1-13.

McCormick, Michael. "Liturgie et guerre des Carolingiens à la première croisade." In: *"Militia Christi" e crociata nei secoli XI-XIII: Atti della undecima settimana internazionale di studio, Mendola, 28 agosta-1 settembre 1989*. Miscellanea del Centro di studi medioevali, 13; Scienze storiche, 48. Milan: Vita e Pensiero, 1992, pp. 209-40.

McCormick, Michael. "The Liturgy of War in the Early Middle Ages: Crisis, Litanies, and the Carolingian Monarchy," *Viator* 15 (1984), 1-23.

McCormick, Michael. "A New Ninth-Century Witness to the Carolingian Mass against Pagans (Paris, B.N., Lat. 2812)," *Revue Benédictine* 97 (1987), 68-86.

McGuire, Brian Patrick. "The Church and the Control of Violence in the Early Middle Ages: Friendship and Peace in the Letters of Gerbert, 982-97." In: *War and Peace in the Middle Ages*. Ed. B.P. McGuire. Copenhagen, 1987, pp. 29-55.

McHardy, Alison. "The Effects of War on the Church: The Case of the Alien Priories in the Fourteenth Century." In: *England and her Neighbours, 1066-1483: Essays in Honour of Pierre Chaplais*. Ed. M. Jones and M. Vale. London, 1989, pp. 277-95.

McHardy, Alison. "The English Clergy and the Hundred Years War," *Studies in Church History* 20 (1983), 171-78.

McHardy, Alison. "Liturgy and Propaganda in the Diocese of Lincoln during the Hundred Years War." In: *Religion and National Identity*. Ed. S. Mews. Oxford, 1982, pp. 215-27.

McNab, Bruce. "Obligations of the Church in English Society: Military Arrays of the Clergy, 1369-1418." In: *Order and Innovation in the Middle Ages: Essays in Honor of Joseph R. Strayer*. Ed. W.C. Jordan et al. Princeton, 1976, pp. 293-314, 516-22.

Meissburger, G. "*De vita christiana*; Zum Bild des christlichen Ritters im Hochmittelalter," *Der Deutschunterricht* 14 (1962), 21-34.

Morisi, A. *La guerra nel pensiero cristiano dalle origini alle crociate*. Florence, 1963.

Muldoon, James. "A Fifteenth-Century Application of the Canonistic Theory of Just War." In: *The Fourth International Congress of Medieval Canon Law*. Ed. Stephen Kuttner. Vatican, 1976, pp. 467-80.

Murphy, Jeffrie G. "The Killing of the Innocent," *The Monist* 57 (1973), 527-50.

Nelson, Janet L. "The Church's Military Service in the Ninth Century: A Contemporary Comparative View?" *Studies in Church History* 20 (1983), 15-30.

Noble, Cheryl. "Political Realism, International Morality, and Just War," *The Monist* 57 (1973), 595-606.

Oberman, H. and James A. Weisheipl. "The *Sermo epincius* Ascribed to Thomas Bradwardine (1346)," *Archives d'histoire doctrinale et littéraire du moyen âge* 33 (1958), 295-329.

Ortega, J.F. "La paz y la guerra en el penasmiento agustiniano," *Revista Española de derecho canónico* 20 (1965), 5-35.

Partner, Peter. *God of Battles: Holy Wars of Christianity and Islam*. London: Harper Collins, 1997.

Pedersen, Jorgen E. "The Unity of Religion and Universal Peace: Nicholas of Cusa and his *De Pace Fidei* (1453)." In: *War and Peace in the Middle Ages*. Ed. B.P. McGuire. Copenhagen, 1987, pp. 195-215.

Poggiaspella, F. "La chiesa la partecipazione dei chierci alla guerra nella legislazione conciliare fino alle Decretali di Gregorio IX," *Ephemerides iuris canonici* 15 (1959), 140-53.

Poggiaspella, F. "La condotta della guerra secundo una disposizione dello III° concilio lateranense," *Ephemerides iuris canonici* 12 (1956), 371-86.

Prinz, Friedrich E. "King, Clergy and War at the Time of the Carolingians." In: *Saints, Scholars and Heroes: Studies in Medieval Culture in Honour of Charles W. Jones.* Ed. M.H. King and W.M. Stevens. Collegeville, 1979, pp. 301-29.

Prinz, Friedrich E. *Klerus und Krieg im frühen Mittelalter: Untersuchungen zur Rolle der Kirche beim Aufbau der Königsherrschaft.* Stuttgart, 1971.

Reeves, Marjorie. "A Note on Prophecy and the Sack of Rome (1527)." In: *Prophetic Rome in the High Renaissance.* Ed. M. Reeves. Oxford, 1992, pp. 271-78.

Regout, R. *La doctrine de la guerre juste de saint Augustin à nos jours d'après les théologiens et les canonistes catholiques.* Paris, 1935.

Renick, Timothy M. "Charity Lost: The Secularization of the Principle of Double Effect in the Just-War Tradition," *The Thomist* 58 (1994), 441-62.

Renna, Thomas. "Monastic Attitudes toward War, 850-1150," *Michigan Academician* 12 (1980), 417-21.

Repgen, Konrad. "Kriegslegitimationen in alteuropa entwurf einer historischen typologie," *Historische zeitschrift* 241 (1985), 27-49.

Reuter, Timothy. "*Episcopi cum sua militia*: The Prelate as Warrior in the Early Stauffer Era." In: *Warriors and Churchmen in the High Middle Ages: Essays Presented to Karl Leyser.* Ed. T. Reuter. London, 1992, pp. 79-94.

Richter, J. "Der Ritter zwischen Gott und Welt: Ein Bild mittelalterlicher Religion bei Hartmann von Aue," *Zeitschrift für Religions- und Geistesgeschichte* 16 (1964), 57-69.

Rosenwein, Barbara H. "Feudal War and Monastic Peace: Cluniac Liturgy as Ritual Aggression," *Viator* 2 (1971), 129-57.

Rubelin, Michel. "Combattant de Dieu ou Combattant du Diable? Le combattant dans les duels judiciaires aux IXe au Xe siècles." In: *Le combattant au moyen âge*. 2nd ed. Histoire ancienne et médiévale, 36. Paris: Publications de la Sorbonne, 1995, pp. 111-20.

Russell, Frederick H. "Innocent IV's Proposal to Limit Warfare." In: *The Fourth International Congress of Medieval Canon Law*. Ed. Stephen Kuttner. Vatican, 1976, pp. 383-99.

Russell, Frederick H. *The Just War in the Middle Ages*. Cambridge: Cambridge University Press, 1975.

Russell, Frederick H. "Love and Hate in Medieval Warfare: The Contribution of Augustine," *Nottingham Medieval Studies* 31 (1987), 108-24.

Russell, Frederick H. "Paulus Vladimiri's Attack on the Just War: A Case Study in Legal Polemics." In: *Authority and Power: Studies on Medieval Law and Government Presented to Walter Ullmann on his Seventieth Birthday*. Ed. B. Tierney and P. Linehan. Cambridge, 1980, pp. 237-54.

Sayers, Jane. "Violence in the Medieval Cloister," *Journal of Ecclesiastical History* 41 (1990), 533-42.

Schmandt, R.H. "The Fourth Crusade and the Just War Theory," *Catholic Historical Review* 61 (1975), 191-221.

Setton, Kenneth M. "Lutheranism and the Turkish Peril," *Balkan Studies* 3 (1962), 133-68.

Sicard, G. "Paix et guerre dans le droit canon du XIIe siècle," *Paix de Dieu et guerre sainte en Languedoc au XIIIe siècle, Cahiers de Fanjeaux* 4 (1969), 72-90.

Solages, B. de. *La théologie de la guerre juste, genèse et orientation*. Paris, 1946.

Southern, Richard W. *Western Views of Islam in the Middle Ages*. Cambridge: Harvard University Press, 1962.

Stehkämper, H. "Ein Ütrechter kanonischer Traktat über Kriegsrecht (1419-20)," *Zeitschrift der Savigny-Stiftung für Rechtsgeschichte, Kanonische Abteilung* 78 (1961), 196-265.

Swanson, R.N. "The Way of Action: Pierre d'Ailly and the Military Solution to the Great Schism," *Studies in Church History* 20 (1983), 191-200.

Swift, Louis, J. "Augustine on War and Killing," *Harvard Theological Review* 66 (1973), 369-83.

Swift, Louis, J. *The Early Fathers on War and Military Service*. Wilmington, 1983.

Swift, Louis, J. "St. Ambrose on Violence and War," *Transactions and Proceedings of the American Philological Association* 101 (1970), 533-43.

Synan, Edward A. "St. Thomas Aquinas and the Profession of Arms," *Mediaeval Studies* 50 (1988), 404-37.

Taft, Robert F. "War and Peace in the Byzantine Divine Liturgy." In: *Peace and War in Byzantinum: Essays in Honor of George T. Dennis, S.J.* Ed. T.S. Miller and J. Nesbitt. Washington, 1995, pp. 17-32.

Tooke, J.D. *The Just War in Aquinas and Grotius*. London, 1965.

Vanderpol, A.M. *Le droit de guerre d'après les théologiens et les canonistes du moyen âge*. Paris and Brussels, 1911.

Vanderpol, A.M. *La doctrine scolastique du droit de guerre*. Paris, 1925.

Verkamp, Bernard J. "Moral Treatment of Returning Warriors in the Early Middle Ages," *Journal of Religious Ethics* 17 (1989), 223-49.

Viscuso, Patrick. "Christian Participation in Warfare: A Byzantine View." In: *Peace and War in Byzantinum: Essays in Honor of George T. Dennis, S.J.* Ed. T.S. Miller and J. Nesbitt. Washington, 1995, pp. 33-40.

Vismara, G. "Problemi storici e istituti giuridici della guerra alto-medievale." In: *Ordinamenti militari in occidente nell'alto medioevo*. Settimane di studio del centro italiano di studi sull'alto medioevo, XV. Spoleto, 1968, II:1126-1200.

Walter, Christopher. "Theodore, Archetype of the Warrior Saint," *Revue des études Byzantines* 57 (1999), 163-210.

Walters, LeRoy. "The Just War and the Crusade: Antitheses or Analogies?" *The Monist* 57 (1973), 584-94.

Wang, A. *Der 'miles christianus' im 16. und 17. Jahrhundert und seine mittelalterliche Tradition: Ein Beitrag zum Verhältnis von sprachlicher und graphischer Bildlichkeit.* Bern and Frankfurt, 1975.

Windass, S. *Le christianisme et la violence.* Paris, 1966.

Wood, Diana. "*Omnino partialitate cessante*: Clement VI and the Hundred Years War," *Studies in Church History* 20 (1983), 179-89.

Woods, David. "Varus of Egypt: A Fictitious Military Martyr," *Byzantine and Modern Greek Studies* 20 (1996), 175-200.

Medieval – Crusades – General

Abulafia, David. "Trade and Crusade, 1050-1250." In: *Cross-Cultural Convergences in the Crusader Period: Essays Presented to Aryeh Grabois on His Sixty-Fifth Birthday.* Ed. Michael Goodich, Sophia Menache, and Sylvia Schein. New York, 1995, pp. 1-20.

Alphandéry, Paul and Louis Dupront. *La Chrétienté et l'idée de croisade.* 2 vols. Paris, 1954, 1959.

Anderson, Gary M., Robert B. Ekelund, Jr., Robert F. Hebert and Robert D. Tollison. "An Economic Interpretation of the Medieval Crusades," *Journal of European Economic History* 21 (1992), 339-63.

Atiya, Aziz Suryal. *The Crusade: Historiography and Bibliography.* Bloomington: Indiana University Press, 1962.

Auffarth, Christoph. "Himmlisches und irdisches Jerusalem: Ein religionswissenschaftlicher Versuch zur Kreuzzugeschatologie," *Zeitschrift für Religionswissenschaft* 1/1 (1993), 25-49; 1/2 (1993), 91-118.

Barber, Malcolm. "How the West Saw Medieval Islam," *History Today* 47.5 (May 1997), 44-50.

Bartlett, W.B. *God Wills It! An Illustrated History of the Crusades.* Stroud: Sutton, 1999.

Beer, Jeanette M.A. "The Letter of Jean Sarrasin, Crusader." In: *Journeys Toward God: Pilgrimage and Crusade*. Ed. B.N. Sargent-Baur. Kalamazoo, 1992, pp. 135-56.

Bender, Karl-Heinz. "La *Geste d'Outremer* ou les epopées des croisades." In: *La croisade: Realités et fictions*. Ed. Danielle Buschinger. Goppingen, 1989, pp. 19-30.

Bennett, Matthew. "First Crusaders' Image of Muslims: The Influence of Vernacular Poetry?" *Forum for Modern Language Studies* 22 (1986), 101-22.

Bennett, Matthew. "Travel and Transport of the Crusades," *Medieval History* 4 (1994), 91-101.

Benvenisti, M. *The Crusaders in the Holy Land*. Jerusalem, 1970.

Boehm, Laetitia. "Gesta Dei per Francos–oder Gesta Francorum: Die Kreuzzüge als historiographisches Problem," *Saeculum* 8 (1957), 43-81.

Brown, E.A.R. and Michael Cothren. "The Twelfth-Century Crusading Window of the Abbey of St. Denis," *Journal of the Warburg and Courtauld Society* 49 (1986), 1-40.

Brundage, James A. "The Crusades: Past Achievements and Future Agenda." In: *The Meeting of Two Worlds: Cultural Exchange between East and West during the Period of the Crusades*. Ed. Vladimir P. Goss. Kalamazoo: Medieval Institute Publications, 1986, pp. 447-53.

Brundage, James A. "'Cruce Signari': The Rite for Taking the Cross in England," *Traditio* 22 (1966), 289-310.

Brundage, James A. Holy War and the Medieval Lawyers." In: *The Holy War*. Ed. T.P. Murphy. Columbus: Ohio State University, 1976, pp. 99-140.

Brundage, James A. Holy War and the Medieval Lawyers. *Medieval Canon Law and the Crusades*. Madison: University of Wisconsin Press, 1969.

Brundage, James A. Holy War and the Medieval Lawyers. "A Note on the Attestation of Crusaders' Vows," *Catholic Historical Review* 52 (1966), 234-39.

Brundage, James A. Holy War and the Medieval Lawyers. "Recent Crusade Historiography: Some Observations and Suggestions," *Catholic Historical Review* 49 (1964), 493-507.

Brundage, James A. Holy War and the Medieval Lawyers. "A Transformed Angel (X 3.31.18): The Problem of the Crusading Monk." In: *Studies in Medieval Cistercian History Presented to Jeremiah F. O'Sullivan.* Spenser, 1971, pp. 55-62.

Brundage, James A. Holy War and the Medieval Lawyers. "The Votive Obligations of Crusaders: The Development of a Canonistic Doctrine," *Traditio* 24 (1968), 77-118.

Brundage, James A. Holy War and the Medieval Lawyers, ed. *The Crusades: A Documentary Survey.* Milwaukee: The Marquette University Press, 1962.

Bull, Marcus. "The Capetian Monarchy and the Early Crusade Movement: Hugh of Vermandois and Louis VII," *Nottingham Medieval Studies* 50 (1996), 25-46.

Buschinger, Danielle. "La signification de la croisade dans la littérature allemande du moyen âe tardif." In: *La croisade: réalités et fictions.* Ed. Danielle Buschinger. Göppinger, 1989, pp. 51-60.

Cahen, Claude. *Orient et occident aux temps des croisades.* Paris: Aubier Montaigne, 1983.

Cahen, Claude. "A propos d'Albert d'Aix et de Richard le Pèlerin," *Moyen âge* 96 (1990), 31-33.

Cahen, S. *La Syrie du nord au temps des croisades.* Paris, 1940.

Cardini, Franco. *Studi sulla storia e sull'idea di crociata.* Rome, 1993.

Chebab, M.H. "Tyr à la époque des croisades," *Bulletin des musée de Beyrouth* 31 (1979).

Cipollone, Giulio. "Le parole, les paroles de Dieu: la guerre sainte (1187-1216)." In: *La guerre, la violence et les gens au Moyen Âge.* I: *Guerre et violence.* Ed. P. Contamine and O. Guyotjeannin. 119e congrès national des sociétés historiques et scientifiques, Amiens, octobre 1994, Section d'histoire médiévale et philologie. Paris, 1996, pp. 25-34.

Cognasso, F. *Storia delle crociate*. Florence, 1967.

Cole, Penny J. "Christians, Muslims, and the 'Liberation' of the Holy Land," *Catholic History Review* 84 (1998), 1-10.

Cole, Penny J. "'O God, The Heathen Have Come Into Your Inheritance' (Ps. 78.I): The Theme of Religious Pollution in Crusade Documents, 1095-1188." In: *Crusaders and Muslims in Twelfth-Century Syria*. Ed. Maya Schatzmiller. Leiden: E.J. Brill, 1993, pp. 84-111.

Cole, Penny J. *The Preaching of Crusades to the Holy Land, 1095-1270*. Cambridge: The Medieval Academy of America, 1991.

Constable, Giles. "The Place of the Crusader in Medieval Society," *Viator* 29 (1998), 377-403.

Constable, Giles. "The Financing of the Crusades in the Twelfth Century." In: *Outremer: Studies in the History of the Crusading Kingdom of Jerusalem*. Ed. Benjamin Z. Kedar. Jerusalem, 1982, pp. 64-88.

Constable, Giles. "Medieval Charters as a Source for the History of the Crusades." In: *Crusade and Settlement: Papers Read at the First Conference of the Society for the Study of the Crusades and the Latin East and Presented to R.C. Smail*. Ed. Peter W. Edbury. Cardiff: University College Cardiff Press, 1985, pp. 73-89.

Cook, Robert Francis. "Crusade Propaganda in the Epic Cycles of the Crusade." In: *Journeys Toward God: Pilgrimage and Crusade*. Ed. B.N. Sargent-Baur. Kalamazoo, 1992, pp. 157-76.

Costello, Con. "Ireland and the Crusades," *Irish Sword* 9 (1969-70), 263-77.

Cramer, V. "Kreuzpredigt und Kreuzzugsgedanke von Bernhard von Clairvaux bis Humbert von Romans." In: *Des Heilige Land in Vergangenheit und Gegenwart*. Cologne, 1939.

Crocker, Richard L. "Early Crusade Songs." In: *The Holy War*. Ed. T.P. Murphy. Columbus, 1976, pp. 78-98.

Daly, W.M. "Christian Fraternity: The Crusaders and the Security of Constantinople, 1097-1204: The Precarious Survival of an Ideal," *Mediaeval Studies* 22 (1960).

Daniel, Norman. "Crusade Propaganda." In: *A History of the Crusades*. Ed. Kenneth M. Setton. Madison: University of Wisconsin Press, 1989, VI:39-97.

Daniel, Norman. "The Legal and Political Theory of the Crusade." In: *A History of the Crusades*. Ed. Kenneth M. Setton. Madison: University of Wisconsin Press, 1989, VI:3-38.

Davies, J.G. "Pilgrimage and Crusade Literature." In: *Journeys Toward God: Pilgrimage and Crusade*. Ed. Barbara N. Sargent-Baur. Studies in Medieval Culture, 30. Kalamazoo: Medieval Institute Publications, 1992, pp. 1-30.

Delaruelle, Étienne. *L'idée de croisade au moyen âge*. Turin, 1980.

Delaruelle, Étienne. "L'idée de croisade chez S. Bernard." In: *Mélanges Saint Bernard*. Dijon, 1954, pp. 53-67.

Deluz, Christiane. "L'accomplissement des temps à Jérusalem." In: *Fin des temps et temps de la fin dans l'univers médiéval*. Sénéfiance, 33. Aix-en-Provence: Centre Universitaire d'Etudes et de Recherches Médiévales d'Aix, 1993, pp. 87-198.

Demouy, Patrick. "L'église de Reims et la croisade aux Xie-XIIe siècles." In: *Les Champenois et la croisade: Actes des IVe journées rémoises, 27-28 novembre 1987*. Ed. Yvonne Bellenger and Danielle Quérel. Paris: Aux Amateurs de Livres, 1987, pp. 19-38.

Dostourian, A.E., ed. *Armenia and the Crusades: Tenth to the Twelfth Centuries*. Lanham, 1993.

Dotson, John E. "Perceptions of the East in Fourteenth-Century Italian Merchants' Manuals." In: *Across the Mediterranean Frontiers: Trade, Politics and Religion, 650-1450: Selected Proceedings of the International Medieval Congress, University of Leeds, 10-13 July 1995, 8-11 July 1996*. Ed. Dionisius A. Agius and Ian Richard Netton. Turnhout: Brepols, 1997, pp. 173-92.

Dufourq, C.-E. "Chrétien et Musulman durant les derniers siècles du moyen âge," *Anuario de estudios medievales* 10 (1980).

Edbury, Peter W. "Chronicles of the Crusade: William of Tyre," *History Today* 38 (June 1988), 24-28.

Edbury, Peter W. *The Kingdom of Cyprus and the Crusades, 1191-1374*. Cambridge: Cambridge University Press, 1991.

Edbury, Peter W. "The Lyon *Eracles* and the Old French Continuations of William of Tyre." In: *Montjoie: Studies in Crusade History in Honour of Hans Eberhard Mayer*. Ed. Benjamin Z. Kedar, Jonathan Riley-Smith, and Rudolf Hiestand. Aldershot, 1997, pp. 139-53.

Edbury, Peter W. "Preaching the Crusade in Wales." In: *England and Germany in the High Middle Ages*. Ed. Alfred Haverkamp and Hanna Vollrath. London: The German Historical Institute, 1996, pp. 221-33.

Edbury, Peter W. "The State of Research: Cyprus Under the Lusignans and Venetians, 1991-98," *Journal of Medieval History* 25 (1999), 57-66.

Edbury, Peter W. "Warfare in the Latin East." In: *Medieval Warfare: A History*. Ed. Maurice Keen. Oxford: Oxford University Press, 1999, pp. 89-112.

Edbury, Peter W. and John Gordon Rowe. *William of Tyre, Historian of Tyre, Historian of the Latin East*. Cambridge: Cambridge University Press, 1981.

Edgington, Susan B. "The Doves of War: The Part Played by Carrier Pigeons in the Crusades." In: *Autour de la première croisade: Actes du Colloque de la Society for the Study of the Crusades and the Latin East (Clermont-Ferrand, 22-25 juin 1995)*. Ed. M. Balard. Paris: Publications de la Sorbonne, 1996, pp. 167-75.

Edgington, Susan B. "From Aachen: A New Perspective on Relations between the Crusaders and Byzantium, 1096-1120," *Medieval History* 4 (1994), 156-69.

Eidelberg, Schlomo. *The Jews and the Crusaders: The Hebrew Chronicles of the First and Second Crusades*. Madison: University of Wisconsin Press, 1977.

Epp, Verena. "Miles und militia bei Fulcher von Chartres und seinen Bearbeitern." In: *"Militia Christi" e crociata nei secoli XI-XIII: Atti della undecima settimana internazionale di studio, Mendola, 28 agosta-1 settembre 1989*. Miscellanea del Centro di studi medioevali, 13; Scienze storiche, 48. Milan: Vita e Pensiero, 1992, pp. 769-84.

Erbstösser, Martin. *The Crusades*. Trans. C.S.V. Salt. Leipzig, 1978.

Evans, Michael R. "Commutation of Crusade Vows: Some Examples from the English Midlands." In: *From Clermont to Jerusalem: The Crusades and Crusader Societies, 1095-1500*. Selected Proceedings of the International Medieval Congress, University of Leeds, 10-13 July 1995. Ed. Alan V. Murray. Turnhout: Brepols, 1998, pp. 219-28.

Favreau-Lilie, Marie-Luise. "The German Empire and Palestine: German Pilgrimages in Jerusalem between the 12th and 16th Century," *Journal of Medieval History* 21 (1995), 321-41.

Favreau-Lilie, Marie-Luise. *Die Italiener im Heiligen Land vom ersten Kreuzzug bis zum Tode Heinrichs von Champagne (1098-1197)*. Amsterdam: Hakkert, 1989.

Flori, Jean. "La caricature de l'Islam dans l'occident médiéval: Origine et signification de quelques stéréotype concernant l'Islam," *Aevum* 66 (1992), 245-56.

Flori, Jean. *Croisade et chevalerie: XIe-XIIIe siècles*. Bibliothèque du Moyen Age, 12. Paris: De Boeck Université, 1998.

Flori, Jean. "Croisade et chevalerie: Convergence idéologique ou rupture?" In: *Femmes. Mariages–Lignages, XIIe-XIVe siècles: Melanges offerts à Georges Duby*. Ed. Jean Dufournet et al. Bibliothèque du Moyen Age, 1. Brussels: De Boeck-Wesmael, 1992, pp. 157-76.

Flori, Jean. "L'église et la guerre sainte de la 'paix de dieu' a la 'Croisade,'" *Annales ESC* 47 (1992), 453-66.

Frenkel, Yehoshua. "The Impact of the Crusades on Rural Society and Religious Endowments: The Case of Medieval Syria." In: *War and Society in the Eastern Mediterranean, 7th-15th Centuries*. Ed. Yaacov Lev. Leiden, 1997, pp. 237-48.

Gabrieli, Francesco. *Storici arabi delle crociate*. Turin: Einaudi, 1957; trans. *Arab Historians of the Crusades*. London: Routledge and Kegan Paul, 1969; trans. *Die Kreuzzüge aus arabischer Sicht*. Zurich: Artemis, 1973.

Gabrieli, Francesco. "The Arabic Historiography of the Crusades." In: *Historians of the Middle East*. Ed. Bernard Lewis and P.M. Holt. Oxford: Oxford University Press, 1962, pp. 98-107.

Gauss, J. "Toleranz und Intoleranz zwischen Christen und Mulsimen in der Zeit vor den Kreuzzügen," *Saeculum* 19 (1968), 362-89.

Gibb, Hamilton A.R. "Notes on the Arabic Materials for the History of the Early Crusade," *Bulletin of the School of Oriental Studies* 7 (1933-35), 738-54.

Giese, Wolfgang. "Untersuchungen zur *Historia Hierosolymitana* des Fulcher von Chartres," *Archiv für Kulturgeschichte* 69 (1987), 62-115.

Gilchrist, John. "The Papacy and War Against 'the Saracens,' 795-1216," *International History Review* 10 (1988), 174-97.

Goitein, S.D. "Geniza Sources for the Crusader Period: A Survey." In: *Outremer: Studies in the History of the Crusading Kingdom of Jerusalem Presented to Joshua Prawer*. Jerusalem, 1982, pp. 306-22.

Goitein, S.D. "Tyre–Tripoli–'Arqua: Geniza Documents from the Beginning of the Crusader Period," *Jewish Quarterly Review* 66 (1975), 69-88.

Gottlob, A. *Kreuzzuganblass und Almosenablass*. Stuttgart, 1906.

Grabois, Aryeh. "Anglo-Norman England and the Holy Land," *Anglo-Norman Studies* 7 (1985), 132-41.

Gumilev, L.N. *Searches for an Imaginary Kingdom: The Legend of the Kingdom of Prester John*. Cambridge: Cambridge University Press, 1987.

Hagspiel, G.H. *Die Führerpersöhnlichkeit im Kreuzzug*. Geist und Werk der Zeiten, 10. Zurich: Fretz und Wasmuth, 1963.

Hamel, Mary. "*The Siege of Jerusalem* as a Crusading Poem." In: *Journeys Toward God: Pilgrimage and Crusade*. Ed. B.N. Sargent-Baur. Kalamazoo, 1992, pp. 177-94.

Hamilton, Bernard. "Ideals of Holiness: Crusaders, Contemplatives, and Mendicants," *International History Review* 17 (1995), 693-712.

Hamilton, Bernard. "The Impact of Crusader Jerusalem on Western Christendom," *Catholic Historical Review* 80 (1994), 695-713.

Hehl, Ernst-Dieter. "Was ist eigentlich ein Kreuzzug?" *Historische Zeitschrift* 259 (1994), 297-336.

Herde, Peter. "Taktiken muslimischer Heere vom ersten Kreuzzug bis 'Ain Djalut (1260) und ihre Einwirkung auf die Schlacht bei Tagliacozzo." In: *Das Heilige Land im Mittelalter: Begegnungsraum zwischen Orient und Okzident.* Ed. Wolfdietrich Fischer and Jürgen Schneider. Neustadt an der Aisch: Degener, 1982, pp. 83-94.

Hiestand, Rudolf. "Kingship and Crusade in Twelfth-Century Germany." In: *England and Germany in the High Middle Ages.* Ed. Alfred Haverkamp and Hanna Vollrath. London: The German Historical Institute, 1996, pp. 235-65.

Hillenbrand, Carole. *The Crusades: Islamic Perspectives.* New York: Routledge, 2000.

Holt, Peter M. *The Age of the Crusades: The Near East from the Eleventh Century to 1517.* London: Longman, 1986.

Holt, Peter M., ed. *The Eastern Mediterranean Lands in the Period of the Crusades.* Warminster, 1977.

Hugenholtz, F.W.N. *De kruistocht in de Noordnederlandse historiographie der middeleeuwen.* Haarlem, 1950.

Ilieva, Annetta and Mitko Delev. "Sclavonia and Beyond: The Gate to a Different World in the Perception of Crusaders (c. 1104-c. 1208)." In: *From Clermont to Jerusalem: The Crusades and Crusader Societies, 1095-1500.* Selected Proceedings of the International Medieval Congress, University of Leeds, 10-13 July 1995. Ed. Alan V. Murray. Turnhout: Brepols, 1998, pp. 153-72.

Irwin, Robert. "Islam and the Crusades, 1096-1699." In: *The Oxford Illustrated History of the Crusades.* Ed. Jonathan Riley-Smith. Oxford: Oxford University Press, 1995, pp. 217-59.

Irwin, Robert. "Muslim Responses to the Crusades," *History Today* 47.4 (Apr 1997), 43-49.

Jordan, William Chester. "The Representation of the Crusades in the Songs Attributed to Thibaud, Count Palatine of Champagne," *Journal of Medieval History* 25 (1999), 27-34.

Kahrl, Stanley J. "Introduction." In: *The Holy War*. Ed. T.P. Murphy. Columbus, 1976, pp. 1-8.

Kedar, Benjamin Z. "Croisade et *Jih ād* vus par l'ennemi: une étude des perceptions mutuelles des motivations." In: *Autour de la première croisade: Actes du Colloque de la Society for the Study of the Crusades and the Latin East (Clermont-Ferrand, 22-25 juin 1995)*. Ed. M. Balard. Paris: Publications de la Sorbonne, 1996, pp. 345-55.

Kedar, Benjamin Z. *Crusade and Mission: European Approaches toward the Muslims*. Princeton: Princeton University Press, 1984.

Kedar, Benjamin Z. *The Franks in the Levant, 11th to 14th Centuries*. London, 1993.

Kernaghan, Pamela. *The Crusades: Cultures in Conflict*. Cambridge: Cambridge University Press, 1993.

Knobler, Adam. "Pseudo-Conversions and Patchwork Pedigrees: The Christianization of Muslim Princes and the Diplomacy of Holy War," *Journal of World History* 7 (1996), 181-97.

Kolia-Dermitzaki, A. "Die Kreuzfahrer und die Kreuzzüge im Sprachbrauch der Byzantiner," *Jahrbuch der Österreichischen Byzantinistik* 41 (1991), 163-88.

Kritzeck, James. *Peter the Venerable and Islam*. Princeton: Princeton University Press, 1964.

Lesourd, Paul and Jean Marie Ramiz. *On the Path of the Crusaders*. Trans. Jerry O'Dell. Ramat-Gan, 1969.

Lev, Yaacov. "Regime, Army and Society in Medieval Egypt, 9th-12th Centuries." In: *War and Society in the Eastern Mediterranean, 7th-15th Centuries*. Ed. Y. Lev. Leiden, 1997, pp. 115-52.

Lewis, Archibald R. *Nomads and Crusaders, A.D. 1000-1368*. Bloomington: Indiana University Press, 1988.

Libertini, Christopher G. "Practical Crusading: The Transformation of Crusading Practice, 1095-1221." In: *Autour de la première croisade: Actes du Colloque de la Society for the Study of the Crusades and the Latin East*

(Clermont-Ferrand, 22-25 juin 1995). Ed. M. Balard. Paris: Publications de la Sorbonne, 1996, pp. 281-91.

Ligato, Giuseppe. "Fra ordini cavallereschi e crociata: 'Milites ad terminum' e 'confraternitates' armate." In: *'Militia Christi' e crociata nei secoli XI-XIII*. Miscellanea del centro di studi medioevali, 13. Milan, 1992, pp. 645-97.

Lilie, Ralph-Johannes. *Byzanz und die Kreuzfahrerstaaten: Studien zur Politik des byantischen Reiches gegenüber den Staaten der Kreuzfahrer in Syrien und Palästina bis zum Vierten Kreuzzug (1096-1204)*. Poikila byzantina, 1. Munich: Fink, 1981.

Lüders, Anneliese. *Die Kreuzzüge im Urteil syrischer und armenischer Quellen*. Berliner byzantinische Arbeiten, 29. Berlin: Akademie-Verlag, 1964.

Macquarrie, Alan. *Scotland and the Crusades, 1095-1560*. Edinburgh: John Donald, 1997.

Madden, Thomas F. *A Concise History of the Crusades*. Lanham: Rowman and Littlefield, 2000.

Maier, Christoph T. "Crisis, Liturgy, and the Crusade in the Twelfth and Thirteenth Centuries," *Journal of Ecclesiastical History* 48 (1997), 628-57.

Maier, Christoph T. *Crusade Propaganda and Ideology: Model Sermons for the Preaching of the Cross*. Cambridge: Cambridge University Press, 2000.

Maier, Christoph T. *Preaching the Crusade: Mendicants, Friars and the Cross*. Cambridge: Cambridge University Press, 1994.

Markowski, Michael. "*Crucisignatus*: Its Origins and Early Usage," *Journal of Medieval History* 10 (1984), 157-65.

Marshall, Christopher J. *Warfare in the Latin East, 1192-1291*. Cambridge: Cambridge University Press, 1992.

Mayer, Hans Eberhard. *Bibliographie zur Geschichte der Kreuzzüge*. Hannover: Hahn, 1960.

Mayer, Hans Eberhard. *Geschichte der Kreuzzüge*. 8th ed. Urban-Taschen-bücher, 86. Stuttgart: Kohlhammer, 1995; trans. *The Crusades*. Oxford: Oxford University Press, 1972.

Mayer, Hans Eberhard. "Literaturbericht über die Geschichte der Kreuz-züge," *Historische Zeitschrift* sonderheft 3 (1969), 641-731.

Mayer, Hans Eberhard and Joyce McLellan. "Select Bibliography of the Crusades." In: *A History of the Crusades*. Ed. Kenneth M. Setton. Madison: University of Wisconsin Press, 1989, VI:511-664.

Menache, Sophie. "The Communication Challenge of the Early Crusades, 1099-1187." In: *Autour de la première croisade: Actes du Colloque de la Society for the Study of the Crusades and the Latin East (Clermont-Ferrand, 22-25 juin 1995)*. Ed. M. Balard. Paris: Publications de la Sorbonne, 1996, pp. 293-314.

Mercuri, Chiara. "San Luigi e la crociata," *Mélanges de l'école françaises de Rome: Moyen âge* 108 (1996), 221-41.

Michaud, Joseph. *Michaud's History of the Crusades*. Trans. W. Robson. London, 1852.

Möhring, Hannes. "Zu der Geschichte der orientalischen Herrscher des Wilhelm von Tyrus: Die Frage der Quellenabhängigkeiten," *Mittellatieni-sches Jahrbuch* 19 (1984), 170-83.

Mol, J.A. "Friese krijgers en de kruistochten," *Jaarboek voor middeleeuw-se gescheidenis* 3 (2000).

Morris, Colin. "Propaganda for War: The Dissemination of the Crusading Ideal in the Twelfth Century," *Studies in Church History* 20 (1983), 79-101.

Morrisson, C. *Les croisades*. 4th ed. Paris, 1984.

Munro, Dana C. "A Crusader," *Speculum* 7 (1932), 321-35.

Munro, Dana C. "The Western Attitude Towards Islam during the Cru-sades," *Speculum* 6 (1931), 329-43.

Murray, Alan V. "Coroscane: Homeland of the Saracens in the Chansons de Geste and the Historiography of the Crusades." In: *Aspects de 'épopée romane: Mentalités–idéologies–intertextualités*. Ed. Hans van Dijk and Willem Noomen. Groningen: Forsten, 1995, pp. 177-84.

Nesbitt, John W. "The Rate of March of Crusading Armies in Europe: A Study and Computation," *Traditio* 19 (1963), 167-81.

Nicolle, David C. *Crusades*. London: Osprey, 1988.

Nicolle, David C. *Knight of Outremer, 1187-1344 AD: Weapons, Armour, Tactics*. Warrior Series. London: Osprey Military, 1996; rpt. *Crusader Knight*. Oxford: Osprey, 1999.

Oldenburg, Zoé. *The Crusades*. Rpt. London: Wiedenfeld and Nicolson, 1998.

Omran, Mahmoud Said. "Truces Between Moslems and Crusaders (1174-1217 A.D.)." In: *Autour de la première croisade: Actes du Colloque de la Society for the Study of the Crusades and the Latin East (Clermont-Ferrand, 22-25 juin 1995)*. Ed. M. Balard. Paris: Publications de la Sorbonne, 1996, pp. 421-41.

Paetow, Louis J. "The Crusading Ardor of John of Garland." In: *The Crusades and Other Historical Essays Presented to Dana C. Munro by His Former Students*. Ed. L.J. Paetow. Freeport, 1928, pp. 207-22.

Partner, Peter. "Guerra santa, crociata e 'jihad': un tentativo di definire alcuni problemi," *Studi storico* 36 (1995), 945-55; trans. "Holy War, Crusade and *Jih ād*: An Attempt to Define Some Problems." In: *Autour de la première croisade: Actes du Colloque de la Society for the Study of the Crusades and the Latin East (Clermont-Ferrand, 22-25 juin 1995)*. Ed. M. Balard. Paris: Publications de la Sorbonne, 1996, pp. 333-43.

Pennington, Kenneth. "The Rite for Taking the Cross in the Twelfth Century," *Traditio* 30 (1974), 429-31.

Pernoud, Régine. *Les hommes de la croisade*. Paris, 1982.

Peters, Edward. "Henry II of Cyprus, *Rex inutilis*: A Footnote to *Decameron* 1.9," *Speculum* 72 (1997), 763-75.

Pflaum, H. "A Strange Crusader's Song," *Speculum* 10 (1935), 337-39.

Pick, L.K. "*Signaculum caritatis et fortitudinis*: Blessing the Crusader's Cross in France," *Revue bénédictine* 105 (1995), 381-416.

Pickering, Oliver. "The Crusades in Leeds University Library's Genealogical History Roll." In: *From Clermont to Jerusalem: The Crusades and Crusader Societies, 1095-1500*. Selected Proceedings of the International Medieval Congress, University of Leeds, 10-13 July 1995. Ed. Alan V. Murray. Turnhout: Brepols, 1998, pp. 251-66.

Platelle, Henri. *Les croisades*. Paris, 1994.

Powell, James M. "Rereading the Crusades," *Journal of International History* 17 (1995), 663-69.

Queller, Donald E. "Review Article–On the Completion of *A History of the Crusades*," *International History Review* 13 (1991), 314-30.

Rheinheimer, M. *Das Kreuzdahrerfürstentum Galiläa*. Frankfurt-am-Main, 1990.

Riant, P. *Expéditions et pèlerinages des Scandinaves en Terre Sainte au temps des croisades*. Paris, 1869.

Riant, P. "Inventaire critique des lettres historiques des croisades," *Archives de l'orient latin* 1 (1881), 9-224.

Richard, Jean. "La chrétienté latine et l'orient aux XIe et XIIe s.," *Etudes d'histoire* (1994), 9-33.

Richard, Jean. *Croisades et Etats Latins d'orient*. London, 1992.

Richard, Jean. *Croisés, missionaires et voyageurs*. London, 1983.

Richard, Jean. *Histoire des croisades*. Paris: Fayard, 1996; trans. *The Crusades, c.1071-c.1291*. Trans. Jean Birrell. Cambridge: Cambridge University Press, 1999.

Richter, Horst. "*Militia Dei*: A Central Concept for the Religious Ideas of the Early Crusades and the German *Rolandslied*." In: *Journeys Toward God: Pilgrimage and Crusade*. Ed. B.N. Sargent-Baur. Kalamazoo, 1992, pp. 107-26.

Riley-Smith, Jonathan. "An Approach to Crusading Ethics," *Reading Medieval Studies* 6 (1980), 3-19.

Riley-Smith, Jonathan. *The Crusades: A Short History*. New Haven: Yale University Press, 1987.

Riley-Smith, Jonathan. "Crusading as an Act of Love," *History* 65 (1980), 177-92.

Riley-Smith, Jonathan. "The Crusading Heritage of Guy and Aimery of Lusignan." In: *Hē Kupros kai hoi Staurophories/Cyprus and the Crusades: Hoi anakoinōseis tou deithnous symposiou "Hē Kupros kai hoi Staurophories", Leukōsia, 6-9 septembriou, 1994/Papers Given at the International Conference "Cyprus and the Crusades", Nicosia, 6-9 September, 1994.* Ed. Nikos Coureas and Jonathan Riley-Smith. Nicosia: Cyprus Research Centre/Society for the Study of the Crusades and the Latin East, 1995, pp. 31-45.

Riley-Smith, Jonathan. "Early Crusaders to the East and the Costs of Crusading, 1095-1130." In: *Cross-Cultural Convergences in the Crusader Period: Essays Presented to Aryeh Grabois on His Sixty-Fifth Birthday.* Ed. Michael Goodich, Sophia Menache, and Sylvia Schein. New York: Peter Lang, 1995, pp. 237-58.

Riley-Smith, Jonathan. "History, the Crusades and the Latin East, 1095-1204: A Personal View." In: *Crusaders and Muslims in Twelfth-Century Syria.* Ed. Maya Schatzmiller. Leiden: E.J. Brill, 1993, pp. 1-17.

Riley-Smith, Jonathan. *What Were the Crusades?* 2nd ed. London, 1992.

Riley-Smith, Jonathan, ed. *The Atlas of the Crusades.* London: Times Books, 1991.

Riley-Smith, Jonathan, ed. *Illustrated History of the Crusades.* Oxford: Oxford University Press, 1995.

Riley-Smith, Louise and Jonathan Riley-Smith. *The Crusades: Idea and Reality, 1095-1274.* London, 1981.

Rogers, Donna M. "Christians and Moors in ¡Ay Jerusalem!." In: *Journeys Toward God: Pilgrimage and Crusade.* Ed. B.N. Sargent-Baur. Kalamazoo, 1992, pp. 127-34.

Rogers, Randall. *Latin Siege Warfare in the Twelfth Century.* Oxford: Clarendon Press, 1992.

Rose, Susan. "Islam Versus Christendom: The Naval Dimension, 1000-1600," *Journal of Military History* 63 (1999), 561-78.

Rosetti, R. "L'histoire militaire des croisades," *Revue internationale d'histoire militaire* 1-2 (1939), 94-95.

Rousset, Paul. *Histoire des croisades*. Paris, 1957.

Rousset, Paul. *Histoire d'une ideologie: la croisade*. Lausanne, 1983.

Runciman, Steven. *A History of the Crusades*. Vol. I: *The First Crusade and the Foundation of the Kingdom of Jerusalem*. New York: Harper and Row, Publishers, 1964.

Runciman, Steven. *A History of the Crusades*. Vol. II: *The Kingdom of Jerusalem and the Frankish East, 1100-1187*. New York: Harper and Row, Publishers, 1965.

Runciman, Steven. *A History of the Crusades*. Vol. III: *The Kingdom of Acre*. New York: Harper and Row, Publishers, 1967.

Russell, Josiah Cox. "Demographic Factors of the Crusades." In: *The Meeting of Two Worlds: Cultural Exchange between East and West during the Period of the Crusades*. Ed. Vladimir P. Gross. Studies in Medieval Culture, 21. Kalamazoo: Medieval Institute Publications, 1986, pp. 53-58.

Saunders, J.J. *Aspects of the Crusades*. Christchurch, 1962.

Savvides, Alexis G.C. "Late Byzantine and Western Historiographers on Turkish Mercenaries in Greek and Latin Armies: The Turcoples/Tourkopouloi." In: *The Making of Byzantine History: Studies Dedicated to Donald M. Nicol*. Ed. Roderick Beaton and Charlotte Roueché. Ashgate: Variorum, 1993, pp. 122-36.

Schein, Sylvia. "Die Kreuzzüge als volkstümlich-messianische Bewegungen," *Deutsches Archiv für Erforschung des Mittelalter* 47 (1991), 119-38.

Schwinges, R.C. *Kreuzzugsideologie und Toleranz: Studien zu Wilhelm von Tyrus*. Monographien zur Geschichte des Mittelalters, 15. Stuttgart: Hiersemann, 1977.

Seidel, Linda V. "Holy Warriors: The Romanesque Rider and the Fight Against Islam." In: *The Holy War*. Ed. T.P. Murphy. Columbus, 1976, pp. 33-77.

Shatzmiller, Maya. "The Crusades and Islamic Warfare: A Re-Evaluation," *Der Islam* 69 (1992), 247-88.

Siberry, Elizabeth. *Criticism of Crusading, 1095-1274*. Oxford: Clarendon Press, 1985.

Siberry, Elizabeth. "Missionaries and Crusaders, 1095-1274: Opponents or Allies?" *Studies in Church History* 20 (1983), 103-10.

Sivan, E. *L'Islam et la croisade: Idéologie et propagande dans les réactions musulmanes aux croisades*. Paris, 1968.

Smail, R.C. *The Crusaders in Syria and the Holy Land*. London, 1973.

Smail, R.C. *Crusading Warfare (1097-1193)*. Cambridge: Cambridge University Press, 1956.

Southern, Richard W. *Western Views of Islam in the Middle Ages*. Cambridge: Harvard University Press, 1962.

Spreckelmeyer, Goswin. *Das Kreuzzugslied des Lateinischen Mittelalters*. Munich, 1974.

Synan, Edward A. "'The Popes' Other Sheep.'" In: *The Religious Roles of the Papacy: Ideals and Realities, 1150-1300*. Ed. C. Ryan. Toronto, 1989, pp. 389-411.

Tate, G. *L'orient des croisades*. Paris, 1991.

Teule, Herman. "The Crusaders in Barhebraeus' Syriac and Arabic Secular Chronicles: A Different Approach." In: *East and West in the Crusader States: Context–Contacts–Confrontations*. Ed. Krijnie Ciggaar, Adelbert Davids, and Herman Teule. Orientalia Lovaniensia analecta, 75. Leuven: Uitgeverij Peeters, 1996, pp. 39-49.

Thompson, Kathleen. "Family Tradition and the Crusading Impulse: The Poitou Counts of the Perche," *Medieval Prospography* 19 (1998), 1-33.

Thouzellier, C. "Hérésie et croisade au xiie siècle," *Revue de l'histoire ecclésiastique* 49 (1954), 855-72.

Tyerman, Christopher. *England and the Crusades, 1095-1588*. Chicago: The University of Chicago Press, 1988.

Tyerman, Christopher. *The Invention of the Crusades*. Toronto: University of Toronto Press, 1998.

Villey, Maurice. *La croisade: Essai sur la formation d'une théorie juridique*. Paris, 1942.

Waas, A. *Geschichte der Kreuzzüge*. 2 vols. Freiburg im Breisgau, 1956.

Wankenne, André. "Les Belges et la croisade," *Etudes classiques* 55 (1987), 163-73.

Watt, W. Montgomery. "Islamic Conceptions of the Holy War." In: *The Holy War*. Ed. T.P. Murphy. Columbus, 1976, pp. 141-56.

White, Lynn, Jr. "The Crusade and the Technological Thrust of the West." In: *War, Technology and Society in the Middle East*. Ed. V. J. Parry and M.E. Yapp. London: Oxford University Press, 1975, pp. 97-112; in: *Medieval Religion and Technology: Collected Essays*. Berkeley and Los Angeles: University of California Press, 1978, pp. 277-96.

Willemart, P. *Les croisades: Mythe et réalité de la guerre sainte*. Verviers, 1972.

Williams, Jay. *Knights of the Crusades*. London: Cassell, 1963.

Wise, Terence. *Armies of the Crusades*. Men-at-Arms Series. London: Osprey Publishing. 1978.

Medieval – Crusades – Origins

Alphandéry, Paul. *La chrétienté et l'idée de croisade*. 2 vols. Ed. A. Dupront. Paris, 1954-59.

Becker, Alfons. *Papst Urban II (1088-1099)*. 2 vols. Monumenta Germaniae Historica Schriften, 19. Stuttgart, 1964, 1988.

Becker, Alfons. "Urbain II, pape de la croisade." In: *Champenois et la croisade: Actes des IVe journées rémonises, 27-28 novembre 1987*. Ed. Yvonne Bellenger and Danielle Quéruel. Publications de la centre de recherche sur la littérature du moyen âge et de la renaissance de l'Université de Reims. Paris: Aux Amateurs de Livres, 1989, pp. 9-17.

Beech, George T. "Urban II, the Abbey of Saint-Florent of Saumur, and the First Crusade." In: *Autour de la première croisade: Actes du Colloque de la Society for the Study of the Crusades and the Latin East*

(Clermont-Ferrand, 22-25 juin 1995). Ed. M. Balard. Paris: Publications de la Sorbonne, 1996, pp. 57-70.

Belch, S.F. "Theologi anonymi utrum bella contra infideles fidelibus licitum sit movere?" *Mediaevalia philosophica Polonorum* 19 (1974), 3-63.

Belke, K. "Phrygia between Byzantines and Seljuks," *Byzantinische Forschungen* 16 (1991), 159-65.

Beumann, H. "Kreuzzugsgedanke und Ostpolitik im hohen Mittelalter." In: *Heidenmission und Kreuzzugsgedanke in der deutschen Ostpolitik des Mittelalters*. Ed. H. Beumann. Darmstadt, pp. 121-45.

Blake, Ernest O. "The Formation of the 'Crusade Idea,'" *Journal of Ecclesiastical History* 21 (1970), 11-31.

Blake, Ernest O and Colin Morris. "A Hermit Goes to War: Peter and the Origins of the First Crusade." In: *Monks, Hermits and the Ascetic Tradition*. Ed. W.J. Sheils. Oxford, 1985, pp. 79-107.

Bull, Marcus. "The Pilgrimage Origins of the First Crusade," *History Today* 47.3 (Mar 1997), 10-15.

Cahen, Claude. "Le campagne de Mantzikert d'après les sources musulmans," *Byzantion* 9 (1934), 628-42.

Cahen, Claude. "En quoi le conquête turque appelait-elle la croisade?" *Bulletin de la faculté des lettres de Strasbourg* 29 (1950-51).

Callahan, Daniel F. "Jerusalem in the Monastic Imaginations of the Early Eleventh Century," *Haskins Society Journal* 6 (1994), 119-27.

Capitani, Ovidio. "Sondaggio sulla terminologia militare in Urbano II." In: *"Militia Christi" e crociata nei secoli XI-XIII: Atti della undecima settimana internazionale di studio, Mendola, 28 agosta-1 settembre 1989*. Miscellanea del Centro di studi medioevali, 13; Scienze storiche, 48. Milan: Vita e Pensiero, 1992, pp. 167-92.

Charanis, Peter. "Byzantium, the West and the Origin of the First Crusade," *Byzantion* 19 (1949), 17-36.

Cheynet, Jean-Claude. "Mantzikert, un désastre militaire?" *Byzantion* 50 (1980), 412-38.

Cowdrey, H.E.J. "The Genesis of the Crusades: The Springs of Western Ideas of Holy War." In: *The Holy War*. Ed. T.P. Murphy. Columbus: Ohio State University, 1976, pp. 9-32.

Cowdrey, H.E.J. "The Gregorian Papacy, Byzantium and the First Crusade." In: *Byzantium and the West, c. 850-1200: Proceedings of the XVIII Spring Symposium of Byzantine Studies*. Ed. J.D. Howard-Johnston. Amsterdam: Hakkert, 1988, pp. 145-69.

Cowdrey, H.E.J. "The Mahdia Campaign of 1087," *English Historical Review* 92 (1977), 1-29.

Cowdrey, H.E.J. "The Origin of the Idea of Crusade," *The International History Review* 1 (1979), 121-25.

Cowdrey, H.E.J. "The Papacy and the Origins of Crusading," *Medieval History* 1 (1991), 48-60.

Cowdrey, H.E.J. "Pope Gregory VII's 'Crusading' Plans of 1074." In: *Outremer: Studies in the History of the Crusading Kingdom of Jerusalem Presented to Joshua Prawer*. Jerusalem, 1982, pp. 27-40.

Cowdrey, H.E.J. "Pope Urban II and the Idea of Crusade," *Studi medievali* ser. 3, 36 (1995), 721-42.

Cowdrey, H.E.J. "Pope Urban II's Preaching of the First Crusade," *History* 55 (1970), 177-88.

Crozet, René. "Le voyage d'Urbain II en France (1095-96) et son importance du point de vue archéologique," *Annales du Midi* 49 (1937), 42-69.

Crozet, René. "Le voyage d'Urbain II et ses négotiations avec le clergé de France (1095-1096)," *Revue historique* 179 (1937), 271-310.

Delaruelle, Étienne. "Essai sur la formation de l'idée de croisade," *Bulletin de littérature ecclésiastique* 42 (1941), 24-45, 86-103; 45 (1944), 13-46, 73-90; 54 (1953), 226-39; 55 (1954), 50-63.

Duncalf, Frederic. "The Councils of Piacenza and Clermont." In: *A History of the Crusades*. Ed. Kenneth Setton. Madison: University of Wisconsin Press, 1969, I:220-52.

Duncalf, Frederic. "The Pope's Plan for the First Crusade." In: *The Crusades and Other Historical Essays Presented to Dana C. Munro by*

His Former Students. Ed. Louis J. Paetow. New York: F.S. Crofts, 1928, pp. 44-56.

Eickhoff, Ekkhard. "Zur Wende von Manzikert." In: *Das andere wahrnehmen: Beiträge zur europäischen Geschichte.* Ed. Martin Kintzinger, Wolfgang Stürner, and Johannes Zahlten. Cologne: Böhlau, 1991, pp. 101-19.

Erdmann, Carl. *Die Entstehung des Kreuzzugsgedankens.* Forschungen zur Kirchen- und Geistesgeschichte, 6. Stuttgart: Kohlhammer, 1935; trans. *The Origin of the Idea of Crusade.* Trans. Marshall W. Baldwin and Walter Goffart. Princeton: Princeton University Press, 1977.

Fedalto, G. *Perché le crociate: Saggio interpretativo.* Bologna, 1980.

Fledelius, Karsten. "The Idea of the Crusades." In: *War and Peace in the Middle Ages.* Ed. B.P. McGuire. Copenhagen, 1987, pp. 252-61.

Fliche, Augustin. "Urbain II et la croisade," *Revue d'histoire de l'église de France* 13 (1927), 289-306.

Flori, Jean. "L'idea di crociata." In: *Piacenza e la prima crociata.* Ed. Pierre Racine. Piacenza: Diabasis, 1995, pp. 15-33.

Flori, Jean. *La première croisade: L'occident chrétien contre l'Islam.* Paris: Editions complexe, 1992.

Flori, Jean. *"Pur eschalcier sainte crestiëenté.* Croisade, guerre sainte et guerre juste dans les anciennes chansons de geste françaises," *Moyen âge,* 5th ser., 5 (1991), 171-87.

Flori, Jean. "Réforme, *reconquista,* croisade: L'idée de reconquête dans la correspondance pontificale d'Alexandre II à Urbain II," *Cahiers de civilisation médiévale (X-XIIe siècle)* 40 (1997), 317-35.

Flori, Jean. "Une ou plusieurs 'première croisade'? Le message d'Urbain II et les plus anciens pogroms d'occident," *Revue historique* 285 (1991), 3-27.

Fornasari, Giuseppe. "Tra assestamento disciplinare e consolidamento istituzionale: un'interpretazione del pontificato di Urbano II." In: *Regensburg, Bayern und Europa: Festschrift für Kurt Reindel zu seinem 70. Gebeurtstag.* Ed. Lothar Kolmer and Peter Segl. Regensburg: Universitätsverlag, 1995, pp. 213-28.

France, John. "Les origines de la première croisade: Un nouvel examen." In: *Autour de la première croisade: Actes du Colloque de la Society for the Study of the Crusades and the Latin East (Clermont-Ferrand, 22-25 juin 1995)*. Ed. M. Balard. Paris: Publications de la Sorbonne, 1996, pp. 43-56.

Friendly, Alfred. *The Dreadful Day: The Battle of Mantzikert, 1071*. London: Hutchinson, 1981.

Gieysztor, A. "The Genesis of the Crusades: The Encyclical of Sergius IV," *Mediaevala et humanistica* 5 (1948), 3-23; 6 (1950), 3-34.

Gilchrist, John T. "The Erdmann Thesis and the Canon Law, 1083-1141." In: *Crusade and Settlement: Papers Read at the First Conference of the Society for the Study of the Crusades and the Latin East and Presented to R.C. Smail*. Ed. Peter W. Edbury. Cardiff: University College Cardiff Press, 1985, pp. 37-45.

Grabois, Aryeh. "Anselme, l'ancien testament en l'idée de croisade." In: *Les mutations socio-culturelles au tournant des XIe-XIIe siècles*. Spicilegium Beccense, 2. Paris: C.N.R.S., 1984, pp. 161-73, 197-200.

Hiestand, Rudolf. "Der Kreuzzug–ein Traum?" In: *Traum und Träumen: Inhalt–Darstellung–Funktionen einer Lebenserfahrung in Mittelalter und Renaissance*. Ed. Rudolf Hiestand. Studia humaniora: Düsseldorfer Studien zu Mittelalter und Renaissance, 24. Dusseldorf: Droste, 1994, pp. 153-85.

Hill, John H. "Raymond of St. Gilles in Urban's Plan of Greek and Latin Friendship," *Speculum* 26 (1951), 265-76.

Housley, Norman. "Crusades Against Christians: Their Origins and Early Development, c.1000-1216." In: *Crusade and Settlement: Papers Read at the First Conference of the Society for the Study of the Crusades and the Latin East and Presented to R.C. Smail*. Ed. Peter W. Edbury. Cardiff: University College Cardiff Press, 1985, pp. 17-36.

Joranson, Einar. "The Great German Pilgrimage of 1064-1065." In: *The Crusades and Other Historical Essays Presented to Dana C. Munro by His Former Students*. Ed. L.J. Paetow. Freeport, 1928, pp. 3-43.

Kuloglu, Abdullah. "The Battle of Malazgirt and the Turkish Expansion in Anatolia," *Revue internationale d'histoire militaire* 46 (1980), 1-14.

Laurent, J. "Des Grecs aux croisés: Etude sur l'histoire d'Edesse entre 1071 et 1098," *Byzantion* 1 (1924), 367-449.

Lounghis, T. "The Failure of the German-Byzantine Alliance on the Eve of the First Crusade," *Diptycha* 1 (1979), 158-67.

Matzke, Michael. "*De origine hospitalorum Hierosolymitanorum*–vom klösterlichen Pilgerhospital zur internationalen Organisation," *Journal of Medieval History* 22 (1996), 1-23.

Morillon, M. "Le voyage d'Urbain II en France, le concile de Clermont et les débuts de la première croisade," *Amis du pays civraisien* n.s. 40 (1980), 11-16.

Morisi, A. *La guerra nel pensiero cristiano dalle origini alle crociate.* Florence, 1963.

Munro, Dana C. "Did the Emperor Alexius Ask for Aid at the Council of Piacenza?" *American Historical Review* 27 (1922), 731-33.

Munro, Dana C. "The Speech of Pope Urban II at Clermont, 1095," *American Historical Review* 11 (1906), 231-42.

Munro, Dana C. *Urban and the Crusaders.* Philadelphia: University of Pennsylvania Press, 1895.

Noth, A. *Heiliger Krieg und heiliger Kampf: Beiträge zur Geschichte der Kreuzzüge.* Bonn, 1966.

Pahlitzsch, Johannes. "Die Idee von der *liberatio orientalium ecclesiarum* bei Urban II." In: *Miszellen aus dem Schülerkreis: Kaspar Elm dargebracht zum 23. septembre 1994.* Berlin: Friedrich-Meinecke-Institut, 1994, pp. 13-23.

Partner, Peter. "Guerra santa, crociate e 'Jihad': Un tentativo di definire alcuni problemi," *Studi storici* 36 (1995), 945-55.

Porter, J.M.B. "Preacher of the First Crusade? Robert of Arbissel after the Council of Clermont." In: *From Clermont to Jerusalem: The Crusades and Crusader Societies, 1095-1500.* Selected Proceedings of the International Medieval Congress, University of Leeds, 10-13 July 1995. Ed. Alan V. Murray. Turnhout: Brepols, 1998, pp. 43-54.

Richard, Jean. "La croisade: l'évolution des conceptions et des stratégies." In: *From Clermont to Jerusalem: The Crusades and Crusader Societies, 1095-1500*. Selected Proceedings of the International Medieval Congress, University of Leeds, 10-13 July 1995. Ed. Alan V. Murray. Turnhout: Brepols, 1998, pp. 3-25.

Richard, Jean. *L'esprit de la croisade*. Paris, 1969.

Richard, Jean. "Urbain II, la prédiction de la croisade et la définition de l'indulgence." In: *Deus qui mutat tempora: Menschen und Institutionen im Wandel des Mittelalters. Festschrift für Alfons Becker zu seinem fünfundsechzigsten Geburtstag*. Ed. Ernst-Dieter Hehl, Hubertus Seibert, and Franz Staab. Sigmaringen: Thorbecke, 1987, pp. 129-35.

Ringel, Ingrid Heike. "Ipse transfert regna et mutat tempora: Beobachtungen zur Herkunft von Dan. 2, 21 bei Urban II." In: *Deus qui mutat tempora: Menschen und Institutionen im Wandel des Mittelalters. Festschrift für Alfons Becker*. Ed. Ernst-Dieter Hehl, Hubertus Seibert, and Franz Staab. Sigmaringen, 1987, pp. 137-56.

Robinson, Ian S. "Gregory VII and the Soldiers of Christ," *History* 58 (1973), 169-92.

Runciman, Steven. "The Pilgrimages to Palestine before 1095." In: *A History of the Crusades*. Ed. Kenneth Setton. Madison: University of Wisconsin Press, 1969, I:68-78.

Somerville, Robert. "The Council of Clermont (1095) and Latin Christian Society," *Archivum historiae pontificiae* 12 (1974), 55-90.

Somerville, Robert. "The Council of Clermont and the First Crusade," *Studia Gratiana* 20 (1976), 325-37.

Somerville, Robert. "The French Councils of Pope Urban II," *Annuarium historiae conciliorum* 2 (1970), 56-65.

Walters, LeRoy. "The Just War and the Crusade: Antitheses or Analogies?" *The Monist* 57 (1973), 584-94.

Medieval – Crusades – First

Abulafia, Anna Sapir. "The Interrelationship between the Hebrew Chronicles of the First Crusade," *Journal of Semitic Studies* 27 (1982), 221-39.

Abulafia, Anna Sapir. "Invectives against Christianity in the Hebrew Chronicles of the First Crusade." In: *Crusade and Settlement: Papers Read at the First Conference of the Society for the Study of the Crusades and the Latin East and Presented to R.C. Smail.* Ed. Peter W. Edbury. Cardiff: University College Cardiff Press, 1985, pp. 66-72.

Adhémar-Labaume, G.J. de. *Adhémar de Monteil, évêque du Puy, légat d'Urbain II, 1079-1098.* Le Puy: Peyriller, Rouchon et Gamon, 1910.

Airaldi, Gabriella. "I Lombardi alla prima crociata." In: *I comuni Italiani nel regno crociato del Gerusalemme.* Ed. Gabriella Airaldi and Benjamin Z. Kedar. Genoa: Università di Genova, 1986, pp. 477-96.

Andenna, G. "I Lombardi e la prima crociata." In: *Piacenza e la prima crociata.* Ed. Pierre Racine. Piacenza: Diabasis, 1995, pp. 67-88.

Andressohn, John C. *The Ancestry and Life of Godfrey of Bouillon.* Bloomington: Indiana University Press, 1947.

Armanski, Gerhard. *Es begann in Clermont: Der erst Kreuzzug und die Genese der Gewalt in Europa.* Geschichte der Gewalt in Europa, 1. Pfaffenweiler: Centaurus-Verlagsgesellschaft, 1995.

Aubé, Pierre. *Godfroi de Bouillon.* Paris: Fayard, 1985.

Auffarth, Christoph. "'Ritter' und 'Arme' auf dem Ersten Kreuzzug: Zum Problem Herrschaft und Religion, ausgehend von Raymond von Aguiliers," *Saeculum* 40 (1989), 39-55.

Bachrach, Bernard. "The Siege of Antioch: A Study in Medieval Demography," *War in History* 6 (1999), 127-46.

Beech, George T. "A Norman-Italian Adventurer in the East: Richard of Salerno, 1097-1112," *Anglo-Norman Studies* 15 (1993), 25-40.

Beech, George T. "The Ventures of the Dukes of Aquitaine into Spain and the Crusader East in the Early Twelfth Century," *Haskins Society Journal* 5 (1993), 61-75.

Bliese, John R.E. "The Motives of the First Crusaders: A Social Psycho-logical Analysis," *Journal of Psychohistory* 17 (1990), 393-411.

Brandt, Coenraad D.J. *Kruisvarders naar Jeruzalem: Geschiedenis van de eerste kruistocht.* Utrecht: W. de Haan, 1950.

Brundage, James A. "Adhemar of Puy: The Bishop and his Critics," *Speculum* 34 (1959), 201-12.

Brundage, James A. "The Army of the First Crusade and the Crusade Vow: Some Reflections of a Recent Book," *Mediaeval Studies* 33 (1971), 334-43.

Brundage, James A. "An Errant Crusader: Stephen of Blois," *Traditio* 16 (1960), 380-95.

Brundage, James A. "Prostitution, Miscegenation and Sexual Purity in the First Crusade." In: *Crusade and Settlement: Papers Read at the First Conference of the Society for the Study of the Crusades and the Latin East and Presented to R.C. Smail.* Ed. Peter W. Edbury. Cardiff: University College Cardiff Press, 1985, pp. 57-65.

Brundage, James A. "St. Anselm, Ivo of Chartres, and the Ideology of the First Crusade." In: *Les mutations socio-culturelles au tournant des XIe-XIIe siècles* (Collcques internationaux de CNRS Le Bec-Hellouin 1982). Paris, 1984, pp. 175-87.

Buckler, Georgina. *Anna Comnena.* London, 1929.

Bull, Marcus. "The Diplomatic of the First Crusade." In: *The First Cru-sade: Origins and Impact.* Ed. Jonathan Phillips. Manchester: University of Manchester Press, 1997, pp. 35-54.

Bull, Marcus. *Knightly Piety and the Lay Response to the First Crusade: The Limousin and Gascony, c.970-c.1130.* Oxford: Oxford University Press, 1993.

Bull, Marcus. "The Roots of Lay Enthusiasm for the First Crusade," *History* 78 (1993), 353-72.

Cahen, Claude. "An Introduction to the First Crusade," *Past and Present* 6 (1954), 6-29.

132   MEDIEVAL – CRUSADES

Cate, James Lea. "The Crusade of 1101." In: *History of the Crusades*. Ed. Kenneth M. Setton. Madison: University of Wisconsin Press, 1969, I:343-67.

Cate, James Lea. "A Gay Crusader," *Byzantion* 16 (1944), 503-26.

Chalandon, Ferdinand. *Histoire de la première croisade jusqu'à l'élection de Godefroi de Bouillon*. Paris: Picard, 1925.

Chazan, Robert. *European Jewry and the First Crusade*. Berkeley and Los Angeles: University of California, 1987.

Chazan, Robert. "The First Crusade as Reflected in the Earliest Hebrew Narrative,"*Viator* 29 (1998), 25-38.

Chazan, Robert. "The Hebrew First Crusade Chronicles," *Revue des études juives* 133 (1974), 235-54.

Chrysostomides, J. "A Byzantine Historian: Anna Comnena." In: *Medieval Historical Writing in the Christian and Islamic Worlds*. Ed. D.O. Morgan. London, 1982, pp. 30-46.

Cizek, Alexandre. "Die umstrittene Feuerprobe des Kreuzfahrers Pierre Barthelemi in der Diachronie der Wunderberichte." In: *La croisade– Réalités et fictions: Actes du colloque d'Amiens 18-22 mars 1987*. Ed. Danielle Buschinger. Goppingen: Kümmerle, 1989, pp. 79-95.

Cohen, Jeremy. "Gzeirot tatnav–ha meorat ve-ha-alihot: sipurei kiddush hashem be-heksheram ha-tarbuti-hevreti," *Zion* 59 (1994), 169-208.

Coupe, Michael D. "Peter the Hermit–A Re-assessment," *Nottingham Medieval Studies* 31 (1987), 37-45.

Cowdrey, H.E.J. "Canon Law and the First Crusade." In: *The Horns of Hattin*. Ed. Benjamin Z. Kedar. London, 1992, pp. 41-48.

Cowdrey, H.E.J. "Cluny and the First Crusade," *Revue Bénédictine* 83 (1973), 285-311.

Cowdrey, H.E.J. "The Gregorian Papacy, Byzantium, and the First Crusade." In: *Byzantium and the West, c. 850-c. 1200*. Ed. J.D. Howard-Johnston. Byzantinische Forschungen, 13. Amsterdam, 1988, pp. 145-69.

Cowdrey, H.E.J. "Martyrdom and the First Crusade." In: *Crusade and Settlement: Papers Read at the First Conference of the Society for the Study of the Crusades and the Latin East and Presented to R.C. Smail.* Ed. Peter W. Edbury. Cardiff: University College Cardiff Press, 1985, pp. 46-56.

Cowdrey, H.E.J. "Pope Urban's Preaching of the First Crusade," *History* 55 (1970), 177-88.

Cutler, Alan. "The First Crusade and the Idea of Conversion," *Muslim World* 58 (1968), 155-64.

Despy, Georges. "Le date de l'accession de Godfroid de Bouillon au duché de Basse-Lotharingie," *Revue Belge de philologie et d'histoire* 36 (1958), 1275-84.

Despy, Georges. "Godefroid de Bouillon, mythes et réalités," *Academie royale de Belgique, bulletin de la classe des lettres et des sciences morales et politiques* ser. 5, 71 (1985), 249-75.

Dorchy, H. "Godefroid de Bouillon, duc de Basse-Lotharinge," *Revue Belge de philologie et d'histoire* 26 (1948), 961-99.

Duncalf, Frederic. "The First Crusade: Clermont to Constantinople." In: *A History of the Crusades.* Ed. Kenneth Setton. Madison: University of Wisconsin Press, 1969, I:253-79.

Duncalf, Frederic. "The Peasants' Crusade," *American Historical Review* 26 (1921), 440-53.

Dupont, André. "Raymond IV de Saint-Gilles et son role en orient pendant la première croisade (1096-1099)," *Bulletin des séances de l'académie de Nîmes* n.s. 47 (1970), 19-21, 24-26.

Edgington, Susan B. "Albert of Aachen Reappraised." In: *From Clermont to Jerusalem: The Crusades and Crusader Societies, 1095-1500.* Selected Proceedings of the International Medieval Congress, University of Leeds, 10-13 July 1995. Ed. Alan V. Murray. Turnhout: Brepols, 1998, pp. 55-68.

Edgington, Susan B. *The First Crusade.* New Appreciations in History, 37. London: Historical Association, 1996.

Edgington, Susan B. "The First Crusade: Reviewing the Evidence." In: *The First Crusade: Origins and Impact.* Ed. Jonathan Phillips. Manchester: University of Manchester Press, 1997, pp. 55-77.

Edgington, Susan B. "Medical Knowledge in the Crusading Armies: The Evidence of Albert of Aachen and Others." In: *The Military Orders: Fighting for the Faith and Caring for the Sick.* Ed. Malcolm Barber. Aldershot: Ashgate, 1994, pp. 320-26.

Edgington, Susan B. "Pagan Peverel: An Anglo-Norman Crusader." In: *Crusade and Settlement: Papers Read at the First Conference of the Society for the Study of the Crusades and the Latin East and Presented to R.C. Smail.* Ed. Peter W. Edbury. Cardiff: University College Cardiff Press, 1985, pp. 90-93.

Epp, Verena. *Fulcher von Chartres: Studien zur Geschichtesschreibung des ersten Kreuzzuges.* Studia humaniora: Düsseldorfer Studien zu Mittelalter und Renaissance, 15. Dusseldorf: Droste, 1990.

Figliuolo, Bruno. "Ancora sui Normanni d'Italia alla prima crociata," *Archivio storico per le province napoletane* 104 (1988), 1-16.

Flesch, Stefan. "Die Verfolgung und Vernichtung der jüdischen Gemeinde von Köln während des Ersten Kreuzzugs." In: *Der Erste Kreuzzug 1096 und seine Folgen: Die Verfolgung von Juden im Rheinland.* Schriften des Archivs der Evangelischen Kirche im Rheinland, 9. Dusseldorf: Archiv der Evangelischen Kirche im Rheinland, 1996, pp. 77-94.

Flori, Jean. "Des chroniques à l'épopée ... ou bien l'inverse (à propos du Picard Pierre l'Ermite)," *Perspectives médiévales* 20 (1994), 36-44.

Flori, Jean. "Du nouveau sur les origines de la première croisade," *Moyen âge* 5th ser. 9 (1995), 103-11.

Flori, Jean. "Faut-il réhabiliter Pierre l'Ermite? (Une réévaluation des sources de la première croisade)," *Cahiers de civilisation médiévale (X-XIIe siècles)* 38 (1995), 35-54.

Flori, Jean. "Guerre sainte et rétributions spirituelles dans la 2e moitié de XI siècle," *Revue d'histoire ecclesiastique* 85 (1990), 617-49.

Flori, Jean. "Mort et martyre des guerriers vers 1100. L'exemple de la première croisade," *Cahiers de civilisation médiévale (Xe-XIIe siècles)* 34 (1991), 121-39.

Flori, Jean. "Pierre l'Ermite et sa croisade–légende et vérité," *Cahiers de clio* 125-26 (1996), 29-39.

Flori, Jean. *La première croisade: L'occident chrétien contre l'Islam (Aux origines des idéologies occidentales)*. Brussels, 1992.

Flori, Jean. "Un problème de méthodologie: La valeur des nombres chez les chroniqueurs du Moyen âge. A propos des effectifs de la première Croisade," *Moyen âge*, 5th ser., 99 (1993), 399-422.

Flori, Jean. "Une ou plusieurs "première croisade"? Le message d'Urbain II et les plus anciens pogroms d'Occident," *Revue historique* 285 (1991), 3-27.

Foreville, R. "Un chef de la première croisade: Arnoul Malecouronne," *Bulletin philologique et historique* (1953-54), 377-90.

Forse, James H. "Armenians and the First Crusade," *Journal of Medieval History* 17 (1991), 13-22.

Foss, Michael. *People of the First Crusade*. London: O'Mara, 1997.

France, John. "Anna Comnena, the *Alexiad*, and the First Crusade," *Reading Medieval Studies* 10 (1984), 20-38.

France, John. "The Capture of Jerusalem," *History Today* 47.4 (Apr 1997), 37-42.

France, John. "The Crisis of the First Crusade: From the Defeat of Kerbogha to the Departure from Arqa," *Byzantion* 40 (1970), 276-308.

France, John. "The Departure of Tatikios from the Crusader Army," *Bulletin of the Institute of Historical Research* 44 (1971), 137-47.

France, John. "The Destruction of Jerusalem and the First Crusade," *Journal of Ecclesiastical History* 47 (1996), 1-17.

France, John. "The Election and Title of Godfrey of Bouillon," *Canadian Journal of History* 18 (1983), 321-29.

France, John. "The First Crusade as a Naval Enterprise," *Mariner's Mirror* 83 (1997), 389-97.

France, John. "Patronage and Appeal of the First Crusade." In: *The First Crusade: Origins and Impact*. Ed. Jonathan Phillips. Manchester: University of Manchester Press, 1997, pp. 5-20.

France, John. "Technology and Success of the First Crusade." In: *War and Society in the Eastern Mediterranean, 7th-15th Centuries*. Ed. Y. Lev. Leiden, 1997, pp. 163-76.

France, John. "The Text of the Account of the Capture of Jerusalem in the Ripoll Manuscript, Bibliothèque Nationale (Latin) 5132," *English Historical Review* 103 (1988), 640-57.

France, John. "The Use of the Anonymous Gesta Francorum in the Early Twelfth-Century Sources for the First Crusade." In: *From Clermont to Jerusalem: The Crusades and Crusader Societies, 1095-1500*. Selected Proceedings of the International Medieval Congress, University of Leeds, 10-13 July 1995. Ed. Alan V. Murray. Turnhout: Brepols, 1998, pp. 29-42.

France, John. *Victory in the East: A Military History of the First Crusade*. Cambridge: Cambridge University Press, 1994.

Ganshof, François Louis. "Recherche sur le lien juridique qui unissait les chefs de la première croisade à l'empereur byzantin." In: *Mélanges offerts à M. Paul-E. Martin*. Paris: Société d'histoire et d'archéologique de Genève, 1962, pp. 49-63.

Giese, Wolfgang. "Die 'lancea Domini' von Antiocha (1098/99)." In: *Fälschungen im Mittelalter: Internationaler Kongreß der Monumenta Germaniae Historica, München, 16.-19. September 1986*. Ed. Wolfram Setz. Schriften der Monumenta Germaniae Historica, 33. Hannover: Hahn, 1988-90, V:485-504.

Gilchrist, John T. "The Perception of Jews in the Canon Law in the Period of the First Two Crusades," *Jewish History* 3 (1988), 9-24.

Goitein, S.D. "Contemporary Letters on the Capture of Jerusalem by the Crusaders," *Journal of Jewish Studies* 3-4 (1952), 162-77.

Golb, N. "New Light on the Persecution of French Jews at the Time of the First Crusade." In: *Medieval Jewish Life: Studies from the Proceedings of the American Academy for Jewish Research*. Ed. R. Chazan. New York: American Academy for Jewish Research, 1976, pp. 334-52.

Grabois, Aryeh. "The Description of Jerusalem by William of Malmesbury: A Mirror of the Holy Land's Presence in the Anglo-Norman Mind," *Anglo-Norman Studies* 13 (1990), 145-56.

Grgin, Borislav. "Odjeci krizarskih radova u Hrvatskoj," *Historijski zbornik* 45 (1993), 139-54.

Hagenmeyer, Heinrich. "Der Brief der Kreuzfahrer an den Pabst und die abendländische Kirche im Jahre 1099 nach der Schlacht bei Askalon," *Forschungen zur deutschen Geschichte* 13 (1873), 400-12.

Hagenmeyer, Heinrich. "Chronologie de la première croisade, 1094-1100," *Revue de l'orient latin* 6 (1898), 214-93, 490-549; 7 (1899), 275-399, 430-503; 8 (1900-01), 318-82.

Hagenmeyer, Heinrich. "Etude sur la Chronique de Zimmern: Renseignements qu'elle fournit sur la première croisade," *Archives de l'orient latin* 2 (1884), 20-36.

Hagenmeyer, Heinrich. *Die Kreuzzugsbriefe aus den Jahren 1088-1100*. Innsbruck, 1901.

Hagenmeyer, Heinrich. *Peter der Eremite: ein kritischer Beitrag zur Geschichte des ersten Kreuzzuges*. Leipzig: Harassowitz, 1879.

Hagenmeyer, Heinrich. *Le vrai et le faux sur Pierre l'Hermite*. Paris: Société bibliographique, 1883.

Head, Constance. "Alexios Komnenos and the English," *Byzantion* 47 (1977), 186-98.

Heermann, O. *Die Gefectsführung abendländischer Heere im Orient in der Epoch des ersten Kreuzzugs*. Marburg, 1888.

Heers, Jacques. "Le implicaziono economiche della prima crociata." In: *Piacenza e la prima crociata*. Ed. Pierre Racine. Piacenza: Diabasis, 1995, pp. 103-24.

Heers, Jacques. *Libérer Jérusalem: La première croisade, 1095-1107*. Paris: Perrin, 1995.

Hemptinne, Thérèse de. "Les épouses des croisés et pèlerins flamands aux XIe et XIIe siècles: l'exemple des comtesses de Flandre Clémence et Sibylle." In: *Autour de la première croisade: Actes du Colloque de la Society for the Study of the Crusades and the Latin East (Clermont-Ferrand, 22-25 juin 1995)*. Ed. M. Balard. Paris: Publications de la Sorbonne, 1996, pp. 83-95.

Hiestand, Rudolf. "Die Erste Kreuzzug in der Welt des ausgehenden 11. Jahrhunderts." In: *Der Erste Kreuzzug und seine Folgen: Die Verfolgung von Juden im Rheinland*. Schriften des Archivs der Evangelischen Kirche im Rheinland, 9. Dusseldorf: Archiv der Evangelischen Kirche im Rheinland, 1996, pp. 1-36.

Hill, John H., and Laurita L. Hill. "Contemporary Accounts and the Later Reputation of Adhemar, bishop of Puy," *Mediaevalia et humanistica* 9 (1955), 30-38.

Hill, John H., and Laurita L. Hill. "The Convention of Alexius Comnenus and Raymond of St. Gilles," *American Historical Review* 58 (1952-53), 322-27.

Hill, John H., and Laurita L. Hill. "Justification historique du titre de Raymond de St. Gilles 'Christiane milice excellentissimus princeps," *Annales du midi* 66 (1954), 101-12.

Hill, John H., and Laurita L. Hill. *Raymond IV, Count of Toulouse*. Syracuse: Syracuse University Press, 1962.

Hill, John H., and Laurita L. Hill. *Raymond IV de Sain-Gilles 1041 (ou 1042)-1105*. Bibliothèque meridionale, ser. 2, 35. Toulouse, 1959.

Hill, Rosalind M.T. "Christian View of the Muslims at the Time of the First Crusade." In: *The Eastern Mediterranean Lands in the Period of the Crusades*. Ed. P.M. Holt. Warminster: Aris and Phillips, 1977, pp. 1-8.

Hill, Rosalind M.T. "Crusading Warfare: A Camp-followers View, 1097-1120," *Proceedings of the Battle Conference on Anglo-Norman Studies* 1 (1978), 75-83.

Hillenbrand, Carole. "The First Crusade: The Muslim Perspective." In: *The First Crusade: Origins and Impact*. Ed. Jonathan Phillips. Manchester: University of Manchester Press, 1997, pp. 130-41.

Housley, Norman. "Jerusalem and the Development of the Crusade Idea, 1099-1128." In: *The Horns of Hattin*. Ed. Benjamin Z. Kedar. London, 1992, pp. 27-40.

Ilieva, Annetta and Mitko Delev. "La conscience des croisés et l'altérité chrétienne: Essai typologique sur les conflits pendant la Première Croisade." In: *Autour de la première croisade: Actes du Colloque de la Society for the Study of the Crusades and the Latin East (Clermont-Ferrand, 22-25 juin 1995)*. Ed. M. Balard. Paris: Publications de la Sorbonne, 1996, pp. 109-18.

Jamison, E.M. "Some Notes on the *Anonymi gesta Francorum*, with Special Reference to the Norman Contingent from South Italy and Sicily in the First Crusade." In: *Studies in French Language and Medieval Literature Presented to Professor Mildred K. Pope*. Manchester: University of Manchester Press, 1939, pp. 195-204.

Jotischky, A.T. "St Gerard of Csanád and the Carmelites: Apocryphal Sidelights on the First Crusade." In: *Autour de la première croisade: Actes du Colloque de la Society for the Study of the Crusades and the Latin East (Clermont-Ferrand, 22-25 juin 1995)*. Ed. M. Balard. Paris: Publications de la Sorbonne, 1996, pp. 143-55.

Katzir, Yael. "The Conquests of Jerusalem, 1099 and 1187: Historical Memory and Religious Typology." In: *The Meeting of Two Worlds: Cultural Exchange between East and West during the Period of the Crusades*. Ed. Vladimir P. Gross. Studies in Medieval Culture, 21. Kalamazoo: Medieval Institute Publications, 1986, pp. 103-13.

Kauffeldt, Rolf. "1096: Erster Kreuzzug und Judenpogrome als Zäsur in der abendländischen Geschichte." In: *Der Erste Kreuzzug und seine Folgen: Die Verfolgung von Juden im Rheinland*. Schriften des Archivs der Evangelischen Kirche im Rheinland, 9. Dusseldorf: Archiv der Evangelischen Kirche im Rheinland, 1996, pp. 105-21.

Knappen, M.M. "Robert II of Flanders in the First Crusade." In: *The Crusades and Other Historical Essays Presented to Dana C. Munro by His Former Students*. Ed. Louis J. Paetow. New York: F.S. Crofts, 1928, pp. 79-100.

Knoch, Peter. *Studien zu Albert von Aachen: Der I. Kreuzzug in der deutschen Chronistik.* Stuttgarter Beiträge zur Geschichte und Politik, 1. Stuttgart: Klett, 1966.

Kohler, Charles. "Un sermon commémoratif de la prise de Jérusalem par les croisés attribué à Foucher de Chartres," *Revue de l'orient latin* 8 (1900-01), 158-64.

Krey, August C. "A Neglected Passage in the Gesta and Its Bearing on the Literature of the First Crusade." In: *The Crusades and Other Historical Essays Presented to Dana C. Munro by His Former Students.* Ed. L.J. Paetow. Freeport, 1928, pp. 57-78.

Krey, August C. "Urban's Crusade, Success or Failure?" *American Historical Revue* 53 (1948), 235-50.

Le Febvre, Yves. *Pierre l'Ermitte et la croisade.* Amiens: Malfère, 1946.

Lilie, Ralph-Johannes. "Anna Komnene und die Lateiner," *Byzantinoslavica* 54 (1993), 169-82.

Lilie, Ralph-Johannes. "Der erste Kreuzzug in der Darstellung Anna Komnenes." In: *Varia II: Beiträge von A. Berger et al.* Poikila Byzantina, 6. Bonn: R. Habelt, 1987, pp. 49-148.

Lobet, Marcel. *Godefroid de Bouillon: Essai de biographie antilégendaire.* Brussels: Les Escrits, 1943.

Loutchitskaja, S. "*Barbarae nationes*: les peuples musulmans dans les chroniques de la Première Croisade." In: *Autour de la première croisade: Actes du Colloque de la Society for the Study of the Crusades and the Latin East (Clermont-Ferrand, 22-25 juin 1995).* Ed. M. Balard. Paris: Publications de la Sorbonne, 1996, pp. 99-107.

Manselli, Raoul. *Italia e Italiani alla prima crociata.* Rome, 1983.

Mayer, Hans Eberhard. "Zur Beurteilung Adhemars von Le Puy," *Deutsches Archiv für Erforschung des Mittelalters* 16 (1960), 547-52.

McFall, J. Arthur. "Ill-Fated Crusade of the Poor People," *Military History* (Feb 1998), 26-32.

McGinn, Bernard. "Iter Sancti Sepulchri: Piety of the First Crusaders." In: *Essays in Medieval Civilization*. Ed. Bede K. Lackner and Kenneth R. Philip. Austin: University of Texas Press, 1978, pp. 33-71.

McGinn, Bernard. "Violence and Spirituality: The Enigma of the First Crusade," *Journal of Religion* 69 (1989), 375-79.

Mentgen, Gerd. "Die Juden des Mittelrhein-Mosel-Gebietes im Hochmittelalter unter besonderer Berücksichtigung der Kreuzzugsverfolgungen." In: *Der Erste Kreuzzug 1096 und seine Folgen: Die Verfolgung von Juden im Rheinland*. Schriften des Archivs der Evangelischen Kirche im Rheinland, 9. Dusseldorf: Archiv der Evangelischen Kirche im Rheinland, 1996, pp. 37-75.

Menzel, Michael. "Gottfried von Bouillon und Kaiser Heraclius," *Archiv für Kulturgeschichte* 74 (1992), 1-21.

Moeller, Charles. "Godefroid de Bouillon et l'avouerie du Saint-Sépulcre." In: *Mélanges Godefroid Kurth: Recueil de mémoires relatifs à l'histoire, à la philologie et à l'archéologie*. Liege: Vaillant-Carmanne, 1908, I:173-83.

Möhring, Hannes. "Graf Emicho und die Judenverfolgungen von 1096," *Rheinische Vierteljahrsblätter* 56 (1992), 97-111.

Morris, Colin. "The Aims and Spirituality of the First Crusade as Seen Through the Eyes of Albert of Aachen," *Reading Medieval Studies* 16 (1990), 99-117.

Morris, Colin. "Martyrs on the Field of Battle Before and During the First Crusade," *Studies in Church History* 30 (1993), 93-104; in: *Martyrs and Martyrologies*. Ed. D. Wood. Oxford, 1993, pp. 93-104.

Morris, Colin. "Peter the Hermit and the Chroniclers." In: *The First Crusade: Origins and Impact*. Ed. Jonathan Phillips. Manchester: University of Manchester Press, 1997, pp. 21-34.

Morris, Colin. "Policy and Visions: The Case of the Holy Lance at Antioch." *War and Government in the Middle Ages: Essays in Honor of J.O. Prestwich*. Ed. J. Gillingham and J.C. Holt. Woodbridge, 1984, pp. 33-45.

Mulinder, Alec. "Albert of Aachen and the Crusade of 1101." In: *From Clermont to Jerusalem: The Crusades and Crusader Societies, 1095-1500*. Selected Proceedings of the International Medieval Congress, University of Leeds, 10-13 July 1995. Ed. Alan V. Murray. Turnhout: Brepols, 1998, pp. 69-77.

Murray, Alan V. "The Army of Godfrey of Bouillon, 1096-1099: Structure and Dynamics of a Contingent on the First Crusade," *Revue Belge de philologie et d'histoire* 70 (1992), 301-29.

Murray, Alan V. "Bibliography of the First Crusade." In: *From Clermont to Jerusalem: The Crusades and Crusader Societies, 1095-1500*. Selected Proceedings of the International Medieval Congress, University of Leeds, 10-13 July 1995. Ed. Alan V. Murray. Turnhout: Brepols, 1998, pp. 267-310.

Murray, Alan V. "The Chronicle of Zimmern as a Source for the First Crusade: The Evidence of Ms. Stuttgart, Württembergische Landesbibliothek, Cod. Don. 580." In: *The First Crusade: Origins and Impact*. Ed. Jonathan Phillips. Manchester: University of Manchester Press, 1997, pp. 78-106.

Murray, Alan V. "Questions of Nationality in the First Crusade," *Medieval History* 1 (1991), 61-73.

Murray, Alan V. "Walther, Duke of Teck: The Invention of a German Hero of the First Crusade," *Medieval Prospography* 19 (1998), 35-54.

Nahon, Gérard. "La communauté juive askenaze face aus pérsecutions des croisades d'après des chroniques hébraïques du XIIe siècle," *Annuaire de l'école des hautes-études–Ve section* 88 (1979-80), 253-58; 90 (1981-82), 259-60.

Nicholson, Robert L. *Tancred: A Study of His Career and Work in Their Relation to the First Cruade and the Establishment of the Latin States in Syria and Palestine*. Chicago: Chicago University Press, 1940.

Petit, Aimé. "Le camp chrétien devant Antioche dans le RPCBB," *Romania* 108 (1987), 503-19.

Phillips, Jonathan. "Who Were the First Crusaders?" *History Today* 47.3 (Mar 1997), 16-22.

Plank, P. "Patriarch Symeon II. von Jerusalem und der erste Kreuzzug: Eine quellenkritische Untersuchung," *Ostkirchliche Studien* 43 (1994), 275-327.

Pontieri, Ernesto. "I Normanni dell'Italia meridionale e la prima crociata," *Archivio storico Italiano* 114 (1956), 3-17.

Porges, Walter. "The Clergy, the Poor, and the Non-Combatants on the First Crusade," *Speculum* 21 (1946), 1-23.

Powell, James M. "Myth, Legend, Propaganda, History: The First Crusade, 1140-ca. 1300."In: *Autour de la première croisade: Actes du Colloque de la Society for the Study of the Crusades and the Latin East (Clermont-Ferrand, 22-25 juin 1995)*. Ed. M. Balard. Paris: Publications de la Sorbonne, 1996, pp. 127-41.

Prawer, Joshua. "The Jerusalem the Crusaders Captured: A Contribution to the Medieval Topography of the City." In: *Crusade and Settlement: Papers Read at the First Conference of the Society for the Study of the Crusades and the Latin East and Presented to R.C. Smail*. Ed. Peter W. Edbury. Cardiff: University College Cardiff Press, 1985, pp. 1-16.

Pryor, John H. "The Oaths of the Leaders of the First Crusade to Emperor Alexius I Comnenus: Fealty, Homage–πιστιζ δονλεια," *Parergon* n.s. 2 (1984), 111-41.

Renna, Thomas. "Bernard of Clairvaux and the Temple of Solomon." In: *Law, Custom, and the Social Fabric in Medieval Europe: Essays in Honor of Bryce Lyon*. Ed. Bernard Bachrach and David Nicholas. Kalamazoo, 1990, pp. 73-88.

Riant, P. "Un dernier triomphe d'Urbain II," *Revue des questions historiques* 34 (1883), 247-55.

Rice, Geoffrey. "A Note on the Battle of Antioch, 28 June 1098: Bohemund as Tactical Innovator," *Parergon* 25 (1979), 3-8.

Richard, Jean. "La confrérie de la croisade: à propos d'un épisode de la première croisade." In: *Etudes de civilisation médiévale (IXe-XIIe siècles): Mélanges offerts à Edmond-René Labande*. Poitiers: CESCM, 1974, pp. 617-22.

Richard, Jean. "Départs de pelèrins et de croisés bourguignons au Xie siècle: à propos d'une charte de Cluny," *Annales de Bourgogne* 60 (1988), 139-43.

Richard, Jean. "La papauté et la direction de la Première Croisade," *Journal des savants* (1960).

Richard, Jean. "Raymond d'Aguilers, historien de la première croisade," *Journal des savants* 3 (1971), 206-12.

Riley-Smith, Jonathan. "Death on the First Crusade." In: *The End of Strife: Papers Selected from the Proceedings of the Colloquium of the Commission international d'histoire ecclésiastique comparée Held at the University of Durham.* Ed. David M. Loades. Edinburgh: T. and T. Clark, 1984, pp. 14-31.

Riley-Smith, Jonathan. "The First Crusade and St. Peter." In: *Outremer– Studies in the History of the Crusading Kingdom of Jerusalem.* Ed. Benjamin Kedar, H.E. Mayer and R.C. Smail. Jerusalem, 1982, pp. 41-63.

Riley-Smith, Jonathan. *The First Crusade and the Idea of Crusading.* Philadelphia: University of Pennsylvania Press, 1986.

Riley-Smith, Jonathan. "The First Crusade and the Persecution of the Jews," *Studies in Church History* 21 (1984), 51-72.

Riley-Smith, Jonathan. *The First Crusaders, 1095-1131.* Cambridge: Cambridge University Press, 1997.

Riley-Smith, Jonathan. "The Motives of the Earliest Crusaders and the Settlement of Latin Palestine, 1095-1100," *English Historical Review* 98 (1983), 721-36.

Rogers, Randall. "Peter Bartholomew and the Role of 'the Poor' in the First Crusade." In: *Warriors and Churchmen in the High Middle Ages: Essays Presented to Karl Leyser.* Ed. Timothy Reuter. London: Hambledon, 1992, pp. 109-22.

Röhricht, Reinhold. *Geschichte des Ersten Kreuzzuges.* Innsbruck: Wagner'sche Universitäts-Buchhandlung, 1901.

Rouche, Michel. "Cannibalisme sacré chez les croisés populaires." In: *La religion populaire: Aspects du Christianisme populaire à travers l'histoire*. Ed. Yves-Marie Hilaire. Lille: Centre interdisciplinaire d'études des religions de l'Université de Lille III, 1981, pp. 29-41.

Rousset, Paul. "Etienne de Blois, croisé fuyard et martyr," *Geneva* n.s. 11 (1963), 183-95.

Rousset, Paul. *Les origines et caractère de la première croisade*. Neuchâtel: Ed. de la Baconnière, 1945.

Runciman, Steven. "The Crusades of 1101," *Jahrbuch der Österreichischen Byzantinischen Gesellschaft* 1 (1951), 3-12.

Runciman, Steven. *The First Crusade*. Cambridge: Cambridge University Press, 1980.

Runciman, Steven. "The First Crusade: Antioch to Ascalon." In: *A History of the Crusades*. Ed. Kenneth Setton. Madison: University of Wisconsin Press, 1969, I:308-41.

Runciman, Steven. "The First Crusade: Constantinople to Antioch." In: *A History of the Crusades*. Ed. Kenneth Setton. Madison: University of Wisconsin Press, 1969, I:280-304.

Runciman, Steven. "The First Crusaders' Journey Across the Balkan Peninsula," *Byzantion* 19 (1949), 207-21.

Runciman, Steven. "The Holy Lance Found at Antioch," *Analecta Bollandiana* 68 (1950), 197-205.

Savvides, Alexis G.C. "The Consolidation of Byzantine Power in Cyprus on the Eve of the First Crusade and the First Decades of the Empire's Relations with the Crusaders." In: *Hē Kupros kai hoi Staurophories/Cyprus and the Crusades: Hoi anakoinōseis tou deithnous symposiou "Hē Kupros kai hoi Staurophories", Leukōsia, 6-9 septembriou, 1994/Papers Given at the International Conference "Cyprus and the Crusades", Nicosia, 6-9 September, 1994*. Ed. Nikos Coureas and Jonathan Riley-Smith. Nicosia: Cyprus Research Centre/Society for the Study of the Crusades and the Latin East, 1995, pp. 3-18.

Savvides, Alexis G.C. "Taticius the Turcopole." In: *X. Türk tarih kongresi, Ankara, 1986: Kongreye sunulan bildriler*, 3. Ankara: Türk Tarih Kurumu Basimevi, 1991, pp. 821-25.

Savvides, Alexis G.C. "Varia Byzantinoturcica, II: Taticios the Turcopole," *Journal of Oriental and African Studies* 3-4 (1993), 235-28.

Schein, Sylvia. "Jérusalem: Objectif originel de la Première Croisade? In: *Autour de la première croisade: Actes du Colloque de la Society for the Study of the Crusades and the Latin East (Clermont-Ferrand, 22-25 juin 1995)*. Ed. M. Balard. Paris: Publications de la Sorbonne, 1996, pp. 119-26.

Schiffman, Sarah. *Heinrich IV und die Bischöfe in ihrem Verhalten zu den deutschen Juden zur zeit des ersten Kreuzzuges*. Berlin: Lichtwitz, 1931.

Schlosser, F.E. "Byzantine Studies and the History of the Crusades: The *Alexiad* of Anna Comnena as a Source for the Crusades," *Byzantinische Forschungen* 15 (1990), 397-406.

Settia, Aldo A. "Un 'lombardo' alla prima crociata tecnologie militari fra occidente e oriente." In: *Società, istituzioni, spiritualità: Studi in onore di Cinzio Violante*. Settimane di studio del centro italiano di studi sull'alto medioevo, XV. Spoleto: Centro Italiano di Studi sull'alto Medioevo, 1994, II:843-55.

Shepard, Jonathan. "Cross Purposes: Alexius Comnenus and the First Crusade." In: *The First Crusade: Origins and Impact*. Ed. Jonathan Phillips. Manchester: University of Manchester Press, 1997, pp. 107-29.

Shepard, Jonathan. "When Greek Meets Greek: Alexius Comnenus and Bohemond in 1097-98," *Byzantine and Modern Greek Studies* 12 (1988), 185-277.

Stemberger, B. "Zu den Judenverfolgungen in Deutschland (zur Zeit der ersten beiden Kreuzzüge)," *Kairos* 20 (1978), 53-72, 151-57.

Sumberg, Lewis A.M. "The 'Tafurs' and the First Crusade," *Mediaeval Studies* 21 (1959), 224-46.

Sybel, Heinrich von. *The History and Literature of the First Crusade*. Trans. Lady Duff Gordon. London, 1861.

Thomas, R.D. "Anna Comnena's Account of the First Crusade: History and Politics in the Reigns of the Emperors Alexius I and Manuel I Comnenus," *Byzantine and Modern Greek Studies* 15 (1991), 269-312.

Thomson, Rodney M. "William of Malmesbury, Historian of the Crusade," *Reading Medieval Studies* 23 (1997), 121-34.

Tuilier, André. "Byzance et la féodalité occidentale. Les vertus guerrières des premiers croisés d'après l'Alexiade d'Anne Comnène." In: *La guerre et la paix: Frontières et violences au moyen âge.* Actes du 101e congrès national des sociétés savantes, Lille, 1976. Paris: Bibliothèque Nationale, 1978, pp. 35-50.

Tyerman, Christopher. "Were There Any Crusades in the Twelfth Century?" *English Historical Review* 110 (1995), 553-77.

Tyerman, Christopher. "Who Went on Crusades to the Holy Land?" In: *The Horns of Hattin.* Ed. Benjamin Z. Kedar. London, 1992, pp. 13-26.

Verbruggen, J.F. "Vrouwen in de eerste kruistocht en in de heldenliederen," *Revue Belge d'histoire militaire* 25 (1983), 181-90.

Waeger, Gerhart. *Gottfried von Bouillon in der Historiographie.* Zurich: Fretz und Wasmuth, 1969.

Ward, John O. "Disaster and Disaster-Response in a Medieval Context: The First Crusade." In: *Disasters: Image and Context.* Ed. Peter Hinton. Sydney Studies in Society and Culture, 7. Sydney: Sydney Association for Studies in Culture, 1992, pp. 105-40.

Wolf, Kenneth Baxter. "Crusade and Narrative: Bohemond and the *Gesta Francorum,*" *Journal of Medieval History* 17 (1991), 207-16.

Wolff, Theodor. *Die Bauernkreuzzüge des Jahres 1096: Ein Beitrag zur Geschichte des ersten Kreuzzuges.* Tubingen: Fues'sche Buchdruckerei, 1891.

Youssef, J.N. "The Battle of Nicaea between the Seldjuk Turks and Peter the Hermit, August 1096 (in the Light of Contemporary Latin and Byzantine Sources." In: *X. Türk tarih kongresi, Ankara, 1986: Kongreye sunulan bildriler,* 3. Ankara: Türk Tarih Kurumu Basimevi, 1991, pp. 991-99.

Zajac, William G. "Captured Property on the First Crusade." In: *The First Crusade: Origins and Impact*. Ed. Jonathan Phillips. Manchester: University of Manchester Press, 1997, pp. 153-86.

Zbinden, Nicolas. *Abendländische Ritter: Griechen und Türken im Ersten Kreuzzug (Zur Problematik ihrer Begegung)*. Texte und Forschungen zur Byzantinisch-neurgriechischen Philologie, 48. Athens: Verlag der Byzantinisch-neurgriechischen Jahrbücher, 1975.

Medieval – Crusades – Second

Asbridge, Thomas. "The Significance and Causes of the Battle of the Field of Blood," *Journal of Medieval History* 23 (1997), 301-16.

Barton, Simon. "A Forgotten Crusade: Alfonso VII of Léon-Castile and the Campaign for Jaén (1148)," *Historical Research* 73 (2000).

Berry, Virginia. "The Second Crusade." In: *A History of the Crusades*. Ed. Kenneth Setton. Madison: University of Wisconsin Press, 1969, I:463-512.

Bolton, Brenda M. "The Cistercians and the Aftermath of the Secon Crusade." In: *The Second Crusade and the Cistercians*. Ed. M. Gervers. New York, 1992, pp. 131-40.

Brundage, James. "St. Bernard and the Jurists." In: *The Second Crusade and the Cistercians*. Ed. M. Gervers. New York, 1992, pp. 25-33.

Bulst-Thiele, Marie Luise. "The Influence of St. Bernard of Clairvaux on the Formation of the Order of the Knights Templar." In: *The Second Crusade and the Cistercians*. Ed. M. Gervers. New York, 1992, pp. 57-65.

Caspar, E. "Die Kreuzzugsbullen Eugens III," *Neues Archiv* 45 (1924).

Constable, Giles. "A Note on the Route of the Anglo-Flemish Crusaders of 1147," *Speculum* 28 (1973), 525-26.

Constable, Giles. "A Report of a Lost Sermon by St. Bernard on the Failure of the Second Crusade." In: *Studies in Medieval Cistercian History Presented to*. Ed. pp. 49-54.

Constable, Giles. "The Second Crusade as Seen by Contemporaries," *Traditio* 9 (1953), 213-79.

Edbury, Peter W. "Looking Back on the Second Crusade: Some Late Twelfth-Century English Perspectives." In: *The Second Crusade and the Cistercians*. Ed. M. Gervers. New York, 1992, pp. 163-69.

Edgington, Susan B. "The Lisbon Letter of the Second Crusade," *Historical Research* 69 (1996), 328-39.

Elisseeff, N. *Nur al Din: un grand prince musulman de Syrie au temps des croisades*. 3 vols. Damascus, 1967.

Erhart, Victoria. "The History of Edessa in the 1140s according to Syriac Historical Sources," *Military and Naval History Journal Forum Proceedings* (Apr 1999), 23-37.

Ferzoco, George. "The Origin of the Second Crusade." In: *The Second Crusade and the Cistercians*. Ed. M. Gervers. New York, 1992, pp. 91-99.

Forey, Alan J. "The Failure of the Siege of Damascus in 1148," *Journal of Medieval History* 10 (1984), 13-23.

Gervers, Michael, ed. *The Second Crusade and the Cistercians*. New York: St. Martin's, 1992.

Gilchrist, John T. "The Perception of Jews in the Canon Law in the Period of the First Two Crusades," *Jewish History* 3 (1988), 9-24.

Grabois, Aryeh. "The Crusade of King Louis VII: a Reconsideration." In: *Crusade and Settlement: Papers Read at the First Conference of the Society for the Study of the Crusades and the Latin East and Presented to R.C. Smail*. Ed. Peter W. Edbury. Cardiff: University College Cardiff Press, 1985, pp. 94-104.

Grabois, Aryeh. "*Militia* and *Malitia*: The Bernardine Vision of Chivalry." In: *The Second Crusade and the Cistercians*. Ed. M. Gervers. New York, 1992, pp. 49-56.

Grabois, Aryeh. "Le pèlerin occidental en Terre Sainte à l'époque des croisades et ses réalités: la relation de pèlerinage de Jean de Wurtzbourg." In: *Etudes de civilisation médiévale (IXe-XIIe siècles. Melanges E.-R. Labande*. Poitiers, 1974, pp. 367-76.

Grabois, Aryeh. "Le privilège de croisade et la régence de Suger," *Revue historique de droit français et étranger* ser. 4, 62 (1964), 458-65.

Guth, Klaus. "The Pomeranian Missionary Journeys of Otto I of Bamberg and the Crusade Movement of the Eleventh to Twelfth Centuries." In: *The Second Crusade and the Cistercians*. Ed. M. Gervers. New York, 1992, pp. 13-23.

Hoch, Martin. "The Choice of Damascus as the Objective of the Second Crusade: A Re-evaluation." In: *Autour de la première croisade: Actes du Colloque de la Society for the Study of the Crusades and the Latin East (Clermont-Ferrand, 22-25 juin 1995)*. Ed. M. Balard. Paris: Publications de la Sorbonne, 1996, pp. 359-69.

Hoch, Martin. "The Crusaders' Strategy Against Fatamid Ascalon and the "Ascalon Project" of the Second Crusade." In: *The Second Crusade and the Cistercians*. Ed. M. Gervers. New York, 1992, pp. 119-28.

Hoch, Martin. *Jerusalem, Damaskus und der Zweite Kreuzzug*. Frankfurt, 1993.

Huyghebaert, Nicholas. "L'Abbé Lionnel de Saint-Bertin à la Seconde Croisade," *Bulletin Trimestriel de la Société Académique des Antiquaires de la Morinie* 20 (1963), 97-113.

Kahl, Hans-Dietrich. "Crusade Eschatology as Seen by St. Bernard in the Years 1146 to 1148." In: *The Second Crusade and the Cistercians*. Ed. M. Gervers. New York, 1992, pp. 35-47.

Katzir, Yael. "The Second Crusade and the Redefinition of *Ecclesia, Christianitas* and Papal Coercive Power." In: *The Second Crusade and the Cistercians*. Ed. M. Gervers. New York, 1992, pp. 3-11.

Leclerq, Jean. "L'encyclique de Saint Bernard en faveur de la croisade," *Revue Bénédictine* 81 (1971), 282-308.

Livermore, H.V. "The 'Conquest of Lisbon' and Its Author," *Portuguese Studies* 6 (1990), 1-16.

Mayr-Harting, Henry. "Odo of Deuil, the Second Crusade and the Monastery of Saint-Denis." In: *The Culture of Christendom: Essays in Medieval History in Commemoration of Denis L.T. Bethell*. Ed. M.A. Meyer. London, 1993, pp. 225-41.

Omran, Mahmoud Said. "King Amalric and the Siege of Alexandria, 1167." In: *Crusade and Settlement: Papers Read at the First Conference of the Society for the Study of the Crusades and the Latin East and Presented to R.C. Smail*. Ed. Peter W. Edbury. Cardiff: University College Cardiff Press, 1985, pp. 191-95.

Phillips, Jonathan. "Hugh of Payns and the 1129 Damascus Crusade." In: *The Military Orders: Fighting for the Faith and Caring for the Sick*. Ed. Malcolm Barber. Aldershot: Ashgate, 1994, pp. 141-47.

Phillips, Jonathan. "Ideas of Crusade and Holy War in *De expugnatione Lyxbonensi* (The Conquest of Lisbon)." In: *Holy Land, Holy Lands, and Christian History*. Ed. Robert Swanson. Studies in Church History, 36. Woodbridge: Boydell Press, 2000, pp. 123-41.

Phillips, Jonathan. "The Murder of Charles the Good and the Second Crusade: Household, Nobility, and Traditions of Crusading in Medieval Flanders," *Medieval Prosopography* 19 (1998), 55-75.

Phillips, Jonathan. "Saint Bernard of Clairvaux, the Low Countries and the Lisbon Letter of the Second Crusade," *Journal of Ecclesiastical History* 48 (1997), 485-97.

Riley-Smith, Jonathan. "Family Traditions and Participation in the Second Crusade." In: *The Second Crusade and the Cistercians*. Ed. M. Gervers. New York, 1992, pp. 101-08.

Riley-Smith, Jonathan. "The Venetian Crusade of 1122-1124." In: *I comuni italiani nel regno crociato di Gerusalemme*. Ed. G. Airaldi and Benjamin Z. Kedar. Genoa, 1986, pp. 339-50.

Rowe, John Gordon. "The Origins of the Second Crusade: Pope Eugenius III, Bernard of Clairvaux and Louis VII of France." In: *The Second Crusade and the Cistercians*. Ed. M. Gervers. New York, 1992, pp. 79-89.

Switten, Margaret. "Singing the Second Crusade." In: *The Second Crusade and the Cistercians*. Ed. M. Gervers. New York, 1992, pp. 67-76.

Turfan, Kemal. "Recherches récentes sur la bataille de Myriokephalon," *Revue internationale d'histoire militaire* 67 (1988), 3-28.

Medieval – Crusades – Third

Baldwin, M.W. *Raymond III of Tripoli and the Fall of Jerusalem (1140-1187)*. Princeton: Princeton University Press, 1936.

Brundage, James A. "The Crusade of Richard I: Two Canonical *Quaestiones*," *Speculum* 38 (1963), 443-52.

Brundage, James A. "Richard the Lion-Heart and Byzantium," *Studies in Medieval Culture* 6-7 (1976), 63-70.

Diverres, Armel. "The Grail and the Third Crusade: Thoughts on *Le Conte del Graal* by Chretien de Troyes," *Arthurian Literature*, X. Ed. Richard Barber. Cambridge, 1990, pp. 13-109.

Ehrenkreutz, A.S. "The Place of Saladin in the Naval History of the Mediterranean Sea in the Middle Ages," *Journal of the American Oriental Society* 75 (1955), 100-16.

Flahiff, George B. "*Deus non vult*: A Critic of the Third Crusade," *Mediaeval Studies* 9 (1947), 162-88.

Flori, Jean. *Richard Couer de Lion: Le roi-chevalier*. Paris: Payot and Rivages, 1999.

Gal, Zvi. "Saladin's Dome of Victory at the Horns of Hattin." In: *The Horns of Hattin*. Ed. Benjamin Z. Kedar. Jerusalem, 1992, pp. 213-15.

Hamblin, William J. "Saladin and Muslim Military Theory." In: *The Horns of Hattin*. Ed. Benjamin Z. Kedar. Jerusalem, 1992, pp. 228-38.

Hamilton, Bernard. "The Elephant of Christ: Raynald of Châtillon," *Studies in Church History* 15 (1978).

Katzir, Yael. "The Conquests of Jerusalem, 1099 and 1187: Historical Memory and Religious Typology." In: *The Meeting of Two Worlds: Cultural Exchange between East and West during the Period of the Crusades*. Ed. Vladimir P. Gross. Studies in Medieval Culture, 21. Kalamazoo: Medieval Institute Publications, 1986, pp. 103-13.

Kedar, Benjamin Z. "The Battle of Hattin Reconsidered." In: *The Horns of Hattin*. Ed. Benjamin Z. Kedar. Jerusalem, 1992, pp. 190-207.

Kessler, Ulrike. *Richard I. Löwenherz: König, Kreuzritter, Abenteurer.* Graz, Vienna, and Cologne: Styria, 1995.

Lyons, Malcolm Cameron and D.E.P. Jackson. *Saladin: The Politics of the Holy War.* Cambridge: Cambridge University Press, 1982.

Markowski, Michael. "Peter of Blois and the Conception of the Third Crusade." In: *The Horns of Hattin.* Ed. Benjamin Z. Kedar. Jerusalem, 1992, pp. 261-69.

Markowski, Michael. "Richard Lionheart: Bad King, Bad Crusader?" *Journal of Medieval History* 23 (1997), 351-65.

Melville, C.P. and M.C. Lyons. "Saladin's Hattin Letter." In: *The Horns of Hattin.* Ed. Benjamin Z. Kedar. Jerusalem, 1992, pp. 208-12.

Möhring, Hannes. *Saladin und der dritte Kreuzzug.* Wiesbaden, 1981.

Möhring, Hannes. "Zwischen Joseph-Legende und Mahdi-Erwartung: Erfolge und Ziele Sultan Saladins im Spiegel zeitgenössicher Dichtung und Weissagung." In: *War and Society in the Eastern Mediterranean, 7th-15th Centuries.* Ed. Y. Lev. Leiden, 1997, pp. 177-224.

Naumann, C. *Der Kreuzzug Kaiser Heinrichs VI.* Frankfurt, 1994.

Nicholson, R.L. *Joscelyn III and the Fall of the Crusader States.* Leiden, 1973.

Nicolle, David C. *Hattin, 1187: Saladin's Greatest Victory.* London: Osprey, 1987.

Paterson, W.F. "The Battle of Arsuf," *Journal of the Society of Archer-Antiquaries* 8 (1965), 20-23.

Regan, Geoffrey. *Lionhearts: Richard I, Saladin, and the Era of the Third Crusade.* New York: Walker & Co., 1999.

Richard, Jean. "1187, Point de départ pour une nouvelle forme de la croisade." In: *The Horns of Hattin.* Ed. Benjamin Z. Kedar. Jerusalem, 1992, pp. 250-60.

Richard, Jean. "An Account of the Battle of Hattin Referring to the Frankish Mercenaries in Oriental Muslim States," *Speculum* 27 (1952), 168-77.

Richard, Jean. "Philippe Auguste, la croisade et le royaume." In: *La France de Philippe Auguste: le temps des mutations : actes du colloque international organiséé par le C.N.R.S. (Paris, 29 septembre-4 octobre 1980)*. Ed. Robert-Henri Bautier. Paris: Editions du Centre national de la recherche scientifique, 1982, pp. 411-24.

Werveke, Hans van. "La contribution de la Flandre et du Hainaut à la troisième croisade," *Moyen âge* 78 (1972), 55-90.

Medieval – Crusades – Fourth and the Latin Kingdom of Constantinople

Andrea, Alfred J. "The Anonymous Chronicler of Halberstadt's Account of the Fourth Crusade: Popular Religiosity in the Early Thirteenth Century," *Historical Reflections* 22 (1996), 447-77.

Andrea, Alfred J. "The *Devastatio Constantinopolitana*, a Special Perspective on the Fourth Crusade: An Analysis, New Edition, and Translation," *Historical Reflections* 19 (1993), 107-49.

Andrea, Alfred J. and Ilona Motsiff. "Pope Innocent III and the Diversion of the Fourth Crusade Army to Zara," *Byzantinoslavica* 33 (1972), 6-25.

Angold, Michael A. *Byzantine Government in Exile*. Oxford, 1975.

Angold, Michael A. "State of Research–The Road to 1204: the Byzantine Background to the Fourth Crusade," *Journal of Medieval History* 25 (1999), 257-78.

Bartlett, W.B. *The Sack of Constantinople and the Fourth Crusade*. Stroud: Sutton Publishing, 2000.

Brand, Charles M. "A Byzantine Plan for the Fourth Crusade," *Speculum* 43 (1968), 462-75.

Carile, A. *Per una storia dell'impero Latino di Constantinopoli, 1204-1261*. Bologna, 1978.

Cigaar, Krijnie. "Flemish Counts and Emperors: Friends and Foreigners in Byzantium." In: *The Latin Empire: Some Contributions*. Ed. V.D. van Aalst and K.N. Cigaar. Hernen, 1990, pp. 33-62.

Frolow, A. *Recherches sur la déviation de la 4e croisade vers Constantinople*. Paris, 1955.

Geanakoplos, D.J. "Greco-Latin Relations on the Eve of the Byzantine Restoration: The Battle of Pelagonia–1259," *Dumbarton Oaks Papers* 7 (1953), 99-141.

Godfrey, John. *1204: The Unholy Crusade*. Oxford, 1980.

Hendrickx, B. "Les Arméniens d'Asie Mineure et de Thrace au début de l'Empire Latin de Constantinople," *Revue des études Armeniennes* 22 (1991), 217-23.

Longnon, J. *Les compagnons de Villehardouin: Recherches sur les croisés de la quatrième croisade*. Geneva, 1974.

Madden, Thomas F. "The Fires of the Fourth Crusade in Constantinople, 1203-04: A Damage Assessment," *Byzantinoslavica* 84/85 (1991-92), 72-92.

Madden, Thomas F. "Vows and Contracts in the Fourth Crusade: The Treaty of Zara and the Attack on Constantinople in 1204," *International History Review* 15 (1993), 441-68.

Maier, Christoph T. "Kirche, Kreuz und Ritual: Eine Kreuzzugspredigt in Basel im Jahr 1200," *Deutsche Archiv für Erforschung des Mittelalters* 55 (1999), 95-115.

Maleczek, W. *Petrus Capuanus*. Vienna, 1988.

Nicol, Donald M. *Byzantium, Venice and the Fourth Crusade*. Athens, 1990.

Queller, Donald E. "Combined Arms Operations and the Latin Conquest of Constantinople." In: *Changing Interpretations and New Sources in Naval History: Papers from the Third U.S. Naval Academy History Symposium*. Ed. R.W. Love, Jr. New York, 1980, pp. 45-57.

Queller, Donald E. *The Fourth Crusade: The Conquest of Constantinople, 1201-1204*. Philadelphia: University of Pennsylvania Press, 1977.

Queller, Donald E., Thomas K. Compton and Donald A. Campbell. "The Fourth Crusade: The Neglected Majority," *Speculum* 49 (1974), 441-65.

Robbert, Louise Buenger. "Rialto Businessmen and Constantinople, 1204-61," *Dumbarton Oaks Papers* 49 (1995), 43-58.

Schmandt, R.H. "The Fourth Crusade and the Just War Theory," *Catholic Historical Review* 61 (1975), 191-221.

Medieval – Crusades – Albigensian

Barber, Malcolm. "Catharism and the Occitan Nobility: The Lordships of Cabaret, Minerve and Termes." In: *The Ideals and Practice of Medieval Knighthood*, III. Ed. C. Harper-Bill and R. Harvey. Woodbridge, 1990, pp. 1-19.

Costen, Michael. *The Cathars and the Albigensian Crusade*. New York: St. Martin's Press, 1997.

Dieulafoy, M.M. "La bataille du Muret," *Mémoires de l'académie des inscriptions et belles lettres* 35.2 (1901), 95-134.

Forey, Alan J. "The Military Orders and Holy War Against Christians in the Thirteenth Century," *English Historical Review* 104 (1989), 1-24.

Goodall, John A. "Simon de Montfort (*c.* 1170-1218) and an Unusual Marshalling of Arms," *Antiquaries Journal* 78 (1998), 433-39.

Gore, Terry L. "Christians Collide in Albigensian Crusade," *Military History* (Oct 1995), 62-68.

Hamilton, Bernard. *The Albigenisan Crusade*. Historical Association Pamphlet, 85. London: Historical Association, 1974.

Hill, Douglas. "Kill Them All . . . God Will Recognize His Own," *MHQ: The Quarterly Journal of Military History* 9 (Win 1997), 99-109.

Kovarik, Robert J. "The Albigensian Crusade: A New View," *Studies in Medieval Culture* 3 (1970), 81-91.

Lacquer, L. de. "L'Albigeois pendant la crise de l'Albigéisme," *Revue de l'histoire ecclésiastique* 29 (1933), 272-315, 586-633, 849-904.

Lamarrigue, Anne-Marie. "La croisade albigeoise vue par Bernard Gui," *Journal des Savants* (1993), 201-73.

Malafosse, J. "Le siège de Toulouse par Simon de Montfort," *Revue des Pyrénées* 4 (1892), 497-522, 725-56.

Pales-Gobilliard, Annette. "Poursuites et déplacements de population après la croisade albigeoise." In: *La guerre, la violence et les gens au Moyen Âge*. I: *Guerre et violence*. Ed. P. Contamine and O. Guyotjeannin. 119e congrès national des sociétés historiques et scientifiques, Amiens, octobre 1994, Section d'histoire médiévale et philologie. Paris, 1996, pp. 51-65.

Racaut, Luc. "The Polemical Use of the Albigensian Crusade during the French Wars of Religion," *French History* 13 (1999), 261-79.

Roquebert, Michel. *Histoire des Cathares: L'essor, la croisade, l'inquisition, XIIIe-XIXe siècles*. Paris: Perrin, 1999.

Strayer, Joseph R. *The Albigensian Crusades*. Ann Arbor: The Unversity of Michigan Press, 1971.

Strayer, Joseph R. "The Political Crusades of the Thirteenth Century." In: *Medieval Statecraft and the Perspectives of History: Essays by Joseph R. Strayer*. Princeton, 1971, pp. 123-58.

Sumption, Jonathan. *The Albigensian Crusade*. London: Faber and Faber, 1978.

Wakefield, W.L. *Heresy, Crusade and Inquisition in Southern France, 1100-1250*. London: Allen and Urwin, 1974.

Medieval – Crusades – Children's

Dickson, Gary. "La genèse de la croisade des enfants (1212)," *Bibliothèque de l'école des chartes* 153 (1995), 53-102.

Dickson, Gary. "Stephen of Cloyes, Philip Augustus, and the Children's Crusade of 1212." In: *Journeys Toward God: Pilgrimage and Crusade*. Ed. B.N. Sargent-Baur. Kalamazoo, 1992, pp. 83-105.

Menzel, Michael. "Die Kinderkreuzzüge in geistes- und sozial-geschichtlicher Sicht," *Deutsche Archiv für Erforschung des Mittelalters* 55 (1999), 117-56.

Raedts, Peter. "The Children's Crusade of 1212," *Journal of Medieval History* 3 (1977), 279-324.

Medieval – Crusades – Hussites

Baum, Wilhelm. *Kaiser Sigismund: Hus, Konstanz und Türkenkrieg*. Graz: Styria, 1993.

Bloom, James J. "The Hussites: Fifteenth Century Armored Wagon Warfare," *Command* 35 (Nov 1995), 36-44.

Durdik, J. *Hussitisches Heerwesen*. Berlin, 1961.

Franz, Lützow. *The Hussite Wars*. London: Dent, 1914.

Fudge, T.A. "'Neither Mine Nor Thine': Communist Experiments in Hussite Bohemia," *Canadian Journal of History* 33 (1998), 26-47.

Heymann, F.G. *John Zizka and the Hussite Revolution*. Princeton, 1955.

Klassen, J. "The Disadvantaged and the Hussite Revolution," *International Review of Social History* 35 (1990), 249-72.

Mörtzsch, Otto. "Heereszugordung gegen die Hussiten vom Jahre 1431," *Zeitschrift für historische Waffenkunde* 8 (1918-20), 80-81.

Mörtzsch, Otto. "Priese der Waffen, Kriegsgeräte und -vorräte zur Zeit der Hussitenkriege in der Mark Meißen und der Lausitz," *Zeitschrift für historische Waffenkunde* 4 (1906-08), 70-75.

Odložilík, Otakar. *The Hussite King: Bohemia in European Affairs, 1440-1471*. New Brunswick: Rutgers University Press, 1965.

Petrin, Silvia. *Der österreichische Hussitenkrieg, 1420-1434*. Militärhistorische Schriftenreihe, 44. Vienna: Heeresgeschichtlichen Museum (Militärwissenschaftliches Institut), 1994.

Seibt, F. *Hussitica: Zur Struktur einer Revolution*. Cologne, 1965.

Smahel, Frantisek. *La révolution hussite: une anomalie historique*. Paris: Presses universitaires de France, 1985.

Wulf, Max von. *Das hussitische Wagenburg*. Berlin: Gustav Schade, 1889.

Żygulski, Zdzisław, Jr. "The Wagon Laager," *Fasciculi archaeologiae historicae* 7 (1994), 15-20.

Medieval – Crusades – Mongols

Allsen, Thomas T. *Mongol Imperialism*. Berkeley and Los Angeles: University of California Press, 1987.

Amitai-Preiss, Reuven. "Mamluk Perceptions of the Mongol-Frankish Rapprochement," *Mediterranean Historical Review* 7 (1992), 50-65.

Amitai-Preiss, Reuven. *Mongols and Mamluks: The Mamluk-Ilkhanid War, 1260-1281*. Cambridge: Cambridge University Press, 1995.

Barfield, Thomas. "The Devil's Horsemen: Steppe Nomadic Warfare in Historical Perspective." In: *Studying War: Anthropological Perspectives*. Ed. S.P. Reyna and R.E. Downs. Langhorne: Gordon and Breach, 1994, pp. 157-82.

Bouvat, L. *L'empire des Mongols*. Paris, 1927.

Boyle, J.A. "The Capture of Isfahan by the Mongols." In: *Atti del convegno internazionale sul tema: la Persia nel medioevo*. Rome, 1971, pp. 331-36.

Burnett, Charles and Patrick Gautier Dalché. "Attitudes towards the Mongols in Medieval Literature: The XXII Kings of Gog and Magog from the Court of Frederick II to Jean de Mandeville," *Viator* 22 (1991), 153-67.

Chambers, James. *The Devil's Horsemen: The Mongol Invasion of Europe*. New York: Atheneum, 1985.

Chambers, James. *Genghis Khan*. Sutton Pocket Biographies. Stroud: Sutton Publishing, 1999.

Grekov, B.D. and A. Iakoubovski. *La horde d'or: La domination Tartare au XIIIe et au XIVe siècle de la Mer Jaune à la Mer Noire*. Trans. F. Thuret. Paris, 1939.

Grousset, R. *The Empire of the Steppes: A History of Central Asia*. New Brunswick, 1970.

Guzman, Gregory G. "The Encyclopedist Vincent of Beauvais and His Mongol Extracts from John of Plano Carpini and Simon of Saint-Quentin," *Speculum* 49 (1974), 287-307.

Halperin, Charles J. *Russia and the Golden Horde*. London, 1985.

Halperin, Charles J. "Russo-Tartar Relations in Mongol Context: Two Notes," *Acta orientalia academiae scientarum Hungaricarum* 51 (1998), 321-39.

Hartog, Leo de. *Russia and the Mongol Yoke: The History of the Russian Principalities and the Golden Horde, 1221-1502*. London: British Academic Press, 1996.

Hookham, H. *Tamburlaine the Conqueror*. London, 1962.

Jackson, Peter. "The Crusade Against the Mongols (1241)," *Journal of Ecclesiastical History* 42 (1991), 1-18.

Jackson, Peter. "The State of Research–The Mongol Empire, 1986-1999," *Journal of the Medieval History* 26 (2000), 189-210.

Jankovich, M. *They Rode into Europe*. Trans. A.A. Dent. London, 1968.

Khazanov, Anatoly M. "Muhammad and Jenghiz Khan Compared: The Religious Factor in World Empire Building," *Proceedings of the British Academy* 82 (1993), 149-69.

Klopprogge, Axel. *Ursprung und Ausprägung des abendländischen Mongolenbildes im 13. Jahrhundert: Ein Versuch zur Ideengeschichte des Mittelalters*. Asiatisch Forschungen, 122. Wiesbaden: Harrassowitz, 1993.

Kwanten, L. *Imperial Nomads: A History of Central Asia, 500-1500*. Leicester, 1979.

Langdon, John S. "Byzantium's Initial Encounter with the Chinggisids: An Introduction to the Byzantino-Mongolica," *Viator* 29 (1998), 95-140.

Manz, Beatrice Forbes. *The Rise and Rule of Tamerlane*. Cambridge Studies in Islamic Civilizations. Cambridge: Cambridge University Press, 1989.

Martin, H.D. "The Mongol Army," *Journal of the Royal Asiatic Society* (1943), 46-85.

Menache, Sophia. "Tartars, Jews, Saracens and the Jewish-Mongol 'Plot' of 1241," *History* 81 (1996), 319-41.

Mongol Conquests, AD 1200-1300, The. Amsterdam: Time-Life Books, 1989.

Morgan, D.O. "The Mongol Armies in Persia," *Der Islam* 56 (1979), 81-96.

Morgan, D.O. *The Mongols*. Oxford, 1986.

Noonan, T.S. "Medieval Russia, the Mongols, and the West: Novgorod's Relations with the Baltic, 1100-1350," *Mediaeval Studies* 37 (1975), 316-39.

Ostrowski, Donald. *Muscovy and the Mongols: Cross-Cultural Influences on the Steppe Frontier, 1304-1589*. Cambridge: Cambridge University Press, 1998.

Peggy, John. "Genghis Khan's Golden Horde," *Army Quarterly and Defence Journal* 128 (Oct 1998), 462-70; 128 (Jan 1999), 69-75.

Poliak, A.N. "The Influence of Chingiz Khan's Yasa upon the General Organization of the Mamluk State," *Bulletin of the School of Oriental and African Studies* 10 (1942), 862-72.

Rady, M. "The Mongol Invasion of Hungary," *Medieval World* 3 (Nov-Dec 1991), 39-46.

Richard, Jean. "Les causes des victoires Mongoles d'après les historiens occidentaux du XIIIe siècle," *Central Asiatic Journal* 23 (1979), 123-33.

Rogers, Greg S. "An Examination of Historians' Explanations for the Mongol Withdrawal from East Central Europe," *East European Quarterly* 30 (1996), 3-26.

Sarnowsky, Jürgen. "The Teutonic Order Confronts the Mongols and the Turks." In: *The Military Orders: Fighting for the Faith and Caring for the Sick*. Ed. Malcolm Barber. Aldershot: Ashgate, 1994, pp. 253-62.

Saunders, J.J. "Matthew Paris and the Mongols." In: *Essays in Medieval History Presented to Bertie Wilkinson*. Ed. T.A. Sandquist and M.R. Powicke. Toronto: University of Toronto Press, 1969, pp. 116-32.

Schmieder, Felicitas. *Europa und die Fremden: Die Mongolen im Urteil des Abendlandes vom 13. bis in das 15. Jahrhundert.* Beiträge zur Geschichte und Quellenkunde des Mittelalters, 16. Sigmaringen: Jan Thorbecke, 1994.

Schütz, Edmond. "The Decisive Motives of Tartar Failure in the Ilkhanid-Mamluk Fights in the Holy Land," *Acta orientalis academiae scientarum hungaricarum* 45 (1991), 3-22.

Sinor, Denis. "The Inner Asian Warriors," *Journal of the American Oriental Society* 101.2 (1981), 133-44.

Sinor, Denis. "The Mongols and Western Europe." In: *A History of the Crusades.* Ed. Kenneth Setton. Madison: University of Wisconsin Press, 1975, III:513-44.

Sinor, Denis. "On Mongol Strategy." In: *Proceedings of the Fourth East Asian Altaistic Conference.* Ed. C. Chieh-hsien. Tainan, 1975, pp. 238-49.

Sinor, Denis. "On Water-Transport in Central Asia," *Ural-Altaische Jahrbücher* 33 (1961), 156-79.

Smith, John Masson, Jr. "Ayn Jalut: Mamluk Success or Mongol Failure?" *Harvard Journal of Asiatic Studies* 44 (1984), 307-45.

Smith, John Masson, Jr. "Mongol Society and Military in the Middle East: Antecedents and Adaptations." In: *War and Society in the Eastern Mediterranean, 7th-15th Centuries.* Ed. Y. Lev. Leiden, 1997, pp. 249-66.

Spuler, B. *Die Mongolen in Iran.* 3rd ed. Berlin, 1968.

Świętosławski, Witold. "Medieval Tartar Military Accessories Finds From the Territory of Poland," *Fasciculi archaeologicae historicae* 7 (1994), 55-59.

Turnbull, Stephen. *The Mongols.* London: Osprey, 1980.

Vernadsky, G.A. *History of Russia.* III: *The Mongols and Russia.* New Haven: Yale University Press, 1953.

Woolman, David S. "Primitive Warriors on Not, the Hardy Mongols of the 12th and 13th Centuries Used the Most Advanced of Tactics," *Military History* (Oct 1995), 12-18.

Medieval – Crusades – Livonian [See also – Military Orders – Teutonic]

Ashcroft, J. "Konrad's 'Rolandslied', Henry the Lion, and the Northern Crusade," *Forum for Modern Language Studies* 20 (1980), 184-208.

Benninghoven, F. "Die Gotlandfeldzuge des deutschen Ordens, 1398-1408," *Zeitschrift für Ostforschung* 13 (1964), 421-77.

Benninghoven, F. "Zur Technik spätmittelalterlicher Feldzuge im Ostbaltikum," *Zeitschrift für Ostforschung* 19 (1970), 631-51.

Birkhan, Helmut. "Les croisades contre des païens de Lituanie et de Prusse: Idéologie et réalité." In: *La croisade: réalités et fictions*. Ed. Danielle Buschinger. Göppinger, 1989, pp. 31-50.

Brundage, James A. "The Thirteenth-Century Livonian Crusade: Henricus de Lettis and the First Legatine Mission of Bishop William of Modena," *Jahrbücher für geschichte Osteuropas* N.F. 20 (1978), 1-9.

Christiansen, Eric. *The Northern Crusades*. 2nd ed. Harmondsworth: Penguin Books, 1997.

Devilliers, L. "Sur les expéditions des comtes de Hainault et de Hollande en Prusse," *Bulletin de la commission royale d'histoire de Belgique* 4th ser. 5 (1878), 127-44.

Ekdahl, Sven. *Die 'Banderia Prutenorum' des Jan Dugosz, eine Quelle zur Schlacht bei Tannenberg*. Gottingen and Zurich, 1976.

Ekdahl, Sven. "Der Krieg zwischen dem Deutschen Orden und Polen-Litauen im Jahre 1422," *Zeitschrift für Ostforschung* 13 (1964), 614-51.

Ekdahl, Sven. *Die Schlacht bei Tannenberg 1410: Quellenkritische Untersuchungen. I: Einführung und Quellenlage*. Berlin, 1982.

Gaier, Claude. "Achats d'armes et expéditions militaires en Prusse et autres lieux du comte Guillaume II de Hainaut (1336-1344)," *Musée d'armes* 65 (1990), 1-16; in: *Armes et combats dans l'univers médiéval*. Liege, 1995, pp. 229-42.

Johnson, Edgar. "The German Crusade on the Baltic." In: *History of the Crusades*. Ed. Kenneth M. Setton. Madison: University of Wisconsin Press, III:545-85.

Markov, Demetrius Dvoichenko de. "The Battle of Tannenburg (Grün-wald) in 1410." In: *XXII. Kongreß der Internationalen Kommission für Militärgeschichte* Acta 22: *Von Crécy bis Mohács Kriegswesen im späten Mittelalter (1346-1526)*. Vienna, 1997, pp. 299-305.

Mazeika, Rasa. "'Nowhere was the Fragility of their Sex Apparent': Women Warriors in the Baltic Crusade Chronicles." In: *From Clermont to Jerusalem: The Crusades and Crusader Societies, 1095-1500*. Selected Proceedings of the International Medieval Congress, University of Leeds, 10-13 July 1995. Ed. Alan V. Murray. Turnhout: Brepols, 1998, pp. 229-48.

Mazeika, Rasa. "Of Cabbages and Knights: Trade and Trade Treaties with the Infidel on the Northern Frontier, 1200-1390," *Journal of Medieval History* 20 (1994), 63-76.

Müller-Hickler, Hans. "Über die Funde aus der Burg Tannenberg," *Zeitschrift für historisches Waffen- und Köstumkunde* 13 (1932-34), 175-81.

Nicolle, David C. *Lake Peipus, 1242: Battle on the Ice*. London: Osprey, 1996.

Paravicini, Werner. *Der Preussenreisen des europaïschen Adels*. Sigmaringen, 1989.

Rowell, S.C. *Lithuania Ascending: A Pagan Empire within East Central Europe*. Cambridge: Cambridge University Press, 1994.

Sterns, Indrikis. "The Teutonic Knights in the Crusader States." In: *History of the Crusades*. Ed. Kenneth M. Setton. Madison: University of Wisconsin Press, 1987, V:315-78.

Urban, William. *The Baltic Crusade*. 2nd ed. Chicago: Lithuanian Research and Studies Center, 1994.

Urban, William. *The Livonian Crusade*. Washington, 1981.

Urban, William. "Medieval Livonian Numismatics," *Journal of Baltic Studies* 24 (1993), 37-52.

Urban, William. "The Organization of Defense of the Livonian Frontier in the Thirteenth Century," *Speculum* 48 (1973), 525-32.

Urban, William. *The Prussian Crusade*. Lanham, 1980.

Urban, William. *The Samogitian Crusade*. Chicago: Lithuanian Research and Studies Center, 1989.

Urban, William. *Tannenburg and After: Lithuania, Poland, and the Teutonic Order in Search of Immortality*. Chicago: Lithuanian Research and Studies Center, 1999.

Urban, William. "The Wendish Princes and the 'Drang nach dem Osten," *Journal of Baltic Studies* 9 (1978), 225-44.

Medieval – Crusades – Later [See also Medieval/Early Modern – Ottoman Turkish Wars]

Abulafia, David. "The Kingdom of Sicily and the Origins of the Political Crusades." In: *Società, istituzioni, spiritualità: Studi in onore di Cinzio Violante*. Ed. Girolamo Arnaldi et al. Spoleto: Centro italiano di studi sull'alto medioevo, 1994, I:65-77.

Arbel, B., Bernard Hamilton, and D. Jacoby, ed. *Latins and Greeks in the Eastern Mediterranean after 1204*. London, 1989.

Atiya, Aziz Suryal. *The Crusade in the Later Middle Ages*. London, 1938.

Aziz, Mohammed A. "La croisade de l'empereur Frédéric II et l'orient latin." In: *Autour de la première croisade: Actes du Colloque de la Society for the Study of the Crusades and the Latin East (Clermont-Ferrand, 22-25 juin 1995)*. Ed. M. Balard. Paris: Publications de la Sorbonne, 1996, pp. 371-78.

Balard, Michel. "Chypre, les republiques maritimes Italiennes et les plans de croisade (1274-1370)." In: *Hē Kupros kai hoi Staurophories/Cyprus and the Crusades: Hoi anakoinōseis tou deithnous symposiou "Hē Kupros kai hoi Staurophories", Leukōsia, 6-9 septembriou, 1994/Papers Given at the International Conference "Cyprus and the Crusades", Nicosia, 6-9 September, 1994*. Ed. Nikos Coureas and Jonathan Riley-Smith. Nicosia: Cyprus Research Centre/Society for the Study of the Crusades and the Latin East, 1995, pp. 97-106.

Birrell, Jean. *Saint Louis: Crusader King of France*. Cambridge: Cambridge University Press, 1992.

Brundage, James A. "Humbert of Romans and the Legitimacy of Crusader Conquests." In: *The Horns of Hattin*. Ed. Benjamin Z. Kedar. Jerusalem, 1992, pp. 302-13.

Coureas, Nicholas. "Cyprus and the Naval Leagues, 1333-58." In: *Hē Kupros kai hoi Staurophories/Cyprus and the Crusades: Hoi anakoinōseis tou deithnous symposiou "Hē Kupros kai hoi Staurophories", Leukōsia, 6-9 septembriou, 1994/Papers Given at the International Conference "Cyprus and the Crusades", Nicosia, 6-9 September, 1994*. Ed. Nikos Coureas and Jonathan Riley-Smith. Nicosia: Cyprus Research Centre/Society for the Study of the Crusades and the Latin East, 1995, pp. 107-24.

Dilke, Oswald and Margaret. "Mapping a Crusade," *History Today* 39 (Aug 1989), 31-35.

Dickson, Gary. "The Crowd at the Feet of Pope Boniface VIII: Pilgrimage, Crusade and the First Roman Jubilee (1300)," *Journal of Medieval History* 25 (1999), 279-307.

Doxey, Gary B. "Norwegian Crusaders and the Balearic Islands," *Scandinavian Studies* 68 (1996), 139-60.

Eddé, Anne-Marie. "Kurdes et Turcs dans l'armée ayyoubide de Syrie de Nord du Nord." In: *War and Society in the Eastern Mediterranean, 7th-15th Centuries*. Ed. Y. Lev. Leiden, 1997, pp. 225-36.

Forey, Alan J. "The Crusading Vows of the English King Henry III," *Durham University Journal* 65 (1973), 229-47.

Forey, Alan J. "Cyprus as a Base for Crusading Expeditions from the West." In: *Hē Kupros kai hoi Staurophories/Cyprus and the Crusades: Hoi anakoinōseis tou deithnous symposiou "Hē Kupros kai hoi Staurophories", Leukōsia, 6-9 septembriou, 1994/Papers Given at the International Conference "Cyprus and the Crusades", Nicosia, 6-9 September, 1994*. Ed. Nikos Coureas and Jonathan Riley-Smith. Nicosia: Cyprus Research Centre/Society for the Study of the Crusades and the Latin East, 1995, pp. 69-79.

Francis, Dominic. "Oliver of Paderborn and his Siege Engine at Damietta," *Nottingham Medieval Studies* 37 (1993), 28-32.

Gottlob, A. *Die päpstlichen Kreuzzugsteuern des 13. Jahrhundert*. Heilgenstadt, 1892.

Hamilton, Bernard. "Eleanor of Castile and the Crusading Movement," *Mediterranean Historical Review* 10 (1995), 92-103.

Herde, Peter. *Karl I von Anjou*. Stuttgart, 1979.

Horowitz, J. "Les exempla au service de la prédication de la croisade au 13e siècle," *Revue d' histoire ecclésiastique* 92 (1997), 367-94.

Housley, Norman. "Cyprus and the Crusades, 1291-1571." In: *Hē Kupros kai hoi Staurophories/Cyprus and the Crusades: Hoi anakoinōseis tou deithnous symposiou "Hē Kupros kai hoi Staurophories", Leukōsia, 6-9 septembriou, 1994/Papers Given at the International Conference "Cyprus and the Crusades", Nicosia, 6-9 September, 1994*. Ed. Nikos Coureas and Jonathan Riley-Smith. Nicosia: Cyprus Research Centre/Society for the Study of the Crusades and the Latin East, 1995, pp. 187-206.

Housley, Norman. "France, England, and the 'National Crusade', 1302-1386. In: *France and the British Isles in the Middle Ages and Renaissance: Essays by Members of Girton College, Cambridge, in Memory of Ruth Morgan*. Ed. G. Jondorf and D.N. Dumville. Woodbridge, 1991, pp. 183-98.

Housley, Norman. "Frontier Societies and Crusading in the Late Middle Ages," *Mediterranean Historical Review* 10 (1995), 104-19.

Housley, Norman. *The Italian Crusades: The Papal-Angevin Alliance and the Crusades Against Christian Lay Powers, 1254-1343*. Oxford: Clarendon Press, 1982.

Housley, Norman. "King Louis the Great of Hungary and the Crusades, 1342-1382," *Slavonic and East European Review* 62 (1984), 192-208.

Housley, Norman. *The Later Crusades, 1274-1580: From Lyons to Alcazar*. Oxford: Oxford University Press, 1992.

Housley, Norman. "The Mercenary Companies, the Papacy, and the Crusades, 1356-1378," *Traditio* 38 (1982), 253-80.

Housley, Norman. "Pope Clement V and the Crusades of 1309-10," *Journal of Medieval History* 8 (1982), 29-43.

Jackson, P. "The Crusades of 1239-41 and their Aftermath," *Bulletin of the School of Oriental and African Studies* 50 (1987), 32-60.

Jordan, William Chester. *Louis IX and the Challenge of the Crusade: A Study in Rulership*. Princeton: Princeton University Press, 1979.

Jordan, William Chester. "Supplying Aigues-Mortes for the Crusade of 1248: The Problem of Restructuring Trade." In: *Order and Innovation in the Middle Ages: Essays in Honor of Joseph R. Strayer*. Ed. W.C. Jordan et al. Princeton, 1976, pp. 165-72, 459-65.

Jorga, N. *Philippe de Mézières 1327-1405 et la croisade au XIVe siècle*. Paris, 1896.

Kedar, Benjamin Z. "The Passenger List of a Crusader Ship, 1250: Towards the History of the Popular Element on the Seventh Crusade," *Studi medievali* 13 (1972), 267-79.

King, D.J. Cathcart. "The Taking of Le Krak des Chevaliers in 1271," *Antiquity* 23 (1949), 83-92.

Laurent, V. "La croisade et la question d'Orient sous le pontificat de Grégoire X," *Revue historique du sud-est européen* 22 (1945).

Lecoy de la Marche, Albert. "La prédiction de la croisade au XIIIe siècle," *Revue des questions historiques* 48 (1890).

Lefevre, R. *La crociata di Tunisi del 1270 nei documenti del distrutto archivio angioino di Napoli*. Rome, 1977.

Le Goff, Jacques. *Saint Louis*. Paris, 1976.

Le Goff, Jacques. "Saint Louis and the Mediterranean," *Mediterranean Historical Review* 5 (1990), 21-43.

Lewis, Archibald R. "The Islamic World and the Latin West, 1350-1500," *Speculum* 65 (1990), 833-44.

Little, Donald P. "The Fall of 'Akkā in 690/1291: The Muslim Version." In: *Studies in Islamic History and Civilization in Honour of Professor David Ayalon*. Ed. Moshe Sharon. Jerusalem, 1986.

Lloyd, Simon. "Crusader Knights and the Land Market in the Thirteenth Century." In: *Thirteenth Century England II*. Ed. P.R. Coss and S.D. Lloyd. Woodbridge, 1988, pp. 119-36.

Lloyd, Simon. "The Crusades of St. Louis," *History Today* 47.5 (May 1997), 37-43.

Lloyd, Simon. "The Lord Edward's Crusade, 1270-2: Its Setting and Significance." In: *War and Government in the Middle Ages: Essays in Honour of J.O. Prestwich*. Ed. J. Gillingham and J.C. Holt. Cambridge, 1984, pp. 120-33.

Lloyd, Simon. "'Political Crusades' in England c. 1215-17 and 1263-5." In: *Crusade and Settlement: Papers Read at the First Conference of the Society for the Study of the Crusades and the Latin East and Presented to R.C. Smail*. Ed. Peter W. Edbury. Cardiff: University College Cardiff Press, 1985, pp. 113-20.

Lloyd, Simon. "William Longspee II: The Making of an English Crusading Hero (Part I)," *Nottingham Medieval Studies* 35 (1991), 41-69.

Lloyd, Simon and Tony Hunt. "William Longspee II: The Making of an English Crusading Hero (Part II)," *Nottingham Medieval Studies* 36 (1992), 79-125.

Lomax, John Phillip. "Frederick II, His Saracens, and the Papacy." In: *Medieval Christian Perceptions of Islam*. Hamden, 1997, pp. 175-97.

Luttrell, Anthony. "The Crusade in the Fourteenth Century." In: *Europe in the Late Middle Ages*. Ed. J.R. Hale, J.R.L. Highfield, and B. Smalley. Evanston: Northwestern University Press, 1965, pp. 122-54.

Luttrell, Anthony. "English Levantine Crusaders, 1363-1367," *Renaissance Studies* 2 (1988), 143-53.

Maddicott, J.R. "The Crusade Taxation of 1268-1270 and the Development of Parliament." In: *Thirteenth Century England II*. Ed. P.R. Coss and S.D. Lloyd. Woodbridge, 1988, pp. 93-117.

Magee, James. "Crusading at the Court of Charles VI, 1388-1396," *French History* 12 (1998), 367-83.

Maier, Christoph T. "Crusade and Rhetoric Against the Muslim Colony of Lucera: Eudes of Châteauroux's *Sermones de Rebellione Sarracenorum Lucherie in Apulia*," *Journal of Medieval History* 21 (1995), 343-85.

Marshall, Christopher J. "The French Regiment in the Latin East, 1254-91," *Journal of Military History* 15 (1989), 301-07.

Mayer, Hans Eberhard. *Kings and Lords in the Latin Kingdom of Jerusalem*. London, 1994.

Morris, Wentworth S. "A Crusader's Testament," *Speculum* 27 (1952), 197-98.

Novara, Filippo di. *Guerra di Federico II in oriente*. Ed. Silvio Melani. Naples, 1994.

Papacostea, Serban. "Byzance et la Croisade au Bas-Danube à la fin du XIVe siècle," *Revue Romaine d'histoire* 30 (1991), 3-21.

Paviot, Jacques. "Angleterre et Bourgogne: deux voies pour la croisade aux 14e et 15 siècles." In: *L'Angleterre et les pays Bourguignons: Relations et comparaisons (XVe-XVIe siècles)*. Neuchâtel: Centre européen d'études Bourguignons (XIVe-XVIe siècles), 1995, pp. 27-35.

Paviot, Jacques. "La dévotion vis-à-vis de la terre sainte au XVe siècle: L'exemple de Philippe le Bon, duc de Bourgogne (1396-1467)." In: *Autour de la première croisade: Actes du Colloque de la Society for the Study of the Crusades and the Latin East (Clermont-Ferrand, 22-25 juin 1995)*. Ed. M. Balard. Paris: Publications de la Sorbonne, 1996, pp. 401-11.

Powell, James M. *Anatomy of a Crusade, 1213-1221*. Philadelphia: University of Pennsylvania Press, 1990.

Powell, James M. "Patriarch Gerold and Frederick II: the Matthew Paris Letter," *Journal of Medieval History* 25 (1999), 19-26.

Powell, James M. "The Role of Women in the Fifth Crusade." In: *The Horns of Hattin*. Ed. Benjamin Z. Kedar. Jerusalem, 1992, pp. 294-301.

Purcell, M. *Papal Crusading Policy, 1244-1291*. Leiden, 1975.

Richard, Jean. "La croisade de 1270, premier 'passage général'?" *Comptes rendus de l'académie des inscriptions* (1989).

Richard, Jean. "L'état de guerre avec l'Egypte et le royaume de Chypre." In: *Hē Kupros kai hoi Staurophories/Cyprus and the Crusades: Hoi anakoinōseis tou deithnous symposiou "Hē Kupros kai hoi Staurophories", Leukōsia, 6-9 septembriou, 1994/Papers Given at the International Conference "Cyprus and the Crusades", Nicosia, 6-9 September, 1994*. Ed. Nikos Coureas and Jonathan Riley-Smith. Nicosia: Cyprus Research Centre/Society for the Study of the Crusades and the Latin East, 1995, pp. 83-95.

Richard, Jean. *Saint Louis: Crusader King of France*. Ed. Simon Lloyd. Trans. J. Birrell. Cambridge, 1992.

Riley-Smith, Jonathan. "The Crusading Heritage of Guy and Aimery of Lusignan." In: *Hē Kupros kai hoi Staurophories/Cyprus and the Crusades: Hoi anakoinōseis tou deithnous symposiou "Hē Kupros kai hoi Staurophories", Leukōsia, 6-9 septembriou, 1994/Papers Given at the International Conference "Cyprus and the Crusades", Nicosia, 6-9 September, 1994*. Ed. Nikos Coureas and Jonathan Riley-Smith. Nicosia: Cyprus Research Centre/Society for the Study of the Crusades and the Latin East, 1995, pp. 31-45.

Saul, Nigel. "Late Medieval Crusading," *History Today* 47.6 (Jun 1997), 23-28.

Schein, Sylvia. "Babylon and Jerusalem: The Fall of Acre, 1291-1995." In: *From Clermont to Jerusalem: The Crusades and Crusader Societies, 1095-1500*. Selected Proceedings of the International Medieval Congress, University of Leeds, 10-13 July 1995. Ed. Alan V. Murray. Turnhout: Brepols, 1998, pp. 141-50.

Schein, Sylvia. *Fideles crucis: The Papacy, the West, and the Recovery of the Holy Lnad, 1274-1314*. Oxford: Oxford University Press, 1991.

Schein, Sylvia. "Philip IV and the Crusade: A Reconsideration." In: *Crusade and Settlement: Papers Read at the First Conference of the Society for the Study of the Crusades and the Latin East and Presented to R.C. Smail*. Ed. Peter W. Edbury. Cardiff: University College Cardiff Press, 1985, pp. 121-26.

Setton, Kenneth M. *The Papacy and the Levant (1204-1571)*. 4 vols. Philadelphia: American Philosophical Society, 1978-85.

Setton, Kenneth M., gen ed. *A History of the Crusades*. Vol. III: *The Fourteenth and Fifteenth Centuries*. Ed. Harry W. Hazard. Madison: University of Wisconsin Press, 1975.

Siberry, Elizabeth. "Criticism of Crusading in Fourteenth-Century England." In: *Crusade and Settlement: Papers Read at the First Conference of the Society for the Study of the Crusades and the Latin East and Presented to R.C. Smail*. Ed. Peter W. Edbury. Cardiff: University College Cardiff Press, 1985, pp. 127-34.

Stacey, Robert C. "Crusades, Crusaders and the Baronial *Gravamina* of 1263-1264." In: *Thirteenth-Century England III*. Ed. P.R. Coss and S.D. Lloyd. Woodbridge, 1991, pp. 137-50.

Strayer, Joseph R. "The Crusades of Louis IX." In: *A History of the Crusades*. II: *The Later Crusades*. Ed. R.L. Woolff and H.W. Hazard. Philadelphia, 1962; in: *Medieval Statecraft and the Perspectives of History: Essays by Joseph R. Strayer*. Princeton, 1971, pp. 159-92.

Strayer, Joseph R. "The Political Crusades of the Thirteenth Century." In: *Medieval Statecraft and the Perspectives of History: Essays by Joseph R. Strayer*. Princeton, 1971, pp. 123-58.

Thorau, Peter. "The Battle of 'Ayn Jalut: a Re-examination." In: *Crusade and Settlement: Papers Read at the First Conference of the Society for the Study of the Crusades and the Latin East and Presented to R.C. Smail*. Ed. Peter W. Edbury. Cardiff: University College Cardiff Press, 1985, pp. 236-39.

Tyerman, C.J. "The Holy Land and the Crusades of the Thirteenth and Fourteenth Centuries," In: *Crusade and Settlement: Papers Read at the First Conference of the Society for the Study of the Crusades and the Latin East and Presented to R.C. Smail*. Ed. Peter W. Edbury. Cardiff: University College Cardiff Press, 1985, pp. 105-12.

Tyerman, C.J. "Marino Sanudo Torsello and the Lost Crusade: Lobbying in the Fourteenth Century," *Transactions of the Royal Historical Society*, 5th ser., 32 (1982), 56-74.

Tyerman, C.J. "Philip V of France, the Assemblies of 1319-20 and the Crusade," *Bulletin of the Institute of Historical Research* 57 (1984), 15-34.

Tyerman, C.J. "Philip VI and the Recovery of the Holy Land," *English Historical Review* 100 (1985), 25-52.

Tyerman, C.J. "Sed Nihil Fecit? The Last Capetians and the Recovery of the Holy Land." In: *War and Government in the Middle Ages: Essays in Honour of J.O. Prestwich*. Ed. J. Gillingham and J.C. Holt. Cambridge, 1984, pp. 170-81.

Wagner, Michael. "Kreuzzug oder Klassenkampf? Zur Sozialgeschichte der französischen Religionskriege im späten 16. Jahrhundert," *Zeitschrift für Historische Forschung* 25 (1998), 85-103.

Walsh, R.J. "Charles the Bold and the Crusade: Politics and Propaganda," *Journal of Medieval History* 3 (1977).

Weiss, Daniel. *Art and the Crusade in the Age of Saint Louis*. Cambridge: Cambridge University Press, 1998.

Willard, Charity Cannon. "Isabel of Portugal and the Fifteenth-Century Burgundian Crusade." In: *Journeys Toward God: Pilgrimage and Crusade*. Ed. B.N. Sargent-Baur. Kalamazoo, 1992, pp. 205-14.

Medieval – Crusades – Crusader Kingdoms

Airaldi, Gabriella and Benjamin Z. Kedar, ed. *I comuni Italiani nel regno crociato di Gerusaleme*. Genoa, 1986.

Amouroux-Mourad, Monique. *Le comté d'Edesse, 1098-1150*. Paris: Paul Geuthner, 1988.

Andressohn, John C. *The Ancestry and Life of Godfrey of Bouillon*. Bloomington: Indiana University Press, 1947.

Asbridge, Thomas. "The Principality of Antioch and the Jabal as-Summaq." In: *The First Crusade: Origins and Impact*. Ed. Jonathan Phillips. Manchester: University of Manchester Press, 1997, pp. 142-52.

Ashtor, Eliyahu. "Il regno crociati e il commercio di Levante." In: *I communi Italiani nel regno crociato di Gerussalemme*. Ed. Gabriella Airaldi and Benjamin Z. Kedar. Genoa, 1986, pp. 1-49.

Attiya, Hussein M. "Knowledge of Arabic in the Crusader States in the Twelfth and Thirteenth Centuries," *Journal of Medieval History* 25 (1999), 203-13.

Aubé, Pierre. *Baudouin IV de Jérusalem, le roi lépreux*. Paris: Pluriel, 1996.

Barber, Malcolm C. "Supplying the Crusader States: The Role of the Templars." In: *The Horns of Hattin*. Ed. Benjamin Z. Kedar. Jerusalem, 1992, pp. 314-26.

Beaumont, André Alden. "Albert of Aachen and the County of Edessa." In: *The Crusades and Other Historical Essays Presented to Dana C. Munro by His Former Students*. Ed. Louis J. Paetow. New York: F.S. Crofts, 1928, pp. 101-38.

Ben-Ami, A. *Social Change in a Hostile Environment: The Crusaders' Kingdom of Jerusalem*. Princeton: Princeton University Press, 1969.

Benvenisti, M. *The Crusaders in the Holy Land*. Jerusalem, 1970.

Boase, T.S.R., ed. *The Cilician Kingdom of Armenia*. New York, 1978.

Brundage, James A. "Marriage Law in the Latin Kingdom of Jerusalem." In: *Outremer–Studies in the History of the Crusading Kingdom of Jerusalem*. Ed. Benjamin Kedar, H.E. Mayer and R.C. Smail. Jerusalem, 1982, pp. 258-71.

Buisson, Ludwig. *Erobererrecht, Vasallität und byzantisches Staatsrecht auf dem ersten Kreuzzug*. Hamburg: Joachim Jungius-Gesellschaft, 1985.

Buisson, Ludwig. "Heerführertum und Erobererrecht auf dem Erstn Kreuzzug," *Zeitschrift der Savigny-Stiftung für Rechtsgechichte. Germanistische Abteilung* 112 (1995), 316-44.

Cahen, Claude. *La Syrie du nord à l'époque des croisades et la principauté franque d'Antioche*. Bibliothèque orientale, 1. Paris: Paul Geuthner, 1940.

Cazel, F.A. "The Tax of 1185 in Aid of the Holy Land," *Speculum* 30 (1955).

Cipollini, G. *Cristianità-Islam. Cattività e liberazione in Nome di Dio: Il tempo di Innovenzo III dopo il 1187*. Rome, 1992.

Cowdrey, H.E.J. "The Latin Kingdom of Jerusalem," *History* 57 (1972), 228-34.

Dajani-Shakeel, Hadia. "Diplomatic Relations between Muslim and Frankish Rulers, 1097-1153 A.D." In: *Crusaders and Muslims in Twelfth-Century Syria.* Ed. Maya Schatzmiller. Leiden: E.J. Brill, 1993, pp. 190-215.

Dickerhof, Harald. "Über die Staatsgründungen des ersten Kreuzzugs," *Historisches Jahrbuch* 100 (1980), 95-130.

Dodu, G. *Histoire des institutions monarchiques dans le royaume Latin de Jerusalem, 1099-1291.* Rpt. New York, 1978.

Edbury, Peter W. *John of Ibelin and the Kingdom of Jerusalem.* Woodbridge: Boydell and Brewer, 1997.

Edbury, Peter W. "Propaganda and Faction in the Kingdom of Jerusalem: The Background to Hattin." In: *Crusaders and Muslims in Twelfth-Century Syria.* Ed. M. Shatzmiller. Leiden: E.J. Brill, 1993, pp. 172-89.

Edgington, Susan B. "Medical Care in the Hospital of St John in Jerusalem." In: *The Military Orders.* Vol. 2: *Welfare and Warfare.* Ed. Helen Nicholson. Aldershot: Ashgate, 1998, pp. 27-34.

Ellenblum, Ronnie. *Frankish Rural Settlement in the Latin Kingdom of Jerusalem.* Cambridge: Cambridge University Press, 1998.

Fedalto, G. *La chiesa latina in oriente.* 3 vols. Verona, 1973-77.

Folda, Jaroslav. *Crusader Manuscript Illumination at Saint-Jean d'Acre, 1275-1291.* Princeton, 1976.

Friedman, Yvonne. "The Ransom of Captives in the Latin Kingdom of Jerusalem." In: *Autour de la première croisade: Actes du Colloque de la Society for the Study of the Crusades and the Latin East (Clermont-Ferrand, 22-25 juin 1995).* Ed. M. Balard. Paris: Publications de la Sorbonne, 1996, pp. 177-89.

Gadolin, Anitra R. "Prince Bohemond's Death and Apotheosis in the Church of San Sabino, Canosa di Puglia," *Byzantion* 52 (1982), 124-53.

Gerish, Deborah. "Ancestors and Predecessors: Royal Continuity and Identity in the First Kingdom of Jerusalem," *Anglo-Norman Studies* 20 (1997), 127-50.

Gerish, Deborah. "The True Cross and the Kings of Jerusalem," *Haskins Society Journal* 8 (1996), 137-55.

Gertwagen, Ruthi. "The Crusader Port of Acre: Layout and Problems of Maintenance." In: *Autour de la première croisade: Actes du Colloque de la Society for the Study of the Crusades and the Latin East (Clermont-Ferrand, 22-25 juin 1995)*. Ed. M. Balard. Paris: Publications de la Sorbonne, 1996, pp. 553-82.

Gindler, Paul. *Graf Balduin I. von Edessa*. Halle: C.A. Kaemmerer, 1901.

Grabois, Aryeh. "The Cyclical Views of History in Late Thirteenth-Century Acre." In: *From Clermont to Jerusalem: The Crusades and Crusader Societies, 1095-1500*. Selected Proceedings of the International Medieval Congress, University of Leeds, 10-13 July 1995. Ed. Alan V. Murray. Turnhout: Brepols, 1998, pp. 131-40.

Hamilton, Bernard. "Baldwin the Leper as War Leader." In: *From Clermont to Jerusalem: The Crusades and Crusader Societies, 1095-1500*. Selected Proceedings of the International Medieval Congress, University of Leeds, 10-13 July 1995. Ed. Alan V. Murray. Turnhout: Brepols, 1998, pp. 119-30.

Hamilton, Bernard. *The Latin Church in the Crusader States: The Secular Church*. London: Variorum, 1980.

Hamilton, Bernard. *The Leper King and His Heirs: Baldwin IV and the Crusader Kingdom of Jerusalem*. Cambridge: Cambridge University Press, 2000.

Hamilton, Bernard. "Review Article: The Crusader Kingdom and Its Guardians," *International History Review* 21 (1999), 104-16.

Hansen, Joseph. *Das Problem eines Kirchenstaates in Jerusalem: Ein Beitrag zur Geschichte der Kreuzzüge*. Luxembourg: Huss, 1928.

Hiestand, Rudolf. "König Balduin und sein Tanzbär," *Archiv für Kulturgeschichte* 70 (1988), 343-60.

Holt, P.M. "Qalawûn's Treaty with Acre in 1283," *English Historical Review* 91 (1976).

Jacoby, David. "Knightly Values and Class Consciousness in the Crusader States of the Eastern Mediterranean," *Mediterranean History Review* 1 (1986), 158-86.

Jacoby, David. *Studies on the Crusader States and on Venetian Expansion.* London, 1989.

Jotischky, A.T. *The Perfection of Solitude: Hermits and Monks in the Crusader States.* Philadelphia, 1995.

Kedar, Benjamin Z. "A Twelfth-Century Description of the Jerusalem Hospital." In: *The Military Orders.* Vol. 2: *Welfare and Warfare.* Ed. Helen Nicholson. Aldershot: Ashgate, 1998, pp. 3-26.

Kedar, Benjamin Z. "The Subjected Muslims of the Frankish Levant." In: *Muslims under Latin Rule, 1100-1300.* Ed. James Powell. Princeton, 1990, pp. 135-74.

La Monte, J.L. *Feudal Monarchy in the Latin Kingdom of Jerusalem.* Cambridge, 1932.

Ligato, Giuseppe. "The Political Meanings of the Relic of the Holy Cross among the Crusaders and in the Latin Kingdom of Jerusalem: an Example of 1185." In: *Autour de la première croisade: Actes du Colloque de la Society for the Study of the Crusades and the Latin East (Clermont-Ferrand, 22-25 juin 1995).* Ed. M. Balard. Paris: Publications de la Sorbonne, 1996, pp. 313-30.

Lilie, Ralph-Johannes. *Byzantium and the Crusader States, 1096-1204: Studies in the Relations of the Byzantine Empire with the Crusader States in Syria and Palestine.* Oxford: Clarendon, 1993.

Lilie, Ralph-Johannes. "Noch einmal zu dem Thema 'Byzanz und die Kreuzfahrerstaaten." In: *Varia I: Beiträge von Ralph-Johannes Lilie und Paul Speck.* Poikila byzantina, 4. Bonn: Habelt, 1984, pp. 121-74.

Matzke, Michael. "De origine Hospitalariorum Hierosolymitanorum: vom klösterlichen Pilgerhospital zur internationalen Organisation," *Journal of Medieval History* 22 (1996), 1-23.

Mayer, Hans Eberhard. "Angevins *versus* Normans: The New Men of King Fulk of Jerusalem," *Proceedings of the American Philosophical Society* 133 (1989), 139-47.

Mayer, Hans Eberhard. *Bistümer, Klöster und Stifte im Königreich Jerusalem.* Stuttgart, 1977.

Mayer, Hans Eberhard. "The Crusader Principality of Galilee between Saint-Omer and Bures-sur-Yvette." In: *Itinéraires d'Orient: Hommages à Claude Cahen, Res Orientales* 6 (1994), 157-67.

Mayer, Hans Eberhard. *Mélanges sur l'histoire du royaume latin de Jérusalem.* Mémoires de l'Academie des Inscriptions et Belles-Lettres, n.s. 5. Paris: Académie des Inscriptions et Belles-Lettres, 1984.

Mayer, Hans Eberhard. "The Origins of the County of Jaffe," *Israel Exploration Journal* 35 (1985), 35-45.

Mayer, Hans Eberhard. "The Origins of the Lordships of Ramla and Lydda in the Latin Kingdom of Jerusalem," *Speculum* 60 (1985), 537-52.

Mayer, Hans Eberhard. "Das Pontifikale von Tyrus und die Krönung der lateinisachen Könige von Jerusalem," *Dumbarton Oaks Papers* 21 (1967), 143-232.

Mayer, Hans Eberhard. "Studies in the History of Queen Melisende of Jerusalem," *Dumbarton Oaks Papers* 26 (1972), 93-182.

Mayer, Hans Eberhard. "The Succession to Baldwin II of Jerusalem: English Impact on the East," *Dumbarton Oaks Papers* 39 (1985), 139-47.

Mayer, Hans Eberhard. "The Wheel of Fortune: Seignorial Vicissitudes under Kings Fulk and Baldwin III of Jerusalem," *Speculum* 65 (1990), 860-77.

Mitchell, Piers D. "The Archaeological Approach to the Study of Disease in the Crusader States, as Employed at Le Petit Gerin." In: *The Military Orders.* Vol. 2: *Welfare and Warfare.* Ed. Helen Nicholson. Aldershot: Ashgate, 1998, pp. 43-50.

Mitchell, Piers D. "Leprosy and the Case of King Baldwin IV of Jerusalem," *International Journal of Leprosy* 61 (1993), 283-91.

Moeller, Charles. "Les flamands du Ternois au royaume latin de Jérusalem." In: *Mélanges Paul Fredericq*. Brussels: H. Lamertin, 1903, pp. 189-202.

Munro, Dana C. *The Kingdom of the Crusaders*. Philadelphia, 1936.

Murray, Alan V. "Baldwin II and his Nobles: Baronial Factionalism and Dissent in the Kingdom of Jerusalem, 1118-1134," *Nottingham Medieval Studies* 38 (1994), 60-85.

Murray, Alan V. "Daimbert of Pisa, the Domus Godefridi and the Accession of Baldwin I of Jerusalem." In: *From Clermont to Jerusalem: The Crusades and Crusader Societies, 1095-1500*. Selected Proceedings of the International Medieval Congress, University of Leeds, 10-13 July 1995. Ed. Alan V. Murray. Turnhout: Brepols, 1998, pp. 81-102.

Murray, Alan V. "Dynastic Continuity or Dynastic Change? The Accession of Baldwin II and the Nobility of the Kingdom of Jerusalem," *Medieval Prosopography* 13 (1992).

Murray, Alan V. "Ethnic Identity in the Crusader States: The Frankish Race and the Settlement of Outremer." In: *Concepts of National Identity in the Middle Ages*. Ed. Simon Forde, Lesley Johnson, and Alan V. Murray. Leeds: Leeds Studies in English, 1995, pp. 59-73.

Murray, Alan V. "The Origins of the Frankish Nobility of the Kingdom of Jerusalem, 1100-1118," *Mediterranean Historical Review* 4 (1989), 281-300.

Murray, Alan V. "The Title of Godfrey of Bouillon as Ruler of Jerusalem," *Collegium medievale* 3 (1990), 163-78.

Nickerson, Michael. "The Seigneury of Beirut in the Twelfth Century and the Brisebarre Family of Beirut-Blanchegarde," *Byzantion* 19 (1949).

Phillips, Jonathan. *Defenders of the Holy Land: Relations between the Latin East and the West, 1119-1187*. Oxford, 1996.

Powell, James M., ed. *Muslims under Latin Rule, 1100-1300*. Princeton: Princeton University Press, 1990.

Prawer, Joshua. *Crusader Institutions*. Oxford: Clarendon Press, 1980.

Prawer, Joshua. *Histoire du royaume Latin de Jérusalem.* 2nd ed. 2 vols. Paris, 1975.

Prawer, Joshua. *The Latin Kingdom of Jerusalem: European Colonialism in the Middle Ages.* London: Weidenfeld and Nicolson, 1972.

Prawer, Joshua. "The Nobility and the Feudal Regime in the Latin Kingdom of Jerusalem." In: *Lordship and Community in Medieval Europe: Selected Readings.* Ed. Frederic Cheyette. New York: Holt, Rinehart, and Winston, Inc., 1968, pp. 156-79.

Prawer, Joshua. "The Settlement of the Latins in Jerusalem," *Speculum* 27 (1952), 490-503.

Pryor, John H. "In subsidium terrae sanctae: Exports of Foodstuffs and War Materiel from the Kingdom of Sicily to the Kingdom of Jerusalem, 1265-1284," *Asian and African Studies* 22 (1988), 127-46.

Richard, Jean. *Le comté de Tripoli sous la dynastie Toulousiane, 1102-1187.* Paris: Paul Geuthner, 1945.

Richard, Jean. "Les comtes de Tripoli de la dynastie antiochénienne et leur vassaux." In: *Crusade and Settlement: Papers Read at the First Conference of the Society for the Study of the Crusades and the Latin East and Presented to R.C. Smail.* Ed. Peter W. Edbury. Cardiff: University College Cardiff Press, 1985.

Richard, Jean. "La féodalité de l'orient Latin et le mouvement communal: un états questions." In: *Structures féodales et féodalisme dans l'occident Mediterranean (Xe-XVe siècles): Collections de l'Ecole française de Rome* 44 (1980), 651-65.

Richard, Jean. *The Latin Kingdom of Jerusalem.* Trans. Janet Shirley. 2 vols. Amsterdam, 1979.

Richard, Jean. "Le paiement des dîmes dans les états des croisés," *Bibliothèque de l'école des chartes* 150 (1992), 71-83.

Richard, Jean. "Le peuplement Latin et Syrien en Chypre au XIIIe siècle," *Byzantinische Forschungen* 7 (1979), 157-73.

Riley-Smith, Jonathan. *The Feudal Nobility and the Kingdom of Jerusalem, 1174-1277.* London, 1973.

Riley-Smith, Jonathan. "The Latin Clergy and the Settlement in Palestine and Syria, 1098-1100," *Catholic Historical Review* 74 (1988), 539-57.

Riley-Smith, Jonathan. "A Note on the Confraternities in the Latin Kingdom of Jerusalem," *Bulletin of the Institute of Historical Research* 44 (1971), 301-08.

Riley-Smith, Jonathan. "Peace Never Established: The Case of the Kingdom of Jerusalem," *Transactions of the Royal Historical Society*, 5th ser., 28 (1972), 87-102.

Riley-Smith, Jonathan. "The Title of Godfrey of Bouillon," *Bulletin of the Institute of Historical Research* 52 (1979), 83-86.

Röhricht, Reinhold. *Die Deutschen im Heiligen Lande*. Innsbruck: Wagner'sche Universitäts-Buchhandlung, 1894.

Rösch, Gerhard. "Der 'Kreuzzug' Bohemonds gegen Dyrrhachium 1107/1108 in der lateinischen Tradition des 12. Jahrhunderts," *Römische historische Mitteilungen* 26 (1984), 181-90.

Rose, Richard B. "The Native Christians of Jerusalem, 1187-1260." In: *The Horns of Hattin*. Ed. Benjamin Z. Kedar. Jerusalem, 1992, pp. 239-49.

Rowe, John Gordon. "Paschal II, Bohemund of Antioch and the Byzantine Empire," *Bulletin of the John Rylands Library* 49 (1966), 165-202.

Salibi, K.S. "The Maronites of Lebanon under Frankish and Mamluk Rule," *Arabica* 4 (1957).

Segal, Judah B. *Edessa, the Blessed City*. Oxford: Clarendon Press, 1970.

Slack, C.K. "Royal Familiares in the Latin Kingdom of Jerusalem, 1100-1187," *Viator* 22 (1991), 15-67.

Smail, R.C. "The Predicament of Guy of Lusignan." In: *Outremer: Studies in the Crusading Kingdom of Jerusalem Presented to Joshua Prawer*. Ed. Benjamin Z. Kedar. Jerusalem, 1982, pp. 159-76.

Talmon-Heller, Daniella. "Arabic Sources on Muslim Villagers under Frankish Rule." In: *From Clermont to Jerusalem: The Crusades and Crusader Societies, 1095-1500*. Selected Proceedings of the International

Medieval Congress, University of Leeds, 10-13 July 1995. Ed. Alan V. Murray. Turnhout: Brepols, 1998, pp. 103-18.

Toll, Christopher. "Arabic Medicine and Hospitals in the Middle Ages: a Probable Model for the Military Orders' Care of the Sick." In: *The Military Orders*. Vol. 2: *Welfare and Warfare*. Ed. Helen Nicholson. Aldershot: Ashgate, 1998, pp. 35-42.

Wilkinson, J. *Jerusalem Pilgrimages, 1099-1185*. Warminster, 1989.

Wollf, Alfred. *König Balduin I. von Jerusalem*. Konigsburg: R. Leupold, 1884.

Yewdale, Ralph B. *Bohemond I, Prince of Antioch*. Princeton, 1924.

Medieval – Declarations of War

DeVries, Kelly. "Medieval Declarations of War: An Example from 1212," *Scintilla* 4 (1987), 20-37.

Medieval – Diplomacy

Allmand, Christopher T. "Diplomacy in Late Medieval England," *History Today* 17 (1967), 546-53.

Chaplais, Pierre. *English Medieval Diplomatic Practice*. 2 vols. London, 1982.

Cuttino, G.P. *English Diplomatic Administration, 1259-1339*. 2nd ed. Oxford: Clarendon Press, 1971.

Cuttino, G.P. *English Medieval Diplomacy*. Bloomington: Indiana University Press, 1985.

Lucas, Henry Stephen. "The Machinery of Diplomatic Intercourse." In: *The English Government at Work, 1327-1336*. Ed. J.F. Willard and W.A. Morris. Cambridge, 1940, I:300-31.

Mattingly, Garrett. *Renaissance Diplomacy*. Harmondsworth: Penguin Books, 1965.

Queller, Donald E. *The Office of Ambassador in the Middle Ages.* Princeton, 1967.

Russell, Joycelyne G. *Diplomats at Work: Three Renaissance Studies.* Stroud: Sutton Publishing, 1992.

Russell, Joycelyne G "The Humanists Converge: The Congress of Mantua (1459)." In: *Diplomats at Work: Three Renaissance Studies.* Stroud: Sutton Publishing, 1992, pp. 51-93

Russell, Joycelyne G. "The Search for Universal Peace: the Conferences at Calais and Bruges in 1521," *Bulletin for the Institute for Historical Research* 44 (1971), 162-93.

Medieval – Eastern Europe (including Russia)

Arrignon, Jean-Pierre. "Le guerrier russe, IXe-XIIIe siècles d'après les données archéologiques." In: *Le combattant au moyen âge.* 2nd ed. Histoire ancienne et médiévale, 36. Paris: Publications de la Sorbonne, 1995, pp. 123-47.

Biskup, Marian. "La guerre de treize ans entre la Pologne et l'Ordre des Chevaliers Teutoniques (1454-66) et son importance dans l'histoire militaire de la Pologne," *Revue internationale d'histoire militaire* 28 (1969), 417-33.

Bon, A. *La morée Franque.* Paris, 1969.

Branzeu, Felician "Vlad l'Empaleur dans la litterature turque," *Revista istorica Romana* 13 (1946), 68-71.

Bury, J.B. "Mutasim's March through Cappadocia in A.D. 838," *Journal of Hellenic Studies* 29 (1909), 120-29.

Dachkévytch, Y.A. "Les Arméniens à Kiev (jusqu'en 1240)," *Revue des études Arméniennes* 10 (1973-74), 305-56.

Diaconu, P. *Les Coumans au Bas-Danube aux XIe aux XIIe siècles.* Bucharest, 1978.

Dircks, Bernhard. "Krieg und Frieden mit Livland (12.-15. Jahrhundert)." In: *Deutsche und Deuteschland aus russischer Sicht, 11.-17. Jahr-*

hundert. Ed. Dagmar Herrmann. Munich: Wilhelm Fink Verlag, 1988, pp. 116-47.

Dogaru, Mircea. *Dracula, împaratul Rasaritului: Gândirea politica si practica miliara în epoca lui Vlad Tepes. Traditie si originalitate.* Bucharest: Editura "Globus", 1995.

Dogaru, Mircea. "Mircea the Great (1386-1418): The Accomplisher of Wallachia and Illustrious Army Commander," *Revue internationale d'histoire militaire* 66 (1987), 107-16.

Dogaru, Mircea. "Les pays roumains et la bataille de Mohács." In: *XXII. Kongreß der Internationalen Kommission für Militärgeschichte Acta 22: Von Crécy bis Mohács Kriegswesen im späten Mittelalter (1346-1526).* Vienna, 1997, pp. 132-44.

Dölger, F. "Die Chronologie des grossen Feldzuges des Kaisers Johannes Tzimiskes gegen die Russen," *Byzantinische Zeitschrift* 32 (1932), 275-92.

Ducellier, A. *La façade maritime de l'Albanie au moyen âge: Durazzo et Valone du XIe au XVe siècle.* Thessaloniki, 1981.

Fennell, J. *The Crisis of Medieval Russia, 1200-1304.* London: Longman, 1983.

Fine, John V.A., Jr. *The Late Medieval Balkans: A Critical Survey from the Late Twelfth Century to the Ottoman Conquest.* Ann Arbor: The University of Michigan Press, 1987.

Fourteen Centuries of Struggle for Freedom. Belgrade: Vojni Muzej, n.d.

Franklin, Simon and Jonathan Shepard. *The Emergence of Rus, 750-1200.* London, 1996.

Giurescu, Constantin C. "Les armées Roumaines dans la lutte pour la défense et l'indépendance du pays, du XIVe au XVIe siècles," *Revue internationale d'histoire militaire* 34 (1975), 5-21.

Grekov, B. *Kiev Rus.* Trans. Y. Sdobnikov. Ed. D. Ogden. Moscow, 1959.

Gultzgoff, V. "La Russie Kiévienne entre la Scandinavie, Constantinople el royaume Franc de Jérusalem," *Revue des études Slaves* 55 (1983), 151-61.

Halperin, Charles J. *Russia and the Golden Horde*. London, 1985.

Halperin, Charles J. "Russo-Tartar Relations in Mongol Context: Two Notes," *Acta orientalia academiae scientarum Hungaricarum* 51 (1998), 321-39.

Henning, Joachim. "Ringwallburgen und Reiterkrieger: Zum Wandel der Militärstrategie im ostsächsisch-slawischen Raum an der Wende vom 9. zum 10. Jahrhundert." In: *Military Studies in Medieval Europe: Papers of the "Medieval Europe Brugge 1997" Conference Volume 11*. Ed. Guy De Boe & Frans Verhaeghe. Zellik: Instituut voor het Archeologisch Patrimonium, 1997, pp. 21-31.

Hoffman, Richard C. "Warfare, Weather, and a Rural Economy: The Duchy of Wroclaw in the Mid-Fifteenth Century," *Viator* 4 (1973), 273-305.

Iorga, N. "Les développement des troupes mercenaires dans les pays roumains des origines à la fin du XVIIIe siècle," *Revue internationale d'histoire militaire* 3 (1939-40), 140-43.

Javaschtschev, Sevo and Rumen Nikolov. "Die Militärstrategie des zweiten bulgarischen Staates (13.-14. Jahrhundert)." In: *XXII. Kongreß der Internationalen Kommission für Militärgeschichte Acta 22: Von Crécy bis Mohács Kriegswesen im späten Mittelalter (1346-1526)*. Vienna, 1997, pp. 263-68.

Kapuścik, J. and W.J. Podgórski. "Les faits d'armes dans la littérature polonaise." In: *Histoire militaire de la Pologne: Problèmes choises*. Ed. W. Bieganski, P. Stawecki, and W. Janusz. Warsaw: Institut d'Histoire, 1970.

Kirpičnikov, Anatolij N. "Die feldschlacht in Altrussland (IX-XIII Jh.)," *Gladius* 9 (1970), 31-51.

Kirpičnikov, Anatolij N. "Nevskaia bitva 1240 goda i ee takičcskie osobennosti," *Fasciculi archaeologicae historicae* 7 (1994), 31-36.

Kirpičnikov, Anatolij N. "Russisk-Skandinaviske forbindelser i IX-XI århundrede illustreret ved våbenfund," *Kuml* (1969), 165-89.

Kirpičnikov, Anatolij N. *Voennoe delo na Rusi v XIII-XV vv.* Leningrad, 1976.

Klein, B., A. Ruttkay, and R. Marsina. *Vojenské dejiny Slovenska: Stručny náčrt do roku 1526*. Bratisalava: RESS s.r.o. Senica, 1994.

Lattimore, O. "The Nomads and South Russia." In: *Byzantine Black Sea*. Birmingham University Symposium, 18-20 March, 1978. Athens, 1978, pp. 193-200.

Lock, Peter W. *The Franks in the Aegean*. London: Longman, 1995.

Martin, J. "Russian Expansion in the Far North, X to mid-XVI Century." In: *Russian Colonial Expansion to 1917*. Ed. M. Rywkin. London, 1988.

Meyendorff, J. *Byzantine and the Rise of Russia*. Cambridge, 1981.

Miller, W. *The Latins in the Levant: A History of Frankish Greece (1204-1566)*. London, 1988.

Miskiewicz, Benon. "Les combats pour la défense des frontières sur l'Odra et la Nysa Lusacienne aux Xe et XIe siècles," *Revue internationale d'histoire militaire* 28 (1969), 403-16.

Nadolski, Andrzej, et al. *Uzbrojenie w Polsce Średniowiecznej, 1350-1450*. Lodz: Polska Akademia Nauk. Instytut Historii Kultury Materialnej, 1990.

Nikžentaitis, Alvydas. "Changes in the Organization and Tactics of the Lithuanian Army in the 13th, 14th, and the First Half of the 15th Century," *Fasciculi archaeologicae historicae* 7 (1994), 45-53.

Noonan, T.S. "Medieval Russia, the Mongols, and the West: Novgorod's Relations with the Baltic, 1100-1350," *Mediaeval Studies* 37 (1975), 316-39.

Olteanu, Stefan. "The Evolution of the Process of Political-Military Organization in the Carpatho-Danubian-Pontic Area in the 4th-13th Centuries," *Revue internationale d'histoire militaire* 66 (1987), 97-106.

Olteanu, Stefan. "Genèse et développement de l'armée permanente chez les Roumains," *Revue internationale d'histoire militaire* 48 (1980), 75-83.

Olteanu, Stefan. "L'organisation de l'armée dans les pays Roumains." In: *Pages de l'histoire de l'armée Roumaine*. Ed. Al. Gh. Savu. Bucharest, 1976, pp. 53-59.

Ostrowski, Donald. *Muscovy and the Mongols: Cross-Cultural Influences on the Steppe Frontier, 1304-1589.* Cambridge: Cambridge University Press, 1998.

Papacostea, Serban. *Românii în secolul XIII-lea, între Cruciada si Imperiul mongol.* Bucharest: Editura Enciclopedica, 1993.

Papacostea, Serban. "Vlad l'Empaleur, prince de la Valachie (1456-1462): Réalité et mythe," *Revue internationale d'histoire militaire* 36 (1977), 202-10.

Paszkiewicz, H. *The Origins of Russia.* London, 1954.

Petrow, P. "1300 Jahre Bulgatien," *Revue internationale d'histoire militaire* 60 (1984), 7-21.

Plewczyński, Marek. "Söldnertruppen in Polen um die Wende des 15. Und 16. Jahrhunderts." In: *XXII. Kongreß der Internationalen Kommission für Militärgeschichte Acta 22: Von Crécy bis Mohács Kriegswesen im späten Mittelalter (1346-1526).* Vienna, 1997, pp. 345-63.

Praga, G. "L'organizzazione militare della Dalmazia nel quattrocentro," *Archivio storico per la Dalmazia* 119 (1936), 463-77.

Pritsak, O. "The Polovcians and Rus," *Archivum Eurasiae medii aevi* 2 (1982), 321-80.

Puś, W. "La chevalerie étrangère au service de la Pologne jusqu'au début du XIVe siècle." In: *Histoire militaire de la Pologne: Problèmes choises.* Ed. W. Bieganski, P. Stawecki, and W. Janusz. Warsaw: Institut d'Histoire, 1970.

Rosetti, R. "Note on Mercenaries: Mercenaries in the Rumanian Army and Rumanian Mercenaries in Foreign Armies," *Revue internationale d'histoire militaire* 5 (1941-45), 34-42.

Seges, Vladimir. "Die Städte in der Slowakei und das Militärwesen an der Wende des Mittelalters." In: *XXII. Kongreß der Internationalen Kommission für Militärgeschichte Acta 22: Von Crécy bis Mohács Kriegswesen im späten Mittelalter (1346-1526).* Vienna, 1997, pp. 238-47.

Shepard, Jonathan. "The Russian Steppe Frontier." In: *Byzantine Black Sea*. Birmingham University Symposium, 18-20 March, 1978. Athens, 1978, pp. 123-33.

Škrivanić, Gavro A. "Bi ka na Tari 1150. godine," *Vesnik* 6-7 (1962), 25-36.

Škrivanić, Gavro A. "Borbe oko Zadra (1105, 1202. i 1345/46. godine)," *Vesnik* 13-14 (1968), 59-80.

Škrivanić, Gavro A. "Rat bosanskog kralja Ostofe sa Dubrovnikom," *Vesnik* 5.2 (1958), 35-60.

Škrivanić, Gavro A. "Ratna veština starih Slovena po svedočanstvu savremenih izvora," *Vesnik* 8-9 (1963), 81-126.

Soulis, G.C. *The Serbs and Byzantium during the Reign of Tsar Stephen Dusan*. Washington, 1984.

Stefanescu, Stefan. "Considerations sur l'histoire militaire Roumaine aux IIIe-XVIe siècles." In: *Pages de l'histoire de l'armée Roumaine*. Ed. Al. Gh. Savu. Bucharest, 1976, pp. 36-52.

Stefanescu, Stefan. "The Draco-Roman Tradition and the 'Barbarian' World," *Revue internationale d'histoire militaire* 48 (1980), 66-74.

Stefanescu, Stefan. "Romanian Countries' Military Effort in their Fight for Independence during the Middle Ages," *Revue internationale d'histoire militaire* 36 (1977), 30-43.

Stoicesu, N. "La levée en masse en Valachie et Moldavie (XIVe-XVIe siècles)." In: *Pages de l'histoire de l'armée Roumaine*. Ed. Al. Gh. Savu. Bucharest, 1976, pp. 60-72.

Tanasoca, N.-S. "Les Mixobarbares et les formations paristriennes du XIe siècle," *Revue Roumaine d'histoire* 12 (1973), 61-82.

Thompson, M.W. *Novgorod the Great*. London, 1967.

Tudor, Gheorghe. "Romanian Medieval Military Thought and Art in the Political and Military Context of Southeast Europe: General Traits and Specific Features," *Revue internationale d'histoire militaire* 66 (1987), 117-26.

Urban, William. "The Organization of Defense of the Livonian Frontier in the Thirteenth Century," *Speculum* 48 (1973), 525-32.

Venedikov, Ivan. *Organisation militaire et administrative de la Bulgarie aux IXe et Xe ss.* Sofia: Presses militaires, 1979.

Vernadsky, G.A. *History of Russia.* II: *Kievan Russia.* New Haven: Yale University Press, 1948.

Vernadsky, G.A. *History of Russia.* III: *The Mongols and Russia.* New Haven: Yale University Press, 1953.

Vernadsky, G.A. *Origins of Russia.* Oxford, 1959.

Wimmer, J. "L'infanterie dans l'armée polonaise aux XVe-XVIIe siècle," In: *Histoire militaire de la Pologne: Problèmes choises.* Ed. W. Bieganski, P. Stawecki, and W. Janusz. Warsaw: Institut d'Histoire, 1970.

Wolff, R.L. "The 'Second Bulgarian Empire': Its Origins and History to 1204," *Speculum* 24 (1949), 167-206.

Woszczyński, B. "Les archives militaires en Pologne." In: *Histoire militaire de la Pologne: Problèmes choises.* Ed. W. Bieganski, P. Stawecki, and W. Janusz. Warsaw: Institut d'Histoire, 1970.

Zachariadou, Elizabeth A. "The Catalans of Athens and the Beginnings of the Turkish Expansion in the Aegean Area," *Studi medievali* 21 (1980), 821-38.

Zakythinos, D.A. *Le despotat grec de Morée: vie et institutions.* London, 1975.

Żygulski, Zdzisław, Jr. "The Winged Hussars of Poland." In: *Arms and Armor Annual: Volume One.* Ed. Robert Held. Northfield: Digest Books, Inc., 1973, pp. 90-103.

Medieval – England

Chew, Helena M. *The English Ecclesiastical Tenants-in-Chief and Knight Service, Especially in the Thirteenth and Fourteenth Centuries.* Oxford: Oxford University Press, 1932.

Connolly, Philomena. "An Account of Military Expenditure in Leinster, 1308," *Analecta hibernica* 30 (1982), 1-5.

Connolly, Philomena. "The Financing of English Expeditions to Ireland, 1361-76." In: *England and Ireland in the Later Middle Ages: Essays in Honour of Jocelyn Otway-Ruthven*. Ed. James F. Lydon. Dublin, 1981, pp. 104-21.

Coss, Peter R. "Knights, Esquires and the Origins of Social Gradation in England," *Transactions of the Royal Historical Society*, 6th ser., 5 (1995), 155-78.

Cuttino, G.P. *English Diplomatic Administration, 1259-1339.* 2nd ed. Oxford: Clarendon Press, 1971.

Cuttino, G.P. *English Medieval Diplomacy*. Bloomington: Indiana University Press, 1985.

Dodds, G.L. *Battles in Britain, 1066-1746*. London: Arms and Armour Press, 1996.

Given, James. *State and Society in Medieval Europe: Gwynedd and Languedoc under Outside Rule*. Ithaca: Cornell University Press, 1990.

Göller, K.H. "War and Peace in the Middle English Romances and Chaucer." In: *War and Peace in the Middle Ages*. Ed. B.P. McGuire. Copenhagen, 1987, 118-45.

Graham, Frank. *Famous Northern Battles*. Rothbury: Butler Publishing, 1988.

Green, J.R. *The Conquest of England*. 3rd ed. 3 vols. London, 1899.

Gwilliam, H.W. "A Thirteenth Century Military Campaign from Worcester," *Worcestershire Archaeology and Local History Newsletter* 34 (1985), 13-14.

Hanawalt, Barbara A. "Violent Death in Fourteenth and Early Fifteenth Century England," *Comparative Studies in Sociology and History* 18 (1976), 297-320.

Harriss, Gerald L. "War and the Emergence of the English Parliament, 1297-1360," *Journal of Medieval History* 2 (1976), 35-56; in: *The Wars of Edward III: Sources and Interpretations*. Ed. Clifford J. Rogers. Wood-bridge: The Boydell Press, 1999, pp. 321-42.

Hollister, C.W. "The Annual Term of Military Service in Medieval England," *Medievalia et humanistica* 13 (1960), 40-47.

Hyams, Paul R. "Feud in Medieval England," *Haskins Society Journal* 3 (1991), 1-21.

Jewell, Helen M. *The North-South Divide: The Origins of Northern Conciousness in England*. Manchester: Manchester University Press, 1994.

Kaeuper, Richard W. *War, Justice, and Public Order: England and France in the Later Middle Ages*. Oxford: Clarendon Press, 1988.

Keen, Maurice H. *England in the Later Middle Ages*. London, 1973.

Keeney, Barnaby C. "Military Service and the Development of Nationalism in England, 1272-1327," *Speculum* 22 (1947), 534-49.

Lloyd, T.H. *England and the German Hanse, 1157-1611: A Study of their Trade and Commercial Diplomacy*. Cambridge: Cambridge University Press, 1991.

Lynch, Andrew. *Malory's Book of Arms: The Narrative of Combat in 'Le Morte Darthur'*. Woodbridge: Boydell and Brewer, 1997.

Morgan, Philip. *War and Society in Medieval Cheshire, 1277-1403*. Manchester: Chetham Society, 1987.

Morris, John E. "Mounted Infantry in Mediaeval Warfare," *Transactions of the Royal Historical Society*, 3rd ser., 8 (1914), 77-102.

Morris, William Alfred. *The Medieval English Sheriff to 1300*. Manchester, 1927.

Morris, William Alfred. "The Office of Sheriff in the Early Norman Period," *English Historical Review* 33 (1918), 145-75.

Norman, A.V.B. and Don Pottinger. *English Weapons and Warfare, 449-1660*. Englewood Hills: Prentice-Hall, Inc., 1979.

Powicke, Michael R. *Military Obligation in Medieval England: A Study in Liberty and Duty*. Oxford: Clarendon Press, 1962.

Prestwich, Michael. *Armies and Warfare in the Middle Ages: The English Experience.* New Haven: Yale University Press, 1996.

Prestwich, Michael. "The English Medieval Army to 1485." In: *The Oxford Illustrated History of the British Army.* Ed. D. Chandler and I. Beckett. Oxford, 1994, pp. 1-24.

Prestwich, Michael. "*Miles in armis strenuus*: The Knight at War," *Transactions of the Royal Historical Society*, 6th ser., 5 (1995), 129-53.

Prestwich, Michael. "Money and Mercenaries in English Medieval Armies." In: *England and Germany in the High Middle Ages.* Ed. Alfred Haverkamp and Hanna Vollrath. London: The German Historical Institute, 1996, pp. 129-50.

Prestwich, Michael. "War and Taxation in England in the XIIIth and XIVth Centuries." In: *Genèse de l'état moderne: Prélèvement et distribution.* Ed. J-Ph. Genet and M. Le Mené. Paris, 1987, pp. 181-92.

Prestwich, Michael. "Was There a Military Revolution in Medieval England?" In: *Recognitions: Essays Presented to Edmund Fryde.* Ed. C. Richmond and I. Harvey. Aberystwyth, 1996, pp. 19-38

Ramsey, J.H. "The Strength of English Armies in the Middle Ages," *English Historical Review* 29 (1914), 221-27.

Rogers, H.C.B. *The Mounted Troops of the British Army, 1066-1945.* London, 1959.

Sandberger, D. *Studien über das Rittertum in England, vornehmlich während des 14. Jahrhunderts.* Berlin, 1937.

Sanders, I.J. *Feudal Military Service in England: A Study of Constitutional and Military Powers of the 'Barones' in Medieval England.* Oxford: Oxford University Press, 1956.

Schlight, John. *Monarchs and Mercenaries: A Reappraisal of the Importance of Knight Service of Norman and Angevin England.* Bridgeport, 1968.

Smail, R.C. "Art of War." In: *Medieval England.* Ed. A.L. Poole. Oxford, 1958.

Suppe, Frederick C. *Military Institutions on the Welsh Marches: Shropshire, 1066-1300.* Woodbridge: The Boydell Press, 1994.

Tait, J. "Knight-Service in Cheshire," *English Historical Review* 57 (1942), 437-59.

Medieval – England – Anglo-Saxon England

Abels, Richard P. *Alfred the Great: War, Kingship and Culture in Anglo-Saxon England*. London: Longman, 1998.

Abels, Richard P. "Bookland and Fyrd Service in Late Saxon England," *Anglo-Norman Studies* 7 (1984), 1-25.

Abels, Richard P. "English Logistics and Military Administration, 871-1066: The Impact of the Viking Wars." In: *Military Aspects of Scandinavian Society in a European Perspective, AD. 1-1300*. Ed. A.N. Jørgensen and B. Clausen. Copenhagen, 1997, pp. 256-65.

Abels, Richard P. "English Tactics, Strategy and Military Organization in the Late Tenth Century." In: *The Battle of Maldon, AD 991*. Ed. D. Scragg. London, 1991, pp. 143-55.

Abels, Richard P. "King Alfred's Peace-Making Strategies with the Vikings," *Haskins Society Journal* 3 (1991), 23-34.

Abels, Richard P. *Lordship and Military Obligation in Anglo-Saxon England*. Los Angeles and Berkeley: University of California Press, 1988.

Abraham, Lenore. "The Devil, the Yew Bow, and the Saxon Archer," *Proceedings of the PMR Conference* 16/17 (1992-93), 1-12.

Alcock, Leslie. "The Organization of Military Expeditions and of Fort Building." In: *Economy, Society and Warfare Among the Britons and Saxons*. Cardiff, 1987, pp. 214-19.

Alcock, Leslie. "Warfare and Poetry among the Northern Britons." In: *Economy, Society and Warfare Among the Britons and Saxons*. Cardiff, 1987, pp. 234-54.

Alcock, Leslie. "The Warfare of Saxons and Britons." In: *Economy, Society and Warfare Among the Britons and Saxons*. Cardiff, 1987, pp. 223-33.

Anderson, Alan O. "Anglo-Scottish Relations from Constantine II to William," *Scottish Historical Review* 42 (1963), 1-20.

Andersson, Theodore M. "The Viking Policy of Ethelred the Unready," *Scandinavian Studies* 59 (1987), 284-95.

Bachrach, Bernard S. and Rutherford Aris. "Military Technology and Garrison Organization: Some Observations on Anglo-Saxon Military Thinking in Light of the Burghal Hidage," *Technology and Culture* 31 (1990), 1-17.

Bell, Alexander. "Notes on Gaimar's Military Vocabulary," *Medium Aevum* 40 (1971), 93-103.

Beresford Ellis, P. *Saxon and Celt: The Struggle for the Supremacy of Britain, AD 410-937*. London, 1993.

Biddle, Martin and Birth Kjølbye-Biddle. "The Repton Stone," *Anglo-Saxon England* 14 (1985), 233-92.

Bliese, John R.E. "Saint Cuthbert and War," *Journal of Medieval History* 24 (1998), 215-41.

Bliese, John R.E. "St. Cuthbert's and St. Neort's Help in War: Visions and Exhortations," *Haskins Society Journal* 7 (1995), 39-62.

Brooks, Nicholas P. "Arms, Status and Warfare in Late-Saxon England." In: *Ethelred the Unready: Papers from the Millenary Conference*. Ed. D. Hill. BAR British Series, 59. Oxford, 1978, pp. 81-103.

Brooks, Nicholas P. "The Development of Military Obligations in Eighth- and Ninth-Century England." In: *England Before the Conquest: Studies in Primary Sources Presented to Dorothy Whitelock*. Ed. P. Clemoes and K. Hughes. Cambridge, 1971, pp. 69-84.

Brooks, Nicholas P. "England in the Ninth Century: The Crucible of Defeat," *Transactions of the Royal Historical Society*, 5th ser., 29 (1979), 1-20.

Brown, Phyllis R. "The Viking Policy of Ethelred: A Response," *Scandinavian Studies* 59 (1987), 296-98.

Bruce-Mitford, Rupert. *The Sutton Hoo Ship-Burial*. 4 vols. London: British Museum, 1975-84.

Campbell, Miles W. "Hypothèses sur les causes de l'ambassade de Harold en Normandie," *Annales Normandie* 27 (1977), 243-65.

Campbell, Miles W. "A Pre-Conquest Norman Occupation of England?" *Speculum* 46 (1971), 21-31.

Campbell, Miles W. "The Rise of an Anglo-Saxon 'Kingmaker': Earl Godwin of Wessex," *Canadian Journal of History* 13 (1978), 17-33.

Cathers, Kerry. "Heirarchy or Anarchy: An Examination of the Leadership Structures Within the Anglo-Saxon Military." In: *The Propagation of Power in the Medieval West: Selected Proceedings of the International Conference, Groningen, 20-23 November 1996*. Ed. M. Gosman, A. Vanderjagt, and J. Veenstra. Groningen, 1997, pp. 97-110.

Cessford, Craig. "Cavalry in Early Bernicia: A Reply," *Northern History* 29 (1993), 185-87.

Christiansen, Eric. "Canute and His World," *History Today* 36 (Oct 1986), 34-39.

Collingwood, W.G. "Arthur's Battles," *Antiquity* 3 (1929).

Cotterill, John. "Saxon Raiding and the Role of the Late Roman Coastal Forts of Britain," *Britannia* 24 (1993), 227-39.

Cross, J.E. "The Ethic of War in Old English." In: *England Before the Conquest: Studies in Primary Sources Presented to Dorothy Whitelock*. Ed. P. Clemoes and K. Hughes. Cambridge, 1971, pp. 269-82.

Cutler, Kenneth E. "The Godwinist Hostages: The Case for 1051," *Annuale medievali* 12 (1971), 70-77.

Dark, K.R. "A Sub-Roman Re-defense of Hadrian's Wall?" *Britannia* 23 (1992), 111-20.

Davidson, Hilda R. Ellis. "The Training of Warriors." In: *Weapons and Warfare in Anglo-Saxon England*. Ed. Sonia Chadwick Hawkes. Oxford, 1989, pp. 11-23.

Davies, John Reuben. "Church, Property and Conflict in Wales, AD 600-1100," *Welsh Historical Review* 18 (1997), 387-406.

Doane, A.N. "Legend, History and Artifice in 'The Battle of Maldon'," *Viator* 9 (1978), 39-66.

Dumville, David N. *Britons and Anglo-Saxons in the Early Middle Ages.* London, 1992.

Dumville, David N. "Ecclesiastical Lands and the Defence of Wessex in the First Viking-Age." In: *Wessex and England from Alfred to Edgar: Six Essays on Political, Cultural, and Ecclesiastical Revival.* Woodbridge, 1992, pp. 29-54.

Evans, Angela Care. *The Sutton Hoo Ship Burial.* London: British Museum, 1986.

Evans, Stephen S. *The Lords of Battle: Image and Relaity of the Comitatus in Dark-Age Britain.* Woodbridge: The Boydell Press, 1997.

Evison, Vera I. *The Fifth-Century Invasions South of the Thames.* London: The Athlone Press, 1965.

Fleming, Robin. "Monastic Lands and England's Defence in the Viking Age," *English Historical Review* 100 (1985), 247-65.

Frank, Roberta. "The Ideal of Men Dying with their Lord in *The Battle of Maldon*: Anachronism or *Nouvelle vague*." In: *People and Places in Northern Europe, 500-1600: Essays in Honour of Peter Hayes Sawyer.* Ed. I. Wood and N. Lund. Woodbridge, 1991, pp. 95-106.

Freeman, Edward August. "On the Life and Death of Earl Godwine," *The Archaeological Journal* 11 (1854), 236-52, 330-44.

Gerchow, Jan. "Prayers for King Cnut: The Liturgical Commemoration of a Conqueror." In: *England in the Eleventh Century: Proceedings of the 1990 Harlaxton Symposium.* Ed. C. Hicks. Stamford, 1992, pp. 219-38.

Gillingham, John. "Thegns and Knights in Eleventh-Century England: Who Was Then the Gentleman?" *Transactions of the Royal Historical Society*, 6th ser., 5 (1995), 129-53.

Godfrey, John. "The Defeated Anglo-Saxons Take Service with the Eastern Emperor," *Proceedings of the Battle Conference on Anglo-Norman Studies* 1 (1978), 63-74.

Grierson, Philip. "The Relations between England and Flanders before the Norman Conquest," *Transactions of the Royal Historical Society* 23 (1941), 71-112.

Hadley, Dawn M. "'And They Proceeded to Plough and to Support Themselves': The Scandinavian Settlement of England," *Anglo-Norman Studies* 19 (1996), 69-96.

Hadley, Dawn M. "Conquest, Colonization and the Church: Ecclesiastical Organization in the Danelaw," *Historical Research* 69 (1996), 109-28.

Halsall, Guy. "Anthropology and the Study of Pre-Conquest Warfare and Society: The Ritual War in Anglo-Saxon England." In: *Weapons and Warfare in Anglo-Saxon England*. Ed. Sonia Chadwick Hawkes. Oxford, 1989, pp. 155-77.

Hare, Kent G. "Apparitions and War in Anglo-Saxon England." In: *The Circle of War in the Middle Ages: Essays on Medieval Military and Naval History*. Ed. Donald J. Kagay and L.J. Andrew Villalon. Woodbridge: The Boydell Press, 1999, pp. 75-86.

Hare, Kent G. "Clerics, War and Weapons in Anglo-Saxon England." In: *The Final Argument: The Imprint of Violence on Society in Medieval and Early Modern Europe*. Ed. Donald J. Kagay and L.J. Andrew Villalon. Woodbridge: The Boydell Press, 1998, pp. 3-12.

Härke, Heinrich. "Early Anglo-Saxon Military Organisation: An Archaeological Perspective." In: *Military Aspects of Scandinavian Society in a European Perspective, AD. 1-1300*. Ed. A.N. Jørgensen and B. Clausen. Copenhagen, 1997, pp. 93-101.

Hawkes, Sonia Chadwick. "Weapons and Warfare in Anglo-Saxon England: An Introduction." In: *Weapons and Warfare in Anglo-Saxon England*. Ed. Sonia Chadwick Hawkes. Oxford, 1989, pp. 1-9.

Hawkes, Sonia Chadwick. "Soldiers and Settlers in Britain, Fourth to Fifth Centuries," *Medieval Archaeology* 5 (1961), 1-70.

Higham, Nicholas J. "Cavalry in Early Bernicia?" *Northern History* 27 (1991), 236-41.

Higham, Nicholas J. *The Death of Anglo-Saxon England*. Stroud: Sutton Publishing, 1997.

Higham, Nicholas J. "King Cearl, the Battle of Chester and the Origins of the Mercian 'Overkingship'," *Midland History* 17 (1992), 1-15.

Higham, Nicholas J. *The Kingdom of Northumbria, AD 350-1100*. Stroud: Sutton Publishing, 1996.

Higham, Nicholas J. "Territorial Organization in Pre-Conquest Cheshire." In: *The Middle Ages in the North-West*. Ed. Tom Scott and Pat Starkey. Liverpool: Leopard's Head Press, 1995, pp. 1-14.

Hill, David and Alexander R. Rumble, ed. *The Defence of Wessex: The Burghal Hidage and Anglo-Saxon Fortifications*. Manchester: Manchester University Press, 1996.

Hines, John. "The Military Context of the *Adventus Saxonum*: Some Continental Evidence." In: *Weapons and Warfare in Anglo-Saxon England*. Ed. Sonia Chadwick Hawkes. Oxford, 1989, pp. 25-47.

Hollister, C. Warren. *Anglo-Saxon Military Institutions on the Eve of the Norman Conquest*. Oxford: Clarendon Press, 1962.

Hollister, C. Warren. "The Five-Hide Unit and the Old English Military Obligation," *Speculum* 36 (1961), 61-74.

Hollister, C. Warren. "Military Obligation in Late-Saxon and Norman England." In: *Ordinamenti militari in occidente nell'alto medioevo*. Settimane di studio del centro italiano di studi sull'alto medioevo, XV. Spoleto, 1968, I:169-86.

Hooper, Jennie. "The 'Rows of the Battle-Swan': The Aftermath of Battle in Anglo-Saxon Art." In: *Armies, Chivalry and Warfare in Medieval Britain and France: Proceedings of the 1995 Harlaxton Symposium*. Ed. M. Strickland. Stamford, 1998, pp. 82-99.

Hooper, Nicholas. "The Aberlemno Stone and Cavalry in Anglo-Saxon England," *Northern History* 29 (1993), 188-96.

Hooper, Nicholas. "Anglo-Saxon Warfare on the Eve of the Conquest: A Brief Survey," *Proceedings of the Battle Conference on Anglo-Norman Studies* 1 (1978), 84-93.

Hooper, Nicholas. "The Anglo-Saxons at War." In: *Weapons and Warfare in Anglo-Saxon England*. Ed. Sonia Chadwick Hawkes. Oxford, 1989, pp.191-202.

Hooper, Nicholas. "The Housecarls in England in the Eleventh Century," *Anglo-Norman Studies* 7 (1984), 161-76; in: *Anglo-Norman Warfare: Studies in Late Anglo-Saxon and Anglo-Norman Military Organization and Warfare*. Ed. M. Strickland. Woodbridge, 1992, pp. 1-16.

Hooper, Nicholas. "Military Developments in the Reign of Cnut." In: *The Reign of Cnut*. Ed. A.R. Rumble. London, 1994, pp. 89-100.

Hudson, Benjamin T. "Cnut and the Scottish Kings," *English Historical Review* 107 (1992), 350-60.

Hudson, Benjamin T. "The Destruction of Gruffudd ap Llywelyn," *Welsh Historical Review* 19 (1991), 331-50.

Hudson, Benjamin T. "The Family of Harold Godwinsson and the Irish Sea Province," *Journal of the Royal Society of Antiquaries of Ireland* 109 (1979), 92-100.

Hughson, Irene. "Pictish Horse Carvings," *Glasgow Archaeological Journal* 17 (1991-92), 53-61.

James, J.W. "Fresh Light on the Death of Gruffudd ap Llywelyn," *Bulletin of the Board of Celtic Studies* 30 (1982-83), 147.

John, Eric. "War and Society in the Tenth Century: The Maldon Campaign," *Transactions of the Royal Historical Society*, 5th ser., 27 (1977), 173-91.

Jones, Michael E. *The End of Roman Britain*. Ithaca: Cornell University Press, 1996.

Jones, Michael E. "The Historicity of the Alleluja Victory," *Albion* 18 (1986), 363-73.

Jones, Michael E. "St. Germanus and the *Adventus Saxonum*," *Haskins Society Journal* 2 (1990), 1-12.

Keynes, Simon. "The Æthelings in Normandy," *Anglo-Norman Studies* 13 (1990), 173-205.

Keynes, Simon. "Cnut's Earls." In *The Reign of Cnut: King of England, Denmark and Norway*. Ed. A.R. Ramble. London, 1994, 43-88.

Keynes, Simon. "The Historical Context of the Battle of Maldon." In: *The Battle of Maldon, AD 991*. Ed. D. Scragg. London, 1991, pp. 81-113.

Kiff, Jennie. "Images of War: Illustrations of Warfare in Early Eleventh-Century England," *Anglo-Norman Studies* 7 (1984), 177-94.

Klausner, David N. "Aspects of Time in the Battle Poetry of Early Britain." In: *The Middle Ages in the North-West*. Ed. Tom Scott and Pat Starkey. Liverpool: Leopard's Head Press, 1995, pp. 85-108.

Kleinschmidt, Harald. "The Old English Annal for 757 and West Saxon Dynastic Strife," *Journal of Medieval History* 22 (1996), 209-24.

Larson, L.M. *The King's Household in England before the Norman Conquest*. Madison, 1904.

Lewis, C.P. "The French in England before the Norman Conquest," *Anglo-Norman Studies* 17 (1994), 123-44.

Linklater, Eric. *The Conquest of England: From the Viking Incursions of the Eighth Century to the Norman Victory at the Battle of Hastings*. New York: Dell Publishing Co., Inc., 1966.

Loyn, Harold R. *Harold, Son of Godwin*. Hastings: The Hastings and Bexhill Branch of the Historical Association, 1966.

Loyn, Henry R. *The Vikings in Britain*. Oxford: Blackwell Publishers, 1994.

Lund, Niels. "The Armies of Swein Forkbeard and Cnut: *Leding* or *Lið*?" *Anglo-Saxon England* 15 (1986), 105-18.

Lund, Niels. *De Danske vikinger i England*. Copenhagen, 1967.

Lund, Niels. *De Hærger og de brænder: Danmark og England i vikingtiden*. Copenhagen, 1993.

Mack, Katherine. "Changing Thegns: Cnut's Conquest and the English Aristocracy," *Albion* 16 (1984), 375-87.

Manley, John. "The Archer and the Army in the Late Saxon Period," *Anglo-Saxon Studies in Archaeology and History* 4 (1985), 223-35.

Maund, K.L. "Cynan ab Iago and the Killing of Gruffudd ap Llywelyn," *Cambridge Medieval Celtic Studies* 10 (1985), 57-65.

Maund, K.L. *Ireland, Wales, and England in the Eleventh Century.* Woodbridge: Boydell and Brewer, 1991.

Maund, K.L. "The Welsh Alliances of Earl Ælfgar of Mercia and his Family in the Mid-Eleventh Century," *Anglo-Norman Studies* 9 (1988), 181-90.

Metcalf, D.M. "Large Danegelds in Relation to War and Kingship: Their Implications for Monetary History, and Some Numismatic Evidence." In: *Weapons and Warfare in Anglo-Saxon England.* Ed. Sonia Chadwick Hawkes. Oxford, 1989, pp. 179-90.

Morris, J. *The Age of Arthur.* London, 1977.

Nicolle, David C. *Arthur and the Anglo-Saxon Wars.* London: Osprey, 1984.

Oda, Takuji. "Alfred '*the Really* Great'–What Happened at the Battle of Ashdown." In: *Essays in Honour of Shinsuke Ando and Haruo Iwasaki.* Ed. Keiko Kawachi and Takami Matsuda. Tokyo, 1997, pp. 10-26.

Owen-Crocker, Gale R. "Hawks and Horse-Trappings: The Insignia of Rank." In: *The Battle of Maldon, AD 991.* Ed. D. Scragg. London, 1991, pp. 220-37.

Peddie, John. *Alfred: Warrior King.* Stroud: Sutton Publishing Limited, 1999.

Pollington, Steven. "'Heart Shall be Keaner': The Argument of Courage at Maldon." In: *Maldon, 991-1991: Reflections on a Battle.* London, 1993.

Prestwich, J.O. "King Æthelhere and the Battle of the Winwaed," *English Historical Review* 83 (1968), 89-95.

Raraty, David G.J. "Earl Godwine of Wessex: The Origins of his Power and his Political Loyalties," *History* 74 (1989), 3-19.

Richards, Julian D. *English Heritage Book of Viking Age England.* London: BCA, 1991.

Ritchie, R.L. Graeme. *The Normans in England before Edward the Confessor*. London, 1948.

Rodger, N.A.M. "Cnut's Geld and the Size of Danish Ships," *English Historical Review* 110 (1995), 392-403.

Rowland, Jenny. "Warfare and Horses in the *Gododdin* and the Problem of Catraeth," *Cambrian Medieval Celtic Studies* 30 (1995), 13-40.

Russell, J.C. "Arthur and the Romano-Celtic Frontier," *Modern Philology* 48 (1950-51).

Sawyer, Peter. "Swein Forkbeard and the Historians." In: *Church and Chronicle in the Middle Ages: Essays Presented to John Taylor*. Ed. I. Wood and G.A. Loud. London, pp. 27-39.

Scragg, Donald. *"The Battle of Maldon."* In: *The Battle of Maldon, AD 991*. Ed. D. Scragg. London, 1991, pp. 15-36.

Searle, Eleanor. "Emma the Conqueror." In: *Studies in Medieval History Presented to R. Allen Brown*. Ed. C. Harper-Bill et al. Woodbridge, 1989, pp. 281-88.

Shadrake, Dan and Susanna Shadrake. *Barbarian Warriors: Saxons, Vikings and Normans*. Brassey's History of Uniforms. London, 1997.

Sleeswyk, André W. "The Ship of Harold Godwinson," *Mariner's Mirror* 61 (1981), 87-91.

Smith, Mary Frances. "Archbishop Stigand and the Eye of the Needle," *Anglo-Norman Studies* 16 (1993), 199-219.

Stafford, Pauline. *Unification and Conquest: A Political and Social History of England in the Tenth and Eleventh Centuries*. London: Edward Arnold, 1989.

Strickland, Matthew. "Military Technology and Conquest: The Anomaly of Anglo-Saxon England," *Anglo-Norman Studies* 19 (1996), 353-82.

Suppe, Frederick C. "Who was Rhys Sais? Some Comments on Anglo-Welsh Relations before 1066," *Haskins Society Journal* 7 (1995), 63-73.

Taylor, Pamela. "The Endowment and Military Obligations of the See of London: A Reassessment of Three Sources," *Anglo-Norman Studies* 14 (1991), 287-312.

Underwood, Richard. *Anglo-Saxon Weapons and Warfare*. Stroud: Tempus Publishing Limited, 1999.

Walker, David. "A Note on Gruffydd ap Llywelyn (1039-63)," *Welsh Historical Review* 1 (1960-63), 83-94.

Walker, Ian W. *Harold: The Last Anglo-Saxon King*. Stroud: Sutton Publishing, 1997.

Walker, Simon. "A Context for 'Brunanburh'? In: *Warriors and Churchmen in the High Middle Ages: Essays Presented to Karl Leyser*. Ed. T. Reuter. London, 1992. pp. 21-39.

Walton, Steven. "Words of Technological Virtue: *The Battle of Brunanburh* and Anglo-Saxon Sword Manufacture," *Technology and Culture* 36 (1995), 987-999.

Whitelock, Dorothy. "The Dealings of the Kings of England with Northumbria in the Tenth and Eleventh Centuries." In: *The Anglo-Saxons: Studies in Some Aspects of their History and Culture Presented to Bruce Dickins*. Ed. P. Clemoes. London, 1959, pp. 70-88.

Wilkinson, Bertie. "Freeman and the Crisis of 1051," *Bulletin of the John Rylands Library* 22 (1938), 3-22.

Wilkinson, Bertie. "Northumbrian Separatism in 1065 and 1066," *Bulletin of the John Rylands Library* 23 (1939), 504-26.

Williams, Ann. "Britain, AD 1000," *History Today* 50.3 (Mar 2000), 35-41.

Williams, Ann. "The King's Nephew: The Family and Career of Ralph, Earl of Hereford." In: *Studies in Medieval History Presented to R. Allen Brown*. Ed. C.Harper-Bill, C.J. Hodlsworth, and J. Nelson. Woodbridge, 1989, pp. 327-43.

Williams, Ann. "Some Notes and Considerations on Problems Connected with the English Royal Succession, 860-1066," *Proceedings of the Battle Conference* 1 (1978), 144-66, 225-33.

Wise, Terence. *Saxon, Viking and Norman Armies*. London: Osprey, 1979.

Woolf, Alex. "Erik Bloodaxe Revisited," *Northern History* 34 (1998), 189-93.

Woolf, R. "The Ideal of Men Dying with their Lords in the 'Germania' and the 'Battle of Maldon'," *Anglo-Saxon England* 5 (1976), 69-81.

Medieval – England – Anglo-Saxon – 1066

Andersen, Per Sveaas. "Harald Hardråde, Danmark og England." In: *Harald Hardråde*. Ed. A. Berg. Oslo, 1966, pp. 95-126.

Ashdown, Margaret. "An Icelandic Account of the Survival of Harold Godwinson." In: *The Anglo-Saxons: Studies in Some Aspects of their History and Culture Presented to Bruce Dickins*. Ed. P. Clemoes. London, 1959, pp. 122-36.

Bachrach, Bernard S. "The Feigned Retreat at Hastings," *Mediaeval Studies* 33 (1971), 344-47.

Bachrach, Bernard S. "On the Origins of William the Conqueror's Horse Transports," *Technology and Culture* 26 (1985), 505-31.

Bachrach, Bernard S. "Some Observations on the Military Administration of the Norman Conquest," *Anglo-Norman Studies* 8 (1985), 1-26.

Barclay, C.N. *Battle 1066*. New York: J.M. Dent and Sons Ltd, 1966.

Barlow, Frank. "The *Carmen de Hastingae proelio*." In: *The Norman Conquest and Beyond*. London, 1983, pp. 189-222.

Barlow, Frank. *Edward the Confessor*. Berkeley and Los Angeles: University of California Press, 1970.

Barlow, Frank. "Edward the Confessor and the Norman Conquest." In: *The Norman Conquest and Beyond*. London, 1983, pp. 99-111.

Barlow, Frank. *The Feudal Kingdom of England, 1042-1216*. London, 1961.

Barlow, Frank. "William I and the Norman Conquest." In: *The Norman Conquest and Beyond*. London, 1983, pp. 129-42.

Barlow, Frank. *William I and the Norman Conquest*. New York: Collier Books, 1965.

Barraclough, E.M.C. "The Flags of the Bayeux Tapestry," *Armi antiche* (1969), 117-24.

Bates, David R. "The Character and Career of Odo, Bishop of Bayeux (1049/50-1097)," *Speculum* 50 (1975), 1-20.

Beech, George T. "The Participation of Aquitanians in the Conquest of England, 1066-1100," *Anglo-Norman Studies* 9 (1986), 1-24.

Bennett, Matthew. "Exploding the Myths of Hastings," *Military Illustrated* (Sept 1996), 25-29.

Bennett, Matthew. "Poetry as History? The 'Roman de Rou' of Wace as a Source for the Norman Conquest," *Anglo-Norman Studies* 5 (1982), 21-39.

Berg, Arno, ed. *Harald Hardråde*. Oslo: Dreyer, 1966.

Bernstein, David. "The Blinding of Harold and the Meaning of the Bayeux Tapestry," *Anglo-Norman Studies* 5 (1982), 40-64.

Berry, Roger. "The Funding of the Norman Conquest and Some Financial Indicators," *Review of the Guernsey Society* 51.1 (1995), 6-11.

Bradbury, Jim. *The Battle of Hastings*. Stroud: Sutton Publishing, 1998.

Bridgeford, Andrew. "Was Count Eustace II of Boulogne the Patron of the Bayeux Tapestry?" *Journal of Medieval History* 25 (1999), 155-85.

Brooks, Nicholas P. and H.E. Walker. "The Authority and Interpretation of the Bayeux Tapestry," *Proceedings of the Battle Conference* 1 (1978), 1-34.

Broüard, Michel de. "Note sur l'appelation 'Guillaume le Conquérant,'" In: *Studies in Medieval History Presented to R. Allen Brown*. Ed. C. Harper-Bill et al. Woodbridge, 1989, pp. 21-26.

Brown, R. Allen. "The Battle of Hastings," *Proceedings of the Battle Conference on Anglo-Norman Studies* 3 (1980), 1-21; In: *Castles, Conquest and Charters: Collected Papers*. Woodbridge, 1989, pp. 264-89; in: *Anglo-Norman Warfare: Studies in Late Anglo-Saxon and Anglo-Norman*

Military Organization and Warfare. Ed. M. Strickland. Woodbridge, 1992, pp. 161-81.

Brown, R. Allen. "Guillaume le Conquérant et son temps." In: *Castles, Conquest and Charters: Collected Papers*. Woodbridge, 1989, pp. 305-15.

Brown, R. Allen. "The Norman Conquest." In: *Castles, Conquest and Charters: Collected Papers*. Woodbridge, 1989, pp. 242-63.

Brown, R. Allen. *The Normans and the Norman Conquest*. 2nd ed. Woodbridge: The Boydell Press, 1985.

Brown, R. Allen. *William the Conqueror and the Battle of Hastings*. London: Pitkin Pictorials, 1982.

Brown, Shirley Ann. "The Bayeux Tapestry: History or Propaganda?" In: *The Anglo-Saxons: Synthesis and Achievement*. Ed. J.D. Woods and D.A.E. Pelteret. Waterloo, 1985, pp. 11-25, 153-54.

Brown, Shirley Ann. "The Bayeux Tapestry: Why Eustace, Odo and William?" *Anglo-Norman Studies* 12 (1989), 7-28.

Brown, Shirley Ann and Michael W. Herren. "The *Adelae comitissae* of Baudri of Bourgeuil and the Bayeux Tapestry" *Anglo-Norman Studies* 16 (1993), 55-73.

Butler, Denis. *1066: The Story of a Year*. London, 1966.

Campbell, Miles W. "An Inquiry into the Troop Strength of King Harald Hardrada's Invasion Fleet of 1066," *American Neptune* 44 (1984), 96-102.

Campbell, Miles W. "Last Viking's Impact: King Harald of Norway Struck England Just before the Norman Conquest," *Military History* 4 (June 1988), 12-17, 66.

Campbell, Miles W. "Note sur les déplacements de Tostig Godwinson en 1066," *Annales de Normandie* 22 (1972), 3-9.

Carter, John Marshall. "The Feigned Flight at Hastings: Birth, Propagation, and the Death of a Myth," *San Jose Studies* (Feb 1978), 95-106.

Carter, John Marshall. "Une réévaluation des interprétations de la fuite simulée d'Hastings," *Annales de Normandie* 45 (1995), 27-34.

Champion, L.G.M. *Les chevaux et les cavaliers de la tapisserie de Bayeux.* Caen, 1907.

Chibnall, Marjorie. *The Debate on the Norman Conquest.* Issues in Historiography. Manchester: Manchester University Press, 1999.

Cholokian, Rouben C. "The Bayeux Tapestry: Is There More to Say?" *Annales de Normandie* 47 (1997), 43-50.

Cigaar, Krijnie and W.J. Aerts. "Byzantine Marginalia to the Norman Conquest," *Anglo-Norman Studies* 9 (1986), 43-70.

Cohen, Marc. "From Throndheim to Waltham to Chester: Viking- and Post-Viking-Age Attitudes in the Survival Legends of Óláfr Tryggvason and Harold Godwinson." In: *The Middle Ages in the North-West.* Ed. Tom Scott and Pat Starkey. Liverpool: Leopard's Head Press, 1995, pp. 143-54.

Cowdrey, H.E.J. "Bishop Ermenfried of Sion and the Penitential Ordinance following the Battle of Hastings," *Journal of Ecclesiastical History* 20 (1969), 225-42.

Cowdrey, H.E.J. "Towards and Interpretation of Bayeux Tapestry," *Anglo-Norman Studies* 10 (1987), 49-65.

Davis, R.H.C. "The *Carmen de hastingae Proelio.*" In: *English Historical Review* 93 (1978), 231-61; in: *From Alfred the Great to Stephen.* London, 1991, pp. 79-100.

Davis, R.H.C. "William of Poitiers and His History of William the Conqueror." in *The Writing of History in the Middle Ages: Essays Presented to Richard William Southern.* Ed. R.H.C. Davis and J.M. Wallace-Hadrill. Oxford, 1981, pp. 71-100.

Deuve, Jean. "Les opérations secrètes des Normands au temps de Guillaume le Conquérant," *Revue de la Manche* 34 (1992), 7-18.

DeVries, Kelly. "The Conflict between Harold and Tostig Godwinson," *Scintilla* 1 (1984), 48-62.

DeVries, Kelly. *The Norwegian Invasion of England in 1066.* Woodbridge: The Boydell Press, 1999.

Dickins, B. "The Late Addition to ASC 1066," *Proceedings of the Leeds Philosophical and Literary Society* 5 (1940), 148-49.

Dolley, M. *The Norman Conquest and the English Coinage*. London, 1966.

Douglas, David C. *The Norman Achievement, 1050-1100*. Berkeley and Los Angeles: University of California Press, 1969.

Douglas, David C. *William the Conqueror*. Berkeley and Los Angeles: University of California Press, 1964.

Dunbabin, Jean. "Geoffrey of Chaumont, Thibaud of Blois and William the Conqueror," *Anglo-Norman Studies* 16 (1993), 101-16.

Farrant, John H. "John Collingwood Bruce and the Bayeux Tapestry," *Archaeologia aeliana* 5th ser., 25 (1997), 109-13.

Faucon, Régis. *Sur les pas de Guillaume le Conquérant*. Paris: Les Nouvelles Editions Latines, 1997.

Fernie, Eric. "The Effect of the Conquest on Norman Architectural Patronage," *Anglo-Norman Studies* 9 (1986), 71-86.

Finn, R. *The Norman Conquest and Its Effects on the Economy, 1066-86*. London, 1971.

Fleming, Robin. *Kings and Lords in Conquest England*. Cambridge: Cambridge University Press, 1991.

Fowler, G.H. "The Devastation of Bedfordshire and the Neighboring Counties in 1065 and 1066," *Archaeologia* 72 (1922), 41-50.

Freeman, Edward August. *The History of the Norman Conquest of England: Its Causes and Results*. 2nd ed. 5 vols. Oxford: Clarendon Press, 1869-75.

Freeman, Edward August. *William the Conqueror*. London: Macmillan and Co. Limited, 1913.

Fry, Plantagenet Somerset. *The Battle of Hastings 1066 and the Story of Battle Abbey*. 1990; London: English Heritage, 1994.

Gade, Kari Ellen. "Einarr Þambarskelfir's Last Shot," *Scandinavian Studies* 67 (1995), 153-62.

Galbraith, V.H. "1066 and All That," *Transactions of the Leicestershire Archaeological and Historical Society* (1967), 1-7.

Garnett, George. "*Franci et Angli*: the Legal Distinctions Between Peoples After the Conquest," *Anglo-Norman Studies* 8 (1985), 109-37.

Gelsinger, Bruce E. "The Battle of Stamford Bridge and the Battle of Jaffa: A Case of Confused Identity?" *Scandinavian Studies* 60 (1988), 13-29.

George, Robert H. "The Contribution of Flanders to the Conquest of England, 1065-1086," *Revue Belge de philologie et d'histoire* 5 (1926), 81-99.

Gibbs-Smith, Charles H. *The Bayeux Tapestry*. London: Phaidon, 1973.

Gibbs-Smith, Charles H. "What the Bayeux Tapestry Does Not Show," *Journal of the Society of Archer-Antiquaries* 8 (1965), 23-25.

Gillingham, John. "William the Bastard at War." In: *Studies in Medieval History Presented to R. Allen Brown*. Ed. C. Harper-Bill et al. Woodbridge, 1989, pp. 141-58; in: *Anglo-Norman Warfare: Studies in Late Anglo-Saxon and Anglo-Norman Military Organization and Warfare*. Ed. M. Strickland. Woodbridge, 1992, pp. 143-60.

Glover, Richard. "English Warfare in 1066," *English Historical Review* 67 (1952), 1-18.

Golding, Brian. *Conquest and Colonisation: The Normans in Britain, 1066-1100*. London: Macmillan, 1994.

Gransden, Antonia. "1066 and All That Revisited," *History Today* 38 (Sept 1988), 47-52.

Gravett, Christopher. *Hastings, 1066: The Fall of Saxon England*. London: Osprey, 1992.

Gravett, Christopher. *Norman Knight, 950-1204 AD*. London: Osprey, 1993.

Hayward, Paul Antony. "Translation-Narratives in Post-Conquest Hagiography and English Resistance to the Norman Conquest," *Anglo-Norman Studies* 21 (1998), 67-93.

Henry, Gilles. *Guillaume le Conquérant*. Paris: France-Empire, 1996.

Higham, Nicholas J. *The Norman Conquest*. Stroud: Sutton Publishing, 1998.

210   MEDIEVAL – ENGLAND

Hinz, Hermann. "Zu zwei Darstellungen auf dem Teppich von Bayeux," *Château Gaillard* 6 (1973), 107-19.

Hollister, C. Warren. "The Norman Conquest and the Genesis of English Feudalism," *American Historical Review* 66 (1961), 641-63.

Hollister, C. Warren, ed. *The Impact of the Norman Conquest*. New York: John Wiley and Sons, Inc., 1969.

Howarth, David. *1066: The Year of Conquest*. New York: The Viking Press, 1977.

Hughes, Shaun F.D. "The Battle of Stamford Bridge and the Battle of Bouvines," *Scandinavian Studies* 60 (1988), 30-76.

Jessee, W. Scott. "The Angevin Civil War and the Norman Conquest of 1066," *Haskins Society Journal* 3 (1991), 101-09.

John, Eric. "Edward the Confessor and the Norman Succession," *English Historical Review* 94 (1979), 241-67.

Kapelle, William E. *The Norman Conquest of the North: The Region and Its Transformation, 1000-1135*. Chapel Hill: University of North Carolina Press, 1979.

Keats-Rohan, K.S.B. "William I and the Breton Contingent in the Non-Norman Conquest 1060-1087," *Anglo-Norman Studies* 13 (1990), 157-72.

Körner, Sten. *The Battle of Hastings, England, and Europe, 1035-1066*. Lund, 1964.

Lemmon, Charles H. "The Campaign of 1066." In: *The Norman Conquest, Its Setting and Impact*. New York: Charles Scribner's Sons, 1966.

Lemmon, Charles H. *The Field of Hastings*. St. Leonards-on-Sea: Budd and Gillat, 1956.

Linklater, Eric. *The Conquest of England: From the Viking Incursions of the Eighth Century to the Norman Victory at the Battle of Hastings*. New York: Dell Publishing Co., Inc., 1966.

Loyn, Henry R. *Anglo-Saxon England and the Norman Conquest*. 2nd ed. London: Longman, 1991.

Loyn, Henry R. *Harold, Son of Godwin*. Hastings: The Hastings and Bexhill Branch of the Historical Association, 1966.

Madou, M.J.H. "'La telle du conquest' en de slag bij Hastings." In: *Oorlog in de middeleeuwen*. Ed. A.J. Brand. Hilversum, 1989, pp. 29-50.

Matthew, D.J.A. "The Effect of the Conquest on England," *History Today* 16 (1966), 678-87.

Matthew, D.J.A. *The Norman Conquest*. London, 1966.

McGuffie, T.H. "October 14th 1066," *History Today* 16 (1966), 670-77.

McLynn, Frank. *1065: The Year of the Three Battles*. London, 1998.

Morillo, Stephen. "Hastings: An Unusual Battle," *Haskins Society Journal* 2 (1990), 96-103.

Morillo, Stephen, ed. *The Battle of Hastings: Sources and Interpretations*. Woodbridge: The Boydell Press, 1996.

Morton, Catherine. "Pope Alexander II and the Norman Conquest," *Latomus* 34 (1995), 362-82.

Nicolle, David C. *Normans*. London: Osprey, 1987.

Oleson, T.J. "Edward the Confessor's Promise of the Throne to Duke William of Normandy," *English Historical Review* 72 (1957), 221-28.

Otter, Monika. "1066: The Moment of Transition in Two Narratives of the Norman Conquest," *Speculum* 74 (1999), 565-86.

Palmer, J.J.N. "The Conqueror's Footprints in Domesday Book." In: *The Medieval Military Revolution: State, Society and Military Change in Medieval and Early Modern Europe*. Ed. A. Ayton and J.L. Price. London, 1995, pp. 23-44.

Reader, Rebecca. "Matthew Paris and the Norman Conquest." In: *The Cloister and the World*. Ed. John Blair and Brian Golding. Oxford, 1996, pp. 118-47.

Renn, Derek F. "Burhgeat and Gonfanon: Two Sidelights from The Bayeux Tapestry," *Anglo-Norman Studies* 16 (1993), 177-98.

Round, J.H. "Military Tenure before the Conquest," *English Historical Review* 12 (1897), 492-94.

Rowe, Elizabeth Ashman. "Historical Invasions/Historiographical Interventions: Snorri Sturluson and the Battle of Stamford Bridge," *Mediaevalia* 17 (1994), 149-76.

Rud, Mogens. *La Tapisserie de Bayeux et la bataille d'Hastings*. Trans. Éric Eydoux. Copenhagen: Christian Ejlers, 1994.

Russell, Josiah Cox. "Demographic Aspects of the Norman Conquest." In: *Medieval Demography: Essays by Josiah C. Russell*. New York, 1987, pp. 125-47.

Schofield, Guy. "The Third Battle of 1066," *History Today* 16 (1966), 688-93.

Searle, Eleanor. "The Abbey of the Conquerors: Defensive Enfeoffment and Economic Development in Anglo-Norman England," *Proceedings of the Battle Conference* 2 (1979), 154-98.

Spear, David S. "Recent Scholarship on the Bayeux Tapestry," *Annales de Normandie* 42 (1992), 221-26.

Stafford, Pauline. "Women and the Norman Conquest," *Transactions of the Royal Historical Society*, 6th ser., 4 (1994), 221-49.

Stenton, Frank M. *William the Conqueror and the Rule of the Normans*. London, 1928.

Strickland, Matthew. "Military Technology and Conquest: The Anomaly of Anglo-Saxon England," *Anglo-Norman Studies* 19 (1996), 353-82.

Swanton, Michael. "The Bayeux Tapestry: Epic Narrative, Not Stichic But Stitched." In: *The Formation of Culture in Medieval Britain: Celtic, Latin and Norman Influences on English Music, Literature, History and Art*. Ed. Françoise H.M. Le Saux. Lampeter, 1995, pp. 149-69.

Taylor, Arnold J. "'BELREM,'" *Anglo-Norman Studies* 14 (1991), 1-23.

Tetlow, Edwin. *Hastings*. New York: Barnes and Noble Books, 1992.

Thacker, Alan. "The Cult of King Harold at Chester." In: *The Middle Ages in the North-West*. Ed. Tom Scott and Pat Starkey. Liverpool: Leopard's Head Press, 1995, pp. 155-76.

Thomas, Hugh M. "The *Gesta Herwardi*, the English, and their Conquerors," *Anglo-Norman Studies* 21 (1998), 213-32.

Thompson, A.I. "The Battle of Stamford Bridge, 1066," *British Army Review* 97 (Apr 1991), 49-52.

Tucker, William E. "Archers at Hastings," *Journal of the Society of Archer-Antiquaries* 8 (1965), 26-32.

Tucker, William E. "The Bayeux Tapestry," *Journal of the Society of Archer-Antiquaries* 8 (1965), 25-26.

Turville-Petre, Gabriel. *Haraldr the Hardruler and His Poets*. Dorothea Coke Memorial Lecture in Northern Studies. London, 1966.

van Houts, Elisabeth M.C. "Hereward and Flanders," *Anglo-Saxon England* 28 (1999), 201-23

van Houts, Elisabeth M.C. "Latin Poetry and the Anglo-Norman Court, 1066-1135: The *Carmen de Hastingae proelio*," *Journal of Medieval History* 15 (1989), 39-62.

van Houts, Elisabeth M.C. "The Memory of 1066 in Written and Oral Traditions," *Anglo-Norman Studies* 19 (1996), 167-79.

van Houts, Elisabeth M.C. "The Trauma of 1066," *History Today* 46.10 (Oct 1996), 9-15.

Walker, Ian W. *Harold: The Last Anglo-Saxon King*. Stroud: Sutton Publishing, 1997.

West, Francis James. "The Colonial History of the Norman Conquest?" *History* 84 (1999), 219-36.

Wheeler, Edd. "The Battle of Hastings: Math, Myth and Melee," *Military Affairs* 52 (1988), 128-34.

Whitelock, Dorothy, David C. Douglas, Charles H. Lemmon, and Frank Barlow. *The Norman Conquest: Its Setting and Impact*. London: Eyre and Spottiswoode, 1966.

Wilkinson, Bertie. "Northumbrian Separatism in 1065 and 1066," *Bulletin of the John Rylands Library* 23 (1939), 504-26.

Williams, Ann. *The English and the Norman Conquest*. Woodbridge: The Boydell Press, 1995.

Williams, Ann. "Land and Power in the Eleventh-Century: The Estates of Harold Godwinson," *Proceedings of the Battle Conference on Anglo-Norman Studies* 3 (1980), 171-87.

Williams, Ann. "Some Notes and Considerations on Problems Connected with the English Royal Succession, 860-1066," *Proceedings of the Battle Conference* 1 (1978), 144-66.

Wise, Terence. *Saxon, Viking and Norman Armies*. London: Osprey, 1979.

Yorke, Barbara. "The Most Perfect Man in History?" *History Today* 49.10 (Oct 1999), 8-14.

Medieval – England – Anglo-Norman

Abels, Richard P. "Sheriffs, Lord-Seeking and the Norman Settlement of the South-East Midlands," *Anglo-Norman Studies* 19 (1996), 19-50.

Alexander, J.J.G. "Ideological Representation of Military Combat in Anglo-Norman Art," *Anglo-Norman Studies* 15 (1993), 1-24.

Barlow, Frank. "The Effects of the Norman Conquest." In: *The Norman Conquest and Beyond*. London, 1983, pp. 151-87.

Barlow, Frank. *The Feudal Kingdom of England, 1042-1216*. London, 1961.

Barlow, Frank. *William Rufus*. Berkeley and Los Angeles: University of California Press, 1983.

Bartlett, Robert J. *England Under the Norman and Angevin Kings, 1075-1225*. The New Oxford History of England. Oxford: Clarendon Press, 2000.

Bates, David R. "The Character and Career of Odo, Bishop of Bayeux (1049/50-1097)," *Speculum* 50 (1975), 1-20.

Bearman, Robert. "Baldwin de Redvers: Some Aspects of a Baronial Career in the Reign of King Stephen," *Anglo-Norman Studies* 18 (1995), 19-46.

Beeler, John H. "XIIth Century Guerilla Campaign," *Military Review* 42 (1962), 39-46.

Beeler, John H. "The Composition of Anglo-Norman Armies," *Speculum* 40 (1965), 398-414.

Beeler, John H. *Warfare in England, 1066-1189*. Ithaca: Cornell University Press, 1966.

Bennett, Matthew. "The Impact of 'Foreign' Troops in the Civil Wars of King Stephen's Reign." In: *War and Society in Medieval and Early Modern Britain*. Ed. Diana Dunn. Liverpool: Liverpool University Press, 2000, pp. 96-113.

Bennett, Matthew. "Wace and Warfare," *Anglo-Norman Studies* 11 (1988), 37-57; in: *Anglo-Norman Warfare: Studies in Late Anglo-Saxon and Anglo-Norman Military Organization and Warfare*. Ed. M. Strickland. Woodbridge, 1992, pp. 230-50.

Bradbury, Jim. "Battles in England and Normandy, 1066-1154." In: *Anglo-Norman Warfare: Studies in Late Anglo-Saxon and Anglo-Norman Military Organization and Warfare*. Woodbridge, 1992, pp. 182-93.

Bradbury, Jim. "The Civil War of Stephen's Reign: Winners and Losers." In: *Armies, Chivalry and Warfare in Medieval Britain and France: Proceedings of the 1995 Harlaxton Symposium*. Ed. M. Strickland. Stamford, 1998, pp. 115-32.

Bradbury, Jim. "The Early Years of the Reign of Stephen." In: *England in the Twelfth Century*. Ed. D. Williams. Woodbridge: Boydell and Brewer, 1990, pp. 17-30.

Bradbury, Jim. *Stephen and Mathilda: The Civil War of 1139-53*. Stroud: Alan Sutton Publishing Limited, 1996.

Brown, R. Allen. *The Origins of English Feudalism*. London, 1973.

Callahan, T., Jr. "Ecclesiastical Reparations and the Soldiers of 'The Anarchy'," *Albion* 10 (1978), 300-18.

Chibnall, Marjorie. "Anglo-French Relations in the Work of Orderic Vitalis." In: *Documenting the Past: Essays in Medieval History Presented to George Peddy Cuttino*. Ed. J.S. Hamilton and P.J. Bradley. Woodbridge, 1989, pp. 5-19.

Chibnall, Marjorie. *The Empress Matilda*. Oxford: Blackwell, 1991.

Chibnall, Marjorie. "Mercenaries and the *Familia Regis* under Henry I," *History* 62 (1977), 15-23; in: *Anglo-Norman Warfare: Studies in Late Anglo-Saxon and Anglo-Norman Military Organization and Warfare*. Ed. M. Strickland. Woodbridge, 1992, pp. 84-92.

Christlelow, Stephanie Mooers. "A Moveable Feast? Itineration and the Centralization of Government under Henry I," *Albion* 28 (1996), 1-13.

Cook, David R. "The Norman Military Revolution in England," *Proceedings of the Battle Conference on Anglo-Norman Studies* 1 (1978), 94-102.

Courtney, Paul. "The Norman Invasion of Gwent: A Reassessment," *Journal of Medieval History* 12 (1986), 297-313.

Crouch, David. *The Reign of King Stephen, 1135-1154*. Harlow: Longman, 2000.

Crouch, David. "Robert, Earl of Gloucester, and the Daughter of Zelophehad," *Journal of Medieval History* 12 (1986), 227-43.

Dalton, Paul. "Aiming at the Impossible: Ranulf II Earl of Chester and Lincolnshire in the Reign of King Stephen." In: *The Earldom of Chester and its Charters*. Ed. A.T. Thacker. Chester, 1991, pp. 109-34.

Dalton, Paul. "Civil War and Ecclesiastical Peace in the Reign of King Stephen." In: *War and Society in Medieval and Early Modern Britain*. Ed. Diana Dunn. Liverpool: Liverpool University Press, 2000, pp. 53-75.

Dalton, Paul. "*In neutro latere*: The Armed Neutrality of Ranulf II Earl of Chester in King Stephen's Reign," *Anglo-Norman Studies* 14 (1991), 40-59.

Davis, H.W.C. "The Anarchy of Stephen's Reign," *English Historical Review* 18 (1903), 630-41.

Davis, R.H.C. "Geoffrey de Mandeville Reconsidered." In: *From Alfred the Great to Stephen.* London, 1991, pp. 203-11; in *English Historical Review* 79 (1964), 299-307.

Davis, R.H.C. *King Stephen, 1135-1154.* Berkeley and Los Angeles: University of California Press, 1967.

Davis, R.H.C. "King Stephen and the Earl of Chester Revised." In: *From Alfred the Great to Stephen.* London, 1991, pp. 213-19; in *English Historical Review* 75 (1960), 654-60.

Davis, R.H.C. "Treaty between William Earl of Gloucester and Roger Earl of Hereford." In: *Medieval Miscellany for D.M. Stenton.* Ed. P.M. Barnes and C.F. Slade. Pipe Roll Society. London, 1968, pp. 139-46.

Davis, R.H.C. "What Happened in Stephen's Reign, 1135-54." In: *From Alfred the Great to Stephen.* London, 1991, pp. 191-202; in *History* 49 (1964), 1-12.

Davis, R.H.C. "William of Poitiers and His History of William the Conqueror." In: *From Alfred the Great to Stephen.* London, 1991, pp. 101-30; in *The Writing of History in the Middle Ages: Essays Presented to Richard William Southern.* Ed. R.H.C. Davis and J.M. Wallace-Hadrill. Oxford, 1981, pp. 71-100.

Douglas, David C. *The Norman Achievement, 1050-1100.* Berkeley and Los Angeles: University of California Press, 1969.

Fernie, E.C. "Architecture and the Effects of the Norman Conquest." In: *England and Normandy in the Middle Ages.* Ed. D. Bates and A. Curry. London, 1994, pp. 105-16.

Fleming, Donald F. "Landholding by *Milites* in Domesday Book: A Revision," *Anglo-Norman Studies* 13 (1990), 83-98.

Fleming, Donald F. "*Milites* as Attestors to Charters in England, 1101-1300," *Albion* 22 (1990), 185-98.

Gillingham, John. "1066 and the Introduction of Chivalry into England." In: *Law and Government in Medieval England and Normandy.* Ed. G. Garnett and J. Hudson. Cambridge, 1994, pp. 31-55.

Gillingham, John. "Thegns and Knights in Eleventh-Century England: Who Was Then the Gentleman?" *Transactions of the Royal Historical Society*, 6th ser., 5 (1995), 129-53.

Golding, Brian. *Conquest and Colonisation: The Normans in Britain, 1066-1100*. London: Macmillan, 1994.

Golding, Brian. "Robert of Mortain," *Anglo-Norman Studies* 13 (1990), 119-44.

Gravett, Christopher. *Norman Knight, 950-1204 AD*. London: Osprey, 1993.

Green, Judith. "Financing Stephen's War," *Anglo-Norman Studies* 14 (1991), 91-114.

Harper-Bill, C. "The Piety of the Anglo-Norman Knightly Class," *Anglo-Norman Studies* 2 (1979), 63-77.

Head, Victor. *Hereward*. Stroud: Alan Sutton Publishing Limited, 1995.

Hill, Rosalind M.T. "The Battle of Stockbridge, 1141." In: *Studies in Medieval History Presented to R. Allen Brown*. Ed. C. Harper-Bill et al. Woodbridge, 1989, pp. 173-77.

Holdsworth, Christopher J. "War and Peace in the Twelfth Century: The Reign of Stephen Reconsidered." In: *War and Peace in the Middle Ages*. Ed. B.P. McGuire. Copenhagen, 1987, pp. 67-93.

Hollister, C. Warren. "The Campaign of 1102 against Robert of Bellême." In: *Studies in Medieval History Presented to R. Allen Brown*. Ed. C. Harper-Bill et al. Woodbridge, 1989, pp. 193-202.

Hollister, C. Warren. "The Knights of Peterborough and the Anglo-Norman Fyrd," *English Historical Review* 77 (1962), 417-36.

Hollister, C. Warren. *The Military Organization of Norman England*. Oxford: Clarendon Press, 1965.

Hollister, C. Warren. "The Norman Conquest and the Genesis of English Feudalism," *American Historical Review* 66 (1961), 641-63.

Hollister, C. Warren. "Military Obligation in Late-Saxon and Norman England." In: *Ordinamenti militari in occidente nell'alto medioevo*. Settimane di studio del centro italiano di studi sull'alto medioevo, XV. Spoleto, 1968, I:169-86.

Hollister, C. Warren. "The Significance of Scutage Rates in Eleventh- and Twelfth-Century England," *English Historical Review* 75 (1960), 577-88.

Holt, J.C. "The End of the Anglo-Norman Realm," *Proceedings of the British Academy* 61 (1975), 223-65.

Hooper, Nicholas. "Edgar the Ætheling: Anglo-Saxon Prince, Rebel and Crusader," *Anglo-Saxon England* 14 (1985), 197-214.

Hudson, John. "The Abbey of Abingdon, Its Chronicle, and the Norman Conquest," *Anglo-Norman Studies* 19 (1996), 181-202.

Johnson-South, Ted. "The Norman Conquest of Durham: Norman Historians and the Anglo-Saxon Community of St. Cuthbert," *Haskins Society Journal* 4 (1992), 85-95.

Kapelle, William E. *The Norman Conquest of the North: The Region and Its Transformation, 1000-1135*. Chapel Hill: University of North Carolina Press, 1979.

Keats-Rohan, K.S.B. "William I and the Breton Contingent in the Non-Norman Conquest 1060-1087," *Anglo-Norman Studies* 13 (1990), 157-72.

King, Edmund J. "The Anarchy of King Stephen's Reign," *Transactions of the Royal Historical Society* 5th ser., 34 (1984).

King, Edmund J. "Dispute Settlement in Anglo-Norman England," *Anglo-Norman Studies* 14 (1991), 115-30.

King, Edmund J. "Mountsorrel and Its Region in King Stephen's Reign," *Huntington Library Quarterly* 44 (1980), 1-10.

King, Edmund J. "Stephen of Blois, Count of Mortain and Boulogne," *English Historical Review* 115 (2000), 271-96.

King, Edmund J. "Waleran, Count of Meulan, Earl of Worcester (1104-1166." In: *Tradition and Change*. Ed. D. Greenway, C. Holdsworth, and J. Sayers. Cambridge, 1985, pp. 165-81.

Le Patourel, John. "The Norman Conquest, 1066, 1106, 1154?" *Anglo-Norman Studies* 1 (1978), 103-20, 216-20.

Mason, J.F.A. "Roger de Montgomery and His Sons (1067-1102)," *Transactions of the Royal Historical Society* 5th ser. 13 (1963), 1-28.

Morillo, Stephen. *Warfare under the Anglo-Norman Kings, 1066-1135.* Woodbridge: The Boydell Press, 1994.

Mortimer, Richard. *Angevin England, 1154-1258.* Oxford: Blackwell, 1994.

Neveux, François. "Quelques aspects de l'impérialisme normand au XIe siècle en Italie et en Angleterre." In: *Les Normands en Méditerranée dans le sillage des Tancréde.* Ed. P. Boulet and F. Neveux. Caen, 1994, pp. 51-62.

Nicolle, David C. *Normans.* London: Osprey, 1987.

Palliser, D.M. "Domesday Book and the 'Harrying of the North'," *Northern History* 24 (1993), 1-23.

Palmer, J.J.N. "The Conqueror's Footprints in Domesday Book." In: *The Medieval Military Revolution: State, Society and Military Change in Medieval and Early Modern Europe.* Ed. A. Ayton and J.L. Price. London, 1995, pp. 23-44.

Palmer, J.J.N. "War and Domesday Waste." In: *Armies, Chivalry and Warfare in Medieval Britain and France: Proceedings of the 1995 Harlaxton Symposium.* Ed. M. Strickland. Stamford, 1998, pp. 256-75.

Prestwich, J.O. "Military Intelligence under the Norman and Angevin Kings." In: In: *Law and Government in Medieval England and Normandy.* Ed. G. Garnett and J. Hudson. Cambridge, 1994, pp. 1-30.

Prestwich, J.O. "War and Finance in the Anglo-Norman State," *Transactions of the Royal Historical Society,* 5th ser., 4 (1954), 19-43; in: *Anglo-Norman Warfare: Studies in Late Anglo-Saxon and Anglo-Norman Military Organization and Warfare.* Ed. M. Strickland. Woodbridge, 1992, pp. 59-83.

Purser, Toby. "William FitzOsbern, Earl of Hereford: Personality and Power on the Welsh Frontier, 1066-1071." In: *Armies, Chivalry and Warfare in Medieval Britain and France: Proceedings of the 1995 Harlaxton Symposium.* Ed. M. Strickland. Stamford, 1998, pp. 133-46.

Reynolds, Susan. "Eadric Silvaticus and the English Resistance," *Bulletin of the Institute of Historical Research* 54 (1981), 102-05.

Rogers, Randall. "Aspects of the Military History of the Anglo-Norman Invasion of Ireland, 1169-1225," *Irish Sword* 16 (1984-86), 135-44.

Round, J.H. *Geoffrey de Mandeville: A Study of the Anarchy*. London: Longmans, Green and Co., 1892.

Rowe, Elizabeth Ashman. "Historical Invasions/Historiographical Interventions: Snorri Sturluson and the Battle of Stamford Bridge," *Mediaevalia* 17 (1994), 149-76.

Russell, Josiah Cox. "Demographic Aspects of the Norman Conquest." In: *Medieval Demography: Essays by Josiah C. Russell*. New York, 1987, pp. 125-47.

Schofield, Guy. "The Third Battle of 1066," *History Today* 16 (1966), 688-93.

Searle, Eleanor. "The Abbey of the Conquerors: Defensive Enfeoffment and Economic Development in Anglo-Norman England," *Proceedings of the Battle Conference* 2 (1979), 154-98.

Searle, Eleanor. "Emma the Conqueror." In *Studies in Medieval History Presented to R. Allen Brown*. Ed. C. Harper-Bill et al. Woodbridge, 1989, pp. 281-88.

Searle, Eleanor. "Women and the Legitimization of Succession at the Norman Conquest," *Proceedings of the Battle Conference on Anglo-Norman Studies* 2 (1979), 159-70.

Shadrake, Dan and Susanna Shadrake. *Barbarian Warriors: Saxons, Vikings and Normans*. Brassey's History of Uniforms. London, 1997.

Southern, Richard W. "The Place of Henry I in English History," *Proceedings of the British Academy* 48 (1962), 127-69.

Strickland, Matthew. "Against the Lord's Anointed: Aspects of Warfare and Baronial Rebellion in England and Normandy, 1075-1265." In: *Law and Government in Medieval England and Normandy*. Ed. G. Garnett and J. Hudson. Cambridge, 1994, pp. 56-79.

Strickland, Matthew. "Slaughter, Slavery or Ransom: the Impact of the Conquest on Conduct in Warfare." In: *England in the Eleventh Century: Proceedings of the 1990 Harlaxton Symposium.* Ed. C. Hicks. Stamford, 1992, pp. 41-59.

Strickland, Matthew. *War and Chivalry: The Conduct and Perception of War in England and Normandy, 1066-1217.* Cambridge: Cambridge University Press, 1996.

Stringer, K.J. *The Reign of Stephen.* London, 1993.

Tanner, Heather J. "The Expansion of the Power and Influence of the Counts of Boulogne under Eustace II," *Anglo-Norman Studies* 14 (1991), 251-86.

Thompson, Kathleen. "Orderic Vitalis and Robert of Bellême," *Journal of Medieval History* 20 (1994), 133-41.

Truax, Jean A. "Anglo-Norman Women at War: Valiant Soldiers, Prudent Strategists or Charismatic Leaders?" In: *The Circle of War in the Middle Ages: Essays on Medieval Military and Naval History.* Ed. Donald J. Kagay and L.J. Andrew Villalon. Woodbridge: The Boydell Press, 1999, pp. 111-26.

van Houts, Elisabeth M.C. "Latin Poetry and the Anglo-Norman Court, 1066-1135: The *Carmen de Hastingae proelio,*" *Journal of Medieval History* 15 (1989), 39-62.

Walker, D. "Miles of Gloucester, Earl of Hereford," *Transactions of the Bristol and Gloucestershire Archaeological Society* 77 (1958), 66-84.

White, G.H. "The Career of Waleran, Count of Meulan and Earl of Worcester (1104-1166)," *Transactions of the Royal Historical Society* 4th ser., 17 (1934), 19-48.

White, G.H. "King Stephen's Earldoms," *Transactions of the Royal Historical Society* 4th ser., 13 (1930), 51-82.

White, Graeme J. "Earls and Earldoms in King Stephen's Reign." In: *War and Society in Medieval and Early Modern Britain.* Ed. Diana Dunn. Liverpool: Liverpool University Press, 2000, pp. 76-95.

White, Graeme J. "The End of Stephen's Reign," *History* 75 (1980).

White, Graeme J. *Restoration and Reform, 1153-1165: Recovery from Civil War in England*. Cambridge, 2000.

Williams, Ann. "The Spoliation of Worcester," *Anglo-Norman Studies* 19 (1996), 383-408.

Williams, A.S. "Norman Lordship in South-east Wales during the Reign of William I," *Welsh Historical Review* 16 (1993), 445-66.

Williams, John Bryan. "Judhael of Totnes: The Life and Times of a Post-Conquest Baron," *Anglo-Norman Studies* 16 (1993), 271-89.

Medieval – England – Angevin Kings

Baker, Derek. "Ailred of Rievaulx and Walter of Espec," *Haskins Society Journal* 1 (1989), 91-98.

Barratt, Nick. "The Revenue of King John," *English Historical Review* 111 (1996), 835-55.

Bartlett, Robert J. *England Under the Norman and Angevin Kings, 1075-1225*. The New Oxford History of England. Oxford: Clarendon Press, 2000.

Beamish, Tufton. *Battle Royal: A New Account of Simon de Montfort's Struggle Against King Henry III*. London: Frederick Muller Limited, 1965.

Beeler, John H. *Warfare in England, 1066-1189*. Ithaca: Cornell University Press, 1966.

Benjamin, R. "A Forty Years War: Toulouse and the Plantagenets, 1156-1196," *Historical Research* 56 (1988), 270-85.

Blaauw, W.H. *The Barons' War including the Battles of Lewes and Evesham*. 2nd ed. London, 1871.

Bradbury, Jim. "Geoffrey V of Anjou, Count and Knight." In: *The Ideals and Practice of Medieval Knighthood*, III. Ed. C. Harper-Bill and R. Harvey. Woodbridge, 1990, pp. 21-38.

Bradbury, Jim. *Stephen and Mathilda: The Civil War of 1139-53*. Stroud: Alan Sutton Publishing Limited, 1996.

Brundage, James A. *Richard Lionheart*. London, 1973.

Burton, D.W. "1264: Some New Documents," *Historical Research* 66 (1993), 317-28.

Carpenter, David. *The Battles of Lewes and Evesham, 1264/65*. British Battlefield Series. Keele: Mercia Publications Ltd., 1987.

Carpenter, David. "King Henry III and the Tower of London," *London Journal* 19 (1995), 95-107.

Carpenter, David. "What Happened in 1258." In: *War and Government in the Middle Ages: Essays in Honour of J.O. Prestwich*. Ed. J. Gillingham and J.C. Holt. Cambridge, 1984, pp. 106-19.

Church, S.D. "The Earliest English Muster Roll, 18/19 December 1215," *Historical Research* 67 (1994), 1-17.

Church, S.D. *The Household Knights of King John*. Cambridge: Cambridge University Press, 1999.

Church, S.D. "The Knights of the Household of King John: A Question of Numbers." *Thirteenth Century England IV*. Ed. P.R. Coss and S.D. Lloyd. Woodbridge, 1991, pp. 151-65.

Cox, D.C. *The Battle of Evesham: A New Account*. Evesham, 1988.

Cox, D.C. "The Battle of Evesham in the Evesham Chronicle," *Historical Research* 62 (1989), 337-45.

Critchley, J.S. "Summonses to Military Service Early in the Reign of Henry III," *English Historical Review* 86 (1971), 79-95.

Crouch, David. "Strategies of Lordship in Angevin England and the Career of William Marshal." In: *The Ideals and Practice of Medieval Knighthood*, II. Ed. C. Harper-Bill and R. Harvey. Woodbridge, 1988, pp. 1-25.

Crouch, David. *William Marshal: Court, Career and Chivalry in the Angevin Empire, 1147-1219*. The Medieval World. London: Longman, 1990.

de Ville, Oscar. "John Deyville: A Neglected Rebel," *Northern History* 34 (1998), 17-40.

Duby, Georges. *William Marshal: The Flower of Chivalry*. Trans. Richard Howard. New York: Pantheon Books, 1984.

Duffy, Séan. "King John's Expedition to Ireland, 1210: The Evidence Reconsidered," *Irish Historical Studies* 30 (1996), 1-24.

Flanagan, Marie Therese. "Strongbow, Henry II and Anglo-Norman Intervention in Ireland." In: *War and Government in the Middle Ages: Essays in Honour of J.O. Prestwich*. Ed. J. Gillingham and J.C. Holt. Cambridge, 1984, pp. 62-77.

Flori, Jean. *Richard Couer de Lion: Le roi-chevalier*. Paris: Payot and Rivages, 1999.

Forey, Alan J. "The Crusading Vows of the English King Henry III," *Durham University Journal* 65 (1973), 229-47.

Gillingham, John. "Conquering Kings: Some Twelfth-Century Reflections on Henry II and Richard I." In: *Warriors and Churchmen in the High Middle Ages: Essays Presented to Karl Leyser*. Ed. T. Reuter. London, 1992, pp. 163-77.

Gillingham, John. "Conquering the Barbarians: War and Chivalry in Twelfth-Century Britain," *Haskins Society Journal* 4 (1992), 67-84.

Gillingham, John. *Richard I*. New Haven: Yale University Press, 1999.

Gillingham, John. "Richard I and the Science of War in the Middle Ages." In: *War and Government in the Middle Ages: Essays in Honour of J.O. Prestwich*. Ed. J. Gillingham and J.C. Holt. Cambridge, 1984, pp. 78-91; in: *Anglo-Norman Warfare: Studies in Late Anglo-Saxon and Anglo-Norman Military Organization and Warfare*. Ed. M. Strickland. Woodbridge, 1992, pp. 194-207; in: *Richard Coeur de Lion: Kingship, Chivalry and War in the Twelfth Century*. London, 1994, pp. 211-26.

Gillingham, John. "Richard I, Galley-Warfare and Portsmouth: The Beginnings of a Royal Navy." In: *Thirteenth Century England VI*. Ed. M. Prestwich, R.H. Britnell and R. Frame. Woodbridge, 1997, pp. 1-15.

Gillingham, John. *Richard the Lionheart*. New York: New York Times Books, 1978.

Gillingham, John. "Some Legends of Richard the Lionheart: Their Development and their Influence." In: *Ricardo Cuor di Leone nella storia e nella leggenda: Accademia Nazionale dei Lincei, colloquio italo-britannico.* Accademia Nazionale dei Lincei, Problemi attuali di scienza e di cultura, 253. Rome, 1981, pp. 35-50; in: *Richard Coeur de Lion: Kingship, Chivalry and War in the Twelfth Century.* London, 1994, pp. 181-92.

Gillingham, John. "War and Chivalry in the *History of William the Marshal.*" In: *Thirteenth Century England II.* Ed. P.R. Coss and S.D. Lloyd. Woodbridge, 1988, pp. 1-13; in: *Anglo-Norman Warfare: Studies in Late Anglo-Saxon and Anglo-Norman Military Organization and Warfare.* Ed. M. Strickland. Woodbridge, 1992, pp. 251-63.

Hauer, S.R. "Richard Coeur de Lion: Cavalier or Cannibal," *Mississippi Folklore Register* 14 (1980), 88-95.

Hays, L. and E.D. Jones. "Policy on the Run: Henry II and Irish Sea Diplomacy," *Journal of British Studies* 29 (1990), 293-316.

Hogg, R. Malcolm. "The Justiciarship and the Battle of Northampton, 1264," *Historical Research* 68 (1995), 88-99.

Holdsworth, Christopher J. "Peacemaking in the Twelfth Century," *Anglo-Norman Studies* 19 (1996), 1-17.

Holt, J.C. "The Loss of Normandy and Royal Finances." In: *War and Government in the Middle Ages: Essays in Honour of J.O. Prestwich.* Ed. J. Gillingham and J.C. Holt. Cambridge, 1984, pp. 92-105.

Holt, J.C. *The Northerners: A Study in the Reign of King John.* 2nd ed. Oxford: Clarendon Press, 1992.

Isaac, Steven. "Defeat from the Jaws of Victory: Stephen of Blois in England." In: *On the Social Origins of Medieval Institutions: Essays in Honor of Joseph F. O'Callaghan.* Ed. Donald J. Kagay and Theresa M. Vann. Leiden: E.J. Brill, 1998, pp. 263-71.

Kessler, Ulrike. *Richard I. Löwenherz: König, Kreuzritter, Abenteurer.* Graz, Vienna, and Cologne: Styria, 1995.

King, James R. "The Friar Tuck Syndrome: Clerical Violence and the Barons' War." In: *The Final Argument: The Imprint of Violence on Society in Medieval and Early Modern Europe*. Ed. Donald J. Kagay and L.J. Andrew Villalon. Woodbridge: The Boydell Press, 1998, pp. 27-52.

Labarge, Margaret Wade. *Simon de Montfort*. London: Eyre and Spottis-woode (Publishers) Ltd., 1962; rpt. Bath: Cedric Chivers Ltd. Portway, 1972.

Laborderie, Olivier de, J.R. Maddicott, and D.A. Carpenter. "The Last Hours of Simon de Montfort: A New Account," *English Historical Review* 115 (2000), 378-412.

Latimer, Paul. "Henry II's Campaign Against the Welsh in 1165," *Welsh Historical Review* 14 (1989), 523-52.

Lawrence, C.H. "The University of Oxford and the Chronicle of the Barons' War," *English Historical Review* 95 (1980).

Maddicott, J.R. *Simon de Montfort*. Cambridge: Cambridge University Press, 1994.

Mason, Emma. "The Hero's Invincible Weapon: An Aspect of Angevin Propaganda." In: *The Ideals and Practice of Medieval Knighthood*, III. Woodbridge, 1990, pp. 121-38.

Mayer, Hans Eberhard. "A Ghost Ship Called *Frankenef*: King Richard I's German Itinerary," *English Historical Review* 115 (2000), 134-44.

New, H. "On the Strategic Movements which Immediately Preceded the Battle of Evesham." *Journal of the British Archaeological Association* 32 (1876), 54-59.

Norgate, K. *John Lackland*. London, 1902.

Norgate, K. *Richard the Lionheart*. London, 1924.

O'Doherty, J.F. "The Anglo-Norman Invasion of 1167-71," *Irish Historical Studies* 1 (1938-39), 154-57.

Oman, W. "The Campaign of Evesham," *Transactions of the Bristol and Gloucestershire Archaeological Society* 32 (1909), 64-83.

Page, Mark. "Cornwall, Earl Richard, and the Barons' War," *English Historical Review* 115 (2000), 21-38.

Painter, Sidney. *The Reign of King John.* Baltimore: Johns Hopkins University Press, 1966.

Painter, Sidney. *William Marshal: Knight-Errant, Baron, and Regent of England.* Baltimore: The Johns Hopkins University Press, 1933; rpt. Toronto: University of Toronto Press, 1971.

Patterson, Robert B. "Bristol: An Angevin Baronial Capital under Royal Siege," *Haskins Society Journal* 3 (1991), 171-81.

Powicke, F.M. *King Henry III and the Lord Edward: The Community of the Realm in the Thirteenth Century.* 2 vols. Oxford, 1947.

Powicke, F.M. *The Loss of Normandy, 1189-1204: Studies in the History of the Angevin Empire.* 2nd ed. Manchester, 1961.

Powicke, Michael R. "Distraint of Knighthood and Military Obligation under Henry III," *Speculum* 25 (1950), 457-70.

Prestwich, J.O. "Military Intelligence under the Norman and Angevin Kings." In: In: *Law and Government in Medieval England and Normandy.* Ed. G. Garnett and J. Hudson. Cambridge, 1994, pp. 1-30.

Prestwich, J.O. "Richard Coeur de Lion: Rex Bellicosus." In: *Ricardo Cuor di Leone nella storia e nella leggenda: Accademia Nazionale dei Lincei, colloquio italo-britannico.* Accademia Nazionale dei Lincei, Problemi attuali di scienza e di cultura, 253. Rome, 1981, pp. 1-15.

Rowlands, Ifor W. "William Marshal, Pembroke Castle and the Historian," *Château Gaillard* 17 (1996), 151-55.

Strickland, Matthew. "Against the Lord's Anointed: Aspects of Warfare and Baronial Rebellion in England and Normandy, 1075-1265." In: *Law and Government in Medieval England and Normandy.* Ed. G. Garnett and J. Hudson. Cambridge, 1994, pp. 56-79.

Strickland, Matthew. "Arms and the Men: War, Loyalty and Lordship in Jordan Fantosme's Chronicle. In: *Medieval Knighthood, IV.* Ed. C. Harper-Bill and R. Harvey. Woodbridge, 1992, pp. 187-220.

Studd, J.R. "The Lord Edward and Henry III," *Bulletin of the Institute for Historical Research* 1 (1977-78), 4-19.

Truax, Jean A. "Winning over the Londoners: King Stephen, the Empress Matilda, and the Politics of Personality," *Haskins Society Journal* 8 (1996), 43-61.

Turner, Ralph V. "Good or Bad Kingship? The Case of Richard Lionheart," *Haskins Society Journal* 8 (1996), 63-78.

Turner, Ralph V. *King John*. London: Longman, 1994.

Turner, Ralph V. "King John's Military Reputation Reconsidered," *Journal of Medieval History* 19 (1993), 171-200.

Valente, Claire. "Simon of Montfort, Earl of Leicester, and the Utility of Sanctity in Thirteenth-Century England," *Journal of Medieval History* 21 (1995), 27-49.

Vincent, Nicholas. "A Roll of Knights Summoned to Campaign in 1213," *Historical Research* 66 (1993), 89-97.

Walker, R.F. "The Supporters of Richard Marshal, Earl of Pembroke, in the Rebellion of 1233-1234," *Welsh Historical Review* 17 (1994-95), 41-65.

Warren, W.L. *Henry II*. London, 1973.

Warren, W.L. *King John*. London: Eyre and Spottiswoode, 1961.

Williams, Daniel. "Simon de Montfort, Earl of Leicester and the Image of Thirteenth Century Chivalry," *Transactions of the Leicester Literary and Philosophical Society* 87 (1993), 7-10.

Young, Charles R. "Divided Loyalties: The Neville Family and the Barons' War against King Henry III, 1264-65." In: *Law, Custom, and the Social Fabric in Medieval Europe: Essays in Honor of Bryce Lyon*. Ed. Bernard Bachrach and David Nicholas. Kalamazoo, 1990, pp. 145-61.

Medieval – England – Edward I and II

Alexander, Graham. "The Battle of Boroughbridge, 16th March 1322," *Battlefield* 4.3 (1998), 3-6.

Black, J.G. "Edward I and Gascony," *English Historical Review* 17 (1902), 518-27.

Campbell, Bruce. "Britain 1300," *History Today* 50.6 (Jun 2000), 10-17.

de Ville, Oscar. "Jocelin Deyville: Brigand, or Man of His Time?" *Northern History* 35 (1999), 27-49.

Freeman, A.Z. "The King's Penny: The Headquarters Paymasters under Edward I, 1295-1307," *Journal of British Studies* 6 (1966), 1-22.

Haines, Roy Martin. "An English Archbishop and the Cerberus of War," *Studies in Church History* 20 (1983), 153-70.

Hepple, Leslie. "Walter le Rey Marchis, a Percy King of Arms, and the Falkirk Roll of 1298," *Archaeologia aeliana*, 5th ser., 24 (1996), 77-82.

Ingamells, Ruth. "The Political Role of the Household Knights of Edward II." In: *Thirteenth Century England V*. Ed. P.R. Coss and S.D. Lloyd. Woodbridge, 1995, pp. 29-35.

King, D.J. Cathcart. "John des Roches: a Fourteenth Century Staff Officer," *Fort* 17 (1989), 3-5.

Lachaud, Frédérique. "Les tentes et l'activité militaire: Les guerres d'Édouard Ier Plantagenet (1272-1307)," *Mélanges de l'école française de Rome: moyen âge* 111 (1999), 443-61.

Leadman, Alex D.H. "The Battle of Boroughbridge," *Yorkshire Archaeological Journal* 7 (1882), 330-60.

Lewis, N.B. "An Early Indenture of Military Service, 27 July 1287," *Bulletin of the Institute of Historical Research* 13 (1935/36), 85-89.

Lewis, N.B. "The English Forces in Flanders, August-November 1297." In: *Studies in Medieval History Presented to F.M. Powicke*. Ed. R.W. Hunt. Oxford, 1948, pp. 310-78

Lewis, N.B. "The Summons of the English Feudal Levy, 5 April 1327." In: *Essays in Medieval History Presented to Bertie Wilkinson*. Ed. T.A. Sandquist and M.R. Powicke. Toronto: University of Toronto Press, 1969, pp. 236-49.

Lydon, James F. "Edward I, Ireland and the War in Scotland, 1303-1304." In: *England and Ireland in the Later Middle Ages: Essays in Honour of Jocelyn Otway-Ruthven*. Ed. James F. Lydon. Dublin, 1981, pp. 43-61.

Maddicott, J.R. *Thomas of Lancaster*. Oxford, 1970.

Moor, C. "Knights of Edward I," *Publications of the Harleian Society* 80-84 (1929-32).

Morris, John E. "Cumberland and Westmorland Military Levies in the Time of Edward I and Edward II," *Transactions of the Cumberland and Westmorland Antiquarian and Archaeological Society* n.s. 3 (1903), 307-27.

Niderost, Eric. "England's Warrior-King Edward I Won Victories Against Such Renowned Foes as Baybars, Llewellyn and Wallace," *Military History* (Dec 1995), 10, 12, 16.

Phillips, J.R.S. *Aymer de Valence, Earl of Pembroke, 1307-1324*. Oxford, 1972.

Powicke, Michael R. "Edward II and Military Obligation," *Speculum* 31 (1956), 92-119.

Powicke, Michael R. "The English Commons in Scotland in 1322 and the Deposition of Edward II," *Speculum* 35 (1960), 556-62.

Powicke, Michael R. "The General Obligation to Cavalry Service under Edward I," *Speculum* 28 (1953), 814-33.

Prestwich, Michael. *Edward I*. London: Guild Publishing, 1988.

Prestwich, Michael. "Military Logistics: the Case of 1322." In: *Armies, Chivalry and Warfare in Medieval Britain and France: Proceedings of the 1995 Harlaxton Symposium*. Ed. M. Strickland. Stamford, 1998, pp. 276-88.

Prestwich, Michael. *The Three Edwards: War and State in England, 1272-1377*. London, 1981.

Prestwich, Michael. *War, Politics and Finance under Edward I*. London: Faber and Faber, Limited, 1972.

Smith, J. Beverley. "Adversaries of Edward I: Gaston de Béarn and Llywelyn ap Gruffudd." In: *Recognitions: Essays Presented to Edmund Fryde*. Ed. C. Richmond and I. Harvey. Aberystwyth, 1996, pp. 55-87.

Thomas, Avril. "Interconnections between the Lands of Edward I: A Welsh-English Mercenary Force in Ireland, 1285-1304," *Bulletin of the Board of Celtic Studies* 40 (1993), 135-47.

Vale, Malcolm. "Edward I and the French: Rivalry and Chivalry." In: *Thirteenth Century England II*. Ed. P.R. Coss and S.D. Lloyd. Woodbridge, 1988, pp. 165-76.

Medieval – England – English/Scottish Conflicts [Cf. Medieval – Scotland]

Anderson, Alan O. "Anglo-Scottish Relations from Constantine II to William," *Scottish Historical Review* 42 (1963), 1-20.

Arthurson, Ian. "The King's Voyage into Scotland: The War that Never Was." In: *England in the Fifteenth Century: Proceedings from the 1986 Harlaxton Symposium*. Ed. D. Williams. Woodbridge, 1987.

Balfour-Melville, E.W.M. *Edward III and David II*. London: Historical Association, 1954.

Barrow, Geoffrey W.S. "The Anglo-Scottish Border," *Northern History* 1 (1966), 21-42.

Barrow, Geoffrey W.S. "The Anglo-Scottish Border: Growth and Structure in the Middle Ages." In: *Grenzen und Grenzregionen*. Ed. W. Haubrichs and R. Schneider. Saarbrücken, 1993, pp. 197-212.

Barrow, Geoffrey W.S. "A Kingdom in Crisis: Scotland and the Maid of Norway," *Scottish Historical Review* 69 (1990), 120-41.

Barrow, Geoffrey W.S. "The Scots and the North of England." In: *The Anarchy of King Stephen's Reign*. Ed. E.J. King. Oxford, 1994, pp. 231-53.

Bell, Graham. "The Siege of Berwick," *Battlefield* 4.3 (1998), 7-10.

Blair, C.H. "Northern Knights at Falkirk, 1298," *Archaeologia aeliana* 4th ser. 25 (1947), 68-114.

Booth, Peter. "Richard Duke of Gloucester and the West March Towards Scotland, 1470-1483," *Northern History* 36 (2000), 233-46.

Brown, A.L. "The English Campaign in Scotland, 1400." In: *British Government and Administration: Studies Presented to S. Chrimes*. Ed. H. Hearder and H.R. Loyn. Cardiff, 1974, pp. 40-54.

Brown, M.H. "The Development of Scottish Border Lordship, 1332-58," *Scottish Historical Review* 77 (1997), 1-22.

Cameron, Sonja and Alasdair Ross. "The Treaty of Edinburgh and the Disinherited (1328-1332)," *History* 84 (1999), 237-56.

Chrimes, S.B., ed. "Some Letters of John of Lancaster as Warden of the East Marches towards Scotland," *Speculum* 14 (1939), 3-27.

Davies, R.R. *Domination and Conquest: The Experience of Ireland, Scotland and Wales, 1100-1300*. Cambridge: Cambridge University Press, 1990.

Duncan, A.A.M. "The Process of Norham, 1291." In: *Thirteenth Century England V*. Ed. P.R. Coss and S.D. Lloyd. Woodbridge, 1995, pp. 207-30.

Freeman, A.Z. "Wall-Breakers and River-Bridgers: Military Engineers in the Scottish Wars of Edward I," *Journal of British Studies* 10 (1976), 1-16.

Gaier, Claude. "The Scottish-English Wars as Seen by the Chronicler Jehan Le Bel from Liège (1326-1361)." In: *Rapports du XIIe congrès de l'association internationale des musées d'armes et d'histoire miltaire, 27 août-1er septembre 1990*. Glasgow, 1993, pp. 63-74.

Goodman, Anthony. "The Anglo-Scottish Marches in the Fifteenth Century: A Frontier Society?" In: *Scotland and England, 1286-1815*. Ed. Roger A. Mason. Edinburgh, 1987, pp. 18-33.

Goodman, Anthony. "Introduction." In: *War and Border Societies in the Middle Ages*. Ed. A. Goodman and A. Tuck. London, 1992, pp. 1-29.

Grant, Alexander. *Independence and Nationhood: Scotland, 1306-1469*. London, 1984.

Grant, Alexander. "Richard III and Scotland." In: *The North of England in the Age of Richard III*. Ed. A.J. Pollard. The Fifteenth Century Series, no. 3. Stroud: Alan Sutton Publishing, 1996, pp. 115-48.

Green, Judith A. "Anglo-Scottish Relations 1066-1174." In: *England and her Neighbours, 1066-1483: Essays in Honour of Pierre Chaplais*. Ed. M. Jones and M. Vale. London, 1989, pp. 53-72.

Green, Judith A. "David I and Henry I," *Scottish Historical Review* 75 (1996), 1-19.

Haskell, Michael. "Breaking the Stalemate: The Scottish Campaign of Edward I, 1303-4." In: *Thirteenth Century England VI*. Ed. Michael Prestwich, Richard Britnell and Robin Frame. Woodbridge: The Boydell Press, 1999, pp. 223-41.

Hay, Denys. "Booty in Border Warfare." In: *Renaissance Essays*. London, 1988, pp. 285-306.

Hay, Denys. "England, Scotland and Europe: The Problem of the Frontier," *Transactions of the Royal Historical Society* 5th ser., 25 (1975), 77-93.

Hill, Rosalind M.T. "An English Archbishop and the Scottish War of Independence," *Innes Review* 22 (1971), 59-71.

Leadman, Alex D.H. "The Battle of Bylands Abbey," *Yorkshire Archaeology Review* 8 (1884), 475-80.

Lomas, Richard. "The Impact of Border Warfare: The Scots and South Tweedside, c.1290-1520," *Scottish Historical Review* 75 (1996), 143-67.

Longley, K.M. "The Scottish Invasion of 1327: A Glimpse of the Aftermath (Wigton Church Accounts, 1328-9)," *Cumberland and Westmorland Archaeological and Antiquarian Society* 2nd ser. 83 (1983), 63-72.

Lydon, James F. "An Irish Army in Scotland, 1296," *Irish Sword* 5 (1962), 184-89.

Lydon, James F. "Irish Levies in the Scottish Wars, 1296-1302," *Irish Sword* 5 (1962), 207-17.

Miller, Edward. *War in the North: The Anglo-Scottish Wars of the Middle Ages*. Hull, 1960.

Neville, Cynthia J. "Keeping the Peace on the Northern Marches in the Later Middle Ages," *English Historical Review* 109 (1994), 1-25.

Neville, Cynthia J. "Local Sentiment and the 'National' Enemy in Northern England in the Later Middle Ages," *Journal of British Studies* 35 (1996), 419-37.

Nicholson, Ranald. *Edward III and the Scots: The Formative Years of a Military Career, 1327-1335.* Oxford: Oxford University Press, 1965.

Nicholson, Ranald. *Scotland: The Late Middle Ages.* Edinburgh, 1974.

Patterson, Raymond Campbell. *For the Lion: A History of the Scottish Wars of Independence.* Edinburgh: John Donald, 1996.

Patterson, Raymond Campbell. *My Wound is Deep: A History of the Later Anglo-Scots Wars, 1380-1560.* Edinburgh: John Donald, 1997.

Prestwich, Michael. "Colonial Scotland." In: *Scotland and England, 1286-1815.* Ed. R.A. Mason. Edinburgh, 1987.

Prestwich, Michael. "Edward I and the Maid of Norway," *Scottish Historical Review* 69 (1990), 157-74.

Prince, Albert E. "The Importance of the Campaign of 1327," *English Historical Review* 50 (1935).

Reid, R.R. "The Office of Warden of the Marches: Its Origin and Early History," *English Historical Review* 32 (1917), 479-96.

Ridpath, George. *The Border History of England and Scotland.* Berwick: Philip Ridpath, 1848.

Rothero, Christopher. *The Scottish and Welsh Wars, 1250-1400.* Men-at-Arms Series. London: Osprey Publishing, 1984.

Schwyzer, Hugo. "Northern Bishops and the Anglo-Scottish War in the Reign of Edward II." In: *Thirteenth Century England VII.* Ed. Michael Prestwich, Richard Britnell and Robin Frame. Woodbridge: The Boydell Press, 1999, pp. 243-54.

Stanford-Reid, W. "Sea Power in the Anglo-Scottish War, 1296-1328," *Mariner's Mirror* 46 (1960), 7-23.

Stell, Geoffrey. "Destruction and Damage: A Reassessment of the Historical and Architectural Evidence." In: *Scotland and War, AD 79-1918.* Ed. Norman Macdougall. Edinburgh: John Donald, 1991, pp. 24-35.

Stones, E.L.G. "The Anglo-Scottish Negotiations of 1327," *Scottish Historical Review* 30 (1951).

Stones, E.L.G. "English Chroniclers and the Affairs of Scotland, 1286-1296." In: *The Writing of History in the Middle Ages: Essays Presented to R.W. Southern.* Ed. R.H.C. Davis, J.M. Wallace-Hadrill, R.J.A.I. Catto, and M.H. Keen. Oxford: Oxford University Press, 1981, pp. 323-48.

Stones, E.L.G. "The English Mission to Edinburgh in 1328," *Scottish Historical Review* 28 (1949), 97-118.

Stones, E.L.G. "The Treaty of Northampton, 1327," *History* n.s. 38 (1953).

Stones, E.L.G. and G.G. Simpson. *Edward I and the Throne of Scotland, 1290-1296.* 2 vols. Oxford, 1978.

Storey, R.L. "Wardens of the Marches of England towards Scotland, 1377-1489," *English Historical Review* 72 (1957).

Strickland, Matthew. "Securing the North: Invasion and the Strategy of Defence in Twelfth-Century Anglo-Scottish Warfare," *Anglo-Norman Studies* 12 (1989), 177-98; in: *Anglo-Norman Warfare: Studies in Late Anglo-Saxon and Anglo-Norman Military Organization and Warfare.* Ed. M. Strickland. Woodbridge, 1992, pp. 208-29.

Stringer, Keith. "King David I (1124-53): the Scottish Occupation of Northern England," *Medieval History* 4 (1994), 51-61.

Summerson, Henry. "The Development of the Laws of the Anglo-Scottish Marches, 1249-1448." In: *Legal History in the Making.* Ed. W. Gordon and T. Fergus. London, 1991, pp. 29-42.

Summerson, Henry. "Responses to War: Carlisle and the West March in the Later Fourteenth Century." In: *War and Border Societies in the Middle Ages.* Ed. A. Goodman and A. Tuck. London, 1992, pp. 155-77.

Thornton, T. "'The Enemy or Stranger, That Shall Invade their Countrey': Identity and Community in the English North." In: *War: Identities in*

Conflict, 1300-2000. Ed. B. Taithe and T. Thorton. Stroud, 1998, pp. 57-72.

Tuck, J. Anthony. *Border Warfare: A History of Conflict on the Anglo-Scottish Border*. London: Her Majesty's Stationery Office, 1979.

Tuck, J. Anthony. "War and Society in the Medieval North," *Northern History* 21 (1985), 33-52.

Watson, Fiona J. "Settling the Stalemate: Edward I's Peace in Scotland." In: *Thirteenth Century England VI*. Ed. M. Prestwich, R.H. Britnell and R. Frame. Woodbridge, 1997, pp. 127-43.

Watson, Fiona J. *Under the Hammer: Edward I and Scotland, 1286-1306*. East Linton: Tuckwell Press, 1998.

Webster, Bruce. "Review Essay: Anglo-Scottish Relations, 1296-1389: Some Recent Essays," *Scottish Historical Review* 74 (1995), 99-108.

Willard, J.F. "The Scotch Raids and the Fourteenth Century Taxation of Northern England," *University of Colorado Studies* 5.4 (1908), 240-42.

Young, Alan. "The Comyns and Anglo-Scottish Relations (1286-1314)." In: *Thirteenth Century England VI*. Ed. Michael Prestwich, Richard Britnell and Robin Frame. Woodbridge: The Boydell Press, 1999, pp. 207-22.

Medieval – England – English/Scottish Conflicts – Bannockburn (battle of)

Mackenzie, William Mackay. *The Battle of Bannockburn: A Study in Mediaeval Warfare*. Glasgow: James MacLehose and Sons, 1913.

Morris, John E. *Bannockburn*. Cambridge: Cambridge University Press, 1914.

Nusbacher, Aryeh. *The Battle of Bannockburn, 1314*. Stroud: Tempus Publishing Ltd., 2000.

Reese, Peter. *Bannockburn: Scotland's Greatest Ever Battlefield Triumph*. Edinburgh: Canongate, 2000.

Medieval – England – English/Scottish Conflicts – Neville's Cross (battle of)

Burne, Alfred H. "The Battle of Neville's Cross," *Durham University Journal* 10 (1948-49), 100-06.

Butler, David. *Battle of Neville's Cross: An Illustrated History*. Durham: Durham City Council, 1996.

Dixon, Marie C. "John de Coupland–Hero to Villain." In: *The Battle of Neville's Cross, 1346*. Ed. David Rollason and Michael Prestwich. Studies in North-Eastern History. Stamford: Shaun Tyas, 1998, pp. 36-49.

Drury, J. Linda. "The Monument at Neville's Cross." In: *The Battle of Neville's Cross, 1346*. Ed. David Rollason and Michael Prestwich. Studies in North-Eastern History. Stamford: Shaun Tyas, 1998, pp. 78-96.

Frame, Robin. "Thomas Rokeby, Sheriff of Yorkshire, the Custodian of David II." In: *The Battle of Neville's Cross, 1346*. Ed. David Rollason and Michael Prestwich. Studies in North-Eastern History. Stamford: Shaun Tyas, 1998, pp. 50-56.

Grant, Alexander. "Disaster at Neville's Cross: The Scottish Point of View." In: *The Battle of Neville's Cross, 1346*. Ed. David Rollason and Michael Prestwich. Studies in North-Eastern History. Stamford: Shaun Tyas, 1998, pp. 15-35.

Hardy, Robert. "The Military Archery at Neville's Cross, 1346." In: *The Battle of Neville's Cross, 1346*. Ed. David Rollason and Michael Prestwich. Studies in North-Eastern History. Stamford: Shaun Tyas, 1998, pp. 112-31.

Johnson, G.A.L. "The Neville's Cross Monument: A Physical and Geological Report." In: *The Battle of Neville's Cross, 1346*. Ed. David Rollason and Michael Prestwich. Studies in North-Eastern History. Stamford: Shaun Tyas, 1998, pp. 97-101.

Lomas, R.A. "The Durham Landscape and the Battle of Neville's Cross." In: *The Battle of Neville's Cross, 1346*. Ed. David Rollason and Michael Prestwich. Studies in North-Eastern History. Stamford: Shaun Tyas, 1998, pp. 66-77.

Prestwich, Michael. "The English at the Battle of Neville's Cross." In: *The Battle of Neville's Cross, 1346*. Ed. David Rollason and Michael Prestwich. Studies in North-Eastern History. Stamford: Shaun Tyas, 1998, pp. 1-14.

Rigg, A.G. "Propaganda of the Hundred Years War: Poems on the Battles of Crecy and Durham (1346): A Critical Edition," *Traditio* 54 (1999), 169-211.

Roberts, Martin. "Neville's Cross: A Suggested Reconstruction." In: *The Battle of Neville's Cross, 1346*. Ed. David Rollason and Michael Prestwich. Studies in North-Eastern History. Stamford: Shaun Tyas, 1998, pp. 102-11.

Rogers, Clifford J. "The Scottish Invasion of 1346," *Northern History* 34 (1998), 51-69.

Rollason, Lynda. "Spoils of War? Durham Cathedral and the Black Rood of Scotland." In: *The Battle of Neville's Cross, 1346*. Ed. David Rollason and Michael Prestwich. Studies in North-Eastern History. Stamford: Shaun Tyas, 1998, pp. 57-65.

White, Robert. "The Battle of Neville's Cross," *Archaeologia aeliana* (1856), 271-303

Medieval – England – English/Scottish Conflicts – Otterburn (battle of)

Goodman, Anthony. "Introduction." In: *War and Border Societies in the Middle Ages*. Ed. A. Goodman and A. Tuck. London, 1992, pp. 1-29.

Grant, Alexander. "The Otterburn War from the Scottish Point of View." In: *War and Border Societies in the Middle Ages*. Ed. A. Goodman and A. Tuck. London, 1992, pp. 30-64.

Reed, James. "The Ballad and the Source: Some Literary Reflections on *The Battle of Otterburn*." In: *War and Border Societies in the Middle Ages*. Ed. A. Goodman and A. Tuck. London, 1992, pp. 94-123.

Tyson, Colin. "The Battle of Otterburn: When and Where was it Fought?" In: *War and Border Societies in the Middle Ages*. Ed. A. Goodman and A. Tuck. London, 1992, pp. 65-93.

Medieval – England – English/Welsh Conflicts

Barrell, A.D.M. and M.H. Brown. "A Settler Community in Post-Conquest Rural Wales: The English of Dyffryn Clwyd, 1294-1399," *Welsh Historical Review* 17 (1994-95), 332-55.

Barrell, A.D.M., M.H. Brown, and R.R. Davies. "Land, Lineage and Revolt in North-East Wales, 1243-1441," *Cambrian Medieval Studies* 29 (1995), 27-51.

Carr, A.D. "An Aristocracy in Decline: The Native Welsh Lords after the Edwardian Conquest," *Welsh Historical Review* 5 (1970/1), 103-29.

Carr, A.D. "Crown and Communities: Collaboration and Conflict." In: *Edward I and Wales*. Ed. Trevor Herbert and Gareth Elwyn Jones. Cardiff, 1988, pp. 123-44.

Carr, A.D. "'The Last and Weakest of His Line': Dafydd ap Gruffydd, the Last Prince of Wales," *Welsh Historical Review* 19 (1999), 375-99.

Carr, A.D. "Madog ap Llywelyn: The Revolt of 1294-5 in Caernarfonshire," *Caernarfonshire Historical Society Transactions* 58 (1997), 35-46.

Chrimes, S.B. *King Edward I's Policy in Wales*. Cardiff, 1969.

Crouch, David. "The March and the Welsh Kings." In: *The Anarchy of King Stephen's Reign*. Ed. E.J. King. Oxford, 1994, pp. 255-89.

Crump, J.J. "The Mortimer Family and the Making of the March." In: *Thirteenth Century England, VI*. Ed. M. Prestwich, R.H. Britnell and R. Frame. Woodbridge, 1997, pp. 117-26.

Davies, R.R. *Conquest, Coexistence, and Change: Wales, 1063-1415*. Oxford, 1987.

Davies, R.R. *Domination and Conquest: The Experience of Ireland, Scotland and Wales, 1100-1300*. Cambridge: Cambridge University Press, 1990.

Davies, R.R. "Edward I and Wales." In: *Edward I and Wales*. Ed. Trevor Herbert and Gareth Elwyn Jones. Cardiff, 1988, pp. 1-10.

Davies, R.R. "Henry I and Wales." In: *Studies in Medieval History Presented to R.H.C. Davis*. Ed. H. Mayr-Harting and R.I. Moore. London, 1985, pp. 133-47.

Davies, R.R. "Kings, Lords and Liberties in the March of Wales, 1066-1272," *Transactions of the Royal Historical Society*, 5th ser., 29 (1979), 41-61.

Davies, R.R. *Lordship and Society in the March of Wales, 1282-1400*. Oxford, 1978.

Davies, R.R. *The Revolt of Owain Glyn Dŵr*. Oxford: Oxford University Press, 1995.

Davies, R.R. "The Survival of the Bloodfeud in Medieval Wales," *History* n.s. 54 (1969), 338-57.

Davies, Wendy. *Wales in the Early Middle Ages*. Leicester, 1982.

Davies, Wendy. "Land and Power in Early Medieval Wales," *Past and Present* 81 (1978), 3-23.

Edwards, John Goronwy. "The Battle of Maes Madog and the Welsh Campaign of 1294-95," *English Historical Review* 39 (1924), 1-12.

Edwards, John Goronwy. "Henry II and the Fight at Coleshill: Some Further Reflections," *Welsh Historical Review* 3 (1967), 251-63.

Edwards, John Goronwy. "The Normans and the Welsh March," *Proceedings of the British Academy* 42 (1956), 155-77.

Gater, Dilys. *The Battles of Wales*. Cardiff: Gewasg Carreg Gwalch, 1991.

Given, James. "The Economic Consequences of the English Conquest of Gwynedd," *Speculum* 64 (1989), 11-45.

Given, James. *State and Society in Medieval Europe: Gwynedd and Languedoc under Outside Rule*. Ithaca: Cornell University Press, 1990.

Griffiths, Rhidian. "Prince Henry and Wales, 1400-1408." In: *Profit, Piety and the Professions in Later Medieval England*. Ed. M. Hicks. Stroud, 1990, pp. 51-61.

Gruffydd, K. Lloyd. "Sea Power and the Anglo-Welsh Wars, 1210-1410," *Maritime Wales* 11 (1987), 28-53.

Henken, Elissa. *National Redeemer: Owain Glyndower*. Ithaca: Cornell University Press, 1996.

Hudson, Benjamin T. "The Destruction of Gruffudd ap Llywelyn," *Welsh Historical Review* 15 (1991), 331-50.

King, D.J. Cathcart. "The Defence of Wales, 1067-1283: The Other Side of the Hill," *Archaeologia Cambrensis* 126 (1977), 1-16.

King, D.J. Cathcart. "Henry II and the Fight at Coleshill," *Welsh Historical Review* 2 (1965), 367-73.

Lloyd, John Edward. *A History of Wales from the Earliest Times to the Edwardian Conquest*. 3rd ed. 2 vols. London, 1939.

Lloyd, John Edward. "Oswestry as a Link Between England and Wales," *Archaeologia Cambrensis* 78 (1923), 196-203.

Lloyd, John Edward. "Wales and the Coming of the Normans (1039-1093)," *Transactions of the Honourable Society of Cymmrodorion* (1899/1900), 122-79.

Mann, Kevin. "The March of Wales: A Question of Terminology," *Welsh Historical Review* 18 (1996), 1-13.

Meisel, Janet. *Barons of the Welsh Frontier: The Corbet, Pantulf and Fitz Warin Families, 1066-1272*. London, 1980.

Morris, John E. *The Welsh Wars of Edward I: A Contribution to Mediaeval Military History, Based on Original Documents*. 1901; rpt. New York: Haskell House Publishers Ltd., 1969; rpt. Stroud: Sutton Publishing, 1996.

Nelson, Lynn H. *The Normans in South Wales, 1070-1170*. London, 1966.

Owens, H. "Warfare in Pre-Edwardian Wales," *Transactions of the Anglesey Antiquarian Society* (1940), 32-45.

Remfrey, Paul M. "The Last Campaign of Rhys ap Gruffydd," *Herefordshire Archaeological News* 62 (1994), 35-48.

Rothero, Christopher. *The Scottish and Welsh Wars, 1250-1400*. Men-at-Arms Series. London: Osprey Publishing, 1984.

Rowlands, Ifor W. "The Edwardian Conquest and its Military Consolidation." In: *Edward I and Wales*. Ed. Trevor Herbert and Gareth Elwyn Jones. Cardiff, 1988, pp. 40-72.

Sandford, G. "Montgomeryshire, in Its Connection with the Marches of Wales," *Montgomeryshire Connections* 12 (1879), 205-38.

Smith, J. Beverley. "Edward II and the Allegiance of Wales," *Welsh Historical Review* 8 (1976-77), 139-71.

Smith, J. Beverley. "Gruffydd Llwyd and the Celtic Alliance," *Bulletin of the Board of Celtic Studies* 26 (1976), 463-78.

Smith, J. Beverley. "Llywleyn ap Gruffudd and the March of Wales," *Byrcheiniog* 20 (1982/83), 9-22.

Smith, J. Beverley. "Welsh Society and Native Power before the Conquest." In: *Edward I and Wales*. Ed. Trevor Herbert and Gareth Elwyn Jones. Cardiff, 1988, pp. 11-39.

Smith, Llinos Beverley. "The Governance of Edwardian Wales." In: *Edward I and Wales*. Ed. Trevor Herbert and Gareth Elwyn Jones. Cardiff, 1988, pp. 73-95.

Stanford, S.C. *The Archaeology of the Welsh Marches*. London, 1980.

Stephenson, David. *The Governance of Gwynedd*. Cardiff, 1984.

Suppe, Frederick C. "The Cultural Significance of Decapitation in High Medieval Wales and the Marches," *Bulletin of the Board of Celtic Studies* 36 (1989), 147-60.

Tout, T.F. "Wales and the March During the Barons' Wars, 1258-1267." In: *Historical Essays*. Ed. T.F. Tout and J. Tait. Manchester, 1907.

Treharne, Cennydd G. "The Conquest of Glamorgan," *Archaeologia cambrensis* 133 (1984), 1-7.

Turvey, R.K. "The Marcher Shire of Pembroke and the Glyndwr Rebellion," *Welsh Historical Review* 15 (1990), 151-68.

Walker, David. "The Norman Settlement in Wales," *Proceedings of the Battle Conference of Anglo-Norman Studies* 1 (1978), 131-43, 222-25.

Williams, Glanmor. "The Church and Monasticism in the Age of Conquest." In: *Edward I and Wales*. Ed. Trevor Herbert and Gareth Elwyn Jones. Cardiff, 1988, pp. 97-122.

Williams, Glanmor. *Owain Glyndŵr*. Cardiff: University of Wales Press, 1993.

Williams, T.W. *The Glyndŵr Rebellion: A Military Study*. Unpublished Thesis. Swansea: University of Wales at Swansea, 1979.

Medieval – England – Wars of the Roses

Allan, Alison. "Yorkist Propaganda: Pedigree, Prophecy and the 'British History' in the Reign of Edward IV." In: *Patronage, Pedigree and Power in Later Medieval England*. Ed. Charles Ross. Gloucester, 1979.

Arthurson, Ian. "Espionage and Intelligence from the Wars of the Roses to the Reformation," *Nottingham Medieval Studies* 35 (1991), 134-54.

Arthurson, Ian. *The Perkin Warbeck Conspiracy, 1491-1499*. Stroud: Sutton, 1997.

Arthurson, Ian and Nicholas Kingwell. "The Proclamation of Henry Tudor as King of England, 3 November 1483," *Historical Research* 63 (1990), 100-06.

Attreed, Lorraine C. "An Indenture between Richard Duke of Gloucester and the Scrope Family of Masham and Upsall," *Speculum* 58 (1983), 1018-25.

Bagley, J.J. *Margaret of Anjou, Queen of England*. London, 1948.

Bazeley, William. "Tewkesbury," *Proceedings of the Bristol and Gloucester Archaeological Society* 26 (1903), 173-93.

Bean, J.M.W. "The Financial Position of Richard, Duke of York." In: *War and Government in the Middle Ages: Essays in Honour of J.O. Prestwich*. Ed. J. Gillingham and J.C. Holt. Cambridge, 1984, pp. 182-98.

Bell, Graham. "Edward IV, Military Genius or Bold Slugger?" *Battlefield* 4.3 (1998), 15-17.

Bennett, Michael J. *The Battle of Bosworth*. New York: St. Martin's Press, 1985.

Bennett, Michael J. "Henry VII and the Northern Rising of 1489," *English Historical Review* 105 (1990).

Bennett, Michael J. *Lambert Simnel and the Battle of Stoke*. New York: St. Martin's Press, 1987

Biggs, Douglas. "'A Wrong Whom Conscience and Kindred Bid Me to Right:' A Reassessment of Edmund of Langley, Duke of York, and the Usurpation of Henry IV," *Albion* 26 (1994), 253-72.

Biggs, Douglas. "The Economic Context." In: *The Wars of the Roses*. Ed. A.J. Pollard. New York, 1988, pp. 41-64.

Blow, Jonathan. "Nibley Green, 1470: The Last Private Battle Fought in England." In: *English Society and Government in the Fifteenth Century*. Ed. C.M.D. Crowder. Edinburgh, 1967, pp. 87-111.

Boardman, A.W. *The Battle of Towton*. Stroud: Sutton Publishing, 1994.

Boardman, A.W. *The Medieval Soldier in the Wars of the Roses*. Stroud: Sutton Publishing, 1998.

Booth, Peter. "Richard Duke of Gloucester and the West March Towards Scotland, 1470-1483," *Northern History* 36 (2000), 233-46.

Boylston, Arthur, Shannon Novak, and Tim Sutherland. "Burials from the Battle of Towton," *Royal Armouries Yearbook* 2 (1997), 136-39.

Brooke, Richard. *Visits to Fields of Battle, in England of the Fifteenth Century*. London, 1857.

Carpenter, Christine. "The Duke of Clarence and the Midlands: A Study in the Interplay of Local and National Politics," *Midland History* 11 (1986), 23-48.

Carpenter, Christine. "The Stonor Circle in the Fifteenth Century." In: *Rulers and Ruled in Late Medieval England: Essays Presented to Gerald Harriss*. Ed. R.E. Archer and S. Walker. London, 1995, pp. 175-200.

Carpenter, Christine. *The Wars of the Roses: Politics and the Constitution in England, c. 1437-1509*. Cambridge: Cambridge University Press, 1997.

Castor, Helen. "'Walter Blount Was Gone to Serve Traytours': The Sack of Elvaston and the Politics of the North Midlands in 1454," *Midland History* 19 (1994), 21-39.

Cherry, Martin. "The Struggle for Power in Mid-Fifteenth-Century Devonshire." In: *Patronage, the Crown and the Provinces in Later Medieval England.* Ed. Ralph A. Griffiths. Gloucester: Alan Sutton, 1981, pp. 123-44.

Chrimes, S.B. *Henry VII.* London: Eyre Methuen Ltd; rpt. New Haven: Yale University Press,1999.

Chrimes, S.B. *Lancastrians, Yorkists and Henry VII.* 2nd ed. London: Macmillan, 1966.

Cook, David R. *Lancastrians and Yorkists: The Wars of the Roses.* London: Longman, 1984.

Crawford, Anne. "The King's Burden?: The Consequences of Royal Marriage in Fifteenth-Century England." In: *Patronage, The Crown, and the Provinces in Later Medieval England.* Ed. Ralph A. Griffiths. Gloucester: Alan Sutton, 1981, pp. 33-56.

Cron, B.M. "Margaret of Anjou and the Lancastrian March on London, 1461," *Ricardian* 11 (Dec 1999), 590-615.

Cunningham, S. "Henry VII and Rebellion in North-Eastern England, 1485-1492: Bonds of Allegiance and the Establishment of Tudor Authority," *Northern History* 32 (1996), 42-74.

Currin, John M. "Henry VII and the Treaty of Redon (1489): Plantagenet Ambitions and Early Tudor Foreign Policy," *History* 81 (1996), 343-58.

Davies, Clifford S.L. "Bishop John Morton, the Holy See and the Accession of Henry VII," *English Historical Review* 102 (1987).

Davies, Clifford S.L. "The Crofts: Creation and Defence of a Family Enterprise under the Yorkists and Henry VII," *Historical Research* 68 (1995), 241-65.

Davies, Clifford S.L. "Richard III, Brittany and Henry Tudor," *Nottingham Medieval Studies* 37 (1993), 110-26.

Davies, Clifford S.L. "The Origins of the Wars of the Roses." In: *The Wars of the Roses.* Ed. A.J. Pollard. New York, 1988, pp. 65-88.

Davies, Clifford S.L. "The Wars of the Roses in the European Context." In: *The Wars of the Roses*. Ed. A.J. Pollard. New York, 1988, pp. 162-85.

Davies, Clifford S.L. "The Church and the Wars of the Roses." In: *The Wars of the Roses*. Ed. A.J. Pollard. New York, 1988, pp. 134-61.

Davis, Virginia. "William Waynflete and the Wars of the Roses," *Southern History* 11 (1989).

Daw, Ben. "Elections to the Order of the Garter in the Reign of Edward IV, 1461-83," *Medieval Prospography* 19 (1998), 187-213.

Dobson, R.B. "Politics and the Church in the Fifteenth-Century North." In: *The North of England in the Age of Richard III*. Ed. A.J. Pollard. The Fifteenth Century Series, no. 3. Stroud: Alan Sutton Publishing, 1996, pp. 1-18.

Dockery, Keith and Richard Knowles. *The Battle of Wakefield*. London: The Richard III Society, 1992.

Dockery, Keith and Richard Knowles. "The Battle of Wakefield," *Ricardian* 9 (Jun 1992).

Dunham, William Huse. "Lord Hastings' Indentured Retainers, 1461-1483: The Lawfulness of Livery and Retaining under the Yorkists and Tudors," *Transactions of the Connecticut Academy of Arts and Sciences* 5 (1955), 1-175.

Dunlop, David. "The 'Masked Comedian': Perkin Warbeck's Adventures in Scotland and England from 1495 to 1497," *Scottish Historical Review* 70 (1991), 97-128.

Dunlop, David. "The 'Redresses and Reparacions of Attemptates': Alexander Legh's Instructions from Edward IV, March-April 1475," *Historical Research* 63 (1990), 340-53.

Dunn, Diana. "Margaret of Anjou, Queen Consort of Henry VI: A Reassessment of her Role, 1445-53." In: *Crown, Government and People in the Fifteenth Century*. Ed. R.E. Archer. Stroud, 1995, pp. 107-43.

Dunn, Diana. "The Queen at War: The Role of Margaret of Anjou in the Wars of the Roses." In: *War and Society in Medieval and Early Modern*

Britain. Ed. Diana Dunn. Liverpool: Liverpool University Press, 2000, pp. 141-61.

Eaton, Mark. "War of the Roses' Second Round," *Military History* (Dec 1996), 66-72.

Elton, Geoffrey R. "Henry VII: Rapacity and Remorse," *Historical Journal* 1 (1958), 21-39.

Elton, Geoffrey R. "Henry VII: A Restatement," *Historical Journal* 4 (1961), 1-29.

Elton, Geoffrey R. "A Revolution in Tudor History?" *Past and Present* 32 (1965), 103-09.

Elton, Geoffrey R. "The Tudor Revolutions: A Reply," *Past and Present* 29 (1964), 26-49.

English Heritage. *The Battlefield of Bosworth Report*. London: Register of Historic Battlefields, 1995.

Evans, H.T. *Wales and the Wars of the Roses*. Cambridge: Cambridge University Press, 1915; rpt. Stroud: Alan Sutton Publishing Limited, 1995.

Fletcher, Doris. "The Lancastrian Collar of Esses: Its Origin and Transformation Down the Centuries." In: *The Age of Richard II*. Ed. James L. Gillespie. New York, 1997, pp. 191-204.

Foss, Peter J. "The Battle of Bosworth: Towards a Reassessment," *Midland History* 13 (1988), 21-33.

Foss, Peter J. *The Field of Redemore: The Battle of Bosworth, 1485*. 2nd ed. Newtown Linford, 1998.

Foss, Peter J. "A Significant Document: The Hinckley-Lyre Agreement (1283) and the Site of the Battle of Bosworth," *Hinckley Historian* 22 (Aut 1988).

Gairdner, J. "The Battle of Bosworth," *Archaeologia* 55.1 (1896).

Gairdner, J. *History of the Life and Reign of Richard III*. Cambridge: Cambridge University Press, 1898.

Gill, Louise. *Richard III and Buckingham's Rebellion*. Stroud: Sutton Publishing, 1999.

Gill, Louise. "William Caxton and the Rebellion of 1483," *English Historical Review* 112 (1997), 105-18.

Gillingham, John. "Introduction: Interpreting Richard." In: *Richard III: A Medieval Kingship*. Ed. J. Gillingham. New York, 1993, pp. 1-20.

Gillingham, John. *The Wars of the Roses: Peace and Conflict in Fifteenth-Century England*. Baton Rouge: Louisiana State University Press, 1981.

Goodman, Anthony. *The Wars of the Roses: Military Activity and English Society, 1452-97*. London: Routledge and Kegan Paul, 1981.

Goodman, Anthony and David Morgan. "The Yorkist Claim to the Throne of Castile," *Journal of Medieval History* 11 (1985), 61-69.

Gransden, Antonia. "Politics and Historiography during the Wars of the Roses." In: *Medieval Historical Writing in the Christian and Islamic Worlds*. Ed. D.O. Morgan. London: School of Oriental and African Studies, University of London, 1982, pp. 125-48.

Grant, Alexander. "Foreign Affairs under Richard III." In: *Richard III: A Medieval Kingship*. Ed. J. Gillingham. New York, 1993, pp. 113-32.

Grant, Alexander. "Richard III and Scotland." In: *The North of England in the Age of Richard III*. Ed. A.J. Pollard. The Fifteenth Century Series, no. 3. Stroud: Alan Sutton Publishing, 1996, pp. 115-48.

Gravett, Christopher. *Bosworth, 1485: Last Charge of the Plantagenets*. London: Osprey, 1999.

Green, Richard Firth. "The Short Version of *The Arrival of Edward IV*," *Speculum* 56 (1981), 324-36.

Griffith, Paddy, ed. *The Battle of Blore Heath, 1459: Documents and Analyses Collected by the Rev. Dr. Brian Swynnerton and William Swinnerton, Especially Featuring a Reprint of the Book by the Same Title by Colonel F.R. Twemlow, First Published in Wolverhampton, 1912*. Nuneaton: Paddy Griffith Associates, 1995.

Griffiths, Ralph A. "Duke Richard of York's Intentions in 1450 and the Origins of the Wars of the Roses." In: *King and Country: England and Wales in the Fifteenth Century*. London, 1991, pp. 277-304.

Griffiths, Ralph A. "The Provinces and the Dominions in the Age of the Wars of the Roses." In: *Estrangements, Enterprise and Education in Fifteenth-Century England*. Ed. Sharon D. Michalove and A. Compton Reeves. The Fifteenth Century Series, no. 5. Stroud: Sutton Publishing, 1998, pp. 1-26.

Griffiths, Ralph A. *The Reign of King Henry VI: The Exercise of Royal Authority, 1422-1461*. Berkeley and Los Angeles: University of California Press, 1981.

Griffiths, Ralph A. "The Trial of Eleanor Cobham: An Episode in the Fall of Duke Humphrey of Gloucester." In: *King and Country: England and Wales in the Fifteenth Century*. London, 1991, pp. 233-52.

Griffiths, Ralph A. and Roger S. Thomas. *The Making of the Tudor Dynasty*. Stroud: Wrens Park Publishing, 1998.

Gross, A. *The Dissolution of the Lancastrian Kingship*. Stamford, 1996.

Gunn, Steven. "Henry VII and Charles the Bold," *History Today* 46 (Apr 1996), 26-33.

Guth, J. DeLloyd. "Climbing the Civil-Service Pole During the Civil War: Sir Reynold Bray (*c.* 1440-1503)." In: *Estrangements, Enterprise and Education in Fifteenth-Century England*. Ed. Sharon D. Michalove and A. Compton Reeves. The Fifteenth Century Series, no. 5. Stroud: Sutton Publishing, 1998, pp. 47-62.

Guth, J. DeLloyd. "Fifteenth-Century England: Recent Scholarship and Future Directions," *British Studies Monitor* 7 (1976-77), 3-50.

Guth, J. DeLloyd. "Richard III, Henry VII and the City: London Politics and the Dun Cowe." In: *Kings and Nobles in the Late Middle Ages: A Tribute to Charles Ross*. Ed. R.A. Griffiths and J. Sherborne. Gloucester, 1986, pp.

Haigh, Philip A. *The Battle of Wakefield, 30 December 1460*. Stroud: Sutton Publishing Limited, 1996.

Haigh, Philip A. *The Military Campaigns of the Wars of the Roses*. Far Stroud: Alan Sutton Publishing Limited, 1995.

Hall, E. *The Union of the Two Noble Families of Lancaster and York*. Menston, 1970.

Halliwell, J.A. "Observations upon the History of Certain Events during the Reign of Edward IV," *Archaeologia* 29 (1842).

Hammond, P.W. *The Battles of Barnet and Tewkesbury*. New York: St. Martin's Press, 1990.

Hammond, P.W. "The Reputation of Richard III." In: *Richard III: A Medieval Kingship*. Ed. J. Gillingham. New York, 1993, pp. 133-49.

Hanham, Alison. *Richard III and His Early Historians, 1483-1535*. Oxford, 1975.

Hanham, Alison. "Text and Subtext: Bishop John Russell's Parliamentary Sermons, 1483-1484," *Traditio* 54 (1999), 300-22.

Harris, O.D. "The Bosworth Commemoration at Dadlington," *Ricardian* 7.90 (Sept 1985).

Harris, O.D. "'... even here, in Bosworth Field': A Disputed Site of Battle," *Ricardian* 7.92 (1986), 194-207.

Harriss, Gerald L. *Cardinal Beaufort: A Study of Lancastrian Ascendency and Decline*. Oxford, 1988.

Hayes, Rosemary C.E. "'Ancient Indictments' for the North of England, 1461-1509." In: *The North of England in the Age of Richard III*. Ed. A.J. Pollard. The Fifteenth Century Series, no. 3. Stroud: Alan Sutton Publishing, 1996, pp. 19-46.

Head, Constance. "Pius II and the Wars of the Roses," *Archivum historiae pontificiae* 8 (1970).

Hedley, Olwen. *Prisoners in the Tower*. Rev. and ed. John McIlwain. London: Pitkin Pictorials, 1994.

Hicks, D. *The Battle of Barnet Quincentenary, 1471-1971: Commemorative Brochure*. Barnet, 1971.

Hicks, Michael A. "The Changing Role of the Wydevilles in Yorkist Politics to 1483." In: *Patronage, Pedigree and Power in Later Medieval England*. Ed. C. Ross. Gloucester: Alan Sutton, 1979.

Hicks, Michael A. "Counting the Cost of War: The Moleyns Ransom and the Hungerford Land-Sales, 1453-87," *Southern History* 8 (1986), 11-35.

Hicks, Michael A. "Descent, Partition and Extinction: The Warwick Inheritance," *Bulletin of the Institute for Historical Research* 52 (1979).

Hicks, Michael A. "Edward IV, the Duke of Somerset and Lancastrian Loyalism in the North," *Northern History* 20 (1984).

Hicks, Michael A. *False, Fleeting, Perjur'd Clarence: George, Duke of Clarence, 1449-78*. Bangor: Headstart History, 1992.

Hicks, Michael A. "The Forfeiture of Barnard Castle to the Bishop of Durham in 1459," *Northern History* 33 (1997), 223-31.

Hicks, Michael A. "From Megaphone to Microscope: The Correspondence of Richard Duke of York with Henry VI in 1450 Revisited," *Journal of Medieval History* 25 (1999), 243-56.

Hicks, Michael A. "A Minute of the Lancastrian Council at York, 20 January 1461," *Northern History* 35 (1999), 214-21.

Hicks, Michael A. "Richard, Duke of Gloucester: The Formative Years." In: *Richard III: A Medieval Kingship*. Ed. J. Gillingham. New York, 1993, pp. 21-38.

Hicks, Michael A. "Richard, Duke of Gloucester and the North." In: *Richard III and the North*. Ed. Rosemary Horrox. Studies in Regional and Local History, 6. Hull: Centre for Regional and Local History, 1986, pp. 11-26.

Hicks, Michael A. *Richard III as Duke of Gloucester: A Study in Character*. Borthwick Paper, 70. York, 1986.

Hicks, Michael A. "The Sources." In: *The Wars of the Roses*. Ed. A.J. Pollard. New York, 1988, pp. 20-40.

Hicks, Michael A. *Warwick the Kingmaker*. Oxford: Blackwell, 1998.

Holmer, Paul Leroy. *Studies in the Military Organization of the Yorkist Kings*. Unpublished dissertation. Minneapolis: University of Minnesota, 1977.

Hooker, James R. "Notes on the Organization and Supply of the Tudor Military under Henry VII," *Huntingdon Library Quarterly* 23 (1959-60), 19-31.

Horrox, Rosemary. "The Government of Richard III." In: *Richard III: A Medieval Kingship*. Ed. J. Gillingham. New York, 1993, pp. 57-74.

Horrox, Rosemary. "Henry Tudor's Letters to England during Richard III's Reign," *Ricardian* 80 (1983), 155-58.

Horrox, Rosemary. "Introduction." In: *Richard III and the North*. Ed. Rosemary Horrox. Studies in Regional and Local History, 6. Hull: Centre for Regional and Local History, 1986, pp. 1-10.

Horrox, Rosemary. "Personalities and Politics." In: *The Wars of the Roses*. Ed. A.J. Pollard. New York, 1988, pp. 89-109.

Horrox, Rosemary. *Richard III: A Study of Service*. Cambridge: Cambridge University Press, 1989.

Horrox, Rosemary. "Richard III and the East Riding." In: *Richard III and the North*. Ed. Rosemary Horrox. Studies in Regional and Local History, 6. Hull: Centre for Regional and Local History, 1986, pp. 82-107.

Horrox, Rosemary. "The State of Research: Local and National Politics in Fifteenth-Century England," *Journal of Medieval History* 18 (1992), 391-403.

Hughes, Jonathan. "'True Ornaments to Know a Holy Man': Northern Religious Life and the Piety of Richard III." In: *The North of England in the Age of Richard III*. Ed. A.J. Pollard. The Fifteenth Century Series, no. 3. Stroud: Alan Sutton Publishing, 1996, pp. 149-90.

Hutton, William. *The Battle of Bosworth Field*. 2nd ed. 1813; rpt. Stroud: Tempus, 1999.

Jack, R.I. "A Quincentenary: The Battle of Northampton, July 10th, 1460," *Northamptonshire Past and Present* 3 (1960-65), 21-25.

Johnson, P.A. *Duke Richard of York, 1411-1460*. Oxford: Clarendon Press, 1988.

Jones, E.W. *Bosworth Field: A Welsh Retrospect*. Liverpool: Modern Welsh Publications, Ltd., 1984.

Jones, Michael K. "Henry VII, Lady Margaret Beaufort and the Orléans Ransom." In: *Kings and Nobles in the Later Middle Ages: A Tribute to Charles Ross*. Ed. R.A. Griffiths and James Sherborne. Gloucester, 1986, pp. 254-73.

Jones, Michael K. "Richard III and the Stanleys." In: *Richard III and the North*. Ed. Rosemary Horrox. Studies in Regional and Local History, 6. Hull: Centre for Regional and Local History, 1986, pp. 27-50.

Jones, Michael K. "Richard III as a Soldier." In: *Richard III: A Medieval Kingship*. Ed. J. Gillingham. New York, 1993, pp. 93-112.

Jones, Michael K. "Somerset, York and the Wars of the Roses," *English Historical Review* 104 (1989), 285-307.

Kendall, Paul Murray. *Warwick the Kingmaker*. London: Cardinal, 1973.

Kendall, Paul Murray, ed. *Richard III: The Great Debate. Sir Thomas More's History of King Richard III and Horace Walpole's Historic Doubts on the Life and Reign of King Richard III*. New York: W.W. Norton and Company, 1965.

Kingsford, Charles Lethbridge. "The Earl of Warwick at Calais in 1460," *English Historical Review* 37 (1922).

Kingsford, Charles Lethbridge. *English Historical Literature in the Fifteenth Century*. 1913; rpt. New York, 1972.

Lacey, Kay. "The Military Organisation of the Reign of Henry VII." In: *Armies, Chivalry and Warfare in Medieval Britain and France: Proceedings of the 1995 Harlaxton Symposium*. Ed. M. Strickland. Stamford, 1998, pp. 234-55.

Lander, J.R. *Conflict and Stability in Fifteenth-Century England*. London: Hutchinson University Library, 1969.

Lander, J.R. *The Wars of the Roses*. London, 1965.

Lee, P.A. "Reflections of Power: Margaret of Anjou and the Dark Side of Queenship," *Renaissance Quarterly* 39 (1986), 183-217.

Leroy, H.P. *Studies in the Military Organization of the Yorkist Kings*. Unpublished dissertation. Minneapolis: University of Minnesota, 1977.

Linnell, B. *The Battle of Tewkesbury, Saturday May 4th 1471*. Cheltenham: The Theoc. Press, 1971.

Luckett, D.A. "The Rise and Fall of a Noble Dynasty: Henry VII and the Lords Willoughby de Broke," *Historical Research* 69 (1996), 254-65.

Markham, Clements R. "The Battle of Wakefield," *Yorkshire Archaeological and Topographical Journal* 9 (1886), 105-23.

Markham, Clements R. "The Battle of Towton," *Yorkshire Archaeological and Topographical Journal* 10 (1889), 1-34.

Maurer, Helen. "Bones in the Tower: A Discussion of Time, Place and Circumstance," *Ricardian* 8 (1990), 474-93; IX (1991), 2-22.

McCulloch, D. and E.D. Jones. "Lancastrian Politics, the French War, and the Rise of the Popular Element," *Speculum* 58 (1983), 95-138.

McFarlane, K.B. "The War of the Roses." In: *England in the Fifteenth Century: Collected Essays*. London, 1981, pp. 231-68.

McNiven, Peter. "Legitimacy and Consent: Henry IV and the Lancastrian Title, 1399-1406," *Mediaeval Studies* 44 (1982), 470-88.

Mercer, M. "Lancastrian Loyalism in the South-West: the Case of the Beauforts," *Southern History* 19 (1997), 42-60.

Morgan, D.A.L. "The House of Policy: The Political Role of the Late Plantagenet Household, 1422-1485." In: *The English Court from the Wars of the Roses to the Civil War*. Ed. D. Starkey. London, 1987.

Morgan, Philip. "'Those Were the Days': A Yorkist Pedigree Roll." In: *Estrangements, Enterprise and Education in Fifteenth-Century England*. Ed. Sharon D. Michalove and A. Compton Reeves. The Fifteenth Century Series, no. 5. Stroud: Sutton Publishing, 1998, pp. 107-17.

Myers, A.R. "The Character of Richard III." In: *English Society and Government in the Fifteenth Century*. Ed. C.M.D. Crowder. Edinburgh, 1967, pp. 112-33.

Myers, A.R. "The Household of Margaret of Anjou, 1452-53." In: *Crown, Household and Parliament in Fifteenth Century England*. Ed. A.R. Myers. London, 1985.

Newman, Christine M. "Order and Community in the North: The Liberty of Allertonshire in the Later Fifteenth Century." In: *The North of England in the Age of Richard III*. Ed. A.J. Pollard. The Fifteenth Century Series, no. 3. Stroud: Alan Sutton Publishing, 1996, pp. 47-66.

Palliser, D.M. "Richard III and York." In: *Richard III and the North*. Ed. Rosemary Horrox. Studies in Regional and Local History, 6. Hull: Centre for Regional and Local History, 1986, pp. 51-81.

Payling, Simon. *Political Society in Lancastrian England: The Greater Gentry in Nottinghamshire*. Oxford: Oxford University Press, 1991.

Phillips, M.J. "The Battle of Bosworth: Further Reflections on the Battle-field Site," *Ricardian* 7.96 (Mar 1987).

Pierce, Hazel. "The King's Cousin: The Life, Career and Welsh Connection of Sir Richard Pole, 1458-1504," *Welsh Historical Review* 19 (1998), 187-225.

Pollard, A.J. "The Characteristics of the Fifteenth-Century North." In: *Government, Religion and Society in Northern England, 1000-1700*. Ed. J.C. Appleby and P. Dalton. Stroud, 1997, pp. 131-43.

Pollard, A.J. "The Crown and the County Palatine of Durham, 1437-94." In: *The North of England in the Age of Richard III*. Ed. A.J. Pollard. The Fifteenth Century Series, no. 3. Stroud: Alan Sutton Publishing, 1996, pp. 67-88.

Pollard, A.J. "Dominic Mancini's Account of the Events of 1483," *Nottingham Medieval Studies* 38 (1994), 152-63.

Pollard, A.J. Introduction: Society, Politics and the Wars of the Roses." In: *The Wars of the Roses*. Ed. A.J. Pollard. New York, 1988, pp. 1-19.

Pollard, A.J. *Late Medieval England, 1399-1509*. Longman History of Medieval England. Harlow: Longman, 2000.

Pollard, A.J. *North-eastern England during the Wars of the Roses: Lay Society, War, and Politics, 1450-1500*. Oxford, 1990.

Pollard, A.J. *Richard III and the Princes in the Tower*. New York: St. Martin's Press, 1991.

Pollard, A.J. "St Cuthbert and the Hog: Richard III and the County Palatine of Durham, 1471-85." In: *Kings and Nobles in the Later Middle Ages: A Tribute to Charles Ross*. Gloucester, 1986.

Pollard, A.J. "The Tyranny of Richard III," *Journal of Medieval History* 3 (1977), 147-65.

Pollard, A.J. *The Wars of the Roses*. New York: St. Martin's Press, 1988.

Powell, Edward. "The Strange Death of Sir John Mortimer: Politics and the Law of Treason in Lancastrian England." In: *Rulers and Ruled in Late Medieval England: Essays Presented to Gerald Harriss*. Ed. R.E. Archer and S. Walker. London, 1995, pp. 83-97.

Powicke, Michael R. "Lancastrian Captains." In: *Essays in Medieval History Presented to Bertie Wilkinson*. Ed. T.A. Sandquist and M.R. Powicke. Toronto: University of Toronto Press, 1969, pp. 371-82.

Priestley, E.J. *The Battle of Shrewsbury, 1403*. Shrewsbury: Shrewsbury and Atcham Borough Council, 1979.

Pugh, T.B. "Richard, Duke of York, and the Rebellion of Henry Holland, Duke of Exeter, in May 1454," *Historical Research* 63 (1990), 248-62.

Pugh, T.B. "Richard Plantagenet (1411-60), Duke of York, as the King's Lieutenant in France and Ireland." In: *Aspects of Late Medieval Government and Society: Essays Presented to J.R. Lander*. Ed. J.G. Rowe. Toronto: University of Toronto Press, 1986, pp. 107-42.

Pugh, T.B. "The Southampton Plot of 1415." In: *Kings and Nobles in the Later Middle Ages: A Tribute to Charles Ross*. Ed. R.A. Griffiths and J. Sherborne. Gloucester, 1986, pp. 62-89.

Ramsey, J.H. *Lancaster and York*. 2 vols. Oxford, 1892.

Rees, David. *The Son of Prophecy: Henry Tudor's Road to Bosworth*. London: Black Raven Press, 1985.

Reeves, A. Compton. "Lawrence Booth: Bishop of Durham (1457-76), Archbishop of York (1476-80)." In: *Estrangements, Enterprise and Education in Fifteenth-Century England*. Ed. Sharon D. Michalove and A. Compton Reeves. The Fifteenth Century Series, no. 5. Stroud: Sutton Publishing, 1998, pp. 63-88.

Reeves, A. Compton. "Some of Humphrey Stafford's Military Indentures," *Nottingham Medieval Studies* 16 (1972), 80-91.

Richardson, Geoffrey. *The Hollow Crowns: A History of the Battles of the Wars of the Roses*. Shipley: Baildon Books, 1996.

Richardson, Thom. "The Bridport Muster Roll of 1457," *Royal Armouries Yearbook* 2 (1997), 46-52.

Richmond, Colin. "1483: The Year of Decision (or Taking the Throne)." In: *Richard III: A Medieval Kingship*. Ed. J. Gillingham. New York, 1993, pp. 39-56.

Richmond, Colin. "1485 And All That, or What Was Going On at the Battle of Bosworth." In: *Richard III: Loyalty, Lordship and the Law*. Ed. P. Hammond. Gloucester: Sutton, 1986.

Richmond, Colin. "The Battle of Bosworth, August 1485," *History Today* 35.8 (1985), 17-22.

Richmond, Colin. "The Earl of Warwick's Domination of the Channel and the Naval Dimension to the Wars of the Roses, 1456-1460," *Southern History* 20/21 (1998-99), 1-19.

Richmond, Colin. "The Nobility and the Wars of the Roses, 1457-1459," *Journal of Historical Sociology* 9 (1996), 395-409.

Richmond, Colin. "Nobility and the Wars of the Roses, 1459-1461," *Nottingham Medieval Studies* 21 (1977), 71-86.

Richmond, Colin. "Propaganda in the Wars of the Roses," *History Today* 42 (Jul 1992), 12-18.

Richmond, Colin. "Richard III, Richard Nixon and the Brutality of Fifteenth-Century Politics." In: *Estrangements, Enterprise and Education in Fifteenth-Century England*. Ed. Sharon D. Michalove and A. Compton Reeves. The Fifteenth Century Series, no. 5. Stroud: Sutton Publishing, 1998, pp. 89-106.

Richmond, Colin. "The Visual Culture of Fifteenth-Century England." In: *The Wars of the Roses*. Ed. A.J. Pollard. New York, 1988, pp. 186-209.

Rosenthal, Joel T. "Other Victims: Peeresses as War Widows, 1450-1500," *History* 72 (1987), 213-30.

Ross, Charles. *Edward IV*. Berkeley and Los Angeles: University of California Press, 1974.

Ross, Charles. *Richard III*. Berkeley and Los Angeles: University of California Press, 1981.

Ross, Charles. "Rumour, Propaganda and Popular Opinion during the Wars of the Roses." In: *Patronage, The Crown, and the Provinces in Later Medieval England*. Ed. Ralph A. Griffiths. Gloucester: Alan Sutton, 1981, pp. 15-32.

Ross, Charles. *The Wars of the Roses: A Concise History*. London: Thames and Hudson, 1976.

Rowse, A.L. *Bosworth Field and the Wars of the Roses*. London, 1966.

Sayer, M. "Norfolk Involvement in Dynastic Conflict, 1467-1471 and 1483-1487," *Norfolk Archaeology*.

Scofield, Cora L. *The Life and Reign of Edward IV, King of England and of France and Lord of Ireland*. 2 vols. London: Longmans, Green and Co., 1923.

Seward, Desmond. *The Wars of the Roses: Through the Lives of Five Men and Women of the Fifteenth Century*. Harmondsworth: Penguin Books, 1996.

Summerson, Henry. "Carlisle and the English West March in the Later Middle Ages." In: *The North of England in the Age of Richard III*. Ed. A.J. Pollard. The Fifteenth Century Series, no. 3. Stroud: Alan Sutton Publishing, 1996, pp. 89-114.

Storey, R.L. *The End of the House of Lancaster*. Gloucester: Alan Sutton, 1986.

Storey, R.L. "Lincolnshire and the Wars of the Roses," *Nottingham Medieval Studies* 14 (1970).

Sutton, Anne F. "The Court and its Culture in the Reign of Richard III." In: *Richard III: A Medieval Kingship*. Ed. J. Gillingham. New York, 1993, pp. 75-92.

Sutton, Anne F. "'A Curious Searcher for Our Public Weal': Richard III, Piety, Chivalry and the Concept of the 'Good Prince'." In: *Richard III:*

Loyalty, Lordship and the Law. Ed. P. Hammond. Gloucester: Sutton, 1986.

Sutton, Anne F. and Livia Visser-Fuchs. "Richard III's Books: VII and VIII. Guido delle Colonne's *Historia Destructionis Troiae* and Geoffrey of Monmouth's *Historia Regum Britanniae* with *The Prophecy of the Eagle* and Commentary: The Interest of these Books to Richard III and Later Owners," *Ricardian* 8 (1990), 403-13.

Sutton, Anne F. and Livia Visser-Fuchs. "Richard III's Books: IX. *The Grandes Chroniques*," *Ricardian* 8 (1990), 494-514.

Sutton, Anne F. and Livia Visser-Fuchs. "Richard III's Books: X. The *Prose Tristan*," *Ricardian* 9 (1991), 23-37.

Sutton, Anne F., Livia Visser-Fuchs, and P.W. Hammond. *The Reburial of Richard, Duke of York, 21-30 July 1476*. London: The Richard III Society, 1996.

Thomson, J.A.F. "The Death of Edward V: Dr. Richmond's Dating Reconsidered," *Northern History* 26 (1990), 207-11.

Thorton, Tim. "A Defence of the Liberties of Cheshire, 1451-2," *Historical Research* 68 (1995), 338-54.

Tudor-Craig, Pamela. "Richard III's Triumphant Entry into York." In: *Richard III and the North*. Ed. Rosemary Horrox. Studies in Regional and Local History, 6. Hull: Centre for Regional and Local History, 1986, pp. 108-16.

Valera, Diego de. "A Spanish Account of the Battle of Bosworth," trans. E.M. Nokes and G. Wheeler, *Ricardian* 2.36 (1972), 1-5.

Visser-Fuchs, Livia. "'Il n'a plus lion ne lieppart, qui vouelle tenir de sa part": Edward IV in Exile, October 1470 to March 1471." In: *L'Angleterre et les pays Bourguignons: Relations et comparaisons (Xve-XVIe siècles*. Neuchâtel: Centre européen d'études Bourguignons (XIVe-XVIe siècles), 1995, pp. 91-106.

Visser-Fuchs, Livia. "The Short Version of the *Arrivall* of Edward IV." *Nottingham Medieval Studies* 36 (1992), 167-227.

Warner, M.W. and Kay Lacey. "Neville vs. Percy: A Precedence Dispute *circa* 1442," *Historical Research* 69 (1996), 211-17.

Watts, John. "*De consulatu stiliconis*: Texts and Politics in the Reign of Henry VI," *Journal of Medieval History* 16 (1990), 251-66.

Watts, John. *Henry VI and the Politics of Kingship*. Cambridge: Cambridge University Press, 1999.

Watts, John. "Ideas, Principles and Politics." In: *The Wars of the Roses*. Ed. A.J. Pollard. New York, 1988, pp. 110-33.

Weir, Alison. *The Princes in the Tower*. New York: Ballantine Books, 1992.

Wigram, Isolde and Marlous Thöne. "A Local Dispute and the Politics of 1483: Two Reactions," *Ricardian* 8 (1990), 414-17.

Wilkinson, Bertie. "Fact and Fancy in Fifteenth-Century English History," *Speculum* 42 (1967), 673-92.

Williams, D.T. *The Battle of Bosworth*. 2nd ed. Leicester: Bosworth Publications, 1984.

Williams, Daniel. "'A place mete for twoo battayles to encountre': The Siting of the Battle of Bosworth, 1485," *Ricardian* 7.90 (1985), 86-96.

Williams, Daniel. "Richard III and His Overmighty Subjects: In Defence of a King." In: *England in the Fifteenth Century: Proceedings of the 1992 Harlaxton Symposium*. Ed. N. Rogers. Stamford, 1994, pp. 56-71.

Williams, Joanna M. "The Political Career of Francis Viscount Lovell (1456-?)," *Ricardian* 8 (1990), 382-402.

Williamson, Hugh Ross. "George, Duke of Clarence," *History Today* 16 (1966), 818-24.

Wise, Terence. *The Wars of the Roses*. Men-at-Arms Series. London: Osprey Publishing, 1983.

Wood, Charles T. *Joan of Arc and Richard III: Sex, Saints, and Government in the Middle Ages*. New York: Oxford University Press, 1988.

Wood, Charles T. "Richard III and the Beginnings of Historical Fiction," *Historian* 54 (1992), 305-14.

Wood, Charles T. "Richard III, William, Lord Hastings and Friday the Thirteenth." In: *Kings and Nobles in the Later Middle Ages: A Tribute to Charles Ross*. Ed. R.A. Griffiths and J. Sherborne. Gloucester, 1986, pp. 155-68.

Woodward, G.W.O. and Michael St. John Parker. *Richard III*. London: Pitkin Pictorials, 1994.

Wright, Edmund. "Henry IV, the Commons and the Recovery of Royal Finance in 1407." In: *Rulers and Ruled in Late Medieval England: Essays Presented to Gerald Harriss*. Ed. R.E. Archer and S. Walker. London, 1995, pp. 65-81.

Yeoman, Frank. "Skeletons in Armour," *Ricardian* 28 (Mar 1970), 8-9.

Medieval – Espionage [See also Hundred Years War – Espionage]

Arthurson, Ian. "Espionage and Intelligence from the Wars of the Roses to the Reformation," *Nottingham Medieval Studies* 35 (1991), 134-54.

Prestwich, J.O. "Military Intelligence under the Norman and Angevin Kings." In: In: *Law and Government in Medieval England and Normandy*. Ed. G. Garnett and J. Hudson. Cambridge, 1994, pp. 1-30.

Medieval – Financing

Allmand, Christopher T. "War and Profit in the Late Middle Ages," *History Today* 15 (1965), 762-69.

Braunstein, P. "Guerre, vivres et transports dans le Haut-Frioul en 1381." In: *Erzeugung, Verkehr und Handel in der Geschichte der Alpenländer, Hervert-Hassinger-Festschrift*. Ed. F. Huter, G. Zwanowetz, and F. Mathias. Innsbruck, 1977, pp. 85-106.

Bridbury, A.R. "Before the Black Death," *Economic History Review* 2nd ser. 30 (1977), 393-410.

Cardini, Franco. "I costi della crociata: L'aspetto economico del progetto di Marino Sanudo il Vecchio (1312-1321)." In: *Studi in memoria di Federigo Melis*. Naples, 1978, II:179-210.

Contamine, Philippe. "Consommation et demande militaire en France et en Angleterre, XIIIe-XVe siècles." In: *Domande e consumi: Livelli e strutture (nei secoli XIII-XVIII: Atti della "Sesta settimana di studio" (27 aprile-3 maggio 1974), Instituto internazionale di storia economica Francesco Datini, Prato*. Florence, 1978, pp. 409-28.

Duby, Georges. "Guerre et société dans l'Europe féodale: la guerre et l'argent." In: *Concetto, storia, miti e immagini del medio evo: Atti del XIV corso internazionale d'alta cultura*. Ed. V. Branca. Florence, 1973, pp. 461-71.

Favier, Jean. *Finance et fiscalité au bas moyen âge*. Paris, 1971; trans. *Gold and Spices: The Rise of Commerce in the Middle Ages*. Trans. Caroline Higgitt. New York: Holmes and Meier, 1998.

Freeman, A.Z. "The King's Penny: The Headquarters Paymasters in the Scottish Wars, 1295-1307," *Journal of British Studies* 6 (1966), 1-22.

Fryde, E.B. "The Financial Policies of the Royal Governments and Popular Resistance to Them in France and England, *c.* 1270-*c.* 1420," *Revue Belge de philologie et d'histoire* 57 (1979), 824-60.

Given, James. "The Economic Consequences of the English Conquest of Gwynedd," *Speculum* 64 (1989), 11-45.

Harriss, Gerald L. *King, Parliament and Public Finance in Medieval England to 1369*. Oxford, 1975.

Hicks, Michael A. "Counting the Cost of War: The Moleyns Ransom and the Hungerford Land-Sales, 1453-87," *Southern History* 8 (1986), 11-35.

Hilton, Rodney H. "Resistance to Taxation and to Other State Impositions in Medieval England." In: *Genèse de l'état moderne: Prélèvement et distribution*. Ed. J-Ph. Genet and M. Le Mené. Paris, 1987, pp. 169-77.

Hoffman, Richard C. "Warfare, Weather, and a Rural Economy: The Duchy of Wroclaw in the Mid-Fifteenth Century," *Viator* 4 (1973), 273-305.

Ladero Quesada, M.A. *Milicia y economia en la guerra de Grenada: el cerco de Baza.* Valladolid, 1964.

Lane, Frederic C. "Economic Consequences of Organized Violence," *Journal of Economic History* 18 (1958), 401-17; in: *Venice and History: The Collected Papers of Frederic C. Lane.* Baltimore, 1966, pp. 412-28.

Lane, Frederic C. "The Economic Meaning of War and Protection." In: *Venice and History: The Collected Papers of Frederic C. Lane.* Baltimore, 1966, pp. 383-98.

Maddicott, J.R. "The English Peasantry and the Demands of the Crown, 1294-1341," *Past and Present* supplement 1 (1975).

Mate, Mavis. "The Impact of War on the Economy of Canterbury Cathedral Priory, 1294-1340," *Speculum* 57 (1982), 761-78.

McFarlane, K.B. "Loans to Lancastrian Kings, the Problem of Inducement." In: *England in the Fifteenth Century: Collected Essays.* London, 1981, pp. 57-78.

Menjot, D. "Le poids de la guerre dans l'économie murcienne, l'exemple de la campagne de 1407-1408 contre Grenade." In: *Miscelanea medieval murciana.* Murcia, 1976, pp. 37-68.

Miller, Edward. "War, Taxation and the English Economy in the Late Thirteenth and Early Fourteenth Centuries." In: *War and Economic Development: Essays in Memory of David Joslin.* Ed. J.M. Winter. Cambridge, 1975, pp. 11-31.

Miskimin, H.A. "L'or, l'argent, la guerre dans la France médiéval," *Annales E.S.C.* 40 (1985), 71-84.

Pavodan, G. "L'económia di guerra di un grande commune del Trecento," *Rivista di storia economica* 5 (1940), 35-42.

Pettengill, John S. "The Impact of Military Technology on European Income Distribution," *Journal of Interdisciplinary History* 10 (1979), 201-25.

Sivéry, Gérard. "L'enquête de 1247 et les dommages de guerre en Tournaisis, en Flandre gallicante et en Artois," *Revue du nord* 59 (1977), 7-18.

Strayer, Joseph R. "The Costs and Profits of War: The Anglo-French Conflict of 1294-1303." In: *The Medieval City*. Ed. H.A. Miskimin, David Herlihy, and A.L. Udovitch. New Haven: Yale University Press, 1977, pp. 269-91.

Strayer, Joseph R. "Notes on the Origin of English and French Export Taxes," *Studia Gratiana* 15 (1972), 399-421.

Taylor, Charles H. "Assemblies of Towns and War Subsidy, 1318-1319." In: *Studies in Early French Taxation*. Ed. Joseph R. Strayer and Charles H. Taylor. Cambridge, 1939, pp. 107-200.

Taylor, Charles H. "French Assemblies and Subsidy in 1321," *Speculum* 43 (1968), 217-44.

Winter, J.M. "Introduction: The Economic and Social History of War." In: *War and Economic Development: Essays in Memory of David Joslin*. Ed. J.M. Winter. Cambridge, 1975, pp. 1-10.

Medieval – France

Allemand, Jean. "Avant-propos à l'étude sur France et Provence." In: *Commission Internationale d'Histoire Militaire. Acta 22: Warfare Throughout the Ages between Small States and Big Powers and Small States Among Themselves*. Tel Aviv: Israel Commission of Military History, 1984, pp. 123-52.

Audouin, E. *Essai sur l'armée royale au temps de Philippe Auguste*. Paris, 1913.

Bémont, Charles. "La campagne de Poitou (1242-1243), Taillebourg et Saintes," *Annales du midi* 5 (1893), 289-314.

Benjamin, R. "A Forty Years War: Toulouse and the Plantagenets, 1156-1196," *Historical Research* 56 (1988), 270-85.

Benoit-Guyod, Henry. "La première armée française: Le ban et arrière-ban des seigneuries," *Revue internationale d'histoire militaire* 25 (1965), 559-61.

Birrell, Jean. *Saint Louis: Crusader King of France*. Cambridge: Cambridge University Press, 1992.

Bonner, Elizabeth. "Scotland's 'Auld Alliance' with France, 1295-1560," *History* 84 (1999), 5-30.

Bordonove, Georges. *Philippe le Bel*. Paris: Éditions Pygmalion/ Gérard Watelet, 1984.

Boutaric, Edgard. *Institutions militaires de la France avant les armées permanentes*. rpt. Geneva, 1978.

Boyer, Majorie Nice. "A Day's Journey in Mediaeval France," *Speculum* 26 (1951), 597-608.

Bur, M.M. "Suger et l'art militaire de son temps," *Académie des inscriptions et belles-lettres* 11 (1994), 689-74.

Caille, J. "Les seigneurs de Narbonne dans le conflit Toulouse-Barcelone au XIIe siècle," *Annales du midi* 97 (1985), 227-44.

Carolus-Barré, Louis. "Le service militaire en Beauvaisis au temps de Philippe de Beaumanoir. L'estaige à Gerberoy et a Beauvais (1271-1277). L'ost de Navarre (1276)." In: *La guerre et la paix: Frontières et violences au moyen âge*. Actes du 101e congrès national des sociétés savantes, Lille, 1976. Paris: Bibliothèque Nationale, 1978, pp. 73-93.

Cazelles, Raymond. "La réglementation de la guerre privée de Saint Louis à Charles V et la precarité des ordonnances," *Revue historique de droit français et étranger* 38 (1960), 530-48.

Champeval, J.B. "Le rôle du ban et arrière-ban du haut Auvergne." In: *L'Auvergne historique, litteraire et artistique: Varia, 1909-1912*. Riom, 1913.

Chaplais, Pierre. "The Making of the Treaty of Paris (1259) and the Royal Style," *English Historical Review* 67 (1952), 235-53.

Chaplais, Pierre. "Le traité de Paris de 1259 et l'inféodation de la Gascogne allodiale," *Moyen âge* 56 (1955), 121-37.

Chédeville, André. "La 'guerre des bourgs': Concurrence châtelaine et patrimoine monastique dans l'ouest de la France (XIe-XIIe siècles)." In: *Campagnes médiévales: L'homme et son espace: Etudes offerts à Robert*

Fossier. Ed. Elisabeth Mornet. Paris: Publications de la Sorbonne, 1995, pp. 501-12.

Chomel, V. "Chevaux de bataille et roncin en Dauphiné au XIVe siècle," *Cahiers d'histoire* 7 (1962), 5-23.

Collins, Roger. "The Basques in Aquitaine and Navarre: Problems of Frontier Government." In: *War and Government in the Middle Ages: Essays in Honour of J.O. Prestwich*. Ed. J. Gillingham and J.C. Holt. Cambridge, 1984, pp. 3-17.

Contamine, Philippe. "L'armée de Philippe Auguste." In: *La France de Philippe Auguste: le temps des mutations : actes du colloque international organiséé par le C.N.R.S. (Paris, 29 septembre-4 octobre 1980)*. Ed. Robert-Henri Bautier. Paris: Editions du Centre national de la recherche scientifique, 1982, pp. 577-93.

Delterre, Michel. "L'action de Philippe le Bel dans les 'Terres de débat' (1294-1301)," *Annales du cercle royale d'histoire et d'archéologie d'Ath* 54 (1995), 39-72.

Demotz, Bernard. "A propos des *clientes* du comte de Savoie aux XIIIe et XIVe siècles." In: *Le combattant au moyen âge*. 2nd ed. Histoire ancienne et médiévale, 36. Paris: Publications de la Sorbonne, 1995, pp. 257-66.

Devos, J.-C. "L'organisation de la defence de l'Artois en 1297." In: *Bulletin philologique et historique (jusqu'en 1715) du comité des travaux historiques et scientifiques, année 1955*. Paris, 1957, pp. 47-55.

Dossat, Yves. "L'Agenais vers 1325, après la campagne de Charles de Valois." In: *La guerre et la paix: Frontières et violences au moyen âge*. Actes du 101e congrès national des sociétés savantes, Lille, 1976. Paris: Bibliothèque Nationale, 1978, pp. 143-54.

Favier, Jean. *Philippe le Bel*. Paris, 1978.

Finó, J.-F. "L'art militaire en France au XIIIe siècle," *Gladius* 8 (1969), 23-37.

Finó, J.-F. "Quelques aspects de l'art militaire sous Philippe Auguste," *Gladius* 6 (1967), 19-36.

France, John. "La guerre dans la France feodale à la fin du IXe au Xe siècle," *Revue Belge d'histoire militaire* 23 (1979), 177-98.

Funck-Brentano, Frantz. *Philippe le Bel et Flandre: Les origines de la guerre de cent ans*. Paris: Honoré Champion, Libraire, 1896.

Gasparri, Stefano. "Les *milites* dans les villes de la Marche de Trévisse (XIe-XIIIe siècles)." In: *Les élites urbaines au moyen âge: XXVIIe congrès de la S.H.M.E.S. (Rome, mai 1996)*. Collection de l'Ecole Française de Rome, 238; Série Histoire Ancienne et Médiévale, 46. Paris: Publications de la Sorbonne, 1997, pp. 55-69.

Given, James. *State and Society in Medieval Europe: Gwynedd and Languedoc under Outside Rule*. Ithaca: Cornell University Press, 1990.

Guilbert, Sylvette. "Combattants pour l'éternité: Représentations de combattants sur les pierres tombales de Châlons-sur-Marne." In: *Le combattant au moyen âge*. 2nd ed. Histoire ancienne et médiévale, 36. Paris: Publications de la Sorbonne, 1995, pp. 267-78.

Guilhiermoz, P. *Essai sur l'origine de la noblesse en France au moyen âge*. Paris, 1902; rpt. New York, 1960.

Guttman, Jon. "Duke's Oath Defied," *Miltiary History* (June 1992), 66-75.

Johrendt, J. *Milites und Militia im 11 Jahrhundert: Untersuchung zur Frühgeschichte der Rittertums in Frankreich und Deutschland*. Nuremburg, 1971.

Kaeuper, Richard W. *War, Justice, and Public Order: England and France in the Later Middle Ages*. Oxford: Clarendon Press, 1988.

Kirkland, D. "The Growth of National Sentiment in France before the Fourteenth Century," *History* 23 (1938-39), 12-24.

Lalou, Elisabeth. "Les questions militaires sous le règne de Philippe le Bel." In: *Guerre et société en France, en Angleterre et en Bourgogne XIVe-XVe siècle*. Ed. P. Contamine, C. Giry-Deloison, and Maurice Keen. Lille, 1991, pp. 37-62.

Lalou, Elisabeth. "Les voyages de Philippe IV le Bel en Normandie." *Les Domfrontais médiéval* 15 (1995), 5-20.

La Presle-Évesque, Alix de. "Le conflit franco-aragonais de la fin du XIIIe siècle et ses conséquences religieuses et politiques." In: *La guerre, la violence et les gens au Moyen Âge*. I: *Guerre et violence*. Ed. P. Contamine and O. Guyotjeannin. 119e congrès national des sociétés historiques et scientifiques, Amiens, octobre 1994, Section d'histoire médiévale et philologie. Paris, 1996, pp. 67-80.

La Roncière, Charles de. "Le blocus continentale de l'Angleterre sous Philippe le Bel," *Revue des questions historiques* n.s. 16 (1896), 402-41.

Le Goff, Jacques. *Saint Louis*. Paris, 1976.

Lewis, Archibald R. *The Development of Southern French and Catalan Society, 718-1050*. Austin: University of Texas Press, 1965.

Lewis, Archibald R. "La féodalité dans le Toulousian et la France méridionale (850-1050)," *Annales du midi* 76 (1964), 247-59.

Lewis, Archibald R. "Observations sur la frontière franco-normande." In: *Le roi de France en son royaume autour de l'an mil*. Paris, 1992, pp. 147-54.

Little, Roger G. *The "Parlement" of Poitiers: War, Government and Policies in France, 1418-1436*. London, 1984.

Lot, Ferdinand. "La langue de commandement dans les armées romaines et le cri de guerre français au moyen âge." In: *Mélanges dédiés à la mémoire de Felix Grat*. Paris, 1946.

Martindale, Jane. "Peace and War in Early Eleventh-Century Aquitaine." In: *Medieval Knighthood, IV*. Ed. C. Harper-Bill and R. Harvey. Woodbridge, 1992, pp. 147-76.

Martindale, Jane. "'His Special Friend'? The Settlement of Disputes and Political Power in the Kingdom of the French (Tenth to Mid-Twelfth Century)," *Transactions of the Royal Historical Society*, 6th ser., 5 (1995), 21-57.

Menache, Sophia. "Philippe le Bel–genèse d'une image," *Revue Belge de philologie et d'histoire* 62 (1984), 689-702.

Michel, Robert. "Les défenseurs des châteaux et des villes fortes dans le Comtat Venaissin," *Bibliothèque de l'école de chartes* 75 (1915), 315-30.

Miskimin, H.A. "L'or, l'argent, la guerre dans la France médiéval," *Annales E.S.C.* 40 (1985), 71-84.

Newman, W.M. *Le domaine royal sous les premiers Capétians (987-1100)*. Paris, 1937.

Notte, Ludovic. "Les ecuries de Robert II, comte d'Artois (vers 1292-1302)," *Revue du nord* 81 (1999), 467-88.

Power, D.J. "French and Norman Frontiers in the Central Middle Ages." In: *Frontiers in Question: Eurasian Borderlands, 700-1700*. Ed. D. Power and N. Standon. London, 1999, pp. 105-27.

Richard, Jean. *Saint Louis: Crusader King of France*. Ed. Simon Lloyd. Trans. J. Birrell. Cambridge, 1992.

Robert, Elisabeth. "Guerre et fortification dans la *Philippide* de Guillaume le Breton: approches archéologiques." In: *Military Studies in Medieval Europe: Papers of the "Medieval Europe Brugge 1997" Conference Volume 11*. Ed. Guy De Boe & Frans Verhaeghe. Zellik: Instituut voor het Archeologisch Patrimonium, 1997, pp. 7-19.

Sevestre, Bernard. "L'ancienne alliance franco-écossaise et le service écossais," *Revue de la Société des Amis du Musée de l'Armée* 99 (1990), 5-21.

Sivéry, Gérard. *Louis VIII: Le lion*. Paris: Fayard, 1995.

Spiegel, Gabrielle M. "'Defense of the Realm': Evolution of a Capetian Propaganda Slogan," *Journal of Medieval History* 3 (1977), 115-33.

Stephenson, Carl. "Les 'aides' des villes françaises aux XIIe et XIIIe siècles," *Moyen âge* 33 (1922), 274-328.

Strayer, Joseph R. "Defence of the Realm and Royal Power in France." In: *Studi in onore di Gino Luzzat*. Milan, 1949, I:289-96; in: *Medieval Statecraft and the Perspectives of History*. Princeton, 1971, pp. 291-99.

Strayer, Joseph R. "France: The Holy Land, the Chosen People, and the Most Christian King." In: *Action and Conviction in Early Modern Europe*. Ed. T. Rabb and J. Seigel. princeton, 1969, pp. 3-16.

Strayer, Joseph R. *The Reign of Philip the Fair*. Princeton: Princeton University Press, 1980.

Tanner, Heather J. "The Expansion of the Power and Influence of the Counts of Boulogne under Eustace II," *Anglo-Norman Studies* 14 (1991), 251-86.

Vale, M.G.A. "The Gascon Nobility and the Anglo-French War, 1294-98." In: *War and Government in the Middle Ages: Essays in Honour of J.O. Prestwich*. Ed. J. Gillingham and J.C. Holt. Cambridge, 1984, pp. 134-46.

van Luyn, Pierre. "Les *milites* dans la France du XIe siècle: Examen des sources narratives," *Moyen âge* 77 (1971), 5-51, 193-238.

White, Stephen D. "'Pactum ... legum vincit et amor judicium': The Settlement of Disputes by Compromise in Eleventh-Century Western France," *American Journal of Legal History* 22 (1978), 281-308.

Wolff, Philippe. "Achats d'armes pour Philippe le Bel dans; a région toulousaine (1295)," *Annales du midi* 61 (1948), 84-91.

Wood, Charles T. *The French Apanages of the Capetian Monarchy, 1224-1328*. Cambridge, 1966.

Medieval – France – Anjou

Jessee, W. Scott. "The Angevin Civil War and the Norman Conquest of 1066," *Haskins Society Journal* 3 (1991), 101-09.

Jessee, W. Scott. "Urban Violence and the *Coup d'état* of Fulk le Réchin in Angers, 1067," *Haskins Society Journal* 7 (1995), 75-82.

Medieval – France – Anjou – Fulk Nerra

Bachrach, Bernard S. "Angevin Campaign Forces in the Reign of Fulk Nerra, count of the Angevins, 987-1040," *Francia* 16/1 (1989), 67-84.

Bachrach, Bernard S. "The Angevin Strategy of Castle Building in the Reign of Fulk Nerra, 987-1040," *American Historical Review* 88 (1983), 533-560.

Bachrach, Bernard S. "The Combat Scupltures at Fulk Nerra's 'Battle Abbey' (c.1005-1012)," *Haskins Society Journal* 3 (1991), 63-80.

272 MEDIEVAL – FRANCE – ANJOU

Bachrach, Bernard S. "The Cost of Castle Building: The Case of the Tower at Langeais, 992-994." In: *The Medieval Castle: Romance and Reality*. Ed. K. Reyerson and F. Powe. Dubuque, 1984, pp. 47-62.

Bachrach, Bernard S. "Enforcement of the *Forma Fidelitatis*: The Techniques Used by Fulk Nerra, Count of the Angevins (987-1040)," *Speculum* 59 (1984), 796-819.

Bachrach, Bernard S. "Fortifications and Military Tactics: Fulk Nerra's Strongholds circa 1000," *Technology and Culture* 20 (1979), 531-49.

Bachrach, Bernard S. *Fulk Nerra, the Neo-Roman Consul, 987-1040: A Political Biography of the Angevin Count*. Berkeley and Los Angeles: University of California Press, 1993.

Bachrach, Bernard S. "Fulk Nerra's Exploitation of the *Facultates monachorum*, ca. 1000." In: *Law, Custom, and the Social Fabric in Medieval Europe: Essays in Honor of Bryce Lyon*. Ed. B. Bachrach and D. Nicholas. Kalamazoo, 1990, pp. 29-49.

Bachrach, Bernard S. "Neo-Roman vs. Feudal: The Heuristic Value of a Construct for the Reign of Fulk Nerra, Count of the Angevins (987-1040)," *Cithara* 30 (1990), 3-30.

Bachrach, Bernard S. "The Pilgrimages of Fulk Nerra, Count of the Angevins, 987-1040." In: *Religion, Culture, and Society in the Early Middle Ages: Studies in Honor of Richard E. Sullivan*. Ed. T.F.X. Noble and J.J. Contreni. Kalamazoo, 1987, pp. 205-17.

Bachrach, Bernard S. "Some Observations on the Origins of Countess Gerberga of the Angevins: An Essay in the Application of the Tellenbach-Werner Prosopographical Method," *Medieval Prosopography* 7 (1986), 1-23.

Bachrach, Bernard S. "A Study in Feudal Politics: Relations between Fulk Nerra and William the Great, 995-1030," *Viator* 7 (1976), 113-21.

Deyres, Marcel. "Les châteaux de Foulque Nerra," *Bulletin monumental* 132 (1974), 7-28.

Medieval – France – Gascony and Guyenne

Bémont, Charles. *La Guyenne pendant la domination Anglaise, 1152-1453*. London, 1920.

Boutruche, Robert. "Anglais et Gascons en Aquitaine du XIIe au XVe siècle: Problèmes d'histoire sociale." In: *Mélanges d'histoire du moyen âge dédiés à la mémoire de Louis Halphen*. Paris: Presses universitaires de France, 1951, pp. 55-60.

Chaplais, Pierre. "Les appels gascons au roi d'Angleterre sous le règne d'Edouard Ier." In: *Economies et sociétés au moyen âge: Mélanges offerts à Edouard Perroy*. Paris, 1973, pp. 382-99.

Chaplais, Pierre. "Le duché-pairie de Guyenne: l'hommage et les services féodaux de 1259 à 1303," *Annales du midi* 69 (1957), 5-38.

Chaplais, Pierre. "Le duché-pairie de Guyenne: l'hommage et les services féodaux de 1303 à 1377," *Annales du midi* 70 (1958), 135-60.

Chaplais, Pierre. "La souveraineté du roi de France et le pouvoir législatif en Guyenne au début du XIVe siècle," *Moyen âge* 64 (1963), 449-69.

Chaplais, Pierre. "Le traité de Paris de 1259 et l'inféodation de la Gascogne allodiale," *Moyen âge* 56 (1955), 121-37.

Drouyn, Leo. *Le Guienne militaire*. 2 vols. Bordeaux, 1865.

Goyheneche, E. "Bayonne port d'embarquement des Navarrais vers la Normandie," *Les cahiers vernonnais* 4 (1964), 107-18.

Kicklighter, J.A. "English Bordeaux in Conflict: The Execution of Pierre Vigier de la Rousselle and Its Aftermath, 1312-24," *Journal of Medieval History* 9 (1983), 1-14.

Kicklighter, J.A. "French Jurisdictional Supremacy in Gascony: One Aspect of the Ducal Government's Response," *Journal of Medieval History* 5 (1979), 127-34.

Labarge, Margaret Wade. *Gascony: England's First Colony, 1204-1453*. London, 1980.

Medieval – France – Normandy

Bates, David R. *Normandy Before 1066*. London, 1982.

Boussard, Jacques. "L'enquête de 1172 sur les services de chevalier en Normandie." In: *Recueil de travaux offerts à Clovis Brunel*. Paris, 1955, I:193-208.

Brown, R. Allen. "The Status of the Norman Knight." In: *War and Government in the Middle Ages: Essays in Honour of J.O. Prestwich*. Ed. J. Gillingham and J.C. Holt. Cambridge, 1984, pp. 18-32; in: *Castles, Conquest and Charters: Collected Papers*. Woodbridge, 1989, pp. 290-305; in: *Anglo-Norman Warfare: Studies in Late Anglo-Saxon and Anglo-Norman Military Organization and Warfare*. Ed. M. Strickland. Woodbridge, 1992, pp. 128-42.

Buisson, L. "Formen normannischer Staatsbildung (9. bis 11. Jahrhundert)." In: *Studien zum mittelalterlichen Lehnwesen*. Lindau and Constance, 1960, pp. 95-184.

Chibnall, Marjorie. "Military Service in Normandy before 1066," *Anglo-Norman Studies* 5 (1982), 65-77; in: *Anglo-Norman Warfare: Studies in Late Anglo-Saxon and Anglo-Norman Military Organization and Warfare*. Ed. M. Strickland. Woodbridge, 1992, pp. 28-40.

David, Charles Wendell. *Robert Curthose, Duke of Normandy*. Cambridge: Harvard University Press, 1920; rpt. New York, AMS Press, n.d.

Davis, R.H.C. "William of Jumièges, Robert Curthose and the Norman Succession," *English Historical Review* 95 (1980), 597-606.

Douglas, David C. *The Norman Achievement, 1050-1100*. Berkeley and Los Angeles: University of California Press, 1969.

Douglas, David C. *William the Conqueror*. Berkeley and Los Angeles: University of California Press, 1964.

Faucon, Régis. *Sur les pas de Guillaume le Conquérant*. Paris: Les Nouvelles Editions Latines, 1997.

Freeman, Edward August. *William the Conqueror*. London: Macmillan and Co. Limited, 1913.

Gamber, Ortwin. "Kataphrakten, Clibanarier, Normannenreiter," *Jahrbuch der Kunsthistorischen Sammlungen in Wien* 64 (1968), 7-44.

Gravett, Christopher. *Norman Knight, 950-1204 AD*. London: Osprey, 1993.

Green, Judith A. "Lords of the Norman Vexin." In: *War and Government in the Middle Ages: Essays in Honour of J.O. Prestwich*. Ed. J. Gillingham and J.C. Holt. Cambridge, 1984, pp. 47-63.

Henry, Gilles. *Guillaume le Conquérant*. Paris: France-Empire, 1996.

Le Patourel, John. *The Norman Empire*. Oxford: Clarendon Press, 1976.

Lewis, Archibald R. "Observations sur la frontière franco-normande." In: *Le roi de France en son royaume autour de l'an mil*. Paris, 1992, pp. 147-54.

Lindsay, Jack. *The Normans and Their World*. London: Hart-Davis, MacGibbon, 1974.

Navel, H. "L'enquête de 1133 sur les fiefs de l'évêche de Bayeux," *Bulletin de la société des antiquaires de Normandie* 42 (1934), 5-80.

Nicolle, David C. *Normans*. London: Osprey, 1987.

Packard, S.R. "The Norman Communes under Richard and John, 1189-1204." In: *Anniversary Essays in Medieval History by Students of Charles Homer Haskins*. Boston, 1929, pp. 231-54.

Power, D.J. "French and Norman Frontiers in the Central Middle Ages." In: *Frontiers in Question: Eurasian Borderlands, 700-1700*. Ed. D. Power and N. Standon. London, 1999, pp. 105-27.

Powicke, F.M. *The Loss of Normandy, 1189-1204: Studies in the History of the Angevin Empire*. 2nd ed. Manchester, 1961.

Prentout, Henri. *Les états provinciaux de Normandie*. 3 vols. Caen, 1925-27.

Prestwich, J.O. "The Military Household of the Norman Kings," *English Historical Review* 96 (1981), 1-35; in: *Anglo-Norman Warfare: Studies in Late Anglo-Saxon and Anglo-Norman Military Organization and Warfare*. Ed. M. Strickland. Woodbridge, 1992, pp. 93-127.

Richard, Isabelle. "Rollon, premier duc de Normandie et son mythe," *Études germaniques* 50 (1995), 691-98.

Sancy, Alain de. *Les ducs de Normandie et les rois de France, 911-1204*. Paris: F. Lanore, 1996.

Strayer, Joseph R. "Knight Service in Normandy in the XIIIth Century." In: *Anniversary Essays in Mediaeval History by Students of Charles Homer Haskins*. Ed. C.H. Taylor. Boston, 1929, pp. 312-27.

Strickland, Matthew. *War and Chivalry: The Conduct and Perception of War in England and Normandy, 1066-1217*. Cambridge: Cambridge University Press, 1996.

Tabuteau, Emily Zack. "Definitions of Feudal Military Obligation in Eleventh Century Normandy." In: *On the Laws and Customs of England: Essays in Honor of Samuel E. Thorne*. Ed. M.S. Arnold. Chapel Hill: University of North Carolina Press, 1981, pp. 18-59.

Wise, Terence. *Saxon, Viking and Norman Armies*. London: Osprey, 1979.

Yver, J. "L'interdiction de la guerre privée dans le très ancien droit normand." In: *Travaux de la semaine d'histoire du droit normand tenue à Guernsey 1927*. Caen, 1928, pp. 307-47.

Medieval – France – Oriflamme

Contamine, Philippe. *L'oriflamme de Saint-Denis aux XIVe et XVe siècles*. Nancy: Université de Nancy II, Institut de Recherche régionale, 1975.

Liebman, C.J. "Un sermon de Philippe de Villette, abbé de Saint-Denis, pour la levée de l'oriflamme (1414)," *Romania* 68 (1944-45), 444-70.

Medieval – Holy Roman Empire

Arnold, Benjamin. *German Knighthood, 1050-1300*. Oxford: Clarendon Press, 1984.

Arnold, Benjamin. *Princes and Territories in Medieval Germany*. Cambridge: Cambridge University Press, 1991.

Auer, Leopold. "Der Kriegsdienst des Klerus unter den sächsischen Kaisern," *Mitteilungen des Instituts für österreichische Geschichtsforschung* 79 (1971), 316-407; 80 (1972), 48-70.

Auer, Leopold. "Zur Kriegswesen unter den früheren Babenberger," *Jahrbuch für Landeskunde von Niederösterreich* 42 (1976), 9-25.

Auer, Leopold. *Die Schlacht bei Mailberg am 12. Mai 1082.* Militärhistorische Schriftenreihe, 31. Vienna: Bundesverlag, 1984.

Auer, Leopold. "Zum spätmittelalterlichen Kriegswesen in den Ostalpenländern." In: *XXII. Kongreß der Internationalen Kommission für Militärgeschichte* Acta 22: *Von Crécy bis Mohács Kriegswesen im späten Mittelalter (1346-1526).* Vienna, 1997, pp. 15-27.

Beck, W. "Bayerns Heerwesen und Mobilmachung im 15. Jahrhundert," *Archivalische Zeitschrift* n.s. 18 (1911), 1-232.

Benninghoven, F. "Die Kriegsdienste der Komturei Danzig um das Jahr 1400." In: *Acht Jahrhunderte Deutscher Orden in Einzeldarstellung: Festschrift ... Marian Tümler.* Ed. P.K. Wieser. Bad Godesberg, 1967, pp. 161-222.

Benninghoven, F. "Probleme der Zahl und Standortverteilung der Livländischen Streitkräfte im ausgehenden Mittelalter," *Zeitschrift für Ostforschung* 12 (1963), 601-22.

Bezzel, O. *Geschichte des Kurpfälzischen Heeres.* I: *Das Heerwesen in Kurpfalz, Pfalzneuburg und Jülich-Berg von seinen Anfängen bis zur Vereinigung von Kurpfalz und Kur-Bayern 1778, nebst Geschichte des Heerwesen in Pfalz-Zweibrücken.* Munich, 1925.

Boshof, Egon. *Ludwig der Fromme.* Darmstadt: Primus Verlag, 1996.

Bottner, R. "Die Wehrorganisation der frühen Babenberger im Einzelgebiet der Bezirke Melk und Scheibbs," *Jahrbuch für Landeskunde von Niederösterriech* 42 (1976), 26-37.

Bowlus, Charles R. "Krieg und Kirche in den Südost-Grenzgrafschaften." In: *Salzburg und die Slawenmission.* Ed. H. Dopsch. Salzburg, 1986, pp. 71-91.

Buttlar, Gertrud. *Die Belagerung des Ladislaus Postumus in Wiener Neustadt, 1452*. Militärhistorische Schriftenreihe, 57. Vienna: Heeresgeschichtlichen Museum (Militärwissenschaftliches Institut), 1986.

Conrad, H. *Geschichte der deutsche Wehrverfassung*. Munich, 1939.

Csendas, Peter. *Wien in den Fehden der Jahre 1461-1463*. Militärhistorische Schriftenreihe, 28. Vienna: Heeresgeschichtlichen Museum (Militärwissenschaftliches Institut), 1974.

Del Treppo, Mario. "Federico II e il Mediterraneo," *Studi storici* 37 (1996), 373-90.

Dienst, Heide. *Die Schlacht an der Leitha, 1246*. Militärhistorische Schriftenreihe, 19. Vienna: Bundesverlag, 1971.

Dieterich, J.R. *Die Taktik in den Lombardenkriegen der Staufer*. Marburg, 1892.

Dihle, Helene. "Das Kriegstagebuch eines deutschen Landsknechts um die Wende des 15. Jahrhunderts," *Zeitschrift für historisches Waffen- und Köstumkunde* 12 (1929-31), 1-11.

Eberbach, O. *Die deutsche Reichsritterschaft in ihrer staatsrechtlich-politischen Entwicklung von den Anfängen bis zum Jahre 1422*. Dresden, 1912.

Ekdahl, Sven. "Über die Kriegsdienst der Freien im Kulmerland zu Anfang des 15. Jahrhunderts," *Preussenland* 2 (1964), 1-14.

Eltis, David. "Towns and Defence in Later Medieval Germany," *Nottingham Medieval Studies* 33 (1989), 91-103.

Erdmann, C. "Die Burgenordnung Heinrichs I," *Deutsches Archiv für Erforschung des Mittelalters* 6 (1943), 59-101.

Fehr, H. "Das Waffenrecht der Bauern im Mittelalter," *Zeitschrift der Savigny-Stiftung für Rechtsgeschichte, Germanistische Abteilung* 35 (1914).

Fleckenstein, Josef. "Friedrich Barbarossa und das Rittertum: Zur Bedeutung der großen Mainzer Hoftage von 1184 und 1188." In: *Festschrift für Hermann Heimpel*. Veröffentlichungen des Max-Planck-Instituts für Geschichte, 36.2. Gottingen, 1972, II:1023-41.

Föhl, W. "Niederrheinische Ritterschaft um Italien des Trecento," *Annalen des historischen Vereins für den Niederrhein* 165 (1963), 73-128.

Franz, G. "Von Ursprung und Brauchtum der Landsknecht," *Mitteilungen des Instituts für österreichische Geschichteforschung* 61 (1953), 79-98.

Frauenholz, E von. *Entwicklungsgeschichte des deutsche Heerwesens.* 3 vols. Munich1935-37.

Freynhagen, W. *Die Wehrmachtverhältnisse der Stadt Rostock im Mittelalter.* Rostock, 1930.

Friesinger, H. "Waffenkunde des 9 und 10 Jahrhunderts aus Niederösterreich," *Archaeologic austriaci* 52 (1972), 43-64.

Furiano, M. "La battaglia di Civitate (1053)," *Archivio storico pugliese* 11 (1949).

Gattermann, G. *Die deutschen Fürsten auf der Reichsheerfahrt: Studien zur Reichskriegsverfassung der Stauferzeit.* Frankfurt, 1956.

Gillingham, J.B. "Frederick Barbarossa: a Secret Revolutionary?" *English Historical Review* 86 (1971), 73-78.

Goldberg, Eric J. "'More Devoted to the Equipment of Battle Than the Splendor of Banquets': Frontier Kingship, Martial Ritual, and Early Knighthood at the Court of Louis the German," *Viator* 30 (1999), 41-78.

Gravett, Christopher. *German Medieval Armies, 1300-1500.* London, 1985.

Gümbel, Albert. "Johann Glöckner von Zittau, ein Nürnberger Festungbaumeister, 1430-1442," *Zeitschrift für historisches Waffen- un Köstumkunde* 9 (1921-22), 11-17.

Haverkamp, Alfred. *Medieval Germany, 1056-1273.* 2nd ed. Oxford: Oxford University Press, 1992.

Hatt, J.J. "Le champ de bataille de Oberhausen (357-1262)," *Bulletin de la faculté des lettres de Strasbourg* 42 (1964), 427-30.

Heinzen, T. "Zunftkämpfe, Zunftherrschaft und Wehrfassung un Köln: Beitrag zum Thema 'Zünfte und Wehrverfassung'," *Veröffentlichungen des Kölnischen Geschichtsverein* 16 (1939).

Helwig, Hellmuth. "Die deutschen Fechtbücher: Eine bibliographische Übersicht," *Börsenblatt für den deutschen Büchhandel, Frankfürter Ausgabe* 55 (1966), 1407-16.

Henning, Joachim. "Ringwallburgen und Reiterkrieger: Zum Wandel der Militärstrategie im ostsächsisch-slawischen Raum an der Wende vom 9. zum 10. Jahrhundert." In: *Military Studies in Medieval Europe: Papers of the "Medieval Europe Brugge 1997" Conference Volume 11.* Ed. Guy De Boe & Frans Verhaeghe. Zellik: Instituut voor het Archeologisch Patrimonium, 1997, pp. 21-31.

Herde, Peter. "Die Schlacht bei Tagliacozzo: Eine historischtopographische Studie," *Zeitschrift für Bayerische Landesgeschichte* 25 (1962), 679-744.

Hiestand, Rudolf. "Pressburg 907: Eine Wende in der Geschichte des ostfränkischen Reiches," *Zeitschrift für bayerische Landesgeschichte* 57 (1994), 1-20.

Hoensch, Jörg K. *Kaiser Sigismund: Herrscher an der Schwelle zur Neuzeit, 1368-1437.* Munich: C.H. Beck, 1996.

Hummelberger, Walter. "Die Waffnung der Bürgerschaft im Spätmittelalter am Beispiel Wien." In: *Das Leben in der Stadt des Spätmittelalters: Internationaler Kongress Krems au der Donau 20. bis 23. September 1976.* Vienna, 1977, pp. 191-206.

Johrendt, J. *Milites und Militia im 11 Jahrhundert: Untersuchung zur Frühgeschichte der Rittertums in Frankreich und Deutschland.* Nuremburg, 1971.

Knussert, R. *Die deutschen Italienfahrten, 951-1220, und die Wehrverfassung.* Ottingen, 1931.

Krieger, Karl-Friedrich. "Obligatory Military Service and the Use of Mercenaries in Imperial Military Campaigns under the Hohenstaufen Emperors." In: *England and Germany in the High Middle Ages.* Ed. Alfred Haverkamp and Hanna Vollrath. London: The German Historical Institute, 1996, pp. 151-68.

Lammers W. *Die Schlacht bei Hemmingstedt: Freies Bauertum und Fürstenmacht in Nordseeraum.* Neuminster, 1953.

Leyser, K.J. "Henry I and the Beginnings of the Saxon Empire," *English Historical Review* 83 (1968), 1-32.

Leyser, K.J. *Rule and Conflict in an Early Medieval Society: Ottonian Saxony*. Bloomington: Indiana University Press, 1979.

Lloyd, T.H. *England and the German Hanse, 1157-1611: A Study of their Trade and Commercial Diplomacy*. Cambridge: Cambridge University Press, 1991.

Lotter, Friedrich. "The Crusading Idea and the Conquest of the Region East of the Elbe." In: *Medieval Frontier Societies*. Ed. R. Bartlett and A. MacKay. Oxford, 1989, 267-306.

Lounghis, T. "The Failure of the German-Byzantine Alliance on the Eve of the First Crusade." *Diptycha* 1 (1979), 158-67.

March, U. "Die holsteinische Heeresorganization im Mittelalter," *Zeitschrift der Gesellschaft für Schleswig-holsteinische Geschichte* 99 (1974), 95-139.

Martin, Paul. "Quelques aspects de l'art de la guerre en Alsace au XIVe siècle," *Revue d'Alsace* 88 (1948), 108-23.

Martin, Paul. "Wehr-, Waffen- und Harnischpflicht der Strassburger Zünfte im 14. Jahrhundert. *Waffen- und Kostümkunde* 34 (1975), 102-08.

Meier-Welcker, Hans. "Das Militärwesen Kaiser Friedrichs II: Landescerteidigung, Heer und Flotte im sizilischen 'Modellstaat'," *Revue internationale d'histoire militaire* 33 (1975), 9-48.

Meissner, G. *Das Kriegswesen der Reichsstadt Nordhausen (1290-1803)*. Berlin, 1839.

Memorial über die Organisation des Kriegswesen der Stadt Worms Ende des XV. Jahrhunderts. In: *Quellen zur Geschichte der Stadt Worms*. Ed. M. Boos. III: *Annalen und Chroniken*. Berlin, 1883, pp. 349-70.

Meyer, H. *Die Militärpolitik Friedrich Barbarossas im Zusammenhang mit seiner Italienpolitik*. Berlin, 1930.

Mörtzsch, Otto. "Das wehrhafte Freiberg im Mittelalter," *Zeitschrift für Historische Waffenkunde* 7 (1915-17), 216-24.

Müller, Hermann. "Waffen und Wehr der stadt Pössneck in Thüringen im 15. Jahrhundert," *Zeitschrift für historisches Waffen- und Köstumkunde* 12 (1929-31), 49-54.

Nell, Martin. *Die Landsknechte: Entstehung der ersten deutschen Infanterie.* Berlin, 1914.

Orth, E. *Die Fehden der Reichsstadt Frankfurt am Main im Spätmittelalter: Fehdrecht und Fehdepraxis im 14. und 15. Jahrhunderts.* Wiesbaden, 1973.

Pauler, Roland. *Die Deutschen Könige und Italien im 14. Jahrhundert: Von Heinrich VII. Bis Karl IV.* Darmstadt: Wissenschaftliche Buchgesellschaft, 1997.

Peball, Kurt. *Die Schlacht bei Dürnkrut am 26. August 1278.* Militärhistorische Schriftenreihe, 10. Vienna: Bundesverlag, 1992.

Pieri, Paolo. "Federigo II di Suevia e la guerra del suo tempo," *Archivio storico pugliese* 13 (1960), 114-31.

Post, P. *Das Kostüm und die ritterliche Kriegstracht in deutschen Mittelalter von 1000-1450.* Berlin, 1939.

Powell, James M. "Patriarch Gerold and Frederick II: the Matthew Paris Letter," *Journal of Medieval History* 25 (1999), 19-26.

Putz, H.H. *Die Darstellung der Schlacht in mittelhochdeutscher Erzähldichtungen von 1150 bis um 1250.* Hamburg, 1971.

Rautenburg, Wilhelm. *Böhmische Söldner im Ordensland Preussen: Ein Beitrag zur Söldnergeschichte des 15. Jahrhunderts, vornehmilch des 13. jährigen Städte-Kriegs 1454-1466.* Hamburg, 1954.

Redlich, Fritz. *The German Military Enterpriser and His Work Forces.* 2 vols. Wiesbaden, 1964-65.

Reuter, Timothy. "Carolingian and Ottonian Warfare." In: *Medieval Warfare: A History.* Ed. Maurice Keen. Oxford: Oxford University Press, 1999, pp. 13-35.

Robinson, Ian S. *Henry IV of Germany.* Cambridge: Cambridge University Press, 2000.

Romeiss, M. "Die Wehrverfassung der Reichsstadt Frankfurt am Main im Mittelalter," *Archiv für Frankfurts-Geschichte und Kunst* (1953), 5-63.

Römer, Christof. *500 Jahre Krieg und Frieden: Braunschweigische Militärgeschichte vom Fehdezeitalter bis zum Ende des Absolutismus.* Braunschweig: Braunschweigischen Landesmuseums, 1982.

Rösener, Werner. "Ministerialität, Vasallität und niederadelige Ritterschaft im Herrschaftsbereich der Markgrafen von Baden vom 11. bis zum 14. Jahrhunderts." In: *Herrschaft und Stand: Untersuchungen zur Sozialgeschichte im 13. Jahrhundert.* Ed. Josef Fleckenstein. Veröffentlichungen des Max-Planck-Instituts für Geschichte, 51. Gottingen, 1977, pp. 40-91.

Sander, E. "Die heeresorganisation Heinrich I," *Historisches Jahrbuch* 59 (1939), 1-26.

Schäfer, Dietrich. "Die *agrarii milites* des Widukind," *Sitzungsberichte des königlichen preussischen Akademie der Wissenschaften* 27 (1905), 569-77.

Schalk, Karl. "Die historische Waffensammlung der Stadt Wien im Zusammenhange mit der militärischen Organisation der Stadt," *Zeitschrift für historische Waffenkunde* 2 (1900-02), 247-51.

Schmidt-Ewald, W. "Das Landesaufgebot im westlichen Thüringen vom 15. bis zum 17. Jahrhundert," *Zeitschrift des Vereins für thüringische Geschichte und Altertumskunde* 36 (1929), 6-58.

Schmitthenner, P. *Das freie Söldnertum im abendländischen Imperium des Mittelalters.* Munich, 1934.

Schmitthenner, P. "Lehnskriegswesen und Söldnertum im abenländischen Imperium des Mittelalters," *Historische Zeitschrift* 150 (1934), 229-67.

Schoenfeld, Edward G. "Freedom and Military Reform in Tenth-Century Saxony." In: *The Circle of War in the Middle Ages: Essays on Medieval Military and Naval History.* Ed. Donald J. Kagay and L.J. Andrew Villalon. Woodbridge: The Boydell Press, 1999, pp. 59-72.

Schultz, J. "Die bürgerliche Dienst- und Wehrpflicht in der Mark Brandenburg," *Jahrbuch für die Geschichte Mittel- und Ostdeutschland* 23 (1974), 270-80.

Schünemann, K. "Deutsche Kriegsführung im Osten während des Mittelalters," *Deutsches Archiv für Erforschung des Mittelalters* (1938), 54-84.

Schürstab, E. *Beschreibung des ersten Markgräflichen Krieges gegen Nürnberg.* Ed. J. Bader. Munich, 1860; rpt. Munich, 1969.

Sprandel, R. "Die Ritterschaft und das Hochstift Würzburg im Spätmittelalter," *Jahrbuch für fränkische Landesforschung* 36 (1976), 117-43.

Sterzel, H. "Das Wolfegger Hausbuch und seine Bedeutung für die Waffenkunde," *Zeitschrift für historische Waffenkunde* 6 (1912-14), 234-29, 280-89.

Stöcklein, H. "Das Landsknechts- und Söldnertum," *Deutsche Soldatenkunde* 1 (1937), 50-62.

Thorau, Peter. "Der Krieg und das Geld: Ritter und Söldner in den Heeren Kaiser Friedrichs II," *Historische Zeitschrift* 268 (1999), 599-634.

Tucci, Hannelore Zug. "I *Victricia castra* di Federico II," *Nuovo rivista storica* 82 (1998), 525-40.

Ulrichs, Cord. *Vom Lehnhof zur Reichsritterschaft Strukturen des fränkischen Niederadels am Übergang vom späten Mittelalter zur frühen Neuzeit.* Vierteljahrschrift für Sozial- und Wirtschaftsgeschichte Beihefte, 134. Stuttgart: Franz Steiner, 1997.

Wehrhafte Stadt: Das Wiener Bürgerliche Zeughaus im 15. Und 16. Jahrhundert. Vienna: Historisches Museum der Stadt Wien, 1986.

Werner, Karl Ferdinand. "Heeresorganisation und Kriegsführung in deutschen Königreich des 10. und 11. Jahrhunderts." In: *Ordinamenti Militari in Occidenti nell'alto medioevo.* Settimane di studio del centro italiano di studi sull'alto medioevo, XV. Spoleto, 1968, I:791-843; in: *Structures politiques du monde franc (VIe-XIIe siècles).* London, 1979.

Zmora, Hillay. *State and Nobility in Early Modern Germany: The Knightly Feud in Franconia, 1440-1567.* Cambridge: Cambridge University Press, 1997.

Zotz, Thomas. "Le jouteur dans la ville: Un aspect des rapports entre noblesse, ville et bourgeoisie en Allemagne au bas moyen âge." In: *Le combattant au moyen âge.* 2nd ed. Histoire ancienne et médiévale, 36. Paris: Publications de la Sorbonne, 1995, pp. 161-67.

Medieval – Hundred Years War – General

Alban, J.-R. "Une révolte des prisonniers de guerre anglaise a Saint-Omer au XIVme siècle," *Bulletin trimestriel de la société académique des antiquaires de la Morinie* 22 (1974), 161-80.

Allmand, Christopher T. *The Hundred Years War: England and France at War c. 1300-c. 1450.* Cambridge: Cambridge University Press, 1988.

Allmand, Christopher T. "Historians Reconsidered: Jean Froissart," *History Today* 16 (1966), 841-48.

Allmand, Christopher T. "Intelligence in the Hundred Years War." In: *Go Spy the Land: Military Intelligence in History.* Ed. K. Neilson and B.J.C. McKercher. Westport, 1992, pp. 31-47.

Allmand, Christopher T. "New Weapons, New Tactics, 1300-1500." In: *The Cambridge Illustrated History of Warfare: The Triumph of the West.* Ed. Geoffrey Parker. Cambridge: Cambridge University Press, 1995, pp. 92-105.

Allmand, Christopher T. "Some Effects of the Last Phase of the Hundred Years War upon the Maintenance of Clergy," *Studies in Church History* 3 (1966), 179-90.

Allmand, Christopher T., ed. *Society at War: The Experience of England and France During the Hundred Years War.* Edinburgh: Oliver and Boyd, 1973; rpt. Woodbridge: The Boydell Press, 1998.

Angers, Denise. "La guerre et le pluralisme linguistique: Aspects de la guerre de cent ans," *Annales de Normandie* 43 (1993), 125-39.

Armstrong, C.A.J. "La double monarchie France-Angleterre et la maison de Bourgogne (1420-1435)," *Annales de Bourgogne* 37 (1965), 81-112.

Artonne, A. "Froissart Historien: Le siège et la prise de la Roche-Vendeix," *Bibliothèque de l'école des chartes* 110 (1952), 89-107.

Bailly, Auguste. *La guerre de cent ans.* Paris, 1943.

Bean, Richard. "War and the Birth of the Nation State," *Journal of Economic History* 33 (1973), 203-21.

Bennett, Matthew. "The Development of Battle Tactics in the Hundred Years War." In: *Arms, Armies and Fortifications in the Hundred Years War*. Ed. A. Curry and M. Hughes. Woodbridge, 1994, pp. 1-20.

Blanchard, Joël. "Écrire la guerre au XVe siècle," *Le moyen français* 24-25 (1989).

Bock, Friedrich. "Some New Documents Illustrating the Early Years of the Hundred Years War (1353-1356)," *Bulletin of the John Rylands Library* 15 (1931), 60-97.

Bonenfant, Paul. *Du meurtre de Montereau au traité de Troyes*. Brussels: Palais des Académies, 1958.

Bossuat, André. *Perrinet Gressart et François de Surienne: Agents de l'Angleterre. Contribution à l'étude des relations de l'Angleterre et de la Bourgogne avec la France, sous le règne de Charles VII*. Paris: Libraire E. Droz, 1936.

Bourassin, Emmanuel. *La France anglaise, 1415-1453: Chronique d'un occupation*. Paris: Libraire Jules Tallandier, 1981.

Bryssel, E. van, ed. "Documents inédits, extraits des coll. du Record Office, concernant les relations entre la Flandre et l'Angleterre sous le règne Edouard III et sous celui de Richard II," *Bulletin de la commission royal d'histoire de Belgique* 3rd series, 9 (1866-67), 501-32.

Burne, Alfred H. *The Agincourt War: A Military History of the Latter Part of the Hundred Years War from 1369 to 1453*. London: Eyre and Spottiswoode, 1956.

Burne, Alfred H. *The Crecy War: A Military History of the Hundred Years War from 1337 to the Peace of Bretigny, 1360*. London: Eyre and Spottiswoode, 1955.

Carolus-Barré, Louis. "Benoit XII et la mission charitable de Bertrand Carit dans les pays devastés du nord de la France: Cambrésis, Vermandois, Thiérarche, 1340," *Mélanges d'archéologie et d'histoire publiés par l'école française de Rome* 62 (1950).

Chaplais, Pierre. "Règlement des conflits internationaux franco-anglais au XIVe siècle (1293-1377)," *Moyen âge*, 4th ser., 6 (1951), 269-302.

Chareyron, N. *Jean le Bel: Le maître de Froissart, Grand imagier de la guerre de cent ans*. Bibliothèque du Moyen Age, vol. 7. Brussels, 1996.

Charles, R. "L'invasion anglaise dans le Maine de 1417 à 1428," *Revue historique et archeologique du Maine* 25 (1889), 62-92, 167-96, 305-27.

Clément-Simon, G. *La rupture du traité de Brétigny et ses consequences en Limousin*. Paris, 1898.

Contamine, Philippe. "Les armées française et anglaise à l'époque de Jeanne d'Arc," *Revue des sociétés savantes de haute-normandie. Lettres et sciences humaines* 57 (1970), 5-33.

Contamine, Philippe. "Les chaînes dans les bonnes villes de France (spécialement Paris), XIVe-XVe siècle." In: *Guerre et société en France, en Angleterre et en Bourgogne XIVe-XVe siècle*. Ed. P. Contamine et al. Lille, 1991, pp. 293-314.

Contamine, Philippe. "De la modernité de la guerre de cent ans: conflit féodal, dynastique ou national?" In: *De Jeanne d'Arc aux guerres d'Italie: Figures, images et problèmes du XVe siècle*. Orléans, 1994, pp. 13-37.

Contamine, Philippe. "La 'France Anglaise' au XVe siècle. Mythe ou réalité?" In: *111e Congrès national des Sociétés savantes, Poitiers, 1986, Histoire médiévale*. T. I: "La France anglaise," pp. 55-84.

Contamine, Philippe. "Froissart: Art militaire, practique et conception de la guerre." In: *Froissart: Historian*. Ed. J.J.N. Palmer. Woodbridge, 1981, pp. 132-44.

Contamine, Philippe. *La guerre de cent ans*. Que Sais-Je? 3rd ed. Paris: Presses Universitaires de France, 1977.

Contamine, Philippe. "The Soldiery in Late Medieval Urban Society," *French History* 8 (1994), 1-13.

Contamine, Philippe. "Structures militaires de la France et de l'Angleterre au milieu du XVe siècle." In: *Das spätmittelalterliche Königtum im europaische Vergleich*. Ed. R. Schneider. Sigmarungen, 1987, pp. 319-34.

Contamine, Philippe. "La théologie de la guerre à la fin du moyen âge: la guerre de cent ans fut-elle une guerre juste?" In: *Jeanne d'Arc: Une époque, un rayonnement*. Paris, 1982, pp. 9-21.

Cormier, Jean-Philippe. "Les effets de la conquête anglaise dans le Domfrontais d'après les comptes de vicomté (1419-1421)." In: *La guerre, la violence et les gens au Moyen Âge*. II: *Guerre et gens*. Ed. P. Contamine and O. Guyotjeannin. 119e congrès national des sociétés historiques et scientifiques, Amiens, octobre 1994, Section d'histoire médiévale et philologie. Paris, 1996, pp. 127-39.

Coulton, G.G. *The Chronicler of European Chivalry*. London, 1930.

Curry, Anne E. *The Hundred Years War*. Houndmills: Macmillan, 1993.

Danbury, Elizabeth. "English and French Artistic Propaganda during the Period of the Hundred Years War: Some Evidence from Royal Charters." In: *Power, Culture, and Religion in France c.1350-c.1550*. Ed. C. Allmand. Woodbridge, 1989, pp. 75-97.

Diller, George T. "*Pour la cause de ce que j'estoie françois*: Langue(s) et loyauté(s) dans les *Chroniques* de Froissart," *Moyen age* (5) 12 (1998), 461-71.

Diller, George T. "Robert d'Artois et l'historicité des *Chroniques* de Froissart," *Moyen Age* 86 (1980), 217-31.

Favier, Jean. *La guerre de cent ans*. Paris: Fayard, 1980.

Fowler, Kenneth. *The Age of the Plantagenet and the Valois: The Struggle for Supremacy 1328-1498*. New York: G.P. Putnam's Sons, 1967; trans. *Le siècle des Plantagenêts et des Valois: La lutte pour la suprématie, 1328-1498*. Paris, 1968.

Fowler, Kenneth. "Froissart: Chronicler of Chivalry," *History Today* 36 (May 1986), 50-54.

Fowler, Kenneth. "News from the Front: Letters and Dispatches of the Fourteenth Century." In: *Guerre et société en France, en Angleterre et en Bourgogne XIVe-XVe siècle*. Ed. P. Contamine, C. Giry-Deloison, and Maurice Keen. Lille, 1991, pp. 63-92.

Gaillard, Philippe. *La bataille d'Anthon: 11 juin 1430*. Annecy-le-Vieux: Historic'one, 1998.

Guesnon, A. "Documents inédits sur l'invasion anglaise et les Etats au temps de Philippe VI et de Jean le Bon," *Bulletin philologique et historique* (1897), 208-59.

Hale, John R. "War and Public Opinion in the Fifteenth and Sixteenth Centuries," *Past and Present* 22 (1962), 18-35.

Harari, Yuval Noah. "Strategy and Supply in Fourteenth-Century Western European Invasion Campaigns," *Journal of Military History* 64 (2000), 297-333.

Hurel, Nathalie. "La représentation et la violence dans l'illustration des Chroniques universalles en rouleau." In: *La guerre, la violence et les gens au Moyen Âge*. I: *Guerre et violence*. Ed. P. Contamine and O. Guyot-jeannin. 119e congrès national des sociétés historiques et scientifiques, Amiens, octobre 1994, Section d'histoire médiévale et philologie. Paris, 1996, pp. 125-35.

Jubault, P. *D'Azincourt à Jeanne d'Arc, 1415-1430*. Amiens: Imprimere Moulat, 1969.

Kirby, J.L. "The Siege of Bourg, 1406." *History Today* 18 (1968), 53-60.

Lassabatère, Thierry. "Théorie et éthique de la guerre dans l'œuvre d'Eustache Deschamps." In: *La guerre, la violence et les gens au Moyen Âge*. I: *Guerre et violence*. Ed. P. Contamine and O. Guyotjeannin. 119e congrès national des sociétés historiques et scientifiques, Amiens, octobre 1994, Section d'histoire médiévale et philologie. Paris, 1996, pp. 35-48.

Leguai, André. *La guerre de cent ans*. Paris, 1974.

Lewis, P.S. "War Propaganda and Historiography in Fifteenth-Century France and England." In: *Essays in Later Medieval French History*. London, 1985, pp. 193-213.

Marsilje, J.W. "De Honderdjarige oorlog; traditie en vernieuwing." In: *Oorlog in de middeleeuwen*. Ed. A.J. Brand. Hilversum, 1989, pp. 141-50.

McRobbie, K. "The Concept of Advancement in the Fourteenth Century in the *Chroniques* of Jean Froissart," *Canadian Journal of History* 6 (1971), 1-19.

Mirot, Léon. "Une tentative invasion en Angleterre pendant la guerre de cent ans," *Revue des études historiques* 81 (1915), 249-87, 417-66.

Neillands, Robin. *The Hundred Years War*. London: Routledge, 1990.

Newhall, Richard Ager. *The English Conquest of Normandy, 1416-1424: A Study in Fifteenth Century Warfare*. New Haven: Yale University Press, 1924.

Offler, H.S. "England and Germany at the Beginning of the Hundred Years' War," *English Historical Review* 54 (1939), 608-31.

Palmer, J.J.N. "Book I (1325-1378) and Its Sources." In: *Froissart: Historian*. Ed. J.J.N. Palmer. Woodbridge, 1981, pp. 7-24.

Palmer, J.J.N. *England, France and Christendom, 1377-99*. Chapel Hill: The University of North Carolina Press, 1972.

Palmer, J.J.N. "Froissart et le Héraut Chandos," *Moyen âge* 88 (1982), 271-92.

Palmer, J.J.N. "The War Aims of the Protagonists and the Negotiations for Peace." In: *The Hundred Years War*. Ed. Kenneth Fowler. London: Macmillan, 1971, pp. 51-74.

Perroy, Edouard. "France, England, and Navarre from 1359 to 1364," *Bulletin of the Institute of Historical Research* 13 (1935/36) 151-60.

Perroy, Edouard. "Historical Revision: Franco-English Relations, 1350-1400," *History* 21 (1937), 148-54; in: *Etudes d'histoire médiévale*. Paris, 1979.

Perroy, Edouard. *La guerre de cent ans*. 6th ed. Paris, 1945; trans. *The Hundred Years War*. Trans. W.B. Wells. New York: Oxford University Press, 1951.

Philippe, Dominique. "Guerre et images de guerre dans la chronique bretonne au XIVe siècle," *Annales de Bretagne et des Pays de l'Ouest* 105 (1998), 35-51.

Poull, G. "La bataille de Bulgnéville, 2 juillet 1431: Ses prisonniers et ses morts," *Les cahiers d'histoire, de biographie et de généalogie* 1 (1965), 10-43.

Racinet, Philippe. "Le rôle de la guerre dans l'évolution des monastères clunisiens aux XIVe et XVe siècles." In: *La guerre, la violence et les gens au Moyen Âge*. II: *Guerre et gens*. Ed. P. Contamine and O. Guyotjeannin. 119e congrès national des sociétés historiques et scientifiques, Amiens, octobre 1994, Section d'histoire médiévale et philologie. Paris, 1996, pp. 89-100.

Raynaud, Christiane. "L'imaginaire de la guerre dans l'histoire du bon roi Alexandre (ms 456 de la collection Dutuit)," *Bulletin des sociétés d'histoire et d'archéologie de la Meuse* 28-29 (1992-93), 61-80.

Rogers, Clifford J. "The Age of the Hundred Years War." In: *Medieval Warfare: A History*. Ed. Maurice Keen. Oxford: Oxford University Press, 1999, pp. 136-60.

Rogers, Clifford J. "The Military Revolutions of the Hundred Years War," *Journal of Military History* 57 (1993), 241-78; in: *The Military Revolution Debate: Readings on the Military Transformation of Early Modern Europe*. Ed. C.J. Rogers. Boulder, 1995, pp. 55-94.

Rogers, Clifford J. "The Offensive/Defensive in Medieval Strategy." In: *XXII. Kongreß der Internationalen Kommission für Militärgeschichte* Acta 22: *Von Crécy bis Mohács Kriegswesen im späten Mittelalter (1346-1526)*. Vienna, 1997, pp. 158-71.

Rowe, B.J.H. "A Contemporary Account of the Hundred Years' War from 1415 to 1429," *English Historical Review* 41 (1926), 504-13.

Salamagne, Alain. "L'attaque des places-fortes au XVe siècle à travers l'exemple des guerres anglo et franco-bourguignonnes," *Revue historique* 289 (1993), 65-113.

Schnerb, Bertrand. *Les Armagnacs et les Bourguignons: La maudite guerre*. Paris: Librairie Académique Perrin, 1988.

Seward, Desmond. *The Hundred Years War: The English in France, 1337-1453*. New York: Atheneum, 1978.

Shears, F.S. *Froissart: Chronicler and Poet*. London: George Routledge and Sons, Ltd., 1930.

Sumption, Jonathan. *The Hundred Years War: Trial By Battle*. Philadelphia: University of Pennsylvania Press, 1991.

Sumption, Jonathan. *The Hundred Years War: Trial By Fire*. London: Faber and Faber, 1999.

Templeman, G. "Two French Attempts to Invade England during the Hundred Years War." In: *Studies in French Language, Literature and History Presented to R.L.G. Ritchie*. Cambridge: Cambridge University Press, 1949, pp. 225-38.

Thibault, Paul R. *Pope Gregory XI: The Failure of Tradition*. Lanham: University Press of America, 1986.

Thompson, Guy Llewelyn. *Paris and Its People Under English Rule: The Anglo-Burgundian Regime 1420-1436*. Oxford: Clarendon Press, 1991.

Thornton, T. "The Alleged French Raid on the Isle of Man, 1377," *Northern History* 35 (1999), 208-13.

Tout, T.F. "Some Neglected Fights between Crécy and Poitiers." In: *Collected Papers of Thomas Frederick Tout*. Manchester, 1934, II:227-31.

Trévédy, J. "La campagne des anglais en France en 1373," *Mémoires de la société d'émulation des Côtes-du Nord* 44 (1906), 1-33.

Tuchman, Barbara W. *A Distant Mirror: The Calamitous 14th Century*. New York: Ballantine Books, 1978.

Tuck, J. Anthony. "Why Men Fought in the Hundred Years War," *History Today* 33 (April 1983), pp. 35-40.

Vale, Malcolm. *War and Chivalry: Warfare and Aristocratic Culture in England, France and Burgundy at the End of the Middle Ages*. Athens: University of Georgia Press, 1981.

Viard, Jules. "Documents Français remis au gouvernement Anglais à la suite du traité de Brétigny," *Bibliothèque de l'école de chartes* 58 (1897), 155-61.

Villaret, Amicie de. *Campagnes des Anglais dans l'Orléanais, la Beauce Chartrain et le Gatinais (1421-1428): L'armée sous Warwick et Suffolk au siège de Montargis. Campagnes de Jeanne d'Arc sur la Loire postérierures au siège d'Orléans*. Orléans: H.Herluison, 1893.

Warner, Mark. "The Anglo-French Dual Monarchy and the House of Burgundy, 1420-1435: The Survival of an Alliance," *French History* 11 (1997), 103-30.

Wright, Nicholas A.R. "Feudalism and the Hundred Years War." In: *Feudalism: Comparative Studies*. Sydney, 1985, pp. 105-23.

Wright, Nicholas A.R. "'Pillagers' and 'Brigands' in the Hundred Years War," *Journal of Medieval History* 9 (1983), 15-24.

Zink, Michel. *Froissart et le temps*. Paris: PUF, 1998.

Medieval – Hundred Years War – Origins [see Medieval – Hundred Years War – Edward III]

Brown, Elizabeth A.R. "The Political Repercussions of Family Ties in the Early Fourteenth Century: The Marriage of Edward II of England and Isabelle of France," *Speculum* 63 (1988), 573-95.

Cazelles, Raymond. *La société politique et la crise de la royauté sous Philippe de Valois*. Paris, 1958.

Chaplais, Pierre. "Le traité de Paris de 1259 et l'inféodation de la Gascogne allodiale," *Moyen âge* 61 (1955), 121-37.

Cuttino, G.P. "Historical Revision: The Causes of the Hundred Years War," *Speculum* 39 (1956), 463-77.

Cuttino, G.P. "The Process of Agen," *Speculum* 19 (1944), 161-78.

Déprez, Eugène. *Les préliminaires de la guerre de cent ans: la papauté, la France et l'Angleterre, 1328-1342*. Paris, 1902.

Dossat, Yves. "L'Agenais vers 1325, après la campagne de Charles de Valois." In: *La guerre et la paix: Frontières et violences au moyen âge*. Actes du 101e congrès national des sociétés savantes, Lille, 1976. Paris: Bibliothèque Nationale, 1978, pp. 143-54.

Funck-Brentano, Frantz. *Philippe le Bel et Flandre: Les origines de la guerre de cent ans*. Paris: Honoré Champion, Libraire, 1896.

Glénisson, J. "L'application de la 'paix' de Paris (1259) en Saintonge, de 1273 à 1293." In: *111e Congrès national des Sociétés savantes, Poitiers, 1986, Histoire médiévale*. T. I: "La France anglaise." Paris, 1988, pp. 191-206.

Kaeuper, Richard W. *War, Justice, and Public Order: England and France in the Later Middle Ages*. Oxford: Clarendon Press, 1988.

Le Patourel, John. "The Origins of the War." In: *The Hundred Years War*. Ed. Kenneth Fowler. London: Macmillan, 1971, pp. 28-50.

Maddicott, John. "The Origins of the Hundred Years War," *History Today* 36 (May 1986), 31-38.

Menache, Sophia. "Mythe et symbolisme au début de la guerre de cent ans: Vers une conscience nationale," *Moyen âge* 89 (1983), 85-97

Ormrod, W.M. "England, Normandy and the Beginnings of the Hundred Years War, 1259-1360." In: *England and Normandy in the Middle Ages*. Ed. D. Bates and A. Curry. London, 1994, pp. 197-213.

Rogers, Clifford J. "A Continuation of the *Manuel d'histoire de Philippe VI* for the Years 1328-39," *English Historical Review* 114 (1999), 1256-66.

Studd, R. "The *privilegiati* and the Treaty of Paris, 1259." In: *111e Congrès national des Sociétés savantes, Poitiers, 1986, Histoire médiévale*. T. I: "La France anglaise." Paris, 1988, pp. 175-89.

Vale, Malcolm. *The Angevin Legacy and the Hundred Years War, 1250-1340*. Oxford: Basil Blackwell, 1990.

Vale, Malcolm. "The Anglo-French Wars, 1294-1340: Allies and Alliances. In: *Guerre et société en France, en Angleterre et en Bourgogne XIVe-XVe siècle*. Ed. P. Contamine, C. Giry-Deloison, and Maurice Keen. Lille, 1991, pp. 15-35.

Vale, Malcolm. "England, France and the Origins of the Hundred Years War." In: *England and her Neighbours, 1066-1483: Essays in Honour of Pierre Chaplais*. Ed. M. Jones and M. Vale. London, 1989, pp. 199-216.

Vale, Malcolm. "The Gascon Nobility and Crises in Loyalty, 1294-1337." In: *111e Congrès national des Sociétés savantes, Poitiers, 1986, Histoire médiévale*. T. I: "La France anglaise." Paris, 1988, pp. 207-16.

Wolff, Philippe. "Un problème d'origines: La guerre de cent ans." In: *Éventail de l'histoire vivante: homage à Lucien Febvre*. Paris, 1953, II:141-8.

Medieval – Hundred Years War – Sluys (battle of)

DeVries, Kelly. "God, Leadership, Flemings, and Archery: Contemporary Perceptions of Victory and Defeat at the Battle of Sluys, 1340," *American Neptune* 55 (1995), 223-42.

Dhondt, André. "1340: de zeeslag in het Zwin," *Croc is ier* 30 (1993), 1-24.

Luce, Siméon. "Le soufflet de l'Écluse et la chanson des pastoureaux normands." In: *La France pendant la guerre de cent ans*. Paris, 1893, pp. 1-15.

Medieval – Hundred Years War – Tournai (siege of)

DeVries, Kelly. "Contemporary Views of Edward III's Failure at the Siege of Tournai, 1340." *Nottingham Medieval Studies* 39 (1995), 70-105.

Rogers, Clifford J. "An Unknown News Bulletin from the Siege of Tournai in 1340," *War in History* 5 (1998), 358-66.

Medieval – Hundred Years War – Crécy (battle of)

Ayton, Andrew. "The English Army and the Normandy Campaign of 1346." In: *England and Normandy in the Middle Ages*. Ed. D. Bates and A. Curry. London, 1994, pp. 253-67.

Contamine, Philippe. "Crécy (1346) et Azincourt (1415): Une comparison." In: *Divers aspects du moyen âge en occident*. Calais, 1977, pp. 29-44.

Kerkhoven, J.G. "Les anglais ont-ils fait usage d'armes à feu à la bataille de Crécy?" *Revue internationale d'histoire militaire* 19 (1957), 323-31.

Morris, John E. "The Archers at Crécy," *English Historical Review* 12 (1897), 427-36.

Rigg, A.G. "Propaganda of the Hundred Years War: Poems on the Battles of Crecy and Durham (1346): A Critical Edition," *Traditio* 54 (1999), 169-211.

Rose, Walther. "König Johann der Blinde von Böhmen und die Schlacht bei Crécy (1346)," *Zeitschrift für historisches Waffenkunde* 7 (1915-17), 37-60.

Viard, Jules. "La campagne de juillet-aôut 1346 et la bataille de Crécy," *Moyen âge*, 2nd ser., 27 (1926), 1-84.

Wailly, Henri de. *Crecy, 1346: Anatomy of a Battle*. Poole, 1987.

Medieval – Hundred Years War – Calais (siege of)

"Compte de Pierre de Ham, dernier bailli de Calais (1346-1347)," ed. Jules-Marie Richard, *Memoires de la commission departementale des monuments historiques du Pas-de-Calais* (1893), 241-58.

DeVries, Kelly. "Hunger, Flemish Participation and the Flight of Philip VI: Contemporary Accounts of the Siege of Calais, 1346-47," *Studies in Medieval and Renaissance History* n.s 12 (1991), 129-81.

Guizot, M. *Édouard III et les bourgeois de Calais ou les Anglais en France (1346-1558)*. Paris: Libraire de L. Hachette et Cio., 1854.

Moeglin, Jean-Marie. "Edouard III et les six bourgeois de Calais," *Revue historique* 292 (1994), 230-67.

Molinier, Émile. *Documents relatifs aux Calaisiens expulsés par Édouard III*. Paris: Alph. Picard, 1878.

Rothero, Christopher. *The Armies of Crécy and Poitiers*. Men-at-Arms Series. London: Osprey Publishing, 1981.

Roncière, Charles de la. "La marine au siège de Calais," *Bibliothèque de l'école de chartes* 58 (1897), 554-78.

Viard, Jules. "Le siège de Calais, 4 septembre 1346-4 aout 1347," *Moyen âge*, 2nd ser., 30 (1929), 124-89.

Medieval – Hundred Years War – Poitiers (battle of)

Autrand, Françoise. "La déconfiture. La bataille de Poitiers (1356) à travers quelques textes français des XIVe et XVe siècles." In: *Guerre et société en France, en Angleterre et en Bourgogne XIVe-XVe siècle*. Ed. P. Contamine, C. Giry-Deloison, and Maurice Keen. Lille, 1991, pp. 93-121.

Barber, Richard. *Edward, Prince of Wales and Aquitaine*. London, 1982.

Beaurepaire, Charles de, ed. "Complainte dur la bataille de Poitiers," *Bibliothèque de l'école de chartes* 12 (1851), 257-63.

Carpentier, Elisabeth. "L'historiographie de la bataille de Poitiers au quatorzième siècle." *Revue historique* 263 (1980), 21-58.

Hewitt, H.J. *The Black Prince's Expedition of 1355 -1357*. Manchester: Manchester University Press, 1958.

Mann, James. *The Funeral Achievements of Edward, the Black Prince*. London, 1950.

Rothero, Christopher. *The Armies of Crécy and Poitiers*. Men-at-Arms Series. London: Osprey Publishing, 1981.

Schlight, John. "Odds Against the Black Prince," *Great Battles* (Mar 1992), 34-41.

Tourneur-Aumont, J.M. *La bataille de Poitiers (1356) et la construction de la France*. Paris: Presses universitaires de France, 1940.

Military – Medieval – Hundred Years War – Aljubarrota (battle of)

Bessa, Carlos Gomes. *Aljubarrota sua evocaçâo em Macau*. Macao: Instituto Cultural de Macau, 1986.

Do Paço, Afonso. "The Battle of Aljubarrota," *Antiquity* 37 (1963), 264-69.

Medieval – Hundred Years War – Agincourt (battle of)

Bennett, Matthew. *Agincourt 1415: Triumph Against the Odds*. Campaign Series. London: Osprey Publishing Ltd., 1991.

Boffa, Serge. "Antoine de Bourgogne et le contingent brabançon à la bataille d'Azincourt (1415), *Revue Belge de philologie et d'histoire* 72 (1994), 255-84.

Contamine, Philippe. *Azincourt*. Paris: René Julliard, 1964.

Contamine, Philippe. "Crécy (1346) et Azincourt (1415): Une comparison." In: *Divers aspects du moyen âge en occident*. Calais, 1977, pp. 29-44.

Delcusse, Claude. *The Battle of Agincourt, Pas de Calais, 25 October 1415*. Agincourt, n.d.

Heath, E.G. "Agincourt," *Journal of the Society of Archer-Antiquaries* 8 (1965), 7-10.

Hibbert, Christopher. *Agincourt*. New York: Dorset Press, 1978.

Hull, Felix. "An Early Kentish Militia Roll," *Journal of the Society of Archer-Antiquaries* 6 (1963), 12-13.

Kerr, Wilfred Brenton. "The English Soldier in the Campaign of Agincourt," *Journal of the American Military Institute* 4 (1940), 209-24.

Loisne, Auguste de. "La bataille d'Azincourt d'après le manuscrit inédit du château de Tramecourt," *Bulletin historique et philologique du comité des travaux historiques et scientifiques* (1897), 70-82.

Malden, A.R. "An Official Account of the Battle of Agincourt," *The Ancestor* 9 (1904), 26-31.

Müller, Wolfgang G. "The Battle of Agincourt in Carol and Ballad," *Fifteenth Century Studies* 8 (1983), 159-78.

Nicolas, Nicholas Harris. *History of the Battle of Agincourt and of the Expedition of Henry the Fifth into France in 1415.* 3rd ed. 1833; rpt. London: H. Pordes, 1971.

Phillpotts, Christopher. "The French Plan of Battle during the Agincourt Campaign," *English Historical Review* 99 (1990), 59-66.

Rothero, Christopher. *The Armies of Agincourt.* Men-at-Arms Series. London: Osprey Publishing, 1981.

"Strongbow". "Historic Doubts on Battle Formations," *Journal of the Society of Archer-Antiquaries* 26 (1983), 45-48.

Medieval – Hundred Years War – Cravant (battle of)

Dousseau, Jean-Michel. *La bataille de Cravant (1423).* Auxerre: Imprimere Moderne, 1987.

Medieval – Hundred Years War – Formigny (battle of)

Joret, Charles. *La bataille de Formigny d'après les documents contemporains.* Paris: Libraire Emile Bouillon, Éditeur, 1903.

Lair, J. *Essai historique et topographique sur la bataille de Formigny (15 avril 1450).* Paris: Honoré Champion, 1903.

Lair, J. *La bataille de Formigny.* Paris: Honoré Champion, 1908.

Lambert, Ch. "Mémoire sur la bataille de Formigny." In: *Pièces sur le Bessin.* Caen: Société Linéenne du Calvados, 1824.

Medieval – Hundred Years War – Castillon (battle of)

Burne, Alfred H. "La bataille de Castillon, 1453: la fin de la guerre de cent ans," *Revue de histoire de Bourdeaux* n.s. 2 (1953), 293-305.

Burne, Alfred H. "The Battle of Castillon, 1453," *History Today* 3 (1953), 249-56.

"Lettre sur la bataille de Castillon en Perigord, 19 juillet 1453," *Bibliothèque de l'école des chartes* 8 191846-47), 245-47.

Medieval – Hundred Years War – England

Armstrong, C.A.J. "Sir John Fastolf and the Law of Arms." In: *War, Literature and Politics in the Late Middle Ages: Essays in Honour of G.W. Coopland*. Ed. C.T. Allmand. Liverpool: University of Liverpool Press, 1975, pp. 46-56.

Ayton, Andrew. "English Armies in the Fourteenth Century." In: *Arms, Armies and Fortifications in the Hundred Years War*. Ed. A. Curry and M. Hughes. Woodbridge, 1994, pp. 21-38; in: *The Wars of Edward III: Sources and Interpretations*. Ed. Clifford J. Rogers. Woodbridge: The Boydell Press, 1999, pp. 303-20.

Ayton, Andrew. "The English Army and the Normandy Campaign of 1346." In: *England and Normandy in the Middle Ages*. Ed. D. Bates and A. Curry. London, 1994, pp. 253-67.

Ayton, Andrew. "Robin Hood and Military Service in the Fourteenth Century," *Nottingham Medieval Studies* 36 (1992), 126-47.

Barber, Richard. *Edward, Prince of Wales and Aquitaine*. London, 1982.

Barber, Richard. "Jean Froissart and Edward the Black Prince." In: *Froissart: Historian*. Ed. J.J.N. Palmer. Woodbridge, 1981, pp. 25-35.

Barnie, John. *War in Medieval English Society: Social Values in the Hundred Years War, 1337-99*. Ithaca: Cornell University Press, 1974.

Baume, Andrew J.L. "L'organisation militaire des seigneuries du duc d'York, 1443-1449," *Cahiers Leopold Delisle* 40 (1991), 37-44.

Bayley, C.C. "The Campaign of 1375 and the Good Parliament," *English Historical Review* 55 (1940), 370-83.

Bittman, K. "La campagne Lancastrienne de 1463," *Revue Belge de philologie et d'histoire* 26 (1948), 1059-88

Bossuat, André. "La littérature de propagande au XVe siècle: La Mémoire de Jean de Rinel, secrétaire du roi d'Angleterre, contre le duc de Bourgogne (1435)," *Cahiers d'histoire* 1 (1956), 131-46.

Bridge, J.C. "Two Cheshire Soldiers of Fortune of the Fourteenth Century: Sir Hugh Calveley and Sir Robert Knolles," *Journal of the Architectural, Archaeological and Historical Society for Chester and North Wales* n.s. 14 (1908).

Brill, Reginald. "The English Preparations before the Treaty of Arras: A New Interpretation of Sir John Fastolf's 'Report,' September, 1435," *Studies in Medieval and Renaissance History* 7 (1970), 211-47.

Campbell, James. "England, Scotland and the Hundred Years War in the Fourteenth Century." In: *Europe in the Late Middle Ages*. Ed. J.R. Hale, J.R.L. Highfield and B. Smalley. Evanston: Northwestern University Press, 1965, pp.; in: *The Wars of Edward III: Sources and Interpretations*. Ed. Clifford J. Rogers. Woodbridge: The Boydell Press, 1999, pp. 207-30.

Carr, A.D. "A Welsh Knight in the Hundred Years War: Sir Gregory Sais," *Transactions of the Honourable Society of Cymmrodorion* (1977), 40-53.

Carr, A.D. "Welshmen in the Hundred Years War," *Welsh Historical Review* 4 (1968), 21-46.

Collins, Hugh. "Sir John Fastolf, John Lord Talbot and the Dispute over Patay: Ambitions and Chivalry in the Fifteenth Century." In: *War and Society in Medieval and Early Modern Britain*. Ed. Diana Dunn. Liverpool: Liverpool University Press, 2000, pp. 114-40.

Curry, Anne E. "English Armies in the Fifteenth Century." In: *Arms, Armies and Fortifications in the Hundred Years War*. Ed. A. Curry and M. Hughes. Woodbridge, 1994, pp. 39-68.

Davies, Clifford S.L. "'Roy de France et roy d'Angleterre': The English Claims to France, 1453-1558." In: *L'Angleterre et les pays Bourguignons: Relations et comparaisons (XVe-XVIe siècles)*. Neuchâtel: Centre européen d'études Bourguignons (XIVe-XVIe siècles), 1995, pp. 123-32.

Fowler, Kenneth. "Les finances et la discipline dans les armées anglaise en France au XIVe siècle." *Les cahiers vernonnais* 4 (1964), 55-84.

Fowler, Kenneth. *The King's Lieutenant: Henry of Grosmont, First Duke of Lancaster, 1310-1361.* New York: Barnes and Noble, Inc., 1969.

Fryde, E.B. "Parliament and the French War, 1336-40." In: *Essays in Medieval History Presented to Bertie Wilkinson.* Ed. T.A. Sandquist and M.R. Powicke. Toronto: University of Toronto Press, 1969, pp. 250-69.

Goodman, Anthony. "The Military Subcontracts of Sir Hugh Hastings, 1380," *English Historical Review* 95 (1980), 114-20.

Griffiths, Ralph A. "The English Realm and Dominions and the King's Subjects in the Later Middle Ages." In: *Aspects of Late Medieval Government and Society: Essays Presented to J.R. Lander.* Ed. J.G. Rowe. Toronto: University of Toronto Press, 1986, pp. 83-106.

Grondeux, Anne. "La présence anglaise en France: Les anglais dans la vallée de la Siene sous la régence du duc de Bedford (1422-1435)," *Journal des savants* (1993), 89-109.

Gruffydd, K. Lloyd. "Maritime Defence and Wales during the Later Middle Ages," *Cymru a'r Môr: Maritime Wales* 18 (1996), 10-32.

Gunn, Steven. "State Development in England and the Burgundian Dominions, c.1460-c.1560." In: *L'Angleterre et les pays Bourguignons: Relations et comparaisons (XVe-XVIe siècles).* Neuchâtel: Centre européen d'études Bourguignons (XIVe-XVIe siècles), 1995, pp. 133-49.

Haines, Roy Martin. "Church, Society and Politics in the Early Fifteenth Century as Viewed from an English Pulpit." In: *Church, Society and Politics.* Ed. D.G. Baker. Oxford, 1975, pp. 143-57.

Harmand, J. "Un document de 1435, concernant Houdan et la fin de l'occupation anglaise dans l'ouest de l'Ile-de-France," *Bulletin de la société nationale des antiquaries de France* (1975), 205-47.

Hay, Denys. "The Divisions of the Spoils of War in Fourteenth-Century England." In: *Renaissance Essays.* London, 1988, pp. 265-83.

Hayes, Richard. "Irish Soldiers at the Siege of Rouen (1418-19)," *Irish Sword* 2 (1954-56), 62-63.

Hewitt, H.J. "The Organization of War." In: *The Hundred Years War*. Ed. Kenneth Fowler. London: Macmillan, 1971, pp. 75-95; in: *The Wars of Edward III: Sources and Interpretations*. Ed. Clifford J. Rogers. Woodbridge: The Boydell Press, 1999, pp. 285-302.

Hill, Rosalind M.T. "Undesirable Aliens in the Diocese of York," *Studies in Church History* 20 (1983), 147-51.

Hudson, W. "Norwich Militia in the Fourteenth Century," *Norfolk Archaeology* 14 (1901), 263-320.

Hughes, Jonathan. "Stephen Scrope and the Circle of Sir John Fastolf: Moral and Intellectual Outlooks." In: *Medieval Knighthood, IV*. Ed. C. Harper-Bill and R. Harvey. Woodbridge: The Boydell Press, 1992, pp. 109-46.

Hughes, Michael. "The Fourteenth-Century French Raids on Hampshire and the Isle of Wight." In: *Arms, Armies and Fortifications in the Hundred Years War*. Ed. A. Curry and M. Hughes. Woodbridge, 1994, pp. 121-44.

Hull, Felix. "An Early Kentish Militia Roll," *Journal of the Society of Archer-Antiquaries* 6 (1963), 12-13.

Jarry, Eugène. "Le compte du siège, la défense et l'effectif de l'armée anglaise," *Mémoires de la société archéologique et historique de Orléanais* 23 (1892), 482-97.

Jones, Michael. "Fortunes et malheurs de guerre: Autour de la rançon du chevalier anglais Jean Bourchier (d. 1400)." In: *La guerre, la violence et les gens au Moyen Âge*. I: *Guerre et violence*. Ed. P. Contamine and O. Guyotjeannin. 119e congrès national des sociétés historiques et scientifiques, Amiens, octobre 1994, Section d'histoire médiévale et philologie. Paris, 1996, pp. 189-208.

Jones, Michael. "The Fortunes of War: The Military Career of John, Second Lord Bourchier (d. 1400)," *Essex Archaeology and History* 26 (1995), 145-61.

Jones, Michael. "John Beaufort, Duke of Somerset and the French Expedition of 1443." In: *Patronage, the Crown and the Provinces in Later*

Medieval England. Ed. Ralph A. Griffiths. Gloucester: Alan Sutton, 1981, pp. 79-102.

Jones, Michael K. "The Relief of Avranches (1439): An English Feat of Arms at the End of the Hundred Years War." In: *England in the Fifteenth Century: Proceedings of the 1992 Harlaxton Symposium.* Ed. N. Rogers. Stamford, 1994, pp.42-55.

Jones, W.R. "The English Church and Royal Propaganda during the Hundred Years War," *Journal of British Studies* 19 (1979), 18-30.

Jones, W.R. "Purveyance for War and the Community of the Realm in Late Medieval England," *Albion* 7 (1975), 300-16.

Kemp, Brian. "English Church Monuments during the Period of the Hundred Years War." In: *Arms, Armies and Fortifications in the Hundred Years War.* Ed. A. Curry and M. Hughes. Woodbridge, 1994, pp. 195-212.

Kingsford, Charles Lethbridge. *English Historical Literature in the Fifteenth Century.* 1913; rpt. New York, 1972.

Kirby, J.L. "The Council of 1407 and the Problem of Calais." In: *English Society and Government in the Fifteenth Century.* Ed. C.M.D. Crowder. Edinburgh, 1967, pp. 71-86.

Lander, J.R. "The Hundred Years War and Edward IV's 1475 Campaign in France." In: *Tudor Men and Institutions: Studies in English Law and Government.* Ed. A.J. Slavin. Baton Rouge, 1972, pp. 70-100.

Lewis, N.B. "The Feudal Summons of 1385," *English Historical Review* 100 (1985), 729-46.

Lewis, N.B. "Indentures of Retinue with John of Gaunt, Duke of Lancaster, Enrolled in Chancery, 1367-1399." In: *Camden Miscellany, XXII.* London, 1964, pp. 77-112.

Lewis, N.B. "The Last Medieval Summons of the English Feudal Levy, 13 June 1385," *English Historical Review* 73 (1958), 1-26.

Lewis, N.B. "The Organization of Indentured Retinues in Fourteenth-Century England," *Transactions of the Royal Historical Society* 4th ser. 27 (1945), 29-39.

Lewis, N.B. "The Recruitment and Organization of a Contract Army, May to November 1337," *Bulletin of the Institute of Historical Research* 37 (1964), 1-19.

Lowe, Ben. *Imagining Peace: A History of Early English Pacifist Ideas, 1340-1560*. University Park: Pennsylvania State University Press, 1997.

Magee, James. "Sir William Elmham and the Recruitment for Henry Despenser's Crusade of 1383," *Medieval Prospography* 20 (1999), 181-90.

McCulloch, D. and E.D. Jones. "Lancastrian Politics, the French War, and the Rise of the Popular Element," *Speculum* 58 (1983), 95-138.

McFarlane, K.B. "A Business-Patrnership in War and Administration, 1421-1445," *English Historical Review* 78 (1963), 290-310; in: *England in the Fifteenth Century: Collected Essays*. London, 1981, pp. 151-74.

McFarlane, K.B. "The Investment of Sir John Fastolf's Profits of War," *Transactions of the Royal Historical Society* 5th ser., 7 (1957), 91-116; in: *England in the Fifteenth Century: Collected Essays*. London, 1981, pp. 175-98.

McFarlane, K.B. "War and Society, 1300-1600: England and the Hundred Years War," *Past and Present* 22 (1962), 3-17.

McHardy, Alison. "The English Clergy and the Hundred Years War," *Studies in Church History* 20 (1983), 171-78.

McHardy, Alison. "Liturgy and Propaganda in the Diocese of Lincoln during the Hundred Years War." In: *Religion and National Identity*. Ed. S. Mews. Oxford, 1982, pp. 215-27.

Mirot, Léon. "Une tentative d'invasion en Angelterre pendant la guerre de cent ans," *Revue des études historiques* 81 (1915), 249-87, 417-66.

Myers, A.R. "The Outbreak of War between England and Burgundy in February 1471," *Bulletin of the Institute of Historical Research* 33 (1960), 114-15.

Newhall, Richard Ager. "Bedford's Ordinance on the Watch of September 1428," *English Historical Review* 50 (1935), 36-60.

Newhall, Richard Ager. "Discipline in an English Army of the Fifteenth Century," *The Military Historian and Economist* 2 (1917), 141-51.

Newhall, Richard Ager. *Muster and Review: A Problem of English Military Administration 1420-1440*. Cambridge: Harvard University Press, 1940.

"Ordinance for Charges of the Castles, North Wales, 2 Edw. III and 5, 6, Hen IV," *Archaeologia Cambrensis*, 3rd ser., 8 (1862), 123-29.

Ormrod, W.M. "The Domestic Response to the Hundred Years War." In: *Arms, Armies and Fortifications in the Hundred Years War*. Ed. A. Curry and M. Hughes. Woodbridge, 1994, pp. 83-102.

Owen, Leonard V.D. *The Connection Between England and Burgundy During the First Half of the Fifteenth Century*. The Stanhope Essay, 1909. Oxford: B. H. Blackwell, 1909.

Palmer. J.J.N. "The Last Summons of the Feudal Army in England (1385), *English Historical Review* 83 (1968), 771-75.

Perroy, Edouard. *L'Angleterre et le grand schisme d'occident: étude sur la politique religieuse de l'Angleterre sous Richard II (1378-1399)*. Paris: Libraire J. Monnier, 1933.

Pistono, Stephen P. "The Petition of Jacob de Smet: A Plea for Reprisals against the English, 1403," *Bulletin de la commission royale d'histoire de Belgique* 142 (1976), 341-51.

Pollard, A.J. *John Talbot and the War in France,1427-1453*. Royal Historical Society Studies in History Series, 35. London: Royal Historical Society, 1983.

Pollard, A.J. *Late Medieval England, 1399-1509*. Longman History of Medieval England. Harlow: Longman, 2000.

Powell, W.R. "Lionel de Bradeham and his Siege of Colchester in 1350," *Essex Archaeology and History* 22 (1991), 67-75.

Powicke, Michael R. "The English Aristocracy and the War." In: *The Hundred Years War*. Ed. Kenneth Fowler. London: Macmillan, 1971, pp. 122-34.

Powicke, Michael R. "Lancastrian Captains." In: *Essays in Medieval History Presented to Bertie Wilkinson*. Ed. T.A. Sandquist and M.R. Powicke. Toronto: University of Toronto Press, 1969, pp. 371-82.

Pratt, D. "Wrexham Militia in the 14th Century," *Transactions of the Denbighshire Historical Society* (1963).

Pratt, John H. *Chaucer and War*. Lanham: Rowman and Littlefield, 2000.

Prince, Albert E. "The Army and Navy." In: *The English Government at Work, 1327-1336*. Ed. J.F. Willard and W.A. Morris. Cambridge, 1940, I:332-93.

Pugh, T.B. "Richard Plantagenet (1411-60), Duke of York, as the King's Lieutenant in France and Ireland." In: *Aspects of Late Medieval Government and Society: Essays Presented to J.R. Lander*. Ed. J.G. Rowe. Toronto: University of Toronto Press, 1986, pp. 107-42.

Richmond, Colin. "Review Article–An English Mafia?" *Nottingham Medieval Studies* 36 (1992), 235-43.

Rigg, A.G. "John of Bridlington's *Prophecy*: A New Look," *Speculum* 63 (1988), 596-613.

Sandberger, D. *Studien über das Rittertum in England, vornehmlich während des 14. Jahrhunderts*. Berlin, 1937.

Saul, Nigel. "Conflict and Consensus in English Local Society." In: *Politics and Crisis in Fourteenth-Century England*. Ed. J. Taylor and W. Childs. London, 1990.

Saul, Nigel. "Great Yarmouth and the Hundred Years War in the Fourteenth Century," *Bulletin of the Institute for Historical Research* 52 (1979), 105-15.

Sherborne, James. "The Defence of the Realm and the Impeachment of Michael de la Pole in 1386." In: *Politics and Crisis in Fourteenth-Century England*. Ed. J. Taylor and W. Childs. London, 1990, pp. 97-116.

Sherborne, James. "Indentured Retinues and English Expeditions to France, 1369-1380," *English Historical Review* 79 (1964), 718-46.

Small, Graeme. "Some Aspects of Burgundian Attitudes towards the English during the Reign of Philip the Good: Georges Chastelain and

His Circle." In: *L'Angleterre et les pays Bourguignons: Relations et comparaisons (Xve-XVIe siècles.* Neuchâtel: Centre européen d'études Bourguignons (XIVe-XVIe siècles), 1995, pp. 15-26.

Talbot, Hugh. *The English Achilles: An Account of the Life and Campaigns of John Talbot, 1ˢᵗ Earl of Shrewsbury (1383-1453).* London: Chatto and Windus, 1981.

Thielmans, Marie-Rose. *Bourgogne et Angleterre: relations politiques et économiques entre les Pays-Bas Bourguignonnes et l'Angleterre, 1435-1467.* Brussels, 1966.

Toulet, Michel. "Le port d'armes dans la 'France Anglaise." In: *111e Congrès national des Sociétés savantes, Poitiers, 1986, Histoire médiévale.* T. I: "La France anglaise," pp. 453-60.

Tout, T.F. "The English Parliament and Public Opinion, 1376-1388." In: *The Collected Papers of T.F. Tout.* Manchester, 1934, II:173-90.

Turville-Petre, Thorlac. "The 'Nation' in English Writings of the Early Fourteenth Century." In: *England in the Fourteenth Century.* Harlaxton Medieval Studies, 3. Ed. Nicholas Rogers. Stamford, 1993, pp. 128-39.

Vale, Malcolm G.A. "England and the Burgundian Dominions: Some Cultural Influences and Comparisons." In: *L'Angleterre et les pays Bourguignons: Relations et comparaisons (XVe-XVIe siècles).* Neuchâtel: Centre européen d'études Bourguignons (XIVe-XVIe siècles), 1995, pp. 7-13.

Vale, Malcolm G.A. "Sir John Fastolf's 'Report' of 1435: A New Interpretation Reconsidered," *Nottingham Medieval Studies* 17 (1973), 78-84.

Walker, Simon. "Janico Dartasso: Chivalry, Nationality and the Man-at-Arms," *History* 84 (1999), 31-51.

Walker, Simon. *The Lancastrian Affinity, 1361-1399.* Oxford: Clarendon Press, 1990.

Walker, Simon. "Profit and Loss in the Hundred Years War: The Subcontracts of Sir John Strother, 1374," *Bulletin of the Institute of Historical Research* 58 (1985), 100-06.

Ward, Jennifer C. "Sir John de Coggeshale: An Essex Knight of the Fourteenth Century," *Essex Archaeology and History* 22 (1991), 61-66.

Williams, E. Carleton. *My Lord of Bedford, 1389-1435: Being a Life of John of Lancaster, First Duke of Bedford, Brother of Henry V and Regent of France*. London: Longmans, 1963.

Wrong, George M. *The Crusade of 1383 Known as That of the Bishop of Norwich*. London: James Parker and Co., 1892.

Wrottesley, George, ed. and trans. "Military Service Performed by Staffordshire Tenants, Temp. R. II." In: *Collections for a History of Staffordshire*, 14. London, 1893, pp. 221-64.

Medieval – Hundred Years War – England – Edward III

Andre, Elsbeth. *Ein Königshof auf Reisen: Der Kontinentaufenthalt Eduards III. von England, 1338-1340*. Cologne: Böhlau, 1996.

Arnold, Janet. "The Jupon or Coat-Armour of the Black Prince in Canterbury Cathedral," *Church Monuments* 8 (1993), 12-24.

Ayton, Andrew. "Edward III and the English Aristocracy at the Beginning of the Hundred Years War." In: *Armies, Chivalry and Warfare in Medieval Britain and France· Proceedings of the 1995 Harlaxton Symposium*. Ed. M. Strickland. Stamford, 1998, pp. 173-206.

Ayton, Andrew. "War and the English Gentry under Edward III," *History Today* 42 (Mar 1992), 34-40.

Ayton, Andrew. *Knights and Warhorses: Military Service and the English Aristocracy under Edward III*. Woodbridge: The Boydell Press, 1994.

Balfour-Melville, E.W.M. *Edward III and David II*. London: Historical Association, 1954.

Barber, Richard. *Edward, Prince of Wales and Aquitaine: A Biography of the Black Prince*. 1978; rpt. Woodbridge: The Boydell Press, 1996.

Bothwell, James. "Edward III and the 'New Nobility': Largesse and Limitation in Fourteenth-Century England," *English Historical Review* 112 (1997), 1111-40.

Bothwell, James. "The Management of Position: Alice Perrers, Edward III, and the Creation of a Landed Estates, 1362-1377," *Journal of Medieval History* 24 (1998), 31-51.

Bryant, W.N. "The Financial Dealings of Edward III with the County Communities, 1330-1360," *English Historical Review* 83 (1968), 760-71.

Fryde, E.B. "Edward III's Wool Monopoly of 1337: A Fourteenth-Century Royal Trading Venture," *History* 37 (1952), 8-24.

Fryde, E.B. "Financial Resources of Edward III in the Netherlands, 1337-40," *Revue Belge de philologie et d'histoire* 45 (1967), 1142-1216.

Fryde, Nathalie B. "Edward III's Removal of His Ministers and Judges, 1340-1," *Bulletin of the Institute of Historical Research* 48 (1975), 149-61.

Gask, George. "The Medical Staff of King Edward the Third." In: *Essays in the History of Medicine.* London, 1950, pp. 77-93.

Harari, Yuval Noah. "Inter-frontal Cooperation in the Fourteenth Century and Edward III's 1346 Campaign," *War in History* 6 (1999), 379-95.

Harvey, J.H. *The Black Prince and His Age.* London, 1976.

Hewitt, H.J. *The Black Prince's Expedition of 1355 -1357.* Manchester: Manchester University Press, 1958.

Hewitt, H.J. *The Organization of War Under Edward III, 1338-62.* Manchester: Manchester University Press, 1966.

Hunt, Edwin S. "A New Look at the Dealings of the Bardi and Peruzzi with Edward III," *Journal of Economic History* 50 (1990), 149-62.

Le Patourel, John. "Edward III and the Kingdom of France," *History* 43 (1958), 173-89; in: *The Wars of Edward III: Sources and Interpretations.* Ed. Clifford J. Rogers. Woodbridge: The Boydell Press, 1999, pp. 247-64.

Lucas, Henry Stephen. "Edward III and the Poet Chronicler John Boendale," *Speculum* 12 (1937), 367-69.

McKisack, May. "Edward III and the Historians," *History* 45 (1960), 1-15.

Morgan, D.A.L. "The Political After-Life of Edward III: The Apotheosis of a Warmonger," *English Historical Review* 112 (1997), 856-81.

Nicholas, David. "The English Trade at Bruges in the Last Years of Edward III," *Journal of Medieval History* 5 (1979), 23-61.

Oberman, H. and James A. Weisheipl. "The *Sermo epincius* Ascribed to Thomas Bradwardine (1346)," *Archives d'histoire doctrinale et littéraire du moyen âge* 33 (1958), 295-329.

O'Connor, Stephen. "Finance, Diplomacy and Politics: Royal Service by Two London Merchants in the Reign of Edward III," *Historical Research* 67 (1994), 18-39.

Ormrod, W.M. "Edward III and His Family," *Journal of British Studies* 26 (1987), 398-422.

Ormrod, W.M. "Edward III and the Recovery of Royal Authority in England, 1340-60," *History* 72 (1987), 4-19.

Ormrod, W.M. "The Personal Religion of Edward III," *Speculum* 64 (1989), 849-77.

Packe, Michael. *King Edward III*. London: Ark Paperbacks, 1983.

Perroy, Edouard. "Édouard III d'Angleterre et les seigneurs Gascons en 1368," *Annales du Midi* 61 (1948-49), 91-96.

Plaisse, André. *A travers le Cotentin: La grande chevauchée guerriere d'Édouard III en 1346*. Cherbourg: Éditions de la Presse de la Manche, 1994.

Prentout, Henri. *La prise de Caen par Édouard III, 1346*. Caen: Henri Delesques, 1904.

Prestwich, Michael. "English Armies in the Early Stages of the Hundred Years War," *Bulletin of the Institute of Historical Research* 56 (1983), 102-13.

Prestwich, Michael. *The Three Edwards: War and State in England, 1272-1377*. London, 1981.

Prince, Albert E. "The Army and Navy." In: *The English Government at Work, 1327-1336*. Ed. James F. Willard and William A. Morris. Cambridge: Mediaeval Academy of America, 1940, I:332-93.

Prince, Albert E. "The Indenture System Under Edward III." In: *Historical Essays in Honour of James Tait*. Ed. J.G. Edwards et al. Manchester, 1933, pp. 283-97.

Prince, Albert E. "A Letter of Edward, the Black Prince, Describing the Battle of Nájera in 1367," *English Historical Review* 41 (1926), 415-18.

Prince, Albert E. "The Payment of Army Wages in Edward III's Reign," *Speculum* 19 (1944), 137-60.

Prince, Albert E. "The Strength of English Armies in the Reign of Edward III," *English Historical Review* 46 (1931), 353-71.

Rogers, Clifford J. "Edward III and the Dialectics of Strategy, 1327-1360," *Transactions of the Royal Historical Society*, 6th ser., 4 (1994), 83-102; in: *The Wars of Edward III: Sources and Interpretations*. Ed. Clifford J. Rogers. Woodbridge: The Boydell Press, 1999, pp. 265-84.

Rogers, Clifford J. *"Werre Cruelle and Sharpe:" English Strategy Under Edward III, 1327-1347*. Unpublished Doctoral Dissertation. Columbus: Ohio State University, 1994.

Rogers, Clifford J., ed. *The Wars of Edward III: Sources and Interpretations*. Woodbridge: The Boydell Press, 1999.

Sherborne, James. "John of Gaunt, Edward III's Retinue and the French Campaign of 1369." In: *Kings and Nobles in the Later Middle Ages: A Tribute to Charles Ross*. Ed. R.A. Griffiths and J. Sherborne. New York, 1986, pp. 41-61.

Templeman, G. "Edward III and the Beginnings of the Hundred Years War," *Transactions of the Royal Historical Society*, 5th ser., 2 (1952), 67-88; in: *The Wars of Edward III: Sources and Interpretations*. Ed. Clifford J. Rogers. Woodbridge: The Boydell Press, 1999, pp. 231-46.

Vale, Juliet. *Edward III and Chivalry: Chivalric Society and Its Context, 1270-1350*. Woodbridge: Boydell and Brewer, 1982.

Wiswall, Frank L. "Politics, Procedure and the 'Non-Minority' of Edward III: Some Comparisons." In: *The Age of Richard II*. Ed. James L. Gillespie. New York, 1997, pp. 7-26.

Ziegler, J.E. "Edward III and Low Country Finances: 1338-1340, With Particular Emphasis on the Dominant Position of Brabant," *Revue Belge de philologie et d'histoire* 61 (1983), 802-17.

Medieval – Hundred Years War – England – John of Gaunt

Burne, Alfred H. "John of Gaunt's Grande Chevauchée," *History Today* 9 (1959), 113-21.

Goodman, Anthony. *John of Gaunt: The Exercise of Princely Power in Fourteenth-Century Europe*. London: Longman, 1992.

Goodman, Anthony. "John of Gaunt: Paradigm of the Late Fourteenth-Century Crisis," *Transactions of the Royal Historical Society*, 5th ser., 37 (1987), 133-48.

Goodman, Anthony. "John of Gaunt: Portugal's Kingmaker," *History Today* 36 (June 1986), 16-21.

Green, Richard Firth. "Jack Philpot, John of Gaunt, and a Poem of 1380," *Speculum* 66 (1991), 294-329.

Lewis, N.B. "Indentures of Retinue with John of Gaunt, Duke of Lancaster, Enrolled in Chancery, 1367-1399." In: *Camden Miscellany, XXII.* London, 1964, pp. 77-112.

Phillpotts, Christopher John. "John of Gaunt and English Policy towards France, 1389-1395," *Journal of Medieval History* 16 (1990), 363-86.

Sherborne, James. "John of Gaunt, Edward III's Retinue and the French Campaign of 1369." In: *Kings and Nobles in the Later Middle Ages: A Tribute to Charles Ross.* Ed. R.A. Griffiths and J. Sherborne. New York, 1986, pp. 41-61.

Stocker, David. "'A Very Goodly House Longging to Sutton ...': A Reconstruction of 'John of Gaunt's Palace', Lincoln," *Lincolnshire History and Archaeology* 34 (1999), 5-15.

Wathey, Andrew. "John of Gaunt, John Pycard and the Amiens Negotiations of 1392." In: *England and the Low Countries in the Late Middle*

Ages. Ed. Caroline Barron and Nigel Saul. New York: St. Martin's Press, 1995, pp. 29-42.

Medieval – Hundred Years War – England – Richard II

Aston, M. "The Impeachment of Bishop Despenser," *Bulletin of the Institute of Historical Research* 38 (1965), 127-48.

Barron, Caroline. "The Deposition of Richard II." In: *Politics and Crisis in Fourteenth-Century England.* Ed. John Taylor and Wendy Childs. London, 1990, pp. 132-49.

Bennett, Michael J. *Richard II and the Revolution of 1399.* Stroud: Sutton Publishing, 1999.

Biggs, Douglas. "A Plantagenet Revolution in Government? The Officers of Central Government and the Lancastrian Usurpation of 1399," *Medieval Prospography* 20 (1999), 191-211.

Bird, Ruth. *The Turbulent London of Richard II.* London, 1949.

Clarke, M.V. and V.H. Galbraith. "The Deposition of Richard II," *Bulletin of the John Rylands Library.* 14 (1930).

Davies, Richard G. "Richard II and the Church in the Years of 'Tyranny,'" *Journal of Medieval History* 1 (1975), 329-62.

Ferris, Sumner. "The Wilton Diptych and the Absolutism of Richard II," *Journal of the Rocky Mountain Medieval and Renaissance Association* 8 (1987), 33-66.

Gillespie, James L. "Richard II: Chivalry and Kingship." In: *The Age of Richard II.* Ed. James L. Gillespie. New York, 1997, pp. 115-38.

Gillespie, James L. "Richard II: King of Battles?" In: *The Age of Richard II.* Ed. James L. Gillespie. New York, 1997, pp. 139-64.

Gillespie, James L. "Richard II's Archers of the Crown," *Journal of British Studies* 18 (1979), 14-29.

Gillespie, James L. "Richard II's Cheshire Archers," *Transactions of the Historic Society of Lancashire and Cheshire* 125 (1975), 1-39.

Gillespie, James L. "Richard II's Knights: Chivalry and Patronage," *Journal of Medieval History* 13 (1987), 143-59.

Given-Wilson, C. "Richard II, Edward II, and the Lancastrian Inheritance," *English Historical Review* 109 (1994), 553-71.

Goodman, Anthony. *The Loyal Conspiracy: The Lords Appellant under Richard II*. London: Routledge and Kegan Paul, 1971.

Hughes, M.E.J. "Counseling the King: Perceptions of Court Politics in Poetry of the Reign of Richard II," In: *France and the British Isles in the Middle Ages and Renaissance: Essays by Members of Girton College, Cambridge, in Memory of Ruth Morgan*. Ed. G. Jondorf and D.N. Dumville. Woodbridge, 1991, pp. 199-206.

Keen, Maurice. "Richard II's Ordinances of War in 1385." In: *Rulers and Ruled in Late Medieval England: Essays Presented to Gerald Harriss*. Ed. R.E. Archer and S. Walker. London, 1995, pp. 33-48.

Leyland, John L. "Knights of the Shire in the Parliament of 1386: A Preliminary Study of Factional Affiliations," *Medieval Prosopography* 9 (1988), 89-104.

Martin, G.H. "Narrative Sources for the Reign of Richard II." In: *The Age of Richard II*. Ed. James L. Gillespie. New York, 1997, pp. 51-70.

Mathew, G. *The Court of Richard II*. London, 1968.

McNiven, Peter. "Rebellion, Sedition and the Legend of Richard II's Survival in the Reigns of Henry IV and Henry V," *Bulletin of the John Rylands Library* 76 (1994), 93-117.

Mott, Roger. "Richard II and the Crisis of July 1397." In: *Church and Chronicle in the Middle Ages: Essays Presented to John Taylor*. Ed. I. Wood and G.A. Loud. London, pp. 165-77.

Palmer, J.J.N. "The Background to Richard II's Marriage to Isabel of France (1396)," *Bulletin of the Institute of Historical Research* 44 (1971), 1-17.

Perroy, Edouard. *L'Angleterre et le grand schisme d'occident: étude sur la politique religieuse de l'Angleterre sous Richard II (1378-1399)*. Paris: Libraire J. Monnier, 1933.

Saul, Nigel. *Richard II*. New Haven: Yale University Press, 1997.

Saul, Nigel. "Richard II: Author of His Own Downfall?" *History Today* 49.9 (Sep 1999), 36-41.

Saul, Nigel. "Richard II, York, and the Evidence of the King's Itinerary." In: *The Age of Richard II*. Ed. James L. Gillespie. New York, 1997, pp. 71-92.

Sayles, G.O. "Richard II in 1381 and 1399," *English Historical Review* 103 (1988), 820-29.

Sherborne, James. "Charles VI and Richard II." In: *Froissart: Historian*. Ed. J.J.N. Palmer. Woodbridge, 1981, pp. 50-63.

Sherborne, James. "Charles VI and Richard II." In: *War, Politics and Culture in Fourteenth-Century England*. Ed. A. Tuck. London, 1994, pp. 155-70.

Sherborne, James. "Perjury and the Lancastrian Revolution of 1399." In: *War, Politics and Culture in Fourteenth-Century England*. Ed. A. Tuck. London, 1994, pp. 131-53.

Sherborne, James. "Richard II's Return to Wales, July 1399." In: *War, Politics and Culture in Fourteenth-Century England*. Ed. A. Tuck. London, 1994, pp. 119-29.

Staley, Lynn. "Gower, Richard II, Henry of Derby, and the Business of Making Culture," *Speculum* 75 (2000), 68-96.

Steel, Anthony. *Richard II*. Cambridge: Cambridge University Press, 1941.

Stouck, Mary-Ann. "Saints and Rebels: Hagiography and Opposition to the King in Late Fourteenth-Century England," *Medievalia et humanistica* n.s. 24 (1997), 75-94.

Stow, George. "Chronicles Versus Records: The Character of Richard II." In: *Documenting the Past: Essays in Medieval History Presented to George Peddy Cuttino*. Ed. J.S. Hamilton and P.J. Bradley. Woodbridge, 1989, pp. 155-76.

Stow, George. "Richard II and the Invention of the Pocket Handkerchief," *Albion* 27 (1995), 221-35.

Stow, George. "Richard II in Jean Froissart's *Chroniques*," *Journal of Medieval History* 11 (1985), 333-45.

Stow, George. "Richard II in John Gower's *Confessio Amantis*: Some Historical Perspectives," *Mediaevalia* 16 (1993), 3-32.

Stow, George. "Richard II in Thomas Walsingham's Chronicles," *Speculum* 59 (1984), 68-102.

Strohm, Paul. *England's Empty Throne: Usurpation and the Language of Legitimation, 1399-1422*. New Haven: Yale University Press, 1998.

Strohm, Paul. "The Trouble with Richard: The Reburial of Richard II and Lancastrian Symbolic Strategy," *Speculum* 71 (1996), 87-111.

Tuck, J. Anthony. "Richard II and the Hundred Years War." In: *Politics and Crisis in Fourteenth-Century England*. Ed. J. Taylor and W. Childs. London, 1990, pp. 117-31.

Walker, Simon. "Richard II's Views on Kingship." In: *Rulers and Ruled in Late Medieval England: Essays Presented to Gerald Harriss*. Ed. R.E. Archer and S. Walker. London, 1995, pp. 49-63.

Wallon, H. *Richard II, épisode de la rivalité de la France et de l'Angleterre* Paris, 1864.

Medieval – Hundred Years War – England – Henry IV [See also Medieval – England – Wars of the Roses]

Biggs, Douglas. "'A Wrong Whom Conscience and Kindred Bid Me to Right:' A Reassessment of Edmund of Langley, Duke of York, and the Usurpation of Henry IV," *Albion* 26 (1994), 253-72.

Kirby, J.L. *Henry IV of England*. London, 1970.

McNiven, Peter. "Legitimacy and Consent: Henry IV and the Lancastrian Title, 1399-1406," *Mediaeval Studies* 44 (1982), 470-88.

Pistono, Stephen P. "Henry IV and the English Privateers," *English Historical Review* 99 (1975), 322-30.

Priestley, E.J. *The Battle of Shrewsbury, 1403.* Shrewsbury: Shrewsbury and Atcham Borough Council, 1979.

Rogers, Alan. "Henry IV, the Commons and Taxation," *Mediaeval Studies* 31 (1969), 44-70.

Rowse, A.L. "The Reign of Henry IV," *History Today* 16 (1966), 601-09, 704-11.

Strohm, Paul. *England's Empty Throne: Usurpation and the Language of Legitimation, 1399-1422.* New Haven: Yale University Press, 1998.

Tuck, J. Anthony. "Henry IV and Europe: A Dynasty's Search for Recognition." In: *The McFarlane Legacy: Studies in Late Medieval Politics and Society.* Ed. R.H. Britnell and A.J. Pollard. New York, 1995, pp. 107-25.

Wright, Edmund. "Henry IV, the Commons and the Recovery of Royal Finance in 1407." In: *Rulers and Ruled in Late Medieval England.* Ed. R.E. Archer and S. Walker. London, 1995.

Wylie, James Hamilton. *The History of England under Henry IV.* 4 vols. 1898; rpt. New York, 1968.

Medieval – Hundred Years War – England – Henry V

Allmand, Christopher T. *Henry V.* Berkeley and Los Angeles: University of California Press, 1992.

Allmand, Christopher T. "Henry V the Soldier, and the War in France." In: *Henry V: The Practice of Kingship.* Ed. G.L. Harriss. Oxford, 1985; rpt. Stroud, 1993, pp. 117-36.

Bradley, Patricia J. "Henry V's Scottish Policy: A Study in Realpolitik." In: *Documenting the Past: Essays in Medieval History Presented to George Peddy Cuttino.* Ed. J.S. Hamilton and P.J. Bradley. Woodbridge, 1989, pp. 177-95.

Catto, Jeremy. "The King's Servants." In: *Henry V: The Practice of Kingship.* Ed. G.L. Harriss. Oxford, 1985; rpt. Stroud, 1993, pp. 75-96.

Catto, Jeremy. "Religious Change under Henry V." In: *Henry V: The Practice of Kingship*. Ed. G.L. Harriss. Oxford, 1985; rpt. Stroud, 1993, pp. 97-116.

Charma, A. "Partie des dons faits par Henri V, roi d'Angleterre, lorsqu'il se fut rendu maître de la Normandie." *Mémoires de la société des antiquaires de Normandie* 23 (1858), 1-23.

Davies, Clifford S.L. "Henry VIII and Henry V: The Wars in France." In: *The End of the Middle Ages? England in the Fifteenth and Sixteenth Centuries*. Ed. J.L. Watts. Stroud, 1998, pp. 235-62.

Gask, George. "The Medical Services of Henry the Fifth's Campaign of the Somme in 1415." In: *Essays in the History of Medicine*. London, 1950, pp. 94-102.

Goodman, A.E. "Responses to Requests in Yorkshire for Military Service under Henry V," *Northern History* 17 (1981), 240-52.

Haines, Roy Martin. "'Our Master Mariner, Our Sovereign Lord:' A Contemporary Preacher's View of King Henry V," *Mediaeval Studies* 38 (1976), 85-96.

Harriss, Gerald L. "Conclusion." In: *Henry V: The Practice of Kingship*. Ed. G.L. Harriss. Oxford, 1985; rpt. Stroud, 1993, pp. 201-10.

Harriss, Gerald L. "Financial Policy." In: *Henry V: The Practice of Kingship*. Ed. G.L. Harriss. Oxford, 1985; rpt. Stroud, 1993, pp. 159-80.

Harriss, Gerald L. "Introduction: the Exemplar of Kingship." In: *Henry V: The Practice of Kingship*. Ed. G.L. Harriss. Oxford, 1985; rpt. Stroud, 1993, pp. 1-30.

Harriss, Gerald L. "The King and his Magnates." In: *Henry V: The Practice of Kingship*. Ed. G.L. Harriss. Oxford, 1985; rpt. Stroud, 1993, pp. 31-52.

Harriss, Gerald L. "The Management of Parliament." In: *Henry V: The Practice of Kingship*. Ed. G.L. Harriss. Oxford, 1985; rpt. Stroud, 1993, pp. 137-58.

Jacob, E.F. *Henry V and the Invasion of France*. London: Hodder and Stoughton Limited, 1947.

Keen, Maurice. "Diplomacy." In: *Henry V: The Practice of Kingship*. Ed. G.L. Harriss. Oxford, 1985; rpt. Stroud, 1993, pp. 181-200.

McFarlane, K.B. "Henry V, Bishop Beaufort and the Red Hat, 1417-21." In: *England in the Fifteenth Century: Collected Essays*. London, 1981, pp. 79-114.

Meron, T. *Henry's Wars and Shakespeare's Laws: Perspectives on the Law of War in the Later Middle Ages*. Oxford, 1993.

Newhall, Richard Ager. "The War Finances of Henry V and the Duke of Bedford," *English Historical Review* 36 (1921), 172-98.

Postel, Raoul. *Siège et capitulation de Bayeux en 1417: Notes pour servir à l'histoire du Bessin pendant la domination anglaise sous l'occupation du roi Henri V*. Caen: Le Gost-Clérisse, Éditeur, 1873.

Powell, Edward. "The Restoration of Law and Order." In: *Henry V: The Practice of Kingship*. Ed. G.L. Harriss. Oxford, 1985; rpt. Stroud, 1993, pp. 53-74.

Puiseux, Léon. *Caen en 1421: appendice au siège de Caen par les anglais en 1417*. Caen: Le Gost-Clérisse, Éditeur, 1860.

Puiseux, Léon. *Siège et prise de Caen par les anglais en 1417: Épisode de la guerre de cent ans*. Caen: Le Gost-Clérisse, Éditeur, 1868.

Puiseux, Léon. *Siège et prise de Rouen par les anglais (1418-1419)*. Caen: Le Gost-Clérisse, Éditeur, 1867.

Roskell, J.S. and F. Taylor. "The Authorship and Purpose of the *Gesta Henrici Quinti*: II," *Bulletin of the John Rylands Library* 54 (1971), 223-40.

Saul, Nigel. "Henry V and the Dual Monarchy," *History Today* 36 (May 1986), 39-44.

Strohm, Paul. *England's Empty Throne: Usurpation and the Language of Legitimation, 1399-1422*. New Haven: Yale University Press, 1998.

Tolmie, Sarah. "*Quia Hic Homo Multa Signa Facit*: Henry V's Royal Entry into London, November 23, 1415." In: *The Propagation of Power in the Medieval West: Selected Proceedings of the International Conference,*

Groningen, 20-23 November 1996. Ed. M. Gosman, A. Vanderjagt, and J. Veenstra. Groningen, 1997, pp. 363-79.

Wylie, James Hamilton. *The Reign of Henry the Fifth*. 3 vols. Cambridge, 1929.

Medieval – Hundred Years War – England – Henry VI [See also Medieval – England – Wars of the Roses]

Beard, C.R. "The Tomb and Achievements of King Henry VI at Windsor." In: *Fragmenta armamentaria*. II: *Miscellanea*, II pt. I. Ed. F.H. Cripps-Day. Frome, 1936.

Cron, B.M. "The Duke of Suffolk, the Angevin Marriage, and the Ceding of Maine, 1445," *Journal of Medieval History* 20 (1994), 77-99.

Griffiths, Ralph A. *The Reign of King Henry VI: The Exercise of Royal Authority, 1422-1461*. Berkeley and Los Angeles: University of California Press, 1981.

McFarlane, K.B. "At the Deathbed of Cardinal Beaufort." In: *England in the Fifteenth Century: Collected Essays*. London, 1981, pp. 115-38.

McKenna, J.W. "Henry VI of England and the Dual Monarchy: Aspects of Royal Political Propaganda, 1422-1432," *Journal of the Warburg and Courtauld Institutes* 28 (1965), 145-62.

Richter, Janice Gordon. "Education and Association: the Bureaucrat in the Reign of Henry VI," *Journal of Medieval History* 12 (1986), 81-96.

Rowe, B.J.H. "King Henry VI's Claim to France: In Picture and Poem," *The Library* 4th ser. 13 (1932), 77-88.

Styles, Dorothy and Christopher T. Allmand. "The Coronations of Henry VI," *History Today* 32 (May 1982), 28-33.

Medieval – Hundred Years War – England – Calais

Baker, Robert L. "The Government of Calais." In: *Order and Innovation in the Middle Ages: Essays in Honor of Joseph R. Strayer*. Ed. W.C. Jordan et al. Princeton, 1976, pp. 207-14, 481-82.

Burley, S.J. "The Victualling of Calais, 1347-65," *Bulletin of the Institute of Historical Research* 31 (1958), 49-57.

Daumet, Georges. *Calais sous la domination Anglaise*. Arras: Répressé-Crépel et Fils, 1902.

Doig, James A. "A New Source for the Siege of Calais in1436," *English Historical Review* 110 (1995), 404-16.

Fons-Melicocq, A. de la., ed. "Documents inédits sur le siège de Calais de 1436," *La Picardie* 4 (1858), 557-62.

Grummitt, David. "The Defence of Calais and the Development of Gunpowder Weaponry in England in the Late Fifteenth Century," *War in History* 7 (2000), 253-72.

Grummitt, David. "The Financial Administration of Calais during the Reign of Henry IV, 1399-1413," *English Historical Review* 113 (1998), 277-99.

Harriss, Gerald L. "The Struggle for Calais: An Aspect of the Rivalry between Lancaster and York," *English Historical Review* 75 (1960), 30-53.

Kirby, J.L. "Calais sous les anglais, 1399-1413," *Revue du nord* 37 (1955), 19-30.

Kirby, J.L. "The Council of 1407 and the Problem of Calais." In: *English Society and Government in the Fifteenth Century*. Ed. C.M.D. Crowder. Edinburgh, 1967, pp. 71-86.

Kirby, J.L. "The Financing of Calais under Henry V," *Bulletin of Historical Research* 23 (1950), 165-77.

Klinefelter, Ralph A., ed. "'The Siege of Calais': A New Text," *Publications of the Modern Language Association* 67 (1952), 888-95.

Lennel, F. *Histoire de Calais*. Vol 2: *Calais sous la domination Anglaise*. Calais, 1910.

Le Patourel, John. "L'occupation anglaise de Calais au XIV siècle," *Revue du nord* 33 (1951), 228-41.

Rainey, John Riley, Jr. *The Defense of Calais, 1436-1477*. Unpublished Dissertation. Rutgers University, 1987.

Thielmans, Marie-Rose, ed. "Une lettre missive inédité de Philippe le Bon concernant le siège de Calais," *Bulletin de la commission royale d'histoire de Belgique* 115 (1950), 285-96.

Medieval – Hundred Years War – France

Allmand, Christopher T. "The Aftermath of War in Fifteenth-Century France," *History* n.s. 61 (1976), 344-57.

Allmand, Christopher T. "Changing Views of the Soldier in Late Medieval France." In: *Guerre et société en France, en Angleterre et en Bourgogne XIVe-XVe siècle*. Ed. P. Contamine, C. Giry-Deloison, and Maurice Keen. Lille, 1991, pp. 171-88.

Allmand, Christopher T. "Entre honneur et bien commun: le témoignage du *Jouvencel* au XV siècle," *Revue historique* 301 (1999), 463-81.

André-Michel, Robert. "Les défenseurs des chateaux et des villes fortes dans le Comtat-Venaissin," *Bibliothèque de l'école de chartes* 75 (1915), 315-30.

Angers, Denise. "Le redressement difficile d'une capitale régionale après la guerre de cent ans: Caen, 1450-1550." In: *Commerce, Finances et Société (XIe-XVIe siècles): Receuil de travaux d'Histoire médiévale offert à M. le Professeur Henri Dubois*. Ed. P. Contamine, T. Dutour, and Bertrand Schnerb. Paris, 1993, pp. 185-97.

Arabeyre, Patrick. "La France et son gouvernement au milieu du XVe siècle d'aprés Bernard de Rosier," *Bibliothèque de l'école des chartes* 150 (1992), 245-85.

Autrand, Françoise. *Pouvoir et société en France, XIVe-XVe siècle*. Paris, 1974.

Avout, J. d'. *La querelle des Armagnacs et des Bourguignons*. Paris, 1943.

Balon, J. "L'organisation militaire des Namurois au XIVe siècle," *Annales de la société archéologique de Namur* 40 (1932), 1-86.

Barnel, Christine. "Symptômes de violence en Provence maritime à la fin du Moyen Âge." In: *La guerre, la violence et les gens au Moyen Âge. I: Guerre et violence*. Ed. P. Contamine and O. Guyotjeannin. 119e congrès national des sociétés historiques et scientifiques, Amiens, octobre 1994, Section d'histoire médiévale et philologie. Paris, 1996, pp. 137-48.

Bataille, Henri. "Vaucouleurs ou l'énigma d'un siège," *Dossiers de archéologie* 34 (May 1979), 56-63.

Battifol, Louis. *Jean Jouvenal, prévôt des marchands de la ville de Paris (1360-1431)*. Paris, 1894.

Beaune, Colette. *The Birth of an Ideology: Myths and Symbols of Nation in Late-Medieval France*. Trans. Susan Ross Huston. Ed. Fredric L. Cheyette. Berkeley and Los Angeles: University of California Press, 1991.

Beaune, Colette. "Histoire et politique: La recherche du texte de la loi salique de 1350 à 1450." In: *La reconstruction après la guerre de cent ans*. Actes du 104e congrès national des sociétés savantes, Bordeaux, 1979. Paris: Bibliothèque Nationale, 1981, I:25-35.

Belleval, René de. *Rôle des nobles et fieffés du baillage d'Amiens convoqués pour la guerre le 25 août 1337*. Amiens, 1862.

Benoit-Guyod, Henry. "La première armée française: Le ban et arrière-ban des seigneuries," *Revue internationale d'histoire militaire* 25 (1965), 559-61.

Berland, J.-M. "Les statuts de réforme du prieuré de la Réole (vers 1472) et la restauration des bâtiments conventuels." In: *La reconstruction après la guerre de cent ans*. Actes du 104e congrès national des sociétés savantes, Bordeaux, 1979. Paris: Bibliothèque Nationale, 1981, I:143-52.

Bertin, Pierre. "Le siège du chateau de Vellexon dans l'hiver 1409-1410," *Revue historique des armées* 27 (1971), 7-18.

Bessen, David M. "The Jacquerie: Class War or Co-opted Rebellion?" *Journal of Medieval History* 11 (1985), 43-59.

Binet, Sylvie. *Jeanne Hachette: l'héroine de Beauvais*. Paris: Tallandier, 1995.

Bonnault, d'Houët, Baron de. *Les francs archers de Compiègne, 1448-1524*. Compiègne: Henry Lefebvre, 1897.

Bordonove, Georges. *Jean le Bon et son temps*. Paris, 1980.

Bossuat, André. "L'idée de nation et la jurisprudence du Parlement de Paris au XVe siècle," *Revue historique* 204 (1950), 54-61.

Bossuat, André. "The Maxim 'The King is Emperor in his Kingdom': Its Use in the Fifteenth Century before the Parlement of Paris." In: *The Recovery of France in the Fifteenth Century*. Ed. P.S. Lewis. Trans. G.F. Martin. New York, 1971, pp. 185-95.

Bossuat, André. "Le parlement de Paris pendant l'occupation anglaise," *Revue historique* 229 (1963), 19-40.

Bossuat, André. "The Re-establishment of Peace in Society during the Reign of Charles VII." In: *The Recovery of France in the Fifteenth Century*. Ed. P.S. Lewis. Trans. G.F. Martin. London, 1971, pp. 60-81, 362-66.

Bourrilly, V.-L. "Duguesclin et le duc d'Anjou en Provence (1368)," *Revue historique* 51 (1926), 161-80.

Boutruche, Robert. *La crise d'une société: seigneurs et paysans du Bordelais pendant la guerre de cent ans*. Paris, 1947.

Boutruche, Robert. "The Devastation of Rural Areas during the Hundred Years War and the Agricultural Recovery of France." In: *The Recovery of France in the Fifteenth Century*. Ed. P.S. Lewis. Trans. G.F. Martin. New York, 1971, pp. 23-59.

Brouwers, D.D. "Indemnités pour dommages de guerre au pays de Namurois en 1432," *Annales de ls société archéologique de Namur* 40 (1932-33), 87-103.

Bruel, François-L. "Inventaire de meubles et de titres trouvés au chateau de Josselin à la mort du connétable de Clisson (1407)," *Bibliothèque de l'école de chartes* 66 (1905), 193-245.

Carolus-Barré, Louis. "Les familiers de Bertrand Du Guesclin d'après 'deux rôles de suppliques' par lui présentés à Urbain V (1366) et à Clément VII (1378)," *Les cahiers vernonnais* 4 (1964), 41-46.

Carolus-Barré, Louis. "Le siège et la délivrance de la ville, 20 mai-25 octobre 1430," *Bulletin de la société historique de Compiègne* 28 (1982), 15-62.

Carpentier, Élisabeth and Jean Glénisson. "La démographie Française au XIVe siècle," *Annales E.S.C.* (1962), 109-29.

Cazelles, Raymond. "Du Guesclin avant Cocherel," *Les cahiers vernonnais* 4 (1964), 33-40.

Cazelles, Raymond. "Les mouvements revolutionnaires du milieu du XIVe siècle et le cycle de l'action politique," *Revue historique* 464 (1962), 279-312.

Cazelles, Raymond. "Le parti navarrais jusqu'à la mort d'Etienne Marcel," *Bulletin philologique et historique* (1960), 839-69.

Cazelles, Raymond. *Société politique, noblesse, et couronne sous Jean le Bon et Charles V.* Geneva, 1982.

Célier, Léonce. "La meurtre du duc Louis d'Orléans dans la chronique du Héraut Berry." In: *Mélanges d'histoire du moyen âge dédiés à la mémoire de Louis Halphen.* Paris: Presses universitaires de France, 1951, pp. 119-23.

Champion, Pierre. *Guillaume de Flavy: Captaine de Compiègne: Contribution à l'histoire de Jeanne d'Arc et à l'étude de la vie militaire et privée au XVe siècle.* Paris: Honoré Champion, 1906.

Champollion-Figeac, Aime. *Louis et Charles, duc d'Orleans.* Paris, 1844.

Chartraire, E. "Jean de Salazar: Écuyer du roi Louis XI, père de l'archevêque de Sens, Tristan de Salazar," *Bulletin de la société archéologique de Sens* 32 (1918), 237-93.

Chavanon, Jules. *Renaud VI de Pons, vicomte de Turenne et de Carlat*. La Rochelle, 1903.

Chevalier, Bernard. *Les bonnes villes de France du XIVe au XVIe siècles*. Paris: Aubier and Montaigne, 1982.

Chevalier, Bernard. "Les écossais dans les armées de Charles VII jusqu'a la bataille de Verneuil." In: *Jeanne d'Arc: Une époque, un rayonnement*. Paris, 1982, pp. 85-9⊆.

Chevalier, Bernard. "L'organisation militaire à Tours au XVe siècle," *Bulletin philologique et historique jusqu'à 1610 du comité des travaux historiques et scientifiques* (1960), pp. 445-59.

Chevalier, Bernard. "Pouvoir royal et pouvoir urbain à Tours pendant la guerre de Cent ans," *Annales de Bretagne* 81 (1974), 365-92, 681-707.

Clin-Meyer, Marie-Véronique. *Isabeau de Bavière, La Reine calomniée*. Paris: Perrin, 1999.

Clin-Meyer, Marie-Véronique, ed. "Mandement de Charles d'Orléans à son trésorier (1414)," *Bulletin d'Association des Amis du Centre Jeanne d'Arc* 10 (1986), 31-32.

Cohen, Esther. "Violence Control in Late Medieval France: The Social Transformation of the Asseurement," *Tijdschrift voor rechtgeschiedenis* 51 (1983), 111-22.

Collin, Hubert. "Les ressources alimentaires en Lorraine pendant la première partie du XIVe siècle, *Bulletin philologique et historique jusqu'à 1610 du comité des travaux historiques et scientifiques* (1971), 37-75.

Contamine, Philippe. "L'armement des populations urbaines à la fin du Moyen Âge: l'exemple de Troyes (1474)." In: *La guerre, la violence et les gens au Moyen Âge. II: Guerre et gens*. Ed. P. Contamine and O. Guyotjeannin. 119e congrès national des sociétés historiques et scientifiques, Amiens, octobre 1994, Section d'histoire médiévale et philologie. Paris, 1996, pp. 59-74.

Contamine, Philippe. "L'armement des populations urbaines dans la France de la fin du moyen âge: L'exemple des habitants de Troyes (1474)," *Fasciculi archaeologiae historicae* 5 (1992), 9-17.

Contamine, Philippe. "Batailles, bannières, compagnies: aspects de l'organisation militaire française pendant la première partie de guerre de cent
ans," *Les cahiers vernonnais* 4 (1964), 19-32.

Contamine, Philippe. "Les derniers mois de la vie de Charles d'Orléans,
d'après un document inédit," *Bulletin d'Association des Amis du Centre
Jeanne d'Arc* 10 (1986), 19-30; in: *De Jeanne d'Arc aux guerres d'Italie:
Figures, images et problèmes du XVe siècle*. Orléans: Paradigme, 1994, pp.
193-204.

Contamine, Philippe. "L'écrit et l'oral en France à la fin du moyen âge:
Note sur l'alphabétisme de l'encadrement militaire." In: *Histoire comparée de l'administration (I've-XVIIIe siècles: Actes du XIVe colloque historique franco-allemand, Tours 27 mars-1er avril 1977*. Ed. W. Paravinci
and K.F. Werner. Munich, 1980, pp. 102-13.

Contamine, Philippe. *De Jeanne d'Arc aux guerres d'Italie*. Orléans:
Paradigme, 1994.

Contamine, Philippe. "De la puissance aux privilèges: doléances de la
noblesse française envers la monarchie aux XIVe et XVe siècles." In: *La
noblesse au moyen âge, XIe-XVe siècles. Essais à la memoire de Robert
Boutruche*. Ed. P. Contamine. Paris, 1976, pp. 235-57.

Contamine, Philippe. "The French Nobility and the War." In: *The Hundred
Years War*. Ed. Kenneth Fowler. London: Macmillan, 1971, pp. 135-62.

Contamine, Philippe. *Guerre, état et société à la fin du moyen âge: Études
sur les armées des rois de France, 1337-1494*. Paris: Mouton, 1972.

Contamine, Philippe. "La musique militaire dans le fonctionnement des
armées: l'exemple français (v. 1300-v. 1550)." In: *XXII. Kongreß der
Internationalen Kommission für Militärgeschichte Acta 22: Von Crécy bis
Mohács Kriegswesen im späten Mittelalter (1346-1526)*. Vienna, 1997,
pp. 93-106.

Contamine, Philippe. "Les pairs de France au sacre des rois (XVe siècle).
Nature et portée d'un programme iconographique." In: *De Jeanne d'Arc
aux guerres d'Italie: Figures, images et problèmes du XVe siècle*. Orléans:
Paradigme, 1994, pp. 111-38.

Contamine, Philippe. "La piété quotidienne dans la haute noblesse à la fin du Moyen Age. L'exemple de Charles d'Orléans (1453-1465)." In: *De Jeanne d'Arc aux guerres d'Italie: Figures, images et problèmes du XVe siècle*. Orléans: Paradigme, 1994, pp. 205-12.

Contamine, Philippe "Une longue vie de chevalier. Jean d'Estouteville, sire de Torcy et de Blainville, grand-maître des arbalétriers de France (vers 1410-1494)." In: *De Jeanne d'Arc aux guerres d'Italie: Figures, images et problèmes du XVe siècle*. Orléans: Paradigme, 1994, pp. 213-44.

Cosneau, E. *Le connétable de Richemont (Artur de Bretagne), 1393-1458*. Paris, 1886.

Courteault, H. *Gaston IV, comte de Foix, vicomte souverain de Béarn, prince de Navarre, 1423-1472*. Toulouse, 1895.

Coville, Alfred. *Les cabochiens et l'ordonnance de 1413*. Paris, 1888.

Coville, Alfred. *Histoire de France*. Vol. 4, pt. 1: *Les premiers Valois et la guerre de cent ans*. Ed. E. Lavisse. Paris, 1900-11.

Coville, Alfred. *Jean Petit: la question du tyrannicide au commencement du XVe siècle*. Paris, 1932.

Currin, John M. "'The King's Army into the Partes of Bretaigne': Henry VII and the Breton Wars, 1489-1491," *War in History* 7 (2000), 379-412.

Delaville le Roulx, J. "La domination bourguignonne à Tours et le siège de cette ville (1417-1418)," *Le cabinet historique* 23 (1877), 161-231.

Déniau, Jean. *La commune de Lyon et la guerre Bourguignonne, 1417-1435*. Lyon, Pierre Masson, 1934.

Denifle, Henri. *La guerre de cent ans et la désolation des églises, monastères et hôpitaux en France vers le milieu du XVe siècle*. Paris, 1897.

Desobry, Jean. "Pour des queues d'hermine: L'abbaye du Mont-Saint-Quentin et la chevauchée de Buckingham (1380)." In: *La guerre, la violence et les gens au Moyen Âge. II: Guerre et gens*. Ed. P. Contamine and O. Guyotjeannin. 119e congrès national des sociétés historiques et scientifiques, Amiens, octobre 1994, Section d'histoire médiévale et philologie. Paris, 1996, pp. 119-26.

Ditcham, Brian G.H. "'Mutton Guzzlers and Wine Bags': Foreign Soldiers and Native Reactions in Fifteenth-Century France." In: *Power, Culture, and Religion in France c.1350-c.1550*. Ed. C. Allmand. Woodbridge, 1989, pp. 1-13.

Dubled, H. "L'artillerie royale Française à l'époque de Charles VII et au début du règne de Louis XI (1437-1469): Les frères Bureau," *Memorial de l'artillerie Française* 50 (1976), 555-637.

Duby, Georges. "The Great Estates in France at the End of the Middle Ages." In: *The Recovery of France in the Fifteenth Century*. Ed. P.S. Lewis. Trans. G.F. Martin. New York, 1971, pp. 312-23.

Dumay, G. "Etat militaire et féodal des baillages d'Autun, Montcenis, Bourbon-Lancy et Semur-en-Brionnais en 1474," *Mémoires de la société éduenne* (1882).

En France après Jeanne d'Arc. Paris: Archives Nationales, 1980.

Etcheverry, Jean-Paul. *Arthur de Richemont le justicier, précurseur, compagnon et successeur de Jeanne d'Arc ou l'honneur d'être Français*. Paris: Editions France-Empire, 1983.

Favreau, Robert. *La ville de Poitiers à la fin du moyen âge*. Paris, 1978.

Fawtier, R. "La crise d'une société durant la guerre de cent ans: A propos d'une livre recent," *Revue historique* 203 (1950), 53-58.

Finó, J.-F. "Les armées française lors de la guerre de cent ans," *Gladius* 13 (1977), 5-23.

Fons-Melicocq, A. de la., ed. "Documents inédits. Péronne durant les guerres de l'invasion anglaise," *La Picardie* 3 (1857), 302-08, 337-47.

Fons-Melicocq, A. de la., ed. "Documents inédits pour servir à l'histoire de la guerre du bien public," *Revue d'histoire et d'archéologie* 4 (1864), 327-33.

Fons-Melicocq, A. de la., ed. "Documents inédits pour servir à l'histoire des guerres le nord de la France et en Belgique (1423-1428)," *Revue d'histoire et d'archéologie* 4 (1864), 107-11.

Fons-Melicocq, A. de la., ed. "Documents inédits pour servir à l'histoire du nord de la France et de la Belgique sous Marie de Bourgogne et

Maximilien d'Autriche (1477-1482)," *Revue d'histoire et d'archéologie* 4 (1864), 410-25.

Fons-Melicocq, A. de la., ed. "Documents inédits pouvant servir a l'histoire de plusieurs villes de Picardie durant les guerres du XVe siècle," *La Picardie* 3 (1857), 409-25.

Fons-Melicocq, A. de la., ed. "Documents inédits. Siège de St.-Riquier–Bataille de Mons-en-Vimeu," *La Picardie* 3 (1857), 145-55.

Fons-Melicocq, A. de la., ed. "Documents inédits sur le siège de Compiègne de 1430," *La Picardie* 3 (1857), 21-29.

Fons-Melicocq, A. de la., ed. "Relation du siège de Ham de 1411, par un Chroniqueuer (anonyme) Bourguignon (XVe siècle)," *La Picardie* 3 (1857), 241-48.

Fournier, Gabriel. "La défense des populations rurales pendant la guerre de cent ans en Basse-Auvergne." In: *Actes du 90ème Congrès national des sociétés savantes: Section d'archéologie*. Paris, 1966, pp. 157-99.

Fowler, Kenneth. "Bertrand du Guesclin–Careerist in Arms?" *History Today* 39 (June 1989), 37-43.

Fowler, Kenneth. "Deux entrepreneurs militaires au XIVe siècle: Bertrand du Guesclin et Sir Hugh Calveley." In: *Le combattant au moyen âge*. 2nd ed. Histoire ancienne et médiévale, 36. Paris: Publications de la Sorbonne, 1995, pp. 243-56.

Garnier, Robert. *Dunois: Le Bâtard d'Orléans (1403-1468)*. Paris: Éditions Fernand Lanore, 1999.

Gibbons, Rachel. "Les conciliatrices au bas Moyen Âge: Isabeau de Bavière et la guerre civile (1401-1415)." In: *La guerre, la violence et les gens au Moyen Âge*. II: *Guerre et gens*. Ed. P. Contamine and O. Guyotjeannin. 119e congrès national des sociétés historiques et scientifiques, Amiens, octobre 1994, Section d'histoire médiévale et philologie. Paris, 1996, pp. 23-33.

Gibbons, Rachel. "Isabeau of Bavaria, Queen of France (1385-1422): The Creation of an Historical Villainess," *Transactions of the Royal Historical Society*, 6th ser., 6 (1996), 51-73.

Gibbons, Rachel. "The Queen as 'Social Mannequin': Consumerism and Expenditure at the Court of Isabeau of Bavaria, 1393-1422," *Journal of Medieval History* 26 (2000), 371-95.

Gicquel, Y. *Olivier de Clisson (1336-1407): Connétable de France ou chef de parti breton?* Paris, 1981.

Girardot, Alain. "La guerre au XIVe siècle: La dévastation, ses modes et ses degrés," *Bulletin de la sociétés d'histoire et d'archéologie de la Meuse* 30-31 (1994-95), 1-32.

Given-Wilson, C. "The Ransom of Olivier du Guesclin," *Bulletin of the Institute of Historical Research* 54 (1981), 17-28.

Goldmann, Catherine. "Papiers et titres de famille dans la guerre: l'exemple des Garencières-Le-Baveux." In: *La guerre, la violence et les gens au Moyen Âge*. II: *Guerre et gens*. Ed. P. Contamine and O. Guyotjeannin. 119e congrès national des sociétés historiques et scientifiques, Amiens, octobre 1994, Section d'histoire médiévale et philologie. Paris, 1996, pp. 75-87.

Grava, Yves. "La guerre au XIVe siècle: Un exemple provençal: Martigues." In: *La guerre et la paix: Frontières et violences au moyen âge*. Actes du 101e congrès national des sociétés savantes, Lille, 1976. Paris: Bibliothèque Nationale, 1978, pp. 179-92.

Grévy-Pons, Nicole. "Propagande et sentiment national pendant le règne de Charles VI: l'exemple de Jean de Montreuil," *Francia* 8 (1979), 127-45.

Grosjean, Georges. *Le sentiment national dans la guerre de cent ans*. Paris: Éditions Bossard, 1928.

Guenée, Bernard. "The History of the State in France at the End of the Middle Ages, as Seen by French Historians in the Last Hundred Years." In: *The Recovery of France in the Fifteenth Century*. Ed. P.S. Lewis. Trans. G.F. Martin. New York, 1971, pp. 324-52.

Guenée, Bernard. *Un meurtre, une société: L'assassinat du duc d'Orléans, 23 Novembre 1407*. Paris: Gallimard, 1992.

Gut, Christian. "Les pays de l'Oise sous la domination anglaise (1420-1435) d'après les registres de la Chancellerie de France." In: *La guerre, la violence et les gens au Moyen Âge*. II: *Guerre et gens*. Ed. P. Contamine and O. Guyotjeannir. 119e congrès national des sociétés historiques et scientifiques, Amiens, octobre 1994, Section d'histoire médiévale et philologie. Paris, 1996, pp. 141-314.

Harmand, J. "Un document de 1435, concernant Houdan et la fin de l'occupation anglaise dans l'ouest de l'Ile-de-France," *Bulletin de la société nationale des antiquaries de France* (1975), 205-47.

Hébert, Michel. "L'armée Provençale en 1374," *Annales du midi* 91 (1979), 5-27.

Hébert, Michel. "Une population en armes: Manosque au XIVe siècle." In: *Le combattant au moyen âge*. 2nd ed. Histoire ancienne et médiévale, 36. Paris: Publications de la Sorbonne, 1995, pp. 215-24.

Henneman, John Bell. "The Military Class and the French Monarchy in the Late Middle Ages, *American Historical Review* 83 (1978), 946-65.

Henneman, John Bell. *Olivier de Clisson and Political Society under Charles V and Charles VI*. Philadelphia: University of Pennsylvania Press, 1996.

Henneman, John Bell. "Reassessing the Career of Olivier de Clisson, Constable of France." In: *Law, Custom, and the Social Fabric in Medieval Europe: Essays in Honor of Bryce Lyon*. Ed. B.S. Bachrach and D. Nicholas. Kalamazoo, 1990, pp. 211-33.

Henneman, John Bell. *Royal Taxation in Fourteenth-Century France: The Captivity and Ransom of John II, 1356-1370*. Philadelphia: The American Philosophical Society, 1976.

Henneman, John Bell. *Royal Taxation in Fourteenth Century France: The Development of War Financing, 1322-1356*. Princeton: Princeton University Press, 1971.

Henneman, John Bell. "Who Were the Marmousets?" *Medieval Prosopography* 5 (1984), 19-63.

Homet, Raquel. "Une conception politique noblaire au temps de la guerre de cent ans," *Journal of Medieval History* 15 (1989), 309-27.

Honoré-Duvergé, Suzanne. "L'origine du surnom de Charles le Mauvais." In: *Mélanges d'histoire du moyen âge dédiés à la mémoire de Louis Halphen*. Paris: Presses universitaires de France, 1951, pp. 345-50.

Honoré-Duvergé, Suzanne. "Participation navarraise à la bataille de Cocherel," *Les cahiers vernonnais* 4 (1964), 99-106.

Huguet, A. "Aspects de la guerre de cent ans en Picardie maritime," *Mémoires de la société des antiquaires de Picardie* 48 (1941); 50 (1944).

"Inventaire de la bastille de l'an 1428," *Revue archeologique* 12 (1855), 321-49.

Jacob, E.F. "The Collapse of France, 1419-20," *Bulletin of the John Rylands Library* 26 (1941-42), 307-26.

Jacob, Yves. *Betrand du Guesclin, connétable de France*. Paris: Tallandier, 1999.

Jäger, G. *Aspekte der Krieges und der Chevalerie im XIVe Jahrhundert in Frankreich: Untersuchungen zu Jean Froissarts Chroniques*. Bern, 1981.

Jamison, D.F. *The Life and Times of Bertrand du Guesclin: A History of the Fourteenth Century*. 2 vols. Charleston, 1864.

Jarousseau, Gérard. "Le guet, l'arrière-guet et la garde en Poitou pendant la guerre de cent ans," *Bulletin de la société des antiquaires de l'ouest* 8 (1965), 159-202.

Jarry, Eugène. "Le compte du siège, la défense et l'effectif de l'armée anglaise," *Mémoires de la société archéologique et historique de Orléanais* 23 (1892), 482-97.

Jarry, Eugène. *La vie politique de Louis de France, duc d'Orleans, 1372-1407*. Paris, 1899.

Jarry, Eugène. "La 'voie de fait' et l'alliance Franco-Milanaise (1386-1395)," *Bibliothèque de l'école de chartes* 53 (1892).

Jarry, Louis, ed. "Deux chansons normandes sur le siège d'Orleans et la mort de Salisbury," *Bulletin de la société archéologique et historique de l'Orleannais* 10 (1893), 359-70.

Jassemin, Henri. *La chambre des comptes de Paris au XVe siècle*. Paris, 1933.

Jones, Michael. "'Bons Bretons et Bon Francoys": The Language and Meaning of Treason in Later Medieval France," *Transactions of the Royal Historical Society* 5th ser. 32 (1982), 91-112.

Jones, Michael. "The Diplomatic Evidence for Franco-Breton Relations, c. 1370-1372," *English Historical Review* 93 (1978), 300-19.

Jones, Michael. "War and Fourteenth-Century France." In: *Arms, Armies and Fortifications in the Hundred Years War*. Ed. A. Curry and M. Hughes. Woodbridge, 1994, pp. 103-20; in: *The Wars of Edward III: Sources and Interpretations*. Ed. Clifford J. Rogers. Woodbridge: The Boydell Press, 1999, pp. 343-64.

"Journal Parisien des années 1412 et 1413," ed. A. Tuetey. *Mémoires de la société de l'histoire de Paris et de l'ile de France* 44 (1917), 163-82.

"Journées Parisiennes de mai-juin 1418 d'après des documents des archives de la couronne d'Aragon, Les," *Annuaire-bulletin de la société de l'histoire de France* 1940, 125-53.

Jusselin, M. "Comment la France se préparait à la guerre de cent ans," *Bibliothèque de l'école des chartes* 73 (1912), 209-36.

Krynen, J. *Idéal du prince et pouvoir royal en France à la fin du moyen âge (1380-1440)*. Paris, 1981.

Labande, L.-H. "L'occupation du Pont-Saint-Esprit par les grandes compagnies (1360-1361)," *Revue historique de Provence* 1 (1901), 79-95, 146-65.

Lacour, René. *Le gouvernement de l'apanage du duc Jean de Berry (1360-1416)*. Paris, 1934.

La Fontenelle de Vaudoré, A.D. de. *Histoire d'Olivier de Clisson, connétable de France*. 2 vols. Paris, 1826.

Lalande, D. *Jean II le Meingre, dit Boucicaut, 1366-1421*. Geneva, 1988.

Lartigaut, J. *Les campagnes du Quercy après la guerre de cent ans* Toulouse, 1978.

Lassabatère, Thierry. "Sentiment national et messianisme politique en France pendant la guerre de Cent Ans, le thème de la fin du monde chez Eustace Deschamps," *Bulletin d'Association des Amis du Centre Jeanne d'Arc* 17 (1993), 27-56.

Lecoy de la Marche, Albert. *Le roi René: sa vie, son administration, ses travaux artistiques et littéraires*. 2 vols. Paris, 1875.

Lefranc, A. *Olivier de Clisson, connétable de France*. Paris, 1898.

Lefrancq, Paul. "Un afforain, pris de corps, hors terre sainte, à Valenciennes en 1445." In: *La guerre et la paix: Frontières et violences au moyen âge*. Actes du 101e congrès national des sociétés savantes, Lille, 1976. Paris: Bibliothèque Nationale, 1978, pp. 375-80.

Leguai, André. *Le Bourbonnais pendant la guerre de cent ans*. Moulins, 1969.

Leguai, André. "Royauté et principautés en France aus XIVe et XVe siècles: L'évolution de leurs rapports au cours de la guerre de cent ans," *Moyen âge* 101 (1995), 121-35.

Leguay, Jean-Pierre. *La ville de Rennes au XVme siècle à travers les comptes des Miseurs*. Rennes: Université de Rennes, Faculté des lettres et sciences humaines, 1968.

Lehoux, Françoise. *Jean de France, duc de Berri (1340-1416)*. 4 vols. Paris, 1966-68.

Le Patourel, John. "The King and the Princes in Fourteenth-Century France." In: *Europe in the Late Middle Ages*. Ed. J.R. Hale, J.R.L. Highfield, and B. Smalley. Evanston: Northwestern University Press, 1965, pp. 155-83.

Le Verdier, P. "Fragment de statue présumée de Du Guesclin," *Bulletin de la commission des des antiquités de la Seine inférieur* (1897-1899), 128-30.

Lewis, Peter S. "The Failure of the French Medieval Estates," *Past and Present* 23 (1962), 3-24; in: *The Recovery of France in the Fifteenth Century*. Ed. Peter S. Lewis. Trans. G.F. Martin. New York, 1971, pp. 294-311; in: *Essays in Later Medieval French History*. London, 1985, pp. 105-26.

Lewis, Peter S. "La 'France anglaise' vue de la France française." In: *111e Congrès national des Sociétés savantes, Poitiers, 1986, Histoire médiévale.* T. I: "La France anglaise," pp. 31-39.

Lewis, Peter S. "France in the Fifteenth Century: Society and Sovereignty." In: *Europe in the Late Middle Ages.* Ed. J.R. Hale, J.R.L. Highfield, and B. Smalley. Evanston: Northwestern University Press, 1965, pp. 276-300.

Lewis, Peter S. "Introduction." In: *The Recovery of France in the Fifteenth Century.* Ed. P.S. Lewis. Trans. G.F. Martin. New York, 1971, pp. 11-22.

Lewis, Peter S. *Later Medieval France: The Polity.* London: Macmillan, 1968.

Lombarès, Michel de. "Patay, 18 juin 1429," *Revue historique de l'armée* 22 (1966), 5-16.

Lomier, Eugene. "Au temps de Jeanne d'Arc. La garde du Pont de Rouen. Document Anglais inédit," *Revue de études historiques* 96 (1930), 377-84.

Longnon, Auguste. *Paris pendant l'occupation anglaise (1420-1436).* Paris: H. Champion, 1878.

Luce, Siméon. *La France pendant la guerre de cent ans: Épisodes historiques et vie privée aux XIVe et XVe siècles.* 2 vols. Paris, 1890, 1893.

Luce, Siméon. *Histoire de Bertrand du Guesclin et de son époque: la jeunesse de Bertrand (1320-64).* Paris, 1876.

Luce, Siméon, ed. "Une pièce de vers sur le siège d'Orléans." In: *La France pendant la guerre de cent ans: Épisodes historiques et vie privée aux XIVe et XVe siècles.* 2nd ed. Paris, 1893, pp. 207-14.

Marscher, E. "Der 'Roi des Ribauds' im französischen Heer," *Zeitschrift für historisches Waffenkunde* 7 (1915-17), 112.

Martin, J.-L. "Une grand seigneur breton en Ile-de-France: Olivier de Clisson," *Bulletin de la société d'émulation des Côtes-du-Nord* 82 (1953).

Martin, Paul. "Quelques aspects de l'art de la guerre en Alsace au XIVe siècle," *Revue d'Alsace* 88 (1948), 108-23.

Mathieu, R. "Les sources de l'histoire de la bataille [Cocherel]," *Les cahiers vernonnais* 4 (1964), 91-98.

McLeod, Enid. *Charles of Orleans: Prince and Poet.* New York: The Viking Press, 1969.

Menkés, F. "Aspect de la guerre de Provence à la fin du XIVe siècle." In: *Économies et sociétés au moyen âge: Mélanges offerts à Edouard Perroy.* Paris, 1973, pp. 465-76.

Michel, Robert. "Les défenseurs des châteaux et des villes fortes dans le Comtat Venaissin," *Bibliothèque de l'école de chartes* 75 (1915), 315-30.

Mirot, Léon. "Dom Bevy et les comptes des tresoriers des guerres. Essai de restitution d'un fonds disparu de la Chambre des Comptes," *Bibliothèque de l'école des chartes* 86 (1925), 245-379.

Miskimin, Harry A. *Money and Power in Fifteenth-Century France.* New Haven: Yale University Press, 1984.

Molinier, Émile. *Étude sur la vie d'Arnoul d'Audrehem, maréchal de France, 1302-1370.* Paris, 1883.

Moranvillé, H. "Le siège de Reims, 1359-1360," *Bibliothèque de l'école de Chartes* 56 (1895), 93-98.

Morel, O. *L'état de siège à Bourg lors de l'invasion de la Bresse en 1468.* Bourg, 1936.

Moshowitz, H.H. "Historical Veracity in the Gilles de Rais File." In: *Fifteenth Century Studies*, I. Ed. G.R. Mermier and E.E. Dubruck. Michigan, 1978.

Niessel, A. "Du Guesclin et les grandes compagnies," *Revue historique des armées* 2.3 (1946), 23-33.

Nollier, Inès. *Isabeau de Bavière, reine de France.* Monaco: Rocher, 1996.

Nordberg, Michael. *Les ducs et la royauté: Études sur la rivalité des ducs d'Orléans et de Bourgogne, 1392-1407.* Upsal, 1964.

Noulons, J. *Ponton de Xaintrailles.* Bordeaux, 1897.

Olland, Hélène. "Un exemple de reconstruction: Colombey-Lès-Choiseul (1485-1550)." In: *La reconstruction après la guerre de cent ans.* Actes du 104e congrès national des sociétés savantes, Bordeaux, 1979. Paris: Bibliothèque Nationale, 1981, I:63-78.

Perroy, Edouard. "Feudalism or Principalities in Fifteenth-Century France." In: *Lordship and Community in Medieval Europe: Selected Readings*. Ed. Frederic L. Cheyette. New York: Holt, Rinehart, and Winston, Inc., 1968, pp. 217-21.

Perroy, Edouard. "Social Mobility Among the French *noblesse* in the Later Middle Ages," *Past and Present* 21 (1962), 25-38.

Plaisse, André. *Charles dit le Mauvais, comte d'Evreux, roi de Navarre, captaine de Paris*. Evreux: Société Libre de l'Eure, 1972.

Plaisse, André. *Un chef de guerre de XVe siècle: Robert de Flocques, baillli royal d'Evreux*. Evreux: Sociéte Libre de l'Eure, 1984.

Plaisse, André. *La délivrance de Cherbourg et du Clos du Cotentin à la fin de la guerre de cent ans*. Cherbourg: Éditions de la Presse de la Manche, 1989.

Plaisse, André and Sylvie Plaisse. *La vie municipale à Évreux pendant la guerre de cent ans*. Evreux: Société Libre de l'Eure, 1978.

Platelle, Henri. "Une révolte populaire à Saint-Amand en 1356." In: *La guerre et la paix: Frontières et violences au moyen âge*. Actes du 101e congrès national des sociétés savantes, Lille, 1976. Paris: Bibliothèque Nationale, 1978, pp. 349-63.

Pocquet du Haut-Jussé, B. "La dernière phase de la vie de Du Guesclin, l'affaire de Bretagne," *Bibliothèque de l'école des chartes* 125 (1967), 142-89.

Pons, Nicole. "La guerre de cent ans vue par quelques polémistes français du XVe siècle," In: *Guerre et société en France, en Angleterre et en Bourgogne XIVe-XVe siècle*. Ed. P. Contamine, C. Giry-Deloison, ad Maurice Keen. Lille, 1991, pp. 143-69.

Pons, Nicole. *"L'Honneur de la couronne de France": Quatre libelles contre les Anglais (vers 1418-vers1429*. Paris: Libraire C. Klincksieck, 1990.

Pons, Nicole. "Information et rumeurs quelques points de vue sur les événements de la Guerre civile en France (1407-1420)," *Revue historique* 297 (1997), 409-33.

Portal, C. "Les insurrections des Tuchins dans les pays de Langue d'oc, vers 1382-1384," *Annales du midi* 4 (1892), 433-74.

Postel, Raoul. *Siège et capitulation de Bayeux en 1417: Notes pour servir à l'histoire du Bessin pendant la domination anglaise sous l'occupation du roi Henri V.* Caen: Le Gost-Clérisse, Éditeur, 1873.

Poulain, A.-G. "Le site de Cocherel," *Les cahiers vernonnais* 4 (1964), 17-18.

Prentout, Henri. *La prise de Caen par Édouard III, 1346.* Caen: Henri Delesques, 1904.

Puiseux, Léon. *Caen en 1421: appendice au siège de Caen par les anglais en 1417.* Caen: Le Gost-Clérisse, Éditeur, 1860.

Puiseux, Léon. *Siège et prise de Caen par les anglais en 1417: Épisode de la guerre de cent ans.* Caen: Le Gost-Clérisse, Éditeur, 1868.

Puiseux, Léon. *Siège et prise de Rouen par les anglais (1418-1419).* Caen: Le Gost-Clérisse, Éditeur, 1867.

Quicherat, Jules. *Rodrigue de Villandrando: L'un des combattants pour l'indépendance française au quinzième siècle.* Paris, 1879.

"Règlement pour la défense du château de Bioule, 18 mars 1347," *Bulletin archéologique* 4 (1846-47), 490-95.

Reynaud, M. "Le service féodal en Anjou et Maine à la fin du moyen âge," *Cahiers d'histoire* 16 (1971), 115-59.

Ribéra-Perville, Claude. "Aspects du mécénat de Louis 1er d'Orléans (d. 1407)." In: *Jeanne d'Arc: Une époque, un rayonnement.* Paris, 1982, pp. 139-48.

Richert, Ernst. *Die Schlacht bei Guinegate.* Berlin, 1907.

Rimboud, Michel. "La paix du Bien public: démesure et marchandages (août-novembre 1465)." In: *La guerre, la violence et les gens au Moyen Âge.* I: *Guerre et violence.* Ed. P. Contamine and O. Guyotjeannin. 119e congrès national des sociétés historiques et scientifiques, Amiens, octobre 1994, Section d'histoire médiévale et philologie. Paris, 1996, pp. 333-44.

Rouquette, J. *Le Rouergue sous les anglais*. Millau, 1887.

Rousten-Verrières, Jean-Marie. "La guerre de cent ans dans l'Albigeois," *Revue du Tarn*, 3rd ser., 144 (1992), 685-718.

Roy, J. *Histoire d'Olivier de Clisson*. Paris, 1872.

Salmon-Legagneur, Emmanuel. "Le souvenir de Jeanne d'Arc, Bertrand du Guesclin et Arthur Richemont à travers la toponymie bretonne contemporaine," *Bulletin d'Association des Amis du Centre Jeanne d'Arc* 16 (1992), 41-58.

Samaran, Charles. "Portrait de Du Guesclin," *Les cahiers vernonnais* 4 (1964), 13-16.

Schnerb, Bertrand. "Un monastère dans la guerre: l'abbaye du Mont-Saint-Éloi (fin XIVe-début XVe siècle." In: *La guerre, la violence et les gens au Moyen Âge*. II: *Guerre et gens*. Ed. P. Contamine and O. Guyotjeannin. 119e congrès national des sociétés historiques et scientifiques, Amiens, octobre 1994, Section d'histoire médiévale et philologie. Paris, 1996, pp. 101-17.

Sené, Elsa. "Un 'miroir du prince' du XVe siècle: l'avis à Yolande d'Aragon, édition critique et commentaire," *Bulletin d'Association des Amis du Centre Jeanne d'Arc* 19 (1995), 145-48.

Sevestre, Bernard. "L'ancienne alliance franco-écossaise et le service écossais," *Revue de la Société des Amis du Musée de l'Armée* 99 (1990), 5-21.

Solon, Paul D. "Popular Response to Standing Military Forces in Fifteenth-Century France," *Studies in the Renaissance* 19 (1972), 78-111.

Stein, Henri. *Charles de France, frère de Louis XI*. Paris, 1919.

Stein, Henri, ed. "Lettres missives des XIVe et XVIe siècle conservées aux archives municipales de la ville de Troyes," *Annuaire-bulletin de la société de l'histoire de France* 1988, 185-234.

Storey-Challenger, Sheila Bredon. *L'administration anglaise du Ponthieu après le traité de Brétigny, 1361-1369*. Trans. R. Petit. Abbeville: Société d'émulation historique et littéraire d'Abbeville, 1975.

Surirey, Henry de Saint-Rémy. *Jean II de Bourbon, duc de Bourbonnais et d'Auvergne*. Paris, 1944.

Taylor, Craig. "Sir John Fortescue and the French Polemical Treatises of the Hundred Years War," *English Historical Review* 114 (1999), 112-29.

Terrier de Loray, Henri-Philippe. *Jean de Vienne, amiral de France (1341-1396)*. Paris, 1977.

Teyssot, Josiane. "Les villes d'Auvergne pendant la guerre de Cent Ans." In: *La guerre, la violence et les gens au Moyen Âge*. II: *Guerre et gens*. Ed. P. Contamine and O. Guyotjeannin. 119e congrès national des sociétés historiques et scientifiques, Amiens, octobre 1994, Section d'histoire médiévale et philologie. Paris, 1996, pp. 49-57.

Thomas, Antoine. "Jean de Salazar et le guet-apens d'Amiens," *Bibliothèque de l'école de chartes* 86 (1925), 122-67.

Thompson, Guy Llewelyn. *Paris and Its People Under English Rule: The Anglo-Burgundian Regime 1420-1436*. Oxford: Clarendon Press, 1991.

Thompson, Guy Llewelyn. "'Monseigneur Saint Denis', his Abbey, and his Town, under the English Occupation, 1420-1436." In: *Power, Culture, and Religion in France c.1350-c.1550*. Ed. C. Allmand. Woodbridge, 1989, pp. 15-35.

Thompson, Guy Llewelyn. "Le régime Anglo-Bourguignon a Paris: Facteurs idéologiques." In: *111e Congrès national des Sociétés savantes, Poitiers, 1986, Histoire médiévale*. T. I: "La France anglaise," pp. 53-60.

Timbal, Pierre-Clément. *La guerre de cent ans vue à travers les registres du Parlement (1337-1369)*. Groupe d'Étude d'Histoire Juridique. Paris: Centre National de la Recherche Scientifique, 1961.

Toudouze, G.G. *Du Guesclin, Clisson, Richemont*. Paris, 1942.

Tucoo-Chala, Pierre. "Froissart dans le Midi Pyrénéen." In: *Froissart: Historian*. Ed. J.J.N. Palmer. Woodbridge, 1981, pp. 118-31.

Tucoo-Chala, Pierre. *Gaston Fébus et la vicomté de Béarn, 1343-1391.* Bordeaux, 1959.

Vaesen, J. "Catalogue du fonds Bourre à la Bibliothèque nationale," *Bibliothèque de l'école des chartes* 45 (1884), 152-79.

Vale, Malcolm. "Warfare and the Life of the French and Burgundian Nobility in the Late Middle Ages." In: *Adelige Sachkultur des Spätmittelalters (Internationaler Kongress, Krems an der Donau, 22. bis 25. September 1980).* Vienna: Österreichische Akademie der Wissenschaften, 1982, pp. 169-94.

Vallez, Anne. "En réserve de la royauté: la vicomté de Pont-Authou." In: *Recueil d'études offert en hommage à Lucien Musset: Cahier des annales de Normandie*, 23 (1990), 393-402.

Verbruggen, J.F. *De slag bij Guinegate, 7 augustus 1479: De verdediging van het graafschap Vlaanderen tegen de koning van Frankrijk, 1477-1480.* Brussels: Koninklijk Legermusuem, 1993.

Verbruggen, J.F. "La tactique de la chevalerie Française de 1340 à 1415," *Publications de l'université de l'état à Elisabethville* 1 (1961), 39-48.

Verger, Jacques. "The University of Paris at the End of the Hundred Years War." In: *Universities in Politics: Case Studies from the Late Middle Ages and Early Modern Period.* Ed. John W. Baldwin and Richard A. Goldthwaite. Baltimore, 1972, pp. 47-78.

Veydarier, Régis. *"Una guerra de layrons*: L'occupation de la Provence par les compagnies de Raymond de Turenne (1393-1399)." In: *La guerre, la violence et les gens au Moyen Âge.* I: *Guerre et violence.* Ed. P. Contamine and O. Guyotjeannin. 119e congrès national des sociétés historiques et scientifiques, Amiens, octobre 1994, Section d'histoire médiévale et philologie. Paris, 1996, pp. 169-88.

Villele, Captaine de. "Aspect militaire de la vie d'une petite cité médiévale: La défense de Belfort à la fin du Moyen âge," *Revue historique des armées* 28 (1972), 7-20.

Wolfe, Michael. "Siege Warfare and the *Bonnes Villes* of France during the Hundred Years War." In: *The Medieval City Under Siege*. Ed. I.A. Corfis and M. Wolfe. Woodbridge, 1995, pp. 49-66.

Wolff, Philippe. "The Armagnacs in Southern France (14th-15th Centuries)," *Bulletin of the Institute for Historical Research* 20 (1945), 186-91.

Wright, Nicholas A.R. "French Peasants in the Hundred Years War," *History Today* 33 (Jun 1983), 38-42.

Wright, Nicholas A.R. *Knights and Peasants: The Hundred Years War in the French Countryside*. Woodbridge: The Boydell Press, 1998.

Wroe, Ann. *A Fool and His Money: Life in a Partitioned Town in Fourteenth-Century France*. New York: Hill and Wang, 1995.

Medieval – Hundred Years War – France – Philip VI

Brown, Elizabeth A.R. "Customary Aids and Royal Fiscal Policy under Philip VI of Valois," *Traditio* 30 (1974), 191-258.

Coville, Alfred. "Poèmes historiques de l'avènement de Philippe de Valois au traité de Calais (1328-1360)." In: *Histoire littéraire de la France*. Paris, 1949, XXXVIII:259-333.

Rogers, Clifford J. "A Continuation of the *Manuel d'histoire de Philippe VI* for the Years 1328-39," *English Historical Review* 114 (1999), 1256-66.

Medieval – Hundred Years War – France – Charles V

Autrand, Françoise. *Charles V: Le sage*. Paris: Fayard, 1994.

Bordonove, Georges. *Charles V le Sage*. Paris: Éditions Pygmalion/ Gérard Watelet, 1985.

Byrne, Donal. "*Rex imago Dei*: Charles V of France and the *Livre des propriétés des choses*," *Journal of Medieval History* 7 (1981), 97-114.

Cazelles, Raymond. *Société politique, noblesse, et couronne sous Jean le Bon et Charles V*. Geneva, 1982.

Delachenal, Roland. *Histoire de Charles V.* 5 vols. Paris, 1909-31.

Henneman, John Bell. "The Age of Charles V." In: *Froissart: Historian.* Ed. J.J.N. Palmer. Woodbridge: Boydell and Brewer, 1981, pp. 36-49.

Miskimin, H.A. "The Last of Charles V: The Background of the Revolts of 1382," *Speculum* 38 (1963), 433-42.

Vallez, Anne. "Un aspect du conflit entre Charles V et Charles de Navarre: le noyautage du Clos de Cotentin par le roi de France, 1365-1378." In: *Recueil d'études offert en hommage au doyen Michel de Boüard.* Annales de Normandie (special volume). Caen, n.d., II:533-48.

Medieval – Hundred Years War – France – Charles VI

Autrand, Françoise. *Charles VI: La folie du roi.* Paris: Fayard, 1966.

Chauveron, R. de. *Des maillotins aux Marmousets: Audoin Chauveron, prévôt du Paris sous Charles VI.* Paris, 1992.

Famiglietti, R.C. *Royal Intrigue: Crisis at the Court of Charles VI, 1392-1420.* New York: AMS Press, 1986.

Gauvard, Claudene. "Le roi de France et l'opinion publique à l'époque de Charles VI." In: *Culture et ideologie dans la genese de l'état moderne.* CNRS 15-17 Octobre 1984. Rome, 1985.

Grévy-Pons, Nicole. "Propagande et sentiment national pendant le règne de Charles VI: l'exemple de Jean de Montreuil," *Francia* 8 (1979), 127-45.

Hindman, Sandra L. *Christine de Pizan's "Epistre Othéa": Painting and Politics at the Court of Charles VI.* Toronto: Pontifical Institute of Mediaeval Studies, 1986.

La Borderie, Arthur le Moyne de. "Lettre de Charles VI, roi de France, aux barons de Bretagne sur la régence du duché (23 aout 1402)," *Revue de Bretagne et de Vendée* 62 (1889), 473-74.

Le Bis, Isabelle. "Pratique de la diplomatie: Un dossier d'ambassadeurs Française sous Charles VI (1400-1403)," *Annuaire-bulletin de la société de l'histoire de France* (1985-1986), 97-215.

Mirot, Léon. *Les insurrections urbaines au début du règne de Charles VI (1380-1383), leurs causes, leurs conséquences*. Paris: Albert Fontemoing, 1905.

Mirot, Léon, ed. "Lettres closes de Charles VI conservées aux archives de Reims et de Tournai," *Moyen âge* 29 (1918), 309-38; 30 (1919), 1-44.

Rey, M. *Le domaine du roi et les finances extraordinaires sous Charles VI, 1388-1413*. Paris, 1965.

Rey, M. *Les finances royales sous Charles VI: Les causes du déficit, 1388-1413*. Paris, 1965.

Sherborne, James. "Charles VI and Richard II." In: *Froissart: Historian*. Ed. J.J.N. Palmer. Woodbridge, 1981, pp. 50-63.

Sherborne, James. "Charles VI and Richard II." In: *War, Politics and Culture in Fourteenth-Century England*. Ed. A. Tuck. London, 1994, pp. 155-70.

Talmant, Pierre. "Le soleil: un emblème redoutable: une lecture typologique de la crise de folie du roi Charles VI," *Journal of Medieval History* 24 (1998), 53-60.

Medieval – Hundred Years War – France – Charles VII

Beaucourt, G. du Fresne de. *Histoire de Charles VII*. 6 vols. Paris, 1881-91.

Bordonove, Georges. *Charles VII le Victorieux*. Paris: Éditions Pygmalion/ Gérard Watelet, 1985.

Bouillé, A. de. *Un conseiller de Charles VII, le maréchal de la Fayette (1380-1463)*. Paris, 1955.

Hunger, V. "Le siège et la prise de Vire par Charles VII en 1450," *Annales de Normandie* 12 (1971), 109-22.

Ilardi, Vincent. "France and Milan: The Uneasy Alliance, 1452-1466." In: *Gli Sforza a Milano e in Lombardia e i loro rapporti con gli stati italiano er europei (1450-1530)*. Milan: Cisalpino-Goliardica, 1982, pp. 405-46.

Ilardi, Vincent. "The Italian League, Francesco Sforza, and Charles VII (1454-1461)," *Studies in the Renaissance* 6 (1959), 129-66.

Petit-Dutaillis, C. *Charles VII, Louis XI, et la minorité de Charles VIII*. Paris, 1981.

Spencer, Mark. *Thomas Basin (1412-1490): The History of Charles VII and Louis XI*. Bibliotheca Humanistica et Reformatorica, 57. Nieuwkoop: De Graaf Publishers, 1997.

Teutey, A. *Les ecorcheurs sous Charles VII*. 2 vols. Montbeliard, 1874.

Vale, M.G.A. *Charles VII*. Berkeley and Los Angeles: University of California Press, 1974.

Vallet, M.A. *Histoire de Charles VII, roi de France et de son époque, 1403-1461*. 3 vols. Paris, 1862-65.

Medieval – Hundred Years War – France – Joan of Arc

Allmand, Christopher T. "L'artillerie de l'armée Anglaise et son organisation à l'époque de Jeanne d'Arc." In: *Jeanne d'Arc: une époque, un rayonment*. Colloque d'histoire médiévale. Orleans–Octobre 1979. Paris, 1982, pp. 73-83.

Anon. "Les derniers vestiges des tourelles où Jeanne d'Arc s'est illustrée, les 7 et 8 mai 1429," *Bulletin de la société archéologique et historique de l'Orléanais* n.s. 1 (1959-60), 75-77.

Anderhuber, Raymond. "Le capitaine de Gaucourt, compagnon de Jeanne d'Arc, et l'histoire meusienne de ses descendants," *Bulletin de la sociétés d'histoire et d'archéologie de Meuse* 30-31 (1994-95), 33-54.

Autin, Marcel. *Jeanne d'Arc à Rouen: son procès–sa mort*. Rouen: n.p., n.d.

Autrand, Françoise. "Le pouvoir et le supernaturel: Jeanne d'Arc en 1429," *Bulletin d'Association des Amis du Centre Jeanne d'Arc* 19 (1995), 5-24.

Auzas, Pierre-Marie. "Mérimée méconnu," *Bulletin d'Association des Amis du Centre Jeanne d'Arc* 9 (1985), 19-29.

Ayroles, Jean-Baptiste-Joseph. *L'Université de Paris au temps de Jeanne d'Arc et la cause de sa haine contre la Libertrice*. Paris: X. Rondelet et Cie, 1902.

Baraude, Henri. "Le siège d'Orléans et Jeanne d'Arc, 1428-1429," *Revue des questions historiques* 80-81 (1906-07), 31-65, 74-112, 395-424.

Barstow, Anne Llewellyn. *Joan of Arc: Heretic, Mystic, Shaman*. Studies in Women and Religion, vol. 17. Lewiston: The Edwin Mellen Press, 1986.

Bataille, Henri. *Vaucouleurs: Les remparts qui ont sauvé Jeanne-d'Arc*. Vosges: Imprimeur-Editeur Fetzer S.A., n.d.

Beaucourt, G. du Fresne de. "Jeanne d'Arc trahie par Chrales VII,"*Revue des questions historiques* (1867), 286-91.

Berents, Dick. "The Resurrection of Joan of Arc." In: *Joan of Arc: Reality and Myth*. Ed. Jan van Herwaarden. Hilversum: Verloren, 1994, pp. 75-96.

Boer, Dick de. "Joan of Arc: The Historical Actuality of a Fascination." In: *Joan of Arc: Reality and Myth*. Ed. Jan van Herwaarden. Hilversum: Verloren, 1994, pp. 7-18.

Boissonade, P. "Une étape capitale de la mission de Jeanne d'Arc," *Revue des questions historiques* 113 (1930), 12-67.

Bordonove, Georges. *Les grandes heures de l'histoire de France: Jeanne d'Arc et la Guerre de Cent Ans*. Paris: Éditions Pygmalion/ Gérard Watelet, 1994.

Boucher de Molandon, M. *Études sur une bastille Anglaise du XVe siècle retrouvée en la commune de Fleury (près Orléans)*. Orléans: Imprimerie d'Alexandre Jacob, 1858.

Boucher de Molandon, M. "Note de Guillaume Girault, Notaire à Orléans en 1429, sur la levée du siège," *Memoires de la société archéologique de Orléannais* 4 (1848), 382-89.

Boucher de Molandon, M. and Adalbert de Beaucorps. *L'armée anglaise vaincue par Jeanne d'Arc sous les murs d'Orléans*. Orléans: H. Herluison, 1892.

Bourguignon, Eug. *Sainte Jeanne d'Arc (la guerrière)*. Bruges: Desclée de Brouwer et Cie., 1928.

Bouteiller, E. de. *Jeanne d'Arc dans les Chroniques Messines de Philippe de Vigneulles*. Orléans: H. Herluison, 1878.

Bouvier, Armand. *Orléans, coeur de la France et Jeanne la libératrice*. Orléans: G. Luzeray. 1929.

Bouzy, Olivier. *Jeanne d'Arc: Mythes et réalités*. Paris: L'Atelier de l'Archer, 1999.

Bouzy, Olivier. "Jeanne d'Arc au Centre Jeanne d'Arc: historiographie, littérature, histoire, *Bulletin d'Association des Amis du Centre Jeanne d'Arc* 19 (1995), 93-144.

Bouzy, Olivier. "Prédiction ou récupération, les prophéties autour de Jeanne d'Arc dans les premiers mois de l'année 1429," *Bulletin d'Association des Amis du Centre Jeanne d'Arc* 14 (1990), 39-47.

Bouzy, Olivier. "Le traité de Jacques Gelu, *De adventu Johanne*," *Bulletin d'Association des Amis du Centre Jeanne d'Arc* 16 (1992), 29-40.

Bouzy, Olivier. "Transcription Errors in Texts of Joan of Arc's History." In: *Fresh Verdicts on Joan of Arc*. Ed. C. Wood and B. Wheeler. New York, 1996, pp. 73-84.

Bruley, Edouard. *Jeanne d'Arc à Orléans*. Orléans: Libraire G. Luzeray, 1929.

Brun, Félix. *Jeanne d'Arc à Soissons: Recherches sur Soissons et le Soissonnais au temps de la Pucelle (1429-1430)*. Paris: Auguste Réty, 1920.

Buchan, Alice. *Joan of Arc and the Recovery of France*. London: Hooder and Stoughton Limited, 1948.

Calemard. "La chevauchée de Jeanne d'Arc et son appel aux habitants de Riom," *Revue politique et parlementaire* 140 (1929), 433-47.

Calmette, Joseph. *Jeanne d'Arc*. Que sais-je? Paris: Presses universitaires de France, 1950.

Candé, Dr. "Sous l'étendard de Jeanne d'Arc: La mort d'un seigneur du Lude, tombé devant Jargeau, le 11 juin 1429," *Revue historique et archéologique du Maine* 82 (1926), 106-14.

Canonge, Général Frédéric. *Jeanne d'Arc guerrière*. Paris: Nouvelles Libraire Nationale, 1907.

Caulier, General. "Jeanne d'Arc," *Revue historique des armées* 9.1 (1953), 7-19.

Champion, Pierre. *Guillaume de Flavy: Captaine de Compiègne: Contribution à l'histoire de Jeanne d'Arc et à l'étude de la vie militaire et privée au XVe siècle*. Paris: Honoré Champion, 1906.

Champion, Pierre. *Jeanne d'Arc*. Paris: Flammarion, 1933.

Charpentier, Jacques. "A propos du procès de Jeanne d'Arc," *Revue de Paris* 70 (1963), 48-52.

Charpentier, Paul. *Histoire du siège d'Orléans, 1428-1429*. Orléans: H. Herluison, 1894.

Chevalier, Ulysse. "L'abjuration de Jeanne d'Arc au cimetière de St-Ouen et l'authenticité de sa formule: Etude critique," *Mémoires de l'academié des sciences de Lyon* 7 (1903), 87-170.

Clin(-Meyer), Marie-Véronique. "Jeanne d'Arc bergère?" *Bulletin d'Association des Amis du Centre Jeanne d'Arc* 10 (1986), 7-8.

Clin(-Meyer), Marie-Véronique. "Joan of Arc and Her Doctors." In: *Fresh Verdicts on Joan of Arc*. Ed. C. Wood and B. Wheeler. New York, 1996, pp. 295-302.

Clin(-Meyer), Marie-Véronique. "Le père de courtoisie," *Bulletin d'Association des Amis du Centre Jeanne d'Arc* 9 (1985), 37-44.

Clin(-Meyer), Marie-Véronique. "Requête de Robinet de Prestreval au comte de Dunois, du 20 mars 1467," *Bulletin d'Association des Amis du Centre Jeanne d'Arc* 9 (1985), 45-47.

Cochard, Th. *Existe-t-il des reliques de Jeanne d'Arc*. Orléans: H. Herluison, 1891.

Colas de la Noue, Ed. *Jeanne d'Arc et le siège d'Orléans*. Angers: Germain and G. Grassin, 1896.

Collet, Lieutenant-Colonel. *Vie militaire de Jeanne d'Arc*. Nancy: Imprimerie Nancéienne, 1919.

Collin, M. *La casemate du bont du pont des Tourelles à Orléans du coté de la Sologne*. Paris: n.p., 1867.

Collin, M. *Les derniers jours du pont des Tourelles à Orléans*. Orléans: H. Herluison, 1875.

Contamine, Philippe. "L'action et la personne de Jeanne d'Arc. L'attitude des princes français à son égard." In: *Des pouvoirs en France, 1300-1500*. Paris, 1992, pp. 109-21.

Contamine, Philippe. "*Henry VI*, première partie, la guerre de cent ans, Jeanne d'Arc." In: *De Jeanne d'Arc aux guerres d'Italie: Figures, images et problèmes du XVe siècle*. Orléans: Paradigme, 1994, pp. 163-78.

Contamine, Philippe. *De Jeanne d'Arc aux guerres d'Italie*. Orléans: Paradigme, 1994.

Contamine, Philippe. "Jeanne d'Arc de Chinon à Paris, l'action militaire, le jeu politique." In: *De Jeanne d'Arc aux guerres d'Italie: Figures, images et problèmes du XVe siècle*. Orléans: Paradigme, 1994, pp. 77-84.

Contamine, Philippe. "Jeanne d'Arc et la prophétie." In: *De Jeanne d'Arc aux guerres d'Italie: Figures, images et problèmes du XVe siècle*. Orléans: Paradigme, 1994, pp. 53-62.

Contamine, Philippe. "Jeanne d'Arc, Rouen, la Normandie," *Etudes Normandes* 44 (1995), 9-27.

Contamine, Philippe. "Jules Quicherat, historien de Jeanne d'Arc." In: *De Jeanne d'Arc aux guerres d'Italie: Figures, images et problèmes du XVe siècle*. Orléans: Paradigme, 1994, pp. 179-92.

Contamine, Philippe. "Mythe et histoire: Jeanne d'Arc, 1429." In: *De Jeanne d'Arc aux guerres d'Italie: Figures, images et problèmes du XVe siècle*. Orléans: Paradigme, 1994, pp. 63-76.

Contamine, Philippe. "Naissance d'une historiographie. Le souvenir de Jeanne d'Arc, en France et hors de France, depuis le 'procès de son innocence' (1455-1456) jusqu'au début du XVIe siècle," *Francia* 15 (1987), 233-56; in: *De Jeanne d'Arc aux guerres d'Italie: Figures, images et problèmes du XVe siècle*. Orléans: Paradigme, 1994, pp. 139-62.

Couget, Henri. *Jeanne d'Arc devant Paris*. Paris: Éditions Spes, 1925.

Crane, Susan. "Clothing and Gender Definition: Joan of Arc," *Journal of Medieval and Early Modern Studies* 26 (1996), 297-320.

Debal, Jacques. "Les fortifications et le pont d'Orléans au temps de Jeanne d'Arc," *Dossiers d'archéologie* 34 (May 1979), 77-92.

Debal, Jacques. "La topographie de l'enceinte fortifiée d'Orléans au temps de Jeanne d'Arc." In: *Jeanne d'Arc: une époque, un rayonment*. Colloque d'histoire médiévale. Orléans–Octobre 1979. Paris, 1982, pp. 23-41.

Desana, Claude. "La première entrevue de Jeanne d'Arc et de Charles VII à Chinon (Mars 1429)," *Analecta Bollandiana* 84 (1966), 113-26.

Desnoyers, M. *Les armes du siège d'Orléans de 1428*. Orléans: H. Herluison, 1884.

DeVries, Kelly. *Joan of Arc: A Military Leader*. Stroud: Sutton Publishing, 1999.

DeVries, Kelly. "The Use of Gunpowder Weaponry By and Against Joan of Arc During the Hundred Years War," *War and Society* 14 (1996), 1-16.

DeVries, Kelly. "A Woman as Leader of Men: A Reassessment of Joan of Arc's Military Career." In: *Fresh Verdicts on Joan of Arc*. Ed. C. Wood and B. Wheeler. New York, 1996, pp. 3-18.

Doncoeur, Père. *La chevauchée de Jeanne d'Arc, 1429*. 3rd ed. Paris: L'Art Catholique, 1928.

Duparc, Pierre. "La délivrance d'Orléans et la mission de Jeanne d'Arc." In: *Jeanne d'Arc: Une époque, un rayonnement*. Paris, 1982, pp. 153-58.

Egan, John. "Joan of Arc–Saint or General?" *Military Illustrated* 140 (Jan 2000), 34-41.

Fanton, Richard. *Les cendres de Jeanne d'Arc*. Paris: J.-B. Baillière and fils, 1891.

ffoulkes, Charles J. "The Armour of Jeanne d'Arc," *The Burlington Magazine* 16 (Dec 1909), 141-46.

Florival, M.A. de. *Le passage de Jeanne d'Arc dans le Ponthieu (1430)*. Abbeville: Imprimerie F. Paillart, 1904.

Fons-Melicocq, A. de la., ed. "Documents inédits sur le siège de Compiègne de 1430," *La Picardie* 3 (1857), 21-29.

Fonssagrives, E. "Jeanne d'Arc et Richemont," *Bulletin de la société polymathique du Morbihan* (1920), 3-20.

Foxwell, Elizabeth. "Saint, Soldier, Spirit, Savior: The Images of Joan of Arc," *Minerva* 12.3 (Fall 1994), 36-46.

Fraikin, Jean. "Was Joan of Arc a 'Sign' of Charles VII's Innocence?" In: *Fresh Verdicts on Joan of Arc*. Ed. C. Wood and B. Wheeler. New York, 1996, pp. 61-72.

Fraioli, Deborah A. "The Literary Image of Joan of Arc: Prior Influences," *Speculum* 56 (1981), 811-30.

Fraioli, Deborah A. *Joan of Arc: The Early Debate*. Woodbridge: The Boydell Press, 2000.

Fraioli, Deborah A. "L'origine des sources écrites et leur fonction pour le *Ditié de Jeanne d'Arc* de Christine de Pisan," *Bulletin d'Association des Amis du Centre Jeanne d'Arc* 17 (1993), 5-18.

Fraioli, Deborah A. "Why Joan of Arc Never Became an Amazon." In: *Fresh Verdicts on Joan of Arc*. Ed. C. Wood and B. Wheeler. New York, 1996, pp. 189-204.

Franq, H.G. "Jean Gerson's Theological Treatise and Other Memoires in Defence of Joan of Arc," *Revue de l'Université d'Ottowa* 41 (1971), 58-80.

Funck-Brentano, Franz. *Jeanne d'Arc chef de guerre*. Paris: Flammarior, 1943.

Gache, Paul. *Sainte Jeanne d'Arc à Vaucouleurs*. Vailly-sur-Sauldre: Éditions Sainte Jeanne d'Arc, 1982.

Gilli, Patrick. "L'épopée du Jeanne d'Arc d'après un document italien contemporaine: éditions et traduction de la lettre du pseudo-Barbaro (1429)," *Bulletin d'Association des Amis du Centre Jeanne d'Arc* 20 (1996), 4-26.

Gonzalez, Elizabeth. "Châtelet ou hôtel? La résidence ducale à Orléans au XVe siècle," *Bulletin d'Association des Amis du Centre Jeanne d'Arc* 18 (1994), 13-22.

Gordon, Mary. *Joan of Arc*. London: Weidenfeld and Nicolson, 2000.

Guerrier, L. *L'age de Jeanne d'Arc à l'époque du siège d'Orléans*. Orléans: P. Pigelet, n.d.

Hanawalt, Barbara A. and Sandra Noakes. "Trial Transcript, Romance, Propaganda: Joan of Arc and the French Body Politic," *Modern Language Quarterly* 57.4 (Dec 1996), 605-31.

Hanotaux, Gabriel. "La mission de Jeanne d'Arc," *Revue des deux mondes*, 7th ser., 50 (Mar-Apr 1929), 88-98.

Harmand, Adrien. *Jeanne d'Arc: ses costumes, son armure. Essai de reconstitution*. Paris: Libraire Ernest Leroux, 1929.

Harty, Kevin J. "Jeanne au cinéma." In: *Fresh Verdicts on Joan of Arc*. Ed. C. Wood and B. Wheeler. New York, 1996, pp. 237-64.

Havard de la Montagne, Philippe. "Rétif de la Bretonne fut-il le biographe de Jeanne d'Arc?" *Bulletin d'Association des Amis du Centre Jeanne d'Arc* 18 (1994), 51-52.

Hellis, M. *La prison de Jeanne d'Arc à Rouen*. Rouen: A. Le Brument, 1865.

Heerwarden, Jan van. "The Appearance of Joan of Arc." In: *Joan of Arc: Reality and Myth*. Ed. Jan van Herwaarden. Hilversum: Verloren, 1994, pp. 19-74.

Hoenselaars, Ton. "La Jeanne d'Arc de Shakespeare et l'art du recyclage." In: *Jeanne d'Arc entre les nations*. Ed. Ton Hoenselaars and Jelle Koopmans. Amsterdam: Rodopi, 1998, pp. 17-32.

Hospes. *Jeanne d'Arc, Grand Capitaine: Sa campagne sur la Loire, la marche sur Reims et Paris*. Orléans: Libraire R. Houzé, 1909.

Hurel-Genin, Nathalie. "Le fragment de parchemin anonyme du Centre Jeanne d'Arc d'Orléans," *Bulletin d'Association des Amis du Centre Jeanne d'Arc* 15 (1991), 39-44.

Jaladon de la Barre, J.-L. *Jeanne d'Arc à Saint-Pierre-le-Moutier et deux juges nivernais à Rouen*. Nevers: Paulin Fay, 1868.

Jarry, Eugène. "Le compte du siège, la défense et l'effectif de l'armée anglaise," *Mémoires de la société archéologique et historique de Orléanais* 23 (1892), 482-97.

Jarry, Louis. *Le compte de L'armée anglaise au siège d'Orléans, 1428-1429*. Orléans: H. Herluison, 1892.

Jarry, Louis, ed. "Deux chansons normandes sur le siège d'Orleans et la mort de Salisbury," *Bulletin de la société archéologique et historique de l'Orleannais* 10 (1893), 359-70.

Jouanique, Marcel. "La chevauchée de Jeanne d'Arc dans le centre," *La revue du centre* 6 (July-Aug 1929), 121-27.

Kelly, H. Ansgar. "Joan of Arc's Last Trial: The Attack of the Devil's Advocates." In: *Fresh Verdicts on Joan of Arc*. Ed. C. Wood and B. Wheeler. New York, 1996, pp. 205-36.

Kelly, H. Ansgar. "The Right to Remain Silent: Before and After Joan of Arc," *Speculum* 68 (1993), 992-1026.

Klein-Rebour, F. "Les fausses Jeanne d'Arc," *Revue historique de l'armée* 17 (1961), 3-9.

Koopmans, Jelle. "Jeanne d'Arc, auteur de sa propre légende." In: *Jeanne d'Arc entre les nations*. Ed. Ton Hoenselaars and Jelle Koopmans. Amsterdam: Rodopi, 1998, pp. 5-16.

Krumeich, Gerd. "Controverses historiographiques autour de la maison de Jeanne d'Arc au XIXe siècle," *Bulletin d'Association des Amis du Centre Jeanne d'Arc* 10 (1986), 33-40.

Lafaye, Claude. "La merveilleuse vie de Jeanne d'Arc," *Bulletin d'Association des Amis du Centre Jeanne d'Arc* 10 (1986), 41-44.

La Martinière, J. de. "Gilles de Rays en face de Jeanne d'Arc," *Bulletin de la société archéologique et historique de l'Orléanais* 21 (1929), 200-06.

Lancesseur, Lt.-Colonel de. *Jeanne d'Arc, chef de guerre: Le génie militaire et politique de Jenne d'Arc, campagne de France, 1429-1430.* Paris: Nouvelles Éditions Debresse, 1961.

Latour, Philippe de. "Jean d'Aulon, Gérard de Saman, ou le combat gascon d'un demi-siècle triomphant," *Bulletin d'Association des Amis du Centre Jeanne d'Arc* 12 (1988), 25-37.

Lefèvre-Pontalis, Germain. "Un détail du siège de Paris par Jeanne d'Arc," *Bibliothèque de l'écoles des chartes* 46 (1885), 5-15.

Lemoine, E.L. *Jeanne d'Arc: chef de guerre.* Paris: Charles-Lavauzell and Cie., 1930.

Lemonnier-Delpy, Marie-Françoise. "Jeanne d'Arc de Joseph Delteil," *Bulletin d'Association des Amis du Centre Jeanne d'Arc* 18 (1994), 53-54; 20 (1996), 43-62.

Lightbody, Charles Wayland. *The Judgements of Joan: Joan of Arc, A Study in Cultural History.* Cambridge: Harvard University Press, 1961.

Liocourt, Ferdinand de. *La mission de Jeanne d'Arc.* 2 vols. Paris: Nouvelle Éditions Latines, 1981.

Lombarès, Michel de. "Patay, 18 juin 1429," *Revue historique de l'armée* 22 (1966), 5-16.

Lomier, Eugene. "Au temps de Jeanne d'Arc. La garde du Pont de Rouen. Document Anglais inédit," *Revue de études historiques* 96 (1930), 377-84.

Luce, Siméon. "Deux documents inédits relatifs a Frère Richard et a Jeanne d'Arc." In: *La France pendant la guerre de cent ans.* Paris, 1893, pp. 195-206.

Luce, Siméon. *Jeanne d'Arc à Domrémy: recherches critiques sur les origines de la mission de la Pucelle.* 2 vols. Paris, 1886.

Luce, Siméon. "Le trésor anglais à Paris en 1431 et le procès de Jeanne d'Arc," *Mémoires de la société de l'histoire de Paris et de l'ile de France* 5 (1878), 299-307.

Lutkas, Anne D. and Julia M. Walker. "PR pas PC: Christine de Pizan's Pro-Joan Propaganda." In: *Fresh Verdicts on Joan of Arc.* Ed. C. Wood and B. Wheeler. New York, 1996, pp. 145-60.

Maleissye, C. de. *Jeanne d'Arc à Rouen en 1913: Les procès, 1431-1456.* Lille: Desclée, De Brouwer et Cie., 1919.

Maleissye, C. de. *Les reliques de Jeanne d'Arc: Ses lettres.* Paris: Libraire Bloud et Cie., 1909.

Mantellier, P. *Histoire du siège d'Orléans.* Orléans: H. Herluison, 1867.

Margolis, Nadia. *Joan of Arc in History, Literature, and Film: A Select, Annotated Bibliography.* New York: Garland Publishing, Inc., 1990.

Margolis, Nadia. "The 'Joan Phenonmenon' and the French Right." In: *Fresh Verdicts on Joan of Arc.* Ed. C. Wood and B. Wheeler. New York, 1996, pp. 265-88.

Marin, Paul. *La génie militaire de Jeanne Darc (siège de Paris, 1429).* Paris: n.p., 1889.

Marin, Paul. *Jeanne d'Arc: tacticien et stratégiste.* 4 vols. Paris: Baudouin, 1889-90.

Marot, Pierre. *Joan of Arc's Birthplace.* Trans. Stan and Rita Morton. Colmar: SAEP, 1979.

Marot, Pierre. *Joan the Good Lorrainer at Domrémy.* Colmar: Editions SAEP, 1981.

Maussabré, F. de, et al. "La chevauchée de Jeanne d'Arc en Berry," *Revue du Berry* 38 (1909), 305-25.

McWebb, Christine. "Joan of Arc and Christine de Pizan: The Symbiosis of Two Warriors in the *Ditié de Jehanne d'Arc.*" In: *Fresh Verdicts on Joan of Arc.* Ed. C. Wood and B. Wheeler. New York, 1996, pp. 133-44.

Merkle, Gertrude H. "Martin le Franc's Commentary on Jean Gerson's Treatise on Joan of Arc." In: *Fresh Verdicts on Joan of Arc.* Ed. C. Wood and B. Wheeler. New York, 1996, pp. 177-88.

Michaud-Fréjaville, Françoise. "L'histoire de Jeanne d'Arc dans quelques rouleaux de Chronologie universelle," *Bulletin d'Association des Amis du Centre Jeanne d'Arc* 15 (1991), 35-37.

Michaud-Fréjaville, Françoise. "Une apothéose de Jeanne d'Arc," *Bulletin d'Association des Amis du Centre Jeanne d'Arc* 17 (1993), 19-26.

Michaud-Fréjaville, Françoise. "Une cité face aux crises: les remparts de la fidélité, de Louis d'Orléans a Charles VII, d'après les comptes de forteresse de la ville d'Orléans (1391-1427)." In: *Jeanne d'Arc: une époque, une rayonment.* Colloque d'histoire médiévale. Orléans–Octobre 1979. Paris, 1982, pp. 43-57.

Michaud-Fréjaville, Françoise. "'Va, va fille de Dieu'. De l'usage du 'tu' et du 'vous' dans les sources concernant Jeanne d'Arc," *Bulletin d'Association des Amis du Centre Jeanne d'Arc* 19 (1995), 25-46.

Michelet, Jules. *Joan of Arc.* Trans. A. Guérard. Ann Arbor: University of Michigan Press, 1957.

Motey, Vicomte du. *Jeanne d'Arc à Chinon et Robert de Rouvres.* Paris: Libraire Ancienne Honoré Champion, 1927.

Olivier, Rene. "La lance, l'epee et la hache (les armes de la Pucelle)," *Les amis de Jeanne d'Arc* 42.3 (1995), 14-21.

Parat, A. *Jeanne d'Arc dans les pays de l'Yonne.* Auxerre: n.p., 1911.

Pernin, C.-R. *Jeanne d'Arc à Troyes.* Paris: Annales Salésiennes, 1894.

Pernoud, Régine. "Christine de Pisan: Une poétesse témoin de son temps," *Bulletin d'Association des Amis du Centre Jeanne d'Arc* 9 (1985), 11-18.

Pernoud, Régine. "Un document nouveau sur Jeanne d'Arc," *La revue de Paris* 67 (June 1960), 101-06.

Pernoud, Régine. "Epilogue: Joan of Arc or the Survival of a People." In: *Fresh Verdicts on Joan of Arc.* Ed. C. Wood and B. Wheeler. New York, 1996, pp. 289-94.

Pernoud, Régine. *J'ai nom Jeanne la Pucelle.* Paris: Gallimard, 1994.

Pernoud, Régine. *Joan of Arc by Herself and Her Witnesses.* Trans. E. Hyams. New York: Dorset Press, 1964.

Pernoud, Régine. *La libération d'Orléans, 8 mai 1429.* Paris: Gallimard, 1969.

Pernoud, Régine. *The Retrial of Joan of Arc: The Evidence at the Trial for Her Rehabilitation.* Trans. J.M. Cohen. London: Methuen And Co., Ltd., 1955.

Pernoud, Régine. *La spiritualité de Jeanne d'Arc*. Paris: Mame, 1992.

Pernoud, Régine. "Sur les traces de Jeanne d'Arc: Archéologie de la guerre de Cent Ans," *Dossiers d'archéologie* 34 (May 1979), 6-10.

Pernoud, Régine and Marie-Véronique Clin. *Joan of Arc: Her Story*. Trans. and rev. J.D. Adams. New York: St. Martin's Press, 1998.

Peyronnet, Georges. "Dans quelle langue les Anglais parlaient-ils à Jeanne d'Arc? Naissance d'un grand conflit de nationalités," *Bulletin d'Association des Amis du Centre Jeanne d'Arc* 16 (1992), 9-28.

Peyronnet, Georges. "En écoutant la 'voix' de Jeanne d'Arc la plus modeste: sainte Marguerite d'Antioche," *Bulletin d'Association des Amis du Centre Jeanne d'Arc* 19 (1995), 47-92.

Peyronnet, Georges. "Gerson, Charles VII et Jeanne d'Arc," *Revue d'histoire écclesiastique* 84 (1989), 334-70.

Peyronnet, Georges. "Jeanne d'Arc et Charles VII: un problème à revoir," *Bulletin d'Association des Amis du Centre Jeanne d'Arc* 12 (1988), 7-23.

Pigeot, Général. "La stratégie de Jeanne d'Arc," *Bulletin de la société archéologique et historique de l'Orléanais* n.s. 1 (1959-60), 67-72.

Pillard, Albert. *Gien dans la vie de Jeanne d'Arc*. Gien: Imprimerie Jeanne-d'Arc, 1955.

Pinzino, Jane Marie. "Speaking of Angels: A Fifteenth-Century Bishop in Defense of Joan of Arc's Mystical Voices." In: *Fresh Verdicts on Joan of Arc*. Ed. C. Wood and B. Wheeler. New York, 1996, pp. 161-76.

Pons, Nicole. "La propagande de guerre française avant l'apparition de Jeanne d'Arc," *Journal des savants* (1982), 191-214.

Poulet, Dom Charles. "Jeanne d'Arc à Chinon. Les causes naturelles et surnaturelles de l'acceptation royale," *Historisch tijdschrift* 1 (1923), 13-21.

Poullain, H. *Essai sur le parcours des routes et chemins suivis par Jeanne d'Arc: Traversant les villes, communes et châteaux depuis Auxerre, Orléans et Blois avant et pendant les premières opérations militaires préparatoires du siège des Tourelles*. Orléans: Imprimerie Auguste Gout et Cie., 1908.

Prévost-Bourré, Jacques. "A propose de la captivité de Jeanne d'Arc: un documnet irréfutable et insuffisant," *Bulletin d'Association des Amis du Centre Jeanne d'Arc* 10 (1986), 9-12.

Quicherat, Jules. *Histoire du siège d' Orléans et des honneurs rendus à la Pucelle*. Paris: Libraire de L. Hachette et Cie., 1854.

Quicherat, Jules. *New Aspects of the Case History of Jeanne d'Arc*. Trans. H.G. Francq. Brandon: Brandon University Press, 1971.

Raillicourt, D. Labarre de. "Jeanne d'Arc à Lagny," *Revue historique des armées* 12.2 (1956), 9-10.

Rankin, Daniel and Claire Quintal, trans. *The First Biography of Joan of Arc with the Chronicle Record of a Contemporary Account*. Pittsburgh: University of Pittsburgh Press, 1964.

Reverseau, Jean-Pierre. "L'armement au temps de Jeanne d'Arc," *Bulletin d'Association des Amis du Centre Jeanne d'Arc* 9 (1985), 31-36.

Robert, Jean-Louis. Images et usages de Jeanne pendant la Seconde Guerre mondiale," *Bulletin d'Association des Amis du Centre Jeanne d'Arc* 20 (1996), 28-42.

Rocolle, Pierre. *Un prisonnier de guerre nommé Jeanne d'Arc*. Paris: Editions S.O.S., 1982.

Rodrigues, Nicole Meyer. "Aspects of Material Culture in the Paris Region at the Time of Joan of Arc." In: *Fresh Verdicts on Joan of Arc*. Ed. C. Wood and B. Wheeler. New York, 1996, pp. 303-14.

Rolland, Monique. *Dunois: Compagnon de Jeanne d'Arc*. Exposition organisée à l'occasion du demi-millénaire de sa mort, 1468-1968. Châteaudun, 1968.

Rucquoi, Adeline. "De Jeanne d'Arc à Isabelle la Catholique: L'image de la France en Castille au XVe siècle," *Journal des savants* (1990), 155-74.

Sackville-West, Vita. *Saint Joan of Arc*. New York: Doubleday, 1991.

Saint-Jean, Jean de (Bernard-Jean Daulon). *Jehanne, 1407-1452*. LeBaule: Impr. La Mouette, 1957.

Salmon-Legagneur, Emmanuel. "Le souvenir de Jeanne d'Arc, Bertrand du Guesclin et Arthur Richemont à travers la toponymie bretonne contemporaine," *Bulletin d'Association des Amis du Centre Jeanne d'Arc* 16 (1992), 41-58.

Sarrazin, A. *Jeanne d'Arc et la Normandie*. Rouen, 1896.

Schibanoff, Susan. "True Lies: Transvestism and Idolatry in the Trial of Joan of Arc." In: *Fresh Verdicts on Joan of Arc*. Ed. C. Wood and B. Wheeler. New York, 1996, pp. 31-60.

Schneider, Édouard. *Jeanne d'Arc et ses lys: La légende et l'histoire*. Paris: Bernard Grasset Éditeur, 1952.

Scott, W.S. *Jeanne d'Arc*. New York: Barnes and Noble Books, 1974.

Sené, Elsa. "Histoire de la maison natale de Jeanne d'Arc à Dorémy," *Bulletin d'Association des Amis du Centre Jeanne d'Arc* 20 (1996), 63-76.

Siège d'Orléans (12 Octobre 1428-8 Mai 1429), Le. Orléans: Centre Jean d'Arc, 1975.

Sorel, Alexandre. *La prise de Jeanne d'Arc devant Compiègne et l'histoire des sièges de la même ville sous Charles VI et Charles VII*. Paris: Alphonse Picard, 1889.

Sorel, Alexandre. *Séjours de Jeanne d'Arc à Compiègne: Maisons ou elle à logé en 1429 et 1430*. Paris: H. Champion, 1888.

Soyer, Jacques. *La bataille de Patay (samedi 18 juin 1429)*. Orléans: n.p., 1913.

Stouff, Louis. "Un pari entre deux Arlésiens à propos de Jeanne d'Arc," *Bulletin d'Association des Amis du Centre Jeanne d'Arc* 10 (1986), 13-18.

Sullivan, Karen. "'I Do Not Name to You the Voice of St. Michael': The Identification of Joan of Arc's Voices." In: *Fresh Verdicts on Joan of Arc*. Ed. C. Wood and B. Wheeler. New York, 1996, pp. 85-112.

Sullivan, Karen. *The Interrogation of Joan of Arc*. Minneapolis: University of Minnesota Press, 1999.

Sullivan, Karen. "'La justice magnanime des Anglais': Les biographes britanniques de Jeanne d'Arc." In: *Jeanne d'Arc entre les nations*. Ed. Ton Hoenselaars and Jelle Koopmans. Amsterdam: Rodopi, 1998, pp. 115-32.

Thérol, J. *L'épée de dieu: Sainte Jeanne d'Arc*. Paris: Les Nouvelles Editions Latines, 1960.

Thibault, Jean. "Un prince territorial au XVe siècle: Dunois, Bâtard d'Orléans," *Bulletin de la sociétés archéologique et historique de l'Orléanais* n.s. 14 (1997), 3-46.

Thomas, Antoine. "Le 'signe royal' et le secret de Jeanne d'Arc," *Revue historique* 103 (1910), 278-82.

Tisset, P. "Capture et rançon de Jeanne d'Arc," *Revue historique de droit français et étranger* 4th ser., 46 (1968), 63-69.

Tourines, Charles Gailly de. "Jeanne d'Arc à Saint-Denys de la Chapelle," *Revue des deux mondes*, 7th ser., 14 (1923), 900-20.

Trask, Willard, ed. and trans. *Joan of Arc in Her Own Words*. New York: Books and Co., 1996.

Trial of Jeanne d'Arc, The. Trans. W.P. Barrett. New York: Gotham House, 1932.

Trial of Joan of Arc, The: Being the Verbatim Report of the Proceedings from the Orleans Manuscript. London: The Folio Society, 1956.

Vale, Malcolm. "Jeanne d'Arc et ses adversaires: Jeanne, victime d'une guerre civile?" In: *Jeanne d'Arc: Une époque, un rayonnement*. Paris, 1982, pp. 203-16.

Valois, N. "Un nouveau témoignage sur Jeanne d'Arc: Réponse d'un clerc Parisien à l'apologie de la pucelle par Gerson," *Annuaire-Bulletin de la société de l'histoire de France* 43 (1906), 161-69.

Vassal, C. de. *La bataille de Patay (18 juin 1429) ou la croix-blon et la croix-Faron: Épisode de la vie de Jeanne d'Arc*. Orléans: H. Herluison, 1890.

Vergnaud-Romagnesi, M. *Document inédit sur le siège d'Orléans par les anglais en 1428 et 1429*. Paris: E. Pannier, 1857.

Vergnaud-Romagnesi, M. *Notice historique sur le fort des Tourelles de l'ancien pont de la ville d'Orléans, où Jeanne d'Arc combattit et fut blessée, sur la découverte de ses restes en juillet 1831*. Paris: Roret Libraire, 1832.

Villaret, Amicie de. *Campagnes des Anglais dans l'Orléanais, la Beauce Chartrain et le Gatinais (1421-1428): L'armée sous Warwick et Suffolk au siège de Montargis. Campagnes de Jeanne d'Arc sur la Loire postérierures au siège d'Orléans*. Orléans: H.Herluison, 1893.

Warner, Marina. "Joan of Arc: A Gender Myth." In: *Joan of Arc: Reality and Myth*. Ed. Jan van Herwaarden. Hilversum: Verloren, 1994, pp. 97-118.

Warner, Marina. *Joan of Arc: The Image of Female Heroism*. Harmondsworth: Penguin Books, 1981.

Waugh, W.T. "Joan of Arc in English Sources of the Fifteenth Century." In: *Historical Essays in Honour of James Tait*. Ed. J.G. Edwards et al. Manchester, 1933, pp. 387-98.

Weiskopf, Steven. "Readers of the Lost Arc: Secrecy, Specularity, and Speculation in the Trial of Joan of Arc." In: *Fresh Verdicts on Joan of Arc*. Ed. C. Wood and B. Wheeler. New York, 1996, pp. 113-32.

Wheeler, Bonnie. "Joan of Arc's Sword in the Stone." In: *Fresh Verdicts on Joan of Arc*. Ed. C. Wood and B. Wheeler. New York, 1996, pp. xi-XVi.

Willard, Charity Cannon. "Early Images of the Female Warrior: Minerva, the Amazons, Joan of Arc," *Minerva* 6 (1988), 1-11.

Wood, Charles T. *Joan of Arc and Richard III: Sex, Saints, and Government in the Middle Ages*. New York: Oxford University Press, 1988.

Wood, Charles T. "Joan of Arc's Mission and the Lost Record of Her Interrogation at Poitiers." In: *Fresh Verdicts on Joan of Arc*. Ed. C. Wood and B. Wheeler. New York, 1996, pp. 19-30.

Medieval – Hundred Years War – France – Louis XI

Bourassin, Emmanuel. *Louis XI: homme d'état, homme privé*. Paris: Tallandier, 1995.

Caillet, Louis. *Etude sur les relations de Louis XI et de la commune de Lyon avec Charles VII et Louis XI (1417-1483)*. Lyons, 1909.

Calmette, J. *Louis XI, Jean II et la révolution catalane*. Toulouse, 1903.

Calmette, J. and G. Périnelle. *Louis XI et l'Angleterre (1461-1483)*. Paris, 1930.

Cauchies, Jean-Marie. *Louis XI et Charles le Hardi: De Péronne à Nancy (1468-1477): le conflit*. Brussels: De Boeck-Université, 1996.

Chevalier, Bernard. "The Policy of Louis XI towards the *Bonnes Villes*: The Case of Tours." In: *The Recovery of France in the Fifteenth Century*. Ed. P.S. Lewis. Trans. G.F. Martin. New York, 1971, pp. 265-93.

Contamine, Philippe. "Louis XI, François II, duc de Bretagne, et l'ordre de Saint-Michel (1469-1470)." In: *Des pouvoirs en France, 1300-1500*. Paris, 1992, pp. 169-90.

Dufournet, Jean. "La génération de Louis XI: quelques aspects," *Moyen âge*, 5th ser., 6 (1992), 227-50.

Gaussin, P.-R. *Louis XI: Un roi entre deux mondes*. Paris, 1976.

Gresser, Pierre. *Le crépuscule du moyen-âge en Franche-Comté*. Besançon: Cêtre, 1992.

Héliot, Pierre. "Louis XI et le Boulonnais," *Bibliothèque de l'école des chartes* 100 (1939), 112-44.

Kendall, Paul Murray. *Louis XI: " . . . the Universal Spider . . . "*. London: Cardinal, 1974.

Leguai, André. "Dijon et Louis XI," *Annales de Bourgogne* 17 (1945), 16-37, 103-15, 145-69, 239-63.

Ourliac, Paul. "The Concordat of 1472: An Essay on the Relations between Louis XI and Sixtus IV." In: *The Recovery of France in the*

Fifteenth Century. Ed. P.S. Lewis. Trans. G.F. Martin. New York, 1971, pp. 102-84.

Perroy, Edouard. "L'artillerie de Louis XI dans la campagne d'Artois," *Revue du Nord* 26 (1943), 171-96, 293-315.

Perroy, Edouard. "L'artillerie royale à la bataille de Montlhery (10 juillet 1465), *Revue historique* 149 (1925), 187-89.

Petit-Dutaillis, Charles. *Charles VII, Louis XI, et la minorité de Charles VIII.* Paris, 1981.

Pouquet du Haut-Jussé, Barthélemy-Amédée. "A Political Concept of Louis XI: Subjection Instead of Vassalage." In: *The Recovery of France in the Fifteenth Century.* Ed. P.S. Lewis. Trans. G.F. Martin. New York, 1971, pp. 196-215.

Salmon, J.H.M. "The Spider King: Louis XI of France," *History Today* 16 (1966), 129-36.

Spencer, Mark. *Thomas Basin (1412-1490): The History of Charles VII and Louis XI.* Bibliotheca Humanistica et Reformatorica, 57. Nieuwkoop: De Graaf Publishers, 1997.

Medieval – Hundred Years War – Brittany

Bellier-Dumaine, C. "L'administration du duché de Bretagne sous le règne de Jean V: les institutions militaires," *Annales de Bretagne* 16 (1900-1901), 112-29.

Choffel, Jacques. *La guerre de succession de Bretagne.* Paris: Fernand Lanore, 1975.

Cintré, R. *Les marches des Bretagne au moyen âge: Économie, guerre et société en pays de frontière (XIVe-XVe siècles).* Pornichet, 1992.

Coativy, Yves. *La Bretagne ducale: La fin du moyen âge.* Paris: J.-P. Giserot, 1999.

Contamine, Philippe. "Louis XI, François II, duc de Bretagne, et l'ordre de Saint-Michel (1469-1470)." In: *Des pouvoirs en France, 1300-1500.* Paris, 1992, pp. 169-90.

Gicquel, Y. *Alain IX de Rohan (1382-1462): Un Grand Seigneur de l'âge d'or de la Bretagne*. Paris, 1986.

Grand, Roger. *Les routiers bretons pendant la guerre de cent ans*. Paris: Libraire Auguste Picard, 1926.

Jones, Michael. "L'armée Bretonne, 1449-1491: Structures et carrieres." In: *The Creation of Brittany: A Late Medieval State*. London, 1988, pp. 351-69.

Jones, Michael. "The Breton Civil War." In: *Froissart: Historian*. Ed. J.J.N. Palmer. Woodbridge, 1981, pp. 64-81.

Jones, Michael. "Breton Nobility in the Service of the State? The Case of Guillaume de Rosnyvinen." In: *Guerre et société en France, en Angleterre et en Bourgogne XIVe-XVe siècle*. Ed. P. Contamine, C. Giry-Deloison, and Maurice Keen. Lille, 1991, pp. 261-292.

Jones, Michael. "Les captaines Anglo-Bretons et les marches entre la Bretagne et le Poitou de 1342 a 1373." In: *111e Congrès national des Sociétés savantes, Poitiers, 1986, Histoire médiévale*. T. I: "La France anglaise," pp. 357-75.

Jones, Michael. "The Diplomatic Evidence for Franco-Breton Relations, c. 1370-1372," *English Historical Review* 93 (1978), 300-19.

Jones, Michael. *Ducal Brittany, 1364-1399: Relations with England and France during the Reign of Duke John IV*. Oxford: Oxford University Press, 1970.

Jones, Michael. "Edward III's Captains in Brittany." In: *England in the Fourteenth Century: Proceedings of the 1985 Harlaxton Symposium*. Ed. W.M. Ormond. Woodbridge, 1986, pp. 99-118.

Jones, Michael. "'Mon Pais et ma Nations': Breton Identity in the Fourteenth Century." In: *War, Literature and Politics in the Late Middle Ages: Essays in Honour of G.W. Coopland*. Ed. C.T. Allmand. Liverpool: University of Liverpool Press, 1975, pp. 144-68.

Jones, Michael. "Nantes au debut de la guerre civile en Bretagne." In: *Villes, bonnes villes, cités et capitales: Mélanges offerts à Bernard Chevalier*. Tours, 1989, pp. 105-20.

Jones, Michael. "Sir John de Hardreshull, King's Lieutenant in Brittany, 1343-5," *Nottingham Medieval Studies* 31 (1987), 76-97.

Kerhervé, J. *L'état breton aux 14e et 15e siècles: Les ducs, l'argent et les hommes*. 2 vols. Paris. 1987.

Knowlson, G.A. *Jean V, duc de Bretagne, et l'Angleterre*. Cambridge, 1964.

Lewis, Peter S. "Of Breton *Alliances* and Other Matters." In: *War, Literature and Politics in the Late Middle Ages: Essays in Honour of G.W. Coopland*. Ed. C.T. Allmand. Liverpool: University of Liverpool Press, 1975, pp. 122-43.

Mollat, G. "Les désastres de la guerre de cent ans en Bretagne," *Annales de Bretagne* 26 (1910-11), 168-201.

Peyronnet, Georges. "Les rélations entre la Bretagne et l'Angleterre sous les ducs de la maison de Montfort d'apres les sources diplomatiques anglaises: État des travaux et directions de recherche." In: *1491: La Bretagne, terre d'Europe*. Ed. J. Kerhervé and T. Daniel. Brest, 1992, pp. 243-49.

Philippe, Dominique. "Guerre et images de guerre dans la chronique bretonne au XIVe siècle," *Annales de Bretagne et des Pays de l'Ouest* 105 (1998), 35-51.

Plaine, F. *Jeanne de Penthièvre, duchesse de Bretagne*. Saint-Brieuc, 1873.

Pocquet du Haut-Jussé, B. "La dernière phase de la vie de Du Guesclin, l'affaire de Bretagne," *Bibliothèque de l'école des chartes* 125 (1967), 142-89.

Pocquet du Haut-Jussé, B. *Philippe le Hardi, régent de Bretagne (1402-1404): Discours de reception à l'Académie de Dijon prononcé dans la seance du 20 décembre 1933*. Dijon, 1933.

Reynaud, M.-R. "Maison d'Anjou et maison(s) de Bretagne (vers 1360-vers 1434)." In: *1491: La Bretagne, terre d'Europe*. Ed. J. Kerhervé and T. Daniel. Brest, 1992, pp. 177-91.

Medieval – Hundred Years War – Burgundy [See also Hundred Years War – Low Countries]

Allan, William. "The Valois Dukes of Burgundy, 1363-1477," *Connoisseur* (Mar 1977), 151-53.

Armstrong, C.A.J. "Les ducs de Bourgogne, interprètes de la pensée politique du 15e siècle," *Annales de Bourgogne* 67 (1995), 5-34.

Arnade, Peter. *Realms of Ritual: Burgundian Ceremony and Civic Life in Late Medieval Ghent*. Ithaca: Cornell University Press, 1996.

Bachrach, David S. "A Military Revolution Reconsidered: The Case of the Burgundian State Under the Valois Dukes," *Essays in Medieval Studies* 15 (1999), 9-17.

Ballard, Mark. "An Expedition of English Archers to Liège in 1467, and the Anglo-Burgundian Marriage Alliance," *Nottingham Medieval Studies* 34 (1990), 152-74.

Ballard, Mark. "'Du sang de Lancestre, je suis extrait . . .': Did Charles the Bold Remain a Loyal Lancastrian?" In: *L'Angleterre et les pays Bourguignons: Relations et comparaisons (XVe-XVIe siècles)*. Neuchâtel: Centre européen d'études Bourguignons (XIVe-XVIe siècles), 1995, pp. 83-90.

Beaulieu, M. and J. Baylé. *Le costume en Bourgogne de Philippe le Hardi à la mort de Charles le Téméraire (1364-1477)*. Paris, 1956.

Bell, Graham. "Charles the Bold and the Killers of Switzerland: The End of Chivalry," *Battlefield* 4 (1998), 3-9.

Bertrand, Anne. "Un seigneur bourguignon en Europe de l'Est: Guillbert de Lannoy (1386-1462)," *Moyen âge* 95 (1989), 293-309.

Bischoff, G. "Institutions judiciaires et centralisation en Haute-Alsace pendant la domination Bourguignonne (1469-1474)," *Publication du Centre européen d'études bourguignonnes (XIVe-XVe siècles)* 30 (1990).

Bömmels, Nicolaus. "Die neusser unter dem Druck der Belagerung." In: *Neuss, Burgund und das Reich*. Neuss: Gesellschaft für Buchdruckerei AG, 1975, pp. 255-88.

Bonenfant, Paul and J. Stengens. "Le role de Charles le Téméraire dans le gouvernement de l'état bourguignonnes en 1465-67," *Annales de Bourgogne* 25 (1953), 7-29, 118-33.

Borchgrave, Christian de. *Diplomaten en diplomatie onder hertog Jan zonder vrees: Impact op de vlaamse politieke situatie.* Kortrijk-Heule: UGA, 1992.

Bossuat, André. "La littérature de propagande au XVe siècle: La Mémoire de Jean de Rinel, secrétaire du roi d'Angleterre, contre le duc de Bourgogne (1435)," *Cahiers d'histoire* 1 (1956), 131-46.

Bourassin, Emmanuel. *Philippe le Bon.* Paris: Tallandier, 1999.

Bousmar, Eric. "La place des hommes et des femmes dans les fêtes de cour Bourguignonnes (Philippe le Bon–Charles le Hardi)." In: *A la cour de Bourgogne le duc, son entourage, son train.* Ed. Jean-Marie Cauchies. Turnhout: Brepols, 1998, pp. 11-32.

Braeckeler, Katharina. "Burgund im Spiegel seiner Kultur." In: *Neuss, Burgund und das Reich.* Neuss: Gesellschaft für Buchdruckerei AG, 1975, pp. 289-322.

Brusten, Charles. *L'armée Bourguignonne de 1465 à 1468.* Brussels: Éditions Fr. Van Muysewinkel, 1954.

Brusten, Charles. "L'armée Bourguignonne de 1465 à 1477," *Revue internationale d'histoire militaire* (1959), 452-66.

Brusten, Charles. "La bataille de Morat," *Publications du centre européen d'études burgundo-médianes* 10 (1968), 79-84.

Brusten, Charles. "Les campagnes Liègeoises de Charles de Téméraire." In: *Liège et Bourgogne. Actes de colloque tenu à Liège les 28, 29 et 30 Octobre, 1968.* Liège, 1972, pp. 81-99.

Brusten, Charles. "Charles le Téméraire et la camp de Lausanne, mars-mai 1476," *Publications du centre européen d'études burgundo-médianes* 14 (1972), 71-81.

Brusten, Charles. "Charles le Téméraire et la campagne de Neuss, 1474-75," *Publications du centre européen d'études burgundo-médianes* 13 (1971), 67-73.

Brusten, Charles. "Les compaignies d'ordonnance dans l'armée Bourguignonne," *Revue internationale d'histoire militaire* 40 (1978), 112-69; in: *Grandson 1476: Essai d'approche d'une action militaire du XVe siècle*. Ed. D. Reichel. Lausanne, 1976, pp. 112-69.

Brusten, Charles. "Les emblèmes de l'armée Bourguignonne de Charles le Téméraire: Essai de classification," *Jahrbuch des bernischen historisches Museum in Bern* 37-38 (1957-58), 118-32.

Brusten, Charles. "La fin des compaignies d'ordonnance de Charles le Téméraire." In: *Cinq-centième anniversaire de la bataille de Nancy (1477): Actes du Colloque organisé par l'institut de recherche régionale en sciences sociales, humaines et économiques de l'Université de Nancy II (Nancy, 22-24 septembre 1977)*. Nancy, 1979, pp. 363-75.

Brusten, Charles. "Les itineraires de l'armée Bourguignonne de 1465 à 1478," *Publications du centre europeen d'études burgundo-medianes* 2 (1960), 55-67.

Brusten, Charles. "A propos des campagnes bourguignonnes, 1475-78," *Publications du centre européen d'études burgundo-médianes* 9 (1967), 79-87.

Brusten, Charles. "Le ravitalillement en vivres dans l'armée Bourguignonne, 1450-1477," *Publications du centre européen d'études burgundo-médianes* 3 (1961), 42-49.

Burgunderbeute und Werke Burgundischer Hofkunst, Die. Bern: Bernisches Historisches Museum, 1969.

Cartellieri, Otto. *The Court of Burgundy: Studies in the History of Civilization*. 1925; rpt. New York: Haskell House Publishers Ltd., 1970.

Cauchies, Jean-Marie. "Baudoin de Bourgogne (v. 1446-1508), bâtard, militaire et diplomatie. Une carrière exemplaire?" *Revue du nord* 77 (1995), 257-81.

Cauchies, Jean-Marie. "Charles le Hardi à Neuss (1474/75): Folie militaire ou contrainte politique," *Publication du centre européen d'études bourguignonnes (XIVe-XVIe siècles)* 36 (1996), 105-15.

Cauchies, Jean-Marie. "La désertion dans les armées bourguignonnes de 1465 à 1476," *Revue Belge d'histoire militaire* 22 (1977-78), 132-48.

Cauchies, Jean-Marie. *Louis XI et Charles le Hardi: De Péronne à Nancy (1468-1477): le conflit.* Brussels: De Boeck-Université, 1996.

Cherrier, Noëlle. "Les chevaux de Philippe le Hardi (1371-1404)," *Annales de Bourgogne* 67 (1995), 107-48.

Chevanne, J. Robert de. *Les guerres en Bourgogne de 1470 à 1475.* Paris, 1934.

Contamine, Philippe. "La Bourgogne du XVe siècle." In: *Des pouvoirs en France, 1300-1500.* Paris, 1992, pp. 61-74.

Contamine, Philippe. "Charles le Téméraire fossoyeur et/ou fondateur de l'État bourguignon?" In: *Des pouvoirs en France, 1300-1500.* Paris, 1992, pp. 87-98.

Contamine, Philippe. "Charles le Téméraire vu par un adversaire de Louis XI, Thomas Basin." In: *Des pouvoirs en France, 1300-1500.* Paris, 1992, pp. 75-85.

David, Henri. "Charles 'le travaillant' quatrième et dernier duc Valois du Bourgogne," *Annales de Bourgogne* 39 (1967), 5-43, 65-85.

Delaville le Roulx, J. "La domination bourguignonne à Tours et le siège de cette ville (1417-1418)," *Le cabinet historique* 23 (1877), 161-231.

Deruelle, Nathalie. "Ouvrages et réparations ordonnés par le duc de Bourgogne dans ses résidences à Arras entre 1401-1417. In: *Arras au moyen âge: histoire et littérature.* Ed. M.-M. Casttellani and J.-P. Martin. Arras, 1994, pp. 53-68.

Deuchler, Florens. *Die Burgundebeute: Inventar der Beutestucke aus den Schlachten von Grandson, Murten und Nancy 1476/77.* Bern: Verlag Stämpfli & Cie, 1963.

Devaux, Jean. "Le rôle politique de Marie de Bourgogne au lendemain de Nancy: vérité ou légende?" *Moyen âge*, 5th ser., 5 (1995), 389-405.

Deviosse, Jean. *Jean le bon.* Paris: Fayard, 1985.

Finot, Jules. *Projet d'expédition contre les turcs préparé par les conseillers du duc de Bourgogne Philippe-le-Bon (janvier 1457)*. Lille: L. Quarré, 1890.

Fons-Melicocq, A. de la. "Les chasses de Philippe-le-Bon, duc de Bourgogne, en Picardie (1419-1467)," *La Picardie* 3 (1857), 439-49.

Fredericq, Paul. *Essai sur le rôle politique et social des ducs de Bourgogne dans les Pays-Bas*. Ghent, 1875.

Garnier, Pierre-Louis. "Les services de la Trésorerie des guerres de la Recette de l'artillerie de Charles le Téméraire," *Revue du nord* 79 (1997), 969-91.

Gilliam, Helmut. Der Neusser Friedensverhandlungen von 1475 und ihre Bedeutung für die Entstehung des Habsburgischen Weltreiches," *Neusser Jahrbuch für Kunst, Kulturgeschichte und Heimatkunde* (1970).

Gilliam, Helmut. "Der neusser Krieg: Wendepunt der europäischen Geschichte." In: *Neuss, Burgund und das Reich*. Neuss: Gesellschaft für Buchdruckerei AG, 1975, pp. 201-54.

Gollut, Loys. *Les mémoires historiques de la république séquanoise et des princes de la Franche-Comté de Bourgougne*. 2nd ed. Arbois, 1846.

Gresser, Pierre. *Le crépuscule du moyen-âge en Franche-Comté*. Besançon: Cêtre, 1992.

Grosjean, Georges. "Die Murtenschlacht: Analyse eines Ereignisses." In: *Actes du Ve centenaire de la bataille de Morat*. Fribourg and Berne, 1976, pp. 35-90.

Grüneisen, H. "Die westlichen Reichsstände in der Auseinandersetzung zwischen dem Reich, Burgund und Frankreich bis 1473," *Rheinische Vierteljahrsblätter* 26 (1961).

Guenée, Bernard. "Les campagnes de lettres qui ont suivi le meurtre de Jean sans Peur, duc de Bourgogne (septembre 1419-février 1420)," *Annuaire-bulletin de la société de l'histoire de France* (1993), 45-64.

Guillaume, M. *Histoire de l'organisation militaire sous les ducs de Bourgogne*. Academie royale de Belgique mémoires couronnes et mémoires des savantes étrangers, 12, n. 8. Brussels, 1848.

Gunn, Steven. "Henry VII and Charles the Bold," *History Today* 46 (Apr 1996), 26-33.

Gunn, Steven. "State Development in England and the Burgundian Dominions, c.1460-c.1560." In: *L'Angleterre et les pays Bourguignons: Relations et comparaisons (XVe-XVIe siècles)*. Neuchâtel: Centre européen d'études Bourguignons (XIVe-XVIe siècles), 1995, pp. 133-49.

Heer, Eugène. "Armes et armures au temps des guerres de Bourgogne." In: *Grandson 1476*. Centre d'histoire et de prospectives militaires, serie recherches de sciences comparées, II. Lausanne, 1976.

Heer, Eugène. "Das Museum der Burgunderkrieg," *Bulletin du Association Suisse pour l'étude des armes et armures* 2 (Nov 1971).

Heimpel, H. Karl der Kühne und Deutschland (mit besonderer Rücksicht auf die Trierer Verhandlungen im Herbst des Jahres 1473," *Elsass-lothringisches Jahrbuch* 21 (1943).

Humbert, Françoise. *Les finances municipales de Dijon du milieu du XIVe siècle à 1477*. Paris. 1961.

Jansma, T.S. "Philippe le bon et la guerre Hollando-Wende (1438-1441)," *Revue du nord* 42 (1960), 5-18.

Kanao, T. "Les messagers du duc de Bourgogne au début du 15e siècle," *Journal of Medieval History* 21 (1995), 195-226.

Kanao, T. "L'organisation et l'enregistrement des messageries du duc de Bourgogne dans les années," *Revue du nord* 76 (1994), 275-98.

Kurz, Hans-Rudolf. "Grandson–2 Mars 1476–le déroulement de la bataille." In: *Grandson 1476*. Centre d'histoire et de prospectives militaires. Serie recherches de sciences comparées, T. II. Lausanne, 1976.

Lachauvelaye, J. "Les armées des trois premiers ducs de Bourgogne," *Mémoires de l'académie des sciences, arts et belles-lettres de Dijon* ser. 3. 6 (1880), 19-335.

Lachauvelaye, J. "Mémoire sur la composition des armées de Charles le Téméraire dans les deux Bourgognes d'après les documents originaux,"

Mémoires de l'academie des sciences, arts et belles-lettres de Dijon 3rd ser., 6 (1880), 139-369.

Lafortune-Martel, Agathe. *Fête noble en Bourgogne au XVe siècle. Le banquet du Faisan (1454): Aspects politiques, sociaux et culturels*. Montreal, 1984.

Lallemand, Alexis. *La lutte des états de Liège contre la maison de Bourgogne, 1390-1492*. Brussels, 1910.

Lange, Joseph. "Pulchra Nussia: Die Belagerung der Stadt Neuss, 1474/75." In: *Neuss, Burgund und das Reich*. Neuss: Gesellschaft für Buchdruckerei AG, 1975, pp. 9-190.

Le Brusque, Georges. "Des chevaliers bouguignons dans les pays du Levant: L'expéditions de Walleran de Wavrin contre les Turcs ottomans (1444-1446) dans les *Anchiennes Cronicques d'Engleterre* de Jean de Wavrin," *Moyen age* 106 (2000), 255-75.

Lecuppre-Desjardin, Elodie. "Le lumières de la ville: recherche sur l'utilisation de la lumière dans les cérémonies bourguignonnes (XIVe-XVe siècles)," *Revue historique* 301 (1999), 23-43.

Léderrey, Ernest. "Les armées de Charles le Téméraire durant les guerres de Bourgogne," *Revue militaire suisse* 107 (1962), 368-82.

Leguai, André. "La conquete de la Bourgogne par Louis XI," *Annales de Bourgogne* 49 (1977), 7-12.

Leguai, André. "Dijon et Louis XI," *Annales de Bourgogne* 17 (1945), 16-37, 103-15, 145-69, 239-63.

Leguai, André. "Un Dijonnais célèbre: Philippe le Bon, duc de Bourgogne," *Bulletin de liaison* 12.1 (1995), 16-20; 12.2. (1995), 12-18.

Leguai, André. "La 'France Bourguignonne' dans le conflit entre la 'France Française' et la 'France Anglaise' (1420-1435)." In: *111e Congrès national des Sociétés savantes, Poitiers, 1986, Histoire médiévale*. T. I: "La France anglaise," pp. 41-52.

Lemaire, Jacques. "Deux poemes bourguignons sur la prise d'Arras en 1492. Un edit de Molinet?" *Revue du Nord* 60 (1978), 57-64.

Loschelder, Josef. "Karls des Kühnen Bild in der Dichtung." In: *Neuss, Burgund und das Reich.* Neuss: Gesellschaft für Buchdruckerei AG, 1975, pp. 337-70.

Marignac, Lucie. "Philippe le Bon et l'ordre de la toison d'or les enjeux d'une référence mythique," *Razo* 12 (1992), 87-112.

Michael, Nicholas. *Armies of Medieval Burgundy, 1364-1477.* Men-at-Arms Series. London: Osprey Publishing, 1983.

Myers, A.R. "The Outbreak of War between England and Burgundy in February 1471," *Bulletin of the Institute of Historical Research* 33 (1960), 114-15.

Nordberg, Michael. *Les ducs et la royauté: Études sur la rivalité des ducs d'Orléans et de Bourgogne, 1392-1407.* Upsal, 1964.

Owen, Leonard V.D. *The Connection Between England and Burgundy During the First Half of the Fifteenth Century.* The Stanhope Essay, 1909. Oxford: B. H. Blackwell, 1909.

Paravicini, Werner. "Der Briefwechsel Karls des Kühnen: Ein Editionsprojekt," *Journal of Medieval History* 11 (1985), 347-64.

Paravicini, Werner. "Die Hofordnungen Herzog Philipps des Guten von Burgund," *Francia* 15 (1987), 183-231.

Paravicini, Werner. *Karl der Kühne: Das Ende des Hauses Burgund.* Göttingen, 1976.

Paravicini, Werner. "Moers, Croy, Burgund: "Eine Studie über den Niedergang des Hauses Moers in der zweiten Hälfte des 15. Jahrhunderts," *Annalen des Historischen Vereins für den Niederrhein* 179 (1978).

Paravicini, Werner. "Structure et fonctionnement de la cour Bourguignonne au XVe siècle." In: *A la cour de Bourgogne le duc, son entourage, son train.* Ed. Jean-Marie Cauchies. Turnhout: Brepols, 1998, pp. 1-32.

Paviot, Jacques. "Jacques de Brégilles, garde-joyaux des ducs de Bourgogne Philippe le Bon et Charles le Téméraire," *Revue du nord* 77 (1995), 313-20.

Paviot, Jacques. "Les navires du duc de Bourgogne Philippe le Bon (vers 1440-1465)." In: *Atti del V convegno internazionale di studi Colombiani: "Navi e navigazione dei secoli XV e XVI.* Genoa, 1990, I:167-95.

Paviot, Jacques. *La politique navale des ducs de Bourgogne, 1384-1482.* Lille: Presses Universitaires de Lille, 1995.

Petit, E. *Itinéraires de Philippe le Hardi et de Jean sans Peur, ducs de Bourgogne (1363-1419), d'après les comptes de depenses de leur hôtel.* Paris, 1888.

Petri, F. "Nordwestdeutschland in der Politik der Burgunderherzöge," *Westfälische Forschungen* 7 (1953-54), 87-92.

Pocquet du Haut-Jussé, B. "Les séjours de Philippe le Hardi, duc de Bourgogne, en Bretagne (1372, 1393, et 1402)," *Mémoires de la société de l'histoire et d'archéologie de Bretagne* 16 (1935).

Prietzel, Malte. "Guillaume Fillastre D.J.: Über Herzog Philipp den Guten von Burgund," *Francia* 24/1 (1997), 83-121.

Quarré, P. "Le roi René prisonnier du duc de Bourgogne à Dijon et son oeuvre de peintre," *Revue du Louvre et des musées de France* (1964), 67-74.

Rapp, F. "Strasbourg et Charles le Hardi: L'ampleur et le prix de l'effort militaire." In: *Cinq-centième anniversaire de la bataille de Nancy (1477): Actes du Colloque organisé par l'institut de recherche régionale en sciences sociales, humaines et économiques de l'Université de Nancy II (Nancy, 22-24 septembre 1977).* Nancy, 1979, pp. 395-414.

Rauzier, Jean. "Les approvisionnements de la cour de Philippe le Hardi, duc de Bourgogne (1371-1384)," *Annales de Bourgogne* 70 (1998), 5-29.

Reichel, Daniel. "Essai d'approche pluridisciplinaire d'une action militaire du XVe siècle." In: *Grandson 1476: Essai d'approche d'une action militaire du XVe siècle.* Ed. D. Reichel. Lausanne, 1976, pp. 214-39.

Reynes-Meyer, Marie-Josèphe. "Dijon sous Charles VIII," *Annales de Bourgogne* 50 (1978), 85-102.

Richard, Jean. "Royal 'Enclaves' and Provincial Boundaries: The Burgundian *Élections.*" In: *The Recovery of France in the Fifteenth Century.* Ed. P.S. Lewis. Trans. G.F. Martin. New York, 1971, pp. 216-41.

Robins, Patricia. "Le mariage de Marguerite d'York et de Charles le Téméraire en 1468," *Handelingen van de koninklijke kring voor oudheidkunde, letteren en kunst van Mechelen* 95 (1991), 75-96.

Roger, Jean-Marc. "Guy le Bouteillier." In: *La guerre et la paix: Frontières et violences au moyen âge.* Actes du 101e congrès national des sociétés savantes, Lille, 1976. Paris: Bibliothèque Nationale, 1978, pp. 271-329.

Roulet, Louis-Edouard. "L'obstacle de la montagne dans les guerres de Bourgogne," *Revue internationale d'histoire militaire* 65 (1988), 91-104.

Roulet, Louis-Edouard. "Présence et engagement des combattants Anglais à Grandson et à Morat." In: *L'Angleterre et les pays Bourguignons: Relations et comparaisons (Xve-XVIe siècles.* Neuchâtel: Centre européen d'études Bourguignons (XIVe-XVIe siècles), 1995, pp. 107-22.

Roulet, Louis-Edouard. "Le Téméraire à Morat: plaidoyer pour une réhabilitation." *Publication du centre Européen d'études Bourguignonnes (XIVe-XVIe s.)* 26 (1986), 39-56.

Schandel, Pascal. "De l'ombre à la lumière: Germain Picavet, bourgeois de Lille, clerc de la gouvernance, scribe occasionnel de Philippe le Bon (1454)," *Revue du nord* 80 (1998), 65-89.

Scherff, Bruno. "Die Ordonnanz Karls des Kühnen von Burgund aus dem Jahre 1473," *Militärgeschichtliche Mitteilungen* 57 (1998), 319-31.

Schiller, David Th. "Auf Hauen und Stechen: im dramatischen 15. Jahrhundert öffnete sich das Tor zur Neuzeit: Mit dem Abstieg der Ritter entstand das moderne Militärwesen," *Visier* (Sept 1995), 148-59.

Schmidt-Sinns, D. *Studien zum Heerwesen der Herzöge von Burgund, 1465-1477.* Unpublished thesis. Gottingen: University of Gottingen, 1966.

Schneebeli, Max. "Das Heer Karls des Kühnen," *Allgemeine schweizerische militarzeitschrift* 126 (1960), 125-35.

Schnerb, Bertrand. *Bulgnéville (1431): L'état bouguignon prend pied en Lorraine.* Paris: Economica, 1993.

Schnerb, Bertrand. "La bataille rangée dans la tactique des armées Bourguignonnes au début du 15e siècle: essai de synthèse," *Annales de Bourgogne* 61 (1989), 5-32.

Schnerb, Bertrand. *L'état Bourguignon, 1363-1477*. Paris: Libraire Académique Perrin, 1999.

Schnerb, Bertrand."Une ordonnance militaire inédite de Charles le Téméraire (26 mars 1473)," *Revue Belge d'histoire militaire* 29 (1991-92), 1-14.

Schnerb, Bertrand. "La préparation des opérations militaires au début du XVe siècle: L'exemple d'un document prévisionnel Bourguignon." In: *Guerre et société en France, en Angleterre et en Bourgogne XIVe-XVe siècle*. Ed. P. Contamine et al. Lille, 1991, pp. 189-96.

Signori, Gabriela. "Ritual und Ereignis: Die Straßburger Bittgänge zur Zeit der Burgunderkriege (1474-1477)," *Historische Zeitschrift* 264 (1997), 281-328.

Small, Graeme. "Some Aspects of Burgundian Attitudes towards the English during the Reign of Philip the Good: Georges Chastelain and His Circle." In: *L'Angleterre et les pays Bourguignons: Relations et comparaisons (XVe-XVIe siècles*. Neuchâtel: Centre européen d'études Bourguignons (XIVe-XVIe siècles), 1995, pp. 15-26.

Sommé, Monique. "L'armée Bourguignonne au siège de Calais de 1436." In: *Guerre et société en France, en Angleterre et en Bourgogne XIVe-XVe siècle*. Ed. P. Contamine et al. Lille, 1991, pp. 197-219.

Sommé, Monique. *Isabelle de Portugal, duchesse de Bourgogne: Une femme au pouvoir au XVe siècle*. Lille: Presses Universitaires du Septentrion, 1998.

Tauch, Max. "Karl der Kühne: Darstellung und Beurteilung in der bildenden Kunst." In: *Neuss, Burgund und das Reich*. Neuss: Gesellschaft für Buchdruckerei AG, 1975, pp. 323-36.

Thielmans, Marie-Rose. *Bourgogne et Angleterre: relations politiques et économiques entre les Pays-Bas Bourguignonnes et l'Angleterre, 1435-1467*. Brussels, 1966.

Treue, Wilhelm. "Umbruch und Übergang." In: *Neuss, Burgund und das Reich*. Neuss: Gesellschaft für Buchdruckerei AG, 1975, pp. 191-200.

Turnbull, Stephen. "Death of a Duke," *Military Illustrated* 144 (May 2000), 24-31.

Vale, Malcolm G.A. "A Burgundian Funeral Ceremony: Olivier de la Marche and the Obsequies of Adolf of Cleves, Lord of Ravenstein," *English Historical Review* 111 (1996), 920-38.

Vale, Malcolm G.A. "England and the Burgundian Dominions: Some Cultural Influences and Comparisons." In: *L'Angleterre et les pays Bourguignons: Relations et comparaisons (XVe-XVIe siècles)*. Neuchâtel: Centre européen d'études Bourguignons (XIVe-XVIe siècles), 1995, pp. 7-13.

Vallière, P.E. de. *Morat: Le siège et la bataille, 1476*. Lausanne: Éditions Spes, 1926.

Vander Linden, H. *Itinéraires de Charles, duc de Bourgogne, Marguerite d'York et Marie de Bourgogne (1467-1477)*. Brussels, 1936.

Vaughan, Richard. "500 Years after the Great Battles," *Bijdragen en mededelingen betreffende de geschiedenis der Nederlanden* 95 (1980), 377-90.

Vaughan, Richard. *Charles the Bold: The Last Valois Duke of Burgundy*. London: Longmans, 1973.

Vaughan, Richard. *John the Fearless: The Growth of Burgundian Power*. London: Longmans, 1966.

Vaughan, Richard. *Philip the Bold: The Formation of the Burgundian State*. London: Longmans, 1962.

Vaughan, Richard. *Philip the Good: The Apogee of Burgundy*. London: Longmans, 1970.

Vaughan, Richard. *Valois Burgundy*. London: Allen Lane, 1975.

Verbruggen, J.F., ed. "Un plan de bataille du duc de Bourgogne (14 september 1417) et la tactique de l'époque," *Revue internationale d'histoire militaire* 20 (1959), 443-51.

Walsh, R.J. "Charles the Bold and the Crusade: Politics and Propaganda," *Journal of Medieval History* 3 (1977).

Weightman, Christine. *Margaret of York: Duchess of Burgundy, 1446-1503*. New York: St. Martin's Press, 1989.

Willard, Charity Cannon. "The Concept of True Nobility at the Burgundian Court," *Studies in the Renaissance* 14 (1967), 33-48.

Wille, Erich. *Die Schlacht von Othée, 23 septembre 1408*. Berlin, 1908.

Wirtgen, Rolf. "In Grandson das Gut . . .: Burgunderbeute und Waffensammlungen auf Schloß Grandson," *Deutsches Waffen Journal* 33 (1997), 752-57.

Medieval – Hundred Years War – Gascony and Guyenne

Bémont, Charles. *La Guyenne pendant la domination Anglaise, 1152-1453*. London, 1920.

Boutruche, Robert. "Anglais et Gascons en Aquitaine du XIIe au XVe siècle: Problèmes d'histoire sociale." In: *Mélanges d'histoire du moyen âge dédiés à la mémoire de Louis Halphen*. Paris: Presses universitaires de France, 1951, pp. 55-60.

Boutruche, Robert. *La crise d'une société: Seigneurs et paysans du Bordelais pendat la guerre de cent ans*. Paris, 1947.

Capra, Pierre. "Les bases sociales du pouvoir anglo-gascon au milieu du XIVe siècle," *Moyen âge*, 4th ser., 30 (1975), 273-99, 447-73.

Carus-Wilson, E.M. "The Effects of the Acquisition and Loss of Gascony on the English Wine Trade," *Bulletin of the Institute for Historical Research* 21 (1947), 145-54.

Chaplais, Pierre. "The Court of Sovereignity of Guyenne (Edward III-Henry VI) and its Antecedents." In: *Documenting the Past: Essays in Medieval History Presented to George Peddy Cuttino*. Ed. J.S. Hamilton and P.J. Bradley. Woodbridge, 1989, pp. 137-53.

Chaplais, Pierre. "Le duché-pairie de Guyenne: l'hommage et les services féodaux de 1303 à 1377," *Annales du midi* 70 (1958), 135-60.

Chaplais, Pierre. "English Arguments concerning the Feudal Status of Aquitaine in the 14th Century," *Bulletin of the Institute for Historical Research* 21 (1946-48), 203-13.

Drouyn, L. *Le Guienne militaire*. 2 vols. Bordeaux, 1865.

Harris, Robin. *Valois Guyenne: A Study of Government and Society in Late Medieval France*. The Royal Historical Society. Woodbridge: The Boydell Press, 1994.

Hubrecht, Georges. "Jurisdictions and Competences in Guyenne after its Recovery by France." In: *The Recovery of France in the Fifteenth Century*. Ed. P.S. Lewis. Trans. G.F. Martin. New York, 1971, pp. 82-101.

Labarge, Margaret Wade. *Gascony: England's First Colony, 1204-1453*. London, 1980.

Lodge, Eleanor C. *Gascony Under English Rule*. London: Methuen and Co. Ltd., 1926.

Morel, Henri. "Une association de seigneurs Gascons au XIVe siècle." In: *Mélanges d'histoire du moyen âge dédiés à la mémoire de Louis Halphen*. Paris: Presses universitaires de France, 1951, pp. 525-34.

Morgan, Philip J. "Cheshire and the Defence of the Principality of Aquitaine," *Transactions of the Historic Society of Lancashire and Cheshire* 128 (1978), 139-60.

Renouard, Yves. *Bordeaux sous les rois d'Angleterre*. Histoire de la Bordeaux, 3. Bourdeaux, 1965.

Renouard, Yves. "Les conséquences de la conquête de la Guienne par le roi de France pour les commerce des vins de Gascogne," *Annales du midi* n.s. 61 (1948), 14-31.

Ribadieu, Henry. *Histoire de la conquète de la Guyenne par les Français de ses antécédents et de ses suites*. Bordeaux: Paul Chaumas, 1866.

Vale, M.G.A. *English Gascony, 1399-1453: A Study of War, Government and Politics During the Later Stages of the Hundred Years' War*. Oxford: Oxford University Press, 1970.

Vale, M.G.A. "The Last Years of English Gascony, 1451-1453." *Transactions of the Royal Historical Society* 5th Series. 19 (1969), 119-38.

Vale, M.G.A. "The War in Aquitaine." In: *Arms, Armies and Fortifications in the Hundred Years War*. Ed. A. Curry and M. Hughes. Woodbridge, 1994, pp. 69-82.

Medieval – Hundred Years War – Low Countries [See also Hundred Years War – Burgundy]

Arnade, Peter. "Crowds, Banners, and the Marketplace: Symbols of Defiance and Defeat during the Ghent War of 1452-1453," *Journal of Medieval and Renaissance Studies* 24 (1994), 471-97.

Balfour-Melville, E.W.M. "Two John Crabbs," *Scottish Historical Review* 39 (1960), 31-34.

Ballard, Mark. "An Expedition of English Archers to Liège in 1467, and the Anglo-Burgundian Marriage Alliance," *Nottingham Medieval Studies* 34 (1990), 152-74.

Blockmans, F. "De erfstrijd tussen Vlaanderen en Brabant in 1356," *Bijdragen en mededelingen betreffende de geschiedenis van Nederland* 69 (1953), 11-16.

Blockmans, Wim. "La position de la Flandre dans le royaume à la fin du XVe siècle." In: *La France de la fin du XVe siècle: Renouveau et apogée*. Ed. Bernard Chevalier and Philippe Contamine. Paris, 1985, pp. 71-89.

Blockmans, Wim. *The Promised Lands: The Low Countries Under Burgundian Rule, 1369-1530*. Ed. Edward Peters. Trans. Elizabeth Fackelman. Philadelphia: University of Pennsylvania Press, 1999.

Blockmans, Wim and Walter Prevenier. *In de ban van Bourgondië*. The Hague: Fibula, 1988.

Boone, Marc. "Destroying and Reconstructing the City: The Inculcation and Arrogation of Princely Power in the Burgundian-Habsburg Netherlands (14th-16th Centuries)." In: *The Propagation of Power in the Medieval West: Selected Proceedings of the International Conference, Groningen, 20-23 November 1996*. Ed. M. Gosman, A. Vanderjagt, and J. Veenstra. Groningen, 1997, pp. 1-33.

Boone, Marc. "Diplomatie et violence d'État. La sentence rendue par les ambassadeurs et conseillers du roi de France, Charles VII, concernant le conflit entre Philippe le Bon, duc de Bourgogne, et Gand en 1452," *Bulletin de la commission royale d'histoire* 156 (1990), 1-54.

Boone, Marc. *Gent en de Bourgondische hertogen, 1385-1453: Een sociaal-politieke studie van een staatsvormingproces.* Brussels, 1990.

Boone, Marc. "Particularisme gantois, centralisme bourguignon et diplomatie française. Documents inédits autour d'un conflit entre Philippe le Hardi, duc de Bourgogne, et Gand en 1401," *Bulletin de la commission royale d'histoire* 152 (1986), 49-113.

Boone, Marc. "Une famille au service de l'Etat bourguignon naissant. Roland et Jean d'Uutkerke, nobles flamands dans l'entourage de Philippe le Bon," *Revue du nord* 77 (1995), 233-55.

Borgnet, Jules. "Troubles du comté de Namur en 1488," *Annales de la société archéologique de Namur* 2 (1851), 27-56.

Brassart, F. "La féodalité dans le nord de la France: Bans et arrière-bans de la Flandre wallonne sous Charles de Téméraire et Maximilien d'Autriche," *Souvenirs de la Flandre wallonne* (1884), 5-78.

Brokken, H.M. "Het beleg van Delft in 1359." In: *De stad Delft: Cultuur en maatschapij tot 1572.* Delft, 1979, pp. 19-22.

Carolus-Barré, Louis. "Compiegne et la guerre, 1414-1430." In: *111e Congres national des Sociétés savantes, Poitiers, 1986, Histoire médiévale, T. I: "La France Anglaise",* pp. 383-92.

Cauchies, Jean-Marie. "Les 'ecorcheurs' en Hainaut (1437-1445)," *Revue Belge d'histoire militaire* 20 (1973-74), 317-39.

Contamine, Philippe. "L'art de la guerre selon Philippe de Clèves, seigneur de Ravenstein (1456-1528): innovation ou tradition?" *Bijdragen en medelingen betreffende de geschiedenis der Nederlanden* 95 (1980), 363-76.

de Graaf, Ronald P. *Oorlog om Holland, 1000-1375.* Hilversum: Verloren, 1996.

Devilliers, L., ed. "Documents relatifs à l'expédition de Guillaume IV contre les Liégeois, 1407-09," *Bulletin de la commission royale d'histoire de Belgique* 4th ser. 4 (1877), 85-120.

De Vos, Luc. "La bataille de Gavere le 23 juillet 1453. La victoire de l'organisation." In: *XXII. Kongreß der Internationalen Kommission für Militärgeschichte* Acta 22: *Von Crécy bis Mohács Kriegswesen im späten Mittelalter (1346-1526)*. Vienna, 1997, pp. 145-57.

DeVries, Kelly. "The Forgotten Battle of Bevershoutsveld, 3 May 1382: Technological Innovation and Military Significance." In: *Armies, Chivalry and Warfare in Medieval Britain and France: Proceedings of the 1995 Harlaxton Symposium*. Ed. M. Strickland. Stamford, 1998, pp. 289-302.

Doumerc, Bernard. "La politique des 'rois-marchands' au XVe siècle: L'enjeu des Flandres." In: *111e Congrès national des Sociétés savantes, Poitiers, 1986, Histoire médiévale*. T. I: "La France anglaise," pp. 61-71.

Dumolyn, J. *De Brugse opstand van 1436-1438*. Courtrai-Heule, 1997.

Dumolyn, J. "Rebelheden ende vergaderinghen: Twee Brugse documenten uit de grote opstand van 1436-1438," *Bulletin de la commission royale d'histoire* 162 (1996), 297-323.

Fons-Melicocq, A. de la., ed. "Documents inédits pour servir à l'histoire de la rébellion des villes de Bruges et de Gand et de plusieurs autres événements de cette époque (1437-1453)," *Revue d'histoire et d'archéologie* 4 (1864), 217-24.

Fons-Melicocq, A. de la., ed. "Documents inédits pour servir à l'histoire des guerres le nord de la France et en Belgique (1423-1428)," *Revue d'histoire et d'archéologie* 4 (1864), 107-11.

Fons-Melicocq, A. de la., ed. "Documents inédits pour servir à l'histoire du nord de la France et de la Belgique sous Marie de Bourgogne et Maximilien d'Autriche (1477-1482)," *Revue d'histoire et d'archéologie* 4 (1864), 410-25.

Fris, V. "La bataille de Gavre," *Bulletin de la société d'histoire et d'archéologie de Gand* 18 (1910), 185-233.

Fryde, E.B. "Financial Resources of Edward I in the Netherlands, 1294-98: Main Problems and Some Comparisons with Edward III in 1337-40," *Revue Belge de philologie et d'histoire* 40 (1962), 1168-87.

Gaier, Claude. "Analysis of Military Forces in the Prinicpality of Liège and the County of Looz from the Twelfth to the Fifteenth Century," *Studies in Medieval and Renaissance History* 2 (1965), 206-61.

Gaier, Claude. "L'apparition de l'infanterie suisse dans la Principauté de Liège à la fin du XVe siècle," *Bulletin de la commission communale d'histoire de l'ancien pays de Liège* 24 (1990), 81-120; in: *Armes et combats dans l'univers médiéval*. Paris: De Boeck Université, 1995, pp. 91-101.

Gaier, Claude. "L'approvisionnement et le régime alimentaire des troupes dans le duché de Limbourg et les terres d'Outre-Meuse vers 1400," *Moyen âge* 74 (1968), 551-75.

Gaier, Claude. "A propos d'un anniversaire: La valeur militaire du 'sanglier des ardennes'," *Revue Belge d'histoire militaire* 26 (1985-86), 1-8.

Gaier, Claude. "Le rôle des armes à feu dans les batailles Liègeoises au XVe siècle," *Le musée d'armes* 51 (1986), 1-12 and *Publication du centre Européen d'études Bourguignonnes (XIVe-XVIe s.)* 26 (1986), 31-37.

Gaier, Claude. "Un étonnant précurseur: le combat du Kriekelerenbosch (17 janvier 1455)," *Revue internationale d'histoire militaire* 24 (1965), 283-87; in: *Armes et combats dans l'univers médiéval*. Liege, 1995, pp. 39-43.

Gérard, Édouard. *Analectes pour servir à l'histoire de la ville de Dinant*. Namur: Jacques Godenne, 1901.

Haegeman, Marc. *De anglofilie in het graafschap Vlaanderen tussen 1379 en 1435: Politieke en economische aspecten*. Anciens Pays et Assemblees d'Etats/Standen en Landen, 90. Kortrijke-Heule: UGA, 1988.

Heerwarden, Jan van. "The War in the Low Countries." In: *Froissart: Historian*. Ed. J.J.N. Palmer. Woodbridge, 1981, pp. 101-17.

Herbenus, Mathieu. "Deux écrits de Mathieu Herbenus sur la destruction de Liège par Charles-le-Téméraire." Ed. E. Bacha. In: *Bulletin de la commission royale l'histoire de Belgique* 76 (1907), 385-90.

Janse, Antheun. "Ambition and Administration: Charles the Bold and the Feudal Levy in Holland." In: *The Propagation of Power in the Medieval West: Selected Proceedings of the International Conference, Groningen, 20-23 November 1996*. Ed. M. Gosman, A. Vanderjagt, and J. Veenstra. Groningen, 1997, pp. 143-62.

Janse, Antheun. *Grenzen aan de macht: De Friese oorlog van de graven van Holland omstreeks 1400*. Hollandse Historische Reeks, 19. The Hague: Stichting Hollandse Historische Reeks, 1994.

Janse, Antheun. "Het leenbezit van de Hollandse ridderschap omstreeks 1475: Een analyse van het register *Valor Feodorum*," *Jaarboek voor middeleeuwse geschiedenis* 1 (1998), 163-204.

Jongkees, A.G. "Holland en de Gentse oorlog van 1452-1453." In: *Bugundica et varia*. Hilversum, 1990, pp. 48-51.

Lallemand, Alexis. *La lutte des états de Liège contre la maison de Bourgogne, 1390-1492*. Brussels, 1910.

Lecuppre-Desjardins, Elodie. "Un modèle de scénographie urbaine: l'exemple des Pays-Bas bourguignons au XVe siècle," *Revue du nord* 81 (1999), 679-88.

Lucas, Henry Stephen. "John Crabbe: Flemish Pirate, Merchant, and Adventurer," *Speculum* 20 (1945), 334-50.

Lucas, Henry Stephen. *The Low Countries and the Hundred Years' War, 1326-1347*. Ann Arbor: University of Michigan Press, 1929.

Lucas, Henry Stephen. "The Sources and Literature on Jacob van Artevelde," *Speculum* 8 (1933), 125-49.

Lyon, Bryce. "The Dividends from War in the Low Countries (1338-1340)." In: *Peasants and Townsmen in Medieval Europe: Studia in honorem Adriaan Verhulst*. Ed. J.-M. Duvosquel and E. Thoen. Ghent, 1995, pp. 693-705.

Maere d'Aertrycke, M. de. "Recherches concernant quelques questions controversées à propos des batailles de Courtrai et de Rosebecque." In: *Annales internationales d'histoire. Congres de Paris, 1900*. 1e section. Paris, 1901, pp. 125-60.

Mohr, Friedrich. *Die Schlacht bei Rosebeke am 27. November 1382: Ein Beitrag zur mittelalterlichen Kriegsgeschichte*. Berlin: Georg Nauck (Fritz Rühe), 1906.

Mol, J.A. "Graaf Willem IV, de Hollands-Friese oorlog van 1344/1345 en de Friese kloosters." In: *Negen eeuwen Friesland-Holland: Gescheidenis van een haat-liefdeverhouding*. Ed. Ph. H. Breuker and A. Janse. Fryske Akademy. Zutphen: Walburg Pers, 1997, pp. 94-108.

Monteuuis, Gustave. "Le siège de Bourbourg en 1383," *Annales du comité flamand de France* 22 (1895), 259-313.

Nicholas, David. *The Van Arteveldes of Ghent: The Varieties of Vendetta and the Hero in History*. Ithaca: Cornell University Press, 1988.

Owen, Leonard V.D. "England and the Low Countries, 1405-1413," *English Historical Review* 28 (1913), 13-33.

Palmer, J.J.N. "England, France, the Papacy and the Flemish Succession, 1361-9," *Journal of Medieval History* 2 (1976), 339-64.

Pauly, Michel. "Une ville en voie d'émancipation: Luxembourg du XIIIe au XVe siècle," *Château Gaillard* 16 (1994), 229-34.

Paviot, Jacques. "Tournai dans l'histoire Bourguignonne." In: *Les grands siècles de Tournai (12e-15e siècles)*. Ed. J. Dumoulin and J. Pycke. Tournai, 1993, pp. 59-80.

Perroy, Edouard. "Louis de Male et les négotiations de paix Franco-anglaise," *Revue Belge de philologie et d'histoire* 27 (1949), 138-50.

Pirenne, Henri. *Histoire de Belgique*. Vol. II: *Du commencement du XIVe siècle à la mort de Charles de Téméraire*. Brussels: Henri Lamertin, 1903.

Pistono, Stephen P. "Flanders and the Hundred Years War: the Quest for the *Trêve marchande*," *Bulletin of the Institute for Historical Research* 49 (1976), 185-97.

Pistono, Stephen P. "Henry IV and the *Vier leden*: Conflict in Anglo-Flemish Relations, 1402-1403," *Revue Belge de philologie et d'histoire* 54 (1976), 458-73.

Pistono, Stephen P. "The Petition of Jacob de Smet: A Plea for Reprisals against the English, 1403," *Bulletin de la commission royale d'histoire de Belgique* 142 (1976), 341-51.

Prevenier, Walter. "Les preturbations dans les relations commerciales Anglo-flamandes entre 1379 et 1407. Causes de désaccord et raisons d'une réconciliation." In: *Economies et sociétés du moyen âge: Melanges Edouard Perroy*. Paris, 1972, pp. 477-97.

Quicke, F. "L'intérêt du point de vue de l'histoire politique, économique et financière, du troisième compte des expéditions militaires d'Antoine de Bourgogne, duc de Brabant et de Limbourg dans le duché de Luxembourg (Ier septembre 1413-24 décembre 1414)," *Publications de la section historique de l'institut grand-ducal de Luxembourg* 64 (1930), 315-468.

Quicke, F. *Les Pays-Bas à la veille de la periode Bourguignonne, 1356-1384: Contribution à l'histoire politique et diplomatique de l'Europe occidentale dans la seconde moitié du XIVe siècle*. Brussels: Éditions Universitaires, les Presses de Belgique, 1947.

"Récueil de documents aux conflits soutenus par les Liègeois contre Louis de Bourbon et Charles le Téméraire, 1458-69," *Bulletin de la commission royale d'histoire de Belgique* 94 (1930), 245-353.

Richert, Ernst. *Die Schlacht bei Guinegate*. Berlin, 1907.

Salamagne, Alain. "La défense des villes des Pays-Bas à la mort de Charles le Téméraire (1477)." In: *La guerre, la violence et les gens au Moyen Âge*. I: *Guerre et violence*. Ed. P. Contamine and O. Guyotjeannin. 119e congrès national des sociétés historiques et scientifiques, Amiens, octobre 1994, Section d'histoire médiévale et philologie. Paris, 1996, pp. 295-307.

Smet, J. de. "L'effectif des milices brugeoises et la population de la ville en 1340," *Revue Belge de philologie et d'histoire* 12 (1933), 631-36.

Tenhaeff, N.B. "Het Stichtse platteland in oorlogstrijd (1481-1483)," *Verspreide geschriften* 1 (1949), 95-118.

Thiry, C., ed. "Les poèmes de langue Française relatifs aux sacs de Dinant et de Liège." In: *Liège et Bourgogne. Actes du colloque tenu à Liège les 28, 29 et 30 Octobre 1968*. Liège, 1972, pp. 101-27.

Thoen, Erik. "Oorlogen en platteland. Sociale en ekonomische aspekten van militaire destruktie in Vlaanderen tijdens de late middeleeuwen en de vroege moderne tijden," *Tijdschrift voor geschiedenis* 91 (1978), 363-78. (Trans. "Warfare and the Countryside: Social and Economic Aspects of the Military Destruction in Flanders during the Late Middle Ages and the Early Modern Period," *Acta historiae Neerlandicae* 13 (1980), 25-39.)

Vale, Malcolm. "The Anglo-French Wars, 1294-1340: Allies and Alliances. In: *Guerre et société en France, en Angleterre et en Bourgogne XIVe-XVe siècle.* Ed. P. Contamine, C. Giry-Deloison, and Maurice Keen. Lille, 1991, pp. 15-35.

van den Brandeler, P., ed. "Rekening der omkosten door die van Dordrecht bij het beleg van Gorinchem in 1407," *Kronijk van het historisch genootschap gevestigd te Utrecht* 3rd ser. 2 (1856), 177-95.

Verbruggen, J.F. "Bewapening en krijgkunst: het Gentse en het Brugse gemeenteleger in 1477-1479," *Militaria Belgica* (1984), 15-23.

Verbruggen, J.F. "De organisatie van de militie te Brugge in de XIVde eeuw," *Annales de la société d'émulation de Bruges* (1950), 163-70.

Verbruggen, J.F. *De slag bij Guinegate, 7 augustus 1479: De verdediging van het graafschap Vlaanderen tegen de koning van Frankrijk, 1477-1480.* Brussels: Koninklijk Legermusuem, 1993.

Verbruggen, J.F. "Vlaamse gemeentelegers tegen Franse ridderlegers in de 14de en 15de eeuw," *Revue Belge d'histoire militaire* 24 (1981), 359-82.

Waale, M.J. *De Arkelse oorlog, 1401-1412: Een politieke, krijgskundige en economische analyse.* Hilversum: Verloren, 1990.

Waale, M.J. "Military and Financial Aspects of Warfare in Holland around 1400," *Journal of Medieval History* 17 (1991), 333-351.

Werveke, Hans van. *Jacques van Artevelde.* Brussels: La Renaissance du Livre, 1943.

Willems, Bart. "Militaire organisatie en staatsvorming aan de vooravond van de Nieuwe Tijd: Een analyse van het conflict tussen Brabant en Maximiliaan van Oostenrijk (1488-1489)," *Jaarboek voor middeleeuwse geschiedenis* 1 (1998), 261-86.

Wrong, George M. *The Crusade of 1383 Known as That of the Bishop of Norwich*. London: James Parker and Co., 1892.

Xhayet, Geneviève. *Réseaux de pouvoir et solidarités de parti à Liège au moyen âge (1250-1468)*. Bibliothèque de la Faculté de Philosophie et Lettres de L'Université de Liège, 269. Geneva: Droz, 1997.

Medieval – Hundred Years War – Normandy

Allmand, Christopher T. "Alan Kirketon: A Clerical Royal Councillor in Normandy during the English Occupation in the Fifteenth Century," *Journal of Ecclesiastical History* 15 (1964), 33-39.

Allmand, Christopher T. "The English and the Church in Lancastrian Normandy." In: *England and Normandy in the Middle Ages*. Ed. D. Bates and A. Curry. London, 1994, pp. 287-97.

Allmand, Christopher T. "The Lancastrian Land Settlement in Normandy, 1417-50," *Economic History Review* 2nd ser., 21 (1968), 461-79.

Allmand, Christopher T. *Lancastrian Normandy, 1415-1450: The History of a Medieval Occupation*. Oxford: Oxford University Press, 1983.

Allmand, Christopher T. "Local Reaction to the French Reconquest of Normandy: The Case of Rouen." In: *The Crown and Local Communities in England and France in the Fifteenth Century*. Ed. J.R.L. Highfield and R. Jeffs. Gloucester, 1981, pp. 146-61.

Allmand, Christopher T. "La Normandie devant l'opinion anglaise à la fin de la guerre de cent ans," *Bibliothèque de l'école de chartes* 128 (1970), 345-68.

Baudot, Marcel. "L'éviction de Normandie des Evreux-Navarre," *Les cahiers vernonnais* 4 (1964), 141-48.

Baudot, Marcel. "Un prieuré de l'Abbaye du Bec-Hellouin dans la tormente de la guerre de cent ans? Le prieuré de St-Lambert à Fontaine-la-Soret," *Annales de Normandie* 43 (1993), 107-23.

Baume, Andrew J.L. "Gisors et la Normandie anglaise, 1419-1449," *Les cahiers de la société historique et géographique du Bassin de l'Epte* 40 (1997), 47-54.

Baume, Andrew J.L. "Lancastrian Normandy and the Calendar of Medieval Warfare." In: *La ronde des saisons: les saisons dans la littérature et la société anglaises au moyen âge*. Ed. Leo Carruthers. Paris: Presses de l'université de Paris-Sorbonne, pp. 61-68.

Baume, Andrew J.L. "Les opérations militaires anglaises pour expulser les compagnies françaises du pays de caux et du vexin normand, 1436-1437." In: *111e Congrès national des Sociétés savantes, Poitiers, 1986, Histoire médiévale*. T. I: "La France anglaise," pp. 393-400.

Baume, Andrew J.L. "Soldats et paysans en Normandie, 1419-1449." *Le monde rural en Normandie*. Annales de Normandie, série des congrès des sociétés historiques et archéologiques de Normandie, 3. Caen: Musée de Normandie, 1998, 275-82.

Beaurepaire, Charles de. *Les états de Normandie sous la domination anglaise*. Rouen, 1859.

Beaurepaire, Charles de. "Fondations pieuses du duc de Bedford à Rouen," *Bibliothèque de l'école des chartes* 34 (1873).

Beaurepaire, Charles de. "Notes sur la prise du château par Ricarville en 1432." In: *Précis des travaux de l'Académie impériale des sciences, belles-lettres et arts de Rouen, 1855-1856*. Rouen: Péron, 1856, pp. 306-43.

Bottin, Georges. "Aspects des guerres en Normandie à la fin du XVe siècle." In: *Les normands et l'armée: actes du XXXe congrès des sociétés historiques et archéologiques de Normandie tenu à Coutances du 19 au 21 octobre 1995, Revue de la manche* 38 (1996), 59-68.

Cheruel, A. *Histoire de Rouen sous la domination anglaise au XVe siècle*. Rouen, 1840.

Contamine, Philippe. "The Norman 'Nation' and the French 'Nation' in the Fourteenth and Fifteenth Centuries." In: *England and Normandy in the Middle Ages*. Ed. D. Bates and A. Curry. London, 1994, pp. 215-34.

Cormier, Jean-Philippe. "Les effets de la conquête anglaise dans le Dom-frontais d'après les comptes de vicomté (1419-1421)." In: *La guerre, la violence et les gens au Moyen Âge*. II: *Guerre et gens*. Ed. P. Contamine and O. Guyotjeannin. 119e congrès national des sociétés historiques et scientifiques, Amiens, octobre 1994, Section d'histoire médiévale et philologie. Paris, 1996, pp. 127-39.

Cormier, Jean-Philippe. "La résistance populaire à l'occupation Anglaise pendant la guerre de cent ans." *Les Domfrontais médiéval* 15 (1995), 49-57.

Curry, Anne E. "L'effet de la libération sur l'armée anglaise: Les problèmes de l'organisation militaire en Normandie, de 1429 à 1435." In: *Jeanne d'Arc: Une époque, un rayonnement*. Paris, 1982, pp. 95-106.

Curry, Anne E. "The First English Standing Army?–Military Organisation in Lancastrian Normandy, 1420-1450." In: *Patronage, Pedigree and Power in Later Medieval England*. Ed. C. Ross. Gloucester, 1979, pp. 193-214.

Curry, Anne E. "Les *"gens vivans sur le païs"* pendant l'occupation anglaise de la Normandie (1417-1450)." In: *La guerre, la violence et les gens au Moyen Âge*. I: *Guerre et violence*. Ed. P. Contamine and O. Guyotjeannin. 119e congrès national des sociétés historiques et scientifiques, Amiens, octobre 1994, Section d'histoire médiévale et philologie. Paris, 1996, pp. 209-21.

Curry, Anne E. "The Impact of War and Occupation on Urban Life in Normandy, 1417-1450," *French History* 1 (1987), 157-81.

Curry, Anne E. "Lancastrian Normandy: The Jewel in the Crown?" In: *England and Normandy in the Middle Ages*. Ed. D. Bates and A. Curry. London, 1994, pp. 253-67.

Curry, Anne E. "The Nationality of Men-at-Arms Serving in English Armies in Normandy and the Pays de Conquête, 1417-1450: A Preliminary Survey," *Reading Medieval Studies* 18 (1992), 135-63.

Curry, Anne E. "The Organisation of Field Armies in Lancastrian Normandy." In: *Armies, Chivalry and Warfare in Medieval Britain and France: Proceedings of the 1995 Harlaxton Symposium*. Ed. M. Strickland. Stamford, 1998, pp. 207-33.

Curry, Anne E. "Le service féodal en Normandie pendant l'occupation anglaise (1417-1450)." In: *111e Congrès national des Sociétés savantes, Poitiers, 1986, Histoire médiévale*. T. I: "La France anglaise," pp. 233-57.

Curry, Anne E. "Towns at War: Relations between the Towns of Normandy and their English Rulers, 1417-1450." In: *Towns and Townspeople in the Fifteenth Century*. Ed. J.A.F. Thomson. Stroud, 1988, pp. 148-72.

Delsalle, Lucien-René. *Rouen et le Rouennais au temps de Jeanne d'Arc*. Rouen: Éditions P'tit Normand, 1982.

Evans, Michael R. "Brigandage and Resistance in Lancastrian Normandy: A Study of the Remission Evidence," *Reading Medieval Studies* 18 (1992), 103-34.

Goulay, Dominique. "La résistance à l'occupant anglais en haute-normandie (1435-1444)," *Annales de Normandie* 36 (1986), 37-55, 91-104.

Goyheneche, E. "Bayonne port d'embarquement des Navarrais vers la Normandie," *Les cahiers vernonnais* 4 (1964), 107-18.

Jones, Michael K. "War on the Frontier: The Lancastrian Land Settlement in Eastern Normandy, 1435-50," *Nottingham Medieval Studies* 33 (1989), 104-21.

Jouet, Roger. "Le Cotentin entre 1394 et 1417: restauration économique ou marasme persistant?" *Annales de Normandie* 20 (1970), 249-65.

Jouet, Roger. *La résistance à l'occupation anglaise en Basse-Normandie, 1418-1450*. Cahier des Annales de Normandie, 5. Caen, 1969.

Le Cacheux, Paul. *La résistance à l'occupation Anglaise en Basse-Normandie (1418-1450)*. Caen, 1969.

Le Cacheux, Paul. *Rouen au temps de Jeanne d'Arc et pendant la domination anglaise (1419-1449)*. Paris, 1931.

Lefèvre-Pontalis, Germain. "Episodes de l'invasion anglaise: La guerre de partisans dans la haute-normandie," *Bibliothèque de l'écoles des chartes* 96 (1936), 102-30.

Léost, Dominique. *Rouen au lendemain de la reconquête française (1449-1455)*. Unpublished masters thesis. Rouen: Université de Rouen, 1986.

Marin, Jean-Yves, ed. *La Normandie dans la guerre de Cent Ans, 1346-1450*. Caen: Musée de Normandie, 1999.

Massey, Robert. "Lancastrian Rouen: Military Service and Property Holding, 1419-49." In: *England and Normandy in the Middle Ages*. Ed. D. Bates and A. Curry. London, 1994, pp. 269-86.

Massey, Robert. "The Land Settlement in Lancastrian Normandy." In: *Property and Politics: Essays in Later Medieval English History*. Ed. A.J. Pollard. Gloucester: A. Sutton, 1984, pp. 76-96.

Masson d'Autume, Madeline de. *Cherbourg pendant la guerre de cent ans de 1354 à 1450*. Cherbourg, 1948.

Mauger, Franck. "Bilan de l'occupation Anglaise (1417-1450) dans les Domfrontais," *Les Domfrontais médiéval* 15 (1995), 48-56.

Mauger, Franck. "Bilan de l'occupation Anglaise dans les Domfrontais. II: le témoignage des assietes de l'aide," *Les Domfrontais médiéval* 16 (1996), 30-43.

Newhall, Richard Ager. *The English Conquest of Normandy, 1416-1424: A Study in Fifteenth Century Warfare*. New Haven: Yale University Press, 1924.

Newhall, Richard Ager. "Henry V's Policy of Conciliation in Normandy, 1417-1422." In: *Anniversary Essays in Medieval History of Students of C.H. Haskins*. Ed. C.H. Taylor. Boston, 1929, pp. 205-29.

Prentout, Henri. *Les états provinciaux de Normandie*. 3 vols. Caen, 1925-27.

Prentout, Henri. *La prise de Caen par Édouard III, 1346*. Caen, 1904.

Puiseux, Léon. *L'émigration normande et la colonisation anglaise en Normandie au XVe siècle*. Paris, 1865.

Puiseux, Léon. "Des insurrections populaires en Normandie pendant l'occupation Anglaise au XVe siècle," *Mémoires de la société des antiquaires de Normandie* 2nd ser. 9 (1851).

Rowe, B.J.H. "Discipline in the Norman Garrisons under Bedford, 1422-35," *English Historical Review* 46 (1931), 194-208.

Rowe, B.J.H. "The Estates of Normandy under the Duke of Bedford, 1422-1435," *English Historical Review* 46 (1931), 551-78.

Rowe, B.J.H. "John, Duke of Bedford and the Norman 'Brigands'," *English Historical Review* 47 (1932), 583-600.

Solon, Paul D. "Valois Military Administration on the Norman Frontier, 1445-1461: A Study in Medieval Reform," *Speculum* 51 (1976), 91-111.

Stratford, J. "John, Duke of Bedford, as Patron in Lancastrian Normandy." In: *Medieval Art, Architecture and Archaeology at Rouen: The British Archaeological Association Conference Transactions for the Year 1986.* Rouen, 1993, pp. 103-04.

Medieval – Hundred Years War – Scotland

Boucher, L. *Les secours écossais au temps de Jeanne d'Arc.* Rouen: Lainé, 1929.

Brander, Michael. *Scottish and Border Battles and Ballads.* New York: Barnes and Noble Books, 1993.

Campbell, James. "England, Scotland and the Hundred Years War in the Fourteenth Century." In: *Europe in the Late Middle Ages.* Ed. J.R. Hale, J.R.L. Highfield and B. Smalley. Evanston: Northwestern University Press, 1965, pp. ; in: *The Wars of Edward III: Sources and Interpretations.* Ed. Clifford J. Rogers. Woodbridge: The Boydell Press, 1999, pp. 207-30.

Chevalier, Bernard. "Les écossais dans les armées de Charles VII jusqu'a la bataille de Verneuil." In: *Jeanne d'Arc: Une époque, un rayonnement.* Paris, 1982, pp. 85-94.

Dunlop, Annie I. *Scots Abroad in the Fifteenth Century.* Historical Association Pamphlet, no. 124. London: The Historical Association, 1942.

Sevestre, Bernard. "L'ancienne alliance franco-écossaise et le service écossais," *Revue de la Société des Amis du Musée de l'Armée* 99 (1990), 5-21.

"The *Vraie Chronique D'Escoce* and Franco-Scottish Diplomacy: An Historical Work by John Ireland," *Nottingham Medieval Studies* 35 (1991), 106-33.

Medieval – Hundred Years War – Spain and Portugal

Ainsworth, Peter F. "Collationnement, montage et *jeu parti*: le début de la campagne espagnole du Prince Noir (1366-67) dans les *Chroniques* de Jean Froissart," *Moyen âge*, 5th ser., 8 (1994), 369-411.

Bessa, Carlos Gomes. "Le Portugal 1383-1385: crise, art militaire et consolidation de l'indépendance." In: *XXII. Kongreß der Internationalen Kommission für Militärgeschichte Acta 22: Von Crécy bis Mohács Kriegswesen im späten Mittelalter (1346-1526)*. Vienna, 1997, pp. 28-50.

Calmette, J. *Louis XI, Jean II et la révolution catalane*. Toulouse, 1903.

Calmette, J. *La question des Pyrénées et la marche d'Espagne au moyen âge*. n.p., 1947.

Castillo Cárceres, Fernando. "Analysis de una batalla: Najera 1367," *Cuadernos de historia de Espana* 73 (1991), 107-46.

Charon, Philippe. "Relations entre les cours de France et de Navarre en 1376-1377," *Bibliothèque de l'école des chartes* 150 (1992), 85-108.

Childs, Wendy R. "Anglo-Portuguese Relations in the Fourteenth Century." In: *The Age of Richard II*. Ed. James L. Gillespie. New York, 1997, pp. 27-50.

Comellas I Solé, Jordi. "L'abastament d'una ciutat en temps de guerra. El setge de Barcelona de 1472," *Acta historica et archaeologica mediaevalia* 18 (1997), 451-71.

Del Campo, A.S. "Sistemas de combate en la iconografia mozarabe y andalusi altomedieval," *Boletin de la Associacion Española de Orientalistas* 22 (1986), 61-87.

Fowler, Kenneth A. "L'emploi des mercenaries par les pouvoirs Ibériques et l'intervention militaire Anglaise en Espagne (vers 1361-vers 1379)."

In: *Realidid e imagines del poder: España a fines de la edad media*. Ed. Adeline Rucquoi. Valladolid, 1988, pp. 23-55.

García, Fermin Miranda. "Felipe y Juana de Évreux y la guerra de Cien Años (1337-1349)." In: *La guerre, la violence et les gens au Moyen Âge*. I: *Guerre et violence*. Ed. P. Contamine and O. Guyotjeannin. 119e congrès national des sociétés historiques et scientifiques, Amiens, octobre 1994, Section d'histoire médiévale et philologie. Paris, 1996, pp. 81-95.

Garcia Moreno, L.A. "Organizacíon militar de Bisancio en la peninsula Ibérica (ss. VI-VII)," *Hispania* 123 (1973), 5-22.

Grassotti, H. "Para la historia del botín y de las parias en Léon y Castilla," *Cuadernos de historia de España* 39-40 (1964), 43-132.

Ladero Quesada, M.A. *Milicia y economia en la guerra de Grenada: el cerco de Baza*. Valladolid, 1964.

Larrayoz-Zarranz, Martin. "Reacción de Carlos el Malo rey de Navarra a la noticia de la Derrota de Cocherel," *Les cahiers vernonnais* 4 (1964), 119-40.

Lopes, Fernão. *The English in Portugal, 1367-87: Extracts from the Chronicles of Dom Fernando and Dom João*. Trans. Derek W. Lomax and R.J. Oakley. Warminster: Aris and Philips Ltd, 1988.

Mahaut, Marie-Claude. "Le rôle pacificateur du Pape Benôit XII dans le conflit de la Castille avec le Portugal (1337-1340)." In: *La guerre et la paix: Frontières et violences au moyen âge*. Actes du 101e congrès national des sociétés savantes, Lille, 1976. Paris: Bibliothèque Nationale, 1978, pp. 225-39.

Major, Richard Henry. *The Life of Prince Henry of Portugal*. 1868; rpt. London, 1967.

Russell, P.E. *The English Intervention in Spain and Portugal in the Time of Edward III and Richard II*. Oxford: Clarendon Press, 1955.

Russell, P.E. "The War in Spain and Portugal." In: *Froissart: Historian*. Ed. J.J.N. Palmer. Woodbridge, 1981, pp. 82-100.

Vann, Theresa M. "Twelfth-Century Castile and its Frontier Strategies." In: *The Circle of War in the Middle Ages: Essays on Medieval Military and Naval History.* Ed. Donald J. Kagay and L.J. Andrew Villalon. Woodbridge: The Boydell Press, 1999, pp. 21-32.

Vaquero, Eloísa Ramírez. "La guerra de los nobles: una sociedad de banderizos en el Pirineo Occidental." In: *La guerre, la violence et les gens au Moyen Âge.* I: *Guerre et violence.* Ed. P. Contamine and O. Guyotjeannin. 119e congrès national des sociétés historiques et scientifiques, Amiens, octobre 1994, Section d'histoire médiévale et philologie. Paris, 1996, pp. 111-24.

Medieval – Hundred Years War – Espionage

Alban, J.R. and C.T. Allmand. "Spies and Spying in the Fourteenth Century." In: *War, Literature and Politics in the Late Middle Ages: Essays in Honour of G.W. Coopland.* Ed. C.T. Allmand. Liverpool: University of Liverpool Press, 1975, pp. 73-101.

Crook, David. "The Confession of a Spy, 1380," *Historical Research* 62 (1989), 346-50.

Griffiths, Ralph A. "A Breton Spy in London, 1425-29." In: *King and Country: England and Wales in the Fifteenth Century.* London, 1991, pp. 221-25.

Medieval – Hundred Years War – Financing

Braunstein, P. "Guerre, vivres et transports dans le Haut-Frioul en 1381." In: *Erzeugung, Verkehr und Handel in der Geschichte der Alpenländer, Hervert-Hassinger-Festschrift.* Ed. F. Huter, G. Zwanowetz, and F. Mathias. Innsbruck, 1977, pp. 85-106.

Bridbury, A.R. "The Hundred Years' War: Costs and Profits." In: *Trade, Government and Economy in Pre-Industrial England: Essays Presented to E.J. Fisher.* Ed. D.C. Coleman and A.H. John. London, 1976, pp. 80-95.

Brouwers, D.D. "Indemnités pour dommages de guerre au pays de Namurois en 1432," *Annales de ls société archéologique de Namur* 40 (1932-33), 87-103.

Brown, Elizabeth A.R. "Customary Aids and Royal Fiscal Policy under Philip VI of Valois," *Traditio* 30 (1974), 191-258.

Bryant, W.N. "The Financial Dealings of Edward III with the County Communities, 1330-1360," *English Historical Review* 83 (1968), 760-71.

Chew, Helena M. "Scutage in the Fourteenth Century," *English Historical Review* 38 (1923), 19-41.

Combes, Jean. "Les donations à la réparation du port d'Aiguesmortes." In: *Mélanges d'histoire du moyen âge dédiés à la mémoire de Louis Halphen.* Paris: Presses universitaires de France, 1951, pp. 125-29.

Contamine, Philippe. "Consommation et demande militaire en France et en Angleterre, XIIIe-XVe siècles." In: *Domande e consumi: Livelli e strutture (nei secoli XIII-XVIII: Atti della "Sesta settimana di studio" (27 aprile-3 maggio 1974), Instituto internazionale di storia economica Francesco Datini, Prato.* Florence, 1978, pp. 409-28.

Contamine, Philippe. "Le coût de la guerre de cent ans en Angleterre," *Annales ESC* 20 (1965), 788-91.

Contamine, Philippe. "La guerre de cent ans in France: une approche économique," *Bulletin of the Institute of Historical Research* 47 (1974), 125-49.

Contamine, Philippe. "Guerre, fiscalité royale et économie en France (deuxième moitié du XVe siècle)." In: *Proceedings of the Seventh International Economic History Congress.* Ed. M.W. Finn. Edinburgh, 1978, II:266-73; in: *Des pouvoirs en France, 1300-1500.* Paris, 1992, pp. 123-30.

Coulon, Laurent. "Un emprunt 'forcé' à Arras en 1433," *Revue du nord* 79 (1997), 939-48.

Doucet, Roger. "Les finances anglaises en France à la fin de la guerre de cent ans, 1413-1435." *Moyen âge*, 2nd ser., 27 (1926), 265-332.

Dupont-Ferrier, Gustave. *Études sur les institutions financières de la France à la fin du moyen âge.* 2 vols. Paris, 1930-32.

Fowler, Kenneth. "Les finances et la discipline dans les armées anglaise en France au XIVe siècle," *Les cahiers vernonnais* 4 (1964), 55-84.

Fryde, E.B. "The Financial Policies of the Royal Governments and Popular Resistance to Them in France and England, *c.* 1270-*c.* 1420," *Revue Belge de philologie et d'histoire* 57 (1979), 824-60.

Genet, J.-P. "Les débuts de l'impôt national en Angleterre," *Annales* 34 (1979), 348-54.

Harriss, Gerald L. *King, Parliament and Public Finance in Medieval England to 1369.* Oxford, 1975.

Hébert, Michel. "Guerre, finances et administration: les Etats de Provence de novembre 1359," *Moyen âge* 83 (1977), 103-30.

Heers, J. "Difficultiés économiques et troubles sociaux en France et en Angleterre pendant la guerre de cent ans: le problème des origines," *Les cahiers vernonnais* 4 (1964), 47-54.

Henneman, John B., Jr. "The Black Death and Royal Taxation in France, 1347-1351," *Speculum* 43 (1968), 405-28.

Henneman, John B., Jr. "Financing the Hundred Years War: Royal Taxation in France in 1340," *Speculum* 42 (1967), 275-98.

Henneman, John B., Jr. "Nobility, Privilege and Fiscal Politics in Late Medieval France," *French Historical Studies* 13 (1983), 1-17.

Henneman, John B., Jr. *Royal Taxation in Fourteenth-Century France: The Captivity and Ransom of John II, 1356-1370.* Philadelphia: The American Philosophical Society, 1976.

Henneman, John B., Jr. *Royal Taxation in Fourteenth Century France: The Development of War Financing, 1322-1356.* Princeton: Princeton University Press, 1971.

Henneman, John B., Jr. "Taxation of Italians by the French Crown, 1311-1363," *Mediaeval Studies* 31 (1969), 15-43.

Humbert, Françoise. *Les finances municipales de Dijon du milieu du XIVe siècle à 1477.* Paris, 1961.

Lardin, Philippe. "Le financement des fortifications dans les principales villes de Normandie (XIV-XV siècles)." In: *Les normands et le fisc: XXIXe congrès des sociétés historiques et archéologiques de Normandie, Elbeuf-*

sur-Seine, 20-23 octobre 1994, Bulletin de la société de l'histoire d'Elbeuf (1996), 47-58.

McFarlane, K.B. "War, the Economy and Social Change: England and the Hundred Years War." In: *England in the Fifteenth Century: Collected Essays*. London, 1981, pp. 139-50.

Miskimin, Harry A. *Money and Power in Fifteenth-Century France*. New Haven: Yale University Press, 1984.

Munro, John H.A. *Wool, Cloth, and Gold: The Struggle for Bullion in Anglo-Burgundian Trade, 1340-1478*. Toronto: University of Toronto Press, 1972.

Myers, A.R. "The Rise and Fall of Jacques Coeur," *History Today* 16 (1966), 445-51, 547-54.

Nederman, Cary J. "Royal Taxation and the English Church: The Origins of William of Ockham's *An princeps*," *Journal of Ecclesiastical History* 37 (1986), 377-88.

Newhall, Richard Ager. "The War Finances of Henry V and the Duke of Bedford," *English Historical Review* 36 (1921), 172-98.

Ormrod, W.M. "The English Crown and the Customs, 1349-63," *Economic Historical Review* 2nd ser. 40 (1987), 27-40.

Perroy, Edouard. "A l'origine d'une économie contractée: les crises du XIVe siècle," *Annales ESC* 4 (1949), 167-82.

Postan, M.M. "The Costs of the Hundred Years War," *Past and Present* 27 (1964), 34-53.

Prestwich, Michael. "War and Taxation in England in the XIIIth and XIVth Centuries." In: *Genèse de l'état moderne: Prélèvement et distribution*. Ed. J-Ph. Genet and M. Le Mené. Paris, 1987, pp. 181-92.

Rey, M. *Le domaine du roi et les finances extraordinaires sous Charles VI, 1388-1413*. Paris, 1965.

Rey, M. *Les finances royales sous Charles VI: Les causes du déficit, 1388-1413*. Paris, 1965.

Sherborne, James. "The Cost of English Warfare with France in the Later Fourteenth Century." In: *War, Politics and Culture in Fourteenth-Century England*. Ed. A. Tuck. London, 1994, pp. 55-70.

Stansfield, Michael. "John Holland, Duke of Exeter and Earl of Huntingdon (d. 1447) and the Costs of the Hundred Years War." In: *Profit, Piety and the Professions in Later Medieval England*. Ed. M. Hicks. Stroud: Sutton Publishing, 1990, pp. 103-18.

Sussman, Nathan. "Debasements, Royal Revenues, and Inflation in France during the Hundred Years' War, 1415-1422," *Journal of Economic History* 53 (1993), 44-70.

Medieval – Hundred Years War – Laws of War (Ransoms)

Armstrong, C.A.J. "Sir John Falstof and the Laws of Arms." In: *War, Literature and Politics in the Late Middle Ages: Essays in Honour of G.W. Coopland*. Ed. C.T. Allmand. Liverpool: University of Liverpool Press, 1975, pp. 46-56.

Bossuat, André. "Les prisonniers de Beauvais et la rançon du poete Jean Regnier, bailli d'Auxerre." In: *Mélanges d'histoire du moyen âge dédiés à la mémoire de Louis Halphen*. Paris: Presses universitaires de France, 1951, pp. 27-32.

Bossuat, André. "Les prisonniers de guerre au XVe siècle: la rançon de Guillaume, seigneur de Châteauvillain," *Annales de Bourgogne* 23 (1951), 7-35.

Bossuat, André. "Les prisonniers de guerre au XVe siècle: la rançon de Jean, seigneur de Rodermack," *Annales de l'Est* 5th ser. 3 (1951), 145-62.

Broome, Dorothy M., ed. and trans. *The Ransom of John I, King of France, 1360-1370*. Camden Miscellany, 14. Camden Third Series, vol. 37. London: Offices of the Society, 1926.

Chaplais, Pierre. "Règlements des conflits internationaux Franco-Anglais au XIVe siècle (1293-1377)," *Moyen âge* 57 (1951), 269-302.

Contamine, Philippe. "Un contrôle étatique croissant: Les usages de la guerre du XIVe au XVIIIe siècle: rançons et butins." In: *Guerre et con-*

currence entre les États européens du XIVe au XVIIIe siècle. Ed. Philippe Contamine. Fondation Européenne de la Science: Les origines de l'État moderne en Europe, XIIIe-XVIIIe siècle. Paris: Presses universitaires de France, 1998, pp. 199-236.

Contamine, Philippe "Rançons et butins dans la Normandie anglaise (1424-1444)." In: *Actes du 101e congès national des sociétés savantes.* Paris, 1978, pp. 241-70.

Given-Wilson, C. "The Ransom of Olivier du Guesclin," *Bulletin of the Institute of Historical Research* 54 (1981), 17-28.

Glénisson, Jean and Victor Deodato da Silva. "La practique et le rituel de la reddition aux XIVe et XVe siècles." In: *Jeanne d'Arc: Une époque, un rayonnement.* Paris, 1982, pp. 113-22.

Henneman, John B. "The French Ransom and Two Legal Traditions," *Studia Gratiana* 15 (1972), 613-30.

Jones, Michael. "Fortunes et malheurs de guerre: Autour de la rançon du chevalier anglais Jean Bourchier (d. 1400)." In: *La guerre, la violence et les gens au Moyen Âge. I: Guerre et violence.* Ed. P. Contamine and O. Guyotjeannin. 119e congrès national des sociétés historiques et scientifiques, Amiens, octobre 1994, Section d'histoire médiévale et philologie. Paris, 1996, pp. 189-208.

Jones, Michael. "The Ransom of Jean de Bretagne, Count of Penthièvre: An Aspect of English Foreign Policy, 1386-8," *Bulletin of the Institute for Historical Research* 111 (1972), 7-26.

Jones, Michael K. "Ransom Brokerage in the Fifteenth Century." In: *Guerre et société en France, en Angleterre et en Bourgogne XIVe-XVe siècle.* Ed. P. Contamine, C. Giry-Deloison, and Maurice Keen. Lille, 1991, pp. 221-35.

Leguai, André. "Le problème des rançons au XVe siècle: la captivité de Jean Ier, duc de Bourbon," *Cahiers d'histoire* 6 (1961), 41-58.

Marchegay, P. "La rançon d'Olivier de Coëtivy," *Bibliothèque de l'école des Chartes* 38 (1877), 5-48.

Perroy, Edouard. "Gras profits et rançons pendant la guerre de cent ans: l'affaire du comte de Denia." In: *Mélanges d'histoire du moyen âge dédiés à la mémoire de Louis Halphen*. Paris: Presses universitaires de France, 1951, pp. 573-80.

Rogers, Alan. "Hoton versus Shakell: A Ransom Case in the Court of Chivalry, 1390-95," *Nottingham Medieval Studies* 6 (1962), 74-108; 7 (1963), 53-78.

Wright, Nicholas A.R. "Ransoms of Non-Combatants during the Hundred Years War," *Journal of Medieval History* 17 (1991), 323-332.

Medieval – Hundred Years War – Mercenaries

Billot, Claudine. "Les mercenaires étrangers pendant la guerre de cent ans comme migrants." In: *Le combattant au moyen âge*. 2nd ed. Histoire ancienne et médiévale, 36. Paris: Publications de la Sorbonne, 1995, pp. 279-86.

Bossuat, André. *Perrinet Gressart et François de Surienne: Agents de l'Angleterre. Contribution à l'étude des relations de l'Angleterre et de la Bourgogne avec la France, sous le règne de Charles VII*. Paris: Libraire E. Droz, 1936.

Bridge, J.C. "Two Cheshire Soldiers of Fortune of the Fourteenth Century: Sir Hugh Calveley and Sir Robert Knolles," *Journal of the Architectural, Archaeological and Historical Society for Chester and North Wales* n.s. 14 (1908).

Contamine, Philippe. "Les compagnies d'aventure en France pendant la guerre de cent ans." In: *Melanges de l'école française de Rome. Moyen âge*. Temps modernes, 87. Rome, 1975, pp. 365-96.

Ditcham, Brian G.H. "'Mutton Guzzlers and Wine Bags': Foreign Soldiers and Native Reactions in Fifteenth-Century France." In: *Power, Culture, and Religion in France c.1350-c.1550*. Ed. C. Allmand. Woodbridge, 1989, pp. 1-13.

Fowler, Kenneth A. "L'emploi des mercenaries par les pouvoirs Ibériques et l'intervention militaire Anglaise en Espagne (vers 1361-vers 1379)." In: *Realidid e imagines del poder: España a fines de la edad media*. Ed. Adeline Rucquoi. Valladolid, 1988, pp. 23-55.

Fowler, Kenneth A. "The Wages of War: the Mercenaries of the Great Companies." In: *Viajeros, peregrinos, mercaderes en el occidente medieval: XVIII semana de estudios medievales*. Estella, 1991, pp. 217-44.

Guigue, C. *Les tard-venus en Lyonnais, Forez et Beaujolais, 1356-1369*. Lyon, 1886.

Labande, L.-H. "L'occupation du Pont-Saint-Esprit par les grandes compagnies (1360-1361)." *Revue historique de Provence* 1 (1901), 79-95, 146-65.

Monicat, Jacques. *Histoire du Velay pendant la guerre de cent ans: Les grandes compagnies en Velay, 1358-1392*. 2nd ed. Paris, 1928.

Quicherat, Jules. *Rodrigue de Villandrando: L'un des combattants pour l'indépendance française au quinzième siècle*. Paris, 1879.

Samaran, Charles. "Pour l'histoire des grandes compagnies: Le 'vuidement' de Chateau-Gontier par les Anglais (1369)." In: *Mélanges d'histoire du moyen âge dédiés à la mémoire de Louis Halphen*. Paris: Presses universitaires de France, 1951, pp. 641-44.

Tucoo-Chala, Pierre. "Une bande de routiers dans la région de Casteljaloux en 1381-1383," *Revue de l'Agenais* (1973), 5-35.

Tuetey, Alexandre. *Les écorcheurs sous Charles VII*. 2 vols. Montbéliard, 1874.

Veydarier, Régis. "*Una guerra de layrons*: L'occupation de la Provence par les compagnies de Raymond de Turenne (1393-1399)." In: *La guerre, la violence et les gens au Moyen Âge*. I: *Guerre et violence*. Ed. P. Contamine and O. Guyotjeannin. 119e congrès national des sociétés historiques et scientifiques, Amiens, octobre 1994, Section d'histoire médiévale et philologie. Paris, 1996, pp. 169-88.

Medieval – Hundred Years War – Navies [See also Military Technology – Premodern – Ships (inc. Warships) – Late Medieval]

Ford, C.J. "Piracy or Policy: The Crisis in the Channel, 1400-1403," *Transactions of the Royal Historical Society*, 5th ser., 29 (1979), 63-77.

Holmes,' G.A. "The 'Libel of English Policy'," *English Historical Review* 76 (1961), 193-216.

Kepler, J.S. "The Effects of the Battle of Sluys upon the Administration of English Naval Impressment, 1340-1434," *Speculum* 48 (1973), 70-77.

Ledieu, Alcius. "Notice sur la *Petite-Trésorière*, navire de guerre acheté par l'Échevinage d'Abbeville en 1479," *Bulletin historique et philologique du comité des travaux historiques et scientifiques* (1897), 99-112.

Merlin-Chazelas, Anne. "La réforme du Clos des Galées de Rouen en 1374," *Revue historique des armées* 1 (1974), 9-23.

Nuñez, José María Blanco. "Las armadas de Castilla y Aragón durante la Guerra de los Cien Años." In: *XXII. Kongreß der Internationalen Kommission für Militärgeschichte Acta 22: Von Crécy bis Mohács Kriegswesen im späten Mittelalter (1346-1526)*. Vienna, 1997, pp. 269-80.

Pistono, Stephen P. "Henry IV and the English Privateers," *English Historical Review* 90 (1975), 322-30.

Richmond, Colin F. "English Naval Power in the Fifteenth Century," *History* 52 (1967), 1-15.

Richmond, Colin F. "The Keeping of the Sea during the Hundred Years War, 1422-1440," *History* 49 (1964), 283-98.

Richmond, Colin F. "The War at Sea." In: *The Hundred Years War*. Ed. Kenneth Fowler. London: Macmillan, 1971, pp. 96-121.

Roncière, Charles de la. "L'invasion anglaise sous Charles VI: Dernières batailles navales," *Revue des questions historiques* n.s. 23 (1900), 56-87.

Rose, Susan, ed. *The Navy of the Lancastrian Kings: Accounts and Inventories of William Soper, Keeper of the King's Ships, 1422-1427*. London, 1982.

Runyan, Timothy J. "Naval Logistics in the Late Middle Ages: The Example of the Hundred Years War." In: *Feeding Mars: Logistics in Western Warfare from the Middle Ages to the Present*. Ed. J.A. Lynn. Boulder, 1993, pp. 79-102.

Runyan, Timothy J. "Ships and Mariners in Later Medieval England," *Journal of British Studies* 16 (1977), 1-17.

Saul, Nigel. "Great Yarmouth and the Hundred Years War in the Four-teenth Century," *Bulletin of the Institute for Historical Research* 52 (1979), 105-15.

Sherborne, James. "The Battle of La Rochelle and the War at Sea, 1372-5," *Bulletin of the Institute of Historical Research* 42 (1969), 17-29.

Sherborne, James. "The English Navy: Shipping and Manpower, 1369-1389," *Past and Present* 37 (1967), 163-75.

Terrier de Loray, Henri-Philippe. *Jean de Vienne, Amiral de France, 1341-1396*. Paris, 1877.

Valentine-Harris, P. "Archers at Sea: the Battle of Winchelsea," *Journal of the Society of Archer-Antiquaries* 27 (1984), 43-44.

Walker, J.A. "John Holand, a Fifteenth-Century Admiral," *Mariner's Mirror* 65 (1979), 235-42.

Warner, G. *The Libelle of Englyshe Polycye: A Poem on the Use of Sea-Power, 1436*. Oxford, 1926.

Medieval – Hundred Years War – Papal Influence

Harvey, Margaret. *England, Rome and the Papacy, 1417-1464: The Study of a Relationship*. Manchester: Manchester University Press, 1993.

Mollat, Guillaume. "La diplomatie pontificale au XIVe siècle." In: *Mélanges d'histoire du moyen âge dédiés à la mémoire de Louis Halphen*. Paris: Presses universitaires de France, 1951, pp. 307-50.

Palmer, J.J.N. and A.P. Wells. "Ecclesiastical Reform and the Politics of the Hundred Years War during the Pontificate of Urban V (1362-70)." In: *War, Literature and Politics in the Late Middle Ages: Essays in Honour of G.W. Coopland*. Ed. C.T. Allmand. Liverpool: University of Liverpool Press, 1975, pp. 169-89.

Wood, Diana. "*Omnino partialitate cessante*: Clement VI and the Hundred Years War," *Studies in Church History* 20 (1983), 179-89.

Medieval – Hundred Years War – Peace and Diplomacy

Allmand, Christopher T. "The Anglo-French Negotiations, 1439," *Bulletin of the Institute of Historical Research* 40 (1967), 1-33.

Allmand, Christopher T. "Diplomacy in Late Medieval England," *History Today* 17 (1967), 546-53.

Autrand, Françoise. "Les artisans de paix face à l'État: La diplomatie pontificale et le conflit franco-anglais au XIVe siècle." In: *Guerre et concurrence entre les États européens du XIVe au XVIIIe siècle.* Ed. Philippe Contamine. Fondation Européenne de la Science: Les origines de l'État moderne en Europe, XIIIe-XVIIIe siècle. Paris: Presses universitaires de France, 1998, pp. 305-38.

Autrand, Françoise. "La paix impossible: les négociations franco-anglaises à la fin du 14e siècle," in "Nicopolis, 1396-1996: Actes du Colloque international," ed. J. Paviot and M. Chauney-Bouillot, *Annales de Bourgogne* 68 (1996), 11-22.

Capra, Pierre. "Le rôle des officiers Bordelais dans l'élaboration et l'application du traité de Brétigny (1354-1361)," *Revue historique de Bordeaux* (1986-87), 19-32.

Chaplais, Pierre. *English Medieval Diplomatic Practice.* 2 vols. London, 1982.

Contamine, Philippe. "Notes sur la paix en France pendant la guerre de cent ans." In: *Rapports du XVe Congrès International des Sciences Historiques.* Bucarest, 1980, pp. 175-86.

Cuttino, G.P. *English Medieval Diplomacy.* Bloomington: Indiana University Press, 1985.

Déprez, Eugène. "La conférence d'Avignon (1344): L'arbitrage pontificale entre la France et l'Angleterre." In: *Essays in Medieval History Presented to T.F. Tout.* Ed. A.G. Little and F.M. Powicke. Manchester, 1925; rpt. New York, 1967, pp. 301-20.

Dickenson, Jocelyn Gledhill. "The Congress of Arras, 1435," *History* 40 (1955), 31-41.

Dickenson, Jocelyn Gledhill. *The Congress of Arras, 1435: A Study in Medieval Diplomacy*. Oxford: Clarendon Press, 1955.

Ferguson, J. *English Diplomacy, 1422-1461*. Oxford, 1972.

Fowler, Kenneth A. "Truces." In: *The Hundred Years War*. Ed. Kenneth Fowler. London: Macmillan, 1971, pp. 184-215.

Gaucher, E. "Les joutes de Saint-Inglevert: Perception et écriture d'un événtement historique pendant la guerre de Cent Ans," *Moyen âge* 102 (1996), 229-43.

Keen, Maurice. "Diplomacy." In: *Henry V: The Practice of Kingship*. Ed. G.L. Harriss. Oxford, 1985, pp. 181-99.

Le Bis, Isabelle. "Pratique de la diplomatie: Un dossier d'ambassadeurs Française sous Charles VI (1400-1403)," *Annuaire-bulletin de la société de l'histoire de France* (1985-1986), 97-215.

Le Patourel, John. "The Treaty of Brétigny, 1360," *Transactions of the Royal Historical Society* 5th ser. 10 (1960), 19-39.

Lowe, Ben. *Imagining Peace: A History of Early English Pacifist Ideas, 1340-1560*. University Park: Pennsylvania State University Press, 1997.

Mérindol, Christian de. "La paix, la justice et la prosperité: des effets du bon gouvernement au milieu du XVe siècle." In: *La guerre, la violence et les gens au Moyen Âge*. I: *Guerre et violence*. Ed. P. Contamine and O. Guyotjeannin. 119e congrès national des sociétés historiques et scientifiques, Amiens, octobre 1994, Section d'histoire médiévale et philologie. Paris, 1996, pp. 345-68.

Mollat, Guillaume. "Innocent VI et les tentatives de paix entre la France et l'Angleterre (1353-1355)," *Revue d'histoire ecclesiastique* 10 (1909), 729-43.

Palmer, J.J.N. "The Anglo-French Peace Negotiations, 1390-1396," *Transactions of the Royal Historical Society* 16 (1966), 81-94.

Palmer, J.J.N. "Articles for a Final Peace between England and France, 16 June 1393," *Bulletin of the Institute of Historical Research* 39 (1966), 180-85.

Palmer, J.J.N. "English Foreign Policy, 1388-99." In: *The Reign of Richard II: Essays in Honour of May McKisack*. Ed. F.R.H. du Boulay and C.M. Barron. London, 1971, pp. 75-107.

Palmer, J.J.N. "The War Aims of the Protagonists and the Negotiations for Peace." In: *The Hundred Years War*. Ed. Kenneth Fowler. London: Macmillan, 1971, pp. 51-74.

Phillpotts, Christopher. "The Fate of the Truce of Paris, 1396-1415," *Journal of Medieval History* 24 (1998), 61-80.

Powicke, Michael R. "War as a Means of Peace: Some Late Medieval Themes." In: *Documenting the Past: Essays in Medieval History Presented to George Peddy Cuttino*. Ed. J.S. Hamilton and P.J. Bradley. Woodbridge, 1989, pp. 217-24.

Rimboud, Michel. "La paix du Bien public: démesure et marchandages (août-novembre 1465)." In: *La guerre, la violence et les gens au Moyen Âge*. I: *Guerre et violence*. Ed. P. Contamine and O. Guyotjeannin. 119e congrès national des sociétés historiques et scientifiques, Amiens, octobre 1994, Section d'histoire médiévale et philologie. Paris, 1996, pp. 333-44.

Wilkinson, Bertie. "The Negotiations Preceding the 'Treaty' of Leake, August 1318." In: *Studies in Mediaeval History Presented to Frederick Maurice Powicke*. Oxford, pp. 333-53.

Medieval – Hundred Years War – Thirty (combat of)

Brush, Henry R. "La bataille de trente anglois et de trente bretons," *Modern Philology* 9 (1911-12), 511-44.

Crapelet, G., ed. *Combat de trente Bretons contre de trente Anglais*. Paris, 1827.

Medieval – Hundred Years War – Conclusion

Keen, Maurice. "The End of the Hundred Years War: Lancastrian France and Lancastrian England." In: *England and her Neighbours, 1066-1483:*

Essays in Honour of Pierre Chaplais. Ed. M. Jones and M. Vale. London, 1989, pp. 297-311.

Léost, Dominique, "Les métiers Rouennais au lendemain de la reconguête Française (1449-1455)," *Annales de Normandie* 43 (1993), 141-53.

Medieval – Hungarian Invasions

D'Haenens, Albert. "Les incursions hongroises dans l'espace belge (954/955)," *Cahiers de civilisation médiévale (Xe-XIIe siècles)* 4 (1961), 423-40.

Dienes, I. *The Hungarians Cross the Carpathians.* Budapest, 1972.

Fasoli, G. *Le incursioni ungare in Europa nel secolo X.* Florence, 1945.

Fodor, István, ed. *The Ancient Hungarians: Exhibition Catalogue.* Budapest: Hungarian National Museum, 1996.

Leyser, Karl. "The Battle at the Lech, 955: A Study in Tenth-Century Warfare," *History* 50 (1965), 1-25.

Macartney, C.A. *The Magyars in the Ninth Century.* Cambridge, 1930.

Siklódi, Csilla, ed. *Between East and West/Über die Grenze zwischen Ost und West.* Budapest: Promptus, 1996.

Székely, G. "Le rôle de l'élément magyar et slave dans la formation de l'état hongrois." In: *L'Europe au Ixe-XIe siècles.* Warsaw, 1968, pp. 225-40.

Medieval – Ireland

Alexander, Graham. "The Battle of Fochart, 1318: The Nemesis of Edward Bruce, The Collapse of Anglo-Norman Ireland," *Battlefield* 4 (1998), 12-14.

Armstrong, O. *Edward Bruce's Invasion of Ireland.* London, 1923.

Bannerman, J. "The Dal Riata and Northern Ireland in the Sixth and Seventh Centuries." In: *Celtic Studies: Essays in Memory of Angus Matheson, 1912-1962*. London, 1968, pp. 1-11.

Butler, George. "The Battle of Piltown, 1462," *Irish Sword* 6 (1963-64), 197-211.

Church, S.D. "The 1210 Campaign in Ireland: Evidence for a Military Revolution," *Anglo-Norman Studies* 20 (1997), 45-58.

Connolly, Philomena. "An Account of Military Expenditure in Leinster, 1308," *Analecta hibernica* 30 (1982), 1-5.

Connolly, Philomena. "The Financing of English Expeditions to Ireland, 1361-76." In: *England and Ireland in the Later Middle Ages: Essays in Honour of Jocelyn Otway-Ruthven*. Ed. James F. Lydon. Dublin, 1981, pp. 104-21.

Davies, R.R. *Domination and Conquest: The Experience of Ireland, Scotland and Wales, 1100-1300*. Cambridge: Cambridge University Press, 1990.

De Paor, M and L. De Paor. *Early Christian Ireland*. London, 1958.

Duffy, Séan. "The 'Continuation' of Nicholas Trivet: A New Source for the Bruce Invasion," *Proceedings of the Royal Irish Academy* 91 C (1991), 303-15.

Duffy, Séan. "The Gaelic Account of The Bruce Invasion, *Cath Fhochairte Brighite*: Medieval Romance or Modern Forgery?" *Seanchas ard macha* 13 (1988), 59-121.

Duffy, Séan. "Ireland's Hastings: The Anglo-Norman Conquest of Dublin," *Anglo-Norman Studies* 20 (1997), 69-85.

Duncan, A.A.M. "The Scots Invasion of Ireland, 1315." In: *The British Isles, 1100-1500: Comparisons, Contrasts and Connections*. Edinburgh, 1988, pp. 100-17.

Ellis, Steven G. "Taxation and Defence in Late Medieval Ireland: The Survival of Scutage," *Journal of the Royal Society of Ireland* 107 (1977), 5-26.

Frame, Robin. "The Bruces in Ireland, 1315-18," *Irish Historical Studies* 19 (1974), 3-37.

Frame, Robin. "The Campaign against the Scots in Munster, 1317," *Irish Historical Studies* 24 (1984-85), 361-72.

Frame, Robin. "The Justiciarship of Ralph Ufford: Warfare and Politics in Fourteenth-Century Ireland," *Studia Hibernica* 13 (1973), 7-47.

Frame, Robin. "Military Service in the Lordship of Ireland, 1290-1360: Institutions and Society on the Anglo-Gaelic Frontier." In: *Medieval Frontier Societies*. Ed. R. Bartlett and A. MacKay. Oxford, 1989, 101-26.

Frame, Robin. "War and Peace in the Medieval Lordship of Ireland." In: *The English in Medieval Ireland*. Ed. James F. Lydon. Dublin, 1984, pp. 118-41.

Hayes-McCoy, G.A. *Irish Battles: A Military History of Ireland*. Belfast: Appeltree Press, 1990.

Hill, James Michael. "The Distinctiveness of Gaelic Warfare, 1400-1750," *European History Quarterly* 22 (1992), 323-45.

Lucas, A.T. "Irish-Norse Relations: Time for a Reappraisal?" *Journal of the Cork Historical and Archaeological Society* 71 (1966), 62-75.

Lydon, James F. "The Braganstown Massacre, 1329," *Journal of the County Louth Archaeological and Historical Society* 19 (1977), 5-16.

Lydon, James F. "An Irish Army in Scotland, 1296," *Irish Sword* 5 (1962), 184-89.

Lydon, James F. "Irish Levies in the Scottish Wars, 1296-1302," *Irish Sword* 5 (1962), 207-17.

Lydon, James F. "The Problem of the Frontier in Medieval Ireland," *Topic* 13 (1967), 5-22.

Lydon, James F., ed. *Law and Disorder in Thirteenth Century Ireland*. Dublin: Four Courts Press, 1997.

MacIomhair, Diarmuid. "Bruce's Invasion and the First Campaign in County Louth," *Irish Sword* 10 (1971-72), 188-212.

MacIomhair, Diarmuid. "The Battle of Fochart, 1318," *Irish Sword* 8 (1967-68), 192-209.

McAulffe, Mary. "The Town House and Warfare in Ireland in the Fourteenth and Fifteenth Centuries," *Irish Sword* 18 (1990-92), 297-302.

McNeill, T.E. "Castles of Ward and the Changing Pattern of Border Conflict in Ireland," *Château Gaillard* 17 (1996), 127-33.

NicGhiollanhaith, A. "Dynastic Warfare and Historical Writing in North Munster, 1276-1350," *Cambridge Medieval Celtic Studies* 2 (1981), 73-89.

Nicholson, Ranald. "A Sequel to Edward Bruce's Invasion of Ireland," *Scottish Historical Review* 42 (1963-64), 30-40.

Ó Cléirigh, Cormac. "Irish Frontier Warfare–A Fifteenth-Century Case Study." In: *XXII. Kongreß der Internationalen Kommission für Militärgeschichte Acta 22: Von Crécy bis Mohács Kriegswesen im späten Mittelalter (1346-1526)*. Vienna, 1997, pp. 179-94.

Ó Cróinín, Dáibhí. *Early Medieval Ireland, 400-1200*. Longman History of Ireland. London: Longman, 1995.

O'Doherty, J.F. "The Anglo-Norman Invasion of 1167-71," *Irish Historical Studies* 1 (1938-39), 154-57.

Ó Néill, Pádraig. "The Impact of the Norman Invasion on Irish Literature," *Anglo-Norman Studies* 20 (1997), 171-85.

Orpen, G.H. *Ireland under the Normans*. London, 1911-12.

Otway-Ruthven, J. "Knight Service in Ireland," *Journal of the Royal Society of Antiquaries of Ireland* 89 (1959), 1-15.

Phillips, J.R.S. "Documents on the Early Stages of the Bruce Invasion of Ireland, 1315-1316," *Proceedings of the Royal Irish Academy* 79 (1979), 247-70.

Ryan, John. "The Battle of Clontarf," *Journal of the Royal Society of Antiquaries of Ireland* 68 (1938), 1-50.

Simms, Katherine. *From Kings to Warlords: The Changing Political Structure of Gaelic Ireland in the Later Middle Ages*. Studies in Celtic History, vii. Woodbridge: Boydell and Brewer, 1987.

Simms, Katherine. "Warfare in the Medieval Gaelic Lordships," *Irish Sword* 12 (1976), 98-108.

Walsh, Paul V. *The Role of Naval Power in the Rise of a National Monarchy: Ireland, 900-1200.* Unpublished Masters Thesis. Philadelphia: Temple University, 1994.

Wyatt, David. "Gruffudd ap Cynan and the Hiberno-Norse World," *Welsh Historical Review* 19 (1999), 595-615.

Medieval – Islam [See also – Crusades]

Agadzhanov, Sergei G. Государство селджукидов и средняя азия в *XI-XII* веках. Moscow: Nauka, 1991.

Agadzhanov, Sergei G. *Der Staat der Seldschukiden und Mittelasien im 11-12 Jahrhundert.* Turkmenenforschung, 17. Berlin: Reinhold Schletzer, 1994.

Akram, A.I. *The Muslim Conquest of Persia.* Rawalpindi, 1976.

Akram, A.I. *The Sword of Allah: Khalid bin al Waleed, His Life and Campaigns.* Karachi, 1970.

Al Jahiz. "Jahiz of Basra to Al-Fath ibn Khaqan on the Exploits of the Turks and the Army of the Khalifate in General," trans. C.T. Harley-Walker, *Journal of the Royal Asiatic Society* (Oct 1915), 631-97.

al-Sarraf, Shihab. "Furusiyya Literature of the Mamluk Period." In: *Furusiyya.* Vol. I: *The Horse in the Art of the Near East.* Ed. D. Alexander. Riyadh: King Abdulaziz Public Library, 1996, pp. 118-35.

Alverny, Marie-Thérèse d'. "La connaissance de l'Islam en occident du IXe au milieu du XII siècle." In: *L'occidente e l'Islam nell'alto medioevo.* Settimane di studi del centro Italiano sull'alto medieovo, 12. Spoleto: Presso la Sede del Centro, 1965, II:577-602.

Amitai-Preiss, Reuven. "The Mamluk Officer Class During the Reign of Sultan Baybars." In: *War and Society in the Eastern Mediterranean, 7th-15th Centuries.* Ed. Y. Lev. Leiden, 1997, pp. 267-300.

André, P.J. "Occupation Byzantine et Turque en Afrique du nord," *Revue internationale d'histoire militaire* 13 (1953), 17-24.

Athamina, Khalil. "Some Administrative, Military and Socio-Political Aspects of Early Muslim Egypt." In: *War and Society in the Eastern Mediterranean, 7th-15th Centuries.* Ed. Y. Lev. Leiden, 1997, pp. 101-14.

Ayalon, David. "Aspects of the Mamluk Phenomenon: The Importance of the Mamluk Institution," *Der Islam* 53 (1976), 196-225.

Ayalon, David. "The Circassians in the Mamluk Kingdom," *Journal of the American Oriental Society* 69 (1949), 135-47.

Ayalon, David. "The Mamluks and Naval Power: A Phase of the Struggle between Islam and Christian Europe," *Proceedings of the Israel Academy of Sciences and Humanities* 1 (1965), 1-12.

Ayalon, David. "The Military Reforms of Caliph al-Mu'taşim." In: *Islam and the Abode of War.* Aldershot: Variorum, 1994, pp. 1-39.

Ayalon, David. "The Muslim City and the Mamluk Military Aristocracy," *Proceedings of the Israel Academy of Sciences and Humanities* 2 (1968), 311-29.

Ayalon, David. "Notes on the Furusiyya Exercises and Games in the Mamluk Sultanate," *Scripta Hierosolymitana* 9 (1961), 31-62.

Ayalon, David. "Payment in Mamluk Military Society," *Journal of Economic and Social History of the Orient* 1 (1958).

Ayalon, David. "Preliminary Remarks on the Mamluk Military Institution in Islam." In: *War, Technology, and Society in the Middle East.* Ed. V.J. Parry and M.E. Yapp. London: Oxford University Press, 1975, pp. 44-58.

Ayalon, David. "Studies in the Structure of the Mamluk Army. I: The Army Stationed in Egypt," *Bulletin of the School of Oriental and African Studies* 15 (1953), 203-28.

Ayalon, David. "Studies in the Structure of the Mamluk Army. II: The Halqa'," *Bulletin of the School of Oriental and African Studies* 15 (1953), 448-76.

Ayalon, David. "Studies in the Structure of the Mamluk Army. III: Holders of Offices Connected with the Army," *Bulletin of the School of Oriental and African Studies* 16 (1954), 57-90.

Bareket, Elingar. "Personal Adversities of Jews during the Period of the Fatimid Wars in Eleventh Century Palestine." In: *War and Society in the Eastern Mediterranean, 7th-15th Centuries*. Ed. Y. Lev. Leiden, 1997, pp. 153-62.

Beckwith, C.I. "Aspects of the Early History of the Central Asian Guard Corps in Islam," *Archivum eurasiae medii aevi* 4 (1984), 29-43.

Beshir, B.J. "Fatimid Military Organization," *Der Islam* 55 (1978), 37-56.

Bianquis, Thierry. "La fortune politique du cavalier turc en Syrie au XIe siècle: Eléments pour l'élaboration d'un *war game*." In: *Castrum 3: Guerre, fortification et habitant dans le monde méditerranéen au moyen âge*. Ed. André Bazzana. Rome: L'école Française de Rome, 1988, pp. 59-66.

Blankinship, K.Y. *The End of the Jihad State*. Albany: State University of New York Press, 1994.

Bombaci, A. "The Army of the Saljuqs of Rum," *Instituto orientale di Napoli annali* n.s. 38 (1978), 343-69.

Bonner, Michael. *Aristocratic Violence and Holy War: Studies in the Jihad and the Arab-Byzantine Frontier*. American Oriental Series, 81. New Haven: American Oriental Society, 1996.

Bosworth, C.E. "Abu 'Amr 'Uthman al-Tarsusi's Sivar al Thughur and the Last Years of Arab Rule in Tarsus (Fourth/Tenth Century)," *Graeco-Arabica* 5 (1993), 183-95.

Bosworth, C.E. "Armies of the Saffarids," *Bulletin of the School of Oriental and African Studies* 31 (1968), 534-54.

Bosworth, C.E. "The City of Tarsus and the Arab-Byzantine Frontiers in Early and Middle Abbasid Times," *Oriens* 33 (1992), 268-86.

Bosworth, C.E. "Ghaznavid Military Organization," *Der Islam* 36 (1960), 37-77.

Bosworth, C.E. *The Ghaznavids*. Edinburgh, 1963.

Bosworth, C.E. *The Later Ghaznavids: Splendour and Decay.* Edinburgh, 1977.

Bosworth, C.E. "Military Organization under the Buyids of Persia and Iraq," *Oriens* 18-19 (1965-66), 143-67.

Bosworth, C.E. "Recruitment, Muster and Review in Medieval Islamic Armies." In: *War, Technology and Society in the Middle East.* Ed. V.J. Parry and M.E. Yapp. London: Oxford University Press, 1975, pp. 59-77.

Bosworth, Edmund. "Armies of the Prophet." In: *Islam and the Arab World: Faith, People, Culture.* New York, 1976, pp. 201-12.

Brett, M. "The Military Interest in the Battle of Haydaran." In: *War, Technology, and Society in the Middle East.* Ed. V.J. Parry and M.E. Yapp. London: Oxford University Press, 1975, pp. 78-88.

Brooks, E.W. "The Arabs in Asia Minor (641-750) from Arabic Sources," *Journal of Hellenic Studies* 18 (1898), 182-208.

Brooks, E.W. "The Campaign of 716-718 from Arabic Sources," *Journal of Hellenic Studies* 19 (1899), 19-33.

Brunschwig, R. *La berberie orientale sous les Hafsides des origines à la fin du XVe siècle.* Paris, 1940-47.

Bulliet, Richard W. *The Camel and the Wheel.* Cambridge: Harvard University Press, 1975.

Bulliet, Richard W. *Conversion to Islam in the Medieval Period: An Essay in Quantitative History.* Cambridge: Harvard University Press, 1979.

Butler, A.J. *The Arab Conquest of Egypt.* 2nd ed. Oxford, 1978.

Cahen, Claude. "L'administration financière de l'armée Fatimide d'après al-Makhzumi," *Journal of Economic and Social History of the Orient* 15 (1972), 163-82.

Cahen, Claude. "Note sur l'esclavage musulman et le dervichisme Ottoman: à propos des travaux récents," *Journal of the Economic and Social History of the Orient* 13 (1970), 211-18.

Cahen, Claude. "La première pénétration turque en Asie Mineur (seconde moitié du XIe s.)," *Byzantion* 18 (1948), 5-67.

Cahen, Claude. "The Turkish Invasion: The Selchükids." In: *A History of the Crusades*. Ed. Kenneth M. Setton. Madison: University of Wisconsin Press, 1969, I:135-76.

Canard, M. "La campagne arménienne du Sultan salguqide Alp Arslan et la prise d'Ani en 1064," *Revue des études arméniennes* n.s.2 (1965), 239-59.

Canard, M. "Le céremonial Fatamite et le céremonial Byzantin," *Byzantion* 21 (1951), 355-420.

Canard, M. "Les relations entre les Mérinides et les Mamelouks au XIVe siècle," *Annales de l'Institut d'ètudes Orientales de la Faculté des lettres d'Alger* 5 (1939-41), pp. 41-81.

Charnay, J.P. "Ethique de guerrier arabe: valeurs classiques et transpositions actuelles," *Revue internationale d'histoire militaire* 49 (1980), 161-70.

Collins, Roger. *The Arab Conquest of Spain, 710-797*. London, 1989.

Constantelos, D.J. "The Moslem Conquests of the Near East as Revealed in the Greek Sources of the Seventh and Eighth Centuries," *Byzantion* 42 (1972), 325-57.

Cook, Michael. *Muhammad*. Oxford: Oxford University Press, 1983.

Cook, Weston F., Jr. *The Hundred Years War for Morocco: Gunpowder and the Military Revolution in the Early Modern Muslim World*. Boulder: Westview Press, 1994.

Cook, Weston F., Jr. "Warfare and Firearms in Fifteenth Century Morocco, 1400-1492," *War and Society* 11 (1993), 25-40.

Crone, Patricia. "Early Islamic World." In: *War and Society in the Ancient and Medieval Worlds: Asia, the Mediterranean, Europe, and Mesoamerica*. Ed. Kurt Raaflaub and Nathan Rosenstein. Washington: Center for Hellenic Studies, 1999, pp. 309-32.

Dachraoui, Farhat. "La captivité d'Ibn Wasul, le rebelle de Sidjilmassa," *Revue internationale d'histoire militaire* 18 (1956), 295-300.

Daniel, Norman. *Islam and the West: The Making of an Image*. Edinburgh: Edinburgh University Press, 1960.

De Moraes Farias, P.F. "The Almoradids: Some Questions Concerning the Character of the Movement during Its Periods of Closest Contact with the Western Sudan," *Bulletin de l'institut fondamentale d'Afrique noir* ser. B, 29 (1967), 794-878.

Donner, Fred McGraw. "Centralized Authority and Military Autonomy in the Early Islamic Conquests." In: *The Byzantine and Early Islamic Near East*. III: *States, Resources and Armies*. Ed. Averil Cameron. Studies in Late Antiquity and Early Islam, 1. Princeton: The Darwin Press, Inc., 1995, pp. 337-60.

Donner, Fred McGraw. *The Early Arabic Conquests*. Princeton: Princeton University Press, 1981.

Douillet, G. "Furusiyya." In: *Encyclopedia of Islam*. 2nd ed. Leiden, 1965, II:952-54.

Elad, A. "The Siege of Al Wasit (132/749)." In: *Studies in Islamic History and Civilization in Honour of Professor David Ayalon*. Ed. M. Sharon. Jerusalem, 1986, pp. 59-90.

Elbeheiry, S. *Les institutions de l'Egypte au temps des Ayyubides*. Lille, 1972.

Frye, R.N. *The Golden Age of Persia: The Arabs in the East*. London, 1975.

Garcin, Jean-Claude. "The Mamluk Military System and the Blocking of Medieval Moslem Society." In: *Europe and the Rise of Capitalism*. Ed. J. Baechler et al. Oxford, 1988, pp. 113-30.

Gaudefoy Demombynes, M. *Syrie à l'epoque Mameloukes d'après les auteurs Arabes*. Paris, 1923.

Gibb, Hamilton A.R. *The Arab Conquests in Central Asia*. London, 1923.

Gordon, Matthew. *The Breaking of a Thousand Swords: A History of the Turkish Military of Samarra, 200-275 AH/815-889 CE*. SUNY Series in Medieval Middle East History. Albany: State University of New York Press, 2001.

Graf, D.F. "The Saracens and the Defence of the Arabian Frontier," *Bulletin of the American Schools of Oriental Research* 209 (1978), 11-26.

Haldon, John F. "Seventh-Century Continuities: the *Ajnād* and the 'Thematic Myth'." In: *The Byzantine and Early Islamic Near East*. III: *States, Resources and Armies*. Ed. Averil Cameron. Studies in Late Antiquity and Early Islam, 1. Princeton: The Darwin Press, Inc., 1995, pp. 379-424.

Haldon, John F. and Hugh Kennedy. "The Arab-Byzantine Frontier in the Eighth and Ninth Centuries: Military Organisation and Society in the Borderlands," *Zbornik radova vizantoloskog instituta* 19 (1980), 79-116.

Harpster, Matthew. "Possible Results of the Muslim Invasion on Merchant Shipping and Shipbuilding Techniques in the Mediterranean." In: *Travel, Technology and Organization in Medieval Europe: Papers of the "Medieval Europe Brugge 1997" Conference Volume 8*. Ed. Guy De Boe & Frans Verhaeghe. Zellik: Instituut voor het Archeologisch Patrimonium, 1997, pp. 7-12.

Hill, Donald R. "The Role of the Camel and the Horse in the Early Arab Conquests." In: *War, Technology and Society in the Middle East*. Ed. V.J. Parry and M.E. Yapp. London: Oxford University Press, 1975, pp. 32-43.

Hodgson, Marshall G.S. *The Order of Assassins: The Struggle of the Early Nizari Ismailis Against the Islamic World*. 's-Gravenhage: Mouton, 1955.

Hourani, Albert. *A History of the Arab Peoples*. Cambridge: The Belknap Press of Harvard University Press, 1991.

Hrochová, Vera. "Byzance et les turcs seljoukides, 1071-1204: Aspects socio-économiques," *Byzantinoslavica* 54 (1993), 142-46.

Hudayl, Ibn. *Gala de caballeros: Bláson de paladines*. Ed. María Jesús Viguerra. Biblioteca de la Literatura y el Pensamiento Hispanícos, 24. Madrid: Editora Nacional, 1977.

Irwin, Robert. "Factions in Medieval Egypt," *Journal of the Royal Asiatic Society* (1986), 228-46.

Ismail, O.S.A. "Mu'tasim and the Turks," *Bulletin of the School of Oriental and African Studies* 29 (1966), 12-24.

Jandora, J.W. "The Battle of Yarmuk: A Reconstruction," *Journal of Asian History* 19 (1985), 8-21.

Jandora, J.W. "Developments in Islamic Warfare: The Early Conquests," *Studia Islamica* 64 (1986), 101-13.

Jandora, J.W. *The March from Medina: A Revisionist Study of the Arab Conquests*. Clifton: Kingston Press, 1990.

Jurji, E.J. "The Islamic Theory of War," *The Moslem World* 30 (1940), 332-42.

Kaegi, Walter E. *Byzantium and the Early Islamic Conquests*. Cambridge: Cambridge University Press, 1992.

Kaegi, Walter E. "Initial Byzantine Reactions to the Islamic Conquest," *Church History* 38 (1969).

Kennedy, Hugh. *The Early Abbasid Caliphate: A Political History*. London, 1981.

Kennedy, Hugh. "The Financing of the Military in the Early Islamic State." In: *The Byzantine and Early Islamic Near East*. III: *States, Resources and Armies*. Ed. Averil Cameron. Studies in Late Antiquity and Early Islam, 1. Princeton: The Darwin Press, Inc., 1995, pp. 361-78.

Kennedy, Hugh. *The Prophet and the Age of the Caliphates: The Islamic Near East from the Sixth to the Eleventh Centuries*. London: Longman, 1986.

Khan, G.M. "The Islamic and Ghaznawide Banners," *Nagpur University Journal* 9 (1943), 106-17.

Khazanov, Anatoly M. "Muhammad and Jenghiz Kham Compared: The Religious Factor in Wolrd Empire Building," *Proceedings of the British Academy* 82 (1993), 149-69.

Kister, M.J. "Al-Hira: Some Notes on its Relation with Arabia," *Arabica* 15 (1968), 143-69.

Kister, M.J. "Mecca and Tamim (Aspects of their Relationship)," *Journal of the Economic and Social History of the Orient* 8 (1965), 113-63.

Kuloglu, Abdullah. "The Anatolian Seljuk State (1077-1308)," *Revue internationale d'histoire militaire* 46 (1980), 15-30.

Lagardère, Vincent. "Évolution de la notion de *djihad* à l'époque almoravide (1039-1147)," *Cahiers de civilisation médiévale (X-XIIe siècle)* 41 (1998), 3-16.

Lambton, A.K.S. "Reflections on the Iqta." In: *Arabic and Islamic Studies in Honour of Hamilton A.R. Gibb.* Leiden, 1965, pp. 358-76.

Landau-Tasseron, Ella. "Features of the Pre-Conquest Muslim Armies in the Time of Muhammad." In: *The Byzantine and Early Islamic Near East.* III: *States, Resources and Armies.* Ed. Averil Cameron. Studies in Late Antiquity and Early Islam, 1. Princeton: The Darwin Press, Inc., 1995, pp. 299-336.

Lassner, J. *The Shaping of 'Abbasid Rule.* Princeton: Princeton University Press, 1980.

Latham, J.D. "The Strategic Position and Defence of Ceuta in the Later Muslim Period," *Islamic Quarterly* 15 (1971), 189-204.

Leaf, W. "Developments in the System of Armorial Insignia during the Ayyubid and Mamluk Periods," *Palestine Exploration Quarterly* 115 (1983), 61-74.

Lev, Yaacov. "Army, Regime, and Society in Fatamid Egypt, 358-487/968-1094," *International Journal of Middle East Studies* 19 (1987), 337-66.

Lev, Yaacov. "The Fatamid Army, A.H. 358-427/968-1036 C.E.: Military and Social Aspects," *Asian and African Studies* 14 (1980), 165-92.

Lev, Yaacov. "Fatamid Policy towards Damascus (358/968-386/996): Military, Political and Social Aspects," *Jerusalem Studies in Arabic and Islam* 3 (1981-82), 165-83.

Lev, Yaacov. "Regime, Army and Society in Medieval Egypt, 9th-12th Centuries." In: *War and Society in the Eastern Mediterranean, 7th-15th Centuries.* Ed. Y. Lev. Leiden, 1997, pp. 115-52.

Lev, Yaacov. *State and Society in Fatamid Egypt.* Arab History and Civilization: Studies and Texts, 1. Leiden: Brill, 1991.

Lewis, Bernard. *The Assassins: A Radical Sect in Islam.* London: Weidenfeld and Nicholson, 1967.

Lewis, Bernard. *Islam from the Prophet Muhammad to the Capture of Constantinople.* Vol. 1: *Politics and War.* New York, 1974.

Lewis, Bernard. "The Isma'ites and the Assasins." In: *A History of the Crusades.* Ed. Kenneth M. Setton. Madison: University of Wisconsin Press, 1969, I:99-132.

Lilie, Ralph-Johannes. "Araber und Themen: Zum Einfluß der arabischen Expansion auf die byzantinische Militärorganization." In: *The Byzantine and Early Islamic Near East.* III: *States, Resources and Armies.* Ed. Averil Cameron. Studies in Late Antiquity and Early Islam, 1. Princeton: The Darwin Press, Inc., 1995, pp. 425-60.

Lings, M. *Muhammad: His Life Based on the Earliest Sources.* London, 1983.

Lokkegaard, Frede. "The Concepts of War and Peace in Islam." In: *War and Peace in the Middle Ages.* Ed. B.P. McGuire. Copenhagen, 1987, pp. 263-81.

Mahdjoub, A. "L'habillement des soldats 'abbasides'," *Bulletin des études Arabes (Algiers)* 8 (1948), 3-5.

Martel-Thoumian, Bernadette. "Les dernières batailles du grand émir Yašbak min Mahdī." In: *War and Society in the Eastern Mediterranean, 7th-15th Centuries.* Ed. Y. Lev. Leiden, 1997, pp. 301-42.

Mayer, L.A. *Saracenic Heraldry.* Oxford, 1933.

Mayerson, P. "The First Muslim Attacks on Southern Palestine (AD 633-4)," *Transactions and Proceedings of the American Philological Association* 95 (1964), 155-99.

Morabia, Alfred. "Gihad et volontaires du combat contre 'l'infidele' dans l'Islam médiéval." In: *Recrutement, mentalités, sociétés: Actes du colloque international d'histoire militaire, 18-22 septembre 1974.* Montpellier, 1974, pp. 9-15.

Morgan, D.O. *Medieval Persia (1040-1797).* London, 1988.

Mottahedeh, R.P. *Loyalty and Leadership in an Early Islamic Society.* Princeton: Princeton University Press, 1980.

Nicolle, David C. *The Armies of Islam, 7th-11th Centuries*. London: Osprey, 1983

Nicolle, David C. "Arms of the Umayyad Era: Military Technology in a Time of Change." In *War and Society in the Eastern Mediterranean, 7th-15th Centuries*. Ed. Y. Lev. Leiden, 1997, pp. 9-100.

Nicolle, David C. "The Capella Palatina Ceiling and the Muslim Military Heritage of Norman Sicily," *Gladius* 16 (1983), 45-145.

Nicolle, David C. "An Introduction to Arms and Warfare in Classical Islam." In: *Islamic Arms and Armour*. Ed. Robert Elgood. London: Scolar Press, 1979, pp. 162-86.

Nicolle, David C. "The Reality of Mamluk Warfare: Weapons, Armour and Tactics," *Al-Masāq* 7 (1994), 77-110.

Nicolle, David C. *Saracen Faris, 1050-1250 AD*. London: Osprey, 1994.

Nicolle, David C. *Sassanian Armies: The Iranian Empire Early 3rd to mid-7th Centuries AD*. Stockport, 1996.

Nicolle, David C. *Yarmuk, 636 AD: The Muslim Conquest of Syria*. London: Osprey Publishing Limited, 1994.

Noth, Albrecht. "Les *ulama* en qualité de guerriers." In: *Saber relgioso y poder político en el Islam: Actas del simposio internacional (Granada, 15-18 octobre 1991*. Madrid: Agencia Española de Cooperación Internacional, 1994, pp. 175-95.

Parry, V.J. "Le manière de combattre." In: *War, Technology and Society in the Middle East*. Ed. V.J. Parry and M.E. Yapp. London: Oxford University Press, 1975, pp. 218-56.

Parry, V.J. "Warfare." In: *Cambridge History of Islam*. Ed. P.M. Holt. Cambridge: Cambridge University Press, 1970, pp. 824-50.

Partner, Peter. *God of Battles: Holy Wars of Christianity and Islam*. London: Harper Collins, 1997.

Peters, R. *Jihad in Medieval and Modern Islam*. Leiden, 1977.

Pipes, D. *Slave Soldiers and Islam: The Genesis of a Military System*. New Haven: Yale University Press, 1981.

Rabie, H. "The Training of the Mamluk Fāris." In: *War, Technology and Society in the Middle East*. Ed. V.J. Parry and M.E. Yapp. London: Oxford University Press, 1975.

Richard, Jean. "Les Turcopoles: Musulmans convertés ou Chrétiens orientaux," *Revue des études Islamiques* 54 (1986), 259-70.

Ritter, H. "*La parure des cavaliers* und die Literatur über die ritterlichen Künste," *Die Islam* 18 (1929).

Robinson, B.W. "A Persian Battle-Piece," *Apollo* 127 (Feb 1988), 77-82.

Rubin, Zeev. "The Reforms of Khurso Anūshirwān." In: *The Byzantine and Early Islamic Near East*. III: *States, Resources and Armies*. Ed. Averil Cameron. Studies in Late Antiquity and Early Islam, 1. Princeton: The Darwin Press, Inc., 1995, pp. 227-97.

Sadeque, S.F. *Baybars I of Egypt*. Oxford, 1956.

Salih, A.H. "Le rôle des bédouins d'Egypte à l'époque Fatimide," *Rivista degli studi orientale* 54 (1980), 51-65.

Scanlon, G.T. *A Muslim Manual of War*. Cairo, 1961.

Setton, Kenneth M. *Western Hostility to Islam and Prophecies of Turkish Doom*. Philadelphia: American Philosophical Society, 1992.

Shaban, M.A. *Islamic History, AD 600-750: A New Interpretation*. Cambridge, 1971.

Shahid, Irfan. *Byzantium and the Arabs in the Fifth Century*. Washington: Dumbarton Oaks, 1989.

Shahid, Irfan. *Byzantium and the Arabs in the Sixth Century*. Vol 1, pt. 1: *Political and Military History*. Washington: Dumbarton Oaks, 1995.

Sharon, M. *Black Banners from the East: The Establishment of the 'Abbasid State–Incubation of a Revolt*. Jerusalem, 1983.

Sharon, M. "The Military Reforms of Abu Muslim, Their Background and Consequences." In: *Studies in Islamic History and Civilization in Honour of Professor David Ayalon*. Ed. M. Sharon. Jerusalem, 1986, pp. 105-43.

Sievers, P. von. "Military, Merchants and Nomads: The Social Evolution of the Syrian Cities and Countryside during the Classical Period, 780-969/164-358," *Der Islam* 56 (1979), 212-44.

Simeonova, Liliana. "In the Depths of Tenth-Century Byzantine Ceremonial: The Treatment of Arab Prisoners of War at Imperial Banquets," *Byzantine and Modern Greek Studies* 22 (1998), 75-104.

Smith, G. Rex. *Medieval Muslim Horsemanship: A Fourteenth-Century Arabic Cavalry Manual*. London: The British Museum, 1979.

Smith, J.M. *A History of the Sarbadar Dynasty, 1336-1381 AD, and Its Sources*. The Hague: 1970.

Smith, S. "Events in Arabia in the 6th Century AD," *Bulletin of the School of Oriental and African Studies* 16 (1954), 425-68.

Sourdel, Dominique. *Medieval Islam*. Trans. J. Montgomery Watt. London: Routledge and Kegan Paul, 1983.

Taha, Abd al Wahid Dhanun. *The Muslim Conquest and Settlement of North Africa and Spain*. London, 1989.

Tantum, G. "Muslim Warfare: A Study of a Medieval Muslim Treatise on the Art of War." In: *Islamic Arms and Armour*. Ed. Robert Elgood. London: Scolar Press, 1979, pp. 187-201.

Terrasse, Henri. "Conséquences d'une invasion Berbère: Le rôle des Almoravides dans l'histoire de l'occident." In: *Mélanges d'histoire du moyen âge dédiés à la mémoire de Louis Halphen*. Paris: Presses universitaires de France, 1951, pp. 673-81.

Thorau, Peter. *The Lion of Egypt: Sultan Baybars I and the Near East in the Thirteenth Century*. Trans. P.M. Holt. London, 1992.

Turan, O. "World Domination among the Medieval Turks," *Studia Islamica* 4 (1955), 77-90.

Vasiliev, Alexander A. *Byzance et les arabes*. 2 vols. Brussels, 1934, 1950.

Vyronis, Speros, Jr. "The Experience of Christians under Seljuk and Ottoman Domination, Eleventh to Sixteenth Century." In: *Conversion and Continuity: Indigenous Christian Communities in Islamic Lands, Eighth to Eighteenth Centuries*. Ed. Michael Gervers and Ramzi Jibran Bikhazi.

Papers in Mediaeval Studies, 9. Toronto: Pontifical Institute of Mediaeval Studies, 1990, pp. 185-216.

Walker, P.E. "A Byzantine Victory over the Fatamids at Alexandretta (971)," *Byzantion* 42 (1972), 431-40.

Weigert, Gideon. "A Note on Hudna: Peace Making in Islam." In: *War and Society in the Eastern Mediterranean, 7th-15th Centuries.* Ed. Y. Lev. Leiden, 1997, pp. 399-406.

Wellhausen, J. *The Arab Kingdom and Its Fall.* Trans. M.Weir. Calcutta: University of Calcutta, 1927.

Zakeri, M. *Sāsānid Soldiers in Early Muslim Society.* Weisbaden: Harrassowitz, 1995.

Zaky, 'Abd al-Rahman. "Military Literature of the Arabs," *Cahiers d'histoire égyptienne* 7 (1955), 149-60.

Zaky, 'Abd al-Rahman. "A Preliminary Bibliography of Medieval Arabic Military Literature," *Gladius* 4 (1965), 107-12.

Zoppoth, G. "Muhammed Ibn Mängli: Ein ägyptischer Offizier und Schriftsteller des 14. Jahrhundherts," *Wiener Zeitschrift für die Kunde des Morgenlandes* 53 (1957), 288-99.

Medieval – Italy [See also – Mercenaries]

Abulafia, David. "Bad Rulership in Angevin Italy: the Sicilian Vespers and their Ramifications," *Haskins Society Journal* 8 (1996), 115-35.

Airaldi, Gabriella. "The Genoese Art of War." In: *Across the Mediterranean Frontiers: Trade, Politics and Religion, 650-1450: Selected Proceedings of the International Medieval Congress, University of Leeds, 10-13 July 1995, 8-11 July 1996.* Ed. Dionisius A. Agius and Ian Richard Netton. Turnhout: Brepols, 1997, pp. 269-82.

Alessandro, V. d'. *Politica e società nella Sicilia Aragonese.* Palermo, 1963.

Amatuccio, Giovanni. "Saracen Archers in Southern Italy," *Journal of the Society of Archer-Antiquaries* 41 (1998), 76-80.

Ancona, C. "Milizie e condottieri." In: *Storia d'Italia*. 5: *I documenti*. Ed. G. Einaudi. Turin, 1973, pp. 642-65.

Ashtor, Eliyahu and Benjamin Z. Kedar. "Una guerra fra Genova e i Mamlucchi negli anni 1380," *Archivio storico Italiano* 133 (1975), 3-44.

Balard, Michel. "Les formes militaires de la colonisation génoise (XIIIe-XVe siècles)." In: *Castrum 3: Guerre, fortification et habitant dans le monde méditerranéen au moyen âge*. Ed. André Bazzana. Rome: L'école Française de Rome, 1988, pp. 67-78.

Barbarich, E. "Gli stradiotti nell'arte militare veneziana," *Rivista di cavalleria* 13 (1904).

Barbero, Alessandro. "L'organizzazione militare del ducato sabaudo durante la guerra di milano," *Societa e storia* 71 (1996), 1-38.

Barlozetti, U. and M. Giuliani. "La prassi guerresca in Toscana." In: *Guerre e assoldati in Toscana, 1260-1364*. Ed. L.G. Boccia and M. Scalini. Florence, 1982, pp. 51-67.

Bautier, Robert-Henri. "Soudoyers d'Outremont à Plaisancce: Leur origine géographique et le mécanisme de leurs emprunts (1293-1330)." In: *La guerre et la paix: Frontières et violences au moyen âge*. Actes du 101e congrès national des sociétés savantes, Lille, 1976. Paris: Bibliothèque Nationale, 1978, pp. 95-129.

Bayley, C.C. *War and Society in Renaissance Florence: The De Militia of Leonardo Bruni*. Toronto: University of Toronto Press, 1961.

Becker, Marvin B. "Changing Patterns of Violence and Justice in Fourteenth- and Fifteenth-Century Florence," *Comparative Studies in Society and History* 18 (1976), 281-96.

Benedetti, A. *Il fatto d'armee del Taro*. Novaro, 1863.

Bertinaria, Pier Luigi. "L'arte militare Italiana dal tardo medio evo al rinascimento." In: *Acta del XVIII Congresso internazionale di storia militare: La scoperta del nuovo mondo e la sua influenza nella storia militare*. Ed. Paolo Alberini and Michele Nones. Turin, 1993, pp. 13-18.

Bianchessi, Silvia. "Cavalli, armi e salnitro fra Milano e Napoli nel secondo quattrocento (1466-1492)," *Nuovo rivista storica* 82 (1998), 541-82.

Blastenbrei, Peter. "The Soldier and His Cardinal: Francesco Sforza and Nicolò Acciapacci, 1438-1444," *Renaissance Studies* 3 (1989), 290-302.

Boccia, Lionella Giorgio. "Le armi medicee negli inventari del Cinquecento." In: *Le arti del principato mediceo* Florence, 1980, pp. 383-405.

Boccia, Lionella Giorgio. *I guerrieri di Avio*. Milan, 1991.

Boccia, Lionella Giorgio and Mario Scalini. "HIC IACET MILES: Immagini guerriere da sepulcri toscani del due e trecento." In: *Guerre e assoldati in Toscana, 1260-1364*. Ed. L.G. Boccia and M. Scabini. Florence: Museo Stibbert, 1983, pp. 81-103.

Boccia, Lionella Giorgio and Mario Scalini, ed. *Guerre e assoldati in Toscana, 1260-1364*. Florence: Museo Stibbert, 1982.

Bowsky, William M. "City and Contado: Military Relationships and Communal Bonds in Fourteenth-Century Siena." In: *Renaissance Studies in Honor of Hans Baron*. Ed. A. Molho and J.A. Tedeschi. DeKalb: Northern Illinois University Press, 1971, pp. 75-98.

Bowsky, William M. *A Medieval Italian Commune: Siena under the Nine, 1287-1355*. Berkeley and Los Angeles: University of California Press, 1981.

Bresc, Henri. "Désertions, regroupements, stratégies dans la Sicile des Vêspres." In: *Castrum 3: Guerre, fortification et habitant dans le monde méditerranéen au moyen âge*. Ed. André Bazzana. Rome: L'école Française de Rome, 1988, pp. 237-46.

Breveglieri, B. "Armamento duecentesco bolognese da statuti e documenti d'archivio," *Bullettino dell'Instituto storico Italiano per il medio evo* 94 (1988).

Brown, T.S. "Settlement and Military Policy in Byzantine Italy." In: *Papers in Italian Archaeology, I: The Lancaster Seminar: Recent Research in Prehistoric, Classical, and Medieval Archaeology*. Ed. H.M. Blake, T.W. Potter, and D.B. Whitehouse. Oxford: British Archaeological Reports, 1978, II:323-38.

Butters, H.C. "Politics and Diplomacy in Late Quattrocento Italy: the Case of the Barons' War (1485-86)." In: *Florence and Italy: Renaissance Studies in Honour of Nicolai Rubenstein*. Ed. P. Denley and C. Elam. London, 1988, pp. 13-31.

Caferro, William. "Italy and the Companies of Adventure in the Fourteenth Century," *Historian* 58 (1996), 795-810.

Caferro, William. "Mercenaries and Military Expenditure: The Costs of Undeclared Warfare in Fourteenth Century Siena," *Journal of European Economic History* 23 (1994), 219-47.

Caferro, William. *Mercenary Companies and the Decline of Siena*. Baltimore: The Johns Hopkins University Press, 1998.

Caggese, R. *Roberto d'Angio e i suoi tempi*. Florence, 1922-30.

Cahen, C. *Le régime féodal de l'Italie normande*. Paris, 1940.

Canestrini, G. "Della milizia italiana dal secolo XIII al XVI," *Archivio storico Italiano* 15 (1851).

Cansacchi, C. "Connestabili ed uomini d'armi della S. Sede nella seconda metà del secolo XV," *Rivista del collegio Araldico* (1943), 5-10, 57-62, 96-105.

Cardini, F. and E. Salvini. *Montaperti 1260: Guerra, società ed errori*. Siena, 1984.

Cardini, Franco, E. Salvini and M. Tangheroni, ed. *Guerra e guerrieri nella Toscana medievale*. Florence, 1990.

Casula, Francesco Cesare. "Gli schiavi sardi della battaglia di Sanluri del 1409." In: *Società, istituzioni, spiritualità: Studi in onore di Cinzio Violante*. Ed. Girolamo Arnaldi et al. Spoleto: Centro Italiano di studi sull'alto medioevo. 1994, I:195-206.

Chamberlain, E.R. "The 'English' Mercenary Companies in Italy," *History Today* 6 (1956), 334-43.

Cherubini, G. *Signori, contadini, borghesi: Ricerche sulla società Italiana del basso medioevo*. Florence, 1974.

Ciampoli, D. *Il capitano del popolo a Siena nel primo trecento*. Siena, 1984.

Ciappelli, Giovanni. "A Trecento Bishop as Seen by Quattrocento Florentines: Sant' Andrea Corsini, His 'Life,' and the Battle of Anghari." In: *Portraits of Medieval and Renaissance Living: Essays in Memory of David Herlihy*. Ed. S.K. Cohn Jr. and S.A. Epstein. Ann Arbor, 1996, pp. 283-98.

Coelho, Edouardo T. "Le armi di Campaldino." In: *Il sabato di S. Barnaba: La battaglia di Campaldino, 11 giugno 1289-1989*. Milan, 1989.

Cohn, Samuel K, Jr. *Creating the Florentine State: Peasants and Rebellion, 1348-1434*. Cambridge: Cambridge University Press, 2000.

Coleman, Edward. "Italy's First Northern League," *History Today* 46.10 (Oct 1996), 6-8.

Corrao, Pietro. "L'aristocrazia militare del primo trecento: Fra dominio e politica," *Archivio storico Siciliano* 4th ser., 23 (1997), 81-108.

Covini, Maria Nadia. *L'esercito del duca: organizzazione militare e istituzioni al tempo degli Sforza (1450-1480)*. Rome: Istituto storico italiano per il medio evo, 1998.

Covini, Maria Nadia. "Liens politiques et militaires dans le système des États italiens (XIIIe-XVIe siècle)." In: *Guerre et concurrence entre les États européens du XIVe au XVIIIe siècle*. Ed. Philippe Contamine. Fondation Européenne de la Science: Les origines de l'État moderne en Europe, XIIIe-XVIIIe siècle. Paris: Presses universitaires de France, 1998, pp. 9-42.

Da Mosto, A. *Ordinamenti militari della soldatesche dello stato Romano dal 1430 al 1470*. Rome, 1903.

Dean, Trevor. "After the War of Ferrara: Relations between Venice and Ercole d'Este, 1484-1505." In: *War, Culture and Society in Renaissance Venice: Essays in Honour of John Hale*. Ed. D.S. Chambers, C.H. Clough and M.E. Mallett. London, 1993, pp. 73-98.

Dieterich, J.R. *Die Taktik in den Lombardenkriegen der Staufer*. Marburg, 1892.

Epstein, Steven A. *Genoa and the Genoese, 958-1528*. Chapel Hill: University of North Carolina Press, 1996.

Fasoli, G. *Le compagnie della armi a Bologna*. Bologna, 1934.

Finlay, Robert. "The Foundation of the Ghetto: Venice, the Jews, and the War of the League of Cambrai," *Proceedings of the American Philosophical Society* 126 (1982), 140-54.

Fiumi, E. *L'impresa di Lorenzo de' Medici contra Volterra (1472)*. Florence, 1948.

Föhl, W. "Niederrheinische Ritterschaft um Italien des Trecento," *Annalen des historischen Vereins für den Niederrhein* 165 (1963), 73-128.

Fontaine, Marie-Madeline. "Comment Pietro del Monte, condottiere Italien, parlait Espagnol," *Bibliothèque d'Humanisme et Renaissance* 54 (1992), 163-73.

Fontaine, Marie-Madeline. *La condottiere Pietro del Monte philosophe et écrivian de la renaissance*. Geneva, 1991.

France, John. "The Battle of Carcano: The Event and Its Importance," *War in History* 6 (1999), 245-61.

Franceschini, G. *I Montefeltro*. Milan, 1970.

Furiano, M. "La battaglia di Civitate (1053)," *Archivio storico pugliese* 11 (1949).

Galletti, A.I. "La società comunale di fronte alla guerra nelle fonti perugine nel 1282," *Bollettino della depputazione di storia patria per l'Umbria* 71 (1974), 35-98.

Gaudenzi, A. *Statuti delle società del popolo di Bologna*. I: *Società della armi*. Rome, 1889.

Gentile, P. "Lo stato Napoletano sotto Alfonso I d'Aragona," *Archivio storico per le provincie napoletane* 62-63 (1937-38).

Green, Louis. *Castruccio Castracani: A Study on the Origins and Character of a Fourteenth-Century Italian Despotism*. Oxford: Clarendon Press, 1986.

Gualdo, G. "I libri delle spese di guerra del Cardinal Albornoz in Italia conservati nell'Archivio Vaticano." In: *El Cardenal Albornoz y el Collegio de España*. Ed. E. Verdera y Tuello. Bologna, 1972, I:577-607.

Hale, John R. "Brescia and the Venetian Militia System in the Cinquecento." In: *Armi e cultura nel bresciano, 1420-1870*. Brescia, 1981, pp. 97-119.

Hale, John R. "War and Public Opinion in Renaissance Italy." In: *Italian Renaissance Studies*. Ed. E.F. Jacob. London, 1960, pp. 94-122; in: *Renaissance War Studies*. London, 1983, pp. 359-88.

Herde, Peter. "Die Schlacht bei Tagliacozzo: Eine historisch-topographische Studie," *Zeitschrift für bayerische Landesgeschichte* 25 (1962), 697-744.

Ilardi, Vincent. "The Assassination of Galeazzo Maria Sforza and the Reaction of Italian Diplomacy." In: *Violence and Civil Disorder in Italian Cities, 1200-1500*. Ed. Lauro Martines. Berkeley and Los Angeles: University of California Press, 1972, pp. 72-103.

Ilardi, Vincent. "The Banker-Statesman and the Condottiere-Prince: Cosimo de' Medici and Francesco Sforza, 1450-1464." In: *Studies in Italian Renaissance Diplomatic History*. London: Variorum, 1986, pp. 1-36.

Ilardi, Vincent. "France and Milan: The Uneasy Alliance, 1452-1466." In: *Gli Sforza a Milano e in Lombardia e i loro rapporti con gli stati italiano er europei (1450-1530)*. Milan: Cisalpino-Goliardica, 1982, pp. 405-46.

Ilardi, Vincent. "The Italian League, Francesco Sforza, and Charles VII (1454-1461)," *Studies in the Renaissance* 6 (1959), 129-66.

Ilardi, Vincent. "Lombard Cattle and Diplomacy in the Fifteenth Century." In: *Studies in Italian Renaissance Diplomatic History*. London: Variorum, 1986, pp. 1-12.

Jacoby, David. *Studies on the Crusader States and on Venetian Expansion*. London, 1989.

Jamme, Armand. "Les soudoyers pontificaux d'Outremont et leurs violences en Italie (1372-1398)." In: *La guerre, la violence et les gens au Moyen Âge*. I: *Guerre et violence*. Ed. P. Contamine and O. Guyotjeannin. 119e congrès national des sociétés historiques et scientifiques, Amiens, octobre 1994, Section d'histoire médiévale et philologie. Paris, 1996, pp. 151-69.

Jarry, Eugène. "La 'voie de fait' et l'alliance Franco-Milanaise (1386-1395)," *Bibliothèque de l'école de chartes* 53 (1892).

Knussert, R. *Die deutschen Italienfahrten, 951-1220, und die Wehrverfassung*. Ottingen, 1931.

Labande, E.R. *Rinaldo Orsini, comte de Tagliacozzo*. Monaco and Paris, 1939.

Lane, Steven G. "Rural Populations and the Experience of Warfare in Medieval Lombardy: The Case of Pavia." In: *The Circle of War in the Middle Ages: Essays on Medieval Military and Naval History*. Ed. Donald J. Kagay and L.J. Andrew Villalon. Woodbridge: The Boydell Press, 1999, pp. 127-36.

Lane, Frederic C. *Venice: A Maritime Republic*. Baltimore, 1973.

Lomax, John Phillip. "Frederick II, His Saracens, and the Papacy." In: *Medieval Christian Perceptions of Islam*. Hamden, 1997, pp. 175-97.

Maire-Vigueur, Jean-Claude. "Guerres, conquête du conado et transformations de l'habitat en Italie centrale au XIIIe siècle." In: *Castrum 3: Guerre, fortification et habitant dans le monde méditerranéen au moyen âge*. Ed. André Bazzana. Rome: L'école Française de Rome, 1988, pp. 271-78.

Mallett, Michael. "Diplomacy and War in Later Fifteenth-Century Italy," *Proceedings of the British Academy* 67 (1981), 267-88.

Mallett, Michael. "L'esercito veneziano in terraferma nel quattrocento." In: *Armi e cultura nel bresciano, 1420-1870*. Brescia, 1981, pp. 181-96.

Mallett, Michael. "The Florentine *Otto di Pratica* and the Beginning of the War of Ferrara." In: *Florence and Italy: Renaissance Studies in Honour of Nicolai Rubenstein*. Ed. P. Denley and C. Elam. London, 1988, pp. 3-12.

Mallett, Michael. *Mercenaries and their Masters: Warfare in Renaissance Italy*. Totowa: Rowman and Littlefield, 1974.

Mallett, Michael. "Preparations for War in Florence and Venice in the Second Half of the Fifteenth Century." In: *Florence and Venice: Comparisons and Relations*. Vol. 1: *Quattrocento*. Florence, 1979, pp. 149-64.

Mallett, Michael. "Some Notes on a Fifteenth-Century *Condottiere* and his Library: Count Antonio da Marsciano." In: *Cultural Aspects of the Italian Renaissance: Essays in Honour of Paul Oskar Kristeller*. Ed. Cecil H. Clough. Manchester: Manchester University Press, 1976, pp. 202-15.

Mallett, Michael. "Venice and its Condottieri, 1404-54." In: *Renaissance Venice*. Ed. J.R. Hale. Totowa, 1973, pp. 121-45.

Mallett, Michael. "Venice and the War of Ferrara, 1482-84." In: *War, Culture and Society in Renaissance Venice: Essays in Honour of John Hale*. Ed. D.S. Chambers, C.H. Clough and M.E. Mallett. London, 1993, pp. 57-72.

Mallett, Michael and J.R. Hale. *The Military Organization of a Renaissance State: Venice, c. 1400 to 1617*. Cambridge: Cambridge University Press, 1984.

Martin, Jean-Marie and Ghislaine Noyé. "Guerre, fortifications et habitants en Italie méridionale du Ve au Xe siècle." In: *Castrum 3: Guerre, fortification et habitant dans le monde méditerranéen au moyen âge*. Ed. André Bazzana. Rome: L'école Française de Rome, 1988, pp. 225-36.

Mazzei, Rita. "Lucca e Firenze: I lucchesi cavalieri di Santo Stefano in età medicea," *Archivio storico italiano* 157 (1999), 269-83.

Meier-Welcker, Hans. "Das Militärwesen Kaiser Friedrichs II: Landes Verteidigung, Heer und Flotte im sizilischen 'Modellstaat'," *Revue internationale d'histoire militaire* 51 (1975), 9-48.

Meyer, H. *Die Militärpolitik Friedrich Barbarossas im Zusammenhang mit seiner Italienpolitik*. Berlin, 1930.

Minieri-Riccio, C. "Memorie della guerra di Sicilia negli anni 1282, 1283, 1284 tratte da'registri angioini del l'Archivio di Stato di Napoli," *Archivio storico per la provinicie napolitane* 1 (1876), 85-105, 285-315, 499-530.

Mirot, Léon. *Sylvestre Budes (13??-1380) et les Bretons en Italie*. Paris, 1898.

Mor, C.G. "La difesa militare delle Capitanata ed i confine della regionale al principio del secolo XI," *Papers of the British School at Rome* 24 (1956), 29-36.

Mosig-Walburg, Karin. "Zur Schlacht bei Singara," *Historia* 48 (1999), 330-84.

Nicolle, David C. "The Capella Palatina Ceiling and the Muslim Military Heritage of Norman Sicily," *Gladius* 16 (1983), 45-145.

Nicolle, David C. *Italian Medieval Armies, 1300-1500*. Men-at-Arms Series. London: Osprey Publishing, 1983.

Nicolle, David C. *Italian Militiaman, 1260-1392: Weapons, Armour, Tactics*. Warrior Series. London: Osprey Military, 1999.

Nicolle, David C. "The Monreale Capitals and the Military Equipment of Later Norman Sicily," *Gladius* 15 (1980), 87-103.

Niese, H. "Zur Geschichte des deutschen Soldrittertums in Italien," *Quellen und Forschungen aus italienischen Archiven und Bibliotheken* 8 (1905), 217-48.

Oerter, Herbert L. "Campaldino, 1289," *Speculum* 43 (1968), 429-50.

Olivia, Gianni. "Des armées citoyennes aux armées communales. L'évolution de l'infanterie en Italie du VIIIe au XIVe siècle." In: *XXII. Kongreß der Internationalen Kommission für Militärgeschichte* Acta 22: *Von Crécy bis Mohács Kriegswesen im späten Mittelalter (1346-1526)*. Vienna, 1997, pp. 70-78.

Paoli, C. *La battaglia di Montaperti*. Siena, 1869.

Patlagean, Evelyne. "Les armes et la cité à Rome du VIIe au XIe siècle, et le modèle européen des trois fonctions sociales," *Mélanges de l'Ecole français de Rome* 36 (1974), 25-62.

Pauler, Roland. *Die Deutschen Könige und Italien im 14. Jahrhundert: Von Heinrich VII. Bis Karl IV.* Darmstadt: Wissenschaftliche Buchgesellschaft, 1997.

Pertici, Petra. "Condottieri senesi e la *Rotta di San Romano* di Paolo Uccello," *Archivio storico Italiano* 157 (1999), 537-62.

Peyronel, Gianfranco. "Un fronte di guerra nel rinascimento esercito sforzesco e communità bresciane nella campagna del 1452-53," *Nuovo rivista storico* 73 (1989), 537-608.

Pezzolo, Luciano. "Armi, ideologia e politica nel cinquecento Veneto: suggestioni di una ricerca." *Publication du centre Européen d'études Bourguignonnes (XIVe-XVIe s.)* 26 (1986), 97-104.

Pieri, Paolo. "Alcune quistioni sopra la fanteria in Italia nel periodo comunale," *Rivista storica Italiana* 45 (1933), 561-614.

Pieri, Paolo. *La crisi militare Italiana nel renascimento*. Naples, 1934.

Pieri, Paolo. "L'evoluzione delle milizie comunali Italiane." In: *Scritti vari*. Ed. P. Pieri. Turin, 1966, pp. 31-91.

Pieri, Paolo. "*Governo et exercito de la militia* di Orso degli Orsini e i *Memoriali* di Diomede Carafa," *Archivio storico per le provincie napoletane* n.s. 19 (1933), 99-212.

Pieri, Paolo. "Milizie e capitani di ventura in Italia nel medio evo," *Atti del reale accademia peloritana di Messina* 40 (1937-38).

Pieri, Paolo. "Le milizie svizzere nel tardo medioevo e nel rinascimento in Italia," *Annali dell facoltà di magistero della Reale Università di Messina* 17 (1939).

Pieri, Paolo. *Il rinascimento e la crisi militare italiana*. Milan, 1952.

Pieri, Paolo. "I sarceni di Lucera nella storia militare medievale," *Archivio storico pugliese* 6 (1954), 94-101.

Pieri, Paolo. "La scienza militare Italiana del renascimento." In: *Scritti vari*. Turin, 1966.

Poisson, Jean-Michel. "Menaces extérieures et mise en défense des zones côtières de la Sardaigne pendant le haut moyen âge." In: *Castrum 3: Guerre, fortification et habitant dans le monde méditerranéen au moyen âge*. Ed. André Bazzana. Rome: L'école Française de Rome, 1988, pp. 49-58.

Racine, Pierre. "Le chevalier des armées communales italiennes." In: *Le combattant au moyen âge*. 2nd ed. Histoire ancienne et médiévale, 36. Paris: Publications de la Sorbonne, 1995, pp. 187-94.

Rasi, Piero. *'Exercitus italicus' e milizie cittadine nell'alto medioevo*. Padua: Casa Editrice Dott Antonio Milani, 1937.

Riga, Antonio. "Desiderio di pace e crisi di coscienza nell'età di Federico II," *Archivio storico italiano* 156 (1998), 211-26.

Ryder, Alan. "The Angevin Bid for Naples, 1380-1480." In: *The French Descent into Renaissance Italy: Antecedents and Effects*. Ed. D. Abulafia. Aldershot: Ashgate, 1995, pp. 55-69.

Sabato di San Barncna, Il: La battaglia di Campaldino, 11 giugno 1289. Milan, 1989.

Sambin, P. "La guerra del 1372-73 tra Venezia e Padova," *Archivio Veneto* 5th ser. 36-39 (1946-47), 1-76.

Schäfer, Karl Heinrich. "Deutsche Ritter und Edelknechte in Italien während des XIV. Jahrhunderts," *Quellen und Forschungen aus dem Gebiet der Geschichte* 15 (1911); 16 (1914); 25 (1940).

Secco d'Arragona, F. "Un giornale della guerra di Ferrara (1482-84), nelle lettere di un condottiero milanese-mantovano," *Archivio storico Lombardo* 84 (1957), 317-45.

Sergi, Giuseppe. "Guerra e popolamento nel 'Regnum Italiae'." In: *Castrum 3: Guerre, fortification et habitant dans le monde méditerranéen au moyen âge*. Ed. André Bazzana. Rome: L'école Française de Rome, 1988, pp. 257-62.

Settia, Aldo A. *Comuni in guerra: armi ad eserciti nell'Italia delle città*. Bologna, 1993.

Settia, Aldo A. "Federico II, il popolo de Cremona e le techniche di combattimento nel secolo XIII," *Studi storici* 37 (1996), 425-43.

Settia, Aldo A. "Gli 'Insegnamenti' di Teodoro di Monferrato e la prassi bellica in Italia all'inizio del Trecento," *Archivio storico italiano* 157 (1999), 667-90.

Settia, Aldo A. "'Pro novis inveniendis': Lo spionaggio militare senese nei 'Libri di Biccherna' (1229-1231)," *Archivio storico italiano* 156 (1998), 3-23.

Soranzo, G. "L'ultima campagna del Gattmelata al servizio della Repubblica veneta (1438-1441)," *Archivio Veneto* 60-61 (1957), 79-114.

Stewart, Paul. "The *Santa Hermandad* and the First Italian Campaign of Gonzalo de Cordoba, 1495-1498," *Renaissance Quarterly* 28 (1975), 29-37.

Stolz, O. *Wehrverfassung und Schützenwesen in Tirol von den Anfängen bis 1918.* Innsbruck, Vienna, and Munich, 1960.

Storti, Francesco. "Istituzioni militari in Italia tra medioevo ed età moderna," *Studi storici* 38 (1997), 257-71.

Swain, Elisabeth Ward. "The Wages of Peace: The *Condotte* of Ludovico Gonzaga, 1436-1478," *Renaissance Studies* 3 (1989), 442-52.

Tabacco, Giovanni. *I liberi del re nell'Italia carolingia e postcarolingia.* Spoleto, 1966.

Tabacco, Giovanni. "Dai possessori dell'età carolinga agli esercitali dell'età longobarda," *Studi medievali* 10 (1969), 211-68.

Tabacco, Giovanni. "Il regno italico nei secoli IX-XI," In: *Ordinamenti militari in occidente nell'alto medioevo.* Settimane di studio del centro italiano di studi sull'alto medioevo, XV. Spoleto, 1968, II:763-90.

Tabacco, Giovanni. "Vassalli, nobili e cavalieri nel-l'Italia precomunale," *Rivista storica italiana* 99 (1987).

Taviani-Carozzi, Huguette. "Une bataille franco-allemande en Italie: Civitate (1053)." In: *Peuples du moyen âge: problèmes d'identification.* Séminare: Sociétés, idéologies et croyances au moyen âge. Ed. Claude Carozzi and Huguette Taviani-Carozzi. Aix-en-Provence: Publications de l'Université de Provence, 1996, pp. 181-211.

Tognetti, Sergio. "L'attività di banca locale di una grande compagnia fiorentina del XV secolo," *Archivio storico italiano* 155 (1997), 595-647.

Troso, Mario. *Le armi in asta: delle fanterie europee (1000-1500).* Novara: Istituto Geographico de Agostini, 1988.

Varanini, Gian Maria. "Mercenari tedeschi in Italia nel Trecento: problemi e linee di ricerca." In: *Kommunikation und Mobilität im Mittelalter: Begegnungen zwischen dem Süden und der Mitte Europas (11.-14. Jahrhundert).* Ed. Siegfried de Rachewiltz and Josef Riedmann. Sigmaringen: Thorbecke, 1995, pp. 159-78.

Vayra, P. "Cavalieri lombardi in Piedmonto nelle guerre del 1229-1230," *Archivio storico Lombardo* 10 (1883), 413-22.

Visconti, E.C. "Ordine dell'esercito ducale sforzesco, 1472-1473," *Archivio storico Lombardo* 3 (1876).

Waley, Daniel P. "The Army of the Florentine Republic from the Twelfth to the Fourteenth Century." In: *Florentine Studies: Politics and Society in Renaissance Florence*. Ed. N. Rubenstein. Evanston, 1968, pp. 70-108.

Waley, Daniel P. "Chivalry and Cavalry at San Gimignano: Knighthood in a Small Italian Commune." In: *Recognitions: Essays Presented to Edmund Fryde*. Ed. C. Richmond and I. Harvey. Aberystwyth, 1996, pp. 39-53.

Waley, Daniel P. "Combined Operations in Sicily, AD 1060-78," *Papers of the British School in Rome* 22 (1954), 118-25.

Waley, Daniel P. "*Condotte* and *Condottieri* in the Thirteenth Century," *Proceedings of the British Academy* 61 (1975), 337-71.

Waley, Daniel P. "Papal Armies in the Thirteenth Century," *English Historical Review* 72 (1957), 1-30.

Webb, Diana M. "Cities of God: The Italian Communes at War," *Studies in Church History* 20 (1983), 111-27.

Wegener, W.J. "'That the Practice of Arms is Most Excellent Declare the Statues of Valiant Men': The Luccan War and Florentine Political Ideology in Paintings by Uccelo and Castagno," *Renaissance Studies* 7 (1992), 29-67.

Wickham, C. *Early Medieval Italy: Central Power and Local Society, 400-1000*. London, 1981.

Zorzi, C. "Un Vicentino alla Corte di Paolo II: Chierighino Chiericati e il suo trattatello della milizia," *Nuovo archivio Veneto* n.s. 30 (1915), 369-434.

Medieval – Italy – Normans

Bennett, Matthew. "Norman Naval Activity in the Mediterranean, c.1060-c.1108," *Anglo-Norman Studies* 15 (1993), 41-58.

Cahen, C. *Le régime féodal de l'Italie normande*. Paris, 1940.

Cuozzo, Errico. "A propos de la coexistence entre Normands et Lombards dans le royaume de Sicile: La révolte féodale de 1160-1162." In: *Peuples du moyen âge: problèmes d'identification*. Séminare: Sociétés, idéologies et croyances au moyen âge. Ed. Claude Carozzi and Huguette Taviani-Carozzi. Aix-en-Provence: Publications de l'Université de Provence, 1996, pp. 45-56.

Cuozzo, Errico. "La *militia neapolitanorum*: Un modello per i *milites* Normanni di aversa," *Mélanges de l'école Français de Rome: moyen âge* 107 (1995), 31-38.

Cuozzo, Errico. *Normanni: nobilità e cavalleria*. Salerno: Gentile, 1995.

Cuozzo, Errico. *"Quei maledetti Normanni": Cavalieri e organizzazione militare nel Mezzogiorno normanno*. Naples, 1989.

Douglas, David C. *The Norman Achievement, 1050-1100*. Berkeley and Los Angeles: University of California Press, 1969.

Douglas, David C. *The Norman Fate, 1100-1154*. London, 1976.

Drell, Joanna H. "Cultural Syncretism and Ethical Identity: The Norman 'Conquest' of Southern Italy and Sicily," *Journal of Medieval History* 25 (1999), 187-202.

Fougerolles, Paula de. "Pope Gregory VII, the Archbishop of Dol and the Normans," *Anglo-Norman Studies* 21 (1998), 47-66.

France, John. "The Occasion of the Coming of the Normans to Southern Italy," *Journal of Medieval History* 17 (1991), 185-205.

Houben, Hubert. *Roger II. von Sizilien: Herrscher zwischen Orient und Okzident*. Darmstadt: Primus, 1997.

Jamin, Christian. "Les Normands d'Italie," *Le Pays d'Auge* 9 (Sept 1996), 19-25.

Loud, G.A. *The Age of Robert Guiscard: Southern Italy and the Norman Conquest*. Harlow: Longman, 2000.

Loud, G.A. "Byzantine Italy and the Normans." In: *Byzantium and the West, c. 850-c. 1200*. Ed. J.D. Howard-Johnston. Byzantinische Forschungen, 13. Amsterdam, 1988, pp. 215-33.

Loud, G.A. "The Church, Warfare and Military Obligation in Norman Italy," *Studies in Church History* 20 (1983), 31-45.

Loud, G.A. "Coinage, Wealth and Plunder in the Age of Robert Guiscard," *English Historical Review* 114 (1999), 815-43.

Loud, G.A. "How 'Norman' Was the Norman Conquest of Southern Italy?" *Nottingham Medieval Studies* 25 (1981), 13-34.

Loud, G.A. "Norman Italy and the Holy Land." In: *The Horns of Hattin*. Ed. Benjamin Z. Kedar. London, 1992, pp. 49-62.

Matthew, Donald. *The Norman Kingdom of Sicily*. Cambridge: Cambridge University Press, 1992.

McQueen, William B. "Relations between the Normans and Byzantium, 1071-1112," *Byzantion* 56 (1986), 427-76.

Mutafian, Claude. "L'enjeu cicilien et les prétensions normandes (1097-1137)." In: *Autour de la première croisade: Actes du Colloque de la Society for the Study of the Crusades and the Latin East (Clermont-Ferrand, 22-25 juin 1995)*. Ed. M. Balard. Paris: Publications de la Sorbonne, 1996, pp. 453-63.

Neveux, François. "Quelques aspects de l'impérialisme normand au XIe siècle en Italie et en Angleterre." In: *Les Normands en Méditerranée dans le sillage des Tancréde*. Ed. P. Boulet and F. Neveux. Caen, 1994, pp. 51-62.

Nicolle, David C. *Normans*. London: Osprey, 1987.

Norwich, John Julius. "The Normans in the South," *History Today* 16 (1966), 694-703.

Taviani-Carozzi, Huguette. *La terreur du monde: Robert Guiscard et la conquête normande en Italie. Mythe et histoire*. Paris: Fayard, 1996.

Waley, Daniel P. "'Combined Operations' in Sicily, A.D. 1060-78," *Papers of the British School in Rome* 22 (1954), 118-25.

Willoughby, Rupert. "The Shock of the New," *History Today* 49 (Aug 1999), 36-42.

Medieval – Laws of War

Armstrong, C.A.J. "Sir John Fastolf and the Law of Arms." In: *War, Literature and Politics in the Late Middle Ages: Essays in Honour of G.W. Coopland*. Ed. C.T. Allmand. Liverpool: University of Liverpool Press, 1975, pp. 46-56.

Chaplais, Pierre. "Règlements des conflits internationaux Franco-Anglais au XIVe siècle (1293-1377)," *Moyen âge* 57 (1951), 269-302.

Conrad, H. "Germanisches Denken im deutschen Kriegsrecht des Mittelalters." In: *Das Bild des Krieges im deutschen Denken*. Ed. A. Fauste. Stuttgart and Berlin, 1941, I:83-103.

Conrad, H. "Das Wehrstrafrecht der germanischen und fränkischen Zeit," *Zeitschrift für die Geschichte der Straftrechtwissenschaft* 56 (1937), 709-34.

Cram, K.G. *Iudicum belli: Zum Rechtscharakter des Krieges im deutschen Mittelalter*. Munster and Cologne, 1955.

Edwards, J. "Hostages and Ransomers," *Medieval World* 8 (Jan-Feb 1993), 17-21.

Erben, Wilhelm. "Schwertleite und Ritterschlag: Beiträge zu einer Rechtsgeschichte der Waffen," *Zeitschrift für historische Waffenkunde* 8 (1918-20), 105-67.

Fehr, H. "Das Waffenrecht der Bauern im Mittelalter," *Zeitschrift der Savigny-Stiftung für Rechtsgeschichte (Germanische Abteilung)* 35 (1914), 111-211, 38 (1917), 1-114.

Glénisson, J. "Notes d'histoire militaire: Quelques lettres de défi du XIVe siècle," *Bibliothèque de l'école de chartes* 107 (1947-48), 235-54.

Grassotti, H. "El deber y el derecho de hacer guerra y pas en Léon y Castilla," *Cuadernos de historia de España* 59-60 (1976), 221-96.

Keen, Maurice H. *The Laws of War in the Late Middle Ages*. London: Routledge and Kegan Paul, 1965.

Keen, Maurice H. "The Laws of War in the Late Middle Ages." In: *Lordship and Community in Medieval Europe: Selected Readings*. Ed. Frederic L. Cheyette. New York: Holt, Rinehart, and Winston, Inc., 1968, pp. 210-15.

Keen, Maurice H. "Treason Trials under the Law of Arms," *Transactions of the Royal Historical Society* 5th ser. 12 (1962), 85-103.

Masi, G. "Un capitulo di storia del diritto internazionale: Alcuni usi di guerra in Italia all'epoca dei communi," *Rivista di storia del diritto Italiano* 28 (1955), 19-37.

Meron, T. *Henry's Wars and Shakespeare's Laws: Perspectives on the Law of War in the Later Middle Ages*. Oxford, 1993.

Pippidi, A. *Contribuitti la studiul legilor razboinlui î evul mediu*. Bucharest, 1974.

Porter, Elizabeth. "Chaucer's Knight, the Alliterative *Morte Arthure*, and Medieval Laws of War: A Reconsideration," *Nottingham Medieval Studies* 27 (1983), 56-78.

Richard, Jean. "Le droit de guerre du noble comtois," *Mémoires de la société pour l'histoire du droit et des institutions des anciens pays bourguignons, comtois et romands* (1948-49), 107-15.

Rosenau, P.U. *Wehrverfassung und Kriegsrecht in der mittelhochdeutschen Epik: Wolfram von Eschenbach, Hartmann von Aue, Gottfried von Strassburg, Der Nibelunge Not, Kridrunepos, Wolfdietrichbruchstück A, König Rother, Salman und Moroff*. Bonn, 1959.

Soldi-Rondinini, G. "Il diritto di guerra in Italia nel secolo XV," *Nuovo rivista storica* 48 (1964), 275-306.

Medieval – Leadership

Beeler, John H. "Towards a Re-Evaluation of Medieval English Leadership," *Journal of British Studies* 3 (1963), 1-10.

Gillingham, John. "Richard I and the Science of War in the Middle Ages." In: *War and Government in the Middle Ages: Essays in Honour of J.O. Prestwich.* Ed. J. Gillingham and J.C. Holt. Cambridge, 1984, pp. 78-91; in: *Anglo-Norman Warfare: Studies in Late Anglo-Saxon and Anglo-Norman Military Organization and Warfare.* Ed. M. Strickland. Woodbridge, 1992, pp. 194-207.

Gillingham, John. "William the Bastard at War." In: *Studies in Medieval History Presented to R. Allen Brown.* Ed. C. Harper-Bill et al. Woodbridge, 1989, pp. 141-58; in: *Anglo-Norman Warfare: Studies in Late Anglo-Saxon and Anglo-Norman Military Organization and Warfare.* Ed. M. Strickland. Woodbridge, 1992, pp. 143-60.

Medieval – Low Countries

Arts, Nico. "Oorlog in Helmond: Archeologische wapenvondsten uit het Oude Huys (circa 1175-1400)," *Brabantse Heem* 47 (1995), 85-91.

Avonds, P. and H.M. Brokken. "Heusden tussen Brabant en Holland (1317-1357): Analyse van een grensconflict," *Varia historica Brabantica* 4 (1975), 1-95.

Avonds, P., H.M. Brokken and Jozef D. Janssens. *Politiek en literatuur: Brabant en de slag bij Woeringen (1288).* Brussels: Centrum Brabantse geschiedenis, Universitaire Faculteiten Sint-Aloysius, 1989.

Baerten, Jean. "La bataille de Worringen (1288) et les villes Brabançonnes, Limbourgeoises et Liégeoises." In: *Villes et campagnes au moyen âge: Mélanges Georges Despy.* Ed. J.-M. Duvosquel and A Dierkens. Brussels, 1991, pp. 71-85.

Beuker, J.R. "Vondsten en plaats van de slag bij Ane," *Nieuwe Drentse Volksalmanak* 97 (1980), 9-15.

Beyaert, Marc. "De algemene militaire evolutie sinds de late middeleeuwen en het Zuid-Nederlandse landleger der XVIe eeuw," *Revue Belge d'histoire militaire* 20 (1973-74), 550-73.

Boffa, Serge. "Les soutiens militaires de Jean Ier, duc de Brabant, à Philippe III, roi de France, durant les expéditions ibériques (1276-1285)," *Revue du nord* 78 (1996), 7-33.

Bruin, Marinus Pieter de and Huib Uil. "La conquête de la Zélande par les Pays-Bas au XIVe siècle: Le role de Rainier Gimaldi, amiral de France, lors du combat naval de Zierikzee (1304)," *Annales monégasques* 10, 65-80.

Bruin, Marinus Pieter de and Huib Uil. "De strijd om Zeeland in de lage landen aan de noordzee van de 11e tot de 14 eeuw: De zeeslag bij Zierikzee in 1304 en het aandeel van Rainer Grimaldi, amiral de France," *Zeeuws tijdschrift* 36 (1986), 24-32.

Cattier, F. "La guerre privée dans le comté de Hainaut," *Annales de la faculté de philosophie de Bruxelles* 1 (1889-90).

de Graaf, Ronald P. *Oorlog om Holland, 1000-1375*. Hilversum: Verloren, 1996.

Dieperink, F.H.J. "De Drentse opstand tegen het bisschoppelijk gezag in 1227." In: *Studiën betreffende de geschiedenis van Oost-Nederland van de diertiende tot de vijftiende eeuw*. Ed. F.H.J. Dieperink, D.Th. Enklaar, and W.J. Alberts. Groningen, 1953, pp. 1-36.

Duby, Georges. *27 juillet 1214: Le dimanche de Bouvines*. Paris, 1973; trans. *The Legend of Bouvines: War, Religion and Culture in the Middle Ages*. Trans. Catherine Tihanyi. Berkeley and Los Angeles: University of California Press, 1990.

Fastes militaires du Pays de Liège. Liege: Musée de l'Art Wallon, 1970.

Formsma, W.J. "De oorlog tussen de Ernerenses en de Uthusenses in de dertiende eeuw," *Groningse Volksalmanak* (1965-1966), 1-16.

Funck-Brentano, Frantz. *Philippe le Bel et Flandre: Les origines de la guerre de cent ans*. Paris: Honoré Champion, Libraire, 1896.

Gaier, Claude. "Analysis of Military Forces in the Prinicpality of Liège and the County of Looz from the Twelfth to the Fifteenth Century," *Studies in Medieval and Renaissance History* 2 (1965), 206-61.

Gaier, Claude. "L'apparition de l'infanterie suisse dans la Principauté de Liège à la fin du XVe siècle." In: *Armes et combats dans l'univers médiéval*. Liege, 1995, pp. 91-101.

Gaier, Claude. *Art et organisation militaires dans la principauté de Liège et dans le comté de Looz au moyen âge*. Académie Royale de Belgique, Classe des Lettres: Mémoires, 59, v. 3. Brussels: Palais des académies, 1968.

Gaier, Claude. "Autour de la bataille de Worringen (1288)," *Moyen âge* 5th ser., 99 (1993), 133-35.

Gaier, Claude. "La bataille de Steppes, 13 octobre 1213." In: *Armes et combats dans l'univers médiéval*. Liege, 1995, pp. 15-25.

Gaier, Claude. "La bataille de Vottem, 19 juillet 1346." In: *Armes et combats dans l'univers médiéval*. Liege, 1995, pp. 27-37.

Gaier, Claude. "Le combat de Visé, 22 mars 1106." In: *Armes et combats dans l'univers médiéval*. Liege, 1995, pp. 11-14.

Gaier, Claude. *Grandes batailles de l'histoire Liegéoise au moyen âge*. Liege, 1980.

Gaier, Claude. "Une manifestation de la tactique moderne: la journée de Zonhoven (3 avril 1490)," *Pallas* (1962), 37-43.

Gaier, Claude. "Mentalité collective de l'infanterie communale liégeoise au Moyen âge," *Revue internationale d'histoire militaire* 30 (1970), 109-19; in: *Armes et combats dans l'univers médiéval*. Liege, 1995, pp. 311-17.

Gaier, Claude. "Le rôle militaire des reliques et de l'étendard de saint Lambert dans la principauté de Liège." In: *Armes et combats dans l'univers médiéval*. Liege, 1995, pp. 337-48.

Ganshof, François Louis. "Etude sur les ministeriales en Flandre Lotharingie," *Mémoires de l'académie royale Belgiques, classe des lettres*. 2nd ser. 20 (1926).

Goosens, J. *Woeringen en de oriëntatie van het Maasland*. Vereniging voor Limburgse Dialect-en Naamkunde, 1988.

Groustra, G.R. *De slach by Starum 1345*. Bolswart, 1978.

Gryse, Piet de. "Militaire verplichtingen te Leuven op het einde van de Middeleeuwen: De organisatie van de stedelijke verdediging." In: *Leven te Leuven in de late middeleeuwen*. Leuven: Peeters, 1998, pp. 33-38.

Heirbaut, Dirk. "De militaire rol van de feodaliteit in het graafschap vlaanderen gedurende de 11de en 12de eeuw," *Revue Belge d'histoire militaire* 29 (1992), 311-18.

Hugenholtz, F.W.N. "Historie en historiografie van de slag aan het Manpad (1304)," *Jaarboek maatschapij Nederlandse letterkunde* (1955), 31-47.

Huyttens, Jules. "Recherches sur l'organisation militaire de la ville de Gand au moyen-âge," *Messager des sciences historiques*, 6th ser., 26 (1858), 413-52.

Janse, Antheun. *Grenzen aan de macht: De Friese oorlog van de graven van Holland omstreeks 1400*. Hollandse Historische Reeks, 19. The Hague: Stichting Hollandse Historische Reeks, 1994.

Jansen, H.P.H. and P.C.M. Hoppenbrouwers. "Military Obligation in Mediaeval Holland. The Burden of the Host," *Acta historiae Neerlandicae* 13 (1980), 1-24.

Janssen, W. "Die Schlacht bei Worringen und die Verbündeten des Herzogs von Brabant," *De Maasgouw* 107 (1988), 251-56.

Janssen, W. and H. Stehkamper. *Der Tag bei Worringen, 5 juni 1288*. Mitteilungen aus dem Stadtarchiv von Köln, 72. Cologne, 1988.

Joris, A. "Remarques sur les clauses militaires des privilèges urbains Liégeois," *Revue Belge de philologie et d'histoire* 37 (1959), 297-316.

Lehnart, Ulrich. *Die Schlacht von Worringen 1288: Kriegführung im Mittelalter: Der Limburger Erbfolgekrieg unter besonderer Berücksichtigung der Schlacht von Worringen, 5.6.1288*. Butzbach-Griedel: AFRA-Verlag, 1993.

Lewis, N.B. "The English Forces in Flanders, August-November 1297." In: *Studies in Medieval History Presented to F.M. Powicke*. Ed. R.W. Hunt. Oxford, 1948, pp. 310-78.

Lucas, Henry Stephen. *The Low Countries and the Hundred Years' War, 1326-1347*. Ann Arbor: University of Michigan Press, 1929.

Mol, J.A. "Hoofdelingen en huurlingen: Militaire innovatie en de aanloop tot 1498." In: *Fryslân, staat en macht, 1450-1650: Bijdragen aan het historisch congres te Leeuwarden van 3 tot 5 juni 1998*. Ed. J. Frieswijk, A.H. Huussen, jr., Y.B. Kuiper and J.A. Mol. Hilversum: Verloren, 1999, pp. 65-84.

Mol, J.A. "Het militaire einde van de Friese vrijheid: de slag bij Laaxum, 10 juni 1498," *Millennium* 13 (1999), 3-20.

Müller, S. "Bella campestria inter episcopos Trajectenses et comites Hollandie," *Bijdragen en mededelingen van het historische genootschap* 11 (1888), 497-508.

Nicholas, David. *The Van Arteveldes of Ghent: The Varieties of Vendetta and the Hero in History*. Ithaca: Cornell University Press, 1988.

Overdiep, G. *De slag bij Ane 1227*. Peize, 1977.

Pirenne, Henri. *Histoire de Belgique*. Vol. II: *Du commencement du XIVe siècle à la mort de Charles de Téméraire*. Brussels: Henri Lamertin, 1903.

Platelle, Henri. "La violence et ses remèdes en Flandre au XIe siècle," *Sacris erudiri* 20 (1971), 101-73.

Poncelet, E. "Les maréchaux d'armée de l'évêché de Liège," *Bulletin de l'institut archaéologique liégeoise* 32 (1902).

Renaud, J.G.N. "Le Comte Florent V comme constructeur de chateaux forts," *Revue internationale d'histoire militaire* 19 (1957), 313-22.

Schaap, H.P. "De slag bij ane (27 juli 1227)," *Nieuwe Drentse volksalmanak* 71 (1954), 131-46.

Schaefke, W., ed. *Der Name der Freiheit 1288-1988: Aspekte Kölner Geschichte von Worringen bis heute*. Cologne, 1988.

Sivéry, Gérard. "L'enquête de 1247 et les dommages de guerre en Tournaisis, en Flandre gallicante et en Artois," *Revue du nord* 59 (1977), 7-18.

Smit, J.G. "De klerk Melis Stoke en Zierikzee in 1304: Een nieuwe archiefvondst," *Kroniek van het land van de zeemeerin* 15 (1990), 31-36.

Stevenson, A. "The Flemish Dimension of the Auld Alliance." In: *Scotland and the Low Countries, 1124-1994.* Ed. G.G. Simpson. East Linton, 1996.

Strubbe, E.I. and J. Craeybeckx. "Statsinrichting en krijgswezen." In: *Algemene geschiedenis der Nederland.* Vol. 4. Utrecht, 1952, pp.

Terlinden, Charles. *Histoire militaire des Belges.* Brussels, 1931.

Thoen, Erik. "Oorlogen en platteland. Sociale en ekonomische aspekten van militaire destruktie in Vlaanderen tijdens de late middeleeuwen en de vroege moderne tijden," *Tijdschrift voor geschiedenis* 91 (1978), 363-78; trans. "Warfare and the Countryside: Social and Economic Aspects of the Military Destruction in Flanders during the Late Middle Ages and the Early Modern Period," *Acta historiae Neerlandicae* 13 (1980), 25-39.

van Houts, Elisabeth M.C. "Hereward and Flanders," *Anglo-Saxon England* 28 (1999), 201-23

van Riel, H. "Herdenking van de slag bij Ane 1227," *Nieuwe Drentse volksalmanak* 95 (1978), 7-25.

van Uytven, R. "Worringen 1288: ridderlijke roem en burgerlijke werkelijkheid," *De Maasgouw* 107 (1988), 257-64.

van Uytven, R. "Woeringen 1288-1988: Brabantse overwinning, maar Keusle triomf," *Bijdragen en mededelingen betreffende de geschiedenis van Nederland* 104 (1989), 224-33.

van Winter, J.M. "The Ministerial and Knightly Classes in Guelders and Zutphen," *Acta historiae Neerlandicae* 1 (1966), 171-86.

Verbruggen, J.F. *Het gemeenteleger van Brugge van 1338 tot 1340 en de namen van de weerbare mannen.* Brussels: Koninklijke Commissie voor Geschiedenis, 1962.

Verbruggen, J.F. "De getalsterkte van de ambachten in het Brugse gemeentleger," *Revue Belge d'histoire militaire* 25 (1984), 461-80.

Verbruggen, J.F. *Het leger en de vloot van de graven van Vlaanderen vanaf het ontstaan tot in 1305.* Brussels: Paleis der Academiën, 1960.

Verbruggen, J.F. "De militaire dienst in het graafschap Vlaanderen," *Tijdschrift voor rechtgeschiedenis* 26 (1958), 437-65.

Verbruggen, J.F. "De militairen: In de middeleeuwen en de bourgondische tijd." In: *Flandria Nostra*. Ed. J.L. Broeckx et al. Antwerp, 1960, V:161-233.

Verbruggen, J.F. "De organisatie van de militie te Brugge in de XIVe eeuw," *Annales de la société d'émulation de Bruges* 87 (1950).

Xhayet, Geneviève. *Réseaux de pouvoir et solidarités de parti à Liège au moyen âge (1250-1468)*. Bibliothèque de la Faculté de Philosophie et Lettres de L'Université de Liège, 269. Geneva: Droz, 1997.

Medieval – Low Countries – Courtrai (battle of)

Baerten, Jean. "La participation d'Arnoul V, comte de Looz, à la bataille des Éperons d'Or (1302)," *Revue Belge de philologie et d'histoire* 35 (1957), 771-77.

Blockmans, Wim. *Een middeleeuwse vendetta: Gent 1300*. Houten: De Haan, 1987.

Debrabandere, F. "Scilt en Vrient," *De Leiegouw* (1977), 361-66.

Delmaire, Bernard. "La guerre en Artois après la bataille de Courtrai (1302-1303)." In: *La guerre et la paix: Frontières et violences au moyen âge*. Actes du 101e congrès national des sociétés savantes, Lille, 1976. Paris: Bibliothèque Nationale, 1978.

Dewilde, B., A. Pauwels, J.F. Verbruggen and F. Warlop. "De kist van Oxford," *De leiegouw* 22 (1980), 163-256; rpt. Kortrijk, 1980.

ffoulkes, Charles J. "A Carved Flemish Chest at New College, Oxford," *Archaeologia* 65 (1914), 113-28.

Funck-Brentano, Frantz. *Mémoire sur la bataille de Courtrai (1302, 11 juillet) et les chroniqueurs qui en ont traité, pour servir à l'historiographie du règne de Philippe le Bel*. Paris: Imprimerie Nationale, 1891.

Gilmour, Brian and Ian Tyers. "Courtrai Chest: Relic or Recent: Reassessment and Further Work: An Interim Report." In: *Papers of the 'Medieval*

Europe Brugge 1997' Conference. Vol 5: *Art and Symbolism in Medieval Europe*. Bruges, 1997, pp. 17-26.

Hall, E.T. "The Courtrai Chest from New College, Oxford, Re-examined," *Antiquity* 61 (1987), 104-07.

Hemmerdinger, Bertrand. "Un curiosum: La bataille de Courtrai (11 juillet 1302)," *Quaderni di stori* 8 (1982), 263-64.

Huyghebaert, J. "De vlaamse slagorde evenwijdig met de Groeningegracht Kortrijk, 11 juli 1302," *Biekorf* 93 (1993), 297-304.

Huyghebaert, N.N. "Onze-Lieve-Vrouw van Groeninge op het slagveld der Gulden Sporen," *De Leiegouw* (1977), 367-87.

Lalou, Elisabeth. "Les questions militaires sous le règne de Philippe le Bel." In: *Guerre et société en France, en Angleterre et en Bourgogne XIVe-XVe siècle*. Ed. P. Contamine, C. Giry-Deloison, and Maurice Keen. Lille, 1991, pp. 37-62.

Luykx, Theo. *Het grafelijk geslacht Dampierre en zijn strijd tegen Filips de Schone*. Leuven, 1952.

Maddens, N. "Een ver gevolg van de guldensporenslag," *De Leiegouw* (1977), 389-97.

Maere d'Aertrycke, M. de. "Recherches concernant quelques questions controversées à propos des batailles de Courtrai et de Rosebecque." In: *Annales internationales d'histoire. Congres de Paris, 1900*. 1e section. Paris, 1901, pp. 125-60.

Marijnissen, R.H. *De "Chest of Courtrai": Een vervalsing van het pasticcio-type*. Brussels: Paleis der Academiën, 1978.

Menache, Sophia. "A Propaganda Campaign in the Reign of Philip the Fair, 1302-03," *French History* 4 (1990), 427-54.

Pirenne, Henri. "La version flamande et la version française de la bataille de Courtrai," *Bulletin de la commission royale de Belgique*, 4th ser., 17 (1890),11-50.

Pirenne, Henri. "La version flamande et la version française de la bataille de Courtrai–Note supplementaire," *Bulletin de la commission royale de Belgique*, 5th ser., 2 (1892), 85-123.

Prevenier, Walter. "Motieven voor leliaardsgezindheid in Vlaanderen in de periode 1297-1305," *De Leiegouw* (1977), 273-88.

Rompaey, J. van. "De publiekrechtelijke achtergrond van de strijd tussen Gwijde van Dampierre en Filips de Schone," *De Leiegouw* (1977), 337-59.

Smet, J.M. de. "Passio francorum secundum flemyngos," *De Leiegouw* (1977), 289-319.

Smet, Jos. de. "Les effectifs Brugeois à la bataille de Courtrai en 1302: Note critique," *Revue Belge de philologie et d'histoire* 8 (1929), 863-70.

Verbruggen, J.F. *1302 in Vlaanderen: De guldensporenslag.* Centre d'Histoire Militaire: Travaux, 13. Brussels: Musée Royal de l'Armée, 1977.

Verbruggen, J.F. "De Brugse effectieven in de slag bij Kortrijk (11 juli 1302): Kritische nota," *Bijdragen voor de geschiedenis der Nederlanden* 11 (1948), 241-47.

Verbruggen, J.F. "De 'Chest of Courtrai': Een oorspronkelije getuigenis over 1302," *Revue Belge d'histoire militaire* 23 (1979-80), 585-608.

Verbruggen, J.F. "Het epos der Vlaamse gemeentenaren: De slag der gulden sporen, 11 juli 1302," *Revue Belge d'histoire militaire* 22 (1977-78), 81-131, 205-29, 285-312.

Verbruggen, J.F. "De historiographie van de guldensporenslag," *De Leiegouw* (1977), 245-72.

Verbruggen, J.F. "De naam guldensporenslag voor de slag bij Kortrijk (11 juli 1302)," *Revue Belge d'histoire militaire* 24 (1982), 701-06.

Verbruggen, J.F. "Pierre de Coninc et Jean Breidel, tribuns brugeois au début du XIVe siècle," *Moyen âge* 76 (1970), 61-89.

Verbruggen, J.F. "Scilt ende vrient," *Revue Belge d'histoire militaire* 23 (1979-80), 311-22.

Verbruggen, J.F. *De slag der guldensporen: Bijdrage tot de geschiedenis van Vlaanderens vrijheidsoorlog, 1297-1305.* Antwerp: N.V. Standaard Boekhandel, 1952.

Verbruggen, J.F. "De slagorde op het Groeningeveld," *Biekorf* 93 (1993), 77-85.

Medieval – Low Countries – Cassel (battle of)

Bovesse, J. "Le Comte de Namur Jean Ier et les événements du comté de Flandre en 1325-1326," *Bulletin de la commission royale d'histoire de Belgique* 131 (1965), 385-454.

Mertens, J. "Zannekin of de evolutie van het beeld van een volksheid," *De Franse Nederlanden-Les Pays-Bas Français* (1978), 24-37.

Nikolaas Zannekin en de slag bij Kassel, 1328-1978: Bijdrage tot de studie van de 14de eeuw en de landelijke geschiedenis van de Westhoek. Diksmuide: Kulturele Raad Diksmuide Werkgroep Zannekin, 1978.

Pirenne, Henri. "Documents relatifs à l'histoire de la Flandre pendant la première moitié du XIVe siècle," *Bulletin de la commission royale d'histoire de Belgique* 7 (1897), 477-93.

Pirenne, Henri. "Un mémoire de Robert de Cassel sur sa participation à la révolte de la Flandre maritime en 1324-1325," *Revue du nord* 1 (1910), 45-50.

Pirenne, Henri. *Le soulèvement de la Flandre maritime de 1323-1328.* Brussels: Libraire Kiessling et Cie., 1900.

Sabbe, J. "De opstand van Brugge tegen graaf Robrecht van Bethune en zijn zoon Robrecht van Kassel in 1321-1322," *Annales de la société d'émulation de Bruges* 107 (1970), 217-49.

Sabbe, J. *Vlaanderen in opstand, 1323-1328: Nikolaas Zannekin, Zeger Janszone en Willem de Deken.* Bruges: Marc Van de Wiele, 1992.

TeBrake, William H. *A Plague of Insurrection: Popular Politics and Peasant Revolt in Flanders, 1323-1328.* Philadelphia: University of Pennsylvania Press, 1993.

Viard, Jules. "La guerre de Flandres (1328)," *Bibliothèque de l'école de chartes* 83 (1922), 362-75.

Medieval – Manuals

Allmand, Christopher T. "France-Angleterre a la fin de la guerre de cent ans: Le 'Boke of Noblesse' de William Worcester." In: *111e Congrès national des Sociétés savantes, Poitiers, 1986, Histoire médiévale.* T. I: "La France anglaise," pp. 103-11.

Bastin, J. "Le traité de Théodore Paléologue dans la traduction de Jean de Vignai." In: *Etudes romanes dédiées à Mario Roques par ses amis, collègues et élèves de France.* Paris, 1946, pp. 77-88.

Bayley, C.C. *War and Society in Renaissance Florence: The De Militia of Leonardo Bruni.* Toronto: University of Toronto Press, 1961.

Bornstein, Diane. "Military Manuals in Fifteenth-Century England," *Mediaeval Studies* 37 (1975), 469-77.

Bornstein, Diane. "Military Strategy in Malory and Vegetius' *De re militari,*" *Comparative Literature Studies* 9 (1972), 123-29.

Bossuat, Robert. "Jean de Rouvroy, traducteur des *Stratagèmes* de Frontin," *Bibliothèque d'humanisme et renaissance* 22 (1960), 273-86, 469-89.

Campbell, Brian. "Teach Yourself How to be a General," *Journal of Roman Studies* 77 (1987), 13-29.

Contamine, Philippe. "The War Literature of the Later Middle Ages: The Treatises of Robert de Balsac and Béraud Stuart, Lord of Aubigny." In: *War, Literature and Politics in the Late Middle Ages: Essays in Honour of G.W. Coopland.* Ed. C.T. Allmand. Liverpool: University of Liverpool Press, 1975, pp. 102-21.

Coopland, G.W. "*Le Jouvencel* (Revisited)," *Symposium* 5 (1951), 137-86.

Dihle, Helene. "Das Kriegstagebuch eines deutschen Landsknechts um die Wende des 15. Jahrhunderts," *Zeitschrift für historisches Waffen- und Köstumkunde* 12 (1929-31), 1-11.

Ermini, G. *I trattati della guerra e della pace di Giovanni da Legnano.* Imola, 1923.

Gallinoni, G. "Di un trattato militare inedito del secolo XV," *Rivista storica Italiana* 40 (1938), 87-90.

Goldbrunner, H.M. "Leonardo Brunis *De militia*: Bemerkungen zur hand-schriftlichen Überlieferung," *Quellen und Forschungen aus italienischen Archiven und Bibliotheken, herausgegeben vom Deutschen Historischen Institut im Rom* 46 (1963), 478-87.

Hall, Bert S. "'So Notable Ordynaunce': Christine de Pizan, Firearms, and Siegecraft in a Time of Transition." In: *Cultuurhistorische Caleidoscoop aangeboden aan Prof. Dr. Willy L. Braekman*. Ghent, 1992, pp. 219-40.

Hils, Hans-Peter. "Handschriften der Fecht- und Ringmeister des Spätmit-telalters," *Waffen- und Köstumkunde* 29 (1987), 107-16.

Hodges, Henry. "The Anonymous in the Later Middle Ages." In: *De rebus bellicis*. Part I: *Aspect of the De rebus bellicis: Papers Presented to Professor E.A. Thompson*. Ed. M.W.C. Hassall. Oxford, 1979, pp. 119-26.

La Rocca, Donald. *The Academy of the Sword: Illustrated Fencing Books, 1500-1800*. New York: Metropolitan Museum of Art, 1998.

Martin, Janet. "John of Salisbury's Manuscripts of Frontinus and Gellius," *Journal of the Warburg and Courtauld Institute* 40 (1977), 1-21.

Mongeau, Rene Guy B. "*Li chevaliers*: Jean de Meun's Translation of *Epitoma rei militaris*." In: *Proceedings of the PMR Conference, 6*. Ed. Joseph C. Schnaubelt and Joseph Reino. Villanova: Villanova University Press, 1985, pp. 89-99.

Peters, J.B. Ward. "The Career of Sex. Julius Frontinus," *Classical Quarterly* 31 (1937), 102-05.

Petersen, Charles C. "The *Strategikon*: A Forgotten Military Classic," *Military Review* 72 (Aug 1992), 66-79.

Rodakiewicz, Erla. "The *Editio princeps* of Roberto Valturio's 'De re militari' in Relation to the Dresden and Munich Manuscripts," *Maso Finguerra* 5 (1940), 15-82.

Singman, Jeffrey L. "The Medieval Swordsman: A Thirteenth-Century German Fencing Manuscript," *Royal Armouries Yearbook* 2 (1997), 129-36.

Soret, David. "Le syndrome de Mars: La guerre selon Christine de Pizan," *Cahiers d'histoire* 40 (1995), 97-113.

Thompson, E.A. *A Roman Reformer and Inventor, being a New Text of the Treatise De rebus bellicis, with a Translation and Introduction.* Oxford: Clarendon Press, 1952.

Upton, Nicholas. *The Essential Portions of Nicholas Upton's De studio militari before 1446.* Trans. John Blount. Ed. Francis Pierrepont Barnard. Oxford: Clarendon Press, 1931.

Willard, Charity Cannon. "Christine de Pizan on Chivalry." In: *The Study of Chivalry: Resources and Approaches.* Ed. H. Chickering and T.H. Seiler. Kalamazoo, 1988, pp. 511-28.

Wright, Nicholas A.R. "Honoré Bouvet and the Abbey of Ile-Barbe," *Recherches de théologie ancienne et médiévale* 39 (1972), 113-26.

Wright, Nicholas A.R. "The *Tree of Battles* of Honoré Bouvet and the Laws of War." In: *War, Literature and Politics in the Late Middle Ages: Essays in Honour of G.W. Coopland.* Ed. C.T. Allmand. Liverpool: University of Liverpool Press, 1975, pp. 12-31.

Zancani, Diego. "Antonio Cornazzano's *De l'integrità de la militare arte.* In: *Chivalry in the Renaissance.* Ed. Sydney Anglo. Woodbridge: The Boydell Press, 1990, pp. 13-24.

Medieval – Manuals – Vegetius

Allmand, Christopher T. "Fifteenth-Century Versions of Vegetius' *De Re Militari.*" In: *Armies, Chivalry and Warfare in Medieval Britain and France: Proceedings of the 1995 Harlaxton Symposium.* Ed. M. Strickland. Stamford, 1998, pp. 30-45.

Bachrach, Bernard S. "The Practical Use of Vegetius' *De re militari* during the Early Middle Ages," *The Historian* 47 (1985), 239-55.

Barnes, Timothy D. "The Date of Vegetius," *Phoenix* 23 (1979), 254-57.

Bornstein, Diane. "Military Strategy in Malory and Vegetius' *De re militari,*" *Comparative Literature Studies* 9 (1972), 123-29.

Bornstein, Diane. "The Scottish Prose Version of Vegetius' *De re militari,*" *Studies in Scottish Literature* 8 (1970-71), 174-83.

Camus, Jules. "Notice d'une traduction française de Végèce faite en 1380," *Romania* 25 (1896), 393-400.

Goffart, Walter. "The Date and Purpose of Vegetius' *De re militari*," *Traditio* 33 (1977), 65-100.

Jones, Charles W. "Bede and Vegetius," *Classical Review* 46 (1932), 248-49.

Knowles, Christine. "A 14th Century Imitator of Jean de Meung: *Jean de Vignay's Translation of the De re militari of Vegetius*," *Studies in Philology* 53 (1956), 452-58.

Legge, M.D. "The Lord Edward's Vegetius," *Scriptorium* 7 (1953), 262-65.

MacCracken, H.N. "Vegetius in English: Notes on the Early Translations." In: *Anniversary Papers by Colleagues and Pupils of George Lyman Kittredge*. Ed. E.S. Sheldon et al. Boston, 1913, pp. 389-403.

Meyer, P. "Les anciens traducteurs français de Végèce et en particulier Jean de Vignai," *Romania* 25 (1896), 401-23.

Sherwood, Foster Hallberg. *Studies in Medieval Uses of Vegetius' Epitoma rei militaris*. Unpublished dissertation. Los Angeles: University of California in Los Angeles, 1980.

Shrader, Charles Reginald. "A Handlist of Extant Manuscripts Containing the *De re militari* of Flavius Vegetius Renatus," *Scriptorium* 33 (1979), 280-305.

Shrader, Charles Reginald. "The Influence of Vegetius' *De re militari*," *Military Affairs* 45 (1981), 167-72.

Shrader, Charles Reginald. *The Ownership and Distribution of the De re militari of Flavius Vegetius Renatus Before the Year 1300*. Unpublished Dissertation. Columbia University, 1976.

Springer, M. "Vegetius im Mittelalter," *Philologus* 123 (1979), 85-90.

Thorpe, L. "Maistre Richard, a Thirteenth-Century Translator of the *De re militari* of Vegetius," *Scriptorium* 6 (1952), 39-50.

Wisman, Josette A. "L'*Epitoma rei militaris* de Végèce et sa fortune au Moyen âge," *Moyen âge* 85 (1979), 13-31.

Wisman, Josette A. "Flavius Renatus Vegetius," *Catalogus translationum et commentariorum: Medieval and Renaissance Latin Translations and Commentaries Annotated Lists and Guides* 6 (1986), 175-84.

Medieval – Mercenaries

Artesi, Renato. "Politica finanziaria e Compagnie di Ventura sotto i Visconti, XIVe secolo," *Armi antichi* (1985), 3-34.

Blastenbrei, Peter. "The Soldier and His Cardinal: Francesco Sforza and Nicolò Acciapacci, 1438-1444," *Renaissance Studies* 3 (1989), 290-302.

Block, W. *Die Condottieri: Studien über die sogenannten "unblutige Schlachten"*. Berlin, 1913.

Boussard, Jacques. "Les mercenaries au XIIe siècle: Henri II Plantagenêt et les origines de l'armée de métier," *Bibliothèque d'école de chartes* 106 (1945-46), 189-224.

Bridge, J.C. "Two Cheshire Soldiers of Fortune in the Fourteenth Century," *Journal of the Chester and North Wales Archaeological Society* n.s. 14 (1908), 112-65.

Brown, Stephen D.B. "Military Service and Monetary Reward in the Eleventh and Twelfth Centuries," *History* 74 (1989), 20-38.

Bueno de Mesquita, D.M. "Some Condottieri of the Trecento and their Relations with Political Authority," *Proceedings of the British Academy* 32 (1946), 219-41.

Burns, Robert Ignatius. "The Catalan Company and the European Powers, 1305-1311," *Speculum* 29 (1954), 751-71.

Caferro, William. "Mercenaries and Military Expenditure: The Costs of Undeclared Warfare in Fourteenth Century Siena," *Journal of European Economic History* 23 (1994), 219-47.

Caferro, William. *Mercenary Companies and the Decline of Siena*. Baltimore: The Johns Hopkins University Press, 1998.

Carrère, Claude. "Aux origines des grandes compaignies: La compaignie catalane de 1302." In: *Recrutement, mentalités, sociétés: Actes du colloque international d'histoire militaire, 18-22 septembre 1974*. Montpellier, 1974, pp. 1-7.

Cecchi, D. "Compagnie di ventura nella Marca," *Studi Macceratesi* 9 (1975), 64-136.

Chamberlain, E.R. "The 'English' Mercenary Companies in Italy," *History Today* 6 (1956), 334-43.

Compagnie di ventura, Le: Catalogo della mostra di arti figurative e armi. Narni, 1970.

Contamine, Philippe. "René II et les mercenaries de la langue germanique: la guerre contre Robert de La Marck, seigneur de Sedan (1496)." In: *Cinq-centième anniversaire de la bataille de Nancy (1477): Actes du Colloque organisé par l'institut de recherche régionale en sciences sociales, humaines et économiques de l'Université de Nancy II (Nancy, 22-24 septembre 1977)*. Nancy, 1979, pp. 377-94.

Croce, B. *Un condottiere Italiano del Quattrocento: Cola di Monforte, conte di Campobasso*. Bari, 1936.

Del Treppo, Mario. "Gli aspetti organizzativi, economici e sociali di una compagna di ventura," *Rivista storica Italiana* 85 (1973), 253-75.

Dinic, M.J. "Spanski najamnici u srpskoj sluzbi," *Zbornik radova visantoloskog instituta* 6 (1960), 15-28.

Elders, E.A. "A Medieval English Mercenary," *Country Life* (Mar 10, 1966), 552-53.

Ferrer i Mallol, M.T. "Mercenaris catalans a Ferrara (1307-17)," *Anuario de estudios medievales* 2 (1965), 15-27.

Fitz-Clarence, C. "Mémoire sur l'emploi des mercenaries mahométans dans les armées chrétiennes," *Journal asiatique* 11 (1827).

Fontaine, Marie-Madeline. "Comment Pietro del Monte, condottiere Italien, parlait Espagnol," *Bibliothèque d'Humanisme et Renaissance* 54 (1992), 163-73.

Fontaine, Marie-Madeline. *La condottiere Pietro del Monte philosophe et écrivian de la renaissance*. Geneva, 1991.

Franceschini, G. "Boldrino da Panicale: Contributo alla storia delle milizie mercenarie Italiane," *Bollettino della deputazione di storia patria dell'Umbria* 46 (1949), 118-39.

Gaupp, Fritz. "The Condottiere John Hawkwood," *History* n.s. 23 (1938-39), 305-21.

Geraud, H. "Les routiers au XIIème siècle," *Bibliothèque de l'école de chartes* 3 (1841-42), 125-47.

Geraud, H. "Mercadier: Les routiers XIIIème siècle," *Bibliothèque de l'école de chartes* 3 (1841-42), 417-43.

Grabski, A.F. "La chevalerie polonaise au service de l'étranger au moyen âge." In: *Histoire militaire de la Pologne: Problèmes choises*. Ed. W. Bieganski, P. Stawecki, and W. Janusz. Warsaw: Institut d'Histoire, 1970.

Green, Louis. *Castruccio Castracani: A Study on the Origins and Character of a Fourteenth-Century Italian Despotism*. Oxford: Clarendon Press, 1986.

Grundmann, H. "Rotten und Brabanzonen: Söldner-Heere im 12. Jahrhundert," *Deutsches Archiv für Erforschung des Mittelalters* 5 (1941-42), 419-92.

Housley, Norman. "The Mercenary Companies, the Papacy, and the Crusades, 1356-1378," *Traditio* 38 (1982), 253-80.

Isaac, Steven. "The Problem with Mercenaries." In: *The Circle of War in the Middle Ages: Essays on Medieval Military and Naval History*. Ed. Donald J. Kagay and L.J. Andrew Villalon. Woodbridge: The Boydell Press, 1999, pp. 101-10.

Iwańczak, Wojciech. "Mercenary Warriors–An Example of the International Relations of Czech Lands," *Fasciculi archaeologicae historicae* 7 (1994), 21-29.

Kidwell, Carol. *Marullus: Soldier Poet of the Renaissance*. London: Duckworth, 1989.

Krieger, Karl-Friedrich. "Obligatory Military Service and the Use of Mercenaries in Imperial Military Campaigns under the Hohenstaufen Emperors." In: *England and Germany in the High Middle Ages*. Ed. Alfred Haverkamp and Hanna Vollrath. London: The German Historical Institute, 1996, pp. 151-68.

La Sizeranne, R. de. *Le vertueux condottière Federigo de Montefeltro, duc d'Urbino, 1422-1482*. Paris, 1927.

Mallett, Michael. "Mercenaries." In: *Medieval Warfare: A History*. Ed. Maurice Keen. Oxford: Oxford University Press, 1999, pp. 209-29.

Mallett, Michael. *Mercenaries and their Masters: Warfare in Renaissance Italy*. Totowa: Rowman and Littlefield, 1974.

Mallett, Michael. "Some Notes on a Fifteenth-Century *Condottiere* and his Library: Count Antonio da Marsciano." In: *Cultural Aspects of the Italian Renaissance: Essays in Honour of Paul Oskar Kristeller*. Ed. Cecil H. Clough. Manchester: Manchester University Press, 1976, pp. 202-15.

Mallett, Michael. "Venice and its Condottieri, 1404-54." In: *Renaissance Venice*. Ed. J.R. Hale. Totowa, 1973, pp. 121-45.

Mens, A. "De 'Brabanciones' of bloeddorstige en plunderzieke avonturiers (XIIe-XIIIe eeuw)." In: *Miscellanea historica in honorem Alberti de Meyer*. Leuven, 1946, I:558-70.

Mirot, Léon. *Sylvestre Budes (13??-1380) et les Bretons en Italie*. Paris, 1898.

Niese, H. "Zur Geschichte des deutschen Soldrittertums in Italien," *Quellen und Forschungen aus italienischen Archiven und Bibliotheken* 8 (1905), 217-48.

Pacella, F. "Un barone condottiero della Calabria del sec. XIV-XV: Nicolò Ruffo, marchese di Cotrone, conte di Catanzero," *Archivio storico per le provincie napoletane* 82 (1964), 45-93.

Pertici, Petra. "Condottieri senesi e la *Rotta di San Romano* di Paolo Uccello," *Archivio storico Italiano* 157 (1999), 537-62.

Pieri, Paolo. "Milizie e capitani di ventura in Italia nel medio evo," *Atti dell'reale Accademia Peloritana di Messina* 40 (1937-38).

Pieri, Paolo. "Le milizie svizzere nel tardo medioevo e nel rinascimento in Italia," *Annali dell facoltà di magistero della Reale Università di Messina* 17 (1939).

Prestwich, Michael. "Money and Mercenaries in English Medieval Armies." In: *England and Germany in the High Middle Ages.* Ed. Alfred Haverkamp and Hanna Vollrath. London: The German Historical Institute, 1996, pp. 129-50.

Puś, W. "La chevalerie étrangère au service de la Pologne jusqu'au début du XIVe siècle." In: *Histoire militaire de la Pologne: Problèmes choises.* Ed. W. Bieganski, P. Stawecki, and W. Janusz. Warsaw: Institut d'Histoire, 1970.

Ricotti, Erole. *Storia delle compagnie di ventura in Italia.* 4 vols. Turin: Pomba, 1893; rpt. Rome, 1965.

Rubio i Lluch, A. "La companya catalana sota el comandament de Teobald de Cepoy (1307-1310)." In: *Miscellania E. Prat de la Riba.* 2 vols. Barcelona, 1923, I:219-70.

Schäfer, Karl Heinrich. "Deutsche Ritter und Edelknechte in Italien während des XIV. Jahrhunderts," *Quellen und Forschungen aus dem Gebiet der Geschichte* 15 (1911); 16 (1914); 25 (1940).

Schlight, John. *Monarchs and Mercenaries.* New York: New York University Press, 1968.

Shepard, Jonathan. "The uses of the Franks in Eleventh-Century Byzantium," *Anglo-Norman Studies* 15 (1993), 275-305.

Simeoni, L. "Note sulle cause e i danni del mercenarismo militare italiano del 1300," *Atti e memorie della Reale Academie di Modena* (1937).

Swain, Elisabeth Ward. "The Wages of Peace: The *Condotte* of Ludovico Gonzaga, 1436-1478," *Renaissance Studies* 3 (1989), 442-52.

Temple-Leader, J. and G. Marcotti. *Sir John Hawkwood (L'Acuto): The Story of a Condottiere.* London, 1889.

Tognetti, Sergio. "L'attività di banca locale di una grande compagnia fiorentina del XV secolo," *Archivio storico italiano* 155 (1997), 595-647.

Trease, Geoffrey. *The Condottieri: Soldiers of Fortune.* New York: Holt, Rinehart and Winston, 1971.

Ugurgieri della Berardenga, C. *Avventuriei alla conquista di feudi e di corone, 1356-1429.* Florence, 1962.

Waley, Daniel P. "*Condotte* and *Condottieri* in the Thirteenth Century," *Proceedings of the British Academy* 61 (1975), 337-71.

Waley, Daniel P. "Le origini della condotta nel duecento e le compagnie di ventura," *Rivista storica italiana* 88 (1976), 531-38.

Medieval – Methodology

Beeler, John H. "The State of the Art–Recent Scholarship in Late Medieval and Early Modern Military History," *Military Affairs* 47 (1983), 141-43.

Burns, Robert Ignatius. "The Significance of the Frontier in the Middle Ages." In: *Medieval Frontier Societies.* Ed. R. Bartlett and A. Mackay. Oxford, 1989, pp. 306-30.

Contamine, Philippe. "La guerre au moyen âge d'après quelques travaux récènts," *Revue internationale d'histoire militaire* 61 (1985), 41-59.

Curry, Anne E. "Medieval Warfare: England and her Continental Neighbours, Eleventh to the Fourteenth Centuries," *Journal of Medieval History* 24 (1998), 81-102.

Medieval – Naval Warfare (See – Medieval Ships and – Hundred Years War – Navies)

Airaldi, Gabriella. "Roger of Lauria's Expedition to the Peloponnese," *Mediterranean Historical Review* 10 (1995), 14-23.

Amari, M. "Su i fuochi da guerra usati nel Mediterraneo nel'XI e XII secoli," *Atti della Reale Academia dei Lincei.* Rome, 1876.

Bennett, Matthew. "Norman Naval Activity in the Mediterranean, c.1060-c.1108," *Anglo-Norman Studies* 15 (1993), 41-58.

Bjork, David K. "Piracy in the Baltic, 1375-1398," *Speculum* 18 (1943), 39-58.

Boyer, Pierre. "Artillerie et tactique navale en Méditerranée au XVIe siècle," *Revue historique des armées* 174 (1989), 110-21.

Brooks, F.W. "The Battle of Damme, 1213," *Mariner's Mirror* 16 (1930), 263-71.

Cheyette, Frederic L. "The Sovereign and the Pirates, 1332," *Speculum* 45 (1970), 40-58.

Christides, Vassilios. "New Light on Navigation and Naval Warfare in the Eastern Mediterranean, the Red Sea and the Indian Ocean (6th-14th Centuries A.D.)," *Nubica* 3 (1994), 3-42.

Davies, Clifford S.L. "The Alleged 'Sack of Bristol': International Ramifications of Breton Privateering, 1484-5," *Historical Research* 67 (1994), 230-39.

Dean, Trevor. "The Sovereign as Pirate: Charles II of Anjou and the Marriage of his Daughter, 1304," *English Historical Review* 111 (1996), 350-56.

DeVries, Kelly. "A 1445 Reference to Shipboard Artillery." *Technology and Culture* 31 (1990), 818-29.

DeVries, Kelly. "The Effectiveness of Fifteenth-Century Shipboard Artillery," *The Mariner's Mirror* 84 (1998), 389-99.

Dotson, John E. "Fleet Operations in the First Genoese-Venetian War, 1264-1266," *Viator* 30 (1999).

Dotson, John E. "Naval Strategy in the First Genoese-Venetian War, 1257-1270," *American Neptune* 46 (1981), 84-90.

Eickhoff, Ekkehard. *Seekrieg und Seepolitik zwischen Islam und Abendland*. Berlin, 1966.

Katele, Irene B. "Piracy and the Venetian State: The Dilemma of Maritime Defense in the Fourteenth Century," *Speculum* 63 (1988), 865-89.

Labrousse, H. "La guerre de course de mer rouge pendant les croisades: Renaud de Chatillon (1182-1183)." In: *Course et piraterie*. XVe Colloque internationale d'histoire maritime. Paris: Colloque internationale d'histoire maritime, 1975.

Lewis, Archibald R. "Northern European Sea Power and the Straits of Gibraltar, 1031-1350." In: *Order and Innovation in the Middle Ages: Essays in Honor of Joseph R. Strayer*. Ed. W.C. Jordan et al. Princeton, 1976, pp. 139-64, 458.

Mira, R. Fullana. "La casa de Lauria en el reino de Valencia." In: *III Congrés de historia de la corona de Aragó, dedicat al periode compres entre la mort de Jaume I i la proclamció del rey Don Ferrán d'Antequerra*. 2 vols. Valencia, 1923.

Mott, Lawrence V. "The Battle of Malta, 1283: Prelude to a Disaster." In: *The Circle of War in the Middle Ages: Essays on Medieval Military and Naval History*. Ed. Donald J. Kagay and L.J. Andrew Villalon. Woodbridge: The Boydell Press, 1999, pp. 145-72.

Pryor, John H. "The Crusade of Emperor Frederick II, 1220-29: The Implications of the Maritime Evidence," *American Neptune* 52 (1992), 113-32.

Pryor, John H. "The Naval Battles of Roger of Lauria," *Journal of Medieval History* 9 (1983), 179-219.

Queller, Donald E. "Combined Arms Operations and the Latin Conquest of Constantinople." In: *Changing Interpretations and New Sources in Naval History: Papers from the Third U.S. Naval Academy History Symposium*. Ed. R.W. Love, Jr. New York, 1980, pp. 45-57.

Reid, W. Stanford. "Sea-power in the Anglo-Scottish War, 1296-1328," *Mariner's Mirror* 46 (1960), 7-23.

Robbert, Louise Buenger. "A Venetian Naval Expedition of 1224." In: *Economy, Society, and Government in Medieval Italy: Essays in Memory of Robert L. Reynolds*. Ed. D. Herlihy, R.S. Lopez and V. Slessarev. Kent: Kent University Press, 1969, pp. 141-51.

Rodgers, William L. *Naval Warfare under Oars, 4th to 16th Centuries: A Study of Strategy, Tactics and Ship Design*. Annapolis: Naval Institute Press, 1939.

Rose, Susan. "Islam Versus Christendom: The Naval Dimension, 1000-1600," *Journal of Military History* 63 (1999), 561-78.

Skinner, Patricia. "Politics and Piracy: the Duchy of Gaeta in the Twelfth Century," *Journal of Medieval History* 21 (1995), 307-19.

Stratos, Andreas N. "The Naval Engagement at Phoenix." In: *Charanis Studies: Essays in Honor of Peter Charanis.* Ed. A.E. Laiou-Thomadakis. New Brunswick, 1980, pp. 221-47.

Valentine-Harris, P. "Archers at Sea: the Battle of Winchelsea," *Journal of the Society of Archer-Antiquaries* 27 (1984), 43-44.

Medieval – Military Obligation (Recruitment; Feudalism)

Bachrach, Bernard S. "Enforcement of the *Forma Fidelitatis*: The Techniques Used by Fulk Nerra, Count of the Angevins (987-1040)," *Speculum* 59 (1984), 796-819.

Barthélemy, Dominique and Stephen D. White. "Debate–The 'Feudal Revolution'," *Past and Present* 152 (Aug 1996), 196-223.

Belleval, René de. *Rôle des nobles et fieffés du baillage d'Amiens convoqués pour la guerre le 25 août 1337.* Amiens, 1862.

Benoit-Guyod, Henry. "La première armée française: Le ban et arrière-ban des seigneuries," *Revue internationale d'histoire militaire* 25 (1965), 559-61.

Bishop, Willard E. "Wages for the Archer Guard," *Journal of the Society of Archer-Antiquaries* 4 (1961), 21-22.

Bisson, Thomas N. "The 'Feudal Revolution,'" *Past and Present* 142 (1994), 6-42.

Bisson, Thomas N. "The Military Origins of Medieval Representation," *American Historical Review* 71 (1966), 1199-1218.

Bosl, K. "*Das ius ministerialium*: Dienstrecht und Lehnrecht im deutschen Mittelalter." In: *Studien zum mittelalterlichen Lehnwesen.* Lindau and Constance, 1960.

Boussard, Jacques. "L'enquête de 1172 sur les services de chevalier en Normandie." In: *Recueil de travaux offerts à Clovis Brunel.* Paris, 1955, I:193-208.

Boussard, Jacques. "Services féodaux, milices et mercenaires dan les armées, en France, aux Xe et XIe siècles." In: *Ordinamenti militari in occidente nell'alto medioevo.* Settimane di studio del centro italiano di studi sull'alto medioevo, XV. Spoleto, 1968, I:131-68.

Boutruche, Robert. *Seigneurie et féodalité.* 2 vols. Paris, 1968-70.

Brassart, F. "La féodalité dans le nord de la France: Bans et arrière-bans de la Flandre wallonne sous Charles de Téméraire et Maximilien d'Autriche," *Souvenirs de la Flandre wallonne* (1884), 5-78.

Brown, Elizabeth A.R. "The Tyranny of a Construct: Feudalism and Historians of Medieval Europe," *American Historical Review* 79 (1974), 1063-88.

Brühl, C.R. *Fodrum, Gistum, Servitium regis: Studien zu den wirtschaftlichen Grundlagen des Königstums (vom 6. bis zur Mitte des 14. Jahrhunderts).* 2 vols. Cologne and Graz, 1968.

Brünner, Heinrich "Der Ritterdienst und die Anfänge des Lehenwesens," *Zeitschrift der Savigny-Stiftung für Rechtsgeschichte, Germanistische Abteilung* 8 (1887), 1-38.

Champeval, J.B. "Le rôle du ban et arrière-ban du haut Auvergne." In: *L'Auvergne historique, litteraire et artistique: Varia, 1909-1912.* Riom, 1913.

Chew, Helena M. *The English Ecclesiastic Tenants-in-Chief and Knight Service.* Oxford, 1932.

Chew, Helena M. "Scutage in the Fourteenth Century," *English Historical Review* 38 (1923), 19-41.

Conrad, H. *Der Gedanke der Allgemeinen Wehrpflicht in der deutschen Wehrverfassung des Mittelalters.* Berlin, 1937.

Coss, Peter R. "Bastard Feudalism Revised," *Past and Present* 125 (1989), 27-64.

Coss, Peter R. "The Formation of the English Gentry," *Past and Present* 147 (1995), 38-64.

Crouch, David, David A. Carpenter and Peter R. Coss. "Debate–Bastard Feudalism Revised," *Past and Present* 131 (May 1991), 165-203.

Duby, Georges. *Les trois ordres ou l'imaginaire du féodalisme*. Paris, 1978; trans. *The Three Orders: Feudal Society Imagined*. Trans. A. Goldhammer. Chicago: University of Chicago Press, 1981.

Frauenholz, E von. *Entwicklungsgeschichte des deutsche Heerwesens*. 3 vols. Munich1935-37.

Ganshof, François Louis. *Feudalism*. Trans. Philip Grierson. 3rd ed. New York: Harper and Row, Publishers, 1964.

Goodman, Anthony. "The Military Subcontracts of Sir Hugh Hastings, 1380," *English Historical Review* 95 (1980), 114-20.

Guilhiermoz, P. *Essai sur l'origine de la noblesse en France au moyen âge*. Paris, 1902; rpt. New York, 1960.

Hicks, Michael A. *Bastard Feudalism*. London: Longman, 1995.

Jones, Michael. "An Indenture between Robert, Lord Mohaut, and Sir John de Bracebridge for Life Service in Peace and War, 1310," *Journal of the Society of Archivists* 4 (1972), 384-94.

Kimball, E.G. "Serjeantry Tenure in Medieval England," *Yale Historical Publications, Miscellany* 30 (1936).

Leicht, P.S. "Gasindi a vassalli," *Rendiconti della reale Accademia nazionale dei Lincei, Scienze morali*, 6th ser. 3 (1927).

Lewis, N.B. "An Early Indenture of Military Service, 27 July 1287," *Bulletin of the Institute of Historical Research* 13 (1935/36), 85-89.

Lewis, N.B. "The Feudal Summons of 1385," *English Historical Review* 100 (1985), 729-46.

Lewis, N.B. "The Last Medieval Summons of the English Feudal Levy, 13 June 1385," *English Historical Review* 73 (1958), 1-26.

Lewis, N.B. "The Organization of Indentured Retinues in Fourteenth-Century England," *Transactions of the Royal Historical Society* 4th ser. 27 (1945), 29-39.

Lewis, N.B. "The Recruitment and Organization of a Contract Army, May to November 1337," *Bulletin of the Institute of Historical Research* 37 (1964), 1-19.

Lewis, N.B. "The Summons of the English Feudal Levy, 5 April 1327." In: *Essays in Medieval History Presented to Bertie Wilkinson.* Ed. T.A. Sandquist and M.R. Powicke. Toronto: University of Toronto Press, 1969, pp. 236-49.

Lewis, P.S. "Decayed and Non-Feudalism in Later Medieval France," *Bulletin of the Institute of Historical Research* 37 (1964), 157-84.

Lübeck, K. "Vom Reichskriegsdienste des Klosters Fulda," *Fuldaer Geschichte-Blätter* (1938), 1-13, 20-32, 45-49.

Lyon, Bryce. "The Feudal Antecedent of the Indenture System," *Speculum* 29 (1954), 503-11.

Lyon, Bryce. *From Fief to Indenture: The Transition from Feudal to Non-Feudal Contract in Western Europe.* Cambridge: Harvard University Press, 1957.

Lyon, Bryce. "The Money Fief under the English Kings," *English Historical Review* 66 (1951), 161-93.

McFarlane, K.B. "Bastard Feudalism," *Bulletin of the Institute for Historical Research* 20 (1943-45), 161-80; in: *England in the Fifteenth Century: Collected Essays.* London, 1981, pp. 1-22.

McFarlane, K.B. "An Indenture of Agreement between Two English Knights for Mutual Aid and Counsel in Peace and War, 5 December, 1298," *Bulletin of the Institute of Historical Research* 38 (1965), 200–10; in: *England in the Fifteenth Century: Collected Essays.* London, 1981, pp. 45-56.

McFarlane, K.B. "Parliament and 'Bastard Feudalism'." In: *England in the Fifteenth Century: Collected Essays.* London, 1981, pp. 1-22.

March, U. "Die holsteinische Heeresorganisation im Mittelalter," *Zeitschrift der Gesellschaft für Schleswig-holsteinische Geschichte* 99 (1974), 95-139.

Massmann, E.H. *Schwertleite und Ritterschlag*. Hamburg, 1932.

Menant, F. "Les écuyers ('scutiferi') vassaux paysans d'Italie du Nord au XIIe siècle." In: *Structures féodales et féodalisme dans l'occident méditerranéen (X-XII siècles): Colloques internationaux du Centre National de la Recherche Scientifique*, no. 588. Paris, 1980, pp. 285-97.

Navel, H. "L'enquête de 1133 sur les fiefs de l'évêché de Bayeux," *Bulletin de la société des antiquaires de Normandie* 42 (1934), 5-80.

Painter, Sidney. "Castle-Guard," *American Historical Review* 40 (1934-35), 450-59.

Parisse, M. *La noblesse lorraine, XI-XIIIe siècles*. 2 vols. Lille, 1976.

Pastoreau, M. "L'origine militaire des armoires." In: *Actes du CIe congrès national des société savantes, Lille 1976: Archéologie et histoire de l'art*. Paris, 1978, pp. 107-18.

Pietzner, F. *Schwertleite und Ritterschlag*. Heidelberg, 1932.

Powicke, Michael R. "Distraint of Knighthood and Military Obligation under Henry III," *Speculum* 25 (1950), 457-70.

Powicke, Michael R. *Military Obligation in Medieval England: A Study in Liberty and Duty*. Oxford: Clarendon Press, 1962.

Reeves, A.Compton. "Some of Humphrey Stafford's Military Indentures," *Nottingham Medieval Studies* 16 (1972), 80-91.

Reuter, Timothy. "The 'Feudal Revolution': Comment 3," *Past and Present* 155 (1997), 177-95.

Reynolds, Susan. *Fiefs and Vassals: The Medieval Evidence Reinterpreted*. Oxford: Oxford University Press, 1994.

Sanders, I.J. *Feudal Military Service in England: A Study of the Constitutional and Military Powers of the 'Barones' in Mediaeval England*. London, 1956.

Schlesinger, W. "Lord and Follower in Germanic Institutional History." In: *Lordship and Community in Medieval Europe: Selected Readings*. Ed. Frederic L. Cheyette. New York, 1968, pp. 64-99.

Schneider, Hugo. *Adel-Burgen-Waffen*. Berne: Francke Verlag, 1967.

Stormer, W. "Früher Adel: Studien zur politischen Führungsschicht im fränkisch-deutschen Reich vom 8. bis 11. Jahrhundert. 2 vols. Stuttgart, 1973.

Strayer, Joseph R. "Feudalism." In: *Dictionary of the Middle Ages*. Ed. J.R. Strayer. New York, 1985, V:52-57.

Tabuteau, Emily Zack. "Definitions of Feudal Military Obligations in Eleventh-Century Normandy." In: *On the Laws and Customs of England: Essays in Honor of Samuel E. Thorne*. Ed. M.S. Arnold et al. Chapel Hill, 1981, pp. 18-59.

Wohlfeil, R. "Adel und neues Heerwesen." In: *Deutscher Adel, 1430-1555: Büdinger Vortrage 1963*. Ed. H. Rossler. Darmstadt, 1965, pp. 203-33.

Wohlfeil, R. "Ritter–Söldnerführer–Offizier: Versuch eines vergleiches." In: *Festschrift Johannes Barmann*. Wiesbaden, 1966, I:45-70.

Zimmermann, J. "Wehrwesen und Zünfte," *Schaffhauser Beiträge zur vaterländischen Geschichte* 38 (1961), 82-90.

Medieval – Military Orders – General

As ordens militares em Portugal: Actas do i encontro sobre ordens militares. Palmela–Setúbal: Câmara Municipal de Palmela, 1991.

Barber, Malcolm. "The Order of Saint Lazarus and the Crusades," *Catholic Historical Review* 80 (1994), 439-56.

Benninghoven, F. *Der Orden der Schwertbrüder*. Cologne, 1965.

Bonet Donato, Maria. "Consideracions sobre el patrimoni dels ordes militars a Catalunya en temps de Ramon Berenguer IV," *Anuario de estudios medievales* 28 (1998), 11-30.

Borchardt, Karl. "Military Orders in East Central Europe: The First Hundred Years." In: *Autour de la première croisade: Actes du Colloque de la Society for the Study of the Crusades and the Latin East (Clermont-Ferrand, 22-25 juin 1995).* Ed. M. Balard. Paris: Publications de la Sorbonne, 1996, pp. 247-54.

Bray, Jennifer R. "The Medieval Military Order of St. Katherine," *Bulletin of the Institute of Historical Research* 56 (1983), 1-6.

Brundage, James A. "A Transformed Angel (X 3.31.18): The Problem of the Crusading Monk." In: *Studies in Medieval Cistercian History Presented to Jeremiah F. O'Sullivan.* Spenser, 1971, pp. 55-62.

Burgtorf, Jochen. "Wind Beneath the Wings: Subordinate Headquarters Officials in the Hospital and Temple from the Twelfth to the Early Fourteenth Centuries." In: *The Military Orders.* Vol. 2: *Welfare and Warfare.* Ed. Helen Nicholson. Aldershot: Ashgate, 1998, pp. 217-24.

Bulst-Thiele, Marie Luise. "Zur Geschichte der Ritterorden und des Konigreichs Jerusalem in 13. Jahrhundert bis zur Schlacht bei La Forbie am 17. Okt 1244," *Deutsches Archiv für Erforschung des Mittelalters* 22 (1966), 197-226.

Burns, Robert Ignatius. "The Friars of the Sack in Barcelona: Financial and Pastoral Profile," *Anuario de estudios medievales* 28 (1998), 419-36.

Burns, Robert Ignatius. "The Friars of the Sack in Valencia," *Speculum* 36 (1961), 435-38.

Cleve, Hertwig. "Kaiser Friedrich II. und die Ritterorden," *Deutsches Archiv für Erforschung des Mittelalters* 49 (1993), 39-73.

Cole, Penny J. "Review Article–The Military Orders in War and Peace," *International History Review* 18 (1996), 620-28.

Contamine, Philippe. "Louis XI, François II, duc de Bretagne, et l'ordre de Saint-Michel (1469-1470)." In: *Des pouvoirs en France, 1300-1500.* Paris, 1992, pp. 169-90.

Contamine, Philippe. "Sur l'ordre de Saint-Michel au temps de Louis XI et de Charles VIII," *Bulletin de la société nationale des antiquaires de France* (1976), 212-36.

Costa, Paula Pinto and António Pestana de Vasconcelos. "Christ, Santiago and Avis: an Approach to the Rules of the Portuguese Military Orders in the Late Middle Ages." In: *The Military Orders*. Vol. 2: *Welfare and Warfare*. Ed. Helen Nicholson. Aldershot: Ashgate, 1998, pp. 251-58.

Costa i Paretas, Maria Mercè. "El segon monestir de Jonqueres i el molí d'En Carbonell," *Anuario de estudios medievales* 28 (1998), 59-74.

De Ayala Martínez, Carlos. "En torno a la filiación disciplinaria de la Orden Militar de Alcántara (siglos XII-XIII)," *Anuario de estudios medievales* 28 (1998), 345-62.

Elm, K. "Kanoniker und Ritter vom Heiligen Grab." In: *Die geistlichen Ritterorden Europas*. Ed. J. Fleckenstein and M. Hellmann. Sigmaringen, 1980, pp. 141-69.

Emery, Richard W. "A Note on the Friars of the Sack," *Speculum* 35 (1960), 591-95.

Favreau-Lilie, Marie-Luise. "The Military Orders and the Escape of the Christian Population from the Holy Land in 1291," *Journal of Medieval History* 19 (1993), 201-27.

Fernandez Izquierdo, Francisco. *La orden militar de Calatrava en el siglo XVI*. Madrid: Biblioteca de Historia CSIC, 1992.

Fleckenstein, Josef. "Friedrich II. und das Rittertum," *Studi medievali*, 3rd ser., 35 (1994), 503-15.

Fleckenstein, Josef and M. Hellmann, ed. *Die geistlichen Ritterorden Europas*. Sigmaringen, 1980.

Forey, Alan J. "The Emergence of the Military Order in the Twelfth Century," *Journal of Ecclesiastical History* 36 (1985), 175-95.

Forey, Alan J. "Literacy and Learning in the Military Orders during the Twelfth and Thirteenth Centuries." In: *The Military Orders*. Vol. 2: *Welfare and Warfare*. Ed. Helen Nicholson. Aldershot: Ashgate, 1998, pp. 185-206.

Forey, Alan J. "The Military Order of St. Thomas of Acre," *English Historical Review* 92 (1977), 481-503.

Forey, Alan J. *The Military Orders: From the Twelfth to the Early Fourteenth Centuries*. Toronto: University of Toronto Press, 1992.

Forey, Alan J. "The Military Orders and Holy War Against Christians in the Thirteenth Century," *English Historical Review* 104 (1989), 1-24.

Forey, Alan J. "Military Orders and Secular Warfare in the Twelfth and Thirteenth Centuries," *Viator* 24 (1993), 79-100.

Forey, Alan J. "The Military Orders and the Ransoming of Captives from Islam (Twelfth to Early Fourteenth Centuries), *Studia monastica* 33 (1991), 259-79.

Forey, Alan J. "The Military Orders and the Spanish Reconquest in the Twelfth and Thirteenth Centuries," *Traditio* 40 (1984), 197-234.

Forey, Alan J. "The Military Orders in the Crusading Proposals of the Late-Thirteenth and Early-Fourteenth Centuries," *Traditio* 36 (1980), 317-45.

Forey, Alan J. "Novitiate and Instruction in the Military Orders during the Twelfth and Thirteenth Centuries," *Speculum* 61 (1986), 1-17.

Forey, Alan J. "The Order of Mountjoy," *Speculum* 46 (1971), 250-66.

Forey, Alan J. "Recruitment to the Military Orders (Twelfth to Mid-Fourteenth Centuries)," *Viator* 17 (1986), 139-71.

Forey, Alan J. "Women and the Military Orders in the Twelfth and Thirteenth Centuries," *Studia monastica* 29 (1987), 63-72.

Gerrard, Christopher. "Opposing Identity: Muslims, Christians and the Military Orders in Rural Aragon," *Medieval Archaeology* 43 (1999), 143-60.

Gonzalvo i Bou, Gener and Manel Salas i Flotats. "Guillem IV de Cervera, cavaller i monjo de Poblet," *Anuario de estudios medievales* 28 (1998), 405-18.

Gutton, F. *La chevalerie militaire en Espagne: L'ordre d'Alcantara*. Paris, 1975.

Gutton, F. *La chevalerie militaire en Espagne: L'ordre de Calatrava*. Paris, 1955.

Gutton, F. *La chevalerie militaire en Espagne: L'ordre de Santiago*. Paris, 1972.

Jan, Libor and Vít Jesenský. "Hospitaller and Templar Commanderies in Bohemia and Moravia: their Structure and Architectural Forms." In: *The Military Orders*. Vol. 2: *Welfare and Warfare*. Ed. Helen Nicholson. Aldershot: Ashgate, 1998, pp. 235-50.

Lock, Peter. "The Military Orders in Mainland Greece." In: *The Military Orders: Fighting for the Faith and Caring for the Sick*. Ed. Malcolm Barber. Aldershot: Ashgate, 1994, pp. 333-39.

Lomax, D.W. *La orden de Santiago, 1170-1275*. Madrid, 1965.

Losse, Michael. "Die Johanniter-Ordensburgen auf den Dodekanes-Inseln Kálymnos und Nísyros (Griechenland)," *Burgen und Schlösser* 37 (1996), 122-26.

Maier, Christoph T. "Strategies of Survival: the Military Orders and the Reformation in Switzerland." In: *The Military Orders*. Vol. 2: *Welfare and Warfare*. Ed. Helen Nicholson. Aldershot: Ashgate, 1998, pp. 355-62.

Martín, J.L. *Orígines de la orden militar de Santiago (1170-1195)*. Barcelona, 1974.

Martínez, Carlos de Ayala. "The *Sergents* of the Military Order of Santiago." In: *The Military Orders*. Vol. 2: *Welfare and Warfare*. Ed. Helen Nicholson. Aldershot: Ashgate, 1998, pp. 225-34.

Mol, Johannes A. "The Beginnings of the Military Orders in Frisia." In: *The Military Orders*. Vol. 2: *Welfare and Warfare*. Ed. Helen Nicholson. Aldershot: Ashgate, 1998, pp. 307-18.

Nicholson, Helen. "Before William of Tyre: European Reports on the Military Orders' Deeds in the East, 1150-1185." In: *The Military Orders*. Vol. 2: *Welfare and Warfare*. Ed. Helen Nicholson. Aldershot: Ashgate, 1998, pp. 111-18.

Nicholson, Helen. "Knights and Lovers: The Military Orders in the Romantic Literature of the Thirteenth Century." In: *The Military Orders: Fighting for the Faith and Caring for the Sick*. Ed. Malcolm Barber. Aldershot: Ashgate, 1994, pp. 340-57.

Nicholson, Helen. *Love, War and the Grail: Templars, Hospitallers and Teutonic Knights in Medieval Epic and Romance, 1150-1500*. History of Warfare, 4. Leiden: Brill, 2001.

Nicholson, Helen. "The Military Orders and the Kings of England in the Twelfth and Thirteenth Centuries." In: *From Clermont to Jerusalem: The Crusades and Crusader Societies, 1095-1500*. Selected Proceedings of the International Medieval Congress, University of Leeds, 10-13 July 1995. Ed. Alan V. Murray. Turnhout: Brepols, 1998, pp. 203-18.

Nicholson, Helen. *Templars, Hospitallers and Teutonic Knights: Images of the Military Orders, 1128-1291*. Leicester: Leicester University Press, 1993.

Nowak, Z.N., ed. *Die Ritterorden zwischen geistlicher und weltlicher Macht in Mittelalter*. Toruń, 1990.

Nowak, Z.N., ed. *Die Rolle der Ritterorden in der Christianisierung und Kolonisierung des Ostseegebiets*. Toruń, 1983.

O'Callaghan, Joseph F. *The Spanish Military Order of Calatrava and its Affiliates*. London, 1975.

Ordres militaires, la vie rurale et le peuplement en Europe occidentale (XIIe-XVIIIe siècles), Les. Auch, 1986.

Porras Arboledas, Pedro Andrés. *La Orden de Santiago en el siglo XV: La provincia de Castilla*. Madrid: Caja Provincial de Ahorros de Jaén and the Comité Español de Ciencias Históricas, 1997.

Ramos, Luis García-Guijarro. "Exemption in the Temple, the Hospital and the Teutonic Order: Shortcomings of the Institutional Approach." In: *The Military Orders*. Vol. 2: *Welfare and Warfare*. Ed. Helen Nicholson. Aldershot: Ashgate, 1998, pp. 289-94.

Reynolds, Michael T. "René of Anjou, King of Sicily, and the Order of the Croissant," *Journal of Medieval History* 19 (1993), 125-61.

Sáinz de la Maza Lasoli, R. *La orden de Santiago en la Corona de Aragón: La encomienda de Montalbán (1210-1327)*. Zaragosa, 1980.

Sánchez Martínez, Manuel. "Las órdenes militares en la cruzada granadina de Alfonso el Benigno (1329-1334)," *Anuario de estudios medievales* 28 (1998), 31-58.

Segura Graíño, Cristina. "Aprovechamientos hidráulicos en las encomiendas de la Orden Militar de Santiago en la Ribera del Tajo (siglos XI al XV)," *Anuario de estudios medievales* 28 (1998), 97-108.

Seward, Desmond. *The Monks of War: The Military Religious Orders*. London: Eyre Methuen, 1972.

Siberry, Elizabeth. "Victorian Perceptions of the Military Orders." In: *The Military Orders: Fighting for the Faith and Caring for the Sick*. Ed. Malcolm Barber. Aldershot: Ashgate, 1994, pp. 365-72.

Simon, Larry J. "The Friars of the Sack and the Kingdom of Majorca," *Journal of Medieval History* 19 (1993), 279-96.

Solano, H. *La Orden de Calatrava en el siglo XV: Los señoríos castellanos de la Orden al fin de la edad media*. Seville, 1978.

Toll, Christopher. "Arabic Medicine and Hospitals in the Middle Ages: a Probable Model for the Military Orders' Care of the Sick." In: *The Military Orders*. Vol. 2: *Welfare and Warfare*. Ed. Helen Nicholson. Aldershot: Ashgate, 1998, pp. 35-42.

Vann, Theresa M. "A New Look at the Foundation of the Order of Calatrava." In: *On the Social Origins of Medieval Institutions: Essays in Honor of Joseph F. O'Callaghan*. Ed. Donald J. Kagay and Theresa M. Vann. Leiden: E.J. Brill, 1998, pp. 93-114.

Waldstein-Wartenberg, B. *Rechtsgeschichte des Maltesordens*. Vienna, 1969.

Waldstein-Wartenberg, B. *Die Vassalen Christi: Kulturgeschichte des Johanniterordens im Mittelalter*. Vienna, 1988.

Wienand, A., ed. *Der Johanniterorden/Der Maltesenorden: Der ritterliche Orden des hl. Johannes vom Spital zu Jerusalem: Seine Geschichte, seine Aufgaben*. 3rd ed. Cologne, 1988.

Wise, Terence and R. Scollins. *The Knights of Christ*. London: Osprey, 1984.

Medieval – Military Orders – Hospitallers

Albuquerque, Martim de. *A ordem de Malta e o mundo/The Order of Malta and the World/L'ordre de Malte et le monde*. Lisbon: Edições Inapa, 1998.

Allen, David F. "The Order of St John as a 'School of Ambassadors' in Counter-Reformation Europe." In: *The Military Orders*. Vol. 2: *Welfare and Warfare*. Ed. Helen Nicholson. Aldershot: Ashgate, 1998, pp. 363-80.

Allen, David F. "Upholding Tradition: Benedict XIV and the Hospitaller Order of St. John of Jerusalem at Malta, 1740-1758," *Catholic Historical Review* 80 (1994), 18-35.

Arnall, Maria Josepa. "El monestir de Sant Pere de Rodes en els protocols notarials de Castelló d'Empúries de 1279," *Anuario de estudios medievales* 28 (1998), 389-404.

Barz, Wolf-Dieter. *Der Malteserorden als Landesherr auf Rhodos und Malta im Licht seiner strafrechtlichen Quellen aus dem 14. und 16. Jahrhundert*. Berlin: Erich Schmidt Verlag, 1990.

Beltjens, Alain. *Aux origines de l'ordre de Malte: De la fondation de l'Hôpital de Jérusalem à sa transformation en ordre militaire*. Brussels: A. Beltjens, 1995.

Borchardt, Karl. "The Hospitallers in Pomerania: Between the Priories of Bohemia and *Alamania*." In: *The Military Orders*. Vol. 2: *Welfare and Warfare*. Ed. Helen Nicholson. Aldershot: Ashgate, 1998, pp. 295-306.

Brundage, James A. "A Twelfth Century Oxford Disputation Concerning the Privileges of the Knights Hospitallers," *Mediaeval Studies* 24 (1962), 153-60.

Cowan, Ian, P.H.R. MacKay, and Alan Maquarrie. *The Knights of St. John of Jerusalem in Scotland*. Edinburgh: Scottish History Society, 1983.

Cozza, Dino Willy. "The Knights of St. John at the End of the Middle Ages." In: *XXII. Kongreß der Internationalen Kommission für Militärgeschichte* Acta 22: *Von Crécy bis Mohács Kriegswesen im späten Mittelalter (1346-1526)*. Vienna, 1997, pp. 281-99.

Delaville le Roulx, Jean. *Les Hospitaliers à Rhodes (1310-1421)*. Paris, 1913; rpt. London, 1974.

Demurger, Alain. "Templiers et Hospitaliers dans les combats de Terre Sainte." In: *Le combattant au moyen âge*. 2nd ed. Histoire ancienne et médiévale, 36. Paris: Publications de la Sorbonne, 1995, pp. 77-92.

Dupuy, Mark. "'An Island Called Rhodes' and the 'Way' to Jerusalem: Change and Continuity in Hospitaller *Exordia* in the Later Middle Ages." In: *The Military Orders*. Vol. 2: *Welfare and Warfare*. Ed. Helen Nicholson. Aldershot: Ashgate, 1998, pp. 343-48.

Edgington, Susan B. "Medical Care in the Hospital of St John in Jerusalem." In: *The Military Orders*. Vol. 2: *Welfare and Warfare*. Ed. Helen Nicholson. Aldershot: Ashgate, 1998, pp. 27-34.

Feliu, Gaspar. "L'administració de la Comanda Hospitalera de Barberà: un llibre de comptes de 1410-1411," *Anuario de estudios medievales* 28 (1998), 187-218.

Fincham, H.W. *The Order of the Hospital of St. John of Jerusalem and its Grand Priory of England*. London, 1933.

Forey, Alan J. "Constitutional Conflict and Change in the Hospital of St. John during the Twelfth and Thirteenth Centuries," *Journal of Ecclesiastical History* 33 (1982), 15-29.

Forey, Alan J. "The Militarization of the Hospital of St. John," *Studia monastica* 26 (1984), 75-89.

Gervers, Michael. *The Hospitaller Cartulary in the British Library (Cotton ms. Nero E VI)*. Toronto: The Pontifical Institute of Mediaeval Studies, 1981.

Goldmann, Z. *Akko in the Time of the Crusades: The Convent of the Order of St. John*. Acre, 1987.

Goñt', Carlos Barquero. "The Hospitallers and the Kings of Navarre in the Fourteenth and Fifteenth Centuries." In: *The Military Orders*. Vol. 2: *Welfare and Warfare*. Ed. Helen Nicholson. Aldershot: Ashgate, 1998, pp. 349-54.

Hamilton, Bernard. "Review Article–The Order of St John of Jerusalem at Malta and its Treasures," *Nottingham Medieval Studies* 35 (1991), 161-65.

Karassava-Tsilingiri, Fotini. "Fifteenth-Century Hospitaller Architecture on Rhodes: Patrons and Master Masons." In: *The Military Orders*. Vol. 2: *Welfare and Warfare*. Ed. Helen Nicholson. Aldershot: Ashgate, 1998, pp. 259-66.

Kollias, E. *The Knights of Rhodes: The Palace and the City*. Athens, 1991.

Lesesma Rubio, M.L. *Templarios y Hospitalarios en el reino de Aragón*. Zaragoza, 1982.

Legras, A.M. *Les commanderies des Templiers et des Hospitaliers de Saint-Jean de Jérusalem en Saintogne et en Aunis*. Paris, 1983.

Luttrell, Anthony. "The Earliest Documents on the Hospitaller *Corso* at Rhodes: 1413 and 1416," *Mediterranean Historical Review* 10 (1995), 177-88.

Luttrell, Anthony. "English Contributions to the Hospitaller Castle at Bodrum in Turkey: 1407-1437." In: *The Military Orders*. Vol. 2: *Welfare and Warfare*. Ed. Helen Nicholson. Aldershot: Ashgate, 1998, pp. 163-72.

Luttrell, Anthony. "Hospitaller Life in Aragon: 1319-1370." In: *God and Man in Medieval Spain: Essays in Honour of J.R.L. Highfield*. Ed. D.W. Lomax and D. Mackenzie. Warminster, 1989, pp. 97-115.

Luttrell, Anthony. "The Hospitallers in Cyprus after 1386." In: *Hē Kupros kai hoi Staurophories/Cyprus and the Crusades: Hoi anakoinōseis tou deithnous symposiou "Hē Kupros kai hoi Staurophories", Leukōsia, 6-9 septembriou, 1994/Papers Given at the International Conference "Cyprus and the Crusades", Nicosia, 6-9 September, 1994*. Ed. Nikos Coureas and Jonathan Riley-Smith. Nicosia: Cyprus Research Centre/Society for the Study of the Crusades and the Latin East, 1995, pp. 125-41.

Luttrell, Anthony. *The Hospitallers in Cyprus, Rhodes, Greece and the West, 1291-1440*. London, 1978.

Luttrell, Anthony. "The Hospitallers' Medical Tradition: 1291-1530." In: *The Military Orders: Fighting for the Faith and Caring for the Sick*. Ed. Malcolm Barber. Aldershot: Ashgate, 1994, pp. 64-81.

Luttrell, Anthony. *Latin Greece, the Hospitallers and the Crusade: 1291-1400*. London, 1982.

Luttrell, Anthony. "Margarida d'Erill, Hospitaller of Alguaire: 1415-1456," *Anuario de estudios medievales* 28 (1998), 219-50.

Madrid y Medina, Ángela. "Aproximación a la atención hospitalaria en la Orden de San Juan: la cofradía de Consuegra," *Anuario de estudios medievales* 28 (1998), 251-62.

Mallia-Milanes, V. *Venice and Hospitaller Malta, 1530-1798: Aspects of a Relationship.* Malta, 1992.

Mallia-Milanes, V., ed. *Hospitaller Malta, 1530-1798: Studies on Early Modern Malta and the Order of St. John of Jerusalem.* Malta, 1993.

Marchal-Verdoodt, M. "Les maisons des Hospitaliers et des Templiers dans l'ancien duché de Brabant au début du XIVe siècle." In: *Hommage au professeur Paul Bonenfant (1899-1965).* Brussels, 1965, pp. 255-66.

Menache, Sophia. "The Hospitallers during Clement V's Pontificate: the Spoiled Sons of the Papacy? In: *The Military Orders.* Vol. 2: *Welfare and Warfare.* Ed. Helen Nicholson. Aldershot: Ashgate, 1998, pp. 153-62.

Miller, Timothy S. "The Knights of Saint John and the Hospitals of the Latin West," *Speculum* 53 (1978), 709-33.

Pérez Castillo, Ana. "Templers i Hospitalers a Catalunya: Documents conservats a l'Arxiu Capitular de la Catedral de Barcelona," *Anuario de estudios medievales* 28 (1998), 3-10.

Phillips, Jonathan. "Archbishop Henry of Reims and the Militarization of the Hospitallers." In: *The Military Orders.* Vol. 2: *Welfare and Warfare.* Ed. Helen Nicholson. Aldershot: Ashgate, 1998, pp. 83-88.

Poutiers, Jean-Christian. *Rhodes et ses Chevaliers, 1306-1523: Approche historique et archéologique.* Brussels: E.S.C.T., 1989.

Pugh, Ralph B. "The Knights Hospitallers as Undertakers," *Speculum* 56 (1981), 566-74.

Riley-Smith, Jonathan. *Hospitallers: The History of the Order of St. John.* London: The Hambledon Press, 1999.

Riley-Smith, Jonathan. *The Knights of St. John in Jerusalem and Cyprus, c.1050-1310.* London, 1967.

Roncetti, M., P. Scarpellini, and F. Tommasi. *Templari e Ospiotalieri in Italia: La chiesa di San Bevignate a Perugia*. Milan, 1987.

Sarnowsky, Jürgen. "'The Rights of the Treasury': the Financial Administration of the Hospitallers on Fifteenth-Century Rhodes, 1421-1522." In: *The Military Orders*. Vol. 2: *Welfare and Warfare*. Ed. Helen Nicholson. Aldershot: Ashgate, 1998, pp. 267-74.

Selwood, Dominic. *Knights of the Cloister: Templars and Hospitallers in Central-Southern Occitania, c.1100-c.1300*. Woodbridge: The Boydell Press, 1999.

Sire, H.J.A. *The Knights of Malta*. New Haven: Yale University Press, 1994.

Spiteri, Stephen C. *Fortresses of the Cross: Hospitaller Military Architecture (1136-1798)*. Valleta: Heritage Interpretation Services, 1994.

Spiteri, Stephen C. *The Palace Armoury: A Study of a Military Storehouse of the Knights of the Order of St. John*. Valetta: The Farsons Foundation, 1999.

Toffolo, Julia. *Image of a Knight: Portrait Prints and Drawings of the Knights of St. John in the Museum of the Order of St. John*. London: The Order of St. John, 1988.

Vann, Theresa M. "A Fourteenth-Century Hospitaller Account Book from Hispania," *Anuario de estudios medievales* 28 (1998), 175-86.

Vann, Theresa M. "Hospitaller Record Keeping and Archival Practices." In: *The Military Orders*. Vol. 2: *Welfare and Warfare*. Ed. Helen Nicholson. Aldershot: Ashgate, 1998, pp. 275-85.

Vatin, Nicolas. *L'order de Saint-Jean-de-Jérusalem, l'empire Ottoman et la Méditerrannée orientale entre les deux sièges de Rhodes, 1480-1522*. Paris: Peeters, 1994.

Winter, Johanna Maria van. "Les seigneurs de Sainte-Catherine à Utrecht: les premiers Hospitalers au nord des Alpes." In: *Autour de la première croisade: Actes du Colloque de la Society for the Study of the Crusades and the Latin East (Clermont-Ferrand, 22-25 juin 1995)*. Ed. M. Balard. Paris: Publications de la Sorbonne, 1996, pp. 239-46.

Medieval – Military Orders – Templars

Barber, Malcolm C. *The New Knighthood: A History of the Order of the Temple*. Cambridge: Cambridge University Press, 1994.

Barber, Malcolm C. "The Origins of the Order of the Temple," *Studia monastica* 12 (1970), 219-40.

Barber, Malcolm C. "Propaganda in the Middle Ages: the Charges Against the Templars," *Nottingham Medieval Studies* 17 (1973), 42-57.

Barber, Malcolm C. "The Social Context of the Templars," *Transactions of the Royal Historical Society*, 5th ser., 34 (1984), 27-46.

Barber, Malcolm C. "Supplying the Crusader States: The Role of the Templars." In: *The Horns of Hattin*. Ed. B.Z. Kedar. Jerusalem, 1992, pp. 314-26.

Barber, Malcolm C. "The Templars and the Turin Shroud," *Catholic Historical Review* 68 (1982), 206-25.

Barber, Malcolm C. *The Trial of the Templars*. Cambridge: Cambridge University Press, 1978.

Barber, Malcolm C. "The Trial of the Templars Revisited." In: *The Military Orders*. Vol. 2: *Welfare and Warfare*. Ed. Helen Nicholson. Aldershot: Ashgate, 1998, pp. 319-28.

Bennett, Matthew. "*La règle du temple* as a Military Manual or How to Deliver a Cavalry Charge." In: *Studies in Medieval History Presented to R. Allen Brown*. Ed. C. Harper-Bill, C.J. Holdsworth and J. Nelson. Woodbridge, 1989, pp. 7-19.

Bramato, F. *Storia dell'ordine dei Templari in Italia*. Rome, 1991.

Bulst-Thiele, Marie Luise. "The Influence of St. Bernard of Clairvaux on the Formation of the Order of the Knights Templar." In: *The Second Crusade and the Cistercians*. Ed. M. Gervers. New York, 1992, pp. 57-65.

Bulst-Thiele, Marie Luise. "Der Prozess gegen den Templeorden." In: *Die geistlichen Ritterorden Europas*. Ed. Josef Fleckenstein and Manfred Hellmann. Vorträge und Forschungen, 26. Sigmaringen, 1980, pp. 375-402.

Bulst-Thiele, Marie Luise. *Sacrae domus militiae Templi Hierosolymitani Magistri: Untersuchungen zur Geschichte des Templeordens 1118/9-1314.* Gottingen, 1974.

Bulst-Thiele, Marie Luise. "Templer in königlichen und päpstlichen." In: *Festschrift Percy Ernst Schramm.* Ed. Peter Classen and Peter Scheibert. Wiesbaden, 1964, I:289-308.

Burton, Janet E. "The Knights Templar in Yorkshire in the Twelfth Century: A Reassessment," *Northern History* 27 (1991), 26-40.

Carcenac, Antoine-Régis. "L'élevage dans le Rouergue méridional au temps des templiers," *Annales du Midi* 103 (1991), 293-306.

Cardini, Franco. *Poveri cavalieri del Cristo: San Bernardo e la fondazione dell'ordine Templare.* Rimini, 1992.

Cerrini, Simonetta. "A New Edition of the Latin and French Rule of the Temple." In: *The Military Orders.* Vol. 2: *Welfare and Warfare.* Ed. Helen Nicholson. Aldershot: Ashgate, 1998, pp. 207-16.

Claverie, Pierre-Vincent. "L'ordre du Temple au coeur d'une crise politique majeure: la *Querela Cypri* des années 1279-1285," *Moyen âge* 104 (1998), 495-511.

Delisle, Leopold. "Mémoire sur les opérations financières des Templiers," *Mémoires de l'Institut National de France: Académie des inscriptions et belles-lettres* 33.2 (1889).

Demurger, Alain. *Brève histoire des ordres religieux-militaires.* Paris, 1997; trans. *A Brief History of Religious Military Orders: Hospitallers, Templars, Teutonic.* Trans. Beryl Degans. Paris, 1997.

Demurger, Alain. "Encore le procès des templiers! A propos d'un ouvrage récent," *Moyen âge*, 5th ser., 5 (1991), 25-39.

Demurger, Alain. "Templiers et Hospitaliers dans les combats de Terre Sainte." In: *Le combattant au moyen âge.* 2nd ed. Histoire ancienne et médiévale, 36. Paris: Publications de la Sorbonne, 1995, pp. 77-92.

Demurger, Alain. *Vie et mort de l'ordre du Temple.* 3rd ed. Paris, 1993.

Edbury, Peter W. "The Templars in Cyprus." In: *The Military Orders: Fighting for the Faith and Caring for the Sick.* Ed. Malcolm Barber. Aldershot: Ashgate, 1994, pp. 189-95.

Forey, Alan J. "The Beginning of Proceedings Against the Aragonese Templars." In: *God and Man in Medieval Spain: Essays in Honour of J.R.L. Highfield.* Ed. D.W. Lomax and D. Mackenzie. Warminster, 1989, pp. 81-96.

Forey, Alan J. *The Templars in the Corona de Aragón.* London, 1973.

Forey, Alan J. "Towards a Profile of the Templars in the Early Fourteenth Century." In: *The Military Orders: Fighting for the Faith and Caring for the Sick.* Ed. Malcolm Barber. Aldershot: Ashgate, 1994, pp. 196-204.

Fuguet Sans, Joan. "Fortificacions menors i altre patrimoni retingut pels Templers després de la permuta de 1294," *Anuario de estudios medievales* 28 (1998), 294-310.

Gaier, Claude. "La valeur militaire des Templiers." In: *Le Temple et Malte: Trésors d'art entre Ourthe et Meuse, Viller-le-Temple.* Liege, 1973, pp. 59-68; in: *Armes et combats dans l'univers médiéval.* Liege, 1995, pp. 47-56.

Gilmour-Bryson, Anne. "Age-Related Data from Templar Trials." In: *Aging and the Aged in Medieval Europe.* Ed. Michael Sheehan. Toronto, 1990, pp. 129-42.

Gilmour-Bryson, Anne. "Sodomy and the Knights Templar," *Journal of the History of Sexuality* 7 (1996), 151-83.

Gilmour-Bryson, Anne. "Testimony of Non-Templar Witnesses in Cyprus." In: *The Military Orders: Fighting for the Faith and Caring for the Sick.* Ed. Malcolm Barber. Aldershot: Ashgate, 1994, pp. 205-11.

Ilieva, Annetta. "The Suppression of the Templars in Cyprus according to the Chronicle of Leontios Makhairas." In: *The Military Orders: Fighting for the Faith and Caring for the Sick.* Ed. Malcolm Barber. Aldershot: Ashgate, 1994, pp. 212-19.

Lesesma Rubio, M.L. *Templarios y Hospitalarios en el reino de Aragón.* Zaragoza, 1982.

Legras, A.M. *Les commanderies des Templiers et des Hospitaliers de Saint-Jean de Jérusalem en Saintogne et en Aunis.* Paris, 1983.

Lema Pueyo, José Angel. "Las confradías y la introducción del Temple en los reinos de Aragón y Pamplona: guerra, intereses y piedad religiosa," *Anuario de estudios medievales* 28 (1998), 311-32.

Luttrell, Anthony. "The Earliest Templars." In: *Autour de la première croisade: Actes du Colloque de la Society for the Study of the Crusades and the Latin East (Clermont-Ferrand, 22-25 juin 1995).* Ed. M. Balard. Paris: Publications de la Sorbonne, 1996, pp. 193-202.

Marchal-Verdoodt, M. "Les maisons des Hospitaliers et des Templiers dans l'ancien duché de Brabant au début du XIVe siècle." In: *Hommage au professeur Paul Bonenfant (1899-1965).* Brussels, 1965, pp. 255-66.

Menache, Sophia. "The Templar Order: A Failed Idea?" *Catholic Historical Review* 79 (1993), 1-21.

Minnucci, G. and F. Sardi, ed. *I Templari; Mito e storia.* Atti del convegno internazionale di studi alla magione Templare di Poggibonsi-Siena, 29-31 maggio 1987. Siena, 1989.

Nicholson, Helen. "Saints or Sinners? The Knights Templar in Medieval Europe," *History Today* 44 (Dec 1994), 30-36.

Nicholson, Helen. "Templar Attitudes towards Women," *Medieval History* 1.4 (1991), 74-80.

Oakeshott, Ewart. "The Templars and the Church," *Park Lane Arms Fair* 15 (1998), 7-10.

Pagarolas i Sabaté, Laureà. "La fi del domini de l'Orde del Temple a Tortosa: La permuta de 1294," *Anuario de estudios medievales* 28 (1998), 269-92.

Partner, Peter. *The Knights Templar and Their Myth.* 2nd ed. Rochester, VT: Destiny Books, 1990.

Pérez Castillo, Ana. "Templers i Hospitalers a Catalunya: Documents conservats a l'Arxiu Capitular de la Catedral de Barcelona," *Anuario de estudios medievales* 28 (1998), 3-10.

Pringle, Denys. "Templar Castles between Jaffa and Jerusalem." In: *The Military Orders*. Vol. 2: *Welfare and Warfare*. Ed. Helen Nicholson. Aldershot: Ashgate, 1998, pp. 89-110.

Read, Piers Paul. *The Templars*. London: Weidenfeld, 1999.

Rigold, Stuart E. *Temple Manor, Rochester, Kent*. London: Her Majesty's Stationery Office, 1975.

Riley-Smith, Jonathan. "The Templars and the Castle of Tortosa in Syria: an Unknown Document concerning the Acquisition of the Fortress," *English Historical Review* 84 (1969), 278-88.

Roncetti, M., P. Scarpellini, and F. Tommasi. *Templari e Ospiotalieri in Italia: La chiesa di San Bevignate a Perugia*. Milan, 1987.

Ruiz-Domènec, José Enrique. "Primeros pasos de la Orden Militar del Temple en Cataluña," *Anuario de estudios medievales* 28 (1998), 263-68.

Selwood, Dominic. *Knights of the Cloister: Templars and Hospitallers in Central-Southern Occitania, c.1100-c.1300*. Woodbridge: The Boydell Press, 1999.

Selwood, Dominic. "Quidam Autem Dubitaverunt: The Saint, the Sinner, the Temple and a Possible Chronology." In: *Autour de la première croisade: Actes du Colloque de la Society for the Study of the Crusades and the Latin East (Clermont-Ferrand, 22-25 juin 1995)*. Ed. M. Balard. Paris: Publications de la Sorbonne, 1996, pp. 221-30.

Serrano Daura, Josep. "L'establiment de l'Orde del Temple a la Tortosa de Síria (segle XIII)," *Anuario de estudios medievales* 28 (1998), 333-44.

Sinclair, Keith V. "The Translations of the *Vitas patrum*, *Thaïs*, *Antichrist*, and *Vision de saint Paul* Made for Anglo-Norman Templars: Some Neglected Literary Considerations," *Speculum* 72 (1997), 741-62.

Upton-Ward, Judi. "The Surrender of Gaston and the Rule of the Templars." In: *The Military Orders: Fighting for the Faith and Caring for the Sick*. Ed. Malcolm Barber. Aldershot: Ashgate, 1994, pp. 179-88.

Walker, John. "Alms for the Holy Land: The English Templars and their Patrons." In: *The Medieval Military Revolution: State, Society and*

Military Change in Medieval and Early Modern Europe. Ed. A. Ayton and J.L. Price. London, 1995, pp. 63-80.

Medieval – Military Orders – Teutonic Knights

Arnold, U., ed. *Von Akken bis Wien: Studien zur Deutschordensgeschichte vom 13. bis zum 20. Jahrhundert: Festschrift zum 90. Geburtstag von Althochmeister P. Dr. Marian Tumler O.T.* Marburg, 1978. March 9, 2000.

Arnold, U., ed. *Zur Wirtschaftsenwicklung des Deutschen Ordens im Mittelalter.* Marburg, 1989.

Arnold, U. and M. Tumler, ed. *Der Deutsche Orden: Von seinem Ursprung bis zur Gegenwart.* Bad Münstereifel, 1992.

Benninghoven, F. "Die Gotlandfeldzuge des deutschen Ordens, 1398-1408," *Zeitschrift für Ostforschung* 13 (1964), 421-77.

Boockmann, Hartmut. *Der Deutsche Orden: Zwölf Kapitel aus seiner Geschichte.* Munich, 1989.

Burleigh, Michael. *Prussian Society and the German Order: An Aristocatic Corporation in Crisis, c. 1410-1466.* Cambridge: Cambridge University Press, 1984.

Demel, Bernhard. "Welfare and Warfare in the Teutonic Order: A Survey." In: *The Military Orders.* Vol. 2: *Welfare and Warfare.* Ed. Helen Nicholson. Aldershot: Ashgate, 1998, pp. 61-74.

Eickels, Klaus van. "Knightly Hospitallers or Crusading Knights? Decisive Factors for the Spread of the Teutonic Knights in the Rhineland and the Low Countries, 1216-1300." In: *The Military Orders.* Vol. 2: *Welfare and Warfare.* Ed. Helen Nicholson. Aldershot: Ashgate, 1998, pp. 75-80.

Eimer, Birgitta. *Gotland unter dem Deutschen Orden und die Komturei Schweden zu Arsta.* Inssbruck: Universitats-verlag Wagner, 1966.

Ekdahl, Sven. "Horses and Crossbows: Two Important Warfare Advantages of the Teutonic Order in Prussia." In: *The Military Orders.* Vol. 2: *Welfare and Warfare.* Ed. Helen Nicholson. Aldershot: Ashgate, 1998, pp. 119-52.

Ekdahl, Sven. "Der Krieg zwischen dem Deutschen Orden und Polen-Litauen im Jahre 1422," *Zeitschrift für Ostforschung* 13 (1964), 614-51.

Ekdahl, Sven. "The Treatment of Prisoners of War during the Fighting between the Teutonic Order and Lithuania." In: *The Military Orders: Fighting for the Faith and Caring for the Sick*. Ed. Malcolm Barber. Aldershot: Ashgate, 1994, pp. 263-69.

Engel, Bernhard, ed. "Nachrichten über Waffen aus dem Tresslerbuche des deutschen Ordens von 1399-1409," *Zeitschrift für historisches Waffenkunde* 1 (1897-99), 195-99, 228-33.

Engel, Bernhard, ed. "Waffengeschichtliche Studien aus dem Deutschordensgebiet," *Zeitschrift für historisches Waffenkunde* 4 (1906-08), 118-25.

Favreau, M.-L. *Studien zur Frühgeschichte des Deutschen Ordens*. Stuttgart, 1974.

Forstreuter, K. *Der Deutsche Orden am Mittelmeer*. Bonn, 1967.

Gaier, Claude. "Quelques particularités de l'armement des chevaliers teutoniques dans le baillage de Germanie inférieure aux XIVe et XVe siècles." In: *Armes et combats dans l'univers médiéval*. Liege, 1995, pp. 151-58.

García, José Manuel Rodríguez. "Alfonzo X and the Teutonic Order: an Example of the Role of the International Military Orders in Mid Thirteenth-Century Castile." In: *The Military Orders*. Vol. 2: *Welfare and Warfare*. Ed. Helen Nicholson. Aldershot: Ashgate, 1998, pp. 319-28.

Heckmann, Dieter. "Zum Leben und Wirkin des livländischen Meisters des Deutschen Ordens Dietrich Torck (1413-1415)," *Blätter für Deutsche Landesgeschichte* 123 (1997), 169-98.

Heinl, Karl. *Fürst Witold von Litauen in seinem Verhältnis zum Deutschen Orden in Preußen während der Zeit seines Kampfes um sein litauisches Erbe, 1382-1401*. Berlin: Eberling, 1925.

Hoensch, Jörg K. "König/Kaiser Sigismund, der Deutsche Orden und Polen-Litauen: Stationen einer problembeladenen Beziehung," *Zeitschrift für Ostforschung* 46.2 (1997), 1-44.

Holst, N. von. *Der Deutsche Ritterorden und seine Bauten von Jerusalem bis Sevilla von Thorn bis Narva.* Berlin, 1981.

Hubatsch, W. *Montfort und der Bildung des Deutschordensstaats im Heiligen Lande.* Gottingen, 1966.

Koncius, Joseph. *Vytautas the Great: Grand Duke of Lithuania.* Miami: Franklin, 1964.

Krollman, C. *The Teutonic Order in Prussia.* Elbing, 1938.

Lückerath, Carl August. *Paul von Rusdorf: Hochmeister des Deutschen Ordens, 1422-1441.* Quellen und Studien zur Geschichte des Deutschen Orderns, 15. Bad Godesberg: Wissenschaftliches Archiv, 1969.

Militzer, Klaus. *Die Entstehung der Deutscheordensballeien im Deutschen Reich.* Marburg, 1981.

Militzer, Klaus. "The Role of Hospitals in the Teutonic Order." In: *The Military Orders.* Vol. 2: *Welfare and Warfare.* Ed. Helen Nicholson. Aldershot: Ashgate, 1998, pp. 51-60.

Mol, J.A. *De Friese Huizen van de Duitse Orde: Nes, Steenkerk en Schoten en hun plaats in het middeleeuwse Friese kloosterlandschap.* Ljouwert: Fryske Akademy, 1991.

Müller, G. *Die Familiaren des Deutschen Ordens.* Marburg, 1980.

Murawski, Klaus Eberhard. *Zwischen Tannenburg und Thorn: Die Geschichte des Deutschen Ordens unter dem Hochmeister Konrad von Erlichshausen, 1441-1449.* Bausteine zur Geschichtswissenschaft, 10-11. Göttinger: Wissenschaftlicher Verlag, 1953.

Nadolski, Andrzej. "Les combattants polonais en lutte contre les Chevaliers Teutoniques à la fin du XIVe et au commencement du XVe siècle." In: *Le combattant au moyen âge.* 2nd ed. Histoire ancienne et médiévale, 36. Paris: Publications de la Sorbonne, 1995, pp. 151-60.

Neitmann, Klaus. *Der Hochmeister des Deutschen Ordens in Preußen— ein Residenzherrscher unterwegs: Untersuchungen zu den Hochmeisteritineraren im 14. und 15. Jahrhundert.* Veröffentlichungen aus der Archiven Preussicher Kulturbesitz, 30. Cologne and Vienna: Böhlau, 1990.

Nickel, Helmut. "Some Heraldic Fragments Found at Castle Montfort/ Starkenberg in 1926, and the Arms of the Grand Master of the Teutonic Knights," *Metropolitan Museum Journal* 24 (1989), 35-46.

Powell, James M. "Frederick II, the Hohenstaufen, and the Teutonic Order in the Kingdom of Sicily." In: *The Military Orders: Fighting for the Faith and Caring for the Sick*. Ed. Malcolm Barber. Aldershot: Ashgate, 1994, pp. 236-44.

Probst, Christian. *Der Deutsche Orden und sein Medizinalwesen in Preussen: Hospital, Firmarie und Artz bis 1525*. Bad Godesberg, 1969.

Rautenburg, Wilhelm. *Böhmische Söldner im Ordensland Preussen: Ein Beitrag zur Söldnergeschichte des 15. Jahrhunderts, vornehmilch des 13. jährigen Städte-Kriegs 1454-1466*. Hamburg, 1954.

Rautenburg, Wilhelm. "Einwirkungen Böhmens auf die Geschichte des Ordenslandes Preußen im späten Mittelalter," *Zeitschrift für Ostforschung* 22 (1973), 626-95.

Sarnowsky, Jürgen. "The Teutonic Order Confronts the Mongols and the Turks." In: *The Military Orders: Fighting for the Faith and Caring for the Sick*. Ed. Malcolm Barber. Aldershot: Ashgate, 1994, pp. 253-62.

Sarnowsky, Jürgen. *Die Wirtschaftsführung des Deutschen Ordens in Preussen (1382-1454)*. Cologne, 1993.

Schloz, K. *Beiträge zur Personengeschichte des Deutschen Ordens in der ersten Hälfte des 14. Jahrhunderts: Untersuchungen zur Herkunft livlandischer und preussischer Deutschordenbrüder*. Munster, 1971.

Sterns, Indrikis. "Crime and Punishment among the Teutonic Knights," *Speculum* 57 (1982), 84-111.

Toomaspoeg, Kristjan. "Les premiers commandeurs de l'ordre Teutonique en Sicile (1202-1291): Évolution de la titulature, origines géographiques et sociales," *Mélanges de l'école française de Rome: moyen âge* 109 (1997), 443-61.

Tumler, P. Marian. *Der Deutschen Orden: Werden, Wachsen und Wirkung bis 1400*. Vienna: Panorama, 1955.

Urban, William. "Roger Bacon and the Teutonic Knights," *Journal of Baltic Studies* 19 (1988), 363-70.

Urban, William. "The Sense of Humor among the Teutonic Knights," *Illinois Quarterly Review* 42 (1979), 40-47.

Urban, William. "The Teutonic Knights and Baltic Chivalry," *Historian* 56 (1994), 519-30.

Vey Mestdagh, J.H. de. *De Utrechtse Balije der Duitse Orde ruim 750 jaar geschiedenis van de Orde in de Nederlanden.* Utrecht, 1988.

Voigt, Johannes. *Geschichte Preussens von den ältesten Zeiten bis zum Untergange der Herrschaft des Deutschen Ordens.* Rpt. Hildesheims: Georg Olms, 1968.

Weise, E. "Der Heidenkampf des deutschen Ordens," *Zeitschrift für Ostforschung* 12 (1963), 420-73, 622-72; 13 (1964), 401-20.

Wojtecki, D. "Der Deutsche Orden unter Friedrich II." In: *Probleme um Friedrich II.* Voträge und Forschungen, 16. Sigmaringen, 1974, pp. 187-224.

Wojtecki, D. *Studien zur Personengeschichte des Deutschen Ordens im 13. Jahrhundert.* Quellen und Studien zur Geschichte des östlichen Europa. Wiesbaden, 1971.

Medieval – Peace Movements (also Peace and Truce of God)

Angermeier, H. *Königtum und Landefriede im deutschen Spätmittelalter.* Munich, 1966.

Angermeier, H. "Landfriedenspolitik und Landfriedensgesetzgebung unter den Staufern." Vorträge und Forschungen, 16. In: *Probleme umm Friedrich II.* Sigmaringen, 1974, pp. 167-86.

Bachrach, Bernard S. "The Northern Origins of the Peace Movement at Le Puy in 975," *Historical Reflections* 14 (1987), 405-21.

Barthélemy, Dominique. *L'an mil et la paix de Dieu: La France chrétienne et féodale, 980-1060.* Paris: Fayard, 1999.

Barthélemy, Dominique. "La Paix de Dieu dans son contexte (989-1041)," *Cahiers de civilisation médiévale* 40 (1997), 3-35.

Bisson, Thomas N. "The Organized Peace in Southern France and Catalonia, ca. 1140-ca. 1233," *American Historical Review* 82 (1977), 290-311.

Bonnaud-Delamare, Roger. "La convention régionale de paix d'Albi de 1191," *Paix de Dieu et guerre sainte en Languedoc au XIIIe siècle, Cahiers de Fanjeaux* 4 (1969), 91-101.

Bonnaud-Delamare, Roger. "Fondements des institutions de paix au XIe siècle." In: *Mélanges d'histoire du moyen âge dédiés à la mémoire de Louis Halphen*. Paris: Presses universitaires de France, 1951, pp. 19-24.

Bonnaud-Delamare, Roger. *L'idée de paix à l'époque carolingienne*. Paris, 1939.

Bonnaud-Delamare, Roger. "Les institutions de paix dans la province ecclésiastique de Reims au XIe siècle," *Bulletin historique et philologique du comitè des travaux historiques et scientifiques, années 1955 et 1956*. Paris, 1957, pp. 143-200.

Bonnaud-Delamare. Roger. "Paix d'Amiens et de Corbie," *Revue du nord* 38 (1956), 169-74.

Bonnaud-Delamare, Roger. "La paix de Dieu en Touraine pendant la première croisade," *Revue d'histoire ecclésiastique* 70 (1975), 749-57.

Bonnaud-Delamare, Roger. "La paix en Aquitaine au XIe siècle," *Recueils de la société Jean Bodin* 14 (1961), 415-87.

Bonnaud-Delamare, Roger. "La paix en Flandre pendant la première croisade," *Revue du nord* 39 (1957), 147-52.

Boüard, Michel de. "Sur les origines de la trêve de Dieu en Normandie," *Annales de Normandie* 9 (1959), 179-89.

Brock, P. *Pacifism in Europe to 1914*. Princeton, 1972.

Callahan, Daniel F. "Adémar de Chabannes et la paix de Dieu," *Annales de midi* 89 (1977), 21-43.

Callahan, Daniel F. "The Peace of God and the Cult of the Saints in Aquitaine in the Tenth and Eleventh Centuries." In: *The Peace of God:*

Social Violence and Religious Response in France Around the Year 1000. Ed. Thomas Head and Richard Landes. Ithaca: Cornell University Press, 1992, pp. 165-83.

Carozzi, Claude. "La tripartition sociale et l'idée de paix au XIe siècle." In: *La guerre et la paix: Frontières et violences au moyen âge.* Actes du 101e congrès national des sociétés savantes, Lille, 1976. Paris, 1978, pp. 9-22.

Conrad, H. "Gottesfrieden und Heerverfassung in der Zeit der Kreuzzüge," *Zeitschrift der Savigny-Stiftung für Rechtgeschichte, Germanischen Abteilung* 61 (1941), 711-26.

Contamine, Philippe. "Notes sur la paix en France pendant la guerre de cent ans." In: *Rapports du XVe Congrès international des sciences historiques.* Bucarest, 1980, pp. 175-86.

Cowdrey, H.E.J. "The Peace and Truce of God in the Eleventh Century," *Past and Present* 46 (1970), 42-67.

Debord, André. "The Castellan Revolution and the Peace of God." In: *The Peace of God: Social Violence and Religious Response in France Around the Year 1000.* Ed. Thomas Head and Richard Landes. Ithaca: Cornell University Press, 1992, pp. 135-64.

Delaruelle, Etienne. "Paix de Dieu et croisade dans la chrétienté du XIIe siècle," *Paix de Dieu et guerre sainte en Languedoc au XIIIe siècle, Cahiers de Fanjeaux* 4 (1969), 51-71.

Duby, Georges. "Guerre et société dans l'Europe féodale: ordannancement de la paix." In: *Concetto, storia, miti e immagini del medio evo: Atti del XIV corso internazionale d'alta cultura.* Ed. V. Branca. Florence, 1973, pp. 449-59.

Duby, Georges. "Les laics et la paix de Dieu." In: *I laici nella "societas christiana" dei secoli XI e XII: Atti della terza settimana internazionale di studio, Mendola 21-27 agosto 1965.* Milan, 1968, pp. 448-61; trans. "Laity and the Peace of God." In: *The Chivalrous Society.* Trans. C. Postan. Berkeley and Los Angeles, 1980, pp. 123-33.

Flori, Jean. "L'église et la guerre sainte de la 'paix de dieu' a la 'Croisade,'" *Annales ESC* 47 (1992), 453-66.

Frassetto, Michael. "Violence, Knightly Piety and the Peace of God Movement in Aquitaine." In: *The Final Argument: The Imprint of Violence on Society in Medieval and Early Modern Europe*. Ed. Donald J. Kagay and L.J. Andrew Villalon. Woodbridge: The Boydell Press, 1998, pp. 13-26.

Ganshof, François Louis. "La paix au très haut moyen âge," *Recueils de la société Jean Bodin* 14 (1961), 397-413.

Gernhuber, J. *Die Landfriedensbewegung in Deutschland bis zum Mainzer Landfrieden von 1235*. Bonn, 1952.

Gernhuber, J. "Staat und Landfrieden im deutschen Reich des Mittelalters," *Recueils de la société Jean Bodin* 15 (1962), 23-77.

Gleiman, Lubomir. "Some Remarks on the Origin of the *Treuga Dei*," *Etudes d'histoire litteraire et doctrinale* (1962), 117-37.

Goetz, Hans-Werner. "Protection of the Church, Defense of the Law, and Reform: On the Purposes and Character of the Peace of God, 989-1038." In: *The Peace of God: Social Violence and Religious Response in France Around the Year 1000*. Ed. Thomas Head and Richard Landes. Ithaca: Cornell University Press, 1992, pp. 259-79.

Grabois, Aryeh. "De la trêve de Dieu à la paix du roi: Etude sur les transformations du mouvement de la paix au XIIe siècle." In: *Mélanges offerts à René Crozet*. Ed. P. Gallais and Y.-J. Riou. Poitiers, 1966, pp. 585-96.

Haines, Keith. "Attitudes and Impediments to Pacificism in Medieval Europe," *Journal of Medieval History* 7 (1981), 369-88.

Head, Thomas. "The Development of the Peace of God in Aquitaine (970-1005)," *Speculum* 74 (1999), 656-86.

Head, Thomas. "The Judgment of God: Andrew of Fleury's Account of the Peace League of Bourges." In: *The Peace of God: Social Violence and Religious Response in France Around the Year 1000*. Ed. Thomas Head and Richard Landes. Ithaca: Cornell University Press, 1992, pp. 219-38.

Head, Thomas and Richard Landes. "Introduction." In: *The Peace of God: Social Violence and Religious Response in France Around the Year 1000*.

Ed. Thomas Head and Richard Landes. Ithaca: Cornell University Press, 1992, pp. 1-20.

Heyn, Udo. *Peacemaking in Medieval Europe: A Historical and Bibliographical Guide*. Regina Guides to Historical Issues. Claremont: Regina Books, 1997.

Hödl, G. "Ein Weltfriedsprogramm um 1300." In: *Festschrift Friedrich Hausmann*. Ed. H. Ebner. Graz, 1977, pp. 217-33.

Hodsworth, Christopher. "Peace-making in the Twelfth Century," *Anglo-Norman Studies* 19 (1996), 1-17.

Hoffmann, H. *Gottesfrieden und Treuga Dei*. Monumenta Germaniae Historia, Schriften, 20. Stuttgart, 1964.

Holdsworth, Christopher J. "Ideas and Reality: Some Attempts to Control and Defuse War in the Twelfth Century," *Studies in Church History* 20 (1983), 59-79.

Holdsworth, Christopher J. "Peacemaking in the Twelfth Century," *Anglo-Norman Studies* 19 (1996), 1-17.

Joris, A. "Observations sur la proclamation de la trêve de Dieu à Liège à la fin du XIe siècle," *Recueils de la société Jean Bodin* 14 (1961), 503-45.

Justus, W. *Die frühe Entwicklung des säkularen Friedensbegriffs in der mittelalterlichen Chronistik*. Cologne and Vienna, 1975.

Keen, Maurice. "War, Peace and Chivalry." In: *War and Peace in the Middle Ages*. Ed. B.P. McGuire. Copenhagen, 1987, pp. 94-117.

Kennelly, Dolorosa. "Medieval Towns and the Peace of God," *Medievalia et humanistica* 15 (1963), 35-53.

Koziol, Geoffrey G. "Monks, Feuds, and the Making of Peace in Eleventh-Century Flanders," *Historical Reflections* 14 (1987), 531-49; in: *The Peace of God: Social Violence and Religious Response in France Around the Year 1000*. Ed. Thomas Head and Richard Landes. Ithaca: Cornell University Press, 1992, pp. 239-58.

Landes, Richard. "Between Aristocracy and Heresy: Popular Participation in the Limousin Peace of God, 994-1033." In: *The Peace of God: Social Violence and Religious Response in France Around the Year 1000*. Ed.

Thomas Head and Richard Landes. Ithaca: Cornell University Press, 1992, pp. 184-218.

Lauranson-Rosaz, Christian. "Peace from the Mountains: The Auvergnat Origins of the Peace of God." In: *The Peace of God: Social Violence and Religious Response in France Around the Year 1000*. Ed. Thomas Head and Richard Landes. Ithaca: Cornell University Press, 1992, pp. 104-34.

Lobrichon, Guy. "The Chiaroscuro of Heresy: Early Eleventh-Century Aquitaine as Seen from Auxerre." In: *The Peace of God: Social Violence and Religious Response in France Around the Year 1000*. Ed. Thomas Head and Richard Landes. Ithaca: Cornell University Press, 1992, pp. 80-103.

Mackinney, Loren C. "The People and Public Opinion in the Eleventh-Century Peace Movement," *Speculum* 5 (1930), 181-206.

Magnou-Nortier, Elisabeth. "The Enemies of Peace: Reflections on a Vocabulary, 500-1100." In: *The Peace of God: Social Violence and Religious Response in France Around the Year 1000*. Ed. Thomas Head and Richard Landes. Ithaca: Cornell University Press, 1992, pp. 58-79.

Magnou-Nortier, Elisabeth. "La place du concile du Puy (vers 994) dans l'évolution de l'idée de paix." In: *Mélanges offerts à Jean Dauvillier*. Toulouse, 1979, pp. 489-506.

Mohrmann, W.D. *Der Landfriede im Ostseeraum während des späten Mittelalters*. Kallmünz, 1972.

Molinié, G. *L'organisation judicaire, militaire et financière des associations de la paix: Etude sur la paix et le trêve de Dieu dans le midi et le centre de la France*. Toulouse, 1912.

Moore, R.I. "Postscript: The Peace of God and the Social Revolution." In: *The Peace of God: Social Violence and Religious Response in France Around the Year 1000*. Ed. Thomas Head and Richard Landes. Ithaca: Cornell University Press, 1992, pp. 308-26.

Pace nel pensiero, nella politica, negli ideali del Trecento, La. Convegni del centro di studi sulla spiritualità medievale, 15. Todi, 1975.

Paxton, Frederick S. "History, Historians, and the Peace of God." In: *The Peace of God: Social Violence and Religious Response in France Around the Year 1000*. Ed. Thomas Head and Richard Landes. Ithaca: Cornell University Press, 1992, pp. 21-40.

Picht, G. and W. Huber. *Was heist Friedensforschung?* Stuttgart, 1971.

Remensnyder, Amy G. "Pollution, Purity, and Peace: An Aspect of Social Reform between the Late Tenth Century and 1076." In: *The Peace of God: Social Violence and Religious Response in France Around the Year 1000.* Ed. Thomas Head and Richard Landes. Ithaca: Cornell University Press, 1992, pp. 280-307.

Renna, Thomas. "The Idea of Peace in the West, 500-1150," *Journal of Medieval History* 6 (1980), 143-67.

Strubbe, E.I. "La paix de Dieu dans le nord de la France," *Recueils de le société Jean Bodin* 14 (1961), 489-501.

Töpfer, Bernhard. "Die Anfänge der 'Treuga Dei' in Nordfrankreich," *Zeitschrift für Geschichteswissenschaft* 9 (1962), 876-93.

Töpfer, Bernhard. "The Cult of Relics and Pilgrimage in Burgundy and Aquitaine at the Time of the Monastic Reform." In: *The Peace of God: Social Violence and Religious Response in France Around the Year 1000.* Ed. Thomas Head and Richard Landes. Ithaca: Cornell University Press, 1992, pp. 41-57.

Töpfer, Bernhard. *Das Kommende Reich des Friedens: Zur Entwicklung chiliasticher Zukunftshoffnungen in Hochmittelalter.* Berlin, 1964.

Vander Linden, H. "Le tribunal de la paix de Henri de Verdun (1082) et la formation de la principauté de Liège." In: *Melanges d'histoire offerts à Henri Pirenne.* Brussels, 1926, II:589-96.

Wallace-Hadrill, J.M. "War and Peace in the Early Middle Ages," *Transactions of the Royal Historical Society* 5th ser. 25 (1975), 57-74; in: *Early Medieval History.* New York, 1976, pp. 19-37.

White, Stephen D. "Feuding and Peace-Making in the Touraine around the Year 1100," *Traditio* 42 (1986), 195-263.

Medieval – Popular Rebellion

Baerten, Jean. "Histoire et sociologie: Les soulèvements populaires aux XIIIème et XIVème siècles dans l'historiographie française." In: *Divers aspects du moyen âge en occident*. Calais, 1977, pp. 136-57.

Bardoel, Agatha. "The Urban Uprising at Bruges, 1280-81: Some New Findings about the Rebels and the Partisans," *Revue Belge de philologie et d'histoire* 72 (1994), 761-91.

Bessen, David M. "The Jacquerie: Class War or Co-opted Rebellion?" *Journal of Medieval History* 11 (1985), 43-59.

Bickle, Peter. "Peasant Revolts in the German Empire in the Late Middle Ages," *Social History* 4 (1979), 223-39.

Blockmans, Wim. "La répression de révoltes urbaines comme méthode de centralisation dans les Pays-Bas Bourguignons," *Publications du centre d'études Bourguignones (XIVe-XVIe siècles* 28 (1988), 5-9.

Brucker, Gene A. "The Ciompi Revolution." In: *Florentine Studies: Politics and Society in Renaissance Florence*. Ed. N. Rubenstein. Evanston, 1968, pp. 314-56.

Cazelles, Raymond. "The Jacquerie." In: *The English Rising of 1381*. Ed. R.H. Hilton and T.H. Aston. Cambridge, 1984, pp. 74-83.

Cohn, Samuel K., Jr. *Creating the Florentine State: Peasants and Rebellion, 1348-1434*. Cambridge: Cambridge University Press, 2000.

Cohn, Samuel K., Jr. "Florentine Insurrections, 1342-1385, in Comparative Perspective." In: *The English Rising of 1381*. Ed. R.H. Hilton and T.H. Aston. Cambridge, 1984, pp. 143-64.

Denton, Jeffrey. "The Second Uprising at Laon and its Aftermath, 1295-98," *Bulletin of the John Rylands Library* 72 (1990), 79-92.

Durvin, Pierre. "Les origines de la Jacquerie à Saint-Leu-d'Esserent en 1358." In: *La guerre et la paix: Frontières et violences au moyen âge*. Actes du 101e congrès national des sociétés savantes, Lille, 1976. Paris: Bibliothèque Nationale, 1978, pp. 365-74.

Fédou, René. "A Popular Revolt in Lyons in the Fifteenth Century: The *Rebeyne* of 1436." In: *The Recovery of France in the Fifteenth Century.* Ed. P.S. Lewis. Trans. G.F. Martin. New York, 1971, pp. 242-64.

François, Martha Ellis. "Revolts in Late Medieval and Early Modern Europe: A Spiral Model," *Journal of Interdisciplinary History* 5 (1974), 19-43.

Freedman, Paul. "The German and Catalan Peasant Revolt," *American Historical Review* 98 (1993), 39-54.

Fryde, E.B. and Nathalie Fryde. "Peasant Rebellion and Peasant Discontents." In: *The Agrarian History of England and Wales.* III: *1348-1500.* Ed. Edward Miller. Cambridge: Cambridge University Press, 1991, pp. 744-819.

Funck-Brentano, Frantz. "Les luttes sociales aux XIVe siècle: Jean Colomb de Bordeaux," *Moyen âge* 10 (1897), 289-320.

Galbraith, V.H. "Thoughts about the Peasants' Revolt." In: *The Reign of Richard II: Essays in Honour of May McKisack.* Ed. F.R.H. DuBoulay and Caroline M. Barron. London, 1971, pp. 46-57.

Goldberg, Eric J. "Popular Revolt, Dynastic Politics, and Aristocratic Factionalism in the Early Middle Ages: The Saxon *Stellinga* Reconsidered," *Speculum* 70 (1995), 467-501.

Gurr, T.R. "Peasant Revolts in the German Empire in the Late Middle Ages," *Social History* 4 (1979), 223-39.

Hanawalt, Barbara A. "Peasant Resistance to Royal and Seigniorial Impositions." In: *Social Unrest in the Late Middle Ages.* Ed. F.X. Newman. Binghamton, 1986, pp. 23-47.

Harvey, I.M.W. *Jack Cade's Rebellion of 1450.* Oxford, 1991.

Herbert, Alisa. "Herefordshire, 1413-61: Some Aspects of Society and Public Order." In: *Patronage, The Crown, and the Provinces in Later Medieval England.* Ed. Ralph A. Griffiths. Gloucester: Alan Sutton, 1981, pp. 103-22.

Holland, P. "The Lincolnshire Rebellion of March 1470," *English Historical Review* 13 (1988), 849-69.

Housley, Norman. "Historiographical Essay–Insurrection as Religious War, 1400-1536," *Journal of Medieval History* 25 (1999), 141-54.

Hugenholtz, F.W.N. *Drie boerenstanden uit de veertiende eeuw: Onderzoek naar het optandig bewustzijn*. 2nd ed. The Hague, 1978.

Hugenholtz, F.W.N. *Ridderkrieg en burgervrede: West Europa aan de vooravond van de Honderdjarige Oorlog*. Bussum: De Haan, 1973.

Ivinskis, Zenonas. *Geschichte des Bauernstandes in Litauen: Von den ältesten Zeiten bis zum Anfang des 16. Jahrhunderts. Beiträge zur sozialen und wirtschaftlichten Entwicklung des Bauernstandes in Litauen im Mittelalter*. Berlin: Eberling, 1933.

Lallemand, Alexis. *La lutte des états de Liège contre la maison de Bourgogne, 1390-1492*. Brussels, 1910.

Leguai, André. "Les révoltes rurales dans royaume de France, du milieu de XIVe siècle à la din du XVe," *Moyen âge*, 4th ser., 37 (1982), 49-76.

Luce, Siméon. *Histoire de Jacquerie*. Paris, 1894.

Luce, Siméon. "Les origines militaires de Jacques bonhomme." In: *La France pendant la guerre de cent ans*. Paris, 1893, pp. 17-32.

Maddern, Philippa C. *Violence and Social Order: East Anglia, 1422-1442*. Oxford: Oxford University Press, 1992.

Maddicott, J.R. "Poems of Social Protest in Early Fourteenth-Century England." In: *England in the Fourteenth Century: Proceedings of the 1985 Harlaxton Symposium*. Ed. W.M. Ormrod. Woodbridge, 1986, pp. 130-44.

McKee, Sally. "The Revolt of St. Tito in Fourteenth-Century Venetian Crete: A Reassessment," *Mediterranean Historical Review* 9 (1994), 174-204.

Medeiros, Marie-Thérèse de. *Jacques et chroniqueurs*. Paris, 1979.

Mirot, Léon. *Les insurrections urbaines au début du règne de Charles VI (1380-1383), leurs causes, leurs conséquences*. Paris, 1905.

Miskimin, H.A. "The Last of Charles V: The Background of the Revolts of 1382," *Speculum* 38 (1963), 433-42.

Mollat, Michel and Philippe Wolff. *Ongles bleus, Jacques, et Ciompi: Les révolutions populaires en Europe aux XIVe et XVe siècles*. Paris, 1970.

Platelle, Henri. "Une révolte populaire à Saint-Amand en 1356." In: *La guerre et la paix: Frontières et violences au moyen âge*. Actes du 101e congrès national des sociétés savantes, Lille, 1976. Paris: Bibliothèque Nationale, 1978, pp. 349-63.

Portal, C. "Les insurrections des Tuchins dans les pays de Langue d'oc, vers 1382-1384," *Annales du midi* 4 (1892), 433-74.

Rebouillat, Marguerite. "La lutte entre les seigneurs de Brancion et Cluny." In: *La guerre et la paix: Frontières et violences au moyen âge*. Actes du 101e congrès national des sociétés savantes, Lille, 1976. Paris: Bibliothèque Nationale, 1978, pp. 333-48.

Rotz, Rhiman A. "Investigating Urban Uprisings with Examples from Hanseatic Towns, 1374-1416." In: *Order and Innovation in the Middle Ages: Essays in Honor of Joseph R. Strayer*. Ed. W.C. Jordan et al. Princeton, 1976, pp. 215-33, 483-94.

Rotz, Rhiman A. "'Social Struggles' or the Price of Power? German Urban Uprisings in the Late Middle Ages," *Archiv für Reformationsgeschichte* 76 (1985), 64-95.

Rotz, Rhiman A. "Urban Uprisings in Germany: Revolutionary or Reformist? The Case of Brunswick, 1374," *Viator* 4 (1973), 207-23.

Scribner, Bob and Gerhard Benecke, ed. *The German Peasant War of 1525: New Viewpoints*. London: George Allen and Unwin, 1979.

Sivéry, Gérard. "L'enquete de 1247 et les dommages de guerre en Tournaisis en Flandre gallicante et en Artois," *Revue du nord* 59 (1977), 7-18.

Vercauteren, Fernand. *Luttes sociales à Liège, XIIIe et XIVe siècles*. 2nd ed. Brussels: La Renaissance du Livre, 1946.

Watts, D.G. "Popular Disorder in Southern England, 1250-1450." In: *Conflict and Community in Southern England: Essays in the Social History of Rural and Urban Labour from Medieval to Modern Times*. Ed. B. Stapleton. New York, 1992, pp. 1-15.

Waugh, Scott. "The Profits of Violence: The Minor Gentry in the Rebellion of 1321-1322 in Gloucestershire and Herefordshire," *Speculum* 52 (1977), 843-69.

Wirz, Matthias. *'Muerent les moignes!' La révolte de Payerne (1420).* Cahiers Lausannois d'Histoire Médiévale, 19. Lausanne: Section d'histoire, Université de Lausanne, 1997.

Wunderli, Richard. *Peasant Fires: The Drummer of Niklashausen.* Bloomington: Indiana University Press, 1992.

Zilverberg, S.B.J. *De Stichtse burgeroorlog.* Zutphen, 1978.

Medieval – Popular Rebellion – Peasants' Revolt of 1381

Aston, Margaret. "Corpus Christi and Corpus Regni: Heresy and the Peasants' Revolt," *Past and Present* 143 (1994), 3-47.

Baker, J.H. "The German Hanse and the Peasants' Revolt of 1381," *Bulletin of the Institute of Historical Research* 57 (1984), 92-98.

Barron, Caroline. *Revolt in London: Eleventh to Fifteenth June 1381.* London, 1981.

Bird, Ruth. *The Turbulent London of Richard II.* London, 1949.

Brooks, Nicholas. "The Organization and Achievements of the Peasants in Kent and Essex in 1381." In: *Studies in Medieval History Presented to R.H.C. Davies.* Ed. H.Mayr Harting and R.I. Moore. London, 1985, pp. 247-70.

Butcher, A.F. "English Urban Society and the Revolt of 1381." In: *The English Rising of 1381.* Ed. R.H. Hilton and T.H. Aston. Cambridge, 1984, pp. 84-111.

Crane, Susan. "The Writing Lesson of 1381." In: *Chaucer's England: Literature in Historical Context.* Ed. B. Hanawalt. Minneapolis, 1992, pp. 201-21.

Crook, David. "Derbyshire and the English Rising of 1381," *Historical Research* 60 (1987), 9-23.

Dobson, R.B. "Remembering the Peasants' Revolt, 1381-1981." In: *Essex and the Great Revolt of 1381: Lectures Celebrating the Six Hundredth Anniversary.* Ed. W.H. Liddell and R.G.E. Wood. Essex Record Office Publications, 84. Chelmsford, 1982, pp. 1-20.

Dobson, R.B. "The Risings in York, Beverley and Scarborough, 1380-81." In: *The English Rising of 1381.* Ed. R.H. Hilton and T.H. Aston. Cambridge, 1984, pp. 112-42.

Dobson, R.B., ed. *The Peasants' Revolt of 1381.* London: Macmillan, 1970.

Dyer, Christopher. "The Causes of the Revolt in Rural Essex." In: *Essex and the Great Revolt of 1381: Lectures Celebrating the Six Hundredth Anniversary.* Ed. W.H. Liddell and R.G.E. Wood. Essex Record Office Publications, 84. Chelmsford, 1982, pp. 21-36.

Dyer, Christopher. "The Rising of 1381 in Suffolk: Its Origins and Participants," *Proceedings of the Suffolk Institute of Archaeology and History* 36 (1988), 274-87.

Dyer, Christopher. "The Social and Economic Background to the Rural Revolt of 1381." In: *The English Rising of 1381.* Ed. R.H. Hilton and T.H. Aston. Cambridge, 1984, pp. 9-42.

Eberhard, Oscar. *Der Bauernaufstand vom Jahre 1381 in der englischen Poesie.* Anglistische Forschungen, 51. Heidelberg, 1917.

Eiden, Herbert. *"In der Knechtschaft werdet ihr verharren . . .": Ursachen und Verlauf des englischen Bauernaufstandes von 1381.* Trier: Trierer Historische Forschungen, 1995.

Eiden, Herbert. "Norfolk, 1382: A Sequel to the Peasants' Revolt," *English Historical Review* 114 (1999), 370-75.

Faith, Rosamund. "The 'Great Rumour' of 1377 and Peasant Ideology." In: *The English Rising of 1381.* Ed. R.H. Hilton and T.H. Aston. Cambridge, 1984, pp. 43-73.

Flaherty, W.E. "The Great Rebellion in Kent in 1381 Illustrated from the Public Records," *Archaeologia cantiana* 3 (1860), 65-96.

Flaherty, W.E. "Sequel to the Great Rebellion in Kent in 1381," *Archaeologia cantiana* 4 (1861), 67-86.

Fryde, E.B. *The Great Revolt of 1381*. Historical Association General Series, 100. London. 1981.

Fryde, E.B. and Nathalie Fryde. "Peasant Rebellion and Peasant Discontents." In: *The Agrarian History of England and Wales*. III: *1348-1500*. Ed. Edward Miller. Cambridge: Cambridge University Press, 1991, pp. 744-819.

Galloway, Andrew. "Gower in his Most Learned Role and the Peasants' Revolt of 1381," *Mediaevalia* 16 (1993), 329-48.

Hansen, Harriet Merete. "The Peasants' Revolt of 1381 and the Chronicles," *Journal of Medieval History* 6 (1980), 393-415.

Harding, Alan. "The Revolt against Justices." In: *The English Rising of 1381*. Ed. R.H. Hilton and T.H. Aston. Cambridge, 1984, pp. 165-93.

Hilton, Rodney H. *Bond Men Made Free: Medieval Peasant Movements and the English Rising of 1381*. London: Maurice Temple Smith Ltd, 1973; rpt. London: Routledge, 1988.

Hilton, Rodney H. "Introduction." In: *The English Rising of 1381*. Ed. R.H. Hilton and T.H. Aston. Cambridge, 1984, pp. 1-8.

Hilton, Rodney H. "The Rising of 1381 in Suffolk," *Proceedings of the Suffolk Institute of Archaeology and History* 36 (1986), 282-85.

Hilton, Rodney H. and H. Fagan. *The English Rising of 1381*. London, 1950.

Justice, Steven. *Writing and Rebellion: England in 1381*. Berkeley and Los Angeles: University of California Press, 1994.

Oman, Charles. *The Great Revolt of 1381*. Oxford, 1906.

Ormrod, W.M. "The Peasants' Revolt and the Government of England," *Journal of British Studies* 29 (1990), 1-30.

Pearsall, Derek. "Interpretative Models for the Peasants' Revolt." In: *Hermeneutics and Medieval Culture*. Ed. Patrick J. Gallacher and Helen Damico. Albany, 1989, pp. 63-70.

Petit-Dutaillis, Charles. "Les prédictions populaires: les lollards et le soulèvement des travailleurs anglais en 1381." In: *Études d'histoire du moyen âge dédiées à Gabriel Monod*. Paris, 1896, pp. 373-88.

Powell, Edgar. *The Rising of 1381 in East Anglia*. Cambridge, 1896.

Prescott, Andrew J. "London in the Peasants' Revolt: A Portrait Gallery," *London Journal* 7 (1981), 125-43.

Raftis, J.Ambrose. "Social Change Versus Revolution: New Interpretations of the Peasants' Revolt of 1381." In: *Social Unrest in the Late Middle Ages*. Ed. F.X. Newman. Binghamton, 1986, pp. 3-22.

Réville, André. *Le soulèvement des travailleurs d'Angleterre en 1381*. Paris, 1898.

Roberts, Eileen. "St. Albans' Borough Boundary and Its Significance in the Peasants' Revolt." In: *The Peasants' Revolt in Hertfordshire: The Rising and Its Background*. Stevenage Old Town, 1981, pp. 126-34.

Ronan, Nick. "1381: Writing in Revolt. Signs of Confederacy in the Chronicle Accounts of the English Rising," *Forum for Modern Language Studies* 25 (1989), 304-14.

Sayles, G.O. "Richard II in 1381 and 1399," *English Historical Review* 103 (1988), 820-29.

Searle, Eleanor and Robert Burghart. "The Defense of England and the Peasants' Revolt," *Viator* 3 (1972), 36-88.

Sparvel-Bayly, J.A. "Essex in Insurrection, 1381," *Transactions of the Essex Archaeological Society* n.s. 1 (1878), 205-19.

Stemmler, Theo. "The Peasants' Revolt in 1381 in Contemporary Literature." In: *Functions of Literature: Essays Presented to Erwin Wolff on His Sixtieth Birthday*. Ed. Ulrich Broich, Theo Stemmler, and Gerd Stratmann. Tubingen, 1984, pp. 21-38.

Tillotson, J.H. "Peasant Unrest in the England of Richard II: Some Evidence from Royal Records," *Historical Studies* (University of Melbourne) 16 (1974-75), 1-16.

Travis, Peter W. "Chaucer's Trivial Fox Chase and the Peasants' Revolt of 1381," *Journal of Medieval and Renaissance Studies* 18 (1988), 185-220.

Tuck, J. Anthony. "Nobles, Commons and the Great Revolt of 1381." In: *The English Rising of 1381.* Ed. R.H. Hilton and T.H. Aston. Cambridge, 1984, pp. 194-212.

Warren, W.L. "The Peasants' Revolt of 1381." In: *English Society and Government in the Fifteenth Century.* Ed. C.M.D. Crowder. Edinburgh, 1967, pp. 41-70.

Wilkinson, Bertie. "The Peasants' Revolt of 1381," *Speculum* 13 (1940), 12-35.

Wood, R.G.E. "Essex Manorial Records and the Revolt." In: *Essex and the Great Revolt of 1381: Lectures Celebrating the Six Hundredth Anniversary.* Ed. W.H. Liddell and R.G.E. Wood. Essex Record Office Publications, 84. Chelmsford, 1982, pp. 85-98.

Medieval – Scandinavia [See also – Vikings]

Byock, Jesse. *Feud in Icelandic Saga.* Berkeley and Los Angeles: University of California Press, 1993.

Cederlöf, Olle. "Apropå: Slaget vid Brunkeberg 1471," *Meddelande* 32 (1971), 5-8.

Ericson, Lars. "Farmers or Mercenaries? The Swedish Army in the late Fifteenth and Early Sixteenth Centuries." In: *XXII. Kongreß der Internationalen Kommission für Militärgeschichte Acta 22: Von Crécy bis Mohács Kriegswesen im späten Mittelalter (1346-1526).* Vienna: Heeresgeschichtliches Museum, 1997, pp. 61-69.

Gelting, Michael H. "Military Organization, Social Power and State Formation in Denmark, 11th-13th Century." In: *Military Aspects of Scandinavian Society in a European Perspective, AD. 1-1300.* Ed. A.N. Jørgensen and B. Clausen. Copenhagen, 1997, pp. 48-54.

Gravett, Christopher. "The Face of Medieval Warfare," *Military Illustrated* 6 (Apr-May 1987), 17-21.

Jørgensen, Anne Nørgård. "Military Organisation and Sea-Defence in Denmark, 200-1200 AD." In: *Military Studies in Medieval Europe: Papers of the "Medieval Europe Brugge 1997" Conference Volume 11.* Ed. Guy De Boe & Frans Verhaeghe. Zellik: Instituut voor het Archeologisch Patrimonium, 1997, pp. 191-96.

Jørgensen, Anne Nørgård. "A Peaceful Discussion of a Martial Topic: The Chronology of Scandinavian Weapon Graves." In: *The Pace of Change: Studies in Early-Medieval Chronology.* Ed. John Hines, Karen Høilund Nielsen, and Frank Siegmund. Cardiff Studies in Archaeology. Oxford: Oxbow Books, 1999, pp. 148-59.

Jørgensen, Anne Nørgård. "Sea Defence in Denmark, AD 200-1300." In: *Military Aspects of Scandinavian Society in a European Perspective, AD. 1-1300.* Ed. A.N. Jørgensen and B. Clausen. Copenhagen, 1997, pp. 200-09.

Musset, L. "Problèmes militaires du monde scandinave (VIIe-XIIe siècle)." In: *Ordinamenti militari in occidente nell'alto medioevo.* Settimane di studio del centro italiano di studi sull'alto medioevo, XV. Spoleto, 1968, I:229-91.

Sawyer, Birgit and Peter Sawyer. *Medieval Scandinavia: From Conversion to Reformation, circa 800-1500.* Minneapolis: University of Minnesota Press, 1993.

Schiotz, Johannes. "L'armée Norvegienne au cours d'un millenaire: Récrutement, stratégic, tactique," *Revue internationale d'histoire militaire* 15 (1955), 273-83.

Sundberg, Ulf. *Medeltidens Svenska krig.* Stockholm: Hjalmarson and Högberg Bokförlag, 1999.

Thordeman, Bengt. *Armour from the Battle of Visby.* 2 vols. Stockholm: Kugl. Vitterhets historie och antikvitels akadmien, 1939-40.

Thordeman, Bengt. *Korsbetningen.* Svensk Fornminnesplatser nr. 14. Uddevalla: Vägledningar utgivna genom riksantikvarieämbetet, 1982.

Thordeman, Bengt. *Invasion på Gotland, 1361: Dikt och verklighet.* Stockholm: Hugo Gebers Förlag, 1944.

Medieval – Scotland [Cf. Medieval – English/Scottish Conflicts]

Aitchison, Nick. *Macbeth: Man and Myth*. Stroud: Sutton, 1999.

Alcock, Leslie. "The Site of the 'Battle of Dunnichen'," *Scottish Historical Review* 75 (1996), 130-42.

Armstrong, A.W. "Sir William Wallace and the Highland Dress," *Scottish Historical Review* 31 (1952), 193-95.

Armstrong, O. *Edward Bruce's Invasion of Ireland*. London, 1923.

Barnes, P. and G.W.S. Barrow. "The Movements of Robert Bruce between September 1307 and May 1308," *Scottish Historical Review* 69 (1990), 46-59.

Barron, E.M. *The Scottish War of Independence*. 2nd ed. Inverness, 1934.

Barrow, Geoffrey W.S. "The Aftermath of War: Scotland and England in the Late Thirteenth and Early Fourteenth Centuries," *Transactions of the Royal Historical Society*, 5th ser., 28 (1972), 103-25.

Barrow, Geoffrey W.S. *The Kingdom of the Scots*. London, 1973.

Barrow, Geoffrey W.S. "Lothian in the First War of Independence, 1296-1328," *Scottish Historical Review* 55 (1976), 151-71.

Barrow, Geoffrey W.S. *Robert Bruce and the Community of the Realm of Scotland*. London: Eyre and Spottiswoode, 1965.

Barrow, Geoffrey W.S. "The Scottish Clergy in the War of Independence," *Scottish Historical Review* 41 (1962), 1-22.

Baudoin-Matuszek, M.N. "Sir James Douglas's Death in Spain, 1330," *Scottish Historical Review* 69 (1990), 84-95.

Bonner, Elizabeth. "Scotland's 'Auld Alliance' with France, 1295-1560," *History* 84 (1999), 5-30.

Brown, Michael. *The Black Douglases: War and Lordship in Late Medieval Scotland, 1300-1455*. East Linton: Tuckwell Press, 1998.

Cameron, Sonya. "Chivalry in Barbour's *Bruce*." In: *Armies, Chivalry and Warfare in Medieval Britain and France: Proceedings of the 1995 Harlaxton Symposium*. Ed. M. Strickland. Stamford, 1998, pp. 13-29.

512 MEDIEVAL

Cruickshank, Graeme. *The Battle of Dunnichen.* 2nd ed. Balgavies: The Pinkfoot Press, 1999.

Davies, R.R. *Domination and Conquest: The Experience of Ireland, Scotland and Wales, 1100-1300.* Cambridge: Cambridge University Press, 1990.

Davis, I.M. *The Black Douglas.* London, 1974.

Duffy, Séan. "The Bruce Brothers and the Irish Sea World, 1306-29," *Cambridge Medieval Celtic Studies* 21 (1991), 55-86.

Duffy, Séan. "The 'Continuation' of Nicholas Trivet: A New Source for the Bruce Invasion," *Proceedings of the Royal Irish Academy* 91 C (1991), 303-15.

Duffy, Séan. "The Gaelic Account of The Bruce Invasion, *Cath Fhochairte Brighite*: Medieval Romance or Modern Forgery?" *Seanchas ard macha* 13 (1988), 59-121.

Duncan, A.A.M. "The Battle of Carham, 1018," *Scottish Historical Review* 55 (1976), 20-28.

Duncan, A.A.M. "The Bruces of Annandale, 1100-1304," *Transactions of the Dumfriesshire and Galloway Natural History and Antiquarian Society* 69 (1994), 89-102.

Duncan, A.A.M. "The Community of the Realm of Scotland and Robert Bruce," *Scottish Historical Review* 45 (1966), 184-201.

Duncan, A.A.M. "The Scots Invasion of Ireland, 1315." In: *The British Isles, 1100-1500: Comparisons, Contrasts and Connections.* Edinburgh, 1988, pp. 100-17.

Duncan, A.A.M. "The War of the Scots, 1306-23," *Transactions of the Royal Historical Society*, 6th ser., 2 (1992), 125-51.

Dunlop, Annie I. *Scots Abroad in the Fifteenth Century.* Historical Association Pamphlet, no. 124. London: The Historical Association, 1942.

Fisher, Andrew. "Wallace and Bruce: Scotland's Uneasy Heroes," *History Today* 39 (Feb 1989), 18-23.

Frame, Robin. "The Bruces in Ireland, 1315-18," *Irish Historical Studies* 19 (1974), 3-37.

Goldstein, R. James. "The Women of the Wars of Independence in Literature and History," *Studies in Scottish Literature* 26 (1991), 271-82.

Goodman, Anthony. "Religion and Warfare in the Anglo-Scottish Marches." In: *Medieval Frontier Societies*. Ed. R. Bartlett and A. Mackay. Oxford, 1989, pp. 245-66.

Gray, D.J. *William Wallace: The King's Enemy*. London: Robert Hale, 1991.

Hill, James Michael. "The Distinctiveness of Gaelic Warfare, 1400-1750," *European History Quarterly* 22 (1992), 323-45.

Kershaw, I. "A Note on the Scots in the West Riding, 1318-1319," *Northern History* 17 (1981), 231-39.

Lomas, Richard. "The Impact of Border Warfare: The Scots and South Tweedside, c.1290-c.1520," *Scottish Historical Review* 75 (1996), 143-67.

Lydon, James F. "The Dublin Purveyors and the Wars in Scotland, 1296-1324." In: *Keimelia: Studies in Medieval Archaeology and History in Memory of Tom Delaney*. Ed. Gearoíd Mac Niocoill and Patrick F. Wallace. Galway, 1988, pp. 435-48.

Lydon, James F. "An Irish Army in Scotland, 1296," *Irish Sword* 5 (1962), 184-89.

Lydon, James F. "Irish Levies in the Scottish Wars, 1296-1302," *Irish Sword* 5 (1962), 207-17.

MacInnes, A.I. "Scotland and the Manx Connection: Relationships of Intermittent Violence, c. 1266-1603," *Proceedings of the Isle of Man Natural History and Antiquarian Society* n.s. 8 (1972-74), 362-77.

MacIomhair, Diarmuid. 'Bruce's Invasion and the First Campaign in County Louth," *Irish Sword* 10 (1971-72), 188-212.

Mackay, James. *William Wallace: Brave Heart*. Edinburgh: Mainstream Publishing, 1995.

Marwick, H. "Naval Defence in Norse Scotland," *Scottish Historical Review* 28 (1949), 1-11.

McGavin, John J. "Robert III's 'Rough Music': Charivari and Diplomacy in a Medieval Scottish Court," *Scottish Historical Review* 74 (1995), 144-58.

McNamee, Colm J. *The Wars of the Bruces: Scotland, England, and Ireland, 1306-1328*. East Linton: Tuckwell Press, 1997.

McNamee, Colm J. "William Wallace's Invasion of Northern England in 1297," *Northern History* 26 (1990), 40-58.

Meehan, Bernard. "The Siege of Durham, the Battle of Carham and the Cession of Lothian," *Scottish Historical Review* 55 (1976), 1-19.

Megaw, B.R.S. "The Scottish Invasion of Man in 1456," *Journal of the Manx Museum* 6 (1957-65), 23-24.

Morrison, A. "The Kingdom of Man and the Isles, 839-1266," *Transactions of the Gaelic Society of Inverness* 58 (1993-94), 425-81.

Neville, Cynthia J. "The Political Allegiance of the Earls of Strathearn during the War of Independence," *Scottish Historical Review* 65 (1986).

Nicholson, Ranald. "The Last Campaign of Robert Bruce," *English Historical Review* 77 (1962), 233-46.

Nicholson, Ranald. *Scotland: The Later Middle Ages*. Edinburgh: Oliver and Boyd, 1979.

Nicholson, Ranald. "A Sequel to Edward Bruce's Invasion of Ireland," *Scottish Historical Review* 42 (1963-64), 30-40.

Phillips, J.R.S. "Documents on the Early Stages of the Bruce Invasion of Ireland, 1315-1316," *Proceedings of the Royal Irish Academy* 79 (1979), 247-70.

Power, R. "The Death of Magnus Barelegs," *Scottish Historical Review* 74 (1994), 216-22.

Power, R. "Magnus Barelegs' Expeditions to the West," *Scottish Historical Review* 65 (1986), 107-32.

Prestwich, Michael. "England and Scotland during the Wars of Independence." In: *England and her Neighbours, 1066-1453: Essays in Honour of Pierre Chaplais*. Ed. M. Jones and M. Vale. London, 1989, pp. 181-97.

Prestwich, Michael. "Victualling Estimates for English Garrisons in Scotland during the Early Fourteenth Century," *English Historical Review* 82 (1967), 536-43.

Reese, Peter. *Wallace: A Biography*. Edinburgh: Canongate, 1996.

Reid, W. Stanford. "Trade, Traders and Scottish Independence," *Speculum* 29 (1954), 210-22.

Scammell, Jean. "Robert I and the North of England," *English Historical Review* 73 (1958), 385-403.

Scott, Ronald McNair. *Robert the Bruce: King of Scots*. New York: Peter Bedrick Books, 1989.

Scott, Tom. *Tales of Sir William Wallace, Guardian of Scotland: Freely Adapted from The Wallas of Blin Hary*. Edinburgh: Gordon Wright Publishing, 1981.

Sevestre, Bernard. "L'ancienne alliance franco-écossaise et le service écossais," *Revue de la Société des Amis du Musée de l'Armée* 99 (1990), 5-21.

Smallwood, T.M. "An Unpublished Early Account of Bruce's Murder of Comyn," *Scottish Historical Review* 54 (1975), 1-10.

Smyth, Alfred P. *Warlords and Holy Men: Scotland, AD 800-1000*. New History of Scotland, i. London, 1984.

Stevenson, A. "The Flemish Dimension of the Auld Alliance." In: *Scotland and the Low Countries, 1124-1994*. Ed. G.G. Simpson. East Linton, 1996.

Stones, E.L.G. "The Submission of Robert Bruce to Edward I c.1301-2," *Scottish Historical Review* 34 (1955), 122-34.

Tuck, J. Anthony. "War and Society in the Medieval North," *Northern History* 21 (1985), 33-52.

William Wallace: Braveheart. London: Pitkin Guides, 1997.

Wood, Stephen. *The Scottish Soldier*. Manchester: Archive Publications Ltd., 1987.

Young, Alan. *Robert the Bruce's Rivals: The Comyns, 1212-1314*. East Linton: Tuckwell Press, 1997.

Young, Alan and Michael J. Stead. *In the Footsteps of Robert Bruce*. Stroud: Sutton Publishing, 1999.

Medieval – Spain and Portugal

Agrait, Nicholás. "The Reconquest during the Reign of Alfonso XI (1312-1350)." In: *On the Social Origins of Medieval Institutions: Essays in Honor of Joseph F. O'Callaghan*. Ed. Donald J. Kagay and Theresa M. Vann. Leiden: E.J. Brill, 1998, pp. 149-65.

Alvira Cabrer, Martín. "La meurte del enemigo en el pleno medievo: cifras e ideología (el modelo de Las Navas de Tolosa)," *Hispania* 55.2: 190 (1995), 403-23.

Amador de los Rios y Villalta, R. "Notas acerca de la batalla de Lucera de la prision de Boabdul in 1483," *Revista des archives, bibliotecas y museos* 16 (1906).

Arié, R. *L'Espagne musulmane au temps des Nasrides (1232-1492)*. Paris, 1973.

Arié, R. *L'Espagne musulmane au bas moyen âge*. Paris, 1992.

Bazzana, André and Pierre Guichard. "Le conquête de la région valenci-enne d'après la chronique de Jacques 1er et les données archéologiques." In: *Castrum 3: Guerre, fortification et habitant dans le monde méditer-ranéen au moyen âge*. Ed. André Bazzana. Rome: L'école Française de Rome, 1988, pp. 21-32.

Beech, George T. "The Ventures of the Dukes of Aquitaine into Spain and the Crusader East in the Early Twelfth Century," *Haskins Society Journal* 5 (1993), 61-75.

Bensch, Stephen P. "From Prizes of War to Domestic Merchandise: The Changing Face of Slavery in Catalonia and Aragon, 1000-1300," *Viator* 25 (1994), 63-93.

Bishko, Charles Julian. "The Castilian as Plainsman: The Medieval Ranching Frontier in La Mancha and Extramadura." In: *The New World Looks at Its History*. Ed. Archibald Lewis and T. McGunn. Austin: University of Texas Press, 1963, pp. 46-69.

Bishko, Charles Julian. "The Spanish and Portuguese Reconquest, 1095-1492." In: *A History of the Crusades*. Ed. Kenneth M. Setton. Madison, 1976, III:299-398.

Blackburn, Donald S. "Collision of Faiths," *Military History* (June 1994), 62-68.

Boffa, Serge. "Les soutiens militaires de Jean Ier, duc de Brabant, à Philippe III, roi de France, durant les expéditions ibériques (1276-1285)," *Revue du nord* 78 (1996), 7-33.

Bonnassie, P. *La Catalogne du milieu du Xe à la fin du XIe siècle: Croissance et mutation d'une société*. 2 vols. Toulouse, 1975-76.

Bramon, Dolors. "La batalla de Albesa (25 de febrero de 1003) y la primera aceifa de 'Abd al-Malik al-Muzaffar (verano del mismo año)," *Anaquel de estudios árabes* 6 (1995), 21-27.

Brett, M. and W. Forman. *The Moors: Islam in the West*. London, 1980.

Brodman, James William. "Fable and Power: The Origins of the Mercedarian Foundation Story," *Journal of Medieval History* 25 (1999), 229-41.

Brodman, James William. "Municipal Ransoming Law on the Medieval Spanish Frontier," *Speculum* 60 (1985), 318-30.

Brodman, James William. *Ransoming Captives in Crusader Spain*. Philadelphia: University of Pennsylvania Press, 1986.

Bronisch, Alexander Pierre. *Reconquista und Heiliger Krieg: Die Deutung des Krieges im christlichen Spanien von den Westgoten bis ins frühe 12. Jahrhundert*. Münster: Aschendorff, 1998.

Burns, Robert Ignatius. "The Catalan Company and the European Powers, 1305-1311," *Speculum* 29 (1954), 751-71.

Burns, Robert Ignatius. "How to End a Crusade: Techniques for Making Peace in the Thirteenth-Century Kingdom of Valencia," *Military Affairs* 35 (1971), 142-48.

Burns, Robert Ignatius. "The Many Crusades of Valencia's Conquest (1225-1280): An Historiographical Labyrinth." In: *On the Social Origins of Medieval Institutions: Essays in Honor of Joseph F. O'Callaghan*. Ed. Donald J. Kagay and Theresa M. Vann. Leiden: E.J. Brill, 1998, pp. 167-77.

Burns, Robert Ignatius. "The Muslim in the Christian Feudal Order: The Kingdom of Valencia, 1240-1280," *Studies in Medieval Culture* 5 (1976), 105-26.

Burns, Robert Ignatius. "Warrior Neighbors: Alfonso El Sabio and Crusader Valencia, an Archival Case Study in his International Relations," *Viator* 21 (1990), 147-202.

Burns, Robert Ignatius and Paul Chevedden. "The Finest Castle in the World," *History Today* 49.11 (Nov 1999), 10-17.

Caille, J. "Les seigneurs de Narbonne dans le conflit Toulouse-Barcelone au XIIe siècle," *Annales du midi* 97 (1985), 227-44.

Casa Genover, Josep and Josep M. Llorens. "Un camp militar medieval a Viladamat (Alt Emporda)," *Annals de l'institut d'estudis Gironins* 33 (1994), 517-26.

Chalmeta, Pedro. "Las campañas califales en al-Andalus." In: *Castrum 3: Guerre, fortification et habitant dans le monde méditerranéen au moyen âge*. Ed. André Bazzana. Rome: L'école Française de Rome, 1988, pp. 33-42.

Clemente Ramos, Julián. "La extremadura musulmana (1142-1248): organización defensiva y sociedad," *Anuario de estudios medievales* 24 (1994), 647-701.

Collins, Roger. *The Arab Conquest of Spain, 710-797*. London, 1989.

Collins, Roger. *Early Medieval Spain: Unity in Diversity, 400-1000*. London, 1983.

Cook, Weston F., Jr. "The Cannon Conquest of Nasrid Spain and the End of the Reconquista," *Journal of Military History* 57 (1993), 43-70.

De Mata Carriazo, J. "Un alcalde entre los cristianos y los moros, en la fronters de Granada," *Andalus* 13 (1948).

De Mata Carriazo, J. "Asiento de la cosas de Ronda, conquista y repartimento de la cuidad por los reyes catolicos (1485-1491)," *Miscelanea de estudios Arabes y Hebraicos* 3 (1954).

De Mata Carriazo, J. "Cartas de la frontera de Granada," *Andalus* 11 (1946).

De Mata Carriazo, J. "Relaciones fronterizas entre Jaen y Granada en el ano 1479," *Revista de archivos, bibliotecas y museos* 61 (1955).

De Mata Carriazo, J. *Los relieves de la guerra de Granada en la Silleria del coro de la Catedral de Toledo*. Granada, 1985.

Diago Hernando, Máximo. "Política y guerra en la frontera castellano-navarra durante la época Trastamara," *Príncipe de Viana* 55 (1994), 527-50.

Doxey, G. "Diplomacy, Trade, and War: Muslim Majorca in International Politics, 1159-81," *Journal of Medieval History* 20 (1994), 39-61.

Echevarria, Ana. *The Fortress of Faith: The Attitude towards Muslims in Fifteenth Century Spain*. Medieval Iberian Peninsula, 12. Leiden: Brill, 1999.

Evans, J., ed. and trans. *The Unconquered Knight: A Chronicle of the Deeds of Don Pero Niño, Count of Buelna*. London, 1928.

Fallows, Noel. *The Chivalric Vision of Alfonso de Cartagena: Study and Edition of the Doctrinal de los caualleros*. Newark, 1995.

Fallows, Noel. *Un texto inédito sobre la caballería del renacimiento español: Doctrina del art de la cauallería de Juan Quijada de Reayo*. Liverpool, 1996.

Fernandez, E.M. "La frontière de Grenade aux environs de 1400," *Moyen âge* 78 (1972), 489-522.

Fernández-Armesto, Felipe. "The Sea and Chivalry in Late Medieval Spain." In: *Maritime History*. I: *The Age of Discovery*. Ed. J.B. Hattendorff. Malabar, 1996, pp. 123-36.

Fernández-Armesto, Felipe. "The Survival of a Notion of *Reconquista* in Late Tenth-and Eleventh-Century León." In: *Warriors and Churchmen in the High Middle Ages: Essays Presented to Karl Leyser*. Ed. T. Reuter. London, 1992, pp. 123-43.

Fernández de Larrea Rojas, Jan Andani. *Guerra y sociedad en Navarra durante la edad media*. Bilbao: Universidad del País Vasco, 1992.

Fernando III y su época. Seville: Diputación Provincial de Sevilla, 1995.

Ferreiro, Alberto. "The Siege of Barbastro, 1064-65," *Journal of Medieval History* 9 (1983), 129-44.

Ferrer i Mallol, M.T. "Mercenaris catalans a Ferrera (1307-17)," *Anuario de estudios medievales* 2 (1965), 155-227.

Fisher, G. *Barbary Legend: War, Trade and Piracy in North Africa, 1415-1830*. Oxford, 1957.

Fletcher, Richard A. *Moorish Spain*. Berkerley and Los Angeles: University of California Press, 1993.

Fletcher, Richard A. *The Quest for El Cid*. Oxford: Oxford University Press, 1989.

Fletcher, Richard A. "Reconquist and Crusade in Spain, c.1050-1150," *Transactions of the Royal Historical Society*, 5th ser., 37 (1987), 31-47.

Gala, A. *Granada de los nazaries*. Barcelona, 1994.

García Fernandez, Manuel. "La infanta Doña María, monja de Sijena, y su política castellana durante la minoría de Alfonso XI (1312-1325)," *Anuario de estudios medievales* 28 (1998), 157-74.

García Fitz, Francisco. *Castilla y Léon frente al Islam: Estrategias de expansíon y tácticas militares (siglos XI-XIII)*. Seville: Universidad de Sevilla, 1998.

Garcia Gómez, E. "Armas, banderas, tièndas de campaña, monturas y correos en los 'Anales de al Hakam II' por 'Isa Rāzā," *Andalus* 32 (1967), 163-79.

Gautier-Dalché, Jean. "En Castile pendant la première moitié du XIIe siècle: les combattants des villes d'entre Duero et Tage." In: *Le combattant au moyen âge*. 2nd ed. Histoire ancienne et médiévale, 36. Paris: Publications de la Sorbonne, 1995, pp. 199-211.

Gautier-Dalché, Jean. "Reconquête et structures de l'habitat en Castille." In: *Castrum 3: Guerre, fortification et habitant dans le monde méditerranéen au moyen âge*. Ed. André Bazzana. Rome: L'école Française de Rome, 1988, pp. 199-206.

Gerrard, Christopher. "Opposing Identity: Muslims, Christians and the Military Orders in Rural Aragon," *Medieval Archaeology* 43 (1999), 143-60.

Glick, T.F. *From Muslim Fortress to Christian Christian: Social and Cultural Change in Medieval Spain*. Manchester: University of Manchester Press, 1995.

Goñi Gaztambide, José. *Historia de la bula de la cruzada en España*. Vitoria, 1958.

Gonzáles de León, Fernando. "'Doctors of Military Discipline': Technical Expertise and the Paradigm of the Spanish Soldier in the Early Modern Period," *Sixteenth Century Journal* 27 (1996), 61-85.

Gonzáles Jiménez, Manuel. "Frontier and Settlement in the Kingdom of Castile (1085-1350)." In: *Medieval Frontier Societies*. Ed. R. Bartlett and A. Mackay. Oxford, 1989, pp. 49-74.

Goodman, Anthony and David Morgan. "The Yorkist Claim to the Throne of Castile," *Journal of Medieval History* 11 (1985), 61-69.

Grunfeld, Foster. "The World of Alfonso X," *MHQ: The Quarterly Journal of Military History* 9 (Spring 1997), 74-81.

Guerrero Lovillo, J. *Las cántigas: Estudio arqueológico de sus miniaturas, alhambra*. Madrid, 1949.

Guiance, Ariel. "To Die for Country, Land or Faith in Castilian Medieval Thought," *Journal of Medieval History* 24 (1998), 313-32.

Harvey, L.P. *Islamic Spain, 1250-1500*. Chicago: University of Chicago Press, 1990.

Hillgarth, J.N. *The Spanish Kingdoms, 1250-1516*. 2 vols. Oxford, 1976-78.

Huici Miranda, Ambrosio. *Las grandes batallas de la reconqusita durante las invasiones africanas (Almoravides, Almohades y Benimerines)*. Madrid, 1956.

Humphries, Paul Douglas. "'Of Arms and Men': Siege and Battle Tactics in the Catalan Grand Chronicles (1208-1387)," *Military Affairs* 49 (1985), 173-78.

Kagay, Donald J. "Columbus as Standardbearer and Mirror of the Spanish Reconquest," *American Neptune* 53 (1993), 254-59.

Kagay, Donald J. "Structures of Baronial Dissent and Revolt under James I (1213-76)," *Medizevistik* 1 (1988), 61-85.

Kamen, Henry. "Clerical Violence in a Catholic Society: The Hispanic World, 1450-1720," *Studies in Church History* 20 (1983), 201-16.

Kennedy, Hugh. *Muslim Spain and Portugal: A Political History of al-Andalus*. London: Longman, 1996.

Lacarra, J.M. "Les villes-frontières dans l'Espagne des Xie-XIIIe siècles," *Moyen âge* 69 (1963), 205-22.

Ladero Quesada, M.A. *Andalucia en el siglo XV: Estudios de historia politica*. Madrid, 1973.

Ladero Quesada, M.A. *Castilla y la conquista del reino de Granada*. Valladolid, 1967.

Ladero Quesada, M.A. "La defense de Granada a raiz de la conquista, Cominezos de un problema," *Miscelanea de estudios arabs y hebraicos* 16-17 (1967-68).

Ladero Quesada, M.A. *Granada: Historia de un país Islámico, 1232-1571*. Granada, 1969.

Lanuza Cano, F. *El ejército en tiempo de los reyes católicos*. Madrid, 1953.

La Presle-Évesque, Alix de. "Le conflit franco-aragonais de la fin du XIIIe siècle et ses conséquences religieuses et politiques." In: *La guerre, la violence et les gens au Moyen Âge*. I: *Guerre et violence*. Ed. P. Contamine and O. Guyotjeannin. 119e congrès national des sociétés historiques et scientifiques, Amiens, octobre 1994, Section d'histoire médiévale et philologie. Paris, 1996, pp. 67-80.

Lévi-Provençal, E. *L'Espagne Musulmane au Xème siècle*. Paris, 1932.

Lewis, Archibald R. "Cataluña como frontera militar (870-1050)," *Anuario de estudios medievales* 51 (1968), 15-29.

Lewis, Archibald R. *The Development of Southern French and Catalan Society, 718-1050*. Austin: University of Texas Press, 1965.

Linehan, Peter. "The Accession of Alfonso X (1252) and the Origins of the War of Spanish Succession." In: *God and Man in Medieval Spain: Essays in Honour of J.R.L. Highfield*. Ed. D.W. Lomax and D. Mackenzie. Warminster, 1989, pp. 59-79.

Linehan, Peter. "The Cid of History and the History of The Cid," *History Today* 37 (Sep 1987), 26-32.

Lomax, D.W. *La orden de Santiago (1170-1275)*. Madrid, 1965.

Lomax, D.W. *The Reconquest of Spain*. London: Longman, 1978.

López de Coca Castañer, José Enrique. "Institutions on the Castilian-Granadan Frontier." In: *Medieval Frontier Societies*. Ed. Robert Bartlett and Angus Mackay. Oxford, 1989, pp. 127-50.

López Pérez, María Dolores. "Sobre la guerra y la paz: El acuerdo entre tremecén y la corona de Aragón (1362)," *Anuario de estudios medievales* 29 (1999), 527-45.

Lourie, Elena. "A Society Organized for War: Medieval Spain," *Past and Present* 35 (1966), 54-76.

Mackay, Angus. "Faction and Civil Strife in Late Medieval Castilian Towns," *Bulletin of the John Rylands Library* 72 (1990), 119-31.

Mackay, Angus. *Society, Economy and Religion in Late Medieval Castile*. London, 1987.

Martín Martín, José Luis. "La frontera Hispano-Portuguesa en la guerra, en la paz y comercio." In: *Las relaciones entre Portugal y Castilla, en la época de los descubrimientos y la expansión colonial, ponencias presentadas al congreso Hispano-Portugués celebrado en Salamanca, 1992*. Ed. Ana María Carabias Torres. Acta Salamanticensia: Estudios Históricos y Geográficos, 92. Salamanca: Ediciones Universidad de Salamanca, 1994, pp. 29-51.

Martín Martín, José Luis. "Origenes de la Orden Militar de Santiago (1170-1195)," *Anuario de estudios medievales* 4 (1967), 571-90.

McCrank, Lawrence J. "The Lost Kingdom of Siurana: Highland Resistance by Muslims to Christian Reconquest and Assimilation in the Twelfth Century." In: *On the Social Origins of Medieval Institutions: Essays in Honor of Joseph F. O'Callaghan*. Ed. Donald J. Kagay and Theresa M. Vann. Leiden: E.J. Brill, 1998, pp. 115-48.

McCrank, Lawrence J. "Norman Crusaders in the Catalan Reconquest: Robert Burdet and the Principality of Tarragona, 1129-55," *Journal of Medieval History* 7 (1981), 67-82.

Menéndez Pidal, R. *La España del Cid*. 5th ed. 2 vols. Madrid, 1956; trans. *The Cid and His Spain*. London, 1971.

Menjot, D. "Le poids de la guerre dans l'économie murcienne, l'exemple de la campagne de 1407-1408 contre Grenade." In: *Miscelanea medieval murciana*. Murcia, 1976, pp. 37-68.

Meyerson, Mark D. *The Muslims of Valencia in the Age of Fernando and Isabel: Between Coexistence and Crusade*. Berkeley and Los Angeles: University of California Press, 1991.

Navarro Palazón, Julio. "La conquista castellana y sus consecuencias: la despoblación de Siyasa." In: *Castrum 3: Guerre, fortification et habitant dans le monde méditerranéen au moyen âge*. Ed. André Bazzana. Rome: L'école Française de Rome, 1988, pp. 207-15.

Nicolle, David C. *Granada, 1492: The Twilight of Moorish Spain*. Campaign Series. London: Osprey Military, 1998.

Nieto Soria, José Manuel. "La nación Española de Roma y la embajada de lcomendador santiaguista Gonzalo de Beteta (1484)," *Anuario de estudios medievales* 28 (1998), 109-22.

Olbes Durán, Carlos. "La batalla de Toro (1476)," *Historia y vída* 326 (1995), 120-27.

Pescador, C. "La caballeria popular en León y Castilla," *Cuadernos de historia de España* 33-34 (1961), 101-238; 35-36 (1962), 56-201; 37-38 (1963), 88-198.

Powers, James F. "The Creative Interaction between Portuguese and Leonese Municipal Military Law, 1055 to 1279," *Speculum* 62 (1987), 53-80.

Powers, James F. "Frontier Competition and Legal Creativity: A Castilian-Aragonese Case Study Based on Twelfth-Century Municipal Military Law," *Speculum* 52 (1977), 465-87.

Powers, James F. "Frontier Military Service and Exemption in the Municipalities of Aragon and Castile," *Military Affairs* 45 (1981), 75-78.

Powers, James F. "Life on the Cutting Edge: The Besieged Town on the Luso-Hispanic Frontier in the Twelfth Century." In: *The Medieval City Under Siege*. Ed. I.A. Corfis and M. Wolfe. Woodbridge, 1995, pp. 17-35.

Powers, James F. "The Origins and Development of Municipal Military Service in the Leonese and Castilian Reconquest, 800-1250," *Traditio* 26 (1970), 91-111.

Powers, James F. *A Society Organized for War: The Iberian Municipal Militias in the Central Middle Ages, 1000-1284*. Berkeley and Los Angeles: University of California Press, 1988.

Powers, James F. "Townsmen and Soldiers: The Interaction of Urban and Military Organization in the Militias of Mediaeval Castile," *Speculum* 46 (1971), 641-55.

Powers, James F. "Two Warrior-Kings and their Municipal Militias: The Townsman-Soldier in Law and Life." In: *The World of Alfonso the Learned and James the Conqueror*. Ed. R.I. Burns. Princeton: Princeton University Press, 1985, pp. 95-129.

Prescott, William H. *The Art of War in Spain: The Conquest of Granada, 1481-1492*. Ed. Albert D. McJoynt. London: Greenhill Books, 1995.

Quiroga, Jorge L. and Mónica R. Lovelle. "La invasióne Árabe y el inicio de la "Reconquista" en el Noroeste de la Península Ibérica (93-251/711-865)." In: *Across the Mediterranean Frontiers: Trade, Politics and Religion, 650-1450: Selected Proceedings of the International Medieval Congress, University of Leeds, 10-13 July 1995, 8-11 July 1996*. Ed. Dionisius A. Agius and Ian Richard Netton. Turnhout: Brepols, 1997, pp. 61-86.

Reilly, Bernard F. *The Contest of Christian and Muslim Spain, 1031-1157*. Oxford: Blackwell, 1992.

Reilly, Bernard F. *The Kingdom of León-Castilla under King Alfonso VII, 1126-1157*. Philadelphia: University of Pennsylvania Press, 1998.

Riesco, Angel. "Vom Kriegsvolk und den mittelalterlichen 'Kriegsscharen' zur modernen spanischen Armee als stabiler, professioneller und repräsentativer Institution des Staates." In: *XXII. Kongreß der Internationalen Kommission für Militärgeschichte* Acta 22: *Von Crécy bis Mohács Kriegswesen im späten Mittelalter (1346-1526)*. Vienna, 1997, pp. 364-85.

Riquer, Martín de. *Caballeros andantes Españoles*. Madrid, 1967.

Riquer, Martín de. *Cavalleria fra realtà e letteratura nel quattrocento*. Bari, 1970.

Riquer, Martín de. *Vida caballeresca en la España del siglo XV*. Madrid, 1965.

Rodríguez García, José Manuel. "Idea and Reality of Crusade in Alfonso X's Reign: Castile and Leon, 1252-1284." In: *Autour de la première croisade: Actes du Colloque de la Society for the Study of the Crusades and the Latin East (Clermont-Ferrand, 22-25 juin 1995)*. Ed. M. Balard. Paris: Publications de la Sorbonne, 1996, pp. 377-90.

Rodriguez-Picavea Matilla, Enrique. "Frontera, soberania territorial y ordenes militares en l apeninsula iberica durante la edad media," *Hispania* 52 (1992), 789-809.

Roigé, Prim Bertram i. "Notes sobre els subsidis de l'església Catalona per a la guerra de Sardinya (1354)," *Anuario de estudios medievales* 29 (1999), 121-39.

Rojas, Gabriel. *La frontera entre los reinos de Sevilla y Granada en el siglo XV (1390-1481): Un ensayo sobre la violencia y sus manifestacions.* Cadiz: Universidad de Cádiz, 1995.

Ruano, E.B. "La participacion extranjera en la guerra de Granada," *Revista de archivos, bibliotecas y Museos* 80 (1977), 679-701.

Rufo Ysern, Paulina. "Participación de Ecija en la guerra de Granada (1482-92)," *Historia, Instituciones, Documentos* 21 (1994), 423-51.

Ruiz-Domènec, José Enrique. "El asedio de Barcelona, según Ermoldo el Negro (Notas sobre el caractér de la guerra en el alta Edad Media)," *Boletin de la Real Academia de Buenas Letras de Barcelona* 37 (1977-78), 149-68.

Sablonier, Roger. *Krieg und Kriegertum in der Crónica des Ramon Muntaner: Eine Studie zum spätmittelalterlichen Kriegswesen aufgrund katalanischer Quellen.* Berne and Frankfurt, 1971.

Sánchez-Albornoz, C. "El ejécito y la guerra en al reino Asturleonés, 718-1037." In: *Ordinamenti militari in occidente nell'alto medioevo.* Settimane di studio del centro Italiano di studi sull'alto medioevo, 15. Spoleto, 1968, I:293-428.

Sánchez Martínez, Manuel. "Guerra, avituallamiento del ejército y carestías en la Corona de Aragón: la provisión de cereal para la expedición granadina de Alfonso el Benigno (1329-1333)," *Historia, Instituciones, Documentos* 20 (1993), 523-49.

Sánchez Prieto, Ana Bélen. *Guerra y guerreros en España: según las fuentes canónicas de la Edad Media.* Madrid, 1990.

Schneidman, J.L. *The Rise of the Aragonese-Catalan Empire, 1200-1350.* London, 1970.

Sénac, Philippe. "La frontière aragonaise aux XIe et XIIe siècles: le mot et la chose *pro defensionem christianorum et confusionem sarracenorum*," *Cahiers de civilisation médiévale (X-XIIe siècle)* 42 (1999), 259-72.

Soler del Campo, Alvaro. "Sistemas de combate en la iconografia Mozarab y Andalusi altomedieval," *Boletín de la asociación Española de orientalistastas* 22 (1986), 61-87.

Stalls, Clay. *Possessing the Land: Aragon's Expansion into Islam's Ebro Frontier under Alfonso the Battler, 1104-1134*. Leiden: E.J. Brill, 1995.

Stewart, P. "The Soldier, the Bureaucrat and Fiscal Records in the Army of Ferdinand and Isabella," *Hispanic American Historical Review* 49 (1969).

Strayer, Joseph R. "The Crusade against Aragon." In: *Medieval Statecraft and the Perspectives of History: Essays by Joseph R. Strayer*. Princeton, 1971, pp. 107-22.

Terrasse, Henri. "L'Espagne Musulmane et l'héritage Wisigothique." *Etudes d'orientalisme dédidées à la mémoire de Lévi-Provençal*. Paris, 1962, pp. 757-66.

Torres, A.P. "Contribución al estudio del ejército en los estados de la Reconquista," *Anuario de historia del derecho Español* 15 (1944), 205-351.

Turnbull, Stephen. "Guns and Granada," *Military Illustrated* 146 (Jul 2000), 32-39.

Ubieto Areta, A. "La guerra en la edad media según los fueros de la linea del tajo," *Saitabi* 16 (1966), 91-210.

Vallvé, J. "España en el siglo VIII: ejercito y sociedad," *Al Andalus* 43 (1978), 51-112.

Velho, Martim. *Estudios criticos sobre a batalha de Ourique*. Lisbon: Sociedade Histórica da Independência de Portugal, 1989.

Vigón, J. *El ejército de los reyes católicos*. Madrid, 1968.

Vogt, John. "Saint Barbara's Legion: Portuguese Artillery in the Struggle for Morocco, 1415-1578," *Military Affairs* 41 (1977), 176-82.

Vones-Liebenstein, Ursula. "Une femme gardienne du royaume? Régentes en temps de guerre (France-Castile, XIIIe siècle)." In: *La guerre, la violence et les gens au Moyen Âge. II: Guerre et gens*. Ed. P. Contamine and O. Guyotjeannin. 119e congrès national des sociétés historiques et scientifiques, Amiens, octobre 1994, Section d'histoire médiévale et philologie. Paris, 1996, pp. 9-22.

Williams, John. "The Making of a Crusade: The Genoese Anti-Muslim Attacks in Spain, 1146-8," *Journal of Medieval History* 23 (1997), 29-53.

Medieval – Surgery (Battlefield)

Allbutt, T. Clifford. *The Historical Relations of Medicine and Surgery to the end of the Sixteenth Century*. London, 1905.

Beck, R. Theodore. *The Cutting Edge: Early History of the Surgeons of London*. London, 1974.

Billroth, Theodore. *Historical Studies on the Nature and Treatment of Gunshot Wounds from the Fifteenth Century to the Present Time*. Trans. C.P. Rhoads. New Haven, 1933.

Castiglioni, Arturo. *A History of Medicine*. Trans. E.B. Krumbhaar. New York, 1941.

Davies, Jonathan. "Arrow Wounds and How to Treat Them: A Short Study of Medieval and Early Renaissance Practice," *Journal of the Society of Archer-Antiquaries* 41 (1998), 6-8.

DeVries, Kelly. "Military Surgical Practice and the Advent of Gunpowder Weaponry," *Canadian Bulletin of Medical History* 7 (1990), 131-46.

Downes, R.M. "What Medicine Owes to War and War Owes to Medicine," *Journal of the Royal Army Medical Corps* 67 (1936), 381-94.

Elmy, D. "Arrow Wounds and Arrow Extraction," *Journal of the Society of Archer-Antiquaries* 35 (1992), 16-17.

Forrest, Richard D. "Development of Wound Therapy from the Dark Ages to the Present," *Journal of the Royal Society of Medicine* 75 (1982), 268-73.

Gabriel, Richard A. and Karen S. Metz. *A History of Military Medicine*. 2 vols. New York: Greenwood, 1992.

Gask, George. "Historical Sketch of the Methods of Treating Wounds in the Chest in War from A.D. 1300 to 1900." In: *Essays in the History of Medicine.* London, 1950, pp. 145-56.

Gask, George. "The Medical Services of Henry the Fifth's Campaign of the Somme in 1415." In: *Essays in the History of Medicine.* London, 1950, pp. 94-102.

Gask, George. "The Medical Staff of King Edward the Third." In: *Essays in the History of Medicine.* London, 1950, pp. 77-93.

Gask, George. "Vicary's Predecessors." In: *Essays in the History of Medicine.* London, 1950, pp. 55-76.

Gravett, Christopher. "The Face of Medieval Warfare," *Military Illustrated* 6 (Apr-May 1987), 17-21.

Halpin, R. "Arrow Wounds and How to Treat Them," *Journal of the Society of Archer-Antiquaries* 42 (1999), 81-85.

Heizmann, Charles L. "Military Sanitation in the Sixteenth, Seventeenth and Eighteenth Centuries," *Annals of Medical History* 1 (1917-18), 281-300.

Howell, H.A.L. "The Army Surgeon and the Care of the Sick and Wounded in British Campaigns during the Tudor and Stuart Periods," *Journal of the Royal Army Medical Corps* 2 (1904), 606-15, 737-45.

Howell, H.A.L. "An Historical Retrospect of the Army Surgeon in Britain, Prior to the Sixteenth Century," *Journal of the Royal Army Medical Corps* 1 (1903), 111-24.

Huard, Pierre and Mirko Drazen Grmek. *Mille ans de chirurgie en occident: Ve-XVe siècles.* Paris, 1966.

Klinger, Charles, Owen H. Wangensteen, and Sarah D. Wangensteen. "Wound Management of Ambroise Paré and Dominique Larrey, Great French Military Surgeons of the 16th and 19th Centuries," *Bulletin of the History of Medicine* 46 (1972), 207-34.

Leonardo, Richard A. *History of Surgery.* New York, 1943.

Lutz, Frank J. "*Das Buch der Buendth-Erztnei* of Heinrich von Pfolsprundt, Member of the German Order," *Janus* 18 (1913), 109-19.

Malgaigne, J.F. *Histoire de la chirurgie en occident depuis le VIe jusqu'au XVIe siècle*. Paris, 1840.

McVaugh, Michael R. "Arnald of Villanova's Regimen Almarie (Regimen castra sequentium) and Medieval Military Medicine," *Viator* 23 (1992), 201-13.

Nicolle, David C. "Wounds, Military Surgery and the Reality of Crusading Warfare: The Evidence of Usamah's Memoires," *Journal of Oriental and African Studies* 5 (1993), 33-46.

Power, D'Arcy. "English Medicine and Surgery in the Fourteenth Century." In: *Selected Writings, 1877-1930*. Oxford, 1931, pp. 29-47.

Quasigroch, Günter. "Die Handprothesen des fränkischen Reichsritters Götz von Berlichingen: Der Landshuter Unfall," *Waffen- und Kostümkunde* 22 (1980), 108-12; 24 (1982), 17-33.

Sigal, Pierre-André. "Les coups et blessures reçus par le combattant à cheval en occident aux XIIe et XIIIe siècles." In: *Le combattant au moyen âge*. 2nd ed. Histoire ancienne et médiévale, 36. Paris: Publications of the Sorbonne, 1990, pp. 171-83.

Stewart, David. "Causes of Disease in the Sixteenth-Century Army," *Journal of the Royal Army Medical Corps* 92 (1949), 35-41.

Stewart, David. "Disposal of the Sick and Wounded of the English Army during the Sixteenth Century," *Journal of the Royal Army Medical Corps* 90 (1948), 30-38.

Stewart, David. "The English Army Surgeon in the Sixteenth Century," *Journal of the Royal Army Medical Corps* 88 (1947), 231-47.

Stewart, David. "Military Surgery in the Sixteenth Century," *Journal of the Royal Army Medical Corps* 92 (1949), 229-37.

Stewart, David. "Sickness and Mortality Rates of the English Army in the Sixteenth Century," *Journal of the Royal Army Medical Corps* 91 (1948), 23-35.

Talbot, Charles H. *Medicine in Medieval England*. London, 1967.

Trueta, J. *The Principles and Practice of War Surgery*. London, 1943.

Watt, James. "Surgeons of the *Mary Rose*: The Practice of Surgery in Tudor England," *Mariner's Mirror* 69 (1983), 3-17.

Webb, Henry J. "English Military Surgery during the Age of Elizabeth," *Bulletin of the History of Medicine* 15 (1944), 261-75.

Wenham, S.J. "Anatomical Interpretations of Anglo-Saxon Weapon Injuries." In: *Weapons and Warfare in Anglo-Saxon England*. Ed. Sonia Chadwick Hawkes. Oxford, 1989, pp. 123-39.

Whipple, Allen O. *The Story of Wound Healing and Wound Repair.* Springfield, Ill., 1963.

Winters, Henri P.J. "Federico da Montefeltro, Duke of Urbino (1422-82): The Story of His Missing Nasal Bridge," *British Journal of Plastic Surgery* 35 (1982), 247-50.

Medieval – Switzerland

Brady, Thomas A., Jr. *Turning Swiss: Cities and Empire, 1450-1550.* Cambridge: Cambridge University Press, 1985.

Deutsch, K.W. and H. Weillenmann. "Die militärische Bewährung eines sozialen Systems: die Schweizer Eidgenossenschaft im 14. Jahrhundert," *Kölner Zeitschrift für Soziologie und Sozialpsychologie.* Sonderheft 12: *Beiträge zur Militärsoziologie.* Cologne, 1968, pp. 38-58.

Elgger, C. von. *Kriegswesen und Kriegskunst der schweizerischen Eidgenossen im 14, 15, und 16 Jahrhundert.* Lucerne, 1873.

Meyer, Bruno. "Die Schlacht am Mortgarten: Verlauf der Schlacht und Absichten der Parteien," *Revue Suisse d'histoire* 16 (1966), 129-79.

Miller, Douglas. *The Swiss at War, 1300-1500.* Men-at-Arms Series. London: Osprey Publishing, 1979.

Müller, Philipp. "Mortgarten: Ein Beitrag zur Waffentechnik." In: *Mitteilungen des historischen Vereins des Kantons Schwyz* 88 (1996), 23-40.

Padrutt, C. *Staat und Krieg im alten Bünden: Studien zur Beziehung zwischen Obrigkeit und Kriegertum in den drei Bünden, vornehmlich im 15. Und 16. Jahrhundert.* Zurich, 1965.

Roulet, Louis-Edouard. "Des Préalpes à l'Europe: le combattant suisse à la fin du moyen âge." In: *XXII. Kongreß der Internationalen Kommission für Militärgeschichte* Acta 22: *Von Crécy bis Mohács Kriegswesen im späten Mittelalter (1346-1526)*. Vienna, 1997, pp. 121-31.

Roulet, Louis-Edouard. "Le Téméraire à Morat: plaidoyer pour une réhabilitation." *Publication du centre Européen d'études Bourguignonnes (XIVe-XVIe s.)* 26 (1986), 39-56.

Sablonier, Roger. "État et structures militaires dans la Confédération autour des années 1480." In: *Cinq-centième anniversaire de la bataille de Nancy (1477): Actes du Colloque organisé par l'institut de recherche régionale en sciences sociales, humaines et économiques de l'Université de Nancy II (Nancy, 22-24 septembre 1977)*. Nancy, 1979, pp. 429-77.

Schaufelberger, W. *Der Alte Schweizer und sein Krieg: Studien zur Kriegsführung vornehmlich im 15. Jahrhundert*. 2nd ed. Zurich, 1966.

Schaufelberger, W. "Zu einer Charakterologie des altschweizerischen Kriegertums," *Schweizerisches Archiv für Volkskunde* 56 (1960), 48-87.

Schaufelberger, W. "Zum Problem der militärischen Integration in der spätmittelalterlichen Eidgenossenschaft," *Allgemeine schweizerische Militärschrift* 136 (1970), 313-28.

Schnitzer, M. *Die Mortgartenschlacht in werdenden schweizerischen National-Bewusstsein*. Zurich, 1969.

Sennhause, A. *Hauptmann und Führung im Schweizer Krieg des Mittelalters*. Bern, 1965.

Stürler, M. von. *Der Laupenkrieg, 1339 und 1340: Kritische Beleuchtung der Tradition als Beitrag zur Läuterung der ältern Bernergeschichte*. Bern: Stämpfli'sche Buchdruckerei, 1890.

Vallière, P.E. de. *Morat: Le siège et la bataille, 1476*. Lausanne: Éditions Spes, 1926.

Widmer, Berthe. "Die Schlacht bei Sempach in der Kirchengeschichte," *Revue Suiss d'histoire* 16 (1966), 180-205.

Winkler, Albert Lynn. *The Swiss at War: The Impact of Society on the Swiss Military in the Fourteenth and FifteenthCenturies.* Unpublished dissertation. Provo: Brigham Young University, 1982.

Medieval – Vikings

Albrethsen, Svend E. "Logistical Problems in Iron Age Warfare." In: *Military Aspects of Scandinavian Society in a European Perspective, AD. 1-1300.* Ed. A.N. Jørgensen and B. Clausen. Copenhagen, 1997, pp. 210-19.

Ambrosiani, Björn. "Birka: Its Waterways and Hinterland." In: *Aspects of Maritime Scandinavia, AD 200-1200: Proceedings of the Nordic Seminar on Maritime Aspects of Archaeology, Roskilde, 13th-15th March, 1989.* Ed. Ole Crumlin-Pedersen. Roskilde: The Viking Ship Museum, 1991, pp. 99-104.

Ambrosiani, Björn. *Birka on the Island of Björkö.* Trans. Helen Clarke. Stockholm: Cultural Monuments in Sweden, 1991.

Andersen, Per Sveaas. "Harald Hardråde, Danmark og England." In: *Harald Hardråde.* Ed. A. Berg. Oslo, 1966, pp. 95-126.

Andersen, Per Sveaas. *Samlingen av Norge og kristningen av landet, 800-1300.* Handbok I Norges historie, 2. Bergen, 1977.

Andersen, Steen Wulff. *The Viking Fortress of Trelleborg.* Trans. Joan F. Davidson. Slagelse: Museet ved Trelleborg, 1996.

Andersson, Theodore M. "The Viking Policy of Ethelred the Unready," *Scandinavian Studies* 59 (1987), 284-95.

Benedikz, B.S. "The Evolution of the Varangian Regiment in the Byzantine Army," *Byzantinische Zeitschrift* 62 (1969), 20-25.

Berg, Arno, ed. *Harald Hardråde.* Oslo: Dreyer, 1966.

Bersu, G. "Three Viking Graves in the Isle of Man," *Journal of the Manx Museum* 6 (1957), 15-18.

Bersu, G. and David Wilson. *Three Viking Graves in the Isle of Man.* London, 1966.

Biddle, Martin and Birth Kjølbye-Biddle. "Repton and the Vikings," *Antiquity* 66 (1992), 36-51.

Biddle, Martin and Birth Kjølbye-Biddle. "The Repton Stone," *Anglo-Saxon England* 14 (1985), 233-92.

Binns, Alan. "Towards a North Sea Kingdom? Viking Age Incursions and Later Attempts to Establish Scandinavian Rule 'West over the Sea'." In: *The North Sea: A Highway of Economic and Cultural Exchange; Character–History*. Ed. Arne Bang-Andersen, Basil Greenhill, and Egil Harald Grude. Stavanger, 1985, pp. 49-62.

Blöndel, Sigfús. *The Varangians of Byzantium*. Trans. B.S. Benedikz. Cambridge, 1978.

Brønsted, Johannes. *The Vikings*. Trans. K. Skov. Harmondsworth: Penguin Books, 1965.

Brown, Phyllis R. "The Viking Policy of Ethelred: A Response," *Scandinavian Studies* 59 (1987), 296-98.

Bugge, Alexander. "The Norse Settlements in the British Islands," *Transactions of the Royal Historical Society*, 4th ser., 4 (1921), 173-210.

Bull, Edv. *Leding: Militær- og finansforfatning i norge i ældre tid*. Christiana (Oslo) and Copenhagen, 1920.

Byock, Jesse. *Feud in Icelandic Saga*. Berkeley and Los Angeles: University of California Press, 1983.

Cassard, Jean-Christophe. *Le siècle des Vikings en Bretagne*. Paris: J.-P. Gisserot, 1996.

Christiansen, Eric. "Canute and His World," *History Today* 36 (Oct 1986), 34-39.

Clapham, J.H. "The Horsing of the Danes," *English Historical Review* 25 (1910), 287-93.

Clark, Philip. *Weapons and Warfare in the Viking Age*. Stroud: Tempus, 1999.

Clarke, Howard B. "The Bloodied Eagle: The Vikings and the Development of Dublin, 841-1014," *Irish Sword* 18 (1990-92), 91-119.

Clarke, Howard B. "The Vikings." In: *Medieval Warfare: A History*. Ed. Maurice Keen. Oxford: Oxford University Press, 1999, pp. 36-58.

Cohen, Marc. "From Throndheim to Waltham to Chester: Viking- and Post-Viking-Age Attitudes in the Survival Legends of Óláfr Tryggvason and Harold Godwinson." In: *The Middle Ages in the North-West*. Ed. Tom Scott and Pat Starkey. Liverpool: Leopard's Head Press, 1995, pp. 143-54.

Coupland, Simon. "The Frankish Tribute Payments to the Vikings and their Consequences," *Francia* 26/1 (1999), 57-75.

Coupland, Simon. "The Rod of God's Wrath or the People of God's Wrath? The Carolingian Theology of the Viking Invasions," *Journal of Ecclesiastical History* 42 (1991), 535-54.

Coupland, Simon and Janet L. Nelson. "The Vikings on the Continent," *History Today* 38 (Dec 1988), 12-19.

Crawford, Iain A. "War or Peace–Viking Colonisation in the Northern and Western Isles of Scotland Reviewed." In: *Proceedings of the Eighth Viking Congress*. Ed. H. Bekker-Nielsen et al. Odense, 1981, pp. 259-69.

Davidson, Hilda R. Ellis. *The Viking Road to Byzantium*. London, 1976.

D'Haenens, Albert. "Les invasions normandes dans l'empire franc au IXe siècle." In: *I Normanni e la loro espansione in Europa nell'alto Medioevo*. Spoleto, 1969, pp. 233-98.

D'Haenens, Albert. *Les invasions normandes, une catastrophe?* Paris: Flammarion, 1970.

Dhondt, J. "La destruction de Valenciennces par les Normands," *Revue historique* 193 (1942-43), 19-21.

Engström, Johan. "The Vendel Chieftains: A Study of Military Tactics." In: *Military Aspects of Scandinavian Society in a European Perspective, AD. 1-1300*. Ed. A.N. Jørgensen and B. Clausen. Copenhagen, 1997, pp. 248-55.

Fell, Clare. "A Viking Spearhead from Kentmere," *Transactions of the Cumberland and Westmorland Antiquarian and Archaeological Society* 56 (1957), 67-69.

Foot, Sarah. "Violence against Christians? The Vikings and the Church in Ninth-Century England," *Medieval History* 1.3 (1991), 3-16.

Foote, Peter G. and David M. Wilson. *The Viking Achievement*. London: Sidgwick and Jackson, 1970.

Frank, Roberta. "Viking Atrocity and Skaldic Verse: The Rite of the Blood-Eagle," *English Historical Review* 99 (1984), 332-43.

Gade, Kari Ellen. "Einarr Þambarskelfir's Last Shot," *Scandinavian Studies* 67 (1995), 153-62.

Garner, H.W. "The Danes on the Rame Peninsula," *Devon and Cornwall Notes and Queries* 38 (1998), 76-83.

Gillmor, Caroll. "War on the Rivers: Viking Numbers and Mobility on the Seine and Loire, 841-886," *Viator* 19 (1988), 79-109.

Graham-Campbell, James. *Cultural Atlas of the Viking World*. Abingdon, 1984; trans. *Atlas du monde viking*. Trans. Isabelle Delvallée. Paris: Ed. du Fanal, 1994.

Graham-Campbell, James. "The Irish Sea Vikings: Raiders and Settlers." In: *The Middle Ages in the North-West*. Ed. Tom Scott and Pat Starkey. Liverpool: Leopard's Head Press, 1995, pp. 59-84.

Graham-Campbell, James. "The Scandinavian Impact: Pagans and Christians," *History Today* 36 (Oct 1986), 24-28.

Graham-Campbell, James and Dafydd Kidd. *The Vikings*. London: The British Museum, 1980.

Griffith, Paddy. *The Viking Art of War*. London: Greenhill Books, 1995.

Hall, Richard. "The Scandinavian Impact: The Vikings as Town Dwellers," *History Today* 36 (Oct 1986), 29-34.

Hanawalt, Emily Albu. "Scandinavians in Byzantium and Normandy." In: *Peace and War in Byzantium. Essays in Honor of George T. Dennis, S.J.* Ed. T.S. Miller and J. Nesbitt. Washington, 1995, pp. 114-22.

Hasse, G. "Les Vikings en Belgique," *Revue Belge d'archéologie et d'histoire de l'art* 5 (1935), 199-210.

Haugen, Einar. "Was Vinland in Newfoundland?" In: *Proceedings of the Eighth Viking Congress*. Ed. H. Bekker-Nielsen et al. Odense, 1981, pp. 3-8.

Haywood, John. *The Penguin Atlas of the Vikings*. Harmondsworth: Penguin, 1995.

Heath, Ian. *The Vikings*. London: Osprey Publishing, 1985.

Hødnebø, Finn. "Who Were the First Vikings? In: *Proceedings of the Tenth Viking Congress*. Ed. J.E. Knirk. Oslo, 1987, pp. 43-54.

Holm, Poul. "Between Apathy and Antipathy: The Vikings in Irish and Scandinavian History," *Peritia* 8 (1994), 151-69.

Hvass, Steen. "Jelling from Iron Age to Viking Age." In: *People and Places in Northern Europe, 500-1600: Essays in Honour of Peter Hayes Sawyer*. Ed. I. Wood and N. Lund. Woodbridge, 1991, pp. 149-60.

Hyenstrand, Ake. "Iconography and Rune Stones: The Example of Sparlösa." In: *People and Places in Northern Europe, 500-1600: Essays in Honour of Peter Hayes Sawyer*. Ed. I. Wood and N. Lund. Woodbridge, 1991, pp. 205-09.

Jones, Gwyn. *A History of the Vikings*. Oxford: Oxford University Press, 1968.

Jørgensen, Anne Nørgård. "Sea Defence in Denmark, AD 200-1300." In: *Military Aspects of Scandinavian Society in a European Perspective, AD. 1-1300*. Ed. A.N. Jørgensen and B. Clausen. Copenhagen, 1997, pp. 200-09.

Kendrick, T.D. *A History of the Vikings*. New York, 1930.

Kendrick, T.D. "A Viking Figure-head from the Scheldt," *British Museum Quarterly* 12 (1938), 73-74.

Kazakevičius, Vytautas. "Some Debatable Questions Concerning the Armament of the Viking Period in Lithuania," *Fasciculi archaeologiae historicae* 7 (1994), 37-44.

Kirpičnikov, Anatolij N. "Russisk-Skandinaviske forbindelser i IX-XI århundrede illustreret ved våbenfund," *Kuml* (1969), 165-89.

Laursen, Jesper. *On the Track of the Vikings in Denmark: Museums and Monuments: An Introduction*. Copenhagen, n.d.

Lifshitz, Felice. "La Normandie carolingienne: essai sur la continuité, avec utilisation de sources négligées," *Annales de Normandie* 48 (1998), 505-24.

Logan, F. Donald. *The Vikings in History*. 2nd ed. London: Harper Collins Academic, 1991.

Loyn, Henry R. *The Vikings in Britain*. Oxford: Blackwell Publishers, 1994.

Lucas, A.T. "Irish-Norse Relations: Time for a Reappraisal?" *Journal of the Cork Historical and Archaeological Society* 71 (1966), 62-75.

Lund, Niels. "Allies of God or Man? The Viking Expansion in a Human Perspective," *Viator* 20 (1989), 45-59.

Lund, Niels. "The Armies of Swein Forkbeard and Cnut: *Leding* or *Lið*?" *Anglo-Saxon England* 15 (1986), 105-18.

Lund, Niels. "Danish Military Organisation." In: *The Battle of Maldon: Fiction and Fact*. Ed. J. Cooper. London, 1993, pp. 109-26.

Lund, Niels. "The Danish Perspective." In: *The Battle of Maldon, AD 991*. Ed. D. Scragg. London, 1991, pp. 114-42.

Lund, Niels. *De Danske vikinger i England*. Copenhagen, 1967.

Lund, Niels. *De Hærger og de brænder: Danmark og England i vikingtiden*. Copenhagen, 1993.

Lund, Niels. "If the Vikings Knew a *Leding*–What Was It Like?" In: *The Twelfth Viking Congress: Developments Around the Baltic and the North Sea in the Viking Age*. Ed. B. Ambrosiani and H. Clark. Stockholm, 1994, pp.100-05.

Lund, Niels. "Is Leidang a Nordic or a European Phenomenon?" In: *Military Aspects of Scandinavian Society in a European Perspective, AD. 1-1300*. Ed. A.N. Jørgensen and B. Clausen. Copenhagen, 1997, pp. 195-99.

Lund, Niels. *Lið, leding og landeværn*. Roskilde, 1996.

Lund, Niels. "Peace and Non-Peace in the Viking Age–Ottar in Biarma-land, the Rus in Byzantium, and Danes and Norwegians in England." In: *Proceedings of the Tenth Viking Congress*. Ed. J.E. Knirk. Oslo, 1987, pp. 255-69.

Malmros, Rikke. "Leding og Skjaldekvad: Det elvte århundredes nordiske krigsflå der, deres teknologi og organisation og deres placering I samfun-det, belyst gennem den samtidige fyrstedigtning," *Aarbøger for nordisk oldkyndigheid og historie* (1985), 89-139.

Malmros, Rikke. "Leiðangr." In *Medieval Scandinavia: An Encyclopedia*. Ed. P. Pulsiano. New York, 1993, pp. 389-90.

Martens, Irmelin. "Norwegian Viking Age Weapons: Some Questions Concerning their Production and Distribution." In: *The Twelfth Viking Congress: Developments Around the Baltic and the North Sea in the Viking Age*. Ed. B. Ambrosiani and H. Clark. Stockholm, 1994, pp. 180-82.

Marwick, H. "Naval Defence in Norse Scotland," *Scottish Historical Review* 28 (1949), 1-11.

Maund, K.L. "'A Turmoil of Warring Princes': Political Leadership in Ninth-century Denmark," *Haskins Society Journal* 6 (1994), 29-47.

McBarron, H.C. and H.L. Peterson. "Viking Warriors circa 1000," *Journal of the Company of Military Collectors and Historians*. 10.3 (Fall 1958), 77-79.

McDougall, Ian. "Discretion and Deceit: A Re-Examination of a Military Strategem in *Egil's Saga*." In: *The Middle Ages in the North-West*. Ed. Tom Scott and Pat Starkey. Liverpool: Leopard's Head Press, 1995, pp. 109-42.

McDougall, Ian. "Serious Entertainments: An Examination of a Peculiar Type of Viking Atrocity," *Anglo-Saxon England* 22 (1993), 201-25.

Morris, Christopher D. "Viking and Native in Northern England." In: *Proceedings of the Eighth Viking Congress*. Ed. H. Bekker-Nielsen et al. Odense, 1981, pp. 223-42.

Munksgaard, E. "A Viking Smith, His Tools and Stock in Trade," *Offa* 41 (1984), 85-89.

Musset, L. *Les invasions: le second assaut contre l'Europe chrétienne (VIe-IXe siècle)*. 2nd ed. Paris, 1971.

Musset, L. "Problèmes militaires du monde scandinave (VIIe-XIIe siècle)." In: *Ordinamenti militari in occidente nell'alto medioevo*. Settimane di studio del centro italiano di studi sull'alto medioevo, XV. Spoleto, 1968, I:229-91.

Nordhagen, Jonas. "Harald og Bysants." In *Harald Hardråde*. Ed. A. Berg. Oslo, 1966, pp. 7-27.

Nørgaard, F., E. Rosedahl, and P. Skovmand, ed. *Aggersborg gennem 1000 år*. Herning, 1986.

Nørlund, Poul. "Quelques remarques sur l'organisation militaire des Vikings," *Revue internationale d'histoire militaire* 16 (1955), 478-85.

Nørlund, Poul. *Trelleborg*. Copenhagen, 1948.

Nørlund, Poul. *Trelleborg*. Nationalmuseets Blå Bøger. Copenhagen: Nationalmuseet, 1968.

Norman, Peter. "Maritime Monuments from the Viking Period and Early Middle Ages in the Kalmarsund Area." In: *Aspects of Maritime Scandinavia, AD 200-1200: Proceedings of the Nordic Seminar on Maritime Aspects of Archaeology, Roskilde, 13th-15th March, 1989*. Ed. Ole Crumlin-Pedersen. Roskilde: The Viking Ship Museum, 1991, pp. 121-30.

Olsen, Olaf. *Fyrkat: The Viking Camp Near Hobro*. The Danish National Museum. 2nd ed. Copenhagen: The National Museum, 1975.

Olsen, Olaf. "The Geometric Viking Fortress," *Château Gaillard* 4 (1969), 185-90.

Olsen, Olaf, Else Rosedahl, and H. Schmidt. *Fyrkat: En jysk vikingborg*. 2 vols. Copenhagen, 1977.

Pedersen, Anne. "Weapons and Riding Gear in Burials–Evidence of Military and Social Rank in 10th Century Denmark?" In: *Military Aspects of Scandinavian Society in a European Perspective, AD. 1-1300*. Ed. A.N. Jørgensen and B. Clausen. Copenhagen, 1997, pp. 123-36.

Poertner, Rudolf. *The Vikings: Rise and Fall of the Norse Sea Kings*. London, 1975.

Poole, R.G. *Viking Poems on War and Peace: A Study in Skaldic Narrative*. Toronto: University of Toronto Press, 1991.

Price, Neil S. "Viking Armies and Fleets in Brittany: A Case Study for Some General Problems," *Vikingsymposium* 10 (1991), 7-24.

Randsborg, Klavs. *The Viking Age in Denmark: The Formation of a State*. London, 1980.

Randsborg, Klavs. "Viking Raiders: The Transformation of Scandinavian Society." In: *Medieval Archaeology: Papers of the Seventeenth Annual Conference of the Center for Medieval and Early Renaissance Studies*. Ed. C.L. Redman. Binghamton, 1989, pp. 23-39.

Richards, Julian D. *English Heritage Book of Viking Age England*. London: BCA, 1991.

Rieck, Flemming and Erik Jørgensen. "Non-military Equipment from Nydam." In: *Military Aspects of Scandinavian Society in a European Perspective, AD. 1-1300*. Ed. A.N. Jørgensen and B. Clausen. Copenhagen, 1997, pp. 220-25.

Roesdahl, Else. "Aggersborg: The Viking Settlement and Fortress," *Château Gaillard* 8 (1977), 269-78.

Roesdahl, Else. "Aggersborg in the Viking Age." In: *Proceedings of the Eighth Viking Congress*. Ed. H. Bekker-Nielsen et al. Odense, 1981, pp. 107-22.

Roesdahl, Else. "The Building Activities of King Harold Bluetooth: Notes of the Dendro-chronological Dating of the Viking Fortress of Trelleborg," *Château Gaillard* 9-10 (1982), 543-46.

Roesdahl, Else. "The Danish Geometrical Viking Fortresses and their Context," *Anglo-Norman Studies* 9 (1986), 209-26.

Roesdahl, Else. *Viking Age Denmark*. Trans. S. Margeson and K. Williams. London, 1982.

Roesdahl, Else. "The Viking Fortress of Fyrkat in the Light of the Object Found," *Château Gaillard* 6 (1973), 195-202.

Roesdahl, Else. *The Vikings*. Trans. S.M. Margeson and K. Williams. Harmondsworth:Penguin Books, 1992.

Rouche, Michel. "The Vikings Versus the Towns of Northern Gaul: Challenge and Response." In: *Medieval Archaeology: Papers of the Seventeenth Annual Conference of the Center for Medieval and Early Renaissance Studies*. Ed. C.L. Redman. Binghamton, 1989, pp. 41-56.

Ryan, John. "The Battle of Clontarf," *Journal of the Royal Society of Antiquaries of Ireland* 68 (1938), 1-50.

Rynne, Etienne. "The Impact of the Vikings on Irish Weapons." In: *Atti del congresso internazionale delle scienze preistoriche e protoistoriche*. Rome, III:181-84.

Sawyer, Birgit. "Women as Bridge-Builders: The Role of Women in Viking-Age Scandinavia." In: *People and Places in Northern Europe, 500-1600: Essays in Honour of Peter Hayes Sawyer*. Ed. I. Wood and N. Lund. Woodbridge, 1991, pp. 211-24.

Sawyer, Birgit and Peter Sawyer. *Medieval Scandinavia: From Conversion to Reformation, circa 800-1500*. Minneapolis: University of Minnesota Press, 1993.

Sawyer, Peter. *The Age of the Vikings*. London: Edward Arnold, 1962.

Sawyer, Peter. "Conquest and Colonization: Scandinavians in the Danelaw and in Normandy." In: *Proceedings of the Eighth Viking Congress*. Ed. H. Bekker-Nielsen et al. Odense, 1981, pp. 123-31.

Sawyer, Peter. "Ethelred II, Olaf Tryggvason, and the Conversion of Norway," *Scandinavian Studies* 59 (1987), 299-307.

Sawyer, Peter. *Kings and Vikings: Scandinavia and Europe, AD 700-1100*. London: Methuen, 1982.

Sawyer, Peter. *Scandinavians and the English in the Viking Age*. H.M. Chadwick Memorial Lecture, 5. Cambridge, 1995.

Sawyer, Peter. "Wics, Kings and Vikings." In: *The Vikings*. Ed. T. Andersson and K.I. Sandred. Stockholm, 1978.

Seaby, W.A. and P. Woodfield. "Viking Stirrups from England and their Background," *Medieval Archaeology* 24 (1980), 87-122.

Searle, Eleanor. "Frankish Rivalries and Norse Warriors," *Anglo-Norman Studies* 8 (1985), 198-213.

Shadrake, Dan and Susanna Shadrake. *Barbarian Warriors: Saxons, Vikings and Normans*. Brassey's History of Uniforms. London, 1997.

Skaare, Kolbjørn. "Harald Hardråde som myntherre." In *Harald Hardråde*. Ed. A. Berg et al. Oslo, 1966, pp. 41-67.

Skovgaard-Petersen, Inge. "Vikingerne I den nyere forskning," *Historisk tidsskrift* (Copenhagen) (12) 5 (1971), 651-721.

Stafford, Pauline. "The Scandinavian Impact: The Danes and the 'Danelaw,'" *History Today* 36 (Oct 1986), 17-23.

Steinnes, A. "Kor gamal er den norsk leidangsskipnaden?" *Syn of segn* (1929), 49-65.

Turville-Petre, Gabriel. *Haraldr the Hardruler and His Poets*. Dorothea Coke Memorial Lecture in Northern Studies. London, 1966.

Vander Linden, H. "Les Normands à Louvain (884-892)," *Revue historique* 124 (1917), 64-81.

Vercauteren, Fernand. "Comment s'est-on défendu, au IXe siècle dans l'empire franc contre les invasions normandes?" In: *Annales du XXXe Congrès de la Féderation archéologique et historique de Belgique*. Brussels, 1936, pp. 117-32.

Wallace, Birgitta Linderoth. "L'anse aux meadows: Gateway to Vinland," *Acta archaeologia* 61 (1990), 166-97.

Wallace-Hadrill, J.M. "The Vikings in Francia." In: *Early Medieval History*. Oxford, 1975, pp. 217-36.

Wheeler, M. *London and the Vikings*. London, 1927.

Williams, Ann. "The Vikings in Essex, 871-917," *Essex Archaeology and History* 27 (1996), 92-101.

Wilson, David M. *Civil and Military Engineering in Viking Age Scandinavia*. London, 1978.

Wilson, David M. "An Early Viking Age Grave from Källby, Lund," *Meddelanden från Lunds Universitets Historiska Museum* (1955), 105-26.

Wilson, David M. *The Vikings and their Origins: Scandinavia in the First Millennium*. London: Thames and Hudson, 1970.

Wise, Terence. *Saxon, Viking and Norman Armies*. London: Osprey, 1979.

Woolf, Alex. "Erik Bloodaxe Revisited," *Northern History* 34 (1998), 189-93.

Wyatt, David. "Gruffudd ap Cynan and the Hiberno-Norse World," *Welsh Historical Review* 19 (1999), 595-615.

Zettel, Horst. *Das Bild der Normannen und der Normanneneinfälle in westfränkischen, östfränkischen und angelsächsischen Quellen des 8. bis 11. Jahrhunderts*. Munich, 1977.

Medieval – Women

Adams, D. "Why There Are So Few Women Warriors," *Behavior Science Research* 18 (1983), 196-212.

Damsholt, Nanna. "War, Women, and Love." In: *War and Peace in the Middle Ages*. Ed. B.P. McGuire. Copenhagen, 1987, pp. 56-66.

Dennis, George T. "Woman Repels Pirates: Note in a Florentine Manuscript," *Byzantine and Modern Greek Studies* 23 (1999), 256-57.

De Pauw, Linda Grant. *Battle Cries and Lullabies: Women in War from Prehistory to the Present*. Norman: University of Oklahoma Press, 1998.

Dufresne, Laura Rinaldi. "Women Warriors: A Special Case from the Fifteenth Century: *The City of Ladies*," *Women's Studies* 23 (1994), 111-31.

Forey, Alan J. "Women and the Military Orders in the Twelfth and Thirteenth Centuries," *Studia monastica* 29 (1987), 63-72.

Hale, John R. "Women and War in the Visual Arts of the Renaissance." In: *War, Literature and the Arts in Sixteenth-Century Europe*. Ed. J.R. Mulryne and M. Shewring. New York, 1989, pp. 43-62.

Mazeika, Rasa. "'Nowhere was the Fragility of their Sex Apparent': Women Warriors in the Baltic Crusade Chronicles." In: *From Clermont to Jerusalem: The Crusades and Crusader Societies, 1095-1500*. Selected Proceedings of the International Medieval Congress, University of Leeds,

10-13 July 1995. Ed. Alan V. Murray. Turnhout: Brepols, 1998, pp. 229-48.

McLaughlin, Megan. "The Woman Warrior: Gender, Warfare and Society in Medieval Europe," *Women's Studies* 17 (1990), 193-209.

Powell, James M. "The Role of Women in the Fifth Crusade." In: *The Horns of Hattin*. Ed. B.Z. Kedar. Jerusalem, 1992, pp. 294-301.

Solterer, Helen. "Figures of Female Militancy in Medieval France," *Signs* 16 (1991), 522-49.

Truax, Jean A. "Anglo-Norman Women at War: Valiant Soldiers, Prudent Strategists or Charismatic Leaders?" In: *The Circle of War in the Middle Ages: Essays on Medieval Military and Naval History*. Ed. Donald J. Kagay and L.J. Andrew Villalon. Woodbridge: The Boydell Press, 1999, pp. 111-26.

Verbruggen, J.F. "Vrouwen in de eerste kruistocht en in de helden-liederen," *Revue Belge d'histoire militaire* 25 (1983), 181-90.

Verbruggen, J.F. "Vrouwen in de middeleeuwse legers," *Revue Belge d'histoire militaire* 24 (1982), 617-34.

Verrier, Frédérique. "Viragoes et gestes féminines dans la littérature italienne du XVIe siècle." In: *La guerre, la violence et les gens au Moyen Âge*. II: *Guerre et gens*. Ed. P. Contamine and O. Guyotjeannin. 119e congrès national des sociétés historiques et scientifiques, Amiens, octobre 1994, Section d'histoire médiévale et philologie. Paris, 1996, pp. 35-46.

Vones-Liebenstein, Ursula. "Une femme gardienne du royaume? Régentes en temps de guerre (France-Castile, XIIIe siècle)." In: *La guerre, la violence et les gens au Moyen Âge*. II: *Guerre et gens*. Ed. P. Contamine and O. Guyotjeannin. 119e congrès national des sociétés historiques et scientifiques, Amiens, octobre 1994, Section d'histoire médiévale et philologie. Paris, 1996, pp. 9-22.

Renaissance

Greene, Thomas. "Renaissance Warfare: A Metaphor in Conflict." In: *The Holy War*. Ed. T.P. Murphy. Columbus, 1976, pp. 157-80.

Hale, John R. *Artists and Warfare in the Renaissance*. New Haven: Yale University Press, 1990.

Hale, John R. "Soldiers in the Religious Art of the Renaissance," *Bulletin of the John Rylands Library* 69 (1987), 166-94.

Murrin, Michael. *History and Warfare in Renaissance Epic*. Chicago: The University of Chicago Press, 1994.

Schnitter, Helmut. "Zu einigen Aspekten der Kriegstechnik und der Kriegskunst in der Renaissance," *Militärgeschichte* 14 (1975), 401-10.

Medieval/Early Modern – Ottoman Turkish Wars (also Hungary)

Ágostan, Gábor. "Az európai hadügyi forradalom és az oszmánok," *Törénelmi Szemle* 37 (1995).

Ágostan, Gábor. "Gunpowder for the Sultan's Army: New Sources on the Supply of Gunpowder to the Ottoman Army in the Hungarian Campaigns of the Sixteenth and Seventeenth Centuries," *Turcica* 25 (1993), 75-96.

Ágostan, Gábor. "Karamania, The Anti-Ottoman Christian Diplomacy and the Non-Existing Hungarian-Karamanid Diplomatic Relations of 1428," *Acta orientalia academiae scientarum Hungaricarum* 48 (1995), 267-74.

Ágostan, Gábor. "Ottoman Artillery and European Military Technology in the Fifteenth and Seventeenth Centuries," *Acta orientalia academiae scientarum Hungaricarum* 47 (1994), 15-48.

Ágostan, Gábor. "Ottoman Gunpowder Production in Hungary in the Sixteenth Century: The *Baruthane* of Buda." In: *Hungarian-Ottoman Military and Diplomatic Relations in the Age of Süleyman the Magnificent*. Ed. G. Dávid and P. Fodor. Budapest, 1994, pp. 149-59.

Ágostan, Gábor. "Ottoman Warfare in Europe, 1453-1826." In: *European Warfare, 1453-1815*. Ed. Jeremy Black. New York: St. Martin's Press, 1999, pp. 118-44.

Ágostan, Gábor. "Párhuzamok és eltérések az oszmán és az európai tüzérség fejlödésében a 15-16 században," *Történelmi szemle* 34.3-4 (1992), 173-98.

Askan, Virginia H. "Locating the Ottomans Among Early Modern Empires," *Journal of Early Modern History* 3 (1999), 103-34.

Askan, Virginia H. "Ottoman War and Warfare 1453-1812." In: *War in the Early Modern World, 1450-1815*. Ed. Jeremy Black. London, 1999, pp. 147-76.

Alföldi, Lászlo M. "The Battle of Mohács, 1526." In: *From Hunyadi to Rákóczi: War and Society in Late Medieval and Early Modern Hungary*. War and Society in Eastern Central Europe, vol. III. Ed. J.M. Bak and B.K. Király. New York: 1982, pp. 189-202.

Babinger, Franz. *Mehmed the Conqueror and His Time*. Trans. Ralph Manheim. Ed. William C. Hickman. Bollingen Series, 96. Princeton: Princeton University Press, 1978.

Bain, R.N. "The Siege of Belgrade by Muhammed II, July 1-23, 1456," *English Historical Review* 7 (1892), 235-42.

Bak, János M. "Politics, Society and Defense in Medieval and Early Modern Hungary." In: *From Hunyadi to Rákóczi: War and Society in Late Medieval and Early Modern Hungary*. War and Society in Eastern Central Europe, vol. III. Ed. J.M. Bak and B.K. Király. New York: 1982, pp. 1-22.

Bak, János M. "The Price of War and Peace in Late Medieval Hungary." In: *War and Peace in the Middle Ages*. Ed. B.P. McGuire. Copenhagen, 1987, pp. 161-78.

Barker, John W. "The Question of Ethnic Antagonisms among Balkan States of the Fourteenth Century. In: *Peace and War in Byzantium. Essays in Honor of George T. Dennis, S.J.* Ed. T.S. Miller and J. Nesbitt. Washington, 1995, pp. 165-77.

Barker, Thomas M. "New Perspectives on the Historical Significance of the Year of the Turk," *Austrian History Yearbook* 19-20 (1983-84), 3-14.

Barta, Gábor. "A Forgotten Theater of War 1526-1528 (Historical Events Preceding the Ottoman-Hungarian Alliance of 1528)." In: *Hungarian-Ottoman Military and Diplomatic Relations in the Age of Süleyman the Magnificent*. Ed. G. Dávid and P. Fodor. Budapest, 1994, pp. 93-130.

Baum, Wilhelm. *Kaiser Sigismund: Hus, Konstanz und Türkenkrieg*. Graz: Styria, 1993.

Bayerle, Gustav. "One Hundred Fifty Years of Frontier Life in Hungary." In: *From Hunyadi to Rákóczi: War and Society in Late Medieval and Early Modern Hungary*. War and Society in Eastern Central Europe, vol. III. Ed. J.M. Bak and B.K. Király. New York: 1982, pp. 227-42.

Beldiceanu, N. "Les Roumans à la bataille d'Ankara," *Südost-Forschungen* 14 (1955), 441-50.

Berckenhagen, Ekhart. "Lepanto 7.10.1571: Blutigster Tag globaler Marinehistorie," *Deutsches Schiffahrtsarchiv* 19 (1996), 105-39.

Betts, R.R. "Central and South-Eastern Europe." In: *The Fall of Constantinople*. London, 1955, pp. 18-24.

Bodnar, Edward W. "Ciriaco d'Ancona and the Crusade of Varna: A Closer Look," *Mediaevalia* 14 (1988), 253-79.

Borosy, András. "Peasants in Arms, 1437-1438 and 1456." In: *From Hunyadi to Rákóczi: War and Society in Late Medieval and Early Modern Hungary*. War and Society in Eastern Central Europe, vol. III. Ed. J.M. Bak and B.K. Király. New York: 1982, pp. 63-80.

Boyer, Pierre. "Armement et alliances au maghreb central dans la première moitié du XVIeme siècle." In: *Commission internationale d'histoire militaire. Acta 6: Montpeillier 2-6 IX 1981*. Montpellier: Commission Française d'Histoire Militaire, 1983, I:77-92.

Bradford, Ernle. *The Great Siege: Malta, 1565*. London: The Reprint Society, 1961.

Bradford, Ernle. *The Sword and Scimitar*. London: Victor Gollancz Ltd., 1974.

Brockman, Eric. *The Two Sieges of Rhodes: The Knights of St. John at War, 1480-1522*. New York: Barnes and Noble Press, 1969.

Brummett, Palmira. "Foreign Policy, Naval Strategy, and the Defence of the Ottoman Empire in the Early Sixteenth Century," *International History Review* 11 (1989), 613-27.

Brummett, Palmira. "The Myth of Shah Ismail Safavi: Political Rhetoric and 'Divine' Kingship." In: *Medieval Christian Perceptions of Islam*. Hamden, 1996, pp. 331-59.

Butler, Lionel. *The Siege of Rhodes, 1480.* Historical Pamphlets, 11. London: Order of St. John, n.d.

Caron, Marie-Thérèse. "17 février 1454: le Banquet du Voeu du Faisan, fête de cour et stratégies de pouvoir," *Revue du nord* 78 (1996), 269-88.

Creasy, E.S. *History of the Ottoman Turks.* London, 1858.

Cvetkova, B. "Analyse des principales sources Ottomanes du XVe siècle sur les campagnes de Vladislav le Varnenien et Jean Hunyadi en 1443-1444," *Studia Albanica* (1968), 137-58.

David, Géza. "Ottoman Administrative Strategies in Western Hungary." In: *Studies in Ottoman History in Honour of Professor V.L. Ménage.* Ed. C. Heywood and C. Imber. Istanbul: Isis Pressm 1994, pp. 31-43.

Dennis, George T. "The Byzantine-Turkish Treaty of 1403," *Orientalia christiana periodica* 33 (1967), 72-88.

Dennis, George T. "The Second Turkish Capture of Thessalonica, 1391, 1394 or 1430?" *Byzantinische Zeitschrift* 57 (1964), 53-61.

Dennis, George T. "Three Reports from Crete on the Situation in Romania, 1401-1402," *Studi Veneziana* 12 (1970), 243-65.

DeVries, Kelly. "The Lack of a Western European Military Response to the Ottoman Invasions of Eastern Europe from Nicopolis (1396) to Mohács (1526)," *Journal of Military History* 63 (1999), 539-59.

Dogaru, Mircea. "Les pays roumains et la bataille de Mohács." In: *XXII. Kongreß der Internationalen Kommission für Militärgeschichte* Acta 22: *Von Crécy bis Mohács Kriegswesen im späten Mittelalter (1346-1526).* Vienna, 1997, pp. 132-44.

Domonkos, Leslie S. "The Battle of Mohács as a Cultural Watershed." In: *From Hunyadi to Rákóczi: War and Society in Late Medieval and Early Modern Hungary.* War and Society in Eastern Central Europe, vol. III. Ed. J.M. Bak and B.K. Király. New York: 1982, pp. 203-26.

Durrieu, Comte L. "La délivrance de la Gréce projetée en France à la France du quinzième siècle," *Revue d'histoire diplomatique* 26 (1912), 333-51.

Ellesmere, Lord. *The Sieges of Vienna by the Turks*. London: John Murray, 1879.

Ellul, Joseph. *1585: The Great Siege of Malta*. Malta: Siggiewi, 1992.

Emecen, Feridun. "The History of an Early Sixteenth Century Migration–Sirem Exiles in Gallipoli." In: *Hungarian-Ottoman Military and Diplomatic Relations in the Age of Süleyman the Magnificent*. Ed. G. Dávid and P. Fodor. Budapest, 1994, pp. 77-91.

Engel, Pál. "János Hunyadi and the Peace 'of Szeged' (1444)," *Acta orientalia academiae scientarum Hungaricarum* 48 (1995), 241-57.

Engel, Pál. "János Hunyadi: The Decisive Years of His Career, 1440-1444." In: *From Hunyadi to Rákóczi: War and Society in Late Medieval and Early Modern Hungary*. War and Society in Eastern Central Europe, vol. III. Ed. J.M. Bak and B.K. Király. New York: 1982, pp. 103-24.

Erendil, M. "Emergence of the Ottoman State: An Outline of the Period between 1299-1453," *Revue internationale d'histoire militaire* 46 (1980), 31-60.

Evert-Kappesowa, H. "La tiare ou le turban," *Byzantinoslavica* 14 (1953), 245-57.

Fabris, Antonio. "From Adrianople to Constantinople: Venetian-Ottoman Diplomatic Missions, 1360-1453," *Mediterranean Historical Review* 7 (1992), 154-200.

Fine, John V.A., Jr. *The Late Medieval Balkans: A Critical Survey from the Late Twelfth Century to the Ottoman Conquest*. Ann Arbor: The University of Michigan Press, 1987.

Fine, John V.A., Jr. "A Tale of Three Fortresses: Controversies Surrounding the Turkish Conquest of Smederevo, of an Unnamed Fortress at the Junction of the Sava and Bosna, and of Bobovac." In: *Peace and War in Byzantium. Essays in Honor of George T. Dennis, S.J.* Ed. T.S. Miller and J. Nesbitt. Washington, 1995, pp. 181-96.

Finkel, Caroline. *The Administration of Warfare: the Ottoman Military Campaigns in Hungary, 1593-1606*. Vienna: VWGÖ, 1988.

Finkel, Caroline. "The Costs of Ottoman Warfare and Defence," *Byzantinische forschungen* 16 (1990), 91-103.

Finot, Jules. *Projet d'expédition contre les turcs préparé par les conseillers du duc de Bourgogne Philippe-le-Bon (janvier 1457)*. Lille: L. Quarré, 1890.Spain

Fischer-Galati, Stephen A. "Ottoman Imperialism and the Lutheran Struggle for Recognition in Germany, 1520-1529," *Church History* 23 (1954), 44-67.

Fodor, Pál. "Ottoman Policy Towards Hungary, 1520-1541," *Acta orientalia academiae scientarum Hungaricarum* 45 (1991), 271-345.

Fodor, Pál and Géza Dávid. "Hungarian-Ottoman Peace Negotiations in 1512-1514." In: *Hungarian-Ottoman Military and Diplomatic Relations in the Age of Süleyman the Magnificent*. Ed. G. Dávid and P. Fodor. Budapest, 1994, pp. 9-45.

Foretic, Vinko. "Turska opsada Korčule g. 1571," *Vesnik* 5.2 (1958), 61-91.

Frejdenberg, Maren. "The Birth of the Ragusan Republic," *Mediterranean Historical Review* 7 (1992), 201-07.

Frey, Linda and Marsha. "Rákóczi and the Maritime Powers: An Uncertain Friendship." In: *From Hunyadi to Rákóczi: War and Society in Late Medieval and Early Modern Hungary*. War and Society in Eastern Central Europe, vol. III. Ed. J.M. Bak and B.K. Király. New York: 1982, pp. 455-66.

Fügedi, Erik. "Medieval Hungarian Castles in Existence at the Start of the Ottoman Advance." In: *From Hunyadi to Rákóczi: War and Society in Late Medieval and Early Modern Hungary*. War and Society in Eastern Central Europe, vol. III. Ed. J.M. Bak and B.K. Király. New York: 1982, pp. 59-62.

Fügedi, Erik. "Two Kinds of Enemies–Two Kinds of Ideology: The Hungarian-Turkish Wars in the Fifteenth Century." In: *War and Peace in the Middle Ages*. Ed. B.P. McGuire. Copenhagen, 1987, pp. 146-60.

Gautier, Paul. "Un récit inédit du siège de Constantinople par les turcs (1394-1402)," *Revue des études byzantines* 23 (1965), 100-17.

Geary, John S. "Arredondo's *Castillo inexpugnable de la fee*: Anti-Islamic Propaganda in the Age of Charles V." In: *Medieval Christian Perceptions of Islam*. Hamden, 1996, pp. 291-311.

Genc, Nevin. "The Administrative Functions of the Timali Sipahis during the Ottoman Classical Age," *Revue internationale d'histoire militaire* 67 (1988), 29-44.

Giurescu, Constantin C. "Les armées roumaines dans la lutte la défense et l'indépendance du pays, du XIVe au XVIe siècle," *Revue internationale d'histoire militaire* 34 (1975), 5-21.

Grant, Jonathan. "Rethinking the Ottoman 'Decline': Military Technology Diffusion in the Ottoman Empire, Fifteenth to Eighteenth Centuries," *Journal of World History* 10 (1999), 179-201.

Griswold, William J. *The Great Anatolian Rebellion, 1000-1020/1591-1611*. Berlin: Klaus Schwarz, 1983.

Grunzweig, Armand. "Philippe le Bon et Constantinople," *Byzantion* 24 (1954), 47-61.

Guilmartin, John Francis, Jr. "Ideology and Conflict: The Wars of the Ottoman Empire, 1453-1606," *Journal of Interdisciplinary History* 18 (1988), 721-47.

Gündisch, Gustav. "Die Türkeneinfälle in Siebenbürgen bis zur Mitte des 15. Jahrhunderts," *Jahrbücher für Geschichte Osteuropas* 2 (1937), 393-412.

Halasi-Kun, Tibor. "Ottoman Toponymic Data and Medieval Boundaries in Southeastern Hungary." In: *From Hunyadi to Rákóczi: War and Society in Late Medieval and Early Modern Hungary*. War and Society in Eastern Central Europe, vol. III. Ed. J.M. Bak and B.K. Király. New York: 1982, pp. 243-50.

Halecki, Oscar. "The Defense of Europe in the Renaissance Period." In: *Didascaliae: Studies in Honor of Anselm M. Albareda, Prefect of the Vatican Library*. Ed. S. Prete. New York, 1961, pp. 121-46.

Hankins, James. "Renaissance Crusaders: Humanist Crusade Literature in the Age of Mehmed II," *Dumbarton Oaks Papers* 49 (1995), 111-207.

Hassenstein, Wilhelm. "Über die Feuerwaffen in der Seeschlacht von Lepanto," *Zeitschrift für historische Waffen- und Köstumkunde* 16 (1940-42), 1-11.

Hegyi, Klára. "The Ottoman Military Force in Hungary." In: *Hungarian-Ottoman Military and Diplomatic Relations in the Age of Süleyman the Magnificent*. Ed. G. Dávid and P. Fodor. Budapest, 1994, pp. 131-48.

Held, Joseph. "Military Reform in Early Fifteenth Century Hungary," *East European Quarterly* 9 (1977), 129-39.

Helgason, Þorsteinn. "Historical Narrative as Collective Therapy: The Case of the Turkish Raid in Iceland," *Scandinavian Journal of History* 22 (1997), 275-90.

Hess, Andrew C. "The Ottoman Conquest of Egypt (1517) and the Beginning of the Sixteenth-Century World War," *International Journal of Middle Eastern Studies* 4 (1973), 55-76.

Hess, Andrew C. "The Road to Victory: The Significance of Mohács for Ottoman Expansion." In: *From Hunyadi to Rákóczi: War and Society in Late Medieval and Early Modern Hungary*. War and Society in Eastern Central Europe, vol. III. Ed. J.M. Bak and B.K. Király. New York: 1982, pp. 179-88.

Hintzen, Johanna Dorina. *De kruistochtplannen van Philips den Goede*. Rotterdam: W.L. and J. Brusse's Uitgevers-Maatschappij, 1918.

Housley, Norman. "Crusading as Social Revolt: The Hungarian Peasant Uprising of 1514," *Journal of Ecclesiastical History* 49 (1998), 1-28.

Housley, Norman. "Frontier Societies and Crusading in the Late Middle Ages," *Mediterranean Historical Review* 10 (1995), 104-19.

Housley, Norman. "King Louis the Great of Hungary and the Crusades, 1342-1382," *Slavonic and East European Review* 62 (1984), 192-208.

Hughes, Quentin and Athanassios Migos. "Rhodes: The Turkish Sieges," *Fort* 21 (1993), 2-17.

Hummelberger, Walter. *Wiens erste Belagerung durch die Türken, 1529*. Militärhistorische Schriftenreihe, 33. Vienna: Heeresgeschichtlichen Museum (Militärwissenschaftliches Institut), 1983.

Hünoglu, Buhanettin. *Türk sihali kuvvetleri tarihi: Fas seferi*. Ankara: Genelkurmay Askeri Tarih ve Stratejik Etüt Baskanligi, 1978.

Inalcik, Halil. "Mehmed the Conqueror (1432-1481) and His Time," *Speculum* 35 (1960), 408-27.

Inalcik, Halil. "Military and Fiscal Transformation in the Ottoman Empire, 1600-1700," *Archivum Ottomanicum* 6 (1980), 283-337.

Inalcik, Halil. *The Ottoman Empire: The Classical Age, 1300-1600*. London, 1973.

Inalcik, Halil. "Ottoman Methods of Conquest," *Studia Islamica* 2 (1954), 103-29.

Ivanics, Mária. "Der Bündnisplan zwischen dem Chan Gazi Giray II. und dem Fürsten Sigismund Báthory aus dem Jahre 1598." In: *Hungarian-Ottoman Military and Diplomatic Relations in the Age of Süleyman the Magnificent*. Ed. Géza Dávid and Pál Fodor. Budapest: Loránd Eötvös University, Department of Turkish Studies/Hungarian Academy of Sciences, Institute of History, 1994, pp. 183-98.

Izeddin, M. "Deux voyageurs du XVe siècle en Turquie: Bertrandon de la Broquière et Pero Tafur," *Journal asiatique* 239 (1951), 159-74.

Jennings, R.C. "Firearms, Bandits, and Gun-Control: Some Evidence on Ottoman Policy Towards Firearms in the Possession of *Reaya*, From Judicial Records of Kayseri, 1600-1627," *Archivum Ottomanicum* 6 (1980), 339-58.

Kafadar, Cemal. "The Ottomans and Europe." In: *Handbook of European History, 1400-1600: Late Middle Ages, Renaissance, and Reformation*. Vol. I: *Structures and Assertions*. Ed. Thomas A. Brady, Jr., Heiko A. Oberman, and James D. Tracy. Leiden: E.J. Brill, 1994; rpt. Grand Rapids: William B Eerdmans Publishing Company, 1996, pp. 589-636.

Káldy-Nagy, Gyula. "The First Centuries of the Ottoman Military Organization," *Acta orientalia academiae scientiarum Hungaricum* 31 (1977), 147-83.

Király, Béla K. "Society and War from Mounted Knights to the Standing Armies of Absolute Kings: Hungary and the West." In: *From Hunyadi to Rákóczi: War and Society in Late Medieval and Early Modern Hungary*.

War and Society in Eastern Central Europe, vol. III. Ed. J.M. Bak and B.K. Király. New York: 1982, pp. 23-58.

Kniewald, Dragutin. "Dubrovčanin Feliks Petančić o ratovanju s Turcima 1502," *Vesnik* 3 (1956), 80-106.

Kniewald, Dragutin. "Feliks Petančić 1502 o putevima kojim valja napasti Turke," *Vesnik* 5.1 (1958), 25-58.

Kortepeter, Carl Max. "The Turkish Question in the Era of the Fifth Lateran Council (1512-1517)." In: *The Ottoman Turks: Nomad Kingdom to World Empire*. Istanbul, 1991, pp. 105-23.

Kubinyi, András. "The Road to Defeat: Hungarian Politics and Defense in the Jagiellonian Period." In: *From Hunyadi to Rákóczi: War and Society in Late Medieval and Early Modern Hungary*. War and Society in Eastern Central Europe, vol. III. Ed. J.M. Bak and B.K. Király. New York: 1982, pp. 159-78.

Kunt, Metin and Christine Woodhead, ed. *Süleyman the Magnificent and His Age: The Ottoman Empire in the Early Modern World*. London: Longman, 1995.

Lacaze, Yvon. "Philippe le Bon et les terres d'empire: La diplomatie bourguignonne a l'oeuvre en 1454-1455," *Annales de Bourgogne* 36 (1964), 81-121.

Lacaze, Yvon. "Politique 'Méditerranéenne' et projets de croisade chez Philippe le Bon: De la chute de Byzance à la victoire chrétienne de Belgrade (mai 1453-juillet 1456)," *Annales de Bourgogne* 41 (1969), 81-132.

Lafortune-Martel, Agathe. *Fête noble en Bourgogne au XVe siècle. Le banquet du Faisan (1454): Aspects politiques, sociaux et culturels*. Montreal: Bellarim, 1984.

Le Brusque, Georges. "Des chevaliers bouguignons dans les pays du Levant: L'expéditions de Walleran de Wavrin contre les Turcs ottomans (1444-1446) dans les *Anchiennes Cronicques d'Engleterre* de Jean de Wavrin," *Moyen age* 106 (2000), 255-75.

Le Roulx, J. Delaville. *La France en Orient au XIVe siècle: Expéditions du Maréchal Boucicaut*. 2 vols. Paris: Ernest Thorin, 1886.

Lewis, Bernard. "Constantinople and the Arabs." In: *The Fall of Constantinople*. London, 1955, pp. 12-17.

Lybyer, Albert H. "Mohammed the Conqueror," *Slavonic and East European Review* 15 (1936-37), 639-48.

Makkai, László. "István Bocskai's Insurrectionary Army." In: *From Hunyadi to Rákóczi: War and Society in Late Medieval and Early Modern Hungary*. War and Society in Eastern Central Europe, vol. III. Ed. J.M. Bak and B.K. Király. New York: 1982, pp. 275-96.

Maksay, Ferenc. "Peasantry and Mercenary Service in Sixteenth-Century Hungary." In: *From Hunyadi to Rákóczi: War and Society in Late Medieval and Early Modern Hungary*. War and Society in Eastern Central Europe, vol. III. Ed. J.M. Bak and B.K. Király. New York: 1982, pp. 261-74.

Manz, Beatrice Forbes. *The Rise and Rule of Tamerlane*. Cambridge Studies in Islamic Civilizations. Cambridge: Cambridge University Press, 1989.

Marinesco, Constantin. "Philippe le Bon, duc de Bourgogne, et la croisade. Deuxième partie (1453-1467)," *Bulletin des études portugaises de l'Institut française de Portugal* ns. 13 (1949), 3-28.

The Maritime Siege of Malta, 1565. London: Her Majesty's Stationery Office, n.d.

Maxim, Mihal. *Tárile Române si Înalta Poartá: Cadrul juridic al relatiilor româno-otomane în evul mediu*. Bucharest: Editura Enciclopedicá, 1993.

Mears, John A. "Influence of the Turkish Wars in Hungary." In: *Asia and the West: Essays in Honour of Donald Lach*. Ed. C.K. Pullapilly and E.J. Vankly. Notre Dame: Notre Dame University Press, 1986.

Menczer, Béla. "The Turk at the Gates: The Hunyad Saga," *History Today* 16 (1966), 174-83.

Migos, Athanassios. "Rhodes: the Knights' Battleground," *Fort* 18 (1990), 5-28.

Moačanin, Nenad. "Haci Mehmed *Ağa* of Požega, God's Special Protégé (ca. 1490-ca. 1580)." In: *Hungarian-Ottoman Military and Diplomatic Relations in the Age of Süleyman the Magnificent*. Ed. Géza Dávid and

Pál Fodor. Budapest: Loránd Eötvös University, Department of Turkish Studies/Hungarian Academy of Sciences, Institute of History, 1994, pp. 171-82.

Mohács emlékezete: A mohácsi csatára vonatkozó legfontosabb magyar, nyugati és török források: A csatahely régészeti felkutatásának eredményei. Bp. Europa K., 1979.

Molinier, Auguste. "Description de deux manuscrits conténant la règle de la *Militia Passionis Jhesu Christi* de Philippe de Mézières," *Archives de l'orient latin* 1 (1881), 335-64.

Morin, Marco. "La battaglia di Lepanto: il determinante apporto dell' artiglieri Veneziana," *Diana armi* 9.1 (1975), 54-61.

Müller, Heribert. *Kreuzzugspläne und Kreuzzugspolitik des Herzogs Philipp des Guten von Burgund.* Gottingen: Vandenhoeck and Ruprecht, 1993.

Murphey, Rhoads. "The Ottoman Attitude towards the Adoption of Western Technology: The Role of *Efrenci* Technicians in Civil and Military Applications." In: *Contributions à l'histoire économique et sociale de l'Empire Ottoman.* Ed. J.-L. Basque-Grammont and P. Dumont. Louvain, 1983.

Murphey, Rhoads. *Ottoman Warfare, 1500-1700.* London: UCL Press, 1999.

Necipoğlu, Gülru. "Süleyman the Magnificent and the Representation of Power in the Context of Ottoman-Hapsburg-Papal Rivalry," *Art Bulletin* 71 (1989), 401-27.

Necipoglu, N. "Economic Conditions in Constantinople during the Siege of Bayezid I (1394-1402)." In: *Constantinople and Its Hinterland.* Ed. C. Mango and G. Dagron. Aldershot: Ashgate, 1995, pp. 157-67.

Nicolle, David C. *The Armies of the Ottoman Turks, 1300-1774.* London: Osprey, 1983.

Niederkorn, Jan Paul. *Die europäischen Mächte und der "Lange Türkenkrieg": Kaiser Rudolfs II (1593-1606).* Archiv für österreichische Geschichte, 135. Vienna: Verlag der österreichischen Akademie der Wissenschaften, 1993.

Niederkorn, Jan Paul. "Zweifrontenkrieg gegen die Osmanen: Iranisch-christliche Bündnispläne in der Zeit des 'Langen Türkenkriegs,' 1593-1606," *Mitteilungen des Instituts für Österreichische Geschichtsforschung* 104 (1996), 310-23.

O'Donnel, Hugo. "Lepanto: Creación, triunfo y consecuecias de la Santa Liga." In: *Felipe II: La monarquía hispánica*. Real monasterio de San Lorenzo de El Escorial, 1 junio-10 octubre, 1998. Madrid: Sociedad Estatal para la Conmemoración de los Centenarios de Felipe II y Carlos V, 1998, pp. 275-83.

Orhon, Nafiz, Fethi Ünsal, and Ihsan Gürsoy. *Ankara Meydan Muharebesi 1402*. Ankara: Turkish General Staff Military History and Strategic Studies Presidency, 1995.

Özbaran, Salih. "The Ottomans' Role in the Diffusion of Fire-arms and Military Technology in Asia and Africa in the 16th Century," *Revue internationale d'histoire militaire* 67 (1988), 77-83.

Palmer, J.A.B. "Fr. Georgius de Hungaria, O.P., and the *Tractatus de moribus condicionibus et nequicia turcorum*," *Bulletin of the John Rylands Library* 34 (1951-52), 44-68.

Palmer, J.A.B. "The Origins of the Janissaries," *Bulletin of the John Rylands Library* 35 (1952-53), 448-81.

Parker, Geoffrey and I.A.A. Thompson. "The Battle of Lepanto, 1571: The Costs of Victory," *Mariner's Mirror* 64 (1978), 13-21; in: *Spain and the Netherlands, 1559-1659: Ten Studies*. 2nd ed. London, 1990, pp. 122-34.

Paschalidou, Efpraxia. "The Walls of Constantinople: an Obstacle to the New Power of Artillery." In: *XXII. Kongreß der Internationalen Kommission für Militärgeschichte Acta 22: Von Crécy bis Mohács Kriegswesen im späten Mittelalter (1346-1526)*. Vienna, 1997, pp. 172-78.

Paviot, Jacques. "'Croisade' bouguignonne et intérêts génois en mer Noire au milieu du XVe siècle," *Studi di storia medioevale e di diplomatica* 12-13 (1992), 135-62.

Perbellini, Gianni. "The Venetian Defences of Cyprus," *Fort* 16 (1988), 7-44.

Perjés, Géza. *The Fall of the Medieval Kingdom of Hungary: Mohács 1526-Buda 1541*. Trans. Márió D. Fenyó. War and Society in East Central Europe, 26. Boulder: Social Science Monographs, 1989.

Perjés, Géza. *Mohács*. Budapest: Magvetö, 1979.

Petkov, Kiril. "England and the Balkan Slavs, 1354-1583: An Outline of a Late-Medieval and Renaissance Image," *Slavonic and East European Review* 75 (1997), 86-117.

Petkov, Kiril. "The Rotten Apple and the Good Apples: Orthodox, Catholics, and Turks in Philippe de Mézières' Crusading Propaganda," *Journal of Medieval History* 23 (1997), 255-70.

Petrovic, Djurdjica. "Fire-arms in the Balkans on the Eve of and after the Ottoman Conquests of the Fourteenth and Fifteenth Centuries." In: *War, Technology and Society in the Middle East*. Ed. V.J. Parry and M.E. Yapp. London: Oxford University Press, 1975, pp. 164-94.

Petrovics, István. "The Role of Towns in the Defence System of Medieval Hungary." In: *La guerre, la violence et les gens au Moyen Âge*. I: *Guerre et violence*. Ed. P. Contamine and O. Guyotjeannin. 119e congrès national des sociétés historiques et scientifiques, Amiens, octobre 1994, Section d'histoire médiévale et philologie. Paris, 1996, pp. 263-71.

Pickles, Tim. *Malta, 1565: Last Battle of the Crusades*. London: Osprey, 1998.

Podhorodecki, Leszek. *Lepanto 1571*. Warsaw: Bellona, 1993.

Polišenský, J.V. "Bohemia, the Turk and the Christian Commonwealth (1462-1620)," *Byzantinoslavica* 14 (1953), 82-108.

Pourmarede, Géraud. "Justifier l'injustifiable l'alliance turque au miroir de la chrétienté (16ième-17ième siècles)," *Revue d'histoire diplomatique* 14 (1997), 217-46.

Rabb, Theodore K. "Artists on War: 'Painter A' and the Battle of Mohacs," *MHQ: The Quarterly Journal of Military History* 9 (Autumn 1996), 28-31.

Raby, Julian. "East and West in Mehmed the Conqueror's Library," *Bulletin du bibliophile* (1987), 297-321.

Raffa, Angelo. "L'argent pour la guerre, la guerre pour l'argent: Politique militaire et commerce en Méditerranée entre Chrétiens et Musulmans au XVIe et XVIIe siècles." In: *Actas do XXIV congresso internacional de historía militar*. Centro cultural de Belém, 24 a 29 de agosto, 1998. Lisbon: Comissão Portuguesa de Historía Militar, 1998, pp. 666-701.

Rázsó, Gyula. *Feldzüge des Königs Matthias Corvinus in Niederösterreich, 1477-1490*. Militärhistorische Schriftenreihe, 24. Vienna: Heeresgeschichtlichen Museum (Militärwissenschaftliches Institut), 1982.

Rázsó, Gyula. "Hungarian Strategy Against the Ottomans (1365-1526)." In: *XXII. Kongreß der Internationalen Kommission für Militärgeschichte* Acta 22: *Von Crécy bis Mohács Kriegswesen im späten Mittelalter (1346-1526)*. Vienna, 1997, pp. 226-37.

Rázsó, Gyula. "The Mercenary Army of King Matthias Corvinus." In: *From Hunyadi to Rákóczi: War and Society in Late Medieval and Early Modern Hungary*. War and Society in Eastern Central Europe, vol. III. Ed. J.M. Bak and B.K. Király. New York: 1982, pp. 125-40.

Römer, Claudia. "Zur Bestellung eines *Mü'ezzin* und *Devrhan* an einer Moschee in Buda im Jahr 971/1564." In: *Hungarian-Ottoman Military and Diplomatic Relations in the Age of Süleyman the Magnificent*. Ed. Géza Dávid and Pál Fodor. Budapest: Loránd Eötvös University, Department of Turkish Studies/Hungarian Academy of Sciences, Institute of History, 1994, pp. 161-70.

Roso, Daniela and Gianni Pedrini. "Solimano il Magnifico a Filippopoli nel 1566," *Studi Veneziani* n.s. 50 (2000), 207-33

Rothenberg, Gerhard E. "Aventinus and the Defense of the Empire against the Turks," *Studies in the Renaissance* 10 (1963), 60-67.

Rothenberg, Gerhard E. "Christian Insurrections in Turkish Dalmatia, 1580-1596," *Slavonic and East European Review* 40 (1961-62), 136-45.

Rubenstein, Nicolai. "Italy." In: *The Fall of Constantinople*. London, 1955, pp. 25-32.

Rúzsás, Lajos. "The Siege of Szigetvár of 1566: Its Significance in Hungarian Social Development." In: *From Hunyadi to Rákóczi: War and Society in Late Medieval and Early Modern Hungary*. War and Society in

Eastern Central Europe, vol. III. Ed. J.M. Bak and B.K. Király. New York: 1982, pp. 251-60.

Sarnowsky, Jürgen. "The Teutonic Order Confronts the Mongols and the Turks." In: *The Military Orders: Fighting for the Faith and Caring for the Sick*. Ed. Malcolm Barber. Aldershot: Ashgate, 1994, pp. 253-62.

Schönherr, Klaus. "Kaiser versus Sultan: Der militärische Konflikt Maximilians II. mit Suleyman, 1564-1566," *Militärgeschichte* n.f. 8 (1998), 3-11.

Setton, Kenneth M. "Lutheranism and the Turkish Peril," *Balkan Studies* 3 (1962), 133-68.

Setton, Kenneth M. *The Papacy and the Levant (1204-1571)*. 4 vols. Philadelphia: American Philosophical Society, 1978-85.

Setton, Kenneth M. "Pope Leo X and the Turkish Peril," *Proceedings of the American Philosophical Society* 113 (1969), 367-424.

Setton, Kenneth M. *Western Hostility to Islam and Prophecies of Turkish Doom*. Philadelphia: American Philosophical Society, 1992.

Shaw, S. *History of the Ottoman Empire and Modern Turkey*. I: *1280-1808*. Cambridge, 1976.

Škrivanić, Gavro A. "Turski pohod na Siget 1566," *Vesnik* 4 (1957), 185-214.

Sousa, Luís and João Tavares. "Os Portugueses e a 'Guerra Justa' no Índico no século XVI." In: *Actas do XXIV congresso internacional de história militar*. Centro cultural de Belém, 24 a 29 de agosto, 1998. Lisbon: Comissão Portuguesa de História Militar, 1998, pp. 727-41.

Stiles, Andrina. *The Ottoman Empire, 1450-1700*. Access to History. London: Hoddes and Stoughton, 1991.

Sugar, Peter F. "The Ottoman Professional Prisoner on the Western Borders of the Empire in the Sixteenth and Seventeenth Centuries." In: *Actes du deuxième congrès international des études du sud-est européen*. Athens, 1972-76, VI:29-40.

Sugar, Peter F. "A Near-Perfect Military Society: The Ottoman Empire." In: *War: A Historical, Political, and Social Study*. Ed. L.L. Farrar, Jr. Santa Barbara: ABC-Clio, 1978, pp. 94-104.

Szakály, Ferenc. "Das Bauerntum und die Kämpfe gegen die Türken bzw. gegen Habsburg in Ungarn im 16.-17. Jahrhundert." In: *Aus der Geschichte der ostmitteleuropäischen Bauernbewegungen*. Ed. G. Heckenast. Budapest, 1977, pp. 251-66.

Szakály, Ferenc. "Die Bilanz der Türkenherrschaft in Ungarn," *Acta historica Hungaricarum* 34 (1988), 63-78.

Szakály, Ferenc. "The Hungarian-Croatian Border Defense System and Its Collapse." In: *From Hunyadi to Rákóczi: War and Society in Late Medieval and Early Modern Hungary*. War and Society in Eastern Central Europe, vol. III. Ed. J.M. Bak and B.K. Király. New York: 1982, pp. 141-58.

Szakály, Ferenc. "Nándorfehérvár, 1521: The Beginning of the End of the Medieval Hungarian Kingdom." In: *Hungarian-Ottoman Military and Diplomatic Relations in the Age of Süleyman the Magnificent*. Ed. G. Dávid and P. Fodor. Budapest, 1994, pp. 47-76.

Szakály, Ferenc. "Phases of Turco-Hungarian Warfare Before the Battle of Mohács (1365-1526)," *Acta orientalia academiae scientiarum Hungaricum* 33 (1979), 65-111.

Szendrey, Thomas. "'Inter Arma . . .' Reflections on Seventeenth-Century Educational and Cultural Life in Hungary and Transylvania." In: *From Hunyadi to Rákóczi: War and Society in Late Medieval and Early Modern Hungary*. War and Society in Eastern Central Europe, vol. III. Ed. J.M. Bak and B.K. Király. New York: 1982, pp. 315-34.

Taparel, Henri. "Geoffroy de Thoisy: Une figure de la croisade bourguignonne au XVe siècle," *Moyen âge*, 5th ser., 2 (1988), 381-93.

Taparel, Henri. "Un épisode de la politique orientale de Philippe le Bon: Les bourguignons en mer noire (1444-1446)," *Annales de Bourgogne* 55 (1983), 5-29.

Taşkiran, Cemalettin. "L'art de guerre dans l'Empire Ottoman et la bataille de Mohács (jusqu'au XVIe siècle)." In: *XXII. Kongreß der Internationalen Kommission für Militärgeschichte* Acta 22: *Von Crécy bis Mohács Kriegswesen im späten Mittelalter (1346-1526)*. Vienna, 1997, pp. 207-17.

Taşkiran, Cemalettin. "Les relations Ottomano-Portugaises au XVIième siècle." In: *Actas do XXIV congresso internacional de história militar*.

Centro cultural de Belém, 24 a 29 de agosto, 1998. Lisbon: Comissão Portuguesa de História Militar, 1998, pp. 133-38.

Teply, K. "Vom Loss osmanischen Gefangener aus dem Grossen Türkenkrieg," *Südost Forschungen* 32 (1973), 33-72.

Tóth, István György. "A Spy's Report about Turkish-Occupied Hungary and Bosnia in 1626: The Journey of the Dalmatian Humanist Athanasio Georgiceo," *Acta orientalia academiae scientarum Hungaricarum* 51 (1998), 185-218.

Turan, O. "World Domination among the Medieval Turks," *Studia Islamica* 4 (1955), 77-90.

Vasić, M. "Die Einfluss den Türkenkriege auf die wirtschaft des osmanischen Grenzgebietes in Serbien und Bosnien, 1480-1536." In: *Wirtschaftlichen Auswirkungen der Türkenkriege*. Ed. O. Pickl Pp. 308-18.

Vatin, Nicolas. *L'order de Saint-Jean-de-Jérusalem, l'empire Ottoman et la Méditerrannée orientale entre les deux sièges de Rhodes, 1480-1522*. Paris: Peeters, 1994.

Veinstein, G. "Some Views on Provisioning in the Hungarian Campaigns of Suleyman the Magnificent." In: *Osmanistische Studien zur Wirtschafts- und sozial geschichte in memoriam V. Baskov*. Ed. H.G. Majer. Wiesbaden, 1986, pp. 177-85.

Vryonis, Speros, Jr. "Byzantine and Turkish Societies and Their Sources of Manpower." In: *War, Technology, and Society in the Middle East*. Ed. V.J. Parry and M.E. Yapp. London: Oxford University Press, 1975, pp. 125-52.

Vryonis, Speros, Jr. "Byzantine Attitudes toward Islam during the Late Middle Ages," *Greek, Roman and Byzantine Studies* 12 (1971), 263-86.

Vryonis, Speros, Jr. "The Byzantine Patriarchate and Turkish Islam," *Byzantinoslavica* 57 (199), I:69-111.

Vryonis, Speros, Jr. *The Decline of Medieval Hellenism in Asia Minor and the Process of Islamization from the Eleventh through the Fifteenth Century*. Berkeley and Los Angeles: University of California Press, 1971.

Vryonis, Speros, Jr. "The Experience of Christians under Seljuk and Ottoman Domination, Eleventh to Sixteenth Century." In: *Conversion and Continuity: Indigenous Christian Communities in Islamic Lands, Eighth to Eighteenth Centuries*. Ed. Michael Gervers and Ramzi Jibran Bikhazi. Papers in Mediaeval Studies, 9. Toronto: Pontifical Institute of Mediaeval Studies, 1990, pp. 185-216.

Vryonis, Speros, Jr. "The Greeks under Turkish Rule." In: *Hellenism and the First Greek War of Liberation (1821-1830): Continuity and Change*. Ed. N. Diamondouros, J. Anton, J. Petropolous, and D. Topping. Thessaloniki, 1976, pp. 45-58.

Vryonis, Speros, Jr. "Religious Change and Continuity in the Balkans and Anatolia from the Fourteenth through the Sixteenth Century." In: *Aspects of the Balkans*. Ed. H. Birnbaum and S. Vryonis, Jr. The Hague, 197), pp. 151-76.

Walsh, R.J. "Charles the Bold and the Crusade: Politics and Propaganda," *Journal of Medieval History* 3 (1977).

Wheatcroft, Andrew. *The Ottomans: Dissolving Images*. Harmondsworth: Penguin Books, 1993.

Williamson, Joan. "Philippe de Mézières and the Idea of Crusade." In: *The Military Orders: Fighting for Faith and Caring for the Sick*. Ed. Malcolm Barber. Aldershot: Ashgate, 1994, 358-64.

Wittek, Paul. *The Rise of the Ottoman Empire*. London, 1938.

Zachariadou, Elizabeth A. "The Catalans of Athens and the Beginnings of the Turkish Expansion in the Aegean Area," *Studi medievali* 21 (1980), 821-38.

Zachariadou, Elizabeth A. "The Conquest of Adrianople by the Turks," *Studi Veneziana* 12 (1970), 211-17.

Zachariadou, Elizabeth A. "The First Serbian Campaigns of Mehemmed II (1454, 1455)." In: *Annali dell'Instito Orientale di Napoli: Scritti in onore di Laura Veccia Vaglieri*. Naples, 1964, pp. 837-40.

Zachariadou, Elizabeth A. "Holy War in the Aegean during the Fourteenth Century." In: *Latins and Greeks in the Eastern Mediterranean after 1204*. Ed. B. Arbel, B. Hamilton, and D. Jacoby. London, 1989, pp. 212-25.

Zachariadou, Elizabeth A. *Romania and the Turks*. London, 1985.

Medieval/Early Modern – Ottoman Turkish Wars – Battle of Nicopolis

Atiya, Aziz Suryal. *The Crusade of Nicopolis*. London: Methuen and Co., Ltd., 1934.

Autrand, Françoise. "La paix impossible: les négociations franco-anglaises à la fin du 14e siècle," in "Nicopolis, 1396-1996: Actes du Colloque international," ed. J. Paviot and M. Chauney-Bouillot, *Annales de Bourgogne* 68 (1996), 11-22.

Contamine, Philippe. "La *Consolation de la desconfiture de Hongrie* de Philippe de Mézières (1396)," in "Nicopolis, 1396-1996: Actes du Colloque international," ed. J. Paviot and M. Chauney-Bouillot, *Annales de Bourgogne* 68 (1996), 35-48.

Housley, Norman. "Le Maréchal Boucicaut à Nicopolis," in "Nicopolis, 1396-1996: Actes du Colloque international," ed. J. Paviot and M. Chauney-Bouillot, *Annales de Bourgogne* 68 (1996), 85-99.

Kintzinger, Martin. "Sigismond, roi de Hongrie, et la croisade," in "Nicopolis, 1396-1996: Actes du Colloque international," ed. J. Paviot and M. Chauney-Bouillot, *Annales de Bourgogne* 68 (1996), 23-33.

Magee, James. "Le temps de la croisade bourguignonne: l'expédition de Nicopolis," in "Nicopolis, 1396-1996: Actes du Colloque international," ed. J. Paviot and M. Chauney-Bouillot, *Annales de Bourgogne* 68 (1996), 49-58.

Nicolle, David C. *Nicopolis, 1396: The Last Crusade*. London: Osprey, 1999.

Palmer, J.J.N. *England, France and Christendom, 1377-99*. Chapel Hill: The University of North Carolina Press, 1972.

Pocquet du Haut-Jussé, B.-A. "Le retour de Nicopolis et la rançon de Jeans san Puer," *Annales de Bourgogne* 9 (1937), 296-302.

Richard, Jean. "Les prisonniers de Nicopolis," in "Nicopolis, 1396-1996: Actes du Colloque international," ed. J. Paviot and M. Chauney-Bouillot, *Annales de Bourgogne* 68 (1996), 75-84.

Rosetti, R. "Notes on the Battle of Nicopolis (1396)," *Slavonic and East European Review* 15 (1936-37), 629-38.

Savage, Henry L. "Enguerrand de Coucy VII and the Campaign of Nicopolis," *Speculum* 14 (1939), 423-42.

Schnerb, Bertrand. "Le contingent franco-bourguignon à la croisade de Nicopolis," in "Nicopolis, 1396-1996: Actes du Colloque international," ed. J. Paviot and M. Chauney-Bouillot, *Annales de Bourgogne* 68 (1996), 59-74.

Šišić, Ferdinand von. "Die Schlacht bei Nicopolis (25. September 1396)," *Wissenschafteliche mitteilungen aus Bosnien under Hecegovina* 6 (1899), 291-327.

Tipton, Charles L. "The English at Nicopolis," *Speculum* 37 (1962), 528-40.

Medieval/Early Modern – Ottoman Turkish Wars – Fall of Constantinople

Antonucci, Michael. "Siege Without Reprieve," *Military History* (April 1992), 42-49.

Balard, M. "Constantinople vue par les témoins du siège de 1453," In: *Constantinople and Its Hinterland.* Ed. C. Mango and G. Dagron. Aldershot: Ashgate, 1995, pp. 169-77.

Betts, R.R. "Central and South-Eastern Europe." In: *The Fall of Constantinople.* London, 1955, pp. 18-24.

Bozkurt, R. "Sultan Mehmet II and the Conquest of Constantinople," *Revue internationale d'histoire militaire* 46 (1980), 61-70.

DeVries, Kelly. "Gunpowder Weaponry at the Siege of Constantinople, 1453." In: *War, Army and Society in the Eastern Mediterranean, 7th-16th Centuries.* Ed. Y. Lev. Leiden, 1996, pp. 343-62.

Dujcev, I. "La conquête turque et la prise de Constantinople dans la littérature slave contemporaine," *Byzantinoslavica* 14 (1953), 14-54.

Evert-Kappesowa, H. "La tiare ou le turban," *Byzantinoslavica* 14 (1953), 245-57.

Grecu, V. "La chute de Constantinople dans la littérature populaire roumaine," *Byzantinoslavica* 14 (1953), 55-81.

Grunzweig, Armand. "Philippe le Bon et Constantinople," *Byzantion* 24 (1954), 47-61.

Guilland, R. "Les appels de Constantin XI Paleologue à Rome et à Venise pour sauver Constantinople (1452-1453)," *Byzantinoslavica* 14 (1953), 226-44.

Inalcik, Halil. "Mehmed the Conqueror (1432-1481) and His Time," *Speculum* 35 (1960), 408-27.

Irmscher, J. "Zeitgenössische deutsche stimmen zum fall von Byzanz," *Byzantinoslavica* 14 (1953), 109-22.

Lybyer, Albert H. "Mohammed the Conqueror," *Slavonic and East European Review* 15 (1936-37), 639-48.

Massignon, Louis. "Textes prémontoires et commentaires mystiques relatifs à la prise de Constantinople par les turcs en 1453 (=858 hég.)," *Oriens* 6 (1953), 10-17.

Nicol, Donald M. *Immortal Emperor: The Life and Legend of Constantine Paleologus, Last Emperor of the Romans*. Cambridge: Cambridge University Press, 1992.

Paulova, M. "L'empire Byzantin et les tchèques avant la chute de Constantinople," *Byzantinoslavica* 14 (1953), 158-225.

Pears, Edwin. *The Destruction of the Greek Empire and the Story of the Capture of Constantinople by the Turks*. 1903; rpt. New York, 1968.

Pertusi, Agostino, ed. "The Anconitan Colony in Constantinople and the Report of Its Consul, Benvenuto, on the Fall of the City." Trans. A. di Candia. In: *Charanis Studies: Essays in Honor of Peter Chanaris*. Ed. A. E. Laiou-Thomadakis. New Brunswick, 1980, pp. 199-218.

Philippides, Marios. "The Fall of Constantinople, 1453: Bishop Leonardo Giustiniani and His Italian Followers," *Viator* 29 (1998), 189-226.

Philippides, Marios. "*Urbs capta*: Early 'Sources' on the Fall of Constantinople (1453)." In: *Peace and War in Byzantium. Essays in Honor of George T. Dennis, S.J.* Ed. T.S. Miller and J. Nesbitt. Washington, 1995, pp. 209-24.

Rubenstein, Nicolai. "Italy." In: *The Fall of Constantinople*. London, 1955, pp. 25-32.

Runciman, Steven. "The Fall of Byzantium." In: *The Fall of Constantinople*. London, 1955, pp. 5-11.

Runciman, Steven. *The Fall of Constantinople, 1453*. Cambridge: Cambridge University Press, 1965.

Şesan, M. "La chute de Constantinople et les peuples orthodoxes," *Byzantinoslavica* 14 (1953), 271-82.

Turková, H. "Le siège de Constantinople d'après le Seyāhatnāme d'Evliyā Čelebī," *Byzantinoslavica* 14 (1953), 1-13.

Wittek, Paul. "Fath Mubin, 'An Eloquent Conquest.' In: *The Fall of Constantinople*. London, 1955, pp. 33-44.

Early Modern – General

Adams, Robert P. *The Better Part of Valor: More, Erasmus, Colet, and Vives, on Humanism, War, and Peace, 1496-1535*. Seattle: University of Washington Press, 1962.

Anderson, M.S. *War and Society in Europe of the Old Regime, 1618-1789*. London: Fontana Press, 1988.

Anglo, Sydney. *The Martial Arts of Renaissance Europe*. New Haven: Yale University Press, 2000.

Arnold, Thomas F. "War in Sixteenth-Century Europe: Revolution and Renaissance." In: *European Warfare, 1453-1815*. Ed. Jeremy Black. New York: St. Martin's Press, 1999, pp. 23-45.

Askgaard, Finn. "Med pike og musket: Fodfolkets fornyelse 1450-1650," *Vaabenhistoriske aarbøger* 17 (1971).

Bak, János M. "Delinquent Lords and Forsaken Serfs: Thoughts on War and Society during the Crisis of Feudalism." In: *Society in Change: Studies in Honour of Bela K. Király.* Ed. S.B. Vardy. Boulder, 1983, pp. 291-304.

Baumann, Reinhard. *Landsknecht: Ihre Geschichte und Kultur vom späten Mittelalter bis zum Drießigjährigen Krieg.* Munich: C.H. Beck, 1994.

Billacois, François. *Le duel dans la société Française des XVIe-XVIIe siècles.* Paris, 1986.

Black, Jeremy. *The Cambridge Illustrated Atlas of Warfare: Renaissance to Revolution, 1492-1792.* Cambridge: Cambridge University Press, 1996.

Black, Jeremy. "Introduction." In: *European Warfare, 1453-1815.* Ed. Jeremy Black. New York: St. Martin's Press, 1999, pp. 1-22.

Black, Jeremy. "Introduction." In: *War in the Early Modern World, 1450-1815.* Ed. Jeremy Black. London, 1999, pp. 1-24.

Bleckwenn, Ruth. "Beziehungen zeischen Soldatentracht und ziviler modischer Kleidung zwischen 1500 und 1650," *Waffen- und Kostümkunde* 16 (1974), 107-18.

Bonny, Richard. *The European Dynastic States, 1494-1600.* Oxford: Oxford University Press, 1991.

Braudel, Fernand. *La Méditerranée et le monde Méditerranéan à l'époque de Philippe II.* 2 vols. Paris, 1949, 1966; trans. *The Mediterranean and the Mediterranean World in the Age of Philip II.* 2 vols. Trans. S. Reynolds. New York: Harper and Row, 1972.

Bridgman, Jon M. "Gunpowder and Governmental Power: War in Early Modern Europe (1494-1825)." In: *War: A Historical, Political and Social Study.* Ed. L.L. Farrar, Jr. Santa Barbara, 1978, pp. 105-11.

Clark, George Norman. *War and Society in the Seventeenth Century.* Cambridge: Cambridge University Press, 1958.

Contamine, Philippe. "Un contrôle étatique croissant: Les usages de la guerre du XIVe au XVIIIe siècle: rançons et butins." In: *Guerre et concurrence entre les États européens du XIVe au XVIIIe siècle.* Ed. Philippe

Contamine. *Fondation Européenne de la Science: Les origines de l'État moderne en Europe, XIIIe-XVIIIe siècle*. Paris: Presses universitaires de France, 1998, pp. 199-236.

Corvisier, André. *Armies and Societies in Europe, 1494-1789*. Trans. Abigail T. Siddall. Bloomington: Indiana University Press, 1979; orig. *Armée et société à la fin du moyen âge*. Paris: Mouton, 1972.

Cotterill, Rowland. "War and Music in the Sixteenth Century." In: *War, Literature and the Arts in Sixteenth-Century Europe*. Ed. J.R. Mulryne and M. Shewring. New York, 1989, pp. 63-77.

Crouzet, D. *Les guerriers de Dieu: La violence au temps des troubles de religion (vers 1525-vers 1610)*. 2 vols. Seyssel: Champ Vallon, 1990.

Delbrück, Hans. *History of the Art of War*. IV: *The Dawn of Modern Warfare*. Trans. Walter J. Renfroe, Jr. Lincoln: University of Nebraska Press, 1990.

Dörnhöffer, Friedrich. "Albrecht Dürer's Fechtbuch," *Jahrbuch der Kunsthistorischen Sammlungen des Allerhöchsten Kaiserhauses* 27 (1907-09).

Dunn, Richard S. *The Age of Religious Wars, 1559-1715*. 2nd ed. New York: W.W. Norton and Company, 1979.

Duchhardt, Heinz. "La guerre et le droit des gens dans l'Europe du XVIe au XVIIIe siècle." In: *Guerre et concurrence entre les États européens du XIVe au XVIIIe siècle*. Ed. Philippe Contamine. Fondation Européenne de la Science: Les origines de l'État moderne en Europe, XIIIe-XVIIIe siècle. Paris: Presses universitaires de France, 1998, pp. 339-64.

Elliott, J.H. *Europe Divided, 1559-1598*. The Fontana History of Europe. London: Collins, 1968.

Fontaine, Marie-Madeline. "Le développement technique des exercices corporels dans la préparation militaire (fin XVe-début XVIe s.)," *Micrologus: natura, scienza e società medievali* 1 (1993), 61-80.

González de Leon, Fernando. "'Doctors of the Military Discipline': Technical Expertise and the Paradigm of the Spanish Soldier in the Early Modern Period," *Sixteenth Century Journal* 27 (1996), 61-85.

Gräf, Holger Th. "Militarisierung der Stadt oder Urbanisierung des Militärs? Ein Beitrag zur Militärgeschichte der frühen Neuzeit zus stadtgeschichtlicher Perspektive." In: *Klio in Uniform? Probleme und Perspektiven einer modernen Militärgeschichte der Frühen Neuzeit.* Ed. Ralf Pröve. Cologne, 1997, pp. 89-108.

Greengrass, Mark. "Introduction: Conquest and Coalescence." In: *Conquest and Coalescence: The Shaping of the State in Early Modern Europe.* Ed. Mark Greengrass. London: Edward Arnold, 1991, pp. 1-24.

Gush, George. *Renaissance Armies, 1480-1650.* Cambridge: Patrick Stephens, 1975.

Hagemann, Karen. "Militär, Krieg und Geschlechterverhältnisse: Untersuchungen, Überlegungen und Fragen zur Militärgeschichte der Frühen Neuzeit," In: *Klio in Uniform? Probleme und Perspektiven einer modernen Militärgeschichte der Frühen Neuzeit.* Ed. Ralf Pröve. Cologne, 1997, pp. 35-88.

Hale, John R. "Andrea Palladio, Polybius and Julius Caesar." In: *Renaissance War Studies.* London, 1983, pp. 471-86.

Hale, John R. *Artists and Warfare in the Renaissance.* New Haven: Yale University Press, 1990.

Hale, John R. "A Humanistic Visual Aid: The Military Diagram in the Renaissance," *Renaissance Studies* 2.2 (Oct 1998), 280-98.

Hale, John R. "International Relations in the West: Diplomacy and War." In: *The New Cambridge Modern History.* Vol. 1: *The Renaissance, 1493-1520.* Ed. G.R. Potter. Cambridge: Cambridge University Press, 1971, pp. 259-91.

Hale, John R. "The Military Education of the Officer Class in Early Modern Europe." In: *Cultural Aspects of the Italian Renaissance: Essays in Honor of Paul Oskar Kristeller.* Ed. C.H. Clough. New York, 1976, pp. 440-61; in: *Renaissance War Studies.* London, 1983, pp. 225-46.

Hale, John R. "Epilogue: Experience and Artifice." In: *War, Literature and the Arts in Sixteenth-Century Europe.* Ed. J.R. Mulryne and M. Shewring. New York, 1989, pp. 190-96.

Hale, John R. "Sixteenth-Century Explanations of War and Violence." In: *Renaissance War Studies*. London, 1983, pp. 335-58.

Hale, John R. "Soldiers in the Religious Art of the Renaissance," *Bulletin of the John Rylands Library* 69 (1987), 166-94.

Hale, John R. "War and Public Opinion in the Fifteenth and Sixteenth Centuries," *Past and Present* 22 (1962), 18-35.

Hale, John R. *War and Society in Renaissance Europe, 1450-1620*. London: Fontana Press, 1985.

Hale, John R. "Women and War in the Visual Arts of the Renaissance." In: *War, Literature and the Arts in Sixteenth-Century Europe*. Ed. J.R. Mulryne and M. Shewring. New York, 1989, pp. 43-62.

Hanlon, Gregory. *The Twilight of a Military Tradition: Italian Aristocrats and European Conflicts, 1560-1800*. London, 1998.

Housley, Norman. "'Pro Deo et patria Mori': le patriotisme sanctifié en Europe, 1400-1600." In: *Guerre et concurrence entre les États européens du XIVe au XVIIIe siècle*. Ed. Philippe Contamine. Fondation Européenne de la Science: Les origines de l'État moderne en Europe, XIIIe-XVIIIe siècle. Paris: Presses universitaires de France, 1998, pp. 269-304.

Jones, Colin. "New Military History for Old? War and Society in Early Modern Europe," *European Studies Review* 12 (1982), 97-108.

Kaiser, David. *Politics and War: European Conflict from Philip II to Hitler*. Cambridge: Harvard University Press, 1990.

Kennedy, Paul. *The Rise and Fall of the Great Powers: Economic Change and Military Conflict from 1500 to 2000*. New York: Vintage Books, 1987.

Kidwell, Carol. *Marullus: Soldier Poet of the Renaissance*. London: Duckworth, 1989.

Kiernan, V.G. "Foreign Mercenaries and Absolute Monarchy." In: *Crisis in Europe, 1560-1660*. Ed. Trevor Aston. Garden City: Doubleday and Company, Inc., 1967.

Kiser, E., et al. "Ruler Autonomy and War in Early Modern Western Europe," *International Studies Quarterly* 39 (1995), 109-38.

Kleinschmidt, Harald. "An Early Case of Social Disciplining: The Lansquenet Mode of Fighting," *Historia juris* 4 (1995).

Kleinschmidt, Harald. "Die Schneckenformation und die Entwicklung der Feuerwaffentaktik von Maximilian I bis zu Elizabeth I," *Publication du centre européen d'études Bourguignonnes* 26 (1985), 105-12.

Kohler, Alfred. "Kriegsorganisation und Kriegführung in der Zeit Karls V," *Historisches Jahrbuch* 11 (1991), 433-51.

Kroener, Bernhard R. "Vom Landsknecht zum Soldaten. Anmerkungen zu Sozialprestige, Selbstverständis und Leistungsfähigkeit von Soldaten in den Armeen des 16. Jahrhunderts." In: *XXII. Kongreß der Internationalen Kommission für Militärgeschichte Acta 22: Von Crécy bis Mohács Kriegswesen im späten Mittelalter (1346-1526)*. Vienna, 1997, pp. 79-92.

Kroener, H. "L'État moderne et la 'société militaire' au XVIIIe siècle." In: *Guerre et concurrence entre les États européens du XIVe au XVIIIe siècle*. Ed. Philippe Contamine. Fondation Européenne de la Science: Les origines de l'État moderne en Europe, XIIIe-XVIIIe siècle. Paris: Presses universitaires de France, 1998, pp. 237-68.

Levy, Jack S. *War in the Modern Great Power System, 1495-1975*. Lexington, 1983.

Lochner, Karl E. *Die Entwicklungensphasen der europäische Fechtkunst*. Vienna, 1953.

Loucas, Ioannis. "La géopolitique de l'occident et l'Hellénisme au début des temps modernes." In: *Actas do XXIV congresso internacional de historía militar*. Centro cultural de Belém, 24 a 29 de agosto, 1998. Lisbon: Comissão Portuguesa de Historía Militar, 1998, pp. 94-104.

Majewski, Wieslaw. "The Polish Art of War in the Sixteenth and Seventeenth Century." In: *A Republic of Nobles: Studies in Polish History to 1864*. Ed. J.K. Fedorowicz. Cambridge, 1982, pp. 179-97.

Mallett, Michael E. "The Art of War." In: *Handbook of European History, 1400-1600: Late Middle Ages, Renaissance, and Reformation*. Vol. I: *Structures and Assertions*. Ed. Thomas A. Brady, Jr., Heiko A. Oberman, and James D. Tracy. Leiden: E.J. Brill, 1994; rpt. Grand Rapids: William B Eerdmans Publishing Company, 1996, pp. 535-62.

Meyer, Jean. "États routes, guerre et espace." In: *Guerre et concurrence entre les États européens du XIVe au XVIIIe siècle.* Ed. Philippe Contamine. Fondation Européenne de la Science: Les origines de l'État moderne en Europe, XIIIe-XVIIIe siècle. Paris: Presses universitaires de France, 1998, pp. 167-98.

Miller, Douglas. *The Landsknechts.* London: Osprey, 1976.

Moor, J.A. de. "Experience and Experiment: Some Reflections Upon the Military Developments in Sixteenth and Seventeenth Century Europe." In: *Exercise of Arms: Warfare in the Netherlands, 1568-1648.* Ed. M. van den Hoeven. Leiden, 1998, pp. 17-32.

Mork, Gordon R. "Flint and Steel: A Study in Military Technology and Tactics in 17th-Century Europe," *Smithsonian Journal of History* (Sum 1970), 171-213.

Murrin, Michael. *History and Warfare in Renaissance Epic.* Chicago: The University of Chicago Press, 1994.

Nell, Martin. *Die Landsknecht: Entstehung der eersten deutschen Infanterie.* Berlin, 1914; rpt. Vaduz: Kraus, 1965.

Nowosadtko, Jutta. "Zur Rolle der stehenden Heere innerhalb der frühneuzeitlichen Gesellschaft." In: *Klio in Uniform? Probleme und Perspektiven einer modernen Militärgeschichte der Frühen Neuzeit.* Ed. Ralf Pröve. Cologne, 1997, pp. 5-34.

Oman, Charles. *A History of the Art of War in the Sixteenth Century.* Rpt. London: Greenhill, 1991.

Parker, Geoffrey. "Dynastic War, 1494-1660." In: *The Cambridge Illustrated History of Warfare: The Triumph of the West.* Ed. Geoffrey Parker. Cambridge: Cambridge University Press, 1995, pp. 146-63.

Parker, Geoffrey. "Warfare." In: *New Cambridge Modern History.* Vol. 13: *Companion Volume.* Ed. Peter Burke. Cambridge: Cambridge University Press, 1979, pp. 201-19.

Polišenský, J.V. and Frederick Snider. *War and Society in Europe, 1618-1648*. Cambridge: Cambridge University Press, 1978.

Porter, Bruce D. *War and the Rise of the State: The Military Foundations of Modern Politics*. New York: The Free Press, 1994.

Potter, David. "Les allemands et les armées françaises au XVIe siècle. Jean-Philippe Rhingrave, Chef de lansquenets: Étude suivie de sa correspondance en France, 1548-1566," *Francia* 20/2 (1993), 1-20; 21/2 (1994), 1-61.

Puddu, R. *Eserciti e monarchie nazionale nei secoli XV-XVI*. Florence, 1975.

Quaas, Gerhard. *Das Handwerk der Landsknecht: Waffen und Bewaffnung zwischen 1500 und 1600*. Militärgeschichte und Wehrwissenschaften, 3. Onasbrück: Biblio Verlag, 1997.

Raudzens, George. "In Search of Better Quantification for War History: Numerical Superiority and Casualty Rates in Early Modern Europe," *War and Society* 15 (1997), 1-30.

Redlich, Fritz. *De praeda militari: Looting and Booty, 1500-1815*. Vierteljahrschrift für Sozial- und Wirtschaftsgeschichte, 39. Wiesbaden: F. Steiner, 1956.

Repgen, Konrad. "What is a 'Religious War'?" In: *Politics and Society in Reformation Europe: Essays for Sir Geoffrey Elton on his Sixty-Fifth Birthday*. Ed. E.I. Kouri and T. Scott. New York, 1987, pp. 311-28.

Ropp, Theodore. *War in the Modern World*. 2nd ed. New York: Collier Books, 1962.

Rovighi, Alberto. "L'impresa di Colombo e l'anno 1492 quali momenti di grande evoluzione dell'arte militare e di inizio dell'era moderna." In: *Acta del XVIII Congresso internazionale di storia militare: La scoperta del nuovo mondo e la sua influenza nella storia militare*. Ed. Paolo Alberini and Michele Nones. Turin, 1993, pp. 125-40.

Schulze, Winfried. *Landesdefension und Staatsverfassung*. Vienna: Böhaus, 1973.

Shimpo, Hideo. "Zur verfassungsgeschichtlichen Bedeutung des Landes-defensionswesens," *Zeitschrift für historische Forschung* 19 (1992), 341-58.

"Talhoffer's *Fechtbuch*," *Royal Armouries Yearbook* 4 (1999), 189-92.

Tallett, Frank. *War and Society in Early-Modern Europe, 1495-1715.* London: Routledge, 1992.

Thompson, I.A.A. "The European Crisis of the 1590s: The Impact of War." In: *The European Crisis of the 1590s: Essays in Comparative History.* Ed. P. Clark. London, 1985, pp. 261-84.

Tilly, Charles. *Coercion, Capital, and the European States, AD 990-1990.* Oxford, 1990.

Trease, Geoffrey. *The Condottieri: Soldiers of Fortune.* New York: Holt, Rinehart and Winston, 1971.

Verrier, Frédérique *Les armes de Minerve: L'humanisme militaire dans l'Italie du XVIe siècle.* Paris: Presses de l'Université de Paris-Sorbonne, 1997.

Wang, A. *Der 'miles christianus' im 16. und 17. Jahrhundert und seine mittelalterliche Tradition: Ein Beitrag zum Verhältnis von sprachlicher und graphischer Bildlichkeit.* Bern and Frankfurt, 1975.

Weigley, Russell F. *The Age of Battles: The Quest for Decisive Warfare from Breitenfeld to Waterloo.* Bloomington: Indiana University Press, 1991.

Wilson, Peter. "European Warfare 1450-1815." In: *War in the Early Modern World, 1450-1815.* Ed. Jeremy Black. London, 1999, pp. 177-206.

Wurm, Helmut. "Wie groß waren Ritter und Landsknechte im 16. Und 17. Jahrhundert? Über Vesuche der Körperhöhenschätzung von Harnischträgern nach Harnischmessungen einschließlich einer genauen Darstellung der möglichen Methoden," *Waffen- und Köstumkunde* 26 (1984), 97-110, 27 (1985), 49-74.

Early Modern – Military Revolution

Adams, Simon. "Tactics or Politics? 'The Military Revolution' and the Hapsburg Hegemony, 1525-1648." In: *Tools of War: Instruments, Ideas, and Institutions of Warfare, 1445-1871.* Ed. John A. Lynn. Urbana, 1990, pp. 28-52; in: *The Military Revolution Debate: Readings on the Military Transformation of Early Modern Europe.* Ed. C.J. Rogers. Boulder, 1995, pp. 253-72.

Arnold, Thomas F. "Fortifications and the Military Revolution: The Gonzaga Experience, 1530-1630." In: *The Military Revolution Debate: Readings on the Military Transformation of Early Modern Europe.* Ed. C.J. Rogers. Boulder, 1995, pp. 201-26.

Ayton, Andrew and J.L. Price. "Introduction: The Military Revolution from a Medieval Perspective." In: *The Medieval Military Revolution: State, Soceity and Military Change in Medieval and Early Modern Europe.* Ed. A. Ayton and J.L. Price. London, 1995, pp. 1-22.

Bean, Richard. "War and the Birth of the Nation State," *Journal of Economic History* 33 (1973), 203-21.

Bérenger, Jean. "Existe-t-il une révolution militaire à l'époque moderne?" In: *La révolution militaire en Europe (XVe-XVIIIe siècles): Actes du colloque organisé le 4 avril 1997 à Saint-Cyr Coëtquidan par le Centre de recherches des Écoles de Coëtquidan, par l'Institut de Recherches sur les Civilisations de l'Occident Moderne (Université de Paris-Sorbonne) et par l'Institut de Stratégie Comparée.* Ed. Jean Bérenger. Coëtquidan: Institut de Stratégie Comparée, 1998, pp. 7-22.

Black, Jeremy. *A Military Revolution? Military Change and European Society, 1550-1800.* Atlantic Highlands: Humanities Press International, Inc., 1991.

Black, Jeremy. "A Military Revolution? A 1660-1792 Perspective." In: *The Military Revolution Debate: Readings on the Military Transformation of Early Modern Europe.* Ed. C.J. Rogers. Boulder, 1995, pp. 95-114.

Braddick, M.J. "An English Military Revolution?" *Historical Journal* 36 (1993), 965-75.

Bridgman, Jon M. "Gunpowder and Governmental Power: War in Early Modern Europe (1494-1825)." In: *War: A Historical, Political and Social Study*. Ed. L.L. Farrar, Jr. Santa Barbara, 1978, pp. 105-11.

Chagniot, Jean. "Critique du concept de révolution militaire." In: *La révolution militaire en Europe (XVe-XVIIIe siècles): Actes du colloque organisé le 4 avril 1997 à Saint-Cyr Coëtquidan par le Centre de recherches des Écoles de Coëtquidan, par l'Institut de Recherches sur les Civilisations de l'Occident Moderne (Université de Paris-Sorbonne) et par l'Institut de Stratégie Comparée*. Ed. Jean Bérenger. Coëtquidan: Institut de Stratégie Comparée, 1998, pp. 23-30.

Cornette, Joël. "La révolution militaire et l'état moderne," *Revue d'histoire moderne et contemporaine* 41 (1994), 696-709.

Corvisier, André. "Conclusion générale." In: *La révolution militaire en Europe (XVe-XVIIIe siècles): Actes du colloque organisé le 4 avril 1997 à Saint-Cyr Coëtquidan par le Centre de recherches des Écoles de Coëtquidan, par l'Institut de Recherches sur les Civilisations de l'Occident Moderne (Université de Paris-Sorbonne) et par l'Institut de Stratégie Comparée*. Ed. Jean Bérenger. Coëtquidan: Institut de Stratégie Comparée, 1998, pp. 149-57.

DeVries, Kelly. "Gunpowder Weaponry and the Rise of the Early Modern State," *War in History* 5 (1998), 127-45.

Downing, Brian M. *The Military Revolution and Political Change: Origins of Democracy and Autocracy in Early Modern Europe*. Princeton: Princeton University Press, 1992.

Duffy, Michael. "Introduction: The Military Revolution and the State, 1500-1800." In: *The Military Revolution and the State, 1500-1800*. Ed. M. Duffy. Exeter, 1980, pp. 1-9.

Eltis, David. *The Military Revolution in Sixteenth-Century Europe*. London: I.B. Tauris Publishers, 1995.

Finer, Samuel E. "State and Nation-Building in Europe: The Role of the Military." In: *The Formation of National States in Western Europe*. Ed. C.Tilly. Princeton, 1975, pp. 84-163.

Guilmartin, John Francis, Jr. "The Miltiary Revolution: Origins and First Tests Abroad." in: *The Military Revolution Debate: Readings on the Military Transformation of Early Modern Europe.* Ed. C.J. Rogers. Boulder, 1995, pp. 299-333.

Hall, Bert S. "Weapons of War and Late Medieval Cities: Technological Innovation and Tactical Changes." In: *Teachnology and Resource Use in Medieval Europe: Cathedrals, Mills and Mines.* Ed, E.B. Smith and M. Wolfe. Aldershot: Ashgate, 1997, pp. 185-208.

Hall, Bert S. and Kelly R. DeVries. "Essay Review–The 'Military Revolution' Revisited," *Technology and Culture* 31 (1990), 500-07.

Jespersen, Knud J.V. "Det 16. århundredes 'militære revolution' og det danske adelsrytteri.–En sammenlignende analyse," *Militärhistorisk Tidskrift* (1981), 3-18.

Jespersen, Knud J.V. "Social Change and Military Revolution in Early Modern Europe: Some Danish Evidence," *Historical Journal* 26 (1983), 1-13.

Jones, Colin. "The Military Revolution and the Professionalisation of the French Army Under the Ancien Regime." In: *The Military Revolution and the State, 1500-1800.* Ed. M. Duffy. Exeter, 1980, pp. 29-48; and In: *The Military Revolution Debate: Readings on the Military Transformation of Early Modern Europe.* Ed. C.J. Rogers. Boulder, 1995, pp. 149-68.

Kingra, Mahinder S. "The *Trace Italienne* and the Military Revolution during the Eighty Years War, 1567-1648," *Journal of Military History* 57 (1993), 431-46.

Le Flem, Jean-Paul. "Diego Garcia de Palacios et l'artillerie: Un précurseur de la balistique moderne?" In: *La révolution militaire en Europe (XVe-XVIIIe siècles): Actes du colloque organisé le 4 avril 1997 à Saint-Cyr Coëtquidan par le Centre de recherches des Écoles de Coëtquidan, par l'Institut de Recherches sur les Civilisations de l'Occident Moderne (Université de Paris-Sorbonne) et par l'Institut de Stratégie Comparée.* Ed. Jean Bérenger. Coëtquidan: Institut de Stratégie Comparée, 1998, pp. 51-64.

Lindegren, Jan. "The Swedish 'Military State', 1560-1720," *Scandinavian Journal of History* 10 (1985), 305-36.

Lynn, John A. "Tactical Evolution in the French Army, 1560-1660," *French Historical Studies* 14 (1985), 176-91.

Lynn, John A. "The *trace italienne* and the Growth of Armies: The French Case," *Journal of Military History* 55 (1991), 297-330; in: *The Military Revolution Debate: Readings on the Military Transformation of Early Modern Europe*. Ed. C.J. Rogers. Boulder, 1995, pp. 169-200.

Mears, John A. "The Emergence of the Standing Professional Army in Seventeenth-Century Europe," *Social Science Quarterly* 50 (1969), 106-15.

Murtagh, Harman. "Ireland, the Military Revolution and the Thirty Years' War." In: *Bellum Tricennale: The Thirty Years War*. XXIIIrd Colloquium of the International Commission of Military History. Prague, 1999, pp. 309-26.

Nouzille, Jean. "Les impériaux aux XVIIe et XVIIIe siècles." In: *La révolution militaire en Europe (XVe-XVIIIe siècles): Actes du colloque organisé le 4 avril 1997 à Saint-Cyr Coëtquidan par le Centre de recherches des Écoles de Coëtquidan, par l'Institut de Recherches sur les Civilisations de l'Occident Moderne (Université de Paris-Sorbonne) et par l'Institut de Stratégie Comparée*. Ed. Jean Bérenger. Coëtquidan: Institut de Stratégie Comparée, 1998, pp. 65-102.

Parker, Geoffrey. "In Defense of *The Military Revolution*." In: *The Military Revolution Debate: Readings on the Military Transformation of Early Modern Europe*. Ed. C.J. Rogers. Boulder, 1995, pp. 337-66.

Parker, Geoffrey. "The Gunpowder Revolution, 1300-1500." In: *The Cambridge Illustrated History of Warfare: The Triumph of the West*. Ed. Geoffrey Parker. Cambridge: Cambridge University Press, 1995, pp. 106-17.

Parker, Geoffrey. *The Military Revolution: Military Innovation and the Rise of the West, 1500-1800*. Cambridge: Cambridge University Press, 1988.

Parker, Geoffrey. "The 'Military Revolution,' 1560-1660–a Myth?" *Journal of Modern History* 48 (1976), 195-214, in: *Spain and the Netherlands, 1559-1659: Ten Studies*. 2nd ed. London, 1990, pp. 86-105; in: *The Military Revolution Debate: Readings on the Military Transformation of Early Modern Europe*. Ed. C.J. Rogers. Boulder, 1995, pp. 37-54.

Parrott, David A. "Strategy and Tactics in the Thirty Years' War: The 'Military Revolution,'" *Militärgeschichtlichte Mitteilungen* 38 (1985), 7-25; in: *The Military Revolution Debate: Readings on the Military Transformation of Early Modern Europe*. Ed. C.J. Rogers. Boulder, 1995, pp. 227-52.

Pernot, Jean-Francis. "'La trace italienne', élements d'approche." In: *La révolution militaire en Europe (XVe-XVIIIe siècles): Actes du colloque organisé le 4 avril 1997 à Saint-Cyr Coëtquidan par le Centre de recherches des Écoles de Coëtquidan, par l'Institut de Recherches sur les Civilisations de l'Occident Moderne (Université de Paris-Sorbonne) et par l'Institut de Stratégie Comparée*. Ed. Jean Bérenger. Coëtquidan: Institut de Stratégie Comparée, 1998, pp. 31-50.

Pettengill, John S. "Firearms and the Distribution of Income: A Neo-Classical Model," *Review of Radical Political Economics* 13 (Summer 1981), 1-11.

Riccioli, J.-L. "Le problème du passage des cours d'eau au XVIIIe siècle." In: *La révolution militaire en Europe (XVe-XVIIIe siècles): Actes du colloque organisé le 4 avril 1997 à Saint-Cyr Coëtquidan par le Centre de recherches des Écoles de Coëtquidan, par l'Institut de Recherches sur les Civilisations de l'Occident Moderne (Université de Paris-Sorbonne) et par l'Institut de Stratégie Comparée*. Ed. Jean Bérenger. Coëtquidan: Institut de Stratégie Comparée, 1998, pp. 115-38.

Roberts, Michael. "The Military Revolution, 1560-1660." In: *Essays in Swedish History*. London, 1967, pp. 195-225; in: *The Military Revolution Debate: Readings on the Military Transformation of Early Modern Europe*. Ed. C.J. Rogers. Boulder, 1995, pp. 13-36.

Rogers, Clifford J. "The Military Revolution in History and Historiography." In: *The Military Revolution Debate: Readings on the Military Transformation of Early Modern Europe*. Ed. C.J. Rogers. Boulder, 1995, pp. 1-10.

Rogers, Clifford J. "'Military Revolutions' and 'Revolutions in Military Affairs': A Historian's Perspective." In: *Toward a Revolution in Military Affairs? Defense and Security at the Dawn of the Twenty-First Century*. Ed. Thierry Gongora and Harald von Riekhoff. Contributions in Military Studies, 197. Westport: Greenwood Press, 2000, pp. 21-34.

Storrs, Christopher and H.M. Scott. "The Military Revolution and the European Nobility, c. 1600-1800," *War in History* 3 (1996), 1-41.

Stradling, R.A. "Review Article–'A Military Revolution': The Fall-Out from the Fall-In," *European History Quarterly* 24 (1994), 271-78.

Thiriet, Jean-Michel. "Le renseignement aux XVIIe et XVIIIe siècles: le cas de Vienne et des États italiens." In: *La révolution militaire en Europe (XVe-XVIIIe siècles): Actes du colloque organisé le 4 avril 1997 à Saint-Cyr Coëtquidan par le Centre de recherches des Écoles de Coëtquidan, par l'Institut de Recherches sur les Civilisations de l'Occident Moderne (Université de Paris-Sorbonne) et par l'Institut de Stratégie Comparée.* Ed. Jean Bérenger. Coëtquidan: Institut de Stratégie Comparée, 1998, pp. 103-14.

Thompson, I.A.A. "'Money, Money, and Yet More Money!' Finance, the Fiscal-State, and the Military Revolution: Spain, 1500-1650." In: *The Military Revolution Debate: Readings on the Military Transformation of Early Modern Europe.* Ed. C.J. Rogers. Boulder, 1995, pp. 273-98.

Thompson, William R. "The Military Superiority Thesis and Ascendency of Western Eurasia in the World System," *Journal of World History* 10 (1999), 143-78.

Topolski, Jerzy. "La réforme militaire en Pologne au XVIIIe siècle." In: *La révolution militaire en Europe (XVe-XVIIIe siècles): Actes du colloque organisé le 4 avril 1997 à Saint-Cyr Coëtquidan par le Centre de recherches des Écoles de Coëtquidan, par l'Institut de Recherches sur les Civilisations de l'Occident Moderne (Université de Paris-Sorbonne) et par l'Institut de Stratégie Comparée.* Ed. Jean Bérenger. Coëtquidan: Institut de Stratégie Comparée, 1998, pp. 139-48.

Early Modern – Military Revolution Abroad (Colonial Warfare)

Almeida, Justino M. de. "A guerra e o encontro de civilizações n' *O Lusíadas.*" In: *Actas do XXIV congresso internacional de história militar.* Centro cultural de Belém, 24 a 29 de agosto, 1998. Lisbon: Comissão Portuguesa de História Militar, 1998, pp. 69-80.

Appleby, John C. "War, Politics, and Colonization, 1558-1625." In: *The Origins of Empire: British Overseas Enterprise to the Close of the Seventeenth Century*. Ed. Nicholas Canny. The Oxford History of the British Empire, I. Oxford: Oxford University Press, 1998, pp. 55-78.

Baquer, Miguel Alonso. "L'éthique de la conquête et la morale des Conquistadores." In: *Acta del XVIII Congresso internazionale di storia militare: La scoperta del nuovo mondo e la sua influenza nella storia militare*. Ed. Paolo Alberini and Michele Nones. Turin, 1993, pp. 19-30.

Bessa, Carlos Gomes. "L'union du Portugal à l'Espagne, 1580-1640: L'expansion du Brésil et le déplacement du méridien de Tordesillas." In: *Acta del XVIII Congresso internazionale di storia militare: La scoperta del nuovo mondo e la sua influenza nella storia militare*. Ed. Paolo Alberini and Michele Nones. Turin, 1993, pp. 439-56.

Blanco Nuñes, Jose Maria. "El encuentro Español con la tierra firme americana." In: *Actas do XXIV congresso internacional de historía militar*. Centro cultural de Belém, 24 a 29 de agosto, 1998. Lisbon: Comissão Portuguesa de Historía Militar, 1998, pp. 139-50.

Braid, Douglas H.P. "Ordnance and Empire: Portugal in the Fifteenth and Sixteenth Century," *Journal of the Ordnance Society* 4 (1992), 55-66.

Bruhn de Hoffmeyer, Ada. "Las armas de los conquistadores. Las armas de los Aztecas," *Gladius* 17 (1986), 5-56.

Chao, Andrés Mas. "L'espace géographique caribien, clef de l'expansion espagnole à la Amerique." In: *Actas do XXIV congresso internacional de historía militar*. Centro cultural de Belém, 24 a 29 de agosto, 1998. Lisbon: Comissão Portuguesa de Historía Militar, 1998, pp. 105-16.

Dogaru, Mircea. "Conquista et reconquista péruviennes: Les causes de désastre militaire inca de Cajamarca." In: *Acta del XVIII Congresso internazionale di storia militare: La scoperta del nuovo mondo e la sua influenza nella storia militare*. Ed. Paolo Alberini and Michele Nones. Turin, 1993, pp. 463-72.

Dogaru, Mircea. "Les conséquences des grandes découvèrtes géographiques portugaises et éspanoles dans la société Roumaine du XVIe siècle." In: *Actas do XXIV congresso internacional de historía militar*.

Centro cultural de Belém, 24 a 29 de agosto, 1998. Lisbon: Comissão Portuguesa de História Militar, 1998, pp. 215-25.

Guilmartin, John Francis, Jr. "The Military Revolution: Origins and First Tests Abroad." in: *The Military Revolution Debate: Readings on the Military Transformation of Early Modern Europe*. Ed. C.J. Rogers. Boulder, 1995, pp. 299-333.

Hassig, Ross. "Aztec Warfare," *History Today* 40 (Feb 1990), 17-24.

Hassig, Ross. *Aztec Warfare: Imperial Expansion and Political Control*. Norman: University of Oklahoma Press, 1988.

Hassig, Ross. *War and Society in Ancient Mesoamerica*. Berkeley and Los Angeles: University of California Press, 1992.

Hassig, Ross. "War, Politics and the Conquest of Mexico." In: *War in the Early Modern World, 1450-1815*. Ed. Jeremy Black. London, 1999, pp. 207-36.

Kupperman, Karen Ordahl. *Indians and English: Facing Off in Early America*. Ithaca: Cornell University Press, 2000.

Lenman, Bruce P. "The Transition to European Military Ascendancy in India, 1600-1800." In: *Tools of War: Instruments, Ideas, and Institutions of Warfare, 1445-1871*. Ed. John A. Lynn. Urbana, 1990, pp. 100-30.

Martinez, Jose Luis. "Artilleros y exploraciones de Hernan Cortes en el pacifico." In: *Atti del v convegno internazionale di studi colombiani: "Navi e navigazione nei secoli XV e XVI"*. Genoa, 1990, I:245-92.

McNeill, William H. "World History and the Rise and Fall of the West," *Journal of World History* 9 (1998), 215-36.

Moro, Tiberio. "L'influenza delle armi nel periodo delle scoperte e della conquista del continente americano." In: *Acta del XVIII Congresso internazionale di storia militare: La scoperta del nuovo mondo e la sua influenza nella storia militare*. Ed. Paolo Alberini and Michele Nones. Turin, 1993, pp. 93-124.

Nester, William R. *The Great Frontier War: Britain, France, and the Imperial Struggle for North America, 1607-1755*. Westport: Praeger, 2000.

Nunes, António Lopes Pires. "Les guerres hollandaises au Brésil du XVIIe siècle: Confrontation de deux écoles militaires." In: *Acta del XVIII Congresso internazionale di storia militare: La scoperta del nuovo mondo e la sua influenza nella storia militare*. Ed. Paolo Alberini and Michele Nones. Turin, 1993, pp. 457-62.

Oberg, Michael Leroy. *Dominion and Civility: English Imperialism and Native America, 1585-1685*. Ithaca: Cornell University Press, 1999.

Parker, Geoffrey. "Joint Stock and Gunshot: European Conquest and Trade, 1500 to 1800," *MHQ* 4 (Sum 1992), 8-17.

Picciuolo, José L. "Expediciones poblacionales españolas en el actual territorio Argentino, siglo XVI." In: *Actas do XXIV congresso internacional de historía militar*. Centro cultural de Belém, 24 a 29 de agosto, 1998. Lisbon: Comissão Portuguesa de Historía Militar, 1998, pp. 151-66.

Raudzens, George. "Military Revolution or Maritime Evolution? Military Superiorities or Transportation Advantages as Main Causes of European Colonial Conquests to 1788," *Journal of Military History* 63 (1999), 631-41.

Raudzens, George. "So Why Were the Aztecs Conquered, and What Were the Wider Implications? Testing Military Superiority as a Cause of Europe's Pre-industrial Colonial Conquests," *War in History* 2 (1995), 87-104.

Raudzens, George. "Debate–Why Did Amerindian Defences Fail? Parallels in the European Invasions of Hispaniola, Virginia and Beyond," *War in History* 3 (1996), 331-52.

Rodger, N.A.M. "Guns and Sails in the First Phase of English Colonization, 1500-1650." In: *The Origins of Empire: British Overseas Enterprise to the Close of the Seventeenth Century*. Ed. Nicholas Canny. The Oxford History of the British Empire, I. Oxford: Oxford University Press, 1998, pp. 79-98.

Sánchez Prieto, Ana Bélen. "Die militärische Macht des kastilischen Adels zur Zeit der Entdeckung Amerikas." In: *Acta del XVIII Congresso internazionale di storia militare: La scoperta del nuovo mondo e la sua influenza nella storia militare*. Ed. Paolo Alberini and Michele Nones. Turin, 1993, pp. 37-44.

Seed, Patricia. "Conquest of the Americas, 1500-1650." In: *The Cambridge Illustrated History of Warfare: The Triumph of the West*. Ed. Geoffrey Parker. Cambridge: Cambridge University Press, 1995, pp. 132-45.

Starkey, Armstrong. "European-Native American Warfare in North America 1513-1815." In: *War in the Early Modern World, 1450-1815*. Ed. Jeremy Black. London, 1999, pp. 237-62.

Thorton, John. "Warfare, Slave-Trading and European Influence: Atlantic Africa 1450-1800." In: *War in the Early Modern World, 1450-1815*. Ed. Jeremy Black. London, 1999, pp. 129-46.

Early Modern – Diplomacy

Bérenger, Jean. "La diplomatie imperiale: personnel et structure." In: *Guerre et pouvoir en Europe au XVIe siècle*. Ed. V. Barrie-Currien. Paris: Veyrier, 1991, pp. 57-77.

Cant, R. "The Embassy of the Earl of Leicester to Denmark in 1632," *English Historical Review* 54 (1939).

Hale, John R. "International Relations in the West: Diplomacy and War." In: *The New Cambridge Modern History*. Vol. 1: *The Renaissance, 1493-1520*. Ed. G.R. Potter. Cambridge: Cambridge University Press, 1971, pp. 259-91.

Mattingly, Garrett. *Renaissance Diplomacy*. Harmondsworth: Penguin Books, 1965.

Paix de Vervins (1598), La. Amiens: Fédération des Société d'Histoire er d'Archéologie de l'Aisne/Société historique et archéologique de Verins et de la Thiérache, 1998.

Reeve, L.J. "Quiroga's Paper of 1631: A Missing Link in Anglo-Spanish Diplomacy during the Thirty Years War," *English Historical Review* 101 (1986).

Russell, Joycelyne G. *The Field of Cloth of Gold: Men and Manners in 1520*. London: Routledge and Kegan Paul, 1969.

Russell, Joycelyne G. *Peacemaking in the Renaissance*. London: Duckworth, 1996.

Russell, Joycelyne G. "The Search for Universal Peace: the Conferences at Calais and Bruges in 1521," *Bulletin for the Institute for Historical Research* 44 (1971), 162-93.

Early Modern – Eastern Europe (including Russia)

Dangl, Vojtech and Vojtech Kopcan. *Vojenské dejiny Slovenska,1526-1711*. Bratisalava: RESS s.r.o. Senica, 1995.

Davies, Brian L. "The Development of Russian Military Power, 1453-1815." In: *European Warfare, 1453-1815*. Ed. Jeremy Black. New York: St. Martin's Press, 1999, pp. 145-79.

Englund, Peter. *The Battle of Poltava*. London: Victor Gollancz, 1992.

Hellie, Richard. "Warfare, Changing Military Technology, and the Evolution of Muscovite Society." In: *Tools of War: Instruments, Ideas, and Institutions of Warfare, 1445-1871*. Ed. John A. Lynn. Urbana, 1990, pp. 74-99.

Iorga, N. "Les développement des troupes mercenaires dans les pays roumains des origines à la fin du XVIIIe siècle," *Revue internationale d'histoire militaire* 3 (1939-40), 140-43.

Jespersen, Knud J.V. "Warfare and Society in the Baltic, 1500-1800." In: *European Warfare, 1453-1815*. Ed. Jeremy Black. New York: St. Martin's Press, 1999, pp. 180-200.

Massa, Isaac. *A Short History of the Beginnings and Origins of These Present Wars in Moscow under the Reign of Various Sovereigns down to the Year 1610*. Trans. G. Edward Orchard. Toronto: University of Toronto Press, 1982.

Millar, Gilbert John. "The Albanians: Sixteenth-Century Mercenaries," *History Today* 26 (1976), 468-72.

Oakley, Stewart P. "War in the Baltic, 1550-1790." Ed. Jeremy Black. In: *The Origins of War in Early Modern Europe*. Edinburgh, 1987, pp. 52-71.

Ostrowski, Donald. *Muscovy and the Mongols: Cross-Cultural Influences on the Steppe Frontier, 1304-1589.* Cambridge: Cambridge University Press, 1998.

Plewczyński, Marek. "Söldnertruppen in Polen um die Wende des 15. Und 16. Jahrhunderts." In: *XXII. Kongreß der Internationalen Kommission für Militärgeschichte Acta 22: Von Crécy bis Mohács Kriegswesen im späten Mittelalter (1346-1526).* Vienna, 1997, pp. 345-63.

Rosetti, R. "Note on Mercenaries: Mercenaries in the Rumanian Army and Rumanian Mercenaries in Foreign Armies," *Revue internationale d'histoire militaire* 5 (1941-45), 34-42.

Rystad, Göran. "The Rise and Fall of the Swedish Empire: The Experience of a Small State as a Great Power in the 17th Century." In: *Commission Internationale d'Histoire Militaire. Acta 22: Warfare Throughout the Ages between Small States and Big Powers and Small States Among Themselves.* Tel Aviv: Israel Commission of Military History, 1984, pp. 247-58.

Safta, Ion. "L'art militaire Roumain à l'époque de la Renaissance, composante originelle de l'art militaire européen." In: *Acta del XVIII Congresso internazionale di storia militare: La scoperta del nuovo mondo e la sua influenza nella storia militare.* Ed. Paolo Alberini and Michele Nones. Turin, 1993, pp. 45-54.

Smith, Dianne L. "Muscovite Logistics, 1462-1598," *Slavonic and East European Review* 71 (1993), 35-65.

Wirtschafter, Elise Kimerling. "Social Misfits: Veterans and Soldiers' Families in Servile Russia," *Journal of Military History* 59 (1995), 215-36.

Żygulski, Zdzisław, Jr. "The Battle of Orsha." In: *Art, Arms and Armour: An International Anthology.* Vol I: *1979-80.* Ed. Robert Held. Chiasso: Acquafresca Editrice, 1979, pp. 108-43.

Early Modern – England

Ambler, R.W. "'Wise and Experimented': Sir William Pelham, Elizabethan Soldier and Landlord, c. 1560-87." In: *The Medieval Military Revo-*

lution: State, Society and Military Change in Medieval and Early Modern Europe. Ed. A. Ayton and J.L. Price. London, 1995, pp. 163-81.

Anglin, Jay P. "The Schools of Defence in Elizabethan London," *Renaissance Quarterly* 37 (1984), 393-410.

Anglo, Sydney. *Images of Tudor Kingship*. London: B.A. Seaby Ltd., 1992.

Barker, Felix. "Sir Philip Sidney and the Forgotten War of 1586," *History Today* 36 (Nov 1986), 40-46.

Beer, Barrett. *Northumberland: The Political Career of John Dudley*. Kent: Kent State University Press, 1973.

Beer, Barrett. *Rebellion and Riot: Popular Disorder in England during the Reign of Edward VI*. Kent: Kent State University Press, 1982.

Bernard, G.W. "Debate–New Perspectives or Old Complexities?" *English Historical Review* 115 (2000), 113-20.

Borman, Tracy. "Untying the Knot? The Survival of the Anglo-Dutch Alliance, 1587-97," *European Historical Quarterly* 27 (1997), 307-38.

Bourgeois, Eugene J., II. "Meeting the Demands of War: Late-Elizabethan Militia Management in Cambidgeshire," *Local Historian* 26 (1996), 130-41.

Boynton, Lindsay. *The Elizabethan Militia, 1558-1638*. London: David and Charles: Newton Abbot, 1971.

Boynton, Lindsay. "The Tudor Provost-Marshal," *English Historical Review* 77 (1962), 437-55.

Bush, Michael. *The Pilgrimage of Grace: A Study of the Rebel Armies of 1536*. Manchester: Manchester University Press, 1996.

Bush, Michael. "Protector Somerset and the 1549 Rebellions: A Post-Revision Questioned," *English Historical Review* 115 (2000), 103-12.

Butler, T. Blake. "King Henry VIII's Irish Army List," *Irish Genealogist* (1937), 3-13, 36-38.

Chancey, Karen. "The Amboyna Massacre in English Politics, 1624-1632," *Albion* 30 (1998), 583-98.

Clark, Peter. "Popular Protest and Disturbance in Kent, 1558-1640," *Economic History Review* n.s. 29 (1976), 365-81.

Cornish, Paul. "The English Soldier of 1544," *Military Illustrated* 46 (Mar 1992), 28-33.

Cornish, Paul. *Henry VIII's Army*. London: Osprey, 1987.

Coward, B. "The Lieutenancy of Lancashire and Cheshire in the Sixteenth and Early Seventeenth Centuries," *Transactions of the Historical Society of Lancashire and Cheshire* 119 (1967), 39-64.

Cruickshank, C.G. *Army Royal: Henry VIII's Invasion of France, 1513*. Oxford: Clarendon Press, 1969.

Cruickshank, C.G. "Dead-Pays in the Elizabethan Army," *English Historical Review* 53 (1938), 93-97.

Cruickshank, C.G. *Elizabeth's Army*. 2nd ed. Oxford: Clarendon Press, 1966.

Cruickshank, C.G. *The English Occupation of Tournai, 1513-1519*. Oxford: Clarendon Press, 1971.

Cruickshank, C.G. *Henry VIII and the Invasion of France*. New York: St. Martin's Press, 1991.

Cruickshank, C.G. "King Henry VIII's Army: Camp," *History Today* 18 (1968), 852-57.

Cruickshank, C.G. "King Henry VIII's Army: Munitions," *History Today* 19 (1969), 40-45.

Darling, Anthony D. "An English Military Camp during Henry VIII's Boulogne Campaign of 1544," *Man at Arms* 6.6 (Nov-Dec 1984), 12-18.

Davies, Clifford S.L. "England and the French War, 1557-59." In: *The Mid-Tudor Polity, c.1540-1560*. Ed. Jennifer Loach and Robert Tittler. London, 1980, pp. 159-85.

Davies, Clifford S.L. "Henry VIII and Henry V: The Wars in France." In: *The End of the Middle Ages? England in the Fifteenth and Sixteenth Centuries*. Ed. J.L. Watts. Stroud, 1998, pp. 235-62.

Davies, Clifford S.L. "Provisions for Armies, 1509-50: A Study in the Effectiveness of Early Tudor Government," *Economic History Review* 2nd ser. 17 (1964), 234-48.

Davies, Clifford S.L. "Tournai and the English Crown, 1513-1519," *Historical Journal* 41 (1998), 1-26.

Davies, G. *The Early Stuarts, 1603-1660*. Oxford History of England. 2nd ed. Oxford: Clarendon Press, 1959.

Davies, M.B. "Suffolk's Expedition to Montdidier, 1523," *Fouad I University: Bulletin of the Faculty of Arts* 7 (1944), 33-43.

Davis, Harold. "John Bende: Soldier and Translator," *Huntington Library Quarterly* 1 (1937-38), 421-26.

Davis, Ralph. "England and the Mediterranean, 1570-1670." In: *Essays in the Economic and Social History of Tudor England in Honour of R.H. Tawney*. Ed. F.J. Fisher. Cambridge, 1961, pp. 117-37.

Dillon, C.H. "The English Soldier of the Sixteenth Century," *Journal of the Society for Army Historical Research* 1 (1921-22), 200-04.

Dodds, G.L. *Battles in Britain, 1066-1746*. London: Arms and Armour Press, 1996.

Douch, H.L., ed. *The Cornwall Muster Roll for 1569*. Bristol: T.L. Stoate, 1984.

Elton, Geoffrey R. "Taxation for War and Peace in Early-Tudor England." In: *War and Economic Development: Essays in Memory of David Joslin*. Ed. J.M. Winter. Cambridge, 1975, pp. 33-48.

Elton, Geoffrey R. "War and the English in the Reign of Henry VIII." In: *War, Strategy and International Politics: Essays in Honour of Sir Michael Howard*. Ed. Lawrence Freedman, Paul Hayes, and Robert O'Neill. Oxford: Oxford University Press, 1992, pp. 1-17.

Falls, Cyril. *Elizabeth's Irish Wars*. 1950; rpt. New York: Barnes and Noble, Inc., 1970.

Falls, Cyril. *Mountjoy: Elizabethan General*. London: Odhams Press, 1955.

Fissel, Mark Charles. "Tradition and Invention in the Early Stuart Art of War," *Journal of the Society for Army Historical Research* 65 (1987), 133-47.

Fissel, Mark Charles. *War and Government in Britain, 1598-1650*. Manchester: Manchester University Press, 1991.

Fletcher, Anthony. *Tudor Rebellions*. London: Longman, 1986.

Fowler, Alastair. "Spenser and War." In: *War, Literature and the Arts in Sixteenth-Century Europe*. Ed. J.R. Mulryne and M. Shewring. New York, 1989, pp. 147-64.

Gichon, Mordechai. "War and Warfare in the Writings of William Shakespeare." In: *XXII. Kongreß der Internationalen Kommission für Militärgeschichte* Acta 22: *Von Crécy bis Mohács Kriegswesen im späten Mittelalter (1346-1526)*. Vienna, 1997, pp. 107-20.

Goring, Jeremy. "The General Proscription of 1522," *English Historical Review* 86 (1971), 681-705.

Goring, Jeremy. "Social Change and Military Decline in Mid-Tudor England," *History* 60 (1975), 185-97.

Green, A.C.F. "The Loss of Calais," *Army Quarterly* 80 (1959-60), 173-78.

Gruffudd, E. "Boulogne and Calais from 1545 to 1559," trans. M. Bryn Davie, *Fouad I: Bulletin of the Faculty of Arts* 12.1 (May 1950).

Gunn, Steven J. *Charles Brandon, Duke of Suffolk, 1485-1545*. Oxford: Blackwell, 1988.

Gunn, Steven J. "The Duke of Suffolk's March on Paris in 1523," *English Historical Review* 121 (1986), 561-634.

Gunn, Steven J. "The French Wars of Henry VIII." In: *The Origins of War in Early Modern Europe*. Ed. Jeremy Black. Edinburgh, 1987, 28-51.

Hale, John R. "Armies, Navies and the Art of War." In: *The New Cambridge Modern History*. Ed. G.R. Elton. II:481-509.

Hale, John R. *The Art of War and Renaissance England*. Washington, 1961.

Hale, John R. *Incitement to Violence? English Divines on the Theme of War, 1578 to 1631.* The Society for Renaissance Studies Occasional Papers, 5. London: The Society for Renaissance Studies, 1978; in: *Renaissance War Studies.* London, 1983, pp. 487-51

Hale, John R. "International Relations in the West: Diplomacy and War." In: *The New Cambridge Modern History.* Ed. G.R. Potter. I:259-291.

Hale, John R. "On a Tudor Parade Ground: The Captain's Handbook of Henry Barrett, 1562." In: *Renaissance War Studies.* London, 1983, pp. 247-84.

Hale, John R. "The True Shakespearean Blank." In: *Renaissance War Studies.* London, 1983, pp. 421-28.

Hammer, P.E.J. "Myth Making: Politics, Propaganda and the Capture of Cadiz in 1596," *Historical Journal* 40 (1997), 621-42.

Hammer, P.E.J. "New Light on the Cadiz Expedition of 1596," *Historical Research* 70 (1997), 182-202.

Hattaway, Hermann H. "Some Aspects of Tudor Military History," *Army Quarterly* 98 (1969), 53-63.

Heath, Ian. *The Irish Wars, 1485-1603.* London: Osprey, 1993.

Hebb, David D. *Piracy and the English Government, 1616-1642.* Aldershot: Scolar Press, 1994.

Jones, Whitney. *The Mid-Tudor Crisis, 1539-1563.* London: Macmillan, 1973.

Kelsey, Harry. *Sir Francis Drake: The Queen's Pirate.* New Haven: Yale University Press, 1998.

Land, Steven K. *Kett's Rebellion: The Norfolk Rising of 1549.* Ipswich: The Boydell Press, 1977.

Lee, C.D. "The Battle of Beachy Head: Lord Torrington's Conduct," *Mariner's Mirror* 80 (1994), 270-89.

Lely, Peter and James Mildren. *Sir Francis Drake.* A National Trust Pocket Book. Norwich: Jarrold and Sons Ltd., 1988.

Loades, David. *Power in Tudor England.* London: Macmillan, 1997.

Lock, Julian. "'How Many Tercios Has the Pope?' The Spanish War and the Sublination of Elizabethan Anti-Popery," *History* 81 (1996), 197-214.

Lowe, Ben. *Imagining Peace: A History of Early English Pacifist Ideas, 1340-1560*. University Park: Pennsylvania State University Press, 1997.

Lowe, Ben. "Religious Wars and the 'Common Peace': Anglican Anti-War Sentiment in Elizabethan England," *Albion* 28 (1996).

Lowe, Ben. "War and the Commonwealth in Mid-Tudor England," *Sixteenth Century Journal* 21 (1990), 171-92.

Lumpkin, Henry. "The Pictures of Henry VIII's Army in Cotton Manuscript Augustus III," *Journal of the Arms and Armour Society* 3 (1959-61), 145-70.

MacCaffrey, Wallace T. "The Newhaven Expedition, 1562-1563," *Historical Journal* 40 (1997), 1-22.

Mackie, J.D. *The Earlier Tudors, 1485-1558*. Oxford: Clarendon Press, 1952.

Manning, Roger B. *Village Revolts: Social Protest and Popular Disturbances in England, 1509-1640*. Oxford, 1988.

Manning, Roger B. "Violence and Social Conflict in Mid-Tudor Rebellions," *Journal of British Studies* 16 (1977), 18-40.

Marshall-Cornwall, James. "An Expedition to Aquitaine, 1512," *History Today* 23 (1973), 640-47.

Marx, Steven. "Shakespeare's Pacifism," *Renaissance Quarterly* 45 (1992), 49-95.

McGurk, John J.N. "Casualties and Welfare Measures for the Sick and Wounded of the Nine Year War in Ireland, 1593-1602," *Journal of the Society for Army Historical Research* 68 (1990), 22-35; 188-204.

McGurk, John J.N. "The Clergy and the Militia, 1580-1610," *History* 60 (1975), 198-210.

McGurk, John J.N. *The Elizabethan Conquest of Ireland*. Manchester: Manchester University Press, 1997.

McKee, Alexander. "Henry VIII as Military Commander," *History Today* 41 (1991), 22-29.

Millar, Gilbert John. "The Landsknecht: His Recruitment and Organization, with Some Reference to the Reign of Henry VIII," *Military Affairs* 35 (1971), 95-99.

Millar, Gilbert John. "Henry VIII's Preliminary Letter of Retainer to Colonel Frederick Von Reiffenberg for the Raising of 1500 Men-At-Arms," *Journal of the Society for Army Historical Research* 67 (1989), 220-25.

Millar, Gilbert John. "Mercenaries Under Henry VIII, 1544-46," *History Today* 27 (1977), 173-82.

Millar, Gilbert John. *Tudor Mercenaries and Auxiliaries, 1485-1547.* Charlottesville: University Press of Virginia, 1980.

Mulryne, J.R. "'Here's Unfortunate Revels:' War and Chivalry in Plays and Shows at the Time of Prince Henry Stuart." In: *War, Literature and the Arts in Sixteenth-Century Europe.* Ed. J.R. Mulryne and M. Shewring. New York, 1989, pp. 165-89.

Neale, John. "Elizabeth and the Netherlands, 1586-87," *English Historical Review* 45 (1930), 373-96.

Nolan, John S. "The Militarization of the Elizabethan State," *Journal of Military History* 58 (1994), 391-420.

Nolan, John S. "The Muster of 1588," *Albion* 23 (1991), 387-407.

Nolan, John S. *Sir John Norreys and the Elizabethan Military World.* Exeter: Exeter University Press, 1997.

Parkinson, E. Malcolm. "Sidney's Portrayal of Mounted Combat with Lances," *Spenser Studies* 5 (1985), 231-305.

Pearce, Brian. "Elizabethan Food Policy and the Armed Forces," *Economic History Review* 12 (1942), 39-49.

Phillips, Gervase. "The Army of Henry VIII: A Reassessment," *Journal of the Society for Army Historical Research* 75 (1997), 9-23.

Ridley, Jasper. *Henry VIII.* London: Constable, 1984.

Robinson, W.R.B. "Knighted Welsh Landowners, 1485-1558: Corrigenda," *Welsh Historical Review* 19 (1999), 517-25.

Rogers, H.C.B. *The Mounted Troops of the British Army, 1066-1945*. London, 1959.

Rowse, A.L. *The Expansion of Elizabethan England*. London: Macmillan, 1955.

Rowse, A.L. *Sir Richard Grenville of the Revenge: An Elizabethan Hero*. London, 1937.

Roy, Ian. "Muster Roll for the Hundred of North Greenhoe (circa 1523)." *Norfolk Records Society* 1 (1931), 41-68.

Roy, Ian. "Towards the Standing Army, 1485-1660." In: *The Oxford Illustrated History of the British Army*. Ed. D. Chandler and I. Beckett. Oxford, 1994, pp. 25-47.

Russell, Joycelyne G. *The Field of Cloth of Gold: Men and Manners in 1520*. London: Routledge and Kegan Paul, 1969.

"Seax." "The Wyatt Rebellion," *Journal of the Society of Archer-Antiquaries* 7 (1964), 19.

Shagan, Ethan H. "Debate–'Popularity' and the 1549 Rebellions Revisited," *English Historical Review* 115 (2000), 121-33.

Shagan, Ethan H. "Protector Somerset and the 1549 Rebellions: New Sources and New Perspectives," *English Historical Review* 114 (1999), 34-63.

Sharp, Buchanan. *In Contempt of All Authority: Rural Artisans and Riot in the West of England, 1586-1660*. Berkeley and Los Angeles: University of California Press, 1980.

Shepard, Alan. "Endless Sacks: Soldiers' Desire in *Tamburlaine*," *Renaissance Quarterly* 46 (1993), 734-53.

Starkey, David, ed. *The Inventory of King Henry VII: Society of Antiquaries MS 129 and British Library MS Harley 1419*. Vol. 1: *The Transcript*. London: Harvey Miller Publications, 1998.

Stoate, T.L., ed. *The Cornwall Military Survey, 1522, with the Loan Books and a Tinners' Muster Roll c. 1535*. Bristol: Lower Court, 1987.

Stoyle, Mark. "Caricaturing Cymru: Images of the Welsh in the London Press of 1642-46." In: *War and Society in Medieval and Early Modern Britain*. Ed. Diana Dunn. Liverpool: Liverpool University Press, 2000, pp. 162-79.

Thomas, Phillip. "Vagabond Soldiers and Deserters at Elizabethan Northampton," *Northamptonshire Past and Present* 9 (1995-96), 101-10.

Tincey, John. "The London Trained Bands, 1588," *Military Illustrated* 14 (Aug-Sept 1988), 15-19; 15 (Oct-Nov 1988), 29-33.

Trim, David J.B. "The Context of War and Violence in Sixteenth-Century English Society," *Journal of Early Modern History* 3 (1999), 233-55.

Trim, David J.B. "The Foundation-Stone of the British Army? The Normandy Campaign of 1562," *Journal of the Society for Army Historical Research* 77 (1999), 71-87.

Waddington, Raymond B. "Elizabeth I and the Order of the Garter," *Sixteenth Century Journal* 24 (1993), 97-113.

Walker, A.F. "Fynnesburie Field 1559," *Journal of the Society of Archer-Antiquaries* 6 (1963), 13.

Walton, C. *History of the British Standing Army, 1600-1700*. London: Harrison, 1894.

Webb, Henry J. *Elizabethan Military Science: The Books and the Practice*. Madison: University of Wisconsin Press, 1965.

Webb, Henry J. "English Military Books, Laws, and Proclamations Published from 1513 to 1610," *Philological Quarterly* 23 (1944), 116-28.

Wernham, R.B. *After the Armada: Elizabethan England and the Struggle for Western Europe, 1588-1595*. Oxford, 1984.

Wernham, R.B. *Before the Armada: The Growth of English Foreign Policy, 1485-1588*. London: Jonathan Cape, 1966.

Wernham, R.B. "Elizabethan War Aims and Strategy." In: *Elizabethan Government and Society: Essays Presented to Sir John Neale*. Ed. S.T. Bindoff, J. Hurstfield, and C.H. Williams. London, 1961, pp. 340-68.

Wernham, R.B. "Queen Elizabeth and the Portugal Expedition of 1589," *English Historical Review* 66 (1951), 1-26, 194-218.

Wernham, R.B. *The Return of the Armadas: The Last Years of the Elizabethan War against Spain, 1595-1603*. Oxford, 1994.

West, Michael. "Spenser's Art of War: Allegory, Military Technology, and the Elizabethan Mock-Heroic Sensibility," *Renaissance Quarterly* 41 (1988), 654-704.`

White, Dean Gunter. "Henry VIII's Irish Kerne in France and Scotland, 1544-1545," *Irish Sword* 3 (1958), 222-24.

Williams, P. "The Welsh Borderland under Queen Elizabeth," *Welsh History Review* 1 (1960).

Williamson, James. "A Tudor Army," *Blackwoods Magazine* 196 (1914), 195-206, 346-58.

Wolffe, Mary. *Gentry Leaders in Peace and War: The Gentry Governments of Devon in the Early Seventeenth Century*. Exeter: Exeter University Press, 1997.

Youings, Joyce. "Bowmen, Billmen and Hackbutters: the Elizabethan Militia in the South West." In: *Security and Defence in South-West England Before 1800*. Ed. R. Higham. Exeter, 1987, pp. 51-68.

Young, Alan. *Tudor and Jacobean Tournaments*. London: Sheridan House, 1987.

Early Modern – England – English Civil War

Abbott, W.C. *A Bibliography of Oliver Cromwell*. Cambridge: Harvard University Press, 1929.

Abram, A. *The Battle of Montgomery, 1644*. Bristol, 1993.

Adair, John. *By the Sword Divided*. London, 1983.

Adamson, John. "The English Context of the British Civil Wars," *History Today* 48.11 (Nov 1998), 23-29.

Ashley, M. *Cromwell's Generals*. London: Cape, 1954.

Atkin, Malcolm. *The Civil War in Worcestershire*. Stroud: Alan Sutton Publishing, 1995.

Atkin, Malcolm and Wayne Laughlin. *Gloucester and the Civil War: A City under Siege*. Stroud: Alan Sutton, 1992.

Bennett, Martyn. *The Civil Wars, 1637-1653*. Stroud: Sutton Publishing, 1998.

Bennett, Martyn. *The Civil Wars Experienced: Britain and Ireland, 1638-1661*. New York: Routledge, 2000.

Bennett, Martyn. *The Civil Wars in Britain and Ireland, 1638-1651*. Oxford, 1997.

Bennett, Martyn. "Dammpnified Villagers: Taxation in Wales during the First Civil War," *Welsh History Review* 19 (1998), 29-43.

Bernard, G.W. "Elton's Cromwell," *History* 83 (1998), 587-607.

Blackwood, B.G. "The Cavalier and Roundhead Gentry of Norfolk," *Local Historian* 26 (1996), 194-208.

Brenner, Robert. "The Civil War Politics of London's Merchant Community," *Past and Present* 58 (1973), 53-107.

Burke, James. "The New Model Army and the Problems of Siege Warfare, 1648-51," *Irish Historical Studies* 27 (1990), 1-29.

Burne, Alfred H. and P. Young. *The Great Civil War: A Military History of the First Civil War, 1642-1646*. London: Eyre and Spottiswoode, 1959.

Carlton, Charles. *Going to Wars: The Experience of the British Civil Wars, 1638-1651*. London: Routledge, 1992.

Clarendon, Edward Hyde. *The History of the Rebellion and Civil Wars in England*. Ed. W.D. Macray. 6 vols. Oxford, 1888.

Courtney, Paul and Yolanda. "A Siege Examined: The Civil War Archaeology of Leicester," *Post-Medieval Archaeology* 26 (1992), 47-90.

Cowley, Abraham. *The Civil War*. Ed. Allan Pritchard. Toronto: University of Toronto Press, 1973.

Donagan, Barbara. "Atrocity, War Crime, and Treason in the English Civil War," *American Historical Review* 99 (1994), 1137-66.

Dore, R.N. "Sir Thomas Myddleton's Attempted Conquest of Powys," *Montgomeryshire Collections* 57 (1961-62), 91-118.

Eales, J. *Puritans and Roundheads: The Harleys of Brampton Bryan and the Outbreak of the English Civil War*. Cambridge, 1990.

Ede-Borrett, Stephen. "The Headgear of Civil War Musketeers," *Journal of the Society for Army Historical Research* 68 (1990), 120-21.

Ede-Borrett, Stephen. "The Length of Colour-Poles During the Seventeenth Century," *Journal of the Society for Army Historical Research* 68 (1990), 66-67.

Ede-Borrett, Stephen. "The Royalist Army at the Second Battle of Newbury, 27 October 1644," *Journal of the Society of Army Historical Research* 77 (1999), 240-49.

Evans, D.E. *Montgomery, 1644*. n.p., 1984-85.

Evans, David and Bryan Sitch. *Beverley Gate: The Birthplace of the English Civil War*. Beverley: Hull High Council, 1991.

Firth, Charles H. *Cromwell's Army*. 4th ed. London: Methuen, 1961.

Firth, Charles H. *Oliver Cromwell*. Oxford: Clarendon Press, 1900.

Friedman, Jerome. "The Battle of the Frogs and Fairford's Flies: Miracle and Popular Journalism During the English Revolution," *Sixteenth Century Journal* 23 (1992), 419-42.

Fuller, P. "Outfitting the New Model Army," *Glenbow* 8.2 (Spr 1988), 10-12.

Furgol, Edward M. *A Regimental History of the Covenanting Armies, 1639-1651*. Edinburgh: John Donald Limited, 1990.

Gardiner, S.R. *History of the Great Civil War, 1642-1649*. 3 vols. London: Longmans, 1886-91.

Garner, A.A. *Boston and the Great Civil War*. London, 1972.

Gaunt, Peter. *The Cromwellian Gazetteer*. Stroud, 1987.

Gaunt, Peter. *Oliver Cromwell*. Oxford: Basil Blackwell, 1996.

Gaunt, Peter. "'One of the Goodliest and Strongest Places that I Ever Looked Upon': Montgomery and the Civil War." In: *War and Society in Medieval and Early Modern Britain*. Ed. Diana Dunn. Liverpool: Liverpool University Press, 2000, pp. 180-204.

Gentles, Ian. "Multiple Kingdoms at War: The 'English' Revolution, 1638-1651," *Journal of British Studies* 35 (1996), 542-47.

Gentles, Ian. "The New Model Officer Corps in 1647: A Collective Portrait," *Social History* 22 (1997), 127-44.

Goodwin, G.N. *The Civil War in Hampshire*. London, 1904.

Harrington, Peter. *Archaeology of the English Civil War*. Shire Archaeology Series, 68. Princes Risborough: Shire Publications Ltd., 1992.

Hill, Christopher. *Intellectual Origins of the English Revolution Revisited*. Oxford: Clarendon Press, 1997.

Hopper, A.J. "The Clubmen of the West Riding of Yorkshire during the First Civil War," *Northern History* 36 (2000), 59-72.

Hughes, Ann. *The Causes of the English Civil War*. 2nd ed. New York: St. Martin's Press, 1998.

Hutton, R. *The Royalist War Effort, 1642-46*. Harlow, 1982.

Kenyon, John and Jane Ohlmeyer, ed. *The Civil Wars: A Military History of England, Scotland, and Ireland, 1638-1660*. Oxford: Oxford University Press, 1998.

Morrill, John. *Revolt in the Provinces: The People of England and the Tragedies of War, 1630-1648*. 2nd ed. London: Longman, 1998.

Newman, P.R. *Atlas of the English Civil War*. London: Routledge, 1998.

Newman, P.R. *The Old Service: Royalist Regimental Colonels and the Civil War, 1642-46*. Manchester: Manchester University Press, 1993.

Newman, Peter. *The Battle of Marston Moor*. Chichester, 1981.

Nusbacher, Aryeh J.S. "Civil Supply in the Civil War: Supply of Victuals to the New Model Army on the Naseby Campaign, 1-14 June 1645," *English Historical Review* 115 (2000), 145-60.

Oakeshott, Ewart. "Deserter or Fugitive?" *Park Lane Arms Fair* 14 (1997), 18-20.

Ohlmeyer, Jane H. *Civil War and Restoration in the Three Stuart Kingdoms: The Career of Randal MacDonnell, Marquis of Antrim, 1609-1683.* Cambridge, 1993.

Ohlmeyer, Jane H. "Irish Privateers during the Civil War, 1642-50," *Mariner's Mirror* 76 (1990), 119-31.

Ohlmeyer, Jane H. "The Wars of the Three Kingdoms," *History Today* 48.11 (Nov 1998), 16-22.

Parker, Michael St. John. *The Civil War, 1642-51*. London: Pitkin Guides, 1993.

Phillips, C.E.L. *Cromwell's Captains*. London: Heinemann, 1938.

Rehberg, Rolf. "Justification of Resistance in Early Modern Revolutions: A Comparison of the German Peasant War, the Dutch Revolt and the British Revolution," *International Politics* 33 (1996), 273-90.

Reid, Stuart. *The Campaigns of Montrose: A Military History of the Civil War in Scotland, 1639 to 1646*. Edinburgh, 1990.

Roberts, Keith. "The London Trained Bands and the English Civil War," *Military Illustrated* 22 (Dec 1989/Jan 1990), 34-38.

Scott, David. "The Barwis Affair: Political Allegiance and the Scots during the British Civil Wars," *English Historical Review* 115 (2000), 843-63.

Spraxton, Judy. *Violence and Religion: Attitudes towards Militancy in the French Civil Wars and the English Revolution*. London: Routledge, 1995.

Stone, Lawrence. "The English Revolution." In: *Preconditions of Revolution in Early Modern Europe*. Ed. R. Forster and J.P. Greene. Baltimore, 1970, pp. 55-108.

Stoyle, Mark. *From Deliverance to Destruction: Rebellion and Civil War in an English City*. Exeter, 1996.

Stoyle, Mark. *Loyalty and Locality: Popular Allegiance in Devon during the English Civil War*. Exeter: Exeter University Press, 1994.

Tennant, P. *Edgehill and Beyond: The People's War in the South Midlands, 1642-45*. Stroud, 1992.

Toynbee, M. and Peter Young. *Croperdy Bridge, 1644*. Kineton, 1970.

Tucker, John and Lewis S. Winstock, ed. *The English Civil War: A Military Handbook*. London: Arms and Armour Press, 1972.

Underdown, D. *Revel, Riot and Rebellion: Popular Politics and Culture in England, 1603-1660*. Oxford, 1985.

Warmington, A.R. *Civil War, Interregnum and Restoration in Gloucestershire, 1640-1672*. Royal Historical Society Studies in History, New Series. Woodbridge: Boydell for the Royal Historical Society, 1997.

Wedgwood, C.V. *The Great Rebellion: The King's War, 1641-1647*. London: Collins, 1958.

Wood, Andy. "Beyond Post-Revisionism?: The Civil War Allegiances of the Miners of Derbyshire 'Peak Country'," *Historical Journal* 40 (1997), 23-40.

Woolford, John. "Charge Signaled by Thunderclap," *Military History* (June 1994), 30-37.

Woolrych, A.H. *Battles of the English Civil War*. London: Batsford, 1961.

Young, Peter. *Edgehill, 1642: The Campaign and the Battle*. Kineton: Roundwood Press, 1967.

Young, Peter. *Naseby*. London, 1985.

Young, Peter. *The English Civil War Armies*. London: Osprey, 1981.

Zaret, David. "Petitions and the 'Invention' of Public Opinion in the English Civil War," *American Journal of Sociology* 101 (1996), 1497-1555.

Early Modern – England – English/Scottish Conflicts

Archbold, W.A.J., ed. "A Diary of the Expedition of 1544," *English Historical Review* 16 (1901), 503-07.

Armitage, David. "Making the Empire British: Scotland in the Atlantic World, 1542-1717," *Past and Present* 155 (1997), 34-63.

Barber, S. "The People of Northern England and Attitudes towards the Scots, 1639-1651," *Northern History* 35 (1999), 93-118.

Bates, Cadwallader J. "Flodden Field," *Archaeologia aeliana* 16 (1892), 351-72.

Bingham, Caroline. *James V, King of Scots, 1512-1542*. London: Collins, 1971.

Bonner, Elizabeth A. "The Genesis of Henry VIII's 'Rough Wooing' of the Scots," *Northern History* 33 (1997), 36-53.

Brander, Michael. *Scottish and Border Battles and Ballads*. New York: Barnes and Noble Books, 1993.

Brown, J.B. "The French Troops in the Borders in 1548," *Transactions of the Hanwick Archaeological Society* (1905), 35-45.

Bruce, Gainsford. "The English Expedition into Scotland in 1542," *Archaeologia aeliana* 3rd ser. 3 (1907), 191-212.

Caldwell, David H. "The Battle of Pinkie." In: *Scotland and War, AD 79-1918*. Ed. Norman Macdougall. Edinburgh: John Donald, 1991, pp. 61-94.

Dickinson, Gladys. "Some Notes on the Scottish Army in the First Half of the Sixteenth Century," *Scottish Historical Review* 28 (1949), 133-45.

Durham, Keith and Angus McBride. *The Border Reivers*. London: Osprey, 1995.

Elliot, Fitzwilliam. *The Battle of Flodden and the Raids of 1513*. Tonbridge: Pallas Armata Reprints, 1991.

Ellis, Steven G. "A Border Baron and the Tudor State: The Rise and Fall of Lord Dacre of the North," *Historical Journal* 35 (1992).

Fissel, Mark Charles. *The Bishops' Wars: Charles I's Campaigns Against Scotland, 1638-1640*. Cambridge: Cambridge University Press, 1994.

Harris, Stuart. "The Fortifications and Siege of Leith: A Further Study of the Map and the Siege in 1560," *Proceedings of the Society of Antiquaries of Scotland* 121 (1991), 359-68.

Head, David. "Henry VIII's Scottish Policy: A Reassessment," *Scottish Historical Review* 61 (1982), 1-24.

Hill, James Michael. *Celtic Warfare, 1595-1763*. Edinburgh: John Donald Ltd., 1986.

Hill, James Michael. "The Distinctiveness of Gaelic Warfare, 1400-1750," *European History Quarterly* 22 (1992), 323-45.

Hill, James Michael. "Killiecrankie and the Evolution of Highland Warfare," *War and History* 1 (1994), 125-39.

Hodgkin, Thomas. "The Battle of Flodden," *Archaeologia aeliana* 16 (1892), 1-44.

Hodgkin, Thomas. *The Wardens of the Northern Marches*. London: John Murray, 1908.

Leather, Gerald F.T. *New Light on Flodden*. Berwick: Berwickshire Naturalists' Club, 1937.

Lomas, Richard. "The Impact of Border Warfare: The Scots and South Tweedside, c.1290-1520," *Scottish Historical Review* 75 (1996), 143-67.

MacKenzie, William Mackay. *The Secret of Flodden*. Edinburgh: Grant and Murray, 1931.

Mackie, J.D. "The English Army at Flodden," *Miscellany of the Scottish History Society* 8 (1951), 35-85.

Martin, Colin J.M. "Ancrum Moor: A Day of Reckoning," *Scots Magazine* 83 (May 1965), 146-52.

McEwen, John. "The Battle of Flodden," *History Today* 8 (1958), 337-45.

Merriman, M. "The Assured Scots: Scottish Collaborators with England during the Rough Wooing," *Scottish Historical Review* 47 (1986), 10-34.

Murray, William. "Flodden: Before and After," *Transactions of the Hawick Archaeological Society* (1913), 38-43.

Patterson, Raymond Campbell. *My Wound is Deep: A History of the Later Anglo-Scots Wars, 1380-1560.* Edinburgh: John Donald, 1997.

Paul, J. Balfour. "Edinburgh in 1544 and Hertford's Invasion," *Scottish Historical Review* 8 (1911), 113-31.

Phillips, Gervase. *The Anglo-Scots Wars, 1513-1550: A Military History.* Woodbridge: The Boydell Press, 1999.

Phillips, Gervase. "The Battle of Pinkie Cleugh: Changing the Face of British Warfare," *Military History* (Aug 1997), 42-48.

Phillips, Gervase. "In the Shadow of Flodden: Tactics, Technology and Scottish Military Effectiveness, 1513-1550," *Scottish Historical Review* 77 (1998), 162-82.

Phillips, Gervase. "Strategy and Its Limitations: The Anglo-Scots Wars, 1480-1550," *War in History* 6 (1999), 396-416.

Pollard, A.F. "The Protector Somerset and Scotland," *English Historical Review* 13 (1898), 464-72.

Reid, Stuart. "Covenanters: Scots Infantry in the 1640s," *Military Illustrated* 19 (June/July 1989), 27-32.

Ridpath, George. *The Border History of England and Scotland.* Berwick: Philip Ridpath, 1848.

Scott, D. "'Hannibal at Our Grades': Loyalists and Fifth Columnists during the Bishops Wars–The Case of Yorkshire," *Historical Research* 70 (1997), 269-93.

Seton, Bruce. "The Flodden Campaign–1513: A Study in Mediaeval Mobilisation in Scotland," *Journal of the Society for Army Historical Research* 3 (1924), 175-91.

Sevestre, Bernard. "L'ancienne alliance franco-écossaise et le service écossais," *Revue de la Société des Amis du Musée de l'Armée* 99 (1990), 5-21.

Sinclair, G.A. "The Scots at Solway Moss," *Scottish Historical Review* 2 (1904), 372-77.

Stell, Geoffrey. "Destruction and Damage: A Reassessment of the Historical and Architectural Evidence." In: *Scotland and War, AD 79-1918.* Ed. Norman Macdougall. Edinburgh: John Donald, 1991, pp. 24-35.

Tuck, J. Anthony. *Border Warfare: A History of Conflict on the Anglo-Scottish Border.* London: Her Majesty's Stationery Office, 1979.

White, Dean Gunter. "Henry VIII's Irish Kerne in France and Scotland, 1544-1545," *Irish Sword* 3 (1958), 222-24.

Wood, Stephen. *The Scottish Soldier.* Manchester: Archive Publications Ltd., 1987.

Early Modern – France

Barbiche, Bernard and Ségolène de Danville-Barbiche. *Sully: L'homme et ses fidèles.* Paris: Fayard, 1997.

Baes, Christian. "La campagne d'Henri II de France dans l'Entre-Sambre-et-Meuse." In: *Les malheurs de la guerre.* I: *De la guerre à l'ancienne à la guerre réglée.* Ed. André Corvisier and Jean Jacquart. Paris: Éditions du CTHS, 1996, pp. 13-26.

Baumgartner, Frederic J. "The Final Demise of the Medieval Knight in France." In: *Regnum, Religio et Ratio: Essays Presented to Robert N. Kingdon.* Ed. J. Friedman. Sixteenth Century Essays and Studies, VIII. Kirksville, Missouri, 1987, pp. 9-17.

Bérenger, Jean. "La Lorraine et La France, 1550-1750." In: *Commission Internationale d'Histoire Militaire. Acta 22: Warfare Throughout the Ages between Small States and Big Powers and Small States Among Themselves.* Tel Aviv: Israel Commission of Military History, 1984, pp. 101-04.

Bonner, Elizabeth. "Scotland's 'Auld Alliance' with France, 1295-1560," *History* 84 (1999), 5-30.

Bouhier, Claude. "Un homme de Mazurin ou un grand marin méconne, l'arrival du Montade (1610-1648)," *Revue historique des armées* 202 (1996), 3-11.

Bourquin, Laurent. *La France au XVIe siècle, 1483-1594.* Paris: Belin, 1996.

Briggs, Robin. *Early Modern France, 1560-1715.* 2nd ed. Oxford: Oxford University Press, 1998.

Charles, Robert-Jean. "La valeur documentaire de l'oeuvre gravé de Tortorel et Perissen: Cap. II: Tortorel et Perissen et la tactique au debut de la seconde moitié du XVIe siècle (1562-1570)," *Bulletin de la société des amis du musée de l'armée* 57 (1956), 37-44.

Chilton, Paul. "Humanism and War in the Work of Rabelais and Montaigne." In: *War, Literature and the Arts in Sixteenth-Century Europe.* Ed. J.R. Mulryne and M. Shewring. New York, 1989, pp. 119-43.

Contamine, Philippe. "La musique militaire dans le fonctionnement des armées: l'exemple français (v. 1300-v. 1550)." In: *XXII. Kongreß der Internationalen Kommission für Militärgeschichte* Acta 22: *Von Crécy bis Mohács Kriegswesen im späten Mittelalter (1346-1526).* Vienna, 1997, pp. 93-106.

Coste, Laurent. "Les malheurs de la Fronde en Entre-deux-Mers." In: *Les malheurs de la guerre.* I: *De la guerre à l'ancienne à la guerre réglée.* Ed. André Corvisier and Jean Jacquart. Paris: Éditions du CTHS, 1996, pp. 131-45.

Davies, Clifford S.L. "England and the French War, 1557-59." In: *The Mid-Tudor Polity, c.1540-1560.* Ed. Jennifer Loach and Robert Tittler. London, 1980, pp. 159-85.

Davies, M.B. "Boulogne and Calais from 1545 to 1550," *Fouad I University: Bulletin of the Faculty of Arts* 12 (1950), 1-90.

Davies, M.B. "The 'Enterprise' of Paris and Boulogne," *Fouad I University: Bulletin of the Faculty of Arts* 11 (1949), 37-95.

Davies, M.B. "Suffolk's Expedition to Montdidier, 1523," *Fouad I University: Bulletin of the Faculty of Arts* 7 (1944), 33-43.

Delord, Jean-François. "Fronton (Haute-Garonne) et les malheurs du temps: vers 1620-vers 1630." In: *Les malheurs de la guerre*. I: *De la guerre à l'ancienne à la guerre réglée*. Ed. André Corvisier and Jean Jacquart. Paris: Éditions du CTHS, 1996, pp. 119-29.

Desplat, Christian. "Louis XIII and the Union of Béarn to France." In: *Conquest and Coalescence: The Shaping of the State in Early Modern Europe*. Ed. Mark Greengrass. London: Edward Arnold, 1991, pp. 68-83.

Dillon, C.H. "Irish Troops at Boulogne in 1544," *Journal of the Society for Army Historical Research* 1 (1922), 81-84.

Follain, Antoine. "Les charges militaires sur les communautés rurales normandes aux XVIe-XVIIe siècles." In: *Les Normands et l'armée: actes du XXXe congrès des Sociétés Historiques et Archéologiques de Normandie tenu à Coutances du 19 au 21 octobre 1995: Revue de la Manche* 38 (1996), 123-32.

Gaier, Claude. "L'opinion des chefs de guerre français du XVIe siècle sur le progrès de l'art militaire," *Revue internationale d'histoire militaire* 29 (1970), 723-46.

Green, A.C.F. "The Loss of Calais," *Army Quarterly* 80 (1959-60), 173-78.

Gunn, Steven J. "The Duke of Suffolk's March on Paris in 1523," *English Historical Review* 121 (1986), 561-634.

Jones, Colin. "The Military Revolution and the Professionalisation of the French Army Under the Ancien Regime." In: *The Military Revolution and the State, 1500-1800*. Ed. M. Duffy. Exeter, 1980, pp. 29-48; and In: *The Military Revolution Debate: Readings on the Military Transformation of Early Modern Europe*. Ed. C.J. Rogers. Boulder, 1995, pp. 149-56.

Jouanna, Arlette. *La France du XVIe siècle: 1483-1598*. Paris: PUF, 1996.

Knecht, Robert J. "Military Autobiographies in Sixteenth-Century France." In: *War, Literature and the Arts in Sixteenth-Century Europe*. Ed. J.R. Mulryne and M. Shewring. New York, 1989, pp. 3-21.

Le Fur, Didier. "Image d'une titulature, Louis XII Père du Peuple," *Bulletin d'Association des Amis du Centre Jeanne d'Arc* 17 (1993), 57-66.

Lot, Ferdinand. *Recherches sur les effectifs des armées Françaises des guerres d'Italie aux guerres de religion, 1492-1562.* Paris, 1962.

Lynn, John A. "Recalculating French Army Growth during the *Grand Siècle*, 1610-1715," *French Historical Studies* 18 (1994), 881-906; in: *The Military Revolution Debate: Readings on the Military Transformation of Early Modern Europe.* Ed. C.J. Rogers. Boulder, 1995, pp. 117-48.

Marshall-Cornwall, James. "An Expedition to Aquitaine, 1512," *History Today* 23 (1973), 640-47.

Michel, Jacques. *Avignon et ses Suisses.* Avignon: Jacques Michel, 1993.

Parrott, David A. "The Causes of the Franco-Spanish War of 1635-59." In: *The Origins of War in Early Modern Europe.* Edinburgh, 1987, pp. 72-111.

Pic, François. "*La gascouigno desoulado*, récit des malheurs de la guerre dans le Sud-Ouest de la France au milieu du XVIIe siècle." In: *Les malheurs de la guerre. I: De la guerre à l'ancienne à la guerre réglée.* Ed. André Corvisier and Jean Jacquart. Paris: Éditions du CTHS, 1996, pp. 147-59.

Potter, David. "The Duc de Guise and the Fall of Calais," *English Historical Review* 118 (1983), 481-512.

Potter, David. "Foreign Policy in the Age of Reformation: French Involvement in the Schmalkaldic War," *Historical Journal* 20 (1977), 525-44.

Potter, David. *War and Government in the French Provinces: Picardy, 1470-1560.* Cambridge: Cambridge University Press, 1993.

Rothrock, G.A. "The Siege of La Rochelle," *History Today* 19 (1969), 752-59, 856-62.

Rozet, A. *L'invasion de la France et le siège de Saint Digier, 1544.* Paris, 1910.

Sevestre, Bernard. "L'ancienne alliance franco-écossaise et le service écossais," *Revue de la Société des Amis du Musée de l'Armée* 99 (1990), 5-21.

Stévenin, Michel. "Une fatalité: les dévastations des gens de guerre dans l'Est de la France (1620-1660): L'exemple de la Champagne." In: *Les malheurs de la guerre. I: De la guerre à l'ancienne à la guerre réglée.*

Ed. André Corvisier and Jean Jacquart. Paris: Éditions du CTHS, 1996, pp. 161-79.

Stradling, R.A. "Olivares and the Origins of the Franco-Spanish War, 1627-1635," *English Historical Review* 101 (1968), 68-94; in: *Spain's Struggle for Europe*. London, 1994, pp. 95-120.

Tallett, Frank. "Church, State, War and Finance in Early-Modern France," *Renaissance and Modern Studies* 36 (1993), 15-35.

Williams, H. Noel. *Henri II*. New York, 1910.

Zeller, Gaston. *La siège de Metz par Charles-Quint*. Nancy, 1943.

Early Modern – France – French Civil Wars (or Wars of Religion)

Andrault, Jean-Pierre. "Une capitale de province sous les armes au temps de la Ligue: la guerre de course menée par Poitiers entre 1589 et 1593." In: *Les malheurs de la guerre*. I: *De la guerre à l'ancienne à la guerre réglée*. Ed. André Corvisier and Jean Jacquart. Paris: Éditions du CTHS, 1996, pp. 39-63.

Bayrou, François. *Henri IV, le roi libre*. Paris: J'ai lu, 1996.

Benedict, P. *Rouen during the Wars of Religion*. Cambridge: Cambridge University Press, 1980.

Bérenger, Jean. "Les armées Françaises et les guerres de religion," *Revue internationale d'histoire militaire* 55 (1983), 11-26.

Carroll, Stuart. *Noble Power during the French Wars of Religion: The Guise Affinity and the Catholic Cause in Normandy*. Cambridge: Cambridge University Press, 1998.

Cassan, Michel. *Le temps des guerres de religion: Le Cas du Limousin (vers 1530-vers 1630)*. Paris: Publisud, 1996.

Castarède, Jean. *Henri IV, le roi vengé*. Paris: France-Empire, 1996.

Cramer, Lucien and Alain Dufour. *La seigneurie de Genève et la maison de Savoie*. IV: *La guerre de 1589*. Geneva: A. Jullien, 1958.

Davies, Joan M. "The Duc de Montmorency, Philip II and the House of Savoy: a Neglected Aspect of the Sixteenth-Century French Civil Wars," *English Historical Review* 105 (1990), 870-92.

Delabarre-Duparcq, Nicolas Edouard de. *L'art militaire pendant les guerres de religion, 1562-1598*. Paris, 1864.

Desachy, Sylvie. "Du captaine au soldat: comportements guerriers en Rouergue pendant les guerres de religion." In: *Les malheurs de la guerre. I: De la guerre à l'ancienne à la guerre réglée*. Ed. André Corvisier and Jean Jacquart. Paris: Éditions du CTHS, 1996, pp. 27-38.

Drune. "Henri IV: chef de guerre," *Revue historique de l'armée* 17.4 (Dec 1961).

Eurich, S. Amada. *The Economics of Power: The Private Finances of the House of Foix-Navarre-Albret during the Religious Wars*. Kirksville: Sixteenth Century Journal, 1994.

Finley-Croswhite, S. Annette. "Confederates and Rivals: Picard Urban Alliances during the Catholic League, 1588-1594," *Canadian Journal of History* 31 (1996), 359-76.

Finley-Croswhite, S. Annette. "Engendering the Wars of Religion: Female Agency during the Catholic League in Dijon," *French Historical Studies* 20 (1997), 127-54.

Holt, Mack P. *The French Wars of Religion, 1562-1629*. Cambridge: Cambridge University Press, 1995.

Horne, Alistair. "Paris for the Price of a Mass," *MHQ* 11 (Sum 1999), 18-29.

Hurpin, Gérard. "Carlos Coloma et l'histoire militaire de la Normandie pendant la Ligue." In: *Les Normands et l'armée: Actes du XXXe congrès historiques et archéologiques de Normandie tenu à Coutances du 19 au 21 octobre 1995. Revue de la manche* 38 (1996).

Jouanna, Arlette, et al. *Histoire et dictionnaire des guerres de religion*. Paris: Laffront, 1998.

Knecht, Robert J. *The French Wars of Religion, 1559-1598*. 2nd ed. London: Longman, 1996.

Leboucq, Karin. "L'administration provincale à l'époque des guerres de religion: Henri III, François d'O et le gouvernement de Basse-Normandie (1579-1588)," *Revue historique* 122 (1998), 345-408.

Love, Ronald S. "'All the King's Horsemen': The Equestrian Army of Henri IV, 1585-1598," *Sixteenth Century Journal* 22 (1991), 510-23.

Love, Ronald S. "A Game of Cat and Mouse: Henri de Navarre and the Huguenot Campaigns of 1584-89," *Canadian Journal of History* 24 (1999), 1-22.

Neale, J.E. *The Age of Catherine de Medici.* New York: Harper Torch-books, 1943.

Parrow, Kathleen A. *From Defense to Resistance: Justification of Violence during the French Wars of Religion.* Transactions of the American Philosophical Society, vol. 83, part 6. Philadelphia: American Philosophical Society, 1993

Pernot, Michel. *Les guerres de réligion.* Paris, 1987.

Racaut, Luc. "The Polemical Use of the Albigensian Crusade during the French Wars of Religion," *French History* 13 (1999), 261-79.

Roberts, Penny. *A City in Conflict: Troyes during the French Wars of Religion.* Manchester: Manchester University Press, 1996.

Slove, Ronald. "A Game of Cat and Mouse: Henri de Navarre and the Hugenot Campaigns of 1584-89," *Canadian Journal of History* 34 (1999), 1-22.

Spraxton, Judy. *Violence and Religion: Attitudes towards Militancy in the French Civil Wars and the English Revolution.* London: Routledge, 1995.

Thierry, Éric. "La guerre et la paix à Vervins de 1589 à 1598." In: *Les malheurs de la guerre. I: De la guerre à l'ancienne à la guerre réglée.* Ed. André Corvisier and Jean Jacquart. Paris: Éditions du CTHS, 1996, pp. 65-75.

Waele, Michel de. "Clémence royale et fidélités Françaises à la fin des Guerres de Religion," *Historical Reflections* 24 (1998), 231-52.

Walker, Anita M. and Edmund H. Dickerman. "The King Who Would Be Man: Henri III, Gender Identity and the Murders at Blois, 1588," *Historical Reflections* 24 (1998), 253-82.

Wolfe, Michael. "Piety and Political Allegiance: The Duc de Nevers and the Protestant Henri IV, 1589-93," *French History* 2 (1988), 1-21.

Wood, James B. *The King's Army: Warfare, Soldiers and Society during the Wars of Religion in France, 1562-1576*. Cambridge: Cambridge University Press, 1996.

Wood, James B. "The Royal Army during the Early Wars of Religion, 1559-1576." In: *Society and Institutions in Early Modern France*. Ed. Mack P. Holt. Athens, 1991, pp. 1-35.

Early Modern – Holy Roman Empire

Adams, Simon. "Tactics or Politics? 'The Military Revolution' and the Hapsburg Hegemony, 1525-1648." In: *The Military Revolution Debate: Readings on the Military Transformation of Early Modern Europe*. Ed. C.J. Rogers. Boulder, 1995, pp. 253-72.

Allmayer-Beck, Johann Christoph and Erich Lessing. *Die kaiserlichen Kriegsvölker: Von Maximilian I. bis Prinz Eugen, 1479-1718*. Munich: C. Bertelsmann, 1978.

Baes, Christian. "Les armées dans les pays-bas à la fin du regne de Charles Quint. Contribution à l'étude de leur administration," *Revue Belge d'histoire militaire* 29 (1991-92), 81-91.

Baes, Christian. "Les armées dans les pays-bas à la fin du regne de Charles Quint. Contribution à l'étude de leur organisation," *Revue Belge d'histoire militaire* 28 (1989-90), 257-68.

Beaufort, Christian. "The Imperial Army in the 17th Century: Troops and Equipment." In: *17th Century War, Weaponry and Politics: International Association of Museums of Arms and Military History, Xth Congress Stockholm 1984* Stockholm, 1984, pp. 121-31.

Brandi, Karl. *The Emperor Charles V*. Trans. C.V. Wedgwood. London, 1939.

Burschel, Peter. "Langspiess und Bettelstab: Leben und Sterben in deutschen Söldnerheeren des 16. Jahrhunderts." In: *Eisenkleider: Plattnerarbeiten aus drei Jahrhunderten aus der Sammlung des Deutschen Historischen Museums*. Berlin: Deutsches Historisches Museum, 1992, pp. 25-30.

Burschel, Peter. *Söldner im Nordwestdeutschland des 16. und 17. Jahrhunderts*. Göttingen: Vandenhoeck and Ruprecht, 1994.

Cohn, Henry J. "Götz von Berlichingen and the Art of Military Autobiography." In: *War, Literature and the Arts in Sixteenth-Century Europe*. Ed. J.R. Mulryne and M. Shewring. New York, 1989, pp. 22-40.

Contamine, Philippe. "René II et les mercenaires de la langue germanique: la guerre contre Robert de La Marck, seigneur de Sedan (1496)." In: *Cinqcentième anniversaire de la bataille de Nancy (1477): Actes du Colloque organisé par l'institut de recherche régionale en sciences sociales, humaines et économiques de l'Université de Nancy II (Nancy, 22-24 septembre 1977)*. Nancy, 1979, pp. 377-94.

Engels, Frederick. *The Peasant War in Germany*. Trans. Moissaye J. Olgin. Ed. D. Riazanov. 2nd ed. New York: International Publishers, 1966.

Erlanger, Ph. *Charles Quint*. Paris: Perrin, 1997.

Franz, G. "Von Ursprung und Brauchtum der Landsknecht," *Mitteilungen des Instituts für österreichische Geschichteforschung* 61 (1953), 79-98.

Friedrichs, Christopher R. *Urban Society in an Age of War: Nördlingen, 1580-1700*. Princeton: Princeton University Press, 1979.

Memorial über die Organisation des Kriegswesen der Stadt Worms Ende des XV. Jahrhunderts. In: *Quellen zur Geschichte der Stadt Worms*. Ed. M. Boos. III: *Annalen und Chroniken*. Berlin, 1883, pp. 349-70.

Mur i Raurell, Anna. "Rocandolfo al servicio de Carlos V: Wilhelm von Rogendorf, comendador de Otos (1481-1541)," *Anuario de estudios medievales* 28 (1998), 363-88.

Nell, Martin. *Die Landsknechte: Entstehung der ersten deutschen Infanterie*. Berlin, 1914.

Pohl, Jürgen. *"Die Profiantirung der keyserlichen Armaden ahnbelangendt": Studien zur Versorgung der kaiserlichen Armee, 1634-35*. Mitteilungen des Österreichischen Staatsarchiv, Sonderband 1. Horn and Vienna: Berger, 1994.

Potter, D.L. "Foreign Policy in the Age of Reformation: French Involvement in the Schmalkaldic War," *Historical Journal* 20 (1977), 525-44.

Quatrefages, René. "Les forces armées et les traités de l'Espagne en Afrique du Nord sous Charles Quint." In: *Commission internationale d'histoire militaire*. Acta 6: *Montpeillier 2-6 IX 1981*. Montpellier: Commission Française d'Histoire Militaire, 1983, I:93-128.

Redlich, Fritz. *The German Military Enterpriser and His Work Forces*. 2 vols. Wiesbaden, 1964-65.

Regele, O. *Der Österreichische Hofskriegsrat 1556-1848*. Vienna: Österreichische Staatsdruckerei, 1949.

Römer, Christof. *500 Jahre Krieg und Frieden: Braunschweigische Militärgeschichte vom Fehdezeitalter bis zum Ende des Absolutismus*. Braunschweig: Braunschweigischen Landesmuseums, 1982.

Rothenberg, Gerhard E. *The Austrian Military Border in Croatia, 1522-1747*. Urbana: University of Illinois Press, 1960.

Rublack, Ulinka. "Wench and Maiden: Women, War and the Pictorial Function of the Feminine in German Cities in the Early Modern Period," *History Workshop* 44 (1997), 1-22.

Schmidt, J. "The Egri Campaign of 1596: Military History and the Problem of Sources." In: *Habsburgisch-Osmanische Bezeihungen*. Ed. A. Tietze. Vienna: VWGO, 1985, pp. 125-44.

Schmidt-Ewald, W. "Das Landesaufgebot im westlichen Thüringen vom 15. bis zum 17. Jahrhundert," *Zeitschrift des Vereins für thüringische Geschichte und Altertumskunde* 36 (1929), 6-58.

Schulze, Winfried. "Die deutschen Landesdefensionen im 16. und 17. Jahrhundert." In: *Staatsverfassung und Heeresfassung in der europäischen Geschichte der frühen Neuzeit*. Ed. Johannnes Kunisch and Barbara Stollberg-Rillinger. Berlin: Duncker and Humbolt, 1986, pp. 129-49.

Tauch, Max, Helmut Gilliam, and Jürgen Huck. *Neuss und der kölner Kriege*. Neuss: Clemens-Sels-Museum, 1986.

618

EARLY MODERN – HOLY ROMAN EMPIRE

Trippenbach, Max. "Johann Jacobi-Tautphoeus von Wallhausen, der erste deutsche Militärschriftsteller (1580-1627)," *Hanauisches Magazin* (1937).

Turek, Eva. *Böhmiska fanor i Statens trofésamling*. Copenhagen: Armémuseum, 1991.

Ulrichs, Cord. *Vom Lehnhof zur Reichsritterschaft Strukturen des fränkischen Niederadels am Übergang vom späten Mittelalter zur frühen Neuzeit*. Vierteljahrschrift für Sozial- und Wirtschaftsgeschichte Beihefte, 134. Stuttgart: Franz Steiner, 1997.

Wehrhafte Stadt: Das Wiener Bürgerliche Zeughaus im 15. Und 16. Jahrhundert. Vienna: Historisches Museum der Stadt Wien, 1986.

Wiesflecker, Hermann. *Kaiser Maximilian I: Das Reich, Österreich und Europa an der Wende zur Neuzeit*. 5 vols. Vienna, 1981.

Wohlfeil, R. "Adel und neues Heerwesen." In: *Deutscher Adel, 1430-1555: Büdinger Vortrage 1963*. Ed. H. Rossler. Darmstadt, 1965, pp. 203-33.

Wohlfeil, R. "Ritter–Söldnerführer–Offizier: Versuch eines vergleiches." In: *Festschrift Johannes Barmann*. Wiesbaden, 1966, I:45-70.

Zeller, Gaston. *La siège de Metz par Charles-Quint*. Nancy, 1943.

Zmora, Hillay. *State and Nobility in Early Modern Germany: The Knightly Feud in Franconia, 1440-1567*. Cambridge: Cambridge University Press, 1997.

Early Modern – Holy Roman Empire – Thirty Years War

1648: Westfaliska freden/1648: Der Westfälische frieden/1648: The Peace of Westphalia. Stockholm: Vasamuseet och Skolostens Slott, 1998.

Åberg, Alf. "Gustav II Adolf och hans skotsa krigare," *Livrustkammaren* 16 (1982), 1-21.

Ahnlund, Nils. "Gustavus Adolphus: The Case of Protestantism and Freedom of Conscience." In: *The Thirty Years' War: Problems of Motive, Extent, and Effect*. Ed. T.K. Rabb. Boston, 1964, pp. 56-59.

Albrecht, Dieter. *Maximilian I. von Bayern, 1573-1651.* Munich: Oldenbourg, 1998.

Asch, Ronald G. *The Thirty Years War: The Holy Roman Empire and Europe, 1618-48.* New York: St. Martin's Press, 1997.

Asch, Ronald G. "Warfare in the Age of the Thirty Years War, 1598-1648." In: *European Warfare, 1453-1815.* Ed. Jeremy Black. New York: St. Martin's Press, 1999, pp. 45-68.

Barata, Manuel. "Portugal and the Thirty Years War." In: *Bellum Tricennale: The Thirty Years War.* XXIIIrd Colloquium of the International Commission of Military History. Prague, 1999, pp. 91-98.

Barker, Thomas M. "Les relations civilo-militaires dans la détermination des objectifs de la politique étrangère notamment des alliances: l'exemple de Wallenstein." In: *Commission internationale d'histoire militaire.* Acta 6: *Montpeillier 2-6 IX 1981.* Montpellier: Commission Française d'Histoire Militaire, 1983, I:157-64.

Batiffol, Louis. "Cardinal Richelieu: A Policy of Justice, Necessity, and Tradition." In: *The Thirty Years' War: Problems of Motive, Extent, and Effect.* Ed. T.K. Rabb. Boston, 1964, pp. 83-86.

Becker, Winfried. "Der Westfälische Friede im historisch-politischen Urteil der Nachwelt," *Zeitschrift für Bayerische Landesgeschichte* 62 (1999), 439-66.

Bělina, Pavel. "The Thirty Years War? In the Margin of the 350th Anniversary of the First Peace Conference of the Early Modern Era in Europe." In: *Bellum Tricennale: The Thirty Years War.* XXIIIrd Colloquium of the International Commission of Military History. Prague, 1999, pp. 301-08.

Beller, E.A. "The Military Expedition of Sir Charles Morgan to Germany, 1627-9," *English Historical Review* 43 (1928).

Bérenger, Jean. "Le siège de Mantoue, 1629-1630," *Mélanges Anne Blanchard.* Montpellier, 1993, pp. 242-67.

Bodin, Per-Arne. "Ryska dokument i Riksarkivet från Gustav II Adolfs tid," *Livrustkammaren* 16 (1983), 116-31.

Bogdan, H. *La guerre de trente ans.* Paris: Perrin, 1996.

Brightwell, P. "Spain and Bohemia: The Decision to Intervene, 1619," *European Studies Review* 12 (1982), 117-41.

Brightwell, P. "Spain, Bohemia and Europe," *European Studies Review* 12 (1982), 371-99.

Brightwell, P. "The Spanish Origins of the Thirty Years War," *European Studies Review* 9 (1979), 270-92.

Bringéus, Nils-Arvid. "Gustav II Adolf och reformationsminnet," *Livrustkammaren* 16 (1984), 181-96.

Broucek, Peter. "Wallenstein und der Gründung des österreichischen Generalstabes." In: *Bellum Tricennale: The Thirty Years War*. XXIIIrd Colloquium of the International Commission of Military History. Prague, 1999, pp. 193-204.

Brzezinski, Richard. *The Army of Gustvaus Adolphus*. I: *Infantry*. London: Osprey, 1991.

Brzezinski, Richard. "British Mercenaries in the Baltic, 1560-1683," *Military Illustrated* 6 (Apr-May 1987), 29-35.

Brzezinski, Richard. "Gustavus Adolphus," *Military Illustrated* 21 (Oct/ Nov 1989), 53-55.

Bulloch, J.M. "A Scoto-Austrian: John Gordon: the Assassinator of Wallenstein," *Transactions of the Banffshire Field Club* (1916-17), 21-27.

Burkhardt, J. *Der Dreißigjährige Krieg*. Frankfurt, 1992.

Burkhardt, J. "Der Dreißigjährige Krieg als frühmoderner Staatsbildungskrieg," *Geschichte in Wissenschaft und Unterricht* 45 (1994), 487-99.

Cederström, Rudolf. *Gustav II Adolf vid Lützen*. Stockholm, 1944.

Chaboche, R. "Les soldats Français de la guerre de trente ans: Une tentative d'approache," *Revue d'histoire moderne et contemporaine* 20 (1973), 10-24.

Corum, James S. "Ascheffenburg under Swedish Occupation during the Thirty Years War." In: *Bellum Tricennale: The Thirty Years War*. XXIIIrd Colloquium of the International Commission of Military History. Prague, 1999, pp. 155-80.

Cozza, Dino Willy. "The Thirty Years' War and its Reflections on Brazil." In: *Bellum Tricennale: The Thirty Years War*. XXIIIrd Colloquium of the International Commission of Military History. Prague, 1999, pp. 273-78.

Croxton, Derek. "The Peace of Westphalia of 1648 and the Origins of Sovereignty," *International History Review* 21 (1999), 569-91.

Croxton, Derek. *Peacemaking in Early Modern Europe: Cardinal Mazarin and the Congress of Westphalia, 1643-1648*. Cranbury: Susquehanna University Press, 1999.

Croxton, Derek. "'The Prosperity of Arms is Never Continual': Military Intelligence, Surprise, and Diplomacy in 1640s Germany," *Journal of Military History* 64 (2000), 981-1004.

Croxton, Derek. "A Territorial Imperative? The Military Revolution, Strategy and Peacemaking in the Thirty Years War," *War in History* 5 (1998), 253-79.

Dangl, Vojtech. "Zu einigen strategischen Fragen der Stellung der Slowaken in dem dreißigjährigen Krieg." In: *Bellum Tricennale: The Thirty Years War*. XXIIIrd Colloquium of the International Commission of Military History. Prague, 1999, pp. 237-42.

Danielsson, Arne. "Gustav II Adolfs hatt," *Livrustkammaren* 16 (1983), 89-115.

Danielsson, Arne. "Det kejserliga kyrassiärregimentet Alt-Piccolominis troféer i Statens Trofésamling," *Meddelande* 49 (1989), 103-10.

Danielsson, Arne. "Nördlingen 1634: Tre bataljmålninger," *Meddelande* 33 (1972), 13-52.

Droysen, Gustav. "Gustavus Adolphus: The Statesmen of 'Realpolitik'." In: *The Thirty Years' War: Problems of Motive, Extent, and Effect*. Ed. T.K. Rabb. Boston, 1964, pp. 52-54.

Duchhardt, Heinz. ed. *Der Westfälische Friede: Diplomatie, politische Zäser, kulturelles Umfeld, Rezeptionsgeschichte*. Munich: Oldenbourg, 1998.

Ekstrand, Gudrun. "Apropos ett Gustav Adolf-porträtt i England," *Livrustkammaren* 16 (1982), 33-41.

Ekstrand, Gudrun. "Nils Brahes tröja," *Livrustkammaren* 13 (1973), 93-105.

Ellenius, Allan. "Gustav Adolf i bildkonsten: från Miles Christianus till nationell frihetssymbol." In: *Gustav II Adolf–350 år efter Lützen*. Ed. Keresti Holmquist. Stockholm: Livrustkammaren, 1982, pp. 91-106.

Ergang, R. *The Myth of the All-Destructive Fury of the Thirty Years War*. Pocono Pines, 1956.

Fidler, Jiři. "The Thirty Years War and the Bohemian Lands." In: *Bellum Tricennale: The Thirty Years War*. XXIIIrd Colloquium of the International Commission of Military History. Prague, 1999, pp. 19-26.

Findeisen, Jörg-Peter. *Gustav II. Adolf von Schweden: Der Erober aus dem Norden*. Graz: Verlag Styria, 1996.

Fletcher, C.R.L. "Gustavus Adolphus: The Christian Gentleman." In: *The Thirty Years' War: Problems of Motive, Extent, and Effect*. Ed. T.K. Rabb. Boston, 1964, pp. 54-56.

Franco, Hermenegildo. "The Battle of the Dunes: End of the Spanish Presence in Europe, Oquendo-Tromp." In: *Bellum Tricennale: The Thirty Years War*. XXIIIrd Colloquium of the International Commission of Military History. Prague, 1999, pp. 279-88.

Freytag, Gustav. "The German Catastrophe." In: *The Thirty Years' War: Problems of Motive, Extent, and Effect*. Ed. T.K. Rabb. Boston, 1964, pp. 1-4.

Friedrich, Carl J. "The Religious Motive Reaffirmed." In: *The Thirty Years' War: Problems of Motive, Extent, and Effect*. Ed. T.K. Rabb. Boston, 1964, pp. 32-35.

Frost, R.I. "Poland-Lithuania and the Thirty Years' War." In: *1648: War and Peace in Europe*. Vol. I: *Politics, Religion, Law and Society*. Ed. K. Bußmann and H. Schilling. Münster and Osnabrück, 1998, pp. 197-205.

Fuhrer, Hans Rudolf. "Das 'Stillesitzen': Zur Problematik der schweizerischen Neutralität im Driessigjährigen Krieg." In: *Bellum Tricennale: The Thirty Years War*. XXIIIrd Colloquium of the International Commission of Military History. Prague, 1999, pp. 99-128.

Fulda, Daniel. "Gewalt gegen Gott und die Natur: Ästhetik und Metaphorizität von Anthropophagieberichten aus dem Dreißigjährigen Krieg." In: *Ein Schauplatz herber Angst. Wahrnehmung und Darstellung von Gewalt im 17. Jahrhundert*. Ed. Markus Meumann and Dirk Niefanger. Göttingen, 1997, pp. 240-69.

Gindely, Anton. "Religion and Politics." In: *The Thirty Years' War: Problems of Motive, Extent, and Effect*. Ed. T.K. Rabb. Boston, 1964, pp. 4-6.

Grönhammar, Ann. "Gustav II Adolfs firande den 6 November–hur svenskar minns det 1982," *Livrustkammaren* 16 (1984), 155-78.

Gutmann, Myron P. "The Origins of the Thirty Years' War," *Journal of Interdisciplinary History* 18 (1988), 749-70.

Hartmann, Anja. *Von Regensburg nach Hamburg: die diplomatischen Beziehungen zwischen dem französischen König und dem Kaiser vom Regensburger Vertrag (13. Oktober 1630) bis zum Hamburger Präliminarfrieden (25. Dezember 1641)*. Münster: Aschendorff Verlag, 1998.

Heckel, M. "Die Krise der Religionsverfassung des Reiches und die Anfänge des Dreißigjährigen Krieges." In: *Gesammelte Schriften: Staat, Kirche, Recht, Geschichte*. Ed. K. Schlaich. Tubingen, 1989, II:970-98.

Higham, Robin. "Some Thoughts on the 30 Years' War." In: *Bellum Tricennale: The Thirty Years War*. XXIIIrd Colloquium of the International Commission of Military History. Prague, 1999, pp. 339-50.

Höfer, Ernst. *Das Ende des Dreißjährigen Krieges*. Cologne: Böhlau Verlag, 1997.

Hofström, Gerhard. "Gustav Vasa i Lübeck," *Livrustkammaren* 9 (1961).

Holmquist, Keresti. "Förord." In: *Gustav II Adolf–350 år efter Lützen*. Ed. Keresti Holmquist. Stockholm: Livrustkammaren, 1982, pp. 5-10.

Huxley, Aldous. "Cardinal Richelieu: The Lust for Money and Power." In: *The Thirty Years' War: Problems of Motive, Extent, and Effect*. Ed. T.K. Rabb. Boston, 1964, pp. 79-83.

Johannesson, Kurt. "Gustav II Adolf som retoriker." In: *Gustav II Adolf– 350 år efter Lützen*. Ed. Keresti Holmquist. Stockholm: Livrustkammaren, 1982, pp. 11-30.

Kaiser, Michael. "'Excidium Magdeburgense': Beobachtungen zur Wahrehmung und Darstellung von Gewalt im Dreißigjährend Krieg." In: *Ein Schauplatz herber Angst. Wahrnehmung und Darstellung von Gewalt im 17. Jahrhundert*. Ed. Markus Meumann and Dirk Niefanger. Göttingen, 1997, pp.43-64.

Kaiser, Michael. *Politik und Kriegführung: Maximilian von Bayern, Tilly und die Katholische Liga im Dreißjährigen Krieg*. Münster: Aschendorff Verlag, 1999.

Kapser, Cordula. *Die Bayerische Kriegsorganisation in der zweiten Hälfte des dreißigjahrigen Krieges, 1635-1648/49*. Schriftenreihe der Vereinigung zur Erforschung der Neueren Geschichte, 25. Münster: Aschendorff, 1997.

Kirchmeier-Andersen, J.C. "Christian IV som taktiker," *Vaabenhistoriske aarbøger* 33 (1987), 63-157; 34 (1988), 5-107.

Klučina, Pertr. "The Thirty Years War Began and Ended in the Czech Lands." In: *Bellum Tricennale: The Thirty Years War*. XXIIIrd Colloquium of the International Commission of Military History. Prague, 1999, pp. 11-18.

Knauer, Martin. "Krieg, Gewalt und Erbauung: Zur Funktion der Todesmahnung in druckgraphischen Bildfolgen des Dreißigjährigen Krieges." In: *Ein Schauplatz herber Angst. Wahrnehmung und Darstellung von Gewalt im 17. Jahrhundert*. Ed. Markus Meumann and Dirk Niefanger. Göttingen, 1997, pp.83-104.

Lagerqvist, Lars O. "Gustav II Adolfs liktag och sorgeläger i Tyskland," *Livrustkammaren* 16 (1982), 42-62.

Langer, Herbert. *Hortus Bellicus: Der Dreissigjährige Krieg: Eine Kulturgeschichte*. Leipzig: Verlag Edition, 1978; trans. *The Thirty Years' War*. Poole: Dorset, 1978.

Lappalainen, Jussi T. "'Ex agmine haccapellorum libera nos Domine': Les 25,000 Finnois dans la Guerre de Trente Ans." In: *Bellum Tricennale: The*

Thirty Years War. XXIIIrd Colloquium of the International Commission of Military History. Prague, 1999, pp. 39-50.

Le Diberder, Georges. "Fraternité d'armes et relations diplomatiques Franco-Suedoises pendant la Guerre de Trent Ans." In: *17ᵗʰ Century War, Weaponry and Politics: International Association of Museums of Arms and Military History, Xth Congress Stockholm 1984* Stockholm, 1984, pp. 61-75.

Lindgren, Mereth. "'Kyrkian til prydning och Gudi til ära': Om kyrkmäl-ningar under Gustav Adolfs tid," *Livrustkammaren* 16 (1983), 61-86.

Livet, Georges. *La guerre de trente ans*. Paris: PUF, 1966.

Lockhart, Paul Douglas. *Denmark in the Thirty Years' War, 1618-1648: King Christian IV and the Decline of the Oldenburg State*. Selinsgrove: Susquehanna University Press, 1996.

Loomis, A.J. "Olivares, the English Catholics and the Peace of 1630," *Revue Belge de philologie et d'histoire* 47 (1969), 1154-66.

Loucas, Ioannis. "La Guerre de Cent Ans et l'espace Grec." In: *Bellum Tricennale: The Thirty Years War*. XXIIIrd Colloquium of the International Commission of Military History. Prague, 1999, pp. 253-64.

Louis, Gérard. "Les misères de la guerre de Trente Ans en Franche-Comté." In: *Les malheurs de la guerre*. I: *De la guerre à l'ancienne à la guerre réglée*. Ed. André Corvisier and Jean Jacquart. Paris: Éditions du CTHS, 1996, pp. 181-.

Lundkvist, Sven. "Gustav Adolf som fältherre." In: *Gustav II Adolf–350 år efter Lützen*. Ed. Keresti Holmquist. Stockholm: Livrustkammaren, 1982, pp. 47-60.

Lynn, John A. "War, Military Forces, and the Formation of French Absolutism, 1635-1659." In: *Bellum Tricennale: The Thirty Years War*. XXIIIrd Colloquium of the International Commission of Military History. Prague, 1999, pp. 65-80.

Malettke, Klaus. "Wallenstein–général, prince d'empire et homme politique dans la guerre de trente ans," *Francia* 20/2 (1993), 21-33.

Mann, G. *Wallenstein*. London, 1976.

Mears, John A. "The Thirty Years' War, the 'General Crisis,' and the Origins of a Standing Professional Army in the Habsburg Monarchy," *Central European History* 21 (1988), 122-41.

Mehring, Franz. "The Marxist View: Economic Causation." In: *The Thirty Years' War: Problems of Motive, Extent, and Effect*. Ed. T.K. Rabb. Boston, 1964, pp. 6-9.

Montgomery, Ingun. "Gustav Adolf och religionen." In: *Gustav II Adolf– 350 år efter Lützen*. Ed. Keresti Holmquist. Stockholm: Livrustkammaren, 1982, pp. 61-78.

Müller, Frank. *Kirsachsen und der Böhmische Aufstand, 1618-1622*. Münster: Aschendorff, 1997.

Murtagh, Harman. "Ireland, the Military Revolution and the Thirty Years' War." In: *Bellum Tricennale: The Thirty Years War*. XXIIIrd Colloquium of the International Commission of Military History. Prague, 1999, pp. 309-26.

Nilsson, Sven A. "Militärstaten i funktion." In: *Gustav II Adolf–350 år efter Lützen*. Ed. Keresti Holmquist. Stockholm: Livrustkammaren, 1982, pp. 31-46.

Nouzille, J. "Les relations entre la France et la Transylvanie pendant la guerre de trente ans: La difficile recherche d'une alliance de revers," *Revue Roumaine d'histoire* 36 (1997), 173-90.

Pagès, Georges. *La guerre de trente ans*. Paris, 1939.

Pagès, Georges. "The War as a Dividing Point Between Medieval and Modern Times." In: *The Thirty Years' War: Problems of Motive, Extent, and Effect*. Ed. T.K. Rabb. Boston, 1964, pp. 20-25.

Paoletti, Ciro. "L'Italie et la guerre de Trente Ans." In: *Bellum Tricennale: The Thirty Years War*. XXIIIrd Colloquium of the International Commission of Military History. Prague, 1999, pp. 243-52.

Parker, Geoffrey. *The Thirty Years' War*. 2nd ed. New York: Military Heritage Press, 1987.

Parrott, David A. "Strategy and Tactics in the Thirty Years' War: The 'Military Revolution,'" *Militärgeschichtlichte Mitteilungen* 38 (1985),

7-25; in: *The Military Revolution Debate: Readings on the Military Transformation of Early Modern Europe*. Ed. C.J. Rogers. Boulder, 1995, pp. 227-52.

Pekař, Josef. "Albrecht von Wallenstein: The Cowardly and Megalomanic Traitor." In: *The Thirty Years' War: Problems of Motive, Extent, and Effect.* Ed. T.K. Rabb. Boston, 1964, pp. 67-70.

Pekař, Josef. "The Turning-Point in Czech History." In: *The Thirty Years' War: Problems of Motive, Extent, and Effect.* Ed. T.K. Rabb. Boston, 1964, pp. 49-51.

Pillorget, René. "France et Bavière au cours de la Guerre de Trente Ans (1618-1648)." In: *Bellum Tricennale: The Thirty Years War*. XXIIIrd Colloquium of the International Commission of Military History. Prague, 1999, pp. 327-38.

Pleiss, Detlev. "Die Friedensquartiere der Schweden und Finnen um Nürnberg 1648/49." *Nürnberg Mitteilungen* 86 (1999), 115-71.

Polišenský, J.V. "Social and Economic Change and the European-Wide War." In: *The Thirty Years' War: Problems of Motive, Extent, and Effect.* Ed. T.K. Rabb. Boston, 1964, pp. 35-42.

Polišenský, J.V. *The Thirty Years War*. Trans. Robert Evans. London: New English Library, 1974.

Porshev, B.F. *Muscovy and Sweden in the Thirty Years' War, 1630-5.* Cambridge, 1995.

Quatrefages, René. "Le plan baltique: le 'Sursaut' espagnol." In: *Bellum Tricennale: The Thirty Years War*. XXIIIrd Colloquium of the International Commission of Military History. Prague, 1999, pp. 51-64.

Queloz, Dimitry. *La défense du Comté de Neuchâtel durant la Guerre de Trente Ans*. Auvernier: Le Roset, 1998.

Queloz, Dimitry. "Les milices du comte de Neuchatel durant Guerre de Trente Ans: organisation, fonctionnement et engangement." In: *Bellum Tricennale: The Thirty Years War*. XXIIIrd Colloquium of the International Commission of Military History. Prague, 1999, pp. 289-300.

Rabb, Theodore K. "The Economic Effects of the War Reviewed." In: *The Thirty Years' War: Problems of Motive, Extent, and Effect*. Ed. T.K. Rabb. Boston, 1964, pp. 42-49.

Rabb, Theodore K. "The Effects of the Thirty Years' War on the German Economy," *Journal of Modern History* 34 (1962), 40-51.

Ranke, Leopold von. "Albrecht von Wallenstein: The Egoistic but Idealistic Seeker of Peace." In: *The Thirty Years' War: Problems of Motive, Extent, and Effect*. Ed. T.K. Rabb. Boston, 1964, pp. 63-67.

Redlich, Fritz. "Contributions in the Thirty Years' War," *Economic History Review* 2nd ser. 12 (1959-60), 247-54.

Redondo Diaz, Fernando. "The Soldier of the Thirty Years War: The Spanish Soldier." In: *Bellum Tricennale: The Thirty Years War*. XXIIIrd Colloquium of the International Commission of Military History. Prague, 1999, pp. 81-90.

Reeve, L.J. "Quiroga's Paper of 1631: A Missing Link in Anglo-Spanish Diplomacy during the Thirty Years War," *English Historical Review* 101 (1986).

Repgen, Konrad. "Die Hauptprobleme der Westfälischen Friedensverhandlungen von 1648 und ihre Lösungen," *Zeitschrift für Bayerische Landesgeschichte* 62 (1999), 400-38.

Ringmar, Erik. *Identity, Interest and Action: A Cultural Explanation of Sweden's Intervention in the Thirty Years War*. Cambridge: Cambridge University Press, 1996.

Roberts, Michael. "Gustaf Adolf and the Art of War." In: *Essays in Swedish History*. London: Weidenfeld and Nicolson, 1966, pp. 56-81.

Roberts, Michael. *Gustavus Adolphus*. 2 vols. London, 1958.

Roberts, Michael. "Gustavus Adolphus: The Practical Stateman." In: *The Thirty Years' War: Problems of Motive, Extent, and Effect*. Ed. T.K. Rabb. Boston, 1964, pp. 59-62.

Roberts, Michael. "The Political Objectives of Gustavus Adolf in Germany, 1632," *Transactions of the Royal Historical Society* 5th ser. 7 (1957).

Rudnert, Sune. "Lik i lasten: En studie en svensk historie-målares framställning av inskeppningen av Gustav II Adolfs lik i Wolgast 1633," *Livrustkammaren* 16 (1984), 133-56.

Runeby, Nils. "'Godh politie och regemente'." In: *Gustav II Adolf–350 år efter Lützen*. Ed. Keresti Holmquist. Stockholm: Livrustkammaren, 1982, pp. 79-90.

Rystad, Göran. "The Problem of Shared Command: The Convention of Frankfurt and the Battle of Nördlingen." In: *Bellum Tricennale: The Thirty Years War*. XXIIIrd Colloquium of the International Commission of Military History. Prague, 1999, pp. 27-38.

Seitz, Heribert. "Värjan och dödskotten," *Livrustkammaren* 16 (1982), 22-32.

Sicken, Bernhard. "Würzburg und der schwedische Griff nach Süddeutschland: Eroberung (1631) und Verlust (1634/35) von Stadt, Feste und Territorium." In: *Bellum Tricennale: The Thirty Years War*. XXIIIrd Colloquium of the International Commission of Military History. Prague, 1999, pp. 129-44.

Srbik, Heinrich Ritter von. "Albrecht von Wallenstein: The Tortured Idealist." In: *The Thirty Years' War: Problems of Motive, Extent, and Effect*. Ed. T.K. Rabb. Boston, 1964, pp. 70-74.

Srbik, Heinrich Ritter von. *Wallenstein's Ende: Ursachen, Verlauf und Folgen der Katastrophe*. Vienna, 1952.

Steinberg, S.H. "The Not So Destructive, Not So Religious, and Not Primarily German War." In: *The Thirty Years' War: Problems of Motive, Extent, and Effect*. Ed. T.K. Rabb. Boston, 1964, pp. 25-32.

Steinberg, S.H. *The 'Thirty Years' War and the Conflict for European Hegemony, 1600-1660*. London, 1966.

Sutherland, N.M. "The Origins of the Thirty Years War and the Structure of European Politics," *English Historical Review* 107 (1992), 587-625.

Tapié, V.L. "Cardinal Richelieu: The Overburdened Statesman Driven by Events." In: *The Thirty Years' War: Problems of Motive, Extent, and Effect*. Ed. T.K. Rabb. Boston, 1964, pp. 86-88.

Taşkiran, Cemalettin. "L'empire Ottoman dans les Guerres de 30 Ans." In: *Bellum Tricennale: The Thirty Years War*. XXIIIrd Colloquium of the International Commission of Military History. Prague, 1999, pp. 145-54.

Theibault, John. "The Demography of the Thirty Years War Re-visited: Günther Franz and his Critics," *German History* 15 (1997), 1-22.

Theibault, John. "The Rhetoric of Death and Destruction in the Thirty Years War," *Journal of Social History* 27 (1993), 271-90.

Thiriet, Jean-Michel. "Les officiers Italiens au service des Habsbourg pendant la Guerre de Trente Ans: Le cas des familles de Bohême-Moravie." In: *Bellum Tricennale: The Thirty Years War*. XXIIIrd Colloquium of the International Commission of Military History. Prague, 1999, pp. 181-92.

Turek, Eva. "Under False Colours: A Case of Missing Identity–Are Those the Colours of Wallenstein or Liechtenstein?" *Meddelande* 56 (1996), 27-49.

Wagner, Eduard. *European Weapons and Warfare, 1618-1648*. Trans. Simon Pellar. London: Octopus Books Limited, 1979.

Wedgwood, C.V. "The Futile and Meaningless War." In: *The Thirty Years' War: Problems of Motive, Extent, and Effect*. Ed. T.K. Rabb. Boston, 1964, pp. 9-20.

Wedgwood, C.V. *The Thirty Years War*. London: Jonathan Cape, 1938.

Weeks, Charles Andrew. "Jacob Boehme and the Thirty Years' War," *Central European History* 24 (1991), 213-21.

Wetterberg, Gunnar. "Förhandlingarna i Onasbrück och Münster, 1644-1648," *Internationella Studier* (1998), 21-39.

Zachar, József. "Ungarn in den Heeren der Habsburger zur Zeit des Dreissigjährigen Krieges." In: *Bellum Tricennale: The Thirty Years War*. XXIIIrd Colloquium of the International Commission of Military History. Prague, 1999, pp. 205-54.

Zhenyu, Yang. "Brief Analysis on the Features of Military Economy of the Thirty Years' War." In: *Bellum Tricennale: The Thirty Years War*. XXIIIrd Colloquium of the International Commission of Military History. Prague, 1999, pp. 265-72.

Early Modern – Ireland

Brady, Claran. "The Captain's Games: Army and Society in Elizabethan Ireland." In: *A Military History of Ireland*. Ed. Thomas Bartlett and Keith Jeffrey. Cambridge: Cambridge University Press, 1996, pp. 136-59.

Brady, Claran. "The Decline of the Irish Kingdom." In: *Conquest and Coalescence: The Shaping of the State in Early Modern Europe*. Ed. Mark Greengrass. London: Edward Arnold, 1991, pp. 94-115.

Carey, Vincent P. "John Derricke's *Image of Irelande*, Sir Henry Sidney, and the Massacre at Mullaghmast, 1578," *Irish Historical Studies* 31 (1999), 305-27.

Duffy, Seán. "Tudor Conquest and Gaelic Collapse: Ireland in the Sixteenth Century." In: *Actas do XXIV congresso internacional de historía militar*. Centro cultural de Belém, 24 a 29 de agosto, 1998. Lisbon: Comissão Portuguesa de Historía Militar, 1998, pp. 117-22.

Falls, Cyril. *Elizabeth's Irish Wars*. 1950; rpt. New York: Barnes and Noble, Inc., 1970.

Falls, Cyril. "The Growth of Irish Military Strength in the Second Half of the Sixteenth Century," *Irish Sword* 2 (1954-56), 103-08.

Gillespie, Raymond. "An Army Sent from God: Scots at War in Ireland, 1642-9." In: *Scotland and War, AD 79-1918*. Ed. Norman Macdougall. Edinburgh: John Donald, 1991, pp. 113-32.

Hardacre, P.H. "Patronage and Purchase in the Irish Standing Army under Thomas Wentworth, Earl of Strafford, 1632-1640," *Journal of the Society for Army Historical Research* 69 (1989), 40-45, 94-104.

Hayes-McCoy, G.A. *Irish Battles: A Military History of Ireland*. Belfast: Appeltree Press, 1990.

Heath, Ian. *The Irish Wars, 1485-1603*. London: Osprey, 1993.

Henry, Gráinne. *The Irish Military Community in Spanish Flanders, 1586-1621*. Dublin: Irish Academic Press, 1992.

Hill, James Michael. *Celtic Warfare, 1595-1763*. Edinburgh: John Donald Ltd., 1986.

Hill, James Michael. "Gaelic Warfare, 1453-1815." In: *European Warfare, 1453-1815*. Ed. Jeremy Black. New York: St. Martin's Press, 1999, pp. 201-23.

Hill, James Michael. "The Origins and Development of the 'Highland Charge' c.1560 to 1646," *Militärgeschichtliche mitteilungen* 53 (1994), 295-307.

Lindley, Keith J. "The Impact of the 1641 Rebellion upon England and Wales, 1641-5," *Irish Historical Studies* 18 (1972), 143-76.

MacCormack, Anthony M. "Internecine Warfare and the Decline of the House of Desmond, c.1510-c.1541," *Irish Historical Studies* 30 (1997), 497-512.

MacCuarta, Brian, ed. *Ulster 1641: Aspects of the Rising*. Belfast: The Institute of Irish Studies, 1993.

McGurk, John J.N. "Casualties and Welfare Measures for the Sick and Wounded of the Nine Year War in Ireland, 1593-1602," *Journal of the Society for Army Historical Research* 68 (1990), 22-35, 188-204.

McKerral, Andrew. "West Highland Mercenaries in Ireland," *Scottish Historical Review* 30 (1951), 1-14.

Morgan, Hiram. *Tyrone's Rebellion*. Dublin: Gill and Macmillan, 1993.

O'Domhnaill, Sean. "Warfare in Sixteenth-Century Ireland," *Irish Historical Studies* 5 (1946-47), 29-54.

Ohlmeyer, Jane H. "Ireland Independent: Confederate Foreign Policy and International Relations during the Mid-Seventeenth Century." In: *Ireland from Independence to Occupation, 1641-1660*. Ed. J.H. Ohlmeyer. Cambridge, 1995, pp. 89-112.

Ohlmeyer, Jane H. "The Wars of Religion, 1603-1660." In: *A Military History of Ireland*. Ed. Thomas Bartlett and Keith Jeffrey. Cambridge: Cambridge University Press, 1996, pp. 160-87.

Pawlisch, Hans S. "Metropolitan Law and Native Property Rights in the English Conquest of Ireland." In: *Actas do XXIV congresso internacional de historía militar*. Centro cultural de Belém, 24 a 29 de agosto, 1998. Lisbon: Comissão Portuguesa de Historía Militar, 1998, pp. 123-32.

Shagan, Ethan H. "Constructing Discord: Ideology, Propaganda, and the English Responses to the Irish Rebellion of 1641,"*Journal of British Studies* 36 (1997), 4-34.

Early Modern – Italy and the Italian Wars [See also Medieval – Italy]

Anglo, Sydney. "Sixteenth-Century Italian Drawings in Federico Ghisliero's *Regole di molti cavagliereschi essercitii*," *Apollo* (Nov 1994), 29-36.

Barbarich, E. "Gli stradiotti nell'arte militare veneziana," *Rivista di cavalleria* 13 (1904).

Benedetti, A. *Il fatto d'armee del Taro*. Novaro, 1863.

Blanchard, Joël. "Political and Cultural Implications of Secret Diplomacy: Commynes and Ferrara in the Light of Unpublished Documents." In: *The French Descent into Renaissance Italy: Antecedents and Effects*. Ed. D. Abulafia. Aldershot: Ashgate, 1995, pp. 231-47.

Brand, C.P. "The Poetry of War in the Italian Renaissance." In: *War, Literature and the Arts in Sixteenth-Century Europe*. Ed. J.R. Mulryne and M. Shewring. New York, 1989, pp. 81-100.

Brandt, F. "Die Schlacht bei Pavia, 1525," *Militärgeschichte* 18 (1979), 73-86.

Bryson, Frederick. *The Sixteenth-Century Italian Duel*. Chicago, 1938.

Chambers, D.S. *The Imperial Age of Venice, 1380-1580*. London, 1970.

Chambers, David. "Francesco II Gonzaga, Marquis of Mantua, 'Liberator of Italy.'" In: *The French Descent into Renaissance Italy: Antecedents and Effects*. Ed. D. Abulafia. Aldershot: Ashgate, 1995, pp. 217-29.

Chao, Andrés Mas. "Cerignola, Bicocca et Pavie: L'arme à feu individuelle comme facteur décisif au combat." In: *XXII. Kongreß der Internationalen Kommission für Militärgeschichte* Acta 22: *Von Crécy bis Mohács Kriegswesen im späten Mittelalter (1346-1526)*. Vienna, 1997, pp. 195-206.

Chastel, André. *The Sack of Rome, 1527*. Trans. Beth Archer. Princeton, 1983.

Chittolini, Giorgio. "Milan in the Face of the Italian Wars (1494-1535): Between the Crisis of the State and the Affirmation of Urban Autonomy." In: *The French Descent into Renaissance Italy: Antecedents and Effects*. Ed. D. Abulafia. Aldershot: Ashgate, 1995, pp. 391-404.

Clough, Cecil H. "Love and War in the Veneto: Luigi da Porto and the True Story of *Giulietta e Romeo*." In: *War, Culture and Society in Renaissance Venice: Essays in Honour of John Hale*. Ed. D.S. Chambers, C.H. Clough and M.E. Mallett. London, 1993, pp. 99-127.

Clough, Cecil H. "The Romagna Campaign of 1494: A Significant Military Encounter." In: *The French Descent into Renaissance Italy: Antecedents and Effects*. Ed. D. Abulafia. Aldershot: Ashgate, 1995, pp. 191-215.

Contamine, Philippe. "À propos du 'voyage de Milan' (février-juillet 1500). Louis de La Trémoille, Louis XII et Ludovic le More." In: *De Jeanne d'Arc aux guerres d'Italie: Figures, images et problèmes du XVe siècle*. Orléans: Paradigme, 1994, pp. 245-62.

Contamine, Philippe. "L'artillerie royale Française à la veille des guerres d'Italie," *Annales de Bretagne* 71 (1964), 221-61.

Covini, Maria Nadia. "Liens politiques et militaires dans le système des États italiens (XIIIe-XVIe siècle)." In: *Guerre et concurrence entre les États européens du XIVe au XVIIIe siècle*. Ed. Philippe Contamine. Fondation Européenne de la Science: Les origines de l'État moderne en Europe, XIIIe-XVIIIe siècle. Paris: Presses universitaires de France, 1998, pp. 9-42.

Dalla Santa, Giuseppe. *La Lega di Cambrai e gli avvenimenti dell'anno 1509 descritti da un mercante veneziano contemporaneo*. Venice, 1903.

Davis, James Cushman. "Shipping and Spying in the Early Career of a Venetian Doge, 1496-1502," *Studi veneziana* 16 (1974), 97-108.

Davis, Robert C. *The War of the Fists: Popular Culture and Public Violence in Late Renaissance Venice*. Oxford: Oxford University Press, 1994.

Dean, Trevor. "After the War of Ferrara: Relations between Venice and Ercole d'Este, 1484-1505." In: *War, Culture and Society in Renaissance Venice: Essays in Honour of John Hale*. Ed. D.S. Chambers, C.H. Clough and M.E. Mallett. London, 1993, pp. 73-98.

De Cardenas y Vicent, Vicente. *El saco de Roma de 1527 por el ejercito de Carlos V*. Madrid, 1974.

Delaborde, H.F. *L'expedition de Charles VIII en Italie: Histoire diplomatique et militaire*. Paris, 1888.

Del Prato, A. "Contributo alla storia della battaglia di Fornovo," *Archivio storico per la province Parmensia* 5 (1915).

Esson, D.M.R. "The Italian Campaigns of Consalvo de Cordoba," *Army Quarterly* 80 (1958-60), 235-46; 81 (1960-61), 105-20.

Finlay, Robert. "Fabius Maximus in Venice: Doge Andrea Gritti, the War of Cambrai, and the Rise of Habsburg Hegemony, 1509-1530," *Renaissance Quarterly* 53 (2000), 988-1031.

Finlay, Robert. "The Foundation of the Ghetto: Venice, the Jews, and the War of the League of Cambrai," *Proceedings of the American Philosophical Society* 126 (1982), 140-54.

Finlay, Robert. "The Immortal Republic: The Myth of Venice during the Italian Wars (1494-1530)," *Sixteenth Century Studies* 30 (1999), 931-44.

Finlay, Robert. "Venice, the Po Expedition, and the End of the League of Cambrai, 1509-1510," *Studies in Modern European History and Culture* 2 (1976), 37-72.

Firpo, Massimo. *Il Sacco di Roma: tra profezia, propaganda politica e riforma religiosa*. Caligari, 1990.

Fischer, G. *Die Schlacht bei Novara (6 June 1513)*. Berlin, 1908.

Foscari, Antonio and Manfredo Tafuri. *L'armonia e i conflitti: La chiesa di San Francisco della Vigna nella Venezia del '500*. Turin, 1983.

Frigo, Daniela, ed. *Politics and Diplomacy in Early Modern Italy: The Structure of Diplomatic Practice, 1450-1800*. Cambridge: Cambridge University Press, 2000.

Gaibi, Agostino. "Un codice manoscritto della fine del '500 che interessa la storia delle armi Italiane," *Armi antiche* (1959), 35-50.

Gilbert, Felix. "Venetian Diplomacy Before Pavia: From Reality to Myth." In: *History: Choice and Commitment*. Cambridge, 1977, pp. 295-321.

Giono, Jean. *Le désastre de Pavie: 24 février 1525*. Paris, 1963; trans. *The Battle of Pavia, 24th February 1525*. Trans. A.E. Murch. London: Peter Owen, 1965.

Gouwens, Kenneth. "Discourses of Vulnerability: Pietro Alcionio's Orations on the Sack of Rome," *Renaissance Quarterly* 50.1 (1997), 38-77.

Hale, John R. "Michiel and the *Tempesta*: the Soldier in a Landscape as a Motif in Venetian Painting." In: *Florence and Italy: Renaissance Studies in Honour of Nicolai Rubenstein*. Ed. P. Denley and C. Elam. London, 1988, pp. 405-18.

Hale, John R. "Military Academies on the Venetian Terrafirma in the Early Seventeenth Century," *Studi Veneziani* 15 (1973), 273-95; and in: *Renaissance War Studies*. London, 1983, pp. 285-308.

Hale, John R. "Printing and the Military Culture of Renaissance Venice." In: *Renaissance War Studies*. London, 1983, pp. 429-70.

Hale, John R. "Renaissance Armies and Political Control: the Venetian Proveditorial System, 1509-1529," *Journal of Italian History* 2 (1979), 11-31.

Hale, John R. "War and Public Opinion in Renaissance Italy." In: *Italian Renaissance Studies*. Ed. E.F. Jacob. London, 1960, pp. 94-122; in: *Renaissance War Studies*. London, 1983, pp. 359-88.

Hanlon, Gregory. "The Decline of a Provincial Military Aristocracy: Siena, 1560-1740," *Past and Present* 155 (1997), 64-108.

Hanlon, Gregory. *The Twilight of a Military Tradition: Italian Aristocrats and European Conflicts, 1560-1800*. London: UCL Press, 1998.

Hardy, E. *Les Français en Italie de 1494 à 1559*. Paris, 1880.

Henninger, Laurent. *Marignan, 1515*. Les Grandes Batailles de l'Histoire, no. 15. Paris: Socomer Éditions, 1991.

Hook, Judith. "Clement VII, the Colonna and Charles V: A Study of the Political Instability of Italy in the Second and Third Decades of the Sixteenth Century," *European Studies Review* 2 (1972), 281-99.

Hook, Judith. "The Destruction of the New 'Italia': Venice and the Papacy in Collision," *Italian Studies* 28 (1973), 10-30.

Hook, Judith. *The Sack of Rome, 1527*. London, 1972.

Kaplan, Paul H.D. "The Storm of War: the Padua Key to Giorgione's *Tempesta*," *Art History* 9 (1986), 405-35.

Kidwell, Carol. "Venice, the French Invasion and the Apulian Ports." In: *The French Descent into Renaissance Italy: Antecedents and Effects*. Ed. D. Abulafia. Aldershot: Ashgate, 1995, pp. 295-308.

Konstam, Angus. *Pavia, 1525: The Climax of the Italian Wars*. London: Osprey, 1996.

Laderchi, L. "La battaglia di Fornovo, 6 Luglio 1495," *Nuovo antologia* (Sept 1916).

La Pilorgerie, J. de. *Campagne et bulletins de la Grande Armée d'Italie commandée par Charles VIII, 1494-5*. Paris, 1886.

Laven, David. "Machiavelli, *italianità* and the French Invasion of 1494." In: *The French Descent into Renaissance Italy: Antecedents and Effects*. Ed. D. Abulafia. Aldershot: Ashgate, 1995, pp. 355-69.

Lenci, A. "L'assedio di Padova del 1509: questioni militari e implicazioni urbanistiche nella strategia difensiva veneziana all'indomani di Agnadello," *Bollentino del Museo Civico di Padova* 63 (1974), 123-55.

Lenzi, M.L. "Fanti e cavalieri nelle prime guerre d'Italia (1494-1527)," *Ricerche storiche* 7.1 (1977), 7-92; 7.2 (1978), 359-415.

Libby, Lester J. "The Reconquest of Padua in 1509 according to the Diary of Girolamo Priuli," *Renaissance Quarterly* 28 (1975), 323-31.

Lot, Ferdinand. *Recherches sur les effectifs des armées Françaises des guerres d'Italie aux guerres de religion, 1492-1562*. Paris, 1962.

Luzio, Alessandro. "I preliminari della Lega di Cambrai concordati a Milano ed a Mantova," *Archivio storico* 38 (1911), 245-310.

Luzio, Alessandro and R. Renier. "Francesco Gonzaga alla battaglia di Fornovo (1495)," *Archivio storico Italiana* 6 (1890).

Luzzati, M. *Una guerra di popolo: Lettere private del tempo dell'assedio di Pisa (1494-1509)*. Pisa, 1973.

Mallett, Michael. *Mercenaries and their Masters: Warfare in Renaissance Italy*. Totowa: Rowman and Littlefield, 1974.

Mallett, Michael. "Personalities and Pressures: Italian Involvement in the French Invasion of 1494." In: *The French Descent into Renaissance Italy: Antecedents and Effects*. Ed. D. Abulafia. Aldershot: Ashgate, 1995, pp. 151-63.

Mallett, Michael and J.R. Hale. *The Military Organization of a Renaissance State: Venice, c. 1400 to 1617*. Cambridge: Cambridge University Press, 1984.

Martinazzi, G. "Occupazione del castelo e della città di Novaro par parte del Duca d'Orleans nel 1495," *Archivio storico Lombardo* 3 (1876).

Mason, Judith. "The Sack of Rome," *History Today* 16 (1966), 400-05.

Massa, E. "La battaglia di Fornovo," *Rivista militare Italiana* (1912).

Niccoli, Ottavia. *Prophecy and People in Renaissance Italy*. Trans. Lydia G. Cochrane. Princeton: Princeton University Press, 1990.

Nicolle, David C. *Fornovo, 1495: France's Bloody Fighting Retreat*. Osprey Military Campaign Series, 43. London: Osprey, 1999.

North, Jonathan. "Rising to Crush an Invader," *Military Heritage* (Apr 2000), 78-85, 98.

Oppel, John W. "Peace vs. Liberty in the Quattrocento: Poggio, Guarino, and the Scipio-Caesar Controversy," *Journal of Medieval and Renaissance Studies* 4 (1974), 221-66.

Partner, Peter. "The Papal State: 1417-1600." In: *Conquest and Coalescence: The Shaping of the State in Early Modern Europe*. Ed. Mark Greengrass. London: Edward Arnold, 1991, pp. 25-47.

Parrott, David A. "The Mantuan Succession, 1627-31: A Sovereignty Dispute in Early Modern Europe," *English Historical Review* 112 (1997), 20-65.

Patria, Ettore. "Discors sur la prise d'Essiglies, 1593," *Armi antiche* (1977), 19-38.

Pepper, Simon. "Castles and Cannon in the Naples Campaign of 1494-95." In: *The French Descent into Renaissance Italy, 1494-95: Antecedents and Effects*. Ed. D. Abulafia. Aldershot: Ashgate, 1995, pp. 263-93.

Petta, Paolo. *Stradioti: Soldati Albanesi in Italia (secolo XV-XIX)*. Lecce: Argo S.c.r.l., 1996.

Peyronnet, Georges. "The Distant Origins of the Italian Wars: Political Relations between France and Italy in the Fourteenth and Fifteenth Centuries." In: *The French Descent into Renaissance Italy: Antecedents and Effects*. Ed. D. Abulafia. Aldershot: Ashgate, 1995, pp. 29-53.

Pieri, Piero. *La crisi militare Italiana nel renascimento*. Naples, 1934.

Pieri, Piero. *Il rinascimento e la crisi militare italiana*. Turin, 1952.

Pieri, Piero. "La scienza militare Italiana del renascimento." In: *Scritti vari*. Turin, 1966

Ryder, Alan. "The Angevin Bid for Naples, 1380-1480." In: *The French Descent into Renaissance Italy: Antecedents and Effects*. Ed. D. Abulafia. Aldershot: Ashgate, 1995, pp. 55-69.

Santalena, Antonio. *Veneti e Imperiali: Treviso al tempo della lega di Cambray*. Venice, 1896.

Santosuosso, Antonio. "Anatomy of Defeat in Renaissance Italy: The Battle of Fornovo in 1495," *International History Review* 16 (1994), 221-50.

Sanudo, M. *La spedizione di Carlo VIII in Italia*. Venice, 1873.

Schaufelberger, Walter. *Marignano: Strukturelle Grenzen eidgenössischer Militärmacht zwischen Mittelalter und Neuzeit*. Frauenfeld: Huber Verlag, 1993.

Seneca, Federico. "Venezia, l'equilibrio politico e la crisi della 'libertà' d'Italia," *Critica storica* 6 (1967), 453-69.

Shaw, Christine. "The Roman Barons and the French Descent into Italy." In: *The French Descent into Renaissance Italy: Antecedents and Effects.* Ed. D. Abulafia. Aldershot: Ashgate, 1995, pp. 249-61.

Stewart, Paul. "The *Santa Hermandad* and the First Italian Campaign of Gonzalo de Córdoba, 1495-1498," *Renaissance Quarterly* 28 (1975), 29-37.

Storti, Francesco. "Istituzioni militari in Italia tra medioevo ed età moderna," *Studi storici* 38 (1997), 257-71.

Taylor, F.L. *The Art of War in Italy, 1494-1529.* Cambridge: Cambridge University Press, 1921.

Usteri, Emil. *Marignano: Die Schickalsjahre 1515/1516 im Blickfeld der Historischen Quellen.* Zurich, 1974.

Zanetti, P. "L'assedio di Padova del 1509 in correlazione alle guerra combattuta nel Veneto dal maggio all'ottobre," *Nuovo archivio veneto* 2 (1891), 5-168.

Early Modern – Low Countries

Baes, Christian. "La campagne d'Henri II de France dans l'Entre-Sambre-et-Meuse." In: *Les malheurs de la guerre.* I: *De la guerre à l'ancienne à la guerre réglée.* Ed. André Corvisier and Jean Jacquart. Paris: Éditions du CTHS, 1996, pp. 13-26.

Beyaert, Marc. "De algemene militaire evolutie sinds de late middeleeuwen en het Zuid-Nederlandse landleger der XVIe eeuw," *Revue Belge d'histoire militaire* 20 (1973-74), 550-73.

Borman, Tracy. "Untying the Knot? The Survival of the Anglo-Dutch Alliance, 1587-97," *European Historical Quarterly* 27 (1997), 307-38.

Boxer, C.R. *The Dutch Seaborne Empire, 1600-1800.* London: Hutchinson, 1966.

Carasso-Kok, M. and J.Levy-van Helm. *Schutters in Holland: kracht en zenuwen van de stad*. Zwolle: Uitgeverij Waanders, 1988.

Cruickshank, C.G. *The English Occupation of Tournai, 1513-1519*. Oxford: Clarendon Press, 1971.

DeSmette, Ph. "Les archers de Saint-Martin à Moustier au XVIe siècle: Vision de l'organisation d'une conferie militaire au travers d'un document normatif," *Revue Belge d'histoire militaire* 30 (1994), 419-39.

De Vos, Luc. "Le siège d'Ostende." In: *Acta del XVIII Congresso internazionale di storia militare: La scoperta del nuovo mondo e la sua influenza nella storia militare*. Ed. Paolo Alberini and Michele Nones. Turin, 1993, pp. 67-80.

Gaier, Claude. "L'apparition de l'infanterie suisse dans la Principauté de Liège à la fin du XVe siècle," *Bulletin de la commission communale d'histoire de l'ancien pays de Liège* 24 (1990), 81-120; in: *Armes et combats dans l'univers médiéval*. Paris: De Boeck Université, 1995, pp. 91-101.

Henry, Gráinne. *The Irish Military Community in Spanish Flanders, 1586-1621*. Dublin: Irish Academic Press, 1992.

Hoof, J.P.C.M. and W. van Klinkert. *'s-Hertogenbosch en Vught: Een militair verleden*. The Hague: Sectie Militaire Geschiedenis KL (SMG), 1993.

Hummelberger, Walter. "Erzherzog Matthias in den Niederlanden (1577-1581)," *Jahrbuch der Kunsthistorischen Sammlungen in Wien* 61 (1965), 91-118.

Israel, Jonathan I. *The Dutch Republic: Its Rise, Greatness, and Fall, 1477-1806*. The Oxford History of Early Modern Europe. Oxford: Clarendon Press, 1995.

Jelsma, Auke. "The 'Weakness of Conscience' in the Reformed Movement in the Netherlands: The Attitude of the Dutch Reformation to the Use of Violence between 1562 and 1574," *Studies in Church History* 20 (1983), 217-29.

Kleinschmidt, Harald. "Tragt die Spieß auf Englisch': Quellen zu den Heeresreformen der Oranier," *Nassauische Annalen* 102 (1991), 67-85.

Neale, John. "Elizabeth and the Netherlands, 1586-87," *English Historical Review* 45 (1930), 373-96.

Tracy, James D. "Herring Wars: The Habsburg Netherlands and the Struggle for Control of the North Sea, ca. 1520-1560," *Sixteenth Century Journal* 24 (1993), 249-72.

van der Hoeven, Marco. "The Republic at War, 1568-1713: An Historical Overview." In: *The Arsenal of the World: The Dutch Arms Trade in the Seventeenth Century*. Ed. Jan Piet Puype and Marco van der Hoeven. Amsterdam: Batavian Lion International, 1996, pp. 7-12.

Vogel, H. Ph. "Arms Production and Exports in the Dutch Republic, 1600-1650." In: *Exercise of Arms: Warfare in the Netherlands, 1568-1648*. Ed. M. van den Hoeven. Leiden, 1998, pp. 197-210.

Early Modern – Low Countries – Dutch Revolt

Alcalá-Zamora y Queipo de Llano, José. "La ruinosa guerra de Flandes." In: *Felipe II: La monarquía hispánica*. Real monasterio de San Lorenzo de El Escorial, 1 junio-10 octubre, 1998. Madrid: Sociedad Estatal para la Conmemoración de los Centenarios de Felipe II y Carlos V, 1998, pp. 308-17.

Bangs, Carl. "Dutch Theology, Trade, and War: 1590-1610," *Church History* 39 (1970), 470-82.

Caldecott-Baird, Duncan. *The Expedition in Holland, 1572-1574. The Revolt of the Netherlands: The Early Struggle for Independence*. London: Seeley Service, 1976.

Doedens, L.L. "'The Day the Nation was Born.' The Battle of Heiligerlee, 1568." In: *Exercise of Arms: Warfare in the Netherlands, 1568-1648*. Ed. M. van den Hoeven. Leiden, 1998, pp. 57-68.

Dorsman, Leen. *1600: Slag bij Nieuwpoort*. Verloren Verleden. Hilversum: Verloren, 2000.

Feld, M.D. "Middle-Class Society and the Rise of Military Professionalism: The Dutch Army, 1589-1609," *Armed Forces and Society* 1 (1975), 419-42.

Geyl, Pieter. *The Revolt of the Netherlands, 1555-1609*. 2nd ed. London: Ernest Benn Limited, 1958.

Gutmann, Myron P. *War and Rural Life in the Early Modern Low Countries*. Princeton: Princeton University Press, 1980.

Israel, Jonathan I. *Conflicts of Empires: Spain, the Low Countries, and the Struggle for World Supremacy, 1585-1713*. London: Hambeldon Press, 1997.

Jong, M.A.G. de. "Dutch Public Finance during the Eighty Years War: The Case of the Province of Zeeland, 1585-1621." In: *Exercise of Arms: Warfare in the Netherlands, 1568-1648*. Ed. M. van den Hoeven. Leiden, 1998, pp. 133-52.

Parker, Geoffrey. *The Army of Flanders and the Spanish Road, 1567-1659*. Cambridge: Cambridge University Press, 1972.

Parker, Geoffrey. "Corruption and Imperialism in the Spanish Netherlands: the Case of Francisco de Lixalde, 1567-1613." In: *Spain and the Netherlands, 1559-1659: Ten Studies*. 2nd ed. London, 1990, pp. 152-63.

Parker, Geoffrey. "The Decision-making Process in the Government of the Catholic Netherlands under the 'Archdukes', 1596-1621." In: *Spain and the Netherlands, 1559-1659: Ten Studies*. 2nd ed. London, 1990, pp. 164-77.

Parker, Geoffrey. *The Dutch Revolt*. 2nd ed. Harmondsworth: Penguin Books, 1985.

Parker, Geoffrey. "The Dutch Revolt and the Polarization of International Politics." In: *Spain and the Netherlands, 1559-1659: Ten Studies*. 2nd ed. London, 1990, pp. 65-82.

Parker, Geoffrey. *The Grand Strategy of Philip II*. New Haven: Yale University Press, 1998.

Parker, Geoffrey. "Mutiny and Discontent in the Spanish Army of Flanders, 1572-1607." In: *Spain and the Netherlands, 1559-1659: Ten Studies*. 2nd ed. London, 1990, pp. 106-21.

Parker, Geoffrey. "Poner una pica en Flandes: la guerre y Felipe II." In: *Felipe II: La monarquía hispánica*. Real monasterio de San Lorenzo de

El Escorial, 1 junio-10 octubre, 1998. Madrid: Sociedad Estatal para la Conmemoración de los Centenarios de Felipe II y Carlos V, 1998, pp. 290-307.

Parker, Geoffrey. *Spain and the Netherlands, 1559-1659: Ten Studies*. 2nd ed. London: Fontana Press, 1990.

Parker, Geoffrey. "Spain, her Enemies and the Revolt of the Netherlands, 1559-1648." In: *Spain and the Netherlands, 1559-1659: Ten Studies*. 2nd ed. London, 1990, pp. 18-44.

Parker, Geoffrey. "War and Economic Change: The Economic Costs of the Dutch Revolt." In: *War and Economic Development: Essays in Memory of David Joslin*. Ed. J.M. Winter. Cambridge, 1975, pp. 49-71; in: *Spain and the Netherlands, 1559-1659: Ten Studies*. 2nd ed. London, 1990, pp. 178-204.

Parker, Geoffrey. "Why Did the Dutch Revolt Last So Long?" In: *Spain and the Netherlands, 1559-1659: Ten Studies*. 2nd ed. London, 1990, pp. 45-64.

Parrott, David A. and Jonathan Israel. "Olivares, the Cardinal-Infante and Spain's Strategy in the Low Countries (1635-1643): The Road to Rocroi." In: *Spain, Europe and the Atlantic World: Essays in Honour of John H. Elliott*. Ed. R.L. Kagan and Geoffrey Parker. Cambridge, 1995, pp. 267-95.

Price, J.L. "A State Dedicated to War? The Dutch Republic in the Seventeenth Century." In: *The Medieval Military Revolution: State, Society and Military Change in Medieval and Early Modern Europe*. Ed. A. Ayton and J.L. Price. London, 1995, pp. 183-200.

Puype, Jan Piet. "Victory at Nieuwpoort, 2 July 1600." In: *Exercise of Arms: Warfare in the Netherlands, 1568-1648*. Ed. M. van den Hoeven. Leiden, 1998, pp. 69-112.

Puype, Jan Piet and A.A. Wiekart. *Van Maurits naar Munster: Tactiek en triomf van het Staatse leger. Catalogus van de voorwerpen op de gelijknamige tentoonstelling in het Legermuseum te Delft, alsmede een reconstructie van de bibliotheek van prins Maurits/From Prince Maurice to the Peace of Westphalia: Tactics and Triumphs of the Dutch Army. Catalogue of Objects in the Exhibition of the Same Name at the Army*

Museum in Delft, and a Reconstruction of he Library of Maurice of Nassau. Delft: Legermuseum, 1998.

Rehberg, Rolf. "Justification of Resistance in Early Modern Revolutions: A Comparison of the German Peasant War, the Dutch Revolt and the British Revolution," *International Politics* 33 (1996), 273-90.

Rowan, Herbert H. "The Dutch Revolt: What Kind of Revolution?" *Renaissance Quarterly* 43 (1990), 170-90.

Schulten, Cornelis. "Une nouvelle approche de Maurice de Nassau." In: *Le soldat, la strategié, la mort: Mélanges Corvisier.* Ed. J. Bérenger. Paris: Économica, 1989, pp. 42-53.

Smit, J.W. "The Netherlands Revolution." In: *Preconditions of Revolution in Early Modern Europe.* Ed. R. Forster and J.P. Greene. Baltimore, 1970, pp. 19-54.

Stradling, R.A. *The Armada of Flanders: Spanish Maritime Policy and European War, 1568-1668.* Cambridge: Cambridge University Press, 1992.

van der Hoeven, Marco. "Introduction." In: *Exercise of Arms: Warfare in the Netherlands, 1568-1648.* Ed. M.van den Hoeven. Leiden, 1998, pp. 1-16.

van der Wee, Herman. "The Economy as a Factor in the Revolt of in the Southern Netherlands." In: *The Low Countries in the Early Modern World.* Aldershot: Ashgate, 1993, pp. 264-78.

van Loo, I.J. "For Freedom and Fortune. The Rise of Dutch Privateering in the First Half of the Dutch Revolt, 1568-1609." In: *Exercise of Arms: Warfare in the Netherlands, 1568-1648.* Ed. M. van den Hoeven. Leiden, 1998, pp. 173-96.

van Nimwegen, O. "Maurits van Nassau and Siege Warfare (1590-1597)." In: *Exercise of Arms: Warfare in the Netherlands, 1568-1648.* Ed. M. van den Hoeven. Leiden, 1998, pp. 113-32.

van Vliet, A.P. "Foundation, Organization and Effects of the Dutch Navy (1568-1609)." In: *Exercise of Arms: Warfare in the Netherlands, 1568-1648.* Ed. M. van den Hoeven. Leiden, 1998, pp. 153-72.

Wagenaar, F.P. "The 'waardgelders' of Den Haag." In: *Exercise of Arms: Warfare in the Netherlands, 1568-1648*. Ed. M.van den Hoeven. Leiden, 1998, pp. 211-30.

Waxman, Matthew C. "Document–Strategic Terror: Philip II and Sixteenth-Century Warfare," *War in History* 4 (1997), 339-48.

Zwitzer, H.L. "The Eighty Years War." In: *Exercise of Arms: Warfare in the Netherlands, 1568-1648*. Ed. M.van den Hoeven. Leiden, 1998, pp. 33-56.

Early Modern – Military Thought

Anglo, Sydney. "Machiavelli as a Military Authority. Some Early Sources." *Florence and Italy: Renaissance Studies in Honour of Nicolai Rubenstein*. Ed. P. Denley and C. Elam. London, 1988, pp. 321-34.

Audley, Thomas. "A Treatise on The Art of War," *Journal of the Society for Army Historical Research* 6 (1927), 65-78, 129-33.

Gat, Azar. "Machiavelli and the Decline of the Classical Notion of the Lessons of History in the Study of War," *Military Affairs* 52 (1988), 203-05.

Gat, Azar. "Montecuccoli: Humanist Philosophy, Paracelsian Science and Military Theory," *War and Society* 6 (1988), 21-31.

Gilbert, Felix. "Machiavelli: The Renaissance of the Art of War." In: *Makers of Modern Strategy*. Ed. E.M. Earle. Princeton, 1944.

Hobohm, M. *Machiavellis Renaissance der Kriegkunst*. 2 vols. Berlin, 1913.

Kubik, Timothy R.W. "Is Machiavelli's Canon Spiked? Practical Reading in Military History," *Journal of Military History* 61 (1997), 7-30.

Margolin, J.C. *Guerre et paix dans la pensée d'Erasme de Rotterdam*. Paris, 1973.

Neill, Donald A. "Ancestral Voices: The Influence of the Ancients on the Military Thought of the Seventeenth and Eighteenth Centuries," *Journal of Military History* 62 (1998), 487-520.

Pascual, Pedro. "El discurso de las armas y las letras en el *aeiou*." In: *XXII. Kongreß der Internationalen Kommission für Militärgeschichte* Acta 22: *Von Crécy bis Mohács Kriegswesen im späten Mittelalter (1346-1526)*. Vienna, 1997, pp. 324-33.

Wicht, Bernard. *L'idée de milice et le modèle suisse dans la pensée de Machiavel*. Lausanne: L'Age d'Homme, 1995.

Wicht, Bernard. "L'idée de souveraineté militaire populaire chez Machiavel: Argument pour une lecture médiévale de l'*art de la guerre*." In: *XXII. Kongreß der Internationalen Kommission für Militärgeschichte* Acta 22: *Von Crécy bis Mohács Kriegswesen im späten Mittelalter (1346-1526)*. Vienna, 1997, pp. 386-96.

Wood, Neal. "Frontinus as a Possible Source for Machiavelli's Method," *Journal of the History of Ideas* 28 (1967), 243-48.

Early Modern – Popular Rebellion

Bak, James, ed. *The German Peasant War of 1525*. London: Frank Cass, 1976.

Bercé, Yves-Marie. *History of Peasant Revolts: The Social Origins of Rebellion in Early Modern France*. Trans. Amanda Whitmore. Ithaca: Cornell University Press, 1990.

Bernard, G.W. "Debate–New Perspectives or Old Complexities?" *English Historical Review* 115 (2000), 113-20.

Bickle, Peter. *The Revolution of 1525: The German Peasants' War from a New Perspective*. Ed. and trans. T.A. Brady and H.C.E. Midelfort. Baltimore: Johns Hopkins University Press, 1981.

Burke, Peter. "The Virgin of the Carmine and the Revolt of Masaniello," *Past and Present* 99 (1983), 3-21.

Bush, Michael. *The Pilgrimage of Grace: A Study of the Rebel Armies of 1536*. Manchester: Manchester University Press, 1996.

Bush, Michael. "Protector Somerset and the 1549 Rebellions: A Post-Revision Questioned," *English Historical Review* 115 (2000), 103-12.

Cornwall, Julian. *Revolt of the Peasantry*. London: Routledge and Kegan Paul, 1977.

Elliott, J.H. "Revolts in the Spanish Monarchy." In: *Preconditions of Revolution in Early Modern Europe*. Ed. R. Forster and J.P. Greene. Baltimore, 1970, pp. 109-30.

Engels, Frederick. *The Peasant War in Germany*. Trans. Moissaye J. Olgin. Ed. D. Riazanov. 2nd ed. New York: International Publishers, 1966.

Forster, Robert and Jack P. Greene. "Introduction." In: *Preconditions of Revolution in Early Modern Europe*. Ed. R. Forster and J.P. Greene. Baltimore, 1970, pp. 1-18.

François, Martha Ellis. "Revolts in Late Medieval and Early Modern Europe: A Spiral Model," *Journal of Interdisciplinary History* 5 (1974), 19-43.

Freedman, Paul. "The German and Catalan Peasant Revolt," *American Historical Review* 98 (1993), 39-54.

Freedman, Paul. "The Hungarian Peasant Revolt of 1514." In: *Grafenauerjev zbornik*. Ed. V. Rajsp. Ljubljana, 1996, pp. 433-46.

Goldstone, Jack A. *Revolution and Rebellion in the Early Modern World*. Berkeley and Los Angeles: University of California Press, 1991.

Gunst, Peter. "Der ungarische Baurenaufstand von 1514." In: *Revolte und Revolution in Europa*. Ed. Peter Bickle. Munich, 1975, pp. 62-83.

Hoppenbrouwers, Peter. "Rebels with a Cause: The Peasant Movements of Northern Holland in the Later Middle Ages." In: *Showing Status: Representation of Social Position in the Late Middle Ages*. Ed. Wim Blockmans and Antheun Janse. Turnhout: Brepols Publishers, 1999.

Housley, Norman. "Historiographical Essay–Insurrection as Religious War, 1400-1536," *Journal of Medieval History* 25 (1999), 141-54.

Hoyer, Siegfried. "Arms and Military Organization in the German Peasant War." In: *The German-Peasant War of 1525–New Viewpoints*. Ed. Bob Scribner and Gerhard Benecke. London, 1979, pp. 98-108.

Ketteringham, John R. "The Material Manifestation of Secular Piety and the Impact of the Lincolnshire Rising of 1536," *Lincolnshire History and Archaeology* 33 (1998), 30-34.

Land, Steven K. *Kett's Rebellion: The Norfolk Rising of 1549*. Ipswich: The Boydell Press, 1977.

MacHardy, Karin J. "The Rise of Absolutism and Noble Rebellion in Early Modern Habsburg Austria, 1570-1620," *Comparative Studies in Society and History* 34 (1992), 407-38.

Mousnier, Roland. "The Fronde." In: *Preconditions of Revolution in Early Modern Europe*. Ed. R. Forster and J.P. Greene. Baltimore, 1970, pp. 131-60.

Oberman, Heiko A. "The Gospel of Social Unrest." In: *The German-Peasant War of 1525–New Viewpoints*. Ed. B. Scribner and G. Benecke. London, 1979, pp. 39-51.

Palmitessa, James R. "The Prague Uprising of 1611: Property, Politics, and Catholic Renewal in the Early Years of Habsburg Rule," *Central European History* 31 (1998), 299-328.

Raeff, Marc. "Pugachev's Rebellion." In: *Preconditions of Revolution in Early Modern Europe*. Ed. R. Forster and J.P. Greene. Baltimore, 1970, pp. 161-202.

Rehberg, Rolf. "Justification of Resistance in Early Modern Revolutions: A Comparison of the German Peasant War, the Dutch Revolt and the British Revolution," *International Politics* 33 (1996), 273-90.

Scott, Tom. "The Peasants' War: A Historiographical Review," *Historical Journal* 22 (1979), 693-720, 953-74.

Scott, Tom. "Reformation and Peasants' War in Waldshut and Environs," *Archiv für Reformationgeschichte* 69 (1978), 82-102; 70 (1979), 140-69.

Scribner, R.W. "The German Peasants' War." In: *Reformation Europe: A Guide to Research*. Ed. Steven Ozment. St. Louis, 1982, pp. 107-33.

Shagan, Ethan H. "Debate–'Popularity' and the 1549 Rebellions Revisited," *English Historical Review* 115 (2000), 121-33.

Shagan, Ethan H. "Protector Somerset and the 1549 Rebellions: New Sources and New Perspectives," *English Historical Review* 114 (1999), 34-63.

Stayer, James. *The German Peasants' War and Anabaptist Community of Goods*. Montreal: McGill-Queen's University Press, 1991.

Szücs, Jenö. "Die Ideologie des Bauernkrieges." In: *Nation und Geschichte: Studien*. Gyoma, 1981, pp. 329-78.

Vice, Roy L. "The Leadership and Structure of the Tauber Band during the Peasants' War in Franconia," *Central European History* 21 (1988), 175-95.

Villari, R. "The Insurrection in Naples of 1585." In: *The Late Italian Renaissance, 1525-1630*. Ed. Eric Cochrane. London: Macmillan, 1970, pp. 305-30.

Early Modern – Scandinavia [See also Early Modern – Thirty Years War]

Artéus, Gunnar. *Till militärstatens förhistoria: Krig, professionalisering och social förändring under Vasasöneras regering*. Stockholm, 1986.

Berg, Jonas and Bo Lagercrantz. "Scottish Soldiers in Swedish Service in the Sixteenth Century," *Dispatch* 119 (1988), 11-13; 120 (1989), 19-20.

Böhme, Klaus-Richard and B. Hugemark. "Tradition and Modernization: Sweden as a Military Power in a Strategically Important Area, 1600-1982." In: *Commission Internationale d'Histoire Militaire. Acta 22: Warfare Throughout the Ages between Small States and Big Powers and Small States Among Themselves*. Tel Aviv: Israel Commission of Military History, 1984, pp. 259-80.

Brzezinski, Richard. "British Mercenaries in the Baltic, 1560-1683," *Military Illustrated* 6 (Apr-May 1987), 29-35.

Cronholm, Gunnar. "Striderna kring Kalmar 1503-1510: Ledning, finansiering, materiel, krigsfolk, underhåll," *Meddelande* 47 (1987), 85-111.

Dyskant, Józef Wiesław. *Oliwa 1627*. Warsaw: Bellona, 1993.

Ericson, Lars. "Farmers or Mercenaries? The Swedish Army in the late Fifteenth and Early Sixteenth Centuries." In: *XXII. Kongreß der Internationalen Kommission für Militärgeschichte* Acta 22: *Von Crécy bis Mohács Kriegswesen im späten Mittelalter (1346-1526)*. Vienna, 1997, pp. 61-69.

Ericson, Lars. "Hemmafrontens revolt: Kravallerna på Stortorget i Stockholm 1623," *Meddelande* 47 (1987), 64-84.

Ericson, Lars. "Det svenska krigståget mot Blekinge i februari 1507," *Meddelande* 40 (1979-80), 5-36.

Hattendorff, Mathias. "Den kongelige befæstede lejr i Fuhlsbüttel–Et ukendt kapitel om Christian IV's strid med Hamburg," *Krigshistorisk tiddskrift* (1996), 3-13.

Hörsfors, Olle. *The Battle of Stångebro: Exhibition Guide*. Linköping: Östergötlands Länsmuseum, 1998.

Hörsfors, Olle. *Stångebro 1598*. Linköping: Östergötlands Länsmuseum, 1998.

Jensen, Frede p. *Danmarks konflikt med Sverige, 1563-1570*. Copenhagen, 1982.

Jespersen, Knud J V. "Det 16. århundredes 'militære revolution' og det danske adelsrytteri.–En sammenlignende analyse," *Militärhistorisk Tidskrift* (1981), 3-18.

Jespersen, Knud J.V. "Rostjeneste, Ridderhaer og Militaer Revolution, 1525-1625," *Krigshistorisk tidsskrift* (1974), 3-38.

Jespersen, Knud J.V. "Slaget ved Lutter am Barenberg 1626." In: *Krigshistorisk tidsskrift*. Copenhagen, 1973.

Jespersen, Knud J.V. "Social Change and Military Revolution in Early Modern Europe: Some Danish Evidence," *Historical Journal* 26 (1983), 1-13.

Jespersen, Knud J.V. "The Wars between Denmark and Sweden, 1563-1721." In: *Commission Internationale d'Histoire Militaire*. Acta 22: *Warfare Throughout the Ages between Small States and Big Powers and Small*

States Among Themselves. Tel Aviv: Israel Commission of Military History, 1984, pp. 238-46.

Johannesson, Kurt. "Gustav Vasa och renässansen," *Livrustkammaren* 15 (1980), 197-264.

Kirchmeier-Andersen, J.C. "Christian IV som taktiker," *Vaabenhistoriske aarbøger* 34 (1988), 5-107.

Krig och fred i Källorna. Stockholm: Årsbok för Riksarkivet och Landsarkiven, 1998.

Liebe, P.I. and E. Borgstrm. *Dansk krigshistorie i det sekstende arhundrede: Litteraturfortegnelse.* Copenhagen: Det kongelige Garnisonbibliothek, 1979.

Lindegren, Jan. "Les hommes, l'argent, les moyens (Danemark, Finlands, Norvège, Suède, XVIe-XVIIIe siècles)." In: *Guerre et concurrence entre les États européens du XIVe au XVIIIe siècle.* Ed. Philippe Contamine. Fondation Européenne de la Science: Les origines de l'État moderne en Europe, XIIIe-XVIIIe siècle. Paris: Presses universitaires de France, 1998, pp. 123-66.

Lundkvist, Sven. "Die schwedischen Kriegs- und Friedensziele, 1632-1648." In: *Krieg und Politik, 1618-1648: Europäische Probleme und Perspektiven.* Ed. K. Repgen. Munich, 1988, pp. 219-41.

Oakley, Stewart P. *War and Peace in the Baltic, 1560-1790.* London, 1992.

Petersen, E. Ladewig. "Christian IVs skånske og norske fæstningsanlæg 1596-1622," *Historisk tidsskrift* 95 (1995), 328-41.

Roberts, Michael. *Gustavus Adolphus.* 2 vols. London, 1958.

Schiotz, Johannes. "L'armée Norvegienne au cours d'un millenaire: Récrutement, stratégic, tactique," *Revue internationale d'histoire militaire* 15 (1955), 273-83.

Sundberg, Ulf. *Svenska krig, 1521-1814.* Stockholm: Hjalmarson and Högberg Bokförlag, 1998.

Wihtol, Erik. "A Fight in the Snow at Joutselkä 1555." In: *XXII. Kongreß der Internationalen Kommission für Militärgeschichte* Acta 22: *Von Crécy bis Mohács Kriegswesen im späten Mittelalter (1346-1526)*. Vienna, 1997, pp. 248-62.

Early Modern – Scotland [See also Early Modern – England – English/Scottish Conflicts]

Bonner, Elizabeth. "Scotland's 'Auld Alliance' with France, 1295-1560," *History* 84 (1999), 5-30.

Cowan, Ian B. "The Marian Civil War, 1567-73." In: *Scotland and War, AD 79-1918*. Ed. Norman Macdougall. Edinburgh: John Donald, 1991, pp. 95-112.

Gillespie, Raymond. "An Army Sent from God: Scots at War in Ireland, 1642-9." In: *Scotland and War, AD 79-1918*. Ed. Norman Macdougall. Edinburgh: John Donald, 1991, pp. 113-32.

Hill, James Michael. "Gaelic Warfare, 1453-1815." In: *European Warfare, 1453-1815*. Ed. Jeremy Black. New York: St. Martin's Press, 1999, pp. 201-23.

McDonald, R. Andrew. "'Treachery in the Remotest Territories of Scotland:' Northern Resistance to the Canmore Dynasty, 1130-1230," *Canadian Journal of History* 34 (1999), 161-92.

Murdoch, S. "The House of Stuart and the Professional Soldier." In: *War: Identities in Conflict*. Ed. B. Taithe and T. Thornton. Stroud, 1998, pp. 37-51.

Early Modern – Spain and Portugal

Asenjo González, María. "Aproximación al estudio de los patrimonios y fortunas de los caballeros de Santiago en Castilla a comienzos del siglo XVI," *Anuario de estudios medievales* 28 (1998), 123-46.

Baquer, Miguel Alonso. "L'éthique de la conquête et la morale des Conquistadores." In: *Acta del XVIII Congresso internazionale di storia militare: La scoperta del nuovo mondo e la sua influenza nella storia militare*. Ed. Paolo Alberini and Michele Nones. Turin, 1993, pp. 19-30.

Chauchadis, Claude. *La loi du duel: Le code du point d'honneur dans l'Espagne des XVe-XVIIe siècles*. Toulouse, 1997.

De Gaury, Gerald. *The Grand Captain, Gonzalo de Cordoba*. London: Longman, 1955.

Dickinson, Robert. "The Spanish Raid on Mount's Bay in 1595," *Journal of the Royal Institution of Cornwall* n.s. 10 (1987-90), 178-86.

Ejercito y la armada de Felipe II ante el IV centenario de su muerte, El. Jornadas de historia militar, 4a. Madrid: Ministerio de Defensa, 1997.

Elliott, J.H. *The Count-Duke of Olivares: The Statesman in an Age of Decline*. New Haven: Yale University Press, 1986.

Elliott, J.H. *Imperial Spain, 1469-1716*. Harmondsworth: Penguin, 1990.

Elliott, J.H. "The Spanish Monarchy and the Kingdom of Portugal, 1580-1640." In: *Conquest and Coalescence: The Shaping of the State in Early Modern Europe*. Ed. Mark Greengrass. London: Edward Arnold, 1991, pp. 48-67.

Fisher, G. *Barbary Legend: War, Trade and Piracy in North Africa, 1415-1830*. Oxford, 1957.

Garcia, A. Ribot. "Les types d'armée en Espagne au début des temps modernes." In: *Guerre et concurrence entre les États européens du XIVe au XVIIIe siècle*. Ed. Philippe Contamine. Fondation Européenne de la Science: Les origines de l'État moderne en Europe, XIIIe-XVIIIe siècle. Paris: Presses universitaires de France, 1998, pp. 43-82.

Goodman, David C. *Power and Penury: Government, Technology and Science in Philip II's Spain*. Cambridge: Cambridge University Press, 1988.

Kamen, Henry. "Clerical Violence in a Catholic Society: The Hispanic World, 1450-1720," *Studies in Church History* 20 (1983), 201-16.

Monteiro, Armando. *Batalhas e cambates da marinha Portuguesa*. Lisbon: Livraria Sá da Costa, n.d.

Newitt, Malyn. "Plunder and the Rewards of Office in the Portuguese Empire." In: *The Military Revolution and the State, 1500-1800*. Ed. M. Duffy. Exeter, 1980, pp. 10-28.

Parker, Geoffrey. *The Grand Strategy of Philip II*. New Haven: Yale University Press, 1998.

Parker, Geoffrey. "Mutiny and Discontent in the Spanish Army of Flanders, 1572-1607." In: *Spain and the Netherlands, 1559-1659: Ten Studies*. 2nd ed. London, 1990, pp. 106-21.

Parker, Geoffrey. *Spain and the Netherlands, 1559-1659: Ten Studies*. 2nd ed. London: Fontana Press, 1990.

Parrott, David A. "The Causes of the Franco-Spanish War of 1635-59." In: *The Origins of War in Early Modern Europe*. Edinburgh, 1987, pp. 72-111.

Parry, J.H. *The Spanish Seaborne Empire*. London: Hutchinson, 1966.

Picciuolo, José L. "Origenes y creación de la caballeria española. Influencia en América (1492-1526)." In: *XXII. Kongreß der Internationalen Kommission für Militärgeschichte* Acta 22: *Von Crécy bis Mohács Kriegswesen im späten Mittelalter (1346-1526)*. Vienna, 1997, pp. 334-44.

Puddu, Raffaele. *El soldado Gentilhombre: Autoretrato de una sociedad guerrera: La España del siglo XVI*. Madrid: Ed. Argos Vergara, 1984.

Quatrefages, René. "A la naissance de l'armée moderne," *Mélanges de la Casa de Velasquez* 13 (1977), 119-59.

Quatrefages, René. *La revolucion militar moderna: El crisol español*. Madrid: Ministerio de defensa, 1996.

Quatrefages, René. *Los tercios españoles, 1567-1577*. Madrid: Fundacion universitaria española, 1979.

Rekarte, Fernando Santamaria. "Intentos de recuperación del reino de Navarra por la dinastia de los Albert (1512-1521)." In: *La guerre, la violence et les gens au Moyen Âge. I: Guerre et violence*. Ed. P. Contamine and O. Guyotjeannin. 119e congrès national des sociétés historiques et scientifiques, Amiens, octobre 1994, Section d'histoire médiévale et philologie. Paris, 1996, pp. 97-109.

Riesco, Angel. "Vom Kriegsvolk und den mittelalterlichen 'Kriegsscharen' zur modernen spanischen Armee als stabiler, professioneller und repräsentativer Institution des Staates." In: *XXII. Kongreß der Internationalen Kommission für Militärgeschichte* Acta 22: *Von Crécy bis Mohács Kriegswesen im späten Mittelalter (1346-1526)*. Vienna, 1997, pp. 364-85.

Simou, Bahija. "Quelques aspects des échanges Maraco-Portugaises au XVIième siècle." In: *Actas do XXIV congresso internacional de historía militar*. Centro cultural de Belém, 24 a 29 de agosto, 1998. Lisbon: Comissão Portuguesa de Historía Militar, 1998, pp. 397-401.

Stradling, R.A. "Olivares and the Origins of the Franco-Spanish War, 1627-1635," *English Historical Review* 101 (1968), 68-94; in: *Spain's Struggle for Europe*. London, 1994, pp. 95-120.

Taşkiran, Cemalettin. "Les relations Ottomano-Portugaises au XVIième siècle." In: *Actas do XXIV congresso internacional de historía militar*. Centro cultural de Belém, 24 a 29 de agosto, 1998. Lisbon: Comissão Portuguesa de Historía Militar, 1998, pp. 133-38.

Terry, Arthur. "War and Literature in Sixteenth-Century Spain." In: *War, Literature and the Arts in Sixteenth-Century Europe*. Ed. J.R. Mulryne and M. Shewring. New York, 1989, pp. 101-18.

Thompson, I.A.A. "'Money, Money, and Yet More Money!' Finance, the Fiscal-State, and the Military Revolution: Spain, 1500-1650." In: *The Military Revolution Debate: Readings on the Military Transformation of Early Modern Europe*. Ed. C.J. Rogers. Boulder, 1995, pp. 273-98.

Thompson, I.A.A. *War and Government in Habsburg Spain, 1560-1620*. London, 1976.

Vincent, Bernard. "Guerre et habitat en Andalousie orientale au XVIe siècle." In: *Castrum 3: Guerre, fortification et habitant dans le monde méditerranéen au moyen âge*. Ed. André Bazzana. Rome: L'école Française de Rome, 1988, pp. 279-86.

Vogt, John. "Saint Barbara's Legion: Portuguese Artillery in the Struggle for Morocco, 1415-1578," *Military Affairs* 41 (1977), 176-82.

Early Modern – Spain – Spanish Armada [See also Military Technology – Premodern – Ships (inc. Warships) – Early Modern]

Adams, Simon. "The Spanish Armada: The Lurch into War," *History Today* 38 (May 1988), 18-25.

Barker, Felix. "The Spanish Armada: If Parma Had Landed," *History Today* 38 (May 1988), 34-41.

Chandler, David G. "England Against Spain, Elizabeth I versus Philip II: A Successful Challenge to Spanish Hegemony?" In: *Acta del XVIII Congresso internazionale di storia militare: La scoperta del nuovo mondo e la sua influenza nella storia militare*. Ed. Paolo Alberini and Michele Nones. Turin, 1993, pp. 31-36.

Courcy Ireland, J. de. "Ragusa and the Spanish Armada of 1588," *Mariner's Mirror* 64 (1978), 251-62.

Croft, Pauline. "English Commerce with Spain and the Armada War, 1558-1603." In: *England, Spain and the Gran Armada, 1585-1604*. Ed. M.J. Rodríguez-Salagado and Simon Adams. Edinburgh, 1991, pp. 236-63.

Fallon, Niall. *The Armada in Ireland*. London, 1978.

Fernández-Armesto, Felipe. *The Spanish Armada: The Experience of War in 1588*. Oxford: Oxford University Press, 1988.

Fernández Duro, Cesáreo. *La Armada invencible*. 2 vols. Madrid, 1884-85.

Fernández Duro, Cesáreo. *La marina de Castilla desde su origen y pugna con la de Inglaterra hasta la refundacion en la Armada Española*. Madrid, 1894.

Gallagher, P. and D.W. Cruickshank, ed. *God's Obvious Design: Papers from the Spanish Armada Symposium, Sligo, 1988*. London: Tamesis Books Limited, 1990.

Martin, Colin and Geoffrey Parker. *The Spanish Armada*. Harmondsworth: Penguin Books, 1989.

Mattingly, Garrett. *The Armada*. Boston: Houghton Mifflin Company, 1959.

O'Donnel, Hugo. "The Army of Flanders and the Invasion of England, 1586-8." In: *Armada, 1588-1988: An International Exhibition to Commemorate the Spanish Armada.* Ed. M.J. Rodríguez-Salgado. London, 1988, pp. 216-35.

O'Donnel, Hugo. "The Requirements of the Duke of Parma for the Conquest of England." In: *God's Obvious Design: Papers from the Spanish Armada Symposium, Sligo, 1988.* Ed. P. Gallagher and D.W. Cruickshank. London: Tamesis Books Limited, 1990, pp. 85-99.

O'Donnel, Hugo, et al. *Los sucesos de Flandres de 1588 en relación con la empresa de Inglaterra.* Madrid, 1988.

Parker, Geoffrey. "If the Armada had Landed." In: *Spain and the Netherlands, 1559-1659: Ten Studies.* 2nd ed. London, 1990, pp. 135-48.

Parker, Geoffrey. "The Spanish Armada: Why the Armada Failed," *History Today* 38 (May 1988), 26-33.

Parker, Geoffrey. "The Worst Kept Secret in Europe? The European Intelligence Community and the Spanish Armada of 1588." In: *Go Spy the Land: Military Intelligence in History.* Ed. K. Neilson and B.J.C. McKercher. Westport, 1992, pp. 49-72.

Pi Corrales, Magdalena de Pazzis. *La orta invencible, 1574: España y las potencias nórdicas.* Madrid, 1983.

Pierson, Peter. "A Commander for the Armada," *Mariner's Mirror* 55 (1969), 383-400.

Pierson, Peter. *Commander of the Armada: The Seventh Duke of Medina Sidonia.* New Haven: Yale University Press, 1989.

Pierson, Peter. "Ragusa and the Spanish Armada," *Mariner's Mirror* 67 (1981), 91-92.

Pollitt, Ronald. "Contingency Planning and the Defeat of the Spanish Armada," *American Neptune* 44 (1984), 25-32; in: *Naval History: The Sixth Symposium of the United States Naval Academy.* Wilmington: Scholarly Resources Inc., 1987, pp. 70-81.

Pollitt, Ronald. "The Spanish Armada and the Mobilization of English Resources, 1570-85." In: *New Interpretations in Naval History: Selected*

Papers from the Eighth Naval History Symposium. Ed. William B. Cogar. Annapolis, 1989, pp. 14-27.

Riaño Lozano, Fernando. *Los medios navales de Alejandro Farnesio (1587-1588).* Madrid, 1989.

Rodríguez-Salgado, M.J. "The Anglo-Spanish War: The Final Episode in the 'Wars of the Roses'?" In: *England, Spain and the Gran Armada, 1585-1604.* Ed. M.J. Rodríguez-Salgado and Simon Adams. Edinburgh, 1991, pp. 1-44.

Rodríguez-Salgado, M.J. "Pilots, Navigation and Strategy in the *Gran Armada.*" In: *England, Spain and the Gran Armada, 1585-1604.* Ed. M.J. Rodríguez-Salgado and Simon Adams. Edinburgh, 1991, pp. 134-72.

Rodríguez-Salgado, M.J., ed. *Armada, 1588-1988: An International Exhibition to Commemorate the Spanish Armada.* Harmondsworth: Penguin Books, 1988.

Rodríguez-Salgado, M.J. and Simon Adams, ed. *England, Spain and the Gran Armada, 1585-1604.* Edinburgh, 1991.

Ryan, A.N. "400 Years Ago: Reflections on the Armada Campaign," *The Historian* 16 (1987), 3-8.

Schneider, Lukas M. "Der Zweifrontenkrieg als Damoklesschwert über England? Schottland in der spanischen Konfliktstrategie während des ersten Armada-Feldzuges von 1588," *Militärgeschichteliche Mitteilungen* 57 (1998), 1-22.

Thompson, I.A.A. "The Armada and Administrative Reform: The Spanish Council of War in the Reign of Philip II," *English Historical Review* 82 (1967), 698-725.

Thompson, I.A.A. "The Invincible Armada." In: *Royal Armada: 400 Years.* London, 1988, pp. 160-74.

Thompson, I.A.A. "The Spanish Armada: Naval Warfare between the Mediterranean and the Atlantic." In: *England, Spain and the Gran Armada, 1585-1604: Essays from the Anglo-Spanish Conferences.* Ed. M.J. Rodriguez Salgado and S. Adams. Edinburgh, 1991, pp. 70-94.

Thompson, I.A.A. "Spanish Armada Gun Procurement and Policy." In: *God's Obvious Design: Papers for the Spanish Armada Symposium.* Ed. P. Gallagher and D.W. Cruickshank. London, 1990, pp. 69-84.

Thompson, I.A.A. "Spanish Armada Guns," *Mariner's Mirror* 61 (1975), 355-71.

Tincey, John. *The Armada Campaign, 1588.* Elite Series, 15. London: Osprey, 1988.

Whiting, Roger. *The Enterprise of England: The Spanish Armada.* New York: St. Martin's Press, 1988.

Early Modern – Switzerland

Baumann, Reinhard. *Georg von Frundsberg.* 2nd ed. Munich: Süddeutscher Verlag, 1991.

Bosson, Clément. "Les soldats de Genève à la fin du XVIe siècle," *Genava* 8 (1960), 197-228.

Brady, Thomas A., Jr. *Turning Swiss: Cities and Empire, 1450-1550.* Cambridge: Cambridge University Press, 1985.

Gente ferocissima: Mercenariat et société en Suisse (XVe-XIXe siècle): Recueil offerts à Alain Dubois. Lausanne: Editions d'en-bas, Chronos, 1997.

Naphy, W.G. "The Price of Liberty: Genevan Security and Defence Spending, 1535-1555," *War in History* 5 (1998), 379-400.

Padrutt, C. *Staat und Krieg im alten Bünden: Studien zur Beziehung zwischen Obrigkeit und Kriegertum in den drei Bünden, vornehmlich im 15. Und 16. Jahrhundert.* Zurich, 1965.

Perdrazzini, Dominic M. "Les capitualations militaires dans les traités d'alliance des anciens états confédérés au regard des théories d'Emer de Vattel (XVIeme-XVIIIeme siècles)." In: *Commission internationale d'histoire militaire.* Acta 6: *Montpeillier 2-6 IX 1981.* Montpellier: Commission Française d'Histoire Militaire, 1983, I:129-36.

Early Modern – Women

Hacker, Barton C. "Women and Military Institutions in Early Modern Europe: A Reconnaissance," *Signs* 6 (1981), 643-71.

Rublack, Ulinka. "Wench and Maiden: Women, War and the Pictorial Function of the Feminine in German Cities in the Early Modern Period," *History Workshop* 44 (1997), 1-22.

Wilson, Peter H. "German Women and War, 1500-1800," *War in History* 3 (1996), 127-16.

Military Technology – General

A engenharia militar e a construção: 350 anos. Lisbon, 1998.

Adams, A. *The History of the Worshipful Company of Blacksmiths: From Early Times Until the Year 1647.* London, 1937.

al-Hassan, Ahmad Y. and Donald R. Hill. *Islamic Technology: An Illustrated History.* Cambridge: Cambridge University Press, 1986.

Anstee, J.W. and L. Biek. "A Study in Pattern Welding," *Medieval Archaeology* 5 (1961), 71-93.

Baumgartner, Frederic J. *From Spear to Flintlock.* Westport, 1991.

Berthelot, Marcellin. "Les compositions incendiaires dans l'antiquité et au moyen âge," *Revue des deux mondes* 4 (1891), 786-822.

Blair, Claude. "Metals in the Service of Mars," *Journal of the Royal Society of Arts* (Nov 1981), 764-81.

Braun, Hans-Joachim. "Militärische und zivile Technik. Wechselwirkungen in historischer Perspektive," *Technikgeschichte* 59 (1992), 299-303.

Brodie, Bernard and Fawn M. *From Crossbow to H-Bomb.* 2nd ed. Bloomington: Indiana University Press, 1973.

Calvo, Felipe A. *La España de los metales: Notas para una historia.* Madrid: Centro Nacional de Investigaciones Metalurgicas, Ciudad Universitaria, 1964.

Cederlöf, Olle. "Ur stridsvagnens historia: Några milstolpar under 5000 ar," *Meddelande* 34 (1973-74), 7-40.

DeVries, Kelly. "Debate–Catapults Are Not Atomic Bombs: Towards a Redefinition of 'Effectiveness' in Premodern Military Technology," *War in History* 4 (1997), 454-70.

Forbes, R.J. *Studies in Ancient Technology*. Leiden: E.J. Brill, 1955.

Girdivan, Hamit. "Development of Military Technics and Technology: Its Impact on Strategy and Tactics (Before the Atomic Bomb)." In: In: *Commission internationale d'histoire militaire*. Acta 2: *The Washington Meeting, August 1975*. Ed. Robin Higham and Jacob W. Kipp. Manhattan: United States Commission on Military History, 1975, pp. 17-22.

Hacker, Barton C. "Military Institutions, Weapons, and Social Change: Toward a New History of Military Technology," *Technology and Culture* 35 (1994), 768-834.

Hall, A.R. "Military Technology." In: *A History of Technology*. Ed. C. Singer et al. Oxford: Clarendon Press., 1957, II:695-730, III:347-82.

Hill, Donald R. *Islamic Science and Engineering*. Edinburgh: Edinburgh University Press, 1993.

Hoppen, A. "Military Engineers in Malta, 1530-1798," *Annals of Science* 38 (1981), 413-33.

Howard, Michael. "Afterword: Tools of War: Concepts and Technology." In: *Tools of War: Instruments, Ideas, and Institutions of Warfare, 1445-1871*. Ed. John A. Lynn. Urbana, 1990, pp. 238-46.

Kjellson, Lennart. "Om vårdkasarna, särskilt de i Östergötland och på Södertörn," *Meddelande* 54 (1954), 35-64.

McNeill, William H. "Men, Machines, and War." In: *Men, Machines and War*. Ed. Ronald Haycock and Keith Neilson. Waterloo: Wilfrid Laurier Press, 1988, pp. 1-20.

McNeill, William H. *The Pursuit of Power: Technology, Armed Force, and Society since A.D. 1000*. Chicago: The University of Chicago Press, 1982.

McNeill, William H. *The Structure of Military-Technical Transformation*. The Harmon Memorial Lectures in Military History, 37. Fort Collins, 1994.

Morton, Louis. "War, Science, and Social Change." In: *The Social Reality of Scientific Myth: Science and Social Change*. Ed. K.H. Silvert. New York, 1969, pp. 22-57.

Nef, John U. *War and Human Progress: An Essay on the Rise of Industrial Civilization*. New York: W.W. Norton and Company, Inc., 1963.

Nowak, T. "La technique des fusées en Pologne jusqu'à la moitié du XIXe siècle." In: *Histoire militaire de la Pologne: Problèmes choises*. Ed. W. Bieganski, P. Stawecki, and W. Janusz. Warsaw: Institut d'Histoire, 1970.

O'Connell, Robert L. *Of Arms and Men: A History of War, Weapons, and Aggression*. Oxford: Oxford University Press, 1989.

Pacey, Arnold. *The Maze of Ingenuity: Ideas and Idealism in the Development of Technology*. 2nd ed. Cambridge: MIT Press, 1992.

Pacey, Arnold. *Technology in World Civilization: A Thousand-Year History*. Cambridge: MIT Press, 1990.

Raudzens, George. "War-winning Weapons: The Measurement of Technological Determinism in Military History," *Journal of Military History* 54 (1990), 403-33.

Richardson, Thom. "Ballistic Testing of Historical Weapons," *Royal Armouries* 3 (1998), 50-52.

Roland, Alex. "Hephaestus and History: Scientists, Engineers, and War in Western Experience." In: *Ethical Issues Associated with Scientific and Technological Research for the Military*. Ed. C. Mithcam and P. Siekevitz. New York, 1989, pp. 51-60.

Roland, Alex. "Science and War," *Osiris*, 2nd ser., 1 (1985), 247-72.

Roland, Alex. "Science, Technology, and War," *Technology and Culture* 36 (1995), S83-S100.

Roland, Alex. "Technology and War: A Bibliographical Essay." In: *Military Enterprise and Technological Change: Perspectives on the American Experience*. Ed. M.R. Smith. Cambridge, 1985, pp. 349-79.

Roland, Alex. "Review Essay: Technology and War: The Historiographical Revolution of the 1980s," *Technology and Culture* 34 (1993), 117-34.

Schubert, H.R. *History of the British Iron and Steel Industry.* London: Routledge and Kegan Paul, 1957.

Smith, Cyril Stanley. "Art, Technology, and Science: Notes on their Historical Interaction" *Technology and Culture* 11 (1970), 493-549.

van Creveld, Martin. *Technology and War: From 2000 B.C. to the Present.* New York: The Free Press, 1989.

Military Technology – Premodern – General

Allan, J.W. *Persian Metal Technology, 700-1300 AD.* London: Ithaca Press, 1979.

Ascherl, Rosemary. "The Technology of Chivalry in Reality and Romance." In: *The Study of Chivalry: Resources and Approaches.* Ed. H. Chickering and T.H. Seiler. Kalamazoo, 1988, pp. 263-312.

Ashtor, Eliyahu. "The Factors of Technological and Industrial Progress in the Later Middle Age." *Journal of European Economic History* 18 (1989), 7-36.

Awty, Brian G. "The Origin of the Blast Furnace," *Historical Metallurgy* 21 (1987), 96-99; 22 (1988), 125-27.

Bartlett, Robert J. "Technique militaire et pouvoir politique, 900-1300," *Annales: économies, sociétés, civilisations* 41 (1986), 1135-59.

Beaver, Daniel R. "Cultural Change, Technological Development, and the Conduct of War in the Seventeenth Century." In: *New Dimensions in Military History: An Anthology.* Ed. R.F. Weigley. San Rafael, 1975, pp. 75-89.

Bellabarba, Sergio. "The Origins of the Ancient Methods of Designing Hulls: A Hypothesis," *Mariner's Mirror* 82 (1996), 259-68.

Canestrini, G. *Arte militare meccanica medievale.* Milan, 1946.

Cleere, Henry, David Crossley, and Bernard Wossam. *The Iron Industry of the Weald*. 2nd ed. Ed. Jeremy Hodgkinson. Cardiff: Merton Priory Press, 1995.

Crivelli, Antonio. *Sull' arte di fabbricare le sciabole di Damasco*. Ed. C. Panseri. Milan: Centro di storia della metallurgia della associazione Italiana di metallurgia, 1963.

Denig, H. *Alte Schmiedekunst Damaszenerstahl*. Kaiserslautern: Institut für pfalzische Geschichte und Volkskunde, 1990.

DeVries, Kelly. *Medieval Military Technology*. Peterborough: Broadview Press, 1992.

Dondi, Giorgio and Marisa Cartesegna. "Cronaca sommaria del Maglio e della Molera di Torino fra il 1564 e il 1632," *Armi antichi* (1984), 45-52.

Eichberg, Henning. *Festung, Zentralmacht und Sozialgeometrie: Kriegsingenieurwesen in den Herzogtümern Bremen und Verden*. Cologne: Böhlau, 1989.

Engel, Bernhard, ed. "Nachrichten über Waffen aus dem Tresslerbuche des deutschen Ordens von 1399-1409," *Zeitschrift für historisches Waffenkunde* 1 (1897-99), 195-99, 228-33.

Engel, Bernhard, ed. "Waffengeschichtliche Studien aus dem Deutschordensgebiet," *Zeitschrift für historisches Waffenkunde* 4 (1906-08), 118-25.

Finó, J.F. "Notes sur la production du fer et la fabrication des armes en France au moyen-age," *Gladius* 3 (1964), 47-66.

Foley, Vernard and G. Marquis. "Milling Before 1540," *Tools and Technology* 5.1 (1982), 1-7.

France, John. "Technology and Success of the First Crusade." In: *War and Society in the Eastern Mediterranean, 7th-15th Centuries*. Ed. Y. Lev. Leiden, 1997, pp. 163-76.

Gaier, Claude. "Aux origines de l'industrie houillère liégeoise: la renommée militaire des mineurs de Liège," *Annales de la fédération archéologique et historique de Belgique, Congrès de Liège* 1 (1968-69), 131-40; in: *Armes et combats dans l'univers médiéval*. Liege, 1995, pp. 79-90.

García Fitz, Francisco. "Tecnología militar y guerra de asedios: La experiencia castellano-leonesa, siglos XI al XIII." In: *Military Studies in Medieval Europe: Papers of the "Medieval Europe Brugge 1997" Conference Volume 11*. Ed. Guy De Boe & Frans Verhaeghe. Zellik: Instituut voor het Archeologisch Patrimonium, 1997, pp. 33-41.

Hägermann, Dieter. "Das Karolingische Imperium–Ein Resultat kriegstechnischer Innovationen? *Technikgeschichte* 59 (1992), 305-17.

Haldon, John F. "Some Aspects of Byzantine Military Technology from the Sixth to the Tenth Centuries," *Byzantine and Modern Greek Studies* 1 (1975), 11-47.

Hall, A.R. "Military Technology." In: *A History of Technology*. Ed. C. Singer et al. Vol. II: *The Mediterranean Civilizations and the Middle Ages, c. 700 B.C. to c. A.D. 1500*. Oxford, 1957, pp. 695-730.

Hall, A.R. "Science, Technology, and Warfare, 1400-1700." In: *Science, Technology, and Warfare: The Proceedings of the Third Military History Symposium, United States Air Force Academy, 8-9 May 1969*. Ed. M.D. Wright and L.J. Paszek. Washington, 1969, pp. 3-47 (including commentaries by J.R. Hale and John B. Wolf).

Hampe, Theodor, ed. "Archivalische Forschungen zur Waffenkunde," *Zeitschrift für historisches Waffenkunde* 4 (1906-08), 146-52, 183-87; 5 (1909-11), 16-23, 154-56.

Harmuth, Egon. "Eine Ziehbank in Tirol," *Waffen- und Kostümkunde* 11 (1969), 33-36.

"Inventaire de la bastille de l'an 1428," *Revue archeologique* 12 (1855), 321-49.

Keene, Derek. "Metalworking in Medieval London: an Historical Survey," *Journal of the Historical Metallurgy Society* 30 (1996), 95-102.

Landels, J.G. *Engineering in the Ancient World*. London: Chatto & Windus, 1978.

Lombard. M. *Les métaux dans l'ancien monde du Ve au XIe siècle*. Paris, 1974.

Long, Pamela O. and Alex Roland. "Military Secrecy in Antiquity and Early Medieval Europe: A Critical Reassessment," *History and Technology* 11 (1994), 259-90.

Ludwig, Karl-Heinz, and Volker Schmidtchen. *Metalle und Macht, 1000-1600*. Berlin: Propylaen Verlag, 1992.

Martin, G. and Vernard Foley. "Weyland the Smith: Some Findings," *Historical Metallurgy* 13 (1979), 38-39.

Melikian-Chirvani, A.S. "Notes sur la terminologie de la metallurgie et des armes dans l'Iran Musulman: A propos de James W. Allan *Persian Metal Technology, 700-1300 AD*," *Journal of the Economic and Social History of the Orient* 24.3 (1981), 310-16.

Menant, F. "La métallurgie Lombarde au moyen âge." In: *Hommes et travail du métal dans les villes médiévales*. Ed. P. Benoit and D. Cailleaux. Paris, 1988, pp. 127-61.

Monreal Y Tejada, L. *Ingenieria militar en las cronicas catalanas*. Barcelona, 1971.

Mork, Gordon R. "Flint and Steel: A Study in Military Technology and Tactics in 17th-Century Europe," *Smithsonian Journal of History* (Sum 1970), 171-213.

Munksgaard, E. "A Viking Smith, His Tools and Stock in Trade," *Offa* 41 (1984), 85-89.

Nicolle, David C. "Medieval Warfare: The Unfriendly Interchange," *Journal of Military History* 63 (1999), 579-99.

O'Neill, B.H. St. J. "Stefan Von Haschenperg: An Engineer to King Henry VIII, and His Work," *Archaeologia* 91 (1945), 137-55.

Panseri, Carlo. "Damascus Steel in Legend and in Reality," *Gladius* 4 (1965), 5-66.

Parsons, William Barclay. *Engineers and Engineering in the Renaissance*. Cambridge, Mass., 1939.

Piaskowski, Jerzy. "Metallographische Untersuchungen zur Eisen- und Stahltechnologie in Haithabu." In: *Ausgrabungen in Haithabu, 18*. Schleswig, 1983, pp. 45-62.

Puraye, Jean. "Il damasco," *Armi antiche* (1967), 103-33.

Rogers, Clifford J. "The Military Revolutions of the Hundred Years War," *Journal of Military History* 57 (1993), 241-78, and in: *The Military Revolution Debate: Readings on the Military Transformation of Early Modern Europe*. Ed. C.J. Rogers. Boulder, 1995, pp. 55-94.

Salin, Édouard. *La civilisation mérovingienne d'après les sépultures, les textes et le laboratoire*. Part 3: *Les techniques*. Paris: Éditions A. et J. Picard et Cie., 1957.

Salin, Édouard. *Le fer à l'époque mérovingienne: Etude technique et archéologique*. Paris, 1943.

Saxtorph, Niels M. "Technical Innovations and Military Change." In: *War and Peace in the Middle Ages*. Ed. B.P. McGuire. Copenhagen, 1987, pp. 216-26.

Schmidtchen, Volker. *Kriegswesen im späten Middelalter: Technik, Taktik, Theorie*. Weinheim: VCH Verlagsgesellschaft mbH/Acta Humaniora, 1984.

Settia, Aldo A. "L'Europeo aggressore: Tecniche militari in occidente alla vigilia della prima crociata," *Studi storici* 38 (1997), 309-22.

Settia, Aldo A. "L'ingegneria militare all'epoca di Federico II," *Studi storici* 32 (1991), 69-85.

Settia, Aldo A. "Un 'lombardo' alla prima crociata tecnologie militari fra occidente e oriente." In: *Società, istituzioni, spiritualità: Studi in onore di Cinzio Violante*. Spoleto, 1994, II:843-55.

Sprandel, R. *Das Eisengewerbe im Mittelalter*. Stuttgart, 1968.

Squilbeck, Jean. "Le travail du métal à Bruxelles." In: *Bruxelles au XVme siècle*. Brussels, 1954, pp. 247-71.

Strickland, Matthew. "Military Technology and Conquest: The Anomaly of Anglo-Saxon England," *Anglo-Norman Studies* 19 (1996), 353-82.

Tylecote, R.F. "The Medieval Smith and His Methods." In: *Medieval Industry*. Ed. D.W. Crossley. London, 1981, pp. 42-50.

Tylecote, R.F., J.N. Austin, and A.E. Wraith. "The Mechanism of the Bloomery Process in Shaft Furnaces," *Journal of the Iron and Steel Institute* (May 1971), 342-63.

Udina Martorell, F. *Ingenieria militar en las cronicas catalanas*. Barcelona, 1971.

van de Walle, A.L.J. "Some Technical Analogies between Building and Other Crafts in the Use of Split Wood during the Middle Ages," *Château Gaillard* 3 (1969), 152-55.

Wadsworth, Jeffrey and Oleg Sherby. "On the Bulat-Damascus Steel Revisited," *Progress in Materials Science* 25 (1980), 35-68.

White, Lynn, Jr. "The Crusade and the Technological Thrust of the West." In: *War, Technology and Society in the Middle East*. Ed. V. J. Parry and M.E. Yapp. London: Oxford University Press, 1975, pp. 97-112; in: *Medieval Religion and Technology: Collected Essays*. Berkeley and Los Angeles: University of California Press, 1978, pp. 277-96.

White, Lynn, Jr. "Cultural Climates and Technological Advance in the Middle Ages." In: *Medieval Religion and Technology: Collected Essays*. Berkeley and Los Angeles: University of California Press, 1978, pp. 217-54.

White, Lynn, Jr. "The Legacy of the Middle Ages in the American Wild West." In: *Medieval Religion and Technology: Collected Essays*. Berkeley and Los Angeles: University of California Press, 1978, pp. 105-20.

White, Lynn, Jr. "Medieval Engineering and the Sociology of Knowledge." In: *Medieval Religion and Technology: Collected Essays*. Berkeley and Los Angeles: University of California Press, 1978, pp. 317-38.

White, Lynn, Jr. *Medieval Technology and Social Change*. Oxford: Clarendon Press, 1962; trans. *Technologie médiévale et transformations sociales*. Paris and The Hague, 1969.

White, Lynn, Jr. "Technology and Invention in the Middle Ages." In: *Medieval Religion and Technology: Collected Essays*. Berkeley and Los Angeles: University of California Press, 1978, pp. 1-22.

Willen, D., Werner Soedel, and Vernard Foley. "The Story of Weyland the Smith: An Ancient Gilchrist-Thomas Process?" *Historical Metallurgy* 10 (1976), 84-86.

Wulf, Max von. *Das hussitische Wagenburg*. Berlin: Gustav Schade, 1889.

Military Technology – Arms and Armor – General

Adamson, Helen. "Armour and Weapons from the Tower of London," *Scottish Art Review* 15.2 (1978), 22-26.

Angelucci, Angelo. *Catalogo della armeria reale*. Turin, 1890.

Armes anciennes des musées de Belgique: Collection Solvay. Brussels, 1972.

Arms and Armour. London: Dutton Vista Pictureback, 1965.

Arnoldi, A.M. *Armi e armature Italiane*. Milan, 1961.

Barker, A.J. *Weapons and Armour*. London: Hamlyn, 1974.

Blackmore, Howard L. *Arms and Armour*. London: Dutton Vista, 1965.

Blair, Claude. "Arms and Armour Collections in and around London," *Bulletin of the American Society of Arms Collectors* 50 (Apr-May 1984), 40-54.

Blair, Claude. *The James A. de Rothschild Collection at Waddesdon Manor: Arms, Armour and Base-Metalwork*. Fribourg: Office du Livre, 1974.

Blair, Claude and Lionella Giorgio Boccia. *Armi e armatura*. Milan, 1981.

Boccia, Lionella Giorgio. "Armi e armature." In: *Il museo Poldi Pezzoli*. Milan: C.R.P.L., 1972, pp. 32-80.

Boccia, Lionella Giorgio. *Il museo Stibbert a Firenze*. Part III: *L'armeria europea*. 2 vols. Milan: Electa Editrice, 1975.

Boccia, Lionella Giorgio and E.T. Coelho. *L'arte dell' armatura in Italia*. Milan: Bramante Editrice, 1967.

Boeheim, Wendelin. *Handbuch der Waffenkunde*. Graz, 1890.

Borg, Alan. *Arms and Armour in Britain.* 2nd ed. London: Her Majesty's Stationery Office, 1979.

Borg, Alan. "Some Recent Acquistions," *Connoisseur* (Jan 1977), 25-30.

Bruhn de Hoffmeyer, Ada. "East and West: Mutual Contribution to Civilisation," *Gladius* 1 (1961), 9-16.

Bull, Stephen. *An Historical Guide to Arms and Armour.* Ed. A.R.E. North. London: Studio Editions, 1991.

Byam, M. *Arms and Armour.* Eyewitness Guides. London: Dorling Kindersley, 1988.

Caldwell, David H. *The Scottish Armoury.* Edinburgh: William Blackwood and Sons Ltd, 1979.

Carpegna, Nolfo di. "La collezione d'armi Odescalchi in Roma," *Waffen- und Kostümkunde* 3 (1961), 63-71.

Catalogus van de tentoonstelling gewijd aan wapens en wapenrustingen behorend tot Belgische privé verzamelingen/Catalogue de l'exposition armes et armures anciennes conservées dans des collections privées belges: Kasteel/Chateau Laarne, September-November 1968. Brussels, 1968.

Collura, Domenico and A.M. Molfino. *Cataloghi del Museo Poldi Pezzoli.* II: *Armi e armature.* Milan: Associazione Amici del Poldi Pezzoli, 1980.

Cortes, J. *Real armeria de Madrid: Guida turistica.* Madrid, 1963.

Credland, Arthur Graves. "The Blowpipe in Europe and the East," *Journal of the Arms and Armour Society* 10 (1980-82), 119-47.

DeGryse, P. *Wapens en harnassen/Armes et armures.* Brussels: Koninklijk Museum van het Leger en van de Krijgsgeschiedenis/Musée royal de l'Armée et d'Histoire militaire, n.d.

Dolínek, Vladimír and Jan Durdík. *The Encyclopedia of European Historical Weapons.* Trans. Petr Nykrýn. London: Hamlyn, 1993.

Duchartre, P.L. *Histoire des armes de chasse et de leurs emplois de la préhistoire à la cartouche les armes et les munitions d'aujourd'hui.* Paris, 1955.

du Pasquier, J. *Armes: Exposition organisée au Musée des Arts décoratives*. Bordeaux: Musée des Arts décoratives, 1980.

Edge, David A. "An Introduction to the Wallace Collection," *Bulletin of the American Society of Arms Collectors* 50 (Apr-May 1984), 3-21.

Edge, David A. *The Wallace Collection: European Arms and Armor*. London: The Trustees of the Wallace Collection, 1992.

Evangelista, Nick. *The Encyclopedia of the Sword*. Westport: Greenwood Press, 1995.

Exhibition of Arms and Armour and Associated Works of Art, December 4-December 14, 1973. London: Howard Ricketts Limited, 1973.

ffoulkes, Charles J. *Armour and Weapons*. Oxford, 1909.

ffoulkes, Charles J. *Inventory and Survey of the Armouries of the Tower of London*. 2 vols. London: His Majesty's Stationery Office, 1916.

Franzoi, Umberto. *Armoury of the Doge's Palace in Venice*. Venice: Stamperia di Venezia, 1966.

Gaier-Lhoest, Claude and Josianne. *Catalogue des armes du Musée Curtius (Ier-XIXe siècle)*. Liege, 1963.

Gamber, Ortwin and C. Beaufort-Spontin. *Curiositäten und Inventionen aus Kunst- und Rüstkammer: Sonderausteilung der waffen-sammlung in des Neuen Burg*. Vienna: Kunsthistorisches Museum, 1978.

Gonchasova, A.A. *The State Armoury in the Moscow Kremlin*. Moscow: State Publishing House, 1969.

Grancsay, Stephen V. *Arms and Armor*. New York: The Odyssey Press, 1964.

Grancsay, Stephen V. "Historical Arms and Armor," *Metropolitan Museum of Art Bulletin* 28 (Mar 1933), 50-57; in: *Arms and Armor: Essays by Stephen V. Grancsay from The Metropolitan Museum of Art Bulletin, 1920-1964*. New York: The Metropolitan Museum of Art, 1986, pp. 111-16.

Grancsay, Stephen V. "Medieval and Renaissance Arms and Armor in the Metropolitan Museum of Art," *Armi antiche* (1960), 3-28.

Grancsay, Stephen V. "The New Armor Hall," *Metropolitan Museum of Art Bulletin* 34 (Jan 1939), 2-7; in: *Arms and Armor: Essays by Stephen V. Grancsay from The Metropolitan Museum of Art Bulletin, 1920-1964*. New York: The Metropolitan Museum of Art, 1986, pp. 215-22.

Grosz, A. and Bruno Thomas. *Katalog der Waffensammlung der Neuen Burg*. Vienna, 1936.

Haenel, E.A. *Kostbare Waffen aus der Dresdener Rüstkammer*. Leipzig, 1923.

Hewitt, J. *Official Catalogue of the Tower Armouries*. London, 1870.

Historische Kriegs- und Jagdwaffen aus den Beständen des Schwarzburger Zeughauses. 2nd ed. Rudolstadt: Staatliche Museen Heidecksburg, 1970.

Historisches Museum Basel: Die Waffensammlung. Eine Wegleitung von Wolfgang Schneewind. Basel: Historisches Museum Basel, 1958.

Krenn, Peter. *The Landeszeughaus of Graz*. Trans. Erika Pauli. Florence: Casa Editrice Bonechi, 1991.

Krenn, Peter. *Die Steirmärkische Landeszeughaus in Graz: Eine Übersicht über seine Geschichte und seine Waffen*. Graz: Landeszeughaus, 1974.

Krenn, Peter and Walter J. Karcheski, Jr. *Imperial Austria: Treasures of Art, Arms and Armor from the State of Styria*. Munich: Prestel-Verlag, 1992.

Lebedynsky, Jaroslav. *Les armes traditionnelles de l'Europe centrale*. La Tour du Pin: Les Editions du Portail, 1996.

Letošniková, Ludiše. *The Armoury at Konopiště*. Prague: Odeon, 1970.

Macoir, G. *Le Musée royal d'armes et d'armures del al Porte de Hal à Bruxelles*. Brussels, 1928.

Maglioli, Vittorio. *Armeria reale di Torino*. Turin, 1959.

Malatesta, E. *Armi e armaiolo*. Rome, 1930.

Mann, James. *An Outline of Arms and Armour in England*. London, 1960.

Martin, Paul. *Armes et armures de Charlemagne à Louis XIV*. Paris: Bibliothèque des Arts, 1967; Germ. trans. *Waffen und Rüstungen von Karl dem Grossen bis zu Ludwig XIV.* Frankfurt, 1967; Eng. trans. *Armour and Weapons.* London, 1968.

Martin, Paul. "La collection d'armes du Musée de Dijon," *Armes anciennes* 12 (1959), 113-21.

Men at Arms: A Guide to the Military Collections at the Castle Museum, York. York: Castle Museum, 1981.

Miller, Yuri, ed. *Russian Arms and Armour.* Leningrad: Aurora Art Publishers, 1982.

Møller, Th. *Gamle Danske Militaer Våben.* Copenhagen: Høst and Søns Forlag, 1963.

Müller, Heinrich. *Das Berliner Zeughaus: Vom Arsenal zum Museum.* Berlin: Deutschen Historischen Museum, 1994.

Musciarelli, L. *Dizionario della armi.* Milan: Arnoldo Mondadori Editore, 1968-70.

Nadolski, Andrzej. "Ancient Polish Arms and Armour," *Journal of the Arms and Armour Society* 4 (1962-1964), 29-39, 170-86.

Nadolski, Andrzej. *Studia nad uzbrojeniem polskim w X, XI, XII w.* Lodz, 1954.

Natta-Soleri, Raffaele. "En visite à l'Armeria Reale de Turin et le but de l'Accademia de San Marciano," *Armi antiche* (1958).

Nickel, Helmut. *Arms and Armor from the Permanent Collection.* New York: Metropolitan Museum of Art, 1991.

Nickel, Helmut. *Arms and Armour Through the Ages.* London: Collins, 1969.

Nickel, Helmut and David Edge. *Wallace Collection, The: Guide to the Armouries.* London: The Trustees of the Wallace Collection, 1982.

Norman, A.V.B. *Arms and Armour.* London: Wiedenfeld and Nicolson, 1964.

Norman, A.V.B. *Arms and Armour in the Royal Scottish Museum.* Edinburgh: Her Majesty's Stationery Office, 1972.

Norman, A.V.B and G.M. Wilson. *Treasures from the Tower of London: An Exhibition of Arms and Armour*. Norwich: Sainsbury Centre for Visual Arts, University of East Anglia, 1982.

Oakeshott, Ewart. *The Archaeology of Weapons: Arms and Armor from Prehistory to the Age of Chivalry*. New York: Barnes and Noble Books, 1960.

Perusini, G. "L'armamento delle cernide friulani all'epoca veneta," *Armi antiche* (1960), 43-74.

Pfaffenbichler, Matthias. "Europäische Waffen im orientalisierenden Stil aus den Beständen der Hofjagd- und Rüstkammer des Kunsthistorischen Museums in Wien." *Waffen- und Köstumkunde* 38 (1999), 117-28.

Reid, William. *The Lore of Arms: A Concise History of Weaponry*. New York: Facts on File Publications, 1976.

Sannibale, Maurizio. *Le armi della collezione Gorga al Museo Nazionale Romano*. Rome: L'Erma di Bretschneider, 1998.

Schalkhausser, Erwin. "Die 'Alte Abteilung' des bayerischen Armeemuseums," *Waffen- und Kostümkunde* 23 (1981), 5-26.

Spiteri, Stephen C. *The Palace Armoury: A Study of a Military Storehouse of the Knights of the Order of St. John*. Valetta: The Farsons Foundation, 1999.

Steuer, Heiko. "Zur Bewaffnung und Sozialstruktur der Merovingerzeit: Ein Beitrag zur Forschungsmethode," *Nachrichten aus Niedersachsens Urgeschichte* 37 (1968), 18-87

Tarassuk, Leonid. "The Collection of Arms and Armour in the State Heritage, Leningrad," *Journal of the Arms and Armour Society* 3 (1959-61), 1-39; 5 (1965-67), 205-61.

Tarassuk, Leonid and Claude Blair, ed. *The Complete Encyclopedia of Arms and Weapons*. London: Batsford, 1982.

Temesváry, Ferenc. *Arms and Armour: The Treasures of the Hungarian National Museum*. Trans. R.D.C. Sturgess. Budapest: Helikon, 1992.

Thomas, Bruno. "Armature e armi bianche." In: *Storia di Brescia*. Brescia: Morcelliana Editrice, 1964, III, pt. XIV:791-815.

Thomas, Bruno. "Die Waffensammlung des Schlossmuseums in Linz." In: *Führer durch die Sammlungen des Schlossmuseums in Linz.* Linz: Schlossmuseum, 1966, pp. 53-65.

Thomas, Bruno and Ortwin Gamber. *Kunsthistorisches Museum Wien. Waffensammlung: Katalog der Leibrüstkammer.* I: *Der Zeitraum von 500 bis 1530.* Vienna, 1976.

Tøjhusmuseets billedbog. Copenhagen: Tøjhusmuseet, 1937.

Tøjhusmuseets billedkatalog for den permanente udstilling. Copenhagen: Tøjhusmuseet, 1962.

Valencia de Don Juan, Juan Crooke y Navarrot, count of. *Catalogo historico descriptivo de la Real Armeria de Madrid.* Madrid, 1898.

Vlădescu, C.M. and C. König. *Muzeul militar central: Catalogue armelor occidentale din secolul al XVI-lea.* Bucharest: Muzeul militar central, 1977.

Wegeli, R. *Inventar der Waffensammlung der bernischen historischen Museums in Bern.* 4 vols. Bern, 1920-48.

Wilkinson, Frederick. *Arms and Armour.* London: A. & C. Black Ltd., 1963; rpt. London: Hamlyn, 1971.

Wintringham, Tom and J.N. Blashford-Snell. *Weapons and Tactics.* Harmondsworth, 1973.

Zbiory Muzeum Wojska Polskiego w Warszawie. Warsaw: Wydawnictwo "Arkady", 1994.

Żygulski, Zdzisław, Jr. *Broń w dawnej Polsce.* Warsaw: Państwowe Wydawnictwo Naukowe, 1975.

Military Technology – Premodern – Arms and Armor – General

Ackerman, R.B. "Armor and Weapons in the Middle English Romances," *Research Studies of the State College of Washington* 7.2 (Jun 1939), 104-18.

Adamczewski, Marek and Zuzanna Poklewska-Patra (tr.). "The Representation of Arms and Armour in Polish Knight Heraldry," *Fasciculi archaeologicae historicae* 7 (1994), 67-75.

Alexander, David. *The Arts of War: Arms and Armour of the 7th to 19th Centuries*. The Nasser D. Khalili Collection of Islamic Art, XXI. London: The Nour Foundation with Azimuth Editions and Oxford University Press, 1992.

Allason-Jones, L. "'Small Finds' from Turrets on Hadrian's Wall." In: *Military Equipment and the Identity of Roman Soldiers: Proceedings of the Fourth Roman Military Equipment Conference*. Ed. J.C. Coulston. British Archaeological Reports International Series, 394. Oxford: BAR, 1988, pp. 197-233.

Angeletti, Glauco. *L'armeria storica di Castel Sant' Angelo*. Rome: Argos, 1991.

Armes anciennes des collections Suisse: Musée Rath. Lausanne: Edition, 1972.

Aroldi, A.M. *Armi e armature Italiane, fino al XVIII secolo*. Milan, 1961.

Arts, Nico. "Oorlog in Helmond: Archeologische wapenvondsten uit het Oude Huys (circa 1175-1400)," *Brabantse Heem* 47 (1995), 85-91.

Ascherl, Rosemary. "The Technology of Chivalry in Reality and Romance." In: *The Study of Chivalry*. Ed. H. Chickering and T.H. Seiler. Kalamazoo, 1989, pp. 263-311.

Ashdown, Charles H. *Armour and Weapons in the Middle Ages*. 3rd ed. London: The Holland Press, 1975.

Ayton, Andrew. "Arms, Armour, and Horses." In: *Medieval Warfare: A History*. Ed. Maurice Keen. Oxford: Oxford University Press, 1999, pp. 186-208.

Barrière-Flavy, C. "Le costume et l'armament du Wisigoth aux Vème et VIème siècles," *Revue des Pryénées* 14 (1902), 125-43.

Bartlett, Clive and Gerry Embleton. "The Medieval Footsoldier, 1460-85," *Military Illustrated* 7 (June-July 1987), 11-18; 8 (Aug-Sept 1987), 10-17; 11 (Feb-Mar 1988), 14-20; 12 (Apr-May, 1988), 39-46.

Baumel, Jutta, Heinz-Werner Lewerken, Dieter Schaal, Werner Schmidt, and Holger Schuckelt. *Dresdner Rüstkammer, Historisches Museum: Meisterwerke aus vier Jahrhunderten*. Dresden: Staatliche Kunstsammlungen, 1992.

Belles armes anciennes: Musée Ducal de Bouillon. Bouillon: Musée de Bouillon, 1971.

Belleval, René de. *Du costume militaire des Français en 1446*. Paris: Aubry, 1866.

Benes, Ctirad. "Waffensammlung auf dem Schlosse Opočno in Böhmen," *Armi antiche* (1966), 149-72.

Bishop, M.C. and J.C.N. Coulston. *Roman Military Equipment from the Punic Wars to the Fall of Rome*. London: B.T. Batsford, 1993.

Blackmore, David. *Arms and Armour of the English Civil Wars*. London: Royal Armouries, 1990.

Blair, Claude. "Arms and Armour from Spain," *Connoisseur* (Aug 1960), 16-20.

Blair, Claude. "The Armourers' Bill of 1581: The Making of Arms and Armour in 16th Century London," *Journal of the Arms and Armour Society* 12 (1986-88), 20-53.

Boccia, Lionella Giorgio. "L'armamento in Toscana dal Millecento al Trecento." In: *Civiltà delle arti minori in Toscana: Atti del I convegno, Arezzo 11-15 maggio 1971*. Florence: Editrice Edam, 1973, pp. 193-212.

Boccia, Lionella Giorgio. "Arms and Armor from the Medici Court," *Bulletin of the Detroit Institute of Arts* 61.1/2 (Sum 1983), 58-64.

Boccia, Lionella Giorgio. *I guerrieri di Avio*. Milan, 1991.

Boccia, Lionella Giorgio. *Il museo Stibbert a Firenze*. Vol. terzo: *L'armeria Europea*. 2 vols. Milan: Electa Editrice, 1975.

Boccia, Lionella Giorgio and Eduardo T. Coelho. "L'armamento di cuoio e ferro nel trecento Italiano," *L'illustrazione Italiana* 1-2 (1972), 24-27.

Boccia, Lionella Giorgio and Eduardo T. Coelho. "Colaccio Beccadelli: an Emilian Knight of about 1340." In: *Arms and Armor Annual: Volume One*. Ed. Robert Held. Northfield: Digest Books, Inc., 1973, pp. 10-27.

Boccia, Lionella Giorgio, F. Rossi and M. Morin. *Armi e armature Lombarde*. Milan, 1980.

Boeheim, Wendelin. *Meister der Waffenschmeidkunst vom XIV bis XVIII Jahrhundert*. Berlin, 1897.

Boni, B. "Lavoro d'armaroli italiani del XV secolo da testimonianze di S. Bernardino da Siena," *La fonderia Italiana* 5.10 (1956), 3-7.

Borg, Alan. "Henry VIII's Call to Arms: The Tudor Gallery in the Tower of London," *Country Life* (May 8, 1975), 1194.

Bosson, Clément. "Le piquier et son armement au XVIIe siècle," *Armes anciennes* 13 (1959), 141-50.

Bosson, Clément. "Quelques armes de l'exposition 'Armes anciennes des Collections Suisses–Genève 1972," *Waffen- und Kostümkunde* 15 (1973), 53-64.

Brewer, Derek. "The Arming of the Warrior in European Literature and Chaucer," *Comparative Literature* 32 (1980), 113-29; in: *Chaucerian Problems and Perspectives: Essays Presented to Paul E. Beichner*. Ed. E. Vasta and Z.P. Thundy. Notre Dame, 1979, pp. 221-43.

Broń średniowieczna z ziem polskich: Katalog/Catalogue of an Exhibition of Medieval Arms and Armour from Poland. Warsaw: Państwowe Muzeum Archeologiczne, 1978.

Brooks, Nicholas P. "Arms, Status and Warfare in Late-Saxon England." In: *Ethelred the Unready: Papers from the Millenary Conference*. Ed. D. Hill. BAR British Series, 59. Oxford, 1978, pp. 81-103.

Brooks, Nicholas P. "Weapons and Armour." In: *The Battle of Maldon, AD 991*. Ed. D. Scragg. London, 1991, pp. 208-19.

Bruce-Mitford, Rupert. *The Sutton-Hoo Ship-Burial*. Vol. 2: *Arms, Armour and Regalia*. London: British Museum Publications Ltd., 1978.

Bruhn de Hoffmeyer, Ada. *Arms and Armour in Spain: A Short Survey.* Vol 1: *The Bronze Age to the End of High Middle Ages.* Madrid: Instituto de Estudios Sobre Armas Antiguas, 1972.

Bruhn de Hoffmeyer, Ada. *Arms and Armour in Spain: A Short Survey.* Vol 2: *From the End of the 12th Century to the Beginning of the 15th Century.* Madrid: Instituto de Estudios Sobre Armas Antiguas, 1982.

Bruhn de Hoffmeyer, Ada. *Military Equipment in the Byzantine Manuscript of Scylitzes in Biblioteca Nacional in Madrid.* Granada: Instituto de Estudios Sobre Armas Antiguas, 1966.

Buttin, François. *Du costume militaire au moyen âge et pendant la renaissance.* Memorias de la Real Academia de Buenas Letras de Barcelona, 12. Barcelona: Real Academia de Buenas Letras, 1971.

Cabalask, Maria and Wanda Mazur. "Średniowieczne militaria z Polski południowej w świetle badań metaloznawczych," *Studia do dziejów dawnego uzbrojenia i ubioru wojskowego* 8 (1982), 5-17.

Caldwell, David H. "Royal Patronage of Arms and Armour Making in Fifteenth and Sixteenth-Century Scotland." In: *Scottish Weapons and Fortifications, 1100-1800.* Ed. David H. Caldwell. Edinburgh: John Donald Publishers Ltd., 1981, pp. 73-93.

Calvert, A.F. *Spanish Arms and Armour.* London, 1908.

Christie, Neil. "Longobard Weaponry and Warfare, A.D. 1-800," *Journal of Roman Military Equipment* 2 (1991), 1-26.

Clark, Jane. "Eliseus Libaerts and His English Connections," *Journal of the Arms and Armour Society* 11 (1983-85), 41-46.

Clarke, Simon and Rick Jones. "The Newstead Pits," *Journal of Roman Military Equipment Studies* 5 (1994), 109-24.

Contamine, Philippe. "L'armement des populations urbaines à la fin du Moyen Âge: l'exemple de Troyes (1474)." In: *La guerre, la violence et les gens au Moyen Âge. II: Guerre et gens.* Ed. P. Contamine and O. Guyotjeannin. 119e congrès national des sociétés historiques et scientifiques, Amiens, octobre 1994, Section d'histoire médiévale et philologie. Paris, 1996, pp. 59-74.

Contamine, Philippe. "L'armement des populations urbaines dans la France de la fin du moyen âge: L'exemple des habitants de Troyes (1474)," *Fasciculi archaeologiae historicae* 5 (1992), 9-17.

Contamine, Philippe. "Aux origines du Musée de l'Armée: une collection d'armes royales à la fin du XVe siècle: exposition d'armes à Amboise et à Paris (1498)," *Revue de la Société des Amis du Musée de l'Armée* 106 (1993), 6-13.

Contat, Pierre. "Quatre pièces de l'équipement militaire des Stockalper (XVIe et XVIIe siècle)," *Vallesia* (1961), 277-82.

Coupland, Simon. "Carolingian Arms and Armor in the Ninth Century," *Viator*. 21 (1990), 29-50.

Creswell, K.A.C. *A Bibliography of Arms and Armour in Islam*. London: Royal Asiatic Society, 1956.

Danielsson, Arne. *Utländska fälttecken utställda i trofékammaren*. Stockholm: Försvarsstabens Reprocentral, 1988.

Dawson, Tim. "*Kremasmata, Kabadion, Klibanion*: Some Aspects of Middle Byzantine Military Equipment Reconsidered," *Byzantine and Modern Greek Studies* 22 (1998), 38-50.

Dillon, Harold A. "Arms and Armour at Westminster, the Tower, and Greenwich, 1547," *Archaeologia* 51 (1888), 219-80.

Dlužnevskaia, Galina V. "Snarjaženie vsadnika i konia stepej Centralnoi-Azii (IX-XII v.)," *Fasciculi archaeologicae historicae* 7 (1994), 9-12.

Edge, David A. and John Miles Paddock. *Arms and Armour of the Medieval Knight*. London: Saturn Books, 1996.

Erben, Wilhelm. "Schwertleite und Ritterschlag: Beiträge zu einer Rechtsgeschichte der Waffen," *Zeitschrift für historische Waffenkunde* 8 (1918-20), 105-67.

Fett, P. "Arms in Norway between AD 400 and 600," *Bergens museums arbok* (1938).

Fernández Pomar, José María. "El Scylitzes de la Biblioteca Nacional de Madrid," *Gladius* 3 (1964), 15-46.

ffoulkes, Charles J. "European Arms and Armour." In: *Social Life in Early England*. London, 1960, pp. 124-38.

Flamm, Hans-Jürgen. "Die Waffensammlung im Germanischen National-museum in Nürnberg," *Deutsches Waffen Journal* (9/1982), 1057-63.

Fowler, G.H. "Munitions in 1224," *Publications of the Bedfordshire Historical Record Society* 5 (1920), 117-32.

Franzoi, Umberto. *Armoury of the Doges Palace in Venice*. Venice: Doges Palace, 1966.

Fritz, Johann Michael. "Über die Waffensammlung der Markgrafen und Grossherzöge von Baden," *Jahrbuch der Staatlichen Kunstsammlungen in Baden-Württemberg* 12 (1975).

Gaibi, Agostino. "Un manoscritto del '600: L'Arte Fabrile, di Antonio Petrini," *Armi antichi* (1962), 111-40.

Gaier, Claude. "L'armement chevaleresque au moyen âge (IXe au XVe siècle)." In: *Catalogue de l'expostion: "Châteaux et chevalerie en Hainaut au moyen âge"*. Musée des Beaux-Arts de Valenciennes, 1995.

Gaier, Claude. *Les Armes*. Typologie des sources de moyen âge. Turnhout: Brepols, 1979.

Gaier, Claude. "Armes et armures dans l'oeuvre épique et historique de Jean d'Outremeuse (XIVe siècle)," *Gladius* 16 (1983), 11-43; in: *Armes et combats dans l'univers médiéval*. Paris: De Boeck Université, 1995, pp. 351-76.

Gaier, Claude. "Arms and Armour Used in Lists Contests in the Burgundian Principalities during the XVth Century," *Livrustkammaren* 19 (1993), 46-61.

Gaier, Claude. "Ce que les illustrations d'un Chroniqueur nous révèlent sur l'armement de sons temps," *Le Vieux-Liège* 136 (Jan-Mar 1962), 124-35; in: *Armes et combats dans l'univers médiéval*. Liege, 1995, pp. 377-86.

Gaier, Claude. "Contribution à l'étude de l'armement au XVe siècle: A propos d'un bas-relief en terre cuite du Musée Curtius à Liège," *Chronique archéologique du pays de Liège* 51 (1960), 37-55.

Gaier, Claude. "Un eventement attendu: la mise en valeur des collections d'armes et d'armures de la Porte de Hal à Bruxelles," *Musée d'armes* 55 (Dec 1987), 2-11.

Gaier, Claude. "Les inscriptions sur les armes anciennes (Xe-XVIIIe siècles)," *Musée d'armes* 85 (1997), 2-32; 87 (1997), 28-32; 91 (1998), 8-13.

Gaier, Claude. "La nostalgie de l'armement ancien à la fin du Moyen âge: un indicateur social?" In: *Studia in honorem M. de Riquer*. Barcelona, 1988, pp. 431-41; in: *Armes et combats dans l'univers médiéval*. Liege, 1995, pp. 319-26.

Gaier, Claude. "A propos d'armes et d'armures de transition (1495-1500): le témoignage pictural du 'Siège de Jérusalem' du Musée de Gand," *Armi antiche* (1962), 93-110.

Gaier, Claude. "Quelques particularités de l'armement des chevaliers teutoniques dans le baillage de Germanie inférieure aux XIVe et XVe siècles." In: *Armes et combats dans l'univers médiéval*. Liege, 1995, pp. 151-58.

Gaier, Claude. "Sculptures mosanes du XIVe siècle datées par l'armement," *Musée d'armes* 18 (1977), 384-85.

Galea, M. *Malta: The Palace of the Grandmasters and the Armoury*. 2nd ed. Valetta: M.J. Publications, 1990.

Gamber, Ortwin. "Geschichte der mittelalterlichen Bewaffung," *Waffen- und Köstumkunde* 34 (1992), 57-70; 35 (1993), 1-22; 36 (1994), 77-97; 37 (1995), 1-26; 39 (1997), 10-24; 40 (1998), 33-62.

Gamber, Ortwin. "Orientalische Einflüsse auf die mittelalterliche Bewaffung Europas," *Kwartalnik historii kultury materialnej* 21 (1973), 273-79.

Gamber, Ortwin. "Ritterspiele und Turnierrüstung im Spätmittelalter." In: *Das ritterliche Turnier im Mittelalter*. Ed. Josef Fleckenstein. Göttingen: Vandenhoeck and Ruprecht, 1985, pp. 513-31.

Gamber, Ortwin. "Some Notes on the Sutton Hoo Military Equipment," *Journal of the Arms and Armour Society* 10 (1980-82), 208-16.

Gamber, Ortwin. "Studien zum Wehrgehänge des Frühmittelalters," *Waffen- und Köstumkunde* 33 (1991), 1-14.

Gamber, Ortwin. "The Sutton Hoo Military Equipment–An Attempted Reconstruction," *Journal of the Arms and Armour Society* 5 (1965-67), 265-89.

Gamber, Ortwin. "Wikingerbewaffnung und spätrömische Waffen Tradition." In: *I Normanni e la loro espansione in Europa nell'alto medioevo.* Settimane di studio del centro italiano di studi sull'alto medioevo, XV. Spoleto, 1969, pp. 767-82.

Gamber, Ortwin. "Der Zeituntershied zwischen Nachricht und Darstellung im Hochmittelalter," *Fasciculi archaeologiae historicae* 5 (1992), 49-52.

Gamber, Ortwin, et al. *Die Rüstkammern: Sammlungen Schloss Ambras, Kunsthistorisches Museum.* Vienna: Kunsthistorisches Museum, 1981.

Ganshof, François Louis. "Armatura (Galbert de Bruges, ch. 106, éd. Pirenne, p. 152)," *Archivum latinitatis medii aevi* 16 (1940), 179-94.

Gausted, F. "Til bevaepningens historie i nordisk folkevandringstid og merovingertid," *Viking tidsskrift for norrøn arkeologi* 30 (1966), 97-131.

Genevoy, R. "Notes sur l'armureie impériale d'Arbois (1495-1509?) et sur les armures de Claude de Vaudrey et de Maximilien Ier au Kunst historisches Museum de Vienne," *Nouvelle revue franc-comtoise* (1955), 208-22.

Gessler, A.E. *Bewaffung, Wehr- und Befestigungswesen zur Zeit der Schlacht bei St. Jakob an der Birs.* Basel, 1944.

Gilliver, Catherine M. "The *De munitionibus castrorum*: Text and Translation," *Journal of Roman Military Equipment* 4 (1993), 33-48.

Giorgetti, Giovanni. *A Guide to the Arms and Armour Collection in Cesta Castle.* San Marino: Editoriale Sammarinese per le Armi Antiche, 1969.

Giraud, J.B., ed. *Documents pour servir à l'histoire de l'armament au moyen âge et à la renaissance.* 2 vols. Lyon, 1895-1904.

Głosek, Marian. "L'état actuel et les perspectives des recherches sur l'armement médiéval en Pologne," *Fasciculi archaeologiae historicae* 5 (1992), 53-60.

Gorelik, M. "Bitva na Vorskle, 1399," *Tseikhgauz* 3 (1994), 21-25.

Gorelik, M. "Kulikovskaya Bitva, 1380: Russki i Zoloturkuinskii Vojni," *Tseikhgauz* 1 (1991), 2-7.

Gorelik, M. "Voini Kievskoi Rusi, IX-XI bb," *Tseikhgauz* 2 (1993), 20-25.

Goring, Jeremy. "The Dress of the English Soldier in the Early Tudor Period," *Journal of the Society for Army Historical Research* 33 (1955), 136-38.

Grabowska, Irena. *Broń w dawnych wiekach/Arms and Armour of Past Centuries*. Cracow: National Museum, 1978.

Granato, Lois R. "The Location of the Armoury in the Italian Renaissance Palace: A Note on Three Literary Sources," *Waffen- und Kostümkunde* 24 (1982), 152-53.

Grancsay, Stephen V. "Arms and Armor from the Theodore Offerman Collection," *Metropolitan Museum of Art Bulletin* 35 (Feb 1940), 30-32; in: *Arms and Armor: Essays by Stephen V. Grancsay from The Metropolitan Museum of Art Bulletin, 1920-1964*. New York: The Metropolitan Museum of Art, 1986, pp. 249-51.

Grancsay, Stephen V. "The Bashford Dean Memorial Collection," *Metropolitan Museum of Art Bulletin* 25 (Apr 1930), 86-94; in: *Arms and Armor: Essays by Stephen V. Grancsay from The Metropolitan Museum of Art Bulletin, 1920-1964*. New York: The Metropolitan Museum of Art, 1986, pp. 59-68.

Grancsay, Stephen V. "The Cloisters Exhibition of Medieval Arms and Armor," *Metropolitan Museum of Art Bulletin* 35 (Sep 1940), 172-75; in: *Arms and Armor: Essays by Stephen V. Grancsay from The Metropolitan Museum of Art Bulletin, 1920-1964*. New York: The Metropolitan Museum of Art, 1986, pp. 253-56.

Grancsay, Stephen V. "The Exhibition of European Arms and Armor–Notes on Some Oriental Pieces," *Metropolitan Museum of Art Bulletin* 26 (Sep 1931), 203-09; in: *Arms and Armor: Essays by Stephen V. Grancsay from The Metropolitan Museum of Art Bulletin, 1920-1964*. New York: The Metropolitan Museum of Art, 1986, pp. 87-91.

Grancsay, Stephen V. "The Illustrated Inventory of Arms and Armor of Emperor Charles V." In: *Homenaje al Prof. Rodriguez-Moñino*. Madrid: Editorial Castalia, 1966, pp. 1-8.

Grancsay, Stephen V. "Mediaeval and Renaissance Arms and Armor in the City of Steel," *Carnegie Magazine* (Oct 1953), 257-61, 265.

Grancsay, Stephen V. "The New Galleries of European Arms and Armor," *Metropolitan Museum of Art Bulletin* n.s. 14 (May 1956), 205-36; in: *Arms and Armor: Essays by Stephen V. Grancsay from The Metropolitan Museum of Art Bulletin, 1920-1964*. New York: The Metropolitan Museum of Art, 1986, pp. 443-63.

Grancsay, Stephen V. "Technical Aspects of Arms and Armour," *Carnegie Magazine* 28 (1954), 65-68.

Guerre au moyen âge, La. Pons: Château de Pons (Charente-maritime), 1976.

Gutowski, Jacek. *Tartar Arms and Armour/Broń i uzbrojenie tatarów*. Katalog Zabytków Tatarskich, tom 1. Warsaw: Res Publica Multiethnica, 1997.

Harbison, P. "Native Irish Arms and Armour in Medieval Gaelic Literature, 1170-1600," *Irish Sword* 12 (1976), 173-99, 270-84.

Hawkes, Sonia Chadwick. "Weapons and Warfare in Anglo-Saxon England: An Introduction." In: *Weapons and Warfare in Anglo-Saxon England*. Ed. Sonia Chadwick Hawkes. Oxford, 1989, pp. 1-9.

Hayward, John F. "Les collections du Palais de Capodimonte, Naples," *Armes anciennes* 1.6 (1956), 121-40.

Hayward, John F. "A Notable Private Collection: XVth and XVIth Century Armour and Swords in the Collection of R.T. Gwynn, Esquire," *The Connoisseur Yearbook* (1954), 34-44.

Hayward, John F. "Notes on the Hearst Collection Formerly at St. Donat's Castle," *Journal of the Arms and Armour Society* 1 (1953), 39-43.

Heer, Eugène. "Armes et armures au temps des guerres de Bourgogne." In: *Grandson 1476*. Centre d'histoire et de prospectives militaires, serie recherches de sciences comparées, II. Lausanne, 1976, pp.

Herben, Stephen J. "Arms and Armor in Chaucer," *Speculum* 12 (1937), 475-87.

Höft, Thomas. *Shiny Shapes: Arms and Armor from the Zeughaus of Graz.* Vienna: Springer-Verlag, 1998.

Hogg, O.F.G. *From Clubs to Cannon.* London: Gerald Duckworth and Co., Ltd., 1968.

Holmes, M.R. *Arms and Armour in Tudor and Stuart London.* 2nd ed. London: Her Majesty's Stationery Office, 1970.

Hummelberger, Walter. "Der Waffensammler," *Waffen- und Kostümkunde* 5 (1963), 99-106; 6 (1964), 50-57.

Hüpper-Dröge, D. *Schild und Speer: Waffen und ihre Bezeichnungen im frühen Mittelalter.* Berne, 1983.

Jakobsson, Theodor. "Ein waffengeschichtlich Wertvoller geschützfund im Armeemuseum von Stockholm," *Zeitschrift für historische Waffen- und Köstumkunde* 17 (1943-44), 124-27.

Javornik, Ivan. "Zaštitno oružje u zbirkama Vojnog muzeja JNA," *Vesnik* 2 (1955), 105-19.

Johannessen, Kåre. "Den militære udrustning i Bayeux-tapetet," *Vaabenhistorisk Aarbog* 40 (1995), 137-68.

Kajzer, L. *Uzbrojenie i ubiór rycerski w średniowiecznej Małopolsce w świetle źródeł ikonograficznych.* Warsaw: Polska Akademia Nauk. Instytut Historii Kultury Materialnej, 1976.

Karcheski, Walter J., Jr. *Arms and Armor in The Art Institute of Chicago.* Boston: Little, Brown and Company, 1995.

Karcheski, Walter J., Jr. *Arms and Armor of the Conquistador, 1492-1600: A Catalogue of Arms and Armor from the Exhibit, First Encounters: Spanish Explorations of the Carribean and United States, 1492-1570.* Miami?: Florida Museum of Natural History, 1990.

Karcheski, Walter J., Jr. "Arms, Armor and Equipment of the 'Trained Bands' of Early 17th Century New England." In: *17th Century War, Weaponry and Politics: International Association of Museums of Arms and Military History, Xth Congress Stockholm 1984* Stockholm, 1984, pp. 267-82.

Karcheski, Walter J., Jr. "Hammerman of the Gods: The Higgins Armory Museum's *Venus at the Forge of Vulcan," Royal Armouries Yearbook* 4 (1999), 32-48.

Kazakevičius, Vytautas. "Some Debatable Questions Concerning the Armament of the Viking Period in Lithuania," *Fasciculi archaeologiae historicae* 7 (1994), 37-44.

Kirpičnikov, Anatolij N. "Новобнаруженные клейма раннесредневековых мечей," *Fasciculi archaeologiae historicae* 5 (1992), 61-82.

Koster, J. "Iets over de bewapening der bewoners van twee Friesche dorpen omstreeks 1600," *De wapen verzamelaar* 8 (1970).

Kottenkamp, F. *History of Chivalry and Ancient Armour.* Trans. A. Löwy. London: Willis and Sotheran, 1857; rpt. London: Brocken Books, 1988.

Krekovič, E. "Military Equipment on the Territory of Slovakia," *Journal of Roman Military Equipment Studies* 5 (1994), 211-25.

Laking, G.F. *The Armoury of Windsor Castle.* London, 1904.

Laking, G.F. *A Record of European Armour and Arms Through Seven Centuries.* 5 vols. London, 1920-22.

Lecestre, Paul. "Notice sur l'arsenal royal de Paris jusqu'à la mort de Henri IV," *Mémoires de la société de l'histoire de Paris et de l'ile de France* 42 (1915), 185-281, 43 (1916), 1-82.

Leppäho, Jorma. *Späteisenzeitliche Waffen aus Finnland: Schwertinschriften und Waffenverzierungen des 9.-12. Jahrhunderts.* Helsinki: Finska Fornminnesföreningens Tidskrift, 1964.

Linn, Irving. "The Arming of Sir Thopas," *Modern Language Notes* 51 (1936), 300-11.

Macmullen, R. "Inscriptions on Armor and the Supply of Arms in the Roman Empire," *American Journal of Archaeology* 64 (1960), 23-40.

Maik, Jerzy. "Military Accessories from Bolesławiec on the Posna," *Fasciculi archaeologicae historicae* 10 (1997), 19-38.

Maindron, G.R. Maurice. *Les armes*. Paris: Quantin, 1890.

Mann, James. "Arms and Armour". In: *The Bayeux Tapestry: A Comprehensive Survey*. 2nd ed. Ed. F. Stenton. London, 1957, pp. 56-69.

Mann, James. "Arms and Armour". In: *Medieval England*. Ed. A.L. Poole. Oxford, 1958, pp. 314-37.

Mann, James. *European Arms and Armour*. 2 vols. Wallace Collection Catalogues. London: Trustees of the Wallace Collection, 1962.

Mann, James. *The Funeral Achievements of Edward, the Black Prince*. London, 1950.

Mann, James. "The Lost Armoury of the Gonzagas," *Archaeological Journal* 95 (1939), 239-336; 100 (1945), 16-127.

Mann, James. *An Outline of Arms and Armour in England from the Early Middle Ages to the Civil War*. 2nd ed. London: Her Majesty's Stationery Office, 1969.

Martin, Paul. *Armes et armures de Charlemagne à Louis XIV*. Paris: Bibliothèque des Arts, 1967; trans. *Armour and Weapons*. London: Herbert Jenkins, 1968.

Martin, Paul. "Les collections militaires du Musée historique de Strasbourg," *Armi antiche* (1965), 31-56.

Martin, Paul. "Wehr-, Waffen-, und Harnischpflichte der Strassburger Zünfte im 14 Jahrhundert," *Waffen- und Köstumkunde* 17 (1975), 102-08.

Mauro, Maurizio. *Armeria della Rocca: mostra di armi antiche*. Mondavio, 1989.

Mauro, Maurizio. *Armi antiche (XIII-XIX): Catalogo della mostra a Palazzo Bosdari, Anacona*. Ancona: Centro Studi per le Armi Antiche, 1978.

Melville, Neil. "The Incised Effigial Stone at Foveran, Aberdeenshire," *Park Lane Arms Fair* 15 (1998), 11-17.

Moro, Tiberio. "Some Considerations on the Armament of the Republic of Venice during the Thirty-Years War Period (1600-1650)." In: *Bellum Tri-*

cennale: The Thirty Years War. XXIIIrd Colloquium of the International Commission of Military History. Prague, 1999, pp. 193-204.

Mostra di armi antiche. I: *Bolletino del Museo Civico di Modena*. Modena: Museo Civico, 1965.

Mot, G.J. "L'arsenal et le parc de matériel à la cité de Carcassone en 1298," *Annales du midi* 68 (1956), 409-18.

Motta, E. "Armaiuoli Milanesi nel periodo Viconteo-Sforzesco," *Archive storico Lombardo* 61 (1914), 187-232.

Nadolski, Andrzej. *Broń i strój rycerstwa polskiego w średniowieczu*. Wroclaw: Zakład Narodowy imiena Ossolińskich, 1979.

Nadolski, Andrzej. "Historia uzbrojenia w badaniach nad kulturą materialną Polski średniowiecznej," *Kwartalnik historii kultury materialnej* R. 19.4 (1971), 625-43.

Nadolski, Andrzej. "Influences balto-slaves dans l'armament des chevaliers teutoniques." In: *Berichte über den II. Internationalen Kongress für Slawische Archäologie*. Berlin, 1973, III:33-36.

Nadolski, Andrzej. *Studia nad uzbrojeniem polskim w X. XI i XII wieku: Acta archaeologica univeristatis Lodziensis*. Lodz, 1954.

Nadolski, Andrzej, et al. *Uzbrojenie w Polsce Średniowiecznej, 1350-1450*. Lodz: Polska Akademia Nauk. Instytut Historii Kultury Materialnej, 1990.

Nickel, Helmut. "About Arms and Armor in the Age of Arthur," *Avalon to Camelot* 1 (Fall 1983), 19-21.

Nickel, Helmut. *Ullstein Waffenbuch: Eine kulturhistorische Waffenkunde mit Markverzeichnis*. Berlin, 1974.

Nicolle, David C. "Armes and Armures dan les épopées des croisades." In: *Les épopées de la croisade*. Ed. K.-H. Bender. Weisbaden, 1987, pp. 17-34.

Nicolle, David C. "Arms and Armor Illustrated in the Art of the Latin East." In: *The Horns of Hattin*. Ed. B.Z. Kedar. Jerusalem, 1992, pp. 327-40.

Nicolle, David C. *Arms and Armour of the Crusading Era, 1050-1350*. 2 vol. White Plains: Kraus International Publications, 1988; 2nd ed. Mechanicsburg: Stackpole Books, 1999.

Nicolle, David C. "Byzantine and Islamic Arms and Armour: Evidence for Mutual Influence," *Graeco-Arabica* 4 (1991), 299-325.

Nicolle, David C. *Early Medieval Islamic Arms and Armour*. Cáceres: Instituto de Estudios sobre Armas Antiguas, 1976.

Nicolle, David C. "An Introduction to Arms and Warfare in Classical Islam." In: *Islamic Arms and Armour*. Ed. Robert Elgood. London: Scolar Press, 1979, pp. 162-86.

Nicolle, David C. "The Monreale Capitals and the Military Equipment of Later Norman Sicily," *Gladius* 15 (1980), 87-103.

Nicolle, David C. "No Way Overland: Evidence for Byzantine Arms and Armour on the 10th-11th Century Tarsus Frontier," *Graeco-Arabica* 226-45.

Nicolle, David C. "The Reality of Mamluk Warfare: Weapons, Armour and Tactics," *Al-Masāq* 7 (1994), 77-110.

Nicolle, David C. "Saljūq Arms and Armour in Art and Literature." In: *The Art of the Seljuqs in Iran and Anatolia: Proceedings of a Symposium Held in Edinburgh in 1982*. Ed. R. Hillenbrand. Costa Mesa, 1994, pp. 247-56.

Nielsen, Kay S. "Riddertidens våben i Damark," *Vaabenhistorisk Aarbøger* 30 (1984), 137-56.

Niox, G.L. *Le Musée de l'Armée: Armes et armures anciennes et souvenirs historiques les plus précieux*. 2 vols. Paris, 1917.

Norman, A.V.B. "Albrecht Dürer: Armour and Weapons," *Apollo* (Jul 1971), 36-39.

Norman, A.V.B. *Arms and Armour*. London: Weidenfeld and Nicholson, 1964.

Norman, A.V.B. *European Arms and Armour Supplement*. London: Balding and Mansell Limited, 1986.

Norman, A.V.B. and Don Pottinger. *English Weapons and Warfare, 449-1660*. Englewood Hills: Prentice-Hall, Inc., 1979.

North, A.R.E. "Arms and Armour from Arundel Castle," *Connoisseur* (Mar 1978), 186-93.

North, A.R.E. "Islamic Arms and Armour," *Connoisseur* (Apr 1976), 274-79.

Nowakowski, Andrzej. *Arms and Armour in the Medieval Teutonic Order's State in Prussia*. Lodz: Oficyna Naukowa, 1994.

Nowakowski, Andrzej. "New Studies on Arms and Armour in Teutonic Prussia: The Present State and the Perspectives," *Fasciculi archaeologiae historicae* 5 (1992), 83-90.

Oakeshott, Ewart. "Arms and Armour in the Fitzwilliam Museum," *Apollo* 126 (July 1987), 20-24.

Oakeshott, Ewart. *European Weapons and Armour from the Renaissance to the Industrial Revolution*. London: Lutterworth Press, 1980.

Oakeshott, Ewart. "A Man-at-Arms of the Late Fifteenth Century," *Park Lane Arms Fair* 4 (1987), 20-22.

Oakeshott, Ewart. "The Paragon of England," *Park Lane Arms Fair* 5 (1988), 15-24.

Oakeshott, Ewart and David Oliver. "The Fitzwilliam Armoury," *Park Lane Arms Fair* 6 (1989), 15-20.

Ortiz, Antonio Domínguez, Concha Herrero Carretero, and José A. Godoy. *Resplendence of the Spanish Monarchy: Renaissance Tapestries and Armor from the Patrimonio Nacional*. New York: Metropolitan Museum of Art, 1991.

Os descobrimentos Portugueses e a Europa do renascimento: A mão que ao ocidente o véu rasgou armaria. XVII exposição europeia de arte, ciência e cultura. Lisbon: Presidência do Conselho de Ministros, 1983.

Peirce, Ian. "Arms, Armour and Warfare in the Eleventh Century," *Anglo-Norman Studies* 10 (1987), 237-57.

Peirce, Ian. "The Knight, His Arms and Armour, c.1150-1250," *Anglo-Norman Studies* 15 (1993), 251-74.

Peirce, Ian. "The Knight, His Arms and Armour in the Eleventh and Twelfth Centuries." In: *The Ideals and Practice of Medieval Knighthood.* Ed. C. Harper-Bi.ll and R. Harvey. Woodbridge, 1986, pp. 152-64.

Petrović, Djurdjica. *Dubrovačko oručje.* Belgrade: Volni Muzej, 1974.

Pfaffenbichler, Matthias. "Europaische Waffen im orientalisierenden Stil aus den Bestanden der Hofjadg- und Rustkammer des Kunsthistorischen Museums in Wein," *Waffen- und Köstumkunde* 38 (1996), 117-28.

Piletić, Dragoslav. "Rekonstrukcija naoružanja rimskog ratnika," *Vesnik* 8-9 (1963), 61-80

Polívka, Miloslav. "Prager Waffenhandwerke des 14. und 15. Jahrhunderts: Zum Stand und zu den Veränderungen in der Hussitenzeit." In: *Das Andere wahrnehmen: Beiträge zur europäischen Geschichte. August Nitschke zum 65. Geburtstag gewidmet.* Ed. Martin Kintzinger, Wolfgang Stürner, and Johannes Zahlten. Cologne: Böhlau, 1991, pp. 309-22.

Post, P. *Das Kostüm und die ritterliche Kriegstracht in deutschen Mittelalter von 1000-1450.* Berlin, 1939.

Post, P. *Kriegs-, Turnier- und Jagdwaffen von frühen Mittelalter bis zum Dreissig-jährigen Krieg: Ein Handbuch der Waffenkunde.* 3rd ed. Berlin, 1929.

Prelle de la Nieppe, E. de. "L'Inventaire de l'armurerie de Guillaume III comte de Hainaut en 1358," *Annales de la société archéologique de l'arrondissement de Nivelles* 7 (1900).

Pribaković, Dušan. "Nekoliko primedbi o oružju na minijaturama kodeska 'Historia Turcica'," *Vesnik* 4 (1957), 115-24.

Pribaković, Dušan. "Prilog hronologiji naoružanja Slovena u VI i VII veku," *Vesnik* 11-12 (1966), 23-67.

Puype, Jan Piet and A.A. Wiekart. *Van Maurits naar Munster: Tactiek en triomf van het Staatse leger. Catalogus van de voorwerpen op de gelijknamige tentoonstelling in het Legermuseum te Delft, alsmede een reconstructie van de bibliotheek van prins Maurits/From Prince Maurice to the Peace of Westphalia: Tactics and Triumphs of the Dutch Army. Catalogue of Objects in the Exhibition of the Same Name at the Army Museum in Delft, and a Reconstruction of he Library of Maurice of Nassau.* Delft: Legermuseum, 1998.

Quaas, Gerhard. *Das Handwerk der Landsknecht: Waffen und Bewaffnung zwischen 1500 und 1600.* Militärgeschichte und Wehrwissenschaften, 3. Onasbrück: Biblio Verlag, 1997.

Rajtár, Ján. "Waffen und Ausrüstungsteile aus dem Holz-Erde-Lager con Iža," *Journal of Roman Military Equipment Studies* 5 (1994), 83-95.

Reitzenstein, Alexander Freiherr von. "Über die Anfänge des Waffensammelns," *Waffen- und Kostümkunde* 11 (1969), 69-75.

Reitzenstein, Alexander Freiherr von. *Der Waffenschmeid: Von Handwerk der Plattner und Büchsenmacher.* Munich: Prestel Verlag, 1964.

Reverseau, Jean-Pierre. "L'armement à la époque de Jeanne d'Arc,"*Dossiers d'archéologie* 34 (1979), 35-46.

Reverseau, Jean-Pierre. *Armes et armures des Montmorency: dossier-exposition.* Paris: Musée de l'Armée, 1993.

Reverseau, Jean-Pierre. "Armes et armures des Montmorency: dossier-exposition departement armes et armures, 18 juin-15 septembre, 1993," *Revue de la Société des Amis du Musée de l'Armée* 106 (1993), 76-81.

Reverseau, Jean-Pierre. *Armes insolites du XVIe au XVIIIe siècle.* Paris: Musée de l'Armée, 1990.

Riquer, Martín de. "El armamento en el 'Roman de Troie' y en la 'Historia Troyana'," *Boletin de la Real Academia Española* 49 (1969), 463-94.

Riquer, Martín de. *L'arnès del cavaller: Armes i armadures catalanes medievals.* Barcelona: Edicions Ariel, 1968.

Riquer, Martín de. "La fecha del 'Ronsasvals' y del 'Rollan a Saragossa' según el armamento," *Boletin de la Real Academia Española* 49 (1969), 211-51.

Rossi, Francesco. *Armi e armaioli Breciani del '400.* Brescia: Ateneo di Brescia, 1971.

Rossi, Francesco. *Guida del museo delle armi 'Luigi Marzoli'*. Brescia: Museo delle armi 'Luigi Marzoli', 1988.

Rossi, Francesco. *Mediaeval Arms and Armour*. Leicester: Magna Books, 1990.

Rossi, Francesco and Nolfo di Carpegna. *Armi antiche dal museo civico L. Marzoli*. Brescia Bramante Editrice, 1969.

Rothero, Christopher. *Medieval Military Dress, 1066-1500*. Poole: Blandford Press, 1983.

Ruttkay, A. "Waffen und Reiterausrüstung des 9. bis zur ersten hälfte des 14. Jahrhunderts in der Slowakei," *Slovenska archeologia* 23 (1975), 191-216.

Rynne, Etienne. "The Impact of the Vikings on Irish Weapons." In: *Atti del congresso internazionale delle scienze preistoriche e protoistoriche*. Rome, III:181-84.

Samling, Davids. *Islamiske våben i dansk privateje*. Copenhagen: Davids Sammling, 1982.

Saxtorph, Niels M. "Technical Innovations and Military Change." In: *War and Peace in the Middle Ages*. Ed. B.P. McGuire. Copenhagen, 1987, pp. 216-26.

Scalini, Mario. "Il 'giubbotto di ferro cesellato a foggia di colletto trinciato con scarselle' di Guidobaldo Della Rovere (1514/1538/1574) e altri resti rovereschi," *Waffen- und Köstumkunde* 39 (1997), 38-50.

Scalini, Mario. "The Weapons of Lorenzo de' Medici." In: *Art, Arms and Armour: An International Anthology*. Vol I: *1979-80*. Ed. Robert Held. Chiasso: Acquafresca Editrice, 1979, pp. 12-29.

Schalk, Karl. "Die historische Waffensammlung der Stadt Wien im Zusammenhange mit der militärischen Organisation der Stadt," *Zeitschrift für historische Waffenkunde* 2 (1900-02), 247-51.

Schedelmann, Hans. "Waffen und Rüstungen," *Keysers Kunst- und Antiquitätenbuch* 2 (1959), 231-77.

Schedelmann, Hans. "Der Waffensammler," *Waffen- und Kostümkunde* 6 (1964), 112-17; 8 (1966), 53-57.

Schedelmann, Hans. "Die Waffensammlung eines Regionalmuseums in der Tschechoslowakei," *Waffen- und Kostümkunde* 7 (1965), 124-32.

Schiedlausky, G. "Das Hohenaschauer Rüstkammarinventar von 1567," *Waffen und Kostümkunde* 4 (1962), 25-34.

Schöbel, Johannes. *Prunkwaffen: Waffen und Rüstungen aus dem Historischen Museum Dresden.* Vienna: Econ-Verlag GMBH, 1973; trans. *Princely Arms and Armour: A Selection from the Dresden Collection.* Altenburg: Editions Leipzig, 1974.

Scott, J.G. *European Arms and Armour at Kelingrove.* Glasgow: Glasgow Museum and Art Galleries, 1980.

Seyrig, H. "Armes et costumes Iraniens de Palmyre," *Syria* 18 (1937), 4-30.

Škrivanić, Gavro A. "Armour and Weapons in Medieval Serbia, Bosnia and Dubrovnik," *Posedna izdanja* 293 (1957).

Sobey, Edwin C. *Castles, Kings and Knights: An Exhibition Exclusively at the South Florida Science Museum.* West Palm Beach, 1988.

Soler del Campo, Alvaro. *La evolucion del armamento medieval en el reino castellano-leones y al-andalus (siglos XII-XIV).* Madrid: Coleccion Adalid. Servicio de Publicaciones del E.M.E., 1993.

Spitzlberger, Georg. *Unvergängliche Harnischkunst: Beiträge zur historischen Waffenkunde.* Landshut: Stadt Landshut (Stadt- und Kreismuseum), 1985.

Stephenson, I.P. *Roman Infantry Equipment: The Later Empire.* Stroud: Tempus Publishing Limted, 1999.

Steuer, Heiko. "Historische Phasen der Bewaffnung nach Aussagen der archäologischen Quellen Mittel- und Nordeuropas im ersten Jahrtausend n. Chr.," *Frühmittelalterliche Studien* 4 (1970), 348-83.

Stratford, Neil. *The Lewis Chessmen and the Enigma of the Hoard.* London: British Museum Press, 1997.

Świętosławski, Witold. "Medieval Tartar Military Accessories Finds From the Territory of Poland," *Fasciculi archaeologicae historicae* 7 (1994), 55-59.

Temesváry, Ferenc. *Arms and Armour: The Treasures of the Hungarian National Museum.* Trans. R.D.C. Sturgess. Budapest: Helikon, 1992.

Terenzi, Marcello. "Le armature di Piero della Francesca," *Commentari* 3 (Jul-Sept 1970), 219-23.

Terenzi, Marcello. *Mostra di armi antiche (sec. XIV-XV): Poppi Castello dei Conti guidi.* Florence: Formatecnica, 1967.

Thomas, Bruno. "Die Augsburger Funeralwaffen Kaiser Karl V," *Waffen- und Kostümkunde* 1 (1959), 28-46.

Thomas, Bruno. "Die Rüstkammer von Stift Kremsmünster in Oberösterreich," *Waffen- und Kostümkunde* 5 (1963), 41-62.

Thomas, Bruno. *Wegweiser durch das Vorarlberger Landesmuseum.* IV: *Waffen.* Bregenz: Vorarlberger Landesmuseum, n.d.

Thomas, Bruno. "Der Wiener Restauierung der überfluteten Florentiner Waffensammlung des Bargello," *Waffen- und Kostümkunde* 11 (1969), 76-88.

Thomas, Bruno, Ortwin Gamber, and Hans Schedelmann. *Arms and Armour of the Western World.* Trans. I. Bolson and W. Reid. London: Thames and Hudson, 1964.

Trapp, Oswald and Mario Scalini. *The Armoury of the Castle of Churburg.* 2nd ed. Churburg: Magnus, 1995.

Uhlemann, Heinz Robert. "Zur Geschichte des brandenburgischen Heerwesens im 16. Und 17. Jahrhundert: Regesten aus Berliner Archiven," *Waffen- und Köstumkunde* 27 (1985), 141-45.

Uhlemann, Heinz Robert. "Orient-Okzident: Gegensätze der Bewaffnung," *Waffen- und Kostümkunde* 13 (1971), 1-12, 97-110.

Underwood, Richard. *Anglo-Saxon Weapons and Warfare.* Stroud: Tempus Publishing Limited, 1999.

Valencia de Don Juan, Juan Crooke y Navarrot, count of. "Bildinventar der Waffen, Rüstungen, Gewänder und Standarten Karl V in der Armeria Real zu Madrid," *Jahrbuch der Kunsthistorischen Sammlungen des allerhöchsten Kaiserhauses in Wien* 10 (1889); 11 (1890).

van der Sloot, R.B.F. *Middeleeuws Wapentuig*. Bussum: C.A.J. van Dishoeck, 1964.

Vlădescu, C.M. "Arme albe şi armuri folosite de oştile române in secolul al XVI-lea," *Studii şi materiale de muzeografie şi istorie militaria, Muzeul Militar Central* 7-8 (1974-75), 151-80.

Vlădescu, C.M., C. König, and D. Popa. *Arme in Muzeele din România.* Bucharest: Editura Meridiave, 1973.

Vlădescu, C.M., C. König, and D. Popa. "Tipuri de arme albi şi armuri oştile române în a dona jumatate a secolului al XV-lea," *Studii şi materiale de muzeografie şi istorie militaria, Muzeul Militar Central* 6 (1973), 58-86.

Wachowski, Krzysztof. "Carolingian Influences on the West Slavs' Arms and Armor," *Fasciculi archaeologicae historicae* 7 (1994), 13-14.

Wagner, Eduard. *European Weapons and Warfare, 1618-1648*. Trans. Simon Pellar. London: Octopus Books Limited, 1979.

Wagner, Eduard, Zoroslava Drobna, and Jan Durdík. *Medieval Costumes, Armour and Weapons*. London: P. Hamlyn, 1989.

Wawrzonowska, Z. *Uzbrojenie i ubiór rycerski Piastów śląskich od XII do XIV w.* Acta Archaeologica Lodziensia, 25. Lodz, 1976.

Wearing, J.M. "Some Examples of Italian Arms and Armour in the Marzoli Collection, Brescia," *Conoisseur* (Nov 1955), 193-96.

Wehrhafte Stadt: Das Wiener Bürgerliche Zeughaus im 15. Und 16. Jahrhundert. Vienna: Historisches Museum der Stadt Wien, 1986.

Wells, W. and A.V.B. Norman. "An Unknown Hercules Tapestry in the Burrell Collection," *Scottish Art Review* 8 (1962), 13-20.

Werner, J. "Frankish Royal Tombs in the Cathedrals of Cologne and Saint Denis," *Antiquity* 38 (1964), 201-16.

White, Lynn, Jr. "The Crusade and the Technological Thrust of the West." In: *War, Technology and Society in the Middle East*. Ed. V.J. Parry and M.E. Yapp. London, 1975, pp. 97-112; in: *Medieval Religion and*

Technology: Collected Essays. Berkeley and Los Angeles: University of California Press, 1978, pp. 277-96.

Wiedemer, Jack Earl. *Arms and Armor in England, 1450-1471: Their Cost and Distribution*. Unpublished dissertation, 1994.

Wilkinson, Frederick. *Antique Arms and Armour*. London: Ward Lock Ltd., 1972.

Willers, J. "Nuremberg Weapons and Armour," *Connoisseur* (Nov 1978), 172-79.

Williams, Alan R. "Roman Arms and Armor: A Technical Note," *Journal of Archaeological Science* (1977), 77-87.

Wirtgen, Rolf. "In Grandson das Gut...: Burgunderbeute und Waffen-sammlungen auf Schloß Grandson," *Deutsches Waffen Journal* 33 (1997), 752-57.

Wozel, Heidrun. *Turniere: Exponate aus dem Historischen Museum zu Dresden*. Berlin: Militärverlag der Deutschen Demokratische Republik, 1979.

Zaky, 'Abd al-Rahman. "Introduction to the Study of Islamic Arms and Armour," *Gladius* 1 (1961), 17-29.

Zijlstra-Zweens, H.M. *Of His Array Telle I No Lenger Tale: Aspects of Costume, Arms and Armour in Western Europe, 1200-1400*. Amsterdam, 1988.

Żygulski, Zdzisław, Jr. "The Battle of Orsha." In: *Art, Arms and Armour: An International Anthology*. Vol I: *1979-80*. Ed. Robert Held. Chiasso: Acquafresca Editrice, 1979, pp. 108-43.

Żygulski, Zdzisław, Jr. "Italian Arms, Armour and Insignia in Poland," *Armi antiche* 8 (1961), 19-44.

Żygulski, Zdzisław, Jr. *Stara broń w polskich zbiorach*. Warsaw: Krajowa Agencja Wydawnicza, 1982.

Military Technology – Premodern – Armor

Ailes, Adrian. "The Knight, Heraldry and Armour: The Role of Recognition and the Origins of Heraldry." In: *Medieval Knighthood, IV*. Ed. C. Harper-Bill and R. Harvey. Woodbridge, 1992, pp. 1-21.

Alexander, D.G. "Decorated and Inscribed Mail Shirts in Metropolitan Museum," *Waffen- und Köstumkunde* 27 (1985), 29-36.

Al-Tarsusi. "Un traité d'armurerie composé pour Saladin," ed. and trans. C. Cahen, *Bulletin d'études Orientales* 12 (1947-48), 103-26.

Anstee, J.W. "Fragments of Roman 'Bronze' Scale Armour from Corbridge," *The Museums Journal* 53 (Nov 1953), 200-02.

Anzelewsky, Fedja. "Erzherzog Maximilians schwere Rossharnisch von 1480," *Waffen- und Kostümkunde* 5 (1963), 77-88.

Anzelewsky, Fedja. "Das Phänomen des Historismus und die frühbarocke Bronzenachbildung einer spätgotischen Rüstung: Ihre Bedeutung für Harischforschung," *Waffen- und Köstumkunde* 36 (1994), 129-36.

Armamento difensivo trecentesco dalle collezioni Carrand e Ressman. Florence: Museo Nazionale del Bargello, 1984.

Armours of Henry VIII: Treasures of the Tower. London: Her Majesty's Stationery Office, 1977.

Aroldi, A.M. "Pompeo della Chiesa ultimo armaiolo milanese," *Armi antiche* 3 (1956), 121-27.

Arnold, Janet. "The Jupon or Coat-Armour of the Black Prince in Canterbury Cathedral," *Church Monuments* 8 (1993), 12-24.

Arwidsson, G. "Armour of the Vendel Period," *Acta archaeologica (Copenhagen)* 10 (1939), 31-59.

Auer, Alfred. "Dictung und Wahrheit: Harnische und Kostüme der Grabmalsfiguren." In: *Ruhm und Sinnlichkeit: Innsbrucker Bronzeguss. Von Kaiser Maximilian I. bis Erzherzog Ferdinand Karl*. Ed. Gert Ammann. Innsbruck: Tiroler Landesmuseum Ferdinandeum, 1996, pp. 140-97.

Augustyniak, Jerzy. "Gantelet–Fragment d'armure datant du XVIe siècle et provenant du château d'Inowłódz, Dép. De Piotrków (Pologne centrale)," *Fasciculi archaeologiae historicae* 2 (1987), 7-9.

Barnes, H.D. "A Fifteenth-Century Armourer's Letter," *Zeitschrift für historische Waffen- und Kostümkunde* 14 (1935-36), 65-66.

Basco, Jean. *The Armour Court*. Toronto: Royal Ontario Museum, 1970.

Beaby, Mark and Thom Richardson. "Hardened Leather Armour," *Royal Armouries Yearbook* 2 (1997), 64-71.

Beaulieu, M. and J. Baylé. *Le costume en Bourgogne de Philippe le Hardi à la mort de Charles le Téméraire (1364-1477)*. Paris, 1956.

Becher, C., Ortwin Gamber, and W. Irtenknauf. *Das Stuttgarter Harnisch-Musterbuch, 1548-1563*. Vienna: Verlag Anton Schroll and Co., 1980.

Blair, Claude. "Church Armour," *Connoisseur* (May 1961), 294.

Blair, Claude. "The Cuirass and the Garniture," *Discovering Antiques* 7 (1970), 160-64.

Blair, Claude. "The Emperor Maximilian's Gift of Armour to Henry VIII and the Silvered and Engraved Armour at the Tower of London," *Archaeologia* 99 (1965), 1-56.

Blair, Claude. *European Armour: circa 1066 to circa 1700*. London: B.T. Batsford, 1958.

Blair, Claude. "Greenwich Armour," *Transactions of the Greenwich and Lewisham Antiquarian Society* 10 (1985), 6-11.

Blair, Claude. "The Informed Eye: King Henry VIII's Silvered and Engraved Armour," *Apollo* 129 (Apr 1989), 266-67.

Blair, Claude. "King Henry VIII's Tonlet Armour," *Journal of the Arms and Armour Society* 15 (1995-98), 85-108.

Blair, Claude. "New Light on Four Alamain Armours," *Connoisseur* (Aug 1959), 17-20; (Dec 1959), 240-44.

Blair, Claude. "Notes on Armour from Chalcis," *Arms and Armour at the Dorchester* (1982), 7-14.

Blakeley, Erik. "Tournament Garniture of Robert Dudley, Earl of Leicester," *Royal Armouries* 2 (1997), 55-63.

Boccia, Lionella Giorgio. "Ancient Italian Pieces in the Kienbusch Collection." In: *Studies in European Arms and Armor: The C. Otto von Kienbusch Collection in the Philadelphia Museum of Art.* Philadelphia: Philadelphia Museum of Art, 1990, pp. 32-65.

Boccia, Lionella Giorgio. "Le armature di Paolo Uccello," *L'arte* 11-12 (Dec 1970), 55-91.

Boccia, Lionella Giorgio. *Le armature di S Maria delle Grazie di Curtatone di Mantova e l'armatura Lombarda del '400.* Bramante: Busto Arsizio, 1982.

Boccia, Lionella Giorgio. *L'arte dell'armature Italiana.* Milan, 1967.

Boccia, Lionella Giorgio. "The Devil's Mask." In: *Art, Arms and Armour: An International Anthology.* Vol I: *1979-80.* Ed. Robert Held. Chiasso: Acquafresca Editrice, 1979, pp. 30-52.

Boccia, Lionella Giorgio. "Gli inventari secenteschi delle armerie medicee: appunti lessicali sull' armamento difensivo." In: *Convegno nazionale sui lessici tecnici del sei e sttecento.* Pisa, 1980, I:319-36.

Boccia, Lionella Giorgio and Claude Blair, ed. *Dizionari terminologici: Armi difensive dal medioevo all'età moderna.* Florence, 1982.

Boccia, Lionella Giorgio and E.T. Coelho. "L'armamento di cuoio e ferro nel trecento Italiano," *L'illustrazione italiani* 1.2 (1972), 24-27.

Boccia, Lionella Giorgio and José-A. Godoy. "La armàdura del Principe Emanuale Filiberto de Saboya (1588-1624)," *Reales sitios* 24, no. 93.3 (1987), 57-68.

Boccia, Lionella Giorgio, F. Rossi, and M. Morin. *Armi e armature Lombarde.* Milan: Electa Editrice, 1980.

Bocheński, Zbigniew. "L'armure en écailles polonaise au XVII siècle," *Armi antiche* 8 (1961), 3-18.

Bocheński, Zbigniew. "Próba określenia genezy Polskiej zbroi husarkiej," *Muzealnictwo wojskowe* 2 (1964), 141-67.

Böhne, Clement. "Werkstofftechnische Fragen bei deutscher Plattnerarbeiten," *Waffen- und Kostümkunde* 3 (1961), 47-53.

Boockmann, Hartmut. "Die Ritter und ihre Harnische." In: *Eisenkleider: Plattnerarbeiten aus drei Jahrhunderten aus der Sammlung des Deutschen Historischen Museums*. Berlin: Deutsches Historisches Museum, 1992, pp. 9-24.

Borg, Alan. "A Crusader in Borrowed Armour: The History of a Museum Piece," *Country Life* (July 18, 1974), 168-69.

Bosson, Clément. "L'armure à cannelures," *Armes anciennes* 2.4 (1958), 89-107.

Bottomley, Ian. "A Remarkable Armour," *Royal Armouries Yearbook* 2 (1997), 144-48.

Brewer, C.W. "Metallographic Examination of Medieval and Post-Medieval Iron Armour," *Historical Metallurgy* 15 (1981), 1-8.

Bruhn de Hoffmeyer, Ada. "Deux armures de rois danois," *Armi antiche* 2 (1955), 3-27.

Buff, A. "Augsburger Plattner Renaissancezeit," *Algemeine Beilage* (1892), 228-30.

Burgess, E. Martin. "Further Research into the Construction of Mail Garments," *Antiquaries Journal* 33 (July-Oct 1953), 193-202.

Burgess, E. Martin. "The Mail-Maker's Technique," *Antiquaries Journal* 33 (1953), 48-55, 193-202.

Burgess, E. Martin. "The Mail Shirt from Sinigaglia," *Archaeological Journal* 37 (1957), 199-205.

Burgess, E. Martin. "A Mail Shirt from the Hearst Collection," *Archaeological Journal* 38 (1958), 197-204.

Burgess, E. Martin. "A Reply to Cyril Stanley Smith on Mail Making Methods," *Technology and Culture* 1.2 (1960), 51-55.

Burgess, E. Martin and H. Russell Robinson. "A 14th-Century Mail Hood in the Royal Scottish Museum, Edinburgh," *Journal of the Arms and Armour Society* 2 (1956-58), 59-65.

Buttin, Charles. *Les bardes articulées au temps de Maximilien Ier: Etude sur l'armament chevaleresque, XVe-XVIe siècles.* Strasbourg, 1930.

Buttin, Charles. "Notes sur les armures à l'épruve (XIVe-XVIe siècle)," *Revue Savoisienne* 42 (1901), 60-92, 150-210.

Buttin, François. "Claude Fauchet, les brigands et la brigadine," *Revue Savoisienne* (1973), 1-30.

Caldwell, David H. "Fragments of a Brigadine from Coldingham Priory, Berwickshire," *Proceedings of the Society of Antiquaries of Scotland* 106 (1977), 219-21.

Cederlöf, Olle. "The Sutton Hoo Ship-Burial and Armour during the Vendel Period," *Journal of the Arms and Armour Society* 1 (1955), 153-64.

Cessford, Craig. "The Borgue Armour and the Dumfriesshire *Spangenhelm,*" *Transactions of the Dumfriesshire and Galloway Natural History and Antiquarian Society* 69 (1994), 73-80.

Clark, G. "Beowulf's Armour," *Journal of English Literary History* 32 (1965), 409-41.

Coulston, J.C.N. "Later Roman Armour, 3rd-6th Centuries, A.D.," *Journal of Roman Military Equipment* 1 (1990), 139-60.

Cripps-Day, F.H. *Fragmenta armamentaria. III: An Introduction to the Study of Greenwich Armour.* Frome, 1944.

Cripps-Day, F.H. *On Armour Preserved in Churches.* London, 1922.

Czarnecka, Katarzyna. "The Re-Use of Roman Military Equipment in Barbarian Contexts: A Chain-Mail Souvenir?" *Journal of Roman Military Equipment Studies* 5 (1994), 245-53.

Daehnhardt, Rainer. "Ein Rüstingsfund des Lissaboner Arsenals," *Waffen- und Köstumkunde* 35 (1993), 57-64.

Dillon, Harold A. *Armour.* Rpt. London: Arms and Armour Press, 1968.

Dillon, Harold A. "The pasguard, garde de cou, Brech-Rand, Stoss-Kragen or Randt, and the volant-piece," *Archaeological Journal* 66 (1900), 129-35, 433.

Dillon, Harold A. "A Letter of Sir Henry Lee, 1590, on the Trial of Iron for Armour," *Archaeologia* 51 (1888), 167-72.

Dinzelbacher, Peter. "Quellenprobleme bei der Erforschung hochmittelalterliche Bewaffnung," *Mediaevistik* 2 (1989), 43-79.

Dondi, Giorgio. "Armures de Pompeo della Cesa à l'Armeria Reale de Turni." In: *Proceedings of the Ninth Triennial Congress of the International Association of Museums of Arms and Military History*. Quantico: Marine Corps Association, 1981, pp. 166-76.

Dondi, Giorgio. "Un corsaletto di barriera di Carlo Emanuele I di Savoia," *Armi antiche* (1980), 3-12.

Dove, Anthony B.L. "On the Prolonged Use of Fifteenth Century Armour," *Riccardian* 4 (June 1977), 12-14.

Dufty, A.R. "Two Paintings from the Reign of Elizabeth I," *Connoisseur* (Jan 1977), 20-24.

Dufty, A.R and W. Reid. *European Armour in the Tower of London*. London, Her Majesty's Stationery Office, 1965.

Eaves, Ian. "The Greenwich Armour and Locking Gauntlet of Sir Henry Lee in the Collection of The Worshipful Company of Armourers and Brasiers," *Journal of the Arms and Armour Society* 16 (1999), 133-64.

Eaves, Ian. "The Jack of Plate." In: *Beeston Castle, Cheshire: A Report on the Excavations, 1968-85*. Ed. Peter Ellis. Archaeological Report, no. 23. London: English Heritage, 1993, pp. 161-64.

Eaves, Ian. "On the Remains of a Jack of Plate Excavated from Beeston Castle in Cheshire," *Journal of the Arms and Armour Society* 13 (1989-91), 81-154.

Eaves, Ian. "The Tournament Armours of King Henry VIII of England," *Livrustkammaren* 19 (1993), 2-45.

Eaves, Ian and Thom Richardson. "The Treytz Armour of Gaudenz von Matsch at Schloss Churburg," *Journal of the Arms and Armour Society* 13 supplement (1990), 1-22.

Eaves, Ian and Thom Richardson. "The Warwick Shaffron," *Journal of the Arms and Armour Society* 12 (1986-88), 217-22.

Edge, David A. "The Greenwich Field Armour of Thomas Sackville, Lord Buckhurst," *Park Lane Arms Fair* 9 (1992), 5-11.

Elwell-Sutton, L.P. "Persian Armour Inscriptions." In: *Islamic Arms and Armour*. Ed. Robert Elgood. London: Scolar Press, 1979, pp. 5-19.

Exhibition of Spanish Royal Armour, Tower of London, 9 April-25 September 1960. London: Her Majesty's Stationery Office, 1960.

Fanger, W. "Innsbrucker Plattnerarbeiten in einer Braunschweiger Sammlung," *Waffen- und Kostümkunde* 22 (1980), 65-70.

Fanger, W. "Stilmerkmale Braunschweiger Plattnerarbeiten." In: *Festschrift zur Ausstellung Bruswiek 1031-Braunschweig 1981: Die Stadt Heinrichs des Löwens von den Anfängen bis zur Gegenwart*. Braunschweig: Städtisches Museum, 1981, pp. 259-74.

ffoulkes, Charles J. "Armour from the Rotunda, Woolwich, Transferred to the Armouries of the Tower, 1927," *Archaeologia* 78 (1928), 61-72.

ffoulkes, Charles J. *The Armourer and His Craft from the XIth to the XVth Century*. London: Methuen, 1912; rpt. New York: Dover Publications, 1988.

ffoulkes, Charles J. "The Armourers' Company of London and the Greenwich School of Armourers," *Archaeologia* 76 (1927), 41-58.

ffoulkes, Charles J. "On Italian Armour from Chalcis in the Ethnological Museum at Athens," *Archaeologia* 62 (1911), 382-90.

ffoulkes, Charles J. "Some Aspects of the Craft of the Armourer," *Archaeologia* 79 (1929), 13-28.

Fischer, Dick. "The Gothic Knight: European Cavalry Armour, Late 15th Century," *Military Illustrated* 70 (Mar 1994), 34-35.

Fliegel, S.N. *The Making of Armour*. Cleveland: Cleveland Museum of Art, 1993.

Frangioni, Luciana. "Una cotta di maglia milanese a Firenze sulla fine del trecento." In: *Studii in memoria di Federigo Melis*. Florence: Giannini Editore, 1978, II:479-95; rpt. *Armi antiche* (1982), 3-18.

Gabra-Sanders, Thea. "Part of a 16th Century Quilted Jack of Plate found at Craigievar Castle, Aberdeenshire," *Journal of the Arms and Armour Society* 14 (1992-94), 147-52.

Gaibi, Agostino. "L'arte bresciana delle armature: Contributo alla storia armi defensive Italiane," *Armi antiche* (1963), 15-50.

Gaier, Claude. "L'armure des chevaliers Templiers, Hospitaliers et Teutoniques dans la région de Liège," *Musée d'armes* 28 (1980), 5-11.

Gaier, Claude. "L'évolution et l'usage de l'armement personnel défensif au pays de Liège du XIIe au XIVe siècle," *Waffen- und Kostümkunde* 4 (1962), 65-86; In: *Armes et combats dans l'univers médiéval*. Liege, 1995, pp. 125-49.

Gamber, Ortwin. "Der Harnisch im 16. Jahrhundert," *Waffen- und Kostümkunde* 41 (1999), 97-120.

Gamber, Ortwin. "Die Harnischgarnitur," *Livrustkammaren* 7 (1955-57).

Gamber, Ortwin. "Eine Harnischgarnitur Maximilians I. von Lorenz Helmschmeid," *Waffen- und Kostümkunde* 1 (1959), 3-15.

Gamber, Ortwin. "Harnischstudien: V: Stilgeschichte des Plattenharnisches von den Anfängen bis um 1440," *Jahrbuch der Kunsthistorischen Sammlungen in Wien* 50 (1953), 53-92.

Gamber, Ortwin. "Harnischstudien: VI: Stilgeschichte des Plattenharnisches von 1440-1510," *Jahrbuch der Kunsthistorischen Sammlungen in Wien* 51 (1955), 31-102.

Gamber, Ortwin. "Der Italienische Harnisch im 16. Jahrhundert," *Jahrbuch der Kunsthistorischen Sammlungen in Wien* 54 (1958), 73-120.

Gamber, Ortwin. "Die Königlich Englische Hofplattnerei Martin von Royne und Erasmus Kirkener," *Jahrbuch der Kunsthistorischen Sammlungen in Wien* 59 (1963), 7-39.

Gamber, Ortwin. "Die Kriegrüstungen Erherzog Ferdinands II. aus der Prager Hofplatternei," *Jahrbuch der Kunsthistorischen Sammlungen in Wien* 68 (1972), 109-52.

Gamber, Ortwin. "Der Plattner Kunz Lochner–Harnische als Zeugnisse Habsburgischer Politik," *Jahrbuch der Kunsthistorischen Sammlungen in Wien* 80 (1984), 35-60.

Gamber, Ortwin. "Die Turnierharnisch zur Zeit König Maximilians I und das Thunsche Skizzenbuch," *Jahrbuch der Kunsthistorischen Sammlungen in Wien* 53 (1957), 33-70.

Gamber, Ortwin, ed. *Glossarium armorum: Arma defensiva*. Graz: Druck- und Verlagsanstalt, 1972.

Genevoy, R. "Notes sur l'armureie impériale d'Arbois (1495-1509?) et sur les armures de Claude de Vaudrey et de Maximilien Ier au Kunst historisches Museum de Vienne," *Nouvelle revue franc-comtoise* (1955), 208-22.

Ghyczy, Paul. "Über Ailettes," *Zeitschrift für historisches Waffen- und Köstumkunde* 12 (1929-31), 242-45.

Gilmour, Brian. "Iron Age Mail in Britain," *Royal Armouries Yearbook* 2 (1997), 26-35.

Godoy, José-A. "Armeros Milaneses en Navarra: La producción de Eugui," *Gladius* 19 (1999), 231-60.

Godoy, José-A. "Notes sur quelques armures du 'Maestro dal Castello'," *Genava* n.s. 35 (1987), 11-34.

Godoy, José-A. "Quelques jalons sur l'influence d'Antonio Tempesta (1555-1630) dans l'art des armuriers," *Genava* n.s. 29 (1981), 107-38.

Gorelik, Michael V. "Oriental Armour of the Near and Middle East from the Eighth to the Fifteenth Centuries as Shown in Works of Art." In: *Islamic Arms and Armour*. Ed. Robert Elgood. London: Scolar Press, 1979, pp. 30-63.

Grancsay, Stephen V. "The Armor of Don Alvaró de Cabrera," *Metropolitan Museum of Art Bulletin* n.s. 10 (June 1952), 275-85; in: *Arms and Armor: Essays by Stephen V. Grancsay from The Metropolitan Museum of Art Bulletin, 1920-1964*. New York: The Metropolitan Museum of Art, 1986, pp. 381-96.

Grancsay, Stephen V. *The Armor of Galiot de Gehouilhac*. Metropolitan Museum of Art Papers, no. 4. New York: Metropolitan Museum of Art, 1937.

Grancsay, Stephen V. "The Armor of Henry I de Montmorency," *Metropolitan Museum of Art Bulletin* 34 (Dec 1939), 284-86; in: *Arms and Armor: Essays by Stephen V. Grancsay from The Metropolitan Museum of Art Bulletin, 1920-1964*. New York: The Metropolitan Museum of Art, 1986, pp. 241-44.

Grancsay, Stephen V. "The Armor of Henry II of France from the Louvre," *Metropolitan Museum of Art Bulletin* n.s. 11 (Oct 1952), 68-80; in: *Arms and Armor: Essays by Stephen V. Grancsay from The Metropolitan Museum of Art Bulletin, 1920-1964*. New York: The Metropolitan Museum of Art, 1986, pp. 395-411.

Grancsay, Stephen V. "Armor with Etching Attributed to Daniel Hopfer," *Metropolitan Museum of Art Bulletin* 34 (Aug 1939), 190-92; in: *Arms and Armor: Essays by Stephen V. Grancsay from The Metropolitan Museum of Art Bulletin, 1920-1964*. New York: The Metropolitan Museum of Art, 1986, pp. 232-37.

Grancsay, Stephen V. "An Augsburg Backplate," *Metropolitan Museum of Art Bulletin* 33 (Aug 1938), 1737-80; in: *Arms and Armor: Essays by Stephen V. Grancsay from The Metropolitan Museum of Art Bulletin, 1920-1964*. New York: The Metropolitan Museum of Art, 1986, pp. 209-12.

Grancsay, Stephen V. *Catalogue of Armor*. Worcester: The John Woodman Higgins Armory, 1961.

Grancsay, Stephen V. "An Element of the Armor of the Queen's Champion," *Metropolitan Museum of Art Bulletin* 31 (Nov 1936), 233-35; in: *Arms and Armor: Essays by Stephen V. Grancsay from The Metropolitan Museum of Art Bulletin, 1920-1964*. New York: The Metropolitan Museum of Art, 1986, pp. 159-62.

Grancsay, Stephen V. "Elements of Armor Made for Christian I of Saxony," *Metropolitan Museum of Art Bulletin* 35 (Oct 1940), 203-04; in: *Arms and Armor: Essays by Stephen V. Grancsay from The Metropolitan Museum of Art Bulletin, 1920-1964*. New York: The Metropolitan Museum of Art, 1986. pp. 256-59.

Grancsay, Stephen V. "Enriched Breastplate and Volant Plate," *Metropolitan Museum of Art Bulletin* 23 (July 1928), 186-89; in: *Arms and Armor: Essays by Stephen V. Grancsay from The Metropolitan Museum of Art Bulletin, 1920-1964*. New York: The Metropolitan Museum of Art, 1986, pp. 28-30.

Grancsay, Stephen V. "The Genouilhac Armor," *Metropolitan Museum of Art Bulletin* 29 (Nov 1934), 190-91; in: *Arms and Armor: Essays by Stephen V. Grancsay from The Metropolitan Museum of Art Bulletin, 1920-1964*. New York: The Metropolitan Museum of Art, 1986, pp. 134-36.

Grancsay, Stephen V. " A Gift of Embossed Armor," *Metropolitan Museum of Art Bulletin* 34 (Apr 1939), 84-88; in: *Arms and Armor: Essays by Stephen V. Grancsay from The Metropolitan Museum of Art Bulletin, 1920-1964*. New York: The Metropolitan Museum of Art, 1986, pp. 227-30.

Grancsay, Stephen V. "A Harness of a King of France," *Metropolitan Museum of Art Bulletin* 35 (Jan 1940), 12-17; in: *Arms and Armor: Essays by Stephen V. Grancsay from The Metropolitan Museum of Art Bulletin, 1920-1964*. New York: The Metropolitan Museum of Art, 1986, pp. 244-49.

Grancsay, Stephen V. "A Historical Horse Armor," *Metropolitan Museum of Art Bulletin* 27 (July 1932), 176-78; in: *Arms and Armor: Essays by Stephen V. Grancsay from The Metropolitan Museum of Art Bulletin, 1920-1964*. New York: The Metropolitan Museum of Art, 1986, pp. 104-07.

Grancsay, Stephen V. "An Historical Spanish Suit of Armour," *Apollo* (Nov 1974), 64-68.

Grancsay, Stephen V. "The Interrelationships of Costume and Armor," *Metropolitan Museum of Art Bulletin* n.s. 7 (Feb 1950), 176-88; in: *Arms and Armor: Essays by Stephen V. Grancsay from The Metropolitan Museum of Art Bulletin, 1920-1964*. New York: The Metropolitan Museum of Art, 1986, pp. 362-77.

Grancsay, Stephen V. "A Jousting Harness," *Philadelphia Museum Bulletin* (Aut 1956), 3-7.

Grancsay, Stephen V. "Just How Good Was Armor," *True* (Apr 1954), 45-47, 89-92.

Grancsay, Stephen V. "Knights in Armor," *Metropolitan Museum of Art Bulletin* n.s. 6 (Feb 1948), 178-88; in: *Arms and Armor: Essays by Stephen V. Grancsay from The Metropolitan Museum of Art Bulletin, 1920-1964.* New York: The Metropolitan Museum of Art, 1986, pp. 313-28.

Grancsay, Stephen V. "Lucio Piccinino, Master Armourer of the Renaissance," *Metropolitan Museum of Art Bulletin* n.s. 22 (Apr 1964), 257-71; in: *Arms and Armor: Essays by Stephen V. Grancsay from The Metropolitan Museum of Art Bulletin, 1920-1964.* New York: The Metropolitan Museum of Art, 1986, pp. 519-36.

Grancsay, Stephen V. "Maximilian Armour," *Metropolitan Museum of Art Bulletin* 23 (Apr 1928), 100-03; in: *Arms and Armor: Essays by Stephen V. Grancsay from The Metropolitan Museum of Art Bulletin, 1920-1964.* New York: The Metropolitan Museum of Art, 1986, pp. 22-26.

Grancsay, Stephen V. "A Maximilian Helmet and Gauntlet Retrieved," *Metropolitan Museum of Art Bulletin* 33 (Dec 1938), 268-71; in: *Arms and Armor: Essays by Stephen V. Grancsay from The Metropolitan Museum of Art Bulletin, 1920-1964.* New York: The Metropolitan Museum of Art, 1986, pp. 212-15.

Grancsay, Stephen V. "Medieval Armor in a Prayer Book," *Metropolitan Museum of Art Bulletin* n.s. 16 (June 1958), 287-92; in: *Arms and Armor: Essays by Stephen V. Grancsay from The Metropolitan Museum of Art Bulletin, 1920-1964.* New York: The Metropolitan Museum of Art, 1986, pp. 463-70.

Grancsay, Stephen V. "A Miniature Portrait of the Earl of Cumberland in Armor," *Metropolitan Museum of Art Bulletin* n.s. 15 (Jan 1957), 120-22; in: *Arms and Armor: Essays by Stephen V. Grancsay from The Metropolitan Museum of Art Bulletin, 1920-1964.* New York: The Metropolitan Museum of Art, 1986, pp. 439-43.

Grancsay, Stephen V. "Museum Armor and a Van Dyck Portrait from Vienna," *Metropolitan Museum of Art Bulletin* n.s. 7 (May 1950), 270-73; in: *Arms and Armor: Essays by Stephen V. Grancsay from The Metropolitan Museum of Art Bulletin, 1920-1964.* New York: The Metropolitan Museum of Art, 1986, pp. 377-81.

Grancsay, Stephen V. "Notes of European Chain Mail," *Metropolitan Museum of Art Bulletin* 23 (Mar 1928), 82-85; in: *Arms and Armor: Essays by Stephen V. Grancsay from The Metropolitan Museum of Art Bulletin, 1920-1964*. New York: The Metropolitan Museum of Art, 1986, pp. 20-22.

Grancsay, Stephen V. "A Renaissance Brigandine," *Metropolitan Museum of Art Bulletin* 37 (1942), 132-36; in: *Arms and Armor: Essays by Stephen V. Grancsay from The Metropolitan Museum of Art Bulletin, 1920-1964*. New York: The Metropolitan Museum of Art, 1986, pp. 282-86.

Grancsay, Stephen V. "A Sixteenth-Century Parade Armor," *Metropolitan Museum of Art Bulletin* 29 (1934), 102-04; in: *Arms and Armor: Essays by Stephen V. Grancsay from The Metropolitan Museum of Art Bulletin, 1920-1964*. New York: The Metropolitan Museum of Art, 1986, pp. 122-27.

Grancsay, Stephen V. "A Stained-Glass Saint Michael in Armor," *Metropolitan Museum of Art Bulletin* 23 (Nov 1928), 268-71; in: *Arms and Armor: Essays by Stephen V. Grancsay from The Metropolitan Museum of Art Bulletin, 1920-1964*. New York: The Metropolitan Museum of Art, 1986, pp. 38-41.

Grancsay, Stephen V. "A Young Prince's Enriched Armor," *Metropolitan Museum of Art Bulletin* 34 (Nov 1939), 260-63; in: *Arms and Armor: Essays by Stephen V. Grancsay from The Metropolitan Museum of Art Bulletin, 1920-1964*. New York: The Metropolitan Museum of Art, 1986, pp. 238-41.

Gravett, Christopher. "Early Tournament Armour," *Livrustkammaren* 19 (1993), 62-88.

Grove, J.P. "A History of English Armour, 1511-1644," *Journal of the Society for Army Historical Research* 36 (Sep 1958), xi-xix.

Harnische. Dresden: Historisches Museum, 1963.

Hayward, John F. "Armour Fit for a King," *Country Life* (Dec 17, 1964), 1706-07.

Hayward, John F. "Armourers and Gunmakers of the French Crown," *Journal of the Arms and Armour Society* 1 (1955), 215-18.

Hayward, John F. "The Armours of the Family of d'Avalos, Marchese di Pescara e del Vasto," *Waffen- und Kostümkunde* 1 (1959), 47-53.

Hayward, John F. "Les collections du Palais de Capodimonte, Naples. V: Les armures," *Armes anciennes* 1.7 (1956), 147-65.

Hayward, John F. *European Armour*. London: Her Majesty's Stationery Office, 1965.

Hayward, John F. "Exhibition of Spanish Royal Armour, Tower of London," *Burlington Magazine* (June 1960), 271.

Hayward, John F. "Filippo Orsoni, Designer, and Caremolo Modrone, Armourer of Mantua," *Waffen- und Kostümkunde* 24 (1982), 87-102.

Hayward, John F. "A Newly Discovered Greenwich Armour," *Connoisseur* 141 (1958), 140-43.

Hayward, John F. "The Revival of Roman Armour in the Renaissance." In: *Art, Arms and Armour: An International Anthology*. Vol I: *1979-80*. Ed. Robert Held. Chiasso: Acquafresca Editrice, 1979, pp. 144-63.

Holmes, Martin. "Genouilhac Reconsidered: A New Theory about a Famous Armour," *Connoisseur* (July 1972), 177-81.

Hummelberger, Walter. "Die Ordnungen der Wiener Plattner und Sarwürcher," *Waffen- und Kostümkunde* 3 (1961), 91-107.

James, Lawrence. "The Cost and Distribution of Armour in the 14th Century," *Transactions of the Monumental Brass Society* 10.4 (Oct 1967), 226-31.

Jarnuszkiewicz, C. "A Note on the Hungarian Pallash: with a Special Reference to an Example in the Wallace Collection," *Journal of the Arms and Armour Society* 6 (1968-70), 179-80.

Javornik, Ivan. "Kratak pregled razvoja zaštitnog oružja," *Vesnik* 1 (1954), 18-29.

Jones, Peter N. "The Attack of Plate Armour by Longbow Arrows," *Château Gaillard* 11 (1983), 167-68.

Jones, Peter N. "A Short History of the Attack of Armour," *Metallurgist and Material Technologist* 16(1984), 247-50.

Karcheski, Walter J., Jr. "An Armour by Pompeo Della Cesa, in the Higgins Armoury Museum, Worcester," *Journal of the Arms and Armour Society* 12 (1986-88), 394-401.

Karcheski, Walter J., Jr. "Notes on a Newly-Identified Armour by the Flemish Master 'MP', in the Smith Art Museum, Springfield, MA," *Journal of the Arms and Armour Society* 11 (1983-85), 307-14.

Karcheski, Walter J., Jr. "The Nuremburg *Stechzeuge* Armours," *Journal of the Arms and Armour Society* 14 (1992-94), 181-217.

Kelly, Francis M. "A Knight's Armour of the Early XIVth Century, Being the Inventory of Raoul de Nesle," *Burlington Magazine* 24.4 (Mar 1905), 457-69.

Kern, Georg Ritter von. "A evolução estilística da armadura canelada/The Stylistic Evolution of the Fluted Armour," *Boletin da sociedade Portuguesa de armas antiguas/Bulletin of the Portuguese Academy of Antique Arms* 1 (1997), 75-77.

Kirpičnikov, Anatolij N. *Snaraženie vsadnika i verschogo konja na Rusi IX-XIII vv.* Leningrad, 1973.

Knowles, Richard. "A Defensive Garment in the Church of Rothwell, West Yorkshire," *Journal of the Arms and Armour Society* 11 (1983-85), 299-305.

Kozhomberdiyev, L. and Y. Khudyakov. "Reconstruction of Ancient Turkic Armour from Sary-Djon Monument." In: *Bulletin no. 17: International Association for the Study of the Cultures of Central Asia (UNESCO).* Moscow, 1990, pp. 56-62.

Krenn, Peter. "Die Grazer Plattner und ihre Werke." In: *Das stierische Handwerk.* Graz, 1970, pp. 273-97.

Krenn, Peter. *Harnisch und Helm: Landeszeughaus Graz, am Steiermärkischen Landesmuseum Joanneum.* Graz: Verlag Hofstetter, 1987.

Lachaud, Frédérique. "Armour and Military Dress in Thirteenth- and Early-Fourteenth-Century England." In: *Armies, Chivalry and Warfare in Medieval Britain and France: Proceedings of the 1995 Harlaxton Symposium.* Ed. M. Strickland. Stamford, 1998, pp. 344-69.

Lachouque, Henri. *Dix siècles de costume militaire*. Paris: Hachette, 1963.

Lacy, Michael S. *Coat of Plates to Brigandine: The Evolution of Cloth Covered Armour, 1250-1500*. Unpublished thesis. Reading: Reading University, 1992.

Landshuter Plattnerkunst: Katalog der Ausstellung Stadtmuseum. Landshut, 1975.

La Rocca, Donald. "The Fico Armours: A Study in Connoisseurship and Secular Iconography," *Journal of the Arms and Armour Society* 13 (1989-91), 1-75.

La Rocca, Donald. "A Notable Group of Late Sixteenth-Century Etched Italian Armour," *Journal of the Arms and Armour Society* 16.4 (Mar 2000), 181-97

La Rocca, Donald. "Notes of the Mail Chausse," *The Journal of the Arms and Armor Society* 15 (1995-98), 69-84.

Larsen, Henrietta M. "The Armor Business in the Middle Ages," *Business History Review* 14 (1940), 49-64.

Lavin, James D. "The Gift of James I to Felipe III of Spain," *Journal of the Arms and Armour Society* 14 (1992-94), 64-88.

Lefort des Ylouses, Emile. "Le sceau de la ville de Fismes en Champagne (1308)," *Revue Française d'héraldique et de sigillographie* 64 (1994), 105-14.

Legge, D.M. "'Osbercs doublez': The Description of Armour in Twelfth Century Chansons de Geste." In: *Société Rançesvals: Proceedings of the Fifth International Conference*. Oxford, 1970, pp. 132-42.

Loades, Mike. "The Wallace Collection's Armour for Man and Horse: Stirring Image of Medieval Chivalry or Sentimental Sham?" *Classic Arms and Militaria* 2.2 (Mar/Apr 1995), 18-23.

Macoir, G. *La salle des armures du Musée de la Porte de Hal à Bruxelles*. Brussels, 1910.

Mann, James. "The Etched Decoration of Armour," *Proceedings of the British Academy* 28 (1942), 17-45.

Mann, James. *European Arms and Armour*. Vol. II: *Armor*. Wallace Collection Catalogues. London: Trustees of the Wallace Collection, 1962.

Mann, James. *Exhibition of Armour Made in the Royal Workshops at Greenwich at the Tower of London*. London: Her Majesty's Stationery Office, 1951.

Mann, James. "A Further Account of the Armour Preserved in the Sanctuary of the Madonna della Grazie," *Archaeologia* 87 (1937), 311-52.

Mann, James. "The Making of Armour," *Parsons Journal* 9.50 (1960), 22-33.

Mann, James. "The Master of the Snails and Dragon-Flies," *Waffen- und Kostümkunde* 3 (1961), 14-27.

Mann, James. "The Nomenclature of Armour," *Transactions of the Monumental Brass Society* 9 (1961), 414-28.

Mann, James. "Notes on the Armour of the Maximilian Period and the Italian Wars," *Archaeologia* 79 (1929), 217-44.

Mann, James. "Notes on the Armour Worn in Spain from the Tenth to the Fifteenth Century," *Archaeologia* 83 (1933), 285-305.

Mann, James. "Notes on the Evolution of Plate Armour in Germany in the Fourteenth and Fifteenth Century," *Archaeologia* 84 (1935), 69-97.

Mann, James. "A Pair of Gothic Cuisses by Jörg Wagner of Innsbruck." In: *Beiträge zur Kunstgeschichte Tirols: Festschrift für Landeskonservator Dr. Oswald Graf Trapp*. Innsbruck: Universitätsverlag Wagner, 1959, pp. 101-03.

Mann, James. "The Sanctuary of the Madonna delle Grazie With Notes on the Evolution of Italian Armour During the Fifteenth Century," *Archaeologia* 80 (1930), 117-42.

Mann, James. "Two Fourteenth-Century Gauntlets from Ripon Cathedral," *Antiquaries Journal* 22 (1942), 113-22.

Maurice, Klaus. "Armour for an Archbishop," *Apollo* (Dec 1970), 474-75.

Melikian-Chirvani, A.S. "The Westward Journey of the Kazhagand," *Journal of the Arms and Armour Society* 11 (1983-85), 8-35.

Metz, Peter. "Ein automatische Tafelspielzeug der Renaissance," *Jahrbuch der Berliner Museen* 12.1 (1970),

Minns, Ellis H. "The Wisby Armour," *Antiquity* 18 (1944), 197-200.

Morello, Giovanni. "Note sulla croce: Armature ed 'abito' dei cavalieri di Malta," *Waffen- und Kostümkunde* 22 (1980), 89-107.

Morrison, Sean. *Armor*. New York: Thomas Y. Crowell Co., 1963.

Nadolski, Andrzej. "Hełm i fragmenty zbroi z XIV wieku znalezione w Siedlatkowie nad Wartą," *Studia i materiały do dziejów dawnego uzbrojenia i ubioru wojskowego* 4 (1969).

Nadolski, Andrzej. "Hełm i fragmenty zbroi z Siedlatków," *Prace i materiały Muzeum Archeologicznego i Etnograficznego w Łodzi* 15 (1968), 89-93.

Nadolski, Andrzej and A. Kosiorek. "Szczątki zbroi średniowiecznej z grodziska w Borówku," *Studia nad kulturą materialną wieków od XIV do XVI: Acta archaeologica Lodziensia* 32 (1986), 33-41.

Nadolski, Andrzej and Z. Wawrzonowska. "Szczątki zbroi ze Spytkowic," *Studia do dziejów dawnego uzbrojenia i ubioru wojskowego* 8 (1982), 19-34.

Neukam, W.G. "Eine Nürnbergersulzbacher Plattenlieferung für Karl IV. in den Jahren 1362-1363: Ein Beitrag zur Nürnberger Waffenfabrikation des 14. Jahrhunderts," *Mitteilungen des Vereins für Geschichte der Stadt Nürnberg* 47 (1956), 124-59.

Newark, Tim. "Decorating Armour: Three Methods of Armour Decoration," *Military Illustrated* 80 (Jan 1995), 26-30.

Nickel, Helmut. "'A harnes all gilte': A Study of the Armor of Galiot de Genouilhac and the Iconography of Its Decoration," *Metropolitan Museum Journal* 5 (1972), 75-124.

Nickel, Helmut. "The Battle of the Crescent," *Metropolitan Museum of Art Bulletin* 24.3 (Nov 1965), 110-27.

Nickel, Helmut. "English Armour in the Metropolitan Museum," *Connoisseur* (Nov 1969), 196-203.

Nickel, Helmut. "Parade Armor for Three Prince Electors in Saxony in the Kienbusch Collection." In: *Studies in European Arms and Armor: The C. Otto von Kienbusch Collection in the Philadelphia Museum of Art.* Philadelphia: Philadelphia Museum of Art, 1992, pp. 10-31.

Nickel, Helmut. "Über Rückensandarten: polnische Husarenflügel, japanische Sashimono und aztiekische Tiahuitzli," *Waffen- und Kostümkunde* 21 (1979), 97-106.

Norman, A.V.B. "Amendments and Additions to the Catalogue of Armour in the Wallace Collection," *Journal of the Arms and Armour Society* 7 (1971-73), 171-230.

Norman, A.V.B. "The Armour on the Van der Goes Altarpiece at Edinburgh," *Journal of the Arms and Armour Society* 2 (1956-58), 116-28.

Norman, A.V.B. "An Early Illustration of Body Armour," *Waffen- und Kostümkunde* 18 (1976).

Norman, A.V.B. "Notes on a Newly Discovered Piece of Fourtenth-Century Armour," *Journal of the Arms and Armour Society* 8 (1974-76), 229-33.

Norman, A.V.B. "A Pauldron in the Scott Collection of Arms and Armour," *Scottish Art Review* 7 (1960), 8-11.

Norris, H.T. "The Hauberk, the Kazāghand, and the cAntar Romance," *Journal of the Arms and Armour Society* 9 (1977-79), 93-101.

Oakeshott, Ewart. *A Knight and His Armour*. London, 1961.

Oberhammer, Vinzenz. "Die Innsbrucker Plattnerkunst," *Tyrol* 6 (1954), 15-26.

Paluka, M.H. *Heraldry and Armor of the Middle Ages*. New York, 1972.

Pasleau, Jean F. *Les armuries Liégeois du XVe au XIXe siècle*. Liege, 1973.

Pfaffenbichler, Matthias. *Medieval Craftsmen: Armourers*. Toronto: University of Toronto Press, 1992.

Piponnier, Françoise. "Textiles et armures," *Fasciculi archaeologicae historicae* 10 (1997), 39-44.

Possio, Vannozzo. "Un artefice del rinascimento: Caremolo di Modrone armarolo dei Gonzaga," *Armi antichi* (1985), 35-56.

Pyhrr, Stuart. "European Armor from the Imperial Ottoman Arsenal," *Metropolitan Museum Journal* 24 (1989), 85-116.

Pyhrr, Stuart. "Some Elements of Armor Attributed to Niccolò Silva," *Metropolitan Museum Journal* 18 (1984), 111-21.

Pyhrr, Stuart and Thom Richardson. "The 'Master of the Snails and Dragonflies' Identified," *Journal of the Arms and Armour Society* 14 (1992-94), 329-63.

Pyhrr, Stuart, José-A. Godoy, and Silvio Leydi. *Heroic Armor of the Italian Renaissance: Filippo Negroli and His Contemporaries*. New York: Metropolitan Museum of Art, 1998.

Randall, Richard H., Jr. "Medieval Armour Proverbs," *Journal of the Arms and Armour Society* 3 (1959-61), 217-19.

Randall, Richard H., Jr. "The Tilting Breastplate of Maximilian II," *Bulletin of the Walters Art Gallery* 18.2 (Nov 1965).

Reid, William. "The Manwood Achievement," *Journal of the Arms and Armour Society* 3 (1959-61), 260-69.

Reid, William. "The Sussex Arm," *Journal of the Arms and Armour Society* 3 (1959-61), 269-70.

Reid, William and M.E. Burgess. "A Habergeon of Westwale," *Antiquaries Journal* 40 (1960), 46-57.

Reitzenstein, Alexander Freiherr von. "Anton Peffenhauser, Last of the Great Armorers." In: *Arms and Armor Annual: Volume One*. Ed. Robert Held. Northfield: Digest Books, Inc., 1973, pp. 72-89.

Reitzenstein, Alexander Freiherr von. "Antoni Peffenhauser," *Waffen- und Kostümkunde* 13 (1971), 111-27.

Reitzenstein, Alexander Freiherr von. "Ein Harnisch Valentin Siebenbürgers in französischen Muzeumbesitz," *Waffen- und Kostümkunde* 15 (1973), 99-108.

Reitzenstein, Alexander Freiherr von. "Eine Harnischbrust des Hans Ringler im Britischen Museum," *Waffen- und Kostümkunde* 7 (1965), 122-23.

Reitzenstein, Alexander Freiherr von. "Die Harnischkammer des Neuburger Schlosses im Jahre 1628," *Waffen- und Kostümkunde* 15 (1973), 146-58.

Reitzenstein, Alexander Freiherr von. "Die Innsbrucker Plattnerkunst," *Kunstchronik* 7.11 (Nov 1954), 305-08, 318-19.

Reitzenstein, Alexander Freiherr von. "Die Innsbrucker Plattnerkunst," *Die Kunst und das Schöne Heim* (1954), 125-29.

Reitzenstein, Alexander Freiherr von. "Die Landshuter Plattner: ihre Ordnung und ihre Meister," *Waffen- und Köstumkunde* 11 (1969), 20-32.

Reitzenstein, Alexander Freiherr von. "Der Landshuter Plattner Matthes Deutsch," *Waffen- und Kostümkunde* 5 (1963), 89-95.

Reitzenstein, Alexander Freiherr von. "Die Landshuter Plattner: Meister Deutsch," *Waffen- und Köstumkunde* 5 (1963), 89-95.

Reitzenstein, Alexander Freiherr von. "Die Landshuter Plattner: Wolfgang und Franz Grosschedel," *Müncher Jahrbuch der bildenden Kunst* 3.5 (1954), 142-53.

Reitzenstein, Alexander Freiherr von. "Die Nürnberger Plattner," *Beiträge zur Wirtschaftgeschichte Nürnbergs* 2 (1967), 700-25.

Reitzenstein, Alexander Freiherr von. "Die Ordnung der Ausburger Plattner," *Waffen- und Köstumkunde* 2 (1960), 96-100.

Reitzenstein, Alexander Freiherr von. "Die Ordnung der Nürnberger Plattner," *Waffen- und Köstumkunde* 1 (1959), 54-85.

Reitzenstein, Alexander Freiherr von. "Ottoheinrichs Harnische." In: *Ottoheinrich: Gedenkschrift zur vierhundertjährigen Wiederkehr seiner Kurfürstenzeit in der Pfalz (1556-1559)*. Heidelberg, 1956, pp. 105-17.

Reitzenstein, Alexander Freiherr von. "Plattner und Maler," *Die Kunst und das Schöne Heim* (Dec 1956), 92-94.

Reitzenstein, Alexander Freiherr von. "Die Plattner von Augsburg." In: *Augusta: Festschrift zum 1,000 jahrgedächtnis der Lechfeldschlacht.* Munich, 1955, pp. 265-72.

Reitzenstein, Alexander Freiherr von. "Der Ringlersche Harnisch des Pfalzgrafen Ottoheinrich," *Anzeiger des Germanisches Nationalmuseums* (1964), 44-56.

Reuck, Anthony de. "Greenwich Revisited: Or Gunpowder and the Obsolescence of Armour." *Journal of the Arms and Armour Society* 15 (1998), 426-43.

Reverseau, Jean-Pierre. "L'armement défensif à la époque de Jeanne d'Arc: L'armure de l'héroine." In: *Jeanne d'Arc: Une époque, un rayonnement.* Paris, 1982, pp. 67-72.

Reverseau, Jean-Pierre. *Les armures des rois de France au Musée de l'Armée.* Saint-Julien-du-Sault dans l'Yonne: Presses Saltusiennes, 1982.

Reverseau, Jean-Pierre. "Les armures des rois de France au Musée de l'Armée," *Waffen- und Kostümkunde* 21 (1979), 3-10.

Reverseau, Jean-Pierre. "The Classification of French Armour by Workshop Styles, 1550-1600." In: *Art, Arms and Armour: An International Anthology.* Vol I: *1979-80.* Ed. Robert Held. Chiasso: Acquafresca Editrice, 1979, pp. 202-19.

Reverseau, Jean-Pierre. "L'habit de guerre des français en 1446: Le manuscrit anonyme fr. 1997 de la Bibliothèque Nationale," *Gazette des beaux arts* 93 (May-June 1979), 181-98.

Reverseau, Jean-Pierre. "Inventaire des armures des rois de France au Musée de l'Armée," *Armi antiche* (1977), 105-39.

Reverseau, Jean-Pierre. "Style et typologie des harnois ducaux selon les comptes de la fin du 14e siècle." In: *Art de la guerre: Technologie et tactique en Europe occidentale à la fin du moyen âge et à la renaissance.* Brussels: Centre Européen d'Etudes Bouruignonnes, 1986, pp. 7-13; and *Revue de la Société des Amis du Musée de l'Armée* 96 (1988), 11-15.

Richardson, Thom. "The Archibald Hauberk," *Royal Armouries Yearbook* 4 (1999), 29-31.

Richardson, Thom. "Armour in the Popham Armoury at Littlecote House," *The London Arms Fair* 38 (1987), 24-28.

Richardson, Thom. "H.R. Robinson's 'Dutch Armour of the 17th Century," *Journal of the Arms and Armour Society* 13 (1989-91), 256-78.

Richardson, Thom. "The Introduction of Plate Armour in Medieval Europe," *Royal Armouries Yearbook* 2 (1997), 40-45.

Riquer, Martín de. "El haubert francés y la loriga castellana." In: *Mélanges de philologie et de littérature romanes offert à Jeanne Wathelet-Willem.* Ed. J. de Caluwe and H. Sépulchre. Liege, 1978, pp. 545-68.

Robinson, H. Russell. *The Armour of Imperial Rome.* London: Arms and Armour Press, 1975.

Robinson, H. Russell. "Problems in Reconstructing Roman Armour," *Bonner Jahrbuch* 172 (1972), 24-35.

Robinson, H. Russell. "Some Examples of Mid-15th Century German Armour," *Journal of the Arms and Armour Society* 2 (1956-58), 136-43.

Robinson, H. Russell. *Treasures of the Tower: Armours of Henry VIII.* London: Her Majesty's Stationery Office, 1977.

Robinson, H. Russell. *What the Soldiers Wore on Hadrian's Wall.* Newcastle-upon-Tyne: Frank Graham, 1976.

Rogers, Hugh C. and Donald J. LaRocca. "A New World Find of European Scale Armor," *Gladius* 19 (1999), 221-30.

Rohr, Alheidis v. "Die Braunschweigischen Prunkharnische des Herzog Julius," *Waffen- und Köstumkunde* 30 (1988), 103-28.

Rothero, Christopher. *Medieval Military Dress, 1066-1500.* Poole: Blandford Press, 1983.

Scalini, Mario. *Armamento difensivo trecentesco dalle collezioni Carrand e Ressman.* Florence: Museo Nazionale de Bargello, 1984.

Scalini, Mario. "La armatura fiorentina del quattrocento e la produzione d'armi in Toscana." In: *Guerra e guerrieri nella Toscana del Rinascimento.* Florence, 1990, pp. 83-126.

Scalini, Mario. "Armature e Corazzai a Monaco di Baveria," *Münchner Jahrbuch der Bildenden Kunst* 3rd ser., 36 (1985), 39-56.

Scalini, Mario. "Note sulla formazione dell' armatura di piastra Italiana, 1380-1420," *Waffen- und Kostümkunde* 22 (1980), 15-25.

Scalini, Mario. "Protezione e segno di distinzione: l'equippaggiamento difensivo del Duecento." In: *Il sabato di San Barnaba*. Milan, 1989.

Schedelmann, Hans. "Ein Rückblick auf den Waffenmarkt des letzen halben Jahrhunderts," *Waffen- und Kostümkunde* 15 (1973), 25-52.

Schneider, Hugo. "Harnischproduktion in der Schweiz am Beispiel von Zürich," *Zeitschrift für Schweizerische Archäologie und Kunstgeschichte* 28 (1971), 175-85.

Schreiner, P. "Zur Ausrüstung des Kriegers im Byzanz, im Kiever Russland und in Nordeuropa nach bildlichen und literarischen Quellen," *Acta universitatis Upsaliencsis, figura* n.s. 19 (1981), 215-36.

Schulze, M. "Das ungarische Kriegergrab von Asprès-lès-Corps," *Jahrbuch des Römisch-Germanischen Zentralmuseums Mainz* 31 (1984), 473-514.

Siebel, G. *Harnisch und Helm in der epischen Dichtungen des 12 Jahrhunderts bis zu Hartemann's "Erek"*. Hamburg, 1968.

Sloot, R.B. van der. "Harnassen uit einde 16e en begin 17e eeuw in de Noordelijke Nederlanden," *Het Nederlandse Kunsthistorisch Jaarboek* (1959), 99-124.

Smith, Cyril Stanley. "Methods of Making Chain Mail (14th to 18th Centuries): A Metallographic Note)," *Technology and Culture* 1 (1959), 60-67.

Soler del Campo, Alvaro. "El armemento medieval Hispano," *Cuadernos de investigacion medieval* 3.6 (1986), 1-51.

Southwick, L. "The Armour Depicted on the Hastings Brass Compared with that on Contemporary Monuments," *Transactions of the Monumental Brass Society* 14 (1988), 173-96.

Spitzlberger, Georg. *Landshuter Plattnerkunst: Ein überblick mit Katalog der Ausstellung vom 14. Juni bis 20. Juli 1975*. Landshut: Stadtmuseum, 1975.

Starke, Heidrun. "Ein Prunkschert der deutschen Frührennaissance," *Dresdener Kunstblätter* 15 (1971), 144-48.

Starley, David Eric. *Medieval Iron and Steel Production: An Assessment of the Changing Technology of European Ferrous Alloy Production, Through the Analysis of Medieval and Renaissance Armour*. Unpublished thesis. Bradford: University of Bradford, 1992.

Steuer, Heiko. "Helm und Ringschwert: Prunkbewaffnung und Rangabzeichen germanischer Krieger," *Studien zur Sachsenforschung* 6 (1987), 189-236.

Stöltzl, Christoph, Gerhard Quaas, Harmut Boockmann, and Peter Burschel. *Eisenkleider: Plattnerarbeiten aus drei Jahrhunderten aus der Sammlung des Deutschen Historischen Museums*. Berlin: Deutsches Historisches Museum, 1992.

Tarassuk, Leonid. "Deux remarquable armures Italiennes du XVIe siècle à l'Ermitage," *Armi antiche* 3 (1956), 23-53.

Tarassuk, Leonid. *Italian Armor for Princely Courts: Renaissance Armor from the Trupin Family Trust and the George F. Harding Collection*. Chicago: The Art Institute of Chicago, 1987.

Terenzi, Marcello. "Armour on a Fresco at Spoleto," *Journal of the Arms and Armour Society* 8 (1974-76), 95-97.

Terenzi, Marcello. "Rundsköldar Tillhörande en Rustning från 600-Talet F. KR," *Meddelande* 31 (1970).

Thomas, Bruno. "L'armatura di guerra e torneo B2 dell' armeria Reale di Torino," *Armi antiche* (1978), 3-30.

Thomas, Bruno. "Harnische für Europas Fürsten: Die Innsbrucker Plattnerkunst," *Merian* 8.8 (1955), 23-27.

Thomas, Bruno. "Die Innsbrucker Plattnerkunst: ein Nachtrag," *Jahrbuch der Kunsthistorischen Sammlungen in Wien* 70 (1974), 179-220.

Thomas, Bruno. "Jakob Topf: Innsbrucker Hofplattner, 1573-1597," *Münchner Jahrbuch der bildenden Kunst* 6.3 (1955), 161-78.

Thomas, Bruno. "Kaiser Ferdinands I Harnisch von Kunz Lochner," *Kunsthistorischen Sammlungen in Wien* 50 (1953), 131-36.

Thomas, Bruno. "Landshuter Plattnerkunst: Rede zur Eröffning der Ausstellung in Landshut am 13.6.1975," *Waffen- und Kostümkunde* 17 (1975), 97-101.

Thomas, Bruno. "Die Münchner Harnischvorzeichnungen des Étienne Delaune für die Emblem- und Schlangen-Garnitur Heinrichs II von Frankreich," *Jahrbuch der Kunsthistorischen Sammlungen in Wien* 56 (1960), 7-62.

Thomas, Bruno. "Die Münchner Harnischvorzeichnungen im Stil François Ier," *Jahrbuch der Kunsthistorischen Sammlungen in Wien* 55 (1959), 31-74.

Thomas, Bruno. "Die Münchner Harnischvorzeichnungen mit Rankendekor des Étienne Delaune," *Jahrbuch der Kunsthistorischen Sammlungen in Wien* 61 (1965), 41-90.

Thomas, Bruno. "Nationalmuseets harnisk fra 1545 et mestervaerk fra Innsbruck," *Vaabenhistoriske aarbøger* 11 (1962).

Thomas, Bruno. "Nürnberger Plattnerkunst in Wien." In: *Anzeiger des Germanischen Museums–Festschrift Ludwig Grote*. Nuremberg, 1963, pp. 89-99.

Thomas, Bruno. "Der Turnier Prunkharnisch für Feld und Turnier B2 des Nürnberger Patriziers Wilhelm Reiter von Boxberg–Meisterwerk von Kolman Helmschmeid zu Augsburg um 1525," *Jahrbuch der Kunsthistorischen Sammlungen in Wien* 73 (1977), 137-54.

Thomas, Bruno. "Two 'Almain Armourers' Identified," *Journal of the Arms and Armour Society* 1 (1953), 13-14.

Thomas, Bruno and Ortwin Gamber. "L'arte milanese dell'armatura." In: *Storia di Milano XI*. Milan, 1958, XI:697-841; rpt. in: Bruno Thomas. *Gesammelte Schriften*. Graz, 1977, II:972-1098.

Thomas, Bruno and Ortwin Gamber. *Die Innsbrucker Plattnerkunst*. Innsbruck: Tiroler Landesmuseum Ferdinandum, 1954.

Thordeman, Bengt. *Armour from the Battle of Visby*. 2 vols. Stockholm: Kugl. Vitterhets historie och antikvitels akadmien, 1939-40.

Ullmann, Konrad. "Ein 'Complementarius' mit seiner Rüstung aus dem Schüttung zu Bremen," *Waffen- und Kostümkunde* 2 (1960), 41-50.

Ullmann, Konrad. "Zur Frage der Stilmerkmale an niederdeutschen Plattnerarbeiten," *Waffen- und Kostümkunde* 5 (1963), 21-40.

van Oeteren, Vincent. "Aspects de l'armure dans les Pays-Bas Bourguignonne ver 1470," *Musée d'armes* 64 (1991), 2-25.

Verreist, Léo. "Les armures et atours d'un chevalier bâtard du XIVe siècle," *Militaria Belgica* 3 (1983), 163-65.

Wagner, Eduard et al. *Medieval Costume, Armour and Weapons (1350-1450)*. Trans. Jean Layton. London, 1958.

Waterer, John W. *Leather and the Warrior*. Northampton: The Museum of Leathercraft, 1981.

Watts, Karen. "The Armour of the Knights of St. John, Malta," *Royal Armouries Yearbook* 3 (1998), 29-43.

Webster, Graham. "A Note on the Roman Cuirass," *Journal of the Arms and Armour Society* 3 (1959-61), 194-97.

Williams, Alan R. "Augsburg Craftsmen and the Metallurgy of Innsbruck Armour," *Journal of the Arms and Armour Society* 14 (1992-94), 121-46.

Williams, Alan R. "The Blast Furnace and the Mass Production of Armour Plate," *History of Technology* 16 (1994), 98-138.

Williams, Alan R. "Experiments with 'Medieval Steel' Plates," *Historical Metallurgy* 32 (1998), 82-86.

Williams, Alan R. "Fifteenth Century Armour from Churburg: A Metallurgical Study/Armature quattrocentesche da Castel Coira: Esame metallografico," *Armi antichi* (1986), 3-82.

Williams, Alan R. "The Gilding of Armour," *Historical Metallurgy* 25 (1992), 86.

Williams, Alan R. "The Grosschedel Family of Armourers of Landshut and their Metallurgy," " *Journal of the Arms and Armour Society* 15 (1995-98), 253-77.

Williams, Alan R. "Italian Armour and Cosimo dei Medici," *Journal of the Arms and Armour Society* 13 (1989-91), 293-315.

Williams, Alan R. "Italian Armour of the 16th Century in the Royal Armoury of Turin: A Metallurgical Note/Armature italiane cinquecentesche nell'America Reale di Torino: Nota di metallografia," *Armi antichi* (1987), 27-76.

Williams, Alan R. "The Knight and the Blast Furnace," *Metals and Materials* 2 (1986), 485-89.

Williams, Alan R. "The Manufacture of Armor in 15th Century Italy, Illustrated by Six Helmets in the Metropolitan Museum of Art," *Metropolitan Museum Bulletin* 13 (1978), 131-42.

Williams, Alan R. "The Manufacture of Armour in Germany: The Metallurgical Evidence from Specimens in German Museums, 14th-17th Centuries," *Waffen- und Köstumkunde* 21 (1988), 90-105.

Williams, Alan R. "The Manufacture of Mail in Medieval Europe: A Technical Note," *Gladius* 15 (1980), 105-34.

Williams, Alan R. "Medieval Armour and Mass Production of Iron." In: *Proceedings of the Conference on Medieval Europe*. York, 1992.

Williams, Alan R. "Medieval Materials for Armour," *Materials Science Club: Bulletin* 56 (Dec 1978), 22-32.

Williams, Alan R. "Medieval Metalworking: Armour Plate and the Advance of Metallurgy," *Chartered Mechanical Engineer* (Sept 1978), 109-14.

Williams, Alan R. "Metallographic Examination of Sixteenth-Century Armour," *Bulletin of the Historical Metallurgy Group* 6.2 (1972), 15-23.

Williams, Alan R. "Metallography and the Manufacture of Armour in Innsbruck," *Waffen- und Köstumkunde* 32 (1990), 53-72.

Williams, Alan R. *Metallurgy of Muslim Armour*. Seminar on Early Islamic Science Monograph, 3. Manchester: Department of Near Eastern Studies, The University of Manchester, 1978.

Williams, Alan R. "Milanese Armour and Its Metallurgy." In: *Military Studies in Medieval Europe: Papers of the "Medieval Europe Brugge 1997" Conference Volume 11*. Ed. Guy De Boe & Frans Verhaeghe. Zellik: Instituut voor het Archeologisch Patrimonium, 1997, pp. 61-70.

Williams, Alan R. "Ottoman Military Technology: the Metallurgy of Turkish Armour." In: *War and Society in the Eastern Mediterranean, 7th-15th Centuries*. Ed. Y. Lev. Leiden, 1997, pp. 363-98.

Williams, Alan R. "Slag Inclusions in Armour," *Historical Metallurgy* 24 (1991), 69-80.

Williams, Alan R. "Slag Inclusions in Armour Plate (1400-1640)." In: *Bloomery Ironmaking during 2000 Years*. Ed. A. Espelund. Trondheim, 1993, III:115-21.

Williams, Alan R. "A Technical Note on Some of the Armour of King Henry VIII and His Contemporaries," *Archaeologia* 106 (1979), 157-65.

Williams, Alan R. and Anthony de Reuck. *The Royal Armoury at Greenwich, 1515-1649: A History of Its Technology*. Royal Armouries Monograph, 4. Leeds: Royal Armouries, 1995.

Wilson, Guy M. "Greenwich Armour in the Portraits of John Michael Wright," *Connoisseur* (Feb 1975), 109-15.

Wilson, Guy M. "The Last of the Knights," *Art and Antiques Weekly* 20.10 (Sept 27, 1975), 25-29.

Woosnam-Savage, Robert C. "The 'AVANT' Armour and R.L. Scott," *Park Lane Arms Fair* 7 (1990), 5-11.

Yeoman, Frank. "Skeletons in Armour," *Ricardian* 28 (Mar 1970), 8-9.

Zaky, 'Abd al-Rahman. "Islamic Armour: An Introduction," *Gladius* 2 (1963), 69-74.

Żygulski, Zdzisław, Jr. "Armour as a Symbolic Form," *Waffen- und Köstumkunde* 26 (1984), 77-96.

Military Technology – Premodern – Armor – Helmets

Addyman, Peter V., Nicholas Pearson and Dominic Tweddle. "The Coppergate Helmet," *Antiquity* 56 (1982), 189-94.

"Anglo-Saxon Helmet from York, Before and After Partial Conservation," *Popular Archaeology* 4.6 (Dec 1982), 8-9.

Arwidsson, G. "A New Scandinavian Form of Helmet from the Vendel-Time," *Acta archaeologica (Copenhagen)* 5 (1934).

Attard, Robert. "Arms and Armour: 6. The Burgonet," *Armourer* 25 (Jan/Feb 1998), 59-60.

Attard, Robert. "Arms and Armour: 4. The Cervelliere and the Bascinet," *Armourer* 21 (Nov-Dec 1997), 60-61.

Attard, Robert. "Arms and Armour: 1. The Great Helm or Heaume," *Armourer* 20 (Mar/Apr 1997), 15-16.

Attard, Robert. "Arms and Armour: 7. Islamic Helmets," *Armourer* 27 (May/Apr 1998), 59-60.

Attard, Robert. "Arms and Armour: 3. The Kettle Hat (Chapel de fer)," *Armourer* 21 (Sep/Oct 1997), 22-23.

Attard, Robert. "Arms and Armour: 2. The Lobster Tail Helmet (Zischeigge)," *Armourer* 21 (May/Jun 1997), 21-22.

Attard, Robert. "Arms and Armour: 5. The Morion," *Armourer* 25 (Jan/Feb 1998), 58-59.

Attard, Robert. "Arms and Armour: 8. The Spangenhelm (also Known as the Conical Helmet)," *Armourer* 28 (Jul/Aug 1998), 58-59.

Begent, P.J. and A.V.B. Norman. "A Garter or a Funerary Helm?" In: *Report of the Society of the Friends of St. George, 1989-1990*. Windsor, 1990, pp. 19-24.

Binns, J.W., E.C. Norton and D.M. Palliser. "The Latin Inscription on the Coppergate Helmet," *Antiquity* 64 (1990), 134-39.

Blair, Claude. "Blithfield Sallet," *Archaeological Journal* 111 (1955), 160-67.

Blair, Claude. "Comments on Dr. Borg's 'Horned Helmet'," *Journal of the Arms and Armour Society* 8 (1974-76), 127-37.

Blair, Claude. "The Lullingstone Helm," *Antiquaries Journal* 78 (1998), 289-305.

Blair, Claude. "A Morion by Caremolo Modrone of Mantua," *Arms and Armour at the Dorchester* (1983), 11-18.

Blair, Claude. "A New-found Greenwich Helmet," *The Connoisseur Yearbook* (1956), 79-84.

Blair, Claude and C.A. Ralegh Radford. "Crediton: The Story of Two Helmets." In: *Studies in European Arms and Armor: The C. Otto von Kienbusch Collection in the Philadelphia Museum of Art*. Philadelphia: Philadelphia Museum of Art, 1992, pp. 152-83.

Bocheński, Zbigniew. "Un groupe de casques hongrois dorés du XVI siècle," *Armi antiche* (1966), 103-39.

Bocheński, Zbigniew. "Supplément au probleme des casques hongrois dorés," *Armi antiche* (1966), 57-60.

Bokhan, Yuras. "The Sallet Type of Helm from Mscislav," *Fasciculi archaeologicae historicae* 10 (1997), 9-12.

Borg, Alan. "The Ram's Horn Helmet," *Journal of the Arms and Armour Society* 8 (1974-76), 138-85.

Bruce-Mitford, Rupert. "The Benty Grange Helmet and Some Other Supposed Anglo-Saxon Helmets." In: *Aspects of Anglo-Saxon Archaeology: Sutton Hoo and Other Discoveries*. New York, 1974, pp. 223-52.

Bruce-Mitford, Rupert. "The Sutton Hoo Helmet–a New Reconstruction," *The British Museum Quarterly* 36 (1970), 120-30; in: *Aspects of Anglo-Saxon Archaeology: Sutton Hoo and Other Discoveries*. New York, 1974, pp. 198-209.

Bruce-Mitford, Rupert. "The Sutton Hoo Helmet-Reconstruction and the Design of the Royal Harness and Sword-Belt: A Reply to Hofrat Dr. Ortwin Gamber with Some Additional Comments on the Sutton Hoo Arms and Armour," *Journal of the Arms and Armour Society* 10 (1980-82), 217-74.

Cessford, Craig. "The Borgue Armour and the Dumfriesshire *Spangenhelm*," *Transactions of the Dumfriesshire and Galloway Natural History and Antiquarian Society* 69 (1994), 73-80.

Chapman, Hugh. "Evidence for a Roman Cavalry Helmet from London." In: *Collecteana Londiniensia: Studies in London Archaeology and History Presented to Ralph Merrifield*. London: London and Middlesex Archaeological Society, 1978, pp. 177-79.

Collet, André. "Dans la salle orientale du Musée de l'Armée: les casques turcs (XVe-XVIe siècle)," *Revue de la Société des Amis du Musée de l'Armée* 106 (1993), 25-31.

Cripps-Day, F.H. "The Nevill Heaume at Birling," *Archaeologia Cantiana* 32 (1917), 317-19.

Curtis, Howard M. *2,500 Years of European Helmets, 800 B.C.-1700 A.D.* North Hollywood: Beinfeld Publishing Inc., 1978.

Dale, Peter. "An English Great Helm, c.1360," *London Arms Fair* (Spring 1975), 30-31.

Dove, Anthony B.L. "A Short Dissertation on the Bellows Visor," *Journal of the Arms and Armour Society* 6 (1968-70), 38-48.

Duns, P. "Notes on a Helmet found at Ancrum Moor," *Proceedings of the Society of Antiquaries of Scotland* 3rd ser., 6 (1895-96), 317-22.

Eaves, Ian. "A Newly Identified Greenwich Helmet in Metropolitan Museum of Art, New York," *Journal of the Arms and Armour Society* 12 (1986-88), 367-93.

Fleury, Michel. "Finding King Charles VI's Golden Helmet," *Apollo* 129 (June 1989), 409-11, 445.

Forgiero, Di C.A. Arnaldo. "The Castel San Angelo Helm," *Journal of the Arms and Armour Society* 1 (1954), 101-02.

Gaier, Claude. "Notes sur les origines de heaume chevaleresque," *Musée d'armes* 31 (1981), 15-22; in: *Armes et combats dans l'univers médiéval*. Liege, 1995, pp. 105-10.

Gamber, Ortwin. "A Funerary Effigy, Grotesque Helmets and the Seusenhofer Workshop," *Apollo* 127 (Feb 1988), 105-07.

Gamber, Ortwin. "Die frühmittelalterlichen Spangenhelme," *Waffen- und Kostümkunde* 24 (1982), 81-86.

Gamber, Ortwin. "Ein Visierhelm der Churburger Rüstkammer." In: *Beiträge zur Kunstgeschichte Tirols: Festschrift für Landeskonservator Dr. Oswald Graf Trapp*. Innsbruck: Universitätsverlag Wagner, 1959, pp. 59-61.

Geßler, E.A. "Der Kalotten-Helm von Chamosen," *Zeitschrift für historische Waffen- und Köstumkunde* 3 (1930), 121-27.

Głosek, Marian and Andrzej Nowakowski. "Średniowieczna przyłbica z Muzeum Okręgowego w Toruniu. Przyczynek do znajomości bałtyjskiego uzbrojenia ochronnego," *Kwartalnik historii kultury materialnej*. nr. 1/80 (1980), 53-61.

Głosek, Marian and Krzysztof Walenta. "The Helm of the Kettle-Hat Type Discovered at the Motte in Leśno, Brusy Commune, Bydgoszcz Province," *Fasciculi archaeologicae historicae* 10 (1997), 13-18.

Grancsay, Stephen V. "An Augsburg Helmet," *Metropolitan Museum of Art Bulletin* 29 (Aug 1934), 130-32; in: *Arms and Armor: Essays by Stephen V. Grancsay from The Metropolitan Museum of Art Bulletin, 1920-1964*. New York: The Metropolitan Museum of Art, 1986, pp. 130-32.

Grancsay, Stephen V. "A Barbarian Chieftain's Helmet," *Metropolitan Museum of Art Bulletin* n.s.7 (June 1949), 272-81; in: *Arms and Armor: Essays by Stephen V. Grancsay from The Metropolitan Museum of Art Bulletin, 1920-1964*. New York: The Metropolitan Museum of Art, 1986, pp. 335-48.

Grancsay, Stephen V. "A Helm for the Baston Course," *Metropolitan Museum of Art Bulletin* 37 (Mar 1942), 60-64; in: *Arms and Armor: Essays by Stephen V. Grancsay from The Metropolitan Museum of Art Bulletin, 1920-1964*. New York: The Metropolitan Museum of Art, 1986, pp. 279-82.

Grancsay, Stephen V. "A Helmet by Kunz Lochner," *Metropolitan Museum of Art Bulletin* 34 (May 1939), 190-92; in: *Arms and Armor: Essays by Stephen V. Grancsay from The Metropolitan Museum of Art Bulletin, 1920-1964*. New York: The Metropolitan Museum of Art, 1986, pp. 230-32.

Grancsay, Stephen V. "A Helmet Made for Philip II of Spain," *Metropolitan Museum of Art Bulletin* n.s. 13 (May 1955), 272-80; in: *Arms and Armor: Essays by Stephen V. Grancsay from The Metropolitan Museum of Art Bulletin, 1920-1964*. New York: The Metropolitan Museum of Art, 1986, pp. 411-21.

Grancsay, Stephen V. "A Maximilian Helmet and Gauntlet Retrieved," *Metropolitan Museum of Art Bulletin* 33 (Dec 1938), 268-71; in: *Arms and Armor: Essays by Stephen V. Grancsay from The Metropolitan Museum of Art Bulletin, 1920-1964*. New York: The Metropolitan Museum of Art, 1986, pp. 212-15.

Grancsay, Stephen V. "A Modern Method of Repairing a Medieval Helmet," *Journal of the Walters Art Gallery* 15-16 (1954), 62-71, 98.

Grancsay, Stephen V. "A Pate Defense of the Emperor Maximilian II," *Metropolitan Museum of Art Bulletin* 26 (May 1931), 125-27; in: *Arms and Armor: Essays by Stephen V. Grancsay from The Metropolitan Museum of Art Bulletin, 1920-1964*. New York: The Metropolitan Museum of Art, 1986, pp. 80-82.

Grancsay, Stephen V. "A Sassanian Chieftain's Helmet," *Metropolitan Museum of Art Bulletin* n.s. 21 (Apr 1963), 253-62; in: *Arms and Armor: Essays by Stephen V. Grancsay from The Metropolitan Museum of Art Bulletin, 1920-1964*. New York: The Metropolitan Museum of Art, 1986, pp. 505-19.

Grancsay, Stephen V. "Sculpture in Steel–A Milanese Renaissance Barbute," *Metropolitan Museum of Art Bulletin* n.s. 21 (Jan 1963), 182-91; in: *Arms and Armor: Essays by Stephen V. Grancsay from The Metropolitan Museum of Art Bulletin, 1920-1964*. New York: The Metropolitan Museum of Art, 1986, pp. 493-505.

Hawkes, Sonia Chadwick, Hilda R. Ellis Davidson, and C. Hawkes. "The Finglesham Man," *Antiquity* 39 (1965), 17-32.

Hayward, John F. "A Renaissance Casque à l'antique," *Connoisseur* (Oct 1954), 116.

Heildinga, H.A. "Een veertiendeeuws vizier." In: *Vondsten onder de Sint Olofskapel: Stadskernonderzoek in Amsterdam*. Amsterdam: Instituut voor Praeen Protohistorie van de Universiteit van Amsterdam, 1972, pp. 9-12.

Hejdová, Dagmar. "Der Sogenannte St. Wenzels-Helm," *Waffen- und Köstumkunde* 7 (1965), 95-110; 8 (1966), 28-54, 95-110; 9 (1967), 28-54; 10 (1968), 15-30.

Holmes, Martin. "A Helmet from Upper Winchendon Buckinghamshire," *Antiquaries Journal* 45 (1965), 183-91.

James, Simon. "Evidence from Dura Europas for the Origins of Late Roman Helmets," *Syria* 63 (1986), 107-34.

Keeble, K. Corey. "Sixteenth Century German Close Helmets in the Royal Ontario Museum," *Canadian Journal of Arms Collecting* 19 (1981), 3-10.

Kirpičnikov, Anatolij N. "Russische Helm aus dem frühen Mittelalter," *Waffen- und Kostümkunde* 15 (1973), 89-98.

Klumbach, Hans. *Römische Helme aus Niedergermanien*. Cologne: Rheinland-Verlag GMBH, 1974.

La Rocca, Donald. "An Embossed Visor in the Kienbusch Collection and Related Examples in the Royal Armoury, Madrid," *Journal of the Arms and Armour Society* 12 (1986-88), 206-11.

Lyne, Malcolm. "Late Roman Helmet Fragments from Richborough," *Journal of Roman Military Equipment Studies* 5 (1994), 97-105.

Makes, Frantisek. "Korrosionsangrepp på en 1500-tals-hjälm genom sönderfall av konserveringsmedel," *Livrustkammaren* 17 (1985), 79-92.

Mann, James. "The Coleshill Helm," *Antiquaries Journal* 13 (1933), 152-54.

Mann, James. "A Tournament Helm in Melbury Sampford Church," *Antiquaries Journal* 20 (1940), 368-79.

Mann, James. "Two Helmets in St. Botolph's Church, Lullingstone, Kent," *Antiquaries Journal* 12 (1932), 136-65.

Menghin, W. "Römische Helme von Theilenhofen, Lkrs. Weissenburg-Gunzenhausen/Mfr," *Anzeiger des Germanischen Nationalmuseums* (1979), 168-69.

Müller, Heinrich and Fritz Kunter. *Europäische Helme aus der Sammlung des Museums für Deutsche Geschichte.* Berlin: Militärverlag der Deutschen Demokratischen Republik, 1971.

Müller, Heinrich and Fritz Kunter. *Europäische Helme.* Berlin, 1984.

Nadolski, Andrzej. "Hełm i fragmenty zbroi z Siedlatków," *Prace i materiały Muzeum Archeologicznego i Etnograficznego w Łodzi* 15 (1968), 89-93.

Nadolski, Andrzej. "Uwagi o wczesnośredniowiecznych hełmach typu 'Wielkopolskiego'," *Materiały muzeum archeologicznego i etnograficznego w Łodzi. Seria archeologiczna* 5 (1960), 99-124.

Nikolić, Desanka. "Neke napomene o specijalnom tipu janičarske kape," *Vesnik* 5.1 (1958), 77-94.

Norman, A.V.B. "A Comparison of Three Helmets," *Waffen- und Kostümkunde* 1 (1959), 16-21.

Painter, K.S. "A Roman Bronze Helmet from Hawkedon, Suffolk," *Antiquaries Journal* 47 (1967), 286-87.

Peterson, Harold L. "A Greenwich Helmet," *Journal of the Arms and Armour Society* 7 (1971-73), 55-56.

Peterson, Harold L. "The Helmet Found at San Gabriel del Yunque, New Mexico," *Journal of the Arms and Armour Society* 1 (1955), 183-86.

Piletić, Dragoslav. "Antički šlemovi–razvojni put i uticaji, s naročitim obzirom na materijal iz naše zemlje," *Vesnik* 13-14 (1968), 29-58.

Piletić, Dragoslav. "Rimski legionarski šlem iz Ćuprije i pitanje determiniranja okvirne hronološke skale rimskih legionarskih šlemova," *Vesnik* 11-12 (1966), 9-22.

Pirling, Renate. "Ein Fränkisches Fürstengrab aus Krefeld-Gellep," *Germania* 42 (1964), 188-216.

Post, Paul. "Der kupferne Spangenhelm: Ein Beitrag zur Stilgeschichte der Völkerwanderungszeit auf waffentechnischer Grundlage," *Bericht der Römisch-Germanischen Kommission* 1951-53 (1954), 115-50.

Quasigroch, Günter. "Die Topfhelm von Dargen," *Waffen- und Kostümkunde* 21 (1979), 11-24.

Reverseau, Jean-Pierre. *Casques royaux fin XIVe début XVe siècle.* Paris: Musée de l'Armée, 1989.

Richardson, Thom. "The Barendyne Helmet," *Royal Armouries Yearbook* 1 (1996), 68-72.

Robinson, H. Russell. "A Converted Helmet and Some Early Barbute and Armets," *Journal of the Arms and Armour Society* 1 (1953), 35-37.

Sandstedt, Fred. "Schischak–Szyszak–Zischägge: Analys av åtta hjälmar av orientalisk typ i Livrustkammaren," *Livrustkammaren* 17 (1985), 1-52.

Schneider, Hugo. "Die Beiden Topfhelm von Madeln," *Zeitschrift für schweizerische Archäologie und Kunstgeschichte* 14 (1953), 24-46.

Schneider, Hugo. "Der Helm von Niederrealta," *Waffen- und Kostümkunde* 9 (1967), 77-90.

Schneider, Hugo. "Zwei Helme aus der Burgruine Innerjuvalta: Zur technischen Konsiervierung der Eisenhütte von Innerjuvalta," *Waffen- und Köstumkunde* 28 (1986), 23-33.

Schöbel, Johannes. *Helm und Schilde.* Dresden: Dresden Historisches Museum, n.d.

Scott, J.G. "Two 14th Century Helms Found in Scotland," *Journal of the Arms and Armour Society* 4 (1962-1964), 68-71.

Siebel, G. *Harnisch und Helm in der epischen Dichtungen des 12 Jahrhunderts bis zu Hartemann's "Erek".* Hamburg, 1968.

Sieblist, Ulrich. "Der vergoldete Spangenhelm und Untersuchungen zu den Herstellungstechniken," *Restaurierung und Museumtechnik* 6 (1985), 23-38.

Spalding, Derek. "An Unrecorded English Helm of c.1370," *Journal of the Arms and Armour Society* 9 (1977-79), 6-9.

Steuer, Heiko. "Helm und Ringschwert: Prunkbewaffnung und Rangabzeichen germanischer Krieger," *Studien zur Sachsenforschung* 6 (1987), 189-236.

Swanton, M.J. "The Manuscript Illustration of Benty Grange Type," *Journal of the Arms and Armour Society* 10 (1980-82), 1-5.

Thomas, Bruno. "Ein ostgotischer Spangenhelm in Libyen," *Waffen- und Kostümkunde* 23 (1981), 1-4.

Thomas, Bruno. "Ein ostgotischer Spangenhelm in Libyen: Nachtrag," *Waffen- und Kostümkunde* 24 (1982), 67-69.

Trapp, Oswald. "Zur Entwicklung der 'Armet-Helme,'" *Zeitschrift für historisches Waffen- und Köstumkunde* 11 (1926-28), 25-29.

"Turneringshejlm: giuoco del ponte," *Våbenhistorisk tidsskrift* 25 (1992), 67.

Tweddle, Dominic. *The Anglian Helmet from 16-22 Coppergate.* 2 vols. The Archaeology cf York, vol. 17: The Small Finds. York: York Archaeological Trust, 1992.

Tweddle, Dominic. *The Coppergate Helmet.* York: York Archaeological Trust, 1984.

Tweddle, Dominic. "The Coppergate Helmet," *Fornvännen* 78 (1984), 105-12.

Vassilatos, Nick. "Middelalderhjelmene fra Chalkis," *Vaabenhistoriske Aarbøger* 47 (1999), 132-44.

Vermeule, C.S. "A Roman Silver Helmet in the Toledo (Ohio) Museum of Art," *Journal of Roman Studies* 50 (1960), 8-11.

Williams, Alan R. "Four Helms of the Fourteenth Century Compared," *Journal of the Arms and Armour Society* 10 (1980-82), 80-102.

Yeoman, Frank. "A Barbuta at Glasgow: A Problem of Identification," *Journal of the Arms and Armour Society* 6 (1968-70), 267-68.

Military Technology – Premodern – Armor – Shields

Bayley, T.D.S. "The Bouchier Shield in Halstead Church," *Essex Archaeological Society's Transactions* n.s. 25 (1955), 80-100.

Denkstein, Vladimir. "The Bohemian Pavise in Turin Armeria Reale Collections," *Armi antiche* (1966), 37-49.

Denkstein, Vladimir. "Pavézy českeho typu I: Studie k dějinám husitské vojenské tradice, jejího rozšíření a vlivu v 15. soletí. Část I," *Sborník národního muzea v Praze* 16.4-5 (1962), 185-228.

Denkstein, Vladimir. "Pavézy českeho typu II: Původ a vývoj pavéz v předhusitske Evrope" *Sborník národního muzea v Praze* 18.3/4 (1964), 107-94.

Denkstein, Vladimir. "Pavises of the Bohemian Type. II: The Origin and Development of Pavises in Pre-Hussite Europe," *Sbornik Národního Muzea y Praze (Acta Musei Nationalis Prague)*, ser. A-Historia, 18 (1964), 149-94.

Denkstein, Vladimir. "Der Zwickauer Pavesen böhmischen Ursprung," *Sächische Heimatblätter* 9 (1958).

Dickinson, Tania, F.S.A. Härke, and Heinrich Härke. "Early Anglo-Saxon Shields," *Archaeologia* 110 (1992), 1-94; rpt. London, 1992.

Dunning, G.C. "The Shield-Boss from Wallingstones, and Notes on Medieval Shields," *Transactions of the Woolhope Naturalists' Field Club* 40.1 (1970), 105-09.

Edwards, Ifor and Claude Blair. "Welsh Bucklers," *Antiquaries Journal* 62 (1982), 74-115.

Evison, Vera I. "Sugar-Loaf Shield Bosses," *Antiquaries Journal* 43 (1963), 38-96.

Felletti, B.M. "Reconstruzione di uno scudo longobardo de Castel Trosini," *Pontificia accademia romano di archeologia, rendiconti* 34 (1961-62), 191-205.

Gaier, Claude. "Le bouclier de Baudouin de Flandre et Hainaut, premier empereur latin de Constantinople," *Musée d'armes* 63 (1990), 2-17; in: *Armes et combats dans l'univers médiéval*. Liege, 1995, pp. 111-23.

Gibson, Geoffrey. "The Pavise in Medieval Europe," *Journal of the Society of Archer-Antiquaries* 21 (1978), 24-26.

Grancsay, Stephen V. "A Shield of Henry II," *Metropolitan Museum of Art Bulletin* 29 (Dec 1934), 212-16; in: *Arms and Armor: Essays by Stephen V. Grancsay from The Metropolitan Museum of Art Bulletin, 1920-1964*. New York: The Metropolitan Museum of Art, 1986, pp. 136-41.

Grancsay, Stephen V. "An Enriched Shield–English or German?" *Metropolitan Museum of Art Bulletin* 23 (Aug 1928), 186-89; in: *Arms and Armor: Essays by Stephen V. Grancsay from The Metropolitan Museum of Art Bulletin, 1920-1964*. New York: The Metropolitan Museum of Art, 1986, pp. 30-33.

Grancsay, Stephen V. "A Fifteenth-Century Painted Shield," *Metropolitan Museum of Art Bulletin* 26 (Jan 1930), 194-96; in: *Arms and Armor: Essays by Stephen V. Grancsay from The Metropolitan Museum of Art Bulletin, 1920-1964*. New York: The Metropolitan Museum of Art, 1986, pp. 71-74.

Grancsay, Stephen V. "A Parade Shield of Charles V," *Metropolitan Museum of Art Bulletin* n.s. 7 (Dec 1948), 122-32; in: *Arms and Armor: Essays by Stephen V. Grancsay from The Metropolitan Museum of Art Bulletin, 1920-1964*. New York: The Metropolitan Museum of Art, 1986, pp. 348-62.

Härke, Heinrich. "Anglo-Saxon Laminated Shields at Petersfinger: A Myth," *Medieval Archaeology* 25 (1981), 141-44.

Härke, Heinrich. "Shield Technology." In: *Early Anglo-Saxon Shields*. Ed. T. Dickinson and H. Härke. London, 1992, pp. 31-54.

Härke, Heinrich. "The Use of the Shield: Combat and Display." In: *Early Anglo-Saxon Shields*. Ed. T. Dickinson and H. Härke. London, 1992, pp. 55-62.

Hayward, John F. "The Sigman Shield," *Journal of the Arms and Armour Society* 2 (1956-58), 21-42.

Javornik, Ivan. "Pregled istoriskog razvitka štita kao zaštitnog oružja, sa naročitim osvrtom na primerke ovog oružja u zbirci Vojnog muzeja JNA," *Vesnik* 4 (1957), 99-114.

Kalmár, János. "Hunyadi Mátyás bécsi hadseregének pajzsai," *Folia archaeologica* 18 (1966-67), 151-93.

Kalus, Ludvik. "Aspects morphologique et technique des boucliers Musulmans," *Gladius* 13 (1977), 25-61.

Kalus, Ludvik. "Un bouclier mamelouk dans le collections du Musée de l'Homme à Paris," *Armi antiche* (1975), 23-28.

Kalus, Ludvik. "Boucliers circulaires de l'orient musulman (évolution et utilisation)," *Gladius* 12 (1974), 59-133.

Kalus, Ludvik. "Inscriptions sur les boucliers circulaires de l'orient musulman," *Gladius* 14 (1978), 59-87.

Kist, J.B. "Twee vijftiende eeuwse schilden in het bezit van het Koninklijk Oudheidkundig Genootschap," *Jaarverslagen Koninklijk Oudheidkundig Genootschap* (1968), 48-50.

Melikian-Chirvani, A.S. "Bucklers, Covers or Cymbals? A Twelfth-Century Riddle from Eastern Iran." In: *Islamic Arms and Armour*. Ed. Robert Elgood. London: Scolar Press, 1979, pp. 97-111.

Nickel, Helmut. *Der mittelalterliche Reiterschild des Abendlandes*. Berlin: Freie Universität, 1958.

Posèq, Avigdor W.G. "Caravaggio's Medusa Shield," *Gazette des beaux arts* 113 (Apr 1989), 170-74.

Pyhrr, Stuart W., Everett Fahy, and Melissa S. Meighan. "A Renaissance Painted Shield Attributed to Girolamo da Trevisa." In: *Studies in European Arms and Armor: The C. Otto von Kienbusch Collection in the Philadelphia Museum of Art*. Philadelphia: Philadelphia Museum of Art, 1992, pp. 96-151.

Schneider, Hugo. "Ein Kampfschild aus dem 14. Jahrhundert," *Waffen-und-Kostümkunde* 23 (1981), 77-86.

Schöbel, Johannes. *Helm und Schilde*. Dresden: Dresden Historisches Museum, n.d.

Schönberg, Alfons Diener von. "Setzschilde der stadt Zwickau aus der werkstatt eines schildmachers von Komatau, 1441," *Zeitschrift für historische Waffen- und Köstumkunde* 17 (1943-44), 45-56.

Škrivanić, Gavro A. "Prilog o izradi i nabavci štitova u Dubrovniku," *Vesnik* 5.1 (1958), 205-07.

van Driel-Murray, C. "A Fragmentary Shield Cover from Caerleon." In: *Military Equipment and the Identity of Roman Soldiers: Proceedings of the Fourth Roman Military Equipment Conference*. Ed. J.C. Coulston. British Archaeological Reports International Series, 394. Oxford: BAR, 1988, pp. 51-66.

Watkin, J.R. "A Medieval Buckler from Hull," *Journal of the Arms and Armour Society* 11 (1983-85), 320-39.

Werner, J. "Ein langobardischer Schild von Ischlan der Alz," *Bayerischer Vorgeschichteblatter* 18-19 (1951-52).

Williams, Richard. "Early Tudor Bucklers with a Note on an Exhibit in Brecon Cathedral," *Radnorshire Society Transactions* 27 (1958), 12-19.

Wilson, Guy M. "Pavises in England," *Royal Armouries Yearbook* 2 (1997), 53-54.

Military Technology – Premodern – Arms – General

Antip, Constantin. "Les armes utilisées par les armées Roumaines dans la première moitie du XVIIe siècle." In: *17ᵗʰ Century War, Weaponry and Politics: International Association of Museums of Arms and Military History, Xth Congress Stockholm 1984* Stockholm, 1984, pp. 171-78.

Arbman, Holger and Nils-Ove Nilsson. "Armes Scandinaves de l'époque Viking en France," *Meddelanden från Lunds Universitets Historiska Museum* (1969), 163-202.

Aylward, J.D. *The English Master of Arms from the Twelfth to the Twentieth Century*. London, 1956.

Blackmore, Howard L. *Hunting Weapons*. London, 1971.

Blair, Claude. *European and American Arms, c.1100-1850*. London: B.T. Batsford, 1962.

Boccia, Lionello Giorgio. *Nove secoli di armi da caccia*. Florence: Editrice EDAM, 1967.

Boccia, Lionello Giorgio and E.T. Coelho. *Armi bianche Italiane*. Milan: Bramante Editrice, 1975.

Boccia, Lionello G. and E.T. Coelho. "L'armamento di cuoio e ferro nel trecento Italiano." In: *L'illustrazione Italiane*. Milan: Bramante Editrice, 1974, pp. 24-37.

Boeheim, Wendelin. *Handbuch der Waffenkunde*. Leipzig, 1890.

Bonnamour, Louis and Annie Dumont. "Les armes romaines de la Saône: état des découvertes et données récentes de fouilles," *Journal of Roman Military Equipment Studies* 5 (1994), 141-54.

Bosson, Clément. "Quelques armes Espagnoles au Musée d'Art et d'Histoire de Genève," *Gladius* 8 (1969), 5-15.

Bouzy, Olivier. "Spatha, framea, ensis: Le vocabulaire de l'armement aux VIIIe -XIIe siècle," *Moyen âge* 105 (1999), 91-107.

Brewer, C.W. "Metallographic Examination of Six Ancient Steel Weapons," *Historical Metallurgy* 10 (1976), 1-10.

Brunner, H. "Die Waffen in der Schatzkammer der Residenz München," *Waffen- und Kostümkunde* 2 (1960), 1-10.

Buttin, Charles. "Les armes prohibées en Savoie sous les royales constitutions," *Revue Savoisienne* 37 (1896), 111-29.

Canby, Courtland. *A History of Weaponry*. London: Leisure Arts Ltd., 1964.

Cirlot, Juan-Eduardo. "La esvatica en arma antiguas: Relaciones iconográficas del símbolo y estimaciones sobre su posible significado," *Gladius* 7 (1968), 45-74.

Clark, Philip. *Weapons and Warfare in the Viking Age*. Stroud: Tempus, 1999.

Collis, J.R. "Burials with Weapons in Iron Age Britain," *Germania* 51 (1973), 121-33.

Del Campo, A.S. "Aportacion al estudio del armamento medieval: un lote de piezas fechadas entre los siglos X-XIII." In: *I congreso de arqueologia medieval Española*. Zaragoza, 1986, pp. 313-29.

Diaconescu, S. and E. Roman. "Probleme privind terminologia armelor medievale in istoriografia românească," *Muzee* 7 (1980), 75-91.

Di Carpegna, Nolfo. *Antiche armi dal sec. IX-XVIII gia Collezione Odes-calchi*. Rome: Ed. De Luca, 1969.

Dondi, Giorgio. "Armi proprie e improprie: la sezione della lame," *Armi antiche* (1983), 23-26.

Echevarria, J.M. *Colleccionismo de armas antiguas*. Madrid: Editorial Everest, 1973.

Erdich, Michael. "Waffen im mitteleuropäischen Barbaricum: Handel oder Politik," *Journal of Roman Military Equipment Studies* 5 (1994), 199-209.

Friesinger, H. "Waffenkunde des 9. und 10. Jahrhunderts aus Niederöster-reich," *Archaeologia austriaca* 52 (1972), 43-64.

Fryer, Douglas J. *Antique Weapons, A-Z*. London: G. Bell and Sons, 1969.

Gaier, Claude. "Les inscriptions sur les armes anciennes (Xe au XVIIIe siècle)," *Musée d'armes* 25.85-86 (1997), 2-32; 25.87 (1997), 28-32; 26.91 (1998), 8-13; 27.94-95 (1999), 25-44.

Gamber, Ortwin. "Die Mittelalterlichen Blankwaffen der Wiener Waf-fensammlung," *Jahrbuch der Kunsthistorischen Sammlungen in Wien* 57 (1961), 1-38.

Gamber, Ortwin. "Die Waffen Kaiser Maximilians I," *Alte und Moderne Kunst* 4.5 (1959), 7-11.

Garcia Fuentes, J.M. "Las armas hispano-musulmanas al final de la Reconquista," *Cronica nova* 3 (1969).

Geßler, E.A. *Die Trutzwaffen der Karolingerzeit vom VIII bis zur XI Jahrhunderts*. Basle, 1908.

Giese, Wolfgang. "Portugiesische Waffenterminologie des XIII. Jahrhun-derts." In: *Miscelânea de estudos en honra de D. Carolina Michaelis de Vasconcellos*. Coimbra, 1930.

Giese, Wolfgang. "Waffen nach den katalanischen Chroniken des XIII. Jahrhunderts," *Volksturm und Kultur der Romanen* 1 (1928), 140-82.

Giese, Wolfgang. "Waffen nach den provenzalischen Epen und Chroniken des XII. und XIII. Jahrhunderts: Beiträge zur Geschichte der Bewaffung

Südfrankreichs im Mittelalter," *Zeitschrift für romanische Philologie* 52 (1932), 351-405.

Giese, Wolfgang. *Waffen nach der spanischen Literatur des 12. und 13. Jahrhunderts.* Hamburg, 1925.

Giese, Wolfgang. "Waffengeschichtliche und terminologische Aufschlüsse aus katalanischen literarischen Denmälern des 14. und 15. Jahrhunderts." In: *Homenatge a Antoni Rubio i Lluch.* Barcelona, 1936, I:33-67.

Giorgetti, G.C. *Inventario delle armi bianche e delle armi da fuoco dei musei della Repubblica di San Marino.* San Marino, 1980.

Gonen, Rivka. *Weapons of the Ancient World.* Cassel's Introducing Archaeology Series, 8. London: Cassel, 1975.

Gradowski, M. and Zdzisław Żygulski, Jr. *Słownik polskiej terminologii uzbrojenia historycznego.* Ministerstwo Kultury i Sztuki, Generalny Konserwator Zabytków, 1982.

Hare, Kent G. "Clerics, War and Weapons in Anglo-Saxon England." In: *The Final Argument: The Imprint of Violence on Society in Medieval and Early Modern Europe.* Ed. Donald J. Kagay and L.J. Andrew Villalon. Woodbridge: The Boydell Press, 1998, pp. 3-12.

Härke, Heinrich. "Changing Symbols in a Changing Society: The Anglo-Saxon Weapon Burial Rite in the Seventh Century." In: *The Age of Sutton Hoo.* Ed. M.O.H. Carver. Woodbridge, 1992, pp. 149-65.

Härke, Heinrich. "Early Saxon Weapon Burials: Frequencies, Distributions and Weapon Combinations." In: *Weapons and Warfare in Anglo-Saxon England.* Ed. Sonia Chadwick Hawkes. Oxford, 1989, pp. 49-61.

Härke, Heinrich. "'Warrior Graves'? The Background of the Anglo-Saxon Weapon Burial Rite," *Past and Present* 126 (1990), 22-43.

Hefner-Alteneck, J.H. von. *Waffen: Ein Beitrage zur historischen Waffenkunde.* 1903; rpt. Graz: Akademische Druck- und Verlagsanstalt, 1969.

Jaeger, Friedrich. "Mittelalterliche Waffenfunde aus der Pfalz," *Zeitschrift für historisches Waffen- und Köstumkunde* 15 (1937-39), 113-16.

Jørgensen, Anne Nørgård. "A Peaceful Discussion of a Martial Topic: The Chronology of Scandinavian Weapon Graves." In: *The Pace of Change:*

Studies in Early-Medieval Chronology. Ed. John Hines, Karen Høilund Nielsen, and Frank Siegmund. Cardiff Studies in Archaeology. Oxford: Oxbow Books, 1999, pp. 148-59.

Joris, Ph. "Quelques armes combinées," *Musée d'armes* 13 (1976), 8-17.

Kalus, Ludvik. "Inscriptions Arabes et Persanes sur les armes musulmanes de la Tour de Londres," *Gladius* 15 (1980), 79-86.

Keller, M.L. *The Anglo-Saxon Weapon Names Treated Archaeologically and Etymologically*. Heidelberg, 1906.

Kirpičnikov, Anatolij N. "Connections between Russia and Scandinavia in the 9th and 10th Centuries, as Illustrated by WeaponFinds." In: *Varangian Problems: Scando-Slavica, Supplementum I*. Copenhagen: Munksgaard, 1970, pp. 50-78.

Kirpičnikov, Anatclij N. *Drevnerusskoye oruzhie IX-XIII vv*. Leningrad: Izdatelstvo "Nauka", 1971.

Kirpičnikov, Anatolij N. "Russische Waffen des 9.-15. Jahrhunderts," *Waffen- und Köstumkunde* 28 (1986), 1-22, 85-129.

Kolias, Taxiarchis G. *Byzantinische Waffen: Ein Beitrag zur byzantinischen Waffenkunde von den Anfängen bis zur lateinischen Eroberung*. Vienna: Verlag des Österreichischen Akademie der Wissenschaftlichen, 1988.

Kordala, Tomasz. "L'arme blanche a un tranchant, du haut moyen âge trouvée à Plock-Podolszyce," *Fasciculi archaeologicae historicae* 4 (1990), 27-30.

Lever, R.A. "Tudor Weapons in Surrey Muster Rolls," *Surrey History* 3.3 (1986-87), 141-44.

Lewerken, H.-W. *Kombinations Waffen des 15.-19. Jahrhunderts*. Berlin: Militärverlag der Deutschen Demokratischen Republik, 1989.

Liebgott, Niels-Knud. *Middelalderns våben*. Copenhagen: Nationalmuseet, 1976.

Mann, James. *European Arms and Armour*. Vol. II: *Arms*. Wallace Collection Catalogues. London: Trustees of the Wallace Collection, 1962.

Martens, Irmelin. "Norwegian Viking Age Weapons: Some Questions Concerning their Production and Distribution." In: *The Twelfth Viking Congress: Developments Around the Baltic and the North Sea in the Viking Age*. Ed. B. Ambrosiani and H. Clark. Stockholm, 1994, pp. 180-82.

Mason, Emma. "The Hero's Invincible Weapon: an Aspect of Angevin Propaganda." In: *The Ideals and Practice of Medieval Knighthood*, III. Ed. C. Harper-Bill and R. Harvey. Woodbridge, 1990, pp. 121-37.

Mileke, Heinz-Peter. "Keramische Waffen," *Waffen- und Kostümkunde* 24 (1982), 64-66.

Mas-Latrie, L. de. "Note des armes existant à l'arsenal de Venise en 1314," *Bibliothèque de l'école de chartes* 25 (1865), 562-66.

Müller, Heinrich. *Historische Waffen: Kurze Entwicklungsgeschichte der Waffen von Frühfeudalismus bis zum 17. Jahrhundert*. Berlin, 1957.

Müller, Heinrich. "Historische Waffen." In: *Einführung in das Studium der Geschichte*. Berlin: Deutscher Verlag der Wissenschaften, 1966, pp. 484-88.

Müller, Heinrich, ed. *Alte Hieb- und Stichtwaffen: Sonderausstellung des Museums für Deutsche Geschichte*. Berlin: Museum für Deutsche Geschichte, 1986.

Müller, Heinrich and F. Kunter. *Europäische Hieb- und Stichwaffen aus der Sammlung des Museums für Deutsch Geschichte*. Berlin, 1981.

Nadolski, Andrzej. *Polish Arms: Side Arms*. Wrocław: Zakład Narodowy imenia Ossolińskich Wydawnictwo, 1974.

Nickel, Helmut. "The Arming of Gawain," *Avalon to Camelot* 2 (Win 1983), 16-19.

Nicolle, David C. "Arms of the Umayyad Era: Military Technology in a Time of Change." In: *War and Society in the Eastern Mediterranean, 7th-15th Centuries*. Ed. Y. Lev. Leiden, 1997, pp. 9-100.

Nicolle, David C. *Islamische Waffen*. Graz, 1981.

Nordman, C.A. "Vapnen in Nordens Forntid," *Nordisk kultur* 12/B (1943), 59-61.

Norheim, Per Terje. *Norske våpenokser gjennom tusen år 800-1800*. Oslo, 1976.

Novak, Rudolf. "Die französischen Waffennamen: Eine Auswahl," *Waffen- und Kostümkunde* 12 (1970), 68-79.

Oakeshott, Ewart. *A Knight and His Weapons*. London, 1964.

Openshaw, Kathleen M. "Weapons in the Daily Battle: Images of the Conquest of Evil in the Early Medieval Psalter," *Art Bulletin* 75 (1993), 17-38.

Petrović, Djurdjica. *Dubrovacko oruzje u XIV veku*. Belgrade, 1976.

Post, P. *Kriegs-, Turnier- und Jadgwaffen vom früher Mittelalter bis zum Dreissig-jahrigen Krieg*. Berlin, 1929.

Pribaković, Dušan. "O srednjevekovnom oružju na umetničkim spomenicima Hrvatske," *Vesnik* 2 (1955), 53-71.

Pribaković, Dušan. "Oružje na zidnom slikarstvu Srbije i Makedonije," *Vesnik* 1 (1954), 53-82.

Pribaković, Dušan and M. Popvic. "Archaeological Finds of Weapons Along the Locality of the Town of Ras Fortification," *Vesnik vojnog muzej* 21-22 (1976), 45-47.

Puype, Jan Piet. "17th Century Terms Concerning Arms, Accessories and Related Subjects." In: *The Arsenal of the World: The Dutch Arms Trade in the Seventeenth Century*. Ed. Jan Piet Puype and Marco van der Hoeven. Amsterdam: Batavian Lion International, 1996, pp. 64-70.

Reitzenstein, Alexander Freiherr von. "Hohenaschauer Waffen," *Waffen- und Kostümkunde* 4 (1962), 34-50.n

Reverseau, Jean-Pierre. "Contribution à létude des armes du Cardinal de Richelieu: L'hypothese d'une nouvelle attribution." In: *17th Century War, Weaponry and Politics: International Association of Museums of Arms and Military History, Xth Congress Stockholm 1984* Stockholm, 1984, pp. 85-97.

Royer, Pierre-Richard. "Introduction à l'étude des arms à inscriptions profanes du Musées de l'Armée," *Revue de la Société des Amis du Musée de l'Armée* 84 (1980), 5-13.

Rynne, Etienne. "The Impact of the Vikings on Irish Weapons." In: *Atti del VI Congresso Internazionale delle Scienze Preistorische e Protoistorische– Roma, 1962*. Rome, 1966, pp. 181-85.

Salas, Alberto M. *Las armas de la Conquista*. Buenos Aries: Emecé, 1950.

Scalini, Mario. "The Weapons of Lorenzo de Medici: An Examination of the Inventory of the Medici Palace in Florence Drawn upon the Death of Lorenzo the Magnificent in 1492." In: *Art, Arms, and Armour*. Ed. Robert Held. Chicago, 1979, pp. 12-29.

Schöbel, Johannes. "Waffen." In: *Deutsche Kunst der Dürer*. Dresden: Ministerium für Kultur Staatliche Kunstsammlungen Dresden, 1971, pp. 331-36.

Scibałło, Feliks. "Późnogotycka zbroja turniejowa w zbiorach wawelskich," *Studia do dziejów Wawelu* 3 (1968), 335-61.

Scott, J.G. "Scottish Arms: Illustrated by Pieces from the Collection in Glasgow Art Gallery and Museum," *Armi antichi* (1963), 51-76.

Seitz, Heribert. *Blankwaffen I: Geschichte und Typenentwicklung im europaischen Kulturnereich. Von der prähistorischen Zeit bis zum Ende des 16. Jahrhunderts*. Brunswick: Klinkhardt and Biermann, 1964.

Seitz, Heribert. *Blankwaffen II: Geschichte und Typenentwicklung im europaischen Kulturnereich. Vom 16. bis 19. Jahrhunderts*. Brunswick: Klinkhardt and Biermann, 1968.

Seitz, Heribert. "Some Traits of the International Expansion of Edged Weapons during the XVIth Century," *Armi antiche* 3 (1956), 3-22.

Sim, David. "The Manufacture of Disposable Weapons for the Roman Army," *Journal of Roman Military Equipment* 3 (1992), 105-19.

Siruni, H.Dj., C. Vlădescu, and Carol König. "Armes Turques du XVe au XIXe siècle du Musée Militaire Centrale de Bucarest," *Studia et acta orientalia* 7 (1968), 277-88.

Solberg, Bergljot. "Weapons." In *Medieval Scandinavia: An Encyclopedia*. Ed. P. Pulsiano. New York, 1993, pp. 718-20.

Stotten, P. "Wandlungen und Gebrauchs der Kriegswaffen im Mittelalter." In: *Die Entwicklung der Kriegswaffer und ihre Zusammenhang mit der Sozialordnung*. Ed. L. von Wiese. Cologne, 1953, pp. 118-33.

Temesváry, Ferenc. *Magyar fegyverek fejlödése a X-XVIII: Század 11*. Budapest: National Museum, 1965.

Thomas, Bruno. "Waffen der Gotik." In: *Die Gotik in Niederösterreich*. Vienna: Österreichische Staatsdruckerei, 1963, pp. 222-26.

Thomas, Bruno. "Die Waffen Kaiser Karls V in Wien," *Alte und Moderne Kunst* 3.11 (1958), 20-24.

Todorovic, Jovan. "Dosadašnja nalazi keltskog oružja na teritoriji Serbije," *Vesnik* 5.2 (1958), 24-34.

Tunis, Edwin. *Weapons: A Pictorial History*. Baltimore: Johns Hopkins University Press, 1999.

Vita, Carlo de. *Dizionari terminologici: armi blanche dal medioevo all'etá moderno*. Brescia: Accademia di Scienze, Lettere ed Arti, 1983.

Vlădescu, C.M. and C. König. "Armele oştilor române în prima jumatate a secolului al XV-lea," *Studii şi materiale de muzeografie şi istorie militaria, Muzeul Militar Cer.tral* 4-5 (1971-72), 63-78.

Voorwinden, N. "Woorden of wapens. Strijdbeschrijvingen in literaire teksten." In: *Oorlog in de middeleeuwen*. Ed. A.J. Brand. Hilversum, 1989, pp. 51-70.

Waffen als Freiburg in den Bund der Eidgenossen trat/Armes datant de l'époque de l'entrée de Fribourg dans la Confederation. Murten: Historisches Museum, 1981.

Wagner, Eduard. *Hieb- und Stichwaffen*. Prague: Artia, 1966.

Wells, H. Bartlett. "Arms in Bruegel's 'Slaughter of the Innocents'," *Journal of the Arms and Armour Society* 4 (1962-64), 193-209.

Wilkinson, Frederick. *Les armes françaises à travers les âges*. Paris: Sélection du Readers Digest, 1972.

Wilkinson-Latham, J. *Discovering Edged Weapons*. Tring: Shire Publications, 1972.

Wilson, Guy M. "The Arms and Weapons of Burgundy in the Fifteenth Century," *Connoisseur* (Mar 1977), 190-97.

Wise, Terence. *European Edged Weapons*. London: Almark Publishing Co., Ltd., 1974.

Zaky, 'Abd al-Rahman. "Medieval Arab Arms." In: *Islamic Arms and Armour*. Ed. Robert Elgood. London: Scolar Press, 1979, pp. 202-12.

Żygulski, Zdzisław, Jr. "Islamic Weapons in Polish Collections and their Provenance." In: *Islamic Arms and Armour*. Ed. Robert Elgood. London: Scolar Press, 1979, pp. 213-38.

Military Technology – Premodern – Arms – Bows and Crossbows

Abraham, Lenore. "The Devil, the Yew Bow, and the Saxon Archer," *Proceedings of the PMR Conference* 16/17 (1992-93), 1-12.

Alm, Josef. *European Crossbows: A Survey*. Trans. H. Bartlett Wells. Ed. G.M. Wilson. Royal Armouries Monograph, 3. London: Trustees of the Royal Armouries, 1994; trans. "Europeiska armborst: En översickt," *Vaaben-historisk aarboger* 5 (1947), 107-255.

Amatuccio, Giovanni. "Saracen Archers in Southern Italy," *Journal of the Society of Archer-Antiquaries* 41 (1998), 76-80.

Ascani, Enrico and Francesco Gorgo. "A Technical Study of the Fresco in the 'St. Sebastian Chapel', Celle Macra, Italy," *Journal of the Society of Archer-Antiquaries* 42 (1999), 86-88.

Atex, Wayne and G. Menes. "The Omnogov Bow," *Journal of the Society of Archer-Antiquaries* 38 (1995), 71-75.

Baker, Dorothea. "Archery in Wall Paintings," *Journal of the Society of Archer-Antiquaries* 15 (1972), 16.

Baker, Dorothea. "Archery on Misericords," *Journal of the Society of Archer-Antiquaries* 6 (1963), 26-27.

Bartlett, Clive. *English Longbowman, 1330-1515 AD*. Warrior Series. London: Osprey, 1995.

Bartlett, Clive and Gerry Embleton. "The English Archer, c.1300-1500," *Military Illustrated* 1 (June/July 1986), 10-17; 2 (Aug/Sept 1986), 14-21.

Benini, Stefano. "The Bow in Italy," *Journal of the Society of Archer-Antiquaries* 36 (1993), 7-13.

Benini, Stefano. "The Bow in Medieval Ferrara," *Journal of the Society of Archer-Antiquaries* 36 (1993), 31.

Bennett, Matthew. "The Impact of English Archery on Later Medieval Tactics." In: *XXII. Kongreß der Internationalen Kommission für Militärgeschichte Acta 22: Von Crécy bis Mohács Kriegswesen im späten Mittelalter (1346-1526).* Vienna, 1997, pp. 51-60.

Betteridge, D.S. "Bow Static Analysis and Optimum Draw Length," *Journal of the Society of Archer-Antiquaries* 40 (1997), 53-58.

Bishop, Willard E. "Wages for the Archer Guard," *Journal of the Society of Archer-Antiquaries* 4 (1961), 21-22.

Blackmore, David and Guy M. Wilson. "Crossbows," *Park Lane Arms Fair* 6 (1989), 6-9.

Blackmore, Howard L. "An Archery Bill for Henry VIII, 1547," *Journal of the Society of Archer-Antiquaries* 32 (1989), 5-8.

Blackmore, Howard L. "The Bow in the British Army, 1627," *Journal of the Society of Archer-Antiquaries* 33 (1990), 4-12.

Blair, Claude. "Medieval Crossbow Bolts in Avignon," *Journal of the Society of Archer-Antiquaries* 35 (1992), 37.

Boie, Achim and H.D. Bader. "Bows Used by the 'Huns'," *Journal of the Society of Archer-Antiquaries* 38 (1995), 28-32.

Bonnault, d'Houët, Baron de. *Les francs archers de Compiègne, 1448-1524.* Compiègne: Henry Lefebvre, 1897.

Booth, Annette Holts. "Crossbow Production at the Archbishop's Palace, Trondheim, Norway," *Journal of the Society of Archer-Antiquaries* 39 (1996), 94-100.

Bosson, Clément. "L'arbaléte," *Les musées de Genève* 13.2 (Feb 1956).

Bosson, Clément. "L'arbaléte," *Gazette des armes* 27 (May 1975), 31-37.

Boudot-Lamotte, Antoine. *Contribution à l'étude de l'archerie musulmane: Principalment d'après le manuscrit d'Oxford Bodléienne Huntington no. 264.* Damascus: Institut Français de Damas, 1968.

Boudot-Lamotte, Antoine. "Kaws." In: *Encyclopedia of Islam* 2nd ed. Leiden, 1978, IV:795-803.

Bowlus, Charles R. "Tactical and Strategic Weaknesses of Horse Archers on the Eve of the First Crusade." In: *Autour de la première croisade: Actes du Colloque de la Society for the Study of the Crusades and the Latin East (Clermont-Ferrand, 22-25 juin 1995).* Ed. M. Balard. Paris: Publications de la Sorbonne, 1996, pp. 159-66.

"Bows of the Nydam Galleys, The: Six Foot Saxon Staves," *Journal of the Society of Archer-Antiquaries* 1 (1958), 7-9.

Bradbury, Jim. *The Medieval Archer.* New York: St. Martin's Press, 1985.

Brown, Robert C. "Observations on the Berkhamstead Bow," *Journal of the Society of Archer-Antiquaries* 10 (1967), 12-17.

Bulanda, E. *Bogen und Pfeil bei den Völkern des Altertums.* Vienna, 1913.

Burns, Robert Ignatius. "The Medieval Crossbow as Surgical Instrument: An Illustrated Case History." In: *Essays on the History of Medicine.* Ed. S. Jarcho. New York, 1976, pp. 64-70.

Buttin, Charles. "La flèche des juges de camp," *Armes anciennes* 1 (1954-55), 57-64.

Calvini, N. *Balestre e balestieri medievali in Liguria.* San Remo, 1982.

Carasso-Kok, M. "Der stede scut: De schuttersgilden in de Hollandse steden tot het einde der zestiende eeuw." In: *Schutters in Holland: Kracht en zenuwen van de stad.* Ed. M. Carasso-Kok. Zwolle, 1988.

Carminati, Franco. "Piedmontese Archery," *Journal of the Society of Archer-Antiquaries* 36 (1993), 49-50.

Cenni, Alessio. "Archery Equipment in the Medici Armoury," *Journal of the Society of Archer-Antiquaries* 41 (1998), 12-18.

Cenni, Alessio. "The Diffusion of the Crossbow in Italian Warfare," *Journal of the Society of Archer-Antiquaries* 42 (1999), 46-54.

Cenni, Alessio. "Wooden Bows in Medieval Italy," *Journal of the Society of Archer-Antiquaries* 39 (1996), 50-51.

Cessford, Craig. "Archery in Medieval Scotland," *Journal of the Society of Archer-Antiquaries* 38 (1995), 68-70.

Coulston, J.C. " Roman Archery Equipment." In: *The Production and Distribution of Roman Military Equipment: Proceedings of the Second Roman Military Equipment Research Seminar.* British Archaeological Reports, International Series, 275. Oxford: BAR, 1985, pp. 220-366.

Credland, Arthur Graves. "Aquatic Shooting with the Crossbow," *Journal of the Society of Archer-Antiquarians* 31 (1988), 20-30.

Credland, Arthur Graves. "Bow and Pike," *Journal of the Society of Archer-Antiquarians* 29 (1986), 4-14.

Credland, Arthur Graves. "The Crossbow and the Law from the Dark Ages to the Present," *Journal of the Society of Archer-Antiquaries* 33 (1990), 51-64.

Credland, Arthur Graves. "Crossbow Guns and Musket Arrows," *Journal of the Society of Archer-Antiquarians* 20 (1977), 5-19.

Credland, Arthur Graves. "A Crossbow Nut from Stray Farm, Holme-on-Spalding Moor, North Humberside," *Journal of the Society of Archer-Antiquaries* 34 (1991), 7-9.

Credland, Arthur Graves. "Crossbow Remains," *Journal of the Society of Archer-Antiquaries* 23 (1980), 12-19; 24 (1981), 9-16; 25 (1982), 16-21.

Credland, Arthur Graves. "The Hunting Crossbow in England from the Time of the Tudors to the End of the Nineteenth Century," *Journal of the Society of Archer-Antiquaries* 30 (1987), 40-60.

Credland, Arthur Graves. "The Longbow in the Sixteenth and Seventeenth Century," *Journal of the Society of Archer-Antiquaries* 32 (1989), 9-23.

Credland, Arthur Graves. "The Medieval War Arrow," *Journal of the Society of Archer-Antiquaries* 25 (1982), 28-35.

Credland, Arthur Graves. "Notes on the Crossbow Spanning Bench," *Journal of the Society of Archer-Antiquaries* 33 (1990), 13-22.

Credland, Arthur Graves. "The Origins and Development of the Composite Bow," *Journal of the Society of Archer-Antiquaries* 37 (1994), 19-39.

Credland, Arthur Graves. "The Pellet Bow in Europe and the East," *Journal of the Society of Archer-Antiquaries* 18 (1975), 13-21.

Credland, Arthur Graves. "The Pellet Bow–A Postscript," *Journal of the Society of Archer-Antiquaries* 21 (1978), 6-8.

Credland, Arthur Graves. "The Tiller Bow," *Journal of the Society of Archer-Antiquaries* 35 (1992), 13-15.

Davies, Jonathan. "The Decline of the Longbow in Elizabethan England," *Journal of the Society of Archer-Antiquaries* 42 (1999), 22-32.

DeSmette, Ph. "Les archers de Saint-Martin à Moustier au XVIe siècle: Vision de l'organisation d'une conferie militaire au travers d'un document normatif," *Revue Belge d'histoire militaire* 30 (1994), 419-39.

DeVries, Kelly. "Catapults Are Not Atomic Bombs: Towards a Redefinition of 'Effectiveness' in Premodern Military Technology," *War in History* 4 (1997), 475-91.

DeVries, Kelly. "Longbow Archery and the Earliest Robin Hood Legends." In: *Robin Hood in Popular Culture: Violence, Transgression, and Justice*. Ed. Thomas Hahn. Woodbridge: D.S. Brewer, 2000, pp. 41-59.

Dini, V. *Dell'antico uso della balestra in Gubbio, San Sepolcro, Massa Maritima e nella Repubblica di San Marino*. Arezzo, 1961.

Dite, Juraj. "Slowakische Jagdarmbürste aus dem 17. Jahrhundert und ihre Besonderheiten," *Waffen- und Kostümkunde* 18 (1976), 40-52.

Dwyer, Bede. "The Closed Quiver," *Journal of the Society of Archer-Antiquaries* 41 (1998), 81-88.

Dwyer, Bede. "Early Archers' Rings," *Journal of the Society of Archer-Antiquaries* 40 (1997), 62-68.

Eguaras, A.M., L.S. Pérez, and E. de Santiago-Simón. "La ballesta naza del museo arqueologico de Granada," *Cuadernos de la Alhambra* 18 (1982).

Ekdahl, Sven. "Die Armbrust im Deutschordensland Preussen zu Beginn des 15 Jahrhunderts." *Fasciculi archaeologiae historicae* 5 (1992), 17-48.

Ekdahl, Sven. "Horses and Crossbows: Two Important Warfare Advantages of the Teutonic Order in Prussia." In: *The Military Orders*. Vol. 2: *Welfare and Warfare*. Ed. Helen Nicholson. Aldershot: Ashgate, 1998, pp. 119-52.

Elmy, D. and W.E. Flewett. "The Assassin's Crossbow," *Journal of the Society of Archer-Antiquaries* 17 (1974), 23-26.

Esper, Thomas. "The Replacement of the Longbow by Firearms in the English Army," *Technology and Culture* 6 (1965), 382-93.

Fabian, G. "An Avar Bow," *Journal of the Society of Archer-Antiquaries* 27 (1984), 30-31.

Fabian, G. "The Hungarian Composite," *Journal of the Society of Archer-Antiquarians* 13 (1970), 12-16.

Featherstone, Donald. *History of the English Longbow*. New York: Barnes and Noble Books, 1967; *The Bowmen of England: The Story of the English Longbow*. London: Jarrolds, 1967.

Flewett, W.E. "The Compound Crossbow" *Journal of the Society of Archer-Antiquaries* 35 (1992), 6-7.

Flewett, W.E. "European Combination Weapons (Crossbow-Firearms)," *Journal of the Society of Archer-Antiquaries* 36 (1993), 51-70.

Flewett, W.E. "Leonardo da Vinci and the Crossbow Lock," *Journal of the Society of Archer-Antiquaries* 24 (1981), 26-30.

Flutre, L.F. "Une arbaleste fait de cor," *Romania* 95 (1974), 309-16.

Foley, Vernard, George Palmer and Werner Soedel. "The Crossbow," *Scientific American* (Jan 1985), 104-10.

Gaier, Claude. "Une illustration du concours de tir à arbalète de Gand en 1527," *Musée d'armes* 62 (1989), 20-21.

Gaier, Claude. "L'invincibilité anglaise et le grande arc après la guerre de cent ans: un mythe tenace," *Tijdschrift voor gescheidenis* 91 (1978),

378-85; in: *Armes et combats dans l'univers médiéval*. Paris: De Boeck Université, 1995, pp. 327-36.

Gaier, Claude. "Quand l'arbalète était une nouveauté. Réflexions sur son rôle militaire du Xe au XIIIe siècle," *Moyen âge* 99 (1993), 201-29; in: *Armes et combats dans l'univers médiéval*. Paris: De Boeck Université, 1995, pp. 159-82.

Gaier-Lhoest, Johanne. "Pointes de flèches et de carreaux du bas moyen âge trouvées dans le lit de la Meuse à Liège," *Armi antichi* (1962), 83-92.

Gaunt, G.D. and E. de Winton. "A Contemporaneous Engraving of a Late 16th Century Archer," *Journal of the Society of Archer-Antiquaries* 20 (1977), 21-22.

Gaunt, G.D. and Ann M. Gaunt. "Mongol Archers of the Thirteenth Century," *Journal of the Society of Archer-Antiquaries* 16 (1973), 18-22.

Gaunt, G.D. and E. McEwen. "Linguistic Associations between Sin and Archery," *Journal of the Society of Archer-Antiquaries* 17 (1974), 17-18.

Géroudet, René. "Les ordnannaces et règlements des arquebusiers Genevois en 1595 et 1671," *Geneva* n.s. 12 (1964), 199-216.

Geßler, E.A. *Die Entwicklung des Geschützwesen in der Schweiz*. Zurich, 1918.

Gibbs-Smith, Charles H. "What the Bayeux Tapestry Does Not Show," *Journal of the Society of Archer-Antiquaries* 8 (1965), 23-25.

Gibson, Geoffrey. "Origins of William Tell," *Journal of the Society of Archer-Antiquaries* 18 (1975), 6-8.

Gilbert, J.M. "Crossbows on Pictish Stones," *Proceedings of the Society of Antiquaries of Scotland* (1975-76), 316-17.

Gillespie, James L. "Richard II's Archers of the Crown," *Journal of British Studies* 18 (1979), 14-29.

Gillespie, James L. "Richard II's Cheshire Archers," *Transactions of the Historic Society of Lancashire and Cheshire* 125 (1975), 1-39.

Giraldus. "The Fletchers and Longbowstringmakers of London," *Journal of the Society of Archer-Antiquaries* 11 (1968), 28-29.

Gizurarson, Bergsteinn. "On the Track of the Horn-Bow from Viking Iceland to Gardariki," *Journal of the Society of Archer-Antiquaries* 41 (1998), 64-72.

Głosek, Marian and L. Kajzer. "Łuk średniowieczny znaleziony w Brzegu," *Silesia antiqua* 19 (1977), 241-50.

Gode, P.K. "The Mounted Bowman on Indian Battlefields–From the Invasion of Alexander (326 BC) to the Battle of Panipat (AD 1761)." In: *Studies in Indian Cultural History*. Ed. P.K. Gode. Poona, 1960, pp. 57-70.

Gohlke, W. "Das Geschützwesen des Altertums und das Mittelalters," *Zietschrift für historisches Waffen und Köstumkunde* 5-6 (1909-14).

Gordon, Henry and Alf Webb. "The Flodden Bow at Archer's Hall, Edinburgh," *Journal of the Society of Archer-Antiquaries* 17 (1974), 15-16.

Gordon, Henry and Alf Webb. "The Hedgeley Moor Bow at Alnwick Castle," *Journal of the Society of Archer-Antiquaries* 15 (1972), 8-9.

Gordon, Henry and Alf Webb. "The Mary Rose Bows at the Tower of London," *Journal of the Society of Archer-Antiquaries* 17 (1974), 19-20.

Haldon, John F. "Solenarion–the Byzantine Crossbow?" *University of Birmingham Historical Journal* 12 (1970), 155-57.

Halpin, Andrew. "Military Archery in Medieval Ireland: Archaeology and History." In: *Military Studies in Medieval Europe: Papers of the "Medieval Europe Brugge 1997" Conference Volume 11*. Ed. Guy De Boe & Frans Verhaeghe. Zellik: Instituut voor het Archeologisch Patrimonium, 1997, pp. 51-60.

Hardy, Robert. "The Archery Equipment in the Mary Rose, Vice-Admiral of Henry VIII's Fleet in 1545," *Popular Archaeology* (Dec 1981), 11-12.

Hardy, Robert. "The Longbow." In: *Arms, Armies and Fortifications in the Hundred Years War*. Ed. A. Curry and M. Hughes. Woodbridge, 1994, pp. 161-82.

Hardy, Robert. *Longbow: A Social and Military History*. 3rd ed. London: Bois d'Arc Press, 1993.

Hardy, Robert. "The Military Archery at Neville's Cross, 1346." In: *The Battle of Neville's Cross, 1346.* Ed. David Rollason and Michael Prestwich. Studies in North-Eastern History. Stamford: Shaun Tyas, 1998, pp. 112-31.

Harmuth, Egon. "Eine arabische Armbrust," *Waffen- und Kostümkunde* 25 (1983), 141-44.

Harmuth, Egon. *Die Armbrust.* Graz: Akadmische Druck- und Verlagsanstalt, 1975.

Harmuth, Egon. *Die Armbrust: Ein Handbuch.* Graz, 1986.

Harmuth, Egon. "Die Armbrustbilder des Haimo von Auxerre," *Waffen und Kostümkunde* 12 (1970), 127-30.

Harmuth, Egon. "Armbrustteile im Röntgenbild," *Waffen- und Kostümkunde* 19 (1977), 129-36.

Harmuth, Egon. "Ein Balestrino," *Waffen- und Kostümkunde* 14 (1972), 31-34.

Harmuth, Egon. "Belt Spanners for Crossbows." In: *Art, Arms and Armour: An International Anthology.* Vol I: *1979-80.* Ed. Robert Held. Chiasso: Acquafresca Editrice, 1979, pp. 100-07.

Harmuth, Egon. "Concerning the One-Foot Crossbow of the High Gothic," *Journal of the Society of Archer-Antiquaries* 28 (1985), 9-12.

Harmuth, Egon. "Zur Einfussarmbrust der Hochgotik," *Waffen- und Kostümkunde* 20 (1978), 47-50.

Harmuth, Egon. "Zur Leistung der mittelalterlichen Armbrust," *Waffen- und Kostümkunde* 13 (1971), 128-36.

Harmuth, Egon. "Zur spanischen Jagdarmbrust," *Waffen- und Kostümkunde* 24 (1982), 60-64.

Harris, P. Valentine. "Archers at Sea: the Battle of Winchelsea," *Journal of the Society of Archer-Antiquaries* 27 (1984), 43-44.

Harris, P. Valentine. "Archery in the First Half of the Fourteenth Century," *Journal of the Society of Archer-Antiquarians* 13 (1970), 19-21.

Harris, P. Valentine. "The Decline of the Longbow," *Journal of the Society of Archer-Antiquaries* 19 (1976), 23-27.

Harris, P. Valentine. "Early Archery from the Minstrels," *Journal of the Society of Archer-Antiquaries* 26 (1983), 39-41.

Harris, P. Valentine. "From Longbow to Crossbow and Back," *Journal of the Society of Archer-Antiquaries* 18 (1975), 9-12.

Harris, P. Valentine. "The Influence of the Story of Robin Hood on Archery," *Journal of the Society of Archer-Antiquaries* 15 (1972), 10-15.

Harris, P. Valentine. "The Longbowman's Stance," *Journal of the Society of Archer-Antiquaries* 16 (1973), 23-26.

Harris, P. Valentine. "The Medieval Bowmen of Cheshire," *Journal of the Society of Archer-Antiquaries* 17 (1974), 23-26.

Hart, Edward A. "Tracing the Butts," *Journal of the Society of Archer-Antiquaries* 39 (1996), 14-15.

Hartley, P.D. "Further Speculations on the Nature of Longbowstrings," *Journal of the Society of Archer-Antiquaries* 29 (1986), 14-15.

Hartley, P.D. "Some Speculations on the Nature of Longbowstrings," *Journal of the Society of Archer-Antiquaries* 27 (1984), 24-25.

Hatto, A.T. "Archery and Chivalry: A Noble Prejudice," *Modern Language Review* 35 (1940), 40-54.

Heath, E.G. "Agincourt," *Journal of the Society of Archer-Antiquaries* 8 (1965), 7-10.

Heath, E.G. "Albrecht Dürer and His Bows and Arrows," *Journal of the Society of Archer-Antiquaries* 5 (1962), 33-35.

Heath, E.G. *Archery: A Military History*. London: Osprey, 1980.

Heath, E.G. "The English Medieval War Arrow," *Journal of the Society of Archer-Antiquaries* 4 (1961), 17-19.

Heath, E.G. *The Grey Goose Wing: A History of Archery*. London: Osprey, 1971.

Heath, E.G., ed. *Bow Versus Gun*. Wakefield: EP Publishing, 1973.

Heer, Eugen. "Notes on the Crossbow in Switzerland." In: *Arms and Armor Annual: Volume One*. Ed. Robert Held. Northfield: Digest Books, Inc., 1973, pp. 56-65.

Hodgkin, A.E. *The Archer's Craft.* 2nd ed. London: Faber and Faber Ltd., 1974.

Hoffman, Dean A. "'With the Shot Y Wyll/Alle Thy Lustes to Full-Fyl': Archery as Symbol in the Early Ballads of Robin Hood," *Neuphilologische Mitteilungen* 86 (1985), 494-505.

Holmer, Paul L. "The Military Crossbow in Yorkist England (1461-1485)," *Journal of the Society of Archer-Antiquaries* 22 (1979), 11-16.

Holt, Alain. "De re saggittarae," *Journal of the Society of Archer-Antiquaries* 29 (1986), 66-68.

Holt, Alain. "De re saggittarae, II," *Journal of the Society of Archer-Antiquaries* 32 (1989), 46-48.

Holt, Alain. "The Elizabethan Shooting Grounds (The Shakespeare Connection)," *Journal of the Society of Archer-Antiquaries* 28 (1985), 3-5.

Hudiakov, U.S. and D. Tseveendorj. "New Finds of Hun Bows in the Altai of the Gobi," *Journal of the Society of Archer-Antiquaries* 36 (1993), 71-76.

Hungerford, Roy C. "Archery and Magic," *Journal of the Society of Archer-Antiquaries* 10 (1967), 6-11.

Hungerford, Roy C. "Bow and Machine," *Journal of the Society of Archer-Antiquaries* 11 (1968), 8-11.

Isles, Fred. "Locating the Ancient Finsbury Fields Archery Marks," *Journal of the Society of Archer-Antiquaries* 7 (1964), 8-13.

Isles, Fred. "A Study of Medieval Crossbow Bolts," *Journal of the Society of Archer-Antiquaries* 5 (1962), 37-38.

Jenkinson, G.P. "Four Centuries of the Crossbow," *Country Life* (Apr 16, 1959), 832-33.

Jessop, Oliver. "European Arrowheads: Evidence for their Technological Development and Geographical Distribution." In: *Military Studies in Me-*

dieval Europe: Papers of the "Medieval Europe Brugge 1997" Conference Volume 11. Ed. Guy De Boe & Frans Verhaeghe. Zellik: Instituut voor het Archeologisch Patrimonium, 1997, pp. 43-50.

Jessop, Oliver. *Medieval Arrowheads: A Study into the Forms of Arrowhead that Occur throughout the British Isles, Using a Collection from Dryslwyn Castle in South Wales as a Case Study*. Unpublished thesis. Durham: University of Durham, 1993.

Jessop, Oliver. "A New Artefact Typology for the Study of Medieval Arrowheads," *Medieval Archaeology* 40 (1996), 192-205.

Jones, Peter N. "The Attack of Plate Armour by Longbow Arrows," *Château Gaillard* 11 (1983), 167-68.

Jones, Peter N. "The Metallography and Relative Effectiveness of Arrowheads and Armor during the Middle Ages," *Materials Characterization* 29 (1992), 111-17.

Jones, Peter N. and Derek F. Renn. "The Military Effectiveness of Arrow Loops: Some Experiments at White Castle," *Château Gaillard* 9-10 (1982), 445-56.

Kaegi, Walter E. "The Contribution of Archery to the Turkish Conquest of Anatolia," *Speculum* 39 (1964), 96-108.

Kaiser, Robert E. "The Medieval English Longbow: Characteristics and Origin," *Journal of the Society of Archer-Antiquaries* 23 (1980), 21-29.

Kirpičnikov, Anatolij N. "Russische Körper-Schutzwaffen des 9.-16. Jahrhunderts," *Zeitschrift für Historische Waffen- und Kostümkunde* 18 (1976), 22-37.

Klopsteg, P.E. *Turkish Archery and the Composite Bow*. 3rd ed. Manchester: Simon Archery Foundation, 1987.

Knighton, Arthur C. "Bow Finds from Caerleon," *Journal of the Society of Archer-Antiquaries* 34 (1991), 15-16.

Lake, Fred. "New Light on the Honourable Artillery Company and Archery in Southwark," *Journal of the Society of Archer-Antiquaries* 10 (1967), 21-28.

Lake, Fred and Hal Wright. *A Bibliography of Archery*. Manchester: The Simon Archery Foundation, 1974.

Lane, Frederic C. "The Crossbow in the Nautical Revolution of the Middle Ages," *Explorations in Economic History* 7 (1969-70), 161-71.

Lanting, J.N., B.W. Kooi, W.A. Casparie, and R. van Hinte. "Bows from the Netherlands," *Journal of the Society of Archer-Antiquaries* 42 (1999), 7-10.

Latham, J.D. "Notes on Mamluk Horse-Archers," *Bulletin of the School of Oriental and African Studies* 32 (1969), 257-67.

Latham, J.D and W.F. Paterson. "Archery in the Lands of Eastern Islam." In: *Islamic Arms and Armour*. Ed. Robert Elgood. London: Scolar Press, 1979, pp. 78-88.

Latham, J.D and W.F. Paterson. *Saracen Archery*. London, 1970.

Loewe, Raphael. "Jewish Evidence for the History of the Crossbow." In: *Les juifs au regard de l'histoire: Mélanges en l'honneur de Bernhard Blumenkranz*. Ed. Gilbert Dahan. Paris: Picard, 1985, pp. 87-107.

Macgregor, A. "Two Antler Crossbow Nuts and Some Notes on the Early Development of the Crossbow," *Proceedings of the Society of Antiquaries of Scotland* (1975-76), 317, 321.

Mactaggart, P. "Hertfordshire Butts," *Journal of the Society of Archer-Antiquaries* 5 (1962), 35-37.

Maglioli, Vittorio. "La balestra," *Armi antiche* 2 (1955), 97-109.

Manfroi, Alessandro. "Bows and Arrows in Anglo-Saxon Heroic Poetry," *Journal of the Society of Archer-Antiquaries* 39 (1996), 68-72.

Manley, John. "The Archer and the Army in the Late Saxon Period," *Anglo-Saxon Studies in Archaeology and History* 4 (1985), 223-35.

Mariën, Michel. "Eléments d'arbalètes," *Militaria Belgica* (1984), 5-14.

Massey, Duncan. "Roman Archery Tested," *Military Illustrated* 74 (Jul 1994), 36-39.

McEwen, E. "Inscriptions on Islamic Composite Bows," *Journal of the Society of Archer-Antiquarians* 13 (1970), 17-18.

McEwen, E. "Persian Archery Texts: Chapter Eleven of Fakhr-i Mudab-bir's Adab al Harb," *Islamic Quarterly* 18 (1974), 76-99.

McGuffie, T.H. "The Long-bow as a Decisive Weapon," *History Today* 5 (1955), 737-41.

McLeod, Wallace, trans. "An Ancient Treatise on Military Archery," *Journal of the Society of Archer-Antiquaries* 5 (1962), 10-11.

McLeod, Wallace, trans. "The Range of the Ancient Bow," *Phoenix* 19 (1965), 1-14.

Megson, Barbara E. "The Bowyers of London, 1300-1550," *London Journal* 18 (1993), 1-13.

Megson, Barbara E. *Such Goodly Company: A Glimpse of the Life of the Bowyers of London, 1300-1600*. London: The Worshipful Company of Bowyers, 1993.

Milleken, E.K. *Archery in the Middle Ages*. London: Macmillan, 1967.

Morris, John E. "The Archers at Crécy," *English Historical Review* 12 (1897), 427-36.

Newark, Tim. "The Knights Never Used Bows: Horse Archery in Western Europe," *Military Illustrated* 81 (Feb 1995), 36-39.

Nickel, Helmut. "Bow and Arrow/Crossbow." In: *Dictionary of the Middle Ages*. Ed. J.R. Strayer. New York, 1982, II:350-54.

Nickel, Helmut. "Ceremonial Arrowheads from Bohemia," *Metropolitan Museum Journal* 1 (1968), 61-93.

Nishamura, D. "Crossbows, Arrow-Guides and the Solenarion," *Byzantion* 58 (1988), 422-35.

Oxley, James E. *The Fletchers and Longbowstringmakers of London*. London: The Worshipful Company of Fletchers, 1968.

Paasch, Jesper Mayntz. "Langbuen," *Våbenhistorisk tidsskrift* 30 (1997), 204-08.

Pancoast, H.S. "The Origins of the Longbow," *Publications of the Modern Language Society* 44 (1929), 47-62.

Parker, Clement C. "Arrow, Eye and King," *Journal of the Society of Archer-Antiquaries* 10 (1967), 30-31.

Paterson, W.F. "An Elizabethan Longbow," *Journal of the Society of Archer-Antiquaries* 17 (1974), 34-35.

Paterson, W.F. *A Guide to the Crossbow*. Ed. Arthur Graves Credland. London, 1990.

Paterson, W.F. "'Mary Rose' Archery Enigmas," *Journal of the Society of Archer-Antiquaries* 28 (1985), 7-8.

Paterson, W.F. "Mary Rose–A Second Report," *Journal of the Society of Archer-Antiquaries* 24 (1981), 4-6.

Paterson, W.F. "A 'Mary Rose' Symposium," *Journal of the Society of Archer-Antiquaries* 26 (1983), 49-51.

Paterson, W.F. "Observations on the Returning Arrow," *Journal of the Society of Archer-Antiquaries* 21 (1978), 14-15.

Paterson, W.F. "Persian Archery of the 14th Century," *Journal of the Society of Archer-Antiquaries* 5 (1962), 23-25; 6 (1963), 20-22.

Paterson, W.F. "The Sassanids," *Journal of the Society of Archer-Antiquaries* 12 (1969), 29-32.

Paterson, W.F. "Shooting Under a Shield," *Journal of the Society of Archer-Antiquaries* 12 (1969), 27-28.

Paterson, W.F. "The Skein Bow," *Journal of the Society of Archer-Antiquaries* 7 (1964), 24-27.

Paterson, W.F. "'Travellers' Tales: A Little Known Museum," *Journal of the Society of Archer-Antiquaries* 18 (1975), 28-31.

Paterson, W.F. "Venetian Archery Equipment," *Journal of the Society of Archer-Antiquaries* 4 (1961), 23-24.

Paterson, W.F. "What is a Composite?" *Journal of the Society of Archer-Antiquaries* 11 (1968), 14-15.

Paterson, W.F. "What is a Longbow?" *Journal of the Society of Archer-Antiquaries* 25 (1982), 36.

Payne-Gallwey, Ralph. *The Crossbow, Medieval and Modern, Military and Sporting: Its Construction, History and Management, with a Treatise on the Balista and Catapult of the Ancients*. London, 1903; rpt. New York: Bramhall House, 1958; trans. *Die Armbrüst*. Trans. Egon Harmuth. Graz, 1963.

Pétrin, Nicole. "Philological Notes on the Crossbow and Related Missile Weapons," *Greek, Roman, and Byzantine Studies* 33 (1992), 262-91.

Petrović, Djurdjica. "Une balestiere marchigiano a Ragusa nel XIV secolo," *Quaderni storici* 13 (1970), 233-45.

Petrović, Djurdjica. "Les premiers nouvelles sur l'exercise des tirs de l'arc à l'arbelète à Raguse au moyen âge," *Vesnik vojni muzej* 17 (1971), 58-59.

Petrović, Djurdjica. "Prve vesti o viteškim igrama u srednjovekovnom Dubrovniku," *Vesnik* 17 (1971), 41-59.

Petrović, Djurdjica. "Samostreli iz zbirke Vojnog muzeja JNA," *Vesnik* 4 (1957), 125-51.

Pope, S.T. *Bows and Arrows*. Berkeley and Los Angeles: University of California Press, 1962.

Poschenburg, V. *Die Schutz- und Trutzwaffen des Mittelalters*. Vienna, 1938.

Pous, Anny de. "Notice sur l'évolution de l'archère dans les châteaux feodaux des Pyrénées Méditerranéenes entre le Xème et le XIVème siècle," *Gladius* 4 (1965), 67-85.

Pratt, P.L. and Robert Hardy. "The Arrow Found in Westminster Abbey in 1878," *Journal of the Society of Archer-Antiquaries* 18 (1975), 22-24.

Rathgen, Bernhard. *Das Geschütz im Mittelalter: Quellenkritische Untersuchungen*. Berlin: VDI-Verlag GMBH, 1928.

Raugh, Harold E., Jr. "The Tactical Employment of Longbowmen by the English during the Hundred Years War," *British Army Review* (Dec 1989), 58-63.

Rausing, G. *The Bow: Some Notes on Its Origins and Development*. Acta Archaeologica Lundensia, series no. 6. Lund, 1967.

Rees, Gareth. "The Longbow's Deadly Secrets," *New Scientist* 138 (June 5, 1993), 24-25.

Reid, William. "A Royal Crossbow in the Scott Collection," *Scottish Art Review* 7.2 (1959), 10-13.

Renn, Derek F. "A Bowstave from Berkhamstead Castle." In: *Hertfordshire Archaeology*. St. Albans, 1971, pp. 72-74.

Riesch, Holger. "Alemannic Bows," *Journal of the Society of Archer-Antiquaries* 37 (1994), 12-18.

Riesch, Holger. "Archery in Renaissance Germany," *Journal of the Society of Archer-Antiquaries* 38 (1995), 63-67.

Riesch, Holger. "'Quod nullus in hostem habeat baculum sed arcum': Pfeil und Bogen als Beispiel für technologische Innovationen der Karolingerzeit," *Technikgeschichte* 61 (1994), 209-26.

Riesch, Holger. "Yew Exploitation and Long-Bow Trade in the 16th Century," *Journal of the Society of Archer-Antiquaries* 39 (1996), 5-13.

Rimer, Graeme. "An Ancient Quiver," *Royal Armouries Yearbook* 3 (1998), 53-56.

Rogers, Clifford J. "The Efficacy of the English Longbow: A Reply to Kelly DeVries," *War in History* 5 (1998), 233-42.

Rohde, Fr. "Die Abzugvorrichtung der frühen Armbrust und ihre Entwicklung," *Zeitschrift für historisches Waffen- und Köstumkunde* 13 (1932-34), 100-02.

Rohde, Fr. "Concerning the Construction of the Crossbow in the Late Middle Ages," *Journal of the Society of Archer-Antiquaries* 19 (1976), 17-20.

Romiti, A. "Le gare di tiro: la balestra, lo schiopetto e lo archibugio." In: *Alcuni giuochi a Lucca al tempo della repubblica*. Lucca, 1981.

Salvemini, G. *I balestrieri del commune di Firenze*. Bari, 1905; rpt. Bologna, 1967.

Sarraf, S. al-. *L'archerie Mamluke (648-924/1250-1517)*. Lille, 1990.

Schimpf, Anselme. "Les statuts de l'arquebuserie Strasbourgeoise," *Armes anciennes* 1 (1954-55), 79-94.

Sebestyen, K. "L'arc et la flèche des Hongrois," *Nouvelle revue de Hongrie* 51 (1934).

Simpson, W.G. "A Medieval Arrowhead from Brough-under-Stainmore," *Transactions of the Cumberland and Westmorland Antiquarian and Archaeological Society* 56 (1957), 158.

Soar, Hugh D. "The Bowyers and Fletchers of Bristowe," *Journal of the Society of Archer-Antiquaries* 32 (1989), 27-36.

Soar, Hugh D. "More Notes on Quivers," *Journal of the Society of Archer-Antiquaries* 42 (1999), 55.

Soar, Hugh D. "The 'Pound and Standard' Arrow," *Journal of the Society of Archer-Antiquaries* 36 (1993), 4-6.

Soar, Hugh D. "Prince Arthur's Knights: Some Notes on a Sixteenth Century Society of Archers," *Journal of the Society of Archer-Antiquarians* 31 (1988), 31-39.

Soar, Hugh D. "Shooting Under the 'Screen': A Medieval French Archery Technique," *Journal of the Society of Archer-Antiquaries* 32 (1989), 63-64.

Soar, Hugh D. "Some Notes on Antique Archery Arm-Guards," *Journal of the Society of Archer-Antiquaries* 33 (1990), 45-50.

Soar, Hugh D. "Tudor Longbows: A Comparative Study," *Journal of the Society of Archer-Antiquaries* 34 (1991), 5-6.

Soler del Campo, Alvaro. "Notas sobre un grupo de ballestas Españolas para el Emperador Maximiliano I de Austria," *Gladius* 19 (1999), 189-96.

Squiers, Granville. "Arrowheads in the London Museum—and Others," *Journal of the Society of Archer-Antiquaries* 2 (1959), 39-40.

Stockton, E.L. "Archery in the Ballads," *Journal of the Society of Archer-Antiquaries* 5 (1962), 40-41.

Strobel, M. "Armbrust vom 13. bis 16. Jahrhundert," *Deutsches Waffen Journal* (April 1991), 526-29.

"Strongbow". "Medieval Archers in Attack," *Journal of the Society of Archer-Antiquaries* 16 (1973), 15-17.

"Strongbow". "More Myths and Mysteries," *Journal of the Society of Archer-Antiquaries* 27 (1984), 34-35.

"Strongbow". "A Somewhat Slanted History," *Journal of the Society of Archer-Antiquaries* 22 (1979), 3-6.

"Strongbow". "Two 15th Century Battle Scenes," *Journal of the Society of Archer-Antiquaries* 21 (1978), 8-10.

Świętosławski, Witold. "Die spätmittelalterlichen Steigbügeltypen aus dem Gebiet Polens," *Fasciculi archaeologiae historicae* 5 (1992), 105-14.

Tackenberg, K. "Über die Schutzwaffen der Karolingerzeit und ihre Wiedergabe in Handsschriften und auf Elfbeinschnitzereien," *Frühmittelalterliche Studien* 3 (1969), 277-87.

Treasures of the Tower: Crossbows. London: Her Majesty's Stationery Office, 1976.

Tucker, William E. "Archers at Hastings," *Journal of the Society of Archer-Antiquaries* 8 (1965), 26-32.

Tucker, William E. "The Bayeux Tapestry," *Journal of the Society of Archer-Antiquaries* 8 (1965), 25-26.

Tucker, William E. "The English Bow in Battle from Hastings to Agincourt," *Journal of the Society of Archer-Antiquaries* 1 (1958), 16-22.

Tucker, William E. "Saint Edmund, Patron Saint of Archers and England," *Journal of the Society of Archer-Antiquaries* 41 (1998), 44-45.

Tucker, William E. "Shakespeare an Archer: as Revealed in his Imagery," *Journal of the Society of Archer-Antiquaries* 30 (1987), 27-39.

van Hinte, Renate. "The Shooters: Prosperous Brothers-at-Arms," *Journal of the Society of Archer-Antiquaries* 15 (1972), 17-21.

van Hinte, Renate. "With Eagle Eye and Steady Hand ... Archery in Haarlem," *Journal of the Society of Archer-Antiquaries* 20 (1977), 36-41.

Walker, A.F. "There's an Archer in Every Pack of Cards," *Journal of the Society of Archer-Antiquaries* 4 (1961), 15-16.

Webb, Alf. "John Malemort–King's Quarreler: The King's 'Great Arsenal'–St. Briavels ard the Royal Forest of Dean," *Journal of the Society of Archer-Antiquaries* 31 (1988), 40-46; 32 (1989), 52-58.

Webb, Alf. "Just Ornament, or Funerary Replica, or Release Aid?" *Journal of the Society of Archer-Antiquaries* 37 (1994), 40-41.

Wilson, Guy M. "An English Sporting Crossbow," *Royal Armouries Yearbook* 2 (1997), 192-94.

Wilson, Guy M. "Stone Crossbows," *London Arms Fair* (Aut 1976), 42-44.

Military Technology – Premodern – Arms – Lances and Spears

Anteins, A. "Die Kurischen Rhombischen Lanzenspitzen mit Damasziertem Blatt," *Gladius* 7 (1968), 5-26.

Barker, Philip. "The *Plumbatae* from Wroxeter." In: *Aspects of the "De rebus bellicis": Papers Presented to Professor E.A. Thompson.* Ed. M.W.C. Hassall. BAR International Series, 63. Oxford, 1987, pp. 97-99.

Buttin, François. "La lance et l'arrêt de cuirasse," *Archaeologia* 99 (1965), 77-178.

Cirlot, Juan-Eduardo. "La evolucion de la lanza en occidente (piezas de hierro de hallstatt al siglo XV)," *Gladius* 6 (1967), 5-18.

Cirlot, Victoria. "Techniques guerrières en Catalogne féodale: le maniement de la lance," *Cahiers de civilisation médiévale (Xe-Xiie siècle)* 28 (1985), 35-43.

Credland, Arthur Graves. "Bow and Pike," *Journal of the Society of Archer-Antiquarians* 29 (1986), 4-14.

Dondi, Giorgio. "Dei lanciari Gounod: Le poche notizie che abbiamo," *Armi antiche* (1983), 13-21.

Ellehauge, Martin. *The Spear Traced Through its Post-Roman Development.* Tøjhusmuseets Skrifter, 5. Copenhagen: N. Olaf Møller, 1948.

Fell, Clare. "A Viking Spearhead from Kentmere," *Transactions of the Cumberland and Westmorland Antiquarian and Archaeological Society* 56 (1957), 67-69.

ffoulkes, Charles J. and E.C. Hopkinson. *Sword, Lance, and Bayonet*. London: Arms and Armour Press, 1967.

Flori, Jean. "Encore l'usage de la lance ... La technique du combat chevaleresque vers l'an 1100," *Cahiers de civilisation médiévale (Xe-XIIe siècle)* 31 (1988), 213-40.

Fois, Graziano. "La 'virga sardescha': Struttura e forma dell'arma," *Waffen- und Köstumkunde* 38 (1996), 87-116.

Gaier, Claude. "A la recherche d'une escrime décisive de la lance chevaleresque: Le'coup de fautre' selon Gislebert de Mons (1168)." In: *Femmes–mariages–lignages XIIe-XIVe siècles: Mélanges offerts à Georges Duby*. Brussels, 1992, pp. 177-96; in: *Armes et combats dans l'univers médiéval*. Liege, 1995, pp. 57-77.

Geßler, E.A. "Eine seltene spätkarolingische Lanzenpitze," *Zeitschrift für historisches Waffen- und Köstumkunde* 11 (1926-28), 66-67.

Hooper, Bari and Brendan O'Connor. "A Bronze Spearhead and its Shaft from the River Thames at Hammersmith," *Archaeological Journal* 133 (1977), 33-37.

Lang, J.T. "A Viking Age Spear-Socket from York," *Medieval Archaeology* 25 (1981), 157-60.

McGuffie, T.H. "The Puissant Pike," *History Today* 11.9 (Sep 1961), 632-36.

Nicolle, David C. "The Impact of the European Couched Lance on Muslim Military Tradition," *The Journal of the Arms and Armour Society* 10 (1980-82), 6-40.

Parkinson, E. Malcolm. "Sidney's Portrayal of Mounted Combat with Lances," *Spenser Studies* 5 (1985), 231-305.

Paulsen, P. "La pointe de lance de Termonde," *Bulletin de la société royale d'archéologique de Bruxelles* (1936).

Ross, D.J.A. "L'originalité de 'Turoldus': le maniement de la lance," *Cahiers de civilisation médiévale* 6 (1963), 127-38

Ross, D.J.A. "Plein sa hanste," *Medium Aevum* 20 (1951), 1-10.

Schwietering, J. "Zur Geschichte von Speer und Schwert im 12 Jahrhundert." In: *Philologische Schriften*. Ed. F. Ohly and M. Wehrli. Munich, 1969, pp. 59-117.

Sherlock, David. *"Plumbatae–*A Note on the Method of Manufacture." In: *Aspects of the "De rebus bellicis": Papers Presented to Professor E.A. Thompson.* Ed. M.W.C. Hassall. BAR International Series, 63. Oxford, 1987, pp. 101-02.

Swanton, M.J. *The Spearheads of the Anglo-Saxon Settlements.* London: The Royal Archaeological Institute, 1973.

Military Technology – Premodern – Arms – Maces

Arnoldi, A.M. "Le armi de botta," *Armi antiche* (1960), 29-42.

Grancsay, Stephen V. "A Gift of Enriched Military Maces," *Metropolitan Museum of Art Bulletin* 33 (Feb 1938), 37-39; in: *Arms and Armor: Essays by Stephen V. Grancsay from The Metropolitan Museum of Art Bulletin, 1920-1964.* New York: The Metropolitan Museum of Art, 1986, pp. 204-07.

Rangström, Lena. "Från stridsklubba till kunglig ordförandeklubba," *Livrustkammaren* 17 (1985), 53-78.

Roe, Fiona E.S. "The Battle-Axes, Mace-Heads and Axe-Hammers from South-West Scotland," *Transactions of the Dumfriesshire and Galloway Natural History and Antiquarian Society* 3rd ser. 44 (1967), 57-80.

Thorne, P.F. "Clubs and Maces in the Bayeux Tapestry," *History Today* 32 (Oct 1982), 48-50.

Military Technology – Premodern – Arms – Slings

Bosman, A.V.A.J. "Pouring Lead in the Pouring Rain: Making Lead Slingshot under Battle Conditions," *Journal of Roman Military Equipment Studies* 6 (1995), 99-103.

Gode, P.K. "The History of the Sling (Gophana) in India and Other Countries between c.300 BC and AD 1900." In: *Studies in Indian Cultural History*. Ed. P.K. Gode. Poona, 1960, pp. 82-91.

Grunfeld, Foster. "The Unsung Sling," *MHQ: The Quarterly Journal of Military History* 9 (Autumn 1996), 50-55.

Mahr, Helmut. "Die Steinschleuder, einer der ältesten Waffen der Menscheit," *Waffen- und Kostümkunde* 6 (1964), 118-29.

Richardson, Thom. "The Ballistics of the Sling," *Royal Armouries Yearbook* 3 (1998), 44-49.

Military Technology – Premodern – Arms – Staff Weapons (also Axes)

Anglo, Sydney. "*Le Jeu de la Hache*: A Fifteenth-Century Treatise on the Technique of Chivalric Axe Combat," *Archaeologia* 109 (1991), 113-28.

Ash, Douglas. "The Fighting Halberd," *Connoisseur* 125 (May 1950), 101-05.

Blair, Claude. "Welsh Bills, Glaives, and Hooks," *Journal of the Arms and Armour Society* 16 (1999), 71-85.

Bleuler, G. "Die Vouge, eine Stangenwaffe des spätern Mittelalters," *Anzeiger für Schweiz, Altertumskunde*, n.s. 3 (1901), 179-82.

Borg, Alan. "Gisarmes and Great Axes," *Journal of the Arms and Armour Society* 8 (1974-76), 337-42.

Bosson, Clément. "La hallebarde," *Geneva* n.s. 3 (1955), 147-82.

Bosson, Clément. "La hallebarde." In: *Guillaume Tell: L'annuaire des armes*. No. 4. Paris: Éditions Crespin, 1980, pp. 7-19.

Bosson, Clément. "Le Morgenstern," *Armi antiche* (1963), 107-40.

Bosson, Clément. "Le piquier." In: *Escalade de Genève, 1602-1980: Recueil du 378e anniversaire.* 6th ser., no. 3. Geneva, 1980, pp. 144-72.

Brown, Rodney Hilton. *American Polearms, 1526-1865: The Lance, Halberd, Spontoon, Pike, and Naval Boarding Weapons.* New Milford: N. Flayderman and Co., Inc., 1967.

Caldwell, David H. "Some Notes on Scottish Axes and Long-Shafted Weapons." In: *Scottish Weapons and Fortifications, 1100-1800.* Ed. David H. Caldwell. Edinburgh: John Donald Publishers Ltd., 1981, pp. 253-314.

Clephan, R. Coltman. "Notes on the 'Goedendag'," *Proceedings of the Society of Antiquaries of Newcastle-upon-Tyne* 9 (1899), 40-43.

Denkstein, Vladimir. "Böhmische Prinksporen aus dem 15. Jahrhundert." In: *Sbornik národního muzea v Praze.* Răa A-Historie, Svazek, 23. Prague, 1969, pp. 166-93.

Devenish, D.C. and W.M. Elliott. "A Decorated Axe-Head of Viking Type from Coventry," *Medieval Archaeology* 11 (1968), 251-52.

Dondi, Giorgio. "Del roncone, del pennato e del cosiddetto scorpione," *Armi antiche* (1976), 11-48.

Ellehauge, Martin. *Certain Phases in the Origin and Development of the Glaive.* Tøjhusmuseet Skrifter, 2. Copenhagen: Nordlundes Bogtrykkeri, 1945.

Enlart, C. "Les armes d'haste de l'homme à pied," *Gazette des armes* 4 (1976), 31-41.

Gaier, Claude. "Une arme d'hast du XVe siècle, présumée liégeoise," *Chronique archéologique du pays de Liege* 55 (1964), 27-34.

Gaitzsch, Wolfgang. "Sichelformige Klingen römischer und frühmittelalterlicher Datierung," *Waffen- und Köstumkunde* 34 (1992), 85-98.

Gamble, James D. *Battle Axes.* Providence: Mowbray Company, 1981.

Géroudet, René. "Notes sur les haches de mineurs Saxons," *Armes anciennes* 1 (1955), 103-08.

Geßler, E.A. "Das Aufkommen der Halbarte von ihrer Entwicklung von der Frühzeit bis in das 15. Jahrhundert," *Revue internationale d'histoire militaire* 3 (1939-40), 144-56.

Geßler, E.A. "Das Aufkommen der Halbarte von ihrer Frühzeit bis zum Ende des 14. Jahrhunderts." In: *Jubiläumsschrift von Dr. Robert Durrer.* Berlin, 1928, pp. 60-79.

Geßler, E.A. "Vom Wurfbeil des 15. Jahrhunderts," *Zeitschrift für historisches Waffen- und Köstumkunde* 11 (1926-28), 249-52.

Ghika, Gregoire and Pierre Contat. "Études sur des glaives valaisans du moyen âge," *Annales Valaisannes* 2nd ser. 25.1-2 (1960), 593-647.

Gordon, Michael. "Axt, Beil, Doloire," *Waffen-und Köstumkunde* 39 (1997), 63-75.

Grancsay, Stephen V. "A State Partisan of Maurice of Nassau," *Metropolitan Museum of Art Bulletin* 23 (Jan 1928), 50-52; in: *Arms and Armor: Essays by Stephen V. Grancsay from The Metropolitan Museum of Art Bulletin, 1920-1964.* New York: The Metropolitan Museum of Art, 1986, pp. 17-20.

Hayes-McCoy, G.A. "The Gallóglach Axe," *Journal of the Galway Archaeological and Historical Society* 17 (1937), 101-21.

Hewitt, John. "Contributions towards the History of Mediaeval Weapons and Military Appliances in Europe: The Goedendag, a Foot-soldier's Weapon of the Thirteenth and Fourteenth Centuries," *Archaeological Journal* 19 (1862), 314-18.

Holmes, Martin R. "Some Hafted Weapons of the Middle Ages," *Archaeological Journal* 91 (1934), 22-31.

Karcheski, Walter J., Jr. "An Ecclesiastical Glaive in the Isabella Stewart Gardner Museum." In: *Fenway Court, 1985.* Boston: Isabella Stewart Gardner Museum, 1986, pp. 50-53.

Karcheski, Walter J., Jr. "A State Halberd of the Guard of Moritz, Landgrave of Hesse-Cassel, in the Higgins Armory Museum," *Journal of the Arms and Armour Society* 16.4 (Mar 2000), 210-21.

Meier, Jürg A. "The Distribution and Origin of the Halberd in Old Zurich," *Journal of the Arms and Armour Society* 8 (1974-76), 98-113.

Meier, Jürg A. "Verbreitung und Herkunft der Halbarte im alten Zürich," *Zürcher Chronik* 2 (1971); *Bulletin du Association Suisse pour l'étude des armes et armures* 1 (May 1971).

Nickel, Helmut. "A Mamluk Axe," *Metropolitan Museum Journal* 5 (1972), 213-25; in: *Islamic Arms and Armour*. Ed. Robert Elgood. London: Scolar Press, 1979, pp. 149-61.

O'Hara, J.G. and A.R. Williams. "The Technology of a 16th Century Staff Weapon," *Journal of the Arms and Armour Society* 9 (1977-79), 198-200.

Paszkiewicz, Mieczyslaw. "Polish War Hammers: Czekai, Nadziak, Obuch," *Journal of the Arms and Armour Society* 8 (1974-76), 225-28.

Puricelli-Guerra, A. "The Glaive and the Bill." In: *Art, Arms and Armour: An International Anthology*. Chiasso, 1979, pp. 2-11; in: *Art, Arms and Armour: An International Anthology*. Vol I: *1979-80*. Ed. Robert Held. Chiasso: Acquafresca Editrice, 1979, pp. 2-11.

Prigge, H. "Steingeschossfunde mittelalterlicher Wurfmaschinen von der Zerstörung der Burg Tannensee bei Buxtehude um 1311," *Zeitschrift für historisches Waffen- und Köstumkunde* 16 (1940-42), 136-42.

Rajković, Ljubinka. "Razvoj helebarde od XIV do XVII veka," *Vesnik* 2 (1955), 120-28.

Roe, Fiona E.S. "The Battle-Axes, Mace-Heads and Axe-Hammers from South-West Scotland," *Transactions of the Dumfriesshire and Galloway Natural History and Antiquarian Society* 3rd ser. 44 (1967), 57-80.

Rose, Walther. "Das mittelalterliche Wurfbeil," *Zeitschrift für historisches Waffenkunde* 2 (1900-02), 239-46.

Rose, Walther. "Das mittelalterliche Wurfbeil und verwandte Wurf-Waffen," *Zeitschrift für historisches Waffen- und Köstumkunde* 10 (1923-25), 151-68.

Schneider, Hugo. "Zur Fabrikation der Halbarte," *Zeitschrift für schweizerische Archäolo.gie und Kunstgeschichte* 19 (1959), 60-65.

Scott, J.G. "An 11th Century War Axe in Dumfries Museum," *Transactions of the Dumfriesshire and Galloway Natural History and Antiquarian Society* 43 (1966), 117-20.

Seifert, Gerhard. "Edged Weapons: The Halberds," *International Arms Review* 1 ( ), 118-25.

Seitz, Heribert. "Ryttarens hammare och yxa," *Livrustkammaren* 14 (1976), 145-76.

Sercer, Marija. *Staro oruzje na motki.* Katalog Muzejskih Zbirki, 7. Zagreb: Povijesni Muzej Hrvatske, 1972.

Snook, George. *The Halberd and Other European Polearms, 1300-1650.* Historical Arms Series, no. 38. Alexandria Bay: Museum Restoration Service, 1998.

Tasić, Nikola. "Dve bakarne bojne sekire sa teritorije NR Srbije," *Vesnik* 5.1 (1958), 193-204.

Thompson, A. Logan. "The Decline of the Armoured Knight. Part 1: The Rise of the Halberd and Emergence of Gunpowder," *Classic Arms and Militaria* 5.2 (Mar/Apr 1998), 34-37.

Troso, Mario. *Le armi in asta: delle fanterie europee (1000-1500).* Novara: Istituto Geographico de Agostini, 1988.

Unger, Josef. "Der vorhussitische Streitflegel aus der Burg Lelekovice," *Castellologica Bohemica* 2 (1991).

van Duyse, Hermann. *Le goedendag, arme flamande: Sa légende et son histoire.* Ghent: J. Vuylsteke, Libraire, 1896.

Verbruggen, J.F. "De goedendag," *Militaria Belgica* (1970), 65-70.

Wilbrand, Wilhelm. "Das eiserne Kampfbeil in der fränkischen Zeit," *Zeitschrift für historisches Waffenkunde* 7 (1915-17), 77-79.

Wilson, David M. "A Frankish Axe-Head from Germany," *British Museum Quarterly* 28.1-2 (1964), 30-32.

Wilson, Guy M. "A Halberd Head from the River Thames," *Park Lane Arms Fair* 2 (1985), 15-20.

Ziggioto, Aldo. "Una bandiera di Trieste all' Armeria Reale di Torino," *Armi antiche* (1977), 39-46.

Military Technology – Premodern – Arms – Swords (also Daggers)

Abrash, Adnan. "The Damascene Swords." In: *17th Century War, Weaponry and Politics: International Association of Museums of Arms and Military History, Xth Congress Stockholm 1984* Stockholm, 1984, pp. 303-49.

Ager, Barry. "A Pattern-Welded Sword from Acklam Wold, North Yorkshire," *Yorkshire Archaeological Journal* 60 (1988), 13-23.

Alexander, D.G. "European Swords in the Collections of Istanbul. Part I: Swords from the Arsenal of Alexandria," *Waffen- und Köstumkunde* 27 (1985), 81-118; "Part II: Swords from the Topkapi and Askeri Museums," *Waffen- und Köstumkunde* 28 (1987), 21-48.

Alexander, D.G. "The Swords of Damascus," *Waffen- und Köstumkunde* 26 (1984), 131-38.

Alexander, David. "Dhu'l-Faqār and the Legacy of the Prophet, Mīrāth Rasūl Allāh," *Gladius* 19 (1999), 157-88.

Ament, H. "Merovingische Schwertgurtel von Typ Weihmörting," *Germania* 52 (1974), 153-61.

Anglo, Sydney. "How to Kill a Man at Your Ease: Fencing Books and the Duelling Ethic." In: *Chivalry in the Renaissance*. Ed. Sydney Anglo. Woodbridge: The Boydell Press, 1990, pp. 1-12.

Anteins, A. "Im Ostbaltikum gefundene Schwerter mit damaszierten Klingen," *Waffen und Kostümkunde* 8 (1966), 111-26.

Arbman, Holger. "Zwei Ingelri-Schwerter aus Schweden," *Zeitschrift für historisches Waffen- und Köstumkunde* 14 (1935-36), 146-49.

Bahnassi, A. "Fabrication des epées de Damas," *Syria* 53 (1976), 281-94.

Bartolotto, Claudio. "Historical and Artistical Studies in the Royal Armoury of Turin: The So-Called 'Sword of Donatello'." In: *Proceedings of the Ninth Triennial Congress of the International Association of Museums of Arms and Military History*. Quantico: Marine Corps Association, 1981, pp. 162-65.

Beard, Charles R. "The Spinola Sword," *Journal of the Arms and Armour Society* 3 (1959-61), 273-83.

Behmer, F. *Das zweischneidige Schwert der Germanischen Völker-wande-rungszeit*. Stockholm, 1939.

Biborski, Marcin. "Römische Schwerter im Gebiet des europäischen Barbaricum," *Journal of Roman Military Equipment Studies* 5 (1994), 169-97.

Blackmore, Howard L. "The Blackamoor Swords," *Royal Armouries Yearbook* 3 (1998), 67-76.

Blair, Claude. "Cesare Borgia's Sword-Scabbard," *Victoria and Albert Museum Bulletin* 2.4 (Oct 1966), 125-36; rpt. London: Her Majesty's Stationery Office, 1969.

Blair, Claude. "The Early Basket-Hilt in Britain." In: *Scottish Weapons and Fortification, 1100-1800*. Edinburgh: John Donald Publishers Ltd., 1981.

Blair, Claude. "An English Sword with an Ottoman Blade in the Swiss National Museum–The Hilt and Scabbard." In: *Blankwaffen/Armes blanches/ Armi bianche/Edged Weapons: Festschrift Hugo Schneider zu seinem 65. Geburtstag*. Ed. Karl Stüber and Hans Wetter. Zurich: Th. Gut and Co. Verlag, 1982, pp. 57-68.

Blair, Claude. "Medieval Swords and Spurs in Toledo Cathedral," *Journal of the Arms and Armour Society* 3 (1959-61), 41-52.

Blair, Claude. "The Papal Sword of Maximilian I of Bavaria," *Waffen- und Köstumkunde* 29 (1987), 117-22.

Blair, Claude. "A Royal Swordsmith and Damascener: Diego de Çaias," *Metropolitan Museum Journal* 3 (1970), 149-98.

Blair, Claude. "Some Swords Associated with Oliver Cromwell," *Park Lane Arms Fair* 12 (1995), 26-33.

Blair, Claude. "The Sword of Estore Visconti," *Waffen- und Kostümkunde* 4 (1962), 112-20.

Blair, Claude. "The Word 'Baselard'," *Journal of the Arms and Armour Society* 11 (1983-85), 193-206.

Blair, Claude. "The Word *Claymore*." In: *Scottish Weapons and Fortifications, 1100-1800*. Ed. David H. Caldwell. Edinburgh: John Donald Publishers Ltd., 1981, pp. 378-87.

Blomquist, R. "Medeltida Svard, Dolkar och Slidor funna i Lund," *Kulturen* (1938), 134-69.

Boeheim, Wendelin. "Die Zweihänder," *Zeitschrift für historisches Waffenkunde* 1 (1897-99), 62-65.

Boesch, Gottfried. "Das kaiserliche Schwert: Die Zerimonialschwerter der urschweizerischen Landammänner," *Geschichtsfreund* 118 (1965), 5-44.

Boesch, Gottfried. "Schwerter aus Uri," *Historisches Neujahrsblatt* (1966), 1-5.

Bone, Peter. "The Development of Anglo-Saxon Swords from the Fifth to the Eleventh Century." In: *Weapons and Warfare in Anglo-Saxon England*. Ed. Sonia Chadwick Hawkes. Oxford, 1989, pp. 63-70.

Bosson, Clément. "Les dagues Suisses," *Geneva* n.s. 12 (1964), 167-98.

Bosson, Clément. "L'épée à deux mains," *Armi antiche* (1976), 49-66.

Bosson, Clément. "L'épée à deux mains." In: *Blankwaffen/Armes blanches/Armi bianche/Edged Weapons: Festschrift Hugo Schneider zu seinem 65. Geburtstag*. Ed. Karl Stüber and Hans Wetter. Zurich: Th. Gut and Co. Verlag, 1982, pp. 45-56.

Bosson, Clément. "Une épée italienne d'environ 1520," *Musées de Genève* n.s. 79 (1967), 6-7.

Bosson, Clément. "Les épées: épée dite 'Colichemarde'," *Bulletin du Association Suisse pour l'étude des armes et armures* 1 (May 1971).

Brandt, A. von. "'Schwerter aus Lübeck': Ein handelsgeschichtliches Rätsel aus der Frühzeit des hansisches Frankreichshandels," *Hansische Geschichtsblätter* 83 (1965), 1-11.

Briggs, Lloyd Cabot. " European Blades in Tuareg Swords and Daggers," *Journal of the Arms and Armour Society* 5 (1965-67), 37-92.

Bruhn de Hoffmeyer, Ada. "From Mediaeval Sword to Renaissance Rapier," *Gladius* 2 (1963), 5-68.

Bruhn de Hoffmeyer, Ada. "From Mediaeval Sword to Renaissance Rapier." In: *Art, Arms and Armour: An International Anthology.* Vol I: *1979-80.* Ed. Robert Held. Chiasso: Acquafresca Editrice, 1979, pp. 52-79.

Bruhn de Hoffmeyer, Ada. "Introduction to the History of the European Sword," *Gladius* 1 (1961), 30-75.

Bruhn de Hoffmeyer, Ada. "Middelalderens islamiske svaerd," *Vaabenhistoriske aarbøger* 8 (1956), 63-80.

Bruhn de Hoffmeyer, Ada. *Middelalderens tveæggede sværd.* 2 vols. Copenhagen: Tøjhusmuseet, 1954.

Bull, Stephen. *European Swords.* Princes Risborough: Shire Publications Limited, 1994.

Buttin, Charles. "Un epée de Charles-Quint," *Armes anciennes* 1 (1954-55), 51-56.

Caneschi, G. "Mostra d'armi bianchi corte," *Armi antiche* (1968), 45-71.

Castle, Egerton. *Schools and Masters of Fence from the Middle Ages to the Eighteenth Century.* 3rd ed. London: Arms and Armour Press, 1969.

Charles, Robert-Jean. "Den franske kårde i det XVI. århundrede," *Vaabenhistoriske aarbøger* 90 (1961), 317-81.

Cirlot, Juan-Eduardo. "Una espada Barcolenesa del Siglo XV?" *Gladius* 10 (1972), 9-13.

Cirlot, Juan-Eduardo. "La espada de la catedral de Barcelona," *Gladius* 3 (1964), 5-14.

Cirlot, Juan-Eduardo. "La espada en la moneda medieval," *Gladius* 8 (1969), 17-22.

Cirlot, Victoria. "La evolucian de la espada en la sociedad Catalana de los siglos XI al XIII," *Gladius* 14 (1978), 9-58.

Cirlot, Victoria. "Un modello de clasificacion de la espada: A proposito de 'The Rapier and Small Sword, 1460-1820' de A.V.B. Norman," *Gladius* 15 (1980), 5-18.

Clark, John. "A Sword of About 1500 from the Thames," *Transactions of the London and Middlesex Archaeological Society* 24 (1973), 159-61.

Clements, John. *Renaissance Swordsmanship: The Illustrated Use of Rapiers and Cut and Thrust Swords*. Boulder: Paladin Press, 1996.

Closs, Adolf and P. Post. "Eine Gruppe mittelalterliche Dolchmesser mit bronzegefäss," *Zeitschrift für historische Waffen- und Köstumkunde* 15 (1937-39), 161-63.

Coe, Michael D. et al. *Swords and Hilt Weapons*. New York: Weidenfeld and Nicolson, 1989.

Collin, B. *The Riddle of a 13th Century Sword-Belt*. East Koyle: The Heraldry Society, 1955.

Coppens, Chris, ed. *En Garde! Scherman verbeeld: Schermboeken uit de Corble-collectie, wapens en attributen*. Leuven, 1998.

Cowen, J.D. "The Southwark Knife Reconsidered," *Antiquaries Journal* 51 (1971), 281-86.

Cowen, J.D. "A Viking Sword from Eaglesfield," *Aracheologia aeliana* 4th ser., 26 (1948), 55-61.

Cowgill, J., J. de Neergaard, and N. Griffith. *Medieval Finds from Excavations in London. I: Knives and Scabbards*. London: Her Majesty's Stationery Office, 1987.

Credland, Arthur Graves. "Some Swords of the English Civil War with Notes on the Origin of the Basket Helm," *Journal of the Arms and Armour Society* 10 (1980-82), 196-205.

Crook, Norman J. "A Note on the Viking Sword," *Canadian Journal of Arms Collecting* 18 (1980), 101-05.

Cubbon, A.M. "A Viking Sword from Ballabrooie, Patrick, with Evidence of Pattern-Welding," *Journal of the Manx Museum* 6.81 (1965), 249-53.

Darling, Anthony D. "Early Scottish Basket-Hilted Swords, c.1600-1700," *Dispatch* 109 (1985), 8-15.

Darling, Anthony D. "A Rare English Sword from Plymouth Colony," *Canadian Journal of Arms Collecting* 20 (1982), 42-56; rpt. Arms Study No. 1. Bloomfield: Museum Restoration Service, 1983.

Davidson, Hilda R. Ellis. "The Ring on the Sword," *Journal of the Arms and Armour Society* 2 (1956-58), 211-26.

Davidson, Hilda R. Ellis. *The Sword in Anglo-Saxon England: Its Archaeology and Literature.* 1962; rpt. Woodbridge: The Boydell Press, 1994.

Di Carpegna, Nolfo. "Edged Weapons in the Odeschalchi Collection," *Apollo* 127 (Feb 1988), 113-16.

Djanpoladian, Roprime and Anatolij N. Kipičnikov. "Mittelalterlicher Säbel mit einer Armenischen Inschrift gefunden im Subpolaren Ural," *Gladius* 10 (1972), 15-23.

Dodds, W. "A Sword Found at Hart, Co. Durham," *Archaeologica aeliana* 4th ser. 44 (1966), 239-42.

Down, Alec and Graham Webster. "A Roman Iron Sword (*gladius*) from Chichester," *Antiquaries Journal* 59 (1979), 402.

Drack, W. "Ein Mittelatèneschwert mit drei Goldmarken von Böttstein (Aargau)," *Zeitschrift für Schweizerische Archäologie und Kunstgeschichte* 15.4 (1954/5), 193-235.

Driel-Murray, C. van. *Zwaardscheden en andere vondsten uit de vierteende eeuw uit de Marktenroute te Leiden.* Leiden, 1988/1989.

Dufty, A.R. *European Swords and Daggers in the Tower of London.* London: Her Majesty's Stationery Office, 1968.

Dunning, G.C. "The Palace of Westminster Sword," *Archaeologia* 98 (1961), 123-58.

Durville, G. "Les épées normandes de l'Ille de Bièce," *Bulletin de la société archéologique et histoire de Nantes et de la Loire-Inférieure* 68 (1928).

Earlshall, Baron of. "Observations of Some Blades Found in Scottish Basket Hilted Swords," *Park Lane Arms Fair* 13 (1996), 30-38.

Ekstrand, Gudrun. "Eine englische Degentasche aus der Rüstkammer Gustavs II. Adolph von Schweden," *Waffen- und Köstumkunde* 10 (1968), 52-61.

Engstrom, Robert, Scott Michael Lankton, and Audrey Lesher-Engstrom. *A Modern Replication Based on the Pattern-Welded Sword of Sutton Hoo.* Kalamazoo: Medieval Institute Publications, 1990.

European Swords and Daggers in the Tower of London. London: Her Majesty's Stationery Office, 1974.

Evangelista, Nick. *The Encyclopedia of the Sword.* Westport: Greenwood Press, 1995.

Evison, Vera I. "A Decorated Seax from the Thames at Keen Edge Ferry," *Berkshire Archaeological Journal* 61 (1963-64), 28-36.

ffoulkes, Charles J. and E.C. Hopkinson. *Sword, Lance, and Bayonet.* London: Arms and Armour Press, 1967.

Fingerlin, Ilse. *Gürtel des hohen und späten Mittelalters.* Munich and Berlin: Deutsche Kunstverlag, 1971.

Forman, James. "The Scottish Dirk," *Canadian Journal of Arms Collecting* 13 (1975), 3-23.

Forman, James. "The Scottish Dirk," *Dispatch* 120 (1989), 10-18.

Forman, James. *The Scottish Dirk.* Historical Arms Series, no. 26. Alexandria Bay: Museum Restoration Service, 1993.

Forman, James. "The Skean dhu: A Gaelic Dagger," *International Arms and Militaria Collector* 10 (1997), 39-42.

Forman, James. "The Stylistic Evolution of the Scottish Dirk," *Canadian Journal of Arms Collecting* 35.3 (Aug 1997), 84-88.

France-Lanord, A. "La fabrication des epées damascées aux époques mérovingienne et carolingienne." In: *Le pays gaumais* (Vireton, 1949).

France-Lanord, A. "La fabrication des epées mérovingiennes et carolingiennes," *Revue de metallurgie* 49 (1952), 411-22.

Gaibi, Agostino. "The Art of the Swordmaker in Brescia," *Journal of the Arms and Armour Society* 5 (1965-67), 332-52.

Gaier, Claude. "L'apparition de l'épée à deux mains dans l'est de la Belgique (XIIIe-XIVe siècles) d'après quelques épitaphiers liégeois," *Bulletin de la société royale "Le vieux Liège"* 157 (1967), 226-30.

Gale, David A. "The Seax." In: *Weapons and Warfare in Anglo-Saxon England*. Ed. Sonia Chadwick Hawkes. Oxford, 1989, pp. 71-83.

Garašanin, Draga. "Mač mošunjskog tipa u Narodnom muzeju u Beogradu," *Vesnik* 5.1 (1958), 9-23.

Geibig, Alfred. *Beiträge zur morphologischen Entwicklung des Schwertes im Mittelalter: Eine Analyse des Fundmaterials vom ausgehenden 8. bis 12. Jahrhundert au Sammlungen der Bundesrepublik Deutschland*. Offa-Bücher, n.b. 71. Neumünster: Karl Wachholtz Verlag, 1991.

Gerino, Giorgio. "Antonio e Federico Piccinino spadari in Milano," *Armi antiche* (1983), 5-11.

Ghika, Gregoire and Pierre Contat. "Etudes sur des glaives valaisans du moyen âge," *Annales valaisannes* 2nd ser., 35 (1960), 593-648.

Girton, T. *The Mark of the Sword: A Narrative History of the Cutlers Company, 1189-1975*. London, 1975.

Głosek, Marian. "Le développement et l'état des recherches sur les épées médiévales en Europe," *Fasciculi archaeologiae historicae* 1 (1986), 33-40.

Głosek, Marian. *Znaki i napisy na mieczach średniowiecznych w Polsce*. Wroclaw: Polska Akademia Nauk. Instytut Historii Kultury Materialnej, 1973.

Głosek, Marian and Leszek Kajzer. "Miecze z napisami grupy DIC w Europie Środkowej," *Kwartalnik historii kultury materialnej* 24.2 (1976), 217-40.

Głosek, Marian and Leszek Kajzer. "The Sword found at Osieczna in Great Poland," *Gladius* 12 (1974), 33-42.

Głosek, Marian and Leszek Kajzer. "Zdobiony miecz średniowieczny znaleziony w Osiecznej pow. Leszno," *Kwartalnik historii kultury materialnej* 23.2 (1975), 279-88.

Głosek, Marian and Leszek Kajzer. "Zu den mittelalterlichen Schwerten der Benedictus-Gruppe," *Waffen- und Kostümkunde* 19 (1977), 117-28.

Głosek, Marian and I. Nadolski. *Miecze sredniowieczne z ziem polskich.* Acta archaeologica Lodziensia, 19. Lodz, 1970.

Gorman, Michael R. "*Ulfberht*: Innovation and Imitation in Early Medieval Swords," *Park Lane Arms Fair* 16 (1999), 7-12.

Grancsay, Stephen V. "A Commemorative Sword of the Thirty Years War," *Metropolitan Museum of Art Bulletin* 25 (Jan 1930), 8-10; in: *Arms and Armor: Essays by Stephen V. Grancsay from The Metropolitan Museum of Art Bulletin, 1920-1964.* New York: The Metropolitan Museum of Art, 1986, pp. 54-55.

Grancsay, Stephen V. "A Damascened Eared Dagger by Diego de Çaias," *Metropolitan Museum of Art Bulletin* 35 (Aug 1940), 160-61; in: *Arms and Armor: Essays by Stephen V. Grancsay from The Metropolitan Museum of Art Bulletin, 1920-1964.* New York: The Metropolitan Museum of Art, 1986, pp. 251-53.

Grancsay, Stephen V. "An Early Short Sword," *Metropolitan Museum of Art Bulletin* 28 (Aug 1933), 138-39; in: *Arms and Armor: Essays by Stephen V. Grancsay from The Metropolitan Museum of Art Bulletin, 1920-1964.* New York: The Metropolitan Museum of Art, 1986, pp. 116-18.

Grancsay, Stephen V. "A French Crusader's Sword Pommel," *Metropolitan Museum of Art Bulletin* 34 (Sep 1939), 211-13; in: *Arms and Armor: Essays by Stephen V. Grancsay from The Metropolitan Museum of Art Bulletin, 1920-1964.* New York: The Metropolitan Museum of Art, 1986, pp. 237-38.

Grancsay, Stephen V. "The Sword of Ambrogio di Spinola," *Metropolitan Museum of Art Bulletin* n.s. 5 (May 1947), 235-39; in: *Arms and Armor: Essays by Stephen V. Grancsay from The Metropolitan Museum of Art Bulletin, 1920-1964.* New York: The Metropolitan Museum of Art, 1986, pp. 293-300.

Grancsay, Stephen V. "A Viking Chieftain's Sword," *Metropolitan Museum of Art Bulletin* n.s. 17 (Mar 1959), 173-81; in: *Arms and Armor: Essays by Stephen V. Grancsay from The Metropolitan Museum of Art Bul-*

letin, 1920-1964. New York: The Metropolitan Museum of Art, 1986, pp. 470-80.

Grancsay, Stephen V. "A Wheellock Dagger for the Court of the Medici." In: *Arms and Armor Annual: Volume One.* Ed. Robert Held. Northfield: Digest Books, Inc., 1973, pp. 48-55.

Haedeke, Hanns-Ulrich. "Das Schwert des heiligen Georg." In: *Blankwaffen/Armes blanches/Armi bianche/Edged Weapons: Festschrift Hugo Schneider zu seinem 65. Geburtstag.* Ed. Karl Stüber and Hans Wetter. Zurich: Th. Gut and Co. Verlag, 1982, pp. 9-16.

Halpin, Andrew. "Irish Medieval Swords *c.* 1170-1600," *Proceedings of the Royal Irish Academy* 86 (1986), 183-230.

Härke, Heinrich. "Knives in Early Saxon Burials: Blade Length and Age at Death," *Medieval Archaeology* 33 (1989), 144-48.

Hazell, P.J. "The Pedite Gladius," *Antiquaries Journal* 61 (1981), 73-82.

Hawkes, Sonia Chadwick and R.I. Page. "Swords and Runes in South-East England," *Antiquaries Journal* 47 (1967), 1-26.

Hayes-McCoy, G.A. "Irish Swords of the Sixteenth Century," *Journal of the Arms and Armour Society* 2 (1956-58), 1-12.

Hayes-McCoy, G.A. *Sixteenth Century Irish Swords in the National Museum of Ireland.* Dublin: The Stationery Office, 1959.

Hayes-McCoy, G.A. "Sixteenth Century Swords Found in Ireland," *Journal of the Royal Society of Antiquaries of Ireland* 78 (1948), 38-54.

Hayward, John F. "The Fountaine Sword: A Sixteenth Century Masterpiece of Sculpture in Iron," *Auction* 3.3 (1969), 37-38.

Hayward, John F. "An Italian Renaissance Sword," *Arms and Armour at the Dorchester* (1982), 15-17.

Horedt, K. "Cu privise la locul de descoperire a sabiel de la Moresti," *Acta Musei Napocensis* 4 (1967), 509-10.

Horedt, K. "Săbiile si spadele din secolul X in bazinul carpatic," *Acta Musei Napocensis* 5 (1968), 422-28.

Ivanov, A. "A Group of Iranian Daggers of the Period from the Fifteenth Century to the Beginning of the Seventeenth, with Persian Inscriptions." In: *Islamic Arms and Armour*. Ed. Robert Elgood. London: Scolar Press, 1979, pp. 64-77.

Jacob, Alain. *Les armes blanches du monde islamique. Armes de poing: Epées, sabres poignards, couteaux*. Paris: Jacques Grancher, 1985.

Jankuhn, H. "Eine Schwertform aus karolingischer Zeit," *Offa* 4.2 (1940).

Janssens, M. "Essai de reconstitution d'un procedé de fabrication des lames d'épées damassées," *Studies in Conservation* 3.3 (Apr 1958), 93-106.

Javornik, Ivan. "Kratak istoriski pregled mača-dvoručnjaka u srednjovekovnom naoružanju," *Vesnik* 5.1 (1958), 59-76.

Jones, Lee A. "The Serpent in the Sword: Pattern-Welding in Early Medieval Swords," *Park Lane Arms Fair* 14 (1997), 7-11.

Kalmár, Johannes V. "Zwei cinquedeen des quattrocento in ungarischen Museen," *Zeitschrift für historische Waffen- und Köstumkunde* 17 (1943-44), 37-44.

Kamniker, K. and Peter Krenn. "Die Zweihander des Landeszeughauses in Graz," *Landesmuseum Joanneum Graz Jahresbericht 1972* n.s. (1974), 129-56.

Keeble, K. Corey. "A 'Grete Sword' in the Royal Ontario Museum, Toronto," *Canadian Journal of Arms Collecting* 31 (May 1993), 48-51.

Keeble, K. Corey. "A 'Sempach' Sword in the Royal Ontario Museum," *Canadian Journal of Arms Collecting* 30 (Nov 1992), 127-29.

Kirpičnikov, Anatclij N. "Inscriptions et marques sur les lames d'épées de l'Europe orientale du IXe au XIIIe siècle." In: *I miedzynzrodowy: Kongres archeologii slowianskiej*. Nadbitka, 1975, pp. 337-51.

Kirpičnikov, Anatolij N. "Der sogenannte Säbel Karls des Grossen," *Gladius* 10 (1972), 69-80.

Kovács, László. "Waffenwechsel vom Säbel zum Schwert: Zur Datierung der ungarischen Gräber des 10.-11. Jahrhunderts mit zweischneidigem Schwert," *Fasciculi archaeologicae historicae* 6 (1993), 45-60.

Kovalčik, R.M. "Ein Schwertdepot aus Spišská Belá und Schalenknaufschwerter aus der Slowakei," *Archeologické rozhledy* 18 (1966), 647-54.

Krenn, Peter. *Schwert und Spiess: Landeszeughaus Graz, am Steiermärkischen Landesmuseum Joanneum.* Graz: Kunstverlag Hofstetter, 1997.

Krenn, Peter and Kurt Kamniker. "Die Dusäggen des Landeszeughauses in Graz," *Waffen- und Kostümkunde* 15 (1973), 139-45.

Kühn, Ulrich. "Das Richtschwert in Bayern," *Waffen- und Kostümkunde* 12 (1970), 89-126.

Künzl, Ernst. "Dekorierte Gladii und Cingula: Eine ikonographische Statistik," *Journal of Roman Military Equipment Studies* 5 (1994), 33-58.

Lang, Janet and Barry Ager. "Swords of the Anglo-Saxon and Viking Periods in the British Museum: A Radiographic Study." In: *Weapons and Warfare in Anglo-Saxon England.* Ed. Sonia Chadwick Hawkes. Oxford, 1989, pp. 85-122.

La Rocca, Donald. *The Academy of the Sword: Illustrated Fencing Books, 1500-1800.* New York: Metropolitan Museum of Art, 1998.

Latham, J. Wilkinson. *The Evolution of Swords.* London: Wilkinson Sword Ltd., 1965.

Lhoste, Jean. *Les épées portées en France: des origines à nos jours.* La Tour du Pin: Editions du Portail, 1997.

Lieber, Elfriede. "Frühe Eisenschnittdegen im Historischen Museum Dresden," *Jahrbuch der Staatlichen Kunstsammlungen Dresden* (1978/79), 117-58.

Lorange, A.L. *Den yngre jernalderens sværd.* Bergen, 1889.

Mann, James. "A European Sword of the Late XIVth Century with an Arabic Inscription," *Eretz-Israel* 7 (1963), 76-77.

Mann, James. "A Fourteenth-Century Sword Found in the River Thames near Dowgate Street," *Antiquaries Journal* 39 (1959), 287-88.

Martindale, Jane. "The Sword on the Stone: Some Resonances of a Medieval Symbol of Power (the Tomb of King John in Worcester Cathedral," *Anglo-Norman Studies* 15 (1993), 199-241.

Maryon, Herbert. "Pattern-Welding and Damascening of Sword Blades," *Studies in Conservation* 5 (1960), 26-37, 52-60.

Mazansky, Cyril. "The Use of Computerised Tomographic X-Rays in the Analysis of a Basket Hilted Sword Relic from the Shipwreck of the *Sea Venture*," *Park Lane Arms Fair* 12 (1995), 18-22.

McAllister, Ronald I. "The Medieval Scottish Sword," *Scotland's Magazine* 64.3 (Mar 1963), 37-39.

McAllister, Ronald I. "The Medieval Scottish Sword: A Monumental History," *Dispatch* 139 (1995), 11-15; 140 (1996), 9-13.

McGrath, J.N. "A Note on the Classification of Celtic Swords," *Journal of the Arms and Armour Society* 7 (1971-73), 263-65.

Melikian-Chirvani. A.S. "An English Sword with an Ottoman Blade in the Swiss National Museum–the Blade." In: *Blankwaffen/Armes blanches/ Armi bianche/Edged Weapons: Festschrift Hugo Schneider zu seinem 65. Geburtstag*. Ed. Karl Stüber and Hans Wetter. Zurich: Th. Gut and Co. Verlag, 1982, pp. 69-78.

Melville, N.H.T. "A Note on the Great Swords in the Burrell Collection," *Dispatch* 114 (1987), 12-13.

Menghin, W. *Das Schwert im frühen Mittelalter*. Wissenschaftliche Beibände zum Anzeiger des Germanischen Nationalmuseums, Nuremburg, Band 1. Stuttgart: Konrad Theiss Verlag, 1983.

Müller, Heinrich and H. Kölling. *Europäische Hieb- und Stichwaffen aus der Sammlung des Museums für Deutsche Geschichte*. Berlin: Militärverlag der Deutschen Demokratische Republik, 1981.

Nadolski, Andrzej. "Pochwa miecza znaleziona w osadzie miejskiej z XI wieku w Gdańsku," *Wiadomości archeologicne* 22.2 (1955), 186-92.

Nadolski, Andrzej. "Szczerbiec–The Polish Coronation Sword," *Journal of the Arms and Armour Society* 6 (1968-70), 183-84.

Navarro, J.M. de. *The Finds from the Site of La Tène*. I: *Scabbards and the Swords found in Them*. London: British Academy, 1972.

Newman, P.R. *A Catalogue of the Sword Collection at York Castle Museum*. York: York Castle Museum, 1985.

Nickel, Helmut. "About the Sword of the Huns and the 'Urepos' of the Steppes," *Metropolitan Museum Journal* 7 (1973), 131-42.

Nickel, Helmut. "A Crusader's Sword: Concerning the Effigy of Jean d'Alluye," *Metropolitan Museum Journal* 26 (1991), 123-28.

Norman, A.V.B. "Additional Material towards a History of the Basket-Hilt," *Journal of the Arms and Armour Society* 15 (1995-98), 403-17.

Norman, A.V.B. *The Rapier and Small Sword, 1460-1820*. London: Arms and Armour Press, 1980.

Norman, A.V.B. "Some Hanger Hilts of the Early Seventeenth Century." In: *Blankwaffen/Armes blanches/Armi bianche/Edged Weapons: Festschrift Hugo Schneider zu seinem 65. Geburtstag*. Ed. Karl Stüber and Hans Wetter. Zurich: Th. Gut and Co. Verlag, 1982, pp. 79-86.

North, A.R.E. "A Late Fifteenth Century Italian Sword," *Connoisseur* (Dec 1975), 238-41.

North, A.R.E. *An Introduction to European Swords*. London: Her Majesty's Stationery Office, 1982.

Oakeshott, Ewart. "Bastard Swords," *Park Lane Arms Fair* 7 (1990), 12-17.

Oakeshott, Ewart. "Beati omnipotensque angeli Christi (Blessed and Omnipotent the Angels of Christ)," *Park Lane Arms Fair* 3 (1986), 5-14.

Oakeshott, Ewart. "Further Notes on a River-Find of 15th Century Swords," *Park Lane Arms Fair* 1 (1984), 7-12.

Oakeshott, Ewart. "The Grip of the Medieval Sword and a Battle near Tagliacozzo," *Park Lane Arms Fair* 11 (1994), 6-13.

Oakeshott, Ewart. "'Hiltipreht!': Name or Invocation," *Park Lane Arms Fair* 12 (1995), 6-11.

Oakeshott, Ewart. "Medieval Swords," *Gun Report* 31.4 (Sep 1985), 18-23; 31.5 (Oct 1985), 18-23; 31.7 (Dec 1985), 18-23; 31.8 (Jan 1986), 18-23; 31.9 (Feb 1986), 14-19; 31.10 (Mar 1986), 14-21; 31.11 (Apr 1986), 16-23; 32.1 (June 1986), 22-32; 32.3 (Aug 1986), 44-53; 32.5 (Oct 1986), 52-62; 32.8 (Jan 1987), 24-32.

Oakeshott, Ewart. "Old Wine in New Bottles," *Park Lane Arms Fair* 8 (1991), 18-21.

Oakeshott, Ewart. *Records of the Medieval Sword*. Woodbridge: Boydell Press, 1991.

Oakeshott, Ewart. "Reflection Upon Some Medieval Swords from the Thames," *Park Lane Arms Fair* 2 (1985), 7-14.

Oakeshott, Ewart. "A River-Find of 15th Century Swords." In: *Blankwaffen/Armes blanches/Armi bianche/Edged Weapons: Festschrift Hugo Schneider zu seinem 65. Geburtstag*. Ed. Karl Stüber and Hans Wetter. Zurich: Th. Gut and Co. Verlag, 1982, pp. 17-32.

Oakeshott, Ewart. "The 'Sempach' Family of Swords," *Park Lane Arms Fair* 4 (1987), 7-15.

Oakeshott, Ewart. "Serpent of Blood," *Park Lane Arms Fair* 8 (1991), 5-11.

Oakeshott, Ewart. "Some Early Examples of the Use of the Ricasso," *Journal of the Arms and Armour Society* 1 (1953), 22-24.

Oakeshott, Ewart. "Some Medieval Sword Pommels: An Essay in Analysis," *Journal of the British Archaeological Association* 14 (1951), 47-62.

Oakeshott, Ewart. "Sword and Rapier," *Park Lane Arms Fair* 9 (1992), 12-18.

Oakeshott, Ewart. *The Sword in the Age of Chivalry*. London, 1964; rpt. Woodbridge: The Boydell Press, 1994.

Oakeshott, Ewart. "The Swords of Castillon," *Park Lane Arms Fair* 10 (1993), 7-16.

Oakeshott, Ewart. "Swords, Warlords and Fish," *Park Lane Arms Fair* 13 (1996), 7-11.

Oakeshott, Ewart. "The Templars and the Church," *Park Lane Arms Fair* 15 (1998), 7-10.

Oakeshott, Ewart. "A War Sword of the XIVth Century in the Guildhall Museum," *Journal of the Arms and Armour Society* 1 (1954), 141-52.

Oliver, David. "Some European Knightly Swords from the Arsenal of Alexandria," *Park Lane Arms Fair* 16 (1999), 13-24.

Pansieri, C. "Ricerche metallographiche sopra una spada da guerra del XII secolo." In: *Associazione Italiana di metallurgia: Documents e contributi.* Milan, 1957, pp. 7-40.

Pansieri, C. *Ricerche metallographiche sopra una spada da guerra del XII secolo: Documenti e contributi per la storia della metallurgia.* Quaderno I. Milan, n.d.

Paulsen, P. *Schwertortbänder der Wikingerzeit.* Stuttgart, 1953.

Peirce, Ian. "The Development of the Medieval Sword, c. 850-1300." In: *The Ideals and Practice of Medieval Knighthood*, III. Ed. C. Harper-Bill and R. Harvey. Woodbridge, 1990, pp. 139-58.

Peirce, Ian and Ewart Oakeshott. "The Sword of Can Grande della Scala," *Park Lane Arms Fair* 17 (2000), 6-8.

Pelaes Valle, Jose Maria. "La espada ropera Española en los siglos XVI y XVII," *Gladius* 16 (1983), 147-99.

Petersen, Jan. "En norsk svertyp fra vikingtiden," *Oldtiden* 7 (1916-18).

Petersen, Jan. *De norske vikingswerd: En typologisk-kronologisk studie over vikingetidens vaaben.* Christiana (Oslo), 1919.

Peterson, Harold L. *Daggers and Fighting Knives of the Western World from the Stone Age till 1900.* London: Herbert Jenkins Ltd., 1968.

Peterson, Harold L. "A Note on a Medieval Sword," *Journal of the Arms and Armour Society* 7 (1971-73), 56-57.

Piaskowski, Jerzy. "Metallographic Examination of Two Damascene Steel Blades," *Journal for the History of Arabic Science* 2 (1978), 3-30.

Piletić, Dragoslav. "O rimskim mačevima," *Vesnik* 1 (1954), 9-17.

Pleiner, Radomír and B.G. Scott. *The Celtic Sword*. Oxford: Clarendon Press, 1993.

Poklewski-Kozieł, Tadeusz. "Schutzwert des Burgwalls von Leczyca in Polen im Lichte der Geschichte des Litauenangriffs im Jahr 1294," *Fasciculi archaeologicae historicae* 10 (1997), 45-50.

Pons, A. "La espada en Mallorca durante el siglo XIV," *Hispania* 11 (1951), 536-606.

Preidel, H. "Die karolingischen Schwerter bei den Westslaven." In: *Gandert-Festschrift*. Berlin, 1959, pp. 128-42.

Radcliffe, A. "Ricciana. II: The Sword of Donatello," *Burlington Magazine* 124 (July 1982), 415-17.

Raddatz, K. "Zum Schwert von Högenäs," *Germania* 34.1/2 (1956), 92-94.

Raid, Ulla. "The Roman Swords from Danish Bog Finds," *Journal of Roman Military Equipment Studies* 5 (1994), 227-41.

Richardson, Thom. "H.R. Robinson's 'Dutch Armour of the 17th Century," *Journal of the Arms and Armour Society* 13 (1989-91), 256-78.

Robinson, B.W. "An Early Islamic Blade," *Journal of the Arms and Armour Society* 1 (1953), 33-35.

Robinson, H.W. "An Iron Age Sword Blade," *Archaeologia aeliana* 4th ser. 46 (1968), 273-75.

Rodolfo, Giacomo. "Una spada del secolo XIV rinvenuta a Carignano nell'alveo del Po," *Armi antiche* 4 (1957), 19-36.

Rodriquez Lorente, J.J. "The XVth Century Ear Dagger: Its Hispano-Moresque Origin," *Gladius* 3 (1964), 67-88.

Rodriquez Lorente, J.J. "El oscuro origen de las dagas o puñales de orejas." In: *II congreso de arqueologia medieval Española*. Madrid, 1987, III:112-14.

Rubi, E.S.R. "Espadas de España," *Arte Español* (1956), 204-24, 237-47.

Rynne, Etienne. "A Classification of Pre-Viking Irish Iron Swords." In: *Studies in Early Ireland: Essays in Honour of M.V. Duignan.* Ed. B.G. Scott. Belfast, 1982, pp. 93-97.

Sarnowska, Wanda. "Miecze wczesnośredniowieczne w Polsce," *Światowit* 21 (1955).

Schneider, Hugo. "Découverte d'une nouvelle épée," *Armes anciennes* 1 (1955), 99-102.

Schneider, Hugo. *Schwerten und Degen: Aus dem Schweizerischen Landesmuseum.* Bern: Schweizerischen Landesmuseum, 1957.

Schneider, Hugo. "Untersuchungen an mittelalterlichen Dolchen aus dem Gebiete der Schweiz," *Zeitschrift für schweizerische Archäologie und Kunstgeschichte* 20 (1960), 91-105.

Schneider, Hugo and Karl Stüber. *Waffen in Schweizerischen Landesmuseum: Griffwaffen I.* Zurich: Orell Füssli Verlag, 1980.

Schwerter und Dolche, Ess- und Schneidgerät. Solingen: Deutsches Klingenmuseum, 1964.

Schwietering, J. "Zur Geschichte von Speer und Schwert im 12 Jahrhundert." In: *Philologische Schriften.* Ed. F. Ohly and M. Wehrli. Munich, 1969, pp. 59-117.

Scott, Jack G. "Three Medieval Swords from Scotland." In: *Scottish Weapons and Fortifications, 1100-1800.* Ed. David H. Caldwell. Edinburgh: John Donald Publishers Ltd., 1981, pp. 10-20.

Seifert, Gerhard. *Schwert, Degen, Säbel.* Hamburg: Helmut Gerhard Schulz, 1962.

Seitz, Heribert. "Saxvapens nomenklatur och des förutsättningar," *Fornvännen* (1963), 20-29.

Seitz, Heribert. "Ett sengotiskt svärd i västerås domkyrka," *Fornvännen* (1959), 11-24.

Seitz, Heribert. "La storta–the Falchion," *Armi antichi* (1963), 3-12.

Seitz, Heribert. *Svärdet och värjan som armévapen.* Kungl. Armémuseums Handböcker. Stockholm, 1955.

Singman, Jeffrey L. "The Medieval Swordsman: A Thirteenth-Century German Fencing Manuscript," *Royal Armouries Yearbook* 2 (1997), 129-36.

Soens, A.L. "Two Rapier Points: Analysing Elizabethan Fighting Methods," *Notes and Queries* n.s. 15.4 (Apr 1968), 127-28.

Stevenson, Robert B.K. "Medieval Bronze Sword-Pommel with Clay Core," *Proceedings of the Society of Antiquaries of Scotland* 106 (1977), 218-19.

Strömberg, M. "Schwertortbänder mit Vogelmotiven der Wikingerzeit," *Meddelanden från Lunds Universitets Historiska Museum* (1951).

Swaryczewski, A. "Granat-sztuka mistrzowska stradomskiego cechu miecznik ów," *Studia do dziejów dawnego uzbrojenia i ubioru wojskowego* 8 (1982), 35-48.

Tarassuk, Leonid. "Daghe e pugnali da duello," *Armi antiche* (1978), 31-64.

Tarassuk, Leonid. "Some Notes on Parrying Daggers and Poniards," *Metropolitan Museum Journal* 12 (1978), 33-54.

Tezcan, Turgay. "Turkish Swords in the Fifteenth Century." In: *Proceedings of the Ninth Triennial Congress of the International Association of Museums of Arms and Military History*. Quantico: Marine Corps Association, 1981, pp. 128-31.

Thiel, Andreas and Werner Zanier. "Römische Dolche–Bemerkungen zu den Fundumständen," *Journal of Roman Military Equipment Studies* 5 (1994), 59-81.

Thompson, A.L. "The Symbolic and Military Significance of the Sword in Britain," *Classic Arms and Militaria* 2.1 (Jan/Feb 1994), 22-6.

Thompson, Logan. *Daggers and Bayonets: A History*. Staplehurst: Spellmount, 1999.

Thompson, Logan. "Ingelrii Sword," *Classic Arms and Armour* 4.1 (Jan/Feb 1997), 21.

Thompson, Logan. "The Sword in Britain," *Classic Arms and Armour* 4.6 (Nov/Dec 1997), 16-19.

Thygesen, Peter. "Sydtysk kårde ca. 1580," *Våbenhistorisk tiddskrift* 13 (1980), 111-12.

Tóth, Z. *Attilas Schwert*. Budapest, 1930.

Tougher, Patrick R. *Basket Hilt Swords, circa 1590-1800*. Washington: Scottish Sword and Shield, 1994.

Uhlemann, Heinz Robert. "Deutsches Klingenmuseum Solingen: Gotische Prunkschwerter und Prunkdolche," *Waffen- und Kostümkunde* 6 (1964), 96-107.

Uhlemann, Heinz Robert. "Die mittelalterlichen Gerichtsschwerter und die späteren Richtschwerter von Passau." In: *Blankwaffen/Armes blanches/Armi bianche/Edged Weapons: Festschrift Hugo Schneider zu seinem 65. Geburtstag*. Ed. Karl Stüber and Hans Wetter. Zurich: Th. Gut and Co. Verlag, 1982, pp. 33-44.

Uhlemann, Heinz Robert. "Peter Monsit me fecit Solingen," *Waffen- und Kostümkunde* 16 (1974), 81-86.

Uhlemann, Heinz Robert. "Über einige Vorschneide- und Kredenzbestecke des Deutschen Klingensmuseums Solingen," *Armi antiche* (1967), 3-26.

Ullmann, K. "Dolchmesser, Dolche und Kurzwehren des 15. und 16. Jahrhunderts im Kern-Raume der Hanse," *Waffen und Kostümkunde* 3 (1961), 1-13, 114-27.

Valentine, Eric. *Rapiers: An Illustrated History and Reference Guide to the Rapiers of the 16th and 17th Centuries and their Companions*. Middlesex: Arms and Armour Press, 1968.

Vinski, Zdenko. "Osvrt na mačeve ranog Srednjeg vijeka u našim krajevima," *Vesnik* 2 (1955), 34-53.

Vinski, Zdenko. "O primjeni rendgenskog snimanja pri istraživanju ranosrednovekovnih mačeva," *Vesnik* 11-12 (1966), 69-88.

Vlassa, N. "Sabia feudala timpurie de la Ernie," *Acta Musei Napocensis* 2 (1965), 669-71.

Walton, Steven. "Words of Technological Virtue: *The Battle of Brunanburh* and Anglo-Saxon Sword Manufacture," *Technology and Culture* 36 (1995), 987-999.

Wathelet-Willem, Jeanne. "L'épee dans les plus anciennes chansons de geste: Etude de vocabulaire." In: *Mélanges offerts à René Crozet à l'occasion de son soixante-dixèime anniversaire.* Ed. P. Gallais and Y.-J. Riou. Poitiers, 1966, I:435-49.

Watkin, J.R. and B.J. Gilmour. "A Late Anglo-Saxon Sword from Gilling West, North Yorkshire," *Medieval Archaeology* 31 (1986), 93-99.

Wegner, Wolfgang. "Ein Schwert von Daniel Hopfer in Germanischen Nationalmuseum in Nürnberg," *Münchner Jahrbuch der bildenden Kunst* 3.5 (1954), 124-30.

Wells, H. Bartlett. "Contributions to the History of the Heat Treatment of Steel (Largely from the Evidence of Sword Blades)," *Journal of the Arms and Armour Society* 6 (1968-70), 217-38.

Wells, H. Bartlett. "Medieval Two-Edged Swords in Rumania," *Journal of the Arms and Armour Society* 2 (1956-58), 265-74.

Wells, H. Bartlett. "A Problem in the Techniques of the Medieval European Swordsmith," *Journal of the Arms and Armour Society* 4 (1962-64), 217-30.

Wever, Franz. "Das Schwert in Mythos und Handwerk," *Arbeitsgemeinschaft für Forschung des Landes Nordrhein Westfalen* 91 (1961), 1-71.

Wilkinson, Frederick. "Two Handed Swords," *London Arms Fair* (Aut 1975), 35-37.

Williams, Alan R. "Methods of Manufacture of Swords in Medieval Europe: Illustrated by the Metallography of Some Examples," *Gladius* 13 (1977), 75-101.

Williams, Alan R. "Seven Swords of the Renaissance from an Analytical Point of View," *Gladius* 14 (1978), 97-127.

Williams, Richard. "A Radnorshire Sword Find," *Radnorshire Society Transactions* 24 (1954), 76-78.

Willis, Tony. "The Fourteenth-Century Scottish Sword," *Journal of the Arms and Armour Society* 15 (1995-98), 1-16.

Willis, Tony. "Scottish 'twa handit Swerdis'," *Park Lane Arms Fair* 13 (1996), 12-25.

Willis, Tony. "A Two Handed Gaelic Irish Sword of the Sixteenth Century,"*Park Lane Arms Fair* 15 (1998), 18-27.

Wilson, David M. "Some Neglected Late Anglo-Saxon Swords," *Medieval Archaeology* 9 (1965), 32-54.

Wilson, Guy M. "Further Notes on Early Basket-Hilted Swords," *Journal of the Arms and Armour Society* 13 supplement (1990), 23-26.

Wilson, Guy M. "Notes on Some Early Basket-Hilted Swords," *Journal of the Arms and Armour Society* 12 (1986-88), 1-19.

Woosnam-Savage, Robert C. "Two Scottish Swords in an English Collection: A Short Note," *Park Lane Arms Fair* 17 (2000), 20-22.

Ypey, J. "Einige Wikingerzeitliche Schwerter aus die Niederlanden," *Offa* 41 (1984), 213-25.

Zaky, 'Abd al-Rahman. "Islamic Swords in the Middle Ages," *Bulletin de l'institut d'Egypte* 36 (1955), 365-79.

Zeki Velidi, A. "Die Schwerter der Germanen nach Arabischen Berichten des 9-11 Jahrhunderts," *Zeitschrift für deutschen Morgenlandischen Gesellschaft* 90 (1926), 19-37.

Military Technology – Premodern – Arms and Armor – Production and Trade

Anting, L. *Tallinskie oruzheincki i ognestrel noe oruzhie XIV-XVI vekov.* Tallin: State Historical Museum of the Estonian S.S. Republic, 1967.

Barron, E.J. "Notes on the History of the Armourers and Brasiers Company," *Transactions of the London Middlesex Archaeological Society* 2 (1911-13), 300-19.

Beks, G. "Dutch Arms for France, 1635-1640." In: *The Arsenal of the World: The Dutch Arms Trade in the Seventeenth Century*. Ed. Jan Piet Puype and Marco van der Hoeven. Amsterdam: Batavian Lion International, 1996, pp. 36-41.

Blair, Claude. "The Armourers' Bill of 1581: The Making of Arms and Armour in Sixteenth-Century London," *Journal of the Arms and Armour Society* 12 (1986-88), 20-53.

Blair, Claude. "A Royal Cutler's Bill of 1547," *Journal of the Arms and Armour Society* 1 (1954), 104-11.

Boeheim, Wendelin. *Meister der Waffenschmeidkunst vom XIV bis XVIII Jahrhundert*. Berlin, 1897.

Brun, Robert. "Notes sur le commerce des armes a Avignon au XIVe siècle," *Bibliothèque de l'école des chartes* 109 (1951), 209-31.

Dillon, Harold A. "An Armourers Bill, Temp. Edward III," *Antiquary* 20 (Jul-Dec 1890).

Dondi, Giorgio. "Dei lanciari Gounod: Le poche notizie che abbiamo," *Armi antiche* (1983), 13-21.

Egg, Erich. "Der Strassburger Goldschmied Josias Barbette," *Waffen und Kostümkunde* 8 (1966), 126-30.

Ekfeldt, Axel. "Some Comments on Swedish Weapons Production in Earlier Times Up until the Present." In: *17th Century War, Weaponry and Politics: International Association of Museums of Arms and Military History, Xth Congress Stockholm 1984* Stockholm, 1984, pp. 295-300.

ffoulkes, Charles J. "The Armourers Company of London and The Greenwich School of Armourers," *Archaeologia* 76 (1927), 41-58.

Finó, J.-F. "Notes sur la production du fer et la fabrication des armes en France au moyen-age," *Gladius* 3 (1964), 47-66.

Fliegel, S.N. *The Making of Armour*. Cleveland: Cleveland Museum of Art, 1993.

Fossati, F. "Per il commercio delle armature e i missaglia," *Archivio storico Lombardo* 59 (1932), 279-97.

Gaibi, Agostino. "Note sulla lavarazione dei metalli in Val Sesia con senni particolari sulle fabbricazione di armi," *Armi antichi* (1960).

Gaibi, Agostino and Pado Gay. "Un manoscritto del 600: L'arte fabrile, di Antonio Petrini," *Armi antiche* (1963), 141-68; (1965), 67-109.

Gaier, Claude. "Un artisanat spécialisé: l'armurerie liégeoise." In: *La Wallonie: Le pays et les hommes, lettres, arts, culture.* Brussels, 1981, IV:198-204.

Gaier, Claude. "Le commerce des armes en Europe au XVe siècle." In: *Armi e cultura nel bresciano, 1420-1870.* Brescia, 1981, pp. 155-68.

Gaier, Claude. "Une enigma: la production 'Belge' d'armures vers l'an 1500 . . . et au-dela," *Musée d'armes* 73-74 (Apr 1993), 3-35.

Gaier, Claude. "L'évolution de l'industrie armurière en Belgique," *Revue universelle des mines, de la metallurgie, des travaux publics, des sciences et des arts appliques à l'industrie* 2 (Jun 1971), 63-74.

Gaier, Claude. *L'industrie et le commerce des armes dans les anciennes principautés belges du XIIIme à la fin du XVme siècle.* Paris: Société d'Edition "Les Belles Lettres". 1973.

Gaier, Claude. "Le problème de l'origine de l'industrie armurière liégeoise au Moyen âge," *Chronique archéologique du pays de Liège* 53 (1962), 22-75; in: *Armes et combats dans l'univers médiéval.* Paris: De Boeck Université, 1995, pp. 191-228.

Gamber, Ortwin. "Kolman Helmschmeid, Ferdinand I. und das Thun'sche Skizzenbuch," *Jahrbuch der Kunsthistorischen Sammlungen in Wien* 71 (1975), 9-38.

Gerino, Giorgio. "Antonio e Federico Piccinino spadari in Milano," *Armi antiche* (1983), 5-11.

Grancsay, Stephen V. "Royal Armorers–Antwerp or Paris?" *Metropolitan Museum of Art Bulletin* n.s. 18 (Sum 1959), 1-7; in: *Arms and Armor: Essays by Stephen V. Grancsay from The Metropolitan Museum of Art Bulletin, 1920-1964.* New York: The Metropolitan Museum of Art, 1986, pp. 480-93.

Hampe, Theodor. "Waffengeschichtliches aus einem Nürnberger Haus und Rechnungsbuch des 15. Jahrhunderts," *Zeitschrift für historisches Waffen- und Köstumkunde* 11 (1926-28), 177-82.

Harmuth, Egon. "Die Armbrustbilder des Haimo von Auxerre," *Waffen und Kostümkunde* 12 (1970), 127-30.

Hartmans, C.A. "Het geweermakersmerk W.S. met kroon, geslagen op de slotplaat van de 17de eeuw en het geweer van Jakob de la Gardie," *Livrustkammaren* 10.3-4 (1964).

Hayward, John F. "Filippo Orsoni, Designer, and Caremolo Modrone, Armourer, of Mantua," *Waffen- und Kostümkunde* 24 (1982), 1-16, 87-102.

James, Simon. "The *fabricae*: State Arms Factories of the Later Roman Empire." In: *Military Equipment and the Identity of Roman Soldiers: Proceedings of the Fourth Roman Military Equipment Conference.* Ed. J.C. Coulston. British Archaeological Reports International Series, 394. Oxford: BAR, 1988, pp. 257-331.

Jong, M.A.G. de. "Arms Trade and Arms Production in Zeeland, 1572-1630." In: *The Arsenal of the World: The Dutch Arms Trade in the Seventeenth Century.* Ed. Jan Piet Puype and Marco van der Hoeven. Amsterdam: Batavian Lion International, 1996, pp. 22-27.

Kessen, A. "Über die Waffenindustrie in Maastricht in früheren Zeiten," *Zeitschrift für historisches Waffen- und Köstumkunde* 15 (1937-39), 57-60.

Larsen, Henrietta M. "The Armor Business in the Middle Ages," *Business History Review* 14 (1940), 49-64.

Marri, Giulia Camerani, ed. *Statuti delle arte dei Corazzai dei Chiavaioli, Ferraioli e Calderai e dei Fabbri di Firenze (1321-1344) con appendice dei marchi di fabbrica dei fabbri, dal 1369.* Florence: Leo S. Olschki, 1957.

Meier, Jürg A. "Die Waffenschmiede von Zürich," *Du: Die Kunstzeitschrift* 9 (1981), 64-66.

Nickel, Helmut. "The Armorers' Shop," *Metropolitan Museum of Art Bulletin* 28.4 (Dec 1969), 183-88.

Nicolle, David C. "Arms Production and the Arms Trade in South-Eastern Arabia in the Early Muslim Period," *Journal of Oman Studies* 5 (1984), 231-38.

Oldenstein, J. "Manufacture and Supply of the Roman Army with Bronze Fittings." In: *The Production and Distribution of Roman Military Equipment: Proceedings of the Second Roman Military Equipment Research*

Seminar. Ed. M.C. Bishop. British Archaeological Review International Series, 275. Oxford: BAR, 1985, pp. 82-93.

Panseri, Carlo. "L'acciaio di Damasco nella leggenda e nella realtà," *Armi antichi* (1962), 3-52.

Pasleau, Jean F. *Les armuries Liégeois du XVe au XIXe siècle*. Liege, 1973.

Petrović, Djurdjica. "Uloga Dubrovnika u snabdevanju srednjovekovne Bosne oruzjem XIV-XV vek," *Radovi* 3 (1973), 67-77.

Reicke, Emil. "Martin Löffelholtz, der Ritter und Techniker," *Mitteilungen des Vereins für Geschichte der Stadt Nürnberg* 31 (1933), 227-39.

Reid, William. "Biscotto me fecit," *Armi antiche* (1966), 3-19.

Reitzenstein, Alexander Freiherr von. "Die beiden Jörg Sorg," *Waffen und Kostümkunde* 8 (1966), 81-86.

Reitzenstein, Alexander Freiherr von. *Der Waffenschmeid: Von Handwerk der Plattner und Büchsenmacher*. Munich: Prestel Verlag, 1964.

Sachse, Manfred. *Damascus Steel: Myth, History, Technology, Applications*. Dusseldorf: Verlag Stahleisen, 1994; trans. *Damaszener Stahl: Mythos, Geschichte, Technik, Anwendung*. Bremerhaven: Wirtschaftsverlag NW, Verlag für neue Wissenschaft Gmbh., 1989.

Sachse, Manfred. "Damaszen Stahl," *Deutsches Waffen Journal* (1981).

Schedelmann, Hans. *Die Grossen Büchsenmacher: Leben, Werke, Marken von 15 bis 19 Jahrhundert*. Brunswick: Klinkhardt and Biermann, 1972.

Scheibe, E. *Studien zur Nürnberger Waffenindustrie von 1450-1550*. Bonn, 1908.

Schneider, Hugo. "Harnischproduktion in der Schweiz am Beispiel von Zürich," *Zeitschrift für Schweizerische Archäologie und Kunstgeschichte* 28 (1971), 175-85.

Schneider, Hugo. "Der Handwerkliche Leistung der Geschützgiesser-Dynastie in Zürich," *Turicum* (Mar 1972), 12–14.

Schneider, Hugo. "Schweizerische Waffenproduktion: Mit einer Verzeichnis schweizerischer Waffenschmiede," *Zeitschrift für schweizerische Archäologie und Kunstgeschichte* 16.4 (1956), 235-48.

Schneider, Hugo. *Schweizer Waffenschmeide vom 15. Bis 20. Jahrhundert.* Zurich: Orell Füssli Verlag, 1976.

Schneider, Hugo. "Suhler Schusswaffenfabrikation in schweizerischer Sicht," *Waffen- und Köstumkunde* 10 (1968), 62-68.

Sherby, Oleg and Jeffrey Wadsworth. "Damascus Steels," *Scientific American* 252.2 (Feb 1985).

Sim, David. "Weapons and Mass Production," *Journal of Roman Military Equipment Studies* 6 (1995), 1-3.

Squilbeck, Jean. "L'iconographie de saint Guillaume et la bannière de la corporation des armuriers de Gand," *Revue Belge d'archéologie et d'histoire de l'art* 29 (1962), 103-18.

Stroobants, A. "De Antwerpse wapenmakers en hun privileges," *Militaria Belgica* (1991), 3-32.

Stroobants, A. "De Brugse wapenmakers en hun privileges," *Militaria Belgica* (1993), 3-36.

Szymczak, Jan. "Some Remarks on the Arms Production in Medieval Poland, 13th-15th Centuries," *Fasciculi archaeologiae historicae* 5 (1992), 91-104.

Thomas, Bruno and Johann Michael Fritz. "Unbekannte Werke spätmittelalterlicher Waffenschmiedekunst in Karlsruhe," *Waffen- und Kostümkunde* 20 (1978), 1-18.

Vettori, I.G. *Gli affreschi cinquecenteschi di Santa Giulio come documenti storici: Quaderni di didattica dei beni culturali.* Bresica: ENAIP, 1978.

Vogel, H.Ph. "List of Arms Traders, 1600-1650." In: *The Arsenal of the World: The Dutch Arms Trade in the Seventeenth Century.* Ed. Jan Piet Puype and Marco van der Hoeven. Amsterdam: Batavian Lion International, 1996, p. 76.

Vogel, H.Ph. "The Republic as Arms Exporter, 1600-1650." In: *The Arsenal of the World: The Dutch Arms Trade in the Seventeenth Century.* Ed. Jan Piet Puype and Marco van der Hoeven. Amsterdam: Batavian Lion International, 1996, pp. 13-21.

Whitelaw, Charles C. *Scottish Arms Makers: A Biographical Dictionary of Makers of Firearms, Edged Weapons and Armour Working in Scotland from the 15th Century to 1870.* Ed. Sarah Barter. London: Arms and Armour Press, 1977.

Military Technology – Premodern – Horses (including harnesses and spurs) [Cf. Medieval – Cavalry]

Ayton, Andrew. "Arms, Armour, and Horses." In: *Medieval Warfare: A History.* Ed. Maurice Keen. Oxford: Oxford University Press, 1999, pp. 186-208.

Ayton, Andrew. *Knights and Warhorses: Military Service and the English Aristocracy under Edward III.* Woodbridge: The Boydell Press, 1994.

Bachrach, Bernard S. "Animals and Warfare in Early Medieval Europe." In: *L'uomo di fronte al mondo animale nell'alto medioevo.* Settimane di studio del centro italiano di studi sull'alto medioevo, xxxi. Spoleto, 1985, pp. 707-51.

Bachrach, Bernard S. *"Caballus et Caballarius* in Medieval Warfare." In: *The Study of Chivalry: Resources and Approaches.* Ed. H. Chickering and T.H. Seiler. Kalamazoo, 1988, pp. 173-212.

Bautier, Anne-Marie. "Contribution à l'histoire du cheval au moyen âge," *Bulletin philologique et historique du comité des travaux historiques et scientifiques* (1976), 209-49.

Bautier, Anne-Marie. "L'élevage du cheval en Europe et specialement en France jusqu'au XIII siècle." In: *Philologique et historique.* Comité archéologique de Senlis. Senlis, 1979-80, pp. 11-19.

Bautier, Robert-Henri and Anne-Marie. "Contribution à l'histoire du cheval au moyen âge: L'élevage au moyen âge et les chevaux de guerre du XIIIe siècle à la guerre de cent ans," *Bulletin philologique et historique du comité des travaux historiques et scientifiques* (1978), 9-75.

Bivar, A.D.H. "Cavalry, Equipment and Tactics on the Euphrates Frontier," *Dumbarton Oaks Papers* 26 (1972), 271-91.

Blair, Claude. "Medieval Swords and Spurs in Toledo Cathedral," *Journal of the Arms and Armour Society* 3 (1959-61), 41-52.

Byrne, Blanche. "The Spurs of King Casimir III and Some Other Fourteenth Century Spurs," *Journal of the Arms and Armour Society* 3 (1959-61), 106-14.

Campo, Alvaro Soler del. "Estudio comparativo de un conjunto de espuelas bajomedievales." In: *II congreso de arqueologia medieval Española*. Madrid, 1987, pp. 180-89.

Champion, L.G.M. *Les chevaux et les cavaliers de la tapisserie de Bayeux*. Caen, 1907.

Chodyński, Antoni Romuald. "Horse Muzzles," *Waffen- und Köstumkunde* 29 (1987), 4-20.

Chomel, V. "Chevaux de bataille et roncin en Dauphiné au XIVe siècle," *Cahiers d'histoire* 7 (1962), 5-23.

Clapham, J.H. "The Horsing of the Danes," *English Historical Review* 25 (1910), 287-93.

Clark, John, ed. *The Medieval Horse and Its Equipment, c.1150-c.1450*. Museum Finds from Excavations in London, 5. London Her Majesty's Stationery Organization, 1995.

Connolly, Peter. "Experiments with the Roman Saddle," *Military Illustrated* 13 (June-July 1988), 26-32.

Contamine, Philippe. "Glanes d'hipponymie médiévale (France, XIVe-XVe siècles)." In: *Commerce, Finances et Société (XIe-XVIe siècles): Receuil de travaux d'Histoire médiévale offert à M. le Professeur Henri Dubois*. Ed. P. Contamine, T. Dutour, and B. Schnerb. Paris, 1993, pp. 369-78.

Davis, R.H.C. "Did Anglo-Saxons have Warhorses?" In: *Weapons and Warfare in Anglo-Saxon England*. Ed. Sonia Chadwick Hawkes. Oxford, 1989, pp. 141-44.

Davis, R.H.C. *The Medieval Warhorse: Origin, Development and Redevelopment*. London: Thames and Hudson, 1989.

Davis, R.H.C. "The Medieval Warhorse." In: *Horses in European Economic History: A Preliminary Canter*. Ed. F.M.L. Thompson. Reading, 1983, pp. 4-20, 177-84.

Davis, R.H.C. "The Warhorses of the Normans." *Anglo-Norman Studies* 10 (1987), 67-82.

Dent, A.A. "Chaucer and the Horse," *Proceedings of the Leeds Philosophical and Literary Society* 9 (1959), 1-12.

Dillon, H.A. "Horse Armour," *Archaeological Journal* 59 (1902), 67-92.

Douillet, G. "Furusiyya." In: *Encyclopedia of Islam*. 2nd ed. Leiden, 1965, II:952-54.

Drugmand, Pierre. "Les éperons à molette du XIVe et XVIIIe siècles," *Militaria Belgica* (1989), 33-42.

Drugmand, Pierre. "Les éperons à pointe, de leur origine au 14e siècle," *Militaria Belgica* (1988), 3-12.

Drugmand, Pierre. "Introduction à l'histoire des éperons européens," *Armi antiche* (1982), 13-32.

Ekdahl, Sven. "Horses and Crossbows: Two Important Warfare Advantages of the Teutonic Order in Prussia." In: *The Military Orders*. Vol. 2: *Welfare and Warfare*. Ed. Helen Nicholson. Aldershot: Ashgate, 1998, pp. 119-52.

Ellis, B.M.A. "Spurs from Sandal Castle." In: *Sandal Castle Excavations, 1964-1973*. Ed. P. Mayes and L.A.S. Butler. Wakefield, 1983, pp. 253-57.

Ernstell, Eva-Sofi. *Streiff: en kunglig häst*. Stockholm: Livrustkammaren, 1999.

Flade, J.E., E. Tylinek, and Z. Samaková. *The Compleat Horse*. London, 1987.

Gillmor, Caroll. "European Cavalry." In: *Dictionary of the Middle Ages*. Ed. J.R. Strayer. New York: Scribners, 1982, II:200-08.

Gillmor, Caroll. "Practical Chivalry: The Training of Horses for Tournaments and Warfare," *Studies in Medieval and Renaissance History* n.s. 13 (1992), 6-29.

Gladitz, Charles. *Horse Breeding in the Medieval World*. Dublin: Four Courts Press, 1997.

Gode, P.K. "The History of the Stirrup in Indian and Foreign Horseman-ship–Between 852 BC and 1948." In: *Studies in Indian Cultural History*. Ed. P.K. Gode. Poona, 1960, pp. 71-81.

Goodall, D.M. *A History of Horse Breeding*. London, 1977.

Graham-Campbell, James. "Anglo-Scandinavian Equestrian Equipment in Eleventh-Century England," *Anglo-Norman Studies* 14 (1991), 77-89.

Grancsay, Stephen V. "A Medieval Sculptured Saddle," *Metropolitan Museum of Art Bulletin* 36 (Mar 1941), 73-76; in: *Arms and Armor: Essays by Stephen V. Grancsay from The Metropolitan Museum of Art Bulletin, 1920-1964*. New York: The Metropolitan Museum of Art, 1986, pp. 267-70.

Grancsay, Stephen V. "A Pair of Spurs Bearing the Bourbon Motto," *Metropolitan Museum of Art Bulletin* 36 (Aug 1941), 170-72; in: *Arms and Armor: Essays by Stephen V. Grancsay from The Metropolitan Museum of Art Bulletin, 1920-1964*. New York: The Metropolitan Museum of Art, 1986, pp. 270-73.

Hayward, John F. "A Fifteenth Century Carved Bone Saddle," *Auction* 2.7 (March 1969), 22-23.

Hewitt, Herbert James. *The Horse in Medieval England*. London: J.A. Allen & Co., Ltd., 1983.

Higham, Nicholas J. "Cavalry in Early Bernicia?" *Northern History* 27 (1991), 236-41.

Hill, Donald R. "The Role of the Camel and the Horse in the Early Arab Conquests." In: *War, Technology and Society in the Middle East*. Ed. V.J. Parry and M.E. Yapp. London, 1975, pp. 32-43.

Hilczerówna, Z. *Ostrogi polskie z X-XIII wieku*. Poznan: Poznańskie Towarzystwo Przyjaciół Nauk, 1956.

Hyland, Ann. *The Medieval Warhorse: From Byzantium to the Crusades*. Stroud: Sutton Publishing, 1994.

Hyland, Ann. *Training the Roman Cavalry: From Arrian's Ars Tactica*. London: Grange Books, 1993.

Jankovich, M. *They Rode into Europe: The Fruitful Exchange in the Arts of Horsemanship Between East and West*. Tr. A. Dent. London, 1971.

Jope, E.M. "The Tinning of Iron Spurs: A Continuous Practice from the Tenth to the Seventeenth Century," *Oxoniensia* 21 (1956), 35-42.

Keefer, Sarah Larratt. "Hwær Cwom Mearh? The Horse in Anglo-Saxon England," *Journal of Medieval History* 22 (1996), 115-34.

Kirpičnikov, Anatolij N. *Snaryazhenie vsadnika i verkhovogo konya na Rusi IX-XIII vv*. Leningrad, 1973.

Kretschmar, M. *Pferd und Reiter im Orient*. Hildesheim, 1980.

Lefebvre des Noëttes,. *L'attelage, le cheval de selle à travers des âges*. Paris, 1931.

Lydon, James F. "The Hobelar: An Irish Contribution to Mediaeval Warfare," *Irish Sword* 2 (1954-56), 12-16.

Mann, James. "A Gothic Horse Armour from Anhalt in the Armouries of the Tower of London," *Waffen- und Kostümkunde* 1 (1959), 22-27.

Megnin, P. *Histoire du harnachement et de ferrure du cheval*. Vincennes, 1904.

Müller-Hickler, Hans. "Sitz und Sattel im Laufe der Jahrhunderte," *Zeitschrift für historisches Waffen- und Köstumkunde* 10 (1923-25), 6-13.

Murphey, Rhoads. "Horsebreeding in Eurasia," *Central and Inner Asian Studies* 4 (1990), 115-31.

Nikolić, Desanka. "Tipološki razvoj mamuze od XIV-XX veka sa osvrtom na zbirku mamuza u Vojnom muzeju JNA," *Vesnik* 3 (1956), 61-79.

Nikolić, Desanka. "Tri tipa vanevropskih mamuza u Vojnom muzeju JNA," *Vesnik* 4 (1957), 171-84.

Nikolić, Desanka. "O zbirci jahacé konjske opreme u Vojnom muzeju JNA," *Vesnik* 1 (1954), 83-105.

Owen-Crocker, Gale R. "Hawks and Horse-Trappings: The Insignia of Rank." In: *The Battle of Maldon AD 991*. Ed. D. Scragg. Manchester, 1991, pp. 220-37.

Schnerb, Bertrand. "Le cheval et les chevaux dans les armées des ducs de Bourgogne au XIVe siècle." In: *Commerce, Finances et Société (XIe-XVIe siècles): Receuil de travaux d'Histoire médiévale offert à M. le Professeur Henri Dubois*. Ed. P. Contamine, T. Dutour, and B. Schnerb. Paris, 1993, pp. 71-87.

Seaby, W.A. and P. Woodfield. "Viking Stirrups from England and their Background," *Medieval Archaeology* 24 (1980), 87-122.

Sinor, Denis. "Horse and Pasture in Inner Asian History," *Oriens extremus* 19 (1972), 171-84.

Smith, G. Rex. *Medieval Muslim Horsemanship: A Fourteenth-Century Arabic Cavalry Manual*. London: The British Museum, 1979.

Sommo, Lorenzo. "La storia dell cinture di castità," *Armi antiche* 1 (1954), 34-43.

Żygulski, Zdzisław, Jr. "Ze studiów nad dawną sztuką siodlarską," *Rozpraw i Sprawozdań Muzeum Narodowego w Krakowie* 5 (1959), 41-110.

Military Technology – Premodern – White Thesis (Stirrups)

Bachrach, Bernard S. "Charles Martel, Mounted Shock Combat, The Stirrup, and Feudalism," *Studies in Medieval and Renaissance History* 7 (1970), 47-75.

Bivar, A.D.H. "The Stirrup and Its Origin," *Oriental Art* n.s. 1.2 (1955), 61-65.

Brünner, Heinrich. "Der Reiterdienst und die Anfänge des Lehnwesens," *Zeitschrift der Savigny-Stiftung für Rechtsgeschichte, Germanistische Abteilung* 8 (1887), 1-38.

Dien, Albert E. "The Stirrup and its Effect on Chinese Military History," *Ars orientalis* 16 (1986), 33-56.

Engmann, J. "Elfenbeinfunde aus Abu Mena," *Jahrbuch für Antike und Christentum* 30 (1987), 172-86.

Gode, P.K. "The History of the Stirrup in Indian and Foreign Horseman-ship–Between 852 BC and 1948." In: *Studies in Indian Cultural History.* Ed. P.K. Gode. Poona, 1960, pp. 71-81.

Hilton, Rodney H. and P.H. Sawyer. "Technical Determinism: The Stirrup and the Plough," *Past and Present* 24 (1963), 90-100.

Littauer, Mary Aitken. "Early Stirrups," *Antiquity* 55 (1981), 99-105.

Ogilvy, J.D.A. "The Stirrup and Feudalism," *The University of Colorado Studies: Series in Language and Literature* 10 (1966), 1-13.

White, Lynn, Jr. "Stirrup, Mounted Shock Combat, Feudalism, and Chival-ry." *Medieval Technology and Social Change*. Oxford: Clarendon Press, 1962, pp. 1-38.

Military Technology – Premodern – Artillery – Catapults

Alm, Josef. "Stockholms stads medeltida artilleri," *Meddelande* 9 (1948), 5-33.

Baatz, Dietwulf. *Bauten und Katapulte des römischen Heeres*. Mavors Roman Army Researches, 11. Stuttgart: F. Steiner, 1994.

Baatz, Dietwulf. "Recent Finds in Ancient Artillery," *Britannia* 9 (1978), 1-17.

Baatz, Dietwulf. "Die Römische Jagdarmbrust," *Archäologisches Korre-spondenzblatt* 21 (1991), 283-90.

Barker, J. "Ancient Arrow-Shooting Machines," *Journal of the Society of Archer-Antiquaries* 42 (1999), 16-21.

Berthelot, Marcellin. "Histoire des machines de guerre et des arts mécha-niques au moyen âge: le livre d'un ingénieur militaire à la fin du XIVe siècle," *Annales de chimie et de physique* 7th ser., 24 (1900), 289-420.

Beffeyte, Renaud. *Les machines de siege au moyen âge*. Castelmoron-sur-Lot: Reanud Beffeyte, 1994.

Chevedden, Paul E. "Artillery in Late Antiquity: Prelude to the Middle Ages." In: *The Medieval City Under Siege*. Ed. I.A. Corfis and M. Wolfe. Woodbridge, 1995, pp. 131-73.

Chevedden, Paul E. "The Artillery of King James I the Conqueror." In: *Iberia and the Mediterranean World of the Middle Ages: Essays in Honor of Robert I. Burns, S.J.* Ed. Paul E. Cheveddan, D.J. Kagay, and P.G. Padilla. Leiden: E.J. Brill, 1996, pp. 179-222.

Chevedden, Paul E. "The Hybrid Trebuchet: The Halfway Step to the Counterweight Trebuchet." In: *On the Social Origins of Medieval Institutions: Essays in Honor of Joseph F. O'Callaghan*. Ed. Donald J. Kagay and Theresa M. Vann. Leiden: E.J. Brill, 1998, pp. 179-222.

Cheveddan, Paul E., Les Eigenbrod, Vernard Foley, and Werner Soedel. "The Trebuchet," *Scientific American* 273 (July 1995), 66-71.

De Poerck, G. "L'artillerie à ressorts médiévale: Notes lexicologiques et étymologiques," *Bulletin Du Cange* 18 (1943-44), 35-49.

Erben, Wilhelm. "Beiträge zur Geschichte des Geschützwesens im Mittelalter," *Zeitschrift für historisches Waffenkunde* 7 (1915-17), 85-102, 117-29.

Finó, J.-F. "Machines et jet médiévales," *Gladius* 10 (1972), 25-43.

Finó, J.-F. "Origines et puissance des machines à balancier médiévales," *Société des antiquités nationales* 11 (1972).

Forrer, Robert. "Römische Geschützkugeln aus Straßburg in Elsaß," *Zeitschrift für historisches Waffenkunde* 7 (1915-17), 243-53.

Francis, Dominic. "Oliver of Paderborn and his Siege Engine at Damietta," *Nottingham Medieval Studies* 37 (1993), 28-32.

Gillmor, Caroll. "The Introduction of the Traction Trebuchet into the Latin West," *Viator*. 12 (1981), 1-8.

Giorgetti, Giovanni. *Le armi antiche*. II: *L'arco, la balestra e le macchine belliche*. Milan: Associazione amatori armi antiche, Museo dell Pusterla di S. Ambrogio, 1964.

Gohlke, W. "Das Geschützwesen des Altertums und des Mittelalters," *Zeitschrift für historische Waffenkunde* 6 (1912-14), 61-65.

Gravett, Christopher. "The Medieval Balista," *London Arms Fair* 46 (Spr 1991), 22-26.

Hacker, Barton C. "Greek Catapults and Catapult Technology: Science, Technology, and War in the Ancient World," *Technology and Culture* 9 (1968), 34-50.

Hansen, Peter Vemming. "Experimental Reconstruction of a Medieval Trébuchet," *Acta Archaeologica* 63 (1992), 189-208.

Hansen, Peter Vemming. *Middelalderens mekaniske apparater til krigsbrug*. Nykøbing F.: Middelaldercentret, 1998.

Hansen, Peter Vemming. "'The Witch with Ropes for Hair'," *Military Illustrated* 47 (Apr 1992), 15-18.

Hansen, Peter Vemming and B. Rayce. "Reconstructing a Medieval Trebuchet," *Military Illustrated* 27 (Aug 1990), 9-11, 14-16.

Harpham, Rex. "Heron's Cheiroballistra (a Roman Torsion Crossbow)," *Journal of the Society of Archer-Antiquaries* 40 (1997), 13-17.

Hill, David. "Siege-craft from the Sixth to the Tenth Century." In: *Aspects of the "De rebus bellicis": Papers Presented to Professor E.A. Thompson*. Ed. M.W.C. Hassall. BAR International Series, 63. Oxford, 1979, 111-17.

Hill, Donald R. "Trebuchets," *Viator* 4 (1973), 99-114.

Holder, Paul. "Roman Artillery," *Military Illustrated* 2 (Aug/Sept 1986), 30-37; 4 (Dec 1986-Jan 1987), 30-37.

Humphreys, P.H. *Engines of War: Replica Medieval Siege Weapons at Caerphilly Castle*. Cardiff: CADW, 1992.

Huuri, Kalervo. *Zur Geschichte des mittelalterichen Geschützwesens*. Helsinki: Societas Orientalis Fennia, 1941.

Johannessen, Kåre. "Middelalderligt artilleri inykøbing," *Våbenhistorisk tidsskrift* 29 (1996), 132-34.

Kalmár, Johann von. "Beiträge zur Geschichte der Kriegsrakete," *Zeitschrift für historisches Waffen- und Köstumkunde* 16 (1940-42), 19-24.

King, D.J. Cathcart. "The Trébuchet and the Other Siege Engines," *Château Gaillard* 9-10 (1982), 457-70.

Krizek, Leonid. "Trebuchet Reconstructions in Czechoslovakia," *Military Illustrated* 47 (April 1992), 19-20.

Liebel, Jean. *Springalds and Great Crossbows*. Trans. Juliet Vale. Royal Armouries Monograph, 5. Leeds: Royal Armouries, 1998.

Marsden, E.W. *Greek and Roman Artillery: Historical Development*. Oxford: Clarendon Press, 1969.

Marsden, E.W. *Greek and Roman Artillery: Technical Treatises*. Oxford: Clarendon Press, 1971.

Needham, Joseph. "China's Trebuchets, Manned and Counterweighted." In: *On Pre-Modern Technology and Science: Studies in Honor of Lynn White, Jr.* Ed. B.S. Hall and D.C. West. Malibu, 1976, pp. 107-45.

Patrick, J.M. *Artillery and Warfare during the Thirteenth and Fourteenth Centuries*. Logan: Utah State University Press, 1961.

Payne-Gallwey, Ralph. *The Crossbow, Medieval and Modern, Military and Sporting: Its Construction, History and Management, with a Treatise on the Balista and Catapult of the Ancients*. London, 1903; rpt. New York: Bramhall House, 1958; trans. *Die Armbrüst*. Trans. Egon Harmuth. Graz, 1963.

Piletić, Dragoslav. "Ratne sprave antike," *Vesnik* 2 (1955), 25-33.

Schmidtchen, Volker. *Mittelalterliche Kriegsmachinen*. Soest: Westfälische Verlagsbuchhandlung, 1983.

Schneider, Rudolf. *Die Artillerie des Mittelalters: Nach den Angaben der Zeitgenossen dargestelt*. Berlin: Weidmannsche Buchhandlung, 1910.

Simms, D.L. "Archimedes and the Invention of Artillery and Gunpowder," *Technology and Culture* 28 (1987), 67-79.

Simms, D.L. "Archimedes' Weapons of War and Leonardo," *British Journal for the History of Science* 21 (1988), 195-210.

Soedel, Werner and Vernard Foley. "Ancient Catapults," *Scientific American*. (March 1979), 150-60.

Tarver, W.T.S. "The Traction Trebuchet: A Reconstruction of an Early Medieval Siege Engine," *Technology and Culture* 36 (1995), 136-67.

Wilkins, Alan. "Reconstructing the *Cheiroballistra*," *Journal of Roman Military Equipment Studies* 6 (1995), 5-59.

Military Technology – Premodern – Artillery – Greek Fire

Arendt, W. von. "Irdene Granaten des 13.-14. Jahrhunderts, die an der Wolga gefunden sind," *Zeitschrift für historisches Waffen- und Köstumkunde* 11 (1926-28), 264-65.

Bradbury, Jim. "Greek Fire in the West," *History Today* 29 (1979), 326-31, 344.

Cheronis, S.D. "Chemical Warfare in the Middle Ages: Kallinkos' 'Prepared Fire'," *Journal of Chemical Education* 14.8 (1937).

Dain, Alphonse. "Appellations grèques du feu grégois." In: *Mélanges de philologie, de littérature et d'histoire anciennes offerts à A. Ernout*. Paris, 1940.

Davidson, Hilda R. Ellis. "The Secret Weapon of Byzantium," *Byzantinische Zeitschrift* 66 (1973), 61-74.

Finó, J.-F. "Le feu et ses usages militaires," *Gladius* 9 (1970), 15-30.

Forrer, Robert. "Archäologisches und Technisches zu der byzantinischen Feuerwaffe des cod. Vat. 1605 vom 11. Jahrhundert," *Zeitschrift für historisches Waffenkunde* 5 (1909-11), 115-22.

Haldane, Douglas. "The Fire-Ship of Al-Sālih Ayyūb and Muslim Use of 'Greek Fire'," In: *The Circle of War in the Middle Ages: Essays on Medieval Military and Naval History*. Ed. Donald J. Kagay and L.J. Andrew Villalon. Woodbridge: The Boydell Press, 1999, pp. 137-44.

Haldon, John F. and M. Byrne. "A Possible Solution to the Problem of Greek Fire," *Byzantinische Zeitschrift*. 70 (1977), 91-99.

Hall, A.R. "A Note on Military Pyrotechnics." In: *A History of Technology*. Ed. C. Singer et al. Vol. II: *The Mediterranean Civilizations and the Middle Ages, c. 700 B.C. to c. A.D. 1500*. Oxford, 1957, pp. 374-82.

Mercier, M. *Le feu grégois, les feux de guerre depuis l'antiquité, la poudre à canon*. Paris, 1952.

Partington, J.R. *A History of Greek Fire and Gunpowder*. Cambridge: W. Heffer and Sons, Ltd., 1960; rpt. Baltimore: Johns Hopkins University Press, 1999.

Pászthory, Emmerich. "Über das 'Griechische Feuer," *Antike Welt* 17 (1986).

Quatremère, E.M. "Observation sur le feu grégois," *Journal asiatique* 4th ser. 15 (1850), 214-74.

Reinaud, Joseph Toussaint and Ildéfonse Favé. *Du feu grégeois, des feux de guerre et des origines de la poudre à canon*. Paris, 1845; *Journal asiatique* 4th ser. 14 (1849), 257-327.

Roland, Alex. "Secrecy, Technology, and War: Greek Fire and the Defense of Byzantium, 678-1204," *Technology and Culture* 33 (1992), 655-79.

Military Technology – Fortifications – General

Bury, John. "Early Writings on Fortifications and Siegecraft, 1502-1554," *Fort* 13 (1985), 5-48.

Bury, John. "The Personification of the Science of Fortification," *Fort* 17 (1989), 7-10.

Floyd, Dale E. *Military Fortifications: A Selective Bibliography*. Westport: Greenwood Press, 1992.

Glossarium artis: Festungen, Fortresses, Fortifications. Munich: K.G. Saur, 1990.

Herman, Marguerita N. *Ramparts: Fortification from the Renaissance to West Point*. New York: Avery Publishing Group, Inc., 1992.

Hogg, Ian V. *Fortress: A History of Military Defense*. New York, 1975.

Hughes, Quentin. "Considerazione e theorie sulla difesa costiera inglese," *Castellum* 25/26 (1986), 25-44.

Hughes, Quentin. *Military Architecture*. 2nd ed. Liphook: Beaufort Publishing Ltd., 1991.

Jones, Richard L.C. "Fortification and Sieges in Western Europe, *c*. 800-1450." In: *Medieval Warfare: A History*. Ed. Maurice Keen. Oxford: Oxford University Press, 1999, pp. 163-85.

Kenyon, John R. *Castles and Artillery Fortifications*. Council for British Archaeology Research Report, 25. London, 1977.

La Croix, Horst de. *Military Considerations in City Planning: Fortifications*. New York, 1972.

Le Pourhiet-Salat, Nicole. *La défence des îles bretonnes de l'Atlantique, des origines à 1860*. 2 vols. Service historique de la Marine. Vincennes, 1983.

Longmate, Norman. *Defending the Island from Caesar to the Armada*. London: Hutchinson, 1989.

McGuffie, T.H. "Fortifications and War," *History Today* (Aug 1956), 352-55.

Muir, Richard. *Castles and Strongholds*. London: Macmillan, 1990.

Neumann, Hartwig. *Festungsbaukunst und Festungsbautechnik*. Koblenz: Bernard and Graefe, 1988.

Piper, O. *Burgen Kunde: Bauwesen und geschichte der burgen zunächst innerhalb des deutschen Sprachgebietes*. Munich, 1912; rpt. Augsburg, 1993.

Salamagne, Alain. "Pour une approche typologique de l'architecture militaire: l'example de la famille monumentale des tours-portes de plan curviligne," *Archéologie médiévale* 18 (1988), 179-213.

Spiteri, Stephen C. "Illustrated Glossary of Military Architecture Terms," *Fort* 21 (1993), 105-14.

Toy, Sidney. *Castles: Their Construction and History*. New York: Dover Publications Inc., 1985; rpt. *Castles: A Short History of Fortifications from 1600 B.C. to A.D. 1600*. London William Heineman, Ltd., 1939.

Toy, Sidney. *A History of Fortification from 3000 B.C. to A.D. 1700*. New York, 1955.

Tuulse, A. *Castles of the Western World*. London, 1958.

Viollet-le-Duc, Eugène Emmanuel. *Military Architecture*. 3rd ed. London: Greenhill Books, 1990.

Wilson, David M. *Moated Sites*. Princes Risborough: Shire Publishing Ltd., 1985.

Military Technology – Premodern – Fortifications – General

Aarts, B. "Early Castles of the Meuse-Rhine Border Region and Some Parallels in Western Europe, c. 1000: A Comparative Approach," *Château Gaillard* 17 (1996), 11-23.

Anderson, Wiliam. *Castles of Europe from Charlemagne to the Renaissance*. London: Paul Elek Ltd., 1970.

Ball, Terry. "Castles on Paper," *Fortress* 2 (Aug 1989), 2-15.

Barker, Philip. "*Rabies archaeologorum*: A Reply," *Château Gaillard* 9-10 (1982), 220-22.

Bennett, Jim and Stephen Johnston. *The Geometry of War, 1500-1750: Catalogue of the Exhibition*. Oxford: Museum of the History of Science, 1996.

Boüard, Michel de. *Manuel d'archéologie médiévale, de la fouille àl'histoire*. Paris, 1975.

Bresc, Henri. "Les normands, constructeurs de châteaux." In: *Les Normands en Méditerranée dans le sillage des Tancréde*. Ed. P. Boulet and F. Neveux. Caen, 1994, pp. 63-75.

Brown, R. Allen. "Castle Gates and Garden Gates." In: *Castles, Conquest and Charters: Collected Papers*. Woodbridge, 1989, pp. 235-37.

Brown, R. Allen. "Les châteaux féodaux." In: *Castles, Conquest and Charters: Collected Papers*. Woodbridge, 1989, pp. 138-48.

Bur, Michel de. *Le château*. Typologie des Sources du Moyen Age Occidental, 79. Turnhout: Brepols, 1999.

Cairns, Conrad. *Medieval Castles*. Cambridge Introduction to World History. Cambridge: Cambridge University Press, 1987.

Charbonnier, Pierre. "Le château seigneurial: protection ou oppression?" In: *La guerre, la violence et les gens au Moyen Âge*. I: *Guerre et violence*. Ed. P. Contamine and O. Guyotjeannin. 119e congrès national des sociétés historiques et scientifiques, Amiens, octobre 1994, Section d'histoire médiévale et philologie. Paris, 1996, pp. 223-32.

Châtelaine, André. *Architecture militaire médiévale: principes élémentaires*. Paris, 1970.

Cherry, J. "Imago castelli: The Depiction of Castles on Medieval Seals," *Château Gaillard* 15 (1990), 83-90.

Contamine, Philippe. "Le château et la guerre." In: *Le château en France*. Ed. J.-P. Babelon. Paris, 1986, pp. 133-46.

Coulson, Charles L.H. "Hierarchism in Conventual Crenellation: An Essay in the Sociology and Metaphysics of Medieval Fortification," *Medieval Archaeology* 26 (1982), 69-100.

Coulson, Charles L.H. "Structural Symbolism in Medieval Castle Architecture," *Journal of the British Archaeological Association* 132 (1979), 73-90.

Counihan, Joan. "The Growth of Castle Studies in England and on the Continent since 1850," *Proceedings of the Battle Conference on Anglo-Saxon Studies* 11 (1989), 77-85.

Cresti, Carlo, Amelio Fara, and Daniela Lamberini, ed. *Achitettura militare nell'Europa del XVI secolo*. Siena: Edizioni Periccioli, 1988.

Debord, André. "*Castrum* et *castellum* chez Adémar de Chabannes," *Archéologie médiévale* 9 (1979), 97-113.

Debord, André. "Châteaux et résidence aristocratique: Réflexions pour la recherche," *Château Gaillard* 13 (1987), 41-51.

Dixon, Philip. "Design in Castle-Building: The Controlling of Access to the Lord," *Château Gaillard* 18 (1998), 47-57.

Donnelly, Mark P. and Daniel Diehl. *Siege: Castles at War*. Dallas: Taylor Publishing Company, 1998.

Ebhard, B. *Der Wehrbau Europas im Mittelalter: Versuch einer Gesamtdarstellung der europäischen Burgen*. 3 vols. Berlin, 1939-58.

Ebner, H. "Die Burg in historiographischen Werken des Mittelalters." In: *Festschrift Friedrich Hausmann*. Ed. H. Ebner. Graz, 1977, pp. 119-51.

Erb, H. "Burgenliteratur und Burgenforschung," *Revue Suisse d'histoire* 8 (1958), 488-530.

Ervynck, A. "Medieval Castles as Top-Predators of the Feudal System: An Archaeozoological Approach," *Château Gaillard* 15 (1990), 151-59.

Faucherre, Nicolas. "Barbacanes, boulevards, ravelins et sutres demi-lunes; inventaire incertain." In: *Aux portes du chateau: Actes du troisième colloque de castellologie*. Paris, 1987, pp. 105-15.

Faucherre, Nicolas. *Places fortes: Bastion du pouvoir*. 4th ed. Paris: Rempart Desclée de Brouwer, 1991.

Faulkner, P.A. "Castle Planning in the Fourteenth Century," *Archaeological Journal* 120 (1963), 215-35.

Flori, Jean. "Châteaux et forteresses aux XIe et XIIe siècles: Etude du vocabulaire des historiens des ducs de Normandie," *Moyen âge* 103 (1997), 261-73.

Gardelles, Pr. J. "Les deux fonctions de la porte dans les châteaux du Moyen âge," In: *Aux portes du chateau: Actes du troisième colloque de castellologie*. Paris, 1987, pp. 11-21.

Gille, Paul. "Fortifications." In: *A History of Technology and Invention: Progress through the Ages*. II: *The First Stages of Mechanization*. Ed. Maurice Daumus. New York: Crown Publishers, Inc., 1969, pp. 464-72.

Hale, John R. "The Early Development of the Bastion: an Italian Chronology, c.1450-c.1534." In: *Europe in the Late Middle Ages*. Ed. J.R. Hale, J.R.L. Highfield and B. Smalley. Evanston: Northwestern University Press, 1965, pp. 466-94.

Hale, John R. *Renaissance Fortification: Art or Engineering?* London: Thames and Hudson, 1977.

Héliot, Pierre. "Un organe peu connu de la fortification médiévale: la gaine," *Gladius* 10 (1972), 45-67.

Higham, Robert. "Public and Private Defence in the Medieval South West: Town, Castle and Fort." In: *Security and Defence in South-West England Before 1800*. Ed. R. Higham. Exeter, 1987, pp. 27-49.

Higham, Robert and Philip A. Barker. *Timber Castles*. London: B.T. Batsford Limited, 1992.

Hinz, Hermann. "Das mobile Haus: Bemerkungen zur Zeitbestimmung durch die Dendrochronologie," *Château Gaillard* 7 (1975), 141-45.

Hinz, Hermann. "Wehrkirchen und Burgenbau," *Château Gaillard* 9-10 (1982), 117-44.

Hubener, Wolfgang. "Romische Wehranlagne an Rhein und Donau als militärgeschichtliche Quelle," *Revue internationale d'histoire militaire* 27 (1968), 175-202.

Jäschke, K.U. *Burgenbau und Landesverteidigung um 900: Überlegungen zur Beispielen aus Deutschland, Frankreich und England*. Sigmaringen, 1975.

Janicaud, G. "Cannonières à obturateur sphérique," *Bulletin monumental* 95 (1936), 372-75.

Jannsen, W. "Die Fleischversorgung auf mittelalterlichen Burgen," *Château Gaillard* 14 (1990), 218-24.

Jannsen, W. "Sozial- und Verfassungsgeschichtliche Problem der Burgen von Motten-typus," *Château Gaillard* 6 (1973), 121-24.

Johnson, Stephen. *Late Roman Fortifications*. Totowa, N.J.: Barnes & Noble, 1983.

Jones, Peter N. and Derek F. Renn. "The Military Effectiveness of Arrow Loops: Some Experiments at White Castle," *Château Gaillard* 9-10 (1982), 445-56.

Kemp, Anthony. *Castles in Colour*. Poole: Blandford Press, 1977.

Kenyon, John R. *Medieval Fortifications*. New York: St. Martin's Press, 1990.

Kenyon, John R. and Michael Thompson. "The Origin of the Word 'Keep'," *Medieval Archaeology* 38 (1994), 175-76.

Kiess, W. *Die Burgen in ihrer Funktion als Wohnbauten: Studien zum Wohnbauten in Deutschland, Frankreich, England, und Italien von 11. bis 15. Jahrhundert.* Munich, 1961.

Kirić, Milan. "Proučavanje naših srednjovekovnih utvrdjenja," *Vesnik* 11-12 (1966), 110-26.

Koehne, Karl. "Burgen, Burgmannen, and Städte. Ein Betrage zur Frage der Bedeutung der ländlichen Grundrenten für die mittelalterliche Stadtentwicklung," *Historishce Zeitschrift* 133 (1926), 1-19.

Lamberini, Daniella. "Practice and Theory in Sixteenth-Century Fortifications," *Fort* 15 (1987), 5-20.

Lander, James. 1984. *Roman Stone Fortifications: Variation and Change from the First Century AD to the Fourth.* BAR International Series, 206. Oxford: British Archaeological Reports.

Liebgott, Niels-Knud. "Brick-Making and Castle-Building," *Château Gaillard* 18 (1998), 109-18.

Luisi, Riccardo. *Scudi di pietra: I castelli e l'arte della guerra tra Medioevo e Rinascimento.* Bari: Laterza, 1996.

Malet, Louis, et al. "Châteaux perdus, châteaux oubliés: A la recherche d'habitats fortifiés médiévaux," *Revue du Tarn* 3rd ser. 145 (1992), 71-95.

Mathieu, James R. "New Methods on Old Castles: Generating New Ways of Seeing," *Medieval Archaeology* 43 (1999), 115-42.n

McNeill, Tom. *Castles.* London: B.T. Batsford Limited/English Heritage, 1992.

Mesqui, Jean. "A propos de la fortification du pont: Pons castri et castrum pontis," *Château Gaillard* 11 (1983), 219-32.

Mesqui, Jean. "La fortification des portes avant la guerre de cent ans: Essai de typologie des défenses des ouvrages d'entrée avant 1350," *Archéologie médiévale* 9 (1981), 203-29.

Meyer, Werner. "Frühe Adelsburgen zwischen Alpen und Rhein." In: *Das ritterliche Turnier im Mittelalter.* Ed. Josef Fleckenstein. Göttingen: Vandenhoeck and Ruprecht, 1985, pp. 571-87.

Meyer, Werner. "Nichte gebaute und unvollendete Burgenlagen im Mittelalter," *Château Gaillard* 14 (1990), 293-304.

Obrecht, Jakob. "Handwerkersspuren am Rohbau der Burg," *Château Gaillard* 18 (1998), 159-69.

Olsen, Olaf. "*Rabies archaeologorum,*" *Château Gaillard* 9-10 (1982), 213-19.

Ottenheym, K.A. "Oorlog rondom kastelen." In: *Oorlog in de middeleeuwen*. Ed. A.J. Brand. Hilversum, 1989, pp. 71-74.

Pernot, Jean-Francis. "Un aspect peu connu de l'oeuvre d'Antoine de Ville, ingénieur du Roi (1596?-1656?): approche d'un type de documents, les gravures des Traités de Fortifications," *Revue historique de armées* (1978), 29-59.

Petrikovits, Harald von. "Fortifications in the North-Western Roman Empire from the Third to the Fifth Centuries AD," *Journal of Roman Studies* 61 (1971), 178-218.

Piboule, Patrick. "Les souterrains médiévaux et leur place dans l'histoire des structures de défense," *Château Gaillard* 9-10 (1982), 237-54.

Pollak, Martha D. *Military Architecture, Cartography and the Representation of the Early Modern City: A Checklist of Treatises on Fortification in the Newberry Library*. Chicago: The Newberry Library, 1991.

Pous, Anny de. "Notice sur l'évolution de l'archère dans les châteaux feodaux des Pyrénées Méditerranéenes entre le Xème et le XIVème siècle," *Gladius* 4 (1965), 67-85.

Ritter, Rudolf. *L'architecture militaire du moyen âge*. Paris, 1974.

Rocolle, Pierre. *Le temps des châteaux forts, Xe-XVe siècle*. Paris, 1994.

Rosetti, R. "Some Medieval Fortifications," *Revue internationale d'histoire militaire* 6 (1946), 90-91.

Salamagne, Alain. "A propos de l'adaptation de la fortification à l'artillerie vers les années 1400: quelques remarques sur les problèmes de vocabulaire, de typologie et de méthode," *Moyen âge* 75 (1993), 809-46.

Schmidtchen, Volker. "Castles, Cannon and Casemates," *Fortress* 6 (Aug 1990), 3-10.

Spiteri, Stephen C. *Fortresses of the Cross: Hospitaller Military Architecture (1136-1798)*. Valleta: Heritage Interpretation Services, 1994.

Tauber, Jürg. "Alltag und Fest auf der Burg im Spiegel der archäologischen Sachquellen." In: *Das ritterliche Turnier im Mittelalter*. Ed. Josef Fleckenstein. Göttingen: Vandenhoeck and Ruprecht, 1985, pp. 588-623.

Taylor, Arnold J. "Castle-Building in Thirteenth-Century Wales and Savoy," *Proceedings of the British Academy* 63 (1977), 265-92.

Thompson, M.W. *The Decline of the Castle*. Cambridge: Cambridge University Press, 1987.

Thompson, M.W. *The Rise of the Castle*. Cambridge: Cambridge University Press, 1991.

Warner, Philip. *The Medieval Castle: Life in a Fortress in Peace and War*. New York: Taplinger Publishing Company, 1971.

Wilcox, R. "Timber Reinforcement in Medieval Castles," *Château Gaillard* 5 (1972), 193-202.

Zdravković, Ivan. "Kratki terenski podaci o našim gradovima," *Vesnik* 6-7 (1962), 247-60.

Military Technology – Premodern – Fortifications – Siege Warfare

André-Michel, Robert. "Les défenseurs des chateaux et des villes fortes dans le Comtat-Venaissin," *Bibliothèque de l'école de chartes* 75 (1915), 315-30.

Aris, Rutherford and Bernard S. Bachrach. "De motu arietum (On the Motion of Batering Rams)," in *Differential Equations, Dynamical Systems, and Control Science: A Festschrift in Honor of Lawrence Markus*. Ed. K.D. Elworthy, W.N. Everitt, and E.B. Lee. New York, 1994, pp. 1-13.

Artonne, A. "Froissart Historien: Le siège et la prise de la Roche-Vendeix," *Bibliothèque de l'école des chartes* 110 (1952), 89-107.

Bachrach, Bernard S. "Medieval Siege Warfare: A Reconnaissance," *Journal of Military History* 58 (1994), 119-33.

Bain, R.N. "The Siege of Belgrade by Muhammed II, July 1-23, 1456," *English Historical Review* 7 (1892), 235-42.

Beaurepaire, Charles de. "Notes sur la prise du château par Ricarville en 1432." In: *Précis des travaux de l'Académie impériale des sciences, belles-lettres et arts de Rouen, 1855-1856.* Rouen: Péron, 1856, pp. 306-43.

Bouteiller, Paul. "Le siège et la prise du Chateau-Gaillard en 1203-1204," *Revue historique des armées* 2.2 (1946), 15-27.

Bradbury, Jim. *The Medieval Siege.* Woodbridge: The Boydell Press, 1992.

Brokken, H.M. "Het beleg van Delft in 1359." In: *De stad Delft: Cultuur en maatschapij tot 1572.* Delft, 1979, pp. 19-22.

Bury, John. "Early Writings on Fortifications and Siegecraft, 1502-1554," *Fort* 13 (1985), 5-48.

Contamine, Philippe. "La guerre de siège au temps de Jeanne d'Arc," *Dossiers de archéologie* 34 (May 1979),; in: *De Jeanne d'Arc aux guerres d'Italie: Figures, images et problèmes du XVe siècle.* Orléans, 1994, pp. 85-95.

Coutil, Léon. "Un témoin du siège de Louviers en 1418, la bombarde de la Haye-le-Comte près de Louviers (Eure): Etude sommaire sur l'artillerie des XIVe et XVe siècles," *Bulletin de la société de Louviers et de sa région* 5 ( ), 17-24.

Delumeau, J. *La peur en Occident, XIVe-XVIIIe siècle: Une cité assiégée.* Paris, 1978.

De Vos, Luc. "Le siège d'Ostende." In: *Acta del XVIII Congresso internazionale di storia militare: La scoperta del nuovo mondo e la sua influenza nella storia militare.* Ed. Paolo Alberini and Michele Nones. Turin, 1993, pp. 67-80.

DeVries, Kelly. "The Impact of Gunpowder Weaponry on Siege Warfare in the Hundred Years War." In: *The Medieval City Under Siege.* Ed. I.A. Corfis and M. Wolfe. Woodbridge, 1995, pp. 227-44.

Duffy, Christopher. *Siege Warfare: The Fortress in the Early Modern World, 1494-1660*. London: Routledge and Kegan Paul, 1979.

Elad, A. "The Siege of Al Wasit (132/749)." In: *Studies in Islamic History and Civilization in Honour of Professor David Ayalon*. Ed. M. Sharon. Jerusalem, 1986, pp. 59-90.

Evans, D.R. "Roman Siege Warfare, II," *Popular Archaeology* 2.5 (Nov 1980), 37-40.

Ferreiro, Alberto. "The Siege of Barbastro, 1064-65," *Journal of Medieval History* 9 (1983), 129-44.

Fons-Meliococq, A. de la. "Relation du siège de Ham de 1411, par un Chroniqueuer (anonyme) Bourguignon (XVe siècle)," *La Picardie* 3 (1857), 241-48.

Freeman, A.Z. "Wall-Breakers and River-Bridgers: Military Engineers in the Scottish Wars of Edward I," *Journal of British Studies* 10 (1976), 1-16.

Gaier, Claude. "Considérations pratiques sur l'attaque et la défense des anciennes places-fortes." In: *Catalogue de l'exposition: "De Bavière à la Citadelle"*. Liege. 1980, pp. 9-18; in: *Armes et combats dans l'univers médiéval*. Paris: De Boeck Université, 1995, pp. 283-96.

Gaier, Claude. "Les moyens d'attaque et de défense des fortifications aux environs de l'an mil," *Bulletin de l'institut archéologique liégeoise* 100 (1988), 61-70; in: *Actes du colloque du Chèvremont*. Liege, 1990, pp. 61-70; in: *Armes et combats dans l'univers médiéval*. Paris: De Boeck Université, 1995, pp. 259-66.

Gravett, Christopher. *Medieval Siege Warfare*. London: Osprey, 1990.

Hall, Bert S. "The Changing Face of Siege Warfare: Technology and Tactics in Transition." In: *The Medieval City Under Siege*. Ed. I.A. Corfis and M. Wolfe. Woodbridge, 1995, pp. 257-75.

Harney, Michael. "Siege Warfare in Medieval Hispanic Epic and Romance." In: *The Medieval City Under Siege*. Ed. I.A. Corfis and M. Wolfe. Woodbridge, 1995, pp. 177-90.

Hebron, Malcolm. *The Medieval Siege: Theme and Image in Middle English Romance*. Oxford: Clarendon Press, 1997.

Hughes, Quentin. "Medieval Firepower," *Fortress* 8 (Feb 1991), 31-43.

Hunger, V. "Le siège et la prise de Vire par Charles VII en 1450," *Annales de Normandie* 12 (1971), 109-22.

Jones, Richard L.C. "Fortification and Sieges in Western Europe, *c.* 800-1450." In: *Medieval Warfare: A History*. Ed. Maurice Keen. Oxford: Oxford University Press, 1999, pp. 163-85.

Kenyon, John R. "Fluctuating Frontiers: Normanno-Welsh Castle Warfare c. 1075 to 1240," *Château Gaillard* 17 (1996), 119-26.

King, D.J. Cathcart. "The Taking of Le Krak des Chevaliers in 1271," *Antiquity* 23 (1949), 83-92.

Kirby, J.L. "The Siege of Bourg, 1406." *History Today* 18 (1968), 53-60.

Lenci, A. "L'assedio di Padova del 1509: questioni militari e implicazioni urbanistiche nella strategia difensiva veneziana all'indomani di Agnadello," *Bollentino del Museo Civico di Padova* 63 (1974), 123-55.

Loomis, Roger Sherman. "The Allegorical Siege in the Art of the Middle Ages," *American Journal of Archaeology* 2nd ser., 23 (1919), 255-69.

Malafosse, J. "Le siège de Toulouse par Simon de Montfort," *Revue des Pyrénées* 4 (1892), 497-522, 725-56.

Mallett, Michael. "Siegecraft in Late Fifteenth-Century Italy." In: *The Medieval City Under Siege*. Ed. I.A. Corfis and M. Wolfe. Woodbridge, 1995, pp. 245-56.

McGlynn, Sean. "Useless Mouths," *History Today* 48.6 (June 1998), 41-46.

Miquel, Jacques. "L'attaque et la défense des portes au Moyen-Age à travers les miniatures et les récits des chroniqueurs." In: *Aux portes du chateau: Actes du troisième colloque de castellologie*. Paris, 1987, pp. 33-49.

Mongeau, Rene Guy B. "Thirteenth-Century Siege Weapons and Machines in *L'art de chevalerie*," *Allegorica* 7 (1987), 123-43.

Monteuuis, Gustave. "Le siège de Bourbourg en 1383," *Annales du comité flamand de France* 22 (1895), 259-313.

Moranvillé, H. "Le siège de Reims, 1359-1360," *Bibliothèque de l'école de Chartes* 56 (1895), 93-98.

Pepper, Simon. "The Underground Siege." *Fort* 10 (1982), 31-38.

Pernot, Jean-Francis. "Guerre de sièges et places fortes." In: *Guerre et pouvoir en Europe au XVIe siècle*. Ed. V. Barrie-Currien. Pp. 129-50.

Postel, Raoul. *Siège et capitulation de Bayeux en 1417: Notes pour servir à l'histoire du Bessin pendant la domination anglaise sous l'occupation du roi Henri V*. Caen: Le Gost-Clérisse, Éditeur, 1873.

Prentout, Henri. *La prise de Caen par Édouard III, 1346*. Caen: Henri Delesques, 1904.

Puiseux, Léon. *Caen en 1421: appendice au siège de Caen par les anglais en 1417*. Caen: Le Gost-Clérisse, Éditeur, 1860.

Puiseux, Léon. *Siège et prise de Caen par les anglais en 1417: Épisode de la guerre de cent ans*. Caen: Le Gost-Clérisse, Éditeur, 1868.

Puiseux, Léon. *Siège et prise de Rouen par les anglais (1418-1419)*. Caen: Le Gost-Clérisse, Éditeur, 1867.

Quenedey, R. "Le siège du Château-Gaillard en 1202-1203," *Bulletin des amis des monuments Rouennais* (1913), 51-89.

Rogers, Randall. *Latin Siege Warfare in the Twelfth Century*. Oxford: Clarendon Press, 1992.

Salamagne, Alain. "L'attaque des places-fortes au XVe siècle à travers l'exemple des guerres anglo et franco-bourguignonnes," *Revue historique* 289 (1993), 65-113.

Sander, E. "Der Belagerungskrieg im Mittelalter," *Historische Zeitschrift* 165 (1941), 99-110.

Sayles, G.O. "The Siege of Carrickfergus Castle, 1315-16," *Irish Historical Studies* (1956-57), 94-100.

Toch, Michael. "The Medieval German City under Siege." In: *The Medieval City Under Siege*. Ed. I.A. Corfis and M. Wolfe. Woodbridge, 1995, pp. 35-48.

Wallacker, B.E. "Studies in Medieval Chinese Siegecraft: The Siege of Ying-Chu'an, AD 548-9," *Journal of Asian Studies* 30 (1971), 611-22.

Warner, Philip. *Sieges in the Middle Ages*. London, 1968; rpt. New York: Barnes and Noble Books, 1994.

Wolfe, Michael. "New Perspectives on Medieval Siege Warfare: An Introduction." In: *The Medieval City Under Siege*. Ed. I.A. Corfis and M. Wolfe. Woodbridge, 1995, pp. 3-16.

Zanetti, P. "L'assedio di Padova del 1509 in correlazione alle guerra combattuta nel Veneto dal maggio all'ottobre," *Nuovo archivio veneto* 2 (1891), 5-168.

Military Technology – Premodern – Fortifications – Early Medieval and Earth-and-Wood Fortifications

Aarts, B. "Early Castles of the Meuse-Rhine Border Region and Some Parallels in Western Europe, c. 1000: A Comparative Approach," *Château Gaillard* 17 (1996), 11-23.

Alcock, Leslie. "Cadbury-Camelot: A Fifteen-year Perspective." In: *Economy, Society and Warfare Among the Britons and Saxons*. Cardiff, 1987, pp. 185-213.

Alcock, Leslie. *Cadbury Castle, Somerset: The Early Medieval Archaeology*. Cardiff: University of Wales Press, 1995.

Alcock, Leslie. "Catalogue of Fortified Sites in Wales and Dummonia." In: *Economy, Society and Warfare Among the Britons and Saxons*. Cardiff, 1987, pp. 168-71.

Alcock, Leslie. "New Perspectives on Post-Roman Forts." In: *Economy, Society and Warfare Among the Britons and Saxons*. Cardiff, 1987, pp. 153-67.

Alcock, Leslie. "The Organization of Military Expeditions and Fort-Building." In: *Economy, Society and Warfare Among the Britons and Saxons*. Cardiff, 1987, pp. 214-19.

Alcock, Leslie. "Reconaissance Excavations on Early Historic Fortifications and Other Royal Sites in Scotland, 1974-84: Excavations at Dunollie Castle, Oban, Argyll, 1978," *Proceedings of the Society of Antiquaries of Scotland* 117 (1987), 1189-1247.

Alexander, Derek. "The Timber-Laced and Timber-Framed Ramparts of Continental Europe," *Fortress* 14 (Aug 1992), 3-13.

Andersen, H. Hellmuth. "Das Danewerk als Ausdruck mittelalterlicher Befestigungskunst," *Château Gaillard* 11 (1983), 9-17.

Andersen, H. Hellmuth. *Das Danewerk im früh- und hochmittelalter.* Flensburg: Museum am Danemwerk, 1995.

Andersen, H. Hellmuth. "Opus Danorum–Befestigungswälle im altdänischen Grenzland," *Archäologie in Deutschland* 3 (1992), 18-21.

Andersen, H. Hellmuth. "Die Ringburgen und die militärische Ereignisgeschichte," *Kuml arbog for Jysk Arkaeologisk Selskab* (1986), 7-19.

Andersen, Steen Wulff. *The Viking Fortress of Trelleborg.* Trans. Joan F. Davidson. Slagelse: Museet ved Trelleborg, 1996.

Aubenas, R. "Les châteaux forts du X et XIe siècles, contribution à l'étude des origines de la féodalité," *Revue historique de droit français et étranger* (1938), 548-86.

Bachrach, Bernard S. "The Angevin Strategy of Castle Building in the Reign of Fulk Nerra, 987-1040," *American Historical Review* 88 (1983), 533-560.

Bachrach, Bernard S. "The Cost of Castle Building: The Case of the Tower at Langeais, 992-994." In: *The Medieval Castle: Romance and Reality.* Ed. K. Reyerson and F. Powe. Dubuque, 1984, pp. 47-62.

Bachrach, Bernard S. "Early Medieval Fortifications in the 'West' of France: A Revised Technical Vocabulary," *Technology and Culture* 16 (1975), 531-69.

Bachrach, Bernard S. "Fortification and Military Tactics: Fulk Nerra's Strongholds *ca* 1000," *Technology and Culture* 20 (1979), 531-49.

Bachrach, Bernard S. and Rutherford Aris. "Military Technology and Garrison Organizaticn: Some Observations on Anglo-Saxon Military Thinking in Light of the Burghal Hidage," *Technology and Culture* 31 (1990), 1-17.

Baker, David. "Mottes, moats and Ringworks in Bedfordshire: Beauchamp Warwick Revisited," *Château Gaillard* 9-10 (1982), 35-54.

Barker, Philip A. "Hen Domen [Powys]," *Current Archaeology* 10 (1988), 137-42.

Barker, Philip A. "Hen Domen, Montgomery: Excavations, 1960-7," *Château Gaillard* 3 (1969), 15-27.

Barker, Philip A. "Timber Castles of the Welsh Border with Special Reference to Hen Domen, Montgomery." In: *Les mondes normandes (VIIIe-XII siècle)*. pp. 135-57.

Barker, Philip A. and Robert A. Higham. *Hen Domen, Montgomery: A Timber Castle on the English-Welsh Border*. London, 1982.

Barker, Philip A. and Robert A. Higham. *Hen Domen, Montgomery: A Timber Castle on the English-Welsh Border. Excavations, 1960-1988: A Summary Report*. Worcester and Exeter: Hen Domen Archaeology Project, 1988.

Bedwin, Owen. "Early Iron Age Settlement at Maldon and the Maldon *burh*: Excavation at Beacon Green, 1987," *Essex Archaeology and History* 23 (1992), 10-24.

Binding, Günther. "Spätkarolingisch-ottonische Pfalzen und Bergen am Niederrhein," *Château Gaillard* 5 (1972), 23-34.

Borremans, R. "Fouille d'une motte féodale à Kontich (prov. d'Anvers, Belgique)," *Château Gaillard* 1 (1964), 9-20.

Cessford, Craig. "Early Medieval Maiden Castle: a Reassessment," *Somerset and Dorset Notes and Queries* 34.344 (1996), 46-49.

Christie, Neil and A. Rushworth. "Urban Fortification and Defensive Strategy in Fifth and Sixth Century Italy: The Case of Terracina," *Journal of Roman Arcaheology* 1 (1988), 73-88.

Coulson, Charles L.H. "Fortresses and Social Responsibility in Late Carolingian France," *Zietschrift für Archäologie des Mittelalters* 4 (1976), 29-36.

Coupland, Simon. "The Fortified Bridges of Charles the Bald," *Journal of Medieval History* 17 (1991), 1-12.

Cox, Barrie. "The Pattern of Old English *Burh* in Early Lindsey," *Anglo-Saxon England* 23 (1994), 35-56.

Dark, K.R. "A Sub-Roman Re-Defence of Hadrian's Wall," *Britannia* 23 (1992), 111-20.

Davison, Brian K. "Early Earthwork Castles: A New Model," *Château Gaillard* 3 (1966), 37-47.

Dearden, Brian. "Charles the Bald's Fortified Bridge at Pîtres (Seine): Recent Archaeological Excavations," *Anglo-Norman Studies* 11 (1988), 107-12.

Dearden, Brian and Anthony Clark. "Pont-de-l'Arche or Pîtres? A Location and Archaeomagnetic Dating for Charles the Bald's Fortifications on the Seine," *Antiquity* 64 (1990), 567-71.

De Meulemeester, Jan. "Les castra carolingiens comme élément de développement urbain: quelques suggestions archéologiques," *Château Gaillard* 14 (1990), 95-120.

De Meulemeester, Jan. "La fortification de terre et son influence sur le développement urbain de quelques villes des Pays-Bas méridionaux," *Revue du Nord* 74 (1992), 13-28.

Deyres, Marcel. "Les châteaux de Foulque Nerra," *Bulletin monumental* 132 (1974), 7-28.

Edwards, Robert W. *The Fortifications of Armenian Cilicia*. Washington: Dumbarton Oaks, 1987.

Ettel, Peter. "Karlburg: Entwicklung eines königlich-bischöflichen Zentralortes am Main mit Burg und Talsiedlung vom 7. bis zum 13. Jahrhundert," *Château Gaillard* 18 (1998), 75-85.

Fehring, G. "Frühmittelalterliche Wehranlagen in Südwestdeutschland," *Château Gaillard* 5 (1972), 37-54.

Fixot, Michel. "Les fortifications de terre et la naissance de la feodalité dans le Cinglais," *Chateau Gailliard* 3 (1966), 61-66.

Fixot, Michel. *Les fortifications de terre et les origines féodales dans le Cinglais*. Caen: Centre de Recherches Archéologiques Médiévales, 1968.

Fournier, Gabriel. "Les campagnes de Pépin le Bref en Auvergne et la question des fortifications rurales au VIIIe siècle," *Francia* 2 (1974), 123-35, 910.

Fournier, Gabriel. "Les enceintes de terre en Auvergne," *Bulletin historique et scientifique de l'Auvergne* 81 (1961), 89-110.

Fournier, Gabriel. "Les forteresses rurales en France à l'époque carolingienne." In: *Actes du CIe congrès national des sociétés savantes, Lille 1976, Archéologie et histoire de l'art*. Paris, 1978, pp. 53-59.

Fox, Cyril. *Offa's Dyke: A Field Survey of the Western Frontier-Works of Mercia in the Seventh and Eighth Centuries A.D.* London, 1955.

Friedrich, R. "Die frühen Perioden der Motte Husterknupp: Neue Untersuchungen zur Keramik," *Château Gaillard* 16 (1994), 207-13.

Gillmor, Caroll. "The Logistics of Fortified Bridge Building on the Seine under Charles the Bald," *Anglo-Norman Studies* 11 (1988), 87-106.

Graham, Brian. "Medieval Timber and Earthwork Fortifications in Western Ireland," *Medieval Archaeology* 32 (1988), 110-29.

Graham, Brian. "Twelfth and Thirteenth Century Earthwork Fortifications in Ireland," *Irish Sword* 17 (1987-90).

Hall, R.A. "The Five Boroughs of the Danelaw: A Review of Present Knowledge," *Anglo-Saxon England* 18 (1989), 149-208.

Haslam, Jeremy. "The Anglo-Saxon Burh at Wigingamere," *Landscape History* 10 (1988), 25-36.

Heidinga, H.A. "The Huneschans at Uddel Reconsidered," *Château Gaillard* 13 (1987), 53-62.

Héliot, Pierre. "Les châteaux-forts en France du Xe au XIIe siècle à la lumière de travaux récents," *Journal des savants*. (1966), 483-515.

Héliot, Pierre. "Sur les résidences princières bâties en France du Xe et XIIe siècle," *Moyen âge* 61 (1955), 27-61, 231-317.

Hensel, W. "Fortifications en bois de l'Europe orientale," *Château Gaillard* 4 (1969), 71-136.

Herrnbrodt, Adolf. "Die frühmittelalterlichen Ringwälle des Rheinlandes," *Château Gaillard* 3 (1969), 67-76.

Herrnbrodt, Adolf. "Stand der frühmittelalterlichen Mottenforschung in Rheinland," *Château Gaillard* 1 (1964), 77-100.

Higham, Robert. "Timber Castles: A Reassessment," *Fortress* 1 (May 1989), 50-60.

Higham, Robert and Philip Barker. *Timber Castles*. London, 1992.

Hill, David. "The Burghal Hidage: The Establishment of a Text," *Medieval Archaeology* 13 (1969), 84-92.

Hill, David and Alexander R. Rumble, ed. *The Defence of Wessex: The Burghal Hidage and Anglo-Saxon Fortifications*. Manchester: Manchester University Press, 1996.

Hubert, J. "Evolution de la topographie et de l'aspect des villes en Gaule du Ve au Xe siècle." In: *La città nell'alto medioevo*. Settimane di studio del centro Italiano di studi sull'alto medioevo, 6. Spoleto, 1959, pp. 529-58, 591-602.

Jankuhn, H. "Ein Burgentyp der späten Wikingerzeit in Nord-friesland und sein historischer Hintergrund," *Zeitschrift der Gesellschaft für schleswig-holsteinische Geschichte* 78 (1954), 1-21.

Janssen, W. "Neue Grabungsergebnisse von der frühmittelalterlichen Niederungsburg bei Haus Meer," *Château Gaillard* 5 (1972), 85-99.

Jäschke, K.U. *Burgenbau und Landesverteidigung um 900: Überlegungen zur Beispielen aus Deutschland, Frankreich und England*. Sigmaringen, 1975.

Jørgensen, Anne Nørgård. "Off-Shore Defensive Works in Denmark, AD 200-1300," *Château Gaillard* 18 (1998), 149-52.

Kaul, Flemming. "Priorsøkke and Its Logistic Implications." In: *Military Aspects of Scandinavian Society in a European Perspective, AD. 1-1300*. Ed. A.N. Jørgensen and B. Clausen. Copenhagen: National Museum of Denmark, 1997, pp. 137-45.

King, D.J. Cathcart and Leslie Alcock. "Ringworks of England and Wales," *Château Gaillard* 3 (1969), 90-127.

Klein, Janice B. "Hillfort Reuse in Gloucestershire, AD 1-700." In: *Medieval Archaeology: Papers of the Seventeenth Annual Conference of the Center for Medieval and Early Renaissance Studies*. Ed. C.L. Redman. Binghamton, 1989, pp. 187-201.

Knight, Jeremy K. "Welsh Fortifications of the First Millennium A.D.," *Château Gaillard* 16 (1994), 277-84.

Lawrence, A.W. "Early Medieval Fortifications Near Rome," *Papers of the British School at Rome* n.s. 19 (1964), 89-122.

Matthys, André. "Les châteaux de Mirwart et de Sugny, centres de pouvoirs aux Xe-XIe siècles." In: *Villes et campagnes au moyen âge: Mélanges Georges Despy*. Ed. J.-M. Duvosquel and A Dierkens. Brussels, 1991, pp. 465-502.

McNeill, T.E. and M. Pringle. "A Map of Mottes in the British Isles," *Medieval Archaeology* 41 (1997), 220-23.

Meyer, Werner. "Frühe Burgen im Lichte der schriftlichen: Quellen und der archäologischen Befunde," *Château Gaillard* 16 (1994), 299-307.

Mogren, Mats. "Northern Timber Castles–Short-Lived But Complex: Some Examples from the Southern Swedish Taiga," *Château Gaillard* 18 (1998), 135-48.

Näsman, Ulf. "Strategies and Tactics in Migration Period Defence: On the Art of Defence on the Basis of the Settlement Forts of Öland." In: *Military Aspects of Scandinavian Society in a European Perspective, AD. 1-1300*. Ed. A.N. Jørgensen and B. Clausen. Copenhagen: National Museum of Denmark, 1997, pp. 146-56.

Nørgaard, F., E. Rosedahl, and P. Skovmand, ed. *Aggersborg gennem 1000 år*. Herning, 1986

Nørlund, Poul. *Trelleborg*. Copenhagen, 1948.

Nørlund, Poul. *Trelleborg*. Nationalmuseets Blå Bøger. Copenhagen: Nationalmuseet, 1968.

Noyé, Ghislaine. "Les fortifications de terre dans la seigneurie de Toucy du Xe au XIIIe siècle: Essai de typologie," *Archéologie médiévale* 6 (1976), 149-217.

Olsen, Olaf. *Fyrkat: The Viking Camp Near Hobro.* The Danish National Museum. 2nd ed. Copenhagen: The National Museum, 1975.

Olsen, Olaf. "The Geometric Viking Fortress," *Château Gaillard* 4 (1969), 185-90.

Olsen, Olaf, Else Rosedahl, and H. Schmidt. *Fyrkat: En jysk vikingborg.* 2 vols. Copenhagen, 1977.

Pesez, Jean-Marie. "Approches méthodologiques d'un recensement général des fortifications de terre médiévales en France," *Château Gaillard* 12 (1985), 79-90.

Pribaković, Dušan. "Neki podaci o gradištima severozapadne Hrvatske," *Vesnik* 3 (1956), 107-42.

Radford, C.A. Ralegh. "The Later Pre-Conquest Boroughs and their Defences," *Medieval Archaeology* 14 (1970), 83-103.

Ramasco, C., G. Giolitto, and M. and P. Scarzella. "Le chiuse Longobardiche tra Dora Baltea e Serra," *Armi antiche* (1975), 3-22.

Randsborg, Klavs. "Viking Raiders: The Transformation of Scandinavian Society." In: *Medieval Archaeology: Papers of the Seventeenth Annual Conference of the Center for Medieval and Early Renaissance Studies.* Ed. C.L. Redman. Binghamton, 1989, pp. 23-39.

Roesdahl, Else. "Aggersborg: The Viking Settlement and Fortress," *Château Gaillard* 8 (1977), 269-78.

Roesdahl, Else. "The Building Activities of King Harold Bluetooth: Notes of the Dendro-chronological Dating of the Viking Fortress of Trelleborg," *Château Gaillard* 9-10 (1982), 543-46.

Roesdahl, Else. "The Danish Geometrical Viking Fortresses and their Context," *Anglo-Norman Studies* 9 (1986), 209-26.

Roesdahl, Else. "Les fortifications circulaires de l'époque viking in Danemark," *Proxima Thulé* 1 (1994), 25-50.

Roesdahl, Else. "The Viking Fortress of Fyrkat in the Light of the Object Found," *Château Gaillard* 6 (1973), 195-202.

Rouche, Michel. "The Vikings Versus the Towns of Northern Gaul: Challenge and Response." In: *Medieval Archaeology: Papers of the Seventeenth Annual Conference of the Center for Medieval and Early Renaissance Studies*. Ed. C.L. Redman. Binghamton, 1989, pp. 41-56.

Schmidt-Thomé, P. "Untersuchungen mit Erdrader in der Niederungsburg von Vörstetten, Landkreis Emmendingen," *Château Gaillard* 16 (1994), 351-54.

Schoenfeld, Edward J. "Anglo-Saxon *Burhs* and Continental *Burgen*: Early Medieval Fortifications in Constitutional Perspective," *Haskins Society Journal* 6 (1994), 49-66.

Siguret, Ph. "Trois mottes de la région de Bellême (Orne)," *Château Gaillard* 1 (1964), 133-48.

Slater, T.R. "Controlling the South Hams: The Anglo-Saxon *Burh* at Halwell," *The Devonshire Association* 123 (1991), 57-78.

Solle, M. "Les bourgwalls en Bohême dans le cadre de l'évolution politique et économique des 8e-11e siècles," *Château Gaillard* 4 (1969), 201-17.

Talbot, Eric J. "The Defences of Earth and Timber Castles." In: *Scottish Weapons and Fortifications, 1100-1800*. Ed. David H. Caldwell. Edinburgh: John Donald Publishers Ltd., 1981, pp. 1-9.

Tarzia, Wade. "No Trespassing: Border Defence in the Táin Bo Cuailge," *Emania* 3 (1987), 28-33.

van Heeringen, Robert M. "The Construction of Frankish Circular Fortresses in the Province of Zeeland (SW Netherlands) in the End of the Ninth Century," *Château Gaillard* 18 (1998), 241-49.

Verbruggen, J.F. "Note sur le sens des mots castrum, castellum, et quelques autres expressions qui désignent des fortifications," *Revue Belge de philologie et d'histoire* 28 (1950), 147-55.

"Voci dell'enciclopedia: Polvere pirica, La," *Armi antiche* 3 (1956), 139-47.

Wilkelmann, W. "*Est locus insignis quo Patra et Lippa fluentant*: Ueber die Ausgrabungen in den karolingischen und ottonischen königsplalzen in Paderhorn," *Château Galliard* 5 (1972), 203-25.

Williams, Ann. "A Bell-house and a Burh-geat: Lordly Residences in England before the Norman Conquest." In: *Medieval Knighthood, IV*. Ed. C. Harper-Bill and R. Harvey. Woodbridge, 1992, pp. 221-40.

Wilson, David M. *Civil and Military Engineering in Viking Age Scandinavia*. London, 1978.

Wilson, David M. "Defence in the Viking Age." In: *Problems in Economic and Social Archaeology*. Ed. G. de G. Sieveking et al. London, 1976, pp. 439-45.

Zadora-Rio, E. "L'enceinte fortifée du Plessis-Grimoult, résidence seigneuriale du XIe siècle," *Château Gaillard* 5 (1972), 227-39.

Zadora-Rio, E. "Les essais de typologie des fortifications de terre médiévale en Europe: bilan et perspective," *Archéologie médiévale* 15 (1985), 191-96.

Military Technology – Premodern – Fortifications – Motte-and-Bailey Castles

Addyman, Peter V. "Excavations at Baile Hill, York," *Château Gaillard* 5 (1972), 7-12.

Armitage, Ella S. *The Early Norman Castles of the British Isles*. London, 1912.

Baker, David. "Mottes, moats and Ringworks in Bedfordshire: Beauchamp Warwick Revisited," *Château Gaillard* 9-10 (1982), 35-54.

Beeler, John H. "Castles and Strategy in Norman and Early Angevin England," *Speculum* 31 (1956), 581-601.

Besteman, Jan G. "Mottes in the Netherlands," *Château Gaillard* 12 (1985), 211-24.

Bonde, Sheila. "Castle and Church Building at the Time of the Norman Conquest." In: *The Medieval Castle: Romance and Reality*. Ed. K. Reyerson and F. Powe. Dubuque, 1984, pp. 84-91.

Borremans, R. "Grimbergen: Fouilles de la motte Senecaberg," *Château Gaillard* 6 (1973), 23-26.

Boüard, Michel de. "La motte." In: *L'archéologie du village médiévale*. Leuven and Ghent, 1967, pp. 25-55.

Boüard, Michel de. "Quelques données archéologiques concernant le premier âge féodal." In: *Les structures sociales de l'Aquitaine, du Languedoc et de l'Espagne au premier âge féodal*. Paris, 1969, pp. 40-51.

Boüard, Michel de. "Quelques données Françaises et Normandes concernant le problème de l'origine des mottes," *Château Gaillard* 2 (1964), 19-26.

Bresc, Henri. "Les normands, constructeurs de châteaux." In: *Les Normands en Méditerranée dans le sillage des Tancréde*. Ed. P. Boulet and F. Neveux. Caen, 1994, pp. 63-75.

Brown, R. Allen. "The Architecture of the Bayeux Tapestry." In: *Castles, Conquest and Charters: Collected Papers*. Woodbridge, 1989, pp. 214-26.

Brown, R. Allen. "The Castles of the Conquest." In: *Castles, Conquest and Charters: Collected Studies*. Woodbridge, 1989, pp. 65-74.

Brown, R. Allen. "An Historian's Approach to the Origins of the Castle in England," *Archaeological Journal* 126 (1969), 131-48; in: *Castles, Conquest and Charters: Collected Papers*. Woodbridge, 1989, pp. 1-18.

Brown, R. Allen. "The Norman Conquest and the Genesis of English Castles," *Château Gaillard* 3 (1969), 1-14; in: *Castles, Conquest and Charters: Collected Papers*. Woodbridge, 1989, pp. 75-89.

Bur, Michel de. "Recherches sur les plus anciennes mottes castrales de Champagne," *Château Gaillard* 9-10 (1982), 55-69.

Counihan, Joan. "Mrs Ella Armitage, John Horace Round, G.T. Clark and Early Norman Castles," *Anglo-Norman Studies* 8 (1985), 73-87.

Darvill, Timothy. "Excavations on the Site of the Early Norman Castle at Gloucester," *Medieval Archaeology* 32 (1988), 1-49.

Davison, Brian K. "The Origins of the Castle in England: The Institute's Research Project," *Archaeological Journal* 124 (1967), 202-11.

Davison, Brian K. "Three Eleventh-Century Earthworks in England: Their Excavation and Implications," *Château Gaillard* 2 (1967), 39-48.

Debord, André. "A propos de l'utilisation des mottes castrales," *Château Gaillard* 11 (1983), 91-99.

Decaëns, Joseph. "De la motte de conquête (XIe siècle) à la seigneurie châtelaine (XIIe siècle): L'exemple de Rivray à Condé-sur-Huisne (Orne)," *Château Gaillard* 16 (1994), 109-20.

De Meulemeester, Jan. "Le château à motte comme chantier: quelques données et réflexions des anciens Pays-Bas méridionaux," *Château Gaillard* 18 (1998), 37-45.

De Meulemeester, Jan. "Le début du château: le motte castrale dans les Pays-Bas méridionaux," *Château Gaillard* 16 (1994), 121-30.

De Meulemeester, Jan. "Mottes castrales du Comté de Flandre: État de la question d'après les fouilles récentes," *Château Gaillard* 11 (1983), 101-15.

De Meulemeester, Jan. "Structures défensives et résidences princières: le châteaux à motte du comté de Looz au XIe siècle," *Château Gaillard* 15 (1990), 101-11.

Demolon, P., E. Louis, J.-F. Ropital. *Mottes et maisons-fortes en Ostrevent médiéval*. Archaeologia Duacensis, 1. Douai: Société Archéologique de Douai, 1988.

Eales, Richard. "Royal Power and Castles in Norman England." In: *The Ideals and Practice of Medieval Knighthood*, III. Ed. C. Harper-Bill and R. Harvey. Woodbridge, 1990, pp. 49-78.

Eddy, M.R. "A Roman Settlement and Early Medieval Motte at Moot Hill, Great Driffield, North Humberside," *East Riding Arcaheology* 7 (1988), 40-51.

English, Barbara. "Towns, Mottes and Ring-works of the Conquest." In: *The Medieval Military Revolution: State, Society and Military Change in*

Medieval and Early Modern Europe. Ed. A. Ayton and J.L. Price. London, 1995, pp. 45-61.

Fixot, Michel. "La motte et l'habitant fortifié en Provence médiévale," *Château Gaillard* 7 (1975), 67-93.

Fournier, Gabriel. "Vestiges de mottes castrales en basse Auvergne: Inventaire provisoire et essai de classement," *Revue de l'Auvergne* 75 (1962), 137-76.

Friedrich, R. and K.-F. Rittershofer. "Die hochmittelalterliche Motte und Niederungsburg von Oberursel-Bommersheim, Hochtanuskreis–Ausgrabungen 1988 bis 1993," *Château Gaillard* 17 (1996), 93-110.

Glasscock, R.E. "Mottes in Ireland," *Château Gaillard* 7 (1975), 95-110.

Graham, Brian. "Medieval Timber and Earthwork Fortifications in Western Ireland," *Medieval Archaeology* 32 (1988), 110-29.

Halbertsma, H. "Les mottes Frisonnes," *Château Gaillard* 7 (1975), 111-25.

Hamroun-Candelier, B., B. Declerq. E. Louis and F. Perreau. *Mottes et maisons-fortes en Artois médiéval*. Douai, 1991.

Harfield, C.G. "A Hand-list of Castles Recorded in the Domesday Book," *English Historical Review* 106 (1991), 371-92.

Higham, Mary C. "The Mottes of North Lancashire, Lonsdale and South Cumbria," *Transactions of the Cumberland and Westmorland Antiquarian and Archaeological Society* 91 (1991), 79-90.

Hodges, Richard. "The Danish Contribution to the Origin of the English Castle," *Acta archaeologia* 59 (1988), 169-72.

Hope-Taylor, Brian. "Norman Castles," *Scientific American* 198 (March 1958), 42-48.

Hope-Taylor, Brian. "The Norman Motte at Abinger, Surrey, and its Wooden Castle." In: *Recent Archaeological Excavations in Britain*. Ed. R.L.S. Bruce-Mitford. New York, 1956.

James, H.F. "Excavations at Montfodo Mount Motte, Ayrshire," *Glasgow Archaeological Journal* 13 (1986), 78-85.

King, D.J. Cathcart. "The Field Archaeology of Mottes in England and Wales: Eine kurze überzicht," *Château Gaillard* 5 (1972), 101-12.

King, D.J. Cathcart. "The Mottes in the Vale of Montgomery," *Archaeologia Cambrensis* 114 (1965), 69-86.

Lefranc, Guy and Francis Perreau. "Mottes et sites fortifiés médiévaux du Pas-de-Calais: Pour la constitution d'une documentation topographique," *Bulletin de la commission départementale d'histoire et d'archéologique du Pas-de-Calais* 12 (1989), 329-44.

Lewis, Carenza. "Paired Mottes in East Chelborough, Dorset." In: *From Cornwall to Caithness: Some Aspects of British Field Archaeology: Papers Presented to Norman V. Quinnell.* Ed. Mark Bowden, Donnie Mackay, and Peter Topping. Oxford, 1989, pp. 159-71.

Louis, E. *Recherches sur le château à motte de Hordain (Nord)*. Archaeologia Duacensis, 2. Douai: Société Archéologique de Douai, 1989.

Maerten, Michel. "Mottes et maisons fortes du Charolais," *Dossiers d'archéologie* 155 (Feb 1991), 32-33.

Mazard, C. "Châteaux à motte et évolution du peuplement: de l'ager au mandement: Quelques exemples dauphinois," *Château Gaillard* 14 (1990), 277-92.

Mouton, D. "L'edification des mottes castrales de Provence, un phénomène durable: Xe-XIIIe siècles," *Château Gaillard* 16 (1994), 309-20.

Müller-Wille, M. *Mittelalterliches Burghügel ('Motten') in nördlichen Rheinland*. Cologne, 1966.

Pindar, A. and B. Dawson. "The Excavation of a Motte and Bailey Castle at Chalgrave, Bedfordshire, 1978," *Bedfordshire Archaeology* 18 (1988), 33-56.

Pringle, Denys. "A Castle in the Sand: Mottes in the Crusader East," *Château Gaillard* 18 (1998), 187-91.

Renn, Derek F. "The First Norman Castles in England (1051-1071)," *Château Gaillard* 1 (1964), 125-32.

Renn, Derek F. "Mottes: A Classification," *Antiquity* 33 (1959), 106-12.

Renn, Derek F. *Norman Castles in Britain*. London, 1968.

Round, J.H. "The Castles of the Conquest," *Archaeologia* 63 (1902), 313-40.

Silvester, R.J. "Tomen Llansantffraid: A Motte Near Rhaeadr Powys," *Medieval Archaeology* 35 (1991), 109-14.

Simpson, G.G. and B. Webster. "Charter Evidence and the Distribution of Mottes in Scotland," *Château Gaillard* 5 (1972), 175-92.

Spurgeon, C.J. "Mottes and Castle Ringworks in Wales." In: *Castles in Wales and the Marches*. Ed. J.R. Kenyon and R. Avent. Cardiff, 1987, pp. 23-50.

Stiesdal, Hans. "Late Earthworks of the Motte and Bailey Type," *Château Gaillard* 4 (1969), 219-20.

Stiesdal, Hans. "Die motten in Dänemark: Eine kurze übersicht," *Château Gaillard* 2 (1967), 94-99.

Taylor, Arnold J. "Evidence for a Pre-Conquest Origin for the Chapels in Hastings and Pevensey Castles," *Château Gaillard* 3 (1969), 144-51; in: *Studies in Castles and Castle Building*. London, 1985, pp. 233-40.

Thompson, M.W. "Excavations in Farnham Castle Keep Surrey, England, 1958-60," *Château Gaillard* 2 (1967), 100-05.

Thompson, M.W. "Motte Substructures," *Medieval Archaeology* 5 (1961), 305-06.

Thompson, M.W. "Recent Excavations in the Keep of Farnham Castle, Surrey," *Medieval Archaeology* 4 (1960), 81-94.

Yeoman, Peter A. "Mottes in North-East Scotland," *Scottish Archaeological Review* 5 (1988), 125-33.

Military Technology – Premodern – Fortifications – Fortified Residences

Bayard, D. "La maison forte de 'La Cologne', à Hargicourt (Aisne)," *Revue archéologique de Picardie* 3/4 (1989), 105-208.

Burnouf, Joëlle. "Butenheim: De le résidence aristocratique du XIe siècle à la maison forte de la fin du moyen âge: Histoire et archéologie de l'echec d'un lignage dans un terroir du sud de l'Alsace," *Château Gaillard* 15 (1992), 61-71.

Demolon, P., E. Louis, J.-F. Ropital. *Mottes et maisons-fortes en Ostrevent médiéval*. Archaeologia Duacensis, 1. Douai: Société Archéologique de Douai, 1988.

Faravel, S. "Une fouille surprise: la maison-forte de Brione à Saint-Germain-d'Esteuil (Gironde)," *Château Gaillard* 14 (1990), 159-74.

Hamroun-Candelier, B., B. Declerq. E. Louis and F. Perreau. *Mottes et maisons-fortes en Artois médiéval*. Douai, 1991.

McNeill, T.E. "The Origins of Tower Houses," *Archaeology Ireland* 19.6.1 (Spr 1992), 13-14.

Murtagh, Ben. "Hatch's Castle, Ardee, County Louth: A Fortified Town House of the Pale," *County Louth Archaeological and Historical Journal* 22, 1, 1989 (1991), 36-48.

Pesez, Jean-Marie. "Maison forte, manoir, bastide, tour, motte, enceinte, moated-site, wasserburg, ou les ensembles en archéologie." In: *La maison forte au moyen âge*. Ed. M. Bur. Paris, 1986, pp. 331-40.

Pesez, Jean-Marie and Françoise Piponnier. "Les maisons-fortes bourguignonne," *Chateau Gaillard* 5 (1972), 143-64.

Pesez, Jean-Marie and Françoise Piponnier. "Villy-le-Moutier: Recherches archéologiques sur un site de maison-forte," *Château Gaillard* 6 (1973), 147-63.

Tranter, Nigel. *The Fortified House in Scotland. I: South-East Scotland*. Edinburgh and London, 1962.

Military Technology – Premodern – Fortifications – Byzantium

Ahrweiler, H. "Les forteresses construites en Asie Mineure face à l'invasion seldjoucide." In: *Akten des XI. Internationalen Byzantinist Kongresses*. Munich, 1960, pp. 182-89.

Crow, James and Alessandra Ricci. "Investigating the Hinterland of Constantinople: Interim Report on the Anastasian Long Wall," *Journal of Roman Archaeology* 10 (1997), 235-62.

Crow, James and Stephen Hill. "Amasra: A Byzantine and Genoese Fortress on the Black Sea," *Fortress* 5 (May 1990), 3-13.

Ersen, Ahmet. "Physical Evidence Revealed During the Cleaning and the Excavations of the Outer Wall of the Land Walls of Constantinople at the Porta Romanus," *Byzantine and Modern Greek Studies* 23 (1999), 102-15.

Foss, Clive and David Winfield. *Byzantine Fortifications: An Introduction.* Pretoria: University of South Africa, 1986.

Pringle, Denys. *The Defence of Byzantine Africa from Justinian to the Arab Conquest: An Account of the Military History and Archaeology of the African Provinces in the Sixth and Seventh Centuries.* 2 vols. British Archaeological Report, 9. Oxford: BAR, 1981.

Rosser, J. "The Role of Fortifications in the Defence of Asia Minor against the Arabs from the Eighth to the Tenth Centuries," *Greek Orthodox Theological Review* 27 (1982), 135-43.

Whittow, Mark. "Rural Fortifications in Western Europe and Byzantium, Tenth to Twelfth Century," *Byzantinische Forschungen* 21 (1995), 57-74.

Military Technology – Premodern – Fortifications – Eastern Europe

Anghel, Gheorghe. "Les forteresses moldaves de l'époque d'Étienne le Grand," *Château Gaillard* 7 (1975), 21-34.

Anghel, Gheorghe. "Fortifications médiévales d'Alba Iulia," *Château Gaillard* 11 (1983), 19-28.

Anghel, Gheorghe. "Les premiers donjons de pierres de Transylvania," *Château Gaillard* 8 (1977), 7-20.

Anghel, Gheorghe. "Quelques considerations concernant le développement de l'architecture des fortifications médiévales roumains du XIIIe au XVIe siècles," *Château Gaillard* 9-10 (1982), 273-92.

Anghel, Gheorghe. "Typologie des églises fortifiées de Roumanie," *Château Gaillard* 9-10 (1982), 13-33.

Bedina, Andrea. "L'eredita di Angelberga: note su strade efortezze del comitato di Bulgaria tra IX e XI secolo," *Nuovo rivista storica* 80 (1996), 614-39.

Bogdanowski, Janusz. "Drei Strategische Stufen eines Mittelalterlichen Verteidigungsnetzes in Polen," *IBI Bulletin* 47 (1990-91), 91-98.

Bogdanowski, Janusz. "Das Neue System des Denkmalschutzes in Polen gegenüber den Alten Verteidigungsbauten," *IBI Bulletin* 47 (1990-91), 19-26.

Bon, A. *La Morée franque: Recherches historiques, topographiques et archéologiques sur la principauté d'Achaïe, 1205-1430.* 2 vols. Paris, 1969.

Budapest: Der mittelalterliche königliche Palast von Buda. Budapest: Kartográfai Vállalat, n.d.

Cabello, J. "Fouilles archéologiques d'un château féodal en Hongrie," *Château Gaillard* 16 (1994), 81-87.

Drda, Petr and Alena Rybora. "L'oppidum de Závist: Construction de la porte principale (D) et sa chronologie," *Památky archeologické* 83/2 (1992), 309-49.

Drechsler-Bižić, Ružica. "Gradine u Lici," *Vesnik* 3 (1956), 36-51.

Durdík, Tomáš. "Anfänge der hochmittelalterlichen Burgen in Böhmen," *Château Gaillard* 16 (1994), 143-53.

Durdík, Tomáš. "Archäologische Belege von Fachwerkkonstruktionen auf böhmischen Burgen," *Château Gaillard* 18 (1998), 59-64.

Durdík, Tomáš. "Baugestalt der Südecke der Burg Lichnice im Zasammenhang mit ihren Anfängen," *Castellologica Bohemica* 2 (1991).

Durdík, Tomáš. "Zum gegenwärtigen Stand der Burgenforschung in Böhmen," *Château Gaillard* 15 (1990), 127-41.

Durdík, Tomáš. "System der königlichen Burgen in Böhmen," *Château Gaillard* 17 (1996), 69-78.

Durdík, Tomáš. "The System of Royal Castles in Bohemia," *IBI Bulletin* 47 (1990-91), 105-06.

Durdík, Tomáš and Pavel Bolina. "Kapellen hochmittelalterlichen Burgen," *Castellologica Bohemica* 2 (1991).

Endre, T. "Vorbericht über die Ausgrabung der festung und des Gräberfeldes von Alsóhetény, 1981-1986: Ergebnisse und umstrittene Fragen," *Archaeoloiai Értesítö* 114-115 (1987-88), 22-61.

Feld, I. "Der Beginn der Adelsburg im mittelalterlichen Königreich Ungarn," *Château Gaillard* 16 (1994), 189-205.

Feld, I. "Spätmittelalterliche Residenzen in Ungarn," *Château Gaillard* 15 (1990), 171-87.

Fügedi, Erik. *Castle and Society in Medieval Hungary, 1000-1437.* Budapest: Akadmeiai Kiado, 1986.

Gabriel, František and Jaroslav Panáček. "Entwicklung der Herrensitze im Oberen Gebiet der Domäne Nové Zámky," *Castellologica Bohemica* 2 (1991).

Gerelyes, I. and I. Feld. "Fundkomplexe des Burgschlosses von Ozara aus der Zeit der Türkenherraschaft," *Communicationes archaeologicae Hungariae* (1986), 161-82.

Gerö, L. *Castles in Hungary.* Budapest, 1969.

Harrison, Peter. "The Fortified and Fortress Churches of Transylvania," *Fortress* 5 (May 1990), 14-26.

Harrison, R.M. "The Long Walls in Thrace," *Archaeologia aeliana* 4th ser. 47 (1963).

Herrmann, Joachim. "Burg und Siedlung in frühgeschichtlicher Zeit Besonderheiten und Modelle im nordwestslawischen Gebiet," *Château Gaillard* 11 (1983), 153-63.

Kostochkin, V. *Krepostnoye zodchestvo drevnii rusi.* Moscow, 1970.

Kuncevičius, Albinus. "First Investigation Records about the Lower Castle Palace of Vilnius Erected by Vytautas, the Grand Duke of Lithuania," *Fasciculi archaeologicae historicae* 7 (1994), 61-66.

Lock, Peter. "Castles and Seigneurial Influence in Latin Greece." In: *From Clermont to Jerusalem: The Crusades and Crusader Societies, 1095-1500*. Selected Proceedings of the International Medieval Congress, University of Leeds, 10-13 July 1995. Ed. Alan V. Murray. Turnhout: Brepols, 1998, pp. 173-86.

Mossakowski, Stanislaw. "The Late Medieval Castles in the Dukedom of Mazovia: Strongholds, Residences, Administrative Centres," *IBI Bulletin* 47 (1990-91), 99-104.

Nenadović, Slobodan. "Prilog proučavanju grada Resave," *Vesnik* 8-9 (1963), 305-22.

Opolovrikov, A.V. and Y.A. *The Wooden Architecture of Russia: Houses, Fortifications, Churches*. London: Thames and Hudson, 1989.

Pepper, Simon. "Fortress and Fleet: The Defence of Venice's Mainland Greek Colonies in the Late Fifteenth Century." In: *War, Culture and Society in Renaissance Venice: Essays in Honour of John Hale*. Ed. D.S. Chambers, C.H. Clough and M.E. Mallett. London, 1993, pp. 29-55.

Petrovics, István. "The Role of Towns in the Defence System of Medieval Hungary." In: *La guerre, la violence et les gens au Moyen Âge*. I: *Guerre et violence*. Ed. P. Contamine and O. Guyotjeannin. 119e congrès national des sociétés historiques et scientifiques, Amiens, octobre 1994, Section d'histoire médiévale et philologie. Paris, 1996, pp. 263-71.

Piletić, Dragoslav. "Arheološka istraživanja na rimskom limesu u Starom Slankamenu," *Vesnik* 4 (1957), 61-73.

Poklewski-Kozieł, Tadeusz. "Le vocabulaire castellologique dans les sources médiévales polonaises et la réalité archéologiques," *Château Gaillard* 18 (1998), 181-85.

Popa, Radu. "Kreuzritterburgen im Südosten Transsilvaniens," *IBI Bulletin* 47 (1990-91), 107-12.

Popa, Radu. "Monuments historiques de Roumanie heritage malheureux et perspectives pour le moment incertaines," *IBI Bulletin* 47 (1990-91), 27-30.

Pribaković, Dušan. "Ostava iz XV veka u Malom gradu smederevske tvrdave," *Vesnik* 6-7 (1962), 55-96.

Rappoport, Pavel. "Russian Medieval Military Architecture," *Gladius* 8 (1969), 39-62.

Seebach, C.H. "Der Stand der Werla-Forschung," *Chateau Gaillard* 5 (1972), 165-73.

Szirmai, Krisztina. "Stratigraphische Beobachtungen in Bereich der spätrömischen Festung von Aquincum," *Communicationes archaeologicae Hungariae* (1988), 49-70.

Zak, Jan. "Mittelalterliche degelförmige Burghügel in Polen," *Château Gaillard* 11 (1983), 289-91.

Zdravković, Ivan. "Kratki terenski podaci o našim gradovima," *Vesnik* 5.1 (1958), 221-44.

Military Technology – Premodern – Fortifications – England (British Islands)

Aberg, F.A. "Recent Research on Medieval Moated Sites in England," *Château Gaillard* 12 (1985), 185-97.

Addyman, Peter V. "Excavations at Ludgershall Castle," *Château Gaillard* 4 (1969), 9-12; 6 (1973), 7-13.

Alban, J.R. "English Coastal Defence: Some Fourteenth Century Modifications within the System." In: *Patronage, the Crown and the Provinces in Later Medieval England.* Ed. Ralph A. Griffiths. Gloucester: Alan Sutton, 1981, pp. 57-78.

Alcock, Leslie, Elizabeth A. Alcock, and Stephen T. Driscoll. "Reconnaissance Excavations on Early Historic Fortifications and Other Royal Sites in Scotland, 3: Dundurn," *Proceedings of the Society of Antiquaries of Scotland* 119 (1990), 9-226.

Armitage, Ella S. *The Early Norman Castles of the British Isles.* London: John Murray, 1912.

Auden, J.E. "Notes on the Church, Castle, and Parish of Shrawardine," *Transactions of the Shropshire Archaeological Society* 2nd ser. 7 (1895), 120-203.

Austin, David. "Barnard Castle, Co. Durham," *Château Gaillard* 9-10 (1982), 293-300.

Avent, Richard. "Castles of the Welsh Princes," *Château Gaillard* 16 (1994), 11-20.

Avent, Richard. *Cestyll Tywysogion Gwynedd/Castles of the Princes of Gwynedd*. Cardiff: Her Majesty's Stationery Office, 1983.

Avent, Richard. *Criccieth Castle, Pennarth Fawr Medieval Hall House, St. Cybi's Well*. Cardiff: Cadw: Welsh Historic Monuments, 1989.

Avent, Richard. *Dolwyddelan Castle, Dolbadarn Castle*. Cardiff: Cadw: Welsh Historic Monuments, 1994.

Avent, Richard. "Laugharne Castle–Excavations, 1976-1988," *Archaeology in Wales*, CBA Grp 2, 28 (1988), 24-27.

Avent, Richard. "The Medieval Development of Laugharne Castle, Dyfed, Wales," *Château Gaillard* 15 (1992), 7-18.

Ayers, Brian S., Robert Smith, and Margot Tillyard. "The Cow Tower, Norwich: A Detailed Survey and Partial Reinterpretation," *Medieval Archaeology* 32 (1988), 184-207.

Baker, David. "Mottes, moats and Ringworks in Bedfordshire: Beauchamp Warwick Revisited," *Château Gaillard* 9-10 (1982), 35-54.

Bamburgh Castle: The Home of Lord and Lady Armstrong and Family. Norwich: Jarrold Publishing, 1994.

Barker, P.A. "Bedford Castle: Some Preliminary Results from Rescue Excavations," *Château Gaillard* 6 (1973), 15-22.

Barker, P.A. "Recent Archaeological Research in Worcester," *Château Gaillard* 4 (1969), 13-18.

Barley, M.W. "Town Defences in England and Wales after 1066." In: *The Plans and Topography of Medieval Towns in England and Wales*. Ed. M.W. Barley. London, 1976, pp. 57-71.

Barton, Ken. "The Principle Fortifications of the Channel Islands before 1750," *Fortress* 3 (Nov 1989), 24-32.

Beeler, John H. "Castles and Strategy in Norman and Early Angevin England," *Speculum* 31 (1956), 581-601.

Beresford, G. "The Excavation of Goltho, Lincs.," *Château Gaillard* 8 (1977), 47-65.

Best, David. *Clitheroe Castle: A Guide.* Preston: Carnegie Publishing, 1990.

Bevis, Trevor. *Castle Acre: Fortress Village.* March, 1990.

Biddle, Martin. "Winchester, 1961-68," *Château Gaillard* 4 (1969), 19-30.

Biddle, Martin. "Wolvesey: the *domus quasi palatium* of Henry of Blois in Winchester," *Château Gaillard* 3 (1969), 28-36.

Bishop, M.C. "The White Wall, Berwick upon Tweed," *Archaeologia aeliana* 5th ser. 20 (1992), 117-19.

Bonde, Sheila. "Castle and Church Building at the Time of the Norman Conquest." In: *The Medieval Castle: Romance and Reality.* Ed. K. Reyerson and F. Powe. Dubuque, 1984, pp. 84-91.

Booth, K. and J. Cronin. "Buckton Castle," *The Greater Manchester Archaeological Journal* 3 (1989), 61-66.

Brannon, N.F. "Excavations at Brackfield Bawn, County Londonderry," *Ulster Journal of Archaeology* 53 (1991), 8-14.

Braun, Hugh. *The English Castle.* 2nd ed. London: B.T. Batsford, 1943.

Brown, R. Allen. *Castles.* Aylesbury: Shire Archaeology, 1985.

Brown, R. Allen. *Castles from the Air.* Cambridge: Cambridge University Press, 1989.

Brown, R. Allen. "Châteaux et societes en Angleterre du XIVe au XVIe siecle." In: *Castles, Conquest and Charters: Collected Papers.* Woodbridge, 1989, pp. 122-37.

Brown, R. Allen. *Dover Castle, Kent.* 2nd ed. London: Her Majesty's Stationery Office, 1974.

Brown, R. Allen. *English Castles.* 3rd ed. London: B.T. Batsford Limited, 1976.

Brown, R. Allen. "Framlingham Castle and Bigod, 1154-1216." In: *Castles, Conquest and Charters: Collected Papers*. Woodbridge, 1989, pp. 187-208.

Brown, R. Allen. "A List of Castles, 1154-1216," *English Historical Review* 74 (1959), 249-80.

Brown, R. Allen. "Le manoir fortifié dans le royaume d'Angleterre." In: *Castles, Conquest and Charters: Collected Papers*. Woodbridge, 1989, pp. 158-62.

Brown, R. Allen. "A Note on Kenilworth Castle: The Change to Royal Ownership." In: *Castles, Conquest and Charters: Collected Papers*. Woodbridge, 1989, pp. 209-13.

Brown, R. Allen. "Royal Castle-Building in England, 1154-1216," *English Historical Review* 70 (1955), 353-98; in: *Castles, Conquest and Charters: Collected Papers*. Woodbridge, 1989, pp. 19-64.

Brown, R. Allen. "Some Observations on the Tower of London." In: *Castles, Conquest and Charters: Collected Papers*. Woodbridge, 1989, pp. 163-76.

Brown, R. Allen. "Lo studio dei castelli medievali in Inghilterra." In: *Castles, Conquest and Charters: Collected Papers*. Woodbridge, 1989, pp. 149-57.

Brown, R. Allen. "The White Tower of London." In: *Castles, Conquest and Charters: Collected Papers*. Woodbridge, 1989, pp. 177-86.

Brown, R. Allen, H.M. Colvin and Arnold J. Taylor, ed. *The History of the King's Works*. 7 vols. London, 1963.

Brown, T. and M.D. Watson. "The Civil War Roushill Wall, Shrewsbury," *Shropshire History and Archaeology: Transactions of the Shropshire Archaeological and Historical Society* 66 (1989), 85-89.

Browne, D.M. and D. Percival. *Newport Castle (Pembrokeshire): An Architectural Study*. Aberystwyth, 1992.

Burnham, Helen. "Test Pits at Aberystwyth Castle, December 1989: Results of Archaeological Recording," *Ceredigion: Journal of the Ceredigion Antiquarian Society* 96 (1989-90), 1-3.

Burrow, Ian. "The Town Defences of Exeter," *Transactions of the Devonshire Association for the Advancement of Science, Literature and Art* 109 (1977), 13-40.

Bush, Robin. *Taunton Castle: A Pictorial History*. Aspects of Somerset History Series, no. 1. Taunton: The Somerset Archaeological and Natural History Society, 1988.

Butler, Lawrence. "Castles of the Welsh Princes in North Wales," *IBI Bulletin* 47 (1990-91), 41-48.

Butler, Lawrence. *Clifford's Tower and the Castles of York*. London: English Heritage, 1997.

Butler, Lawrence. *Denbigh Castle and Town Walls*. Cardiff: CADW, 1990.

Butler, Lawrence. "Dolforwyn Castle, Montgomery, Powys: First Report, the Excavations, 1981-86," *Archaeologia Cambrensis* 138 (1990), 78-98.

Butler, Lawrence. "Dolforwyn Castle, Powys," *Current Archaeology* 120 (1990), 418-23.

Butler, Lawrence. "Dolforwyn Castle, Powys, Wales: Excavations, 1981-84," *Château Gaillard* 12 (1985), 167-77.

Butler, Lawrence. "Dolforwyn Castle, Powys, Wales: Excavations, 1985-90," *Château Gaillard* 15 (1990), 73-82.

Butler, Lawrence. "Masons' Marks in Castles: A Key to Building Practices," *Château Gaillard* 18 (1998), 23-28.

Butler, Lawrence. "The Origins of the Honour of Richmond and its Castles," *Château Gaillard* 16 (1994), 69-80.

Butler, Lawrence. *Pickering Castle, North Yorkshire*. London: English Heritage, 1993.

Butler, Lawrence. *Sandal Castle, Wakefield: The History and Archaeology of a Medieval Castle*. Wakefield: Wakefield Historical Publications, 1991.

Bythell, Duncan and Martin Leyland. *Durham Castle*. 2nd ed. Durham: University College, Durham and Jarrold Publishing Norwich, 1992.

Caldwell, David H. "A Sixteenth-Century Group of Gun Towers in Scotland," *Fort* 12 (1984), 15-24.

Caldwell, David H. "Tantallon Castle, East Lothian: A Catalogue of Finds," *Proceedings of the Society of Antiquarians of Scotland* 121 (1991), 335-57.

Cantwell, Anthony and Peter Sprack. "The Sandown Bay Defences," *Fortress* 7 (Nov 1990), 51-59.

Caple, C. "The Castle and Lifestyle of a 13th Century Independent Welsh Lord: Excavations at Dryslwyn Castle, 1980-1988," *Château Gaillard* 14 (1990), 47-60.

Carpenter, D.A. "King Henry III and the Tower of London," *London Journal* 19 (1995), 95-107.

Chibnall, Marjorie. "Orderic Vitalis on Castles." In: *Studies in Medieval History Presented to R. Allen Brown*. Ed. C. Harper-Bill et al. Woodbridge, 1989, pp. 43-56.

Chitty, L.F. "Interim Notes on Subsidiary Castle Sites West of Shrewsbury," *Transactions of the Shropshire Archaeological Society* 53 (1949/50), 83-90.

Clark, George T. *Mediaeval Military Architecture in England*. 2 vols. London: Wyman and Sons, 1884.

Cleggett, David A.H. *History of Leeds Castle and Its Families*. Maidstone: Leeds Castle Foundation, 1992.

Clifford's Tower, York. London: English Heritage, 1987.

Coad, Jonathan G. *Book of Dover Castle and the Defences of Dover*. English Heritage. London: B.T. Batsford/English Heritage, 1995.

Coad, Jonathan G. "Excavation at Castle Acre, Norfolk," *Château Gaillard* 8 (1977), 79-86.

Coad, Jonathan G. "Recent Work at Castle Acre Castle," *Château Gaillard* 11 (1983), 55-67.

Coad, Jonathan G. *Walmer Castle and Gardens*. London: English Heritage, 1992.

Collard, Mark. "Excavations at Desborough Castle, High Wycombe" *Records of Buckinghamshire* 30 (1988), 15-41.

Conqueror's Castle: The Story of Britain's First Norman Castle. Hastings: Hastings Corporation, n.d.

Cope, J. *Castles in Cumbria.* Milnthorpe, 1991.

Copeland, T. *Kenilworth Castle: A Handbook for Teachers.* London: English Heritage, 1990.

Copeland, T. *Rochester Castle: A Handbook for Teachers.* London: English Heritage, 1990.

Corfe Castle, Dorset. London: National Trust, 1987.

Cornforth, J. "Inverary Castle, Argyllshire: The Seat of the Duke of Argyll," *Country Life* (June 15, 1978), 1734-37.

Coulson, Charles L.H. "Battlements and the Bourgeoise: Municiple Status and the Apparatus of Urban Defence in Later-Medieval England." In: *Medieval Knighthood, V.* Ed. S. Church and R. Harvey. Woodbridge, 1995, pp. 119-95.

Coulson, Charles L.H. "The Castle of the Anarchy." In: *The Anarchy of King Stephen's Reign.* Ed. E. King. Oxford, 1994, pp. 67-92.

Coulson, Charles L.H. "Cultural Realities and Reappraisals in English Castle-Study: The State of Research," *Journal of Medieval History* 22 (1996), 171-208.

Coulson, Charles L.H. "Freedom to Crenellate by Licence: An Historiographical Revision," *Nottingham Medieval Studies* 38 (1994), 86-137.

Coulson, Charles L.H. "The French Matrix of the Castle-Provisions of the Chester-Leicester Conventio," *Anglo-Norman Studies* 17 (1994), 65-86.

Coulson, Charles L.H. "Some Analysis of the Castle of Bodiam, East Sussex." In: *Medieval Knighthood, IV.* Ed. C. Harper-Bill and R. Harvey. Woodbridge, 1992, pp. 51-107.

Coulson, Charles L.H. "Specimens of Freedom to Crenellate by Licence," *Fortress* 18 (Aug 1993), 3-23.

Crone, Anne and Richard Fawcett. "Dendrochronology, Documents and the Timber Trade: New Evidence for the Building History of Stirling Castle, Scotland," *Medieval Archaeology* 42 (1998), 68-87.

Cruden, Stewart. *The Scottish Castle*. Edinburgh: Nelson, 1960.

Cumming, W. "Grange Castle," *Journal of the County Kildare Archaeo-logical Society* 17 (1991), 222-25.

Cunliffe, Barry. *Portchester Castle*. The Portsmouth Papers, 1. Ports-mouth: Portsmouth City Council, 1967.

Curnow, P.E. "The Wakefield Tower, Tower of London," *Château Gaillard* 8 (1977), 87-101.

Curnow, P.E. "The Wakefield Tower, Tower of London." In: *Ancient Monuments and their Interpretation: Essays Presented to A.J. Taylor*. Ed. Mr. Apted, et al. London, 1977, pp. 155-76.

Curnow, P.E and E.A. Johnson. "St-Briavels Castle," *Château Gaillard* 12 (1985), 91-114.

Curwen, J.F. *Castles and Towers*. Cumberland and Westmorland Archae-ological and Antiquarian Society, extra series 13. Kendal, 1913.

Davies, S.M. and A.H. Graham. "Trowbridge Castle Excavations, 1988: An Interim Report," *Wiltshire Archaeological and Natural History Maga-zine* 83 (1990), 50-56.

Davison, Brian. *Old Wardour Castle, Wiltshire*. London: English Heritage, 1999.

Dixon, Philip. *Aydon Castle*. London: English Heritage, 1988.

Dixon, Philip. "The Donjon of Knaresborough: The Castle as Theatre," *Château Gaillard* 14 (1990), 121-40.

Dixon, Philip. "From Hall to Tower: The Change in Seigneurial Houses on the Anglo-Scottish Border after c.1250." In: *Thirteenth Century England IV*. Ed. P.R. Coss and S.D. Lloyd. Woodbridge, 1992, pp. 85-107.

Dodd, A. and P. Moss. "The History of Brimpsfield Castle and the Giffard Family," *Glevensis* 25 (1991), 34-37.

Dollen, Busso von der. "Die Entwicklung der Burgenbaus in Irland seit der anglo-normannischen Eroberung," *Burgen und Schlösser* 37.2 (1996), 50-58.

Drage, Christopher. "Nottingham Castle," *Château Gaillard* 11 (1983), 117-27.

Drage, Christopher. *Nottingham Castle: A Place Full Royal*. Nottingham: Thoroton Society of Nottinghamshire, 1989.

Drewett, Peter. "Excavations at Lewes Castle, East Sussex, 1985-1988," *Sussex Archaeological Collections* 130 (1992), 69-106.

Dunning, Robert. *Somerset Castles*. Tiverton: Somerset Books, 1995.

Dunster Castle, Somerset. 2nd ed. London: National Trust, 1988.

Eales, Richard. "Castles and Politics in England, 1215-1224." In: *Thirteenth-Century England*, II. Ed. P.R. Coss and S.D. Lloyd. Woodbridge, 1988, pp. 23-43.

Eales, Richard. "Royal Power and Castles in Norman England." In: *The Ideals and Practice of Medieval Knighthood*, III. Ed. C. Harper-Bill and R. Harvey. Woodbridge, 1990, pp. 49-78.

Emery, Anthony. "Ashby de la Zouche Castle," *Nottingham Area Proceedings* (1989), 63-71.

Emery, Anthony. "The Development of Raglan Castle and Keeps in Late Medieval England," *Archaeological Journal* 132 (1975), 151-86.

Emery, Anthony. "Kirby Muxloe Castle," *Nottingham Area Proceedings* (1989), 72-77.

Evans, David and Brian Sitch. *Beverley Gate: the Birthplace of the English Civil War*. Beverley: Hull City Council and Hutton Press, 1990.

Ewart, G. "Dundonald Castle–Recent Work," *Château Gaillard* 16 (1994), 167-78.

Everson, Paul. "Bodiam Castle, East Sussex: Castle and Its Designed Landscape," *Château Gaillard* 17 (1996), 79-84.

Eyton, R.W. "The Castles of Shropshire and Its Borders," *Transactions of the Shropshire Archaeological Society* 10 (1887), 10-33.

Fairclough, Graham. "Edingham Castle: The Military and Domestic Development of a Northumbrian Manor. Excavations 1978-80: Interim Report," *Château Gaillard* 9-10 (1982), 373-87.

Fairclough, Graham. *Framlingham and Orford Castles: A Handbook for Teachers*. London: English Heritage, 1990.

Fairclough, Graham. "Meaningful Constructions–Spatial and Functional Analysis of Medieval Buildings," *Antiquity* 66 (1992), 348-66.

Farleigh Hungerford Castle. London: Her Majesty's Stationery Office, 1970.

Fawcett, Richard. "Castle and Church in Scotland," *Château Gaillard* 18 (1998), 87-92.

Fawcett, Richard. *St. Andrews Castle*. Ed. Chris Tabraham. Edinburgh: Historic Scotland, 1992.

Fawcett, Richard. *Stirling Castle*. 2nd ed. Edinburgh: Historic Scotland, 1995.

Fawcett, Richard. "Stirling Castle: the King's Old Building and the Late Medieval Royal Planning," *Château Gaillard* 14 (1990), 175-94.

Flack, S. and T. Gregory. "Excavations at Brancaster, 1985," *Norfolk Archaeology* 40 (1988), 164-70.

Flanagan, Marie Therese. "Anglo-Norman Change and Continuity: The Castle of Telach Cail in Delbna," *Irish Historical Studies* 28 (1993), 385-89.

Forde-Johnston, J. *Castles and Fortifications of Britain and Ireland*. London: J.M. Dent & Sons, 1977.

Foreman, Martin. "The Defences of Hull," *Fortress* 2 (Aug 1989), 36-45.

Fowler, Kenneth A. "Investment in Urban Defence: The Frontier Regions of France and England during the Fourteenth Century." In: *Investimenti e civilità, sec. XIII-XVIII*. 9th Study Week of the Francesco Datini International Institute for Economic History. Prato, 1977.

Fraser, C.M. "The Town Ditch of Newcastle Upon Tyne," *Archaeologia aeliana* 4th ser. 39 (1961), 381-83.

Freeman, A.Z. "A Moat Defensive: The Coast Defense Scheme of 1295," *Speculum* 42 (1967), 442-62.

Frere, S.S., S. Stow, and P. Bennett. *The Archaeology of Canterbury. II: Excavations on the Roman and Medieval Defences of Canterbury.* Maidstone: Kent Archaeological Society, 1982.

Fry, Plantagenet Somerset. *British Medieval Castles.* London, 1974.

Furtado, Paul et al. *Ordnance Survey Guide to Castles in Britain.* 2nd ed. London: Hamlyn/Ordnance Survey, 1988.

Gerrard, S. "Carew Castle, Pembrokeshire Coast National Park." In: *Archaeology in National Parks.* Ed. R.F. White and R. Iles. Leybrun, 1991, pp. 47-54.

Gerrard, S. "The Carew Castle Project, 1986-90," *Fortress* 6 (Aug 1990), 45-50.

Gill, Alan Thomas. "Castell Morgraig," *Caerphilly* 5 (Dec 1995), 19-27.

Gillespie, James L. "Dover Castle: Key to Richard II's Kingdom?" *Archaeologia Cantiana* 105 (1988), 179-96.

Gilyard-Beer, R. "De Ireby's Tower in Carlisle Castle." In: *Ancient Monuments and their Interpretation: Essays Presented to A.J. Taylor.* Ed. Mr. Apted, et al. London, 1977, pp. 191-210.

Good, George L. and Christopher J. Tabraham. "Excavations at Smailholm Tower, Roxburghshire," *Proceedings of the Society of Antiquaries of Scotland* 118 (1988), 231-66.

Goodman, Anthony. "The Defence of Northumberland: a Preliminary Survey." In: *Armies, Chivalry and Warfare in Medieval Britain and France: Proceedings of the 1995 Harlaxton Symposium.* Ed. M. Strickland. Stamford, 1998, pp. 161-72.

Gordon Slade, H. "Glamis Castle, 1372-1626: From Medieval Hunting Lodge to Feudal Castle and Renaissance Palace," *Château Gaillard* 16 (1994), 233-39.

Graham, Brian. "Twelfth and Thirteenth Century Earthwork Fortifications in Ireland," *Irish Sword* 17 (1987-90).

Grant, A. and C. *The Castle Companion: A Guide to Historical Castles of South Wales.* Pontypool, 1991.

Gravett, Christopher. "Kitchens and Keeps," *Royal Armouries Yearbook* 3 (1998), 168-75.

Gray, Madeline. "Castles and Patronage in Sixteenth-Century Wales," *Welsh Historical Review* 15 (1991), 481-93.

Grenter, S. "Holt Castle," *Archaeology in Clwyd* 10 (1988), 6-8.

Guide to Tutbury Castle, Staffordshire, A. London: Duchy of Lancaster, 1990.

Hale, John R. "Defence of the Realm, 1485-1558." In: *The History of the King's Works*. Ed. R. Allen Brown, H.M. Colvin and Arnold J. Taylor. London, 1963, IV.2:367-401.

Hale, John R. "Tudor Fortifications, 1485-1558." In: *Renaissance War Studies*. London, 1983, pp. 63-98.

Hall, Michael. "Chirk Castle," *Country Life* 186 (July 16, 1992), 54-57.

Hamilton, Andrew. *Nottingham's Royal Castle*. 4th ed. Nottingham: Nottingham Civic Society, n.d.

Hammond, Peter. *Her Majesty's Royal Palace and Fortress of the Tower of London*. London: Historic Royal Palaces, 1987.

Harbottle, Barbara. *The Castle of Newcastle upon Tyne*. Newcastle: Society of Antiquaries of Newcastle upon Tyne, 1977.

Harbottle, Barbara. "The Castle of Newcastle upon Tyne: Excavations, 1973-79," *Château Gaillard* 9-10 (1982), 407-18.

Harbottle, Barbara. "The Town Wall of Newcastle Upon Tyne: Consolidation and Excavation in 1968," *Archaeologia aeliana* 4th ser 47 (1969), 71-95.

Harrington, Peter. "English Civil War Fortifications," *Fort* 15 (1987), 39-60.

Harris, Nathaniel. *Castles of England Scotland and Wales: A Guide and Gazetteer*. London: George Philip, 1991.

Harris, Stuart. "The Fortifications and Siege of Leith: A Further Study of the Map and the Siege in 1560," *Proceedings of the Society of Antiquaries of Scotland* 121 (1991), 359-68.

Harvey, John H. *English Medieval Architects*. London, 1954.

Harvey, John H. *Henry Yevele, c. 1320 to 1400: The Life of an English Architect*. London: B.T. Batsford Ltd., 1944.

Haselgrove, Colin, R. Leon Fitts, Percival Turnbull, and Steven Willis. "Excavations in Tofts Field, Stanwick, North Yorkshire, 1988," *Universities of Durham and Newcastle upon Tyne Archaeological Reports* 12 (1988), 29-34.

Haslam, Charlotte. "Landmarks of Coastal Defense," *Fortress* 4 (Feb 1990), 3-12.

Hay, Malcolm. *Westminister Hall and the Medieval Kings*. London: British Museum Press, 1995.

Hayden, A. "Excavation on the Line of the Medieval Town Defences of Loughrea, County Galway," *Journal of the Galway Archaeological and Historical Society* 41 (1987-88), 104-13.

Healy, E. *Bunratty Castle and Folk Park*. Bunratty Castle, 1991.

Healy, E. *Castles of County Cork*. Cork: Mercier Press, 1988.

Héliot, Pierre. "L'évolution des donjons dans le nord-ouest de la France et de l'Angleterre au XIIe siècle," *Bulletin archéologique du comité des travaux historiques et scientifiques* n.s. 5 (1969), 141-94.

Héliot, Pierre. "La genèse des châteaux de plan quadrangulaire en France et en Angleterre," *Bulletin de la société nationale des antiquaires de France* (1965), 238-57.

Hicks, Michael A. "The Forfeiture of Barnard Castle to the Bishop of Durham in 1459," *Northern History* 33 (1997), 223-31.

Higham, Robert A. "Devon Castles: An Annotated List," *Devon Archaeological Society Proceedings* 46 (1988), 142-48.

Higham, Robert A. "Early Castles in Devon (1068-1201)," *Château Gaillard* 9-10 (1982), 101-16.

Higham, Robert A. and Ann Hamlin. "Bampton Castle, Devon: History and Archaeology," *Devon Archaeological Society Proceedings* 48 (1990), 101-10.

Higham, Robert A. and S. Goddard. "Great Torrington Castle," *Proceedings of the Devon Archaeological Society* 45 (1987), 97-103.

Hislop, Malcolm. "The Date of the Warkworth Donjon," *Archaeological aeliana* 5th ser. 19 (1991), 79-92.

Hislop, Malcolm. "John of Gaunt's Building Works at Dunstanburgh Castle," *Archaeologia aeliana*, 5th ser., 23 (1995), 139-44.

Hodges, Richard. "Origins of the English Castle," *Nature* 333 (1988), 112-13.

Hodgson, John. *Southampton Castle*. Southampton City Museums Arcaheology Series. Horndean: Milestone Publications, n.d.

Hogg, A.H.A. and D.J.Cathcart King. "Early Castles in Wales and the Marches," *Archaeologia Cambrensis* 112 (1963), 77-124.

Hogg, A.H.A. and D.J.Cathcart King. "Masonry Castles in Wales and the Marches," *Archaeologia Cambrensis* 116 (1967), 71-132.

Holbrook, Neil and Aileen Fox. "Excavations in the Legionary Fortress at Bartholomew Street East, Exeter, 1959," *Proceedings of the Devon Archaeological Society* 45 (1987), 23-57.

Holland, E.O. *Corfe Castle: History and Guide*. Norwich: Jarrold and Sons Ltd., 1967.

Holland, Patrick. "The Anglo-Normans and their Castles in County Galway." In: *Galway History and Society: Interdisciplinary Essays on the History of an Irish County*. Ed. Gerard Moran and Raymond Gillespie. Dublin: Geography Publications, 1996, pp. 1-26.

Horsman, Valerie. "Eynsford Castle: A Reinterpretation of the Early History in the Light of Recent Excavtions," *Arcaheologia Cantania* 105 (1988), 39-55.

Hughes, Michael. "Hampshire Castles and the Landscape: 1066-1216," *Landscape History* 11 (1989), 27-60.

Jackson, Michael. *Castles of Cumbria*. Carlisle: Carel Press, 1990.

Jackson, Michael. *Castles of Shropshire*. Shrewsbury: Shropshire Libraires, 1988.

James, Terrence. "Carmarthen's Civil War Defences: Discoveries at Carmathen Greyfriars Excavations, 1983-1990," *The Carmarthenshire Antiquary* 27 (1991), 21-30.

Johnson, Christopher and Alan Vince. "The South Bail Gates of Lincoln," *Lincolnshire History and Archaeology* 27 (1992), 12-16.

Johnson, D. Newman. "Tymon–A Lost Pale Castle Recorded." In: *Keimelia: Studies in Medieval Archaeology and History in Memory of Tom Delaney*. Ed. Gearoid MacNiocaill and Patrick F. Wallace. Galway: Galway University Press, 1988, pp. 557-72.

Johnson, Paul. *Castles of England, Scotland and Wales*. London: Weidenfeld and Nicholson, 1989.

Johnson, Stephen. *Conisbrough Castle, South Yorkshire*. London: Her Majesty's Stationery Office, 1984.

Jones, G.R.J. "The Defences of Gwynedd in the Thirteenth Century," *Transactions of the Caernarvonshire Historical Society* 30 (1969), 29-43.

Jones, Siân. *Walk the Southampton Walls: A DIY Guide to the Old Town*. Southampton: Southampton City Council, n.d.

Jones, T.L. *Ashby de la Zouch Castle, Leicestershire*. 2nd ed. London: English Heritage, 1993.

Jope, E.M. "The Scottish Castle," *The Scottish Historical Review* 43 (1964), 148-54.

Juddery, J.Z., M. Stoyle, and P. Thomas. *Exeter City Defences: Expenditure on the Walls and Gates Recorded in the Receivers' Accounts, 1339-1450; 1450-1570; 1570-1600; 1600-1650*. Exeter Museums Archaeological Field Unit Report, 89.09; 89.10; 89.15; 88.14. Exeter: Exeter Museums Archaeological Field Unit, 1988.

Jude, James. *Hurst Castle: An Illustrated History*. Stanbridge: Dovecote Press, 1986.

Keen, Laurence. "The Umfravilles, the Castle and the Barony of Prudhoe, Northumberland," *Anglo-Norman Studies* 5 (1982), 165-84.

Keister, John L. "Southsea Castle in Portsmouth Was Part of Coastal Defence," *Artilleryman* 15.3 (Summer 1994), 33-35.

Kennaway, Mary. *Fast Castle: The Early Years*. Edinburgh: Edinburgh Archaeological Society, 1992.

Kent, Peter. *Fortifications of East Anglia*. Lavenham: Terence Dalton, 1988.

Kenyon, John R. "Artillery and the Defences of Southampton circa 1360-1660," *Fort* 3 (Spr 1977; Rev. ed., 1993), 21-30.

Kenyon, John R. "Coastal Artillery Fortification in England in the Late Fourteenth Century." In: *Arms, Armies and Fortifications in the Hundred Years War*. Ed. A. Curry and M. Hughes. Woodbridge, 1994, pp. 145-50.

Kenyon, John R. "Early Artillery Fortifications in England and Wales," *Fort* 1 (1976; Rev. ed., 1993), 33-36.

Kenyon, John R. "Early Artillery Fortifications in England and Wales: A Preliminary Survey," *Archaeological Journal* 138 (1981), 205-40.

Kenyon, John R. "Early Gunports: A Gazateer," *Fort* 4 (Aut 1977; Rev. ed., 1995), 75-85.

Kenyon, John R. "Fluctuating Frontiers: Normanno-Welsh Castle Warfare c. 1075 to 1240," *Château Gaillard* 17 (1996), 119-26.

Kenyon, John R. "The Gunloops at Raglan Castle, Gwent." In: *Castles in Wales and the Marches. Essays in Honour of D.J. Cathcart King*. Ed. J.R. Kenyon and R. Avent. Cardiff: University of Wales Press, 1996, pp. 143-60.

Kenyon, John R. *Kidwelly Castle*. 2nd ed. Wales: CADW, 1990.

Kenyon, John R. *Medieval Fortifications*. New York: St. Martin's Press, 1990.

Kenyon, John R. "Ordnance and the King's Fortifications in 1547-48: Society of Antiquaries MS 129, Folios 250-374," *Archaeologia* 107 (1982), 165-213.

Kenyon, John R. *Raglan Castle*. Cardiff: CADW, 1988.

Kenyon, John R. "The State of the Fortifications in the West Country in 1623," *Fort* 16 (1988), 45-52.

Kenyon, John R., ed. *Castles, Town Defences, and Artillery Fortifications in Britain: A Bibliography, 1945-74*. London: Council for British Archaeology, 1978.

Kerrigan, Paul M. "Fortifications in Tudor Ireland, 1547-1603," *Fortress* 7 (Nov 1990), 27-39.

Kershaw, Mary J. *Knaresborough Castle*. Harrogate: Harrogate Museum and Arts, 1998.

King, D.J. Cathcart. *The Castle in England and Wales: An Interpretative History*. Portland: Areopagitica Press, 1988.

King, D.J. Cathcart. *Castellarium Anglicanum: An Index and Bibliography of the Castle in England, Wales, and the Islands*. 2 vols. Millwood, 1983.

King, D.J. Cathcart. "Pembroke Castle," *Château Gaillard* 8 (1977), 159-69.

Kinsley, Gavin. "Excavation on the Supposed Site of Civil War Redoubt 11B, Newark-on-Trent, Nottinghamshire," *Transactions of the Thoroton Society* 102 (1988), 78.

Klingelhöfer, Eric. "Castles Built in Air: Spenserian Architecture in Ireland." In: *Military Studies in Medieval Europe: Papers of the "Medieval Europe Brugge 1997" Conference Volume 11*. Ed. Guy De Boe & Frans Verhaeghe. Zellik: Instituut voor het Archeologisch Patrimonium, 1997, pp. 149-54.

Klingelhöfer, Eric. "The Renaissance Fortifications at Dunboy Castle, 1602: A Report of the 1989 Excavations," *Journal of the Cork Historical and Archaeological Society* 97 (1992), 85-96.

Knight, Jeremy K. *Chepstow Castle and Port Wall, Runton Church, Chepstow Bulwarks Camp*. Cardiff: CADW, 1991.

Knight, Jeremy K. "Excavation at Montgomery Castle, Part I: Documentary Evidence, Structures and Excavated Features," *Archaeologia Cambrensis* 141 (1992), 97-180.

Knight, Jeremy K. "Excavation at Montgomery Castle, Part II: Metal Finds," *Archaeologia Cambrensis* 142 (1993), 182-242.

Knight, Jeremy K. "Montgomery: A Castle of the Welsh March, 1223-1649," *Château Gaillard* 11 (1983), 169-82.

Knight, Jeremy K. "Newport Castle," *Monmouthshire Antiquary* 7 (1991), 17-42.

Knight, Jeremy K. *The Three Castles: Grosmont Castle, Skenfrith Castle, White Castle, Hen Gwrt Moated Site*. Cardiff: CADW, 1991.

Knight, Jeremy K. "Usk Castle and its Affinities." In: *Ancient Monuments and their Interpretation: Essays Presented to A.J. Taylor*. Ed. Mr. Apted, et al. London, 1977, pp. 139-54.

Knight, Jeremy K. "Welsh Fortifications of the First Millennium A.D.," *Château Gaillard* 16 (1994), 277-84.

Lapper, Ivan and Geoffrey Parnell. *Landmarks in History: The Tower of London, A 2000-Year History*. Oxford: Osprey Publishing, 2000.

Leach, Roger H. "Aspects of the Medieval Defences of Bristol: The Town Wall, the Castle Barbican and the Jewry." In: *From Cornwall to Caithness: Some Aspects of British Field Archaeology: Papers Presented to Norman V. Quinnell*. Ed. Mark Bowden, Donnie Mackay, and Peter Topping. Oxford, 1989, pp. 235-50.

Leask, Harold G. "Castles and Their Place in Irish History," *Irish Sword* 10 (1971-72), 235-44.

Leeds Castle, Maidstone, Kent. 2nd ed. London: Leeds Castle Foundation, 1994.

Le Patourel, John. "Fortified and Semi-fortified Manor Houses," *Château Gaillard* 9-10 (1982), 187-96.

Le Patourel, John. "Fortified and Semi-Fortified Manor Houses in Eastern and Northern England in the Later Middle Ages." In: *La maison forte au moyen âge*. Ed. M. Bur. Paris, 1986, pp. 17-30.

Le Patourel, John. "Moated Sites of Yorkshire: A Survey and Its Implications," *Chateau Gaillard* 5 (1972), 121-32.

Le Patourel, John. "Les sites fossoyés et leurs problèmes: l'organisation de la recherche en Grand-Bretagne," *Revue du nord* 58 (1976), 571-92.

Lewis, J.M. "Recent Excavations at Loughor Castle (South Wales)," *Château Gaillard* 7 (1975), 147-57.

Lloyd, J.D.K. and Jeremy K. Knight. *Montgomery Castle*. 2nd ed. Cardiff, 1981.

Longley, David. "The Excavation of Castell, Porth Trefadog, Coastal Promontory Fort in North Wales," *Medieval Archaeology* 35 (1991), 64-85.

Lynn, C.J. "Some Thirteenth Century Castle Sites in the West of Ireland: Note on a Preliminary Reconnaissance," *Journal of the Galway Archaeological and Historical Society* 40 (1985-86), 90-113.

MacIvor, Iain. "Artillery and Major Places of Strength in the Lothians and the East Border, 1513-1542." In: *Scottish Weapons and Fortifications, 1100-1800*. Ed. David H. Caldwell. Edinburgh: John Donald Publishers Ltd., 1981, pp. 94-152.

MacIvor, Iain. *Balvenie Castle*. Edinburgh: Her Majesty's Stationery Office, 1988.

MacIvor, Iain. *Blackess Castle*. Edinburgh: Her Majesty's Stationery Office, 1989.

MacIvor, Iain. "Craignethan Castle, Lanarkshire: an Experiment in Artillery Fortification." In: *Ancient Monuments and their Interpretation: Essays Presented to A.J. Taylor*. Ed. Mr. Apted, et al. London, 1977, pp. 239-61.

Mackenzie, William Mackay. *The Mediaeval Castle in Scotland*. London: Methuen and Co., 1927.

Maekawa, Kaname. "A Deserted Medieval Village and the Formation of a Fortified Town in Cambridgeshire, England." In: *Rural Settlements in Medieval Europe: Papers of the "Medieval Europe Brugge 1997" Conference Volume 11*. Ed. Guy De Boe & Frans Verhaeghe. Zellik: Instituut voor het Archeologisch Patrimonium, 1997, pp. 243-52.

Mahany, C. "Excavations at Stamford Castle," *Château Gaillard* 8 (1977), 223-45.

Malin, Tim and Alison Taylor. "Cambridge Castle Ditch," *Proceedings of the Cambridge Antiquarian Society* 80 (1991), 1-6.

Manley, John. "Excavations at Caergwrle Castle, Clwyd, North Wales: 1988-1990," *Medieval Archaeology* 38 (1994), 83-133.

Manley, John. "The Outer Enclosure on Caergwrle Hill, Clwyd," *Journal of the Flintshire Historical Society* 33 (1992), 13-20.

Manning, Conleth. "Dublin Castle: The Building of a Royal Castle in Ireland," *Château Gaillard* 18 (1998), 119-22.

Manning, W.H. *Report on the Excavations at Usk, 1965-1976: The Fortress Excavations, 1972-74*. Cardiff: University of Wales Press, 1989.

Maxwell-Irving, Alistair M.T. "Early Firearms and Their Influence on Military and Domestic Architecture of the Border," *Proceedings of the Society of Antiquaries of Scotland* 103 (1970-71), 192-224.

Maxwell-Irving, Alistair M.T. "Hoddom Castle: A Reappraisal of Its Architecture and Place in History," *Proceedings of the Society of Antiquaries of Scotland* 117 (1987), 183-217.

Maxwell-Irving, Alistair M.T. "Lochwood Castle: A Resume," *Transactions of the Dumfrieshire Natural History and Antiquarian Society* 3rd ser. 65 (1990), 93-99.

Mayers, O. and L.A.S. Butler. *Sandal Castle Excavations: A Detailed Archaeological Report, 1963-74*. Wakefield: Wakefield Corporation, 1983.

McAulffe, Mary. "The Town House and Warfare in Ireland in the Fourteenth and Fifteenth Centuries," *Irish Sword* 18 (1990-92), 297-302.

McCarthy, M.R., H.R.T. Summerson, and R.G. Annis. *Carlisle Castle: A Survey and Documentary Evidence*. English Heritage Archaeological Report, no. 18. London: English Heritage, 1990.

McNeill, T.E. *Castles in Ireland*. London, 1997.

McNeill, T.E. "The Castle of Castlereagh, County Down," *Ulster Journal of Archaeology* 50 (1987), 123-27.

McNeill, T.E. "Castles of Ward and the Changing Pattern of Border Conflict in Ireland," *Château Gaillard* 17 (1996), 127-33.

McNeill, T.E. "Early Castles in Leinster," *Journal of Irish Archaeology* 5 (1989/90), 57-64.

McNeill, T.E. *English Heritage Book of Castles*. London: B.T.Batsford, 1992.

McNeill, T.E. "The Great Towers of Early Irish Castles," *Anglo-Norman Studies* 12 (1989), 99-117.

McNeill, T.E. "Hibernia pacata et castellata," *Château Gaillard* 14 (1990), 261-76.

McNeill, T.E. "The Outer Gate House at Dunamase Castle, Co. Laois," *Medieval Archaeology* 37 (1993), 236-39.

Meek, Marion. *Dunluce Castle*. Edinburgh: Gordon Lyall Associates, n.d.

Mein, A.G. "Excavations at Trostrey Castle: A Summary, 1984-1988," *Monmouthshire Antiquary* 5, pt. 3 (1985-88).

Merriman, M. "The Forts of Eyemouth: Anvils of British Union?" *Scottish Historical Review* 67 (1988), 142-55.

Middleton, Arthur E. *An Account of Belsay Castle in the County of Northumberland*. 1910; rpt. Stocksfield: Spredden, 1990.

Miket, Roger and David L. Roberts. *The Mediaeval Castles of Skye and Lochalsh*. Portree: Maclean Press, 1990.

Miles, T.J. and A.D. Saunders. "King Charles Castle, Tresco, Scilly," *Post-Medieval Archaeology* 4 (1970).

Miller, Keith. "Beverley, North Bar," *Archaeological Journal* 141 (1985), 23-25.

Miller, Keith. "Beverley Town Defences," *Archaeological Journal* 141 (1985), 21-22.

Milner, Lesley. "Warkworth Keep, Northumberland: A Reassessment of Its Plan and Date." In: *Medieval Architecture and Its Intellectual Context: Studies in Honour of Peter Kidson*. Ed. Eric Fernie and Paul Crossley. London, 1990, pp. 219-28.

Mitchell, Keith L. *Fast Castle: A History from 1602*. Edinburgh: Edinburgh Archaeological Field Society, 1989.

Morley, Beric M. "Aspects of Fourteenth-Century Castle Design." In: *Collectanea historica: Essays in Memory of Stuart Rigold*. Ed. A. Detsicas. Maidstone, 1981, pp. 104-13.

Morley, Beric M. *The Castles of Pendennis and St. Mawes*. London: English Heritage, 1988.

Morley, Beric M. *Henry VIII and the Development of Coastal Defence*. London: Her Majesty's Stationery Office, 1976.

Morris, Richard. "The Architecture of Arthurian Enthusiasm: Castle Symbolism in the Reigns of Edward I and His Successors." In: *Armies, Chivalry and Warfare in Medieval Britain and France: Proceedings of the 1995 Harlaxton Symposium*. Ed. M. Strickland. Stamford, 1998, pp. 63-81.

Morton, Catherine. *Bodiam Castle, Sussex*. Plaistow: The National Trust, n.d.

Munby, Julian. *Stokesay Castle*. London: English Heritage, 1993.

Murtagh, Ben. "The Bridge Castle, Thomastown, County Kilkenny." In: *Keimelia: Studies in Medieval Archaeology and History in Memory of Tom Delaney*. Ed. Gearoid MacNiocaill and Patrick F. Wallace. Galway: Galway University Press, 1988.

Musson, C.R. and C.J. Spurgeon. "Curt Llechrhyd, Llanelwedd: An Unusual Moated Site in Central Powys," *Medieval Archaeology* 32 (1988), 97-109.

Newark on Trent: The Civil War Siegeworks. London: Her Majesty's Stationery Office, 1964.

Nolan, John. "The Castle of Newcastle upon Tyne after c1600," *Archaeologia aeliana* 5th ser. 18 (1990), 79-126.

Nolan, John, R. Fraser, R.B. Harbottle, and F.C. Burton. "The Medieval Town Defences of Newcastle upon Tyne: Excavation and Survey, 1986-87," *Arcaeologia aeliana* 17 (1989), 29-78.

Oakeshott, Ewart. *A Knight and his Castle*. London, 1965.

Official Guide to Windsor Castle, The. Windsor: Oxley and Son, 1953.

O'Keeffe, Tadhy. "The Archaeology of Norman Castles in Ireland. Part 2: Stone Castles," *Archaeology Ireland* 4.4 (Win 1990).

O'Keeffe, Tadhy. "The Castle of Tullow, Co. Carlow," *Journal of the Kildare Archaeological Society* 16.5 (1985-86), 528-29.

O'Keeffe, Tadhy. "Rathnageeragh and Ballyhoo: A Study of Stone Castles of Probable Fourteenth to Early Fifteenth Century Date in County Carlow," *Journal of the Royal Society of Antiquaries of Ireland* 117 (1987), 26-49.

O'Mahoney, Cathy, A.C. Thomas, and S. Hartgroves. "Tintagel Papers," *Cornish Studies* 16 (1988), 5-96.

O'Murchada, D. "The Castle of Dun Mic Oghmainn and the Overlordship of Carbery," *Journal of the Cork Historical and Archaeological Society* 93 (1988), 73-82.

O'Neill, B.H.St.J. *Castles and Cannon: A Study of Early Artillery Fortifications in England.* Oxford: Oxford University Press, 1960.

O'Neill, B.H.St.J. *The History of Castle Cornet, Guernsey.* 2nd ed. Guernsey: States of Guernsey Ancient Monuments Committee, 1981.

O'Neill, B.H.St.J. "Stefan von Haschenperg, an Engineer to King Henry VIII and His Work," *Archaeologia* 91 (1945), 137-55.

O'Rahilly, Celie. "Recent Research in Limrick City," *Archaeology Ireland* 2.4 (1988), 140-44.

Owen, John. "Caerphilly Castle–A Modified Plan," *Caerphilly* 5 (Dec 1995), 36-40.

Painter, Sidney. "English Castles in the Early Middle Ages: Their Number, Location, and Legal Position," *Speculum* 10 (1935), 321-32.

Palliser, D.M. "Town Defences in Medieval England and Wales." In: *The Medieval Military Revolution: State, Society and Military Change in Medieval and Early Modern Europe*. Ed. A. Ayton and J.L. Price. London, 1995, pp. 105-20.

Parkes, Cathy. *Archaeological Fieldwork in the Isles of Scilly, March 1990: Early Batteries on the Garrison, St. Mary's*. Truro: Cornwall Archaeological Unit, Cornwall County Council, 1990.

Parnell, Geoffrey. "Ordnance Storehouses at the Tower of London, 1450-1700," *Château Gaillard* 17 (1998), 171-79.

Parnell, Geoffrey. "The Rise and Fall of the Tower of London," *History Today* 42 (Mar 1992), 13-19.

Parnell, Geoffrey. *The Tower of London*. London: English Heritage/Batsford, 1993.

Parnell, Geoffrey. *The Tower of London: Past and Present*. Stroud: Sutton Publishing, 1998.

Parnell, Geoffrey. "The White Tower Reconsidered," *Royal Armouries* 3 (1998), 162-67.

Parry, Charles. "Survey and Excavation at Newcastle Emlyn Castle," *Carmarthenshire Antiquary* 23 (1987), 11-27.

Patterson, B.H. *A Military Heritage: A History of Portsmouth and Portsea Town Fortifications*. Fort Cumberland and Portsmouth Militaria Society, 164. Portsmouth, 1985.

Peers, Charles. *Kirby Muxloe Castle, Leistershire*. London: English Heritage, 1957.

Peers, Charles. *Richmond Castle, Yorkshire*. London: English Heritage, 1981.

Pettifer, Adrian. *English Castles: A Guide by Counties*. Woodbridge: The Boydell Press, 1995.

Pictorial History of the Tower of London, A. London: Pitkin Pictorials Ltd., n.d.

Place, Christopher. "A Medieval Gate in the Earthworks Surrounding the 'Little Park', Arundel, West Sussex," *Sussex Archaeological Collections* 130 (1992), 130-39.

Platt, Colin. *The Castle in Medieval England and Wales*. 1981; rpt. New York: Barnes and Noble Books, 1996.

Platt, Colin. *Dover Castle*. London: English Heritage, 1988.

Platt, Colin and Mike McCarthy. *Carlisle Castle*. London: English Heritage, 1992.

Port, Graham. *Scarborough Castle*. London: English Heritage, 1989.

Pounds, N.J.G. *The Medieval Castle in England and Wales: A Social and Political History*. Cambridge: Cambridge University Press, 1990.

Powell, W.R. "The Medieval Hospitals at East and West Tilbury and Henry VIII's Fortifications," *Essex Archaeology and History* 19 (1988), 154-58.

Preston-Jones, Ann and Peter Rose. "Week St. Mary, Town and Castle," *Cornish Archaeology* 31 (1992), 143-53.

Prestwich, Michael. "English Castles in the Reign of Edward II," *Journal of Medieval History* 8 (1982), 159-78.

Prestwich, Michael. "Isabella de Vescy and the Custody of Bamburgh Castle," *Bulletin of the Institute of Historical Research* 44 (1971), 148-52.

Priddy, Deborah. "Pleshy Castle–The Northern Bailey: Excavations at the Village Hall Site, 1987," *Essex Archaeology and History* 19 (1988), 166-75.

Pringle, Denys. "'Cadzow Castle' and 'The Castle of Hamilton': An Archaeological and Historical Conundrum," *Château Gaillard* 15 (1990), 277-94.

Pringle, Denys. *Craigmillar Castle*. Edinburgh: Her Majesty's Stationery Office, 1989.

Pugh, P.B. and A.D. Saunders. *Old Wardour Castle, Wiltshire*. London: Her Majesty's Stationery Office, 1968.

Purser, Toby Scott. "Castles of Herefordshire, 1066-1135," *Medieval History* 4 (1994), 72-90.

Pye, Andrew R. *Berry Head Fort, Brixham: An Archaeological Assessment*. Exeter Museums Archaeological Field Unit Report, 89.04. Exeter, 1989.

Pye, Andrew R. and Frederick W. Woodward. *The Historic Defences of Plymouth*. Truro: Cornwall County Council, 1996.

Radford, C.A. Ralegh. *Acton Burnell Castle, Shropshire*. London: Her Majesty's Stationery Office, 1977.

Radford, C.A. Ralegh. "Acton Burnell Castle." In: *Studies in Building History: Essays in Recognition of the Work of B.H.St.J. O'Neil*. Ed. E.M. Jope. London, 1961, pp. 94-103.

Radford, C.A. Ralegh. *Goodrich Castle, Herefordshire*. London: Her Majesty's Stationery Office, 1958.

Rahtz, Philip et al. *Cadbury Congresbury, 1968-73: A Late Post-Roman Hilltop Settlement in Somerset*. BAR British Series, 223. Oxford, 1992.

Rees, William. *Caerphilly Castle and Its Place in the Annals of Glamorgan*. 2nd ed. Caerphilly: D. Brown and Sons Ltd., 1974.

Reid, John. "Niddry Castle Revisited," *Archaeology Today* 9.3 (1988), 38-45.

Reid, John and A. Kelly. "Niddry Castle," *Scottish Archaeology Gazette* 17 (1988), 18-27.

Renn, Derek F. "An Angevin Gatehouse at Skipton Castle (Yorkshire, West Riding)," *Château Gaillard* 7 (1975), 173-82.

Renn, Derek F. "The Anglo-Norman Keep, 1066-1138," *Journal of the British Archaeology Association*, 3rd series 23 (1960), 1-23.

Renn, Derek F. *Caerphilly Castle*. Cardiff: Cadw: Welsh Historic Monuments, 1989.

Renn, Derek F. "Canterbury Castle: A Case Study," *Château Gaillard* 11 (1983), 253-55.

Renn, Derek F. "The Castles of Rye and Winchelsea," *Archaeological Journal* 136 (1979), 193-202.

Renn, Derek F. "The Earliest Gunports in Britain?" *Archaeological Journal* 125 (1968), 301-03.

Renn, Derek F. "The *Enceinte* Wall of Quarr Abbey," *Fort* 8 (1980), 5-6.

Renn, Derek F. "English Fortification in 1485," *Château Gaillard* 13 (1987), 169-79.

Renn, Derek F. *Framlingham and Orford Castles*. London: English Heritage, 1988.

Renn, Derek F. *Goodrich Castle*. London: English Heritage, 1993.

Renn, Derek F. "Hen Domen Compared: The Evidence for Wooden Castle Buildings in Britain and Normandy." In: *From Roman Town to Norman Castle: Essays in Honour of Philip Barker*. Ed. A. Burl. Birmingham: University of Birmingham Department of Extra-Mural Studies, 1988.

Renn, Derek F. *Kenilworth Castle*. London: English Heritage, 1991.

Renn, Derek F. *Norman Castles in Britain*. London: John Baker, 1968.

Renn, Derek F. "The Southampton Arcade." *Medieval Archaeology* 8 (1964), 226-28.

Renn, Derek F. and Richard Avent. *Flint Castle, Ewloe Castle*. Cardiff: Cadw: Welsh Historic Monuments, 1995.

Richardson, J.S. and Margaret E. Root. *Stirling Castle*. Edinburgh: Her Majesty's Stationery Office, 1972.

Rigold, Stuart E. *Nunney Castle, Somerset*. London: Her Majesty's Stationery Office, 1957.

Rigold, Stuart E. *Portchester Castle, Hampshire*. 3rd ed. London: Her Majesty's Stationery Office, 1965.

Rigold, Stuart E. "Recent Investigations into the Earliest Defences of Carisbrooke Castle, Isle of Wight," *Château Gaillard* 3 (1969), 128-38.

Rigold, Stuart E. "Timber Bridges at English Castles and Moated Sites," *Château Gaillard* 6 (1973), 183-93.

Roberts, Ian. *Pontefract Castle*. Wakefield: West Yorkshire Archaeology Service, 1990.

Robinson, David M. and Roger S. Thomas. *Wales: Castles and Historic Places*. Cardiff: Welsh Historic Monuments, 1990.

Rose, Peter. "Bossiney Castle," *Cornish Archaeology* 31 (1992), 138-42.

Rowland, T.H. *Medieval Castles, Peles and Bastles of Northumberland*. Morpeth, 1987.

Rowlands, I.W. "King John, Stephen Langton and Rochester Castle, 1213-15." In: *Studies in Medieval History Presented to R. Allen Brown*. Ed. C. Harper-Bill et al. Woodbridge, 1989, pp. 267-79.

Rowlands, Ifor W. "William Marshal, Pembroke Castle and the Historian," *Château Gaillard* 17 (1996), 151-55.

Rowse, A.L. *The Tower of London in the History of the Nation*. London: Cardinal, 1974.

Royal Commission on Historical Monuments (England). *York Castle*. London: Her Majesty's Stationery Office, 1973.

Ruckley, N.A. "Water Supply of Medieval Castles in the United Kingdom," *Fortress* 7 (Nov 1990), 14-26.

Ryder, Peter F. "The Cow Port at Berwick upon Tweed," *Archaeologia aeliana* 5th ser 20 (1992), 99-116.

Ryder, Peter F. "The Gatehouse of Morpeth Castle, Northumberland," *Archaeologia aeliana* 5th ser. 20 (1992), 63-77.

Salter, M. *The Castles and Moated Mansions in Shropshire*. Wolverhampton, 1989.

Salter, M. *The Castles and Moated Mansions in Staffordshire and the West*. Wolverhampton, 1989.

Salter, M. *Castles and Stronghouses of Ireland*. Malvern: Folly Publications, 1993.

Saul, Nigel. "Bodiam Castle," *History Today* 45 (Jan 1995), 16-21.

Saunders, Andrew D. "The Cow Tower, Norwich: An East Anglian Bastile?" *Medieval Archaeology* 29 (1985), 109-19.

Saunders, Andrew D. *Fortress Britain: Artillery Fortification in the British Islands and Ireland*. Liphook: Beaufort Publishing, 1989.

Saunders, Andrew D. *Norham Castle*. London: English Heritage, 1998.

Saunders, Andrew D. "Norham Castle and Early Artillery Defences," *Fort* 25 (1997), 37-59.

Saunders, Andrew D. *Tynemouth Priory, Castle, and Twentieth Century Fortifications*. London: English Heritage, 1993.

Sayles, G.O. "The Siege of Carrickfergus Castle, 1315-16," *Irish Historical Studies* (1956-57), 94-100.

Scarborough Castle. London: English Heritage, 1989.

Scott, J.G. "The Hall and Motte at Courthill, Dalry, Ayrshire," *Proceedings of the Society of Antiquaries of Scotland* 119 (1990), 271-78.

Sharpe, Adam. "Treyn Dinas: Cliff Castles Reconsidered," *Cornish Archaeology* 31 (1992), 65-68.

Shelby, Lon R. "Guines Castle and the Development of English Bastioned Fortifications," *Château Gaillard* 3 (1969), 139-43.

Shelby, Lon R. *John Rogers: Tudor Military Engineer*. Oxford: Clarendon Press, 1967

Shelley, Andy. "Norwich Castle Bridge," *Medieval Archaeology* 40 (1996), 217-26.

Shepherd, Elizabeth. "Recent Excavations at Norwich Castle." In: *Military Studies in Medieval Europe: Papers of the "Medieval Europe Brugge 1997" Conference Volume 11*. Ed. Guy De Boe & Frans Verhaeghe. Zellik: Instituut voor het Archeologisch Patrimonium, 1997, pp. 187-90.

Sherlock, David. "Aydon Castle Kitchen and Its Roof," *Archaeologia aeliana* 5th ser. 25 (1997), 71-86.

Sherlock, S.J. "Excavations at Castle Hill, Castleton, North Yorkshire," *Archaeological Journal* 64 (1992), 41-47.

Shortt, H. de S. *Old Sarum: Illustrated Guide*. London: Her Majesty's Stationery Office, 1965.

Simpson, W. Douglas. "'Bastard Feudalism' and Later Castles," *Antiquaries Journal* (1946), 145-71.

Simpson, W. Douglas. "Brough-under-Stainmore: The Castle and the Church," *Cumberland and Westmorland Archaeological and Antiquarian Society* 2nd ser. 46 (1946), 223-95.

Simpson, W. Douglas. *Castles from the Air*. London, 1949.

Simpson, W. Douglas. "Claves castri: The Role of the Gatekeeper in Scottish Medieval Castle," *Château Gaillard* 15 (1990), 319-24.

Simpson, W. Douglas. "Dunstanburgh Castle," *Archaeologia aeliana* 4th ser. 16 (1939), 31-48.

Simpson, W. Douglas. "Further Notes on Dunstanburgh Castle," *Archaeologia aeliana* 4th ser. 27 (1949), 1-28.

Simpson, W. Douglas. *Huntly Castle, Aberdeenshire*. Edinburgh: Her Majesty's Stationery Office, 1960.

Simpson, W. Douglas. "The Tower-Houses of Scotland." In: *Medieval Archaeology: Papers of the Seventeenth Annual Conference of the Center for Medieval and Early Renaissance Studies*. Ed. C.L. Redman. Binghamton, 1989, pp. 229-42.

Simpson, W. Douglas. "Warkworth: A Castle of Livery and Maintenance," *Archaeologia aeliana* 4th ser. 15 (1938), 115-36.

Skipton Castle. Norwich: Jarrold and Sons Ltd., 1991.

Slade, H. Gordon. "Fyvie Castle, Aberdeenshire, Scotland," *Château Gaillard* 12 (1985), 151-66.

Smith, C. *The Exchequer Gate, Denbigh: A Report on Excavations in 1982 and 1983*. Newcastle upon Tyne, 1988.

Smith, V.T.C. *Defending London's River: The Story of the Thames Fortifications, 1540-1945*. Rochester: North Kent Books, 1985.

Spurgeon, C.J. "The Castles of Glamorgen: Some Sites and Theories of General Interest," *Château Gaillard* 13 (1987), 203-26.

Spurgeon, C.J. "The Castles of Montgomeryshire," *Montgomeryshire Collections* 59 (1965/6), 1-59.

Spurgeon, C.J. "Gwyddgrug Castle (Forden) and the Gorddwr Dispute in the Thirteenth Century," *Montgomeryshire Collections* 57 (1961/2), 125-36.

Stafford Castle: A Brief History. Stafford: Stafford Borough Council, 1989.

Stalley, Roger. "The Anglo-Norman Keep at Trim: Its Architectural Implications," *Archaeology Ireland* 6.4.22 (Win 1992), 16-19.

Steane, Kate. "Excavations at Ratley Castle, 1968-73," *Transactions of the Birmingham and Warwickshire Archaeological Society* 96 (1989-90), 5-26.

Stell, Geoffrey. "Late Medieval Defences in Scotland." In: *Scottish Weapons and Fortifications, 1100-1800*. Ed. David H. Caldwell. Edinburgh: John Donald Publishers Ltd., 1981, pp. 21-54.

Stenton, Frank M. "The Development of the Castle in England and Wales." In: *Social Life in Medieval England*. Ed. G. Barraclough. London, 1960, pp. 96-123.

Stevenson, Janet H. "The Castles of Marlborough and Ludgershall in the Middle Ages," *The Wiltshire Archaeological and Natural History Magazine* 85 (1992), 70-79.

Stocker, David. "The Shadow of the General's Armchair," *Archaeological Journal* 149 (1992), 415-20.

Stocker, David and Alan Vince. "The Early Norman Castle at Lincoln and a Re-evaluation of the Original West Tower of Lincoln Cathedral," *Medieval Archaeology* 41 (1997), 223-33.

Storey, Randall. "The Tower of London and the *garderobe armorum*," *Royal Armouries Yearbook* 3 (1998), 176-83.

Stoyle, M. *Civil War Defences Between Eastgate and Southgate, Exeter*. Exeter Museums Archaeological Field Unit Report, 88.03. Exeter: Exeter City Council, 1988.

Stoyle, M. *The Civil War Defences of Exeter and the Great Parliamentary Siege of 1645-46*. Exeter Museums Archaeological Field Unit Report, 90.26. Exeter: Exeter City Council, 1990.

Stoyle, M. *Exeter City Defences Project: Documentary Evidence for the Civil War Defence of Exeter, 1642-43*. Exeter: Exeter City Council, 1988.

Suppe, Frederick C. "Castle Guard and the Castlery of Clun," *Haskins Society Journal* 1 (1989), 123-34.

Suppe, Frederick C. "The Garrisoning of Oswestry, a Baronial Castle on the Welsh Marches." In: *The Medieval Castle: Romance and Reality*. Ed. K. Reyerson and F. Powe. Dubuque, 1984, pp. 63-78.

Sweeney, Mary M. *A History of Buckden Towers*. 4th ed. Rushden: Stanley L. Hunt, 1990.

Sweetman, P. David. "Archaeological Excavations at Ballymote Castle, County Sligo," *Journal of the Galwey Archaeological and Historical Society* 40 (1985-86), 114-24.

Sweetman, P. David. "Aspects of Early Thirteenth Century Castles in Leinster," *Château Gaillard* 15 (1990), 325-45.

Sweetman, P. David. "Dating Irish Castles," *Archaeology Ireland* 6.4.22 (Win 1992), 8-9

Sweetman, P. David. "The Development of Trim Castle in the Light of Recent Research," *Château Gaillard* 18 (1998), 223-30.

Sweetman, P. David. *The Medieval Castles of Ireland*. Woodbridge: Boydell and Brewer, 2000.

Symons, David, "Weoley Castle, Northfield, in 1424," *Birmingham and Warwickshire Archaeological Transactions* 93 (1983-84), 45-56.

Tabraham, Christopher J. *Edinburgh Castle*. Edinburgh: Historic Scotland, 1994.

Tabraham, Christopher J. *Scottish Castles and Fortifications*. Edinburgh: Her Majesty's Stationery Office, 1986.

Tabraham, Christopher J. "The Scottish Medieval Tower-house as Lordly Residence in the Light of Recent Excavation," *Proceedings of the Society of Antiquaries of Scotland* 118 (1988), 267-76.

Tabraham, Christopher J. "Smailholm Tower: A Scottish Laird's Fortified Residence on the English Border," *Château Gaillard* 13 (1987), 227-38.

Tabraham, Christopher J. "Two Dogs and a Bone: The Story of Roxborough Castle," *Château Gaillard* 17 (1996), 165-67.

Tabraham, Christopher J. and George L. Good. "The Artillery Fortification at Threave Castle, Gallowey." In: *Scottish Weapons and Fortifications*,

1100-1800. Ed. David H. Caldwell. Edinburgh: John Donald Publishers Ltd., 1981, pp. 55-72.

Tatton-Brown, T. "Medieval Building Stone at the Tower of London," *London Archaeologist* 6, 13 (1991), 361-66.

Taylor, Arnold J. "The Building of Flint: A Postscript." In: *Studies in Castles and Castle Building*. London, 1985, pp. 165-72.

Taylor, Arnold J. "The Date of Clifford's Tower, York." In: *Studies in Castles and Castle Building*. London, 1985, pp. 241-47.

Taylor, Arnold J. "Master Bertram, *Ingeniator Regis*." In: *Studies in Medieval History Presented to R. Allen Brown*. Ed. C. Harper-Bill et al. Woodbridge, 1989, pp. 289-315.

Taylor, Arnold J. "Military Architecture." In: *Medieval England*. Ed. A.L. Poole. Oxford, 1958, II:98-127.

Taylor, Arnold J. *Raglan Castle, Monmouthshire*. London: Her Majesty's Stationery Office, 1950.

Taylor, C., P. Everson, and R. Wilson-North. "Bodiam Castle, Sussex," *Medieval Archaeology* 34 (1990), 155-57.

Teasdale, J.A. "An Archaeological Investigation of the Town Wall between St. Andrew's Street and St. Andrew's Courtyard, Newcastle upon Tyne," *Archaeologia aeliana* 5th ser. 27 (1999), 29-43.

Thomas, Avril. *The Walled Towns of Ireland*. 2 vols. Dublin: Irish Academic Press, 1992.

Thompson, A.H. "Military Architecture." In: *Medieval England*. 2nd ed. Oxford: Clarendon Press, 1958, I:.

Thompson, A.H. *Military Architecture in England during the Middle Ages*. Oxford: Oxford University Press, 1912.

Thompson, M.W. "The Architectural Significance of the Building Works of Ralph, Lord Cromwell (1394-1456)." In: *Collectanea historica: Essays in Memory of Stuart Rigold*. Ed. A. Detsicas. Maidstone, 1981, pp. 156-62.

Thompson, M.W. "The Green Knight's Castle." In: *Studies in Medieval History Presented to R. Allen Brown*. Ed. C. Harper-Bill et al. Woodbridge, 1989, pp. 317-25.

Thompson, M.W. *Kenilworth Castle, Warwickshire*. London: Her Majesty's Stationery Office, 1977.

Thompson, M.W. *Military Architecture in England during the Middle Ages*. Oxford, 1912.

Thompson, M.W. "The Military Interpretation of Castles," *Archaeological Journal* 151 (1994), 439-45.

Thompson, M.W. "A Suggested Dual Origin for Keeps," *Fortress* 15 (Nov 1992), 3-16.

Thompson, M.W. "Three Stages in the Construction of the Hall at Kenilworth Castle, Warwickshire." In: *Ancient Monuments and their Interpretation: Essays Presented to A.J. Taylor*. Ed. M.R. Apted et al. London, 1977, pp. 211-18.

Tolley, R.J. "Stokesay Castle, Shropshire: the Repair of a Major Monument," *Transactiosn of the Association for Studies in the Conservation of Historic Buildings* 15 (1990), 3-24.

Tower of London, The. London: Her Majesty's Stationery Office, 1974.

Toy, Sidney. *The Castles of Great Britain*. London: William Heineman, 1953.

Toynbee, Margaret. "King James II of Scotland: Artillery and Fortification," *The Stewarts* 11 (1962), 157-62.

Tranter, Nigel. *The Fortified House in Scotland*. I: *South-East Scotland*. Edinburgh and London, 1962.

Tranter, Nigel. *Tales and Traditions of Scottish Castles*. Glasgow: Neil Wilson Publishing, 1982.

Turner, D.J. "Bodiam, Sussex: True Castle or Old Soldier's Dream House?" In: *England in the Fourteenth Century: Proceedings of the 1985 Harlaxton Symposium*. Ed. W.J. Ormond. Woodbridge, 1986, pp. 267-79.

Turner, Hilary L. *Town Defences in England and Wales: An Architectural and Documentary Study, AD 900-1500*. London: John Baker, 1971.

Turner, R. *Lamphey Bishop's Palace, Llawhaden Castle, Carswell Medieval House, Carew Cross*. Cardiff: CADW, 1991.

Turner, Rick C. "The Medieval Palaces of the Bishops of St Davids, Wales." In: *Military Studies in Medieval Europe: Papers of the "Medieval Europe Brugge 1997" Conference Volume 11*. Ed. Guy De Boe & Frans Verhaeghe. Zellik: Instituut voor het Archeologisch Patrimonium, 1997, pp. 217-25.

Walker, David. "Gloucestershire Castles," *Transactions of the Bristol and Gloucestershire Archaeological Society* 109 (1991), 5-23.

Warner, Philip. *A Guide to Castles in Britain: Where to Find Them and What to Look For*. London: New English Library, 1976.

Watson, B. "The Norman Fortress on Ludgate Hill in the City of London, England: Recent Excavations, 1986-90," *Château Gaillard* 15 (1990), 335-45.

Weaver, John. *Middleham Castle*. London: English Heritage, 1993.

Weaver, John. *Richmond Castle and Easby Abbey*. London: English Heritage, 1989.

Weightman, M. Scott. *Castles of Northumberland*. London: Pitkin Guides, 1997.

White, Peter. "Castle Gateways during the Reign of Henry II," *Antiquaries Journal* 76 (1996), 241-47.

Wilcox, R. "Timber Reinforcement in Medieval Castles," *Château Gaillard* 5 (1972), 193-202.

Williams, John H. "Excavations at Brougham Castle, 1987," *Transactions of the Cumberland and Westmoreland Antiquarian and Archaeological Society* 92 (1992), 105-21.

Wilson, P.R. "Excavations at Helmsley Castle," *Yorkshire Archaeological Journal* 61 (1989), 29-33.

Woodward, F.W. *Drake's Island*. Devon Archaeology, 5. Exeter: Devon Archaeological Society, 1991.

Woodward, F.W. *Plymouth's Defences: A Short History*. Ivybridge: F.W. Woodward, 1990.

Yeoman, Peter A. "Edinburgh Castle: Iron Age Fort to Garrison Fortress," *Fortress* 4 (Feb 1990), 22-26.

Young, C.-J. "Carisbrooke Castle to 1100," *Château Gaillard* 11 (1983), 281-88.

Military Technology – Premodern – Fortifications – England – Late Roman

Austin, Paul. *Bewcastle and Old Penrith: A Roman Outpost Fort and a Frontier Vicus*. Cumberland and Westmorland Archaeological Society, Research Series, 6. 1991.

Austin, Paul. "Burgh-by-Sands," *Current Archaeology* 10 (1988), 10-19.

Baddeley, Colin. "Mancetter, Roman Legionary Fortress," *West Midlands Archaeology* 34 (1991), 3-12.

Bellhouse, R.L. "Hadrian's Wall: The Forts at Drumburgh," *Transactions of the Cumberland and Westmorland Antiquarian and Archaeological Society* 89 (1989), 33-36.

Bellhouse, R.L. "Roman Sites on the Cumberland Coast: Hadrian's Wall, the Fort at Bowness-on-Solway. A Reappraisal," *Transactions of the Cumberland and Westmorland Antiquarian and Archaeological Society* 88 (1988), 33-54.

Berry, J. and D.J.A. Taylor. "The Roman Fort at Halton Chesters: A Geophysical Survey," *Archaeologia aeliana* 5th ser. 25 (1997), 51-60.

Bidwell, P.T. and N. Holbrook. *Hadrian's Wall Bridges*. English Heritage Archaeological Report, 9. London, 1989.

Bidwell, P.T., Roger Miket, and Bill Ford, ed. *Portae cum turribus: Studies of Roman Fort Gates*. BAR British Series, 206. Oxford, 1988.

Birley, Eric. *Chesters Roman Fort, Northumberland*. London: Her Majesty's Stationery Office, 1982.

Birley, Eric. *Corbridge Roman Station (Corstopitum)*. London: Her Majesty's Stationery Office, 1954.

Bishop, M.C. and J.N. Dore. *Corbridge: Excavations of the Roman Fortification and Town, 1947-80*. London: Historic Buildings and Monuments Commission for England, 1988.

Blaylock, S.R. *Exeter City Defences: Excavation and Survey on the City Walls from the North Gate to the Castle, 1987-88*. Part 1: *Roman*. Exeter Museums Archaeological Field Unit Report, 88.13. Exeter, 1988.

Blood, K. and M.C.B. Bowden. "The Roman Fort of Haltonshesters: An Analytical Field Survey," *Archaeologia aeliana* 5th ser. 18 (1990), 55-62.

Bowden, M.C.B. and K. Blood. "The Roman Fort at Rudchester: An Analytical Field Survey," *Achaeologia aeliana* 5th ser. 19 (1991), 25-31.

Carrington, P. "The Plan of the Legionary Fortress at Chester: Further Comparisons," *Journal of the Chester Archaeological Society* 69 for 1986 (1988), 7-18.

Caruana, I.D. "Carlisle: Excavation of a Section of the Annexe Ditch of the First Flavian Fort, 1990," *Britannia* 23 (1992), 45-109.

Chapman, Hugh, Jenny Hall, and Geoffrey Marsh. *The London Wall Walk*. London: Museum of London, 1985.

Charlesworth, Dorothy. "The Turrets on Hadrian's Wall." In: *Ancient Monuments and their Interpretation: Essays Presented to A.J. Taylor*. Ed. Mr. Apted, et al. London, 1977, pp. 13-26.

Cotterill, John. "Saxon Raiding and the Role of the Late Roman Coastal Forts of Britain," *Britannia* 24 (1993), 227-39.

Cracknell, Stephen. "Alcester's Roman Defences: Excavations at the Gateway Supermarket Site, 1986," *West Midlands Archaeology* 34 (1991), 3-12.

Crow, J.G. "An Excavation of the North Curtain Wall at Housesteads, 1984," *Archaeologia aeliana* 5th ser. 16 (1988), 61-124.

Crow, J.G. *Housesteads*. London: English Heritage, 1989.

Crow, J.G. "A Review of Current Research on the Turrets and Curtain of Hadrian's Wall," *Britannia* 23 (1991), 59-63.

Crow, James and Mark Jackson. "The Excavation of Hadrian's Wall at Sewingsheds and the Discovery of a Long Cist Burial," *Archaeologia aeliana* 5th ser. 25 (1997), 61-69.

Crow, Jim. "Peel Gap," *Current Archaeology* 10 (1988), 14-17.

Cunliffe, Barry. *Portchester Castle*. The Portsmouth Papers, 1. Portsmouth: Portsmouth City Council, 1967.

Donaldson, G.H. "Thoughts on a Military Appreciation of the Design of Hadrian's Wall," *Arcaheologia aeliana* 5th ser. 16 (1988), 125-38.

Evans, D.R. and V.M. Metcalf. *Roman Gates, Caerleon*. London: Oxbow, 1992.

Hadrian's Wall: A Souvenir Guide to the Roman Wall. 2nd ed. London: English Heritage, 1989.

Harbottle, R., R. Fraser, and F.C. Burton. "The Westgate Road Milecastle, Newcastle-upon Tyne," *Britannia* 19 (1988), 153-62.

Heywood, Brenda. "The Roman Fort at Penydarren, Glamorgan," *Bulletin of the Board of Celtic Studies* 38 (1991), 167-91.

Hill, P.R. "Hadrian's Wall: Some Aspects of its Execution," *Archaeological aeliana* 5th ser. 19 (1991), 33-39.

Hill, P.R. "The Stone Wall Turrets of Hadrian's Wall," *Archaeologia aeliana* 5th ser. 25 (1997), 27-49.

Hill, P.R. and Brian Dobson. "The Design of Hadrian's Wall and Its Implications," *Archaeological aeliana* 5th ser. 20 (1992), 27-52.

Holbrook, N. "A Watching Brief at the Roman Fort of Benwell-Condercum, 1990," *Archaeological aeliana* 5th ser. 19 (1991), 41-45.

Hurst, J.D., R. Roberts, and S. Woodiwiss. "A Possible Second Roman Fort at Droitwich," *Transactions of the Worcestershire Archaeological Society* 11 (1988), 23-28.

Johnson, Stephen. *English Heritage Book of Hadrian's Wall*. London: B.T. Batsford/English Heritage, 1989.

Johnson, Stephen. "Recent Work on Hadrian's Wall," *Fortress* 1 (May 1989), 3-13.

Johnson, Stephen. *Roman Fortifications on the "Saxon Shore"*. London: Her Majesty's Stationery Office, 1977.

Jones, Dilwyn and J.B. Whitwell. "Survey of the Roman Fort and Multi-Period Settlement Complex at Kirmington on the Lincolnshire Wolds: A Non-Destructive Approach," *Lincolnshire History and Archaeology* 26 (1991), 57-62.

Knight, Jeremy K. *Caerleon Roman Fortress*. Cardiff: CADW, 1988.

Mann, J.C. "The Function of Hadrian's Wall," *Archaeologia aeliana* 5th ser. 18 (1990), 51-54.

Mann, J.C. "The History of the Antonine Wall–a Reappraisal." *Proceedings of the Society of Antiquaries of Scotland* 118 (1988), 101-37.

Mason, D.J.P. "The Roman Site at Heronbridge, near Chester: Aspects of Civilian Settlement in the Vicinity of Legionary Fortresses in Britain and Beyond," *Archaeological Journal* 145 (1988), 123-37.

Maxfield, Valerie A. "The Army and the Land in the Roman South West." In: *Security and Defence in South-West England Before 1800*. Ed. R. Higham. Exeter, 1987, pp. 1-25.

Maxfield, Valerie A. "Hadrian's Wall in Its Imperial Setting," *Archaeologia aeliana* 5th ser. 18 (1990), 1-28.

Maxfield, Valerie A., ed. *The Saxon Shore: A Handbook*. Exeter, 1989.

Monaghan, J.P. "A Roman Marching Camp and Native Settlement at Newton Kyme, Tadcaster," *Yorkshire Archaeological Journal* 63 (1991), 51-58.

Start, D., N. Redhead, and J. Roberts. "Excavation and Conservation at Castleshaw Roman Forts," *The Greater Manchester Archaeological Journal* 3 (1989), 45-55.

Walthew, C.V. "Length-Unit in Roman Military Planning: Inchtuthil and Colchester," *Oxford Journal of Archaeology* 7 (1988), 81-98.

Whitworth, Alan. "The Housesteads Bastle," *Archaeologia aeliana* 5th ser. 18 (1990), 127-29.

Wooliscroft, D.J. "The Outpost System of Hadrian's Wall," *Transactions of the Cumberland and Westmorland Archaeology Society* 88 (1988), 23-28.

Wooliscroft, D.J. "Signalling and the Design of Hadrian's Wall," *Archaeologia Aeliana* 17 (1989), 5-20.

Wooliscroft, D.J. and S.A.M. Swain. "The Roman 'Signal' Tower at Johnson's Plain, Cumbria," *Transactions of the Cumberland and Westmorland Antiquarian and Archaeological Society* 91 (1991), 19-29.

Wooliscroft, D.J, S.A.M. Swain, and N.J. Lockett. "Barcombe B: A Second Roman 'Signal' Tower on Barcombe Hill," *Archaeologia aeliana* 5th ser. 20 (1992), 57-62.

Military Technology – Premodern – Fortifications – England – Edward I's Welsh Castles

Avent, Richard. "The Castles Built by King Edward I in Wales between 1277 and 1300," *IBI Bulletin* 47 (1990-91), 49-58.

Avent, Richard. *Criccieth Castle, Pennarth Fawr Medieval Hall House, St. Cybi's Well*. Cardiff: Cadw: Welsh Historic Monuments, 1989.

Bullinga, Nicki. "Kastelenbouw in Wales: Engelse koningen versus Welshe prinsen," *Spiegel historiael* 30 (1995), 356-60.

Edwards, J. Goronwy. "Edward I's Castle-Building in Wales," *Proceedings of the British Academy* 32 (1946), 15-81.

Hughes, Quentin. "Medieval Firepower," *Fortress* 8 (Feb 1991), 31-43.

Humphreys, P.H. *Castles of Edward the First in Wales*. London: Her Majesty's Stationery Office, 1983.

Kightly, Charles. *A Royal Palace in Wales: Caernarfon*. Cardiff: Cadw: Welsh Historic Monuments, 1991.

Mathieu, James R. "A New Interpretation of Caernarfon Castle," *Medieval Life* 9 (1998), 11-15.

Neaverson, Ernest. *Mediaeval Castles in North Wales*. Liverpool: Liverpool University Press, 1947.

Rogers, Alan. "Edward I and the Castles of Wales," *History Today* 19 (1969), 445-52.

Taylor, Arnold J. *Beaumaris Castle*. Ed. Richard Avent. 2nd ed. Cardiff: Cadw: Welsh Historic Monuments, 1985.

Taylor, Arnold J. "Building at Caernarvon and Beaumarais in 1295-6." In: *Studies in Castles and Castle Building*. London, 1985, pp. 139-44.

Taylor, Arnold J. *Caernarfon Castle and Town Walls*. Ed. M.R. Apted. 3rd ed. Cardiff: Cadw: Welsh Historic Monuments, 1993.

Taylor, Arnold J. "Castle-building in Wales in the Later Thirteenth Century: The Prelude to Construction." In: *Medieval Archaeology: Papers of the Seventeenth Annual Conference of the Center for Medieval and Early Renaissance Studies*. Ed. C.L. Redman. Binghamton, 1989, pp. 104-33; in: *Studies in Building History: Essays in Recognition of the Work of B.H.St.J. O'Neil*. London, 1961, pp. 104-33.

Taylor, Arnold J. *Conwy Castle and Town Walls*. 3rd ed. Cardiff: Cadw: Welsh Historic Monuments, 1990.

Taylor, Arnold J. "The Conwy Particulars Accounts for Nov. 1285-Sept. 1286." In: *Studies in Castles and Castle Building*. London, 1985, pp. 145-54.

Taylor, Arnold J. "The Date of Caernarvon Castle." In: *Studies in Castles and Castle Building*. London, 1985, pp. 129-38.

Taylor, Arnold J. "The Dismantling of Conwy Castle." In: *Studies in Castles and Castle Building*. London, 1985, pp. 155-63.

Taylor, Arnold J. *Harlech Castle*. Ed. Richard Avent. 2nd ed. Cardiff: Cadw: Welsh Historic Monuments, 1988.

Taylor, Arnold J. "Harlech Castle: The Dating of the Outer Enclosure." In: *Studies in Castles and Castle Building*. London, 1985, pp. 173-75.

Taylor, Arnold J. *The History of the King's Work in Wales, 1277-1330*. London, 1973.

Taylor, Arnold J. "Master James of St. George," *English Historical Review* 65 (1950), 433-57.

Taylor, Arnold J. *Rhuddlan Castle*. 4th ed. Cardiff: Cadw: Welsh Historic Monuments, 1987.

Taylor, Arnold J. "The Town and Castle of Conwy: Preservation and Interpretation," *Antiquaries Journal* 75 (1995), 339-63.

Taylor, Arnold J. *The Welsh Castles of Edward I*. London: The Hambledon Press, 1986.

Walker, R.F. "Two Fourteenth-Century Surveys of Aberstwyth Castle," *Ceredigion* 12 (1995), 3-22.

Military Technology – Premodern – Fortifications – France

Alauzier, L. d'. "Les meurtriès triples du château de Berry," *Provence historique* 6 (1956), 16-20.

Andru, O, M. Colardelle, J.-P. Moyne, and E. Verdel. "Les châteaux de la baronnie de Clermont et la marche delphino-savoyard," *Château Gaillard* 17 (1996), 25-37.

Bachrach, Bernard S. "The Angevin Strategy of Castle Building in the Reign of Fulk Nerra, 987-1040," *American Historical Review* 88 (1983), 533-560.

Bachrach, Bernard S. "The Cost of Castle Building: The Case of the Tower at Langeais, 992-994." In: *The Medieval Castle: Romance and Reality*. Ed. K. Reyerson and F. Powe. Dubuque, 1984, pp. 47-62.

Bachrach, Bernard S. "Fortification and Military Tactics: Fulk Nerra's Strongholds circa 1000," *Technology and Culture* 20 (1979), 531-49.

Barbier, Pierre. *La France féodale*. Vol. 1: *Châteaux-forts et eglises fortifées*. Saint-Brieuc:Les presses bretonnes, 1968.

Barral i Altet, Xavier. "L'enceinte urbaine de Dinan." In: *Dinan au moyen âge*. Dinan, 1986, pp. 73-100.

Barthélemy, Dominique. "Castles, Barons, and Vavassors in the Vendômois and Neighboring Regions in the Eleventh and Twelfth Centuries." In: *Cultures of Power: Lordship, Status, and Process in Twelfth-Century Europe*. Ed. Thomas N. Bisson. Philadelphia: University of Pennsylvania Press, 1995, pp. 56-68.

Barzic, Ernest le. *La Roche-Derrien et ses environs: Le barbe Narcisse Quellien*. Rennes, n.d.

Bataille, Henri. *Vaucouleurs: Les remparts qui ont sauvé Jeanne-d'Arc*. Vosges: Imprimeur-Editeur Fetzer S.A., n.d.

Baudin, Pierre. "Une famille châtelaine sur les confins normanno-manceaux: les Géré (Xe-XIIIe s)," *Antiquités nationales* 22 (1992), 309-56.

Baudry, Marie-Pierre. "Le château du Coudray-Salbert," *Antiquités nationales* 23/24 (1991), 137-212.

Baudry, Marie-Pierre. "Le château du Coudray-Salbert," *Bulletin archéologique du comité des travaux historiques et scientifiques* n.s. 23-24 (1991), 137-212.

Baylé, Jeanne. "Mise en défense du chateau de Montaillou au début du XVe siècle," *Bibliothèque de l'école des chartes* 129 (1971), 113-19.

Beaurepaire, Charles de. "Note sur le château de Longueville," *Bulletin de la comission des antiquités de la Seine inférieure* 12 (1900-02), 343-54.

Bécet, Marie. "Comment on fortifiat une petite ville pendant la guerre de cent ans: les fortifications de Chablis au XVe siècle," *Annales de Bourgogne* 21 (1949), 7-30.

Bécet, Marie. "Les fortifications de Chablis au XVe siècle (comment on fortifiait une petite village pendant la guerre de cent ans)," *Annales de Bourgogne* 21 (1949), 7-30.

Bellart, G. and F. Maisan. *Les fortifications d'Arras du XIIe siècle au XVe siècle*. Arras, 1976.

Bentley, James. *Fort Towns of France: The Bastides of the Dordogne and Aquitaine*. London: Tauris Parke Books, 1993.

Berman, Constance H. "Fortified Monastic Granges in the Rouergue." In: *The Medieval Castle: Romance and Reality*. Ed. K. Reyerson and F. Powe. Dubuque, 1984, pp. 125-46.

Besnard, Charles-Henri. "Le château de Fougères," *Bulletin monumental* 76 (1912), 5-21.

Blieck, Gilles and Laurence Vanderstraeten. "Recherches sur les fortifications de Lille au moyen âge," *Revue du Nord* 70 (1988), 107-22.

Blondel, L. "L'architecture militaire au temps de Pierre II de Savoie: Les donjons circulaires," *Geneva* 13 (1935), 271-321.

Bois, M., M.P. Feuillet, P.Y. Laffont, C. Mazard, J.M. Poisson, and E. Sirot. "Approche des plus anciennes formes castrales dans le royaume de Bourgogne-Provence (Xe-XIIe siècles)," *Château Gaillard* 16 (1994), 57-68.

Bonde, Sheila. *Fortress-Churches of Languedoc: Architecture, Religion, and Conflict in the High Middle Ages*. Cambridge: Cambridge University Press, 1994.

Bonville, Essonne. "La château de Farcheville," *Bulletin monumentale* 146.4 (1988), 355-57.

Boüard, Michel de. "Les petites enceintes circulaires d'origine médiévale en Normandie," *Château Gaillard* 1 (1964), 21-35.

Bourin-Derruau, Monique. "Valeur stratégique et valeur symbolique des fortifications castrales en Bas-Languedoc (XIe-XIIIe siècle)." In: *Castrum 3: Guerre, fortification et habitant dans le monde méditerranéen au moyen âge*. Ed. André Bazzana. Rome: L'école Française de Rome, 1988, pp. 99-106.

Bouteiller, Paul. "Le siège et la prise du Chateau-Gaillard en 1203-1204," *Revue historique des armées* 2.2 (1946), 15-27.

Bouvier, A., E. Faure-Boucharlat, J. Monnier, et al. "La motte castrale de Décines-Charpieu (Rhone)," *Archéologie médiévale* 22 (1992), 231-307.

Brillaud, A. "Découvertes archéologiques au château de Dampierre-sur-Boutonne (Charente-Maritime)," *Bulletin monumental* 147 (1989), 247-48.

Bruard, Yves. "L'amélioration de la défense et les transformations des châteaux du Bourbonnais pendant la guerre de cent ans," *Comptes rendus de l'académie des inscriptions* (1972), 518-40.

Bruard, Yves. "Le château de Gisors: Principales campagnes de construction," *Bulletin monumental* 116 (1958), 243-65.

Bruard, Yves. "La cité de Carcassonne: La Citadelle ou château comtal," *Congrès archéologique de France* 131 (1973), 516-32.

Bruard, Yves. "La cité de Carcassonne: Les enceintes fortifiées," *Congrès archéologique de France* 131 (1973), 496-515.

Bruard, Yves. "La position stratégique des châteaux du Bourbonnais au moyen âge," *Bulletin monumental* 110 (1952), 101-18.

Buisson, Gilles. "Les maisons fortes du Mortainais du XVIe siècle à nos jours." In: *Châteaux et châtelains en Normandie: Cahiers Léopold Delisle.* 40 (1991), 49-58.

Bur, Michel de. "Le château d'Epinal et ses relations avec l'espace urbain," *Château Gaillard* 15 (1992), 45-59.

Bur, Michel de. "Fouilles à Vanault-le-Châtel, Bilan provisoire," *Château Gaillard* 6 (1973), 27-41.

Burnouf, Joëlle. "Butenheim: De le résidence aristocratique du XIe siècle à la maison forte de la fin du moyen âge: Histoire et archéologie de l'echec d'un lignage dans un terroir du sud de l'Alsace," *Château Gaillard* 15 (1992), 61-71.

Burnouf, Joëlle and J. Decäens. "La fin du château de Saint-Vaast-sur-Seulles (Calvados)," *Château Gaillard* 12 (1965), 23-37.

Butler, R.M. "Late Roman Town Walls in Gaul," *Archaeological Journal* 116 (1959), 25-50.

Canons et murailles: histoire et évolution de l'architecture défensive dans la région toulonnaise. Toulon, 1990.

Cantié, G. "Le site castral du Dognon (Limousin, France)," *Château Gaillard* 16 (1994), 89-99.

Cazes, Jean-Paul. "Un village castral de la Plaine Lauragaise Lasbordes (Aude)," *Archéologie du Midi médiéval* 8-9 (1990-1991), 3-25.

Chapelot, Jean. "Le château de Vincennes, un jalon essentiel dans l'histoire de l'architecture fortifée de la seconde moitie du XIVe siècle," *Revue de la société des amis de Musée de l'Armée* 109 (1995), 29-37.

Chapelot, Jean and Elisabeth Lalou, ed. *Vincennes: Aux origines de l'état moderne.* Actes du colloque scientifique sur les Capétians et Vincennes au moyen âge. Paris: Presses de l'école normale supérieure, 1996.

Chapu, Ph. "Les donjons rectangulaires du Berry," *Château Gaillard* 1 (1964), 37-51.

Châteaux normands de Guillaume le Conquerant à Richard Coeur de Lion: Exposition organisée par la Musée de Normandie. Caen, 1987.

Châteaux of the Loire, The. Blois: Valoire Publications, 1995.

Châtelaine, André. *Châteaux et guerriers de la France au moyen âge.* II: *Evolution architecturale et essai d'une typologie.* Strasbourg, 1981.

Châtelaine, André. *Châteaux forts: Images de pierre des guerres médiévales.* 4th ed. Paris: Rempart Desclée de Brouwer, 1991.

Châtelaine, André. *Donjons romans des Pays d'Ouest: Étude comparative sur les donjons romans quadrangulaires de la France de l'Ouest.* Paris: Picard, 1973.

Châtelaine, André. "Essai de typologie des donjons romans quadrangulaires de la France de l'Ouest," *Château Gaillard* 6 (1973), 43-57.

Châtelaine, André. "Recherche sur les châteaux de Philippe Auguste," *Archéologie médiévale* 21 (1991), 115-61.

Cherrier, N. "Châteaux et frontières et espaces forestiers à l'est du Poitou du Xe au début du XIIIe siècle," *Château Gaillard* 17 (1996), 45-52.

Cheyette, Frederic L. "The Castles of the Trencavels: A Preliminary Aerial Survey." In: *Order and Innovation in the Middle Ages: Essays in Honor of Joseph R. Strayer.* Ed. W.C. Jordan et al. Princeton, 1976, pp. 255-72, 498-99.

Clauzel, Denis. "Lille et ses remparts à la fin du Moyen Âge (1320-1480)." In: *La guerre, la violence et les gens au Moyen Âge.* I: *Guerre et violence.* Ed. P. Contamine and O. Guyotjeannin. 119e congrès national des sociétés historiques et scientifiques, Amiens, octobre 1994, Section d'histoire médiévale et philologie. Paris, 1996, pp. 273-93.

Cleary, Simon Esmonde, Michael Jones, and Jason Wood. "The Late Roman Defences at Saint-Bertrand-de-Comminges (Haute Garonne): Interim Report," *Journal of Roman Archaeology* 11 (1998), 343-54.

Cloulas, Ivan. *Les châteaux de la Loire au temps de la Renaissance.* Paris: Hachette, 1996.

Colardelle, Michel, et al. "Le chantier de construction de l'habitat fortifié de Charavines (France, XIe siècle)," *Château Gaillard* 18 (1998), 29-35.

Colardelle, Michel and Chantal Mazard. "Les mottes castrales et l'évolution des pouvoirs dans les Alpes du Nord: Aux origines de la seigneurie," *Château Gaillard* 11 (1983), 69-89.

Colardelle, Michel and E. Verdel. "L'habitat immergé de Colletière à Charavines (Isère)," *Château Gaillard* 14 (1990), 77-94.

Collin, Hubert. "État des châteaux du comte de Bar en Lorraine en 1336." In: *La guerre et la paix: Frontières et violences au moyen âge.* Actes du 101e congrès national des sociétés savantes, Lille, 1976. Paris: Bibliothèque Nationale, 1978, pp. 155-77.

Collin, Hubert. "Un lieu d'intérêt militaire au moyen âge: Le confluent de la Meurthe et de la Moselle," *Annales de l'est,* 5th ser., 16 (1964), 163-78.

Collin, Hubert. "Les plus anciens châteaux de la region de nancy, en Lorraine: Dieulouard, Mousson, Prény, Vaudémont," *Château Gaillard* 2 (1967), 27-38.

Collin, M. *La casemate du bont du pont des Tourelles à Orléans du coté de la Sologne.* Paris: n.p., 1867.

Collin, M. *Les derniers jours du pont des Tourelles à Orléans.* Orléans: H. Herluison, 1875.

Colombet, A. "Les églises fortifées de la Bourgogne: à propos d'une étude récente," *Annales de Bourgogne* 31 (1959), 250-58.

Contamine, Philippe. "Les chaînes dans les bonnes villes de France (spécialement Paris), XIVe-XVe siècle." In: *Guerre et société en France, en Angleterre et en Bourgogne XIVe-XVe siècle*. Ed. P. Contamine et al. Lille, 1991, pp. 293-314.

Contamine, Philippe. "Un château dans la tourmente: Saint-Germain-en-Laye." In: *De Jeanne d'Arc aux guerres d'Italie: Figures, images et problèmes du XVe siècle*. Orléans: Paradigme, 1994, pp. 97-110.

Contamine, Philippe. "Les fortifications urbaines en France à la fin du Moyen âge: aspects financiers et économiques," *Revue historique* 260 (1978), 23-47.

Contenson, L. de "Les remparts de Rennes," *Bulletin monumental* 71 (1907), 431-44.

Cornon, Raymond. "Dinan," *Bulletin monumental* 107 (1949), 172-86.

Corvisier, Christian. "L'architecture et l'âe des églises fortifiées: L'exemple de l'Est de la Picardie." In: *Les malheurs de la guerre*. I: *De la guerre à l'ancienne à la guerre réglée*. Ed. André Corvisier and Jean Jacquart. Paris: Éditions du CTHS, 1996, pp. 77-98.

Corvisier, Christian. "Le donjon-porte castral en France à la fin du Moyen âge. Emergence d'un thème architectural." In: *Aux portes du chateau: Actes du troisième colloque de castellologie*. Paris, 1987, pp. 71-83.

Couanon, Philippe. "Pour une typologie fonctionnelle des donjons de pierre: l'exemple du Limousin." In: *Sites défensifs et sites fortifiés au Moyen âge entre Loire et Pyrénées: Actes du premier colloque Aquitania, Limoges, 20-22 mai 1987*. Aquitania, supplément 4. Bordeaux, 1990, pp. 115-22.

Coulson, Charles L.H. "Castellation in the County of Champagne in the 13th Century," *Château Gaillard* 9-10 (1982), 347-64.

Coulson, Charles L.H. "Community and Fortress-Politics in France in the Lull before the Hundred Years War in English Perspective," *Nottingham Medieval Studies* 40 (1996), 80-108.

Coulson, Charles L.H. "The Impact of Bouvines upon the Fortress-Policy of Philip Augustus." In: *Studies in Medieval History Presented to R. Allen Brown*. Ed. C. Harper-Bill et al. Woodbridge, 1989, pp. 71-80.

Coulson, Charles L.H. "'National' Requisitioning for 'Public' Use of 'Private' Castles in Pre-Nation State France." In: *Medieval Europeans: Studies in Ethnic Identity and National Perspectives in Medieval Europe*. Ed. Alfred P. Smyth. New York: St. Martin's Press, 1998, pp. 119-36.

Coulson, Charles L.H. "Rendability and Castellation in Medieval France," *Château Gaillard* 6 (1973), 59-67.

Coulson, Charles L.H. "The Sanctioning of Fortresses in France: 'Feudal Anarchy' or 'Seignorial Amity'?" *Nottingham Medieval Studies* 42 (1998), 38-104.

Coulson, Charles L.H. "Valois Powers Over Fortresses on the Eve of the Hundred Years War." In: *Armies, Chivalry and Warfare in Medieval Britain and France: Proceedings of the 1995 Harlaxton Symposium*. Ed. M. Strickland. Stamford, 1998, pp. 147-60.

Coutil, Léon. *Le Château-Gaillard*. Les Andelys, 1906.

Crozet, R. "Les églises fortifiées du Poitou, de l'Angoumois, de l'Aunis et de la Saintogne: Conclusion d'une enquête," *Bulletin de la société des antiquaires de l'ouest* 4th ser., 1 (1951), 813-20.

Curnow, P.E. "Some Developments in Military Architecture c. 1200: Le Coudray-Salbart," *Proceedings of the Battle Conference on Anglo-Norman Studies* 2 (1979), 42-62.

Cursente, B. *Les castelnaux de la Gascogne médiévale*. Bordeaux, 1980.

Cursente, B. "Castrum et territoire dans la Gascogne du XIIIe siècle," *Château Gaillard* 15 (1990), 91-100.

Cursente, B. "Les habitats fortifiés en Gascogne: une mise à jour." In: *Habitats fortifiés et organisation de l'espace en Mediterranée médiévale*. Ed. A. Bazzana, P. Guichard and J.M. Poisson. Lyon, 1983, pp. 57-61.

Darnas, I. "Le *castrum* de Calberte (Lozère)," *Château Gaillard* 16 (1994), 101-07.

Debal, Jacques. "La topographie de l'enceinte fortifiée d'Orléans au temps de Jeanne d'Arc." In: *Jeanne d'Arc: une époque, un rayonment*. Colloque d'histoire médiévale. Orléans–Octobre 1979. Paris, 1982, pp. 23-41.

Debord, André. "*Castrum* et *castellum* chez Adémar de Chabannes," *Archéologie médiévale* 9 (1979), 97-113.

Debord, André. "Châteaux et société dans la Rouergue médiéval (Xe-XIIIe siècle)," *Château Gaillard* 14 (1990), 7-28.

Debord, André. "Fouille du *castrum* d'Andone, à Villejoubert," *Château Gaillard* 7 (1975), 35-48.

Decaëns, Joseph. "De la motte de conquête (XIe siècle) à la seigneurie châtelaine (XIIe siècle): L'exemple de Rivray à Condé-sur-Huisne (Orne)," *Château Gaillard* 16 (1994), 109-20.

Decaëns, Joseph. "Les châteaux de la vallée de l'huisne dans le perche," *Anglo-Norman Studies* 17 (1994), 1-20.

Decaëns, Joseph. "L'enceinte fortifiée de Sébécourt (Eure)," *Château Gaillard* 7 (1975), 49-65.

Decaëns, Joseph. "Les origines du village et du château de Saint-Vaast-sur-Seulles (Calvados)," *Anglo-Norman Studies* 10 (1987), 83-100.

Deléage, A. "Les forteresses de la Bourgogne franque," *Annales de Bourgogne* 3 (1931), 162-68.

Delisle, Leopold. *Histoire du chateau et des sires de Saint-Sauveur-le-Vicomte*. 2 vols. Paris, 1867.

Demolon, P., H. Halbout, E. Louis, and M. Louis-Vanbauce. *Douai, cité médiévale: Bilan d'archéologie et d'histoire*. Archeologia Duacensis, 3. Douai, 1990.

Deville, A. *Histoire de Château-Gaillard et du siège qu'il soutint en 1203-1204*. Rouen, 1829.

Deville, Jean Achille. *Histoire du château d'Arques*. Rouen: Imprimé Chez Nicétas Periaux, 1839.

Deville, Jean Achille. *Notice sur le château d'Arques*. 8th ed. Rouen: Imprimère de H. Boissel, 1866.

Deyres, Marcel. "Les châteaux de Foulque Nerra," *Bulletin monumental* 132 (1974), 7-28.

Dieulafoy, M. *Le Château Gaillard et l'architecture militaire au XIIIe siècle*. Paris: Libraire C. Klincksieck, 1898.

Dion, A. de. "Note sur le château de Boves-les-Amiens," *Bulletin monumental* (1867), 435-45.

Drouyn, Leo. *La Guienne militaire: Histoire et description des villes fortifiées, forteresses et châteaux*. 2 vols. Bordeaux, 1865.

Dubois, R. and G. Sangnier. "Le château de Saint-Pol: Essai de reconstitution d'après les documents et les fouilles de 1936-1938," *Bulletin de la commission départemtentale des monuments historiques du Pas-de Calais* 7 (1941-46), 415-52.

Ducrot, Janine. *Chateau de Pierrefonds*. Trans. G. Capner. Paris: Nouvelles Editions Latines, n.d.

Dufaÿ, Bruno. "Le château-fort de La Madeline à Chevreuse (Yvelines, France) la fouille archéologique, une approche fondamentale." In: *Military Studies in Medieval Europe: Papers of the "Medieval Europe Brugge 1997" Conference Volume 11*. Ed. Guy De Boe & Frans Verhaeghe. Zellik: Instituut voor het Archeologisch Patrimonium, 1997, pp. 131-38.

Durand, Philippe. "L'entrée du petit château au XVe siècle à travers l'exemple du Montmorillonnais." In: *Aux portes du chateau: Actes du troisième colloque de castellologie*. Paris, 1987, pp. 85-95.

Durand, Philippe. "La protection religieuse de l'entrée du château à l'époque romane en Haut-Poitou," *Cahiers de civilisation médiévale* 31 (1988), 201-12.

Durlewanger, Armand. *The Royal Chateau of Chinon*. Trans. Stan and Rita Morton. Colmar: S.A.E.P., 1982.

Emden, Wolfgang van. "The Castle in Some Works of Medieval French Literature." In: *The Medieval Castle: Romance and Reality*. Ed. K. Reyerson and F. Powe. Dubuque, 1984, pp. 1-26.

Enaud, F. *Les châteaux forts en France*. Paris, 1958.

Enlart, Camille. *Manuel d'archéologie Française depuis les temps méro-vingiens jusqu'à la renaissance*. II: *Architecture militaire*. 3rd ed. Paris, 1932.

Erlande-Brandenburg, Alain. "L'architecture militaire au temps de Philippe Auguste: une nouvelle conception de la défense." In: *La France de Philippe Auguste: le temps des mutations: actes du colloque international organiséé par le C.N.R.S. (Paris, 29 septembre-4 octobre 1980)*. Ed. Robert-Henri Bautier. Paris: Editions du Centre national de la recherche scientifique, 1982, pp. 595-604.

Erlande-Brandenburg, Alain and Bertrand Jestaz. *Le château de Vincennes*. Caisse Nationale des Monuments Historiques et des Sites. Paris: Picard, 1989.

Faravel, S. "Une fouille surprise: la maison-forte de Brione à Saint-Germain-d'Esteuil (Gironde)," *Château Gaillard* 14 (1990), 159-74.

Faravel, S., Ch. Sreix, and Ch. Martin. "Premiers résultats des fouilles du château de Lauzun (Lot-et-Garonne, France) ou la redécouverte d'un donjon roman en Aquitaine," *Château Gaillard* 16 (1994), 179-88.

Faucherre, Nicolas. "Les défenses." In: *Le Monst-Saint-Michel: Histoire et imaginaire*. Paris: Anthèse/Éditions du Patrimoine, 1998, pp. 144-55.

Faucherre, Nicolas and Jean Mesqui. "Le château de Châtillon-Coligny," *Bulletin monumental* 146 (1988), 73-108.

Faucon, Régis. *Falaise*. Paris: Nouvelles Editions Latines, n.d.

Feuillide, J.-G.C. *Le chateau de Ham: Son histoire, ses seigneurs et ses prisonniers*. 2nd ed. Paris, 1842.

Finó, J.-F. *Forteresses de la France médiévale: construction, attaque, défense*. 3rd ed. Paris: Picard, 1977.

Fixot, Michel. "A la recherche des formes les plus anciennes de la fortification privée en Provence: l'enceinte du domaine de Cadrix (Commune de Saint-Maximim, Var)," *Château Gaillard* 9-10 (1982), 389-406.

Fixot, Michel. "La motte et l'habitant fortifié en Provence médiévale," *Château Gaillard* 7 (1975), 67-93.

Flambard-Héricher, Anne-Marie. "La construction dans la basse vallée de la Seine: l'exemple du château de Vatteville-la-Rue (Seine-Maritime)," *Château Gaillard* 18 (1998), 93-102.

Flambard-Héricher, Anne-Marie. "Constructions et habitats fortifiés: Vatteville-la-Rue (Seine-maritime), le Vieux Château," *Archéologie médiévale* 26 (1996), 317-18.

Flambard-Héricher, Anne-Marie. "Le 'Vieux Château' de Vatteville-la-Rue (Seine-Maritime), première approche archéologique," *Château Gaillard* 17 (1996), 85-89.

Fliche, Augustin. "Aigues-Mortes," *Congrès archéologique de France* 108 (1951), 90-103.

Floquet, C. *Châteaux et manoirs bretons des Rohan*. Loudéac, 1989.

Fons-Melicocq, A. de la. "Notice sur la ville et le chateau de Ham (Somme)," *Mémoires de la société des antiquaires de Picardie* 2 (1844/45), 273-94.

Fons-Melicocq, A. de la. "Relation du siège de Ham de 1411, par un Chroniqueuer (anonyme) Bourguignon (XVe siècle)," *La Picardie* 3 (1857), 241-48.

Forts, Philippe des. "Rambures," *Congrès archéologique de France* 99 (1936), 445-58.

Forts, Philippe des. "Le château de Rambures (Somme)," *Bulletin monumental* 67 (1903), 240-66.

Fournier, Gabriel. "Chartes de franchise et fortifications villageoises en basse Auvergne au XIIIe siècle." In: *Les libertés urbaines et rurales du XIe au XIVe siècle: Actes du colloque international de Spa, 1966*. Brussels: Prov Civitate, 1968, pp. 223-44.

Fournier, Gabriel. *Le château dans la France médiévale: Essai de sociologie monumentale*. Paris: Aubier Montaigne, 1978.

Fournier, Gabriel. "Le château du Puiset au début du XIIe siècle et sa place dans l'évolution de l'architecture militaire," *Bulletin monumental* 122 (1964), 355-74.

Fournier, Gabriel. *Châteaux, villages et villes d'Auvergne au XVe d'après l'armorial de Guillaume Revel*. Geneva and Paris, 1973.

Fournier, Gabriel. "La dèfense des populations rurales pendant la guerre de cent ans en basse Auvergne." In: *Actes du XCe congrès national des sociétés savantes, Nice 1965, Section d'archéologie*. Paris, 1966, pp. 157-99.

Fournier, Gabriel. "Les enceintes de terre en Auvergne," *Bulletin historique et scientifique de l'Auvergne* 81 (1961), 89-110.

Fournier, Gabriel. "Les fortifications de la Basse-Auvergne au milieu du XVe siècle, d'après l'Armorial de Revel," *Château Gaillard* 5 (1972), 55-64.

Fowler, Kenneth A. "Investment in Urban Defence: The Frontier Regions of France and England during the Fourteenth Century." In: *Investimenti e civilità, sec. XIII-XVIII*. 9th Study Week of the Francesco Datini International Institute for Economic History. Prato, 1977.

Gardeau, L. "Les châteaux des confins du Périgord et du Libournais au moyen âge," *Bulletin philologique et historique (jusqu'à 1610) du comitédes travaux historiques et scientifiques* (1957), 407-22.

Gardelles, Jacques. *Les châteaux du moyen âge dans la France du Sud-Ouest: La Gascogne anglaise du 1216 à 1327*. Paris: Arts et Méchaniques Graphiques, 1973.

Gardelles, Jacques. "Du manoir au château fort en Gascogne anglaise au début de la guerre de cent ans (1337-60)." In: *Actes du CIe congrès national des sociétés savantes, Lille 1976*. Paris, 1978, pp. 119-29.

Gaudu, G. "La tour de Cesson," *Bulletin de la société d'émulation des Côtes-du-Nord* 82 (1953), 63-74.

Gauthiez, Bernard. "Hypotheses sur la fortification de Rouen au onzieme siècle. Le donjon, la tour de Richard II et l'enceinte de Guillaume," *Anglo-Norman Studies* 14 (1991), 61-76.

Gay, Marie-Thérèse. "La maison forte dans le comte de Bourgogne au moyen âge: aspects juridiques." In: *La maison forte au moyen âge*. Ed. M. Bur. Paris, 1986, pp. 215-28.

Gay, Victor. *Glossaire archéologique du moyen âge et de à renaissance.* 2 vols. Paris, 1887, 1928.

Gazenbeek, Michiel. "Le site castral d'Aubagne," *Archéologie du Midi médiévale* 8-9 (1990-1991), 27-37.

Gebelin, François. *Les châteaux de France.* Paris, 1962.

Genicot, Leopold, ed. *Le grand livre des châteaux de Belgique.* I: *Châteaux forts et châteaux-fermes.* Brussels, 1976.

Gimouvez, O. and L. Schneider. "Un castrum des environs de l'an mil en Languedoc central: le Rocher des Vierges à Saint-Saturnin (Hérault)," *Archéologie du Midi médiévale* 6 (1988), 101-22.

Giuliato, G. "Les premiers châteaux dans les pays du sel en Lorraine (Xe-XIIe siècle)," *Château Gaillard* 16 (1994), 215-32.

Gomart, Charles. "La capucin de la tour de Ham," *La Picardie* 3 (1857), 450-52.

Grand, R. "L'architecture militaire en Bretagne jusqu'à Vauban," *Bulletin monumental* 109 (1951), 237-71, 357-88; 110 (1952), 7-49.

Grandjean, Marcel. "Le château de Vufflens (vers 1415-vers 1430): Notes sur sa construction, son ésthetique et sa valeur défensive," *Zeitschrift für schweizerische Archäologie und Kunstgeschichte* 52 (1995), 89-136.

Gregg, E.M. *Urban Finance and Defence Spending at Nantes during the Fifteenth Century.* Unpublished dissertation. New Haven: Yale University, 1977.

Hajdu, Robert. "Castles, Castellans, and the Structure of Politics in Poitou, 1152-1271, *Journal of Medieval History* 4 (1978), 27-53.

Harbaville, M. "Chateau de Bailleulmont en Artois," *La Picardie* 3 (1857), 433-38.

Harrison, Peter. "Church Fortifications in La Thiérache," *Fort* 22 (1994), 3-26.

Hayez, Anne-Marie. "Travaux à l'enceinte d'Avignon sous les pontificats d'Urbain V et de Grégoire XI." In: *La guerre et la paix: Frontières et violences au moyen âge*. Actes du 101e congrès national des sociétés savantes, Lille, 1976. Paris: Bibliothèque Nationale, 1978, pp. 193-223.

Héliot, Pierre. "L'âge du château de Carcassonne," *Annales du Midi* 78 (1966), 7-21.

Héliot, Pierre. "Boulogne-sur-Mer," *Congrès archéologique de France* 99 (1936), 349-71.

Héliot, Pierre. "Le Chateau-Gaillard et les fortresses des XIIe et XIIIe siècles," *Château Gaillard* 1 (1964), 53-75.

Héliot, Pierre. "Les châteaux-forts en France du Xe au XIIe siècle à la lumière de travaux récents," *Journal des savants*. (1966), 483-515.

Héliot, Pierre. "L'évolution des donjons dans le nord-ouest de la France et de l'Angleterre au XIIe siècle," *Bulletin archéologique du comité des travaux historiques et scientifiques* n.s. 5 (1969), 141-94.

Héliot, Pierre. "La genèse des châteaux de plan quadrangulaire en France et en Angleterre," *Bulletin de la société nationale des antiquaires de France* (1965), 238-57.

Héliot, Pierre. "Sur les résidences princières bâties en France du Xe et XIIe siècle," *Moyen âge* 61 (1955), 27-61, 231-317.

Higounet, C. "Bastiden und Grenzen." In: *Altständisches Bürgertum*. Ed. H. Stoob. Darmstadt, 1978, I:173-98.

Higounet, C. "Esquisse d'une géographie des châteaux des Pyrenées françaises." In: *I° congreso internacional de Pirineistas del Instituto de Estudios Pirenaicos*. Saragossa, 1950.

Hubert, J. "La frontière occidentale du comté de Champagne du XIe au XIIIe siècle." In: *Recueil de travaux offerts à M. Clovis Brunel*. Paris, 1955, II:14-29.

Jarousseau, Gérard. "Le guet, l'arrière-guet et la garde en Poitou pendant la guerre de Cent Ans," *Bulletin de la société des antiquaires de l'ouest* (1965), 159-202.

Jones, Michael. "The Defence of Medieval Brittany: A Survey of the Establishment of Fortified Towns, Castles and Frontiers from the Gallo-

Roman Period to the End of the Middle Ages," *Archaeological Journal* 138 (1981), 149-204.

Jones, Richard. "Les fortifications municipales de Lisieux dans les chroniques et dans les comptes (première moitié du XVe siècle)." In: *La guerre, la violence et les gens au Moyen Âge*. I: *Guerre et violence*. Ed. P. Contamine and O. Guyotjeannin. 119e congrès national des sociétés historiques et scientifiques, Amiens, octobre 1994, Section d'histoire médiévale et philologie. Paris, 1996, pp. 235-44.

Joubert, A. "Le château de Ramefort de Gennes et ses seigneurs aux XIVe et XVe siècles, d'apres des documents inédits," *Revue historique et archéologique du Maine* 22 (1887), 387-99.

Kiener, F. Le problème historique des châteaux forts en Alsace," *Revue d'Alsace* 88 (1948), 5-23.

La Borderie, Arthur le Moyne de. "Récueil de documents rélatifs aux monuments de l'architecture militaire du moyen-âge en Bretagne," *Bulletin archéologique de l'Association Bretonne* 12 (1893-94), 135-206.

Lardin, Philippe. "Le financement des fortifications dans les principales villes de Normandie (XIV-XV siècles)." In: *Les normands et le fisc: XXIXe congrès des sociétés historiques et archéologiques de Normandie, Elbeuf-sur-Seine, 20-23 octobre 1994, Bulletin de la société de l'histoire d'Elbeuf.* Special Bulletin (1996), 47-58.

Lartigaut, J. "Les lieux fortifiés dans la partie occidentale du Quercy au XVe siècle," *Annales du midi* 79 (1967), 5-18.

Le Cain, Bérengère and Dominique Pitte. "La casemate de la porte d'Arras à Rouen: une relecture," *Bulletin des amis des monuments rouennais* (1996), 85-94.

Lefranc, Guy and Francis Perreau. "Mottes et sites fortifiés médiévaux du Pas-de-Calais: Pour la constitution d'une documentation topographique," *Bulletin de la commission départementale d'histoire et d'archéologique du Pas-de-Calais* 12 (1989), 329-44.

Leguay, Jean-Pierre. *Un réseau urbain au moyen âge: les villes du duché de Bretagne aux XIVème et XVème siècles*. Paris: Maloine S.A, 1988.

Le Maho, Jacques. "L'apparition des seigneuries châtelaines dans le Grand-Caux à l'époque ducale," *Archéologie médiévale* 6 (1976), 5-148.

Le Maho, Jacques. "De la *curtis* au château: l'exemple du Pays de Caux," *Château Gaillard* 8 (1977), 171-83.

Le Maho, Jacques. "Genèse d'une fortification seigeuriale: Les fouilles de la motte de Mirville (Xie-XIIe siècles)," *Château Gaillard* 11 (1983), 183-91.

Lemoine, Astrid. "Chennebrun, un bourg castral au coeur des conflits Franco-Normands du XIIe siècle," *Annales de Normandie* 48 (1998), 525-44.

Le Pogam, Pierre-Yves. "Un chantier exmplaire: Le Palais Royal de Rouen," *Antiquités nationales* 23/24 (1991), 213-47.

Lorren, C. "La demeure seigneuriale de Rubercy," *Château Gaillard* 8 (1977), 185-92.

Louise, Gérard. "Châteaux et frontière seigneuriale au XIe siècle: l'exemple du Saosnois aux confins de la seigneurie de Bellême et du comté du Maine," *Château Gaillard* 14 (1990), 225-46.

Louise, Gérard. "Les maisons fortes du bocage Normand (XIIe-XVe siècles)." In: *La maison forte au moyen âge*. Ed. M. Bur. Paris, 1986, pp. 31-42.

Marcille, Catherine and Nicolas Faucherre. "La fouille des jardins du Carrousel à Paris: une contribution à la connaissance de l'enceinte dite de Charles V." In: *Military Studies in Medieval Europe: Papers of the "Medieval Europe Brugge 1997" Conference Volume 11*. Ed. Guy De Boe & Frans Verhaeghe. Zellik: Instituut voor het Archeologisch Patrimonium, 1997, pp. 155-65.

McKenzie, A. Dean. "French Medieval Castles in Gothic Manuscript Painting." In: *The Medieval Castle: Romance and Reality*. Ed. K. Reyerson and F. Powe. Dubuque, 1984, pp. 199-214.

Mersier, Albert. *Histoire et description du Chateau-fort de Ham détruit par les Allemands en 1917*. Caen: A. Olivier, 1921.

Mesqui, Jean. "Le château de Gisors aux XIIe et XIIIe siècles," *Archéologie médiévale* 20 (1990), 253-317.

Mesqui, Jean. *Châteaux et encientes de la France médiévale: De la défense à la résidence.* 2 vols. Paris, 1991.

Mesqui, Jean. "Châteaux et princes de la guerre de cent ans, 1350-1450." In: *Le château en France.* Ed. J.-P. Babelon. Paris, 1986, pp. 103-19.

Mesqui, Jean. *Châteaux forts et fortifications en France.* Paris, 1997.

Mesqui, Jean. "Les enceintes de Crécy-en-Brie et la fortification dans l'Ouest du comté de Champagne et de Brie au XIIIe siècle," *Mémoires publiés par la féderation des sociétés historiques de Paris et de l'Ile-de-France* 30 (1979), 7-86.

Mesqui, Jean. "La fortification dans le Valois du XIe au XVe siècle et le rôle de Louis d'Orléans," *Bulletin monumentale* 135 (1977), 109-49.

Mesqui, Jean. "Parements à bossage dans la fortification et le génie civil en France au moyen âge," *Château Gaillard* 13 (1987), 97-126.

Mesqui, Jean. *Provins: La fortification d'une ville au moyen âge.* Bibliothèque de la société Française d'archéologie, 11. Paris, 1979.

Mesqui, Jean and C. Ribéra-Pervillé. "Les châteaux de Louis d'Orléans et leurs architects (1391-1407)," *Bulletin monumental* 138 (1980), 293-345.

Metzler, Jeannot and John Zimmer. "Récentes recherches archéologiques au château de Vianden," *Château Gaillard* 12 (1985), 115-25.

Michaud-Fréjaville, Françoise. "Une cité face aux crises: les remparts de la fidélité, de Louis d'Orléans a Charles VII, d'après les comptes de forteresse de la ville d'Orléans (1391-1427)." In: *Jeanne d'Arc: une époque, une rayonment.* Colloque d'histoire médiévale. Orléans–Octobre 1979. Paris, 1982, pp. 43-57.

Michel, Robert. "La défense d'Avignon sous Urbain V et Grégoire XI," *Mélanges d'archéologie et d'histoire* 30 (1910), 129-45.

Michel, Robert. "Les défenseurs des châteaux et des villes fortes dans le Comtat Venaissin," *Bibliothèque de l'école de chartes* 75 (1915), 315-30.

Mortet, V. and Paul Deschamps. *Recueil des textes relatifs à l'histoire de l'architecture et à la condition des architectes en France au moyen âge*. 2 vols. Paris, 1911-29.

Mot, G.J. "L'arsenal et la parc de matériel à la cité de Carcassonne en 1298," *Annales du Midi* 68 (1956), 409-18.

Mouton, D. "L'edification des mottes castrales de Provence, un phénomène durable: Xe-XIIIe siècles," *Château Gaillard* 16 (1994), 309-20.

Mussat, André. "Le château de Vitré et l'architecture des châteaux bretons du XIVe au XVIe siècle," *Bulletin monumetal* 133 (1975), 131-64.

Mussat, André. "La singularité Bretonne." In: *Châteaux et sociétés du XIVe au XVIe siècle: Actes des premières rencontres internationales d'archéologie et d'histoire de Commarque*. Perigeux, 1986, pp. 119-30.

Mussat, André. "Tradition militaire et plaisance dans la seconde moitié du XVe siècle." In: *Le château en France*. Ed. J.-P. Babelon. Paris, 1986, pp. 121-32.

Mussot-Goulard, Renée. "Les foyers du site castrale de Luzan en Gascogne," *Château Gaillard* 13 (1987), 143-55.

Mussot-Goulard, Renée. "Le motte castrale de Luzan: premiers résultats," *Château Gaillard* 12 (1985), 199-209.

Ollivier, Gilles. "A propos du plan de Dinan à la fin du moyen âge." In: *Dinan au moyen âge*. Dinan, 1986, pp. 343-51.

Painter, Sidney. "Castellans of the Plain of Poitou in the Eleventh and Twelfth Centuries." *Speculum* 39 (1956), 243-57.

Patria, Ettore. "Ercole Negro di Sanfront Architetto ducale a Exilles: Osservazioni sull'articolo 'Les activités de l'ingenieur piémartais Ercole Negro en France (1566-1597)," *Armi antiche* (1973), 253-73.

Perroy, Edouard. "Les châteaux du Roannais du XIe au XIIIe siècle," *Cahiers de civilisation médiévale* 9 (1966), 13-27.

Pesez, Jean-Marie and Françoise Piponnier. "Les maisons-fortes bourguignonne," *Chateau Gaillard* 5 (1972), 143-64.

Pesez, Jean-Marie and Françoise Piponnier. "Villy-le-Moutier: Recherches archéologiques sur un site de maison-forte," *Château Gaillard* 6 (1973), 147-63.

Piboule, Patrick. "Nouvelles recherches sur le site de la Motte de la Chapelle à Doué-la-Fontaine," *Château Gaillard* 15 (1990), 263-76.

Piponnier, Françoise and Jean-Michel Poisson. "La tour d'Essertines," *Château Gaillard* 9-10 (1982), 527-42.

Pitte, Dominique and Bernard Gauthiez. *Le château de Philippe Auguste: Nouvelles recherches*. Rouen, n.d.

Poisson, Jean-Michel. "La bastide de Gironville (Fort-Sarrazin, Ambronay, Ain)," *Château Gaillard* 12 (1985), 225-36.

Poisson, Jean-Michel. "L'érection de châteaux dans la Sardaigne pisane (XIIIe siècle) et ses conséquences sur la réorganisation du réseau des habitats," *Château Gaillard* 14 (1990), 351-66.

Poisson, Jean-Michel. "Recherches archéologiques sur un site fossoyé du XIVe siècle: la bastide de Gironville ('Fort-Sarrazin', Ambronay, Ain)," *Château Gaillard* 12 (1984), 225-34.

Pous, Anny de. "L'architecture militaire occitane (IXe-XIVe siècles)," *Bulletin archéologique du comité des travaux historiques et scientifiques* n.s. 5 (1969), 41-139.

Pradalié, G. "Les tours médiévales des Pyrénées Garonnaises," *Château Gaillard* 14 (1990), 367-74.

Prarond, E. "Rambures," *La Picardie* 4 (1858), 299-307, 406-13, 451-57, 513-20, 563-68.

Prevel, L. "Le château de Blain: sa description, son histoire," *Annales de la Société Académique de Nantes et du Département de la Loire Inférieure* 40 (1869), 5-149.

Queney, Daniel. *Histoires d'un chateau: Promenade d'un "passe-muraille" et quelques anecdotes, suivies du catalogue de l'iconographie du Château de Dieppe, présentée en exposition du 20 November 1993 au 28 Février 1994*. Dieppe: Chateau-Musée de Dieppe, 1993.

"Règlement pour la défense du château de Bioule, 18 mars 1347," *Bulletin archéologique* 4 (1846-47), 490-95.

Renoux, Annie. "Le château des Comtes de Champagne à Montfélix (Chavot) et son impact sur l'environnement (Xe-XIIIe siècle)." In: *Military Studies in Medieval Europe: Papers of the "Medieval Europe Brugge 1997" Conference Volume 11*. Ed. Guy De Boe & Frans Verhaeghe. Zellik: Instituut voor het Archeologisch Patrimonium, 1997, pp. 119-30.

Renoux, Annie. *Fécamp du Palais Ducal au Palais de Dieu: Bilan historique et archéologique des recherches menées sur le site du château des ducs de Normandie*. Paris: Editions du Centre National de la Recherche Scientifique, 1990.

Renoux, Annie. "Recherches historiques et archéologiques sur le château du Fécamp, ancien palais des ducs de Normandie," *Château Gaillard* 7 (1975), 183-200.

Reynaud, J.-F., E. Faure, and B. Mandy. "Etude archéologique des chapelles castrales de St.-Germain-d'Ambérieu et de Gisors," *Château Gaillard* 6 (1973), 165-81.

Richard, Jean. "Le château dans la structure féodale de la France de l'Est au XIIème siècle." In: *Probleme des 12. Jahrhunderts*. Stuttgart, 1968, pp. 169-76.

Richard, Jean. "Châteaux, châtelains et vassaux en Bourgogne aux XIe et XIIe siècles," *Cahiers de civilisation médiévale* 3 (1960), 433-47.

Richard, Jean. "Quelques idées de François de Surienne sur la défense des villes à propos de la fortification de Dijon (1461)," *Annales de Bourgogne* 16 (1944), 36-43.

Rigaudiere, Albert. "Le financement des fortifications urbaines en France du milieu du XIVe siècle à la fin du XVe siècle," *Revue historique* 273 (1985), 19-95.

Ritter, Rudolf. *Châteaux, donjons et places fortes en France*. Strasbourg, 1953.

Robert, Elisabeth. "Guerre et fortification dans la *Philippide* de Guillaume le Breton: approches archéologiques." In: *Military Studies in Medieval Europe: Papers of the "Medieval Europe Brugge 1997" Conference Volume 11*. Ed. Guy De Boe & Frans Verhaeghe. Zellik: Instituut voor het Archeologisch Patrimonium, 1997, pp. 7-19.

Rocolle, Pierre. *2000 ans de fortification française.* 2 vols. Paris, 1973.

Rohan, A. de. *Le château de Josselin.* Rennes, 1985.

Role, Raymond E. "Aigues-Mortes: French Window to the Sea," *MHQ* 12 (Aut 1999), 50-57.

Rolland, Franck. "Un mur oublié: le rempart du XIIIe siècle à Avignon," *Archéologie médiévale* 19 (1989), 173-208.

Sailhan, Pierre. "Typologie des archères et canonnières: Les archères des châteaux de Chauvigny," *Bulletin de la société des antiquaires de l'Ouest et des musées de Poitiers*, 4th ser., 14 (1978), 511-41.

Salamagne, Alain. "Les années 1400: La genèse de l'architecture militaire bourguignonne ou la définition d'un nouvel espace urbain," *Revue Belge d'histoire militaire* 26 (1986), 325-44, 405-34.n

Salamagne, Alain. "Les fortifications médiévales de la ville du Quesnoy," *Revue du nord* 63 (1981), 997-1008.

Salamagne, Alain. "Pour une approche typologique de l'architecture militaire: l'example de la famile monumentale des tours-portes de plan curviligne," *Archéologie médiévale* 18 (1988), 179-213.

Salch, Charles-Laurent. *L'atlas des châteaux forts en France.* Strasbourg, 1980.

Salch, Charles-Laurent. *L'atlas des villes et villages fortifiés en France (moyen âge).* Strasbourg, 1978.

Salch, Charles-Laurent. *La clef des châteaux forts d'Alsace: Dictionairre architecture, guerre et vie quotidienne dans les châteaux forts.* Lichtenberg: Lettrimage, 1995.

Salch, Charles-Laurent. *Dictionnaire des châteaux de l'Alsace médiévale.* Strasbourg: Éditions Publitotal, 1976.

Salch, Charles-Laurent. *Dictionnaire des châteaux et des fortifications du moyen âge en France.* Strasbourg, 1979.

Salet, Francis. "Najac," *Congrès archéologique de France* 100 (1938), 170-202.

Sartre, Josiane. *Châteaux "brigue et pierre" en Picardie.* Paris, 1973.

Schaad, Daniel and Georges Soukiassian. "*Encraoustos*: un camp militaire romain à Lugdunum civitas Convenarum (Saint Bernard de Comminges)," *Acquitainia* 8 (1990), 99-120.

Scuvée, Frédéric. "Le château féodal de Saint Sauveur-le-Vicomte," *Heimdal* 22 (1976-77), 20-38.

Seillier, Claude. "Tours Romaines et médiévales de l'enceinte de Boulogne-sur-Mer," *Histoire et archéologie du Pas-de-Calais* 13/1 (1992), 73-78.

Seraphin, Gilles. "Les chapelles-porteries dans les châteaux romans." In: *Aux portes du chateau: Actes du troisième colloque de castellologie*. Paris, 1987, pp. 23-31.

Seydoux, Philippe. *Fortresses médiévales du nord de la France*. Bellegarde: Editions de la Morande, 1979.

Sochon, Serge. *Château Gaillard*. Condé-sur-Noireau: Éditions Charles Corlet, 1985.

Soulange-Bodin, Henry. *Les châteaux de Bourgogne*. Paris, 1942.

Taylor, Arnold J. "The Castle of St. Georges-d'Espéranche." In: *Studies in Castles and Castle Building*. London, 1985, pp. 29-43.

Teyssot, Josiane. "Les forteresses urbaines: les châteaux de Riom et de Montferrand en Auvergne aux XIV-XVe siècle," *Château Gaillard* 18 (1998), 231-38.

Tomkinson, John. "The Henrician Bastions of Guines Castle," *Fort* 26 (1998), 121-41.

Trabut-Cussac, J.-P. "Bastides ou forteresses?" *Moyen âge* (1954), 81-135.

Turrel, Claude. *Metz: Deux mille ans d'architecture militaire*. Metz: Editions Serpenoise, 1986.

Ubregts, W. "Quelques idées sur la castellologie Lotharingienne," *Château Gaillard* 8 (1977), 287-97.

Ubregts, William and Frans Doperé. "La chapelle castrale du château de Corroy au XIIIe siècle," *Château Gaillard* 17 (1996), 169-73.

Uwe, Albrecht. *Von der Burg zum Schloss: franzosische Schlossbaukunst im Spätmittelalter.* Worms: Wernerische Verlagsgessellschaft, 1986.

Vaivre, Jean-Bernard de. "Le château de Posanges," *Congrès archéologique de France* 144 (1986), 211-34.

Vale, M.G.A. "Seigneurial Fortification and Private War in Later Medieval Gascony." In: *Gentry and Lesser Nobility in Later Medieval Europe.* Ed. M. Jones. Gloucester, 1986, pp. 133-58.

Vallery-Radot, Jean. "Compte-rendu suivi d'une note sur l'enceinte quadrangulaire du donjon du château de Caen," *Bulletin monumentale* 121 (1963), 65-72.

Vallery-Radot, Jean. "Le donjon de Philippe-Auguste à Villeneuve-sur-Yvonne et son devis," *Château Gaillard* 2 (1964), 106-12.

Vallery-Radot, Jean. "Loches," *Congrès archéologique de France* 106 (1949), 111-25.

Vallery-Radot, Jean. "La tour blanche d'Issoudun (Indre)," *Château Gaillard* 1 (1964), 149-60

Vannier, Daniel. *Beaugency.* Beaugency: n.p., 1991.

Vedrès, G. *Châteaux de Bourgogne.* Paris, 1948.

Villele, Captaine de. "Aspect militaire de la vie d'une petite cité médiévale: La défense de Belfort à la fin du Moyen âge," *Revue historique des armées* 28 (1972), 7-20.

Viollet-le-Duc, Eugène Emmanuel. *Dictionnaire raisonné de l'architecture Française du XIe au XVIe siècle.* 8 vols. Paris: Bance, 1858-75.

Whiteley, Mary. "Les pieces privées de l'appartement du roi au château de Vincennes," *Bulletin monumental* 148 (1990), 83-85.

Will, R. "L'architecture des châteaux alsaciens du moyen âge: Essai de classification," *Revue d'Alsace* 100 (1961), 110-19.

Willsdorf, C. "L'apparition des châteaux alsaciens en Haute Alsace d'après les textes (1000-1200)." In: *Actes du CIe Congrès national des sociétés savantes, Lille 1976, Archéologie et histoire de l'art.* Paris, 1978, pp. 61-76.

Wimet, Pierre-André. "Restauration du château de Boulogne au XVe siècle," *Bulletin de la commission départementale d'histoire et d'archéologique du Pas-de-Calais* 12 (1988), 253-58.

Wirth, J. *Les châteaux forts alsaciens du XIIe au XIVe siècle: Etude architecturale*. I: *XIIe et première moitié du XIIIe siècle*. Strasbourg, 1975.

Wolfe, Michael. "Building a Bastion in Early Modern History," *Proceedings of the Western Society for French History* 25 (1998), 36-48.

Wright, Nicholas A.R. "The Fortified Church at Chitry," *Fort* 19 (1991), 5-10.

Yver, J. "Les châteaux-forts en Normandie jusqu'au milieu du XIIe siècle: contribution à l'étude du pouvoir ducal," *Bulletin de la société antiquaires de Normandie* 53 (1955-56), 28–115.

Military Technology – Premodern – Fortifications – Germany and Switzerland

Arnold, Susanne. "Anlage und Ausbau der Landesfestung Schorndorf (Rems-Murr-Kreis) im 16. Jahrhundert," *Château Gaillard* 16 (1994), 7-10.

Arnold, Susanne. "Befunde von Brückenkonstruktionen aus Holz zn zwei mittelalterlichen Burgställen in Nordwürttemberg," *Château Gaillard* 18 (1998), 7-11.

Atkinson, Catherine. *Celle–Eine Wehrhafte stadt: Ausgrabung an der ehemaligen Stadbefestigung vor dem Hintergrund der frühneuzeitlichen Festungsgeschichte*. Celle: Bormann-Museum, 1989.

Aujourd'hui, Rolf d'. "Die Basler Stadtbefestigung im Hochmittelalter: Neüe archäologische Befunde," *Château Gaillard* 12 (1985), 179-84.

Baraville, R. *Burgen und Schlösser der Steiermark*. Graz, 1961.

Bechthold, André and Alfons Zettler. "Burgen am Oberrhein," *Château Gaillard* 17 (1996), 39-44.

Bechthold, André and Alfons Zettler. "Gelnhausen: eine Großbaustelle Friedrich Barbarossas," *Château Gaillard* 18 (1998), 13-22.

Bill, J. "Archäologische Spuren der willentlichen Zerstörung von Luzerner Städten und Burgen im Mittelalter," *Château Gaillard* 16 (1994), 45-55.

Bill, J. and J. Manser. "Die ehemaligne Richstätte des Standes Luzern in Emmen, 1562-1789 und der dazugehörige Wasenplatz," *Château Gaillard* 14 (1990), 29-46.

Biller, T. "Mörsberg/Morimont im Sundgau: Das Ende des Burgenbaues zwischen Symbolik und Funktion," *Château Gaillard* 15 (1992), 33-44.

Binding, Günther. "Burg Broich in Mülheim an der Ruhr," *Château Gaillard* 4 (1969), 31-44.

Binding, Günther. "Holzankerbalken im Mauerwerk mittelalterlicher Burgen," *Château Gaillard* 8 (1977), 69-77.

Blondel, L. *Châteaux de l'ancien diocèse de Genèva.* Geneva, 1956.

Bohnsack, D. "Das Fundament eines steinernen Rundturmes des 11. Jahrhunderts in der Hamburger Altstadt," *Château Gaillard* 2 (1967), 1-6.

Borger, H. "Archäologische Untersuchungen in rheinischen Stadtkernen," *Château Gaillard* 2 (1967), 7-18.

Bruhns, L. *Hohenstaufenschlösser in Deutschland und Italien.* Königstein in Taunus, 1959.

Burg Forchtenstein. Forchtestein: Verwaltung der Burg Forchenstein, 1963.

Büttner, H. "Zur Burgenbauordnung Heinrichs I," *Blätter für deutsche Landesgeschichte* 92 (1956), 1-17.

Eltis, David. "Towns and Defence in Later Medieval Germany," *Nottingham Medieval Studies* 33 (1989), 91-103.

Ericsson, Ingolf. "Befestige Adelssitze am Sehlendorfer Binnensee, Holstein," *Château Gaillard* 11 (1983), 129-37.

Ewald, J. "Die St. Arbogast-Kirche in Muttenz bei Basel," *Château Gaillard* 8 (1977), 103-20.

Fabini, Hermann. "Kirchenburgen in Siebenbürgen, ein Netzwerk gegen aussere Bedrohung und zur Erhaltung der eigenen Identität," *IBI Bulletin* 47 (1990-91), 113-16.

Fehring, Günter P. "Die Alte Burg oberhalb der frühmittelalterlichen Kirchenfamilie zu Unterregenbach," *Château Gaillard* 6 (1973), 69-81.

Fehring, Günter P. "Burg und Klosterkirche Grosskomburg im Mittelalter: Ergebnisse der Grabungen, 1965-1971," *Château Gaillard* 15 (1990), 161-69.

Fehring, Günter P. "Grabungen in Siedlungsbereichen des 3. bis 13. Jahrhunderts sowie an Töpferöfen der Wüstung Wülfinger am Kocher," *Château Gaillard* 3 (1969), 48-60.

Fehring, Günter P. "Kirchenlagen und ein Herrensitz des frühen und hohen Mittelalters in Unterregenbach," *Château Gaillard* 2 (1967), 49-61.

Fehring, Günter P. "Slawische und frühdeutsche Wehranlagen in Bereich des Lübeckers Beckens," *Château Gaillard* 9-10 (1982), 83-99.

Feldkamp, Heinz. *Die Schwanenburg zu Kleve*. Cleves: Freinde der Schwanenburg, 1994.

Fischer, H. *Burgbezirk und Stadtgebiet in deutschen Süden*. Vienna and Munich, 1956.

Fock, H. "Le château fort de Burg-Reuland," *Château Gaillard* 17 (1996), 91-92.

Friedrich, R. and K.-F. Rittershofer. "Die hochmittelalterliche Motte und Niederungsburg von Oberursel-Bommersheim, Hochtanuskreis–Ausgrabungen 1988 bis 1993," *Château Gaillard* 17 (1996), 93-110.

Genoux, A. *Les remparts de Fribourg au moyen âge*. Fribourg, 1960.

Gerlach, Stefan. "Die kleinen Befestigungsanlagen des Mittelalters in Unterfranken," *Château Gaillard* 12 (1985), 143-49.

Grimm, P. *Der Vor- und Frühgeschichtlicher Burgwälle der Bezirke Halle und Magdeburg*. Berlin, 1958.

Gringmuth-Dallmer, E. "Deutsche und slawische Burgen in einem Grenzraum beiderseits der Mittelelbe (Altmark und Elbe-Havel-Gebiet)," *Château Gaillard* 17 (1996), 111-17.

Großmann, G.U. "Neue Forschungen zum Schloßbau des 16. Jahrhunderts im Weserraum," *Château Gaillard* 16 (1994), 241-47.

Haase, C. "Die mittelalterliche Stadt als Festung." In: *Die Stadt des Mittelalters*. I: *Begriff, Entstehung und Ausbreitung*. Ed. C. Haase. Darmstadt, 1969, pp. 377-407.

Heiligman, Jorg. *Der 'Alb-Limes': Ein Beitrag zur romischen Besetzungsgeschichte Südwestdeustchlands*. Stuttgart: Theiss, 1990.

Heine, Hans-Wilhelm. "Zu Burgen der Salierzeit in Niedersachsen," *Château Gaillard* 15 (1990), 189-204.

Heine, Hans-Wilhelm. "Ergebnisse und Probleme einer systematischen Aufnahme und Bearbeitung mittelalterlicher Wehranlagen," *Château Gaillard* 8 (1977), 121-34.

Heine, Hans-Wilhelm. "Grabungen am Klusberg bei Volksen (Einbeck, Ldkr Nordheim) zur Erschliessung einer frühbis hochmittelalterlichen Befestigung," *Archäologisches Korrespondenzblatt* 18.4 (1989), 397-405.

Heine, Hans-Wilhelm. "Die 'Posteburg' bei Schmarrie, Landkreis Schaumburg," *Château Gaillard* 18 (1998), 103-08.

Heine, Hans-Wilhelm. "Ringwall und Burg zwischen Mittelweser und Leine," *Château Gaillard* 11 (1983), 139-51.

Hejna, A. "Zu den Anfängen der Fürsten- und Herrensitze in Böhmen," *Château Gaillard* 4 (1969), 137-38.

Helmig, Guido. "Basel–Etappen der Befestigung einer Stadt." In: *Military Studies in Medieval Europe: Papers of the "Medieval Europe Brugge 1997" Conference Volume 11*. Ed. Guy De Boe & Frans Verhaeghe. Zellik: Instituut voor het Archeologisch Patrimonium, 1997, pp. 173-86.

Henning, Joachim. "Ringwallburgen und Reiterkrieger: Zum Wandel der Militärstrategie im ostsächsisch-slawischen Raum an der Wende vom 9. zum 10. Jahrhundert." In: *Military Studies in Medieval Europe: Papers of the "Medieval Europe Brugge 1997" Conference Volume 11*. Ed. Guy De Boe & Frans Verhaeghe. Zellik: Instituut voor het Archeologisch Patrimonium, 1997, pp. 21-31.

Hering, E. *Befestige Dörfer in südwestdeutschen Landschaften (mit besonderer Berückstigung des Rhein-Main Gebietes) und ihre Bedeutung für die Siedlungsgeographie*. Frankfurt, 1934.

Herrnbrodt, Adolf. "Die Ausgrabung der Motte Burg Meer in Büderich bei Düsseldorf," *Château Gaillard* 2 (1967), 49-61.

Herrnbrodt, Adolf. "Die Hardtburg bei Stotzheim, Landkreis Euskirchen," *Château Gaillard* 4 (1969), 139-56.

Hinz, Hermann. "Burgenlandschaften und Siedlungskunde," *Château Gaillard* 5 (1972), 55-83.

Högl, Lukas. "Die Grottenburg von Malvaglia," *Château Gaillard* 9-10 (1982), 175-86.

Hotz, Walter. *Pfalzen und Burgen der Stauferzeit. Geschichte und Gestalt.* Darmstadt: Wissenschaftliche Buchgesellschaft, 1981.

Jacobi, Louis. *Das Kastell Heftrich.* Frankfurt: Tanusklub Stammklub e Verlag, 1990.

Janssen, Brigitte and Walter Janssen. *Burgen, Schlösser und Hofesten in Kreis Neuss.* 3rd ed. Neuss, 1997.

Janssen, Walter. "Ausgrabungen auf dem Burgberg von Castell östlich von Würzburg und die Entstehung der frühen Adelsburg im Mainfranken," *Château Gaillard* 16 (1994), 261-75.

Janssen, Walter. "Burg und Siedlung als Probleme der Rheinischen Wüstungsforschung," *Château Gaillard* 3 (1969), 77-89.

Janssen, Walter. "Die Tomburg bei Rheinbach, Landkreis Bonn," *Château Gaillard* 4 (1969), 163-78.

Kempke, T., H.H. Andersen, W. Groenman-van Wateringe, and W. Erdmann. "Forschungsprobleme um den slawischen Burgwall Alt Lübeck 11," *Lübecker Schriften zur Archäologie und Kulturgeschichte* 13 (1988), 9-166.

Klebel, E. *Mittelalterliche Burgen und ihr Recht.* Vienna, 1953.

Klemm, Bernard. "Die Aufgabe Rekonstruktion Historischer Hallenhauser in der Alstadt con Gorlitz," *IBI Bulletin* 47 (1990-91), 11-18.

Klemm, Bernard. "Burgen und Burgwarde längs der Elbe in der Mark Meisen," *IBI Bulletin* 47 (1990-91), 85-90.

Koch, K.-H. "Existierte ein eisenzeitliches Befestigungssystem im Gebiet der Treverer?" *Archäologisches Korrespondenzblatt* 18.2 (1988), 169-82.

Kortüm, K. "Ein archäologischer Aufschluss im Kastellvicus von Jagsthausen, Kreis Heilbronn," *Fundberichte au Baden-Wurttemberg* 13 (1988), 325-49.

Kramer, D. "Frühe Burgen zwischen Mur und Lafnitz: Ein archäologisch-historischer Vorbericht über die Entwicklung des Burgenbaues in der Oststeiermark," *Château Gaillard* 15 (1990), 217-29.

Kunstmann, H. *Mensch und Burg: Burgenkundliche Betrachtungen an Ostfränkischen Wehrlangen.* Wurzburg, 1967.

Lemmens, Gerard. *Die Schwanenburg Kleve.* Munich: Deutschen Kunstverlag, 1990.

Lutë, Dietrich. "Grabungen in der Burg der Bischöfe von Speyer in Bruchsal, Landkreis Karlsruhe," *Château Gaillard* 11 (1983), 207-18.

Lutz, Dietrich. "Zur Geschichte des Kreises Schwäbisch Hall," *Château Gaillard* 15 (1990), 231-46.

Lutz, Dietrich. "Neue Ergebnisse der Grabungen in der Ruine Mandelberg bei Pfalzgrafenweiler im Nordschwarzwald, verbunden mit dem Versuch der landesgeschichtlichen Einordnung," *Château Gaillard* 14 (1990), 247-60.

Lutz, Dietrich. "Die Ruine Mandelberg bei Bösingen im Nordlichen Schwarzwald," *Château Gaillard* 12 (1985), 127-41.

Lutz, Dietrich. "Die Wasserburg Eschelbronn bei Heidelberg," *Château Gaillard* 8 (1977), 193-222.

Meckseper, Carl. "Die Bergfriede von Besigheim und Reichenberg," *Château Gaillard* 9-10 (1982), 199-212.

Meyer, Werner. "Die 'Alte Schloss' von Bümpliz: ein mittelalterlicher Adelssitz," *Château Gaillard* 7 (1975), 159-72.

Meyer, Werner. "Zur Auflassung der Burgen in der spätmittelalterlichen Schweiz," *Château Gaillard* 12 (1985), 11-21.

Meyer, Werner. "Burg, Stadt, Residenz und Territorium," *Château Gaillard* 15 (1990), 247-52.

Meyer, Werner. "Burgengründungen: Die Suche nach dem Standort," *Château Gaillard* 18 (1998), 123-34.

Meyer, Werner. "Grenzbildung und Burgenbau," *Château Gaillard* 17 (1996), 135-45.

Meyer, Werner. "Höchalpine Wüstungen in der Schweiz," *Château Gaillard* 9-10 (1982), 483-95.

Meyer, Werner. "Die Holzbauten auf der Frohburg," *Château Gaillard* 8 (1977), 247-68.

Meyer, Werner. *Der mittelalterliche Adel und sein Burgen im ehemaliger Fürstbistum Basel.* Basel, 1962.

Meyer, Werner. "Die mittelalterliche Burg als Wirtschaftszentrum," *Château Gaillard* 13 (1987), 127-42.

Meyer, Werner. "'Salbüel': Eine hochmittelalterliche Holzburg im Kanton Luzern/Schweiz," *Château Gaillard* 11 (1983), 233-41.

Møller, E. "Der Turm von Ribe," *Château Gaillard* 4 (1969), 179-83.

Mruzek, H.J. *Gesalt und Entwicklung der feudalen Eigenbefestigung im Mittelalter.* Berlin, 1973.

Nelson, W.A. "Bellinzona," *Fortress* 12 (Feb 1992), 43-50.

Neumann, E.G. "Burg Altendorf Ruhr: Grabungen, Bauuntersuchungen und vorläufiges Ergebnis," *Chateau Gaillard* 5 (1972), 133-41.

Neumann, E.G. "Wohtürme und Motten zwischen Lippe und Ruhr," *Château Gaillard* 6 (1973), 137-45.

Neumann, Hartwig. *Zitadelle Jülich.* 2nd ed. Jülich, 1977.

Neumann, Hartwig. "The Study of Fortifications in Germany," trans. Anthony Kemp, *Fort* 3 (Spr 1977; Rev. ed., 1993), 35-51.

Nuber, A.H. "DieGrabung auf dem Marktplatz von Heilbronn," *Château Gaillard* 2 (1967), 73-78.

Orbrecht, J. "Der Hexenturm von Sarnen Erebnisse einer Bauuntersuchung," *Château Gaillard* 14 (1990), 321-40.

Orbrecht, J. "Die Rekonstruktion des Obergadens auf dem Doerfliturm von Silenen im Kanton Uri," *Château Gaillard* 15 (1990), 253-62.

Patze, H., ed. *Die Burgen im deutschen Sprachraum: Ihre Rechte- und Verfassungsgeschichtliche Bedeutung.* 2 vols. Sigmaringen, 1976.

Piepers, W. "Einzelfragen zur Burgenforschung," *Château Gaillard* 2 (1967), 79-86.

Probszt-Ohstorff, Gunther. "Die militarische Bedeutung des Grazer Schlossberger," *Revue internationale d'histoire militaire* 14 (1955), 147-60.

Rothe, H.W. *Burgen und Schlösser in Thüringen.* Frankfurt, 1960.

Sarnowski, Tadeusz. "Zur Statuenausstattung romischer Stabsgebaude: neue Funde aus den Principia des Legionslagers Novae," *Bonner Jahrbücher* 189 (1989), 97-102.

Sayn-Wittgenstein, F., Prinz zu. *Reichstädte.* Munich, 1965.

Schafer, H. "Burg Amlishagen: Vorbericht über archaeologische Untersuchungen, 1984-1986," *Château Gaillard* 13 (1987), 175-88.

Schmid, Beate. "Die Ruine Landskron in Oppenheim am Rhein," *Château Gaillard* 18 (1998), 207-09.

Schmidt-Thomé, P. "Grenzbefestigungen und Linienverschanzungen im südlichen Oberrheingebiet," *Château Gaillard* 17 (1996), 157-63.

Schmidt-Thomé, P. "Eine Grottenburg am Isteiner Klotz," *Château Gaillard* 13 (1987), 189-201.

Schmidt-Thomé, P. "Die Stadtbefestigung von Freiburg im Breisgau zum Ende der Zähringerzeit: Neue archäologische Befunde," *Château Gaillard* 14 (1990), 375-92.

Schneider, A. "Burgen und Befestigungsanlagen des Mittelalters in Bodenseekreis: Eine Bestamdsaufnahme," *Fundserichte am Baden Wurthemberg* 14 (1989), 515-668.

Schnurbein, Seigmar von. "Der neue Plan des valentinischen Kastells Alta Ripa (Altrip)," *Bericht der Römisch-Germanischen Kommission* 70 (1989), 507-26.

Schock-Werner, Barbara. "Die Burg Kaiser Karls IV. in Lauf: Residenz eines geplanten neuen Territoriums?" *Bohemia* 39 (1998), 253-64.

Scholkmann, B. "Ein neu entdecker Sitz der Pfalzgrafen von Tübingen: Ergebnisse zur vorklosterzeitlichen Besiedlung am Platz des Ehemaligen Zisterzienserklosters Bebenhausen: Ein Vorbericht," *Château Gaillard* 15 (1990), 295-317.

Schönberger, Hans, Heinz-Jürgen Köhler, and Hans-Günther Simon. "Neue Ergebnisse zur Geschichte des Kastells Oberstimm," *Bericht der Römisch-Germanischen Kommission* 70 (1989), 243-319.

Seberich, F. *Die Stadtbefestigung Würzburgs.* 2 vols. Wurzburg, 1962-63.

Sieber, H. *Schlösser und Herrensitze in Mecklenburg.* Frankfurt, 1960.

Sölter, W. "Archäologische Ausgrabungen in der ehemaligen Stiftskirche St. Chrysanthus und Daria zu Münstereifel," *Château Gaillard* 2 (1967), 87-93.

Sommer, C.S. "Kastellvicus und Kastell: Untersuchungen zum Zumantel im Taunus und zu den Kastellvici in Obergermanien und Rätien," *Fundberichte au Baden-Wurttemberg* 13 (1988), 457-711.

Tauber, Julius. "Die Burguine Riedfluh: Wirtschaftsgeschichtliche Aspekte," *Château Gaillard* 13 (1987), 239-51.

Tauber, Julius. "Die Oedenburg," *Château Gaillard* 9-10 (1982), 547-56.

Tillmann, C. *Lexikon der deutschen Burgen und Schlösser.* 4 vols. Stuttgart, 1958-61.

Troll, Thaddäus. *Burgen un Deutschland.* Kunzelsau: Sigloch Edition, 1979.

van de Walle, A.L.J. "Über die besondere Problematik und Methode der mittelalterlichen Hausbauforschung in Städten," *Château Gaillard* 2 (1967), 113-19.

Waescher, H. *Feudalburgen in den Bezirken Halle und Magdeburg*. 2 vols. Berlin, 1962.

Weber, G. "Neus zur Befestigung des Oppidums Tarodunum, Gde. Kirchzarten, Kreis Breisgau Hochschwarzwald," *Fundserichte am Baden Wurthemberg* 14 (1989), 14 (1989), 273-88.

Wuelfing, O.E. *Burgen der Hohenstaufen in der Pfalz und im Elsass*. Dusseldorf, 1958.

Wuelfing, O.E. *Burgen der Hohenstaufen in Schwaben, Franken und Essen*. Dusseldorf, 1960.

Zettler, Alfons. "Die Burgen im mittelalterlichen Breisgau," *Château Gaillard* 16 (1994), 355-63.

Zeune, Joachim. "Castellology in Bavaria," *Fortress* 5 (May 1990), 27-34.

Military Technology – Premodern – Fortifications – Italy

Agnello, G. "L'archittetura militare e religiosa dell'età sveva," *Archivio storico Pugliese* 13 (1960), 146-76.

Agnello, G. "L'archittetura religiosa, militare e civile dell'età normanna," *Archivio storico Pugliese* 12 (1959), 159-96.

Agnello, G. *L'archittetura sveva in Sicilia*. Rome, 1935.

Amoretti, Guido. "La citadella di Torino," *Armi antiche* 8 (1961), 45-66.

Amoretti, Guido. "Torino nel suo sviluppo dalla città romana alla piazzaforte militare settecentesca," *Armi antiche* (1967), 151-78.

Andrews, D. "Richerche archeologiche nel castello di Montereale Valcellina (Pordenone): Campagne di scavo del 1983, 1984, 198, 1986," *Archeologia medievale* 14 (1987), 89-156.

Arslan, E.A. et al. "Scavi di Monte Barro, commune di Galbiate, Como, 1986-87," *Archeologia medievale* 15 (1988), 177-252.

Bedini, E., A.P. Bianchimani, F. Redi, and P. Volante. "Santa Maria a Monte (Pisa): rapporto preliminare, 1985-86," *Archeologia medievale* 14 (1987), 319-38.

Bruhns, L. *Hohenstaufenschlösser in Deutschland und Italien*. Königstein in Taunus, 1959.

Bury, John. "Benedetto da Ravenna (c.1485-1556)," *Fort* 22 (1994), 27-38.

Caruso, Enrico. "Il castello normanno-suevo di Salemi (TP)," *Mélanges de l'école Française de Rome: Moyen âge* 110 (1998), 665-90.

Cherasco, Maria Carla Visconti. "Le château de Carrù," *IBI Bulletin* 47 (1990-91), 35-38.

Chiesa, Françoise. "Les donjons Normands d'Italie: une comparison," *Mélanges de l'écoie françaises de Rome: Moyen âge* 110 (1998), 317-39.

Christie, Neil and A. Rushworth. "Urban Fortification and Defensive Strategy in Fifth and Sixth Century Italy: The Case of Terracina," *Journal of Roman Archaeology* 1 (1988), 73-88.

Ciampoltrini, G. and P. Notini. "Montecatino (Val Freddana, co. Lucca): scavi 1986 nell'area del castello: Notizia prelminare," *Archeologia medievale* 14 (1987), 255-66.

Coates-Stephens, Robert. "The Walls and Aqueducts of Rome in the Early Middle Ages, A.D. 500-1000," *Journal of Roman Studies* 88 (1998), 166-78.

Conti, P.M. "Limiti urbani ed organizzazione defensiva nell' Italia tardo antica e alto medioevale." In: *Studi in onore Eugenio Dupré Theseider*. Rome, 1974, II:561-72.

Corretti, Alessandro. "Il palazzo fortificato di Entella," *Mélanges de l'école Française de Rome: Moyen âge* 110 (1998), 591-606.

Covini, Maria Nadia. "Castelli, fortificazioni e difesa locale: Le strutture difensive degli stati regionali nell'italia centro-settentrionale fra XIV e XV secolo." In: *Castrum 3: Guerre, fortification et habitant dans le monde méditerranéen au moyen âge*. Ed. A. Bazzana. Rome, 1988, pp. 135-41.

Cusin, F. "Per la storia del castello medioevale." *Rivista storico Italiana* (1939), 491-542.

Dechert, M.S.A. "The Military Architecture of Francesco di Giorgio in Southern Italy," *Journal of the Society of Architectural Historians* 49.2 (1990), 83-85.

De Rossi, G.M. *Torri e castelli medievali della campagna romana*. Rome, 1969.

Di Liberto, Rosa. "Il castello di Calatubo: Genesi e caratteri di un inedito impianto fortificato siciliano fra l'XI ed il XII secolo," *Mélanges de l'école Française de Rome: Moyen âge* 110 (1998), 607-63.

English, Edward D. "Urban Castles in Medieval Siena: The Sources and Images of Power." In: *The Medieval Castle: Romance and Reality*. Ed. K. Reyerson and F. Powe. Dubuque, 1984, pp. 175-98.

Fiecconi, A. "Luoghi fortificati e strutture edilizie nel Fabrianese nei secoli XI-XIII," *Nuovo rivisti storica* 59 (1975), 1-54.

Fiorilla, Salvina. "Gela medievale: territorio, città e fortificazioni; popolazione, economia e scambi commerciali," *Sicilia archeologica* 29 (1996), 167-80.

Flambard-Héricher, Anne-Marie. "Un instrument de la conquête et du pouvoir: Les châteaux normands de Calabre. L'exempple de Scribla." In: *Les Normands en Méditerranée dans le sillage des Tancréde*. Ed. P. Boulet and F. Neveux. Caen, 1994, pp. 89-109.

Flambard-Héricher, Anne-Marie. "Les réserves alimentaires du château de Scibla au XVe siècle et les pratiques culturales dans la vallée du Crati (Calabre, Italie)," *Archéologie médiévale* 23 (1993), 269-85.

Forti, Carlo L. "Le fortificazioni a Genova," *La Casana* 3 (1976), 22-29.

Francovich, Riccardo and Marco Milanese, ed. "Ko scavo archeologico di Montarrenti e i problemi dell'incastellamento medievale: experienze a confronto: atti del colloquio internazionale," *Archeologia medievale* 16 (1989), 9-288.

Guicciardini, P. "Castelli e rocche della Toscana," *Emporium* 20 (1917).

Guidi, G.Guidoni. "Notizie preliminari su alcuni ritrovamenti effetuati a Firenzie: Piazza della Liberta, N Viale S Lavagini: la Fortezza da Basso," *Ul archaeol medievale* 15 (1988), 407-15.

Hahn, H. *Hohenstaufen Burgen in Süditalien*. Ingelheim, 1961.

Hale, John R. "The Argument of Some Military Title Pages of the Renaissance." In: *Renaissance War Studies*. London, 1983, pp. 211-24.

Hale, John R. "The Early Development of the Bastion: An Italian Chronology." In: *Europe in the Late Middle Ages*. Ed. J.R. Hale. Evanston, Ill., 1965, pp. 466-94; in: *Renaissance War Studies*. London, 1983, pp. 1-30.

Hale, John R. "The End of Florentine Liberty: the Fortezza da Basso." In: *Renaissance War Studies*. London, 1983, pp. 31-62.

Hale, John R. "The First Fifty Years of a Venetian Magistry: The *Provveditori alle Fortezze*." In: *Renaissance War Studies*. London, 1983, pp. 159-88.

Hale, John R. "Francesco Tensini and the Fortification of Vicenza." In: *Renaissance War Studies*. London, 1983, pp. 99-158.

Hale, John R. *Renaissance Fortification: Art or Engineering?* London, 1977.

Hale, John R. "To Fortify or Not to Fortify? Machiavelli's Contribution to a Renaissance Debate." In: *Renaissance War Studies*. London, 1983, pp. 189-210.

Haseloff, A. *Die Bauten der Hohenstaufen in Unter-italien*. 5 vols. Leipzig, 1912-26.

Hook, Judith. "Fortifications and the End of the Sienese State," *History* 62 (1977), 372-87.

Houben, Hubert. "Il castello di Brindisi nell'età di Federico II e di Carlo I d'Angiò," *Archivio storico Pugliese* 50 (1997), 69-88.

Knaak, Alexander. "Das Kasell von Augusta–Neue baugeschichtliche Erkenntnisse." In: *Military Studies in Medieval Europe: Papers of the "Medieval Europe Brugge 1997" Conference Volume 11*. Ed. Guy De Boe & Frans Verhaeghe. Zellik: Instituut voor het Archeologisch Patrimonium, 1997, pp. 107-18.

La Croix, Horst de. "The Literature on Fortification in Renaissance Italy," *Technology and Culture* 4 (1963), 30-50.

Lamberini, Daniela. "The Military Architecture of Giovanni Battista Belluzzi," *Fort* 14 (1986), 5-16.

Law, John E. "The Cittadella of Verona." In: *War, Culture and Society in Renaissance Venice: Essays in Honour of John Hale*. Ed. D.S. Chambers, C.H. Clough and M.E. Mallett. London, 1993, pp. 9-27.

Lawrence, A.W. "Early Medieval Fortifications Near Rome," *Papers of the British School at Rome* n.s. 19 (1964), 89-122.

Lesnes, Élisabeth. "Châteaux du XIVe siècle en Sicile occidentale: Typologie, influences," *Mélanges de l'école Française de Rome: Moyen âge* 110 (1998), 701-18.

Liusi, Riccardo. "Du château-fort à la fortresse: une brève histoire de l'architecture militaire italienne du XIe au XVIe siècle," *Médiévales* 26 (1994), 103-121.

Lo Cascio, P. and Ferdinando Maurici. "Pizzo Mirabella (Palermo): un insediamento militare di età sveva," *Sicilia archeologica* 27 (1994), 93-107.

Lopez, Guido, Aurora Scotti Tosini, Laura Mattoli Rossi. *The Sforza Castle, Milan*. Milan: Electa, 1986.

Marchesi, Pietro. *Fortezze Veneziana, 1508-1797*. Milan: Rusconi Immagini, 1984.

Martegani, Arnaldo. "Strade Romane e castelli in Brianza," *Revista archaeologica dell'antica provincia e diacesi di Como* 171 (1989), 317-28.

Martin, Jean-Marie and Ghislaine Noyé. "Guerre, fortifications et habitants en Italie méridionale du Ve au Xe siècle." In: *Castrum 3: Guerre, fortification et habitant dans le monde méditerranéen au moyen âge*. Ed. André Bazzana. Rome: L'école Française de Rome, 1988, pp. 225-36.

Maurici, Ferdinando. "Il Castel Maniace di Siracusa: Nuova ipotesi di interpretazione di un monumento svevo," *Mélanges de l'école Française de Rome: Moyen âge* 110 (1998), 691-700.

Maurici, Ferdinando. "Il castello di Roccella," *Sicilia archeologica* 27 (1994), 49-75.

Mauro, Maurizio. *Castelli rocche torri cinte fortificate della Marche.* Ravenna: Istituto Italiano Dei Castelli, 1992.

Molinari, Alessandra. "Tipologia, caratteri costruttivi e committenza dei castelli siciliani tra musulmani, Normanni e Suevi: Il caso di Segesta/Calata-barbaro nella Sicilia occidentale (secc. XII-XIII)," *Mélanges de l'école Française de Rome: Moyen âge* 110 (1998), 577-89.

Noyé, Ghislaine. "Le château de Scribla et les fortifications normandes du bessin de Crati." In: *Societa potere e populo nel'età de Ruggero II (III Giornate normanno-suevi, Bari 1977).* Rome, 1979.

Parrott, David A. "The Utility of Fortifications in Early Modern Europe: Italian Princes and their Citadels, 1540-1640," *War in History* 7 (2000), 127-53.

Pepper, Simon. "Castles and Cannon in the Naples Campaign of 1494-95." In: *The French Descent into Renaissance Italy, 1494-95: Antecedents and Effects.* Ed. D. Abulafia. Aldershot: Ashgate, 1995, pp. 263-93.

Pepper, Simon. "Italian Renaissance Fortifications: A Bibliographical Note," *Fort* 1 (1976; Rev. ed., 1993), 29-31.

Pepper, Simon and Nicholas Adams. *Firearms and Fortifications: Military Architecture and Siege Warfare in Sixteenth-Century Siena.* Chicago: University of Chicago Press, 1986.

Pepper, Simon and Quentin Hughes. "Fortifications in Late 15th Century Italy: The Treatise of Francesco di Giorgi Martini." In: *Papers in Italian Archaeology, I: The Lancaster Seminar: Recent Research in Prehistoric, Classical, and Medieval Archaeology.* Ed. H.M. Blake, T.W. Potter, and D.B. Whitehouse. Oxford: British Archaeological Reports, 1978, II:541-67.

Perbellini, Gianni. "The Use of Castle Networks in Northern Italian Medieval Defence Strategies," *IBI Bulletin* 47 (1990-91), 67-78.

Perbellini, Gianni and Lino Vittorio Bozzetto. *Verona la pizzaforte ottocentesca nella cultura europea.* Verona: Architetti Verona, 1990.

Pesez, Jean-Marie. "Sicile arabe et Sicile normande: châteaux arabes et arabo-normands," *Mélanges de l'école Française de Rome: Moyen âge* 110 (1998), 561-76.

Pezzini, Elena. "Un tratto della cinta muraria della città di Palermo," *Mélanges de l'école Française de Rome: Moyen âge* 110 (1998), 719-71.

Pinto, Giuliano. "La guerra e le modificazioni dell'habitat nelle campagne dell'italia centrale (toscana e umbria, secc. XIV e XV)." In: *Castrum 3: Guerre, fortification et habitant dans le monde méditerranéen au moyen âge*. Ed. A. Bazzana. Rome, 1988, pp. 247-55.

Poisson, Jean-Michel. "Caractères originaux et 'modèles' importés dans l'architecture militaire médiévale de l'aire méditerranéenne," *Mélanges de l'école Française de Rome: Moyen âge* 110 (1998), 549-60.

Pollak, Martha D. *Turin, 1564-1680: Urban Design, Military Culture, and.* Chicago: University of Chicago Press, 1991.

Pringle, Denys. "A Group of Medieval Towers in Tuscania," *Papers of the British School at Rome* n.s. 29 (1974), 179-223.

Raimondo, Chiara, Kristjan Toomaspoeg, and Roberto Spadea. "La Castella (Crotone) tra XII e XVI secolo: Indagine sulla torre," *Mélanges de l'école françaises de Rome: Moyen âge* 110 (1998), 473-98.

Redi, F. "L'arsenale medievale di Pisa." In: *Arsenali e città nel'Occidenti europeo*. Ed. E. Concina. Rome, 1987.

Redi, F. "Ripafratta (Pisa)," *Archeologia medievale* 15 (1988), 417-38; 16 (1989), 425-98.

Rizzone, Vittorio Giovanni. "La torre Sant'anna e la chiesa ipogeica a San Martino delle Scale (Palermo)," *Sicilia archeologica* 29 (1996), 181-94.

Roggero, M.F. "Palazzo Madam a Turin," *IBI Bulletin* 47 (1990-91), 31-34.

Role, Raymond E. "*Le Mura*: Lucca's Fortified Enceinte," *Fort* 25 (1997), 83-110.

Rubenstein, Nicolai. "Fortified Enclosures in Italian Cities under *Signori*." In: *War, Culture and Society in Renaissance Venice: Essays in Honour of John Hale*. Ed. D.S. Chambers, C.H. Clough and M.E. Mallett. London, 1993, pp. 1-8.

Sàlita, Eleonora. "Una città 'Turrita'? Milano e le sue torri nel medioevo," *Nuovo rivista storica* 80 (1996), 293-338.

Santoro, Lugio. *Le mura di Napoli*. Rome: Instituto italiano dei castelli, 1984.

Santoro, Lugio. "Le système dèfensif sous l'Empereur Frédéric II dans l'Italie du Sud Souabe," *IBI Bulletin* 47 (1990-91), 79-84.

Schiavina, Lorenzo. "Rocca di Monte Poggiola–Forli," *IBI Bulletin* 47 (1990-91), 39-40.

Schmiedt, G. "Città e fortificazioni nei rilievi aerofotografici." In: *Storia d'Italia*. V.I: *Documenti*. Turin, 1973, I:121-257.

Settia, Aldo A. "Crisi della sicurezza e fortificazioni di rifugio nelle campagne dell'Italia settentrionale." In: *Castrum 3: Guerre, fortification et habitant dans le monde méditerranéen au moyen âge*. Ed. André Bazzana. Rome: L'école Française de Rome, 1988, pp. 263-70.

Settia, Aldo A. "Fortificazioni colletive nei villagi medievali dell'alta Italia: ricetti, ville forti, recinti," *Bollettino storico-bibliografico subalpino* (1976), 527-617.

Severini, G. *Architteture militare di Giuliano da Sangallo*. Pisa, 1970.

Somma, Maria Carla. "Strutture fortificate altomedievali in Italia Centrale: L'esempio della Marisca tra VIII ed XI secolo." In: *Military Studies in Medieval Europe: Papers of the "Medieval Europe Brugge 1997" Conference Volume 11*. Ed. Guy De Boe & Frans Verhaeghe. Zellik: Instituut voor het Archeologisch Patrimonium, 1997, pp. 83-95.

Spanu, Pier Giorgio. "Il Castello di Monreale in Sardegna." In: *Military Studies in Medieval Europe: Papers of the "Medieval Europe Brugge 1997" Conference Volume 11*. Ed. Guy De Boe & Frans Verhaeghe. Zellik: Instituut voor het Archeologisch Patrimonium, 1997, pp. 97-106.

Stiesdal, Hans. "Mittelalterliche Türme in der Römischen Campagne," *Château Gaillard* 11 (1983), 269-79.

Tabarelli, Gian Maria. "'Ideal' and Fortified Cities of the Renaissance." In: *Art, Arms and Armour: An International Anthology*. Vol I: *1979-80*. Ed. Robert Held. Chiasso: Acquafresca Editrice, 1979, pp. 164-81.

Tamasco, Clemente. "La rocca di Verrua-Savoia," *Armi antiche* (1966), 173-247.

Taylor, Arnold J. "Three Early Castles in Sicily: Motta Camastra, Sperlinga and Petralia Soprana," *Château Gaillard* 7 (1975), 209-14.

Trapp, Oswald. *Churburg*. Trans. Peter Marsh-Hunn. Munich: Verlag Schnell and Steiner, 1986.

Tullio, Amedeo. "Le torri del duomo di Cefalù: Esplorazione archeologica, 1985-1986," *Sicilia archeologica* 28 (1995), 143-59.

van Bergeijke, Herman. "Francesco Tensini and the Defenses of Modena," *Fort* 18 (1990), 29-42.

Viganò, Marino, ed. *Architetti e ingegneri militari italiani all'estero dal XV al XVIII secolo*. Rome: Castella 44, 1994.

Volpi, G. *Rocche e fortificazioni del ducato di Urbino (1444-1502): L'esperienza martiniana e l'architettura militare di "transizione"*. Fossombrone, 1982.

Weller, A.S. *Francesco di Giorgio, 1439-1501*. Chicago, 1943.

Willemsen, C.A. *Die Bauten der Hohenstaufen in Süditalien: Neue Grabungs und Forschungsergebnisse*. Cologne, 1968.

Woods-Marsden, Joanna. "Images of Castles in the Renaissance: Symbols of 'Signoria'/Symbols of Tyranny," *Art Journal* 48 (1989), 130-37.

Military Technology – Premodern – Fortifications – Low Countries

Bauer, T.C. "Batenburg Castle (The Netherlands)," *Château Gaillard* 16 (1994), 21-32.

Beeckmans, Luk. "Militaire archaeologica uit de burcht van Herzele," *Handelingen Zottegems Genootschap voor Geschiedenis* 5 (1991), 273-78.

Berckmans, O., J.Cl. Ghislain, and William Ubregts. "Le donjon roman d'Enghien," *Château Gaillard* 9-10 (1982), 329-46.

Besteman, Jan G. "Mottes in the Netherlands," *Château Gaillard* 12 (1985), 211-24.

Blieck, Gilles. "Les fortifications de Lille en Flandre au bas Moyen Âge: approche archéologique et historique." In: *Military Studies in Medieval Europe: Papers of the "Medieval Europe Brugge 1997" Conference Volume 11*. Ed. Guy De Boe & Frans Verhaeghe. Zellik: Instituut voor het Archeologisch Patrimonium, 1997, pp. 167-71.

Bourdeaux, Michel. *Citadel of Dinant: History and Guide*. Dinant: L. Bourdeaux-Capelle, n.d.

Bragard, Philippe. *Le château des comtes de Namur: Autopsis d'une forteresse médiévale*. Namur: Les amis de la citadelle de Namur, 1990.

Bult, E.J. "Moated Sites in their Economical and Social Context in Delfland," *Château Gaillard* 13 (1987), 21-40.

Callebaut, Dirk. "La château des comtes à Gand," *Château Gaillard* 11 (1981), 45-54.

Callebaut, Dirk and L. Millis. "Le castrum de Petegem et le système défensif le long de l'Escaut au haut moyen âge," *Château Gaillard* 9-10 (1982), 71-82.

Cominada-Voorhan, A.M.G. *Loevestein: een fort aan de grens van Holland*. Zutphen: Stichting Vrienden van het slot Loevestein, Gorichem, De Walburg Pers, 1989.

Coolen, Georges. "Le Chateau de Saint Omer," *Bulletin trimestriel de la société academique des antiquaries de la Morine* 22 (Mar 1974), 181-93.

Dekker, C. "Les châteaux dans la principauté ecclésiastique d'Utrecht, dans leur contexte politique et social," *Château Gaillard* 13 (1987), 5-20.

Deprez, R. "La politique castrale dans la principauté de Liège du Xe au XIVe siècle," *Moyen âge* 65 (1959), 501-38.

De Meulemeester, Jan. "Châteaux et frontière: quelques réflexions sur les principautés territoriales des anciens Pays-Bas méridionaux," *Château Gaillard* 17 (1996), 53-59.

De Meulemeester, Jan. "Le début du château: le motte castrale dans les Pays-Bas méridionaux," *Château Gaillard* 16 (1994), 121-30.

De Meulemeester, Jan. "Défenses cotiéres de la Flandre maritime: Formes circulaires," *Château Gaillard* 9-10 (1982), 365-72.

De Meulemeester, Jan. "Maisons fortes: une perspective flamande." In: *La maison forte au moyen âge*. Ed. M. Bur. Paris, 1986, pp. 87-94.

De Meulemeester, Jan. "Mottes castrales du Comté de Flandre: État de la question d'après les fouilles récentes," *Château Gaillard* 11 (1983), 101-15.

De Meulemeester, Jan. "Structures défensives et résidences princières: le châteaux à motte du comté de Looz au XIe siècle," *Château Gaillard* 15 (1990), 101-11.

De Meulemeester, Jan and J. Zimmer. "Castellum Lucilinburhuc: Archäotopographische Vorschläge zur Entstehung und Entwicklung der Stadt Luxembourg," *Château Gaillard* 15 (1990), 113-26.

De Meulemeester, Jan, André Matthys and Jan-Michel Poisson. "Structures emmottées: une comparison d'exemples fouillés récemment en Belgique et en Rhône-Alpes." In: *Military Studies in Medieval Europe: Papers of the "Medieval Europe Brugge 1997" Conference Volume 11*. Ed. Guy De Boe & Frans Verhaeghe. Zellik: Instituut voor het Archeologisch Patrimonium, 1997, pp. 139-48.

Deshoulières, F. "Les premiers donjons de pierre dans le département du Cher," *Bulletin monumental* 106 (1948), 49-61.

Des Marez, G. "Fortifications de la frontière du Hainaut et du Brabant au XIIe siècle," *Annales de la société royale d'archéologie de Bruxelles* (1914), 12-45.

Doperé, Frans and William Ubregts. *De donjon in Vlaanderen: Architectuur en wooncultuur*. Acta Archaeologica Lovaniensia, Monographiae 3. Leuven, 1991.

Doperé, Frans and William Ubregts. "La fin de donjon résidentiel dans nord de la Belgique," *Château Gaillard* 14 (1990), 141-58.

Dunan, M.F. "Les châteaux forts du comté de Luxembourg et les progrès dans leur défense sous Jean l'Aveugle, 1309-1346," *Publications de la section historique de l'institute grand-ducal de Luxembourg* 70 (1950), 9-276.

Engelbrecht, W.F.K. "A Bastioned Entrenchment in Holland," *Fort* 16 (1988), 5-6.

Gaier, Claude. "La fonction stratégico-défensive du plat pays au moyen âge dans la région de la Meuse moyenne," *Moyen âge* 69 (1963), 753-71; in: *Armes et combats dans l'univers médiéval*. Paris: De Boeck Université, 1995, pp. 267-82.

Genicot, Leopold F. *Groot kastelenboek van België: Burchten en hofsteden*. Brussels, 1976.

Groesbeek, J.W. *Middeleeuwse kastelen van Noord-Holland*. Haarlem, 1981.

Guide to the Castle of the Counts of Flanders, Ghent. Ghent: Dienst Archeologie en Historische Monumenten van de Stad Gent, 1976.

Heidinga, H.A. "The Huneschans at Uddel Reconsidered," *Château Gaillard* 13 (1987), 53-62.

Hoek, C. "La maison forte aux pays-bas." In: *La maison forte au moyen âge*. Ed. M. Bur. Paris, 1986, pp. 113-36.

Hoekstra, Tarquinius J. "Vredenburg Castle at Utrecht (1529-1577)," *Château Gaillard* 9-10 (1982), 145-74.

Hoekstra, Tarquinius J., M.D. de Weerd, and S.L. Wynia, ed. *Het romeinse castellum te Utrecht* Utrecht: Universiteit van Amsterdam, 1989.

Hoffsummer, P. and A., and B. Wery. "Naissance, transformations et abandon de trois places fortes des environs de Liège," *Château Gaillard* 13 (1987), 63-80.

Janse, H. and Th. van Straalen. *Middeleeuwse stadswallen en stadspoorten in de lage landen*. Zaltbommel, 1974.

Janssen, H.L. "The Archaeology of the Medieval Castle in the Netherlands. Results and Prospects for Future Research." In: *Medieval Archaeology in the Netherlands: Studies Presented to H.H. van Regteren Altena*. Ed. J.C. Besteman et al. Van Gorcum, 1990, pp. 219-64.

Janssen, H.L. "The Castles of the Bishop of Utrecht," *Château Gaillard* 8 (1977), 135-57.

Joustra, Arjen and Diederik Six. "Elmina," *Bulletin van de Koninklijke Nederlandse oudheidkundige bond (KNOB)* 88.6 (1989), 15-17.

Lavalleye, J. "Le château de Courtrai: Contribution à l'histoire de l'architecture militaire en Belgique," *Annales de la société royale d'archéologie de Bruxelles* 35 (1930), 157-68.

Libois, Raoul, Jacques Jeanmart, and Philippe Jaumin. *Houx (Yvoir) en zijn middeleeuws kasteel van Poilvache*. 2nd ed. Everhailles-Yvoir: De Vrienden van Poilvache, 1993.

Margue, M. "Pouvoir princier et peuplement: aux origines de la ville de Luxembourg," *Château Gaillard* 16 (1994), 285-98.

Moerman, Ingrid W.L. "Le château de Leyde," *Château Gaillard* 14 (1990), 305-20.

Moerman, Ingrid W.L. "La demeure des comtes de Hollande à La Haye," *Château Gaillard* 9-10 (1982), 497-507.

Morreau, L.J. *Bolwerk der Nederlanden: De vestingwerken van Maastricht sdert het begin van de 13e eeuw*. Assen, 1979.

Olde Meierink, B., ed. *Kastelen en ridderhofsteden in Utrecht*. Utrecht, 1995.

Ozinga, L.R.P., T.J. Hoekstra, M.D. de Weerd, and S.L. Wynia, ed. *Het romeinse castellum te Utrecht*. Universiteit van Amsterdam, Albert Egges van Giffen Instituut voor Praeen Protohistorie, Studies in Praeen Protohistorie, 3. Utrecht: Broese Kemink, 1989.

Pauly, Michel. "Une ville en voie d'émancipation: Luxembourg du XIIIe au XVe siècle," *Château Gaillard* 16 (1994), 229-34.

Pierard, Christiane. "Les premières fortifications de Mons," *Revue Belge d'histoire militaire* 23 (1979-80), 681-94.

Polak, M. and S.L. Wynia. "The Roman Forts at Vechten, a Survey of the Excavations, 1829-1989," *Oudheidkundige mededelingen* 71 (1991), 125-56.

Renaud, J.G.N. "Le donjon dans les châteaux des Pays-Bas," *Château Gaillard* 1 (1964), 101-23.

Renaud, J.G.N. "Het middeleeuwse kasteel te Heusden," *Brabants jaarboek* (1949), 45-55.

Renaud, J.G.N. "Quelques remarques concernant le 'Hunneschans' au Lac d'Uddel," *Château Gaillard* 4 (1969), 191-99.

Roosens, Ben. "The Transformation of the Medieval Castle into an Early Modern Fortress in the 16th Century. Some Examples from the Southern Border of the Low Countries: Gravelines, Renty and Namur," *Château Gaillard* 17 (1998), 193-206.

Salamagne, Alain. "La défense des villes des Pays-Bas à la mort de Charles le Téméraire (1477)." In: *La guerre, la violence et les gens au Moyen Âge*. I: *Guerre et violence*. Ed. P. Contamine and O. Guyotjeannin. 119e congrès national des sociétés historiques et scientifiques, Amiens, octobre 1994, Section d'histoire médiévale et philologie. Paris, 1996, pp. 295-307.

Schuyf, Judith. "Moated Sites in Brabant (Netherlands)," *Château Gaillard* 11 (1983), 257-67.

Trimpe Burger, J.A. "The Geometrical Fortress of Oost-Souburg (Zeeland)," *Château Gaillard* 7 (1975), 215-19.

Ubregts, William. "Le château de Corroy," *Château Gaillard* 9-10 (1982), 265-69.

van de Walle, A.L.J. "Le château des Comtes de Flandres à Gand: Quelques problèmes archéologiques," *Château Gaillard* 1 (1964), 161-69.

van den Broecke, J.P. *Middeleeuwse kastelen van Zeeland: Bijzonderheden over verdwenen burchten en ridderhofsteden*. Delft, 1978.

van Doorne, Geert. *Omtrent het Gravensteen in Gent*. Brussels: Gemeentekrediet, 1992.

van Hoof, Joep P.C.M.M. "Forts in the Netherlands (c.1500-1945)," *Revue internationale d'histoire militaire* 58 (1984), 97-126.

van Hoof, Joep P.C.M.M. *Langs wal en Bastion: Hoogtepunten uit de Nederlandse vestingbouw*. Utrecht: Uitgeverij Matrijs, 1991.

van Lennep, J. and W.J. Hoofdijk. *Merkwaardige kasteelen in Nederland*. 5 vols. Amsterdam, 1854.

van Reijen, Paul. *Middeleeuwse kastelen in Nederland*. Haarlem, 1973.

Verhaeghe, Frans. "Les sites fossoyés du moyen âge en basse et moyenne Belgique: état de la question." In: *La maison forte au moyen âge*. Ed. M. Bur. Paris, 1986, pp. 55-86.

Verstegen, S.V. "The Castle Cannenburg as a Centre of Noble Power in the 16th Century: Properties or Privileges?" *Château Gaillard* 13 (1987), 253-62.

Vries, K. de. "De middeleeuwse stad als defensiegemeenschap weerspiegeld in de Noordnederlandse stadsrechten uit de voor Bourgondische tijd," *Rechtsgeleerd magazijn Themis* 18 (1957), 384-97.

Waha, Michel de. "Châteaux et paysage dans la Hainaut médiéval." In: *Peasants and Townsmen in Medieval Europe: Studia in honorem Adriaan Verhulst*. Ed. J.-M. Duvosquel and E. Thoen. Ghent, 1995, pp. 463-92.

Waha, Michel de. "Du sens politique des portes castrales et urbaines en Hainaut au Moyen âge." In: *Aux portes du chateau: Actes du troisième colloque de castellologie*. Paris, 1987, pp. 51-69.

Waha, Michel de. "Habitats 'seigneuriaux' et paysage dans le Hainaut médiéval." In: *La maison forte au moyen âge*. Ed. M. Bur. Paris, 1986, pp. 95-112.

Zimmer, John. "Le château de Larochette (Grande-Duché de Luxembourg): Le maison de Créhange, une résidence seigneuriale du XIVe siècle," *Château Gaillard* 14 (1990), 393.

Zimmer, John. "Die Wahl einer Burgbaustelle: die Beispiele von Luxemburg, Vianden, Befort und Fels," *Château Gaillard* 18 (1998), 257-68.

Military Technology – Premodern – Fortifications – Mediterranean

Hoppen, A. *The Fortification of Malta by the Order of St. John, 1530-1798*. Edinburgh: Scottish Academic Press, 1979.

Hughes, Quentin. "Give Me the Time and I Will Give You Life: Francesco Laparelli and the Building of Valletta, Malta, 1565-1569," *Town Planning Review* 49 (1978), 61-74.

Hughes, Quentin. *Malta: A Guide to the Fortifications*. Valletta: Said International, 1993.

Hughes, Quentin. "The Military Life of a Fortress: Malta Since the Sixteenth Century," *Fortress* 3 (Nov 1989), 11-23.

Kollias, E. *The City of Rhodes and the Palace of the Grand Master: From the Early Christian Period to the Conquest by the Turks (1522)*. Athens, 1988.

Kollias, E. *The Knights of Rhodes: The Palace and the City*. Athens, 1991.

Migos, Athanassios. "Rhodes: the Knights' Background," *Fort* 18 (1990), 5-28.

Molin, Kristian. "Fortifications and Internal Security in the Kingdom of Cyprus, 1191-1426." In: *From Clermont to Jerusalem: The Crusades and Crusader Societies, 1095-1500*. Selected Proceedings of the International Medieval Congress, University of Leeds, 10-13 July 1995. Ed. Alan V. Murray. Turnhout: Brepols, 1998, pp. 187-99.

Perbellini, Gianni. "The Venetian Defences of Cyprus," *Fort* 16 (1988), 7-44.

Rosser, J. "Excavations at Saranda Kolones, Paphos, Cyprus, 1981-1983," *Dumbarton Oaks Papers* 39 (1985), 80-97.

Spiteri, Stephen C. *Discovering the Fortifications of the Order of St. John in Malta*. Valleta: Said International Ltd., 1988.

Spiteri, Stephen C. *Fortresses of the Cross: Hospitaller Military Architecture (1136-1798)*. Valleta: Heritage Interpretation Services, 1994.

Spiteri, Stephen C. *The Knights' Fortifications: An Illustrated Guide of the Fortifications Built by the Knights of St. John in Malta*. 2nd ed. Balzan: Arkadia, 1990.

Military Technology – Premodern – Fortifications – Middle Eastern (including Crusader Castles)

Abel, A. "La citadelle eyyubite de Bosra Eski Cham," *Annales archéologiques arabes Syriennes* 6 (1956).

Ayalon, David. "Hisar: The Mamluk Sultanate." In: *Encyclopedia of Islam*. 2nd ed. Leiden, 1971, III:472-76.

Battista, A. and B. Bagatti. *La fortezza saracena del Monte Tabor: AH 609-15/AD 1212-18*. Jerusalem, 1976.

Bazzana, André. "Approche d'une typologie des édifices castraux de l'ancien Sharq-al-Andalus," *Château Gaillard* 9-10 (1982), 301-28.

Bazzana, André. "Le château d'Alcala de Chivert," *Château Gaillard* 8 (1977), 21-46.

Boase, T.S.R. *Castles and Churches of the Crusading Kingdom*. London: Oxford University Press, 1967.

Boase, T.S.R. "Military Architecture in the Crusader States in Palestine and Syria." In: *A History of the Crusades*. Vol IV: *The Art and Architecture of the Crusader States*. Ed. H.W. Hazard. Madison, 1977, pp. 140-64.

Chevedden, Paul E. "Fortifications and the Development of Defensive Planning in the Latin East," In: *The Circle of War in the Middle Ages: Essays on Medieval Military and Naval History*. Ed. Donald J. Kagay and L.J. Andrew Villalon. Woodbridge: The Boydell Press, 1999, pp. 33-44.

Creswell, K.A.C. "Fortification in Islam before AD 1250," *Proceedings of the British Academy* 38 (1952), 89-125.

Crusaders' Fortress in Palestine, A: A Report of Explorations Made by the Museum, 1926. New York: Metropolitan Museum of Art, 1927.

Deschamps, Paul. *Les châteaux des croisés en Terre Sainte*. 3 vols. Paris, 1934-73.

Edwards, Robert W. *The Fortifications of Armenian Cilicia*. Washington, 1987.

Ellenblum, Ronnie. "Three Generations of Frankish Castle-Building in the Latin Kingdom of Jerusalem." In: *Autour de la première croisade: Actes du Colloque de la Society for the Study of the Crusades and the Latin East (Clermont-Ferrand, 22-25 juin 1995)*. Ed. M. Balard. Paris: Publications de la Sorbonne, 1996, pp. 517-47.

Eydoux, H.-P. "L'architecture militaire des Francs en orient." In: *Le château en France*. Ed. J.P. Babelon. Paris, 1986, pp. 61-77.

Fedden, R. *Crusader Castles: A Brief Study in the Military Architecture of the Crusades*. London, 1950.

Fedden, R. and J. Thomson. *Crusader Castles*. London, 1977.

Foss, Clive. *Survey of Medieval Castles of Anatolia*. 2 vols. Oxford, 1985.

Frye, R.N. "The Sassanian System of Walls for Defence." In: *Studies in Memory of Gaston Weit*. Ed. M. Rosen-Ayalon. Jerusalem, 1977, pp. 7-15.

Gardiner, Robert. "Crusader Turkey: The Fortifications of Edessa," *Fortress* 2 (Aug 1989). 23-35.

Hanisch, Hanspeter. *Die ayyubidischen Toranlagen der Zitadelle von Damaskus: ein Beitrag zur Kenntnis des mittelalterlichen Festungsbauwesens in Syrien* (Wiesbaden, 1996).

Hanisch, Hanspeter. "Der Nordostabschnitt der Zitadelle von Damaskus," *Damaszener Mitteilungen* 7 (1993), 233-96.

Hanisch, Hanspeter. "Der Nordwestturm der Zitadelle von Damaskus," *Damaszener Mitteilungen* 5 (1991), 183-233.

Hanisch, Hanspeter. "Die seldschukischen Anlagen der Zitadelle von Damaskus," *Damaszener Mitteilungen* 6 (1992), 479-99.

Harper, Richard P. and Denys Pringle. "Belmont Castle, 1987: Second Preliminary Report of Excavations," *Levant* 21 (1988), 47-61.

Hazard, H.W. *The Art and Architecture of the Crusader States*. Madison, 1977.

Huygens, R.B.C. "Un nouveau texte du traité *De constructione castri Saphet*," *Studi medievali* 3rd ser. 6 (1965), 355-85.

Jacoby, David. "Crusader Acre in the Thirteenth Century: Urban Layout and Topography," *Studi medievali*, 3rd ser. 20.1 (1979), 1-45.

Johns, C.N. "Excavations at Pilgrims' Castle, 'Atlit (1932): The Ancient Tell and the Outer Defences of the Castle," *Quarterly of the Department of Aniquities in Palestine* 3, no. 4 (1933), 145-64.

Kennedy, Hugh. *Crusader Castles*. Cambridge: Cambridge University Press, 1994.

King, D.J. Cathcart. "The Defenses of the Citadel of Damascus: a Great Mohammedan Fortress of the Time of the Crusades," *Archaeologia* 94 (1951), 57-96.

Lawrence, T.E. *Crusader Castles*. London, 1936; rpt. London: Michael Haag, 1986.

Lezine, Alexandre. "Deux ribat du sahel Tunisien," *Revue internationale d'histoire militaire* 18 (1956), 279-88.

Luttrell, Anthony. "English Contributions to the Hospitaller Castle at Bodrum in Turkey: 1407-1437." In: *The Military Orders*. Vol. 2: *Welfare and Warfare*. Ed. Helen Nicholson. Aldershot: Ashgate, 1998, pp. 163-72.

Marino, Luigi, et al. "The Crusader Settlement in Petra," *Fortress* 7 (Nov 1990), 3-13.

Megaw, Peter. "A Castle in Cyprus Attributable to the Hospital?" In: *The Military Orders: Fighting for the Faith and Caring for the Sick*. Ed. Malcolm Barber. Aldershot: Ashgate, 1994, pp. 42-51.

Megaw, Peter. "Supplementary Excavations on a Castle Site at Paphos, Cyprus, 1970-1971," *Dumbarton Oaks Papers* 26 (1972), 322-44.

Molin, Kristian. "The Non-Military Functions of Crusader Fortifications, 1187-*circa* 1380," *Journal of Medieval History* 23 (1997), 367-88.

Müller-Wiener, Wolfgang. *Castles of the Crusades*. London, 1966.

Nicolle, David C. "Ain Habis–The Cave de Sueth," *Archéologie médiévale* 18 (1988), 113-40.

Nicolle, David C. "Saracen Strongholds," *Military Illustrated* 83 (Apr 1995), 25-29.

Parker, S. Thomas. "The Roman Limes in Jordan." In: *Studies in the History and Archaeology of Jordan*. Ed. Adnan Hadidi. Amman, 1987, pp. 151-64.

Petersen, Andrew. "Early Ottoman Forts on the Darb al-Hajj," *Levant* 21 (1989), 97-117.

Porëe, Brigitte. "Guerre, fortification et habitat dans le territoire d'Acre (XIIe-XIIIe siècles)." In: *La guerre, la violence et les gens au Moyen*

Âge. I: *Guerre et violence*. Ed. P. Contamine and O. Guyotjeannin. 119e congrès national des sociétés historiques et scientifiques, Amiens, octobre 1994, Section d'histoire médiévale et philologie. Paris, 1996, pp. 245-61.

Pringle, Denys. "A Castle in the Sand: Mottes in the Crusader East," *Château Gaillard* 18 (1998), 187-91.

Pringle, Denys. "Crusader Castles: The First Generation," *Fortress* 1 (May 1989), 14-25.

Pringle, Denys. *The Red Tower*. London, 1986.

Pringle, Denys. "Templar Castles between Jaffa and Jerusalem." In: *The Military Orders*. Vol. 2: *Welfare and Warfare*. Ed. Helen Nicholson. Aldershot: Ashgate, 1998, pp. 89-110.

Pringle, Denys. "Templar Castles on the Road to the Jordan." In: *The Military Orders: Fighting for the Faith and Caring for the Sick*. Ed. Malcolm Barber. Aldershot: Ashgate, 1994, pp. 148-66.

Pringle, Denys. "Towers in Crusader Palestine," *Château Gaillard* 16 (1994), 335-50.

Pringle, Denys. "Town Defences in the Crusader Kingdom of Jerusalem." In: *The Medieval City Under Siege*. Ed. I.A. Corfis and M. Wolfe. Woodbridge, 1995, pp. 69-122.

Razi, Zvi and Eliot Braun. "The Lost Crusader Castle of Tiberias." In: *The Horns of Hattin*. Ed. B.Z. Kedar. Jerusalem, 1992, pp. 216-27.

Rice, D.S. "Medieval Harran: Studies in Topography and Monuments, I," *Anatolian Studies* 2 (1952), 36-84.

Riley-Smith, Jonathan. "The Templars and the Castle of Tortosa in Syria: an Unknown Document concerning the Acquisition of the Fortress," *English Historical Review* 84 (1969), 278-88.

Roll, Israel. "Medieval Apollonia-Arsuf: A Fortified Coastal Town in the Levant of the Early Muslim and Crusader Periods." In: *Autour de la première croisade: Actes du Colloque de la Society for the Study of the Crusades and the Latin East (Clermont-Ferrand, 22-25 juin 1995)*. Ed. M. Balard. Paris: Publications de la Sorbonne, 1996, pp. 595-606.

Rosser, J. "Crusader Castles of Cyprus," *Archaeology* 39.4 (July-Aug 1986), 40-47.

Sauvaget, Jean. "La citadelle de Damas," *Syria* 11 (1930), 59-90, 216-41.

Sauvaget, Jean. "Notes sur les défenses de marine de Tripoli," *Bulletin du Musée de Beyrouth* 2 (1938), 1-25.

Smail, R.C. "Crusaders' Castles of the Twelfth Century," *Cambridge Historical Journal* 10 (1951), 133-49.

Soudel-Thomine, J. "Burdj: Military Architecture in the Islamic Middle East." In: *Encyclopedia of Islam*. 2nd ed. Leiden, 1960, I:1315-18.

Terrasse, Henri. "Burdj: Military Architecture in the Muslim West." In: *Encyclopedia of Islam*. 2nd ed. Leiden, 1960, I:1318-21.

Terrasse, Henri. "Hisn: The Muslim West." In: *Encyclopedia of Islam*. 2nd ed. Leiden, 1960, III:498-501.

Military Technology – Premodern – Fortifications – Scandinavia

Back, Birgit Arfwidsson. *Visborgs fall*. Karlstad: Press' Förlag, 1980.

Cinthio, E. "Preliminary Report on Excavations of a Proposed Royal Manor and Palace in Dalby, Scania, Sweden," *Château Gaillard* 4 (1969), 49-52.

Dahl, Bjørn Westerbeek. "Fästningsanläg ved Hals indtil 1687." In: *Fra Himmerland og Kjär Herred*. Copenhagen, 1992, pp. 3-34.

Drake, K. "Sperren oder Öffnungen? Drei Burgen an den Grenzen Schwedens im 14. JH." *Château Gaillard* 17 (1996), 61-68.

Drake, K. "Stadt-Burg-Stadt Hämeelina," *Château Gaillard* 16 (1994), 131-42.

Ekroll, Øystein. "Norwegian Medieval Castles: Building on the Edge of Europe," *Château Gaillard* 18 (1998), 65-74.

Engberg, N. "Borren and Nœsholm: Two Examples of Danish Castle-Building," *Château Gaillard* 16 (1994), 155-65.

Ericsson, Ingolf. "Wehrbauten des Mittelalters in der süddänischen Inselregion," *Château Gaillard* 15 (1990), 143-49.

Gardborg, G.J. and P.O. Welin. *Finlands medeltida borgar*. Esbo: Schildets, 1993.

Hansson, Hans. *Stockholms stadsmurar*. Stockholm: Klichéer Ljungbergs Klichéanstalt, 1956.

Heertz, Johannes. "Danish Medieval Drawbridges," *Château Gaillard* 9-10 (1982), 419-31.

Heertz, Johannes. "The Excavation at Solvig, a Danish Crannog in Southern Jutland: A Preliminary Report on the Years 1965, 66 and 69," *Château Gaillard* 6 (1973), 33-95.

Heertz, Johannes. "Further Excavations at Solvig: A Preliminary Report on the Years 1970-1972," *Château Gaillard* 6 (1973), 97-105.

Heertz, Johannes. "Gjorslev: A Castle Built in the Name of the Cross," *Château Gaillard* 16 (1994), 249-60.

Heertz, Johannes. "Kalundborg, a Danish Medieval Foritfied Town and Castle," *Château Gaillard* 14 (1990), 195-217.

Heertz, Johannes. "Some Early Sixteenth Century Fortifications in Denmark," *Château Gaillard* 12 (1985), 49-68.

Heertz, Johannes. "Some Examples of Medieval Hypocausts in Denmark," *Château Gaillard* 7 (1975), 127-39.

Herteig, A.E. "Mediaeval Archaeological Research in Norway: Some Achievements and Prospects," *Château Gaillard* 4 (1969), 157-62.

Hinz, Hermann. "Die ostskandinavischen Wehrkirchen," *Château Gaillard* 11 (1983), 165-66.

Hinz, Hermann. "Die Schwedischen Kirchenkastale auf Gotland," *Château Gaillard* 9-10 (1982), 433-44.

Jantzen, C. "Timbered Fortresses in Northern Jutland from 14th Century," *Château Gaillard* 15 (1990), 205-15.

Jensen, V. "Koldinghus: A Danish Border Castle of the Late Middle Ages," *Château Gaillard* 13 (1987), 81-95.

Jørgensen, Anne Nørgård. "Off-Shore Defensive Works in Denmark, AD 200-1300," *Château Gaillard* 18 (1998), 149-52.

Liebgott, Niels-Kund. *Dansk middelalder arkaeologi*. Copenhagen, 1989.

Liebgott, Niels-Knud. "An Outline of Danish Castle Studies," *Château Gaillard* 11 (1983), 193-206.

Liebgott, Niels-Kund. "Pedensborg: The Interpretation of a Danish Fortified Site from the 12th Century," *Château Gaillard* 9-10 (1982), 471-81.

Lind, Hans, Viveka Löndahl, and Susanne Pettersson. "The Unknown Castle–Archaeological Aspects of Lordship, Household and Rural Environment." In: *Military Studies in Medieval Europe: Papers of the "Medieval Europe Brugge 1997" Conference Volume 11*. Ed. Guy De Boe & Frans Verhaeghe. Zellik: Instituut voor het Archeologisch Patrimonium, 1997, pp. 197-208.

Lonroth, Erik. "Sweden's Coastal Defence from the Vikings to the Period of Lasting Peace," *Revue internationale d'histoire militaire* (1973/1975), 13-22.

Mogren, Mats. "Northern Timber Castles–Short-Lived But Complex: Some Examples from the Southern Swedish Taiga," *Château Gaillard* 18 (1998), 135-48.

Ödman, A. "Forest Castles in Northern Scania," *Château Gaillard* 16 (1994), 321-28.

Olausson, Michael. "Fortified Manors in the Migration Period in the Eastern Part of Central Sweden–a Discussion of Politics, Warfare and Architecture." In: *Military Aspects of Scandinavian Society in a European Perspective, AD. 1-1300*. Ed. A.N. Jørgensen and B. Clausen. Copenhagen, 1997, pp. 157-68.

Olsen, Rikke Agnete. "Big Manors and Large-Scale Farming in the Late Middle Ages," *Château Gaillard* 13 (1987), 157-67.

Olsen, Rikke Agnete. "The Buildings on Danish Moated-Sites in the 15th and 16th Centuries," *Château Gaillard* 9-10 (1982), 509-26.

Olsen, Rikke Agnete. "Castle, Manor and Society in the Danish Middle Ages," *Château Gaillard* 14 (1990), 341-50.

Olsen, Rikke Agnete. "Danish Medieval Castles at War," *Château Gaillard* 9-10 (1982), 223-35.

Olsen, Rikke Agnete. "The Danish Royal Castles in the Late Middle Ages: Fortresses or Administrative Centres?" *Château Gaillard* 12 (1985), 65-76.

Olsen, Rikke Agnete. "Hammerhaus on Bornholm–Or Who Owned the Archbishops Castle?" *Château Gaillard* 17 (1996), 146-49.

Olsen, Rikke Agnete. "Late Medieval Manor Houses in Northern Jutland," *Château Gaillard* 11 (1983), 243-52.

Olsson, Martin. *Kalmar slotts historia.* 4 vols. Stockholm, 1944-65.

Olsson, Martin. *Kalmar slotts kyrkor.* Stockholm, 1968.

Rieck, Flemming. "Aspects of Coastal Defence in Denmark." In: *Aspects of Maritime Scandinavia, AD 200-1200: Proceedings of the Nordic Seminar on Maritime Aspects of Archaeology, Roskilde, 13th-15th March, 1989.* Ed. Ole Crumlin-Pedersen. Roskilde: The Viking Ship Museum, 1991, pp. 83-96.

Roesdahl, Else. "The End of Viking-Age Fortifications in Denmark, and What Followed," *Château Gaillard* 12 (1985), 39-47.

Schulz, Rainer. "Stolpe, eine Turmberg des späten 12. Jahrhunderts an der Oder: Eine Befestigung der Dänen in Pommern gegen die Markgrafen von Brandenburg?" *Château Gaillard* 18 (1998), 211-21.

Sinisalo, Antero. *Olavinlinna Castle.* Trans. Sonja Tirkkonen and Stephen Condit. Olavininna: The Guild of St. Olaf, 1988.

Stiesdal, Hans. "Die ältesten Danischen Donjons," *Château Gaillard* 8 (1977), 279-86.

Stiesdal, Hans. "Eriksvolde," *Château Gaillard* 9-10 (1982), 255-64.

Stiesdal, Hans. "The Medieval Palatium in Denmark: Some Recent Discoveries at Tranekaer Castle," *Château Gaillard* 7 (1975), 201-07.

Wahl, Hannu-Matti. "Kexholms slott: 700-årig historia från karelsk befäst centralort till svensk fästning," *Meddelande* 55 (1995), 11-52.

Wessman, Monica. *Kalmar Castle.* Trans. Susan Shom-Bäckman, 1997.

Wille-Jørgensen, Dorthe. "Recent Excavations at Vordingborg Castle," *Château Gaillard* 18 (1998), 251–56.

Military Technology – Premodern – Fortifications – Spain and Portugal (and New World holdings)

Aguirre, Javier Martínez de. "Localizachión de los castillos reales medievales cd Pintano y Artajo (Navarre)," *Castillos de España* 100 (Feb 1993), 49-52.

Alcocer Martinez, M. *Castillos y fortalezas del antique reine de Granada.* Tangier, 1941.

Aparicio, Cristóbal Guitart. "Consideraciones sobre plazas fuertes y castillos españoles ante la frontera de Portugal," *Castillos de España* 100 (Feb 1993), 35-42.

Araguas, Philippe. "Les châteaux des marches de Catalogne et Ribagorce (950-1100)," *Bulletin Monumental* 137 (1979), 205-34.

Araguas, Philippe. "Le réseau castral en Catalogne vers 1350." In: *Castrum 3: Guerre, fortification et habitant dans le monde méditerranéen au moyen âge.* Ed. André Bazzana. Rome: L'école Française de Rome, 1988, pp. 113-22.

Arnold, Thomas F. "Fortifications and the Military Revolution: The Gonzaga Experience, 1530-1630." In: *The Military Revolution Debate: Readings on the Military Transformation of Early Modern Europe.* Ed. C.J. Rogers. Boulder, 1995, pp. 201-26.

Avila Vega, Antonio. "El abandono como medio de defensa de un castillo," *Castillos de España* 99 (1992).

Avila y Diaz-Ubierna, G. *Castillos de la provincia de Burgos.* Burgos, 1961.

Barroca, M. Jorge and A.J. Cardosa Morais. "A terre e o castelo: una experiencia arqueologica em Aguiar da Pena," *Portugalia* 6-7 (1985-86), 35-58.

Bazzana, André. "Le début du château dans l'Espagne septentrionale," *Château Gaillard* 16 (1994), 33-43.

Bazzana, André. "Forteresses du royaume nasride de Grenade (XIIIe-XVe siècles): la défense des frontières," *Château Gaillard* 11 (1983), 29-43.

Bazzana, André. "Le *hisn et les ma āqil* dans l'organisation du peuplement musulman d'al-Andalus," *Château Gaillard* 15 (1992), 19-31.

Bogart, Charles H. "The Fortaleza del Real Felipe in Peru," *Fort* 17 (1989), 27-36.

Bordeje, F. *Castles Itinerary in Castila: Guide to the Most Interesting Castilian Castles*. Madrid, 1965.

Bruard, Yves. "De l'importance historique et de la valeur des ouvrages fortifiés en Vielle-Castile au XVe siècle," *Moyen âge* 63 (1957), 59-86.

Burns, Robert Ignatius and Paul E. Chevedden. "The Finest Castle in the World," *History Today* 49.11 (Nov 1999), 10-17.

Castellano, M. a Agueda. "Situación jurídica de las donaciones gallega y portuguesa de Alfonso VI," *Castillos de España* 100 (Feb 1993), 43-44.

Cayetano, Carmen and José Maria Sanz Garcia. "Las murallas de Madrid quo vio Wyngaerde en 1562," *Castillos de España* 97 (Dec 1990), 36-46.

Cressier, Patrice. "Fonction et évolution du réseau castral en Andalousie orientale: le cas de l'Alpujarra." In: *Castrum 3: Guerre, fortification et habitant dans le monde méditerranéen au moyen âge*. Ed. André Bazzana. Rome: L'école Française de Rome, 1988, pp. 123-34.

Del Estal, Juan Manuel. "Vicisitudes del castillo satiaguista de Negra, en el reino de Murçia, bajo la Corona de Aragón (1296-1304)," *Anuario de estudios medievales* 28 (1998), 75-96.

Diaz-Plaja, Fernando. *Los castillos de España y sus fantasmas*. Madrid: Maeve S.A., 1986.

Durand, Robert. "Guerre et fortification de l'habitat au Portugal aux XIIe et XIIIe siècles." In: *Castrum 3: Guerre, fortification et habitant dans le monde méditerranéen au moyen âge*. Ed. André Bazzana. Rome: L'école Française de Rome, 1988, pp. 179-86.

Elduque, José María Estables. "Castellos del Alto Gállego," *Castillos de España* 100 (Feb 1993), 23-34.

Escudero Cuesta, Jose and Cesar N. Rodriguez Achutegui. "El castillo de Triana: Análisis tipológico y geoestratégico," *Castillos de España* 99 (1992).

Espino Nuño, Jesus. "La sede de una encomienda Calatrava: El castillo de Manzanares (Ciudad Real)," *Castillos de España* 99 (1992).

Fernandez Pombo, Alejandro. "El castillo de Mora (Toledo)," *Castillos de España* 97 (Dec 1990), 17-22.

Font Rius, José-Maria. "Les modes de détention de châteaux dans la "vielle catalogne" et ses marches extérieures du début du IXe au début du XIe siècle." In: *Les structures sociales de l'Aquitaine, du Languedoc et de l'Espagne au premier age féodal*. Paris, 1969, pp. 63-77.

Fornals, Francisco. "Fortifications in Minorca," *Fortress* 12 (Feb 1992), 23-32.

Fornals, Francisco. *Torres de defensa y atalayas de Menorca*. Mahon: Museo Militar de Menorca, 1989.

Fuguet Sans, Joan. "Fortificacions menors i altre patrimoni retingut pels Templers després de la permuta de 1294," *Anuario de estudios medievales* 28 (1998), 294-310.

Gómez, Fermin de los Reyes. "Sistema defensivo de Cuéllar (Segovia)," *Castillos de España* 100 (Feb 1993), 58-61.

Grassotti, H. "Sobre la retenencia de castillos en la Castilla medieval," *Bulletin de l'institut historique Belge de Rome* 44 (1974), 283-99.

Guitart Aparicio, Cristóbal. "Consideraciones sobre plazas fuertes y castillos Españoles ante la frontera de Portugal," *Castillos de España* 100 (1993), 35-42.

Izquierdo Benito, Ricardo. "Una ciudad de fundación musulmana: Vascos." In: *Castrum 3: Guerre, fortification et habitant dans le monde méditerranéen au moyen âge*. Ed. André Bazzana. Rome: L'école Française de Rome, 1988, pp. 163-72.

Jiménez Esteban, Jorge. "Casa fuerte de la Bujeda (Guadalajara)," *Castillos de España* 99 (1992).

Martinena Ruiz, Juan José. *Castillos reales de Navarra (siglos XIII a XVI)*. Pamplona: Gobierno de Naverra, 1994.

Martínez de Aguirre, Javier. "Localización de los castillos reales medievales de Pintano y Artajo (Navarra)," *Castillos de España* 100 (1993), 49-52.

Miquel Vives, Marina and Josep Santesmases Ollé. "Els castells del Gaià, entre l'Islam i els comtats Catalans," *L'Avenç* 180 (1994), 36-38.

Molénat, Jean-Pierre. "Villes et forteresses musulmanes de la région toldéane disparues après l'occupation chrétienne (XIIe-XVe siècles)." In: *Castrum 3: Guerre, fortification et habitant dans le monde méditerranéen au moyen âge*. Ed. André Bazzana. Rome: L'école Française de Rome, 1988, pp. 215-24.

Monreal Marti de Riquer, L. *Els castells medievales de Catalunya*. Barcelona, 1958.

Moreira, Rafael. *A arquitectura militar na expansão Portugues*. Lisbon: Comissão Nacional para as Comemorações dos Descobrimentos Portugueses, 1994.

Moreira, Rafael, Carlos Lemos, Augusto Pereira Brandão, and Miguel Sanches de Baena. *História das fortificações portuguesas no mundo*. Lisbon: Publicações Alfa, 1991.

Norris, H.T. "Caves and Strongholds from the Moorish Period around the Rock of Gibraltar," *Maghreb Review* 9 (1984), 39-45.

Pardo de Guevara y Valdés, Eduoardo. "Monterrey: Un castillo, un linaje, una historia," *Castillos de España* 100 (Feb 1993), 56-57.

Passini, Jean. "L'habitat fortifié dans la Canal de Berdún, Aragon (Xe-XIIe siècles)." In: *Castrum 3: Guerre, fortification et habitant dans le monde méditerranéen au moyen âge*. Ed. André Bazzana. Rome: L'école Française de Rome, 1988, pp. 91-98.

Requena, Fermin. "La Fortaleza de Bibastro," *Castillos de España* 97 (Dec 1990), 46-57.

Reyes Gómez, Fermín de los. "Sistema defensivo de Cuéllar (Segovia)," *Castillos de España* 100 (1993), 58-61.

Ruibal, Amador. "Una forteleza en trance de desparición: el castillo de Vioque," *Castillos de España* 100 (Feb 1993), 45-48.

Salas, Rodolfo Segovia. *Las fortificiones de Cartagana*. Bogota: Tercer Mundo Editors, 1992.

Sánchez, Ramón Ruiz de Conejo. "La torre de fusileria de Canfranc," *Ejercito* 619 (Aug 1991), 89-93.

Sanmarti, Enric, Pere Castaner, and Joaquim Tremoleda. "La secuencia histórico-topográfica de las murallas del sector meridional de Emporion," *Madrider Mitteilungen* 29 (1988), 191-99.

Sanz Polo, Antonia. "El castillo de Molina de Aragón: Expediente de reedificación en 1836," *Castillos de España* 97 (Dec 1990), 3-10.

Sarthou-Carreres, C. *Castillos de España*. 4th ed. Madrid, 1963.

Sebastian Fabuel, Vincente. "Castellologia valenciana en la comarca de la Serrania (Valencia)," *Castillos de España* 97 (Dec 1990), 11-16.

Serra-Rafols, C., J. de Camp i Arboix, and P. Catala i Roca. *Els castells catalans*. 3 vols. Barcelona, 1967.

Terrasse, Henri. "Les forteresses de l'Espagne musulmane," *Boletin de la real academia de la historia* 134 (1954).

Torres Balbás, L. "Cáceres y su Cerca Almohade," *Andalus* 13 (1948), 446-72.

Torres Delgado, C. "El ejercito y las fortificaciones del reino Nazari di Granada." In: *Gladius: Las armas en la historia* (Madrid, 1988), 197-217.

Touri, Abd el-Aziz, André Bazzana, and Patrice Cressier. "La qasba de Shafshāwan." In: *Castrum 3: Guerre, fortification et habitant dans le monde méditerranéen au moyen âge*. Ed. André Bazzana. Rome: L'école Française de Rome, 1988, pp. 153-62.

Valdés Fernández, Fernando. "Ciudadela y fortificacíon urbana: el caso de Badajoz." In: *Castrum 3: Guerre, fortification et habitant dans le monde méditerranéen au moyen âge*. Ed. André Bazzana. Rome: L'école Française de Rome, 1988, pp. 143-52.

Valor Piechotta, Magdalena and Nuria Casquete de Prado Sagrera. "El castillo de Cumbres Mayores (Huelva): una aproximación a la arquitectura militar segunda mitad del siglo XII,' *Historia, Instituciones, Documentos* 21 (1994), 473-99.

Vara, Consuelo. "El castillo de Puebla Almenara hasta el siglo XVI," *Castillos de España* 97 (Dec 1990), 23-32.

Villena Pardo, Leonardo. "El castillo Español," *Gladius* 4 (1965), 87-106.

Villena Pardo, Leonardo. "El castillo Español," *Armi antiche* (1966), 82-106.

Villena Pardo, Leonardo. "Glosario de términos castellológicos medievales en lenguas románicas," *Castillos de España* 71 (1971), 77-92.

Villena Pardo, Leonardo. "The Iberian Strategical Castle," *IBI Bulletin* 47 (1990-91), 59-66.

Villena Pardo, Leonardo. "Sobre la defensas verticales en España: tipología y terminología comparadas." In: *Castrum 3: Guerre, fortification et habitant dans le monde méditerranéen au moyen âge*. Ed. André Bazzana. Rome: L'école Française de Rome, 1988, pp. 107-12.

Villena Pardo, Leonardo. "La Torre de doña Blanca, Obra militar o religiosa?" *Castillos de España* 97 (Dec 1990), 33-35.

Weissmuller, A.A. *Castles from the Heart of Spain*. London, 1967.

Williams, Mora-Figueroa. "El Alcázar Real de Carmona (Sevilla): La muralla exterior y su flanqueo," *Archivio Hispalense* 2nd ser., 80 (1997), 637-52.

Zapatero, Juan Manuel. *Les fortalezas de Puerto Cahallo*. Madrid: Servicio Historico Militar, 1988.

Zozaya, Juan. "Evolución de un yacimento: el castillo de Gormaz (Soria)." In: *Castrum 3: Guerre, fortification et habitant dans le monde méditerranéen au moyen âge*. Ed. André Bazzana. Rome: L'école Française de Rome, 1988, pp. 173-78.

Zozaya, Juan. "The Fortifications of al-Andalus." In: *Al-Andalus: The Art of Islamic Spain*. Ed. J.D. Dodds. New York, 1992, pp. 63-73.

Military Technology – Premodern – Ships (including Warships) – General

Adam, P. "Conclusions sur les développements des techniques nautiques médiévales," *Revue d'histoire économique et sociale* 54 (1976), 560-67.

Ahrweiler, H. *Byzance et la mer: La marine de la guerre, la politique et les institutions maritimes de Byzance au VIIe-XVe siècles*. Paris: Presses Universitaires de France, 1966.

Anderson, R.C. *Oared Fighting Ships: From Classical Times to the Coming of Steam*. London: Percival Marshall, 1962.

Anderson, Romula and R.C. *The Sailing Ship*. London, 1976.

Bass, George F. *Archaeology Under Water*. Harmondsworth: Penguin Books, 1970.

Charnack, John. *History of Marine Architecture*. 3 vols. London, 1801.

Clowes, William Laird. *The Royal Navy: A History for the Earliest Times to the Present*. 7 vols. London, 1897-1903.

De Jong, J.C. *Geschiedenis van het Nederlandsche zeewesen*. 2nd ed. 5 vols. Haarlam, 1858-62.

Dotson, John E. "The Economics and Logistics of Galley Warfare." In: *The Age of the Galley: Mediterranean Oared Vessels since Pre-Classical Times*. Ed. J. Morrison. London, 1995.

George, James L. *History of Warships from Ancient Times to the Twenty-First Century*. Annapolis: Naval Institute Press, 1998.

Gonzalez-Aller Hierro, José Ignacio. *España en la mar una historia milenaria*. Madrid: Lunwer, 1998.

Hourani, G.F. *Arab Seafaring in the Indian Ocean in Ancient and Early Medieval Times*. Princeton: Princeton University, 1951.

Keegan, John. *The Price of Admiralty: The Evolution of Naval Warfare*. Harmondsworth: Penguin Books, 1988.

Kosiary, E. *Wojny na Bałtyku X-XIX*. Gdansk, 1978.

La Roncière Charles de. *Histoire de la marine Française*. 3rd ed. Paris, 1914.

McGrail, Séan. *Ancient Boats in N.W. Europe: The Archaeology of Water Transport to AD 1500*. Longman Archaeology Series. London: Longman, 1987.

Modelski, G. and William R. Thompson. *Seapower in Global Politics, 1494-1988*. London, 1988.

Mollat, Michel. *Les sources de l'histoire maritime en Europe du moyen âge au XVIII siècle*. Paris: S.E.V.P.E.N., 1962.

Morales Belda, Francisco. *La marina de Al-Andalus*. Barcelona: Ariel, 1970.

Morales Belda, Francisco. *La marina vándala: Los asdingos en España*. Barcelona: Ariel, 1969.

Mott, Lawrence V. *The Development of the Rudder: A Technological Tale*. College Station: Texas A&M Press, 1997.

Nicolas, Nicholas Harris. *History of the Navy to the French Revolution*. 2 vols. London, 1847.

Nylen, Erik. *Bygden, skeppen och havet*. Stockholm: Almqvist and Wiksell, 1973.

Oppenheim, M. *A History of the Administration of the Royal Navy and of Merchant Shipping in Relation to the Navy*. London, 1896; rpt. New York, 1961.

Steffy, J. Richard. *Wooden Ship Building and the Interpretation of Shipwrecks*. College Station: Texas A&M Press, 1994.

Suárez Fernández, Luis. *Navegación y comercio en el golfo de Viscaya*. Madrid: Consejo Superior de Investigaciones Cientificas, Escuela de Estudios Medievales, 1959.

Military Technology – Premodern – Ships (including Warships) – Late Antiquity

Bellabarba, Sergio. "The Origins of the Ancient Methods of Designing Hulls: A Hypothesis," *Mariner's Mirror* 82 (1996), 259-68.

Bill, Jan. "Iron Nails in Iron Age and Medieval Shipbuilding." In: *Crossroads in Ancient Shipbuilding: Proceedings of the Sixth International Symposium on Boat and Ship Archaeology, Roskilde 1991*. Ed. C. Westerdahl. Oxford, 1994, pp. 55-63.

Black, Eve and David Samuel. "What were Sails Made of?" *Mariner's Mirror* 77 (1991), 217-26.

Camp, L. Sprague de. "The Unsinkables," *Technology and Culture* 10 (1969), 422-23.

Casson, Lionel. *The Ancient Mariners: Seafarers and Sea Fighters of the Mediterranean in Ancient Times*. 2nd ed. Princeton: Princeton University Press, 1991.

Casson, Lionel. *Ships and Seafaring in Ancient Times*. 2nd ed. Austin: University of Texas Press, 1994.

Casson, Lionel. *Ships and Seamanship in the Ancient World*. Princeton: Princeton University Press, 1971.

Christides, Vassilios. "Milaha: In the Pre-Islamic and Early Medieval Periods." In: *Encyclopedia of Islam*. 2nd ed. Leiden, 1991, VIII:40-46.

Christides, Vassilios. "Some Remarks on the Mediterranean and Red Sea Ships in Ancient and Medieval Times. II: Merchant-Passenger vs. Combat Ships," *Tropsis* 2 (1987), 87-99.

Czech, Kenneth P. "Bridge to the Enemy: Faced by Rams at Sea, the Romans Tried a Seagoing Deterrant," *Military History* (June 1992), 26-31.

Dolley, R.H. "The Warships of the Later Roman Empire," *Journal of Roman Studies* 38 (1948), 47-53.

Doorninck, Frederick H. van. "New Evidence Concerning Developments in Anchor and Hull Construction Technology during the Roman and Byzantine Periods." In: *Changing Interpretations and New Sources in*

Naval History: Papers from the Third United States Naval Academy History Symposium. Ed. R.M. Love, Jr. New York, 1980, pp. 26-33.

Evans, Laurence. "Food, Transport, and Policy: Roman Maritime Logistics." In: *Changing Interpretations and New Sources in Naval History: Papers from the Third United States Naval Academy History Symposium.* Ed. R.M. Love, Jr. New York, 1980, pp. 10-25.

Foucher, Louis. "Les galères de Themetra," *Revue internationale d'histoire militaire* 18 (1956), 271-77.

Frost, Honor. "Stone Anchors: A Reassessment Reassessed," *Mariner's Mirror* 79 (1993), 449-58.

Guilmartin, John Francis, Jr. "The Galley in Combat," *MHQ: The Quarterly Journal of Military History* 9.2 (Winter 1997), 20-21.

Lane, Frederic C. "From Biremes to Triremes," *Mariner's Mirror* 29 (1963), 48-50.

Marsden, Peter. "Ships of the Roman Period and After in Britain." In: *A History of Seafaring Based on Underwater Archaeology.* Ed. G. F. Bass. New York, 1972, pp. 113-31.

McGrail, Séan. "Early Frame-First Methods of Building Wooden Boats and Ships," *Mariner's Mirror* 83 (1997), 76-80.

Morrison, John S. "Identifying Hellenistic and Roman Warship Types." In: *New Aspects of Naval History.* Ed. C.L. Symonds. Annapolis, 1981, pp. 3-12.

Rougé, Jean. *Ships and Fleets of the Ancient Mediterranean.* Trans. Susan Frazer. Middletown: Wesleyan University Press, 1981.

Shaw, Joseph W. "Greek and Roman Harbourworks." In: *A History of Seafaring Based on Underwater Archaeology.* Ed. G. F. Bass. New York, 1972, pp. 87-112.

Throckmorton, Peter. "Romans on the Sea." In: *A History of Seafaring Based on Underwater Archaeology.* Ed. G. F. Bass. New York, 1972, pp. 65-86.

Military Technology – Premodern – Ships – Medieval – General (including Warships)

Ahweiler, H. *Byzance et le mer: la marine de guerre, la politique et les institutions maritimes de Byzance aux VIIe-XVe siècles.* Paris: Presses Universitaires de France, 1966.

Alonso, Fernando. "Traditional Clinker and Carvel Techniques in the Northwest of Spain." In: *Carvel Construction Technique: Skeleton-first, Shell-first.* Ed. R. Reinders and K. Paul. London, 1991, pp. 103-11.

Bass, George F. "Underwater Archaeology and Medieval Mediterranean Ships." In: *Medieval Archaeology: Papers of the Seventeenth Annual Conference of the Center for Medieval and Early Renaissance Studies.* Ed. C.L. Redman. Binghamton, 1989, pp. 139-54.

Bill, Jan. "Iron Nails in Iron Age and Medieval Shipbuilding." In: *Cross-roads in Ancient Shipbuilding: Proceedings of the Sixth International Symposium on Boat and Ship Archaeology, Roskilde 1991.* Ed. C. Westerdahl. Oxford, 1994, pp. 55-63.

Bill, Jan. "Ship Construction: Tools and Techniques." In: *A History of Ships.* Vol. 4: *Cogs, Caravels and Galleons.* Ed. Richard Unger. London: Conway Maritime, 1994, pp. 151-59.

Brooks, F.W. "The Cinque Ports," *Mariner's Mirror* 15 (1929), 142-91.

Christensen, Arne Emil. "Boat Finds from Bryggen." In: *The Bryggen Papers, Main Series,* I. Ed. Asbjørn E. Herteig. Bergen, 1985, pp. 47-278.

Christensen, Arne Emil. "A Medieval Ship Model," *International Journal of Nautical Archaeology and Underwater Exploration* 16 (1987), 68-70.

Christides, Vassilios. "Ibn al-Manqali (Mangli) and Leo VI: New Evidence on Arabo-Byzantine Ship Construction and Naval Warfare," *Byzantinoslavica* 56 (1995), 1:83-96.

Christides, Vassilios. "Naval History and Naval Technology in Medieval Times: The Need for Interdisciplinary Studies," *Byzantion* 58 (1988), 9-32.

Christides, Vassilios. "New Light on the Transmission of Chinese Naval Technology to the Mediterranean World: The Single Rudder," *Mediterranean Historical Review* 10 (1995), 64-70.

Christides, Vassilios. "Some Remarks on the Mediterranean and Red Sea Ships in Ancient and Medieval Times I: A Preliminary Report," *Tropsis* 1 (1986), 75-82.

Christides, Vassilios. "Some Remarks on the Mediterranean and Red Sea Ships in Ancient and Medieval Times II: Merchant-Passenger vs. Combat Ships," *Tropsis* 2 (1987), 87-99.

Christides, Vassilios. "The Transmission of Chinese Maritime Technology by the Arabs to Europe," *American Neptune* 52 (1992), 38-45.

Conway, T.M. "Two Curious Ships in British Library Add. MS 24189," *Mariner's Mirror* 78 (1992), 327-30.

Cras, Hervé. "La guerre navale en manche et en basse mer du nord au moyen âge." In: *Divers aspects du moyen âge en occident*. Calais, 1977, pp. 45-54.

Crumlin-Pedersen, Ole. "Medieval Ships in Danish Waters." In: *Crossroads in Ancient Shipbuilding: Proceedings of the Sixth International Symposium on Boat and Ship Archaeology, Roskilde, 1991*. Ed. C. Westerdahl. Oxford, 1994, pp. 65-72.

Crumlin-Pedersen, Ole. "Ship Types and Sizes, AD 800-1400." In: *Aspects of Maritime Scandinavia, AD 200-1200: Proceedings of the Nordic Seminar on Maritime Aspects of Archaeology, Roskilde, 13th-15th March, 1989*. Ed. Ole Crumlin-Pedersen. Roskilde: The Viking Ship Museum, 1991, pp. 69-82.

Crumlin-Pedersen, Ole. "The Vikings and the Hanseatic Merchants: 900-1450." In: *A History of Seafaring Based on Underwater Archaeology*. Ed. G. F. Bass. New York, 1972, pp. 181-204.

Degryse, R. "Van koggen en koggeschepen in Vlaanderen en elders (12e-15e eeuw)," *Handelingen voor het genootschap voor geschiedenis te Brugge* 129 (1992), 65-93.

Dotson, John E. "Treatises on Shipbuilding before 1650." In: *A History of Ships*. Vol. 4: *Cogs, Caravels and Galleons*. Ed. Richard Unger. London: Conway Maritime, 1994, pp. 160-68.

Farrell, A.W. "The Use of Iconographic Material in Medieval Ship Archaeology." In: *The Archaeology of Medieval Ships and Harbours in Northern Europe: Papers Based on those Presented to an International Symposium on Boat and Ship Archaeology at Bremerhaven in 1979*. Ed. S. McGrail. BAR International Series, 66. Greenwich, 1979, pp. 227-46.

Fernández-Armesto, Felipe. *Before Columbus: Exploration and Colonisation from the Mediterranean to the Atlantic, 1229-1492*. London, 1987.

Fourquin, Noël M.H. "Galères du moyen-âge." In: *Quand voguaient les galères*. Paris: Musée de la Marine, 1990, pp. 67-87.

Friel, Ian. "Archaeological Sources and the Medieval Ship: Some Aspects of the Evidence," *International Journal of Nautical Archaeology and Underwater Exploration* 12 (1983), 41-62.

Friel, Ian. *The Good Ship: Ships, Shipbuilding and Technology in England, 1200-1520*. Baltimore: The Johns Hopkins University Press, 1995.

Frost, Honor. "Stone Anchors: A Reassessment Reassessed," *Mariner's Mirror* 79 (1993), 449-58.

Gillmer, Thomas. "The Capability of the Single Square Sail Rig: A Technical Assessment." In: *The Archaeology of Medieval Ships and Harbours in Northern Europe: Papers Based on those Presented to an International Symposium on Boat and Ship Archaeology at Bremerhaven in 1979*. Ed. S. McGrail. BAR International Series, 66. Greenwich, 1979, pp. 167-81.

Gillmer, Thomas. "The Importance of Skeleton-first Ship Construction to the Development of the Science of Naval Architecture." In: *Carvel Construction Technique: Skeleton-first, Shell-first*. Ed. R. Reinders and K. Paul. London, 1991, pp. 89-96.

Godal, Jon. "Maritime Archaeology Beneath Church Roofs." In: *Crossroads in Ancient Shipbuilding: Proceedings of the Sixth International Symposium on Boat and Ship Archaeology, Roskilde, 1991*. Ed. C. Westerdahl. Oxford, 1994, pp. 271-78.

Guilmartin, John Francis, Jr. "The Galley in Combat," *MHQ: The Quarterly Journal of Military History* 9.2 (Winter 1997), 20-21.

Hutchinson, Gillian. *Medieval Ships and Shipping*. Rutherford: Fairleigh Dickinson University Press, 1994.

Jackson, Richard P. "From Profit-Sailing to Wage-Sailing: Mediterranean Owner-Captains and their Crews during the Medieval Commercial Revolution," *Journal of European Economic History* 18 (1989), 605-28.

Lethbridge, T.C. "Shipbuilding." In: *A History of Technology*. Ed. C. Singer et al. Vol. II: *The Mediterranean Civilizations and the Middle Ages, c. 700 B.C. to c. A D. 1500*. Oxford, 1957, pp. 563-88.

Lewis, Archibald R. and Timothy J. Runyan. *European Naval and Maritime History, 300-1500*. Bloomington: Indiana University Press, 1985.

Lezzi, Maria Teresa. "L'arche de Noé en forme de bateau: naissance d'une tradition iconographique," *Cahiers de civilisation médiévale (X-XIIe siècles)* 37 (1994). 301-24.

Marsden, Peter. "The Medieval Ships of London." In: *The Archaeology of Medieval Ships and Harbours in Northern Europe: Papers Based on those Presented to an International Symposium on Boat and Ship Archaeology at Bremerhaven in 1979*. Ed. S. McGrail. BAR International Series, 66. Greenwich, 1979, pp. 83-92.

Menezes, José de Vasconcellose. *Os marinheiros e o almirantado: elementos para a história da marinha (Séc XII-XVI)*. Lisbon: Academia de Marinha, 1989.

Merrien, Jean. *La vie des marins au moyen âge: Des Vikings aux galères*. Rennes: Terres de brume, 1994.

Mollat, Michel. *Les sources de l'histoire maritime en Europe du moyen âge au XVIIIe siècle*. Paris: S.E.V.P.E.N., 1962.

Mollat du Jordain, Michel. "L'état Capétian en quête d'une force navale." In: *Histoire militaire de la France*. I: *Des origines à 1715*. Ed. Philippe Contamine. Paris, 1992, pp. 107-23.

Mollat du Jordain, Michel. "The French Maritime Community: A Slow Progress up to the Social Scale from the Middle Ages to the Sixteenth Century," *Mariner's Mirror* 69 (1983), 115-28.

Mollat du Jordain, Michel. "Les marines et la guerre sur mer le nord et l'ouest de l'Europe (jusqu'au XIIe siècle)." In: *Ordinamenti militari in occidente nell'alto medioevo*. Settimane di studio del centro italiano di studi sull'alto medioevo, XV. Spoleto, 1968, II:1009-42.

Murray, K.M.E. "Shipping." In: *Medieval England*. Ed. A.L. Poole. Oxford, 1958, I:168-95.

Nicolle, David C. "Shipping in Islamic Art: Seventh through Sixteenth Century AD," *The American Neptune* 49 (1989), 168-97.

Pryor, John H. "From Dromon to Galea: Mediterranean Bireme Galleys, ca. 700-1300." In: *The Age of the Galley*. Ed. J. Morrison. London: Conway Maritime, 1995, pp. 101-16, 206-16.

Pryor, John H. *Geography, Technology, and War: Studies in the Maritime History of the Mediterranean, 649-1571*. Cambridge: Cambridge University Press, 1988.

Randsborg, Klavs. "Seafaring and Society–in South Scandinavian and European Perspective." In: *Aspects of Maritime Scandinavia, AD 200-1200: Proceedings of the Nordic Seminar on Maritime Aspects of Archaeology, Roskilde, 13th-15th March, 1989*. Ed. Ole Crumlin-Pedersen. Roskilde: The Viking Ship Museum, 1991, pp. 11-22.

Reinders, Reinder. "Medieval Ships: Recent Finds in the Netherlands." In: *The Archaeology of Medieval Ships and Harbours in Northern Europe: Papers Based on those Presented to an International Symposium on Boat and Ship Archaeology at Bremerhaven in 1979*. Ed. S. McGrail. BAR International Series, 66. Greenwich, 1979, pp. 35-43.

Rodger, N.A.M. "The Naval Service of the Cinque Ports," *English Historical Review* 111 (1996), 636-51.

Rodger, N.A.M. *The Safeguard of the Sea: A Naval History of Britain, 660-1649*. New York: W.W. Norton and Company, 1997.

Rodgers, William L. *Naval Warfare under Oars, 4ᵗʰ to 16ᵗʰ Centuries: A Study of Strategy, Tactics and Ship Design.* Annapolis: Naval Institute Press, 1939.

Rose, Susan. "The Wall of England 1000-1500." In: *The Oxford Illustrated History of the Royal Navy.* Ed. J.R. Hil. Oxford, 1995, pp. 1-23.

Runyan, Timothy J. "Merchantmen to Men-of-War in Medieval England." In: *New Aspects of Naval History.* Ed. C.L. Symonds. Annapolis, 1981, pp. 33-40.

Runyan, Timothy J. "The Organization of Royal Fleets in Medieval England." In: *Ships, Seafaring and Society: Essays in Maritime History.* Ed. T.J. Runyan. Detroit, 1987, pp. 37-52.

Sandurra, Enrico. "The Maritime Republics: Medieval and Renaissance Ships in Italy." In: *A History of Seafaring Based on Underwater Archaeology.* Ed. G. F. Bass. New York, 1972, pp. 205-24.

Steffy, J. Richard. "The Medieval Cargo Ship: Evidence from Nautical Archaeology." In: *New Aspects of Naval History.* Ed. C.L. Symonds. Annapolis, 1981, pp. 13-19.

Steffy, J. Richard. "The Mediterranean Shell to Skeleton Transition: A Northwest European Parallel?" In: *Carvel Construction Technique: Skeleton-first, Shell-first.* Ed. R. Reinders and K. Paul. London, 1991, pp. 1-9.

Suttor, Marc. "Sources et méthodes pour l'histoire de la navigation fluviale: L'exemple de la Meuse," *Le moyen âge* 96 (1990), 5-24.

Taylor, E.G.R. *The Haven-Finding Art: A History of Navigation from Odysseus to Captain Cook.* London, 1956.

Unger, Richard W. "Admiralties and Warships of Europe and the Mediterranean, 1000-1500." In: *Changing Interpretations and New Sources in Naval History.* Ed. R.W. Love. Jr. New York, 1980, pp. 34-44.

Unger, Richard W. *The Art of Medieval Technology: Images of Noah the Shipbuilder.* New Brunswick: Rutgers University Press, 1991.

Unger, Richard W. *The Ship in the Medieval Economy, 600-1600.* London: Croom Helm, 1980.

Unger, Richard W. "Warships and Cargo Ships in Medieval Europe," *Technology and Culture* 22 (1981), 233-52.

Unger, Richard W., ed. *Cogs, Caravels and Galleons: The Sailing Ship, 1000-1650*. London: Conway Maritime, 1994.

Villain-Gandossi, Christiane. "Le navire médiéval à travers les minatures des manuscrits français." In: *The Archaeology of Medieval Ships and Harbours in Northern Europe: Papers Based on those Presented to an International Symposium on Boat and Ship Archaeology at Bremerhaven in 1979*. Ed. S. McGrail. BAR International Series, 66. Greenwich, 1979, pp. 195-224.

Villain-Gandossi, Christiane, S. Busuttil, and P. Adam, ed. *Medieval Ships and the Birth of Technological Societies*. 2 vols. Valleta, 1989-91.

Waites, B. "The Fighting Galley," *History Today* 18 (1968), 337-43.

White, Lynn, Jr. "The Diffusion of the Lateen Sail." In: *Medieval Religion and Technology: Collected Essays*. Berkeley and Los Angeles: University of California Press, 1978, pp. 255-60.

Williamson, David. *The Mariners of Ancient Wessex: A Brief Maritime History of Central Southern England Up to the Reign of Henry VIII*. Southampton, 1998.

Military Technology – Premodern – Ships – Medieval – Early Medieval

Agius, Dionisius A. "Historical-Linguistic Reliability of Muqaddasī's Information on Types of Ships." In: *Across the Mediterranean Frontiers: Trade, Politics and Religion, 650-1450: Selected Proceedings of the International Medieval Congress, University of Leeds, 10-13 July 1995, 8-11 July 1996*. Ed. Dionisius A. Agius and Ian Richard Netton. Turnhout: Brepols, 1997, pp. 303-29.

Bachrach, Bernard S. "The Questions of King Arthur's Existence and of Romano-British Naval Operations," *Haskins Society Journal* 2 (1990), 13-28.

Basch, L. "Navires et bateaux coptes: état des questions en 1991," *Graeco-Arabica* 5 (1993), 23-62.

Bruce-Mitford, Rupert. *The Sutton Hoo Ship-Burial*. 4 vols. London: British Museum, 1975-84.

Dove, C.E. "The First British Navy," *Antiquity* 45 (1971), 15-20.

Ellmers, Detlev. *Frühmittelalterliche Handelsschifffahrt in Mittel- und Nordeuropa*. Neumünster, 1972.

Evans, Angela Care. *The Sutton Hoo Ship Burial*. London: British Museum, 1986.

Filipowiak, Wladyslaw. "Shipbuilding at the Mouth of the River Odra (Oder)." In: *Crossroads in Ancient Shipbuilding: Proceedings of the Sixth International Symposium on Boat and Ship Archaeology, Roskilde, 1991*. Ed. C. Westerdahl. Oxford, 1994, pp. 83-96.

Gifford, Edwin and Joyce. "The Sailing Performance of Anglo-Saxon Ships as Derived from the Building and Trials of Half-Scale Models of the Sutton Hoo and Graveney Ship Finds," *Mariner's Mirror* 82 (1996), 131-53.

Goodburn, D.M. "Anglo-Saxon Boat Finds from London, Are They English?" In: *Crossroads in Ancient Shipbuilding: Proceedings of the Sixth International Symposium on Boat and Ship Archaeology, Roskilde, 1991*. Ed. C. Westerdahl. Oxford, 1994, pp. 97-104.

Harpster, Matthew. "Possible Results of the Muslim Invasion on Merchant Shipping and Shipbuilding Techniques in the Mediterranean." In: *Travel, Technology and Organization in Medieval Europe: Papers of the "Medieval Europe Brugge 1997" Conference Volume 8*. Ed. Guy De Boe & Frans Verhaeghe. Zellik: Instituut voor het Archeologisch Patrimonium, 1997, pp. 7-12.

Haywood, John. *Dark Age Naval Power: A Re-assessment of Frankish and Anglo-Saxon Seafaring Activitiy*. London: Routledge, 1991.

Hill, David. "An East Anglian Penny of About 830: The Earliest Representation of an Anglo-Saxon Ship," *Mariner's Mirror* 80 (1994), 326-27.

Hooper, Nicholas. "Some Observations on the Navy in Late Anglo-Saxon England." In: *Studies in Medieval History Presented to R. Allen Brown*. Ed. C. Harper-Bill et al. Woodbridge, 1989, pp. 203-13; in: *Anglo-Norman Warfare: Studies in Late Anglo-Saxon and Anglo-Norman*

Military Organization and Warfare. Ed. M. Strickland. Woodbridge, 1992, pp. 17-27.

Jones, Michael E. "The Literary Evidence for Mast and Sail during the Anglo-Saxon Invasions," *Studies in Medieval and Renaissance History* n.s. 13 (1992), 31-67.

Jones, Michael E. "The Logistics of the Anglo-Saxon Invasions." In: *Naval History: The Sixth Symposium of the United States Naval Academy.* Ed. D.M. Masterson. Wilmington: Scholarly Resources Inc., 1987, 62-69.

Kreutz, Barbara M. "Ships, Shipping, and the Implications of Change in the Early Medieval Mediterranean," *Viator* 7 (1976), 79-109.

Lev, Yaacov. "The Fatamid Navy, Byzantium and the Mediterranean Sea 909-1036 C.E./2977-427 A.H.," *Byzantion* 54 (1984), 220-52.

Lewis, Archibald R. *Naval Power and Trade in the Mediterranean, AD 500-1100.* Princeton: Princeton University Press, 1951.

Lindow, John. "Sailing and Interpreting the Ships on the Gotland Stones," *American Neptune* 53 (1993), 39-50.

Marsden, Peter et al. "A Late Saxon Logboat from Clapton, London Borough of Hackney," *International Journal of Nautical Archaeology and Underwater Exploration* 18 (1989), 89-111.

McGrail, Seán and Owain Roberts. "A Romano-British Boat from the Shores of the Severn Estuary," *Mariner's Mirror* 85 (1999), 133-46.

Smolarek, Przemyslaw. "Aspects of Early Boatbuilding in the Southern Baltic Region. In: *Crossroads in Ancient Shipbuilding: Proceedings of the Sixth International Symposium on Boat and Ship Archaeology, Roskilde 1991.* Ed. C. Westerdahl. Oxford, 1994, pp. 77-81.

Stratos, Andreas N. "The Naval Engagement at Phoenix." In: *Charanis Studies: Essays in Honor of Peter Charanis.* Ed. A.E. Laiou-Thomadakis. New Brunswick, 1980, pp. 221-47.

van Doorninck, Frederick. "Byzantium, Mistress of the Sea, 330-641." In: *A History of Seafaring Based on Underwater Archaeology.* Ed. G. F. Bass. New York, 1972, pp. 133-57.

van Doorninck, Frederick. "Did Tenth-Century Dromons Have a Waterline Ram? Another Look at Leo, *Tactica*, XIX, 69," *Mariner's Mirror* 79 (1993), 387-92.

Military Technology – Premodern – Ships – Medieval – Viking

Atkinson, Ian. *The Viking Ships*. Cambridge: Cambridge University Press, 1979.

Binns, Alan. "Ships and Shipbuilding." In: *Medieval Scandinavia: An Encyclopedia*. Ed. P. Pulsiano. New York, 1993, pp. 578-80.

Binns, Alan. "The Ships of the Vikings, were they "Viking Ships"? In: *Proceedings of the Eighth Viking Congress*. Ed. H. Bekker-Nielsen et al. Odense, 1981.

Bonde, Niels and Arne Emil Christensen. "Dendochronological Dating of the Viking Age Ship Burials at Oseberg, Gokstad and Tune, Norway," *Antiquity* 67 (1993), 575-83.

Brøgger, A.W. and Haakon Shetelig. *Vikingskipene: deres forgjengere og etterfølgere*. Oslo, 1950; trans. *The Viking Ships: Their Ancestry and Evolution*. Trans. Katherine John. Oslo, 1951.

Christensen, Arne Emil. "Scandinavian Ships from Earliest Times to the Vikings." In: *A History of Seafaring Based on Underwater Archaeology*. Ed. G. F. Bass. New York, 1972, pp. 159-79.

Christensen, Arne Emil. "Viking Age Rigging, A Survey of Sources and Theories." In: *The Archaeology of Medieval Ships and Harbours in Northern Europe: Papers Based on those Presented to an International Symposium on Boat and Ship Archaeology at Bremerhaven in 1979*. Ed. S. McGrail. BAR International Series, 66. Greenwich, 1979.

Christensen, Arne Emil. "Viking Age Ships and Shipbuilding," *Norwegian Archaeology Review* 15 (1982), 19-28.

Crumlin-Pedersen, Ole. "Experimental Boat Archaeology in Denmark." In: *Aspects of Maritime Archaeology and Ethnography*. Ed. Seán Murphy. Portsmouth: National Maritime Museum, 1984, pp. 97-121.

Crumlin-Pedersen, Ole. "Large and Small Warships of the North." In: *Military Aspects of Scandinavian Society in a European Perspective, AD. 1-1300*. Ed. A.N. Jørgensen and B. Clausen. Copenhagen, 1997, pp. 184-94.

Crumlin-Pedersen, Ole. *Viking-Age Ships and Shipbuilding in Hedeby/ Haithbu and Schleswig*. Ships and Boats of the North, 2. Schleswig: Archäologische Landesmuseum der Christian-Albrecht-Universität/ Wikinger-Museum Haithbu and Roskilde: National Museum of Denmark/Viking Ship Museum, 1997.

Crumlin-Pedersen, Ole. "Viking Shipbuilding and Seamanship." *Proceedings of the Eighth Viking Congress*. Ed. H. Bekker-Nielsen, Peter Foote, and Olaf Olsen. Odense, 1981, pp. 271-86.

Crumlin-Pedersen, Ole. "The Viking Ships of Roskilde." In: *Aspects of the History of Wooden Shipbuilding*. Portsmouth: National Maritime Museum, 1970, pp. 7-23.

Crumlin-Pedersen, Ole. "The Vikings and the Hanseatic Merchants: 900-1450." In: *A History of Seafaring Based on Underwater Archaeology*. Ed. G. F. Bass. New York, 1972, pp. 181-204.

Damgård-Sørenson, Tinna. *The Viking Ship Museum in Roskilde*. Roskilde: Vikingeskibshallen, 1995.

Hale, John R. "The Viking Longship," *Scientific American* 278 (Feb 1998), 56-63.

Lindow, John. "Sailing and Interpreting the Ships on the Gotland Stones," *American Neptune* 53 (1993), 39-50.

Marcus, G.J. "The Evolution of the Knörr," *Mariner's Mirror* 41 (1955), 115-22.

Marwick, H. "Naval Defence in Norse Scotland," *Scottish Historical Review* 28 (1949), 1-11.

Myhre, Bjørn. "Boathouses and Naval Organization." In: *Military Aspects of Scandinavian Society in a European Perspective, AD. 1-1300*. Ed. A.N. Jørgensen and B. Clausen. Copenhagen, 1997, pp. 169-83.

Nicolaysen, N. *Langskibet fra Gokstad*. Oslo, 1881.

Olsen, Olaf and Ole Crumlin-Pedersen. *Five Viking Ships from Roskilde Fjord*. Trans. B. Bluestone. Copenhagen, 1978.

Olsen, Olaf and Ole Crumlin-Pedersen. "The Skuldelev Ships (II): A Report of the Final Underwater Excavation in 1959 and the Slavaging Operation in 1962," *Acta archaeologica* 38 (1967), 73-174.

Roberts, Owain. "Descendants of Viking Boats." In: *Cogs, Caravels and Galleons: The Sailing Ship, 1000-1650*. Ed. Richard W. Unger. London: Conway Maritime, 1994, pp. 11-28.

Roberts, Owain. "Viking Sailing Performance." In: *Aspects of Maritime Archaeology and Ethnography*. Ed. Seán McGrail. Portsmouth: National Maritime Museum. 1984, pp. 123-51.

Rodger, N.A.M. "Cnut's Geld and the Size of Danish Ships," *English Historical Review* 110 (1995), 392-403.

Sayers, William. "The Etymology and Semantics of Old Norse *knorr* 'cargo ship': The Irish and English Evidence," *Scandinavian Studies* 68 (1996), 279-90.

Simek, Rudolf. *Die Schiffsnamen, Schiffsbezeichnungen und Schiffsken-ningar im Altnordischen*. Vienna, 1982.

Thorvildsen, Knud. *The Viking Ship of Ladby*. The Danish National Museum. Copenhagen: The National Museum, 1975.

Military Technology – Premodern – Ships – Medieval – William the Conqueror's Fleet

Bachrach, Bernard S. "On the Origins of William the Conqueror's Horse Transports," *Technology and Culture* 26 (1985), 505-31.

Gillmor, Caroll. "Naval Logistics of the Cross-Channel Operation, 1066," *Anglo-Norman Studies* 7 (1985), 221-43.

Graindor, M. "Le débarquement de Guillaume en 1066: un coup de maître de la marine normande," *Archaeologia* 30 (1969).

Grainge, Christine and Gerald Grainge. "The Pevensy Expedition: Brilliantly Executed Plan or Near Disaster?" *Mariner's Mirror* 79 (1993), 261-73.

Houts, Elisabeth M.C. van. "The Ship List of William the Conqueror," *Anglo-Norman Studies* 10 (1987), 159-83.

Laporte, J. "Les opérations navales en Manche et Mer du Nord pendant l'année 1066," *Annales de Normandie* 17 (1967), 3-42.

Lee, C.D. "England's Naval Trauma: 1066," *Mariner's Mirror* 80 (1994), 208-09.

Neumann, J. "Hydrographic and Ship-Hydrodynamic Aspects of the Norman Invasion, AD 1066," *Anglo-Norman Studies* 11 (1989), 221-243.

Roberts, Owain T.P. "The Bayeux Tapestry Sails," *Mariner's Mirror* 61 (1981), 287-88.

Rodger, N.A.M. "The Norman Invasion of 1066," *Mariner's Mirror* 80 (1994), 459-63.

Sleeswyk, André W. "Different Functions of Hand Reefs on Nordic Square Sails," *Mariner's Mirror* 61 (1981), 288-89.

Sleeswyk, André W. "The Ship of Harold Godwinson," *Mariner's Mirror* 61 (1981), 87-91.

Military Technology – Premodern – Ships – Medieval – High Medieval (see – Naval Warfare)

Airaldi, Gabriella. "Roger of Lauria's Expedition to the Peloponnese," *Mediterranean History Review* 10 (1995), 15-23.

Anderson, R.C. "English Galleys in 1295," *Mariner's Mirror* 14 (1928), 220-41.

Ayalon, David. "The Mamluks and Naval Power: A Phase of the Struggle between Islam and Christian Europe," *Proceedings of the Israel Academy of Sciences and Humanities* 1 (1965), 1-12.

Balard, M. *La mer noire et la Romanie Génoise (XIIIe-XVe siècles)*. London, 1989.

Brooks, F.W. "The Battle of Damme, 1213," *Mariner's Mirror* 16 (1930), 263-71.

Brooks, F.W. "The Cinque Ports' Feud with Yarmouth in the Thirteenth Century," *Mariner's Mirror* 19 (1933), 27-51.

Brooks, F.W. *The English Naval Forces, 1199-1272*. Manchester, 1932.

Brooks, F.W. "The King's Ships and Galleys, Mainly under John and Henry III," *Mariner's Mirror* 15 (1929), 15-48.

Brooks, F.W. "Naval Administration and the Raising of Fleets under John and Henry III," *Mariner's Mirror* 15 (1929), 351-90.

Brooks, F.W. "Naval Armament in the Thirteenth Century," *Mariner's Mirror* 14 (1928), 114-31.

Byrne, E.H. *Genoese Shipping the Twelfth and Thirteenth Centuries*. Cambridge, 1930.

Cederlund, C.O. "The Find of a 700 Year Old Cog at Oskarhamn, Sweden, and its Documentation: A Work and Planning Report." In: *Carvel Construction Technique: Skeleton-first, Shell-first*. Ed. R. Reinders and K. Paul. London, 1991, pp. 154-60.

Cohen, W. *Die Geschichte der normannisch-sicilischen Flotte unter der Regieruing Rogers I. und Rogers II*. Breslau, 1910.

Di Stefano, Giovanni. "La galea mediowvale di Camarina: notizie preliminari," *Sicilia archeologia* 27 (1994), 87-92.

Dotson, John E. "Fleet Operations in the First Genoese-Venetian War, 1264-1266," *Viator* 30 (1999), 165-80.

Dotson, John E. "A Problem of Cotton and Lead in Medieval Italian Shipping," *Speculum* 57 (1982), 52-62.

Ehrenkreutz, A.S. "The Place of Saladin in the Naval History of the Mediterranean Sea in the Middle Ages," *Journal of the American Oriental Society* 75 (1955), 100-16.

Fermoy, B.E.R. "A Maritime Indenture of 1212," *English Historical Review* 41 (1926), 556-59.

Fernández-Armesto, Felipe. "Naval Warfare after the Viking Age, *c.* 1100-1500." In: *Medieval Warfare: A History*. Ed. Maurice Keen. Oxford: Oxford University Press, 1999, pp. 230-52.

Finke, H. "Die Seeschlacht am Kap Orlando (1299 Juli 4)," *Historische Zeitschrift* 134 (1926), 257-66.

Foerster Laures, Federico. "La tactica de combata de las flotas catalano-aragonesas del siglo XIII, segun la describe Ramon Muntaner (1265-1315)," *Revista de historia naval* 16 (1987), 23-36.

Foerster Laures, Federico. "The Warships of the Kings of Aragon and their Fighting Tactics during the 13th and 14th Centuries AD," *International Journal of Nautical Archaeology and Underwater Exploration* 16 (1987), 19-29.

Fourquin, Noël M.H. "A Medieval Shipbuilding Estimate (c. 1273)," *Mariner's Mirror* 85 (1999), 20-29.

France, John. "The First Crusade as a Naval Enterprise," *Mariner's Mirror* 83 (1997), 389-97.

Freeman, A.Z. "Wooden Walls: The English Navy in the Reign of Edward I." In: *Changing Interpretations and New Sources in Naval History*. Ed. R.W. Love. Jr. New York, 1980, pp. 58-67.

Friel, Ian. "The Building of the Lyme Galley, 1294-1296," *Dorset Natural History and Archaeological Society Proceedings* 108 (1986), 41-44.

Gelsinger, Bruce E. "Some Unusual Ships in Thirteenth-Century Norway," *Mariner's Mirror* 67 (1981), 173-80.

Gillingham, John. "Richard I, Galley-Warfare and Portsmouth: The Beginnings of a Royal Navy." In: *Thirteenth Century England VI*. Ed. M. Prestwich, R.H. Britnell and R. Frame. Woodbridge, 1997, pp. 1-15.

Gruffydd, K. Lloyd. "Sea Power and the Anglo-Welsh Wars, 1210-1410," *Maritime Wales* 11 (1987), 28-53.

Halphen, Louis. "La conquête de la Méditerranée par les Européens au XIe et au XIIe siècles." In: *Melanges d'histoire offerts à Henri Pirenne*. Brussels, 1926, I:175-80.

Hamblin, William J. "The Fatimid Navy during the Crusades: 1099-1124," *American Neptune* 46 (1986), 77-83.

Ireland, John DeCoucy. "In Search of the Ships that Brought the Normans to Ireland in 1169," *Mariner's Mirror* 72 (1986), 82-84.

Jamison, E. *Admiral Eugenius of Sicily*. London, 1957.

Jenkins, H.J.K. "Medieval Fenland Stone Barges: A Fragment of Evidence," *Mariner's Mirror* 79 (1993), 458-60.

Johnson, Charles. "London Shipbuilding, A.D. 1295," *Antiquaries Journal* 7 (1927), 424-37.

Lixa Filgueiras, Octavio. "Gelmirez and the Reconversion of the W. Peninsular Shipbuilding Tradition (XIth-XIIth Centuries)." In: *Carvel Construction Technique: Skeleton-first, Shell-first*. Ed. R. Reinders and K. Paul. London, 1991, pp. 32-41.

Meier-Welcker, Hans. "Das Militärwesen Kaiser Friedrichs II: Landes Verteidigung, Heer und Flotte im sizilischen 'Modellstaat'," *Revue internationale d'histoire militaire* 51 (1975), 9-48.

Mollat du Jourdain, Michel. "Philippe-Auguste et la mer." In: *La France de Philippe Auguste: le temps des mutations: actes du colloque international organiséé par le C.N.R.S. (Paris, 29 septembre-4 octobre 1980)*. Ed. Robert-Henri Bautier. Paris: Editions du Centre national de la recherche scientifique, 1982. pp. 605-23.

Mott, Lawrence V. "Ships of the 13th-Century Catalan Navy," *International Journal of Nautical Archaeology and Underwater Exploration* 19 (1990), 101-12

Pérez-Embid, Florentino. "La marina real Castellana en el siglo XII," *Anuario de estudios medievales* 6 (1969), 141-85.

Pérez-Embid, Florentino. "La marina real Castellana en el siglo XIII." In: *Estudios de historia martíma*. Ed. Ed. Francisco Morales Padrón. Seville, 1979, pp. 71-127.

Pryor, John H. "The Crusade of Emperor Frederick II, 1220-29: The Implications of the Maritime Evidence," *American Neptune* 52 (1992), 113-32.

Pryor, John H. "The Galleys of Charles I of Anjou, King of Sicily, ca. 1269-84," *Studies in Medieval and Renaissance History* 14 (1993), 33-103.

Pryor, John H. "The Mediterranean Round Ships, ca. 1000-1300." In: *A History of Ships*. Vol. 4: *Cogs, Caravels and Galleons*. Ed. Richard Unger. London: Conway Maritime, 1994, pp. 59-76.

Pryor, John H. "The Naval Architecture of Crusader Transport Ships and Horse Transports Revisited," *Mariner's Mirror* 76 (1990), 255-73.

Pryor, John H. "The Naval Architecture of Crusader Transport Ships: A Reconstruction of Some Archetypes for Round-hulled Sailing Ships," *Mariner's Mirror* 70 (1984), 171-219, 275-92, 363-86.

Pryor, John H. "The Naval Battles of Roger of Lauria," *Journal of Medieval History* 9 (1983), 179-219.

Pryor, John H. "Transportation of Horses by Sea during the Era if the Crusades: Eighth Century to 1285 A.D.," *Mariner's Mirror* 68 (1982), 9-27, 103-25.

Pryor, John H. and Sergio Bellabarba. "The Medieval Muslim Ships of the Pisan Bacini," *Mariner's Mirror* 73 (1990), 99-113.

Robbert, Louise Buenger. "A Venetian Naval Expedition of 1224." In: *Economy, Society and Government in Medieval Italy: Essays in Memory of Robert I Reynolds*. Ed. D. Herlihy, R.S. Lopez, and V. Slessarev. Kent: Kent University Press, 1969, pp. 141-51.

Stanford-Reid, W. "Sea Power in the Anglo-Scottish War, 1296-1328," *Mariner's Mirror* 46 (1960), 7-23.

Steffy, J. Richard. "The Reconstruction of the Eleventh Century Serçe Liman Vessel: A Preliminary Report." In: *Ships, Seafaring and Society: Essays in Maritime History*. Ed. T.J. Runyan. Detroit, 1987, pp. 1-36.

Tinniswood, J.T. "English Galleys, 1272-1377," *Mariner's Mirror* 35 (1949), 276-315.

Weir, Michael. "English Naval Activities, 1242-1243," *Mariner's Mirror* 58 (1972), 85-92.

Whitwell, R.J. and Charles Johnson. "The 'Newcastle' Galley," *Archaeologia aeliana* 4th ser., 2 (1926), 142-96.

Military Technology – Premodern – Ships – Medieval – Late Medieval

Abello, A. Udina. "Los costes de las galeras en el siglo XV: La galera *Sant Narcis* destinada a las communicaciones con Italia," *Anuario de estudios medievales* 10 (1980), 733-36.

Anderson, R.C. "English Galleys in 1295," *Mariner's Mirror* 14 (1928), 220-41.

Anderson, R.C. "The Grace de Dieu of 1446-86," *English Historical Review* 34 (1919), 584-86.

Barker, Richard. "Perspectives on the Fifteenth Century Ship." In: *Congresso internacional Bartolomeu Dias e a sua época Actas*. Vol. II: *Navegaçoes na segunda metade do século XV*. Porto, 1989, pp. 201-22.

Barker, Richard. "Shipshape for Discoveries, and Return," *Mariner's Mirror* 78 (1992), 433-47.

Baykowski, Uwe. "The Kieler Hanse-Cog–A Replica of the Bremen Cog." In: *Crossroads in Ancient Shipbuilding: Proceedings of the Sixth International Symposium on Boat and Ship Archaeology, Roskilde, 1991*. Ed. C. Westerdahl. Oxford, 1994, pp. 261-64.

Beaurepaire, Charles de. "Recherches sur l'ancien clos des galées de Rouen." In: *Précis analytique de l'académie impériale des sciences, belles-lettres et arts de Rouen pendant l'année 1863-64*. Rouen, 1864, pp. 238-75.

Bellabarba, Sergio. "The Ancient Methods of Designing Hulls," *Mariner's Mirror* 79 (1993), 274-92.

Bellabarba, Sergio. "The Square-rigged Ship of the *Fabrica de Galere* Manuscript," *Mariner's Mirror* 74 (1988), 113-30, 225-39.

Bello León, Juan Manuel. "Repercusiones de la piratería Mediterránea y Atlántica en el comercio exterior Castellano a finales de la edad media." In: *Across the Mediterranean Frontiers: Trade, Politics and Religion, 650-1450: Selected Proceedings of the International Medieval Congress, University of Leeds, 10-13 July 1995, 8-11 July 1996*. Ed. Dionisius A. Agius and Ian Richard Netton. Turnhout: Brepols, 1997, pp. 283-301.

Bernard, Jacques. *Navires et gens de mer à Bordeaux (vers 1400-vers 1550)*. 3 vols. Paris, 1968.

Bruijn, Jaap R. "Les États et leurs marines de la fin du XVIe siècle à la fin du XVIIIe siècle." In: *Guerre et concurrence entre les États européens du XIVe au XVIIIe siècle*. Ed. Philippe Contamine. Fondation Européenne de la Science: Les origines de l'État moderne en Europe, XIIIe-XVIIIe siècle. Paris: Presses universitaires de France, 1998, pp. 83-122.

Brummett, Palmira. *Ottoman Seapower and Levantine Diplomacy in the Age of Discovery*. Albany, 1994.

Burwash, Dorothy. *English Merchant Shipping, 1460-1540*. Toronto: University of Toronto Press, 1947.

Charanis, Peter. "Piracy in the Aegean during the Reign of Michael VIII Palaeologus," *Annuaire de l'institut de philologie et d'histoire orientales et slaves* 10 (1950), 27-136.

Childs, Wendy R. "The *George* of Beverley and Olav Olavesson: Trading Conditions in the North Sea in 1464," *Northern History* 31 (1995), 110-22.

Cipolla, Carlo M. *Guns and Sails in the Early Phase of European Expansion, 1400-1700*. London: Collins, 1965.

Clark, Richard, et al. "Recent Work on the R. Hamble Wreck near Bursledon, Hampshire," *International Journal of Nautical Archaeology and Underwater Exploration* 22 (1993), 21-22.

Corvisier, André. "L'art militaire au temps de la lutte entre les grandes puissances pour la suprématie sur la nouveau monde au XVIIe siècle." In: *Acta del XVIII Congresso internazionale di storia militare: La scoperta del nuovo mondo e la sua influenza nella storia militare*. Ed. Paolo Alberini and Michele Nones. Turin, 1993, pp. 81-92.

Davis, James Cushman. "Shipping and Spying in the Early Career of a Venetian Doge, 1496-1502," *Studi veneziana* 16 (1974), 97-108.

Ditchburn, David. "Piracy and War at Sea in Late Medieval Scotland." In: *Scotland and the Sea*. Ed. T.C. Smout. Edinburgh, 1992, pp. 35-58.

Dotson, John E. "Merchant and Naval Influences on Galley Design at Venice and Genoa in the Fourteenth Century." In: *New Aspects of Naval History*. Ed. C.L. Symonds. Annapolis, 1981, pp. 20-32.

Dotson, John E. "Safety Regulations for Galleys in Mid-Fourteenth-Century Genoa: Some Thoughts on Medieval Risk Management," *Journal of Medieval History* 20 (1994).

Doumerc, Bernard. "La crise structurelle de la marine Vénitienne au XVe siècle: Le problème du retard des *Mude*," *Annales: Economies, sociétés, civilisations* 40 (1985), 605-23.

Edwards, Clinton R. "Design and Construction of Fifteenth-Century Iberian Ships: A Review," *Mariner's Mirror* 78 (1992), 419-32.

Elbl, Martin Malcolm. "The Portuguese Caravel and European Shipbuilding: Phases of Development and Diversity," *Revista da universidade de Coimbra* 32 (1985), 543-72.

Ellmers, Detlev. "The Cog of Bremen and Related Boats." In: *The Archaeology of Medieval Ships and Harbours in Northern Europe*. Ed. S. McGrail. BAR International Series, 66. Oxford, 1979, pp. 1-15.

Fernández-Armesto, Felipe. "Naval Warfare after the Viking Age, *c.* 1100-1500." In: *Medieval Warfare: A History*. Ed. Maurice Keen. Oxford: Oxford University Press, 1999, pp. 230-52.

Fernández-Armesto, Felipe. "The Sea and Chivalry in Late Medieval Spain." In: *Maritime History*. I: *The Age of Discovery*. Ed. J.B. Hattendorff. Malabar, 1996, pp. 123-36.

Fernández Duro, Cesáreo. *Armada Española desde la union de los Reinos de Castilla y Aragon*. 9 vols. Madrid, 1895-1903.

Ferrer I Mallol, M.-T. "Els corsaris castellans i la campanya de Pero Niño al Mediterrani (1404): Documentos sobre *El Victorial*," *Anuario de estudios medievaíes* 5 (1968), 265-338.

Francisco Moura, Carlos. "Portuguese Caraveloes." In: *Carvel Construction Technique: Skeleton-first, Shell-first*. Ed. R. Reinders and K. Paul. London, 1991, pp. 190-94.

Freeman, A.Z. "Wooden Walls: The English Navy in the Reign of Edward I." In: *Changing Interpretations and New Sources in Naval History*. Ed. R.W. Love. Jr. New York, 1980, pp. 58-67.

Friel, Ian. "The Carrack: The Advent of the Full Rigged Ship." *Cogs, Caravels and Galleons: The Sailing Ship, 1000-1650*. Ed. Richard W. Unger. London: Conway Maritime, 1994, pp. 77-90.

Friel, Ian. "Henry V's *Grace Dieu* and the Wreck in the R. Hamble near Bursledon, Hampshire," *International Journal of Nautical Archaeology* 22 (1993), 3-19.

Friel, Ian. "Winds of Change? Ships and the Hundred Years War." In: *Arms, Armies and Fortifications in the Hundred Years War*. Ed. A. Curry and M. Hughes. Woodbridge, 1994, pp. 183-94.

Fritze, F. and G. Krause. *Seekriege der Hanse*. Berlin, 1989.

Gilliodts-Van Severen, L. "La marine militaire de Bruges au XIVe siècle," *La Flandre* 12 (1881), 291-318.

Gruffydd, K. Lloyd. "Sea Power and the Anglo-Welsh Wars, 1210-1410," *Maritime Wales* 11 (1987), 28-53.

Guilmartin, John Francis, Jr. "The Early Provision of Artillery Armament on Mediterranean War Galleys," *Mariner's Mirror* 59 (1973), 257-80.

Harris, Jonathan. "Bessarion on Shipbuilding," *Byzantinoslavica* 55 (1994), II:291-303.

Hobbs, Doreen. "Royal Ships and their Flags in the Late Fifteenth and Early Sixteenth Centuries," *Mariner's Mirror* 80 (1994), 388-94.

Hocquet, Jean Claude. "Productivity Gains and Technological Change. Venetian Naval Architecture at the End of the Middle Ages," *Journal of European Economic History* 24 (1995), 537-56.

Hoheisel, Wolf-Dieter. "A Full-Scale Replica of the Hanse Cog of 1380." In: *Crossroads in Ancient Shipbuilding: Proceedings of the Sixth Interna-*

tional Symposium on Boat and Ship Archaeology, Roskilde, 1991. Ed. C. Westerdahl. Oxford, 1994, pp. 257-60.

Hrabak, Bogumil. "Gusarstvo i presretanje pri plovidbi u Jadranskom i Jonskom moru u drogoj polovini XV veka," *Vesnik* 4 (1957), 83-98.

Hutchinson, Gillian. "Henry V's Warship *Grace Dieu*." In: *The Archaeology of Ships of War*. Ed. M. Bound. Oxford, 1995, pp. 22-25.

Jacoby, David. "Les gens de mer dans la marine de guerre venitienne de la mer égée aux XIVe et XVe siècles." In: *Le genti del mare mediterraneo, a cura di R. Ragota*. Naples, 1981, I:169-201.

Jones, Michael. "Two Exeter Ship Agreements of 1303 and 1310," *Mariner's Mirror* 53 (1967), 315-19.

Jongkees, A.G. "Armement et action d'une flotte de guerre: la contribution des comtés maritimes à l'armée générale des pays de Par-Deçà en 1477." *Publications du centre Européen d'études Bourguignonnes (XIVe-XVIe s.)* 26 (1986), 71-86; in: *Burgundica et Varia*. Hilversum, 1990, pp. 302-18.

Lane, Frederic C. "The Economic Meaning of the Invention of the Compass," *American Historical Review* 68 (1963), 605-17.

Lane, Frederic C. "Merchant Galleys, 1300-34: Private and Communal Operation," *Speculum* 38 (1963), 179-205.

Lane, Frederic C. "Naval Architecture about 1550," *Mariner's Mirror* 20 (1934), 24-49; in *Venice and History: The Collected Papers of Frederic C. Lane*. Baltimore, 1966, pp. 163-88.

Lane, Frederic C. "Technology and Productivity in Seaborne Transportation." In: *Trasporti e sviluppo economico, secoli XIII-XVIII*. Ed. A. V. Marx. Florence, 1986, pp. 233-44.

Lane, Frederic C. *Venetian Ships and Shipbuilding of the Renaissance*. Baltimore: The Johns Hopkins University Press, 1934.

Lane, Frederic C. "Venetian Shipping during the Commerical Revolution," *American Historical Review* 38 (1933), 219-39; in *Venice and History: The Collected Papers of Frederic C. Lane*. Baltimore, 1966, pp. 3-24.

Laughton, L.G. Carr. "The Great Ship of 1419," *Mariner's Mirror* 9 (1923), 83-87.

Law, John. "On the Social Explanation of Technical Change: The Case of the Portuguese Maritime Expansion," *Technology and Culture* 28 (1987), 227-53.

Law, John. "Technology and Heterogeneous Engineering: The Case of Portuguese Expansion." In: *The Social Construction of Technological Systems: New Directions in the Sociology and History of Technology*. Ed. W.E. Bijker, T.P. Hughes and T.J. Pinch. Cambridge, 1987, 111-34.

Ledieu, Alcius. "Notice sur la *Petite-Trésorière*, navire de guerre acheté par l'Échevinage d'Abbeville en 1479," *Bulletin historique et philologique du comité des travaux historiques et scientifiques* (1897), 99-112.

L'Hour, Michel and Elisabeth Veyrat. "The French Medieval Clinker Wreck from Aber Wrac'h." In: *Crossroads in Ancient Shipbuilding: Proceedings of the Sixth International Symposium on Boat and Ship Archaeology, Roskilde, 1991*. Ed. C. Westerdahl. Oxford, 1994, pp. 165-80.

L'Hour, Michel and Elisabeth Veyrat. "A Mid-15th Century Clinker Boat Off the North Coast of France, the Aber Wrac'h I Wreck: A Preliminary Report," *The International Journal of Nautical Archaeology and Underwater Exploration* 18 (1989), 285-98.

Luttrell, Anthony. "The Earliest Documents on the Hospitaller *Corso* at Rhodes: 1413 and 1416," *Mediterranean Historical Review* 10 (1995), 177-88.

Luttrell, Anthony. "Late Medieval Galley Oarsmen." In: *La genti del mare mediterraneo*. Ed. R. Ragosta. Naples, 1981, I:87-101.

Lyon, Eugene. "The *Niña*, the *Santa Cruz*, and Other Caravels as Described in the *Libro de Armadas* and Other Spanish Records," *American Neptune* 53 (1993), 239-46.

Mallett, Michael. *The Florentine Galleys in the Fifteenth Century*. Oxford, 1967.

Manwaring, G.E. "The Safeguard of the Sea, 1442," *Mariner's Mirror* 9 (1923), 376-79.

Marcus, G.J. "The Mariner's Compass: Its Influence upon Navigation in the Later Middle Ages," *History* n.s. 41 (1956), 16-24.

Martinez-Valverde, C. "La nota marinera en la crónica de Don Pero Niño," *Revista de historia naval* 8 (1985), 18-20.

McKee, Alexander. "The Influence of British Naval Strategy on Ship Design: 1400-1850." In: *A History of Seafaring Based on Underwater Archaeology*. Ed. G. F. Bass. New York, 1972, pp. 225-52.

Meale, Carol M. "The *Libelle of Englyshe Polycye* and Mercantile Literary Culture in Late-Medieval London." In: *London and Europe in the Later Middle Ages*. Ed. J. Boffey and P. King. London, 1995, pp. 181-227.

Merlin-Chazelas, Anne. "Quelques notes sur le clos de galées," *Bulletin des amis des monuments Rouennais* (1958-1970).

Moens, W.J.C. "Nederlandsche schippers en hum schepen uit de XVe eeuw," *De Nederlandsche leeuw* 13 (1895).

Mollat du Jourdain, Michel. *Le commerce maritime normand à la fin du moyen âge*. Paris, 1952.

Mollat du Jourdain, Michel. "Les enjeux maritimes de la guerre de cent ans." In: *Histoire militaire de la France*. I: *Des origines à 1715*. Ed. Philippe Contamine. Paris, 1992, pp. 153-69.

Mollat du Jourdain, Michel. "Essai d'orientation pour l'étude de la guerre de course et la piraterie (XIIIe-XVe siècles)," *Anuario de estudios medievales* 10 (1980), 743-49.

Moore, Alan. "Accounts and Inventories of John Starlyng, Clerk of the King's Ships to Henry IV," *Mariner's Mirror* 4 (1914), 20-26, 167-73.

Moore, Alan. "A Barge of Edward III," *Mariner's Mirror* 6 (1920), 229-42.

Moortel, Aleydis van de. "The Conctruction [sic] of a Cog-Like Vessel in the Late Middle Ages." In: *Carvel Construction Technique: Skeleton-first, Shell-first*. Ed. R. Reinders and K. Paul. London, 1991, pp. 42-46.

Mott, Lawrence V. "Medieval Ship Graffito in the Palau Reial Major at Barcelona," *Mariner's Mirror* 76 (1990), 13-21.

Mott, Lawrence V. "Square-Rigged Galleys of the Late Fifteenth Century," *Mariner's Mirror* 73 (1987), 49-54.

Nance, R. Morton. "The Ship of the Renaissance," *Mariner's Mirror* 41 (1955), 180-92, 281-98.

O'Donnel, Hugo. "Las galeras renacentistas en sus aspectos militaires y la táctica naval en el Mediterraneo." In: *XXII. Kongreß der Internationalen Kommission für Militärgeschichte Acta 22: Von Crécy bis Mohács Kriegswesen im späten Mittelalter (1346-1526)*. Vienna, 1997, pp. 312-23.

Palou i Miquel, Hug. "La regulació de la navegació comercial per mar en temps de guerra: L' ordinació de Pere III de 1356," *Anuario de estudios medievales* 29 (1999), 775-801.

Parry, J.H. *The Establishment of the European Hegemony: 1415-1715*. 3rd ed. New York, 1959.

Paviot, Jacques. "Les navires du duc de Bourgogne Philippe le Bon (vers 1440-1465)." In: *Atti del V convegno internazionale di studi Colombiani: "Navi e navigazione dei secoli XV e XVI*. Genoa, 1990, I:167-95.

Paviot, Jacques. *La politique navale des ducs de Bourgogne, 1384-1482*. Lille: Presses Universitaires de Lille, 1995.

Phillips, Carla Rahn. "The Caravel and the Galleon." In: *Ships, Seafaring and Society: Essays in Maritime History*. Ed. T.J. Runyan. Detroit, 1987, pp. 91-114.

Pritchard, Violet. "Some English Medieval Ship Graffiti," *Mariner's Mirror* 73 (1987), 318-20.

Proctor, David J. "A Late Fifteenth-Century Venetian Galley Builder and his Beliefs." In: *Atti del V convegno internazionale di studi columbiani: "Navi e navigazione dei secoli XV e XVI*. Genoa, 1990, I:229-43.

Prynne, M.W. "Henry V's *Grace Dieu*," *Mariner's Mirror* 54 (1968), 115-28.

Reid, W. Stanford. "Sea-power in the Anglo-Scottish War, 1296-1328," *Mariner's Mirror* 46 (1960), 7-23.

Richmond, Colin F. "The Earl of Warwick's Domination of the Channel and the Naval Dimension to the Wars of the Roses, 1456-1460," *Southern History* 20/21 (1998-99), 1-19.

Richmond, Colin F. "English Naval Power in the Fifteenth Century," *History* 52 (1967), 1-15.

Richon, Louis. "Le navire de la cathédrale de Bayonne," *Neptunia* 157 (1985), 27-41.

Rieth, Eric. "La question de la construction navale à franc-bord au Ponant," *Neptunia* 160 (1985), 8-21.

Robson, J.A. "The Catalan Fleet and Moorish Sea-Power (1337-1344)," *English Historical Review* 74 (1959), 386-408.

Roelofsen, C.G. "L'evolution de la flotte 'Bourguignonne' aux XVe et XVIe siècles: quelques remarques sur l'introduction du canon dans la guerre maritime et son influence." *Publication du centre Européen d'études Bourguignonnes (XIVe-XVIe s.)* 26 (1986), 87-95.

Rose, Robert. "The Anti-Hogging Hull of the Cog of Bremen," *Mariner's Mirror* 63 (1977), 108.

Rose, Susan. "Henry V's *Grace Dieu* and Mutiny at Sea: Some New Evidence," *Mariner's Mirror* 63 (1977), 3-7.

Rose, Susan, ed. *The Navy of the Lancastrian Kings: Accounts and Inventories of William Soper, Keeper of the King's Ships, 1422-1427.* London, 1982.

Ruddock, Alwyn A. *Italian Merchants and Shipping in Southampton, 1270-1600.* Southampton, 1951.

Runyan, Timothy J. "The Cog as Warship." In: *Cogs, Caravels and Galleons: The Sailing Ship, 1000-1650.* ed. Robert Gardiner. London: Conway Maritime, 1994, pp. 47-58.

Runyan, Timothy J. "Ships and Fleets in Anglo-French Warfare, 1337-1360," *American Neptune* 46 (1986), 91-99.

Salisbury, W. "The Woolwich Ship," *Mariner's Mirror* 47 (1961), 81-90.

Sandurra, Enrico. "The Maritime Republics: Medieval and Renaissance Ships in Italy." In: *A History of Seafaring Based on Underwater Archaeology.* Ed. G. F. Bass. New York, 1972, pp. 205-24.

Scammell, G.V. "English Merchant Shipping at the End of the Middle Ages: Some East Coast Evidence," *Economic History Review* 13 (1961), 327-41.

Scammell, G.V. "Shipowning in England *circa* 1450-1550," *Transactions of the Royal Historical Society* 5th ser. 12 (1962), 105-22.

Sherborne, James. "English Barges and Balingers of the Late Fourteenth Century," *Mariner's Mirror* 63 (1977), 109-14.

Sherborne, James. "The English Navy: Shipping and Manpower 1369-1389," *Past and Present* 37 (1967), 163-75.

Sicking, Louis. "Die offensive Lösung: Militärische Aspekte des Holländischen Ostseehandels im 15. und 16. jahrhundert," *Hansische Geschichtsblätter* 117 (119), 39-51.

Škrivanić, Gavro A. "Prilog proučavanju brodova omiških gusara," *Vesnik* 3 (1956), 52-60.

Smith, Julian A. "Percursors to Peregrinus: The Early History of Magnetism and the Mariner's Compass in Europe," *Journal of Medieval History* 18 (1992), 21-74.

Spont, A. "La marine Française sous le régne de Charles VIII," *Revue des questions historiques* 62 (1894).

Stanford-Reid, W. "Sea Power in the Anglo-Scottish War, 1296-1328," *Mariner's Mirror* 46 (1960), 7-23.

Suárez Fernández, Luis. *Navigación y comercio en el Golfo de Vizcaya: un estudio sobre la politica marinera de la Casa de Trastámara.* Madrid, 1959.

Tangheroni, Marco. "Transporti navali e commercio marittimo nell'Italia del Quattrocentro," *Revista d'historia medieval* 3 (1992), 27-53.

Tiesen, Michael. "A Medieval Clinker-Built Wreck at Hundevika, Norway." In: *Crossroads in Ancient Shipbuilding: Proceedings of the Sixth*

International Symposium on Boat and Ship Archaeology, Roskilde, 1991. Ed. C. Westerdahl. Oxford, 1994, pp. 73-76.

Tinniswood, J.T. "English Galleys, 1272-1377," *Mariner's Mirror* 35 (1949), 276-315.

Tipping, Colin. "Cargo Handling and the Medieval Cog," *Mariner's Mirror* 80 (1994), 3-15.

Turner, W.J. Carpenter. "The Building of the *Gracedieu*, *Valentine* and *Falconer* at Southampton, 1416-1420," *Mariner's Mirror* 40 (1954), 55-72.

Turner, W.J. Carpenter. "The Building of the *Holy Ghost of the Tower*, 1414-1416, and her Subsequent History," *Mariner's Mirror* 40 (1954), 270-81.

Turner, W.J. Carpenter. "Southampton as a Naval Centre, 1414-1458." In: *Collected Essays on Southampton*. Ed. J.B. Morgan and P. Peberdy. Southampton, 1958, pp. 38-47.

Unali, Anna. "Considerazioni sulla pirateria e sulla corsa musulmana e cristiana all'epoca della conquista portoghese di Ceuta (1415)," *Anuario de estudios medievales* 24 (1994), 557-81.

Unger, Richard W. "Alfred Thayer Mahan, Ship Design, and the Evolution of Sea Power in the Late Middle Ages," *International History Review* 19 (1997), 505-21.

Unger, Richard W. "Dutch Ship Design in the Fifteenth and Sixteenth Centuries," *Viator* 4 (1973), 387-411.

Unger, Richard W. "Northern Ships and the Late Medieval Economy: Columbus and the Medieval Maritime Tradition," *American Neptune* 53 (1993), 247-53.

Unger, Richard W. "Marine Paintings and the History of Schipbuilding." In: *Art in History/History in Art*. Ed. J. DeVries and D. Frieburg. Santa Monica, 1991, pp. 74-93.

Unger, Richard W. "Northern Ships and the Late Medieval Economy," *American Neptune* 53 (1993), 247-53.

Unger, Richard W. "Portuguese Shipbuilding and the Early Voyages to the Guinea Coast." In: *Vice-Almirante A. Teixeira Da Mota in memoriam.* Lisbon, 1987, I:229-49.

Unger, Richard W. "Scheepvaart in de Noordelijke Nederlanden." In: *Algemene geschiedenis der Nederland.* Bussum, 1979, VI.

Unger, Richard W. "The Technical Development of Shipbuilding and Government Policies in the Fifteenth and Sixteenth Centuries." In: *Atti del v convegno internazionale di studi colombiani: "Navi e navigazione nei secoli XV e XVI".* Genoa, 1990, I:197-211.

Unger, Richard W. "The Tonnage of Europe's Merchant Fleets, 1300-1800," *American Neptune* 52 (1992), 247-61.

Unger, Richard W. "Warships and Cargo Ships in Medieval Europe," *Technology and Culture* 22 (1981), 233-52.

Unger, Richard W. "Wooden Shipbuilding in Dordrecht," *Mededelingen van de nederlandse vereingen voor zeegescheidenis* 30 (1975), 5-19.

Unger, Richard W. "Wooden Shipbuilding in Zeeland." In: *Ships and Ship-building in the North Sea and Atlantic, 1400-1800.* Aldershot: Ashgate, 1997, #5. (Trans. Of "Houten scheepsbouw in Zeeland," *Zeeuws tijdschrift* 26.4/5 (1976), 130-34.)

van de Moortel, Aleydis. "Functional Analysis of a Small Zuyderzee Cog." In: *Crossroads in Ancient Shipbuilding: Proceedings of the Sixth International Symposium on Boat and Ship Archaeology, Roskilde, 1991.* Ed. C. Westerdahl. Oxford, 1994, pp. 117-24.

van Oosten, F.C. and M. Bosscher. "He taktisch gebruik van het zeilschip," *Marineblad* 80 (1970), 997-1035

Verbruggen, J.F. "Een krijgsvloot, uitgerust door de stad Brugge, in 1316," *Het leger. De natie* 5 (1950), 505-11.

Verbruggen, J.F. "De vlaamse vloot in 1304," *Standen en landen* 4 (1952).

Ward, Robin. "Cargo Handling and the Medieval Cog," *Mariner's Mirror* 80 (1994), 327-31.

Ward, Robin. "A Surviving Charter-Party of 1323," *Mariner's Mirror* 81 (1995), 387-401.

Warner, G. *The Libelle of Englyshe Polycye: A Poem on the Use of Sea-Power, 1436*. Oxford, 1926.

Waters, David W. "Columbus's Portuguese Inheritance," *Mariner's Mirror* 4 (1992), 385-405.

Waters, David W. "The Intellectual Challenge of Oceanic Navigation in the XVth Century." In: *Congresso internacional Bartolomeu Dias e a sua época Actas*. Vol. II: *Navegaçoes na segunda metade do século XV*. Porto, 1989, pp. 141-59.

Whitewell, R.J. and Charles Johnson. "The Newcastle Galley," *Archaeologia aeliana* 4th ser. 2 (1926), pp. 142-96.

Military Technology – Premodern – Ships (including Warships) – Early Modern

Barnby, Henry. "The Algerian Attack on Baltimore, 1631," *Mariner's Mirror* 56 (1970), 27-31.

Baumber, M.L. "The Navy and the Civil War in Ireland, 1641-1643," *Mariner's Mirror* 57 (1971), 385-97.

Baumber, M.L. "The Navy and the Civil War in Ireland, 1643-46," *Mariner's Mirror* 75 (1989), 255-68.

Baumber, M.L. "Parliamentary Naval Politics, 1641-49," *Mariner's Mirror* 82 (1996), 398-408.

Bernard, Jacques. *Navires et gens de mer à Bordeaux (vers 1400-vers 1550)*. 3 vols. Paris, 1968.

Bernard, Jacques. "Les types de navires Ibériques et leur influence sur la construction navale dans les ports du sud-ouest de la France (xve-xvie siècles)." In: *Les aspects internationaux de la découverte océanique aux XVe et XVIe siècles*. Ed. M. Mollat and P. Adams. Paris, 1968, pp. 195-220.

Blake, W. and J. Green. "A Mid-XVIth Century Portuguese Wreck in the Seychelles," *International Journal of Nautical History and Underwater Archaeology* 15 (1986).

Bonner, Elizabeth. "The Recovery of St. Andrews Castle in 1547: French Naval Policy and Diplomacy in the British Isles," *English Historical Review* 111 (1996), 578-98.

Bono, Salvatore. *I corsari Barbareschi*. Turin, 1964.

Boulind, Richard. "Ships of Private Origin in the Mid-Tudor Navy: the *Lartigue*, the *Salamander*, the *Mary Willoughby*, the *Bark Aucher* and the *Galley Blanchard*," *Mariner's Mirror* 59 (1973), 385-408.

Boxer, C.R. *The Dutch Seaborne Empire, 1600-1800*. London: Hutchinson, 1966.

Boyer, Pierre. "Artillerie et tactique navale en Méditerranée au XVIe siècle," *Revue historique des armées* 174 (1989), 110-21.

Bracewell, C.W. *The Uskoks of Senj: Piracy, Banditry and Holy War in the Sixteenth-Century Adriatic*. Ithaca: Cornell University Press, 1992.

Bradford, Ernle. *The Story of the Mary Rose*. London: Hamish Hamilton, 1982.

Bruijn, Jaap R. *The Dutch Navy of the Seventeenth and Eighteenth Century*. Columbia: University of South Carolina Press, 1993.

Brummett, Palmira. *Ottoman Seapower and Levantine Diplomacy in the Age of Discovery*. Albany, 1994.

Burwash, Dorothy. *English Merchant Shipping, 1460-1540*. Toronto: University of Toronto Press, 1947.

Capp, Bernard. *Cromwell's Navy: The Fleet and the English Revolution, 1648-1660*. Oxford, 1989.

Casada Soto, José Luis. "Atlantic Shipping in Sixteenth-Century Spain and the 1588 Armada." In: *England, Spain and the Gran Armada, 1585-1604*. Ed. M.J. Rodríguez-Salagado and Simon Adams. Edinburgh, 1991, pp. 95-132.

Casada Soto, José Luis. *Los barcos españoles del siglo XVI y la Gran Armada de 1588*. Madrid, 1988.

Cerezo Martínez, Ricardo. *Las armadas de Felipe II*. Madrid, 1988.

Cerezo Martínez, Ricardo. *La proyección marítima de España en la época de los Reyes Católicos*. Madrid, 1991.

Cipolla, Carlo M. *Guns and Sails in the Early Phase of European Expansion, 1400-1700*. London: Collins, 1965.

Cogswell, Thomas. "Prelude to Ré: The Anglo-French Struggle over La Rochelle, 1624-1627," *History* 71 (1986), 1-21.

Coindreau, Roger. *Les corsaires de Salé*. Paris, 1948.

Corbett, Julian S. *Drake and the Tudor Navy*. 2nd ed. 2 vols. London: Longman, 1899.

Corbett, Julian S. *England in the Mediterranean: A Study of the Rise and Influence of British Power within the Straits, 1603-1713*. 2nd ed. 2 vols. London, 1917.

Davies, Clifford S.L. "The Administration of the Royal Navy under Henry VIII: The Origins of the Navy Board," *English Historical Review* 80 (1965), 268-88.

Davies, Clifford S.L. "Sixteenth Century Administration," *Mariner's Mirror* 55 (1969), 310.

De Beer, E.S. "The Lord High Admiral and the Administration of the Navy," *Mariner's Mirror* 13 (1927), 45-50.

Dietz, B. "The Huguenot and English Corsairs during the Third Civil War in France, 1568 to 1570," *Proceedings of the Huguenot Society* 19 (1952-58), 278-94.

Duffy, Michael. "The Foundations of British Naval Power." In: *The Military Revolution and the State, 1500-1800*. Ed. M. Duffy. Exeter, 1980, pp. 49-85.

Dyer, Florence E. "The Elizabethan Sailorman," *Mariner's Mirror* 10 (1924), 133-46.

Dyer, Florence E. "Reprisals in the Sixteenth Century," *Mariner's Mirror* 21 (1935), 187-97.

Dyer, Florence E. "The Ship-Money Fleet," *Mariner's Mirror* 23 (1937), 198-209.

Dyskant, Józef Wiesław. *Oliwa 1627*. Warsaw: Bellona, 1993.

Ejercito y la armada de Felipe II ante el IV centenario de su muerte, El. Jornadas de historia militar, 4a. Madrid: Ministerio de Defensa, 1997.

Ewen, C. *Captain John Ward, "Arch-Pirate"*. Paignton, 1939.

Ewen, C. *The Golden Chalice: A Documented Narrative of an Elizabethan Pirate*. Paignton, 1939.

Ewen, C. "Organized Piracy round England in the Sixteenth Century," *Mariner's Mirror* 35 (1949), 29-42.

Fairclough, Keith. "Navigational Devices along the River Lea, 1600-1767," *Transactions of the Newcomen Society* 64 (1992-93), 21-40.

Fasano-Guarini, Elena. "Au XVIe siècle: Comment naviguent les galères," *Annales: E.S.C.* 16 (1961).

Fernández Duro, Cesáreo. *Armada Española desde la union de los Reinos de Castilla y Aragon*. 9 vols. Madrid, 1895-1903.

Fernández Duro, Cesáreo. *La marina de Castilla desde su origen y pugna con la de Inglaterra hasta la refundacion en la Armada Española*. Madrid, 1894.

Fowler, Elaine W. *English Sea Power in the Early Tudor Period, 1484-1558*. Ithaca, 1965.

Gardiner, C. Harvey. *Naval Power in the Conquest of Mexico*. Austin: University of Texas Press, 1956.

Glete, Jan. *Navies and Nations: Warships, Navies and State Building in Europe and America, 1500-1860*. 2 vols. Stockholm, 1993.

Glete, Jan. *Navies and State Building in Europe and America, 1500-1860*. 2 vols. Stockholm: Almqvist and Wiksall, 1993.

Glete, Jan. "Warfare at Sea 1450-1815." In: *War in the Early Modern World, 1450-1815*. Ed. Jeremy Black. London, 1999, pp. 25-52.

Guerot, Max, Eric Reith, Jean-Marie Gassend, and Bernard Lou. *Le navire genois de Villefranche: un naufrage de 1516*. Paris: Editions du Centre National de la Récherche Scientifique, 1989.

Guilmartin, John Francis, Jr. "The Early Provision of Artillery Armament on Mediterranean War Galleys," *Mariner's Mirror* 59 (1973), 257-80.

Guilmartin, John Francis, Jr. *Gunpowder and Galleys: Changing Technology and Mediterranean Warfare at Sea in the Sixteenth Century*. Cambridge: Cambridge University Press, 1974.

Guilmartin, John Francis, Jr. "The Logistics of Warfare at Sea in the Sixteenth Century: The Spanish Perspective." In: *Feeding Mars: Logistics in Western Warfare from the Middle Ages to the Present*. Ed. J.A. Lynn. Boulder, 1993, pp. 109-36.

Goodman, David C. *Spanish Naval Power, 1589-1665: Reconstruction and Defeat*. Cambridge: Cambridge University Press, 1997.

Gunn-Graham, T. Iain. "The Marine Engravings of Peter Bruegel the Elder," *American Neptune* 58 (1998), 329-41.

Hale, John R. "Men and Weapons: The Fighting Potential of Sixteenth Century Venetian Galleys." In: *Renaissance War Studies*. London, 1983, pp. 309-34.

Harding, Richard. *The Evolution of the Sailing Navy, 1509-1815*. London: Macmillan, 1995.

Harding, Richard. "Naval Warfare, 1453-1815." In: *European Warfare, 1453-1815*. Ed. Jeremy Black. New York: St. Martin's Press, 1999, pp. 96-117.

Hassenstein, Wilhelm. "Über die Feuerwaffen in der Seeschlacht von Lepanto," *Zeitschrift für historische Waffen- und Köstumkunde* 16 (1940-42), 1-11.

James, Alan. "The Development of French Naval Policy in the Seventeenth Century: Richelieu's Early Aims and Ambitions," *French History* 12 (1998), 384-402.

Kist, Bas. "Historische archeologie–Oostindiëvaarders–techniek," *Liedschrift* 8 (1992), 43-58.

Konstam, R.A. "16th Century Naval Tactics and Gunnery," *International Journal of Nautical Archaeology and Underwater Exploration* 17 (1988), 17-23.

Kvarning, Lars-Åke and Bengt Ohrelius. *Vasa: Kungens skipp.* 4th ed. Stockholm: Atlantis, 1998.

Lane, Frederic C. "Naval Architecture about 1550," *Mariner's Mirror* 20 (1934), 24-49; in *Venice and History: The Collected Papers of Frederic C. Lane.* Baltimore, 1966, pp. 163-88.

Lane, Frederic C. "Venetian Shipping during the Commerical Revolution," *American Historical Review* 38 (1933), 219-39; in *Venice and History: The Collected Papers of Frederic C. Lane.* Baltimore, 1966, pp. 3-24.

Laughton, L.G. Carr. "Early Tudor Ship-Guns," *Mariner's Mirror* 46 (1960), 242-85.

Laughton, L.G. Carr. "Hull Projection," *Mariner's Mirror* 26 (1940), 55-60.

Lee, C.D. "The Battle of Beachy Head: Lord Torrington's Conduct," *Mariner's Mirror* 80 (1994), 270-89.

L'Hour, M, L. Long, and F. Reith. "The Wreck of the 'Experimental' Ship of the 'Oost-Indische Companie': the Mauritius (1609)," *International Journal of Nautical Archaeology* 19 (1990).

Loades, David. *The Tudor Navy.* Aldershot: Scolar Press, 1992.

Macdougall, Norman. "'The greattest scheip that ewer saillit in Ingland or France': James IV's 'Great Michael'." In: *Scotland and War, AD 79-1918.* Ed. Norman Macdougall. Edinburgh: John Donald, 1991, pp. 36-60.

Maddens, N. "De Vlaamse oorlogsvloot tijdens de regering van Keizer Karel V," *Revue Belge d'histoire militaire* 22 (1977-78), 389-98.

Mafrici, Mirella. *Mezzogiorno e pirateria nell'età moderna (secoli XVI-XVIII).* Naples: Edizioni Scientifiche Italiane, 1995.

Matz, Erling. *Vasa, 1620.* Ed. Katarina Villner. Trans. Clare James. Sabon: Ljungföretagen, n.d.

McKee, Alexander. "The Influence of British Naval Strategy on Ship Design: 1400-1850." In: *A History of Seafaring Based on Underwater Archaeology.* Ed. G. F. Bass. New York, 1972, pp. 225-52.

Mollat du Jordain, Michel. *Les sources de l'histoire maritime en Europe du moyen âge au XVIIIe siècle*. Paris: S.E.V.P.E.N., 1962.

Monteiro, Armando. *Batalhas e cambates da marinha Portuguesa*. Lisbon: Livraria Sá da Costa, n.d.

Olesa Muñido, Francisco-Felipe. *La galera en la navegación y el combate*. 2 vols. Madrid, 1971.

Olesa Muñido, Francisco-Felipe. *La organización naval de los estados Mediterráneos y en especial de España durante los siglos XVI y XVII*. 2 vols. Madrid, 1968.

Otero Lana, Enrique. *Los corsarios Españoles durante la decadencia de los Austrias*. Madrid: Editorial Navale, 1992.

Padfield, Peter. *Maritime Supremacy and the Opening of the Western Mind: Naval Campaigns the Shaped the Modern World, 1588-1782*. New York: Overland Press, 1999.

Parker, Geoffrey. "The *Dreadnought* Revolution of Tudor England," *Mariner's Mirror* 82 (1996), 269-300.

Parker, Geoffrey. "Ships of the Line, 1500-1650." In: *The Cambridge Illustrated History of Warfare: The Triumph of the West*. Ed. Geoffrey Parker. Cambridge: Cambridge University Press, 1995, pp. 120-31.

Parry, J.H. *The Age of Reconnaissance: Discovery, Exploration and Settlement 1450 to 1650*. London, 1963.

Parry, J.H. *The Establishment of the European Hegemony: 1415-1715*. 3rd ed. New York, 1959.

Parry, J.H. *The Spanish Seaborne Empire*. London: Hutchinson, 1966.

Pedrosa, Fernando Alberto Gomes. "La marine de guerre Portugaise en Amérique au XVIe siècle." In: *Acta del XVIII Congresso internazionale di storia militare: La scoperta del nuovo mondo e la sua influenza nella storia militare*. Ed. Paolo Alberini and Michele Nones. Turin, 1993, pp. 61-66.

Penn, C.D. *The Navy under the Early Stuarts*. 2nd ed. Portsmouth and London, 1920.

Pérez-Mallaína, Pablo E. *Spain's Men of the Sea: Daily Life on the Indies Fleets in the Sixteenth Century*. Trans. Carla Rahn Phillips. Baltimore: Johns Hopkins University Press, 1998.

Peterson, Mendel L. "Traders and Privateers across the Atlantic: 1492-1733." In: *A History of Seafaring Based on Underwater Archaeology*. Ed. G. F. Bass. New York, 1972, pp. 253-80.

Petrotin-Dumon, A. "The Pirate and the Emperor: Power and the Law on the Seas, 1450-1850." In: *The Political Economy of Merchant Empires*. Cambridge, 1991, pp. 196-227.

Phillips, Carla Rahn. "The Caravel and the Galleon." In: *Ships, Seafaring and Society: Essays in Maritime History*. Ed. T.J. Runyan. Detroit, 1987, pp. 91-114.

Phillips, Carla Rahn. "The Evolution of Spanish Ship Design from the Fifteenth to the Eighteenth Century," *American Neptune* 53 (1993), 229-38.

Phillips, Carla Rahn. *Six Galleons for the King of Spain: Imperial Defense in the Seventeenth Century*. Baltimore: Johns Hopkins University, 1986.

Phillips, Carla Rahn. *Los Tres Reyes: The Short Life of an unlucky Spanish Galleon*. Minneapolis: University of Minnesota Press, 1990.

Pi Corrales, Magdalena de Pazzis. *Felipe II y la lucha por el dominio del mar*. Madrid, 1989.

Podhorodecki, Leszek. *Lepanto 1571*. Warsaw: Bellona, 1993.

Pollentier, F. *De admiraliteit en de oorlog ter zee onder de aartshertogen (1596-1609)*. Brussels, 1972.

Powell, J.R. *The Navy in the English Civil War*. London, 1962.

Quintrell, Brian. "Charles I and the Navy in the 1630s," *Seventeenth Century* 3 (1988), 159-79.

Riaño Lozano, Fernando. *Los medios navales de Alejandro Farnesio (1587-1588)*. Madrid, 1989.

Rodger, N.A.M. "Guns and Sails in the First Phase of English Colonization, 1500-1650." In: *The Origins of Empire: British Overseas Enterprise to the Close of the Seventeenth Century.* Ed. Nicholas Canny. The Oxford History of the Brit sh Empire, I. Oxford: Oxford University Press, 1998, pp. 79-98.

Roelofsen, C.G. "L'evolution de la flotte 'Bourguignonne' aux XVe et XVIe siècles: que ques remarques sur l'introduction du canon dans la guerre maritime et son influence." *Publication du centre Européen d'études Bourguignonnes (XIVe-XVIe s.)* 26 (1986), 87-95.

Ruddock, Alwyn A. *Italian Merchants and Shipping in Southampton, 1270-1600.* Southampton, 1951.

Rule, Margaret. *The Mary Rose: The Excavation and Raising of Henry VIII's Flagship.* London: Conway Maritime Press, 1982.

Rule, Margaret. "The Sinking of the Mary Rose," *History Today* 32 (Sep 1982), 27-36.

Rule, Margaret and C.T.C. Dobbs. "The Tudor Warship *Mary Rose*: Aspects of Recent Research." In: *The Archaeology of Ships of War.* Ed. M. Bound. Oxford, 1995, pp. 26-29.

Russo, Flavio. *Guerra di corso.* 2 vols. Rome: Stato Maggiore dell'Esercito–Ufficio Storico, 1997.

Saturnino Monteiro, Armando da Silva. "The Decline and Fall of Portuguese Seapower. 1583-1663," *Journal of Military History* 65 (2001), 9-20.

Scammell, G.V. "European Seamanship in the Great Age of Discovery," *Mariner's Mirror* 68 (1982), 357-76.

Scammell, G.V. "Shipowning in England *circa* 1450-1550," *Transactions of the Royal Historical Society* 5th ser. 12 (1962), 105-22.

Scammell, G.V. "The Sinews of War: Manning and Provisioning English Fighting Ships, 1550-1650," *Mariner's Mirror* 73 (1997), 3-13.

Scammell, G.V. "War at Sea under the Early Tudors: Some Newcastle upon Tyne Evidence," *Archaeological aeliana* 38-39 (1960-61), 73-205.

Sicking, Louis. "Die offensive Lösung: Militärische Aspekte des Holländischen Ostseehandels im 15. und 16. jahrhundert," *Hansische Geschichtsblätter* 117 (119), 39-51.

Sicking, Louis. *Zeemacht en onmacht: Maritieme politiek in de Nederlanden, 1488-1558*. Bijdragen tot de Nederlanden Marinegeschiedenis, 7. Amsterdam: Institut voor Maritieme Historie, 1998.

Smith, Roger C. *Vanguard of Empire: Ships of Exploration ain the Age of Columbus*. Oxford: Oxford University Press, 1993.

Stradling, R.A. *The Armada of Flanders: Spanish Maritime Policy and European War, 1568-1668*. Cambridge: Cambridge University Press, 1992.

Unger, Richard W. "Design and Construction of European Warships in the Seventeenth and Eighteenth Centuries." In: *Les marines de guerre européens XVII-XVIII siècles*. Ed. M. Acerra, J. Merins, and J. Meyer. Paris, 1986, pp. 21-34.

Unger, Richard W. "Four Dordrecht Ships of the Sixteenth Century," *Mariner's Mirror* 6 (1975), 109-16.

Unger, Richard W. "Marine Paintings and the History of Schipbuilding." In: *Art in History/History in Art*. Ed. J. DeVries and D. Frieburg. Santa Monica, 1991, pp. 74-93.

Unger, Richard W. "Portuguese Shipbuilding and the Early Voyages to the Guinea Coast." In: *Vice-Almirante A. Teixeira Da Mota in memoriam*. Lisbon, 1987, I:229-49.

Unger, Richard W. "The Technical Development of Shipbuilding and Government Policies in the Fifteenth and Sixteenth Centuries." In: *Atti del v convegno internazionale di studi colombiani: "Navi e navigazione nei secoli XV e XVI"*. Genoa, 1990, I:197-211.

Unger, Richard W. "The Tonnage of Europe's Merchant Fleets, 1300-1800," *American Neptune* 52 (1992), 247-61.

Unger, Richard W. "Wooden Shipbuilding in Dordrecht," *Mededelingen van de nederlandse vereingen voor zeegescheidenis* 30 (1975), 5-19.

Unger, Richard W. "Wooden Shipbuilding in Zeeland." In: *Ships and Shipbuilding in the North Sea and Atlantic, 1400-1800*. Aldershot: Ashgate, 1997, #5. (Trans. Of "Houten scheepsbouw in Zeeland," *Zeeuws tijdschrift* 26.4/5 (1976), 130-34.)

van Vliet, A.P. *Vissers en kapers: De zeevisserij vanuit het Maasmondge-bied en de Duinkerker kapers (ca. 1580-1648)*. The Hague: Stichting Hollandse Historische Reeks, 1994.

Waters, David W. "The Elizabethan Navy and the Armada of Spain," *Mariner's Mirror* 25 (1949), 90-138.

Weber, R.E.J. *De beveiliging van de zee tegen europeesche en barbarische zeerovers, 1609-1621*. Amsterdam, 1936.

Wilson, Garth. "Computer Documentation and Analysis of Historical Ship Design." In: *Crossroads in Ancient Shipbuilding: Proceedings of the Sixth International Symposium on Boat and Ship Archaeology, Roskilde 1991*. Ed. C. Westerdahl. Oxford, 1994, pp. 265-69.

Young, Alan. "The Emblematic Decoration of Queen Elizabeth's Warship the *White Bear*," *Emblematica* 3 (1988), 65-77.

Military Technology – Premodern – Courtly Engineers

Bechmann, Roland. "Villard de Honnecourt: A Medieval Leonardo," *Apollo* 129 (Apr 1989), 232-41, 296-97.

Berg, Theresia and Udo Friedrich. "Wissenstradierung in spätmittelalterlichen Schriften zur Kriegskunst: Der 'Bellifortis' des Konrad Kyeser und das anonyme 'Feuerwerk'." In: *Wissen für den Hof: Der spätmittle alterliche Verschriftungsprozeß am Beispiel Heidelberg im 15. Jahrhundert*. Ed. J.-D. Müller. Munich, 1994, pp. 169-212.

Berthelot, Marcellin. "Les compositions incendiaires dans l'antiquité et au moyen âge," *Revue des deux mondes* 4 (1891), 786-822.

Berthelot, Marcellin. "Histoire des machines de guerre et des arts méchaniques au moyen âge: le livre d'un ingénieur militaire à la fin du XIVe siècle," *Annales de chimie et de physique* 7th ser., 24 (1900), 289-420.

Berthelot, Marcellin. "Le livre d'un ingenieur militaire à la fin du XIVe siècle: Appareils et recettes relatifs aux arts de la guerre au moyen âge, d'après un ouvrage de Conrad Kyeser, intitule *Bellifortis*; manuscrit écrit entre les années 1395 et 1405, appartenant à la bibliothèque de l'Université royale de Gottingue," *Journal des Savants* 1900, 1-15.

Berthelot, Marcellin. "Pour l'histoire des arts mécaniques et de l'artillerie vers la fin du moyen âge," *Annales de la chimie et de physique* 6th ser. 24 (1891), 433-521.

Boni, Bruno. *Leonardo da Vinci e le fecnica fusoria.* Milan, 1973.

Buttin, François. "Les propulseurs de Léonard de Vinci," *Bulletin de la société préhistorique Française* 61 (1964), 56-64.

Dibner, Bern. *Leonardo Da Vinci: Machines and Weaponry.* Norwalk: Burndy Library, 1974.

Fara, Amelio. *Leonardo e l'architettura militare.* Florence: Giunti, 1997.

Feldhaus, Franz M. "Geschützkonstruktionen von Leonardo da Vinci," *Zeitschrift für historische Waffenkunde* 6 (1912-14), 128-34.

Flewett, W.E. "Leonardo, the Goldsmith, and the 'Plaything of Princes'," *Journal of the Arms and Armour Society* 16 (1998), 14-57.

Gille, Bertrand. "Etudes sur les manuscrits d'ingénieurs du XVe siècle," *Techniques et civilisations* 5 (1956), 77-86, 216-23.

Gille, Bertrand. *Les ingénieurs de la Renaissance.* Paris: Hermann, 1964; trans. *Engineers of the Renaissance.* Cambridge: Massachusetts Institute of Technology Press, 1966.

Grassi, Giulio. "Ein Kompendium spätmittelalterlicher Kriegstechnik aus einer Handschriftenmanufaktur (ZBZ. Ms. Rh. hist. 33b)," *Technikgeschichte* 63.3 (1996), 195-217.

Hall, A.R. "Guido's Texaurus, 1335." In: *On Pre-Modern Technology and Science: A Volume of Studies in Honor of Lynn White Jr.* Ed. Bert S. Hall and Delno C. West. Malibu, 1976, pp. 11-35.

Hall, Bert S. "Der Meister sol auch kennen schreiben und lesen: Writings about Technology ca. 1400-ca. 1600 A.D." In: *Early Technologies.* Invited Lectures on the Middle East at the University of Texas at Austin, vol. 3. Ed. D. Schmandt-Besserat. Los Angeles, 1979, pp. 47-57.

Hall, Bert S. "Production et diffusion de certains traités de techniques au moyen âge." In: *Les arts mécaniques au moyen âge.* Cahiers d'études médiévales, VII. Montreal, 1982, pp. 147-70.

Hall, Bert S. *The So-Called "Manuscript of the Hussite Wars' Engineer" and Its Technological Milieu: A Study and Edition of Codex latinus Monacensis 197, part 1.* Unpublished dissertation. Los Angeles: University of California at Los Angeles, 1971.

Monreal Y Tejada, L. *Ingenieria militar en las cronicas catalanas.* Barcelona, 1971.

Parsons, William Barclay. *Engineers and Engineering in the Renaissance.* Cambridge: The M.I.T. Press, 1939.

Pepper, Simon and Quentin Hughes. "Fortifications in Late 15th Century Italy: The Treatise of Francesco di Giorgi Martini." In: *Papers in Italian Archaeology, I: The Lancaster Seminar: Recent Research in Prehistoric, Classical, and Medieval Archaeology.* Ed. H.M. Blake, T.W. Potter, and D.B. Whitehouse. Oxford: British Archaeological Reports, 1978, II:541-67.

Prager, Frank D. and Gustina Scaglia. *Mariano Taccola and his Book 'De Ingeneis'.* Cambridge: Massachusetts Institute for Technology, 1972.

Reti, Ladislao, and Bern Dibner. *Leonardo Da Vinci: Technologist.* Norwalk: Burndy Library, 1969.

Rodakiewicz, Erla. "The *Editio princeps* of Roberto Valturio's 'De re militari' in Relation to the Dresden and Munich Manuscripts," *Maso Finguerra* 5 (1940), 15-82.

Scaglia, Gustina, ed. "A Miscellany of Bronze Works and Texts in the *Zibaldone* of Buonaccorso Ghiberti," *Proceedings of the American Philosophical Association* 120 (1976), 485-513.

Simms, D.L. "Archimedes' Weapons of War and Leonardo," *British Journal for the History of Science* 21 (1988), 195-210.

White, Lynn, Jr. "Kyeser's *Bellifortis*: The First Technological Treatise of the Fifteenth Century," *Technology and Culture* 10 (1969), 436-41.

Military Technology – Premodern – Gunpowder Weapons – European

Åhslund, Bengt. "The Saltpetre Boilers of the Swedish Crown." In: *Gunpowder: The History of an International Technology*. Ed. Brenda Buchanan. Bath: Bath University Press, 1996, pp. 163-82.

Allen, Geoffrey and David Allen. *The Guns of Sacramento*. London: Robin Garton, 1978.

Allmand, Christopher T. "L'artillerie de l'armée Anglaise et son organisation à l'époque de Jeanne d'Arc." In: *Jeanne d'Arc: une époque, un rayonment*. Colloque d'histoire médiévale. Orleans–Octobre 1979. Paris, 1982, pp. 73-83.

Allmand, Christopher T. "New Weapons, New Tactics, 1300-1500." In: *The Cambridge Illustrated History of Warfare: The Triumph of the West*. Ed. Geoffrey Parker. Cambridge: Cambridge University Press, 1995, pp. 92-105.

Alm, Josef. "Stockholms stads medeltida artilleri," *Meddelande* 9 (1948), 5-33.

Angelucci, Angelo. *Documenti inediti per la storia delle armi da fuoco Italiane*. Graz: Akademische Druck- und Verlagsanstalt, 1972.

Anting, L. *Tallinskie oruzheincki i ognestrel noe oruzhie XIV-XVI vekov*. Tallin: State Historical Museum of the Estonian S.S. Republic, 1967.

Archibald, C.D. "Observations on Some Ancient Pieces of Ordnance, and Other Relics, Discovered in the Island of Walney, in Lancashire," *Archaeologia* 28 (1840), 373-92.

Arendt, Wsewolod. "Zwei Escopettes des historischen Museums in Moskau," *Zeitschrift für historisches Waffen- und Köstumkunde* 13 (1932-34), 223.

Arendt, Wsewolod. "Zwei mittelalterliche Hakenbüchsen," *Zeitschrift für historisches Waffen- und Köstumkunde* 13 (1932-34), 42-44.

Armstrong, Douglas R. "A Bronze Saker for England's King Henry VIII: The Recovery and Conservation of an Owyn Gun Cast in 1543, Lost to Shipwreck ca. 1580 Near the Bahamas Island," *Journal of the Ordnance Society* 6 (1994), 9-22.

Armstrong, Douglas R. "A Wrought Iron Gun for Early 16th Century Sea Service," *Journal of the Ordnance Society* 9 (1997), 27-48.

Ashtor, Eliyahu. "L'artiglieria veneziana e il commercio di levante," In: *Armi e cultura nel bresciano, 1420-1870.* Brescia, 1981, pp. 141-54.

Awty, Brian G. "The Arcana Family of Cesena as Gunfounders and Military Engineers." *Transactions of the Newcomen Society* 59 (1987-88), 61-80.

Awty, Brian G. "Parson Levett and English Cannon Founding," *Sussex Archaeological Collections* 127 (1989), 133-45.

Ayalon, David. "A Reply to J.R. Partington," *Arabica* 10 (1963), 64-79.

Baarman, D. "Die 'Faule Magd' der Königlichen Arsenalsammlung zu Dresden," *Zeitschrift für historische Waffenkunde* 4 (1906-08), 229-35.

Bailey, Sarah Barter. "Information Relating to the Operation of the Early Cast-Iron Gun Industry, from a Manuscipt Account Book in the Collection of the Royal Armouries," *Journal of the Ordnance Society* 3 (1991), 11-24.

Bailey, Sarah Barter. "The Royal Armouries 'Firework Book.'" In: *Gunpowder: The History of an International Technology.* Ed. Brenda Buchanan. Bath: Bath University Press, 1996, pp. 57-86.

Barker, Richard. "A Glance at Ricochet," *Journal of the Ordnance Society* 10 (1998), 1-16.

Barker, Richard. "A Gun-List from Portuguese India," *Journal of the Ordnance Society* 8 (1996), 52-71.

Barker, Richard. "A Miscellany," *Journal of the Ordnance Society* 2 (1990), 72-77.

Barker, Richard. "A Proportional Ordinance for Ordnance?" *Journal of the Ordnance Society* 11 (1999), 21-29.

Bas, Begoña. "Fireworks for the Community: The Use of Windpower and Simple Techniques in Galicia." In: *Gunpowder: The History of an International Technology.* Ed. Brenda Buchanan. Bath: Bath University Press, 1996, pp. 137-52.

Baxter, D.R. "The Development of the Blunderbuss in England," *Armi antiche* (1965), 135-52.

Baxter, D.R. *Superimposed Load Firearms, 1360-1860.* Hong Kong, 1966.

Bedford, Clay P. and Stephen V. Grancsay. *Early Firearms of Great Britain and Ireland.* New York: Metropolitan Museum of Art, 1971.

Beeler, John H. "Cannon." In: *Dictionary of the Middle Ages.* Vol. 2. Ed. J. Strayer. pp. 64-66.

Bellamy, Christopher. "The Firebird and the Bear: 600 Years of the Russian Artillery," *History Today* 32 (Sep 1982), 16-20.

Bemmann, Rudolf. "Die Artillerie der Reichsstadt Mühlhausen in Thüringen," *Zeitschrift für historische Waffenkunde* 5 (1909-11), 104-10.

Bennett, G.E. "The Mechanism of the Wheel-lock," *Journal of the Arms and Armour Society* 1 (1953), 14-22.

Benoît, Paul. "Artisans ou combattants? Le cannoniers dans le royaume de France à la fin du moyen âge." In: *Le combattant au moyen âge.* 2nd ed. Histoire ancienne et médiévale, 36. Paris: Publications de la Sorbonne, 1995, pp. 287-96.

Berg, Theresia and Udo Friedrich. "Wissenstradierung in spätmittelalterlichen Schriften zur Kriegskunst: Der 'Bellifortis' des Konrad Kyeser und das anonyme 'Feuerwerk'." In: *Wissen für den Hof: Der spätmittle alterliche Verschriftungsprozeß am Beispiel Heidelberg im 15. Jahrhundert.* Ed. J.-D. Müller. Munich, 1994, pp. 169-212.

Beritić, Lukša. *Dubrovačka artiljerija.* Belgrade: Vojni Muzej, 1960.

Berthelot, Marcellin. "Les compositions incendiaires dans l'antiquité et au moyen âge," *Revue des deux mondes* 4 (1891), 786-822.

Berthelot, Marcellin. "Pour l'histoire de l'artillerie et des arts méchaniques vers la fin du moyen âge," *Annales de chimie et de physique* 6th ser., 24 (1891), 433-521.

Blackmore, Howard L. *The Armouries of the Tower of London.* I: *Ordnance.* London: Her Majesty's Stationery Office, 1976.

Blackmore, Howard L. "The Boxted Bombard," *Antiquaries Journal* 67 (1987), 86-96.

Blackmore, Howard L. "Elizabethan Toy Guns," *Park Lane Arms Fair* 6 (1989), 10-14.

Blackmore, Howard L. "Master Jacobo's Culverin, 1517," *Journal of the Arms and Armour Society* 12 (1986-88), 312-44.

Blackmore, Howard L. "The Oldest Dated Gun," *Canadian Journal of Arms Collecting* 34.2 (May 1996), 39-47.

Blackmore, Howard L. "The Take-Down Gun," *Journal of the Ordnance Society* 2 (1990), 1-4.

Blair, Claude. "The Breadalbane Gun," *Journal of the Arms and Armour Society* 14 (1992-94), 218-30.

Blair, Claude. "A Further Note on the Early History of the Wheel-Lock," *Journal of the Arms and Armour Society* 4 (1962-64), 187-88.

Blair, Claude. "Further Notes on the Origins of the Wheellock." In: *Arms and Armor Annual: Volume One*. Ed. Robert Held. Northfield: Digest Books, Inc., 1973, pp. 28-47.

Blair, Claude. "A New Carriage for Mons Meg," *Journal of the Arms and Armour Society* 5 (1965-67), 431-52.

Blair, Claude. "New Light on the Early History of the Wheel-lock in Italy," *Waffen- und Köstumkunde* 37 (1995), 27-52.

Blair, Claude. "A Note on the Early History of the Wheel-Lock," *Journal of the Arms and Armour Society* 3 (1959-61), 221-56.

Blair, Claude. "Simon and Jacques Robert and Same Early Snaphance Locks/Simon e Jacques Robert e alcune piastre a pietra focaia primitive," *Armi antichi* (1988-89), 33-88.

Blair, Claude. "A 16th Century English Snaphance Gun," *Park Lane Arms Fair* 2 (1985), 21-26.

Blair, Claude. "'Stammt das Radschloß aus Friaul?': A Reply," *Waffen- und Köstumkunde* 41 (1999), 29-34.

Blair, Claude. "Walter de Milemete's Illustrations of Cannon," *Waffen- und Köstumkunde* 36 (1994), 137-39.

Blair, Claude, ed. *Pollard's History of Firearms*. Feltham, 1983.

Bleckwenn, Ruth. "Seidengewebe des 14. Und 15. Jahrhunderts auf Pulverflaschen im Landeszeughaus Graz," *Waffen- und Köstumkunde* 30 (1988), 41-59.

Boccia, Lionello Giorgio. "Gli archibusi a ruota del Bargello." In: *L'illustrazione Italiana*. Milan: Bramante Editrice, 1974, pp. 84-110.

Boeheim, Wendelin. "Studie über die Entwicklung des Geschützwesens in Deutschland," *Zeitschrift für historisches Waffenkunde* 1 (1897-99), 57-62.

Böhne, Clement. "Über Kanonenrohre," *Waffen- und Kostümkunde* 6 (1964), 66-73.

Bonaparte, Louis Napoleon and I. Favé. *Études sur le passé et l'avenir de l'artillerie*. 6 vols. Paris, 1846-71.

Boothroyd, Geoffrey. "The Birth of the Scottish Pistol." In: *Scottish Weapons and Fortifications, 1100-1800*. Ed. David H. Caldwell. Edinburgh: John Donald Publishers Ltd., 1981, pp. 315-38.

Bosson, Clément. "Une arquebuse à mèche du debut du XVIe siècle," *Musées de Genève* 89 (1968), 17-18.

Bosson, Clément. "La mis à feu et l'amélioration de la balistique dans l'arme portative," *Armi antiche* (1971), 117-76; (1972), 79-111; (1973), 191-218.

Bosson, Clément. "Que sait-on de l'haquebute?" *Armes anciennes* 2.1 (1957), 17-22.

Boureulle, P. de. "La poudre-a-feu et l'artillerie des Valois," *Annales de société d'emulation du departement des Vosges* (1877), 396-414.

Boyer, Pierre. "Artillerie et tactique navale en Méditerranée au XVIe siècle," *Revue historique des armées* 174 (1989), 110-21.

Brackenbury, Henry. "Ancient Cannon in Europe. Part I: From Their First Employment to A.D. 1350," *Proceedings of the Royal Artillery Institution*," 4 (1865), 287-308.

Brackenbury, Henry. "Ancient Cannon in Europe. Part II: From A.D. 1351 to A.D. 1400," *Proceedings of the Royal Artillery Institution*," 5 (1867), 1-37.

Bragard, Philippe. "Un exemple de la transformation de la poliorétique au XVe siècle: le premier siège au canon à Namur (1488)," *Revue Belge d'histoire militaire* 31 (Mar-June 1995), 117-52.

Braid, Douglas H.P. "Gun Boring from the Solid," *Transactions of the Newcomen Society* 58 (1986-87), 45-58.

Braid, Douglas H.P. "Ordnance and Empire: Portugal in the Fifteenth and Sixteenth Century," *Journal of the Ordnance Society* 4 (1992), 55-66.

Braid, Douglas H.P. "Ordnance and Freedom of Thought: The Development of Gunmaking in Bohemia, 1350-1450," *Journal of the Ordnance Society* 5 (1993), 75-94.

Brown, Ruth Rhynas. "Guns Carried on the East Indiamen, 1600-1800," *International Journal of Nautical Archaeology* 19 (1990).

Brown, Ruth Rhynas. "Tal-y-bont Gunner's Rule," *Journal of the Ordnance Society* 2 (1990), 71-72.

Brown, Ruth Rhynas and Jan Piet Puyper. "'A Great Gun Wherein a Man May Sit Upright:' The King of Acheen's 'Great Peece'," *Journal of the Arms and Armour Society* 14 (1992-94), 153-62.

Bull, Stephen. "Pearls from the Dungheap: English Saltpetre Production, 1590-1640," *Journal of the Ordnance Society* 2 (1990), 5-10.

Bury, J.B. "The Early History of the Explosive Mine." *Fort* 10 (1982), 23-30.

Buttin, Charles. "La platine à rouet Française au XVIIe siècle," *Armes anciennes* 1 (1955), 109-13.

Caldwell, David H. "The Dresden Pistols, 1598," *Dispatch* 107 (1983), 14.

Caldwell, David H. "A Hagbut of Crok from Corr, County Armagh," *Ulster Journal of Archaeology* 39 (1976), 53-55.

Caldwell, David H. "The Lutiger Gun Barrel and the Manufacture of Long Guns in 16th Century Scotland," *Park Lane Arms Fair* 4 (1987), 16-19.

Caldwell, David H. "The Royal Scottish Gun Foundry in the Sixteenth Century." In: *From the Stone Age to the 'Forty-Five': Studies Presented to R.B.K. Stevenson*. Ed. A. O'Connor and D.V. Clarke. Edinburgh: John Donald Ltd., 1983, pp. 427-49.

Carman, W.Y. *A History of Firearms from the Earliest Times to 1914*. London, 1955.

Carpenter, Austin C. *Cannon: The Conservation, Reconstruction and Presentation of Historic Artillery*. Exeter: Halsgrove Press, 1993.

Cartesegna, Marisa and Piero Choman Ruiz. "La 'Polverera' di Torino: Archeologia industriale in Piemonte," *Armi antiche* (1980), 13-54.

Caruana, Adrian B. *The History of English Sea Ordnance*. I: *The Age of Evolution, 1523-1715*. Rotherfield: Jean Boudroit Publications, 1994.

Caruana, Adrian B. "The Painting of Gun Carriages," *Journal of the Ordnance Society* 2 (1990), 78-81.

Caruana, Adrian B. *Tudor Artillery, 1485-1603*. Historical Arms Series, 30. Alexandria Bay: Museum Restoration Service, 1992.

Catalogue of the Museum of Artillery in the Rotunda at Woolwich. I: *Ordnance*. II: *Personal Arms*. London: Her Majesty's Stationery Office, 1963.

Cederlöf, Olle. "'Finbanker': Om Svenska exportkanoner och deras engelska förebilder, 1550-1700," *Meddelande* 48 (1988), 97-134.

Cederlöf, Olle. "Framladdade automat- och repetervapen: Två utvecklingslinjer, 1360-1860," *Meddelande* 47 (1987), 197-221.

Cederström, Rudolf. "Dürers Kanonenwinde," *Zeitschrift für historische Waffenkunde* 5 (1909-11), 258-59.

Chidsey, Donald Barr. *Goodbye to Gunpowder: An Informal History of Gunpowder from Its Introduction in the Fourteenth Century to the Atom Bomb*. London: Alvin Redman, 1964.

Cipolla, Carlo M. *Guns and Sails in the Early Phase of European Expansion, 1400-1700*. London, 1965.

Clephan, R. Coltman. "The Military Handgun of the Sixteenth Century," *Archaeological Journal* 67 (1910), 109-50.

Clephan, R. Coltman. "The Ordnance of the Fourteenth and Fifteenth Centuries." *Archaeological Journal* 68 (1911), 49-138.

Clephan, R. Coltman. *An Outline of the History and Development of Hand Firearms, from the Earliest Period to about the End of the Fifteenth Century.* London, 1906.

Clephan, R. Coltman. "An Outline of the History of Gunpowder and That of the Hand-Gun, from the Earliest Epoch of the Earliest Records to the End of the Fifteenth Century," *Archaeological Journal* 66 (1909), 145-70.

Contamine, Philippe. "L'artillerie royale Française à la veille des guerres d'Italie," *Annales de Bretagne* 71 (1964), 221-61.

Contamine, Philippe. "Les industries de guerre dans la France de la Renaissance: l'exemple de l'artillerie." *Revue historique* 271 (1984), 249-80.

Cook, Weston F., Jr. "The Cannon Conquest of Nasrid Spain and the End of the Reconquista," *Journal of Military History* 57 (1993), 43-70.

Cook, Weston F., Jr. *The Hundred Years War for Morocco: Gunpowder and the Military Revolution in the Early Modern Muslim World.* Boulder: Westview Press, 1994.

Cook, Weston F., Jr. "Warfare and Firearms in Fifteenth Century Morocco, 1400-1492," *War and Society* 11 (1993), 25-40.

Cottaz, M. *L'arme à feu portative française.* Paris: Éditions Albert Morance, 1971.

Coutil, Léon. "Un témoin du siège de Louviers en 1418, la bombarde de la Haye-le-Comte près de Louviers (Eure): Etude sommaire sur l'artillerie des XIVe et XVe siècles," *Bulletin de la société de Louviers et de sa région* 5 ( ), 17-24.

Credland, Arthur Graves. "Crossbow Guns and Musket Arrows," *Journal of the Society of Archer-Antiquarians* 20 (1977), 5-19.

Credland, Arthur Graves. "Fire Shafts and Musket Arrows from the Fifteenth to Twentieth Centuries," *Journal of the Society of Archer-Antiquarians* 29 (1986), 34-51.

Crocker, Glenys. *The Gunpowder Industry.* 2nd ed. Princes Risborough: Shire Publishing Ltd., 1999.

Curbastro, Gualberto Ricci and Marcello Terenzi. "Alla riscoperta della bombarda di Rignano Flaminio," *Armi antiche* (1974), 61-74.

Daehnhardt, Rainer. "Início do fabrico de armas de fogo no mundo Português, 1450-1650/Early Gunmaking in the Portuguese World, 1450-1650," *Boletin da sociedade Portuguesa de armas antiguas/Bulletin of the Portuguese Academy of Antique Arms* 1 (1997), 5-30.

Dannecker, Peter and Joachim von Wlassaty. "Combat anno 1399," *Deutsches Waffen Journal* 10/81 (1981), 1444-47.

Delmaire, Bernard. "L'artillerie d'Aire au XVe siècle." *Société académique des antiquaires de la Morine* 22 (1973), 99-113.

Dedenroth-Schou, Poul. "Hundrede Konger: To kanonserier fra Christian IV's tid," *Vaaben historiske aarbøger* 20 (1974), 61-96.

De Poerck, G. "L'artillerie à ressorts médiévale: Notes lexicologiques et étymologiques," *Bulletin Du Cange* 18 (1943-44), 35-49.

Deroko, Aleksandar. "Quelques mots sur les plus anciens gros canons turcs," *Armi antiche* (1963), 169-78.

Deroko, Aleksandar. "Најстарије ватрено оружје у средыековној срљији: Допуна писаним историјским подацима," *Glas de l'académie Serbe des sciences et des arts, tome CCXLVI, Classe des sciences sociales* 9 (1961).

Deters, Friedrich. *Die englischen Angriffswaffen zur Zeit der Einführung der Feuerwaffen (1300 bis 1350).* Heidelberg, 1913.

DeVries, Kelly. "A 1445 Reference to Shipboard Artillery." *Technology and Culture* 31 (1990), 818-29.

DeVries, Kelly. "Early Modern Military Technology: New Trends and Old Ideas (a Bibliographical Essay)," *Liedschrift* 8 (1992), 73-88.

DeVries, Kelly. "The Effectiveness of Fifteenth-Century Shipboard Artillery," *The Mariner's Mirror* 84 (1998), 389-99.

DeVries, Kelly. "The Forgotten Battle of Bevershoutsveld, May 3, 1382: Technological Innovation and Military Significance." In: *Armies, Chivalry and Warfare: Harlaxton Medieval Studies, VII*. Ed. M. Strickland. Stamford, 1998, pp. 280-94.

DeVries, Kelly. "Gunpowder and Early Gunpowder Weapons." In: *Gunpowder: The History of an International Technology*. Ed. Brenda Buchanan. Bath: Bath University Press, 1996, pp. 121-36.

DeVries, Kelly. "Gunpowder Weaponry and the Rise of the Early Modern State," *War in History* 5 (1998), 127-45.

DeVries, Kelly. "Gunpowder Weaponry at the Siege of Constantinople, 1453." In: *War, Army and Society in the Eastern Mediterranean, 7th-16th Centuries*. Ed. Y. Lev. Leiden, 1996, pp. 343-62.

DeVries, Kelly. "Military Surgical Practice and the Advent of Gunpowder Weaponry," *Canadian Bulletin of Medical History* 7 (1990), 131-46.

DeVries, Kelly. "The Technology of Gunpowder Weaponry in Western Europe during the Hundred Years War." In: *XXII. Kongreß der Internationalen Kommission für Militärgeschichte Acta 22: Von Crécy bis Mohács Kriegswesen im späten Mittelalter (1346-1526)*. Vienna, 1997, pp. 285-98.

DeVries, Kelly. "The Use of Gunpowder Weaponry By and Against Joan of Arc During the Hundred Years War," *War and Society* 14 (1996), 1-16.

Di Carpegna, Nolfo. *Armi da fuoco della Collezione Odescalchi*. Rome: Ed. Marte, 1968.

Di Carpegna, Nolfo. *Brescian Firearms from Matchlock to Flintlock: A Compendium of Names, Marks and Works Together with an Attempt at Classification*. Rome: Edizioni de Luca, 1997.

Dieters, Friedrich. *Die englischen Angriffswaffen zur Zeit der Einführung der Feuerwaffen (1300 bis 1350)*. Heidelberg, 1913.

Dite, Tibor. "Stammt das Radschloss aus Deutschland oder aus Italien?" *Waffen- und Kostümkunde* 17 (1975), 109-20.

Dittrich, Reinhart and Peter Krenn. "Die Handfeuerwaffen des Landeszeughauses in Graz," *Waffen- und Köstumkunde* 35 (1993), 23-44; 36 (1994), 98-116; 40 (1998), 49-66.

Dolleczek, Anton. *Geschichte der Österreichischen Artillerie von den frühesten Zeiten bis zur Gegenwart.* 1887; rpt. Graz: Akademische Druck- und Verlagsanstalt, 1973.

Dubled, H. "L'artillerie royale Française à l'époque de Charles VII et au début du règne de Louis XI (1437-1469): Les frères Bureau," *Memorial de l'artillerie Française* 50 (1976), 555-637.

Dupre, M., ed. "Inventaires de l'artillerie du château de Blois en 1418, 1421 et 1434," *Revue des sociétés savantes des départements* 4th series, 5 (1867), 311-17.

Eaves, Ian. "Further Notes on the Pistol in Early 17th Century England," *Journal of the Arms and Armour Society* 8 (1974-76), 269-329.

Eaves, Ian. "Some Notes on the Pistol in Early 17th Century England," *Journal of the Arms and Armour Society* 6 (1968-70), 277-344.

Edwards, Peter. "Gunpowder and the English Civil War," " *Journal of the Arms and Armour Society* 15 (1995-98), 109-31.

Egg, E. *Der Tiroler Geschützguss, 1400-1600.* Inssbruck: Universitätsverlag Wagner, 1961.

Egg, E., J. Jobé, H. Lachouque, P.E. Cleator, and D. Reichel. *Guns: An Illustrated History of Artillery.* Lausanne: Patrick Stephens Ltd., 1971.

Ellis, John. *The Social History of the Machine Gun.* Baltimore: Johns Hopkins University Press, 1975.

Engel, Bernhard. "Zwei mittelalterliche Büchsen," *Zeitschrift für historisches Waffenkunde* 2 (1900-02), 301-02.

Eriksen, Egon. "Miniaturer og middelalderskyts," *Vaaben historiskaarbøger* 8 (1955-56), 5-24.

Esper, Thomas. "The Replacement of the Longbow by Firearms in the English Army," *Technology and Culture* 6 (1965), 382-93.

Essenwein, August von. *Quellen zur Geschichte der Feuerwaffen.* 2 vols. 1877; rpt. Graz: Akademische Druck- und Verlagsanstalt, 1969.

Evrard, René. "Wauthier Godefroid le premier fondeur de canons de fer," *Industrie: Revue de la Féderation des Industries Belges* (Jun 1955), 401-04.

Fawtier, R., ed. "Documents inédits sur l'organisation de l'artillerie royale au temps de Louis XI." In: *Essays in Medieval History Presented to Thomas Frederick Tout.* Ed. A.G. Little and F.M. Powicke. Manchester, 1925, pp. 367-78.

Feldhaus, Franz M. "Die älteste Darstellung eines Pulvergeschützes," *Zeitschrift für historisches Waffenkunde* 5 (1909-11), 92.

Feldhaus, Franz M. "Ein Feuerangriff um 1290," *Zeitschrift für historisches Waffenkunde* 7 (1915-17), 236-37, 337-40; 8 (1918-20), 36-37.

Feldhaus, Franz M. "Geschützkonstruktionen von Leonardo da Vinci," *Zeitschrift für historische Waffenkunde* 6 (1912-14), 128-34.

Feldhaus, Franz M. "Der Pulvermönch Berthold 1313 oder 1393?" *Zeitschrift für historisches Waffenkunde* 4 (1906-08), 286.

Feldhaus, Franz M. "Die Serpantinen und Kanonen von Metz im Krieg 1324," *Zeitschrift für historisches Waffenkunde* 7 (1915-17), 203-05.

Feldhaus, Franz M. "Verfaßte Abraham von Memmingen das Feuerwerkbuch?" *Zeitschrift für historische Waffenkunde* 5 (1909-11), 27-28.

Feldhaus, Franz M. "Was wissen wir von Berthold Schwarz?" *Zeitschrift für historisches Waffenkunde* 4 (1906-08), 65-69.

ffoulkes, Charles J. *The Gun-Founders of England with a List of English and Continental Gun-Founders from the XIV to the XIX Centuries.* Cambridge, 1937; rpt London: Arms and Armour Press, 1969.

Finlayson, W.H. "Mons Meg." *Scottish Historical Review* 27 (1948), 124-26.

Finó, J.-F. "L'artillerie en France à la fin du moyen âge." *Gladius* 12 (1974), 13-31.

Fischler, Gustav. "Über Pulverproben früherer Zeiten," *Zeitschrift für historisches Waffen- und Köstumkunde* 11 (1926-28), 49-57.

Fleischhauer, Werner. "Eine Radschlossbüchse von Hieronymous Bortstorffer und Caspar Spät," *Waffen und Kostümkunde* 9 (1967), 70-72.

Foley, Vernard. "The Invention of the Wheellock," *Journal of the Arms and Armour Society* 11 (1983-85), 207-48.

Foley, Vernard. "Leonardo and the Invention of the Wheellock," *Scientific American* 288 (1998), 96-100.

Foley, Vernard and Keith Perry. "In Defense of *Liber Igneum*: Arab Alchemy, Roger Bacon, and the Introduction of Gunpowder into the West," *Journal for the History of Arabic Science* 3 (1979), 200-18.

Foley, Vernard and Susan Canganelli. "Proposal for a New Earliest Matchlock," *Journal of the Arms and Armour Society* 13 (1989-91), 161-72.

Fons-Melicocq, A. de la. "Histoire de l'artillerie de la ville de Lille aux XIVe, XVe et XVIe siècles," *Revue du Nord* 2 (1854), 307-13.

Forestié, F. "Hughes de Cardaillac et la poudre à canon," *Bulletin archéologique de la société archéologique de Tarn-et-Garonne* 39 (1901), 93-132, 185-222, 297-312.

Forman, James D. *The Blunderbuss, 1500-1900.* Historical Arms Series, no. 32. Alexandria Bay: Museum Restoration Service, 1994.

Forrer, Robert. "Die ältesten gotischen ein- und mehrläufigen Faustrohrstreitkolben," *Zeitschrift für historische Waffenkunde* 4 (1906-08), 55-61.

Forrer, Robert. "Geschützminiaturen aus den Mss. 'Christine de Pisan' und 'Histoire de Charles Martel,'" *Zeitschrift für historisches Waffenkunde* 7 (1912-14), 277-80.

Forrer, Robert. "Gotische und exotische Stangenbüchsen in Drehgabeln," *Zeitschrift für Historische Waffenkunde* 7 (1915-17), 333-36.

Forrer, Robert. "Ein Kalender für König Matthias Corvinus mit Dartellungen gotischer Büchsenschützen," *Zeitschrift für historische Waffenkunde* 8 (1918-20), 221-40.

Forshell, Helena. *Bronze Cannon Analysis: Alloy Composition Related to Corrosion Picture*. Armémuseum, rapport nr 2. Stockholm: Liber Tryck, 1984.

Frantzen, Ole Louis. *Dansk landartilleri, 1400-2000*. Copenhagen: Tøjhusmuseet, 1997.

Frantzen, Ole Louis. "Rigens marsk Anders Billes broncemortér fra 1647," *Vaabenhistoriske aarbøger* 32 (1986), 13-29.

Frantzen, Ole Louis, Michael H. Mortensen, Niels M. Probst, and Sven E. Thiede. *Dansk søartilleri, 1400-2000*. Copenhagen: Tøjhusmuseet, 1999.

Fromont, A. and A. de Meunynck. *Histoire de canonniers de Lille*. 2 vols. Lille, 1892.

Fuchs, Walter. "Zwei hinterindische Stangenbüchsen in Drehgabeln," *Zeitschrift für historisches Waffen- und Köstumkunde* 16 (1940-42), 246-48.

Gabriel, Erich. *Die Hand- und Faustfeuerwaffen der Habsburgischen Heere*. Vienna: Österreichischer Bundesverlag, 1990.

Gaibi, Agostino. "Appunti sull'origine e sulla evoluzione meccanica degli apparecchi di accensione delle armi da fuoco portatili," *Armi antiche* 3 (1956), 81-120; 4 (1957), 37-66.

Gaibi, Agostino. "Armi da fuoco Italiane all'Ermitage," *Armi antiche* (1970), 65-80; (1973), 165-90.

Gaibi, Agostino. *Le armi da fuoco portatili Italiane*. Milan, 1962.

Gaibi, Agostino. "I Franzini: Inventori, forgiatori di canne, archibugiari Italiano," *Armi antiche* (1971), 95-116.

Gaibi, Agostino. "La polvere pirica (Voci dell'enciclopedia)," *Armi antiche* 3 (1956), 13947.

Gaibi, Agostino. "Un raro cimelio piemontese del trecento: Ritrovamento di una 'bombardella' di ferro presso il Castello di Verrua Savoia," *Armi antiche* (1966), 29-35.

Gaibi, Agostino. "Il serpentino (Nuovo contributo alla storia degli apparecchi di accensione delle armi da fuoco)," *Armi antiche* (1969), 3-12.

Gaier, Claude. "Un cas précoce de normalisation des pièces d'artillerie: 1447," *Musée d'armes* 28 (Sept 1980), 12-13.

Gaier, Claude. "Historique des systèmes de mise à feu," *Musée d'armes* 3 (1973), 9-11; 4 (1974), 12-13; 5 (1975), 14-16; 6 (1975), 19-21; 7 (1975), 13-18.

Gaier, Claude. "Maître Jean Bovy, Pyrotechnicien liégeois du XVIe siècle," *Musée d'armes* 13 (1976), 18-21.

Gaier, Claude. "The Origin of Mons Meg," *Journal of the Arms and Armour Society* 5 (1965-67), 425-31.

Gaier, Claude. "Qui a inventé la poudre?" *Musée d'armes* 72 (1992), 15-20; in: *Armes et combats dans l'univers médiéval*. Paris: De Boeck Université, 1995, pp. 183-87.

Gaier, Claude. "Le rôle des armes à feu dans les batailles Liègeoises au XVe siècle," *Musée d'armes* 51 (1986), 1-12 and *Publication du centre Européen d'études Bourguignonnes (XIVe-XVIe s.)* 26 (1986), 31-37.

Galperin, Peter. "Mons Meg: en vittig dame," *Våbenshistorisk tidsskrift* 26 (1993), 214-20.

Gamber, Ortwin. "Grundriss einer Geschichte der Schutzwaffen der Altertums," *Jahrbuch der Kunsthistorischen Sammlungen in Wien* 62 (1966), 7-70.

Gandilhon, Rene, ed. "Le personnel de l'artillerie royale en 1491 d'après un compte inédit," *Annales du Midi* 54 (1942), 102-07.

Garnier, Joseph. *L'artillerie des ducs de Bourgogne d'après les documents conservés aux archives de la Cote-d'Or*. Paris: Honoré Champion, 1895.

Garnier, Pierre-Louis. "Les services de la Trésorerie des guerres de la Recette de l'artillerie de Charles le Téméraire," *Revue du nord* 79 (1997), 969-91.

Gay, Paolo. "Della nomenclatura delle bocche da fuoco antiche: Gli esemplari custoditi nel Museo Nazionale d'Artiglieria di Torino," *Armi antiche* 2 (1955), 64-80.

Gay, Paolo. "Il nuovo ordinamento della Ia sezione 'artiglierie e materiali relativi' del Museo Nazionale d'Artiglieria di Torino," *Armi antiche* 1 (1954), 58-64.

Geßler, E.A. "Eine Basler Handbüchse aus dem Anfang des 16. Jahrhundert," *Zeitschrift für historisches Waffen- und Köstumkunde* 11 (1926-28), 14.

Geßler, E.A. "Beiträge zum altschweizerischen Geschützwesen: Die großen Geschütze aus dem Zeughausbestand der Stadt Basel," *Zeitschrift für historische Waffenkunde* 6 (1912-14), 3-12, 50-61.

Gille, Paul. "Weaponry, 1500-1700." In: *A History of Technology and Invention: Progress through the Ages.* II: *The First Stages of Mechanization.* Ed. Maurice Daumus. New York: Crown Publishers, Inc., 1969, pp. 473-92.

Giogetti, G. *Storia delle armi da fuoco.* Milan: Luciano Ferriani, 1960.

Girardot, Alain. "Fondeurs d'artillerie et sidérurgistes, une direction de recherche? In: *Mines carrières et métallurgie dans la France médiévale.* Actes du colloque de Paris, 19, 20, 21 juin 1980. Ed. P. Benoit and P. Braunstein. Paris, 1983.

Glage, Wolfgang. "Herzog-Erich-Pistole, Braunschweig um 1505-1515," *Deutsches Waffen Journal* (1/1983), 52-55.

Godoy, José-A. *Armes à feu, XVe-XVIIe siècle: Catalogue du Musée d'Art et d'Histoire, Geneve.* Milan: Bramante Editrice, 1993.

Goetz, Dorothea. *Die Anfänge der Artillerie.* Berlin: Militärverlag der Deutschen Demokratischen Republik, 1985.

Gohlke, W. "Das Geschützwesen des Altertums und des Mittelalters," *Zeitschrift für historische Waffenkunde* 6 (1912-14), 61-65.

Gohlke, W. "Nichtmetallische Geschützrohre," *Zeitschrift für historische Waffenkunde* 5 (1909-11), 141-49.

González Tascón, Ignacio, Juan Carlos Jiménez Barrientos, Dolores Romero Muñoz, and Amaya Sáenz Sanz. "The Manufacture of Gunpowder in Spain and Latin America from the Sixteenth to the Eighteenth Centuries."

In: *Gunpowder: The History of an International Technology*. Ed. Brenda Buchanan. Bath: Bath University Press, 1996, pp. 183-202.

Goold Walker, G. *The Honourable Artillery Company, 1537-1987*. 3rd ed. London: The Honourable Artillery Company, 1987.

Grancsay, Stephen V. "A Hapsburg Gun," *Metropolitan Museum of Art Bulletin* 29 (Oct 1934), 173-75; in: *Arms and Armor: Essays by Stephen V. Grancsay from The Metropolitan Museum of Art Bulletin, 1920-1964*. New York: The Metropolitan Museum of Art, 1986, pp. 132-34.

Grancsay, Stephen V. "A Saxon Wheellock Pistol," *Metropolitan Museum of Art Bulletin* 32 (Nov 1937), 248-51; in: *Arms and Armor: Essays by Stephen V. Grancsay from The Metropolitan Museum of Art Bulletin, 1920-1964*. New York: The Metropolitan Museum of Art, 1986, pp. 198-200.

Grancsay, Stephen V. "A Wheellock Dagger for the Court of the Medici." In: *Arms and Armor Annual: Volume One*. Ed. Robert Held. Northfield: Digest Books, Inc., 1973, pp. 48-55.

Grancsay, Stephen V. "A Wheellock Pistol Made for the Emperor Charles V," *Metropolitan Museum of Art Bulletin* n.s. 6 (Dec 1947), 117-22; in: *Arms and Armor: Essays by Stephen V. Grancsay from The Metropolitan Museum of Art Bulletin, 1920-1964*. New York: The Metropolitan Museum of Art, 1986, pp. 308-13.

Green, J. "Note on Guns from the VOC Ship *Batavia*, Wrecked Off the Western Australian Coast in 1629," *International Journal of Nautical Archaeology and Underwater Exploration* 17 (1988), 103-04.

Grummitt, David. "The Defence of Calais and the Development of Gunpowder Weaponry in England in the Late Fifteenth Century," *War in History* 7 (2000), 253-72.

Guilmartin, John Francis, Jr. "Ballistics in the Black Powder Era." In: *British Naval Armaments*. Ed. R.D. Smith. London, 1989, pp. 73-98.

Guilmartin, John Francis, Jr. "The Earliest Shipboard Gunpowder Ordnance: An Analysis of Technical Parameters and Tactical Capabilities." In: *Actas do XXIV congresso internacional de história militar*. Centro cultural de Belém, 24 a 29 de agosto, 1998. Lisbon: Comissão Portuguesa de História Militar, 1998, pp. 315-28.

Guilmartin, John Francis, Jr. "Early Modern Naval Ordnance and European Penetration of the Caribbean: the Operational Dimension," *International Journal of Nautical Archaeology and Underwater Exploration* 17 (1988), 35-54.

Guilmartin, John Francis, Jr. "The Early Provision of Artillery Armament on Mediterranean War Galleys," *Mariner's Mirror* 59 (1973), 257-80.

Guilmartin, John Francis, Jr. *Gunpowder and Galleys: Changing Technology and Mediterranean Warfare at Sea in the Sixteenth Century.* Cambridge: Cambridge University Press, 1974.

Gümbel, Albert. "Johann Glöckner von Zittau, ein Nürnberger Festungbaumeister, 1430-1442," *Zeitschrift für historisches Waffen- un Köstumkunde* 9 (1921-22), 11-17.

Gusler, Wallace B. and James D. Lavin. *Decorated Firearms, 1540-1870, from the Collection of Clay P. Bedford.* Williamsburg: The Colonial Williamsburg Foundation, 1977.

Gwynn, R.T. "The Breadalbane Gun," *Journal of the Arms and Armour Society* 14 (1992-94), 364-66.

Hale, John R. "Gunpowder and the Renaissance: An Essay in the History of Ideas." In: *From Renaissance to Counter-Reformation: Essays in Honour of Garrett Mattingly.* Ed. Charles H. Carter. London, 1966, pp. 113-44; in: *Renaissance War Studies.* London, 1983, pp. 389-420.

Hall, Bert S. "The Corning of Gunpowder and the Development of Firearms in the Renaissance." In: *Gunpowder: The History of an International Technology.* Ed. Brenda Buchanan. Bath: Bath University Press, 1996, pp. 87-120.

Hall, Bert S. "'So Notable Ordynaunce': Christine de Pizan, Firearms, and Siegecraft in a Time of Transition." In: *Cultuurhistorische Caleidoscoop aangeboden aan Prof. Dr. Willy L. Braekman.* Ghent, 1992, pp. 219-40.

Hall, Bert S. *Weapons and Warfare in Renaissance Europe: Gunpowder, Technology, and Tactics.* Baltimore: The Johns Hopkins University Press, 1997.

Hall, Bert S. "Weapons of War and Late Medieval Cities: Technological Innovation and Tactical Changes." In: *Teachnology and Resource Use in*

Medieval Europe: Cathedrals, Mills and Mines. Ed, E.B. Smith and M. Wolfe. Aldershot: Ashgate, 1997, pp. 185-208.

Hall, Nicholas. "Building and Firing a Replica *Mary Rose* Port Piece," *Royal Armouries Yearbook* 3 (1998), 57-66.

Hassenstein, Wilhelm. *Das Feuerbuch von 1420.* Munich, 1941.

Hassenstein, Wilhelm. "Über die Feuerwaffen in der Seeschlacht von Lepanto," *Zeitschrift für historische Waffen- und Köstumkunde* 16 (1940-42), 1-11.

Hayward, John F. "Armourers and Gunmakers of the French Crown," *Journal of the Arms and Armour Society* 1 (1955), 215-18.

Hayward, John F. *The Art of the Gunmaker.* 2nd ed. 2 vols. London: Barrie and Rockliff, 1965; trans. *Die Kunst der alten Büchsenmacher.* 2 vols. Hamburg and Berlin: Verlag Paul Parey, 1968.

Hayward, John F. "The Decoration of Firearms in the Sixteenth and Seventeenth Centuries," *Bulletin of the American Society of Arms Collectors* 29 (Spr 1974), 2-9.

Hayward, John F. "English Firearms of the 16th Century," *Journal of the Arms and Armour Society* 3 (1959-61), 117-41.

Heath, E.G., ed. *Bow Versus Gun.* Wakefield: EP Publishing, 1973.

Heer, Eugène. *Der neue Støckel: Internationales Lexikon der Büchsenmacher, Feuerwaffenfabrikanten und Armbrustmacher von 1400-1900.* 3 vols. Schwäbischen Hall: Journal-Verlag, 1978-82.

Held, Robert. "Scottish Miquelet Pistol–1623," *Dispatch* 112 (1986), 13-14.

Henderson, Dave. "Power Unparalleled: Gunpowder Weapons and the Early *Furioso*," *Schifanoia: notizie dell'Instituto di studi rinascimentali di Ferrera* 13-14 (1992), 109-31.

Hennessy, N. St. John. "The Dublin Breech-Loading Swivel Gun," *Journal of the Ordnance Society* 3 (1991), 1-4.

Henrard, Paul. "Documents pour servir à l'histoire de l'artillerie en Belgique. Les fondeurs d'artillerie," *Annales de l'academie d'archéologie de Belgique* 45 (1889),.

Henrard, Paul. *Histoire de l'artillerie en Belgique depuis son oringe jusqu'au règne d'Albert et d'Isabelle.* Brussels: Libraire Européen de C. Muquardt, 1865.

Henry, Chris. "The Itchenor Gun," *Royal Armouries Yearbook* 1 (1996), 92-94.

Hernandez, Prisco R. "The Operational Use of Artillery in the War of Granada, 1482-1492," *Field Artillery* (Jul-Aug 1999), 14-17.

Hewitt, J. "Mons Meg, The Ancient Bombard, Preserved at Edinburgh Castle," *Proceedings of the Royal Artillery Institution*," 4 (1865), 25-29.

Hildred, Alexzandra. "The King's Ship: A Study in Strategic Ordnance," *International Journal of Nautical Archaeology and Underwater Exploration* 17 (1988), 55-56.

Hime, Henry W.L. *Gunpowder and Ammunition: Their Origin and Progress.* London, 1904.

Hime, Henry W.L. *The Origin of Artillery.* London: Longmans, Green and Co., 1915.

Hoff, Arne. "Stammt das Radschloß aus Braunschweig?" *Waffen- und Köstumkunde* 30 (1988), 61-67.

Hoff, Arne. "Scottish Pistols in Scandinavian Collections," *Journal of the Arms and Armour Society* 1 (1955), 199-214.

Hogg, Ian. *A History of Artillery.* London: Hamlyn, 1974.

Hogg, O.F.G. *Artillery: Its Origin, Heyday and Decline.* London: C. Hurst and Co., 1970.

Hogg, O.F.G. "The Board of Ordnance," *Journal of the Royal Artillery Institution* 57 (1930-31), 190-207.

Hogg, O.F.G. "The Dawn of Ordnance Administration," *Journal of the Royal Artillery Institution* 59 (1932-33), 427-47.

Hogg, O.F.G. *English Artillery, 1326-1716*. London: Royal Artillery Institution, 1963.

Hogg, O.F.G. "The 'Gunner' and Some Early Masters of Ordnance," *Journal of the Royal Artillery Institution* 62 (1935-36), 463-73.

Hogg, O.F.G. *The Royal Arsenal: Its Background, Origin, and Subsequent History*. 2 vols. London: Oxford University Press, 1963.

Hogg, O.F.G. "Some Notes on Old Artillery," *Journal of the Royal Artillery* 82.3 (Jul 1955), 170-91.

Hoir, S. de. "Guns in Medieval and Tudor Ireland." *Irish Sword* 15 (1982-83), 76-88.

Howard, Frank. "Early Ship Guns. Part I: Built-up Breech Loaders," *Mariner's Mirror* 72 (1986), 439-53.

Howard, Frank. "Early Ship Guns. Part II: Swivels," *Mariner's Mirror* 73 (1987), 49-55.

Howard, Robert A. "The Evolution of the Process of Powder Making from an American Perspective." In: *Gunpowder: The History of an International Technology*. Ed. Brenda Buchanan. Bath: Bath University Press, 1996, pp. 3-24.

Howlett, Richard. "Norwich Artillery in the Fourteenth Century," *Norfolk Archaeology* 16 (1903), 46-75.

Hunter, Joseph. "Proofs of the Early Use of Gunpowder in the English Army," *Archaeologia* 32 (1897), 379-87.

Jacobs, Karl. *Beiträge aur Geschichte der Feuerwaffen am Niederheine bis zum Jahre 1400*. Bonn: Peter Hanstein, 1910.

Jacobsen, Michael A. "A Sforza Miniature by Cristoforo da Preda," *Burlington Magazine* 116 (1974), 91-96.

Jähns, M. *Entwicklungsgeschichte der alten Trutzwaffen, mit einem Anhange über die Feuerwaffen*. Berlin, 1899.

Jexlev, Thelma and Ebba Waaben. "Fortegnelse over rigets skyts og Våbenforråd 1597," *Vaabenhistoriske aarbøger* 34 (1988), 109-63.

Johannsen, Otto. "Die Anwendung des Gußeisens im Geschützwesen des Mittelalters und der Renaissance," *Zeitschrift für historisches Waffen- und Köstumkunde* 8 (1918-20), 1-20.

Johannsen, Otto. "Eine mittelalterliche Hakenbüchse," *Zeitschrift für historisches Waffen- und Köstumkunde* 16 (1940-42), 158-60.

Johannsen, Otto. "Die Quellen zur Geschichte des Eisengusses im Mittelalter und in der neueren Zeit bis zum Jahre 1530," *Archiv für die Geschichte der Naturwissenschaften und der Technik* 3 (1912), 365-94; 6 (1915), 127-41; 8 (1918), 66-81.

Jones, Michael. "L'utilisation de la poudre à canon et de l'artillerie dans le duché de Bretagne avant 1400: la preuve documentaire," *Mémoires de la Société d'Histoire et d'Archéologie de Bretagne* 69 (1992), 163-72.

Jong, M.A.G. de. "Saltpetre Trade on the Amsterdam Staple Market, 1600-1625." In: *The Arsenal of the World: The Dutch Arms Trade in the Seventeenth Century*. Ed. Jan Piet Puype and Marco van der Hoeven. Amsterdam: Batavian Lion International, 1996, pp. 42-46.

Joris, Ph. "Quelques armes combinées," *Musée d'armes* 13 (1976), 8-17.

Juel, A. "Über Kanonenrohre," *Waffen- und Kostümkunde* 7 (1965), 64-65.

Kaestlin, J.P. *Catalogue of the Museum of Artillery in the Rotunda at Woolwich*. Part I: *Ordnance*. 2nd ed. Manchester: Her Majesty's Stationery Office, 1970.

Kalmár, Johannes. "Stachelbomben des XVI. Jahrhunderts," *Zeitschrift für historisches Waffen- und Köstumkunde* 13 (1932-34), 189-90.

Keen, Maurice H. "The Changing Scene: Guns, Gunpowder, and Permanent Armies." In: *Medieval Warfare: A History*. Ed. Maurice Keen. Oxford: Oxford University Press, 1999, pp. 273-91.

Kempers, R.T.W. "Haakbussen uit Nederlands bezit," *Armamentaria* 11 (1976), 75-97; trans. "Haquebuts from Dutch Collections," *Journal of the Arms and Armour Society* 11 (1983-85), 56-89.

Kennard, A.N. "A Civil War Hand Grenade," *Bradford Antiquary* n.s. 39 (1958), 191-93.

Kennard, A.N. *Gunfounding and Gunfounders: A Directory of Cannon Founders from Earliest Times to 1850*. London: Arms and Armour Press, 1986.

Kenyon, John R. "Artillery and the Defences of Southampton circa 1360-1660," *Fort* 3 (Spr 1977; Rev. ed., 1993), 21-30.

Kerkhoven, J.G. "Les anglais ont-ils fait usage d'armes à feu à la bataille de Crécy?" *Revue internationale d'histoire militaire* 19 (1957), 323-31.

King, Edward. "An Account of an Old Piece of Ordnance, which Some Fishermen Dragged Out of the Sea near the Goodwin Sands, in 1775," *Archaeologia* 5 (1779), 147-59.

Kist, J.B. "The Dutch East India Company's Ships' Armament in the 17th and 18th Centuries: An Overview," *International Journal of Nautical Archaeology and Underwater Exploration* 17 (1988), 101-02.

Klein, Herbert. "Die salzburgischen Büchsenmeister des 14. jahrhunderts," *Zeitschrift für historische Waffen- und Köstumkunde* 15 (1937-39), 141-47.

Kleinschmidt, Harald. "Die Schneckenformation und die Entwicklung der Feuerwaffentaktik von Maximilian I bis zu Elizabeth I," *Publication du centre européen d'études Bourguignonnes* 26 (1985), 105-12.

Kleinschmidt, Harald. "Using the Gun: Manual Drill and the Proliferation of Portable Firearms," *Journal of Military History* 63 (1999), 601-41.

Konstam, R.A. "16th Century Naval Tactics and Gunnery," *International Journal of Nautical Archaeology and Underwater Exploration* 17 (1988), 17-23.

Kramer, Gerhard. *Berthold Schwarz: Chemie und Waffentechnik im 15. Jahrhundert*. Munich: Deutsches Museum, 1995.

Kramer, Gerhard. "*Das Feuerwerkbuch*: Its Importance in the Early History of Black Powder." In: *Gunpowder: The History of an International Technology*. Ed. Brenda Buchanan. Bath: Bath University Press, 1996, pp. 45-56.

Krenn, Peter. *Gewehr und Pistole/Rifles and Pistols: Landeszeughaus Graz, am Steiermärkischen Landesmuseum Joanneum*. Graz: Kunstverlag Hofstetter, 1990.

Krenn, Peter. "Was leisteten die alten Handfeuerwaffen? Ergebnisse einer Ausstellung des Landeszeughauses in Graz," *Waffen- und Köstumkunde* 32 (1990), 35-52.

Krenn, Peter, ed. *Von Alten Handfeuerwaffen: Entwicklung, Technik, Leistung*. Graz: Landeszeughaus, 1989.

Krenn, Peter, Paul Kalaus, and Bert Hall. "Material Culture and Military History: Test-Firing Early Modern Small Arms," *Material History Review* 42 (Fall 1995), 101-09.

Kuyper, F.W.H. *Geschiedenis der Nederlandsche artillerie van de vroegste tijden tot op heden*. 5 vols. Nijmegen, 1869-74.

Lacabane, L. "De la poudre à canon et de son introduction en France," *Bibliothèque de l'école de chartes* 2nd ser., 1 (1844), 28-57.

Larchey, L. "Les ribauequins du manuscrit de Colmar," *Revue Alsacienne* 13 (1890), 585-92.

Laughton, L.G. Carr. "Early Tudor Ship-Guns," *Mariner's Mirror* 46 (1960), 242-85.

Laughton, L.G. Carr. "Hull Projection," *Mariner's Mirror* 26 (1940), 55-60.

Lavin, James D. "An Examination of Some Early Documents Regarding the Use of Gunpowder in Spain," *Journal of the Arms and Armour Society* 4 (1962-64), 163-69.

Lavin, James D. "La influencia italiana en la arcabucería Española," *Armi antiche* (1965), 111-26.

Lefroy, Brigadier-General. "On Two Large English Cannon of the Fifteenth Century, Preserved at Mont S. Michel in Normandy," *Proceedings of the Royal Artillery Institution*," 4 (1865), 10-24.

Lehner, Heinz. "Die sachsischen Militarpistolen und revolver, 1564-1883," *Deutsches Waffen Journal* (Feb 1990), 186-93.

Lenk, Torsten. "Two French Wheel-Lock Guns," *Journal of the Arms and Armour Society* 2 (1956-58), 113-14.

Lewendon, R.J. "The Leather Gun if Gustavus Adolphus of Sweden in the Rotunda Collection at Woolwich." In: *17ᵗʰ Century War, Weaponry and Politics: International Association of Museums of Arms and Military History, Xth Congress Stockholm 1984* Stockholm, 1984, pp. 113-19; *Journal of the Royal Artillery* 112 (1985).

Lewendon, R.J. "The Mary Rose Cannon." In: *Proceedings of the Ninth Triennial Congress of the International Association of Museums of Arms and Military History.* Quantico: Marine Corps Association, 1981, pp. 177-84.

Lewerken, H.-W. *Kombinations Waffen des 15.-19. Jahrhunderts.* Berlin: Militärverlag der Deutschen Demokratischen Republik, 1989.

Lewis, Michael. *Armada Guns: A Comparative Study of English and Spanish Armaments.* London: George Allen and Unwin Ltd., 1961.

Lhotsky, Alphons. "Die 'Lauerpfeif' als Geschichtsdenkmal," *Zeitschrift für historische Waffen- und Köstumkunde* 15 (1937-39), 261-63.

Liebe, G. "Die sociale Wertung der Artillerie," *Zeitschrift für historische Waffenkunde* 2 (1900-02), 146-51.

Liebnitz, Klaus. "Die Manuskripte des Walter de Milemete," *Waffen- und Köstumkunde* 34 (1992), 117-31.

Lindsay, Merrill K. "Gunpowder, or How It All Didn't Start," *Armi antiche* (1966), 133-61.

Lloyd, Christopher. "Sussex Guns," *History Today* 23 (1973), 785-91.

Lombarès, Michel de. *Histoire de l'artillerie Française.* Paris, 1985.

López Martín, Francisco Javier. "Un cañon de Cristobál Frisleva en el Museo Naval de Madrid," *Gladius* 19 (1999), 197-220

Lugs, J. *Ručni palné zbrané.* 2 vols. Prague, 1956.

Lupi, Gianoberto. "Gli Alberghetti, dinastia di artiglieri e conditori di cannoni," *Diana armi* 7.8 (Aug 1973).

Lupi, Gianoberto. "Una regina per Ercole," *Diana armi* 20.1 (Jan 1986), 96-98.

MacIvor, Iain. "Artillery and Major Places of Strength in the Lothians and the East Border, 1513-1542." In: *Scottish Weapons and Fortifications, 1100-1800.* Ed. David H. Caldwell. Edinburgh: John Donald Publishers Ltd., 1981, pp. 94-152.

Madlić, Josif. "Konzervacija bronzanih pušaka–kukača iz XV veka," *Vesnik* 6-7 (1962), 279-84.

Maeßer, W. "Suhl und Lüttich als Großerzeuger von Schußwaffen," *Zeitschrift für historisches Waffenkunde* 7 (1915-17), 254-61.

Mahoney, Dhira B. "Malory's Great Guns." *Viator* 20 (1989), 291-310.

Mallet, Robert. "On the Physical Conditions Involved in the Construction of Artillery, and on Some Hitherto Unexplained Causes of the Destruction of Cannon in Service." *Transactions of the Royal Irish Academy* 23 (1856), 141-436.

Manchester, William. *The Arms of Krupp, 1587-1968.* New York: Bantam Books, 1970.

Marscher, E. "Der 'Roi des Ribauds' im französischen Heer," *Zeitschrift für historisches Waffenkunde* 7 (1915-17), 112.

Martin, Colin J.M. "Incendiary Weapons from the Spanish Armada Wreck *La Trinidad Valencera*, 1588," *International Journal of Nautical Archaeology* 23 (1994), 207-17.

Martin, Colin J.M. "A 16th Century Siege Train: The Battery Ordnance of the 1588 Spanish Armada," *International Journal of Nautical Archaeology and Underwater Exploration* 17 (1988), 57-74.

Martin, Paul. "L'artillerie et la fonderie de canons de Strasbourg du XIVe au XVIIIe siècle," *Armi antiche* (1967), 71-90.

Martinez, Jose Luis. "Artilleros y exploraciones de Hernan Cortes en el pacifico." In: *Atti del v convegno internazionale di studi colombiani: "Navi e navigazione nei secoli XV e XVI".* Genoa, 1990, I:245-92.

Mataloni, Francc. "Le scomode cavalcate di Belzebú: Il cannone el medioevo," *Diana armi* 4.3 (1970).

Maxwell-Irving, Alistair M.T. "Early Firearms and Their Influence on Military and Domestic Architecture of the Border," *Proceedings of the Society of Antiquaries of Scotland* 103 (1970-71), 192-224.

McElvogue, Douglas M. "An Analysis and Description of Firearms and Associated Artefacts Off a Late Sixteenth-Century Vessel Wrecked Off Alderney, Channel Islands," *Journal of the Arms and Armour Society* 16.4 (Mar 2000), 198-209.

McElvogue, Douglas M. "Ordnance from a Late 16th Century Wreck, Alderney," *Journal of the Ordnance Society* 11 (1999), 1-17.

Meier, Jürg A. "Notizen zur Geschichte der Handfeuerwaffen in der Schweiz 14.-16. Jh. (Unter besonderer Berücksichtigung von Schaffhausen und Bern)," *Revue* n.s. 4 (Sep 1985), 193-214, 6 (Jun 1986), 289-304.

Melero, María Jesús. "La evolución y empleo del armamento a bordo de los buques entre los siglos XIV al XIX," *Militaria* 5 (1993), 45-66.

Mercier, M. *Le feu grégois, les feux de guerre depuis l'antiquité, la poudre à canon*. Paris, 1952.

Meyrick, Samuel Rush. "Observations upon the History of Hand Fire-arms, and their Appurtenances," *Archaeologia* 22 (1829), 59-105; Rpt; Richmond: Richmond Publishing Co., Ltd., 1971.

Montu, C. *Storia dell'artiglieri italiana*. Rome, 1934.

Morillo, Stephen. "Guns and Government: A Comparative Study of Europe and Japan," *Journal of World History* 6 (1995), 75-106.

Morin, Marco. "Armi da fioco particolari nelle collezioni dei Musei Italiani: Una pepperbox del XVIo secolo," *Diana armi* 4.2 (1970).

Morin, Marco. "Armi da fioco particolari nelle collezioni dei Musei Italiani: Le pistole de Corsaro," *Diana armi* 5.2 (1971).

Morin, Marco. "La battaglia di Lepanto: il determinante apporto dell' artiglieri Veneziana," *Diana armi* 9.1 (1975), 54-61.

Morin, Marco. "La bombarde del maestro Ferlino," *Diana armi* 9.6 (1975), 59-63.

Morin, Marco. "The Origins of the Wheellock: A German Hypothesis." In: *Art, Arms and Armour: An International Anthology*. Vol I: *1979-80*. Ed. Robert Held. Chiasso: Acquafresca Editrice, 1979, pp. 80-99.

Morin, Marco. "Per la mia Venezia," *Diana armi* 8.7 (July 1974), 59-64.

Morin, Marco. "Una pistola del 1546 nell' Armeria del Consiglio dei Dieci," *Diana armi* 9 (1975), 56-60.

Mörtzsch, Otto. "Einige Bestallungen von fürstlichen Büchsenmeistern, Schützenmeistern und Pfeilstickern," *Zeitschrift für historische Waffenkunde* 5 (1909-11), 321-23.

Müller, Heinrich. *Alte Geschütze: Kostbare Stücke aus der Sammlung des Museums*. Berlin: Museum für Deutsche Geschichte, 1969.

Müller, Heinrich. *Deutsche Bronzegeschützrohre, 1400-1750*. Berlin: Deutscher Militärverlag, 1968.

Müller, Heinrich. *Guns, Pistols, Revolvers: Hand-Firearms from the 14th to the 19th Centuries*. Leipzig: Edition Leipzig, 1980.

Müller, Heinrich. "Kanonen und Vogelgesang: Vogeldarstellungen auf alten Geschutzröhren," *Der Falke* 13.1 (1966), 16-22.

Munday, John. *Naval Cannon*. Princes Risborough: Shire Publishing Ltd., 1998.

Napoleon-Bonaparte, Louis and Ildéfonse Favé. *Études sur le passé et l'avenir de l'artillerie*. 6 vols. Paris, 1846-71.

Neal, W. Keith and D.H.L. Back. *Great British Gunmakers, 1540-1740*. Historical Firearms, 5. Norwich, 1984.

Neuhaus, August. "Der Geschützgiesser Oswald Baldner," *Zeitschrift für historisches Waffen- und Köstumkunde* 13 (1932-34), 199-204.

Nida, C.A. von. "Die Steinbüchsen," *Zeitschrift für historisches Waffen- und Köstumkunde* 10 (1923-25), 117-21.

Nikolaus, Alfred. "The Preservation of the 'Faule Magd': An Example of the Care of the National Cultural Heritage of the German Democratic Republic." In: *Proceedings of the Ninth Triennial Congress of the Inter-*

national Association of Museums of Arms and Military History. Quantico: Marine Corps Association, 1981, pp. 206-15.

Nonte, George C. *Firearms Encyclopedia*. London: Wolf Publishing Ltd., 1973.

Norman, A.V.B. "Notes on Some Early Representations of Guns and on Ribaudekins," *Journal of the Arms and Armour Society* 8 (1975), 234-27.

O'Neill, B.H.St.J. *Castles and Cannon: A Study of Early Artillery Fortifications in England*. Oxford: Oxford University Press, 1960.

Padfield, Peter. *Guns at Sea*. London: Hugh Evelyn, 1973.

Parker, Geoffrey. "The Gunpowder Revolution, 1300-1500." In: *The Cambridge Illustrated History of Warfare: The Triumph of the West*. Ed. Geoffrey Parker. Cambridge: Cambridge University Press, 1995, pp. 106-17.

Parnell, Geoffrey. "Ordnance Storehouses at the Tower of London, 1450-1700," *Château Gaillard* 17 (1998), 171-79.

Partington, J.R. *A History of Greek Fire and Gunpowder*. Cambridge: W. Heffer and Sons, Ltd., 1960; rpt. Baltimore: Johns Hopkins University Press, 1999.

Pasquali-Lasagni, Alberto and Emilio Stefanneli. "Note di storia dell'artigliera nel secoli XIV-XV," *Archivio della reale deputazione romana di studia patria* 60 (1937), 149-89.

Patria, Ettore. "Il tiro al tavolazzo," *Armi antiche* (1980), 55-76.

Pearse, Richard. "The Use of the Matchlock When Mounted," *Journal of the Society for Army Historical Research* 44 (1966), 201-04.

Pederby, Bo. "Sancta Barbara–artilleriets skyddshelgon," *Meddelande* 47 (1987), 288-94.

Pedrosa, Fernando G. "A artilharia naval portuguesa no século XVI." In: *Actas do XXIV congresso internacional de historía militar*. Centro cultural de Belém, 24 a 29 de agosto, 1998. Lisbon: Comissão Portuguesa de Historía Militar, 1998, pp. 329-33.

Peine, Selmar. *St. Barbara, die Schuzheilige der Bergleute und der Artillerie, und ihre Darstellung in der Kunst*. Freiberg, 1896.

Pepper, Simon. "Castles and Cannon in the Naples Campaign of 1494-95." In: *The French Descent into Renaissance Italy, 1494-95: Antecedents and Effects*. Ed. D. Abulafia. Aldershot: Ashgate, 1995, pp. 263-93.

Pepper, Simon. "The Underground Siege." *Fort* 10 (1982), 31-38.

Pepper, Simon and Nicholas Adams. *Firearms and Fortifications: Military Architecture and Siege Warfare in Sixteenth-Century Siena*. Chicago: University of Chicago Press, 1986.

Perroy, Edouard. "L'artillerie de Louis XI dans la campagne d'Artois," *Revue du Nord* 26 (1943), 171-96, 293-315.

Perroy, Edouard. "L'artillerie royale à la bataille de Montlhery (10 juillet 1465), *Revue historique* 149 (1925), 187-89.

Peterson, Harold L. *Round Shot and Rammers*. Harrisburg: Stackpole Books, 1969.

Petrović, Djurdjica. "Fire-arms in the Balkans on the Eve of and after the Ottoman Conquests of the Fourteenth and Fifteenth Centuries." In: *War, Technology and Society in the Middle East*. Ed. V.J. Parry and M.E. Yapp. London, 1975, pp. 164-94.

Petrović, Djurdjica. "Puškarski zanat u Metohiji," *Vesnik* 2 (1955), 81-104.

Petrović, Djurdjica and Dušanka Bojanić-Lukač. "Dobijanje šalitre u Makedoniji od polovine XVI do polovine XIX veka," *Vesnik* 10 (1964), 23-58.

Pettengill, John S. "Firearms and the Distribution of Income: A Neo-Classical Model," *Review of Radical Political Economics* 13 (Summer 1981), 1-11.

Pfaffenbichler, Matthias. "Die graphischen Vorlagen zum Werk des Büchsenschäfters Hans Schmidt von und zu Helding: Eine Untersuchung zur Waffenkunde als Kunstwissenschaft," *Waffen- und Köstumkunde* 30 (1988), 69-83.

Phillips, Gervase. "Longbow and Hackbutt: Weapons Technology and Technology Transfer in Early Modern England," *Technology and Culture* 40 (1999), 576-93.

Pinti, Paolo. "La artigilieri del Museo Marzoli a Brescia. Parte prima: artigilieri pesanti," *Armi antichi* (1988-89), 153-86.

Pinti, Paolo. "Artiglierie medievali," *Diana armi* 19.9 (Sep 1985), 40-43; 19.10 (Oct 1985), 85-87.

Poncin, D. *De la science au Moyen âge. Archéologie balistique*. Antwerp, 1885.

Post, Paul. "Die frühste Geschützdarstellung von etwa 1330," *Zeitschrift für historische Waffen- und Köstumkunde* 15 (1937-39), 137-41.

Post, Paul. "Eine mittelalterliche Geschützkammer mit Ladung im Berliner Zeughaus," *Zeitschrift für historische Waffen- und Köstumkunde* 9 (1921-22), 117-21.

Probst, Christian. "Saltpetereinfuhr und Saltpetersieder im Deutschordensland Preussen," *Waffen- und Kostümkunde* 7 (1965), 60-64.

Puype, Jan Piet. "Dutch Firearms from the 17th Century." In: *The Arsenal of the World: The Dutch Arms Trade in the Seventeenth Century*. Ed. Jan Piet Puype and Marco van der Hoeven. Amsterdam: Batavian Lion International, 1996, pp. 71-75.

Puype, Jan Piet. "Het embleem van Lodewijk van Gruuthuse." In: *Lodewijk van Gruuthuse: Mecenas en europees diplomaat, ca. 1427-1492*. Ed. Maximiliaan P.J. Martens. Bruges, 1992, pp. 93-108.

Puype, Jan Piet. "Notes on an Early 17th Century Flintlock Target Gun," *Waffen- und Kostümkunde* 22 (1980), 27-38.

Pyhrr, Stuart W. "Elements from Two Medici Guns," *Armi antichi* (1986), 83-90.

Radisavljević, Slobodan. "Neka razmatranja o pušci fitiljači," *Vesnik* 1 (1954), 30-52.

Radisavljević, Slobodan. "Neki podaci o kolašicama," *Vesnik* 3 (1956), 148-60.

Radisavljević, Slobodan. "Prilog proučavanju porekla pištolja," *Vesnik* 4 (1957), 152-70.

Rathgen, Bernhard. *Das Aufkommen der Pulverwaffe*. Munich, 1925.

Rathgen, Bernhard. "Das Drehkraftgeschütz in Deutschland," *Zeitschrift für historische Waffenkunde* 8 (1918-20), 54-67.

Rathgen, Bernhard. "Das Drehkraftgeschütz im Streite der Meinungen," *Zeitschrift für historische Waffen- und Köstumkunde* 10 (1923-25), 47-59.

Rathgen, Bernhard. "Feuer- und fernwaffen des 14. jahrunderts in Flandern." *Zeitschrift für historisches Waffenkunde* 7 (1915-17), 275-306.

Rathgen, Bernhard. *Die feuer- und fernwaffen in Naumburg von 1348-1449.* Naumburg: H. Sielings Buchdruckerei, 1921.

Rathgen, Bernhard. "Frankfurter Prunkgeschütze und ihre Meister," *Zeitschrift für historisches Waffen- un Köstumkunde* 9 (1921-22), 83-108.

Rathgen, Bernhard. *Das Geschütz im mittelalter: Quellenkritische untersuchungen.* Berlin: VDI-Verlag GMBH, 1928.

Rathgen, Bernhard and Karl Heinrich Schäfer. "Feuer- und fernwaffen beim päpstlichen Heere im 14. Jahrhundert." *Zeitschrift für historisches Waffenkunde* 7 (1915-17), 1-15.

Reimer, Paul. "Die älteren Hinterladungsgeschütze," *Zeitschrift für Historische Waffenkunde* 2 (1900-02), 3-9, 39-43.

Reimer, Paul. "Die Erscheinung des Schusses und seine bildliche Darstellung," *Zeitschrift für historische Waffenkunde* 2 (1900-02), 393-402, 435-41.

Reimer, Paul. "Das Geschützprobieren," *Zeitschrift für historische Waffenkunde* 2 (1900-02), 71-74.

Reimer, Paul. "Nochmals: Die älteren Hinterladungsgeschütze," *Zeitschrift für Historische Waffen- und Köstumkunde* 9 (1921-22), 194-99.

Reimer, Paul. "Das pulver und die ballistischen Anschauungen im 14. und 15. Jahrhundert," *Zeitschrift für historische Waffenkunde* 1 (1897-99), 164-66.

Reimer, Paul. "Vom Schwartzpulver," *Zeitschrift für historische Waffenkunde* 4 (1906-08), 367-83.

Reinaud, Joseph Toussaint and Ildéfonse Favé. *Du feu grégeois, des feux de guerre et des origines de la poudre à canon.* Paris, 1845; *Journal asiatique* 4th ser. 14 (1849), 257-327.

Reitzenstein, Alexander Freiherr von. "Die Feuerwaffen in der Rüstkammer von Pfalz-Neuburg 1628 und 1654," *Waffen- und Kostümkunde* 23 (1981), 87-100.

Reuck, Anthony de. "Greenwich Revisited: Or Gunpowder and the Obsolesence of Armour," *Journal of the Arms and Armour Society* 15 (1995-98), 426-43.

Reverseau, Jean-Pierre. "Un pistolet à rouet signé de Cisteron à Figeac, vers 1630-1640," *Revue de la Société des Amis du Musée de l'Armée* 106 (1993), 68-71.

Richardson, Thom. "Venetian Cannon in the Askeri Müze, Istanbul," *Ordnance Society Newsletter* 1 (1987), 4-7.

Riederer, Josef. "Metallanalysen von Geschützbronzen," *Waffen- und Kostümkunde* 14 (1972), 49-56.

Rimer, Graeme. "Early Handguns," *Royal Armouries Yearbook* 1 (1996), 73-78.

Rimer, Graeme and David Blackmore. "Firearms in the Popham Armoury at Littlecote House," *Park Lane Arms Fair* 3 (1986), 19-24.

Ritter, Karl. "Aufbau und Herstellung der Schmiedeeisernen Steinbüchsen des Mittelalters," *Technische mitteilungen Krupp* 5 (1938), 113-27.

Robert, L. *Catalogue des collections composant le Musée d'Artillerie en 1889.* 4 vols. Paris, 1889-93.

Röder, Ernst. "Aus der Waffensammlung des Germanischen Nationalmuseums. 1. Die Tannenberger Büchse," *Zeitschrift für historische Waffenkunde* 3 (1902-05), 97-102.

Röder, Ernst. "Eine Hakenbüchse des 15. Jahrhunderts," *Zeitschrift für historisches Waffen- und Köstumkunde* 11 (1926-28), 265.

Rodger, N.A.M. "Elizabethan Naval Gunnery," *Mariner's Mirror* 61 (1975), 353-54.

Rodger, N.A.M. "Guns and Sails in the First Phase of English Colonization, 1500-1650." In: *The Origins of Empire: British Overseas Enterprise to the Close of the Seventeenth Century*. Ed. Nicholas Canny. The Oxford History of the British Empire, I. Oxford: Oxford University Press, 1998, pp. 79-98.

Rodriguez, M.R Marco. "Arcabuz Turco y Retaco Japonés en la Museo Arqueológico Nacional, Madrid," *Gladius* 14 (1978), 89-96.

Roelofsen, C.G. "L'evolution de la flotte 'Bourguignonne' aux XVe et XVIe siècles: quelques remarques sur l'introduction du canon dans la guerre maritime et son influence." *Publication du centre Européen d'études Bourguignonnes (XIVe-XVIe s.)* 26 (1986), 87-95.

Rogers, H.C.B. *Artillery through the Ages*. London: Seeley Service and Co., Ltd., 1971.

Roland, C. "L'artillerie de la ville de Binche, 1362-1420." *Bulletin de la société royale paléontologique et archéologique de l'arrondissement judicaire de Charleroi* 23 (1954), 17-38.

Roosens, B. "De keizerlijke artillerie op het einde van de regering van Karel V," *Revue Belge d'histoire militaire* 23 (1979-80), 117-46.

Roth, Rudi. "Um 'Leão" Português de 48 libras de 1594/A Portuguese 48 pounder 'Leão' of 1594," *Boletin da sociedade Portuguesa de armas antiguas/Bulletin of the Portuguese Academy of Antique Arms* 1 (1997), 51-63.

Roth, Rudi. "The Measuring of Cannons," *Journal of the Ordnance Society* 1 (1989), 51-62.

Roth, Rudi. "The 'Mons Meg' Cannon Story Has Become Legend Over its 500 Years," *Artilleryman* 9.1 (Win 1987).

Roth, Rudi. "The Orford Gun," *Journal of the Ordnance Society* 7 (1995), 79-92.

Roth, Rudi. "A Proposed Standard in the Reporting of Historic Artillery," *The International Journal of Nautical Archaeology and Underwater Exploration* 18 (1989), 191-202.

Roth, Rudi. "The Renaissance Man," *Journal of the Ordnance Society* 6 (1994), 1-8.

Rothbert, H. "Wann und wo ist die Pulverwaffe erfunden?" *Blätter für deutsche Landesgeschichte* 89 (1952), 84-86.

Royer, Pierre-Richard. "Aspects techniques de l'évolution des armes à feu àrouets géminés d'après les exemples du Musée de l'Armée," *Waffen- und Köstumkunde* 27 (1985), 3-12.

Ruhmann, Jenö. "Gunpowder for the Defence of the City: Sopron from the Sixteenth Century." In: *Gunpowder: The History of an International Technology*. Ed. Brenda Buchanan. Bath: Bath University Press, 1996, pp. 157-62.

Rule, Margaret and Alexzandra Hildred. "Armaments from the 'Mary Rose'," *Antique Arms and Militaria* 4 (May 1994), 15-24.

Saint-Rémy, Surirey de. "The Manufacture of Gunpowder in France (1702), Part I: Saltpetre, Sulphur and Charcoal," trans. D.H. Roberts, *Journal of the Ordnance Society* 5 (1993), 47-55.

Salamagne, Alain. "A propos de l'adaptation de la fortification à l'artillerie vers les années 1400: quelques remarques sur les problèmes de vocabulaire, de typologie et de méthode," *Moyen âge* 75 (1993), 809-46.

Salgado, Augusto António Alves. "Portuguese Naval Carriages in the Late 16th Century," *Journal of the Ordnance Society* 11 (1999), 31-33.

Sanchez Morales, Narciso. "Los cañones de Carlos V," *Gladius* 8 (1969), 63-69.

Schaal, Dieter. *Katalog Dresdener Büchsenmacher 16.-18 Jahrhundert.* Dresden: Historisches Museum, 1975.

Schalkhausser, Erwin. "Bronzegeschütze des 16. Jahrhunderts im Bayerischen Armeemuseum," *Waffen- und Kostümkunde* 19 (1977), 1-24.

Schalkhausser, Erwin. "Die Handfeuerwaffen des Bayerischen National-museums," *Waffen- und Kostümkunde* 8 (1966), 1-12; 9 (1967), 1-27, 117-30; 10 (1968), 31-46, 127-33; 11 (1969), 48-59; 12 (1970), 135-46; 14 (1972), 57-73.

Schalkhauser, Erwin. "Die Handfeuerwaffen des Bayerischen National-museums," *Waffen- und Kostümkunde* 13 (1971), 137-46.

Schalkhauser, Erwin. "Peter Peck, ein Münchner Büchsenmacher der 16. Jahrhunderts," *Waffen- und Kostümkunde* 16 (1974), 21-40.

Schalkhausser, Erwin. "Peter Peck, the Emperor's Gunsmith." In: *Art, Arms and Armour: An International Anthology.* Vol I: *1979-80.* Ed. Robert Held. Chiasso: Acquafresca Editrice, 1979, pp. 182-201.

Schedelmann, Hans. *Die Grossen Büchsenmacher: Leben, Werke, Marken von 15 bis 19 Jahrhundert.* Brunswick: Klinkhardt and Biermann, 1972.

Schimpf, Anselme. "L'arquebuserie Strasbourgeoise," *Armi antiche* (1971), 3-34; (1972), 3-38.

Schmidtchen, Volker. *Bombarden, Befestigungen, Büchsenmeister: Von den ersten Mauerbrechern des Spätmittelalters zur Belagerungsartillerie der Renaissance. Eine Studie zur Entwicklung der Militärtechnik.* Dusseldorf: Droste Verlag, 1977.

Schmidtchen, Volker. "Castles, Cannon and Casemates," *Fortress* 6 (Aug 1990), 3-10.

Schmidtchen, Volker. *Die feuerwaffen des deutschen Ritterordens bis zur Schlacht bei Tannenberg 1410: Beistände, Funktion und Kosten dargestellt Anhand der Wirtschaftsbücher des Ordens von 1374 bis 1410.* Lüneburg: Nordostdeutsches Kulturwerk, 1977.

Schneider, Hugo. *Aus dem Schweizerischen Landesmuseum. I: Schutzwaffen aus sieben Jahrhunderten.* Bern, 1953.

Schneider, Hugo. "Schweizerische Büchsenmacherei," *Armi antichi* (1963), 91-103.

Schneider, Hugo. "Schweizerische Handfeuerwaffen. Stand der Forschung." *Waffen- und Kostümkunde* 13 (1971), 40-51.

Schneider, Rudolf. *Die Artillerie des Mittelalters: Nach den Angaben der Zeitgenossen dargestelt.* Berlin: Weidmannsche Buchhandlung, 1910.

Schneider, Rudolf. "Eine byzantinische Feuerwaffe," *Zeitschrift für historisches Waffenkunde* 5 (1909-11), 83-86.

Schubert, H.R. "The First Cast-Iron Cannon Made in England." *Journal of the Iron and Steel Institute* 146 (1942), 131P-140P.

Schubert, H.R. "The Superiority of English Cast-Iron Cannon at the Close of the Sixteenth Century," *Journal of the Society for Army Historical Research* 3 (1924), 85-86.

Scrive-Bertin, M. "Les canonniers Lillois avant 1483," *Bulletin de la commission historique du departement du Nord* 19 (1890), 119-91.

Seel, Wolfgang. "Altpreußische Saltpeterwirtschaft," *Waffen- und Kostümkunde* 25 (1983), 31-41.

Segre, Michael. "Schuss–und kein Treffer: Die schweren Anfänge der wissenschaftlichen Balistik," *Kultur & Technik* 18.1 (1994), 30-33.

Simmons, Joe J., III. "Early Modern Wrought-Iron Artillery: Macroanalyses of Instruments of Enforcement," *Materials Characterization* 29 (1992), 129-38.

Simmons, Joe J., III. "Lidded-breech Wrought-iron Swivel Gun at Southsea Castle, Portsmouth, England," *Journal of the Ordnance Society* 1 (1989), 63-68.

Simmons, Joe J., III. "Replication of Early 16th Century Shot-Mould Tongs," *Journal of the Ordnance Society* 3 (1991), 5-10.

Simmons, Joe J., III. "Wrought-Iron Ordnance: Revealing Discoveries from the New World," *International Journal of Nautical Archaeology and Underwater Exploration* 17 (1988), 25-34.

Simms, D.L. "Archimedes and the Invention of Artillery and Gunpowder," *Technology and Culture* 28 (1987), 67-79.

Singer, Dorothea Waley. "On a 16th Century Cartoon Concerning the Devilish Weapon Gunpowder: Some Medieval Reactions to Guns and Gunpowder," *Ambix* 7 (1959), 25-33.

Sixl, P. "Entwickelung und Gebrauch der Handfeuerwaffen." *Zeitschrift für Historische Waffenkunde* 1 (1897-99), 112-17, 137-41, 182-84, 199-202, 220-28, 248-56, 276-82, 300-06; 2 (1900-02), 13-16, 44-48, 77-79, 116-19, 163-70, 264-69, 316-20, 386-87, 407-17, 441-48; 3 (1902-05), 231-36, 269-71, 285-89, 327-29, 361-65; 4 (1906-08), 24-27, 84-88.

Sixl, P. "Zur Geschichte des Schiesswesens der Infanterie," *Zeitschrift für Historische Waffenkunde* 2 (1900-02), 327-37, 374-80.

Škrivanić, Gavro A. "Prilozi za proučavanje razvoja vatrenog oružja," *Vesnik* 2 (1955), 72-80.

Sloane, Hamish. "A Pair of Pistols by Robert Alison of Dundee–1635," *Dispatch* 117 (1988), 45-47.

Sloane, Hamish. "The 'Sinclair' Pistols, circa. 1600 to 1625," *Dispatch* 111 (1986), 8-10.

Sloane, Hamish and James B. McKay. "The People's Palace Pistol, *circa* 1600-1625," *Dispatch* 102 (Spring 1983), 17-20.

Smith, Robert D. "Artillery and the Hundred Years War: Myth and Interpretation." In: *Arms, Armies and Fortifications in the Hundred Years War*. Ed. A. Curry and M. Hughes. Woodbridge, 1994, pp. 151-60.

Smith, Robert D. "Early Cast-Iron Guns with Particular Reference to Guns on the Isle of Man," *Journal of the Ordnance Society* 3 (1991), 25-46.

Smith, Robert D. "HM Tower Armouries: Wrought Iron Cannon Project," *Historical Metallurgy* 19 (1985), 193-95.

Smith, Robert D. "Port Pieces: The Use of Wrought-Iron Guns in the Sixteenth Century," *Journal of the Ordnance Society* 5 (1993), 1-10.

Smith, Robert D. "The Reconstruction and Firing Trials of a Replica of a 14th-Century Cannon," *Royal Armouries Yearbook* 4 (1999), 86-94.

Smith, Robert D. "A Sixteenth-Century Bronze Cannon from London," *Royal Armouries Yearbook* 2 (1997), 107-12.

Smith, Robert D. "Towards a New Typology for Wrought Iron Ordnance." *International Journal of Nautical Archaeology and Underwater Exploration* 17 (1988), 5-16.

Smith, Robert D. "A Turkish Gun," *Ordnance Society Newsletter* 2 (Mar 1988), 16-17.

Smith, Robert D. "Wrought-Iron Swivel Guns." In: *The Archaeology of Ships of War*. Ed. M. Bound. Oxford, 1995, pp. 104-13.

Smith, Robert D. and Ruth Rhynas Brown. "The Bodiam Mortar," *Journal of the Ordnance Society* 1 (1989), 3-22.

Smith, Robert D. and Ruth Rhynas Brown. *Mons Meg and Her Sisters*. Royal Armouries Monograph, 1. London: Trustees of the Royal Armouries, 1989.

Smith, Robert D. and Brian Gilmour. "A Wrought-Iron Handgun: A Preliminary Report," *Ordnance Society Newsletter* 5 (Dec 1988), 6-8.

Smith, Ronald Bishop. *A 16ᵗʰ Century Portuguese Swivel Gun in the British Museum*. Lisbon, 1995.

Smith, Ronald Bishop. *An Early 16ᵗʰ Century Wrought Iron Cannon in Goa*. Lisbon, 1996.

Sommé, Monique. "L'artillerie et la guerre de frontière dans le nord de la France de 1477 à 1482." *Publication du centre Européen d'études Bourguignonnes (XIVe-XVIe s.)* 26 (1986), 57-70.

Sommé, Monique. "Les mesures dans l'artillerie Bourguignonne au XVe siècle," *Cahiers de metrologie* 7 (1989), 43-53.

Spencer, Michael G. "An Archaic Wheellock," *Journal of the Arms and Armour Society* 10 (1980-82), 176-81.

Spencer, Michael G. "Early Wheellock Firearms at Chirk Castle," *Journal of the Arms and Armour Society* 15 (1995-98), 17-21.

Spencer, Michael G. "Early Wheellock Firearms with Autormatically-Opening Pan-Covers," *Journal of the Arms and Armour Society* 10 (1980-82), 206-07.

Spencer, Michael G. "The English Flintlock and the English Civil War," *Journal of the Arms and Armour Society* 14 (1992-94), 89-109.

Spencer, Michael G. "A Note on the 'Portuguese' Wheellock," " *Journal of the Arms and Armour Society* 15 (1995-98), 220-37.

Spencer, Michael G. "Some Wheellocks with English Associations," *Park Lane Arms Fair* 13 (1996), 26-29.

Stern, Walter M. "Gunmaking in Seventeenth-Century London," *Journal of the Arms and Armour Society* 1 (1954), 55-100.

Sterzel, H. "Die 'Dulle Griet' von Gent," *Zeitschrift für Historische Waffenkunde* 7 (1915-17), 324-25.

Stevenson, Robert B.K. "The Return of Mons Meg from London, 1828-1829." In: *Scottish Weapons and Fortifications, 1100-1800.* Ed. David H. Caldwell. Edinburgh: John Donald Publishers Ltd., 1981, pp. 419-41.

Stewart, Richard Winship. *The English Ordnance Office, 1585-1625: A Case Study in Bureaucracy.* London: Royal Historical Society, 1996.

Stradonitz, Stephan Kekule von. "Ein Geschütz von Meister Pegnitzer und sein Besteller," *Zeitschrift für historisches Waffen- und Köstumkunde* 13 (1932-34), 9-12.

Streubel, Johannes. "Die Konservierung der 'Faulen Magd': Ein Beispiel für die Pflege nationalen Kulturgutes in der Deutschen Demokratischen Republik," *Waffen- und Köstumkunde* 25 (1983), 54-58.

Susane, G. *Histoire de l'artillerie Française.* Paris, 1874.

Sutton, Anne F. and Livia Visser-Fuchs. "Richard of Gloucester and *la grosse bombarde,*" *Ricardian* 10.134 (1996), 461-65.

Svenningsen, Sten. "En kommentar til artiklen om aeldre danske militaer-pistoler i sidste Aarbog (XXVI)," *Våbenhistorisk tiddskrift* 13 (1980), 130-31.

Świętosławski, Witold. "Koszt broni palnej i jej uzycia w panstwie krzyżackim w Prussach na poczatku XV wieku," *Studia i materialy do historii wojskowosci* 35 (1993), 19-31.

Tarassuk, Leonid. "The Earliest Military-Issue Pistol," *Waffen- und Kostümkunde* 20 (1978), 137-42.

Tarassuk, Leonid. "Introduction de la platine à silex *à la française* dans les armes à feu russes," *Armi antiche* (1965), 3-14.

Tarassuk, Leonid. "Model of a Basilisk by Petrus de Arena," *Metropolitan Museum Journal* 24 (1989), 189-97.

Tarassuk, Leonid. "Scenes from *Orlando Furioso* on a Powder Horn," *Armi antiche* (1982), 3-12.

Teesdale, Edmund B. *Gunfounding in the Weald in the Sixteenth Century*. Royal Armouries Monograph, 2. London: Trustees of the Royal Armouries, 1991.

Thierbach, M. *Die geschichtliche Entwickelung des Handfeuerwaffen bearbeitet nach den in den deutschen Sammlungen noch corhandenen Originalen*. Dresden, 1886.

Thierbach, M. "Die Handfeuerwaffen der sächsischen Armee," *Zeitschrift für historische Waffenkunde* 3 (1902-05), 90-96.

Thierbach, M. "Ueber die erste Entwicklung der Handfeuerwaffen," *Zeitschrift für historisches Waffenkunde* 1 (1897-99), 129-33.

Thierry-Marjollet, Philippe. *Le développment de l'artillerie dans les armées bourguignonnes*. Dijon: Thierry-Marjollet, 1993.

Thomas, Bruno. "Die Artillerie im triumphzug Kaiser Maximilians I," *Zeitschrift für historische Waffen- und Köstumkunde* 15 (1937-39), 229-35.

Thomas, Bruno. *Hans Schmidt von und zu Helding: Der "kunstreiche" Büchsenschäfter von Ferlach (um 1600-1669)*. Klagenfurt: Verlag des Geschichtesvereins für Kärnten, 1982.

Thomas, Bruno. "Hans Schmidt zu Ferlach, 1628: Die silberne Jagdbüchse Erzherzog Leopolds V. von Österreich." In: *Unica Austriaca*. Vienna, 1960, III:110-12.

Thompson, A. Logan. "The Decline of the Armoured Knight. Part 1: The Rise of the Halberd and Emergence of Gunpowder," *Classic Arms and Militaria* 5.2 (Mar/Apr 1998), 34-37.

Thompson, A. Logan. "The Decline of the Armoured Knight. Part 2: How Feudal Armoured Cavalry Became Obsolete, the Response of Feudal Aristocracy to their Defeats," *Classic Arms and Militaria* 5.3 (May/Jun 1998), 32-36.

Thompson, A. Logan. "Gunpowder!" *Military Modelling* (Jan 1996), 28-31.

Thompson, I.A.A. "Spanish Armada Gun Procurement and Policy." In: *God's Obvious Design: Papers for the Spanish Armada Symposium*. Ed. P. Gallagher and D.W. Cruickshank. London, 1990, pp. 69-84.

Thrush, A. "The Ordnance Office and the Navy, 1625-40," *Mariner's Mirror* 77 (1991), 339-54.

Tittmann, Wilfried. "Die Eltzer Büchsen pfeile von 1331/2," *Waffen- und Köstumkunde* 36 (1994), 117-28; 37 (1995), 53-64.

Tittmann, Wilfried. "Entgegnung auf Claude Blair: 'Stammt das Radschloß aus Friaul?: A Reply'," *Waffen- und Köstumkunde* 41 (1999), 35-40.

Tittmann, Wilfried. "Die Geschützdarstellungen des Walter de Milemete von 1326," *Waffen- und Köstumkunde* 35 (1993), 145-47.

Tittmann, Wilfried. "Der Mythos vom 'Schwarzen Berthold,'" *Waffen- und Köstumkunde* 25 (1983), 17-30.

Tittmann, Wilfried. "Stammt das Radschloß aus Friaul?" *Waffen- und Köstumkunde* 39 (1995), 25-37.

Tomalin, D., J. Cross, and D. Motkin. "An Alberghetti Bronze Minion and Carriage from Yarmouth Roads, Isle of Wight," *International Journal of Nautical Archaeology and Underwater Exploration* 17 (1988), 75-86.

Tout, T.F. "Firearms in England in the Fourteenth Century." *English Historical Review* 26 (1911), 666-702; rpt. *Firearms in England in the Fourteenth Century*. London: Arms and Armour Press, 1968.

Toynbee, Margaret. "King James II of Scotland: Artillery and Fortification," *The Stewarts* 11 (1962), 157-62.

Towes, R.M. and P. McCree. "A Note on Drakes," *Journal of the Ordnance Society* 6 (1994), 39-47.

Trench, Charles Chenevix. "From Arquebus to Rifle: The Pursuit of Perfection," *History Today* 23 (1973), 407-17.

Trenschel, Hans-Peter. "Drei Geschützfragmente aus der Bungunderbeute," *Jahrbuch des Bernischen Historischen Museums in Bern* 47-48 (1967-1968), 9-60.

Trollope, Charles. "The Guns of the Queen's Ships during the Armada Campaign," *Journal of the Ordnance Society* 6 (1994), 23-38.

T'Sas, Francois. "Dulle Griet. La grosse bombarde de Gand, et ses souers." *Armi antiche* 1969, 13-57.

Turnbull, Stephen. "Guns and Granada," *Military Illustrated* 146 (Jul 2000), 32-39.

Uhlemann, Heinz Robert. "Älteste verzierte Bronzerohre," *Waffen- und Kostümkunde* 11 (1969), 136-41.

Uhlemann, Heinz Robert. "Berliner Büchsenmacher," *Waffen- und Kostümkunde* 15 (1973), 132-38.

Vale, M.G.A. "New Techniques and Old Ideals: The Impact of Artillery on War and Chivalry at the End of the Hundred Years War." In: *War, Literature and Politics in the Late Middle Ages: Essays in Honour of G.W. Coopland.* Ed. C.T. Allmand. Liverpool: University of Liverpool Press, 1975, pp. 57-72.

van den Brink, Jan M. "A Late Medieval Hackbut," *Journal of the Arms and Armour Society* 6 (1968-70), 241-43.

van Wakeren, A.I. "English Cast Iron Guns: A Dutch Trade, 1609-1640." In: *The Arsenal of the World: The Dutch Arms Trade in the Seventeenth Century.* Ed. Jan Piet Puype and Marco van der Hoeven. Amsterdam: Batavian Lion International, 1996, pp. 28-35.

Vaux de Foletier, Francois de. *Galiot de Genouillac, Mâitre de l'artillerie de France (1465-1516).* Paris, 1925.

Vigon, Jorge. *Historia de la artillería española.* 3 vols. Madrid: Instituto Jeronimo Zurita, 1947.

Vogt, John. "Saint Barbara's Legion: Portuguese Artillery in the Struggle for Morocco, 1415-1578," *Military Affairs* 41 (1977), 176-82.

Volpicella, L. "Le artiglierie di Castel Nuovo nell'anno 1500," *Archivio storico per le provincie Napoletane* 35 (1910), 308-48.

Waale, M.J. "Vuurwapens in de Noordelijke Nederlanden in de middeleeuwen," *Spiegel historiael* 27 (1992), 304-09.

Walker, Robert, Richard Dunham, Alexzandra Hildred, and Margaret Rule. "Analytical Study of Composite Shot from the Mary Rose," *Historical Metallurgy* 23 (1989), 84-90.

Wannenmacher, Leonie and Ulrike Rader. "Buchsenmacherei in Essen 1470 bis 1815," *Deutsches Waffen Journal* (May 1987), 700-04.

Weber, Ingrid. "Modelle zu den figürlichen Reliefs am Geschützrohr 'Die schöne Taube' ehemals Zeughaus Berlin," *Waffen- und Kostümkunde* 11 (1969), 129-36.

Wedler, R. "Die Namen der Kanonen Maximilians I.," *Beiträge zur Namenforschung* n.s. 2 (1967), 169-78.

Weidhagen-Hallerdt, Margareta. *Med byssa och kanon om Stockholms medeltida försvarsvapen visade på Stockholms Medeltidsmuseum.* Särtryck ur Stadsvandringar, 14. Årsbok: Stockholms stadsmuseum, 1991.

Weiss, Walter. "Suhler Handfeurwaffen im 16. Jahrhundert," *Natur und Heimat* 8.2 (Feb 1959), 74-77.

Wenzel, Ernst. "Beiträge zur Kenntnis des alt-Magdeburger Geschützwesens," *Zeitschrift für historisches Waffen- und Köstumkunde* 13 (1932-34), 279-87.

Wettendorfer, Eduard. "Zur Technologie der Steinbüchsen," *Zeitschrift für historische Waffen- und Köstumkunde* 15 (1937-39), 147-54.

Wild, Heinz Walter. "Black Powder in Mining–Its Introduction, Early Use, and Diffusion over Europe." In: *Gunpowder: The History of an International Technology.* Ed. Brenda Buchanan. Bath: Bath University Press, 1996, pp. 203-18.

Wilinbachow, W. "Note on the History of the Initial Period of the Use of Firearms in Slavonic Countries," *Kwartalnik historii techniki* 8 (1963), 215-35.

Wilkinson, Frederick. *Les armes à feu.* Paris: Libraire Larousse, 1972.

Wilkinson, Frederick. "Matchlocks and Blunderbusses," *Discovering Antiques* 15 (1970), 351-55.

Wilkinson-Latham, R.J. *Discovering Artillery.* Tring: Shire Publications, 1972.

Willers, J.K.W. *Die Nürnberger Handfeuerwaffe bis zur Mitte des 16. Jahrhunderts: Entwicklung, Herstellung, Absatz nach archivalischen Quellen*. Schriftenreihe des Stadtarchivs Nürnberg. Nuremberg: Buchhandlung Korn und Berg, 1973.

Williams, Alan R. "The Production of Saltpetre in the Middle Ages," *Ambix* 22 (1975), 125-33.

Williams, Alan R. "Some Firing Tests with Simulated Fifteenth-Century Handguns," *Journal of the Arms and Armour Society* 8 (1974), 114-20.

Wilson, Guy M. "The Commonwealth Gun," *International Journal of Nautical Archaeology and Underwater Exploration* 17 (1988), 87-100.

Wilson, Guy M. "Military Target Practice in England," *Royal Armouries Yearbook* 1 (1996), 79-80.

Wilson, Guy M. "The Threat of the Handgun in Elizabethan England," *Royal Armouries Yearbook* 1 (1996), 117-18.

Wlassaty, Joachim von. "Combat anno 1399: Welche Schlussleistung besass die Tannenberg-Büchse?" *Deutsches Waffen Journal* (1977), 716-21.

Wlassaty, Joachim von. "Nachlaß der Raubritter," *Deutsches Waffen Journal* (1999), 978-84.

Yablonskaya, Helen. "English 17th-Century Firearms in the Kremlin Armoury Chamber," *Royal Armouries Yearbook* 4 (1999), 49-61.

Zylbergeld, Léon. "L'artillerie de la ville de Bruxelles au milieu du XVe siècle d'apres un inventaire de 1451-1452," *Revue Belge d'histoire militaire* 23 (1979-80), 609-46.

Military Technology – Premodern – Gunpowder Weapons – Non-European

Ágostan, Gábor. "Gunpowder for the Sultan's Army: New Sources on the Supply of Gunpowder to the Ottoman Army in the Hungarian Campaigns of the Sixteenth and Seventeenth Centuries," *Turcica* 25 (1993), 75-96.

Ágostan, Gábor. "Ottoman Artillery and European Military Technology in the Fifteenth and Seventeenth Centuries," *Acta orientalia academiae scientarum Hungaricarum* 47 (1994), 15-48.

Ágostan, Gábor. "Ottoman Gunpowder Production in Hungary in the Sixteenth Century: The *Baruthane* of Buda." In: *Hungarian-Ottoman Military and Diplomatic Relations in the Age of Süleyman the Magnificent.* Ed. G. Dávid and P. Fodor. Budapest, 1994, pp. 149-59.

Ágostan, Gábor. "Párhuzamok és eltérések az oszmán és az európai tűzérség fejlődésében a 15-16 században," *Történelmi szemle* 34.3-4 (1992), 173-98.

Ayalon, David. *Gunpowder and Firearms in the Mamluk Kingdom: A Challenge to a Mediaeval Society.* London, 1956.

Barker, Richard. "A Gun-List from Portuguese India," *Journal of the Ordnance Society* 8 (1996), 52-71.

Barker, Richard and A.H. Fonseca de Castro. "Livrio Primeiro do Governo do Brasil, 1607-1633," *Journal of the Ordnance Society* 7 (1995), 18-26

Brown, Delmer M. "The Effect of Firearms on Japanese Warfare, 1543-98," *Far Eastern Quarterly* 7 (1947), 236-53.

Brown, M.L. *Firearms in Colonial America: The Impact on History and Technology, 1492-1792.* Washington: Smithsonian Institute Press, 1980.

Davis, Tenny L. and James R. Ware. "Early Chinese Military Pyrotechnics," *Journal of Chemical Education* 24 (1947), 522-37.

Favez, J. Frederich. "Fighting Fire with Firearms: The Anglo-Powhatan Arms Race in Early Virginia," *American Indian Culture and Research Journal* 3 (1979).

Gommans, Jos. "Warhorse and Gunpowder in India c. 1000-1850." In: *War in the Early Modern World, 1450-1815.* Ed. Jeremy Black. London, 1999, pp. 105-28.

Goodrich, L. Carrington and Feng Chia-Sheng. "The Early Development of Firearms in China," *Isis* 36 (1946), 114-23, 250-51.

Gwei-Djen, Lu, Joseph Needham and Phan Chi-Hsing. "The Oldest Representation of a Bombard." *Technology and Culture* 29 (1988), 594-605.

Hess, Andrew C. "Firearms and the Decline of Ibn Khaldun's Military Elite." *Archivum Ottomanicum* 4 (1972), 173-99.

Imamura, Nobuya. "Introduction of the Japanese Arquebus and Its Tactics: On the Anniversary of Vasco da Gama's Discovery of a Sea Route to India." In: *Actas do XXIV congresso internacional de historía militar.* Centro cultural de Belém, 24 a 29 de agosto, 1998. Lisbon: Comissão Portuguesa de Historía Militar, 1998, pp. 171-77.

Inalcik, Halil. "The Socio-political Effects of the Diffusion of Fire-arms in the Middle East." In: *War, Technology and Society in the Middle East.* Ed. V.J. Parry and M.E. Yapp. London, 1975, pp. 195-217.

Işiksal, T. "Gunpowder in Ottoman Documents of the Last Half of the Sixteenth Century," *International Journal of Turkish Studies* 2 (1981-1982), 81-91.

Jennings, R.C. "Firearms, Bandits, and Gun-Control: Some Evidence on Ottoman Policy Towards Firearms in the Possession of *Reaya*, From Judicial Records of Kayseri, 1600-1627," *Archivum Ottomanicum* 6 (1980), 339-58.

Khan, Iqtidar Alam. "Coming of Gunpowder to the Islamic World and North India: Spotlight on the Role of the Mongols," *Journal of Asian History* 30 (1996), 27-45.

Khan, Iqtidar Alam. "Early Use of Cannon and Musket in India, AD 1442-1526." *Journal of the Economic and Social History of the Orient* 24 (1981), 146-64.

Khan, Iqtidar Alam. "Origin and Development of Gunpowder Technology in India, AD 1250-1500." *Indian Historical Review* 42 (1977), 20-29.

Khan, Iqtidar Alam. "The Role of the Mongols in the Introduction of Gunpowder and Firearms to South Asia. In: *Gunpowder: The History of an International Technology*. Ed. Brenda Buchanan. Bath: Bath University Press, 1996, pp. 33-44.

Kleinschmidt, Harald. "Using the Gun: Manual Drill and the Proliferation of Portable Firearms," *Journal of Military History* 63 (1999), 601-41.

Ling, Wang. "On the Invention and Use of Gunpowder and Firearms in China," *Isis* 37 (1947), 160-78.

Needham, Joseph. "The Epic of Gunpowder and Firearms: Developing from Alchemy." In: *Science and Traditional China: A Comparative Perspective*. Cambridge: Harvard University Press, pp. 27-56.

Needham, Joseph. *Gunpowder as the Fourth Power, East and West*. Hong Kong: Hong Kong University Press, 1985.

Needham, Joseph. *Science and Civilization in China*. Vol. 5, part 7: *Military Technology: The Gunpowder Epic*. Cambridge: Cambridge University Press, 1986.

Pan, Jixing. "The Origin of Rockets in China." In: *Gunpowder: The History of an International Technology*. Ed. Brenda Buchanan. Bath: Bath University Press, 1996, pp. 25-32.

Perrin, Noel. *Giving Up the Gun: Japan's Reversion to the Sword, 1543-1879*. Boulder: Shambala Publications, 1980.

Rathgen, Bernhard. "Die Pulverwaffe in Indien." *Ostasiatische Zeitschrift* 12 (1925), 11-30, 196-217.

White, G. "Firearms in Africa: An Introduction." *Journal of African History* 12 (1971), 173-84.

Williams, Alan R. and A.J.R. Paterson. "A Turkish Bronze Cannon in the Tower of London," *Gladius* 17 (1986), 185-205.

Zaky, 'Abd al-Rahman. "Gunpowder and Arab Firearms in Middle Ages," *Gladius* 6 (1967).

INDEX OF AUTHORS' NAMES

HISTORY
OF WARFARE

History of Warfare presents the latest research on all aspects of military history. Publications in the series will examine technology, strategy, logistics, and economic and social developments related to warfare in Europe, Asia, and the Middle East from ancient times until the early nineteenth century. The series will accept monographs, collections of essays, conference proceedings, and translation of military texts.

1. HOEVEN, M. VAN DER (ed.). *Exercise of Arms*. Warfare in the Netherlands. 1568-1648. 1997. ISBN 90 04 10727 4
2. RAUDZENS, G. (ed.). *Technology, Disease and Colonial Conquests, Sixteenth to Eighteenth Centuries*. Essays Reappraising the Guns and Germs Theories. 2001. ISBN 90 04 11745 8
3. LENIHAN P. (ed.). *Conquest and Resistance*. War in Seventeenth-Century Ireland. 2001. ISBN 90 04 11743 1
4. NICHOLSON, H. *Love, War and the Grail*. 2001. ISBN 90 04 12014 9
5. BIRKENMEIER, J.W. *The Development of the Komnenian Army: 1081-1180*. 2002. ISBN 90 04 11710 5
6. MURDOCH, S. (ed.) *Scotland and the Thirty Years' War, 1618-1648*. 2001. ISBN 90 04 12086 6
7. TUYLL VAN SEROOSKERKEN, H.P. VAN. *The Netherlands and World War I*. Espionage, Diplomacy and Survival. 2001. ISBN 90 04 12243 5
8. DEVRIES, K. *A Cumulative Bibliography of Medieval Military History and Technology*. 2002. ISBN 90 04 12227 3

ISSN 1385–7827